A History of Private Bill Legislation, Volume 2

Frederick Clifford

PRIVATE BILL LEGISLATION.

VOL. II.

A

HISTORY

OF

Private Bill Legislation.

BY

FREDERICK CLIFFORD,

OF THE MIDDLE TEMPLE,

BARRISTER-AT-LAW.

IN TWO VOLUMES.

VOL. II.

LONDON:

BUTTERWORTHS, 7, FLEET STREET,

Law Publishers to the Queen's most excellent Majesty.

MANCHESTER: MEREDITH, RAY & LITTLER.
EDINBURGH: T. & T. CLARK; BELL & BRADFUTE.
DUBLIN: HODGES, FIGGIS & CO., GRAFTON STREET.
CALCUTTA: THACKER, SPINK & CO. MELBOURNE: G. ROBERTSON & CO.

1887.

LONDON :

PRINTED BY C. F. ROWORTH, GREAT NEW STREET, FETTER LANE—E.C.

Dedication

(BY ROYAL PERMISSION)

TO

THE QUEEN.

———◆———

MADAM,

During the fifty years of your Majesty's Reign, nearly Eleven thousand Local and Personal Statutes have been passed by the Imperial Parliament, and received your Majesty's Assent. To the vast undertakings completed by Railway and other Companies, and the money expended upon the faith of these Statutes, is due in large measure within this period a social and industrial Progress throughout the United Kingdom of which History affords hardly any other example.

No less memorable during the same fifty years have been the great Sanitary and other Works, together with the numerous Parks, Baths, Picture Galleries, Libraries, and Public Buildings, provided by Local Authorities under Local Acts, adding materially thereby to the health, *comfort and enjoyment of your Majesty's subjects in their ever-growing towns, and accomplishing these ends by measures of local self-government in harmony with the best English traditions.*

Within the same period Parliament has cheapened, expedited and greatly improved its procedure upon Local and Personal Bills. These Volumes attempt, for the first time, to describe the changes thus made and trace the History of that Private Legislation which, working quietly, is but little noticed, although it has done so much for the public good.

Your Majesty has been graciously pleased to accept the Dedication of my Work. That it may prove one not unfitting memorial of an auspicious Era in a renowned and beneficent Reign is the earnest hope of,

Madam,

Your Majesty's most faithful Subject,

THE AUTHOR.

PREFACE

———◆———

Owing to representations made in the progress of this Work, material additions have been made in the Chapters relating to Local Authorities and the London Water Companies. Volume II. thus considerably exceeds in size its companion volume, but the Author hopes that its usefulness may be correspondingly increased, and that, although not so intended, it may serve as a Jubilee record of the Queen's reign.

The Author's grateful acknowledgments are due to the many official personages, legal agents, town clerks, and secretaries of public bodies, whom it was necessary to consult in preparing portions of this Volume, for aid and information courteously afforded.

1, Plowden Buildings, Temple,
December, 1886.

CONTENTS.

———◆———

VOL. II.

—

CHAPTER VII.

CHAPTER VIII.

CHAPTER IX.

CHAPTER X.

CHAPTER XI.

CHAPTER XII.

CHAPTER XIII.

CHAPTER XIV.—PART I.

CHAPTER XIV.—PART II.

CHAPTER XV.

CHAPTER XVI.

CHAPTER XVII.

CHAPTER XVIII.

CHAPTER XIX.

CHAPTER XX.

CHAPTER XXI.

CHAPTER XXII.

CHAPTER XXIII.

CHAPTER XXIV.

CHAPTER XXV.

APPENDIX A.

DRAINAGE, WATER SUPPLY AND PROTECTION AGAINST FLOODS AT HULL, A.D. 1402.

APPENDIX B.

SANITARY CONDITION OF MERTHYR TYDFIL, 1845-85.

A History of

PRIVATE BILL LEGISLATION.

———◆———

CHAPTER VII.

HIGHWAYS: ROADS: BRIDGES: FERRIES.

On no subject of domestic legislation has Parliament bestowed more time and labour than on the making, improvement, and maintenance of our highways and roads. From the earliest times, public and private Acts without end have been passed for this purpose. Besides the many measures now obsolete or repealed, there were, in 1885, in the Statute Book thirty-three public Acts which, in whole or in part, still regulated highways in England,[1] and fifty which, dating from the year 1822, applied to turnpike roads. The 3,800 private Turnpike Acts have already been briefly mentioned.[2] To these must be added many annual public Acts which put an end to turnpike trusts in different localities, and continued others. There have also been Acts confirming more than two hundred Provisional Orders,[3] passed to arrange the debts of these unlucky trusts, extinguish arrears of interest, allow compositions, and generally make the best of some very disastrous investments. The list is not even yet exhausted, for many Acts of a local nature relating to highways, especially those between London and Holyhead, and other arterial roads, are printed among the public general Acts, in this summary not included.[4]

Public and private legislation regulating highways and roads.

---

[1] And, according to the Report (p. 1) of the Lords' Committee on Highways, in 1881, there had then been upwards of 700 judicial decisions upon cases arising under these Acts.

[2] *Ante*, I. p. 5.

[3] See Chronological Table of Statutes, 9th ed., 1884, App. 17, pp. 1276-7.

[4] Ib. p. 1261.

Local Turn-
pike Trust
Acts.

In the long and dreary array of Turnpike Trust Acts there is nothing which calls for detailed notice. But some attention is due to the causes which led to so enormous a claim upon the time and care of Parliament, and which also led Parliament to sanction the maintenance of our roads by a local system of tolls on traffic. In attempting this explanation reference must be made to a few of the numerous public measures, the trial and failure of which, through a course of many centuries, ended in a fresh experiment by means of private legislation, and in quite as signal a failure. At common law the duty of keeping highways in repair generally rested with the parishes, unless by prescription this duty attached to townships or districts, or to owners of estates *ratione tenuræ* or *clausuræ*. From this burden at common law parishes and townships were not relieved by Acts authorizing turnpikes. According to judicial decisions, these special Acts merely provided additional means for the discharge of what was a public obligation, to be performed, failing other means, by local rates.[1] In cases, therefore, where highways were converted into turnpike roads, and afterwards fell out of repair, the only parties liable to indictment were the road authorities of the parish or township, though, after conviction, they had a remedy against the turnpike trustees.[2] From the earliest times, however, as well as in the latest, there is ample proof how difficult it was to enforce the theoretical liability of parishes, and either to make or maintain good roads, especially through poor and sparsely-populated districts.[3] Some examples are here collected which illustrate this difficulty.

[1] *Rex* v. *Inhabitants of St. George, Hanover Square*, 3 Campbell's Reports, 222; *Bussey* v. *Storey*, 1 Neville & Manning, 639.

[2] This remedy, however, could only be enforced if the Court were satisfied that the securities of creditors of the trust would not be endangered thereby (3 Geo. IV. c. 126, s. 110). See *Rex* v. *Nethergong*, 2 Barnewall & Alderson, 179.

[3] Even in 1878 there were 788 parishes in England with fewer than fifty inhabitants, and 6,000 parishes containing fewer than 300 inhabitants (Commons' Committee on Highways, 1878). When repairs depended on parishes such as these, no

One of the first entries on the Rolls of Parliament, in the Hawarden, A.D. 1278. year 1278, allows the abbot and men of Chester to cut and sell wood and make clearings between Hawarden and Montalt (Montem Altum), on condition of their making a road a league in length.[1] Again, in 1290, Walter Good- Licence to take toll asked for, A.D. 1290. lake, of Wallingford, asks[2] for a licence to take toll on carts conveying merchandize upon the road between Jowemersh and Newenham, for the repair of this road (Walter Godelak de Walinford petit aliquam consuetudinem dari de qualibet carecta de marcandisis transeuntibus per viam[3] inter Jowe- mersh et Newenham, propter profunditatem, ad emendationem ejusdem vie). An unfavourable answer was returned to this petition, "Rex nihil inde faciet:" but such licences were not unusual.

In 1304, a road leading to Salisbury was placed in charge of the bishop with a view to its more effectual repair.[4] Upon Tolls farmed on roads in Cumberland. petition by John Wake, in 1306, he was allowed to farm the King's toll levied between Soulewath and Arturet, in

wonder our highways two or three centuries ago were in the condition described by Macaulay (*ante*, I. pp. 4–5), or by Defoe, who, in his Tour through Great Britain (written in 1724) says that trees bought in Sussex for the royal dockyard were drawn on "tugs" by twenty-two oxen, and even then were sometimes two or three years in reaching Chatham. He adds, that in a village, not far from Lewes, he saw a lady of good quality drawn to church in her coach by six oxen, "the way being so stiff that no horses could go in it."

[1] In the original, "via, seu tren-chata, habens in latitudinem unam leucam;" but length, not breadth, must here be meant. "Leuca" has been rendered by its later equivalent of a league; originally it seems to have been used for a measurement of 1,500 paces.

[2] 1 Rot. Parl. p. 48.

[3] Mediæval writers mention five kinds of ways: *semita* (Fr. *sentier*), a half-road, or pathway, four feet wide; *carreria* (via quam carrus transire potest), a road eight feet wide, sufficient for the passing of one cart; *via*, an ordinary road, six-teen feet broad; *cheminus*, or via major, thirty-two feet wide, in which a pedagium or toll was sometimes levied; and *via regia*, sixty-four feet wide, still known as the King's high-way, in which two vehicles might pass and sixteen armed horsemen ride abreast. *Via ferrata* meant one of the lines of Roman road by which those great road-makers kept their hold on conquered provinces; *calcetum*, or *via munita*, was a paved causeway, *lapidibus confecta*. Du-cange; & D'Arnis' Lexicon Med. et Inf. Lat., *passim*.

[4] 1 Rot. Parl. 174.

Cumberland, at the rental then paid into the Treasury by the sheriff of that county.[1] A commission was issued in 1314-15, upon petition from inhabitants of Huntingdon and the Isle of Ely, to take evidence on oath in presence of the Bishop of Ely, upon a question whether he was not bound to repair and maintain the causeway (calcetum) of Horheth, then broken and impassable, the petitioners alleging that this great injury to them and their neighbours had happened through the bishop's default, although he levied on vessels passing under the bridge a toll properly applicable for repairs of the bridge and causeway.[2] A petition in 1321-25,

from Thomas Wake, lord of Lydell, prayed the King to order his burgesses of Hull not to make any new road upon the petitioner's land, and to disuse any roads they had made there while he was under age. This petitioner was told that he must resort to the common law for his remedy.[3] A curious complaint was made, in 1320, by the master and

brethren of St. Bartholomew's Hospital: that whereas Henry III. granted to them, for the support of poor people, two fish out of every load passing over London Bridge, the sheriffs of London, Nicholas Pyket and Nigel Drury, exacted a toll of one-tenth upon these fish.

A special commission was issued in 1394-5, upon petition in Parliament, to inquire into an alleged extortion by servants of the constable of Nottingham Castle, in levying fourpence a load upon each cart passing along a highway through Sherwood Forest, and conveying charcoal, notwithstanding a verdict given against such levy.[4] It was also provided, in 1404, that the mayor and burgesses of Calais should not charge more toll on carts coming for staple ware than was usual in the time of Edward III.[5] But this was probably a market toll.

---

[1] 1 Rot. Parl. 199 ; 35 Edw. 1.
[2] Ib. 314.
[3] Ib. 420. Both at common law and by statute, under certain conditions, private land may still be taken and used for purposes of a public highway.
[4] 3 Rot. Parl. 330 ; 18 Rich. II.
[5] 3 Ib. 555 ; 6 Hen. IV.

When parishes were poor, and other means were not available, large powers were lodged with sheriffs, who might, upon presentment in their "tournes,"[1] make a general levy for repairs and maintenance of roads, causeways, and bridges. A complaint made in Parliament, in the year 1406, shows that these powers were sometimes abused.[2] The Commons, spiritual as well as temporal (Item, suplient humblement les communes de votre roiaume, si bien espirituelx come temporelx), set forth that many sheriffs procured feigned presentments that divers roads, bridges, and causeways were in bad repair, with intent to levy on abbots, priors, and secular persons, some ten pounds, some more, some less. These levies were made by officers called "out-riders," who allowed no delay and no appeal (les ditz amerciaments levont par lour ministres appellez outryders, saunz delaye, ou ascun responce des parties), although the roads, bridges and causeways in question were sufficient, standing in no need of repair. For this unwarrantable charge and great grievance, the Commons prayed a prompt remedy, suggesting that the legality of such presentments should be tested in the Court of King's Bench, before any levies under them were made. To this prayer the King's answer was that the common law should take its course, and the sum levied be reasonable (Soit la commune leye tenuz, et les amerciaments resonables en ce cas).

Power of sheriffs upon presentment, to levy for repairs of roads, causeways, and bridges.

Sheriffs' officers called "out-riders."

---

[1] The sheriff's tourn was an ancient court of record, held twice a year before the sheriff in different parts of the county in turn. King Alfred, in his Dom Bec, or *Liber judicialis*, collected and codified then existing customs for the guidance of this court, as well as of the court baron, the county court and court leet. Magna Carta mentions the sheriff's tourn, which was the great court leet of the county, the court leet proper being held but once a year, and in a particular hundred, lordship or manor. All free-holders within the jurisdiction were bound, if required, to attend the jury of the leet or tourn, and it was their duty to present, besides crimes and misdemeanors, all common nuisances and matters injurious to the King's peace and the common good. See Stephen's Com. 8th ed., IV., 316, *et seq.* From these presentments came, no doubt, the abuses mentioned in the text.

[2] 3 Rot. Parl. 598; 7 & 8 Hen. IV.

Statute of
Winchester,
1385.

The statute of Winchester,[1] passed about the year 1385, is an early instance of general legislation affecting highways. This statute was for the abatement of robberies, murders, burnings, and theft, which were declared to be more frequent than they had been heretofore ; and with a view to greater security in travel, it was " commanded that highways leading from one market town to another, shall be enlarged wherever

Highways to
be cleared of
underwood,
dykes, &c.

bushes, woods, and dykes be, so that there be neither dyke, tree, nor bush, whereby a man may lurk to do hurt within 200 feet on either side of the way."[2] There was a proviso that this command should " not extend unto ashes nor unto great trees, so as it be clear underneath. And if by default of the lord that will not abate the dyke, underwood or bushes in manner aforesaid, any robberies be done therein, the lord shall be answerable for the felony ; and if murder be done, the lord shall make a fine at the King's pleasure. And if the lord be not able to fell the underwood, the country shall aid him therein. And the King willeth that in his demesne

Royal de-
mesnes in-
cluded.

lands and woods, within his forest and without, the ways shall be enlarged as before is said.   And if, peradventure, a park be near to the highway, it is requisite that the lord shall set back his park a space of 200 feet from the high-ways, or that he make such a wall, dyke, or hedge, that offenders may not pass, nor return to do evil."

Roads be-
tween Abing-
don and
Dorchester,
A.D. 1421.

In the collection published by the Record Commission, the earliest statute relating to any local ways is one passed in 1421, for repairing a road and bridges at Burford and Culhamford, between Abingdon and Dorchester.[3] It recites that, as hath been shown in this Parliament, by petition from the commonalty, the road passing through a manor of the abbot of Abingdon, along which the King's liege subjects

---

[1] 13 Edw. I.

[2] Mounted highwaymen were products of a later civilization. A statute of 1692 gave a highwayman's horse to the person who apprehended him, and the executors of any person killed in apprehending him could claim a reward (4 Will. & Mary, c. 8, ss. 3, 6).

[3] 9 Hen. V., st. 2, c. 11, printed in 2 Stat. of Realm, p. 211.

have enjoyed free passage from time out of memory (ont euz lour cariage et franc passage, sibien ove charettes come ove lour chivalx, biens, chatieux et marchandises, du temps dont memorie ne court), was lately by increase of water so much surrounded, that no one could pass there without danger; until certain inhabitants of Abingdon, out of their own proper goods and by alms from neighbouring people, made bridges at Burford and Culhamford, and enlarged and repaired this road, with assent of the abbot and convent, planting upon the banks of the ditches certain trees called poplars and willows, for use in mending the road upon necessary occasions in time to come.

Then, with assent of the Lords, and at the commonalty's request, it is ordained and established that the bridges and road (the breadth of which is carefully specified) shall be and remain for ever common bridges and a common road to all persons whatsoever there passing, or desiring to pass, as well on horseback as on foot, and with all manner of carriages. Next, leave is given to all the King's liege subjects for ever to repair and renew the bridges and road, plant new trees, dig for clay, marl, gravel and earth in the ditches, and at all reasonable times cut branches and shoots from the trees to repair the bridges and road (a passage which throws some light on the old method of road-making and mending) without impediment or impeachment, any title or interest of the abbot and convent notwithstanding. There is a saving of the King's rights, with a reservation to the abbot and convent, and their successors, of their existing liberties and franchises within and upon the bridges, road, passages, waters and ditches, and also of any fishery in water beneath the bridges and in the ditches for ever. (Salve toutfoitz le droit du Roi, et salvez auxi as ditz abbe et covent et a lours successours, lour libertees et franchises dedeins et en les ponts, chemyn, passages, eaues et fosses avantditz, sicome ils avoient a devant en les

Dedication of road.

Saving rights of Crown and abbot.

ditz chemyn, soil et eaue, et auxi toute la pescherie en
leaue desoutz les ditz ponts et en les fosses suisditz perpetuel-
ment.)

Although in the Act just cited there was a specific dedication of this local road to public use, no specific provision was
made for its maintenance, which, instead of being thrown
upon the parish, seems to have been left as one of those
general duties which are usually discharged by nobody.
More than a century afterwards the need for some better
system was felt by Parliament; and in 1555 compulsory
labour for repairs of roads was sanctioned by the first
Highway Act.[1] It directed constables and churchwardens
in every parish throughout the realm, yearly during Easter
week, to "call together a number of the parochians,"
and choose two honest persons to serve for one year
as surveyors and orderers of works for amending parish
highways leading to any market town. These surveyors
were authorised to require occupiers of land, at each Midsummer, to attend with wains or carts, in proportion to their
holdings, such carts being furnished after the custom of
the country with oxen, horses, or other cattle, and necessaries, in charge of two able men. All other householders,
cottagers and labourers, able to work, and not being servants hired by the year, were to furnish work in their own
persons or by deputy, bringing with them "such shovels,
spades, pikes, mattocks, and other tools and instruments, as
they do make their own fences and ditches withall." Work
was to be carried on for four days, of eight hours each,
unless otherwise directed by supervisors; and constables and
churchwardens were "openly in the church to give knowledge" of appointed days. Fines for default were to be
imposed at leets, or quarter sessions, and to be collected by
constables, with an allowance to them of eightpence in the
pound, and one shilling for clerks of the peace or stewards
of any leet.

Forced labour for road-mending, A.D. 1555.

Fines for default.

[1] 2 & 3 P. & M. c. 8.

This Act, limited to seven years, was continued in 1562-3[1] 5 Eliz. c. 13.
for twenty years, and its provisions were made more effectual
by powers given to supervisors to take road materials from
any quarries, or in default of such, to dig in adjoining lands,
without leave from owners, for gravel, sand, or cinder.
They were not, however, to dig in any man's garden, orchard
or meadow; and pits must not exceed a certain size and
must be filled up after use. Supervisors were authorized to Power of road supervisors.
turn into private ditches any springs or watercourses which
prevented an effective mending of highways; and adjoining owners were required to scour, repair and keep low
their dykes, fences and hedges, and also to cut down all
trees and bushes growing in highways. Lastly, the annual
working period for forced labour was extended from four to
six days; and easier methods were enacted for punishing
defaults and recovering penalties.

An early Road Act, in 1576, related to highways and Repair of roads near Oxford.
bridges near Oxford.[2] Mainly through floods, these were
said to be so decayed and impaired that travellers were
much annoyed and encumbered, and country people were
not able without danger to bring to market corn, grain,
victuals, and other necessaries, so that dearth was likely to
ensue both in university and city. It was, therefore, enacted Statute labour proportioned to holding.
that each occupier of land within five miles of Oxford
should provide, for repairs of roads within one mile of the
city, wains or draught carts in proportion to the size of his
holding, furnished after the custom of the country with oxen,
horse, or other cattle, and with able men to load and unload:
and every other householder, cottager, or labourer (being no
hired servant), was to find and send one sufficient labourer,
with tools proper for mending, repairing, and upbuilding
any decayed bridges and ways. Supervisors were appointed
by the Vice-Chancellor, mayor and justices, under whose
direction occupiers and other persons liable, or their deputies,

[1] By 5 Eliz. c. 13.   [2] 18 Eliz. c. 20.

were, for six whole days, to render service by hand or carriage, in such places and in such wise as should be appointed,

Penalties applied towards repairs.

subject on default to daily penalties; these to be applied in mending bridges and causeways. Following the precedent of 1562-3, supervisors were empowered, under certain restrictions, to enter private lands and dig for " gravel, sand, rubbish, stone, or cinder," and other things.

Injury to roads by southern ironworks.

One objection to ironworks in Kent, Sussex and Surrey was their wholesale consumption of timber, and the frequent enactments against this southern industry have already been mentioned.[1] " In short time " our ancestors feared, timber trees in England would be "utterly consumed and wasted" if iron manufactures were encouraged. Another hardly less serious indictment against these works was their destruction of neighbouring highways by the carriage of heavy loads of metal and fuel. It was, therefore, provided, in 1585, that, for every ton of material carted by them upon roads within the three counties, occupiers of ironworks should repair these roads with certain quantities of gravel and stones, as the justices directed.[2]

Highway Act, 1662.

In 1662, a century after the last Highway Act, Parliament declared[3] that former laws and statutes for mending and repairing common and public highways in this realm had been found ineffectual, by means whereof and the extraordinary burdens carried upon waggons and other carriages, divers highways were become dangerous and almost impassable. Churchwardens and constables, or tithingmen in every parish, were therefore directed to choose surveyors yearly on the Monday or Tuesday in Easter week, giving public notice hereof in church, immediately after the end of morning prayer.[4] These surveyors were

Appointment of road surveyors.

---

[1] *Ante*, I. pp. 31-2.

[2] 27 Eliz. c. 19 ; and see 39 Eliz. c. 19, and 7 Geo. III. c. 42, s. 57. Individuals are still liable for repairs of roads if they occasion any extraordinary traffic. (See 41 & 42 Vict. c. 77, s. 23.)

[3] 14 Car. II. c. 6.

[4] By 7 Will. IV. & 1 Vict. c. 45, printed notices on church doors were substituted for all statutory notifications during divine service in church.

to view highways, consider what repairs were wanting, estimate the cost, and then, helped by two or more substantial householders, might assess "every inhabitant rated to the poor, and every occupier of lands and houses, and all tithes impropriate or appropriate, portions of tithes, coal mines, and other mines, saleable underwoods, stock, goods, or other personal estate, not being household stuff." No rate was to exceed sixpence in the pound in any one year; and 20*l.* in money, goods, stock, or other personal estate, was to be rated equally to 20*s.* a year in lands.

Property assessed.

This, then, was the view taken in 1662 as to the incidence of rating, and the respective burdens which should be borne by real and personal property. Before becoming valid, each assessment was to be allowed by a justice of the peace. Surveyors were to abate nuisances; and as the statute labour system appeared to be faulty, they were authorized to hire labour, or direct persons chargeable under older Acts to send their wains or carts. These persons were to be paid, according to customary rates, "for such work as they shall do over and above what" by law they were required to do in mending highways. No occupiers could be assessed both for land and for stock feeding or employed upon it. There were the usual powers to surveyors to dig for gravel on private land, excepting gardens and orchards, where road materials could not be had from commons. In order to prevent undue wear of roads, the number of draught horses or oxen used in waggons was limited. After September 29, 1662, no travelling waggon wherein any goods were drawn for hire, except carts or carriages employed upon husbandry or carrying manure, hay, coal, chalk, timber for shipping, materials for building, stones of all sorts, or ammunition or artillery for the King's service, could go in any highway with "above seven horse-beasts, whereof six shall draw in pairs, and not with above eight oxen, or six oxen and two horse-beasts, nor shall at any time carry above 20 cwt. between October 1 and May 1, nor above 30 cwt. between May 1 and

Paid labour on roads.

Restrictions to prevent undue wear of roads.

October 1." Other restrictions were imposed as to quantities of corn and other produce; wheels were not to be less in breadth than four inches in the tyre. This Act did not exempt owners and occupiers of ironworks within the wilds (*sic*)[1] of Surrey, Sussex, or Kent from making such special contributions towards road repair as they were then bound to make under statute. Lastly, there was a proviso that where lands were let, occupiers and not owners were to pay road assessments, unless any agreement existed to the contrary.

As general legislation failed to secure good roads, attempts were again made to supply a remedy by means of special Acts, with special provisions. One of these became law

Nonsuch and Kingston, A.D. 1605-6. in 1605-6, and applied to a road between Nonsuch and Kingston, over which traffic to the King's houses at Nonsuch, Richmond, Oatlands and Hampton Court necessarily passed. In this Act there is no mention of forced labour, but after a recital that the parishes in which these roads lie are

Parishes being unable to repair, the hundreds charged. unable to repair them, owners and occupiers in the hundreds of Kingston, Emlinbridge, Copthorne, Effingham, Wallington, Wotton and Reigate (the borough of Reigate excepted), are charged with the repair, by rates upon lands and tenements, such rates to be fixed by justices at sessions. No limit of rating is imposed, and no mode of repair prescribed. Overseers are to carry out the Act, and means of levying rates are provided.[2]

High road from London to York. This was a public statute, though of local application. Another, passed in 1663, did not trust to the Highway Act of the previous year, but introduced fresh methods,

Turnpike Act, A.D. 1663. and is usually described as the first Turnpike Act.[3] It applied to such parts of the ancient highway from London to York as were within the counties of Hertford, Cambridge,

[1] Wealds. See 27 Eliz. c. 19.
[2] 3 Jac. I. c. 19.
[3] 15 Car. II. c. 1. Though generally known as a public Act, its title is entered in the roll of private Acts (see 5 Stat. of Realm, 436, where the full text is given from the original in the Parliament office).

and Huntingdon. This road, the Act recited, was very ruinous, and almost impassable, "by reason of great and many loads which are weekly drawn in waggons," especially barley and malt, coming to Ware, and so conveyed to London "by water, as by other carriages, both from the north parts, and also from Norwich, St. Edmunds Bury, and Cambridge to London." Another recital was "that the ordinary course appointed by the laws and statutes of this realm is not sufficient" for effectual repairs of this road, "neither are the inhabitants through which the road doth lie of ability to repair the same without some other provision of moneys." Justices in each county were, therefore, to appoint surveyors, who should provide road materials, and require persons chargeable under the general law to send waggons and labour; and it was again enacted that, for extra work, such waggons and labour should be paid "according to the usual rate of the country." In order to furnish funds, the old system of tolls was revived. Collectors were to be appointed by the road surveyors, with power to levy, "for every horse, one penny; for every coach, sixpence; for every waggon, one shilling; for every cart, eightpence; for every score of sheep or lambs, one half-penny, and so in proportion for greater numbers; for every score of oxen or neat cattle, fivepence; for every score of hoggs, twopence"; but no person having once paid toll, and returning the same day with the same horse, coach, waggon, or other carriage, or with cattle, was to pay a second time.

Payment for waggons and labour.

Tolls.

Three places were appointed for collecting tolls, one in each county, at Wades-Mill, Hertford; Caxton, Cambridge; and Stilton, Huntingdon. Upon refusal to pay, a collector might distrain or detain the thing liable. Collectors were to account to surveyors; these to justices at Quarter Sessions; defaulters might be imprisoned till accounts were rendered. As the moneys collected would not raise a sufficient stock to pay for repairs, surveyors, with the justices'

Tolls to be mortgaged, or rates

levied to supply deficit.

assent, were authorized to mortgage tolls; and if money could not be so borrowed, a rate might be made at Quarter Sessions, and paid over to the surveyors. There were elaborate provisions for the effectual carrying out of these powers. Other clauses in favour of agriculture exempted occupiers or others, in specified localities, conveying "stones, sand, lime, or gravel, dung, mould, and compost of any nature or kind whatsoever, brick, chalk, or wood," and provided "that they and all carts, with hay or corn in the straw, at hay-time or harvest, ploughs, harrows, and other implements of husbandry, and all other things whatsoever, employed in the husbanding, stocking, and manuring of their several and respective lands, in the several and respective parishes, shall pass to and fro" free of toll. Soldiers on their march, and all persons riding post, were also exempted. The Act was to continue for eleven years, and if before that time the roads were sufficiently mended, all rates and tolls were to cease. In 1663, and following Sessions, private Acts were also passed providing for repairs of highways in the same counties.

General Act of 1670.

In 1670 Parliament again confessed the failure of general legislation. What was called "an additional Act" was passed in that year for better amending highways "now generally spoiled" by neglect as well as by an "unreasonable" loading of waggons and other carriages. Surveyors were enjoined to cause all Acts of Parliament relating to highways to be properly executed. More stringent provisions were also made with a view to prevent wear and tear by loaded waggons.[1] It was now enacted that, subject to the exceptions of 1663, waggons should not have "above five horse-beasts at length, and if any shall draw with a greater number of horses or oxen, they shall all draw in pairs, that is to say, two abreast." Instead of leaving assessments for repairs to be made by surveyors, justices at Quarter Sessions, if "fully satisfied" that highways,

[1] 22 Car. II. c. 12.

Exemptions in favour of husbandry.

causeways, or bridges in any parish, township, or hamlet within their jurisdiction would "not be sufficiently amended, repaired and supported by means of the laws now in force without help of this Act" might order a rate for this purpose to be laid upon all inhabitants rateable to the poor. As before, assessments were not to exceed "sixpence in the pound of yearly value" for real estate, and sixpence for every pound of personal estate.

In the legislation of 1663 sanctioning tolls on roads, there was a revival of powers not, indeed, new, but never before elaborated, or, indeed, clothed in statutory form, because previous tolls had generally been imposed only by royal licence, or by ordinance. Wearied, it may be, by its repeated failures to induce parochial and other authorities to charge the rates for adequate repairs, Parliament now tried this alternative method.

In the reign of William III. the system of tolls was extended by various statutes, which differed little from provisions already noticed. But the combined system of forced labour, and partial payment for such labour, was once more varied in an Act of 1695-6 for repairing highways between London and Harwich,[1] which required teams, waggons, and labour from all persons liable to furnish them, but provided that these services should be paid for according to the usual rate, instead of allowing merely for over-work. Another new provision was, that no person so liable should be compelled to travel above four miles from his dwelling-house, for the purpose of repairing a highway, or to work above two days in any one week, "nor at any time in seed time, hay time, or corn harvest." Receivers of tolls were to be appointed by justices at Quarter Sessions; the rates to be levied were specified; and for collecting them, "a turnpike[2] or otherwise," as the justices should determine,

Tolls and statute labour, Will. III.

Turnpikes set up.

---

[1] 7 & 8 Will. III. c. 9. See also c. 26 of the same session, for repairing roads between Wymondham and Attleborough, Norfolk.

[2] This is the first statutory mention of "Turnpike," which, according to Johnson, was originally a cross of two bars armed at the end with pikes, and turning on a pin, to prevent the passage of horses.

was to be set up in some convenient places between Brent-wood and Ingatestone, or near to Mountnessing. This Act was to continue for fifteen years unless the highways were sooner amended. During this period road surveyors, under order of Quarter Sessions, might borrow money secured on authorized tolls, paying six per cent. interest.

Loans secured by tolls.

At a later period most Acts relating to local roads contained recitals "that the ordinary course appointed by the laws" was not sufficient to provide for their repair, and that inhabitants of adjoining places were unable to do so. An Act for amending a road between Northfleet, Gravesend, and Rochester[1] extended, to five miles, the distance within which persons were required to furnish labour. As this road was very narrow, summary power was given to justices of Kent, at Quarter Sessions, to widen any part of it, so that the ground taken in did not exceed ten yards in breadth, that no house should be pulled down, and no part of any garden, orchard, court, or yard taken. Power was again given to surveyors, by order of Quarter Sessions, to mortgage tolls, paying interest at six per cent.

Road between North-fleet, Graves-end, and Rochester.

During the reigns of Queen Anne, George I. and George II., local Acts to maintain roads by tolls gradually increased in number. From the first they were unpopular, and in 1728 it was necessary to pass a general Act[2] against "ill-designing and disorderly persons" who "have in several parts of this kingdom associated themselves together, both by day and by night, and cut down, pulled down, burnt, and otherwise destroyed several turnpike gates and houses which have been erected by authority of Parliament for repairing divers roads by tolls, thereby preventing such tolls from being taken, and lessening the security of divers of her Majesty's good subjects for considerable sums of money which they have advanced upon credit of the said Acts, and deterring others from making like advances." Severe punishments were imposed upon offenders breaking down any turnpike: upon convic-

Unpopularity of turnpikes.

---

[1] 10 Anne, c. 16.   [2] 1 Geo. II. st. 2, c. 19.

tion, without discretion on the part of justices, they were to be sent for three months to the common gaol or house of correction, and also whipped at the market cross.

Before the last century closed, there arose a general desire to mend our roads by means of tolls, and to revive and apply throughout England and Wales, by private Acts, the legislation of 1663, itself a revival of ancient systems.[1] The

Extension of turnpike system.

[1] Between 1760 and 1774, a period of fourteen years, there were 452 local Acts for altering, widening and improving roads by means of tolls. In the sixteen years from 1785 to 1800, there were 643, and from 1800 to 1809, there were 419 such Acts, most of which constituted new turnpike trusts or continued old ones. But, owing to imperfect skill in road-making, even some early turnpikes earned maledictions from travellers like Arthur Young, who, in his Six Months' Tour (published in 1770), thus mentions a Wigan turnpike :— "I know not in the whole range of language terms sufficiently expressive to describe this infernal road." He cautions all travellers "to avoid it as they would the devil." "They will here meet with ruts, which I actually measured, four feet deep, and floating with mud from a wet summer; what, therefore, must it be after a winter?" Of a Warrington turnpike he speaks as "a paved road, most infamously bad; any person would imagine the people of the country had made it with a view to immediate destruction." Other turnpikes in northern England are condemned as strongly. Even so lately as the year 1833, when Sir Henry Parnell published his Treatise on Roads, he laments their grievous defects in England, though in Ireland, since an Act of 1763 which placed them under grand juries, roads were everywhere in good con-

dition. In the Scotch Highlands a similar result was secured by a Parliamentary Commission of 1803, under which Mr. Telford constructed 875 miles of road, and 1,117 bridges, the expense being defrayed in equal proportions by Parliamentary grants and local contributions. In 1815, Mr. Telford was also employed under a Parliamentary Commission for improving the Holyhead road, with a view to facilitate communication with Ireland. (See 55 Geo. III. c. 152, and 59 Geo. III. c. 30, which consolidated several local trusts into one body.) In 1830 a House of Commons' Committee reported (see App. IV. to Sir Henry Parnell's Treatise) that these Commissioners had received 759,718*l.*, of which sum 338,518*l.* was granted by Parliament, without any condition for repayment, for works in North Wales; and 394,114*l.* was granted by Parliament, or advanced on loan by the Exchequer Bill Loan Commissioners, towards building the Menai and Conway Bridges, making a new road across Anglesey, and improving the road between London and Shrewsbury. The Committee were of opinion that these works "afforded an example of road-making on perfect principles, and with complete success;" and they place on record "their high sense of the public and permanent benefit which has resulted from the unexampled exertions of Sir Henry Parnell, in discharging his duties as a Commis-

objects were, first, a better repair of roads; secondly, a shifting of part, at least, of the burden of maintenance from rate-payers who might not use them for vehicles, to persons who really did so use them. With increased trade, communication between town and town, and between town and country, grew more frequent, with need for better means of communication. There was no prophet to foretell that, just as the science of road-making was perfected, and travel behind well-appointed teams upon smooth macadamized ways became a delight, iron roads would supersede those of macadam, divert traffic, and inflict disastrous losses on all persons who had lent money to the new turnpike trusts. For the time, these trusts looked and were an unmixed public benefit. Parliament forwarded the good work with equal zeal and goodwill; and the result of its labours was that 1,116 trusts were created, 3,800 Turnpike Acts passed, and 22,000 miles of good turnpike roads were made, dotted by nearly 8,000 toll-houses, toll-gates or side-bars. In 1838, these turnpike roads cost 1,122,000*l.* a-year for repairs and management; the trusts had accumulated a debt of over nine millions; 84 trusts had paid no interest on loans for several years, and in several instances clamorous creditors had exercised their statutory power of seizing tolls, leaving no fund applicable for repairs or management.[1] But this decay of turnpikes was preceded by a period of usefulness and fair prosperity.

While each turnpike trust was the creature of a local Act, and subject to its special provisions, certain general rules embodied in public statutes applied to all turnpike roads.

Public Acts regulating turnpike roads.

In the reign of George II., no fewer than eleven general measures were passed regulating this new local legislation

sioner of the Holyhead road, and from the great skill displayed by Mr. Telford in overcoming the seemingly insuperable difficulty of erecting a bridge over the Menai Strait, and also in every other work which he has executed." Sir Henry was an honorary member of the Institution of Civil Engineers.

[1] Royal Commission on Roads, 1840; Report, p. 9. Com. Committee of 1839 on Turnpike Trusts, pp. 3, 4.

in small matters or in great. In the next reign public
measures of the same nature were still more plentiful; and
indeed, if trade was to prosper, no subject had stronger
claims on Parliament than that of improved communications.
An Act was passed in 1767 "to explain, amend, and reduce
into one" statute "the general laws now in being for regulating turnpike roads in this kingdom."[1] But in 1773 it
was found that existing laws for the general regulation of
turnpike roads were "in some respects ineffectual," and they
were accordingly again amended.[2] Similar discoveries of
defects requiring amendment continued to be made in every
succeeding reign.

Some provisions in these regulating statutes[3] may be
rapidly sketched. Road trustees, for example, required
a certain property qualification. County justices, through
whose jurisdiction a road passed, were ex-officio members
of the trust; licensed victuallers and retailers of intoxicat-
ing liquors were disqualified from acting. Trustees might,
under certain restrictions, purchase land for roads, and widen,
divert, and improve them, making use of private property,
and, as in the case of highways, taking materials from adjoining land. There were elaborate provisions relating to
meetings of the trustees, their clerks, treasurers, surveyors,
and other officers, and accounts. Where, through failure
of income, as too often happened, the obligation of the
parish for repairs revived, these accounts were open for
inspection by ratepayers,[4] a privilege from which, it is to be
feared, they seldom derived much practical benefit. Tolls
were generally regulated by breadth of wheels.[5] Wear and
tear of roads being also affected by weight of load, as well as

Appointment and powers of trustees.

Tolls.

---

[1] 7 Geo. III. c. 40. Before it came
5 Geo. III. c. 38, and 6 Geo. III. c. 43.

[2] 13 Geo. III. c. 84.

[3] Among them, in and after the
year 1822, were:—3 Geo. IV. c. 126;
4 Geo. IV. c. 95; 7 & 8 Geo. IV. c. 24;
9 Geo. IV. c. 77; 13 & 14 Vict. c. 79;
30 & 31 Vict. c. 121; 31 & 32 Vict.
c. 99; 34 & 35 Vict. c. 115; 40 & 41

Vict. cc. 64, 66. The Home Secretary's powers over turnpike roads
were transferred to the Local Government Board by 38 & 39 Vict. c. 55,
s. 343 (sched. 5, pt. 3).

[4] 30 & 31 Vict. c. 121, s. 5.

[5] 3 Geo. IV. c. 126, ss. 7-11; 4
Geo. IV. c. 95, ss. 5, 6, 10, 19.

by breadth of wheels, additional tolls were imposed for over-weight, and weighing machines therefore had to be provided at each toll-house.[1]

Exemptions.

Foot passengers were in no case charged with toll. Among many exemptions were horses and carriages of the Sovereign and Royal family, of soldiers, volunteers, and yeomanry, and of police. Following old statutes, another class of exemptions applied to implements of husbandry, horses employed in husbandry, the carriage of agricultural produce, cattle going to pasture, and, in certain cases, to waggons carrying manure or lime. Horses and carriages were free when conveying persons to or from church on Sundays, or to or from funerals, or when conveying ministers of religion engaged in ministerial duty.[2] A similar privilege attached to horses and carriages conveying materials for roads; or vagrants, prisoners, or mails; or persons to or from county elections. Trustees might lease tolls, and generally did so; they could reduce and afterwards advance tolls within the maximum imposed by their special Act, or

Toll-houses.

allow compositions for one year. Their toll-gates and toll-houses were exempted from rates, and one characteristic provision was that by residence in toll-houses collectors were not to gain a settlement,[3] an illustration of parochial watchfulness in 1823-4 against possible additions to poor-rates.

Loans were always raised by mortgage of the tolls allowed under local Acts.[4] In the early days of turnpike trusts, before railways diminished traffic on roads, and when mail and stage coaches, post-chaises, and private vehicles were the only means of inland transit, this security was thought good, and

Deficits in trust income.

money was easily found. With the railway period came a necessity for continued legislation, in order to supply deficits in income. It was then enacted that, if two-thirds

---

[1] Provisions on this head will be found in the two Acts last cited, and in 2 & 3 Will. IV. c. 124; 4 & 5 Will. IV. c. 81; and 2 & 3 Vict. c. 46.
[2] 3 Geo. IV. c. 126, ss. 32-3; 20 & 21 Vict. c. 81, s. 14.

[3] 3 Geo. IV. c. 126, s. 51; 4 Geo. IV. c. 95, s. 31.
[4] 14 & 15 Vict. c. 38; 24 & 25 Vict. c. 46; 38 & 39 Vict. c. 55, s. 343, sch. 5, pt. 3.

of the creditors assented, the Local Government Board, by provisional order, might reduce the rate of interest. Trustees and executors were also enabled to accept a composition for debts due.[1]

Parliament viewed with natural sympathy the increasing difficulties of turnpike trustees. In 1821, a Committee of the House of Commons recommended that all turnpike continuance Bills should be exempted from fees, then a heavy charge upon such measures. This recommendation was repeated by another Committee in 1827,[2] and was afterwards carried out by scheduling any continuations of expiring trusts in an annual public statute. With a view to economy and better management, a general consolidation of trusts was suggested by more than one Committee.[3] In 1839, the House of Commons appointed a committee to ascertain "how far the formation of railroads may affect the interest of turnpike trusts, and the creditors of such trusts." It required no particular acumen to discover that railway extensions "must seriously diminish the revenue" of turnpike trusts, which suffered also from steam vessels plying on rivers and as coasting traders. Even then transit by mechanical power afloat or on rail was cheaper than by animal power on roads ; and the Committee doubted whether trade would ever revert to its former channels.[4] Like their predecessors, they recommended unions of trusts, including all roads within a radius of fifteen miles. In the following year Royal Commissioners were appointed to make a similar investigation. Besides a consolidation of trusts, they advocated a State loan to pay

Parliamentary inquiries, 1821—1840.

[1] 16 & 17 Vict. c. 135, s. 5 ; 17 & 18 Vict. c. 58, s. 4.

[2] Com. Committee of 1827 on Turnpike Trust Renewal Bills.

[3] Lords' Committee, 1833 ; Com. Committee, 1836. This plan was adopted with excellent results in the case of metropolitan turnpike trusts north of the Thames, which were consolidated in 1827 by a public Act (7 Geo. IV. c. 142, amended by 10 Geo. IV. c. 59, and 26 & 27 Vict. c. 78.

All these Acts were repealed in 1871 by 34 & 35 Vict. c. 115, s. 13). Sir James McAdam, a well-known authority on road-making, was superintendent of these metropolitan roads in 1839. The highways of South Wales were also regulated by 23 & 24 Vict. c. 68. The Highway Act of 1835 (5 & 6 Will. IV. c. 50) did not apply to any turnpike or other road managed under a local Act.

[4] Report, p. 3.

off the whole debt of the trusts, at a fair valuation.[1]   But a Committee of the House of Commons had already suggested the expediency of abolishing turnpike tolls, and with an evident leaning that way, Parliament did not adopt any of the palliatives which were suggested.

Statute
labour.

Meanwhile the embarrassments of turnpike trusts had been seriously increased by public legislation. At common law, when a highway was out of repair, parishioners were bound to reinstate it by actual labour.[2] It will be seen that the common law was supplemented by repeated statutes, extending the area within which labour must be supplied, defining the terms of such supply, and adding to any available funds by assessments. Later Highway Acts allowed statute labour to be compounded for in money. Trustees of turnpike roads were also authorized to call for a portion of statute duty from parishes in aid of tolls; and in this case, too, a compulsory money payment was substituted. In 1835, however, the Highway Act[3] abolished forced labour on roads, and turnpike trustees lost from this source a revenue estimated by competent authority at 200,000l. a year.[4]

Limited duration of Turnpike Acts.

Following old precedents which have been quoted, all local Acts authorizing tolls had been passed for a limited period, generally twenty-one years, as an experiment, and with a view to secure a periodical revision of the powers of each trust; or in a vain hope that revenue would so far exceed outlay as to free the roads from debt during the specified term. From time to time these local Acts were continued as they were about to

Their gradual discontinuance after 1871.

expire; but in 1871, when turnpikes had been condemned as wasteful[5] and impolitic, the annual public statute, while con-

---

[1] Report, p. 11.

[2] Royal Commission of 1840; Report, p. 6.

[3] 5 & 6 Will. IV. c. 50.

[4] Com. Committee of 1839; Evidence of Sir James McAdam, p. 35. By 2 & 3 Vict. c. 81, turnpike trustees, in certain cases, were allowed for a short period to draw upon parochial funds to supplement tolls;

but this Act expired in 1841. In Scotland, statute labour was abolished, along with tolls and bridge-money, by the Roads and Bridges Act, 1878 (41 & 42 Vict. c. 51, s. 33), which provided that turnpike roads should become highways and be open free to all traffic.

[5] It was reckoned that every turnpike cost about 25l. annually. In

tinuing some, fixed short terms for the abolition of large numbers of trusts.[1] Along with this arrangement for a gradual discontinuance of tolls, there were provisions for the taking over of roads by highway and sanitary authorities; an assessment and apportionment of trust debts by the Local Government Board after request from highway authorities, who were authorized to borrow money for this purpose; and a rateable distribution of funds in hand among creditors.[2] In the course of another generation turnpikes will only survive as a name, but some account of the prominent place they once occupied in legislation, and of the great social and economic influence they exercised in this country for more than a century, was indispensable in these pages.[3]

Provision for debts.

Bridges were regarded as of even greater importance than roads, for the expense of maintaining them was part of that *trinoda necessitas* to which, by ancient law, every man's estate was subject, namely, *expeditio contra hostem, arcium constructio, et pontium reparatio*.[4] As a rule, unless

Bridges part of the trinoda necessitas.

some places the tolls proved insufficient to pay the staff of trusts; and in Norfolk, of 15,000*l.* a year collected by tolls, only 7,000*l.* was expended on roads.—Lords' Com. of 1881 on Highway Acts; Report, p. 20.

[1] 34 & 35 Vict. c. 115. This Act contains eleven schedules filled with the names of condemned trusts.

[2] 35 & 36 Vict. c. 85, s. 15; 36 & 37 Vict. c. 90, ss. 15, 16; 37 & 38 Vict. c. 95, s. 11; 39 & 40 Vict. c. 39, s. 10.

[3] As turnpikes were discontinued, the whole expense of maintaining roads fell upon ratepayers. In 1878 this charge was distributed over a wider area, and half the expense of disturnpiked and certain other roads was placed upon county rates. The Highway Act of 1862 (25 & 26 Vict. c. 61) authorized county justices to divide counties into districts for a more convenient management of highways. Several counties, however, have re-

sisted the formation of highway districts, preferring the old system of parochial management, which is a popular system, gives to parishioners the management of their own affairs, and secures economy by placing administration in the hands of those whose immediate interest it is to keep down rates. When a parish is merged in a larger area, a waywarden is not so attentive to economy, as he knows that his neighbours in other districts share the payment. At present, roads are managed under the parochial system (Act of 1835), the district system (Acts of 1862 and 1864), and a system partly permissive, partly compulsory, under the Act of 1878.—Report of Lords' Committee of 1881 on Highways.

[4] 1 Blackstone's Com. 357. The last of these duties, however, was often postponed in favour of the two former.

County or hundred liable.

individuals were liable to repair bridges *ratione tenuræ*, the obligation rested on counties or hundreds, but sometimes by prescription a parish was liable. In this case a statute of 1530-1[1] authorized agreements between counties and parishes for the execution of repairs by the former. At common law the liability of a county or hundred extended not only to bridges, but to roads over bridges and their approaches. Parishes, however, are now called upon to repair roadways over all bridges built since 1835, though counties are still subject to maintain " walls, banks, or fences of raised causeways and raised approaches to any bridge, or the land arches thereof."[2]

Ancient bridges made by distraints.

From the year 1297 numerous public statutes have been passed relating to bridges. The earliest provision for making them was by distraint, or levy, the necessity of this work being held to justify extraordinary measures. These levies were regarded with jealousy, and the great charter of 1297 provided that they should not be made indiscriminately : "No town nor freeman shall be distrained to make bridges or embankments but such as of old times and of right were bound to make them (*nisi qui ab antiquo et de jure facere debent*), in the time of King Henry our grandfather."[3] An impatience of local taxation, and a lively desire to avoid it, are by no means modern characteristics. But this was not the only hindrance to an effectual support of bridges, for in many parts of the realm, according to

Difficulty in proving obligation to maintain, 1530-1.

recitals in an Act of 1530-1, it could not " be known or proved what hundred, riding, wapentake, city, borough, town, or parish, nor what person certain or body politic " was bound to replace or maintain bridges, so that these often remained long in decay. It was therefore ordered that bridges situated outside the boundaries of cities and corporate towns should be made or maintained by inhabitants of the county or riding, or if within municipal limits, then by

[1] 22 Hen. VIII. c. 5.
[2] 5 & 6 Will. IV. c. 50, s. 21.
[3] 25 Edw. I. (Mag. Cart.), c. 15 (9 Hen. III. in Ruffhead).

inhabitants of those places. From this statute it also appears that the Court of Queen's Bench, upon information or indictment, had been accustomed to direct that bridges should be made or repaired by the responsible parties. This remedy, however, was cumbrous and expensive. Justices, therefore, in every shire, city, or borough, were authorized[1] to enquire and determine, at general sessions of the peace, as to "all manner of annoyances of bridges broken in highways to the damage of the King's liege people," and upon every presentment before them, to make like orders as the Court of King's Bench were wont to make, or as should seem in their discretion to be necessary, for a speedy repair of such bridges.

Charity aided in the construction of works, for want of which life was often lost and communication delayed. Lands were sometimes devised to keep up certain bridges, and an Act of 1671 conferred upon trustees of these lands power to lease and make the best of them.[2] In 1530-1, provision was made for the appointment of bridge surveyors, with allowances;[3] and upon them, as upon surveyors of highways, compulsory powers to obtain materials for repairs were then and afterwards conferred under certain conditions.[4] Several modern statutes gave to other bodies the ancient powers of the Sheriff's tourn as to presentments when highways or bridges were in flagrant disrepair.[5]

Lands devised for support of bridges.

Surveyors.

Presentments.

Notwithstanding many attempts by general legislation to maintain these essential links of communication, some examples of particular bridges now to be cited will show that the law, as for repairs of highways, was often appealed to in vain, and then bridge-tolls, or pontage, became indispensable, with the abuses to which grants of this nature were naturally exposed.

In early petitions from the Commons, preserved among the rolls of Parliament, there are repeated complaints of faulty

---

[1] 22 Hen. VIII. c. 5, s. 1.
[2] 22 Car. II. c. 12, s. 2; 14 Geo. II. c. 33.
[3] 22 Hen. VIII. c. 5, ss. 3, 6.
[4] 43 Geo. III. c. 59, s. 1; 54 Geo. III. c. 90; 55 Geo. III. c. 143, ss. 1-4; 5 & 6 Will. IV. c. 50, s. 22.
[5] 12 Geo. II. c. 29, s. 13; 53 Geo. III. c. 110, s. 2; 55 Geo. III. c. 143, s. 5.

Derwent and
Ribble
bridges.

Cockermouth
bridges car-
ried away by
floods.

Boston.

Windsor.

Division of
Holland in
Lincolnshire.

bridges. Thus, in the year 1302, inhabitants of Walton-en-la-Dale represented that certain bridges[1] over the rivers Derwent and Ribble were broken, and prayed the King to grant them a right of pontage for five years, presumably for the purpose of repairing these bridges. Their request was granted, the reply indicating that it was a matter to be dealt with by the King alone (*coram rege*).[2] A like petition in 1304, from burgesses of Cockermouth, asked the King for a grant of pontage, " ad reparationem trium pontium ejusdem burgi, qui asportati fuerant per cretinum aque ante Natale hoc anno."[3] A concession for five years was accordingly given to them (Fiat per quinquennium). On a petition from the Duke of Brittany and Earl of Richmond, rights of pontage were conceded to them for three years to repair a bridge at Boston.[4] In 1306, some poor inhabitants of Windsor alleged that their bridge was unfit for passage of carriages or horses (nimis est debilis, nam nulla carecta seu aliqui equi possint transire ibidem absque magno periculo). As no rents or other sure funds were applicable to repairs, the petitioners asked for pontage for eight years, but the King would only grant it for five.[5]

A bridge and causeway in the division of Holland, in Lincolnshire, was declared, in 1306, by the warden (custos pontis), whose name is not given, to be a source of great danger to passengers, through damage done by floods. He, therefore, begged the King to allow aid towards the cost of repairs by a toll to be levied on carts, horses and merchandize crossing the bridge (aliquod certum auxilium capiendum de carectis, equis et mercandisis). In reply, the King allowed pontage to be taken for seven years, but made the prior of Sempringham warden of the bridge, and charged him to make all necessary repairs.[6] The new warden proved no more efficient or trustworthy than his predecessor; for in

---

[1] The old spelling is brig, brigg, or brigge.

[2] 1 Rot. Parl. 154 ; 30 Edw. I.

[3] Ib. 160 ; 33 Edw. I.

[4] Ib. 165.

[5] Ib. 193 ; 35 Edw. I.

[6] Ib. 199 ; 35 Edw. I.

1330, certain men of Kesteven and Holland charged the prior with misappropriating tolls, and declared that he had removed several bridges from the causeway, so that no persons could now pass one way or the other, on horse or on foot, without risk of death, but had to hire boats, to their great cost and delay.[1] Therefore, the petitioners asked that good and sufficient auditors should be appointed to inspect the prior's accounts, during the time he had collected and received the tolls, and that any money found due from him upon this account should be applied in repairing the causeway and bridges. (Q'il pleise a notre Seigneur le roi et a son conseil ordiner que bons et suffisantz auditours soient assignez d'oir l'accompte le dit priour, de tut le temps q'il ad este coillour et receiviour des ditz paiages et custumes, et ce qe trove serra qe le dit priour devra sur cet accompte soit mis en amendement des ditz chausee et pontz.) To this a reply in Latin was given that certain trusty persons should be appointed to enquire into the petitioners' complaints, to take evidence, and to do, further, what justice demanded.

Alianora, widow of Henry Percy, stated, in 1315, that, as executrix of Sir Richard Arundel, she had undertaken the reconstruction of Wetherby Bridge, a work which Sir Richard had desired to complete as a benefaction. For want of this bridge many people and much cattle had perished, and there was great injury to trade. Lady Alianora prayed for pontage to help this good work, and Edward II. granted it for three years, on condition that upon enquiry no adverse interests were found.[2] In like manner, William de Latimer, lord of Jarmi, obtained a right to levy tolls for five years to renew a bridge across the Tees, connecting roads which led towards Scotland. This work was intended by William de Latimer for the repose of his wife's soul, and for common profit to all people passing (pur l'alme Madame sa Cum-

Marginal notes:
Alleged misapplication of tolls by prior of Sempringham.

Prayer for audit of accounts.

Wetherby bridge, A.D. 1315.

Bridge over Tees.

---

[1] 2 Rot. Parl. 32; 4 Edw. III.   [2] 1 Rot. Parl. 340.

paygne, qe est a Dieu comaundez, e pur comun profit des gentz passauntz).[1]

Commission of enquiry, 1314-15, as to bridges in Notts.

On petition from inhabitants of Nottinghamshire in 1314-15, a commission was appointed to enquire into their complaint that the Sheriff of Nottingham had applied to his own use fines and funds properly applicable to repairs of county bridges and causeways. Owing to this default the petitioners alleged that these bridges and causeways were broken and destroyed, to the great loss of people accustomed to use them, and a common danger. Three Commissioners, Edmund D'Eynecourt, John de Crumbewell, and Lambert de Trykingham, or any two of them (Edmund D'Eynecourt being one), were to examine this alleged default, and see that justice was done.[2]

The post of collector of tolls must have been one of some value, for a statute of 1467-8 [3] reserved all rights possessed by " our well-beloved Rauff Machon, squire of our household," under letters patent granting to him " the office of collector and receiver of custom and toll, to us growing by the passage over the brigge, called Newnham Brigge, beside our town of Calais, as well of men, as of beasts, goods, merchandizes, and of all manner of things, which over and under the said brigge should pass, for his life, with all manner of fees and rewards, in value twenty marks by year."

Engineers will be interested in a petition for a Bill, sanctioned in 1442, which contains the earliest statutory record of a draw-bridge for the passing of vessels.[4] In-

Turnbrigg, in Snaith parish, West Riding.

habitants of the counties of York, Lincoln, Nottingham, and Derby, " meekly beseech the wise and discreet Commons " in Parliament, concerning a timber bridge called Turnbrigg, in the parish of Snaith, in Yorkshire. This

[1] 1 Rot. Parl. 468 ; Annis incertis, Edw. I. and Edw. II.

[2] 1 Rot. Parl. 333 ; 8 Edw. II.

[3] 7 & 8 Edw. IV.; 5 Rot. Parl. 911.

[4] But in the fourteenth century old London Bridge was provided with a draw-bridge, and in 1334, pontage was exacted from merchants of Picardy for raising and drawing the bridge when their vessels passed with merchandize. Liber Albus (Rolls' Series), Int. p. 50.

bridge crossed a stream called the Dike, on which passed all manner of ships charged with wool, lead, stone, timber, victuals, fuel, and other merchandize. The bridge, however, was "so low, so near the stream, so narrow, and so strait in the arches, that there is, and of long time hath been, a right perilous passage, and oft times perishing of divers ships." At times, indeed, "there may no ships pass under this bridge by the space of half a year or more; and also a great part of the counties to the said river adjoining is yearly, by the space of twenty miles or more, surrounded with water, by cause of lowness and straightness of the bridge," to the great hurt and damage of the King in his customs and subsidies, and also of his merchants and other liege subjects. Considering the premises, therefore, the King was asked to grant to "the beseechers," by authority of Parliament, as follows:—

"That hit shall be lefulle to what sum ever person or persons of the seid shires that will at theire owne costages take away the seid brigge, and ther with and profites thereof, and in othir wise, newe edifie and bilde another brigge there, *Authority to build new bridge.* lengere in lengthe by the quantity of V yerdes called the Kynge's standard, and in hieght a yerd and a half by the same yerd higher than the seid brigge that standes ther nowe, as well for passage of all maner shippes comyng thereto, and voidance of water under the brigge, as for passage of man, best and cariage, over the newe brigge so to be made, with a draght lef[1] contenyng the space of IV *Drawbridge for passing ships.* fete called Paules fete in brede, for the voidyng thorough of the mastes of the shippes passinge under the newe brigg; and that every shipmen that wol passe under the seid brigg with their shippes may lawfully lifte up and close such lef att ther pleser; and that the mayster of evry shippe paie *Toll for raising the leaf.* for every liftyng of the seid lef Is. to the lord of the soille for the time beyng; and that no maner of person or persons her after lette nor stoppe the seid passage of ships or cours of water with stone, piles or any other disceyte in any wise in the water called Dike; and also that the shipmen passyng *Towing allowed on either bank.* by the seid streem or water myght have lawfully halyng and drayng be them or their servauntes with lynes, and to festyn their vesseles on the bankes and the grounde of

---

[1] A movable flap or leaf.

either partie of the Dike, like as thei have used of old tyme; and atte what tyme the brigge be so made, who sum ever will amend the seid newe brigge, that hit be repared and amended in the same lenght, hieght, and brede, with the seid lef, and who sum ever will make any otheir brigge ther, after that newe brigge so made, that they make hit of the same lenght, hieght, and brede, with a lef for to be opened in the forme aforeseid, as the same newe brigge shall be made; and that it be leful to the makers of the newe brigge to have free entry and issue, with their tymbre, cariage and other stuffe for the makyng of the seid newe brigge, opon the wast and the soille joynyng to the brigge. For the lofe of Godd and in waye of charite."

With the usual advice and assent of Lords and Commons, the King granted the prayer of this petition in all points (graunt tout le contenue en icell petition en toutz pointz).[1]

Exemptions from levy for making bridges. Sometimes we find exemptions pleaded from the general levy made upon surrounding property, for repairs of bridges. Thus, in 1335, the King's poor liege men living in the forest of Macclesfield, and there holding lands in his ancient demesne, in return for certain services, complained that bailiffs of the Earl of Chester had called upon them to contribute towards a levy for building Chester Bridge (un mise fait pur la fessour del pount de Cestr'), though the petitioners held no land from the Earl, and owed him no service, but, on the contrary, by their tenure upon part of the royal demesne within the forest, were relieved from all such levies and tolls.[2] From statements in this petition, certain lands in Cheshire were, it appears, "geldable,"[3] by ancient custom, for rebuilding the bridge: but these were lands in cultivation, and were liable at a time when there was no cultivated land within the forest of Macclesfield. The petitioners asked his Majesty to direct the justices of Chester that his heritage and demesne[4] should not be subjected to this charge without his express command. Accordingly, the Earl

[1] 5 Rot. Parl. 44; 20 Hen. VI.
[2] 2 Rot. Parl. 94; 9 Edw. III.
[3] *Ante*, I. p. 397 (n.).

[4] See Bacon's Abridgment, tit. Ancient Demesne, for an account of privileges and exemptions enjoyed under this tenure.

was ordered to enquire into this complaint, that justice might be done.

In 1383-4, a similar claim to exemption on behalf of Great Grandesden and Wells, county Huntingdon, was made by Edmund, Earl of March, who held those places in right of his wife. Great Grandesden and Wells formed part of the manor of Gloucester, which, with all towns and tenants belonging thereto, had, time out of mind, enjoyed freedom from toll, pontage, passage-money, and all other dues in the kingdom (est quite de tolnen, pontages, passages et toutes autres custumes parmy le roialme d'Engleterre, et ad este de temps dont il n'y ad memorie). Nevertheless, process had been taken out in the King's Bench against tenants in these places to contribute towards re-making Huntingdon Bridge, contrary to their immunity and franchise, and against the rights of the earl, who therefore prayed his Majesty and the Lords of Parliament to put a stop to such process, or grant some other remedy. This Bill, or petition, was sent into Chancery with directions that right should be done.[1]

Huntingdon bridge, exemption from aid to rebuild.

An order was made by the King in Parliament, in the year 1339, upon petition by the prior of St. Neot's, that good and loyal men should be appointed to survey a bridge and causeway there, broken and carried away by floods, and to enquire who was bound to renew and maintain the same, and what the work would cost, and to return their report into Chancery (de combien le pount et le chauce purront estre refaitz et repasaillez; et ceo q'ils aueront trove, face retourner en la Chauncellerie).[2]

Commission of enquiry, A.D. 1339.

Another plan for a better maintenance of bridges was suggested in 1376 by inhabitants of Nottingham, and the counties of Lincoln and Derby. They represented that a bridge across the Trent, called Heybeth-Brigg, had no funds applicable for its maintenance, and depended on

Proposed incorporation of wardens for bridge across Trent.

[1] 3 Rot. Parl. 177.   [2] 2 Rot. Parl. 111; 13 Edw. III.

voluntary and charitable offerings. It was then in so ruinous a condition that many lives were lost in attempts to cross the river, people mounted being drowned, both man and harness, as well as those in carts. They, therefore, prayed the King in Parliament to grant them letters patent appointing two wardens, one for the county, the other for the town of Nottingham, with perpetual succession, and power to receive gifts of lands, tenements, and rents, to be applied in maintaining the bridge. This proposal was not allowed, the King's answer being, "Le roi se ent adviser."[1]

Rochester bridge, 1391.

Rochester bridge, spanning the Medway on the highway between London and Dover, was naturally one of the chief structures of this kind in England. Special provision was made for its maintenance in very early times; and in 1391, during certain proceedings in Parliament, an obligation of this nature is mentioned which dated beyond memory, and attached to certain persons, towns, and districts in Kent. In 1391, Robert Knokes and John of Cobham petitioned the King and his Council in Parliament on the subject of a new bridge, reciting this ancient obligation, which required all persons and places charged with the duty of maintenance to appoint two bridge-wardens. But to uphold the ancient bridge had been found so heavy a burden upon the persons and places responsible that they were well-nigh crushed under it (q'ils sont bien pres destruitz et aniantez). By a great depth of salt water and rough waves around its piers, the bridge was then nearly destroyed, and there was no hope of restoring it. Moved by the great loss and danger to all persons crossing from Strood to Rochester, the two petitioners had, at their own great cost, built a new bridge of stone, near the site of the old bridge. This new bridge, in course of time, would need repair, and they asked the King that these repairs should be borne by persons and places now responsible for

Ancient obligation to maintain.

New bridge of stone.

---

[1] 2 Rot. Parl. 350; 50 Edw. III.

the old bridge. Further, in consideration of insufficient means at their disposal, the two wardens should be autho- Incorporation of wardens. rized to receive and hold any lands, tenements, or rents devised to them by will for the support of the bridge, up to an annual value of five hundred marks, the laws of mortmain notwithstanding, with power to them and their successors to sue and be sued.[1]

This petition was "read in full Parliament," and the King, with assent of Parliament, granted all that was asked for, except that the annual value of lands to be held by the wardens was reduced from five to three hundred marks. There must, however, have been some demur to this transfer of the charge, or some doubt of its validity, for, six years afterwards, in 1397, the Commons represented to Richard II. Petition of 1397. that the ancient bridge at Rochester was formerly of wood (estoit nadgairs faitz de maeresme);[2] but a new bridge of stone had been built on a safer site (le dit pount est fait de nouvel de pere, et en un meilleur et pluis seure lieu q'il estoit devant). They, therefore, prayed that all persons in Kent, who owed rent or were bound by any custom, prescription, or duty (qi feurent tenuz ou devoient ascun rente, custumes, prestation, ou autre duete), to repair and maintain the ancient bridge, should be bound to pay in like proportion towards the new bridge; a just and reasonable prayer which the King at once granted (Quele prier semble au roy juste et resonable, et ad ottroie a la priere avant dit).[3] In 1421 an Act was passed confirming letters Letters patent confirmed by Act, 1421. patent of Richard II. to this effect, and incorporating the wardens of the new bridge, with a common seal and perpetual succession.[4]

In 1485 an Act was passed for enabling inhabitants of the Isle of Thanet to build a bridge at Sarre Ferry. The preamble shows the care with which special legislation was

---

[1] 3 Rot. Parl. 289–90; 15 Rich. II.
[2] Mireame, or maeresme, was the Norman word for timber.
[3] 3 Rot. Parl. 354; 21 Rich. II.
[4] 4 Rot. Parl. 149; 9 Hen. V.

watched at this period, and also records some physical changes which have occurred in the Isle [1] :—

Forasmuch as the Isle of Tenet (*sic*), in the county of Kent, lying upon the high sea on the east and north parts thereof, and to the river of salt water leading from a place called Northmouth, joining the sea, to a place within the shire called Sarre, and from thence to the town and haven of Sandwich, and so forth to the sea on the west and south parts of the isle, out of time of mind, hath been enclosed and environed with the sea and river; at which place, called Sarre, by all this time, hath been had and used a passage, and a ferry, called Sarre ferry, over the said river, by a ferry boat, out of the isle into the country of the shire of Kent, for all manner of persons, beasts, corn, and other things, to pass and be conveyed at all seasons, to and from the same isle and country; by which same ferry also, when enemies afore this time have arrived, and purposed to have arrived in the isle, the people of the same country lightly have been conveyed and might be conveyed into the isle to resist all such enemies for defence and tuition [2] of the isle. It is so now that, by change of the course of the sea, which hath fortuned in years

late passed, the river at the place called Sarre, where the ferry and passage was had and used, is so swared, [3] grown, and highed with wose, [4] mud, and sand, that now no ferry or other passage may be there, nor in any other place nigh adjoining and convenient, to or from the isle, by boat or otherwise, but only at high spring floods, and that not passing an hour at a tide, to the great hurt and impoverishing of the possessioners, landholders, owners, and inhabitants of the isle and country, and by likelihood in time of war great jeopardy and fear of loss of the isle, if enemies should fortune to arrive in the same."

Considering the premises, and "intending the common weal, tuition, safeguard, and defence of every part of this his realm," the King, with assent and authority from Parliament, empowered the inhabitants of Thanet to build a

bridge at Sarre Ferry, " of such reasonable length, height, and large space between the arches thereof, that boats and lighters

---

[1] 6 Rot. Parl. 331 ; 1 Hen. VII.

[2] Here used in its primary meaning of protection.

[3] Probably meaning sluggish, from

the A.-S. swær, heavy; the current not being strong enough to prevent silting.

[4] Silted up with ooze, &c.

may pass to and fro under the same, at any time hereafter
when the water may happen to increase and be sufficient"
for their passage. After the bridge was completed, the
Chancellor was directed to appoint Commissioners who Commissioners to pre-
pare scheme
of assessment
for maintain-
ing bridge.
should make provision for repairs and maintenance of the
bridge and approaches, but no lands were to be charged
except those in Thanet, and only inhabitants of the isle.
At any future time the Chancellor might appoint other
Commissioners, being justices, to discover means of restoring the haven; and if these Commissioners found that it Bridge to be
removed if
found to inter-
fere with
haven.
injured the haven, they might even order that the bridge
should be removed.

Ferries were subjects of similar complaints to those made Ferry across
the Humber.
respecting tolls upon roads and bridges. In 1314-15, the
Commons petitioned the King in Parliament to abate certain
extortionate dues levied at the ferry across the Humber,
between Barton and Hessle, such dues amounting to double
those which had usually been paid for horse and foot passengers. Enquiry and redress were ordered in this case.[1]

[1] 1 Rot. Parl. 319; 8 Edw. II.

CHAPTER VIII.

WATER SUPPLY OF LONDON :—THE CITY CONDUITS : WATER-
WORKS AT LONDON BRIDGE : THE NEW RIVER.

Early sources of supply.

BEFORE the year 1235-6 London drew ample stores of water from streams flowing near to or within the city bounds. Then, and till a much later period, the river-side population found in "silver" Thames a pure and abundant beverage. In more distant streets, sources more accessible were at hand. Such were the brooks and bournes, the names of which still survive in Walbrook, Holborn (formerly Oldebourne), and Langbourne. Besides

Wells and streams

running streams, Fitz-Stephen,[1] the earliest historian of London, in his often-quoted description of the city, written during the latter half of the twelfth century, mentions with enthusiasm the sweet, wholesome and clear springs rising in its northern suburbs : " Sunt etiam circa Londoniam ab Aquilone suburbani fontes præcipuæ, aqua dulci, salubri, perspicua, et ' per claros rivo trepidante lapillos.' " Among them he refers to Holy Well, Clerken Well, and St. Clement's Well (" fons sacer, fons clericorum, fons sancti Clementis "), then much visited by scholars and city youths in their walks on summer evenings. Stow says that in his time " every street and lane " had " divers fair wells " and springs, which served the city with " sweet and fresh water."[2] He also speaks of Flete river, or river of the Wells, so named in a charter granted by William the Conqueror to the college of St. Martin-le-Grand, and once navigable to Oldbourne bridge.[3]

[1] Stephanides, or Fitz-Stephen, was a monk of Canterbury, and wrote a biography of Thomas-à-Becket.

[2] Survey, p. 8. Stow's " Survey " was written in 1598. The references in the text are to an edition of 1633.

[3] Stow, p. 9.

As its population "mightily increased," streams within the city became foul, and citizens were "forced to seek fresh waters abroad."[1] In London, as in other cities, the obligation of furnishing water, and of furnishing it gratuitously, rested on the corporation. Accordingly, in the reign of Henry III., they obtained leave to construct conduits,[2] bringing water from the Tyburn, at Paddington. **The Tyburn.** Royal letters patent, bearing date 1236, set forth that this grant was "for the profit of the city, and good of the whole realm thither repairing: to wit, for the poor to drink, and the rich to dress their meat."[3] Many small conduits existed in various thoroughfares; but, according to Stow, the first cistern of lead, castellated with stone, in the City of London, called the Great Conduit in West Cheap, was begun to be built in 1285.[4] Into this open fountain, or cistern, was brought water from the Tyburn. From the same brook the monks at Westminster were supplied by pipes. In 1432, Tyburn water was taken to another point in the city, at the expense of Sir John Wells, Mayor; in 1438 it was carried from the same source into Fleet Street and Aldermanbury by Sir William Eastfield, Mayor; and streams at Highbury were brought into Cripplegate.[5] Such gifts, or benefactions, were not then uncommon. They distinguished a term of office, or were offered in charity; and there

[1] Stow, p. 11.

[2] In early writings and records, "conduit" is used in a double sense, meaning both the channel through which the water passed, and the stand-pipe or fountain at which it was made to stream forth for public use.

[3] Stow, p. 11. These quaint terms in the grant often recur in subsequent documents alluding to the Tyburn source of supply. (See *post*, pp. 41, 60).

[4] The Great Conduit of 1285 was situated at the west end of the present Poultry. There was an earlier conduit in Cheapside, for we read in the Anglo-Norman Chronicles of London (p. 237): — "This year (1273-4) came King Edward I. and his wife from the Holy Land; and were crowned at Westminster on the Sunday next after the Feast of the Assumption of Our Lady (August 15): and the conduit in Chepe ran all the day with red wine and white wine to drink, for all such as wished."

[5] Survey, p. 12.

could be no better work of charity than one which increased the common stock of pure and wholesome water, free to every citizen.

City records[1] mention Tyburn conduit in the year 1237, when a convention or compact was entered into between the citizens of London and merchants of Amiens, Corby, and Nesle, in Picardy. Until then these merchants had not the privilege of landing their merchandize, and could only sell it on board their vessels. Under the compact of 1237 they were allowed to unload, and warehouse within the city, their cargoes of woad,[2] garlic, and onions, and

100l. paid towards Tyburn conduit by Picardy merchants.

[1] There have been irreparable losses of civic books and records in London. Lord Protector Somerset, a bold robber, "borrowed," in 1552, three cartloads, never to be returned. Cotton, the antiquary, was an ungrateful and no less impudent pilferer, blazoning his shame by placing his coat of arms on the volumes he appropriated. But a French historian (M. Jules Delpit, "Collection Générale des Documents Français en Angleterre," p. 61) is still able to say, that "no city in the world possesses a collection of archives so ancient and so complete as the collection at Guildhall." Happily, it may be added, through the public spirit and liberality of the Corporation, no city has made its records more accessible to students. Quotations in this and the following chapters are from :—(1) Liber Custumarum (A.D. 1154–1171) compiled about the year 1320. (2) Liber Albus, compiled in 1419. These two works form part of the Rolls' Series. (3) An Analytical Index to civic records known as the Remembrancia, consisting of nine MS. volumes of correspondence, covering the period from 1579 to 1664. This index has been published, with valuable notes, by the Guildhall Library Committee, under the authority of the Corporation. The well-known office of Remembrancer was created in 1570. (4) Riley's Memorials of London Life from A.D. 1276 to 1419, founded on the Letter-books of the Corporation for this period. These letter-books commence about 140 years before the journals of the Common Council, which date from 1416. (5) The same author's translation of the Anglo-Norman "Croniques de Londres." The originals of the earlier records are in mediæval Latin or Norman-French. All inquirers into the social and municipal history of ancient London owe a deep debt of gratitude to the late Mr. H. T. Riley, of the Inner Temple, who edited the Rolls' Series, entitled "Londoniensis," and whose unwearied industry and great learning are conspicuous in every page of the volumes above mentioned.

[2] At this period, and indeed long previously, woad was largely imported from Picardy and the Hanse towns. By public enactments it was to be the only medium employed for dyeing woollen cloths blue-black. (Liber Albus, Int. 88).

to sell the same within the city, and to carry them beyond
the city by land or by water. For these and other privileges
the merchants, besides an annual payment of fifty marks,
gave 100*l*. towards the Tyburn conduit, which was then
in course of building (cent livres desterlings au conduyt
del ewe de la funtayne de Tybourne amener en la cite de
Loundre).[1]

A conduit in the Ward of Chepe is mentioned in the
Coroner's roll of the City of London, A.D. 1278.[2] Whether
each conduit had its keeper does not appear. Such an officer
was appointed to take charge of the Great Conduit; and in
1310 he was required to take oath that he would "well and
trustily, with the greatest diligence, cause the conduit to be
kept so that neither brewers nor fishmongers shall waste
the water thereof, nor will he sell the water to any one,
by night or by day, on pain of losing his freedom."[3] This
oath must mean that he would not take fees or sell water
for his private profit; for it appears by an entry in the city
letter-books, A.D. 1312, that the keeper of the conduit, with
two other persons, "were sworn before the Mayor and Aldermen to receive from brewers, cooks, and fishmongers the
moneys which, at their discretion, upon such brewers, cooks,
and fishmongers they shall assess, for the easement which
they have from water of the conduit in Chepe. And such
moneys they will trustily expend on the repair and maintenance thereof; and on being requested will give a faithful
account."[4] At this period, therefore, though supplies for
domestic use were free, a charge was made for water used
for trade purposes. Three keepers were sworn in 1325, and
keys of the conduit were delivered to them, from which we
may infer that the supply was restricted within certain
hours. Some months afterwards two of these keepers were
removed, for no cause assigned, and others appointed in

Marginal notes: The Great Conduit in Chepe. — Keepers of the conduit, oath taken by. — Charge for water used for trade purposes.

[1] Liber Custumarum, pp. 64-66.
[2] Riley's Mem. p. 14.
[3] Ib. pp. 77-78; 4 Edw. II.
[4] Ib. p. 107.

their stead.[1]   One item in the Chamberlain's accounts, A.D. 1329, is "for cleansing and repairing the springs"; probably those of Tyburn supplying the conduit.[2]

In the Liber Albus there are several entries between the years 1309-16, and subsequently, showing that the city brewers, who must have been numerous, took so much water from the Great Conduit that the supply of their fellow-citizens ran short.[3]   We find specific complaint made to the Mayor, Sheriffs, and Aldermen, in 1337, by John de Snefield, Thomas Kesteven, and other neighbours dwelling around Cheap, "that the commonalty of the city cannot be served with water from the conduit as it used to be served, because that men who keep brew-houses in the streets and lanes near the conduit send day after day, and night after night, their brewers with their vessels called 'tynes,' and make the ale which they sell with the water thereof; and so in like manner they make malt with the same water, to the loss of the commonalty."   Therefore, the complainants asked "that this common damage may be corrected, and the conduit from henceforth kept for the public good, as of old it used to be kept."   Further we read that "talk and converse being had hereon, order was given in full court by the Mayor, Sheriffs, and Aldermen, that if in future any such vessel as those aforesaid should chance to be brought to be filled at the conduit, the keepers should not allow it to be taken away, but retain it in their own possession for the benefit of the conduit."[4]   In the same year the keepers account for 6l. 6s. 6d. received as quittances, &c., for tynes and tankards.[5]

Complaint of excessive supply to brewers, A.D. 1337.

[1] Riley's Mem. p. 149.

[2] Ib. p. 177.

[3] I. Liber Albus, 582 et seq. Ordinatio quod brasiatores non consumant aquam conductus.

[4] Letter-book of Corporation, 11 Edw. III.; Riley's Mem. p. 200.

[5] Tynes were large tubs. Tankards were smaller tubs or pails, used by the London water-carriers, and holding about three gallons; they were shaped large at the bottom, narrowing to the mouth, and were fitted with an iron handle.   In 1276, the Coroner's roll of the city recorded an inquest on Henry Grene, water-carrier, drowned in the Thames at the hythe of Castle Baynard, in

These restrictions did not deter the brewers, for, in 1345, Further complaints, A D. 1345. "it was shown by William de Iford, Common Serjeant, on behalf of the commonalty, that whereas of old a certain conduit was built in the midst of the City of London that so rich and middling persons therein might have water for preparing their food, and the poor for their drink : the water aforesaid was now so wasted by brewers and persons keeping brew-houses and making malt, that in these modern times it will no longer suffice for rich and middling, or for poor persons, to the loss of the whole community. And for avoiding such common loss it was by the Mayor and Aldermen agreed, the commonalty assenting thereto, that such brewers, or persons keeping brew-houses or making malt, shall in future no longer presume to brew or make malt with water from the conduit. And if any one hereafter shall presume to make ale with the water of the conduit, or to make malt with the same, he is to lose the tankard or tyne with which he shall have carried water from the conduit, and 40*d.* the first time, to the use of the commonalty ; the tankard or tyne, and half a mark, the second time ; and the third time he is to lose the tankard or tyne, and 10*s.*, and further he is to be committed to prison, at the discretion of the Mayor and Aldermen there to remain."[1]

It is probable that, in spite of these ordinances, the city authorities were loth to lose the revenue derived from brewers and other tradesmen for water. An account rendered by keepers of the Great Conduit, in 1350, shows that water was still supplied for trade purposes, and that the following payments were received "to the use of the conduit" :— "From the house of Cecily Foune, for two years, 11*s.* 8*d.* ; Assessment on houses for water for trade purposes. from the house of Thomas Beater, for two years, 13*s.* 4*d.* ; from the house of John Albon in the Poultry, for two years,

---

attempting to fill his tankard. (Riley's Mem. p. 6.)   :

[1] Letter-book of Corporation, 19 Edw. III. ; Riley's Mem. p. 225.

10s.; from Roger Brewer, at Mayden-en-la-hope,[1] one year empty, 6s. 8d.; from the house of Simon the founder, one year empty, 5s.; from the house of Maiot, the brew-wife, one year empty, 6s.; from the house of John Goby in the Poultry, for one year, 6s. 8d.; from Roger atte Broke, for the first year, 6s. 8d.; from Patrick Leddred, for the first year, 6s. 8d.; from the house of Dame Cecily Wrastelyng-worthe, for one year, 5s. Total, 3l. 17s. 8d. Also, received for tankards of persons whose names are unknown, 11l. 15s. 4d." Then the names of three persons in the Poultry and three in Chepe are returned as defaulters. An account of ex-

Repairs of conduit.

penditure includes the following items:—"For repairing the fountain head, 33s. 6d.; examining the conduit when it was slandered for poison (esclandre de poyson), by com-mand of the mayor, 32s. 2d." There are various jobs of mending pipes; cleansing and washing the fountain-head; closing and opening the conduit,[2] and candles; hire of two vadlets twenty-four days to collect the money for the tan-kards, the vadlets[3] receiving sixpence per day; hire of a house for putting the tankards in, for one year, 10s.; paid for two irons for stamping the tankards, 2s. 6d.[4]

Brewers, &c. supplied, A.D. 1415.

It appears from a later record, in 1415, that brewers, and other traders requiring a large supply of water, rented the fountain and upper pipe of the great conduit. Com-plaint was again made that "they do draw water for their brewing out of the pipes that run below in the conduit, whereby the common people are oftentimes greatly impeded." It was therefore ordained "that no one of the brewers or other persons who rent the fountains and great upper pipe of

[1] Sign of the Maid in the Hoop. It may be inferred from this account that there was an assessment on the houses of brewers and other persons using water in trade, as well as a payment for tankards filled from the conduit for the same purpose.

[2] It was probably closed and locked up at night.

[3] Vadlets, vadlette; a term used both in the Liber Custumarum and Liber Albus; a groom or serving-man: hence varlet and valet.

[4] Letter-book of Corporation, 24 Edw. III.; Riley's Mem. p. 264.

the conduit shall from henceforth draw any water from the small pipes below on pain of paying to the Chamber of the Guildhall 6s. 8d. every time that he shall be lawfully convicted thereof."[1]

. Pipes conveying water to the Great Conduit were laid from Tyburn to Constitution Hill, thence to "the Mews"[2] near Charing Cross, and afterwards through the Strand and Fleet Street. As the pipes were exposed at certain points, they were sometimes broken by frost or accident, and the water then caused great damage. Complaint to this effect was made to the Mayor and Aldermen in the year 1388, by inhabitants of Fleet Street, who alleged that "the water found its way into their houses, and flooded their cellars." They urged that the pipes should be covered, so as to protect them from fracture; and they were allowed to furnish such covering[3] at their own costs and charges, on condition of its removal if it were found at any time to injure the aqueduct.[4] Probably the pipes which burst were those at the spot at which water was drawn, as these would necessarily be above ground. This conjecture is strengthened by the fact that "the good men of the neighbourhood" only received permission to make a pent-house at a given point of the aqueduct, namely, "opposite to the house and tavern" "of John Walworthe, vintner, which are situate near to the hostel of the Bishop of Salisbury."[5] The covering thus made to the conduit in Fleet Street must have had some architectural pretensions, for a licence to add a pinnacle was granted by the Corporation towards the end of the 14th century.[6]

Course of channel from Tyburn to Cheapside.

---

[1] Letter-book, 3 Hen. V.; Riley's Mem. p. 617.

[2] The royal stables, where also the King's falcons were "mewed" or confined.

[3] Aventum, in modern French auvent, which Mr. Riley translates pent-house. (Mem. p. 503.)

[4] Letter-book of Corporation, 11 Rich. II.

[5] This inn, or London house of the Bishops of Salisbury, stood on the site of Salisbury Court, Fleet Street. (Riley's Mem. p. 504, n)

[6] Concessio erectionis Pinnaculi conductus de Flete-strete. (Liber Albus, I. 686)

New conduit
provided by
ward of Far-
ringdon
Within.

While the Corporation were responsible for a supply of water, supplemental works were occasionally made at the expense of a portion of the citizens. Thus, in 1390, certain "substantial men of the ward of Farndone (Farringdon) Within, and other citizens of London, for the common advantage and easement, at their own costs and charges," proposed " to make and build a water conduit near to the church of St. Michael-le-Quern, in the West-chepe of London, supplied by the great pipe of the conduit."[1] They therefore asked leave of the Mayor and Aldermen, who consented, providing that the intended work should not injure the Great Conduit; and the reputable men who thus applied gave security that the work should be removed if found harmful.

The Thames
as a source of
supply.

Water car-
riers and
carters.

Besides the city conduits, the Thames was a never-failing source of supply, and its waters were largely used.[2] A numerous body of men, the water-carriers,[3] performed useful and necessary functions by filling their tankards from the conduits or river, and supplying the houses of citizens for a small remuneration. There were also carts which conveyed water in greater quantities from the Thames.

[1] Letter-book of Corporation, A.D. 1390; Riley's Mem. p. 521.

[2] In one year (1325–1326) of great drought, we read in the Anglo-Norman Chronicles of London (p. 261) that, "for want of fresh water, the tide from the sea prevailed to such a degree that the water of the Thames was salt; so much so that many folks complained of the ale being salt." Perhaps this complaint may explain the brewers' eagerness to be supplied with fresh spring water from the Great Conduit. Unless care were taken to take water from the river at certain states of the tide only, a similar complaint might be justly made at any season.

[3] The water-carriers, or tankard-bearers, had a guild, with a hall in Bishopsgate Street; their "rules, ordinances and .statutes, made by the rulers, wardens, and fellowship of the Brotherhood of St. Christopher, of the water-bearers of London," are dated October, 1496. See their petition against the laying-on of pipes or "quills" of water to private dwellings, *post*, p. 61. As the supply grew scarce, or the demand increased, there were frequent disputes among the "cobs," as these water-carriers were called, for precedence in filling their tankards; and the Lord Mayor forbade them to take clubs and staves, with which they sometimes enforced their claims.

In the city ordinances made after the year 1275, but probably before the Great Conduit in Cheapside was opened, there is a regulation that for carts taking water from Dowgate or Castle Baynard to Cheap the charge should be three half-pence; if they went beyond Cheap, twopence; if they stopped short of Cheap, one penny farthing[1] (Item, charette[2] qe meisne ewe de Dowegate a Chepe, preigne 1 denier obole; de Chastal Baynarde a Chepe, 11 deniers; et sils ne veignent mye a Chepe, 1 denier quart). In 1342 complaint was made to the Mayor and Aldermen that, when the tide served for fetching water from the Thames, various lanes and passages leading thereto were blocked by persons claiming a right of way, who demanded a toll from water-carriers and others. At this period, the land water, when not disturbed by freshets, must have been tolerably pure. Thames salmon were plentiful, and in the year 1390 we find the citizens complaining in Parliament that, owing to dams and weirs, salmon could no longer, as in the reign of Edward III., be bought in London for sixteen, eighteen, or twenty pence apiece, and the best for two shillings.[3]

Various civic ordinances and enactments in Parliament at this period tend to destroy our faith in the general purity of the river and its fitness for drinking. The Corporation did what they could to prevent pollution by repeated but ineffectual orders that refuse should not be thrown into its waters.[4] Edward III. wrote in most peremptory terms to the Mayor and Sheriffs, A.D. 1357, pointing out the dangers of pestilence from accumulations of filth

Pollution of the Thames.

[1] Liber Albus, I. p. 730.

[2] Whence chariot, from the Gaelic "carruca." In Tyndale's and other old versions of the Bible, instead of "waggons" (Num. vii. 3) we find charettes.

[3] 3 Rot. Parl. 282; 14 Rich. II.

[4] See, however, in Liber Albus, 270, a remarkable civic edict, in the reign of Edw. I., forbidding barber-surgeons, under penalties, to attract customers by exposing in their windows blood taken from patients, and requiring them to dispose of it by carrying it privately to the Thames (et qe nul barbier ne soit si ose ne si hardy qil mette sank en lour fenestres en apiert ou en view des gentz; mais pryvement le facent porter a Thamise).

on the river banks.[1] In 1345, the Mayor and Aldermen themselves, at a congregation held in Guildhall, found that Thames water in Dowgate Dock "had become so corrupted" by filth thrown there that water-carriers accustomed to fill their tankards from this dock "were no longer able to serve the commonalty, to their great loss." Orders were,

Penalties for casting refuse into the river. therefore, given for cleansing the dock.[2] Again, in 1357, the Corporation ordered "that no man shall take, or cause to be carried, any manner of rubbish, earth, gravel, or dung, from out of his stable or elsewhere, to throw and put the same into the rivers of Thames and Flete, or into the fosses around the city walls; and as to refuse that is found in streets and lanes, the same shall be carried and taken elsewhere out of the city by carts, as heretofore, or else by the rakyers (street-sweepers) to certain spots, that the same may be put into dung-boats (donge-botes), without throwing anything into the Thames, for avoiding the filthiness that is increasing in the water and upon the banks of the Thames, to the great abomination and damage of the people. And if any one shall be found doing to the contrary hereof, let him have the prison for his body, and other heavy punishment as well, at the discretion of the Mayor and Aldermen."[3] Similar orders were made in 1375.

Ordinance in Parliament, A.D. 1392-3. An ordinance of Parliament, made in 1392-3 on a petition from the citizens, would not promote purity in the Thames.[4] Owing to complaints of nuisance a few years previously, London butchers had then been forbidden to kill, within the city or certain defined limits, any cattle or other stock (grosses bestes, veeles, berbys,[5] ne porkes). The citizens represented that great inconvenience had been caused by this prohibition, and prayed that the Mayor and Aldermen might be allowed to appoint a suitable place within the city

[1] *Post*, p. 244.
[2] Letter-book of Corporation, 19 Edw. III.; Riley's Mem. p. 222.
[3] Ib., 31 Edw. III.; Riley's Mem.

p. 299.
[4] 3 Rot. Parl. 282; 14 Rich. II.
[5] Berbrees, or berbets (brebis), was the old Norman word for sheep.

for slaughtering, and for removing offal (pur l'occasion des bestes sus ditz, et pur la voidance des fimes, fetures, issues, et entrails). In reply, Richard II. ordered that a slaughter-house should be built on the Thames bank near the house of Robert de Paris, and that butchers should carry thither the offal of all beasts killed by them in the city, and should there cut it up into small pieces, and cast it into the middle of the river, taking it in boats at the commencement of ebb-tide.[1] On the other hand, by the same ordinance, all filth and rubbish (fymes, ordures, mukes, rubbouses, ou lastage) on either bank of the river between Westminster and the Tower of London was to be removed before the feast of Pentecost, and was on no account to be thrown into the river between the two points mentioned, under a penalty of four pounds.

Butchers' offal thrown into river.

In one instance a great conventual house within the city walls provided a water-supply of its own. In the year 1432, the prior and convent of the Charterhouse (le priour et covent del meason de la salutation de Nostre Dame d'ordre de Charthous, joust foundrez), represented to Henry VI., in Parliament, their great want of water.[2] A short time previously the King had, by letters patent, allowed John Ferriby and his wife, Margery, to grant to the Charterhouse a fountain, and land surrounding it, in the town of Islington (en la vill' de Iseldon). The prior and convent were now allowed to utilize this gift by making a conduit under the highway in leaden pipes from the fountain to their house, with power to hold this conduit, when made, for ever, the Statute of Mortmain notwithstanding (et qu'ils puissent mesme le conduit, ensi fait, tenir a eux et lour successours a toutz jours, le statuit de noun aliener terres a mort mayn noun obstant). The grantors reserved a rent of twelve pence per annum, and also all profits of pasturage.

Supply of the Charterhouse from Islington, A.D. 1432.

[1] 3 Rot. Parl. 306 ; 16 Rich. II.
[2] 10 Hen. VI. ; 4 Rot. Parl. 394. Great mansions also sometimes had

a private supply (see London Water Act of 1543-4, *post*, p. 50).

Water supply of city by Corporation solely.

In the fifteenth and sixteenth centuries we come again upon evidence that the water supply of London concerned the Corporation, as a work for the common good.[1] In 1439 the Abbot of Westminster granted to the Mayor and Citizens of London, and their successors, one head of water, containing twenty-six perches in length and one in breadth, together with all springs in the manor of Paddington, for a peppercorn rent; and this grant was confirmed by Henry VI. In the next century additional conduits were constructed by the Corporation in various thoroughfares: at London Wall, in 1500; at Bishopsgate, in 1513; in Coleman Street, in 1528. At Aldgate, long known for its pure water, a conduit was also built, in 1535, by means of a grant of money from the Common Council. But the water yielded from these and other sources, old and new, proved inadequate; and the Corporation now found that Parliamentary powers were necessary for replenishing their supplies.

First London Water Act, 1543.

London did not obtain its first Water Act until 1543,[2] two years after that of Gloucester.[3] In the preamble to their

---

[1] For surreptitiously tapping the conduit where it passed his door, and conveying the water into a private well, thereby causing "a lack of water" to his fellow-citizens, civic records relate that William Campion, of Fleet Street, was, in 1478, imprisoned for a time upon sentence pronounced by the Lord Mayor and Aldermen, and was then further punished in the following mediæval fashion :—Being set upon a horse, a vessel like unto a conduit was placed upon his head, and kept filled with water, which ran down his person from small holes made for the purpose, and kept him continually drenched. In this condition he was taken round to the city conduits, where his offence was proclaimed, as a warning to other citizens.

[2] 35 Hen. VIII. c. 10. In 3 Hen. VIII. (1511) a Bill "concernens conductus aquarum" passed the House of Commons, and was read a second and third time, with amendments, in the Lords, but was then stopped, the entry in the Lords' Journals (I. 15) being "Domini volunt superinde advisari." The Commons' Journals are not extant for this period, and the scanty records of the other House do not show whether the Bill was one of general application or referred to the London conduits.

[3] Ante, Vol. I. p. 9. Some of the Gloucester provisions are repeated in the London Act.

Act, the Corporation take care to mention their ancient conduits; and the advantages of a good and abundant water-service are set forth in fresh and vigorous terms:

"Forasmuch as it is very commodious, necessary and profitable to all cities, towns and inhabitations to have sweet and wholesome running waters and springs, to serve the same for their businesses and necessities, and specially within great towns and cities, to be conveyed by conduits and fountains; whereunto requireth abundance and copiosity for serving the inhabitants of the same; whereof the City of London *Failure of* hath been before this time well furnished and abundantly *ancient* served, till now of late, either for faintness of the springs, or *sources.* for the dryness of the earth, the accustomed courses of the waters coming from the old springs and ancient heads are sore decayed, diminished and abated, and daily more and more be like to disappear and fail, to the great discommodity and displeasure both of the citizens and inhabitants within the city and suburbs, as to all other persons having recourse to the same, and also to the great decay of the city, if speedy remedy be not soon foreseen and provided:

"For remedy whereof Sir William Bowyer, Knight, now *Services of* Mayor of the said City, intending and pondering the same *Sir W. Bow-* necessity, much willing to help and relieve the city and *yer, Mayor,* suburbs with new fountains and fresh springs for the com- *new supply.* modity (advantage) of the King's subjects, calling to him as well divers grave and expert persons of his brethren and other of the commonalty of the city, as other persons in and about the conveyance of water well experimented, hath not only by diligent search and exploration found out divers great and plentiful springs at Hampstead Heath, Marybon, Hackney, Muswell Hill, and divers places within five miles of the city, very meet, propice and convenient to be brought and conveyed to the same, but also hath laboured, studied, and devised the conveyance thereof by conduits, vaults and pipes to the city, and otherwise to his great travail and labour and pains, and also to the great charges and costs of the citizens; which good and profitable purpose cannot sort to conclusion nor take good effect without the aid and consent of the King's Majesty and of this High Court of Parliament."

Then come enacting words authorizing the Corporation at *Power to Cor-* all and every time and times thereafter to enter upon lands, *poration to enter lands* whether belonging to the King (but in this case the royal *and appro-* assent must be first obtained), or to any other person or *priate water.*

corporate body, in order to search for springs, "so that it be
not in houses, gardens, orchards, or places enclosed with
stone, brick, or mud walls;" and there to dig pits, trenches,
and ditches, and erect heads, lay pipes, and make vaults. The
servants of the Corporation are to have free ingress, egress,
and regress, in order to repair works, convey water, and
find new springs, without interruption from owners. But
within one month after breaking any ground they must

Compensation to owners. pay to owners "as much money for the same digging and
breaking as shall be adjudged and taxed by the deter-
mination and judgment of three or four indifferent men,
to be assigned by the Lord Chancellor for the time being,
under the King's commission." Non-payment by the Corporation within ten days will be visited by a fine of 13s. 4d., over
and above the sum assessed. If the commissioners do not
agree, and reasonable amends or satisfaction be not made by
the Corporation, claimants are to have their lawful remedy
by action of trespass, and may recover damages accordingly.
Penalties are in like manner imposed on all persons resisting
the Corporation or their officers in carrying out the Act.

Supply of private mansions not to be interfered with. No water or spring now or hereafter conveyed by pipes
or trenches to private mansions, for necessary use by their
household, is to be taken or interfered with. On the other
hand, no person must, "by any way, deceit, mean or other
crafty contrivance, undermine, diminish, withdraw, or abate
any spring or springs" appropriated for use by the citizens.

Clauses saving rights of Bishop of Westminster and town of Hampstead. A protecting clause saves any rights of the Bishop of Westminster, as "lord and very owner" of Hampstead Heath;
and if the Corporation make use of any spring or springs
there, they are required to pay yearly to the Bishop one
pound of pepper in acknowledgment. Another protecting
clause forbids the Corporation to meddle with a spring at the
foot of Hampstead Hill "now closed in with brick for the
ease, commodity, and necessary use of inhabitants of Hampstead;" and the Bishop of Westminster reserves to himself
and his successors the right to any water in lands on the

left side of the highway leading from Hampstead towards Hendon, for the use of Manor Place, in Hampstead.

This statute contains only seven clauses; three had sufficed for the Gloucester Act. Reasonable respect, it will be seen, is paid to all rights of property, represented by owners and occupiers of land taken or interfered with; but, subject to this reservation, the health and necessities of the citizens are recognized as paramount. There are no powers to impose rates on inhabitants taking water. The Act, indeed, implied an obligation resting on the Corporation to provide a supply, not laid to houses, but made free to all comers by open conduits or public fountains in the streets.

No rating powers in Act.

Free supply contemplated.

For some cause, which does not appear, the Corporation of London allowed nearly fifty years to pass before they exercised the powers obtained in 1543. A scheme was then carried out to use the Hampstead springs for an improved water supply, and also for flushing the Fleet brook or dike. According to Stow, this brook had been scoured and cleansed in 1502, "so that boats with fish and fuel were rowed to Fleet bridge and Oldbourne bridge, as they of old time had been accustomed, which was a great commodity to all the inhabitants in that part of the city." Then he adds:—"In the year 1589 was granted a fifteen (poundage rate) by a Common Council of the City for the cleansing of this (Fleet) brook or dike. The money, amounting to a thousand marks, was collected; and it was undertaken that, by drawing divers springs about Hampsted Heath into one head and course, both the city should be served of fresh water in all places of want; and also that by such a 'follower' as men call it" (flow or flush of water), "the channel of this river should be scoured into the river of Thames. But much money being therein spent, the effect failed, so that the brook, by means of continual encroachments upon the banks, and by casting of soilage into the stream, is now become worse cloyed than ever it was before."[1]

Powers of Act not exercised till 1589.

Springs at Hampstead brought to scour Fleet brook or dike.

[1] Stow, pp. 9, 10.

Meanwhile, fresh attempts had been made by the city authorities or by private benevolence to meet an increased demand for fresh water. In 1546 the Common Council voted money for conveying water from Hoxton to a public conduit at Lothbury. In the same year, Lambe, a gentleman said to belong to the Chapel Royal of Henry VIII., generously undertook the charge of bringing water from several springs in leaden pipes, a distance of two thousand yards, to a public conduit, built by him at Snow Hill, at a cost of 1,500*l*.[1] Conduits were also formed in 1568 and 1583, at Dowgate, Fish Street Hill, and elsewhere ; these contained water drawn from the Thames. But London had now outgrown a system of public fountains and water carriers. It appeared, too, that no sufficient supply could be procured from such neighbouring springs as were still uncontaminated. In this exigency, a foreign adventurer, one Peter Morice,[2] a Dutchman, in the service of Sir Christopher Hatton, undertook to bring water from the Thames, pumping it to a higher level than that of the river, and supplying, not only public fountains, but private houses.

In the mayoralty of Sir James Hawes, in 1574, an agreement was made between Morice and the Corporation, for the conveyance of water from the Thames to certain specified places around Leadenhall, with a view also to supply private houses there. Towards this work, the Corporation agreed to give 100*l*., with other privileges, also providing land for the erection of engines. For some reason, after paying 50*l*. of the stipulated sum, the Corporation hesitated to complete this agreement. Morice, who by reason of his employment under Sir Christopher Hatton, whatever it may have been, enjoyed powerful protection, thereupon prevailed on the Lords of the Council to write to the Mayor, Aldermen and Commonalty, in 1580, stating that Morice had " disbursed the sum of 200*l*. in

New conduits, 1546-83.

Peter Morice.

Agreement between Corporation and Morice, 1574.

[1] Stow, pp. 93, 356, where is given a punning epitaph upon Lambe on his tomb in St. Faith's Church under Paul's. His name and work still live in Lambe's Conduit Street.

[2] The name appears as Morryce, Moryce, Morice, Morris.

preparing piles and stones for the foundation," and desired to proceed with the work. Their Lordships, therefore, "requested to be certified as to the grounds of the city in refusing to complete the agreement;"[1] an unwarrantable interference, which, at some periods of civic history, would have been strongly resented.

Owing probably to this remonstrance, the works were continued, but they must have lagged, and the Corporation complained of delay, for in May, 1580, we find Sir Christopher Hatton writing to the Mayor to request that Morice might have further time for carrying out the works.[2] There is proof that they were finished, and were successful; for in 1582, Bernard Randolph, common serjeant of the city, agreed to advance money,[3] as a charitable gift "towards bringing water out of the Thames, by an engine to be constructed by Peter Morice, from London Bridge to Old Fish Street, in like manner as he had already brought the water to Leadenhall, and by the way to supply the private houses of the citizens." This offer had been approved by the Court of Aldermen, and licensed by the Common Council, inasmuch as the work "would profit the whole city, and be no hindrance to the poor water-bearers, who would still have as much work as they were able to perform, so far as the water of the conduits would satisfy." Mr. Randolph appears to have delayed payment until he received the Lord Chancellor's assent; and in December, 1582, the Lord Mayor wrote to request this assent, stating that Morice had proceeded on the faith of receiving this money, but had meanwhile "entangled himself with bonds and bargains," so that "the work would be in peril of failing, and the benefit to the city, both in cases of fire and infection, would be lost."[4]

Before this work of private benevolence was contemplated,

Successful supply of streets around Leadenhall.

Proposed supply at Old Fish Street, A.D. 1582.

Arches of London

---

[1] Remembrancia, p. 551. The letter is dated Nonsuch, July 5, 1580.

[2] Remembrancia, p. 551.

[3] Stow (p. 94) says the amount was 700*l.*, and was given by Randolph to the Fishmongers' Company for the purposes mentioned in the text.

[4] Remembrancia, p. 553.

Bridge leased
to Morice.
the Corporation had, in 1581, granted to Morice a lease for
500 years, at a nominal rent reserved, of the first arch of
London Bridge for the erection of a waterwheel.[1] Two years
afterwards, the second arch was leased to him for the same
term. At first the supply from the London Bridge works
was confined to a district parallel with the Thames, and not
extending far from it, for the rise of ground and imperfect
machinery for pumping caused difficulties in giving a continuous supply at any distance from the river, especially
through wooden pipes, which were unable to resist heavy
pressure. Considerable pressure must, however, have been
obtained on occasions, for Stow relates that, after the second
arch was leased, the Mayor and Aldermen came down to
see an experiment by Morice, who succeeded in throwing
water " over the steeple of St. Magnus's church, before which
time no such thing was known in England. It was done by
a mill, and was the first waterwork to supply the city with
Thames water, and this water-mill furnished the neighbouring
parts of the city as far as Gracechurch Street." The further history of the Morice family and their successors belongs
to a later period. It is stated that Peter Morice received
large grants from the Corporation to help him to complete
his waterworks.[2] In the Act for rebuilding the city in 1667,
it was provided that his grandson, Thomas Morris (*sic*) should
have power to rebuild with timber his waterhouse adjoining
London Bridge, for supplying the city with water, " as it
for almost this hundred years hath done."[3]

Transfer of
water supply
from munici-
pality to
private ad-
venturers.
Such was the rise of the first private undertaking on record
which supplied water for private profit. The London Bridge
works enjoyed considerable vitality, for they lasted as long as the

---

[1] Morice obtained motive power by
using the tidal ebb and flow, his water-
wheels pumping the water into receivers. In the *Philosophical Trans-
actions* for 1731 an account of the
engines then existing at London
Bridge is given by Mr. Beighton,
who says they may be " justly
esteemed as good as any in Europe,"
and "are far superior to those so
much famed at Marly, in France."

[2] Remembrancia, p. 551, n.

[3] 18 & 19 Chas. II. c. 8, s. 39.

bridge itself, a period of nearly 250 years, but at no period did the adventurers reap any great gains. They were soon confronted by formidable competitors, possessed of greater capital, selling purer water, and able to send it by gravitation to higher levels than could be reached by pumping from the river. Until 1581, it will be seen, the water supply of London had rested solely with the Corporation, and was undertaken by them not for the sake of revenue, but as a municipal duty which devolved upon all municipal bodies anxious to promote the health and comfort of their fellow-citizens. In furthering the plans of Morice and his co-adventurers the Corporation did not foresee, and could hardly be expected to foresee, how great a power they were beginning to transfer to private hands. As yet, however, they did not wholly relinquish an acknowledged duty.

An Act of 1571, "for bringing the river of Lea to the north side of the City of London,"[1] has sometimes been cited as an attempt to improve the water supply of London. But there is no mention of such an object in any part of this Act. Its preamble shows that the Corporation of London, in obtaining powers to make a new cut or river, hoped thereby to cheapen provisions in the city by facilitating communication; and its recitals are limited to the advantages which "many grave and wise men" expected from the proposed works, "for the navigation of barges and other vessels, for the caryag (*sic*) and conveying as well of all merchandises, corn and victuals as other necessaries from Ware, and all other places near the river, into London." Of a different character, however, was a statute of 1606,[2] which authorized the Corporation to bring "a fresh stream of running water to the north parts of the City of London from the springs of Chadwell and Amwell, and other springs in the county of

Acts obtained by Corporation of London relating to New River.

Act of 1606.

---

[1] 13 Eliz. c. 18.   [2] 3 Jac. I. c. 18.

Hertford not far distant from the same, which upon view is found very feasible, and like to be profitable to many." This water was to be brought within the city by a trench not broader than ten feet throughout its entire length. Owners were to receive compensation, and in default of agreement such compensation was to be assessed by sixteen Commissioners, appointed by the Lord Chancellor. Care was taken that these Commissioners should be impartial by providing that four of them should reside in each of the counties of Middlesex, Hertford and Essex, and four should be chosen from the City of London. Having made this " trench, channel, cut or river," the Corporation were to maintain it, repair breaches, and from time to time scour and cleanse it; but the chief authority over it was vested in the Commissioners of Sewers.

Amending Act, 4 Jac. I. Nothing was said or provided as to any use to be made of the water when conveyed into the city. Nor was anything done under this Act, but that water-works were contemplated is clear from an Act of the following Session,[1] which recited that, "upon view of the grounds through which the waters are to pass by men of skill, and upon advised consideration," it was "thought more convenient and less damage to the ground that the running water be brought and conveyed in and through a trunk or vault of brick or stone inclosed, and in some places where need is, raised upon arches, than in an open trench or sewer." But as doubts had arisen whether the operative words used in 1606 would authorise the construction of a trunk or vault of brick or stone, such authority was now given to the Corporation, who might either enclose this trunk or vault in the earth, or might raise it upon arches.

Opposition in House of Commons. There was strong opposition to the Bill of 1606. A Captain Edmund Colthurst claimed compensation in respect of some prior rights he had acquired in this project. He

[1] 4 Jac. I. c. 12.

appears to have been employed by the Corporation to make plans for a supply of water from the Hertfordshire springs, and there must have been some plausible ground for his claims, as they were recognized by both Houses. In the Commons, where the Bill originated, it was referred to a Committee consisting of the knights of Hertford, Essex, and Middlesex, and twenty-five other members, among whom were the brothers Middleton and Sir William Bowyer. An order was also made that Captain Colthurst should be heard before the Committee. On the third reading, May 20, the House divided, sixty voting in its favour and forty-nine against it. The following note is entered in the Journals:—"Mr. Recorder, in the name of the Lord Mayor and the State of the City, hath promised that they will submit themselves to such order for recompence to be given to Captain Colthurst as the Lord Chancellor shall set down."[1] Two days afterwards the Bill was sent to the Lords with the message "that some recompence may be considered by the City to Captain Colthurst."

Claims of Capt. Colthurst.

In the Lords, after a second reading, the Bill was referred to a Committee of fourteen prelates and peers, the Archbishop of Canterbury, Lord Treasurer, Lord Chamberlain, Earl of Salisbury, Earl of Exeter, Bishops of London, Winchester and Hereford, with Lords Morley, Hunsdon, St. John, Compton, Petre, and Dennye.[2] The Committee were directed to meet on a Saturday, at two o'clock; and, as was not unusual at this period, one of the Judges, Mr. Justice Daniell, with Serjeant Crooke, were directed to attend the sitting. No time was lost, for on the following Monday the Bill was "returned to the House by the Lord Treasurer, the second of the Committees,[3] with a proviso thought meet to be added, which proviso was pre-

Bill in House of Lords.

Judge and serjeant-at-law assisting Committee.

---

[1] 1 C. J. p. 310; May 20, 1606.
[2] 2 L. J. 441; May 24, 1606.

[3] That is, the second in official rank of the *comites*, the peers associated to serve on the Committee.

sently twice read, and thereupon appointed to be ingrossed in parchment."

Upon the third reading, which was at once taken, " a motion was made by the Earl of Exeter, and other of the Lords, that some order might be taken for recompence to be yielded unto Colthurst, who had been heretofore employed by the Lord Mayor and citizens of London about the work of bringing a fresh stream of running water to the north parts of the city. And thereupon the Earl of Exeter and Lord Bishop of Hereford were appointed presently to call before them the Recorder of London, together with the said

The Recorder and Colthurst called before two peers deputed to hear them.

Colthurst, and to deal with the Recorder in behalf of the City, for such recompence to be made unto Colthurst as aforesaid; who being called before their lordships accordingly, answer was made by the Recorder (and so signified by the said Lords to the House) that he had no authority from the City to offer or yield to any particular recompence; but that the Lord Mayor and citizens were content to submit themselves to such order as the Lord Chancellor should be pleased to make therein. Whereupon it was desired by the House that stay should be made hereafter by the Lord Chancellor for granting any commission under the great seal of England upon any matter concerning the Bill, until such recompence should be made unto Colthurst, for his travail and pains in the aforesaid work, as his Lordship should think reasonable." [1]

The Corporation transfer their powers to Hugh Middleton.

No long time passed before the Corporation abandoned the powers confided to them. By deeds dated 1609 and 1611, they transferred these powers to Hugh Middleton,[2] and there

---

[1] 2 L. J. 442; May 26, 1606. The effect of this resolution was to stop the Corporation from the exercise of any compulsory powers to acquire land, as land not agreed for could only be taken under the Act upon assessment of its value by Commissioners appointed by the Lord Chancellor (ante, p. 56).

[2] In March, 1608, a year before the arrangement with Middleton, Colthurst offered to carry out the works; but the Court of Aldermen were of opinion that he had not the necessary means, and therefore refused his application. We may pre-

is a letter dated in 1609, after the first of these indentures, written by the Lord Mayor to the Lords of the Council, informing them that "Mr. Hugh Middleton, goldsmith, had undertaken, as deputy to this city, to perform" the work, and requesting their lordships to instruct all justices of the peace in Herts and Middlesex "to assist him and his men all in their power."[1]

We may now for a time leave Middleton and the formidable task he had undertaken, and return to the conduits, on which the city still depended for its chief supply of drinking water. While the citizens generally obtained water from these public fountains, some noblemen and other persons having mansions in the city, or near the course of the conduit from Tyburn, obtained leave to lay a small pipe, or "quill,"[2] connecting the conduit with their mansions or grounds. An instance of this nature occurs A.D. 1582, when the Marquis of Winchester writes to the Mayor and Aldermen that his grandfather, Lord Treasurer of England, had been licensed by the Corporation to lay certain conduit pipes for the use of his house in Broad Street, nigh Bishopsgate, "which pipes ran through divers men's grounds;" and as these pipes had become decayed, application is made for leave to substitute a brick vault for passage of the water on paying to the city 20s. of yearly rental.[3]

Pipes from the city conduits to private mansions.

Marquis of Winchester, A.D. 1582.

---

sumc that he had then received the compensation awarded by the Lord Chancellor.

[1] Remembrancia, p. 555.

[2] Probably, as the name implies, a pipe not exceeding a goose quill in diameter. There would thus be a check upon the quantity taken. What this quantity was may be gathered from an entry in the civic letter book, dated June 2, 1618:— "Alice, Countess of Derby, allowed a quill of water, &c. from the city's main pipe, to yield three gallons an hour, at her dwelling-house in St.

Martin's Lane."

[3] Remembrancia, 552. William Paulet, first Marquis of Winchester, obtained possession of the dissolved Priory of St. Augustine (Austin Friars) in 1540, and on the site and gardens built a large mansion, called Winchester House, which was taken down in 1865. He married a daughter of Sir William Capel, Lord Mayor in 1503 and 1509, from whose residence, in the parish of St. Bartholomew, Capel Court takes its name (ib. n.).

Towards the end of the sixteenth century, when water was less abundant, or there was a greater demand for it, these licences were watched with jealousy by the commonalty, and

Lord Cobham, A.D. 1592. were given sparingly. In 1592 Lord Cobham asked for a quill of water from the conduit at Ludgate for use in "his house within the Blackfriars." This request was laid before the Court of Aldermen. Meanwhile the Lord Mayor wrote suggesting that for the present nothing could be done, but that the city were in treaty with one Frederick Genibella,[1] skilled in water-works, for the erection of a wind-mill at the fountain-head to increase the supply. If this plan succeeded, the request might be granted; evidently it did not succeed, for in 1594, we find the request again urged, and supported by a letter from Lord Burghley.[2]

Essex House, in the Strand, A.D. 1601. Other letters are preserved from Lady Essex and Lady Walsingham in 1601 asking for "a continuance of the pipe of water formerly granted to the Lord Admiral for use in Essex-house." These requests were supported by the Earl of Suffolk, Lord Chamberlain. The Lord Mayor's answer was to the effect that, water in the city conduits having become very low, it had been found necessary to cut off several "quills" formerly allowed to Essex House and other mansions. "Moreover, complaints had been made of an extraordinary waste of water in Essex House, it being taken not only for dressing meat, but for the laundry, stable, and other offices which might be otherwise served."[3] To Lord

Lord Fenton, A.D. 1613. Fenton who, in 1613, asked for "a quill of water out of the city's great pipe for his house near Charing Cross," the Lord Mayor wrote regretting that this request must be refused, "on account of a frequent failure by the conduits to supply

---

[1] From a note in Remembrancia (p. 554), we learn that, in 1591, Genebelli, an Italian, submitted to the Lords of the Council a scheme which would, as he alleged, cleanse the filthy ditches in the city, such as Houndsditch and Fleet ditch;

bring into them plenty of wholesome, clear water for use by the citizens; and also help to put out fires, enabling twenty-five or thirty persons to do the work of 300.

[2] Remembrancia, p. 554.

[3] Ib. 554.

sufficient water to the city, by reason whereof the Corporation were frequently visited with complaints and clamours, especially from the poor."

As grants of "quills" conferred privileges which brought no revenue to the Corporation, while the common stock of water was diminished, these popular murmurs were well-founded. A vested interest was also affected, and made itself heard both in the city and in Parliament. A curious petition, bearing no date, but probably drawn up early in the reign of James I., was presented to the House of Commons from "the whole company of the poore water tankard-bearers of the City of London and suburbs thereof, they and their families being 4,000 in number, living and relieved thereby."[1] This quaintly-worded petition throws so much light upon the ancient water-supply of the city that it is given here without abridgment :— *Petition of tankard-bearers, or water-carriers, to Parliament.*

"Among the great multitude of poore distressed people of this kingdom, with joyful hearts and lifted-up hands to heaven, we, your petitioners, have just cause to say 'Blessed be the Lord God of Israel that moved the heart of his gratious Majestie, to call so honorable an assembly in Parliament, which will not suffer Gehazi to take tallents of silver, nor change of rayments, but that every one may sit under his own olive-tree, and anoint himself with the fat thereof.' Wee, poore miserable people labouring hardly for a poore living, under great burthens, have the bread taken out of our children's mouthes, and our owne, both contrary to good lawes established, and all equity and good conscience.

"For, most honourable Assembly, to make this their grievance plaine, that they are matters of truth, and no suggestions or inforcements : There was in the Parliament holden in 35th yeare of King Henry VIII. an Act made *Case founded on 35 Hen. VIII. c. 10.*

---

[1] A copy is preserved in the Guildhall Library. This spacious and well-managed library, free to all comers, and open in the evening as well as throughout the day, is in every way worthy of its ancient origin and of the City of London. In restoring and maintaining it upon so liberal a basis, the Corporation have conferred a priceless boon upon readers and students, and have their reward in the intelligent appreciation of its value shown at all hours by thronged benches.

and provided concerning the repayring, making and amending of the conduits in London, and that sweete, holsome
running waters, and fresh springs might be conveyed by
conduits and fountaines to the said conduits in London, and
whereof the said city had been before time well furnished,
and abundantly served.

Proviso in Act against interference with public user.

"In the said Act there was a carefull proviso[1] that it should
not be lawfull for the said Lord Maior nor Commonaltie, nor
to their successors or ministers, to take away any water or
spring now brought, or hereafter to be brought or conveyed,
by pypes or trenches, to the mansion of any person or persons, nor for any person or persons, by any way, deceipt, meane,
or any other craftie conueiance, to vndermine, minish, withdraw, or abate any spring, or springs, found or hereafter to
be found, brought or conveyed to the city whereby the water
shall be minished, stopped, abated, or otherwise altered from
his dew course and conveyance to the conduits in London.

"That the water brought to the citie by vertue of the said
Act is the most wholsome, purest and sweetest water com-
ming to the city is not to be doubted or disputable; and
**Water inter-
cepted before
reaching
public foun-
tains.**
(there is) sufficient store thereof at the spring heads. And
yet, notwithstanding the Act, most of the water is taken and
kept from the conduits in London by many private branches
and cockes, cut and taken out of the pipes, which are layed
to convey the same to the conduits, and laid into private
houses and dwellings, both without and within the city;
whereby it is drawne out of the wayes, and many times
suffered to runne at waste, to the generall grievance of all
good citizens, and all others repayring to the same, having
their meat dressed with other waters, neither so pure nor
holsome, as the conduit water is, as common experience
teacheth; contrary to the true intent of the same statute.

"There are, as was confessed by the city's plumber, one
Mr. Randall, fifteen branches or cockes laid into private
houses, and drawn from the conduits, contrary to the proviso in the Act; and three branches or cockes laid by himself
**Inquiry sug-
gested, and
evidence to
be produced.**
without warrant, only for his owne private gain. By what
warrant the others were granted to particular persons, and
taken from the common conduits, we humbly desire that
first the said Randall may be sent for and examined, and
afterwards such other persons as we shall produce, besides
many others, who may privately take in water out of our
maine pipes, and as yet unknown to the petitioners.

**Supply to
Newgate.**
"Secondly, the water granted unto Newgate, for use of
that house only, is carried forth daily by five men to many

[1] *Ante*, p. 50.

es, which tankerd-bearers keepe no houres, but work
inually,[1] and so exhaust and draw away the water from
other conduits.

The Lady Swinnerton is allowed but two gallons every houre
ill president, and against the proviso of 35 Henry VIII.).
that branche is so great as (that) it yieldeth thirteene
lons and better every hour, for it hath beene tried, which
ny times runneth at waste. If this one branch or cocke
hin this city doth or may draw away above a thousand
lons extraordinarily from the conduits in a weeke, what
ong so many branches without the city, where lesse care
iad, is to be taken into your honourable consideration.

"Fourthly, the water that now serveth Aldermanbury
iduit doth belong to the pipes of Cheapside, and was
ely cut out of the same, and that water which should or
ould serve that conduit of Aldermanbury is wholly stopt
given to private houses by the way.

"Fifthly, Cornehill and Gracious[2] Street men complayn-
g for want of water in their conduits, there was three
oures in a day abated by the Chamberlayne of the city,
t the request of the plumber, from the conduits in Cheap-
ide, thereby to furnish them with the more store, being ill-
erved, by the same pipes. But yet Cornehill and Gracious
Street conduits have never a whit more water, nor the houres
yet restored to the conduits in Cheapside.

"Sixthly, one of the maine and chiefest pipes runneth
inder part of St. Martin's Lane and the Coven Garden, in
which places there are lately erected many new buildings
nd dwellings of bricke, and it is supposed that digging
eeper for the foundations, and finding the pipes, they may
ake some private branches out of their due course.

"Your petitioners doe humbly desire (for that there is great
lefect of water in the said conduits; and that it is a generall
grievance to the whole city; and that divers complaints have
been made by your petitioners for redresse, but no reliefe
can be procured, who are utterlie remedilesse, but by this
Honourable Assembly), that we the petitioners may be permitted to preferre our Bill into this Honourable House for
remedie of this grievance, and as in duty we are bounden,

Lady Swin-
nerton's case:
waste alleged.

Aldermanbury
conduit.

Short supply
at Cornhill
and Grace-
church Street.

Supposed ab-
straction of
water.

[1] Probably these water-carriers
were not of the craft, and so did not
comply with any rules laid down by
the company. When not engaged
in serving Newgate, they seem to
have taken water to private houses
out of the hours prescribed for regular tankard-bearers.

[2] Gracechurch. When James I.
entered London, on his accession,
some verses in his honour were hung
upon the conduits in "Grateous"
Street, and elsewhere.

so we will daily pray, that God may blesse all your cou
to the benefit of all succeeding ages." [1]

Applications
to tap the city
conduits.

We may assume that, before appealing to Parliamen
water-carriers had appealed, and ineffectually, to the
poration, with whom originated all licences for "qu
Some applicants for these privileges were supported by
persons about the Court, who brought to bear upon
Corporation an influence which, in those days, it was diffi
to withstand. Thus, in spite of the poor tankard-bear
gratuitous services from the city conduits continued,
until a much later period city records contain repeated ap
cations of the kind already mentioned. Among the suit

Sir Francis
Bacon, A.D.
1617.

were Sir Francis Bacon, in 1617, "for a lead pipe fr
the city's main pipe for supply of water to York House

Sir H. Vane,
A.D. 1637.

Sir Henry Vane, in 1637, "for a quill of water for his hou

Denzil Holles.

at Whitehall;" and Denzil Holles[2] requesting a quill "fo
the use of his son and daughter at their residence in St.
Martin's Lane."

The last records of this nature are of 1662-4. In 1662

York House,
Strand.

the Earl of Manchester writes that York House in the
Strand has been appointed as a residence for the Russian
Ambassador, and desires that water-pipes belonging to the
city, bringing water to that house, shall be repaired. On
two occasions the Duke of Albemarle requests, first, that
the Court of Aldermen will "take measures to supply the

The Mews.

Mews with water as heretofore, which is so essentially
necessary for the King's service," and afterwards that a
quill of water shall be supplied "for the gentlemen of
the horse at the Mews' Gate." After its occupation by the
Russian Ambassador, York House was tenanted by the

Duke of
Buckingham.

Duke of Buckingham, who renews the stereotyped application. Lastly, the Earl of Northumberland complains, in

Earl of
Northumber-
land, A.D.
1664.

March, 1664, that "he has been lately deprived of the con-

[1] There is no trace of this petition
in the Journals of the House of Commons.

[2] One of the five members whom
Charles I. attempted to arrest in 1642.

duit water which has always served Northumberland House at Charing Cross," and requests that he may be allowed a quill of water from the city pipes which pass his residence.[1]

After his appointment as deputy of the Corporation, Middleton's troubles began. So great was the objection to the proposed work by landowners through whose estates it passed that in the year 1610 a Bill was brought into the House of Commons to repeal the New River Acts.[2] At this period the Commons' journals are so scanty that they throw no light upon the reasons urged for such a repeal.[3] But the landowners' petition, on which the Bill was founded, alleged, among other evils, that their meadows would be turned into bogs and quagmires, and their arable land become " squalid ground;" that their farms would be " mangled," and their fields cut up into "quillets" and small pieces; that the " cut " was no better than a deep ditch, dangerous to men[4] and cattle, and upon sudden rains would inundate the adjoining land, to the ruin of many poor people; that the church would be wronged in its tithe, and the highway between London and Ware made impassable; and that all this mischief would be done, not by the Corporation, who now would have nothing to do with the business, but by Mr. Middleton, to whom they had made an irrevocable transfer of their powers, and who was exercising them " for his own private benefit."[5]

The Bill was referred to a Committee, on which two of the brothers Middleton served.[6] On June 30 there is the

Marginal notes: Landowners' opposition, 1610. Bill to repeal New River Acts. Bill referred to Committee.

---

[1] Remembrancia, p. 561.

[2] 1 C. J. 429.

[3] " L. 1. Repeal of the Acts for the river from Ware " is the brief reference to the first reading of this Bill, May 18, 1610.

[4] James I. lived to experience this danger. In January, 1622, he was riding with his son Prince Charles, on the bank of the New River, in Theobalds' Park, when his horse stumbled, and the King was thrown into the river, disappearing under the thin ice. On being dragged out, "there came much water from his mouth and body."

[5] Smiles's Life of Middleton, pp. 111-12, quoting from the Domestic Calendar of State Papers, vol. 78, in the Record Office.

[6] 1 C. J. 442; June 22, 1610.

following entry:—"Sir John Savill—touching the bill of the New River. A petition from gentlemen of the country that attend; to meet this afternoon; to make choice of ten."

Ten members appointed to view.

At the next meeting of the House "Sir H. Poole reporteth the choice of ten; to survey and certify according to the former order of the House;"[1] but there is no record of this order. We gather, however, that the business of the ten members was to survey and certify as to the damage which would be suffered by petitioning landowners if the works were carried out. On July 16, the journals report:—"Ten men reported by Sir H. Poole to view the River. Not to go till the next session. Mr. Alford, Sir William Stroud, Sir George Rivers, Sir Roger Owen, Sir Dudley Diggs, Sir Thomas Holcroft, Sir Edward Montague, Sir Thomas Beaumont, Mr. Talbot Bowos, Sir Warwick Heale; to view, the next Session."[2] But this delay was fatal to the proposed inquiry, for Parliament was prorogued July 23, and did not meet again until April 5, 1614, when the New River was finished and opened.

Prorogation.

Proposed supply of London from the Lea, at Hackney, A.D. 1610.

A fact of some interest in the history of the London water supply has hitherto escaped notice, and must have been an additional source of uneasiness to Middleton. In the same Session in which the opposing landowners were trying to repeal the New River Acts, a competitive scheme was carried through Parliament, and seriously threatened the interests of the Corporation, or their deputy. There is reason for assuming that this scheme, which contemplated the supply of London from the river Lea, was favoured by James I. His interest in the reclamation of land has already been mentioned.[3] Morice's works had shown that the supply of water might be made profitable to private adventurers. James I. also had a motive, and not a selfish motive, for the success of this plan of 1610. He had founded and endowed at Chelsea a College of Divinity, "of his most royal and zealous care for the defence of the true religion now established within this

College of Divinity at Chelsea.

[1] 1 C. J. 444-45.　　　[2] 1 C. J. 450.　　　[3] *Ante*, I. p. 11.

realm of England, and for the refuting of errors and heresies repugnant unto the same." The King had endowed this College with some land, and by letters patent had authorized it to receive other land by gift and bequest to the yearly value of 3,000*l.* Benefactions, however, were not abundant, and the College appears to have been straightened for means.

In this position, the Provost and Fellows were led to believe that they might enrich their college by imitating the example of Morice, and by forestalling Middleton or the Corporation. Accordingly, they obtained an Act in 1610,[1] "for bringing fresh streams of water by engine from Hackney Marsh to the City of London, for the benefit of Chelsea Hospital."[2] This Act, in fact, authorized the Provost and Fellows to become a water company, and speculate in supplying the City of London with water drawn from the Lea at Hackney. They were to cut into that river on the side nearest the city, by a trench not exceeding ten feet wide, and convey the water, and also that of any adjacent springs, "through certain little gutters, or trenches, or pots, or pipes under the ground, into one pit, pond or head of convenient largeness to be made in some place apt for the same." Having thus, "by art and sleight of their engines and water-wheels," raised the water to such height as they thought requisite, the undertakers were enabled to convey it "in close pipes under the ground into the City of London and the suburbs thereof, for the perpetual maintenance and sustentation of the Provost and Fellows, and their successors, by the rent to be made of the said waters." They were also authorized to lay and repair the necessary pipes in any land, and also, but in these cases not without consent, through houses, gardens or orchards, or through any corn-fields while the corn was growing. All damages for

7 Jac. I. c. 9.

[1] 7 Jac. I. c. 9.
[2] There is a very curt note of this bill in 1 C. J. 446, and an entry that ten members were appointed "to view the ditch," as the Lea is disrespectfully called. The Act provides that the contemplated works shall not draw from the river such an amount of water as to interfere with the navigation. No funds are provided to defray the outlay.

ground taken, or injuries done, were to be assessed in the way then usual, by Commissioners of the Lord Chancellor's appointment.

Probable
reasons of
Corporation
for relinquish-
ing the New
River under-
taking.

It may be that the Corporation took alarm at a scheme, which was no doubt contemplated in 1609, and was put forward, with the King's sanction and encouragement, in support of an institution of his own creation. They may, therefore, have been the more willing to part with their statutory powers. Or the Corporation may have been discouraged by the opposition of landowners, or by the engineering difficulties which Middleton had met with, and by the unknown cost of an aqueduct forty miles long, with some 160 bridges. Part of the city had also by this time been supplied from the London Bridge works, and the Corporation may have supposed that they would be committed to an expenditure for an object already in part accomplished. Whatever causes influenced them, they did not seek to regain the position they had surrendered, and thus a second private undertaking for the supply of London with water became firmly established. Falling short of money, Mid-

Jas. I. be-
comes partner
in New River.

dleton applied to the King, who, in 1611,[1] agreed to furnish one-half the outlay in bringing the New River to north London, and in distributing water, on condition of receiving one moiety of the undertaking and of its annual

Advantages
to Middleton
of Royal
favour.

profits. For Middleton this arrangement had advantages beyond the mere command of funds which it gave him. He

[1] Articles of agreement between the King and Middleton were dated November 5, 1611, and were confirmed by an elaborate grant under the Great Seal in May of the year following. An abstract of the grant is given in Smiles (pp. 116-17) from the original in the Record Office. It is so called because the King grants to Middleton and his assigns exclusive rights to bring water from the Hertfordshire springs, with a right of way for that purpose through any Royal manors, parks and lands; and his Majesty stipulates for himself and his successors to assent to any Act or Acts of Parliament which may be necessary for confirming and enlarging the powers obtained by the Corporation of London, and by them assigned to Middleton. Entries in the Pell records show that the payments made on the King's account were 8,609l. 14s. 6d., so that the total expenditure was 17,219l. 9s. (Ib. pp. 118-19.) But see post, pp. 117-18.

could now feel secure that the Chelsea scheme would not be carried out, for James I. was not likely to allow competition with an undertaking in which he had invested money. The whole influence of King and Court, also, might now be counted upon to counteract the jealousies and rivalries called forth by the near completion of the New River works,[1] and to secure something even more than fair play for the speculation. It was not long before this influence was effectually exercised.

There is no trace in city records of any application by Middleton to the Corporation for means to complete the New River. James I. had become familiar with the works during his residence at Theobalds, his favourite retreat near Enfield. Middleton was shrewd enough to know that the King's interest would be a tower of strength to any enterprise,[2] and was all the more necessary here since his Majesty was a landowner through whose park the New River ran.[3] There is reason, therefore, to believe that, probably upon some encouragement received, the Court jeweller's first application for pecuniary aid was to the King. Of the Corporation he had no cause to complain, and, as far as we know, never did complain. One article of the agreement of 1609 was that Middleton should finish the works within four years. In 1610 he asked for an extension of time, and five years more were granted to him, on the ground of

Middleton's relations with Corporation.

Extension of time granted by Corpora-

[1] Stow (p. 12), who surveyed the works during their progress, mentions these jealousies as one of the obstacles which Middleton encountered:—"For if those enemies to all good endeavours, danger, difficulty, impossibility, detraction, contempt, scorn, derision, yea, and desperate despight, could have prevailed by their accursed and malevolent interposition, either before, at the beginning, in the very birth of proceeding, or in the least stolen advantage of the whole prosecution, this work of so great worth had never been accomplished." See also the poetic address delivered at the opening ceremony, *post*, p. 71.

[2] In a project for reclaiming marsh land in Wales, afterwards suggested to Middleton, he wrote, "First of all his Majesty's interest must be got." (See letter given at p. 148 of Smiles's Life of Middleton).

[3] The statutory powers granted to the Corporation included a right to cut through the King's Park.

tion for com-
pleting New
River.

difficulties interposed by occupiers and owners of the lands required.[1] In the same year the Corporation helped him to oppose the Bill for repealing the New River Acts, and sent a deputation of Aldermen, accompanied by the Town Clerk and Remembrancer, to wait upon the Home Secretary, Chancellor of the Exchequer, and other ministers, representing the importance of the New River "for the preservation of health in the city," and adding that "the stream had already been brought onward about ten miles at the charges of Mr. Hugh Middleton, the City's deputy, amounting already to the sum of 3,000l. and more."[2]

Loan of
3,000l. to
Middleton by
Corporation.

In September, 1614, the Corporation, at his request, granted him a loan of 3,000l. for three years, "in consideration of the benefit likely to accrue to the City from his New River." This loan was not repaid in 1634, three years after Middleton's death, for in October of that year, upon a memorial from his widow, the Common Council remitted 1,000l. of the amount due, as well for her "present comfort" as in consideration of the public benefit conferred on the City by the New River, and of losses alleged to have been sustained by Sir Hugh through breaches in the water pipes on the occasion of divers great fires.[3] As a mark of their esteem for his public services, a "great jewel" was given to him by the Lord Mayor and his brother Aldermen, and is mentioned in his will. That the Corporation were justly annoyed at an unwarrantable interference by the King in 1616-17,[4] on behalf of his co-partner, and in furtherance of his own interest, cannot be doubted; but no such feeling is reflected in the records of their dealings with Middleton.

New River
Head opened,
A.D. 1613.

Having obtained the necessary funds, Middleton was able to complete the works, and the water was let into the reser-

---

[1] Journals of Common Council, February 27, 1610; Smiles, 114.

[2] Ib. May 25, 1610; Smiles, 113.

[3] Smiles, pp. 128, 150, n. The New River water had proved of great service at fires, and had been freely given for public use on those occasions.

[4] Post, p. 73-4.

voir at the New River head, in the parish of Clerkenwell, on September 29, 1613. Sir John Swinnerton was then Lord Mayor; Sir Thomas Middleton, brother of Sir Hugh,[1] was Lord Mayor elect. Both were present at the opening, with the Recorder, some Aldermen and citizens. Sixty labourers, wearing green caps, and handsomely dressed, marched twice round the reservoir to the sound of drums and trumpets. Stopping before the civic dignitaries, one of these labourers read some rude verses, of which the following are not without interest :—

> " Long have we laboured, long desir'd and pray'd
> For this great work's perfection ; and by th' aid
> Of Heaven, and good men's wishes, 'tis at length
> Happily conquered by cost, art and strength ;
> And after five years' dear expense in days,
> Travail and pains, beside the infinite ways
> Of malice, envy, false suggestions,
> Able to daunt the spirits of mighty ones,
> In wealth and courage, this work so rare,
> Only by one man's industry, cost and care,
> Is brought to blest effect, so much withstood,
> His only aim the City's general good."

The poet naturally proclaims the royal favour shown to a work which had won for Middleton

> " The King's most gracious love. Perfection draws
> Favour from Princes, and from all applause."

[1] Sir Hugh was knighted in 1613, and made a baronet in 1622, James I. directing that the usual fees, amounting to 1,095l., should be remitted. The patent recited that the dignity was conferred—(1) "for bringing to the City of London, with excessive charge and greater difficulty, a new cut or river of fresh water, to the great and inestimable preservation thereof ; (2) for reclaiming 'out of the bowels of the sea' land in Brading Haven, in the Isle of Wight ; and (3) for finding out, with a fortunate and prosperous skill, exceeding industry, and no small charge, in the county of Cardigan, a royal and rich mine, from whence he hath extracted many silver plates which have been coined in the Tower of London for current money of England."—Smiles, 143–4, quoting Sloane M.S. (British Museum), and Calendar of Domestic State Papers, October 19, 1622.

And the workmen are not forgotten:

> " Clerk of the work, reach me the book to show
> How many arts from such a labour flow."
> [*All this he readeth in the Clerk's book.*]
> " First, here's the Overseer, this tried man,
> An ancient soldier, and an artisan.
> The Clerk, next him Mathematician,
> The Master of the timber-work takes place .
> Next after these ; the Measurer, in like case,
> Bricklayer and Engineer ; and after these
> The Borer and the Pavior.   Then it shows
> The Labourers next ; Keeper of Amwell head,
> The Walkers last : so all their names are read.
> Yet these but parcels of six hundred more
> That (at one time) have been employed before.
> Yet these in sight, and all the rest, will say,
> That all the week they had their royal pay."
> [*At the opening of the sluice.*]
> " Now for the fruits then :—Flow forth, precious spring,
> So long and dearly sought for, and now bring
> Comfort to all that love thee ; loudly sing,
> And with thy crystal murmurs strook together,
> Bid all thy true well-wishers welcome hither."

At these words the flood-gates flew open, and the stream ran gallantly into the cistern, drums and trumpets sounding, ordnance firing, and the people shouting joyously.[1]

Letter from Lords of Council to Corporation, A.D. 1616.

Some correspondence, dated three years after this ceremony, shows that the Corporation were suspected of being indifferent to the success of Middleton's adventure, while James I. naturally desired that his investment should yield a return.   Long accustomed to receive water, as a municipal privilege, without payment, the citizens did not hasten to take the New River supply into their houses.   Clearly the Corporation could not be held responsible for this condition of things.   Yet in 1616,[2] the Lords of the Council made it the subject of a long letter to the Mayor and Aldermen, which reads like an admonition or even a reprimand.   The Corporation were reminded

---

[1] Stow gives the whole of these verses and a brief description of the ceremony.

[2] December 23.   Remembrancia, pp. 556–7.

of the two Acts passed "upon humble suit made to Parliament on behalf of the City of London," authorizing the New River project. Then their lordships added that Middleton, "being by Act of Common Council authorized and deputed to perform the work, had expended large sums of money in purchasing ground through which the water was to pass, making bridges and other works; and that with such difficulty, on account of opposition and disturbances of the country, that if the King had not favoured and supported the undertaking, Middleton would have sunk under the burden, and never have completed his work." His Majesty had been moved by the Aldermen to sanction the passage of the water through his parks. Moreover, the statutes had for their object the general good and profit in a use of sweet and wholesome water, as well as a preservation of the city from fire, of which there had been good experience there several times last summer. Yet " the King and Council had been informed that but few persons took the water. It was not to be supposed that two Acts of Parliament and an Act of Common Council had been passed, so much concerning the health and safety of the city, to no use or purpose except the prejudice of such as were by the city deputed to undertake the work, and who had deserved so well of the public. His Majesty had therefore commanded, and the Lords of the Council requested the Court of Aldermen to provide, by Common Council or otherwise, that all such houses in the city and liberties as, either of necessity or convenience, might use the same water, should be required to do so."

Middleton's outlay and difficulties recounted.

The King's favour and support.

Corporation commanded to require citizens to take New River water.

This high-handed proceeding on the part of James I. shows that Middleton was well advised in enlisting the King as a partner in his undertaking. What notice, if any, the Corporation took of the royal mandate does not appear; they certainly had no legal power to compel the citizens to take and pay for New River water. But this was not a solitary instance of the King's care to secure business for his co-

Proposed
lease of city
water-house
and works at
Dowgate,
A.D. 1617.

adventurers and save them from competition. In 1617 certain brewers and others, in the parish of St. Giles, Cripplegate, applied to the City Lands Committee for a lease of a water-house and works at Dowgate belonging to the City,[1] offering to maintain these works, serve the conduit with water, and defray the expense of pumping, on condition that they were allowed to lay pipes to convey any surplus water into their brew-houses without Cripplegate. The City Lands Committee recommended that a lease should be granted, especially as the brewers " were willing to take in Middleton's water for their other uses and to pay reasonable rates for the same." Middleton, however, was not satisfied with this arrangement, and his influence at Court brought from the Lords of the Council another letter,[2] in which their lordships state that they had been informed of the brewers'

New works at
London
Bridge for
supply of
Southwark
hindered by
Jas. I.

application, " and although they did not doubt that due regard would be had to his Majesty's pleasure, signified upon a former similar occasion, for the stay of a house intended to be erected on London Bridge for the conveyance of water to Southwark, to the prejudice of his waterworks at Islington," yet since the new stream, brought at great cost from the springs of Chadwell and Amwell, was of great consequence for his Majesty's service, and deserved all due encouragement, the Lords of the Council " deemed it expedient to

Similar pro-
hibition of
intended
works at
Dowgate.

require that stay should be made of any intended waterworks at Dowgate, the more so since the brewers could so conveniently be supplied from the new stream."

A minute watch was thus kept by the Court upon all proceedings which might prejudice the New River Company;

Effect of
Court influ-
ence.

and this unjust and arbitrary influence was even used to prevent Morice and the Corporation from furnishing a better supply of Thames water to the population on both banks of the river. When such means were used to check

---

[1] These works must have been constructed by Morice, at the expense of the Corporation, for pumping water from the Thames.

[2] February 27, 1617. Remembrancia, p. 558.

free competition, and force unwilling consumers to take water from one favoured source, Middleton and his co-adventurers,[1] however enterprising and otherwise worthy to rank as benefactors of the city, could hardly fail to be unpopular there. The Corporation must also by this time have sorely repented that they had allowed their own scheme to fall into private hands and become, through royal favour, an instrument of injustice and coercion. Under the Stuarts, however, corporate bodies were used to harsh and arbitrary dealing; and their time to resent it was yet to come.

Meanwhile the Lords of the Council were not without opportunities of effectually meeting any neglect of their suggestions. In a vain hope of keeping up that free supply of water from their ancient fountains to which the citizens had been accustomed, the Corporation, in 1633, were obliged to apply for an Order in Council, authorizing their officers to search the courses of the main pipes which supplied water to their conduits, with power " to remedy all defects or abuses occasioned by the erection of buildings, &c., over the same; cut off all unauthorized branches; and cause mains to be diverted, where necessary, at the expense of owners of any buildings erected over them."[2] This Order was granted. Again, in the following year, Mayor, Commonalty, and citizens petitioned the Lords of the Council, setting forth that they "had formerly been at great charge to bring fresh and sweet water, in leaden pipes, from the manors of Tyburn and Marylebone, to certain conduits in the city." Much of this water had of late years been taken away, "whereby the city had been in great want, and the poor had sustained much misery." The Corporation had lately begun "to bring part of the waste water from the Roundhead, near Tyburne, to the storehouse near the Ban-

Marginal notes:
Old supplies by conduits improved, A.D. 1633.

Jas. I. opposes attempt by Corporation to increase

---

[1] There were seventy-two shares, of which one-half belonged to Jas. I.; and soon after the completion of the New River, Middleton sold twenty-eight of his thirty-six shares, in order to obtain the capital for his mining operations in Wales.

[2] Remembrancia, p. 559.

supplies from Tyburn, A.D. 1634.

queting-house, and had disbursed great sums of money in digging, laying of leaden pipes, and providing materials, but were now stayed by the King's command;" and they prayed the Council to mediate with his Majesty for permission to finish this work.[1]

Conduits obstruct traffic, and sites changed.

After Morice had completed his waterworks at London Bridge, and the New River was opened in 1613, the citizens no longer depended on their old conduits. Before 1633, the public fountains, or cisterns, in Cheapside, Cornhill, Fleet Street, and other thoroughfares, were removed to sites where they interfered less with passing traffic. At the same period many private houses in the city appear to have been served either by Morice or Middleton, and the civic historian could

Services to private houses, circa 1633.

write:—"What with the spring water coming from the several spring heads through the streets of the city to public cisterns; the New River waters from Chadwell and Amwell; and the Thames water, raised by several engines or water-houses, there is not a street in London but one or other of those waters runs through it in pipes conveyed under ground; and from those pipes there is scarce a house whose rent is 15*l.* or 20*l.* a year but hath the convenience of water brought into it by small leaden pipes laid into the great ones. And for smaller tenements, such as are in courts and alleys, there is generally a cock or pump common to the inhabitants; so that I may boldly say there is never a city in the world so well served with water."

Inspecting the conduits.

According to ancient custom, the conduits were visited once a year by the Mayor, Aldermen, and some Masters and Wardens of the City Companies, who went with their friends on horseback, and the ladies in waggons.

[1] April 11, 1634. An Order in Council on this subject was issued in the following month, but its effect is not stated.—Remembrancia, p. 559. That James I. should have even delayed an attempt by the Corporation to improve their gratuitous supply of water, from ancient sources, shows the lengths to which he went in support of his own and of Middleton's interest.

There was a city banqueting house, used at these visits, and situated near a small bridge over the Tyburn stream, upon land afterwards occupied by Stratford Place, Oxford Street. Under this banqueting house were cisterns to receive water from the streams which supplied the city.[1] Stow gives a pleasant description of one such inspection of the conduits, on September, 18, 1562:—"And afore dinner they hunted the hare and killed her, and thence to dinner at the head of the conduit. There was a good number entertained with good cheer by the Chamberlain; and after dinner they went to hunting the fox. There was great cry for a mile, and at length the hounds killed him at the end of St. Giles's. Great hollowing at his death, and blowing of hornes; and thence the Lord Mayor, with all his company, rode through London to his place in Lombard Street." Good cheer in 1562.

All the city conduits, particularly leaden pipes and cisterns, suffered severely in the great fire of London in 1666. An eye-witness describes the effect of the flames, in the figurative language of his day. The conduits, he says, "stood like so many little but strong forts, to confront and give check to the great enemy; and as enemies are wont to deal with castles, thought impregnable, by attempting to carry them by storm, so went the fire to work with these little castles of stone, which were not easy for it to burn down (witness their standing to this day): and spoiled them, or almost spoiled them, by melting the leaden channels through which their supplies of water came. It was as if the fire had been angry with the poor old tankard-bearers, both men and women, for propagating the contrary element."[2] The city conduits in the great fire of 1666.

[1] Both the banqueting-house and reservoir are mentioned in the civic letter-book of 1634, *ante*, pp. 75-6. This house was taken down in 1737, and the cisterns were arched over.

[2] Abridged from Rolle's Account of the Burning of London in 1666. The 18 & 19 Chas. II. c. 8, "An Act for rebuilding the City of London" after the great fire, provided (sect. 20) that, as "the freedom and openness of the street conduceth much to the advancement of trade, and the ornament of the city," all or any conduits then standing in the high streets might, by order of Common Council, be removed and set up in any other public place within the city.

Water reve-
nue of Cor-
poration
charged in
favour of city
orphans.

Down to the year 1694, however, the Corporation of London continued to furnish water from their conduits within the city; and they must then have derived some revenue from this source, for by a statute of 1694, all the aqueducts, and right of bringing and conveying water, were charged with payment of an annual sum by way of interest in favour of "the orphans of the city," to whom the Corporation ": by reason of sundry accidents, and public calamities," had become indebted "in a much greater sum of money than they are able to satisfy and pay, unless some assistance be given them for the same." From this charge water supplied to public conduits, hospitals, halls, and prisons in the city was excepted.[1]

Sale of civic
springs and
conduits at
Tyburn to
Bishop of
London, A.D.
1812.

Until the year 1812, the Corporation of London continued to exercise their rights in Tyburn springs, usually leasing their conduits to tenants, who sold water to inhabitants of western London. In 1812, however, an Act was passed[2] confirming an agreement under which the Bishop of London, and lessees of the episcopal estate at Paddington, bought from the Corporation these springs, together with "the conduits, conduit heads, pipes, drains, wells, sewers, ditches, trenches, vaults, cisterns and suspirals containing or conveying the said waters, or any of them, to the City of London and suburbs." The purchase-money was 2,500*l.*; and it was provided that, after payment, any of the works might be discontinued, and the course of water diverted at the purchasers' option. By this agreement and statute the Corporation broke the last link which had so long connected them with the water supply of London.

[1] 5 & 6 Will. & M. c. 10, s. 2; an Act to relieve "the orphans and other creditors of the City of London." By sect. 25, Morice's water- works at London Bridge were also excepted from this charge.
[2] 52 Geo. III. c. 193.

CHAPTER IX.

WATER SUPPLY OF LONDON (*continued*) :—BILLS AND PROJECTS
IN THE SEVENTEENTH AND EIGHTEENTH CENTURIES:
EXTENSION OF LONDON BRIDGE WATERWORKS: YORK
BUILDINGS, CHELSEA, AND LAMBETH COMPANIES: DRINK-
ING WATER FROM CANALS: THE GRAND JUNCTION, SOUTH
LONDON, KENT, WEST MIDDLESEX, AND EAST LONDON
COMPANIES: COMPETITION BETWEEN NEW AND OLD
UNDERTAKINGS, 1810-17: PARTITION OF DISTRICTS:
INCREASE IN WATER RATES: UNLIMITED POWERS OF COM-
PANIES: MARYLEBONE PAROCHIAL WATERWORKS BILLS,
1818-19.

WE may now take leave of the city conduits, which had
served their purpose for more than five hundred years. The
legislation, and projects brought before Parliament, during
the remainder of the seventeenth century, must be rapidly
traced. In 1619, James I. granted letters patent incorporating the New River Company under the title of " The Governor
and Company of the New River brought from Chadwell and
Amwell to London."[1] That the Company were viewed with
little favour in Parliament may be inferred from their fruitless attempts to confirm these letters patent by statute. A

Letters patent to New River Company, 1619.

---

[1] One of the privileges granted by
this charter was that the adventurers
should hold their property from the
Crown in free and common socage,
the effect of which was to make each
proprietor's share a freehold estate.
As the undertaking in its early days
yielded no return, Charles I., in the
year 1630, re-granted to the Company the thirty-six King's shares,
representing a moiety of the whole
capital, in consideration of an annual
payment of 500*l*. This sum is still
paid into the Exchequer, and attaches
to the King's shares as a "clog" or
charge. The thirty-six shares were
sold by the Company on the general
account, and the proceeds applied to
an extension of works. Middleton
stipulated that James I. should have
no part in the management in respect
of his interest. This condition still
applies to King's shares. Both
King's and adventurers' shares are
now much subdivided.

Statutory
confirmation
sought in
1621;
Bill to this effect, "and for granting liberties to the Company" was read a first time in the House of Commons in 1621,[1] but advanced no further.

and in 1623.
A similar measure, introduced in 1623, met with the same fate.[2] Against another Bill, brought forward in the same Session, "for ratifying and confirming his Majesty's charter to the Company of Gold Wire-drawers of the City of London," Sir William Strode spoke, because it would "confirm a monopoly by Act of Parliament;" and this objection may have reflected the mind of the House of Commons upon the New River Bill, which had the additional demerit of being in great part a royal monopoly.[3] It was referred to

Sir Edward
Coke's
opinion.
a Committee on the motion of Sir Edward Coke, and obtained the support of this great lawyer as "a very good Bill, preventing one great mischief that hangs over the City: *nimia potatio, frequens incendium.*"[4] The letters patent were ordered to be brought to this Committee, which met in the Star Chamber; but they do not seem to have reported to the House, and the Bill dropped.

Confirming
Bill of 1642.
In 1642 a Bill to confirm the letters patent was re-introduced, but the time was not favourable to any measure supposed to enjoy royal countenance, and again the Bill went no further than a first reading.[5] There has since been no express statutory recognition of the Company's charter. The first Act subsequent in date which applied to them was one

Act of 1738.
passed in 1738,[6] to carry out an arrangement under which they were allowed to take water from the Lea upon payment

---

[1] 1 Com. Journ. 611; May 7, 1621.

[2] Ib. 727; March 4, 1623.

[3] A Bill against monopolies was much discussed in 1621.

[4] 1 Com. Journ. 745. The members of the Committee were:—Secretary Calvert, Mr. Treasurer, Mr. Comptroller, Sir Edward Coke, Mr. Recorder, Sir J. Saville, Mr. Shervyle, Sir Charles Morrison, Sir Robert Killegrue, Mr. Noye, Sir Thomas Cheeke, Sir Wm. Udall, Sir Thomas Middleton, Sir Francis Crane, Secretary Cottington, Sir Arthur Capell, Mr. Oliver, Sir Henry Poole, Sir J. Walter, Mr. Cooke, Sir Gilbert Jerrard and Mr. Maynard; with the knights and burgesses of Essex, Middlesex, Herts and London.

[5] 2 Com. Journ. 554; May 3, 1642.

[6] 12 Geo. II. c. 32.

of an annual sum towards improving the navigation. Indirectly, this Act does recognize the status of the New River Company, because it is an Act not only "for ascertaining, preserving and improving the navigation of the river Lea," but "for enabling the Governor and Company of the New River the better to supply the cities of London and Westminster, and liberties and suburbs thereof, with good and wholesome water."

Several proposals for new water undertakings were made during the reign of Charles I. In 1640 a Bill was promoted for "bringing a new stream of fresh water to the cities of London and Westminster from the river of Colne." After its second reading in the House of Lords the Bill was referred to a Committee of twenty-one peers and prelates, with Mr. Justice Heath as "assistant"; five to be a quorum. It appears that at this time 18,000*l.* had been raised by a lottery "for bringing a new river to London and Westminster from Hoddesdon, in Hertfordshire." The House of Lords resolved that this plan was "insufficient," and as the 18,000*l.* "lay dispersed in several men's hands," it was expedient that this money "should be paid into some responsible hand." It was therefore ordered "that Mr. Justice Heath and Sir Joseph Wolstonholme do examine in whose custody the 18,000*l.* is, and that it be called in and deposited in the Chamber of London, there to remain until further order of this House; and Mr. Attorney-General to have notice not to release any bonds of any parties who have any part of the 18,000*l.* in their hands, until the money be paid in as aforesaid; and further, that the petitions of Sir Walter Roberts and Edward Forde shall be heard at the sitting of the Lords' Committee for the aqueduct aforesaid."[1] This was the Colne project, but it fell through.

In the following Session the Hoddesdon plan came before

Bill of 1640: water from the Colne.

18,000l. raised by lottery for bringing water from Hoddesdon.

Bill of 1641: water from Hoddesdon.

---

[1] 4 Lords' Journ. 153; 16 Chas. I.; Feb. 6, 1640.

the House of Commons and was embodied in a Bill "for bringing certain springs of water from Hoddesdon, in Hertfordshire, to the cities of London and Westminster, in a close aqueduct of brick, stone, lead, or timber." The Bill was referred to a Committee, of which Sir Thomas Middleton was a member,[1] but did not go beyond the Committee stage.

Bill of 1664: water from Hyde Park. Another unsuccessful scheme was submitted to the House of Commons in 1664, under the title of "a Bill for the continuance and enjoyment of certain waters brought from and about Hide Park to Westminster and places adjacent." This Bill was also referred to a Committee, on which vested interests were represented by Mr. Morice; and the Committee met on an appointed day "in the Speaker's chamber: to summon and hear all persons concerned; and to send for persons, papers, and records."[2] Afterwards no further mention of the scheme appears in the Journals.

York Buildings Water Company, 1676. Two or three plans at this period were launched successfully. In the year 1676 Charles II. granted letters patent to a company of adventurers enabling them to raise a joint-stock capital to purchase lands, and construct engines and other works, on the site of York House and garden, near the Strand, for supplying Westminster and adjoining places **Bill of 1690.** with Thames water.[3] In 1690 the company petitioned Parliament for a Bill, on the ground that they had carried out their supply under these letters patent, but found that they could not let on lease or properly manage their undertaking, notwithstanding its convenience to the public, **Opposition of vested interests.** without statutory powers.[4] The New River Company succeeded in obtaining from the promoters a proviso saving their rights. Petitions asking for similar protection were presented by two owners of separate water undertakings

[1] 2 Com. Journ. 161; May 29, 1641.

[2] 8 Ib. 541; April 2, 1664.

[3] Ralph Bucknall and Ralph Wayne were specially named in this licence, which was limited to a term of 99 years.

[4] 10 Com. Journ. 458. The company's works were at the bottom of Villiers Street. They had been burnt down some time before 1690.

established without Parliamentary powers, " Hugh Merchant, proprietor or lessee of Marybone Waterwork," [1] and " Charles Rampaine and others, proprietors of waterworks for raising Thames water for use in St. Margaret's parish." [2]   Both petitions were referred to a Committee on the Bill, which was afterwards re-committed, with two additional members, showing that its provisions must have undergone considerable discussion.[3]   In January, 1691, the Act of 1691. Bill passed to incorporate these proprietors, and encourage, carry on, and settle their waterworks at York Buildings; and they were authorized to take water out of the Thames, and lay and repair pipes for its distribution.[4]   This company continued to supply a district adjacent to the Strand for a period of nearly 150 years.

With authority from the Corporation, several " waterhouses " were established on the river-bank by private speculators in East London to pump drinking-water from the Thames.   In 1681 Charles II. by letters patent granted to Thomas Neale and his assigns the privilege of constructing works on land at Shadwell to supply inhabitants of the manors of Stepney and East Smithfield.   Ten years afterwards an Act passed the House of Lords, was brought down to the Commons, and received the Royal assent, " for incorporating the proprietors of waterworks in the parish of St. Paul's, Shadwell, and for encouraging, carrying on, and settling the said waterworks." [5]   These proprietors were authorized to construct waterworks and waterhouses, take water from the Thames, lay pipes and branches in the streets, and open passages for the supply of water so obtained.[5] This company supplied Wapping, the Tower Hamlets, and other places too remote to be served from the New River. The north-west suburbs of London obtained a stock of water

Shadwell Waterworks Company, 1681.

----

[1] He was probably lessee of the old city conduits under the Corporation; see *ante*, p. 78.

[2] 10 Com. Journ. 502, 503; December 9 and 12, 1690.

[3] Ib. 508.

[4] 2 Will. & Mary (Sess. 2), c. 24.

[5] 3 Will. & Mary, c. 37.

Supply of Hampstead and Holloway.

in 1692 through a company of adventurers, who took over from the Corporation their unused or partially used powers conferred by the Act of 1543-4.[1] This company afterwards made certain ponds and reservoirs at Hampstead, to be filled by rain water and by some of the springs which the Corporation had been authorized to appropriate. For some years during the early part of the eighteenth century, they appear to have served parts of Westminster and of intermediate districts; but as population increased in northern London their supply proved insufficient, and the company were forced to contract their area. Up to the year 1813-14 they still continued to furnish water to houses situated at the south end of the Tottenham Court Road.

Extension of waterworks at London Bridge.

Early in the eighteenth century the waterworks at London Bridge were considerably extended. The Corporation had already leased two arches to Morice and his successors for a term of five hundred years. In 1701, no longer apprehensive of a royal prohibition, as in 1616,[2] the Lord Mayor and Commonalty leased to these adventurers,[3] for 381 years, a fourth arch of the bridge, for the erection of another water-wheel. In 1761 they let on lease a third arch for a term of 321 years; six years afterwards the fifth arch from the north end was let to this company for 315 years, in order to afford an improved supply in the city, and the second arch from the south end to serve the Borough. Before this period Southwark chiefly depended on water which flowed from the Thames into a pond at St. Mary Overies, and James I., in the New River interest, had vetoed any improvement upon this simple means of supply.

[1] 35 Hen. VIII. c. 10; *ante*, pp. 48-51.

[2] *Ante*, pp. 73-4.

[3] In 1703 Thomas and John Morris (sic), surviving representatives of the original grantee, sold the greater part of their interest in the London Bridge works to Richard Soame and others for the sum of 38,000*l.*, the property being divided into 300 shares, and the management vested in a court of assistants. When the company was dissolved in 1822, the shares had been increased to 1,500.

A project submitted to Parliament in 1719 encountered much opposition from landowners and possessors of water rights. It proposed to draw from several sources, including the Colne, Gade, Bulborne, Chesham, and other streams. In the House of Commons a petition from the adventurers was referred to a Committee of sixty members, and all representatives of Bucks, Middlesex, and Herts. Before this Committee a principal witness was Mr. Thomas Acherley, whose evidence may be summarised here as an example of engineering testimony given a hundred and fifty years since. He told the Committee " that he had been twenty years a surveyor of lands, mines, levels, and throwing out waters, and had surveyed the grounds between London and the rivers mentioned, from station to station, at every fifty or sixty yards' distance, with proper levelling instruments, and did find, by the level, that those rivers, and also the river Lea, about Whethamstead, lay about a hundred feet higher than the lowest pond at Milford farm, called Hampstead ponds, which lowest pond was about twenty feet higher than the top of Mountague House in Great Russell Street ; and that the waters of those rivers might be brought to serve the town higher than any house in London and Westminster." As to quantity, one of these rivers would suffice for the ends proposed. But the adventurers would not rely on or exhaust one source ; some parts drawn from each river, and united into one trench or canal, would not only yield water enough for "inhabitants of London, Westminster, Southwark, and villages and places lying about," but would also give to the royal palaces, and particularly the royal palace and gardens at Kensington, a service of water, which, as far as water could do so, would "make these places delightful ; and that, too, at reasonable rates." Inconsiderable damage would be occasioned by the undertaking to meadows and mills,[1] because any water drawn away might be replaced by

Project of 1719 : water from the Colne and other sources.

Engineering evidence.

Compensation water.

---

[1] 19 Com. Journ. 297 ; March 9, 1719.

opening new and cleansing old springs, which abounded along the course of these rivers.

Dr. Halley,
Astronomer
Royal, A.D.
1720.

Another scientific witness was Dr. Edmund Halley, then secretary to the Royal Society, and in the following year appointed Astronomer Royal. In his opinion such an undertaking was practicable; in quantity of water it would prove sufficient, and its source was twice as high as that of the New River. The fall would be at least three feet in every mile; and he "undertook to effect the undertaking if he were employed." After hearing this evidence the Committee resolved that the promoters had made good the allegations in their petition, and that the undertaking would be "convenient and beneficial for inhabitants of

Leave given
for Bill.

London and Westminster, and parts adjacent." Leave was therefore given to bring in a Bill, and Mr. Carteret, Lord William Powlett, Mr. Freman, and Mr. Plumer, were ordered

Hostile peti-
tions of mill-
owners.

to prepare and introduce it.[1] Opposing petitions then came from owners and occupiers of mills on the Colne, in and near Uxbridge, who declared that the proposed diversion of water "must totally destroy all mills on this river, or so weaken the river that mills will be of little use to grind corn; and though the water, so diverted, may be of service to the city of Westminster, and parts adjacent, yet far greater will be the damage to the city of London when they shall want bread." Then, too, as the petitioners alleged, Uxbridge Market would be spoiled, the town in general impoverished, the vent of corn much lessened, and thousands of families ruined.[2]

Other owners, complaining of injury to their property, were the Earls of Bridgwater and Essex. On the other hand, inhabitants of Westminster petitioned in favour of the Bill, declaring that an improved supply of water was

Bill dropped.

"much wanted in those parts." The House of Commons ordered that they should be heard by counsel,[3] as

[1] 19 Com. Journ. 298.   [3] Ib. 321.
[2] Ib. 315–16.

well as opponents; but the adventurers were discouraged, and did not carry their Bill to a second reading. In 1720 they asked leave to re-introduce it, but the House rejected their prayer.[1]

During the same Session of 1720, another set of adventurers proposed to bring into London and Westminster plenty of good and wholesome water "from one or more streams or rivers that run by or near the village of Drayton," having, "at their great pains and charges, found ways and means" of conveying such water. After being ordered to lie on the table in the House of Commons, where it remained for a whole month, their petition for a Bill was referred to a Committee on February 7.

Project of 1720: water from streams near Drayton.

Scientific witnesses were on this occasion more numerous than in 1719. Among them were Dr. Desaguliers, Capt. Robinson, Mr. Osmond, "and other mathematicians." Cowley and Heatham streams were to be chief sources of supply, Cowley alone being expected to yield three times as much as the New River. Levels had been taken by "Mr. Dean, a mathematical instrument maker," with two other witnesses, who were "a check one upon the other, and used to compare their observations every night," always finding them to agree. These observations proved that water from Drayton might be conducted into a reservoir, whence the highest parts of London and Westminster might be served very plentifully. On the whole, the Committee thought that these cities were insufficiently supplied with water, and that leave should be given to bring in a Bill.

Scientific evidence.

Favourable report of Committee on petition.

This report did not come before the House till April 26, when an order was made that it should be considered "in a full House" on the following Monday morning. It then appeared that some interests were affected, amongst others, his Majesty's gardens and waterworks at Hampton Court,

Vested interests affected.

---

[1] 19 Com. Journ. 417.

the Duke of Somerset's powder and other mills on the
Thistleworth river, and certain paper and leather mills on
the Heatham streams, near a village called Poyle; but the
undertakers alleged that no substantial injury would be
occasioned by their project, and that their diversion of water
from the Thames " would not alter its depth by half an
inch." They also engaged to dredge and deepen the shallows. A debate arose on a motion to bring in the Bill; and
then, as it appeared that "his Majesty's interests might be
concerned," there was an adjournment.[1] On May 9, his
Majesty acquainted the House that he had no objection to
the Bill, provided that certain measures were taken, at the
adventurers' charge, to ensure a regular supply of water to

Bill intro-
duced.

Hampton Court. Leave was then given to bring in the
Bill.

Complaints of
injury to
navigation.

Among several petitions against it, was one from "dealers
in timber, barge-owners, and barge-masters on the river of
Thames," who alleged that navigation would be greatly
damaged if a new river were brought to London by diverting
streams that now flowed into the Thames near Staines. Even
now barges were frequently forced to lie aground a month
at a time for want of water to carry them over the shallows,
to the petitioners' great expense and detriment, and also to

Abingdon
and Henley.

the injury of traders in London. Abingdon and Henley,
through their corporations, alleged that their trade chiefly
depended on water carriage, and that they would be impoverished if navigation in the Thames were further impeded.

Owners of
land and
mills.

There were five petitions from gentlemen, farmers, and owners
of land and mills, suggesting a common origin, and alleging,
substantially in the same terms, that if the Bill should
become law " it would be not only prejudicial, but utter ruin
to many of them." On the other side were three favourable
petitions from barge-masters, who thought that, if the ad-

[1] 19 Com. Journ. 526-7; April 24, 1720.

venturers carried out their undertaking to deepen existing shallows, navigation in the Thames would be improved rather than obstructed; and from directors of the Sun and Hand-in-Hand Fire Insurance Offices, setting forth the destruction of houses from fire "for want of an early service of water from the fire-plugs,"[1] and praying the House to encourage all attempts to extend the water supply of London.[2]

Fire insurance offices support Bill.

At subsequent sittings of the House fresh opponents came forward. The Corporation of London, as Conservators of the Thames, complained of interference with navigation; and on June 12, six other petitions were presented from Egham, Chertsey, Hertford, Ware, Colnebrook, and St. Albans, whose "great corn-market, whence London receives large supplies of meal and flour, would be ruined if the adventurers, who had cast their eye upon these poor streams," were allowed their way.[3] Owners and occupiers along the river banks complained that their estates and holdings "would sink in value." Inhabitants "of the ancient and great corn-market town of Hemel Hempstead" found that they would suffer material injury;[4] the Chancellor, Masters and Scholars of Oxford University also joined in the outcry against adventurers who would obstruct the current of the river, and "greatly prevent a supply to the University of all sorts of provisions and necessaries for their subsistence, so enhancing prices, to the University's great detriment." The Corporation of Oxford represented that "for many years last past they had been put to great charge in maintaining locks,

Corporation of London oppose.

Local opposition.

University and city of Oxford.

---

[1] Down to the year 1805, the New River Company could not serve water above the ground floor in any part of London. All their mains were of wood, and at night the water was shut off to prevent waste, which was enormous. If a fire broke out, it was necessary to send to the New River head with instructions to turn on the water; and a watchman was kept to look out. (Com. Committee of 1821 on Metropolitan Water Supply; evidence of Mr. Mylne, pp. 6, 8).

[2] 19 Com. Journ. 580-1.

[3] Ib. 587.

[4] Ib. 592.

weirs, and turnpikes,[1] for supporting navigation in the Thames, which would be made impracticable by this Bill, to the great discouragement of their city's trade."

Up to this time there is no record in Parliament of a private Bill which had aroused such determined and widespread antagonism. At length the struggle began. On June 12, after one adjournment, a motion was made that the Bill "be read a second time upon Thursday morning next." There was, no doubt, a debate, but it is not recorded. The only entry in the journals is—"The House divided. The yeas go forth.[2] Yeas, 41: Noes, 45. Tellers for the yeas, Lord Tyrconnell, Mr. Younge. Tellers for the Noes, Mr. Bertie, Mr. Corrance. So it passed in the negative." This was no defeat of the Bill, but only a refusal to read it on the early day which its promoters desired to fix. On June 20, the Bill was read a second time. Nearly all its opponents had asked to be heard by counsel, but they now gave place to the Corporation of London, whose counsel were first heard at the bar, and afterwards counsel for the Bill, witnesses being examined on both sides. A motion then made, "that the Bill be committed," was negatived without division or debate;[3] and all the efforts and outlay of the adventurers went for nothing.

After the failure of these attempts to procure water from tributaries of the Thames, Parliament was asked to sanction a plan for taking water from the Thames itself, at a point near Chelsea, where vested interests were not likely to be touched. A petition for a Bill to incorporate a body of adventurers for this purpose came before the House of Commons in 1721, the proposed area of supply being "the city of Westminster, and parts adjacent," a description conveniently vague. A Committee to whom this petition was referred heard evidence in support of it. Mr. James Scanlan,

Margin notes:

Motion to fix second reading defeated.

Motion for commitment negatived.

Chelsea Water Bill, 1721.

Evidence for Bill.

---

[1] In early statutes and records this word is used to signify a toll-bar across rivers as well as roads.

[2] That is, into the lobby, the Noes remaining in the House.

[3] 19 Com. Journ. 602–4.

" mathematician," was the chief witness. He said he had surveyed and levelled the ground ; and, with engines worked by tidal reflux, the adventurers could raise any quantity of water to the necessary height, without any injury to navigation.   They proposed to make one large reservoir, of about ten acres, to hold from five to ten feet of water, according to different changes of tide; this could be enlarged to thirty or forty acres if required.   Another witness, Mr. Watts, said that land between the river and Oliver's Mount, which they would make use of, belonged to Sir Richard Grosvenor, with whom an agreement had been made.

Lord Molesworth was Chairman of the Committee, who reported that there was a great scarcity of water in Westminster, and that the undertaking was practicable, would not injure the navigation, and might be of great use and benefit to the public.[1] In the House the Bill was received with favour, and passed rapidly through its various stages. After a second reading it was referred to another Committee consisting of all the representatives of Middlesex, together with seventy-one nominated members.   Among these occur the names of Mr. Walpole, Mr. Pulteney, Lord Stanhope, Lord Molesworth, Lord Morpeth, Mr. Pitt, and Mr. Pelham.[2] Three days afterwards the Bill was brought back with amendments, which were adopted by the House, along with a clause protecting the rights, property and jurisdiction of the city of London.[3]   On February 9 it was passed and sent to the Lords, who returned it with verbal amendments on the 19th.   In striking contrast to the project last recorded, the Bill went through its several stages without a single opposing petition.

This Act " for better supplying the city and liberty of Westminster, and parts adjacent, with water,"[4] gave birth to a new and powerful company.   Its preamble set forth a

Bill reported by Committee.

Second Committee.

---

[1] 19 Com. Journ. 727; January 25, 1721.

[2] Ib. 736 ; February 5, 1721.

[3] Ib. 739.

[4] 8 Geo. I. c. 26.

Chelsea
Waterworks
Company.

great increase of buildings and inhabitants in and about Westminster, and divers other places in the county of Middlesex, so that "there are greater occasions for water, for the safety and necessary uses of the inhabitants, than are supplied by waterworks now in being;" and it sanctioned "one or more cut or cuts" from the Thames "at any convenient places between the grounds belonging to the Royal Hospital at Chelsea, and the houses or grounds commonly called the Neat Houses,"[1] into canals and ponds proper for receiving the water, which was thence to be raised and conveyed "into convenient reservatories" (*sic*), to be erected at any place between Oliver's Mount and Hyde Park. Col. John Fane, Col. Richard Molesworth, Col. James Otway, Col. Robert Gardner, and Sir Andrew Chadwick, were constituted commissioners and trustees for designing and carrying on the authorized works, and for maintaining and preserving them; and the King might incorporate them and others, under the great seal, into one body under the title of the Governor and Company of Chelsea Waterworks, with perpetual succession. Power was given to the commissioners and

Works clause. their successors "to open, dig, cut, make, erect, raise, and from time to time to repair, preserve, and maintain, alter, scour, and cleanse all such sewers, trenches, watercourses, canals, waterworks, pits, dams, banks, walls, arches, sluices, flood-gates, engines, pipes, cisterns, ponds, and other works, devices, and buildings," which should be made "for conducting and using water for the purposes of the Act, through or under any roads, highways or streets, or in, through, under or over any ground" purchased by the company.

---

[1] A name said to be derived from the Crown manor of Neyte or Neate, which gave its name to Knightsbridge. The Neat Houses, and their gardens, on the banks of the Thames, were formerly places of entertainment. Pepys, in his Diary (Aug. 1, 1667), writes:—"After the play, we went into the house, and spoke with Knipp, who went abroad with us by coach to the Neat Houses in the way to Chelsea; and there, in a box in a tree, we sat and sang, and talked and eat; my wife out of humour, as she always is when this woman is by."

No compulsory powers were granted. Before the commissioners meddled with, cut, dug, or altered lands, they were first to agree with owners or tenants; but pipes might be laid in any highway or road, and "in any streets, passages, or common grounds, or places in or about Westminster, and parts adjacent." There were no restrictions whatever upon rates to be charged for water, or indeed any mention of rates. Upon requisition from "the major part of the inhabitants of any courts, squares, or other places" into which water was brought under the Act, the commissioners were bound, at their own charges, to provide "pipes standing upright, in the likeness of pumps, to be ready on all occasions for better conveying water into engines for extinguishing accidental fires." There were clauses protecting the rights of the New River and York Buildings Water Companies, as well as those of the Corporation of London. A provision inspired, no doubt, by recent experiences of South Sea bubbles, and other stock jobbing concerns, is worth quoting:—"And for preventing all sinister practices, or abuses of the design of this Act, be it enacted . . . that it shall not be lawful for any person or persons whatsoever having any stock or share in the said undertaking to transfer or assign the same before or until such time as water be brought into the grand reservatory or reservatories intended to be at or near Oliver's Mount." The Act consists of only fifteen clauses.

Area of supply.

Stand-pipes for use in case of fires.

Dealings in shares prohibited until completion of works.

A charter under this Act was granted on March 8, 1723, incorporating the undertakers, the first Governor being Sir Thomas Hewett; the Deputy Governor, Col. Robert Gardner. These officers, and each director, were required to "take a corporate oath" before a Master in Chancery, to the following effect:—"I, A. B., do faithfully promise that in the office of [Governor or otherwise] of the Corporation called the Governor and Company of Chelsea Waterworks, I will give my best advice and assistance for the support and good government of the said Corporation, and I will faith-

Charter of incorporation.

Oath of governor and directors.

fully and honestly demean myself, and execute the said office, according to the best of my skill and understanding."

Capital of company, 40,000*l.*

No money powers were contained in the Act, but their charter authorized the Corporation to raise by subscription a joint stock not exceeding 40,000*l.* This capital was not divided into shares of any specified amount. There was a curious provision prohibiting the company under heavy penal-

Company restrained from banking and other business.

ties, or risk of revocation of their charter, "from inter-meddling or interfering with the business or affairs" of the Bank of England, by discounting bills, keeping banking accounts, or issuing notes payable on demand, or any way using the banking trade or business, or dealing in any bullion, gold or silver, or any goods, wares, or merchandize. A like prohibition extended to any acts in prejudice of two charters granted in 1720, for assurance of ships and merchandize at sea, and for lending money on bottomry.

Increase of capital, 1736.

In 1736, the small authorized capital had been expended, and a considerable debt incurred. A supplementary charter was then obtained, enabling the company to increase their capital by 20,000*l.*

Schemes of 1723-4: the Gultchwell springs.

Renewed attempts were made in 1723-4, to obtain statutory powers for schemes more directly competing with the New River. Mr. Acherley proposed on this occasion to supply the western parts of London and Westminster with water from springs at Gultchwell, which feed the river Colne, and obtained some support from petitioners who had been hostile to his former plan. Substantially the same opposition, however, was offered from Uxbridge, Reading, and other places, on the ground of interference with water rights, and with navigation in the Thames. The

Commons' Committee on petition for Bill.

adventurers' petition was referred to a Committee in the House of Commons, and much evidence was taken. Mr. Rowley, "master of mechanics to his Majesty," stated that the fall from Gultchwell springs to Cavendish Square would be thirty-five feet; that the intended reservoir in

Marylebone Fields might be easily supplied; and that the springs would yield about a thousand tuns of water an hour. For the first time, in an engineering scheme considered by Parliament, we find evidence taken as to the cost of proposed works; and engineers will be interested in contrasting estimates for excavation in 1723 with those at the present day. "Capt. Perry said a canal thirty miles long would cost ten shillings a rod digging, at four feet deep, and sixteen feet and a-half broad, provided it were good ground." Mr. Hoar confirmed this estimate, adding that a canal in bad ground would cost for digging twelvepence a yard, and in good ground threepence a yard; an average of sevenpence halfpenny a yard, "so that, by computation, the digging, one mile with another, would cost 370*l.*, or thereabouts."

Evidence as to estimated cost of works.

Another new feature in a Parliamentary inquiry was that, before the same Committee, a competitive scheme was placed by a second body of adventurers, who proposed to bring water to Marylebone Fields from streams near Drayton, a source suggested in 1721. A point alleged in its favour was that the necessary cut or new river would be shorter than Mr. Acherley's. After examining many witnesses for and against both schemes, the Committee reported that both were "practicable," and that the western districts of London were still greatly in want of water. Upon a division, it was ordered by 43 yeas against 36 noes, that the Committee's report should be considered by a Committee of the whole House. After several adjournments, the House, on March 12, 1723, resolved itself into Committee, but no report was made, and the two schemes came to nothing.[1]

Competitive scheme: streams near Drayton.

Both schemes reported as practicable.

Considered in Committee of whole House.

By repeated decisions the House of Commons had shown a clear disinclination to sanction interference with these affluents of the Thames for a supply of water to London. Undaunted, however, by previous failures, two similar schemes were put forward in 1724-5, and were sharply contested. A petition

Schemes of 1724-6.

[1] 20 Com. Journ. 292.

to supply the cities of London and Westminster, and parts adjacent, with water from the Cowley streams was referred,

Committee to consider petition.

on November 19, 1724, to a Committee consisting of more than fifty nominated members (among whom was the Master of the Rolls, Sir Joseph Jekyll), with all the members for Middlesex, as well as for London and Westminster.[1] It was an open Committee, and all that came were to have voices. In January, after the holidays, an opposing petition was presented by barge-masters of Wallingford, who asked to be heard by counsel. In the ordinary course such petitions would be referred to a Committee on a Bill, but here the Bill had not yet been introduced. A motion was made that the opposing petition should be referred to the Committee who were considering the adventurers' petition. Opinion was evenly balanced, for the motion was only carried by a majority of one, 93 against 92 votes.[2] There must have been a strong feeling to call together so full a House upon a discussion of the preliminary stages to a private Bill.

Competing scheme for supply from Cowley river.

At the same sitting, another set of adventurers petitioned for leave to construct a new river, or canal, navigable for boats and other vessels, also from Cowley river, below Uxbridge, to Oxford Square, in the parish of St. Marylebone. At the same time the river Colne was to be made navigable to Watford, and the west of London supplied with good and wholesome water, without prejudice to anybody. A motion

Petition referred to Committee.

to refer this petition to the same Committee, who were considering the petitions already noticed, was negatived, and a new Committee was appointed of more than twenty members, including the Attorney-General, with the members for Middlesex and the City. As before, all that came were to have voices; and, like the other Committee, they were authorized to send for persons, papers, and records.

[1] 20 Com. Journ. 343; November 19, 1724. [2] Ib. 372; January 18, 1725.

Many witnesses were examined. They had taken levels from Cowley stream " to the pavement of Lord Harcourt's hall door in Oxford Square," and found a sufficient fall. The intended river was to be about thirty feet wide, and five feet deep; by the abstraction of water the Thames would not be lowered in depth by so much as the thickness of a five-shilling piece. The Committee reported that, in their opinion, the adventurers had fully proved their allegations, but a motion for leave to bring in a Bill was negatived by a decisive majority of 133 votes to 72.[1]

Scheme approved by Committee; rejected by House.

The scheme referred to the first Committee was next dealt with. From the Cowley stream there was to be a canal which, in its "meanders," would be twenty miles long. Compensation water was provided for mill-owners, but mills were to be turned from undershot to overshot mills. After hearing much evidence, the Committee came to four distinct resolutions : that (1) there was great want of water in London and Westminster; (2) the plan proposed was practicable ; (3) it might be executed without damage to mill-owners on the Cowley stream ; (4) no damage would be done to navigation in the Thames. These resolutions were communicated to the House of Commons, and, on question put, were agreed to. On a motion for leave to bring in a Bill, Mr. Chancellor of the Exchequer communicated his Majesty's assent, "as far as it would affect the water of Hampton Court." [2] This reception seemed of good augury. Meanwhile petitions had been presented for and against the scheme, some leather dressers and tanners at Poyle Mill again complaining that they would suffer great injury through abstraction of water, that the adventurers proposed to give them no satisfaction, and that the Crown would lose 700l. a year in duties now paid by them.

Evidence on petition.

Resolutions of Committee adopted by House.

On February 18, the Bill having been introduced, the House heard counsel for and against it, and it was then

Second reading.

---

[1] 20 C. J. 382; January 26, 1725.   [2] Ib. 385; January 28, 1725.

read a second time.[1]   Immediately afterwards petitions were read from millers on the Colne, landowners, and the leather dressers and tanners at Poyle Mill.   Counsel against the Bill were next heard, and after examining several witnesses summed up their evidence.   By this time the House were tired of the subject, but a motion to adjourn the further hearing was negatived by thirty to twenty votes, and counsel were recalled and allowed to examine another witness.[2]   Next day the House again divided upon a question whether counsel should be further heard on the following Monday, and an affirmative decision was come to by 120 to 88 votes.   So far the promoters had triumphed over many obstacles, and a considerable majority of the House were clearly in their favour.   But one of the mischances frequent in Parliamentary strife was now to befall them.   On the day appointed, counsel for the Bill " examined several witnesses, went through their evidence, and summed up the same."   Opposing counsel then replied.   A motion to commit the Bill was next made, but was defeated by forty votes against thirty-four.   It was probably a division snatched against the Bill in the absence of its usual supporters.[3]

A scheme was prepared in 1730 to supply London and Westminster, and parts adjacent, with water from the rivers Colne, Gade, Bulborne, Chesham Water, and Lea, under the title of " The Company of St. Alban's Waters."   But, like so many of its predecessors, the plan came to nothing.   Again, in 1766, " several noblemen and gentlemen " tried their fortune in the House of Commons with a plan for serving the west end of London and Westminster with water from the Colne.   Previous failures they attributed to the injury which mill-owners would suffer if water were taken above Uxbridge.   They therefore proposed to take it from a point called Hobart's Mill, three miles below Uxbridge, by a cut navigable for

Counsel and evidence at bar of House.

Motion for committal negatived.

Supply proposed from the Colne, 1730, and 1766.

---

[1] 20 Com. Journ. 415.   [3] Ib. 418 ; February 22, 1725.
[2] Ib. 416.

boats, barges, and other vessels, to Williams's farm-house, Marylebone. They were willing to make adequate satisfaction to any mill-owners who might be injured; and if their plan were sanctioned by Parliament they had "a proposal pending for an agreement with the Governor and Company of Chelsea Waterworks for uniting the petitioners' undertaking with that company, and making them one united company with a joint stock."[1] So hostile was the House to this scheme that even the bringing-up of the petition was opposed, though it was carried by twenty-nine to nine votes. The petition was afterwards referred to a Committee, along with several opposing petitions, but no report was presented by the Committee, and the plan therefore dropped.

Fusion contemplated with Chelsea Company.

Failure of scheme.

A curious proposal was made in the same Session by a city merchant, Thomas Long, to make and maintain in Moorfields a reservoir, from which water might be drawn on the breaking out of fires, the proprietors of the London Bridge waterworks being under covenant to keep this reservoir full when made. A part of the scheme was to build around the reservoir houses then "much wanted for substantial inhabitants and merchants;" the site being "at present unoccupied and a receptacle for idle and disorderly persons." A motion to refer this petition to a Committee was carried by 100 votes to 37,[2] and a month afterwards the Committee was revived, but no report was presented.

Proposed reservoir in Moorfields.

While water rights and other interests on the Colne were protected against attack, the Lea was surrendered as a source of supply for East London. An Act was obtained in 1748 by George Montgomerie, Thomas Byrd and Ezra Patching, authorizing them " to complete an undertaking for furnishing the inhabitants of Stratford, West Ham, Bow, Bromley, Mile End, Stepney, and other parishes and places adjacent" with water from the river Lea; " and for better

Supply from the Lea for East London.

[1] 30 Com. Journ. 584; February 16, 1766. [2] Ib. 481; January 22, 1766.

securing their property in such undertaking."[1]   One condition imposed upon the adventurers, as in the Chelsea Act, was that they should erect, without charge, in convenient spots to be fixed by the respective vestries, stand-pipes for a free delivery of water in case of fires.   Twelve years after

Supply in East London in 1762.

this Act was passed, parts of East London were still badly served with water, as was shown by evidence given before the House of Commons in 1762, upon a Bill promoted by "several adventurers and undertakers" for serving Hackney from the Lea.   The only supply of the inhabitants was then derived from pumps and rain water; in dry weather, carts brought round for sale water taken from the Lea.   The New River Company had refused to serve Hackney unless they were guaranteed "an annual payment of 250*l.*," but this very moderate sum the inhabitants were unable or unwilling to provide.   Mr. Smeaton was engineer of the scheme, and was examined before a Committee in its favour.   Leave was afterwards given by the House to Mr. Wilkes, Mr. Buller, and Mr. Alderman Harley to introduce a Bill, but it did not pass.

South London.

South London was first supplied with water under statutory powers by the Lambeth Water Company, who obtained their Act in 1785.[2]   Their petition for a Bill represented that inhabitants of Lambeth and parts adjacent were in great want of water for domestic use, and liable to heavy losses from fire; and that certain persons had "agreed to raise a fund for the establishment of an engine and other

Subscription for purposes of Act.

necessary works."   They had not applied to the House of Commons until "the last day for receiving petitions for private Bills was past, because a subscription for the fund requisite for establishing such engine and works was not filled till after that day."   But as the summer months

---

[1] 21 Geo. II. c. 8.   The three adventurers named in the Act had set on foot works in the year 1743, and pumped water from the Lea by

a steam - engine on Newcomen's principle.

[2] 25 Geo. III. c. 89.

were "most proper for erecting this engine," petitioners asked the House to relax its rule, and this indulgence was granted. There was no opposition to their Bill,[1] and the subscribers were accordingly incorporated as "The Company of Proprietors of Lambeth Waterworks," with power to supply "the parish of Lambeth, and parts adjacent," with water from the Thames, to make cuts into the river, erect engines, waterhouses, or other devices upon any ground they might purchase or rent, lying 300 yards from the river bank, between Westminster Bridge and the parish of Christchurch, and make and maintain any reservoir that might be necessary for keeping and receiving water. A clause, introduced, it would seem, for the protection of local authorities rather than of competing water undertakings, prevented the Company from laying down pipes in any of the then paved streets in the parishes of St. George and St. Saviour, Southwark. The company's share capital was 4,800*l.*, divided into 32 shares of 150*l.* each; and no person was to hold more than four shares, unless they came to him by will or act of law. If the first subscriptions were not sufficient, a further sum of 4,800*l.* might be raised. These were clearly the days of modest estimates and outlay.

Lambeth Water Works Company.

Area of supply.

Restriction from laying pipes in paved streets in Southwark.

Capital.

When canals were made around London, it occurred to the projectors that, as water must be provided for navigation, it might also be supplied at a profit for public consumption. Thus the Grand Junction Canal Company, in their Act of 1798,[2] obtained powers to make subsidiary works, in order to furnish good and wholesome water in Paddington and adjacent districts. In like manner a company which, in 1801, proposed to cut a canal from Croydon to Deptford were authorised to supply drinking water in Croydon, Dulwich, Streatham, Norwood, and Sydenham.[3] The Surrey Canal Com-

Drinking water from canals.

Grand Junction.

Croydon.

Surrey.

[1] 40 Com. Journ. 925; May 3, 1785.

[2] 38 Geo. III. c. 33.

[3] 41 Geo. III. c. 127. This canal

pany were allowed similar powers in Bermondsey, Camberwell, New Cross, Rotherhithe, and Walworth.[1]

Twenty years after the Lambeth Act had passed, another company was formed to supply parts of the same district, and other places in South London. The usual petition, on which a Bill was to be founded in the House of Commons, set forth a great want of good water among the growing population of Camberwell, and parts of Lambeth, Bermondsey, Rotherhithe, Deptford, Newington, Walworth, Kennington, Stockwell, Clapham, Peckham, Peckham Rye, Dulwich, and places adjacent; a wide district, extending into two counties. Water was to be procured from the Thames. Engines and works were proposed at Kennington Green, or near Vauxhall creek, or at a creek close to Cumberland Tea Gardens.[2] Upon a report by a Committee to whom this petition was referred, that the Standing Orders relative to Bills for making aqueducts had been complied with, and that witnesses had been heard in proof of the petitioners' allegations, a Bill was allowed to be brought in by Lord

William Russell and Sir John Frederick. Existing water companies were then aroused, and opposing petitions promptly presented by the Croydon Canal, Surrey Canal, and Lambeth Companies, in defence of their vested interests. Trustees

of roads, also, for the first time appeared, alleging injury to thoroughfares "from the manner of laying down and amending" water pipes; a statement for which there was ample reason, owing to frequent leakage from the wooden mains then in use.

There was a prolonged inquiry before the Committee, which was open to all members, and counsel were heard for

---

was bought by the London and Croydon Railway Company. (See 5 & 6 Will. IV. c. 10.)

[1] 48 Geo. III. c. 99. According to a recital in a subsequent Act of 1811 (51 Geo. III. c. 170), the company had then been unable to raise any capital for the construction of waterworks.

[2] 60 Com. Journ. 11; January 22, 1805.

all opposing petitioners. It was not till May 31 that the Committee reported. They then acquainted the House that the allegations in the preamble had not been proved to their satisfaction. Such a finding by a Committee would now be fatal to any Bill. In this instance the Committee went on to report that they "had gone through part of the Bill, and made several amendments thereunto." Upon a motion that their report be taken into consideration on a future day, a three months' amendment was defeated by 51 votes to 9, and a copy of the minutes of evidence taken by them was ordered to be printed and laid before the House,[1] which thus resolved to take the matter into its own hands. On June 17, the House, by a majority of 41 to 16 votes, disagreed with an amendment made by the Committee, and sent back the Bill to them.[2] On July 3, the Bill passed the House of Commons, after having been under consideration there for more than five months. It was soon despatched by the Lords, who received it on July 4, read it a second time, and committed it on the next day; while the Committee reported it, through the Duke of Norfolk, five days afterwards, showing by their amendments that they had considered it with minuteness. To all these amendments the House of Commons agreed on July 11; and next day came the Royal assent.

The Act thus obtained bears clearer traces of a tenderness for vested interests than any other Water Act passed up to that period. One provision, due to opposition from the Lambeth Company, did not, indeed, shut out the new-comers from the whole parish of Lambeth, but specified exact limits which they must not overpass there.[3] In the House of Lords, they were forbidden to furnish any supply within the county of Kent. In that House there was a hostile appearance by representatives of two patentees who had obtained from William III. in 1699 an exclusive right to supply inhabitants within the Royal manors of East

South London Water Works Act, 1805.

Existing rights protected.

---

[1] 60 Com. Journ. 333.   [3] 45 Geo. III. c. 119, s. 17.
[2] Ib. 385.

Greenwich and Sayes Court. These petitioners also obtained protection, and the new company were restrained from invading their district.[1] But a sufficient area was left, for the company might supply the whole of Camberwell, with parts of Bermondsey, Rotherhithe, Lambeth, Newington, Walworth, Kennington, Stockwell, Clapham, Peckham, Peckham Rye, " and other places." [2] A saving clause was given to the Surrey Canal Company; and in the interest of other canal companies it was provided that no cut or communication made by the company " with the river Thames, or with any navigable canal or railway," should be made " a conveyance for goods, wares or merchandize." [3] No water was, under any circumstances, to be taken from the Wandle or Ravensbourne, or from any of their springs, streams, or feeders.[4]

Area of supply.

Competition with canals forbidden.

There had been a formidable opposition by landowners, whose influence was shown in various provisions. No roving powers were given, as in some previous Water Acts, to make reservoirs wherever the company pleased, if they could only buy the necessary land. Here the company were allowed to construct no other reservoirs, or watercourses leading to them, than those shown on a deposited map; [5] and to an intended reservoir in the parish of Camberwell it was necessary to obtain previous consents from the Bishop of the diocese, and the patron and vicar of St. Giles respectively.[6] The Act was not to be construed so as to authorize engines worked by fire or steam in any place where in law they would be deemed a nuisance. No land belonging to the Prince of Wales, the Archbishop of Canterbury, or Mr. Joseph Windham, was to be taken without their consent. Full recompense and satisfaction were to be made for all tithes, both great and small, taken for the proposed works. A long clause regulated any opening of roads, so that as

Landowners.

Reservoirs.

Nuisances.

Tithes.

Roads.

---

[1] 45 Geo. III. c. 119, s. 66.
[2] Ib. s. 15.
[3] Ib. ss. 65, 70.
[4] Ib. s. 71.
[5] Ib. s. 16.
[6] Ib. s. 18.

little injury as possible should be done to them. Lastly, Capital.
the company's capital was fixed at 50,000*l*., but they might
raise 30,000*l*. additional among themselves, or by mortgage.

In other parts of South London enterprise was busy in
the same direction. A Bill was promoted in 1808 by a body Kent Water
of adventurers, who sought for power to supply Greenwich, Works Company, 1808-9.
Plumstead, Woolwich, Deptford, Blackheath, and other
places in the counties of Kent and Surrey, from waterworks
constructed at Ravensbourne marshes, Greenwich, and at
Blackheath; but this Bill was opposed and defeated by proprietors of the Ravensbourne Waterworks at Deptford, whose
rights had been protected by a clause in the South London
Act. It is noteworthy that this result was not due to com- Standing
petition but to several Standing Order objections taken by Order objections.
the petitioners. Among other defaults, the promoters had
not published notices of their intended application to Parliament in any Kentish newspapers; they had not deposited
with the Clerk of the Peace for Surrey a plan of their proposed aqueducts; and in the plan annexed to their petition
for leave to bring in a Bill their proposed line of aqueducts
was not shown.[1] These objections were fatal. In 1809 the
Bill was re-introduced, and there was renewed opposition
from proprietors of the Ravensbourne works. During the
progress of their Bill, however, the promoters agreed to
purchase this undertaking. Their Bill then passed without
further opposition,[2] though their area of supply was confined
to certain parts of Deptford, Greenwich, New Cross, Lewisham, Rotherhithe, "and not elsewhere,"[3] but including any
districts served by the purchased works.

Woolwich was omitted from the Kent Company's district,
because in the same Session a Bill passed, enabling Commis- Improvement
sioners under a local Act[4] at Woolwich to supply the town Commissioners at
and parish with water. This was the main object of a sioners at

---

[1] 63 Com. Journ. 321.
[2] 49 Geo. III. c. 139.
[3] Ib. s. 41.

[4] 47 Geo. III. sess. 2, c. 111; a
paving, lighting, and watching Act.

Woolwich enabled to supply water.

measure[1] which is of interest as an early effort by a local authority within the metropolitan area to revert to old methods of providing water for inhabitants, instead of leaving this work to private enterprise. This Act is also remark-

Charge for water assessed on rating.

able as being the first to fix charges for water and base assessments upon rating. Every occupier rated at or under 20*l.* was to pay 20*s.* yearly, and one shilling for every pound of additional rate. Consumers were to pay quarterly in advance. For trade purposes charges were to be settled by

Application of surplus revenue.

agreement. If any surplus remained from water revenue after paying interest on money borrowed, and expenses, it was to be applied towards relieving the poor of Woolwich.[2] The powers of this Act were sufficient; unfortunately they were never exercised.

South London Waterworks Bill, 1810.

Dissatisfied with their district, the South London Company tried to extend it, in 1810, to "the parishes of Newington; St. George's, Southwark; St. Mary, Lambeth; Christchurch, and parts adjacent." A Bill promoted for this object passed successfully through a Committee to which it was referred, but was strongly opposed by the Lambeth and Kent Companies, and though their opposition failed in Committee, they prevailed on the House of Commons to reject the Bill before its third reading by sixty votes to thirty-two.[3]

Holloway and Highbury.

A large part of the population in North London were without any regular supply of water before the year 1810, in consequence of the New River Company's refusal to extend their mains to new houses built around Holloway and Highgate. An Act was therefore obtained in 1810,[4] to supply Upper and Lower Holloway, Highbury, Canonbury, Upper Islington, "and their respective vicinities." A large well and reservoir was made at Holloway for the collection and storage of water, to be obtained by pumping

[1] 48 Geo. III. c. 146.
[2] Ib. s. 12.
[3] 65 Com. Journ. 283; April 13, 1810.
[4] 50 Geo. III. c. 150.

from deep springs there. After some money, however, had been spent in erecting machinery and constructing works, the New River Company determined to extend their system to this district. As the new association had obtained no exclusive rights of supply, and their expenditure largely exceeded the original estimates, they were unable to face a competition begun by older and wealthier rivals, and abandoned their undertaking.

It soon appeared, as might have been expected, that the business of a water and a canal company could not be advantageously combined. In South London the canal companies exercised their powers, if at all, to a very limited extent. The Grand Junction Canal Company employed Mr. Rennie to draw up plans for water works, but in the year 1811 they thought it expedient, in consideration of a rent reserved, to transfer their rights under their Act of 1798 to certain proprietors, who were incorporated as the Grand Junction Waterworks Company,[1] with power to raise 150,000*l.*, and a further like amount, if necessary, for a supply of water to " the parish of Paddington and parishes and streets adjacent." One section in the Act of 1811 provided that every furnace used by the company should be so constructed as to consume its own smoke; that every chimney should have its shaft at least 130 feet above the ground-level, and " that the smoke issuing therefrom shall not at any one time exceed the quantity of smoke usually issuing from the chimneys of twenty-four fires for domestic uses." On breach of this provision, any such chimney or furnace might be dealt with as a common nuisance. No furnace or steam engine could be erected within a quarter of a mile of the Edgware Road without the consent of Mr. Edward Berkely Portman, his heirs or assigns. Lessees or tenants upon the Bishop of London's estate at Paddington were to be supplied at ten per cent. below any average rates taken by

Grand Junction Waterworks Company, 1811.

Consumption of smoke.

---

[1] 51 Geo. III. c. 169.

which Parliament must have contemplated, and, indeed, had expressly sanctioned, when it permitted the West Middlesex Company to enter London in 1810.[1] To this competition Parliament trusted as a protection for consumers, who, in all other respects, were left at the mercy of the companies. There was no limit to profits, no restriction upon rates, no basis fixed on which rates should be charged; companies were not bound to supply any consumer, and might, therefore, be as capricious and arbitrary as they pleased, without appeal. But in many leading thoroughfares there were mains belonging to two companies, and sometimes even three; and when consumers could change their water company almost as easily as their baker, low charges and considerate treatment seemed certain, unless in the event of a combination which experience has shown to be still more certain under such conditions.

Shadwell and West Ham Companies. The end which might have been expected first came about in East London. Both the Shadwell and West Ham undertakings, it will be seen, enjoyed a respectable antiquity.[2] No distinct line of separation had been drawn between them. Each company, therefore, attempted to supply the same district. A competition ensued, which proved so injurious to both that they at last agreed upon a division of territory, and were thus enabled to charge remunerative rates. Neither **London Docks Company with powers of water supply.** enterprise, however, lived long into the century. In 1800, the London Docks Company demolished some 1,500 houses within the Shadwell district. By a clause in their Act,[3] this company were therefore compelled to purchase the Shadwell Waterworks, and were authorized to take the supply of water into their own hands. Competition with the West Ham Company was then renewed, and as it threatened to destroy all hopes of profit from either undertaking, negotiations were opened by the dock directors, and ended in an application by them to Parliament for statutory

---

[1] *Ante*, p. 109.
[2] *Ante*, pp. 83, 99.
[3] 39 & 40 Geo. III. c. 47.

powers to purchase the West Ham works. Their application succeeded in 1807.[1]

This consolidation of interests in East London led to fears of monopoly, and subscriptions were raised towards a rival project. Accordingly, after an ineffectual attempt in 1806, an Act was obtained in the following Session,[2] in spite of opposition from the New River and other rivals, constituting the East London Waterworks Company, and enabling them to supply from the river Lea at Old Ford the eastern and northern districts and about twenty adjacent parishes and hamlets.[3] Having, however, obtained these powers, the new company used them, not in furtherance of the wholesome competition which was expected, but in order to secure monopoly. They therefore entered into an arrangement with the London Docks Company to purchase the consolidated Shadwell and West Ham undertakings for a sum of 130,000*l.* This agreement was confirmed by Parliament in 1808;[4] and the Dock Company were no doubt glad to be relieved from a business so different from that for which they had been associated. From 1808, East London, for purposes of water supply, was thus handed over to the East London Company, subject, in part, to rivalry from the New River and London Bridge Companies. Down to the year 1815, the East London and New River Companies carried on a " destructive " competition for business.[5] Both had mains in the same streets;

East London Waterworks Company, 1807.

Competition of East London and New River Companies.

---

[1] 47 Geo. III. c. 5.

[2] 47 Geo. III c. 72.

[3] Such was the eagerness at this period to invest in water undertakings, that, before any dividend was paid, the East London Company's 100*l.* shares were at 60*l.* premium, and gradually increased in value till they commanded a premium of 130*l.*

[4] 48 Geo. III. c. 8.

[5] Commons' Committee of 1821 on Metropolitan Water Supply: evidence of Mr. Joseph Steevens, Engineer of East London Company,

pp. 59, 60. Some incidents of this competition may be gathered from the following questions :—" Was not the competition used as a means of reducing rates and sometimes of evading them altogether ?—It was to a considerable extent. *Q.* Was it not usual for tenants from half-year to half-year to refuse payment of their water-rates, and dare the company to take any measure to recover what was owing ?—Very frequently so. *Q.* Threatening to resort to the other company, and so shift

consumers changed frequently from one company to another, being tempted by lower prices or other inducements, so that streets were constantly broken up; and their outlay was so large that neither company could supply the common district to a profit.

South London,

On the other side of the Thames the South London Company complained that, whereas they were confined within a specified district, the Lambeth Company could, and did, compete with them in that district, to their great loss.[1] In a joint Memorial, dated January 10, 1845, to the Health of Towns[2] Commissioners, the Southwark and Vauxhall Companies (not then amalgamated), refer to some disastrous results of competition in South London. They state that, prior to 1834, they, with the Lambeth Company, were possessed of charters "which more or less permitted or encouraged competition;" and after Acts obtained by them in 1834, this competition "was in full activity during the years 1839, 1840 and 1841, and has only completely ceased since 1842." They sum up the results of this struggle as follows :—

Waste of capital in competition.

" An immense expenditure of capital in utter waste; double or treble sets of mains and pipes being laid down in districts where one set would better have served the inhabitants. An enormous annual outlay, equally in utter waste,

from one to the other when payment was demanded ?—Yes. Many of them were so unreasonable as to declare that unless the company would be at the expense of breaking up the pavement and thawing the pipes during a frost, they would go to the other company. Q. In consequence of the lenity shown to poor tenants, did your arrears of rates increase to a large amount ?—From 15,000l. to 20,000l." In other words, the company feared to drive their poorer customers to another source of supply by enforcing arrears. Water consumers then clearly enjoyed an independence very far removed from their existing status.

[1] Ib. : evidence of Mr. Marshall, Secretary of South London Water Company, pp. 63-6.

[2] Supplement to Second Report of Commissioners on the State of Large Towns and Populous Districts, pp. 116-118. This Memorial was in opposition to a Bill, of which notice had been given, for supplying South London, and some parts north of the Thames, with water from the Wandle, culverts being carried down that river, on both sides, from its source to its junction with the Thames, to intercept all drainage.

in the salaries of canvassers and commission to agents, who procured tenants; in the bills of plumbers who changed the service-pipes of tenants from one set of mains to another; in the charges of taking up and relaying roads and pavements on the like occasions;[1] in double and treble sets of turncocks and pipe-layers; and, as the climax of absurdity, a payment of all parochial and district rates in every parish on all the pipes of all the companies in proportion to the capital expended on assumed profits or interest, which it is needless to say had no existence. These expenses being accompanied by a great reduction of rates, the result was such as might have been anticipated; one of the companies, overwhelmed with difficulties and debts, ceased to pay dividends to its shareholders; the other, too, must shortly have arrived at the same condition; and the total return on more than half a million of capital expended has not since been, and is not now, more than $2\frac{3}{5}$ per cent. per annum."

When such were the results of competition to undertakings of large capital and resources, it may easily be supposed that smaller water companies suffered still more severely. By conditions in their leases, the London Bridge Company on the northern bank were restricted to the city, but, in fact, supplied many hundred houses outside, in Goodman's Fields and Whitechapel, the old Artillery Ground, Spitalfields, and parts of Shoreditch. They therefore came into direct conflict with the New River and East London Companies, both of whom gave water of better quality,[2] and could send it to higher levels. No effective supply could be given from London Bridge at a greater elevation than one story; and as houses now began to be built with cisterns and conveniences at higher levels than had before been usual, a high pressure service was naturally preferred by consumers. From these

London Bridge works.

[1] The expenditure of the three companies for these three items alone, namely, canvassing and commission, plumbers' bills, and taking up and relaying pavements, &c. amounted, in the year 1841, to not less than 4,300*l.*

[2] In the Committee of 1821, the London Bridge Company's Secretary was asked — "Is not your water the most inferior of all the water supplied by other works?"—"So far from being inferior, in many instances distillers take our water in preference to any other. Some people may prefer the New River, but there are many that think our water vastly softer than the New River, and take it in preference." Q. "Is it not so soft that it is not drinkable?" — "I never think of drinking it." (Ev. p. 16.)

causes, and encroachments on their district, the London Bridge Company were not prosperous, and in 1820 their 100*l.* shares had sunk to one-half that value.

York Buildings Waterworks.

Another small and early adventure suffered from similar causes. The York Buildings Waterworks Company had undergone many vicissitudes since their grant of letters patent by Charles II. They did not confine themselves to a supply of water, but speculated in the purchase of forfeited estates, and in 1742 were appellants in a case heard in the House of Lords, as lessees of certain lead-mines in Argyle and Peebles, for which they had covenanted to pay " a sixth dish or part" of all ore dug, and a rental of 3,600*l.* a year. Whether from these or other ill-advised speculations, the company's affairs became seriously embarrassed. Having raised money by an issue of bonds secured on their joint-stock property, they were unable to pay the accruing interest, or discharge the principal, and assigned their common seal to some of their principal creditors. Afterwards, their affairs being thrown into Chancery, their waterworks were vested in trustees, with power to let the works on lease, and apply any proceeds in liquidation of debts.[1] The undertaking was then leased to a private individual. His representatives continued to supply water until the year 1810, when the lease was purchased by a new company, with a capital increased from 8,400*l.* to 75,000*l.*

In 1812, fresh capital was raised, wooden pipes were replaced by a complete system of iron mains and services, a large steam-engine was put up for pumping, and works were constructed in the river-bed which would have enabled the company to supply about 10,000 houses. Unfortunately, however, for the new proprietors who had shown this enterprise, other water companies now began to compete with

[1] In 1777, an Act passed (17 Geo. III. c. 24), "for expediting the sale of estates in Scotland belonging to the York Buildings Company, for the relief of their creditors." Among other property bought by the company were the Panmure, Brechin, Marischall, Kilsyth, Linlithgow, Fingask, Kinnaird, and Southesk estates. (See Reports of Commons' Committees, 1732-5.)

them for business; and the York Buildings Company, hemmed in by powerful neighbours, could not hold their own. Their district was common to those of the New River, Chelsea, and Grand Junction Companies. "In some cases these companies threatened to work for nothing; they said 'We have plenty of money. What we want is a numerical rental; and when we have got that we will turn you out of the field.'" Such was the evidence given in 1821, with natural bitterness, by a gentleman who had been for 21 years secretary of what was then a defunct association, ruined by a competition which, in the Haymarket and in Piccadilly among other places, was carried on by the larger companies with a determination to secure business, whether at remunerative rates or not.[1] In 1818, the York Buildings undertaking disappeared: its works and plant were bought by the New River Company for 32,000l.

Undertaking absorbed by New River Company.

It was, however, between four companies in the west and north-west that competition was most keen, and was carried on with the greatest bitterness. At this period the New River Company had spread themselves over most of the northern suburbs, and penetrated to the west, where growing wealth and population promised them rich returns. Here, however, they met with formidable rivals. The Chelsea and Grand Junction were already in partial possession, and by their Act of 1810, the West Middlesex took root in the same districts, commissioned, it may almost be said, by Parliament to compete there with existing companies.[2] These new-comers had appealed to the vestries to support their Bill of 1810, undertaking "not only to lay down iron pipes throughout the whole of their service, and thereby save to each parish the expense and inconvenience so incessantly occasioned in taking up pavements on account of the wear and bursting of wooden pipes, but to give a most ample supply of perfectly settled soft water for domestic

Competition of New River and West Middlesex Companies.

Advantages promised by West Middlesex Company.

---

[1] Commons' Committee of 1821 on Metropolitan Water Supply: Evidence of Mr. James Dupin, 23–5.
[2] *Ante*, pp. 109–10.

purposes, and to make such arrangements with the different fire offices as shall ensure an instantaneous supply of water for use by engines wherever fires happen."[1] Having obtained their Act, and completed their works in 1811, the West Middlesex directors at once began to fulfil their mission by active hostilities. "In justice to themselves, as well as for the information of the public," they thought it was " incumbent on them concisely to state," among other advantages they were able to hold out to consumers, " that their supply is derived from the bed of the river Thames, from off a fine gravelly bottom, thirteen miles above London Bridge, pure as it comes from the country, of superior excellence and unlimited in quantity, and that it is received in reservoirs, which, if it had any sediment to deposit, in times of rain or otherwise, would transmit it perfectly clear and bright to their tenants."[2] Their next circular, dated October 16, 1811, was of a more aggressive character. They now stated that, in addition to the advantages of purer water and higher pressure, they were "enabled to supply their tenants at lower rates than those adopted by any existing establishment." Then they continued :—

" It is doubtless on this account that Parliament has of late thought fit to incorporate so many new water companies; by whose competition, as the supply must of course increase, a corresponding diminution could not fail to take place in the price of the commodity.

General reduction of water rates through competition.

"The West Middlesex Company have a pride in forwarding, thus early in their career, the provident designs of the Legislature; nor are they withheld from the performance of this duty, though aware of the clamour likely to be raised by those whom their example will compel (and compel them it must) to a proportionate reduction in their demands. They feel confident that a discerning community will at once perceive, in such proposed reduction, the natural effect of a widened competition, and that by holding forth every fair encouragement to the West Middlesex Company, the public

[1] Letter of West Middlesex Water Company, dated February 14, 1810, to the vestries of St. Giles's-in-the- Fields, and St. George's, Bloomsbury.

[2] Circular of August 21, 1811.

will enable them to continue in the market; their expulsion from which, by the operation of the unerring principle above adverted to, must infallibly produce, first the re-establishment, and eventually an augmentation of present prices. . . .

"Postscript, Nov. 1.—That which was predicted in the above address has actually occurred. The different water companies are now offering to reduce their prices. It is sufficiently evident to what cause this reduction is attributable; and the directors of the West Middlesex Company rely with increased confidence on the liberal support of the public."

This and other attacks brought the New River Company into the lists with a long "address to the occupiers of houses supplied with water" by them. Some of the facts mentioned in it are of historical interest :— *Reply by New River Board.*

"The present opposition to the New River Company, and the unjust representations of their conduct, have rendered it a duty to make this appeal, and to show their claims upon the public.

"They have served the Metropolis with water nearly two centuries, at rates which have at no time yielded them above 6¼ per cent., and for many years past not 5 per cent., on their capital; whether it be estimated by the original cost of their works, by the actual value of those works, and of the company's stock-in-trade in its present state, or by the prices which the present proprietors have paid for their shares. The property of the company has advanced less beyond its original value than any species of real property since the commencement of their undertaking. *Water supplied hitherto with moderate profits to company.*

"The absurd report that their shares (seventy-two in number) originally cost only 100*l.* each, needs no other refutation than the statement that their water was brought to London through an aqueduct of forty miles in length. The formation of their works in the time of the original projector, Sir Hugh Middleton, cost, according to the best authorities, 500,000*l.*;[1] and they yielded no dividend for twenty years. *Alleged cost of New River in Middleton's time.*

---

[1] Cf. estimate founded on the moiety of the original expenditure paid by James I. (*ante*, p. 68, *n.*). It will be remembered, however, that the company resold the thirty-six King's shares, after their surrender by Charles I. for an annual "clog," and applied the proceeds in extending their works. In 1821, the New River Company furnished a Committee of the House of Commons with an estimate of their capital expenditure, which included 369,600*l.* "for original purchase of the

"The New River actually discharges above 214,000 hogs-heads of water in every twenty-four hours into the town; the prices received for this water, and the average rate of rents for its use, will show the extreme cheapness with which an abundant supply of one of the greatest conveniences of life has been afforded by the company to the public; and how little they deserve the imputation of abusing the advantage of a market without competition. Comparing the whole quantity supplied in the year at 214,000 hogsheads per day, with the gross annual receipts of the company, the gross price received for their water does not exceed two shillings for each hundred hogsheads. The average rental upon the houses supplied is something less than twenty-seven shillings per annum, or about sixpence per week for each house; the most numerous class of private houses is supplied at less than one-third of this rate, this depression of the rate in favour of the poorer inhabitants being, of course, compensated by a rise on the higher class of houses proportioned to their magnitude, and to the greater abundance of the supply."

Average water-rate per house.

These facts, the directors hoped, would show that the New River Company were not, as had been represented, an oppressive monopoly. They would also show what foundation there was for hopes of large returns from a speculative investment of money in new waterworks. Then the directors pointed to the advantage they enjoyed, in their reservoir at Islington, of a natural elevation of eighty-five feet above the level of the Thames, with a further height of thirty-five feet to which New River water was raised there by powerful machinery. "If," they added, "the rental of the New River Company has been hitherto such as to have afforded, with these advantages, a bare interest on its capital, the most

Advantage of natural pressure by gravitation.

springs of Chadwell and Amwell; remuneration to millers upon river of Lea; purchase of land for formation of river; excavation of ground; levelling and puddling of banks; timber and brick wharfing at various places on banks eighty miles long; embankment of various valleys; and tunnelling at five guineas a yard:" 15,700*l*. for 157 brick, timber, and iron bridges; 8,120*l*. for 57 culverts; 6,000*l*. for "the purchase of 60 acres of land adjoining the river at various places;" purchase of land for reservoirs, ponds and heads cisterns, and their construction, 108,300*l*. The total outlay down to 1820, including 32,000*l*. paid for the York Buildings Waterworks, was 1,115,500*l*.

sanguine adventurer will hardly look for a better return where every ton of water must be raised by steam to a height of 120 feet to bring it on a level with the present power of the New River Company. Whether water so raised can be profitably sold at the rate of two shillings for every hundred hogsheads, is matter of no difficult computation for those who are at all acquainted with the powers of steam engines, and the expenses of maintaining and working them." To their numerous tenants[1] the directors promised "that whatever be the expense, or reduction of fair profit to the company, they shall be supplied as effectually, in every respect, and at as low a price as they can possibly be, by any other water company." In conclusion, they trusted that their tenants "will honour them with their support until an opportunity has been given of showing that the company's resources are abundantly sufficient to furnish and continue to them every advantage which has been holden out by any of its competitors."[2]

By no means disinclined to return to the fray, the West Middlesex directors issued a reply of almost equal length[3], twitting the New River Company with apprehensions of an utter overthrow of their monopoly, and attempting an elaborate refutation of their financial statement :—

Reply of West Middlesex board.

"The New River directors do not condescend to specify the amount of capital on which the company have divided '6¼, and for many years past not more than 5 per cent.;' but, estimated in either of two modes suggested by themselves, it must be enormous. 500,000l., it seems, were expended in bringing their water to London, through an aqueduct of forty miles; and as 'the works yielded no dividend for twenty years' the real amount of this outlay may be fairly stated at 1,500,000l. Taking, however, as a more correct mode of computation, the cost of shares to the actual proprietors, or the sums at which they have been rated in bequests and inheritances for the last thirty years, which

New River finances examined.

---

[1] In publications of this period, persons supplied with water were generally described as tenants of the water company.

[2] Circular of February 27, 1812, by New River board.

[3] Circular of April 27, 1812, by West Middlesex board.

may be moderately averaged at 12,000*l.* each, this sum multiplied by seventy-two, the number of shares, will make a capital to be divided upon of near 900,000*l.* But this is not all. On the system of wooden pipes, adopted by the New River Company, which require constant repairs and renovation, together with river charges, &c., the annual expenditure incurred by them exceeds 50,000*l.*; so that upwards of 104,000*l.* per annum must be levied upon the community before the proprietors can divide six per cent. on their capital, the lowest rate of profit certainly, upon which any trade can be carried on with advantage. How does the case stand at the present day? By the progress of the arts during the last two centuries (from the whole benefit of which the New River Company would willingly exclude the public), steam engines and other mechanical powers are capable of forcing a level of sufficient elevation to supply the upper stories of every house in London; and though our ancestors, to whom these things were unknown, were compelled to go forty miles in search of a similar, though not an equal, facility, it does not seem very reasonable that the present race should be assessed, in order to make good to their representatives this now superfluous expenditure. About half of the New River capital, taken at 900,000*l.*, would suffice to construct works adequate to the supply of its actual tenants; while under the system of iron pipes, the same might be administered at a third of its annual expenditure. It follows that a new company, when in equal service, would be able, on the same scale of profits, to undersell the New River Company in that proportion.

Steam pumping contrasted with gravitation.

"Thus, then, it appears with what little reason the directors of the New River Company take credit with the public for the cheap rate at which they have served the Metropolis. Cheapness is a relative term: that article has reached its minimum, which, being brought to market at the least possible cost, is sold at the lowest profit; but if an unnecessary expense be incurred in bringing it thither, the article is comparatively dear; it matters not how small may be the rate of profit to the dealer."[1]

Cheapness of New River supply denied.

[1] Among other curious productions of this period are cards introducing "deputations," who waited on consumers to solicit their custom on behalf of rival companies. Here is one specimen:—"A deputation from the West Middlesex Water-works Company to solicit the favour of your custom and support for that establishment. The water supplied by this company is of the purest and softest quality, being taken from the Thames near Hammersmith, and filtered in spacious reservoirs. The superior powers of their works enable them also to deliver it to the

Meanwhile, as we have seen,[1] the Grand Junction Canal Company thought the time opportune for exercising their powers to provide water in Paddington and the neighbourhood; powers which had lain dormant since the year 1798. In 1810, therefore, they also issued a notice to the public that works were in progress which would ensure a supply, " far superior to any other in this Kingdom," yielding " an abundance of pure and excellent soft water," and carried down Oxford Street in " a grand main, at present casting, thirty inches in diameter." This supply would be afforded by a separate company,[1] for whom they paved the way in this notice. They assured the public that the water in their canal was " unequalled in the Metropolis." It had been " analysed and found excellent for all culinary and domestic purposes." It was also " lighter," and contained " less foreign matter than Thames water." New reservoirs were being made, and new streams of water introduced, which would enable the company not only to perform their engagement of supplying 40,000 houses, but to meet any demand that might arise. Hence, it was obvious that their undertaking would confer great public benefit, and the proprietors hoped for liberal support.[2] In 1811, when the Grand Junction Waterworks Company were incorporated, they renewed this appeal, giving testimonials founded upon analyses of the canal water, and promising to lay it on free of expense to their tenants. Extending their works beyond Paddington into Marylebone and the neighbourhood, they

Grand Junction Waterworks Company.

tops of the highest houses, by which the great expense and labour attendant on the use of force pumps is avoided. N.B.—The necessary change of pipes is made without expense to those who may favour the company with their orders." In another card the company add — " The peculiar softness of the Thames water need not be dwelt on; nor is it necessary to make a comparison between the salubrity of a supply drawn from the first river in Europe, and that which is deposited from streams unpurified by tide, and rendered turbid by the draining of marshy lands into a confined canal."

[1] *Ante,* p. 107.

[2] Advertisement headed " Grand Junction Waterworks," and dated November 15, 1810.

were able to compete there not only with the New River, but with the Chelsea and West Middlesex Companies.

Proposed amalgamation of New River and West Middlesex Companies, 1816.
Such serious losses were sustained by the parties to this competition, that, in 1815, the New River and West Middlesex Companies agreed to amalgamate their respective undertakings, and a Bill to this effect was submitted to Parliament in the Session of 1816. The petition for leave to introduce it contained elaborate reasons why such a Bill was necessary in the interests of the two companies, and would not be inconsistent with public interests.

Reasons for amalgamation.
" Under the pressure upon their present capital, the New River and West Middlesex Companies are not only deprived of the means of deriving an adequate return of profit thereon, but have incurred and are subjected to the continuance of great losses, whilst, at the same time, the public are exposed to inconvenience and danger through frequent removals of the pavement." The two companies " find it impossible to continue their respective establishments for the service and convenience of the public under the losses to which they are at present exposed. Much less can they, in their present relative situations as distinct and independent companies (unless by subjecting the public to a considerable increase of water rates), engage in the further enormous expense of completing their respective systems with iron pipes, the superiority of which over wooden pipes is so fully established, and the substitution of the one for the other so earnestly desired by the various parishes through which their pipes pass. But being desirous that the Metropolis should have perfected and perpetuated establishments of so useful and unrivalled a nature, it is expedient, for the attainment of so desirable an end, that the companies should be united, and form one company, under such provisions, and subject to such restrictions as will afford a fair and reasonable profit to the united company, but at the same time effectually secure the public from monopoly."[1]

Bill put off for six months.
On a motion for its second reading, this Bill was negatived without a division.[2] Probably the two companies were not keen for its success, in view of another arrangement then

[1] 70 Com. Journ. 43–4 ; February, 15, 1816.   [2] Ib. 230 ; March 20, 1816.

pénding, and afterwards applied, without authority from Parliament, to the whole Metropolis north of the Thames. This was a partition of districts, agreed upon between the companies: the same obvious method of settling differences as was adopted some years afterwards by rival gas companies throughout London. First to shake hands were the New River and East London Companies, who, on November 9, 1815, executed a formal agreement of amity and peace. It recited that, on account of difficulties and losses experienced by both contracting parties through competition in the same districts, they had respectively agreed to relinquish their right to supply water, the one to the east, the other to the west, of a certain line described in a schedule and plan annexed, each making over to the other all pipes and plant lying in the district relinquished. On an estimate of the respective value of this plant, a balance had been found in favour of the East London Company of 7,151*l*. As a fair equivalent, the New River Company agreed to transfer to the East London Company an annual rental of 715*l*., after the rate of ten years' purchase upon the capital sum found due. Then the deed contained mutual assignments of the plant thus abandoned, and mutual covenants, under penalties, at no time thereafter to supply water within the district allotted to each other.[1] Partition treaties to the same effect were made by the New River Company with their competitors in the western districts, but not till the close of the year 1817. In these cases there were no formal agreements, and each company reserved the right of re-entering their relinquished territory if they thought proper.[2] In each instance the boundary line was drawn, not merely for convenience of limits or nearness to sources of supply, but with

Marginal notes: Partition of districts. In East London, 1815. In West London, 1817.

[1] This agreement is set forth, in substance, by Commons' Committee of 1821 on Metropolis Water Supply, App. pp. 202–5.

[2] Minutes of Evidence, ib. p. 9.

But having sold their mains and pipes in the district surrendered, no company could re-enter it without new works (pp. 46, 47).

a view to secure to each company a certain rental previously agreed upon.[1]

This division of territory was made without reference to consumers, some of whom naturally felt much aggrieved on finding themselves suddenly transferred to a new source of supply, instead of one which they preferred.[2] From the companies' point of view a concentration of interests was easily defended. A statement made by the New River Company to the Marylebone Vestry in 1818, gave a most natural and reasonable explanation. During the previous eight years, they said, they had "sustained very heavy losses in the service of those quarters of the town into which the works of the new water companies" had been generally introduced. They believed those companies had suffered as severely; and experience having proved that there was not a sufficient demand to make a return to all, each company had withdrawn within certain limits, "with a view of extricating themselves from a situation which was tending very rapidly to the utter ruin of all their establishments." Similar explanations were given by the West Middlesex and Grand Junction directors.

Limitation of districts explained by companies.

Local authorities might rejoice to find that the same streets would no longer be broken up by two or three water companies. Consumers, however, had no such reason for approving of the new arrangements. Parliament thought it had protected their interests by encouraging competition, and had therefore imposed no restrictions in their favour. The companies had now, by a private understanding, put an end to competition. An increase of rates, amounting to about twenty-five per cent., with an additional charge for high pressure service, was the almost immediate result of this new combina-

Position of consumers.

Increase of water rates.

---

[1] This, at least, was the basis of the agreement with the West Middlesex Company. Commons' Committee of 1821; Min. of Ev. p. 31.

[2] Ib. pp. 84-5. The first intimation of the change was a notice, similar to one issued by the West Middlesex Company (January 16, 1818), that "the New River and Chelsea Waterworks being withdrawn from the western parts of the town," the directors had adopted measures for supplying consumers.

tion. A storm of indignation then arose in Western London. Consumers, however, found themselves with no redress against over-charge, and their supplies might be, and were, cut off without appeal. They were especially indignant with the new companies, which had held out a hope of low charges, and had appealed to consumers as their champions against monopoly. Obeying the natural law of self-interest, these companies had now made common cause with their rivals, and had used competition only as the stepping-stone to a new monopoly.

Public feeling in Marylebone found expression through the vestry, who, in 1818, promoted a Bill for the establishment of parochial waterworks, or, as an alternative, enabling the vestry to contract with any water company for a supply to the parish. A parochial committee had previously suggested that the vestry should "take into their most serious consideration the possibility of supplying the parish with water from an establishment of their own, upon the same principle that this parish was originally paved, when a sum of 200,000*l.* was borrowed on bond to carry such measure into effect, and has been all redeemed and paid off." By this plan, consumers would be secured against any undue charge for water; in course of time the cost of works would be discharged; and then the only outlay would be the cost of service. *Marylebone Parochial Waterworks Bill, 1818.*

A petition for a Bill was accordingly presented by the vestry to the House of Commons. It stated that Marylebone had hitherto been supplied by the Chelsea, New River, West Middlesex, and Grand Junction Water Companies, the result of their competition being abundant water at reduced rates. An arrangement had now been made by these four companies for their own pecuniary benefit, whereby the New River and Chelsea Companies withdrew from the entire parish, leaving the West Middlesex in possession of the greater part of it, the Grand Junction only continuing to supply a small portion on its western side. Thus competition had ceased; consumers were compelled to take water from the only company *Reasons assigned for Bill.*

left in the district, who might make what charges they pleased and impose what terms they pleased; and the parish was "delivered over to the mercy and discretion of perpetually fluctuating boards, who might make such exorbitant demands as would materially depreciate the value of property, operate as an oppressive tax, and create a monopoly contrary to the ancient and fundamental laws of the realm." For several years past the parishioners had been put to an expenditure of many thousands a year, owing to the destruction of pavements by these water companies, after giving credit for sums paid by them towards repairs; and thereby the parochial rates had been greatly increased. Under these circumstances Parliament was asked to authorize the vestry for the time being to contract with any water company for a supply, for any term, with power to make and assess a parochial rate to defray the expenses; or to form a parochial establishment for supplying the parish with water, with power to borrow a sum of money upon the security of the rates for this purpose, and provide a sinking fund for the discharge of any debt.[1]

Leave was given to introduce a Bill for these objects, and it was read a first time. Petitions against it were presented by the Chelsea and West Middlesex Companies, and a petition from inhabitants in the same interest set forth objections which later experience has made familiar. "To erect parochial waterworks," it was said, "established and maintained by funds derived from rates to be assessed by the vestry, would virtually have the effect of rendering the inhabitants partners in a trading concern." An outlay of several hundred thousand pounds would be necessary, to be raised on the security of the rates. There was a risk of loss, and of charges far exceeding those of water companies; and competition by private undertakings would be destroyed. Probably the Bill was promoted without any

Marginal notes:

Cost to parish of taking up pavement for water purposes.

Bill introduced: opposition to.

---

[1] 73 Com. Journ. 243; April 14, 1818.

serious resolve to pass it, and rather with a view to exert pressure upon the companies. It was in the end withdrawn, after a first reading, in hopes of an amicable arrangement, but no arrangement was come to. In the House of Lords this subject attracted notice. Replying to the Earl of Lauderdale, Lord Eldon, then Chancellor, said that the Legislature, in passing the different Acts for supplying London with water, must be presumed to have intended the creation of a competition; and if this object had been defeated by a combination between the several companies to establish a monopoly, he wished their lordships to understand that it was perfectly within the competence of Parliament to set that matter right.[1] A second Bill was promoted by the vestry in 1819, their object then being "to regulate and control the supply of water in the parish of Marylebone." But this Bill also came to nothing.

Withdrawal of Bill.

Statement by Lord Chancellor Eldon in House of Lords.

Parochial Bill of 1819.

As the water companies could not but feel that Parliament would soon interpose, two of them, the West Middlesex and Grand Junction Companies, resolved to forestal any such intervention by a measure of their own. They, therefore, in 1819, submitted a joint Bill "to regulate the supply of water" by them, and "limit the rates to be charged for such supply." There was a recital that the two companies were not then limited to any maximum charge, and could not be compelled to afford a supply, and the Bill professed to cure the former defect by a curious limitation, not of the rate to individual consumers, but of the aggregate rate charged in any district. This aggregate rate was not to exceed 25 per cent. above any sum charged in the year 1810, except on houses built since that period. Thus, subject to general limits, individual cases would still be left to the companies' discretion. For the purpose of ascertaining that the rates of 1810 were not exceeded in any district, the companies' rate-books for that year were to be deposited with the vestries. There was

Companies' Bill, 1819.

Proposed limit of aggregate rate in district.

Limitation of profits.

---

[1] Hansard, April 3, 1818.

also, for the first time, a proposal to restrict profits to ten per cent.[1] This Bill was warmly opposed by vestries and inhabitants in districts affected, on the ground that the regulations imposed were arbitrary, and the new rates higher than had before been charged. The Bill was before a Committee of the Commons for four days, and passed that House. It then came before a Committee of the Lords, of which Lord Donoughmore was Chairman.[2] This Committee passed **Bill dropped.** the preamble, but limited the rates to those of 1810. As this alteration in a money clause by the Lords affected the privileges of the Commons, the Bill was dropped on its return to the latter House; but the promoters were not likely, under any circumstances, to accept so vital a change.

[1] Bill 25, Session 1819.

[2] The rule that ratepayers are represented by local authorities did not then apply, for Mr. Weale, a ratepayer, addressed the Lords' Committee against the Bill, as well as counsel for the Marylebone Vestry. Mr. Weale took an active part in this and the subsequent agitation down to 1821, and in the Guildhall Library are four large folio volumes of newspaper-cuttings, pamphlets, broadsides, and MS., evidently compiled by him, to which I am indebted for much information.

CHAPTER X.

WATER SUPPLY OF LONDON (*continued*):—PROFITS OF COM-
PANIES, AND THEIR CHARGES, DOWN TO 1827: WOODEN
PIPES: DEFECTIVE SERVICE: PARLIAMENTARY INQUIRIES,
1821 AND 1828: POLLUTED SOURCES OF SUPPLY: ROYAL
COMMISSION, 1827-8: MR. TELFORD'S SCHEME, 1834:
RENEWED INQUIRIES BY PARLIAMENT, 1834 AND 1840:
BILL OF GOVERNMENT TO CONSOLIDATE COMPANIES, 1851:
METROPOLIS WATER ACT, 1852: QUANTITY AND QUALITY
OF WATER: REPORTS AND INQUIRIES, 1856-69: PLANS
OF SUPPLY, 1840-84: DISPUTED PURITY OF RIVER WATER:
CONSTANT SUPPLY: METROPOLIS WATER ACT, 1871: EX-
TINCTION OF FIRES: ATTEMPTS TO TRANSFER WATER
SUPPLY TO PUBLIC BODIES: METROPOLIS WATERWORKS
PURCHASE BILL, 1880: ASSESSMENT OF WATER RENTS:
INCREASED VALUE OF WATER UNDERTAKINGS.

ALTHOUGH the companies failed in obtaining a statutory
confirmation of higher rates, they were left with unlimited
powers in their respective districts; and complaints by consumers and by local authorities being brought before Parliament, a Committee was appointed by the House of *Commons'*
Commons in 1821 "to inquire into the past and present *Committee, 1821.*
supply of water to the Metropolis, and the laws relating
thereto." From evidence given before this Committee, and *Profits of*
from other sources, some information may be gleaned of the *water com-*
profits of shareholders in London water companies down to *panies down to 1821.*
1821. Upon the whole, these profits were by no means
excessive. Early records of the two oldest companies, the
London Bridge and New River, were both destroyed by
fire.[1] From 1790, however, to 1820, the highest dividend *London*
paid on the London Bridge undertaking was three per cent.; *Bridge works.*
the lowest was two per cent.

---

[1] Those of the New River Company were so destroyed in 1769.

New River.   During the first nineteen years after their works were completed, the annual profits of the New River Company amounted to no more than about 13s. a share. No dividend was paid till the year 1633, when the profits were 3l. 4s. 2d.; and the accumulated profits being added to this sum, each share received 15l. 3s. 3d. In 1640, the dividend rose to 33l. In 1680, it was 145l. From the year 1770, there is a complete record. In that year each share produced in round numbers (after payment of property tax), 255l.; ten years afterwards, 316l.; in 1790, 400l.; in 1800, 463l.; and in 1810, 465l. Then, under the stress of competition, profits fell in 1811 to 282l., and continued falling until, in 1814, they were only 23l.[1] per share. We can easily understand the directors' anxiety to stop a competition which had led to such results as these. After the arrangement with the East London Company in 1815, and still more after 1818, there was a revival of dividends, which in 1820 reached 266l., still a long way in rear of the old prosperity. It will be remembered that, according to a statement made by the board in 1812, during two centuries their shareholders had at no time received more than six and a quarter per cent., and for many years not five per cent., on their capital.[2]

York Buildings Company.   Another ancient body of water-traders, the York Buildings Company, only paid two dividends of 1l. a share each after their final reconstitution, and that was out of capital. Their last bonâ fide dividend was one of four per cent. in 1804, though in 1789 they divided 10l. per share; in 1790, and 1791, 7l. 10s.; and in 1792, 8l. The original shares were 100l., but in their prosperous days the company put upon them a nominal value of 250l.[3] From the year 1723 to 1737, shareholders of the Chelsea Company received no dividends; from 1737 to 1741, their joint profits were 1,600l. a

Chelsea Company.

---

[1] Some of these figures are given by the Committee of 1821; they are repeated, with additions, by the Committee of 1828 (App. p. 53).

[2] *Ante*, p. 117.

[3] Commons' Committee of 1821; Evid. p. 23.

year; from 1741 to 1753, dividends were again suspended; between 1753 and 1770, the shareholders divided 1,200*l.* a year; between 1770 and 1796, 1,600*l.*; between 1798 and 1808, 2,000*l.* a year; between 1808 and 1820, 2,400*l.* a year; " or not quite one and a quarter per cent. on the sum expended for engines, reservoirs, and pipes, and four per cent. on the first capital of 70,000*l.*, 60,000*l.* of which was expended previously to the year 1735."[1] The East London works at Old Ford were not completed till 1811, and until then this company were unable to undertake any new supply, but they obtained a rental from the transfer to them of the Shadwell and West Ham works, and out of this gross rental a dividend of three per cent. was paid in 1809. This was really a dividend out of capital. Other half-yearly dividends of from four to five per cent. per annum were also paid out of capital up to the years 1813 and 1814, when no dividend was paid. In 1815-16, two per cent. per annum was divided out of net rental; in 1817, two and a half; in 1818, three per cent.; in 1819, three and a half. The shares were then forty per cent. below par, and so remained for some years. For two years, 1820-2, there was no dividend.[2]

A similar story of early discouragement may be told of the Lambeth Company.   For ten or eleven years after their incorporation in 1785 no dividend was paid, but between 1817 and 1820, there was a yearly dividend of from 40*l.* to 70*l.*, averaging 55*l.*   For six years previously there was no dividend.[3] Their competitors, the South London Company, incorporated in 1805, had made no profits, and the shareholders had received no dividends, up to 1820.[4] The old

Marginal notes: East London. / Lambeth Company. / South London, and Borough works.

[1] Commons' Committee of 1828; App. Report, p. 48.

[2] Commons' Committee of 1821; evidence of Mr. Pickering, Secretary to East London Water Company, pp. 61-2; and App. to Report of Committee of 1828, p. 58.

[3] Committee of 1821; evidence of Mr. Simpson, Engineer, and Mr. Nelthorpe, Secretary to Lambeth Water Company, pp. 66-8.

[4] Ib.; evidence of Mr. Marshall, Secretary of South London Company, pp. 63-6. Down to 1828 the shareholders had only received two dividends, each of three per cent. (Commons' Committee of 1828; App. p. 61.)

Borough waterworks, established without Parliamentary powers about the year 1758, did not pay one per cent. upon their capital.[1] In the partition of districts arranged in 1817, the West Middlesex were allotted a rental of 15,000*l.* A first dividend of 4*l.* per share was declared in 1810, but it was paid out of capital. At different times other dividends of 12,400*l.* were paid out of capital, but this amount was afterwards written off from capital in the company's books. Before the partition, at a time when companies were fighting for business, and "the contest between them was very acrimonious," the West Middlesex had no real dividends, nor for some time afterwards.[2] No dividends were paid to the Grand Junction proprietors from 1810 to 1818. In 1819 they received 1*l.* 5*s.* per share; in 1820, 12*s.* 6*d.*[3]

These examples will suggest that in any estimate of the present position of London water companies fair allowance must be made for their early difficulties. Nor, judged by modern standards, can their charges, before the inquiry of 1821, be deemed excessive. For example, including sixty-eight public buildings, the total number of houses supplied in 1821 by the London Bridge Company was 10,417. Of these houses, 4,229 paid 20*s.* and under per annum; 5,835 from 20*s.* to 50*s.*; 157 from 50*s.* to 5*l.*; 128 from 5*l.* to 20*l.* These were lower rates than had been charged twenty years before. According to a statement by the New River board, their average rental upon houses in the year 1812 was "something less than 27*s.* per annum, or about sixpence per week for each house," and "the most numerous

Margin notes:
West Middlesex.

Grand Junction.

Charges of companies.

---

[1] Commons' Committee of 1828; App. p. 66.

[2] Commons' Committee of 1821; evidence of Mr. Knight, Secretary of West Middlesex Company, pp. 31-3. We must read by the light of this explanation the company's statement to the Committee of 1828 (App. p. 39), that from 1806 to 1819 the shareholders received no dividends; in 1819, 1*l.* 15*s.* per share; in 1820-1, 2*l.*; gradually reaching, in 1828, 3*l.* per share.

[3] For three years after 1820 the dividends were 2*l.* 10*s.* per share; in 1825-8 they rose to 3*l.* (Commons' Committee of 1828; App. p. 42.)

class of private houses" was "supplied at less than one-third of this rate."[1] The average rates per house charged by six companies, in the years 1820 and 1827, are shown in the following table[2]:—

Average water rate per house in 1820-27.

Names of Companies.	1820.			1827.		
	Houses supplied.	Rate per House.	Gross Income.	Houses supplied.	Rate per House.	Gross Income.
		s.	£		*s.*	£
West Middlesex	10,350	47	24,252	14,500	51	37,000
Grand Junction	7,180	57	20,153	7,809	61	24,702
Chelsea	8,631	35	15,150	12,409	30	18,589
East London..........	32,071	22	35,358	42,000	21	45,442
New River............	52,082	25	67,275	66,600	28	96,657
Lambeth	11,487	16	9,335	15,987	16	12,370

In competing with their younger rivals, it will be gathered that the older companies were at a disadvantage, for a great part of their plant was out of date and required renewal. As we have seen, the London Bridge Company could not afford to replace their wooden mains by iron. In 1810 the New River Company had about 400 miles of wooden pipes in the London streets, and renewed on an average about twenty miles of these pipes every year. In 1816 they had 257 miles of wooden mains and services, which, with necessary fittings, cost more than 128,000*l*.[3] By the substitution of iron, to

Cost of replacing wooden by iron mains.

[1] *Ante*, p. 118. Water was first supplied by the New River Company by leasing for twenty-one years the easement of inserting pipes of half-an-inch bore into their main service pipes, subject in each instance to the payment of 1*l.* 6*s.* 8*d.* yearly, and one year's rent in advance. In Nelson's History of Islington is quoted the grant of a lease for this term to a citizen and his wife of "a pipe or quill of half an inch bore, for the service of their yarde and kitchine,"

by means of "tooe of the smallest swan-necked cookes," in consideration of the yearly sum of 26*s.* 8*d.* Reckoning by the value of money in 1616, this rate may not have been unremunerative.

[2] These figures are taken from the comparative returns printed at p. 68, App. to Report of Commons' Committee of 1828.

[3] Commons' Committee of 1821 App. p. 212.

which this company were driven during the struggle in 1816, these wooden mains became worthless, and a new expenditure of 125,000*l.* for iron mains became necessary.[1]

The new companies founded their appeals for public support, in part, upon their power to give a high-pressure service, by means of new engines and pumping machinery, so as to send water to the top of the highest houses in their districts. The older companies, besides their wooden pipes, which gave way under any unusual strain, had rude appliances for pumping. At London Bridge it was necessary to assist the water-wheels by a steam-engine, in order to meet demands for higher service. At first the New River Company used a windmill for pumping. A horse-engine was then substituted, and about the year 1737 a steam-engine was set up. In 1787, Messrs. Boulton and Watts patented an improved steam-engine, and agreed with the company to supply one for pumping, being repaid by a profit on the coals. A water-wheel was erected in 1789 which threw up as much water as supplied Islington.

In spite of these improvements, the inability of the New River Company to serve water above the ground floor, through the frequent bursting of their wooden pipes, disabled them from effective competition in many cases. It was

---

[1] The first iron main in London was laid by the Chelsea Water Company in 1746. It was a 12-inch main, and cost 2,740*l.* (Committee of 1821, p. 178.) It was estimated by the engineer of the New River Company that the waste by leakage from wooden pipes, and by their bursting under pressure, was about one-fourth of the total quantity of water supplied. (Ib.; evidence of Mr. W. C. Mylne, p. 179.) Stone pipes were tried by the Grand Junction Water Company, as being purer carriers of water than either wood or iron, but they could not withstand the pressure and had to be taken up, at a loss of 10,800*l.* to the water company, and of a still larger sum to the company who had manufactured these pipes and guaranteed their stability. (Ib. p. 170.) In 1814, the price of a 4-inch iron pipe laid down complete was 11*s.* 3*d.* per yard; the price of a wooden pipe of the same diameter was 5*s.* 2*d.* per yard. There was a saving, however, on the larger iron pipes, as it was impossible to obtain tubes in wood of a larger diameter than seven inches.

found that wooden pipes gave way in all directions when New River. the pumping-engines began to work. Owing to defects arising from this and other causes, houses were sometimes left for days, and even a week, without water; and numerous houses were untenanted because of irregular service. In populous centres it was necessary to have several mains lest one should give way. For example, there were nine lines of wooden pipes passing down Goswell Street, side by side.[1] These were replaced by one iron main, of a diameter sufficient to carry the whole supply.[2] However good timber might be when laid down, it decayed rapidly in certain soils, and could not be trusted there for more than two years. Repairs of wooden pipes were therefore very costly.[3] It may be that the New River mains and works justified an early criticism of Sir Christopher Wren, that they were not so laid as to give an effective service in high portions of the northern suburbs.[4] Works of more modern design were free

---

[1] Commons' Committee on Metropolitan Water Supply, 1821, p. 38. These details are summarised from evidence given by the New River Company's engineer, Mr. W. C. Mylne, who succeeded his father in that office in 1811. Smeaton had previously filled the same post.

[2] The first iron pipes used were flanch-pipes screwed together, and so forming one rod. It was found that these, from contraction, generally pulled themselves asunder at intervals of about 300 yards. Socket-pipes were then introduced, and these failures avoided.

[3] Mr. Simpson, who had been engineer of the Chelsea Company since 1783, estimated the average life of a wooden pipe at fifteen years. Leakage from wooden pipes was about one-seventh more than from iron. Wooden pipes of seven inches diameter were commonly used. They cost, in 1821, about 8s. a yard. An iron 12-inch pipe, equal to three wooden pipes of seven inches, then cost from 30s. to 35s. a yard. (Evid. pp. 12, 13.)

[4] In the *Gentleman's Magazine* for March, 1753 (Vol. 23, p. 114), is a curious paper by Sir Christopher Wren, not published in his collected works, called "Thoughts concerning the Distribution of the New River Water," in which he mentions the feeble flow in Soho and the higher parts of London, and suggests improvements. "As all cities are built by time and chance, and not by mathematical designs, so the distribution of this noble aqueduct hath fallen by chance into the present economy, which, although it serves pretty well the turn, is capable of improvement," &c.

from this disadvantage, though, according to later standards, their service was far from satisfactory.

Service of West Middlesex Company. In 1820, the West Middlesex Company had a low service four times a week, and a high service three days a week; their supply on these days lasted two or three hours. Marylebone was their chief district. Water was raised by engines from the Thames to a reservoir 122 feet above the river level, and, for high service, was there pumped over a thirty-feet stand-pipe. For this high service, which included everything six feet and a-half above the street level, an additional charge was made. **Grand Junction.** In 1820, the Grand Junction Company also had both a high and low service, their supply being given four or seven days a week, continued from half an hour to an hour at a time. The company's engineer estimated that in 1810 the supply per house in London was one hogshead per day, or 324 gallons.[1] He attributed increased consumption to the greater luxury of the times, an increase in closets and stables, and a greater waste. Up to September, 1820, the company drew water from the canal which gave them their name. Afterwards they pumped from the Thames, at Chelsea, into a reservoir at Paddington over two miles from the river. The height of this upper reservoir from the Thames at high water of spring tides was 88 feet, and water was there pumped 61 feet higher. From their reservoirs an ordinary low service was performed early in the day; later, for service to cisterns standing eight or ten feet above the street level, water was taken direct from the Thames, **East London.** without passing through any reservoir.[2] The East London Company made no distinction between high and low service. Their average supply, in 1820, was reckoned at about 135 gallons a day to each house, including manufac-

[1] Commons' Committee on Metropolitan Water Supply, 1821; Evidence of Mr. W. Anderson, p. 35. These and similar estimates of consumption are clearly loose and untrustworthy.

[2] Ib., Evid. p. 45.

tories. A considerable portion of this water, however, ran to waste, through an absence of proper appliances in the low class of houses in East London. Generally, services were given four days a week, lasting from one to two hours at a time. In the South London Company's South London. district the estimated average supply was 288 gallons a day to each house, including manufactories, of which there were many in Bermondsey. Water was pumped from the Thames, each house having an average service of only an hour a day; the highest point which the company could serve with their engines was 65 feet above the level of their reservoirs near the river. Into these reservoirs water flowed at each tide.[1] Another undertaking in South London was Southwark. the Southwark, which, in 1820, belonged to one proprietor only, Mr. Edwards. Its district bordered on that of the London Bridge Company in Southwark, with which it was in rivalry. A supply of about 64,000 gallons a day was taken from the river. There was no reservoir; water was pumped into a cistern about twenty feet high, by a single engine of 18-horse power. All mains were of wood, and in many streets there were four lines of wooden pipes. It will be gathered that the business thus carried on was not large.

Though these and similar imperfections in the water service Inquiry of of London would have justified complaint, little was said 1821. on these topics by witnesses who were examined in 1821. Their evidence was almost wholly directed to the increase of charges, and the monopoly established by division into districts, in each of which one company was now supreme, while a consumer could enforce no complaint as to price, quality, or method of supply, and indeed could not require any company to supply him at all. One witness was in advance of his time, and his opinions deserve to be cited here.

[1] Commons' Committee of 1821;   Secretary of South London Water Evidence of Mr. M. C. Marshall,   Company, pp. 63-6.

Water supply by local authorities advocated.

Water, he said, in effect, being, like light and air, an element necessary to existence, and not merely one of many articles of subsistence or convenience, like corn or coal, ought not to be supplied for profit. It should not be left to be the subject of free trade, or protected trade, or indeed of any trade. Neither should domestic consumption be checked by high rates. A supply should be profuse rather than sufficient; to the poor it should be gratuitous. Waterworks should be in the hands of local authorities. The cost of construction and of delivery should be defrayed out of local revenue, raised by an equitable assessment on property. If the water supply of London had been vested, as it ought to have been, in a local board, or in commissioners, the expense of several concurrent organizations and sets of works might have been saved. A single establishment would have met all public wants and convenience; no higher rates would have been imposed than were required to discharge actual outlay; and this necessary of life would have been received by the inhabitants at the lowest possible charge. They could not so receive it while the supply was left to trading companies, whose first object must be the realization of profits, by limiting quantity or enhancing rates.[1]

Report of Commons' Committee, 1821.

To the level of this evidence the Committee of 1821 could not rise. Their inquiry was more important than any hitherto made on the subject entrusted to them, but their report was confined to narrow issues. It caused much disappointment among those consumers who had expected a sweeping condemnation of the companies. The Committee admitted that a partition of districts by the water companies was a measure of self-preservation, though they thought it of a nature to excite public alarm and discontent, especially when

Increased charges.

followed soon after by increased charges, amounting to 25 per cent. for ordinary service, with additional charges for

---

[1] Commons' Committee of 1821 on Metropolitan Water Supply; Evidence of Mr. James Weale, p. 70 *et seq.* *Ante*, p. 128 (*n*).

high or extra service.[1]   During the competition the West
Middlesex and Grand Junction Companies had pledged
themselves to supply their respective districts at the rates of
1810, or even at lower rates, including high pressure, with
a more abundant and certain supply for ordinary service.   It
was now natural for consumers to recall those pledges, and
contrast them with the increased tariff enforced by the companies as soon as they obtained a monopoly of their respective
districts.   Such pledges were "rash and unqualified," subjecting the companies in question to a "charge of culpable
precipitancy, if not of intentional delusion."[2]   The Committee,
however,—and this was a vital point in the matter referred
to them,—did not declare the increase demanded to be unreasonable, nor, on the other hand, did they feel themselves
qualified to decide that this specific increase should be sanctioned.[2]   It is clear that they thought there had been a
mistake in policy by Parliament in not imposing maximum   Restriction by
rates, and restrictive regulations, when the companies were   Parliament.
first incorporated.   But as their capital was "already irre-
trievably engaged," the companies were entitled to liberal
consideration, and restriction should be carried no further
than was "warranted by the clearest evidence."[3]

In the opinion of the Committee, there had been a material   Improved
improvement in the water supply of London, which was now   supply.
more certain and regular, and reached districts until lately
dependent upon wells, while, as to quantity, each house now
received a proportion of about five parts to four compared
with its former service.   The Committee had "no hesitation"
in saying "that the present supply of water to London is
very superior to that enjoyed by any other city in Europe."
Having brought themselves to this conclusion, they were
not prepared to admit that the consumers' demand for a
return to the old rates of 1810 was a fair demand, or would

[1] Commons' Committee on Metro-   [2] Ib. p. 5.
politan Water Supply, Report, p. 4.   [3] Ib. pp. 5-6.

yield the companies an adequate return for their existing supply. On the other hand, the companies should submit their accounts to Parliament, so that the effect of any increased water rents might be watched; consumers should be protected against further and indefinite increases; and there should be some tribunal to which they might appeal against any arbitrary withdrawal of their supply.[1]

No monopoly originally intended by Parliament.

That Parliament never intended to confer a monopoly on any one of the Metropolitan Water Companies was clear to the Committee. Before 1810, the London Bridge, New River, and Chelsea works, with those of three smaller companies, in 1821 no longer existing, supplied all London north of the Thames. "None of them," however, "had any legal privilege in the nature of a monopoly," though "each possessed a monopoly in effect through the greater part of the district which it supplied." Their works were often intermixed, owing to gradual extensions, and in those districts the inhabitants could choose the company whose

Competition as applied to water companies.

source of supply they preferred. The principle of the Acts which incorporated the East London, West Middlesex, and Grand Junction Companies was to encourage competition, by which alone "a perfect security can be had for good supply."[2] But from the peculiar nature of water undertakings, the Committee were of opinion that, in its application to them, the principle of competition must be "guarded by checks and limits," in order to render it effectual without risk of destruction to the competing parties, and thereby ultimately of serious injury to the public. In ordinary

[1] Commons' Committee of 1821 on Metropolitan Water Supply, pp. 7–8.
[2] So, when examined in 1828, before a Committee of the House of Commons on the Metropolitan Water Supply, Mr. Clay, M.P., then chairman of the Grand Junction Waterworks Company, acknowledged the possibility and salutary influence of competition. "I am myself most distinctly of opinion that the dread of public disapprobation, and the certainty of competition, will hold over every company (as it always has over ours) a sufficient check." (Min. of Evid. p. 30.)

cases, the Committee explained, competition adjusts supply
to demand, and sellers may go out of the market as well as
come into it. But in trades carried on by large capital,
vested in fixed machinery, and furnishing a commodity of
the same quality, of no value but for consumption on the
spot, sellers are confined to one market, and new comers
can only obtain business " by underbidding each other down
to the point of ruin." Such had been the result of the recent
protracted competition. That the companies should have
sought to avoid ruinous losses by a partition of territory
looked at first sight a combination against the public, but was
from their own point of view natural and prudent.

To carry out their chief recommendations, the Committee suggested a Bill, limited in duration to four years,
restraining the companies from any advance beyond the
25 per cent. already imposed for ordinary service, leaving
charges for service at high pressure to be settled by agreement, and fixing, as far as was practicable, any rates for
water used for trade purposes.[1] Notwithstanding local circumstances which might distinguish the respective companies,
such as " differences of elevation, distance from the source of
supply, a more or less scattered distribution," or different
classes of houses taking water, the Committee would not
attempt to fix a separate maximum for each company. There
had been complaints that the Grand Junction Company
had altered the proportions of water rental throughout
their district, alleging inequalities of assessment in the old
rates. It would be just that consumers should have a right
of appeal against such surcharges. As to competition, the
experiment had been tried and had failed; but the Committee distinctly reserved for Parliament a right, if occasion
should call for it, to encourage "any other undertakings by
which it may plainly appear that a better or cheaper supply
can be furnished, none of the companies having any claim to

Remedial measure suggested.

Right of Parliament to sanction competing undertakings.

---

[1] Report, p. 8.

an exclusive privilege of any sort."[1]　Meanwhile, Parliament must leave the companies "something worth having," which would tempt other persons to undertake similar services.　But with proper checks, the Committee thought that the prudence of the companies, and a due sense of their own interests, would suffice to make such steps unnecessary.　A concluding suggestion was, that any measure introduced to regulate the companies should be "considered with that liberality which belongs to the national character."

Public Bill of 1821.

A public Bill embodying these recommendations was brought into the House of Commons in June, 1821.　It was called a Bill "for further regulating the supply of water to the cities of London and Westminster, and parts adjacent thereto north of the Thames," and, among other provisions, proposed to restrict the rates for ordinary service, and for high service.　It gave the water companies certain powers of entry to inspect pipes, and prevent waste and leakage; compelled owners or occupiers to provide cisterns and proper fittings; relieved owners from any payment of rates for unoccupied houses; required the companies to supply new houses or streets adjoining houses and streets already supplied by them; and prohibited them from cutting off

Water referees.

water, except in certain specified cases.　Another proposal, afterwards adopted, in substance, as a means of controlling a supply of gas,[2] was the annual appointment of two Referees, one by vestries and one by water companies, to hear and decide upon complaints made either by companies or by consumers.[3]　These Referees were only to take cognizance of complaints after application made to the companies, and refusal of redress by them.　In like manner consumers were

[1] Report, p. 10.

[2] City of London Gas Act, 1868, *ante*, Vol. I., p. 229.

[3] If the vestries did not agree in nominating the same referee, the names of all the nominees were to be written on slips of paper, placed in a glass urn, and the first drawn was to act for the year.　In the city of London separate referees were to be appointed.

allowed an opportunity of complying with any demands by companies. The Referees were to decide whether any regulations imposed by companies were reasonable, and also as to sufficiency of supply, cases of alleged waste, amount of rent, and other questions. Provision was made for enforcing their awards; but the value of this new tribunal was destroyed by a proviso that companies might still bring actions, suits, or other proceedings in any Courts then open to them, and might thus oust the jurisdiction of the Referees, unless there had been an express decision by them. In every year the water companies' accounts were to be laid before Parliament, showing income, expenditure, and dividends, with other particulars. As an experiment, the Bill was to be in force for four years. *Accounts.*

Though this measure would have imposed some useful restrictions on the water companies, it failed to satisfy those persons who had taken part in the agitation of 1820-1, and met with so cold a reception, both in and out of Parliament, that it was not proceeded with. As the companies were careful to avoid any flagrant abuse of their powers, agitation against them died out for a few years. New and legitimate cause for discontent then arose. It is remarkable that, during the heated discussions of 1820-1, hardly a word was said against the quality of Thames water except that pumped at London Bridge;[1] and the Committee of 1821 pronounced the water supply of London to be better than that of any city in Europe. In 1826-7, however, there arose well-founded complaints of pollution in the tidal waters of the Thames.[2] An influential public meeting *Failure of public Bill.* *Quality of water drawn from the Thames.* *Public meeting, 1827.*

[1] *Ante*, p. 113, n.

[2] See especially a pamphlet anonymously published in 1827 (written by Mr. J. Wright), called "The Dolphin; or, Grand Junction Nuisance: proving that seven thousand families in Westminster and its suburbs are supplied with water in a state offensive to the sight, disgusting to the imagination, and destructive to health." "The Dolphin" was a name given by the water companies to a small wooden erection, somewhat resembling a martello tower, which they placed in the river to enclose and to indicate the source or head from which, by means of a steam engine, their supply was ob-

was held in April, 1827, at which Sir Francis Burdett, M.P., presided, and the Marquis of Salisbury, the Earls of Jersey, Sefton, Tankerville, Hardwicke, and Rosslyn, Lord Auckland, Lord Wharncliffe, Mr. Samuel Rogers, Mr. John Murray, and several members of Parliament, were present. Resolutions were passed, and petitions to Parliament adopted, denouncing the existing sources of supply, and praying for inquiry.[1]

Royal Commission, 1827–8.

Owing to political changes at this period, there was not sufficient time for a Parliamentary inquiry, but a Royal Commission was appointed on June 4, 1827, after motions carried in both Houses. The Commissioners were Dr. P. M. Roget, a physician, Professor W. T. Brande, a chemist, and Mr. Telford, C.E. To make their report intelligible, it is necessary to describe shortly the position of the companies at this period, and the sources from which they drew their

tained. The Grand Junction Company's dolphin was near Chelsea Hospital, not far from the mouth of the great Ranelagh sewer. (Royal Commission of 1828 on Metropolitan water supply; App. to Report, p. 124.) At p. 134 there is a sketch showing the position of the dolphin and of the Ranelagh sewer and Chelsea Hospital. The Grand Junction directors, however, said :—"The 'great Ranelagh sewer' is not a sewer at all, or only in a very minute degree in proportion to the volume of its waters. It has but recently acquired the name of the Ranelagh sewer, upon being taken under the jurisdiction of the Commissioners of Sewers. Its old name was Westbourne brook. It rises on the west side of Hampstead Hill, flows through the fields beyond Kilburn, past Westbourne Green, and taking there the name of the Bayswater stream, supplies the water for the Serpentine river. From the park it

passes by Knightsbridge to Chelsea, where it falls into the Thames between the hospital and the company's works. The only sewer water it receives is between the Park and Chelsea." Remarks of Directors, April 16, 1827, upon resolutions passed at a meeting at Willis's Rooms, April 9.

[1] One of the resolutions, reproduced in the petition, was as follows :—"That the water taken up from the River Thames at Chelsea, for use by inhabitants of the western portion of the metropolis, being charged with the contents of the great common sewers, the drainings from dunghills and lay-stalls, the refuse of hospitals, slaughter-houses, colour, lead, and soap works, drugmills, and manufactories, and with all sorts of decomposed animal and vegetable substances, rendering the water offensive and destructive to health, ought no longer to be taken up by any of the water companies from so foul a source."

supplies.   The New River Company had, in 1822, absorbed their ancient rivals at London Bridge.   In that year, when old London Bridge was demolished, an Act was passed[1] for removing the London Bridge Waterworks.   It recited that the great fall of water, and obstructions occasioned by these works, projecting, as they did, into the river from both banks, made all navigation through the bridge at particular states of the tide dangerous to life and property. With a view, therefore, to a removal of these works, and proper compensation of the proprietors, Parliament sanctioned an arrangement by which the Committee of Assistants (as the managers of the London Bridge works were termed) surrendered to the Corporation of London all leases granted to their predecessors in title.   At the same time they transferred to the New River Company their water wheels, machinery, property, plant, and goodwill of their business north of the Thames, receiving in return 10,000*l.* from the Corporation, and from the New River Company annuities amounting to 3,750*l.*, or 2*l.* 10*s.* per annum upon each of the 1,500 shares into which the capital of the London Bridge undertaking had been divided.   As, under the respective leases, there were unexpired terms of about 260 years, the annuities were limited to this period, dating from October 1, 1822. This arrangement was carried out by a deed dated September 28, 1822.   The Borough portion of the undertaking was conveyed to the proprietor of the Southwark works for an annual sum of 1,060*l.*; and the two undertakings were consolidated under the name of the Southwark Waterworks.

It was a public gain that the two oldest works taking water from the Thames, those at London Bridge and York Buildings, should give way to a supply from purer sources.   In 1827-8, the New River Company took two-thirds of their

Removal of London Bridge works.

Southwark Waterworks.

Sources of supply, 1827-8.

New River.

---

[1] 3 Geo. IV. c. 109, repealing 29 Geo. II. as to the waterworks.

supply from their springs at Chadwell, and one-third from an arm of the river Lea; but, as a reserve, they had an engine and works at Broken Wharf, Thames Street, by which they were occasionally able to serve parts of their district with Thames water, when, from long-continued droughts, severe frosts, or other accidental causes, the flow of the New River was impeded.[1]   In quantity, however, the Thames water bore a very trifling proportion to that obtained from comparatively

East London.   untainted sources twenty miles from London.   The East London Waterworks were situated at Old Ford, on the Lea; but as the tide of the Thames flowed a mile beyond Old Ford, and the company's supply was taken at ascending tides, the water closely resembled that of the Thames.[2]

We come now to works situated on the Thames.   Those of

West Middlesex.   the West Middlesex Company were at Barnes, higher up the river than the works of any other company.   The Chelsea

Chelsea.   Company's supply was taken from a point about a quarter

Grand Junction.   of a mile east of Chelsea Hospital.   In 1810, the Grand Junction Company had promised an exceptional quality of water, chiefly "derived from the rivers Colne and Brent, and from an immense reservoir of nearly a hundred acres, fed by streams in the Vale of Ruislip;" and, as we have seen, they had published analyses showing that this water was "lighter and contained less foreign matter than Thames water."   In fact, however, the company derived their supply not directly from the streams mentioned, but from the canal at Paddington, which was, in part, fed from these sources.   Moreover, in 1819, instead of taking water from the Grand Junction Canal, the company were allowed by Parliament[3] to substitute a supply taken from the Regent's Canal, the proprietors of which had, in 1812, been authorized to draw water from the Thames for navigation. Afterwards the Grand Junction Company took their supply

[1] Royal Commission of 1828; Report, r. 84.
, ntine r.

[2] Ib.
[3] 59 Geo. III. c. 111.

direct from the Thames at Chelsea. On its southern bank, the Lambeth Company pumped water into their mains *Lambeth.* direct from the river opposite Hungerford; the South Lon- *South* don supplied consumers with water taken at the foot *London.* of Vauxhall Bridge; the Southwark works drew water in *Southwark.* mid-stream between Southwark and London Bridge.[1] To this description we need only add that, between Chelsea and the Tower, the source of supply for two northern and three southern companies, more than 130 common sewers emptied *Sewers* *flowing into* themselves into the river on its north bank alone, not *Thames, 1828.* including "the refuse of colour, lead, gas, soap works, drug mills, and manufactories of various descriptions."[2]

A well-known chemist, Dr. Bostock, was employed by the *Report of* Commissioners to make a series of analyses, and "to ascertain *Royal Com-* *mission, 1828.* how far the water of the Thames contiguous to or in the neighbourhood of London is in a state proper for being employed in diet and other domestic purposes." Dr. Bostock reported that "when free from extraneous substances," the water of the Thames was "in a state of considerable purity." He added:—"But as it approaches the metropolis it becomes loaded with a quantity of filth, which renders it disgusting to the senses, and improper to be employed in the preparation of food." With this testimony before them, the Commissioners came to some very mild conclusions. During the last ten or twelve years, they reported, the quality of Thames water within the London district had suffered a gradual deterioration. They were of opinion that the supply to the Metropolis was "susceptible of, and requires, improvement; that many of the complaints respecting the quality of the water are well-founded; and that it ought to be derived from other sources than those now resorted to, and guarded by such restrictions as shall at all times ensure its cleanliness and purity."[3]

[1] Royal Commission of 1828; Report, p. 6.

[2] Ib.; App. p. 148; statement of Mr. Wright.

[3] Report, p. 11.

Committee
of House of
Commons,
1828.

The Commissioners had originally been instructed to suggest new and better methods or sources of supply, but they were afterwards directed not to prosecute this large branch of inquiry. In 1828, their report was referred to a Committee of the House of Commons, who were appointed to inquire into the same subject, and also into the amount of rates paid for water throughout London. This Committee

Suggestion
of other
sources than
the Thames.

unanimously approved the Commissioners' opinion that a purer source than the Thames should be found, and recommended that Mr. Telford should be instructed to make surveys, and prepare a plan for supplying the whole of London

Rates charged
by companies.

with wholesome water. As to rates, the Committee found that, while the water rental of 1821 was itself an increase of 25 per cent. upon that of 1810, there had been since 1821 another increase of 44,000l. a year in charges on the north

Various
methods of
assessment.

side of the Thames alone. Another evil was that no two companies agreed in their mode of rating. "On the contrary, as the amount is unlimited, so is the proportion altogether uncertain. It is not regulated either by the quantity of water consumed, or by the distance to which it is conveyed, but appears to be in every instance left solely to the agents of the different companies to charge as they shall think fit."[1]

Reluctance of
Government
to interfere.

When the Royal Commissioners' report came before the House of Commons, Mr. Peel, then Home Secretary, said the Government did not intend to interfere any further,

---

[1] Report, p. 5. By sect. 27 of an Act of 1826 (7 Geo. IV. c. 140), the Grand Junction Company were authorized to levy a scale of rates which would have added from 50 to 300 per cent. to their existing charges. From evidence given in 1828 by the Chairman, it appeared that this scale had been introduced, contrary to their wish, at the instance of Lord Shaftesbury, Chairman of Committees in the House of Lords, in order to impose a maximum limit of charge. (Min. of Evid. p. 30.) But the company had not acted upon the clause, which, according to Mr. Clay, was objectionable, because "it proposes a scale according to rents, which would be a very inadequate criterion of the remuneration to which the company are entitled for water supplied." (Ib. p. 29.)

but would leave the remedy to private enterprise.[1] After
further agitation the Government were induced to sanction the Committee of 1828, but some time passed before
Mr. Telford, as that Committee suggested, was asked
by the Treasury to submit plans for an improved supply;
and it was not until February, 1834, that this engineer's
report was completed. He advised that there should be no
interference with the New River and East London Companies, but that the northern districts of London, then
served from the Thames by the Grand Junction, West
Middlesex, and Chelsea Companies, should be supplied from
the river Verulam, or St. Alban's river. A covered aqueduct
was to convey the whole stream, " should it ever be required,"
from Bushey Mill, near Watford, to Primrose Hill, termi-
nating there in a set of extensive receiving and distributing
reservoirs, at a height of 146 feet above high-water mark.
From these reservoirs each of the three companies might be
supplied separately, in given proportions. Including compensation to mill-owners, the purchase of land, and all other
charges, these works would cost 786,000*l.* On the south
side, Mr. Telford proposed to construct an aqueduct from the
Croydon branch of the river Wandle, at Beddington Park, to
reservoirs on Clapham Common, from which the Lambeth,
South London, and Southwark Companies might be supplied,
at a cost of 391,000*l.*[2]

Mr. Telford's plan, 1834.

Thus, at an expense of about 1,178,000*l.*, according to

Cost of scheme.

[1] 19 Hansard, 771-4; May 19,
1828. Mr. Peel said the objection
against Thames water "was one
rather of feeling than of just or
serious alarm." If an improved
supply were required, it should be
left to private enterprise. " Why
was it to be supposed that, if the
public were dissatisfied, another
company would not arise, making a
purer supply the basis of its prospectus? He did not mean to hold
out any encouragement to such a
speculation, much less offer any inducement to it." Nor did he think
it would be prudent for the Government to interfere in the appointment
of engineers who were to point out
the manner in which individuals
should invest their property.

[2] Report of Mr. Telford, C.E.,
February, 1834, "on the means of
supplying the Metropolis with pure
water." (House of Commons' Paper,
No. 176.)

Mr. Telford's plan, the Thames, as a source of supply, would have been abandoned, and London might have received an ample stock of pure water, through six water companies, without disturbing their existing works, and at a comparatively small expense in adapting mains.   Four years previously, anticipating a similar inquiry by Government Commissioners, the Grand Junction directors had suggested that, when these Commissioners had ascertained the best mode of obtaining a supply, "the only course that could be pursued to avoid a ruinous waste of capital, and a consequent loss to the public," was "that Government should advance the sum requisite to bring water to a spot from whence the companies could receive it into their several works, upon the security of their respective incomes, as has been done in other public undertakings; that the outlay should be under supervision by some Parliamentary authority; and that the increase of rates to be charged by each company should be no more than the proportion of interest they should respectively pay to Government."[1]   But the Government were not disposed either to lend money, or incur responsibility.   Mr. Telford's report was practically shelved by reference, in the same Session, to an unwieldy Committee, at first composed of 32 members, and afterwards increased to 52.[2]   This Committee were not appointed till May 7, 1834, and continued their inquiry till August 7, when they found themselves unable to do more than submit to the House the evidence they had taken, and suggest their re-appointment in the next Session, advice which was not followed.

In 1840, the House of Lords appointed a Committee upon the same subject, but, after considering many schemes, in-

Side notes:

Proposed State loan to water companies.

Commons' Committee, 1834.

Lords' Committee, 1840.

---

[1] Directors' Report, March 11, 1830, quoted by Mr. Telford, p. 5.

[2] Among the members were Sir Francis Burdett, Dr. Lushington, Mr. Hume, Viscount Howick, Mr. Brougham, Mr. Cayley, Viscount Morpeth, Mr. Edward Buller, Mr. Clay, and Mr. Grote.   Mr. Hanbury Tracy acted as Chairman.

cluding one for obtaining water from artesian wells near Watford, this Committee also did no more than report to the House the evidence they had taken.

No legislation followed these inquiries. Mr. Telford's plan was much questioned by witnesses examined before both Committees, the six companies admitting that it might be well to go higher up the Thames, but stoutly maintaining that, by means of filtration and subsidence, the water drawn from this source would be better than that from either the Verulam or Wandle. Indirectly, good service was rendered by Parliament in urging upon the companies the necessity of improvements. In 1831 the Grand Junction Company promoted a Bill for obtaining water from the river Colne. It was stopped pending Mr. Telford's report, and, upon further consideration, the company resolved still to take water from the Thames, but asked for powers to shift their works from Chelsea to a point between Kew and Richmond. Their Bill was much discussed in both Houses in 1835. For seven days it occupied the consideration of a Lords' Committee, and at length became law.[1] A site was sanctioned at a short distance above Kew Bridge, on the Surrey side; at an expense of 120,000*l.* works were constructed there; and water was pumped through a main nearly six miles long to reservoirs at Paddington, where it was filtered before delivery. The Chelsea Company contented themselves with the construction of filter-beds at Chelsea, capable of filtering daily nearly two million gallons. This material improvement was carried out in 1829. Previously, two-thirds of the company's supply were pumped into the houses of consumers direct from the Thames.

Drawing their supply from the Thames at Hammersmith, beyond reach, as they contended, of London sewage, the West Middlesex Company had strenuously protested against

Improvements made by companies.

West Middlesex.

---

[1] 5 & 6 Will. IV. c. 95.

Mr. Telford's plan, classing them with the five companies whose "dolphins" were situated between Chelsea and London Bridge. They even suggested that, by separate mains, they should pump a supply from Hammersmith to each of these five companies.[1] Meanwhile, they constructed settling reservoirs, and the New River Company followed this example.

East and South London.

In 1829, the East London Company obtained statutory powers[2] to go higher up the Lea, beyond reach of tides from the Thames. The South London Company, who drew their supply from Vauxhall, altered their style in 1834 to the Vauxhall Waterworks Company, and at the same time obtained a considerable extension of district.[3] In the same Session the old Borough works, then privately owned, were incorporated as the Southwark Waterworks Company, and

Amalgamation of Southwark and Vauxhall Companies, 1845.

their source of supply was changed to Battersea.[4] Some ten years later the separate history of each of these companies closed by their amalgamation as the Southwark and Vauxhall Waterworks Company,[5] and their joint works were then established at Battersea. Lastly, in 1834, the Lambeth

Lambeth, 1834.

Company were dissolved, and the proprietors re-united into a new company under their old name, with authority to raise fresh capital; and they were required, within four years, to supply no water which had not been effectually purified by filtration.[6]

These palliatives succeeded in lulling apprehension for a time, but an outbreak of cholera in 1848-9 directed public attention anew to sanitary defects in London as well as in large provincial towns, and led to a mass of inquiry and legislation.[7] Better drainage and sewerage were then

[1] Lords' Committee of 1840; Evidence.
[2] 10 Geo. IV. c. 117.
[3] 4 & 5 Will. IV. c. 78.
[4] Ib. c. 79.
[5] 8 & 9 Vict. c. 69.

[6] 4 & 5 Will. IV. c. 7, s. 86.
[7] See also Reports made in 1844 and 1845 by a Royal Commission on Health of Towns, which recommended a consolidation under one management of the water and drain-

forced upon local authorities, but in London, as elsewhere, the result was simply a transfer of pollution from houses and streets to streams and rivers.[1] In its tidal flow the Thames became less fitted than ever to furnish water for drinking purposes. A general Board of Health had been created in 1848,[2] and in 1850 this body recommended that the Thames should be abandoned as a source of supply, and that water for the Metropolis should be taken from the Bagshot sands and lower greensands of Surrey.[3] They also stated that there were, in 1850, about 18,000 houses in the Metropolis receiving no supply of water, the inhabitants being dependent on wells more or less polluted, or on neighbours, from whom they begged it or bought it at so much a bucket-full.

Increased pollution of rivers.

General Board of Health.

Instead of the nine companies then supplying the Metropolis, the Board were of opinion that one combined management should be substituted. Had there then been a municipality in London, or a governing body exercising authority over the whole Metropolitan area, the Board would have suggested that the water supply should be transferred to this central body. As, however, there was no such authority, they were of opinion that " public responsibility to the ratepayers would be best secured through Parliament."[4]

Combined management in water supply suggested by Board.

age of the Metropolis. A Royal Commission was also appointed in 1847 upon the sanitary state of the Metropolis, the Public Health Act, 1848, being one result of these inquiries.

[1] " It had long been penal to allow any solid matter to pass into the drains, but, with a better supply of water, the idea that all solid matter should be at once washed into the drains prevailed, and was at length made compulsory. By the increase of population, the quantity of house drainage was at the same time largely increased." (Committee on London Water Bills, 1867; Report, p. 6.) Common sewers were not unknown in the seventeenth century (see Acts of 18 & 19 Chas. II. c. 8, and 22 & 23 Chas. II. c. 17); but few of those in London are much more than a century old. Before that time, the common carriers for sewage were channels open to the street. Until an ample supply of water was given, such sewers as existed could have been, in dry weather, no better than elongated cesspools.

[2] This Board was reconstituted in 1854, and continued in existence till 1858.

[3] Report on Metropolitan Water Supply [1218], with appendices [1218-4].

[4] Report, p. 285.

Government Bill for amalgamation of water companies, 1851.

Acting upon this view, the Government brought in a Bill, in the year 1851, to amalgamate all the Metropolitan water companies, under State supervision. Sir George Grey, then Home Secretary, took charge of this measure. Competition, he said, could no longer be trusted. Parliament had relied on it, in sanctioning new companies, but the result was combination, with irresponsible management, and no security as to quality of water, mode of service or cost. Sir George was not prepared to sanction the creation of a Board, appointed and paid by the Government. If, he said, there had been a municipality in London, or if such a representative system could be provided, the best way would be to act through its means, as in Liverpool and other large towns; and such an agency would be more satisfactory to ratepayers

Consolidation of capital with limited dividend.

than any other. In the absence of such a representative body, the only practical alternative was a consolidation of existing companies. Their capital would be valued by arbitration or otherwise. Its amount having been ascertained and apportioned, he proposed that the dividend on this consolidated stock should be five per cent., rising to a maximum of six per cent. in case of a reduction in the rates of supply according to a scheduled scale. Any subsequent surplus should be applied to similar reductions. It was further proposed to limit charges, and place the united company under

Power of purchase reserved to Government.

the control of Government, to whom was reserved powers of purchasing the company's rights, at any time, on a fixed basis. The Home Secretary might also direct the amalgamated company to obtain water from any new source, if this step were found expedient on sanitary grounds. There were minor provisions requiring the company to furnish water for cleansing streets and sewers, and for other public purposes. Other clauses secured an official audit, and authorized the Treasury from time to time to revise and reduce rates.[1]

---

[1] Speech of Sir George Grey, April 29, 1851; 116 Hansard, 309–19.

This Bill met with a determined opposition in the House of Commons, from Sir Benjamin Hall, Mr. Baillie Cochrane, Viscount Ebrington, and other members, who thought the terms proposed too favourable to the companies. No opposition to the principle of the measure was offered by any water company. Indeed, one of their chief representatives in Parliament stated that, in his opinion, there were good reasons for placing a supply of water under municipal control, instead of leaving it in the hands of individuals.[1] Stress was laid on the view taken by the Board of Health that the cost of water to London, which in 1851 was about 450,000l. a year, might be reduced to one-half, with a constant and purer supply.[2] It was argued that any valuation of the companies' interests should be based on a state of competition, such as the Legislature intended to secure, and not on combinations entered into by the companies for their own benefit in defiance of the Legislature. The Bill, it was added, would increase by five millions the cost of water, without increasing or improving the supply. These and other arguments, with which Par-

[1] Sir William Clay (116 Hansard, 337). A passage in a pamphlet written by him was quoted in debate:—"There is no doubt that the water service should be, wherever practicable, vested in the hands, not of individuals, but of some authorities, municipal or other, acting on behalf of the public. For thus vesting it there are reasons which seem to me to be conclusive. 1. A supply of water, abundant and of good quality, is so absolutely essential, not only to public health, but even to public morals, that it would appear on this account alone to fall within that class of functions which Government is bound to take upon itself. 2. There is a great and obvious convenience in the supply of water being vested in the same authority in any locality as the paving and sewerage. 3. There is, perhaps, no other mode by which the public can be perfectly protected against the possible occurrence of some of those evils to which monopoly has been found to lead. The cost of water will, or, at all events, ought to be less to the consumer. . . . 4. There is nothing in the character of a water supply which places it beyond the range of those functions which public authorities may conveniently discharge. There is no commercial acuteness required, no buying and selling, no watching of markets."

[2] A company was projected in 1851 to supply the metropolis with soft water, constantly laid on, for a capital outlay of under two millions.

liament again became familiar when a proposal to purchase was made thirty years afterwards, had such influence that, on its second reading, the Bill was only carried by a majority of sixteen.[1]

Second reading.

Such a reception was not of favourable augury. In fact the House saw no more of this Bill. It was referred, with other measures promoted by the water companies, to a Committee of which Sir James Graham was chairman. This Committee sat for six weeks, and heard a cloud of witnesses, but towards the middle of July was not half-way through its chief business. Many advocates were found for a system of water supply under local administration rather than by any consolidated private body, while the companies now ceased to favour the Bill. Under these circumstances there was no hope of any practical result from inquiry. Next Session the Home Secretary left the task of initiating legislation to Lord Seymour, then First Commissioner of Works, and a member of the Cabinet, who brought forward a measure on wholly different lines. He rejected the proposal of the Board of Health to abandon the Thames and rely on water drawn from the Surrey sands. In his view the Thames beyond reach of the tide was a very fit source of supply, and there should be covered reservoirs with filtration. He was against another proposal of the Board: management by a commission, with Parliamentary responsibility. Government, acting through commissioners, could not superintend such a work satisfactorily. As to a fusion of companies, with concentrated management, it might be desirable, but he did not think it was incumbent on Parliament to demand such a combination. "All that it behoved Parliament to do was to require that water should be supplied of good quality, in sufficient quantity, and at a cheap rate. The companies had better be left to act separately, or in conjunction, as they should find best." Lord Seymour was also against a supply of water by municipalities. For

Reference to Committee.

Lord Seymour's Bill, 1852.

[1] 117 Hansard, 510.

the proper carrying out of this work he "had more hopes from companies than he had from municipal corporations."[1]

This was an entire reversal of the policy suggested by Sir George Grey, but after further inquiry[2] it was adopted by Parliament. By the Metropolis Water Act, 1852, it was provided that no company supplying the Metropolis should take water for domestic use from the Thames below Teddington lock, or from any tributary of the Thames within range of the tide.[3] Every store reservoir within five miles of St. Paul's was to be covered, unless the water were filtered after leaving the reservoir; and all water for domestic use was to be effectually filtered before distribution, unless it were pumped from wells direct into a covered reservoir.[4] If twenty inhabitant householders found fault with the quantity or quality of water supplied to them, the Board of Trade might appoint a competent person to inquire and report, with power to examine and inspect the works; and, if the Board believed this complaint to be well founded, the company were bound, after notice, to remove the cause of it within a reasonable time.[5]

Powers were at once obtained by the respective companies to satisfy the conditions of this general Act. Since 1809,[6] the Chelsea Company had not been before Parliament. They were authorized in 1852 to remove their works from Chelsea Reach, take water from the Thames at Seething Wells, in the parish of Kingston, and raise fresh capital for this purpose.[7] At the same time Parliament, taking advantage of their application, limited their rates,[8] defined their district,[9] required them to afford a constant supply after a certain

Margin notes: Metropolis Water Act, 1852. As to quantity and quality of water. Acts obtained in 1852. Removal of works to higher points of Thames.

[1] 119 Hansard, February 6, 1852. Speech on motion for leave to introduce Bill.

[2] Commons' Committee on Metropolis Waterworks, 1852. They issued two volumes of evidence.

[3] 15 & 16 Vict. c. 84. A year's grace was given to the Chelsea Company.

[4] 15 & 16 Vict. c. 84, ss. 1–4.

[5] Ib. ss. 9–13.

[6] 49 Geo. III. c. 157.

[7] 15 & 16 Vict. c. 156.

[8] Ib. s. 60.

[9] Ib. s. 15.

interval, and introduced various other provisions for the
public good.[1] Corresponding provisions were inserted in all
other Water Acts of the same Session. Two statutes, of
1852-3, regulated the East London Company's supply,
transferring its source to a higher point in the Lea, and
diverting drainage and sewerage.[2] This company had not
been before Parliament since 1829.[3] The Grand Junction
Company were enabled to take a supply from the Thames
at Hampton and construct additional works.[4] In 1852, the
New River Company were also authorized to make filtering
reservoirs and otherwise improve their supply.[5] From Battersea, the Southwark and Vauxhall Company migrated to
Hampton.[6] The last Act of the West Middlesex Company
was dated 1813.[7] They had been prohibited in 1806 from
taking water from the Thames west of Kew Bridge. This
policy was now reversed, and their source of supply transferred to Hampton.[8] As the Lambeth Company, in 1848, had
set the example of moving higher up the river by removing
their works to a point above Kingston,[9] they were not obliged
to obtain fresh powers in 1852. Drawing their supplies from
wells in the chalk, the Kent Company were also exempt from
the necessity of new legislation.

Reports and
inquiries,
1856-69.

Although purer water was thus secured, an increased discharge of sewage into the upper waters of the Thames soon
disturbed the general satisfaction with these changes. Some
reports to the Board of Health[10] caused such uneasiness
that the Government set on foot further inquiries. A

[1] The Waterworks Clauses Act,
1847, was also incorporated in all
the Metropolitan Water Acts of the
Session.

[2] 15 & 16 Vict. c. 164 ; 16 & 17
Vict. c. 166.

[3] 10 Geo. IV. c. 117.

[4] 15 & 16 Vict. c. 157.

[5] Ib. c. 160.

[6] Ib. c. 158.

[7] 53 Geo. III. c. 36.

[8] 15 & 16 Vict. c. 159.

[9] 11 & 12 Vict. c. 7.

[10] Report by the Board's medical
officer (Mr. Simon) on the last two
cholera epidemics of London, as
affected by the consumption of impure water ; 1856. Report on micro-
scopical examination of the Metropolitan water supply, by Dr. Hill
Hassall ; 1857.

Royal Commission on the pollution of rivers was appointed in 1865,[1] to inquire generally "how far the present use of rivers or running waters in England, for the purpose of carrying off the sewage of towns and populous places, and the refuse arising from industrial processes and manufactures, can be prevented without risk to public health, or serious injury to such processes and manufactures." This Commission issued three reports.[2] It was re-constituted in 1868, and then made six reports.[3]

In 1866-7, another Royal Commission was appointed to ascertain "what supply of unpolluted and wholesome water can be obtained, by collecting and storing water in the high grounds of England and Wales, either by the aid of natural lakes or by artificial reservoirs, at a sufficient elevation for the supply of large towns; and to report, firstly, which of such sources are best suited for the supply of the Metropolis and its suburbs; and, secondly, how the supply from the remaining sources may be most beneficially distributed among the principal towns." A second warrant directed the Commissioners "to inquire into the present water supply to the Metropolis, and whether there are other districts, in addition to the high districts of England and Wales, from which a good supply of unpolluted and wholesome water can be obtained."[4] This Commission reported in June, 1869.[5]

Two years before the appearance of this report, a Com- mittee of the House of Commons, sitting to adjudicate upon

---

[1] The Commissioners were Mr. Robert Rawlinson, Mr. Thornhill Harrison, and Mr. J. T. Way.

[2] The first, which appeared in 1866, dealt with the Thames; the second, in 1867, with the Lea. A map in the latter report illustrated the connection between an outbreak of cholera in East London and the water at Old Ford.

[3] The Commissioners were Sir William Dennison, Mr. E. Frankland, and Mr. Chalmers Morton. Their

sixth report on the domestic water supply of Great Britain did not appear till 1874.

[4] The Commissioners were the Duke of Richmond and Gordon, Sir John Thwaites (then Chairman of the Metropolitan Board of Works), Colonel Drury Harness, Sir Benjamin Phillips, Mr. T. Elliott Harrison, and Mr. Joseph Prestwich.

[5] Report [4169]; Evidence and Appendix, with plans [4169—I.-II.].

Water Bills, 1867.

certain East London Water Bills, was instructed to inquire into " the operation and results " of the Act of 1852. They took much evidence, and made a lengthened and valuable report. In their opinion, the Thames water supply, both in quantity and quality, was " so far satisfactory that there was no ground for disturbing the arrangements made under the Act of 1852."[1] Any attempt to do so would, they thought, " only end in entailing a waste of capital, and an unnecessary charge upon owners and occupiers of property in the Metropolis."

Estimated consumption of Thames water, A.D. 1927.

At the date of this inquiry the quantity of Thames water drawn each day by the five companies using this source was close on forty-seven million gallons, the estimated number of persons then supplied by these companies being 1,369,000. Assuming that this population doubled within sixty years, the quantity of water then required, at the same rate per head, would not exceed a hundred million gallons daily. Having, doubtless, in their minds the great and costly works proposed for bringing water from other and more distant sources, the Committee recalled a consideration sometimes forgotten, " that a present expenditure, with compound interest at the commercial rate of five per cent., is equivalent to an expenditure of more than eight times the amount at the end of sixty years, and is subject to the risks of the works not being required at all, or not being found best adapted to the state of facts which may then exist."[2] Was

Adequacy of supply in Thames for future wants.

such an outlay, incurred with these serious risks, called for by any probable failure in quantity of existing sources? According to evidence which the Committee saw no reason to doubt, " the smallest quantity of water known to flow down the Thames at the source of supply, in the driest time on record, exceeds three hundred and fifty million gallons in a day, and the maximum flow in a time of flood exceeds twenty-

[1] Report (Commons' Paper, 399 of 1867), p. 9. Mr. Ayrton presided over this Committee. Their labours deserve warm acknowledgment.

[2] Report, p. 8.

five thousand million gallons, while the daily average flow in the dry season may be estimated at five hundred million gallons. If, therefore, at any future period increased population should render it necessary to make provision for a greater supply of water than could be conveniently drawn from the Thames in dry seasons, it could be adequately made by storing up in reservoirs in the valley of the Thames a portion of the flood water, which now yields in a single day a sufficient supply for a whole year." [1]

Storage reservoirs for flood water of Thames.

From their springs at Amwell, the New River Company, in 1866, drew about four million gallons of water daily, and from the Lea about eighteen and a quarter millions. The Lea also furnished the East London Company with nearly nineteen million and a half gallons daily, and this company were authorized in 1867 [2] to supplement their supply by taking from the Thames at Sunbury ten million gallons daily, and as much flood water as they desired for storage purposes. In 1867, the population supplied by these two companies was estimated at 1,458,570. With the means of supply they possessed, and with further storage reservoirs, [3] the Committee were satisfied that there would be an abundant provision of water for the population of East London for many years to come. [4] They formed a similar conclusion upon the resources of the North Kent Company, which, since 1852, had abandoned the river Ravensbourne, and in 1867 supplied a population of 237,000 with over six million gallons daily from deep wells sunk in the chalk. This quantity, it appeared, might easily be doubled.

Water drawn in 1866-7 from springs and the river Lea.

As to quality, the Committee quoted from a report made in 1856 to the Board of Health by Mr. A. W. Hofmann, chemist to the Museum of Practical Geology, and Mr.

Favourable report on quality of Thames water in 1867.

---

[1] Report, p. 8.
[2] 30 & 31 Vict. cc. 148–9.
[3] Mr. Rendel estimated that reservoirs capable of holding 6,212,500,000 gallons might be constructed in the valley of the Lea for 530,000l.
[4] Report, pp. 9, 10.

Lindsay Blyth, lecturer on Natural Philosophy at St. Mary's Hospital, who found that water then supplied to London from the Thames contained no more than one-half of the organic matter present in the year 1851. A minute analysis made in 1867, and laid before the Committee,[1] convinced them "that, as far as chemical science and other means of comparison admit, the quality of the water drawn from the Thames has been still further improved, and may be advantageously compared with the water generally supplied to towns in England."[2] Owing to the report in 1866 of the Rivers Pollution Commission, a measure had been passed[3] to hinder the flow of crude sewage or of other noxious matter into the river, and much was hoped from this measure, though it did not extend to tributaries beyond three miles of their junction with the Thames. Of the quality of water supplied by the New River and East London Companies, the Committee gave an equally favourable opinion. They were convinced that, as far as chemical or other science afforded the means of judging, this water was not only wholesome, but compared satisfactorily with that furnished to other places.[4] As to the quality of the North Kent water, no question had ever arisen.

Royal Commission on Water Supply, 1867-9.

A storehouse of information on these and kindred questions is the report made in 1869 by the Royal Commissioners on Water Supply. In conformity with their instructions they examined several schemes submitted to them for

---

[1] It will be found in Appendix No. 3 to Report. But the Committee observe that chemical and other science fails to detect the presence of impurities in water which may prejudicially affect the health of consumers. Hence they lay stress on the necessity of preventing contamination from sewage. On the other hand, "the power of running water to purify itself is stated to be so great that, notwithstanding the quantity of drainage flowing into the Thames and the Lea and their tributaries, these rivers, aided by the animal and vegetable life with which they abound, are capable of purifying their waters so as to render them perfectly wholesome when they reach the consumer, after undergoing the filtration to which they are subjected." (Report, pp. 13–14.)

[2] Report, p. 8.

[3] 29 & 30 Vict. c. 89, ss. 63-9.

[4] Report, p. 11.

a supply of water to London. These may be shortly indicated. About the year 1840 Mr. Robert Stephenson suggested a recourse to water underlying the chalk around Watford. In 1851 there were two reports to the General Board of Health on a supply from soft-water springs in the Surrey sands.[1] In 1856, Mr. J. F. Bateman proposed to form collecting grounds and reservoirs in the mountainous districts of North Wales, south of Snowdon, conveying water to London by an artificial conduit.[2] These works, yielding two hundred and thirty million gallons a day, would have cost 11,400,000*l.* Messrs. Hemans and Hassard would have appropriated the water of Thirlmere and other lakes in Cumberland, bringing it to London, a distance of 270 miles, by conduits, tunnels, and iron pipes, and supplying *en route* various manufacturing districts in Lancashire and the Potteries. For two hundred and fifty million gallons a day the estimated cost was 13,500,000*l.* Mr. Hamilton Fulton's plan was to tap the upper sources of the Wye in Mid Wales, constructing six reservoirs and a conduit 180 miles long, to bring two hundred and thirty million gallons a day, at an approximate cost of 9,000,000*l.* Mr. Remington suggested the Derbyshire hills for a gathering ground, with collecting works on the river Dove, and a conduit, 135 miles long, to Barnet Hill, bringing a hundred million gallons daily, at a cost of 5,000,000*l.*

Several plans were submitted for bringing water from other than mountainous districts in England and Wales. Mr. McLean proposed to embank and canalize the Thames above Medmenham, between Henley and Great Marlow, forming in the river channel a series of impounding reservoirs. He expected to obtain two hundred million gallons daily, at a cost, estimated in 1849-50, of about

Margin notes: Plans for supply of London. From mountainous districts of England and Wales. From upper waters of Thames and Lea.

[1] By the Hon. W. Napier (1371 of 1851); and by Mr. Rammell, Superintending Inspector of Board of Health (345 of 1851).

[2] A pamphlet explaining this plan was published in November, 1856.

It was further explained and criticised in the course of evidence taken by the Commission. Part I. in their Report of 1869 deals with this and other projects mentioned in the text.

1,500,000*l.*, excluding the cost of pumping. Mr. Bailey Denton would have collected water from the higher parts of the Thames basin, but embracing also the rivers Lea, Wey and Mole. These sources, made more certain by storage reservoirs, would afford a supply of two hundred million gallons daily, with means of future increase, at a cost of 5,320,000*l.*, which included intercepting drains for sewage. To the Medmenham plan the Commissioners saw objections on the ground of expense, inferior quality of water, and because it would deprive the thirty-seven miles of river between Medmenham and Hampton of a large proportion of its dry weather volume. But they were of opinion that the methods of storage suggested in both the foregoing plans were valuable, and would deserve consideration whenever it became necessary to draw an increased quantity of water from the Thames. Another suggestion, by Mr. T. C. Brown, involved a dual system of supply. He would have taken water from the Upper Thames, from six to nine million gallons daily, for drinking purposes only. Mr. Bravender's plan was to supplement existing supplies by collecting water in the valleys of the Churn, the Colne (Gloucester), the Windrush and the Ock, and delivering it to the respective companies through a conduit or pipes. Mr. R. W. Mylne confined his project to the upper drainage area of the Lea, collecting and impounding streams and chalk springs in that district, with principal reservoirs at Enfield Chase. An increased supply of twenty-eight million gallons daily would thus be afforded, at a cost of 1,250,000*l.* This plan seemed to the Commissioners to present some ingenious and novel features, and would deserve consideration if there were any future need for enlarging and improving the supply from the Lea.

Subsidiary sources, chalk springs. There were other projects by the Rev. J. C. Clutterbuck, Mr. Homersham, Mr. P. W. Barlow, and Mr. R. Meeson, for using the chalk formations in the Thames basin as subsidiary means of supply. Mr. Homersham would have

abandoned the Thames as a source of supply for domestic
consumption, depending entirely upon this spring water, and
softening it by Dr. Clark's process. Mr. Barlow proposed
a tunnel twenty miles long parallel with the river, from
Lewisham to Gravesend, thereby obtaining sixty million
gallons a day. According to Mr. Meeson, springs in the
chalk at Grays, in Essex, would have furnished ten million
gallons a day. Mr. Thomas Hennell hoped to bring daily
fourteen million gallons from the chalk and Bagshot sands
around Basingstoke and Farnham, using the Basingstoke
canal as a channel, aided by storage reservoirs, until it
reached a point near Weybridge. A conduit constructed
thence would have delivered its water to the companies at
Thames Ditton, in extension of their existing supply. Mr.
G. W. Ewens drew attention to certain springs in the
chalk between Emsworth and Bedhampton, near Chichester.
Lastly, Mr. Telford McNeil submitted plans for a supply
of two hundred million gallons a day, at a cost of about
6,000,000l., by intercepting Thames water at Teddington,
pumping it to a height of from 200 to 380 feet, and
conveying it in an open channel to the Bagshot sands.
Through these it was then to be made to filter, and be conveyed in closed conduits to Norwood and Hampstead for
distribution.

To these projects may be added two of later date. In
the year 1877, Sir Frederick Bramwell and Mr. Easton,
in conjunction with Sir Joseph Bazalgette, engineer to the
Metropolitan Board of Works, reported, at the Board's
request, upon the London water supply. They found that
the existing supply was generally satisfactory for all except
drinking and culinary purposes and the extinction of fires.
Their plan was a separate supply of pure water, pumped from
the chalk into four reservoirs on the northern and southern
heights of London, and thence distributed for domestic use,[1]

Later projects.

Separate supply for drinking, and for extinguishing fires.

[1] Two gallons of water per head
daily are stated to be a "most liberal
allowance" for drinking and cooking,
including not only water used in

at a pressure which would also give an effective service from hydrants for fire extinction.   Of this separate service, including house fittings and hydrants, the estimated cost was 5,500,000*l.* Looking at the language of old grants and other documents already cited,[1] there seems little doubt that, in early times, citizens of London were expected to take conduit water only for drinking and cooking, using well or Thames water for all other household purposes.

A report made to the Local Government Board in July, 1884, by Mr. J. T. Harrison, suggested that London might be supplied with pure water from the chalk, equal to " at least double the volume of water at present withdrawn from the Thames."[2]   In this plan the cost of the necessary land, and of works for collecting water and conveying it to the several companies at their pumping stations at Hampton, is set down at only 700,000*l.* A comparison of this sum with the aggregate capital of the five companies which now draw their whole supply from the Thames is suggestive.[3] All these companies take water from the same reach of the river.

Opinions of Royal Commission, 1869.
After examining the plans submitted to them, and hearing much evidence, the Royal Commissioners came to conclusions substantially agreeing with those of the Committee of 1867. They thought that some of the projects for bringing water by aqueducts from Wales and Cumberland were practicable, but had doubts as to estimates, and doubted, also, whether London ought to depend on sources of supply so far removed. Looking nearer home, they were of opinion that the rivers Thames and Lea, with the chalk wells, and springs in the lower greensand, would furnish " a supply sufficient for

---

saucepans, but that used in washing vegetables and fish, and in otherwise preparing food for cooking. Two gallons per head daily would be only seven or eight million gallons for the whole Metropolis; but the plan under notice allowed sixteen millions.

(Paper read before British Association, by Sir F. Bramwell and Mr. Easton, August 20, 1877.)

[1] *Ante,* pp. 37, 41, 60.
[2] Com. Paper, 27, Session 1884.
[3] *Post,* p. 197.

any probable increase of the Metropolitan population."[1]   In
their view, two hundred million gallons a day was "the
highest demand that need be reasonably looked forward to."[2]
If, however, London increased so as to call for a larger
supply, the Thames, supplemented by reservoirs for storing
flood waters, would give two hundred and twenty million
gallons, the Lea fifty million, and the chalk springs of South
and South-east London thirty million; a total of three hundred million gallons daily.   Even with their then existing
statutory powers, the companies represented themselves as
able to supply one hundred and eighty million gallons daily.

Supply available from existing sources.

While existing sources would thus yield a sufficient quantity of water, the Commissioners also thought that, when
efficient measures were adopted for excluding sewage and
other pollutions from the Thames, the Lea, and their tributaries, and for ensuring perfect filtration, water taken from
these sources would be "perfectly wholesome, and of suitable
quality for the supply of the Metropolis."[3]   As to the minute
organic matter contained in this water, varying with the
seasons, there was much conflict of evidence, but the Commissioners found no reason for believing that the presence
of a small quantity of organic matter in drinking water is
necessarily prejudicial to health.

Quality of drinking water from the Thames and Lea.

In 1885, as twenty years before, this controversy between
chemists still continues.   On one side it is urged that, while
great improvements have been made since 1869, town-sewage
still finds its way into the upper waters of the Thames
and Lea, though in a purified form.   By irrigation, by in-

Continued controversies as to quality of river water.

[1] The Commissioners looked forward to a population of 4,500,000 to
5,000,000 as "a very remote contingency."   According to Sir Francis
Bolton's Report for September, 1885,
the estimated population supplied
within the districts of the London
water companies was then 5,183,000.

[2] This was a maximum summer
consumption.   The actual daily sup-

ply during August, 1885, averaged
167,771,000 gallons.

[3] The Committee of 1871, to whom
the Metropolitan Water Bill of that
Session was referred, came to the
same conclusion, reporting that, if
properly filtered, water supplied
from the Thames might be made
suitable for all domestic purposes.

termittent downward filtration, and by various methods of chemical treatment, river water is improved in appearance and even in chemical quality; yet, it is alleged, not one of these processes can guarantee the exclusion from the Thames or Lea of noxious ingredients which are capable of spreading zymotic disease.[1] Further, it is objected, from small towns and villages, comprising great part of the population of the Thames valley, that river still receives much raw sewage, together with the effluents from sewage works constructed by larger towns. Indeed, the expense of any plan for totally excluding sewage-matter from rivers is so great as to make such a plan practically impossible; the task of banishing these and other objectionable pollutions from the Thames and other rivers is pronounced "an entirely hopeless one;" and "there is nothing in the subsequent treatment to which river water is subjected by the companies which will ensure the removal of matters of this description."[2]

Alleged self-purifying power of running water.

On the other side, these objections are described as fanciful. The self-purifying power of running water, mentioned by the Committee of 1867, has now, it is said, "become more than ever a matter of positive demonstration."[3] In 1869, the Royal Commissioners stated that this purifying process was "not a mere theoretical speculation," and that they had "abundant practical evidence of its real action on the Thames and other rivers." An examination of water supplied from the Thames during 1881-3 shows a gradual yearly diminution in the proportion of organic matter; a result attributed in large measure to

[1] Professor Frankland's Report to the Registrar-General on analyses of water supplied by the London Companies during the year 1883.

[2] Ib. Professor Frankland adds:— "I am informed that several of the water companies are now impressed with the necessity of ultimately abandoning the rivers Thames and Lea as sources of water supply, and some of them have already completed works for utilizing subterraneous waters which have undergone natural filtration through great thicknesses of gravel and sand, whilst others are sinking deep wells into the chalk."

[3] Report to the London Companies on the water supplied by them during 1883, by Mr. Crookes, Mr. Odling, and Dr. Tidy.

increased efforts made by the companies to improve their Organic matter in drinking water. processes for filtering and subsidence.[1]   There is said to be "absolutely no chemical evidence to indicate that the minute proportion of organic matter present in water" supplied to London from the Thames differs, "either in quantity or kind, from the natural organic matter of the river, as met with, for instance, at Lechlade, where the main stream of the Thames is formed." Moreover, the difference in the quantity of organic matter present in Thames and other drinking water is small, and that quantity is itself infinitesimal.   According to the mean of monthly analyses made in 1883, the organic matter contained in Thames water supplied to London was under three-tenths of a grain per gallon, while the organic matter in water supplied to Glasgow from Loch Katrine, and to Birmingham, which receives a water mixed in varying proportions from reservoir, stream and well, was about two-and-a-half-tenths of a grain per gallon.[2]

This controversy is likely to continue; and though, judging Public feeling against river water for drinking. by the results of Parliamentary and official inquiry, the weight of authority is, on the whole, in favour of the existing river supply, the numberless contaminations to which it must ever be subject will keep alive a desire that new sources should be substituted for the drinking water of London. Such a desire may rest on sentiment alone; and water supplied from the Thames, as the Royal Commissioners reported in 1869, may be generally good and wholesome.   But this

[1] In their annual report for 1884-5 (p. 123), the Local Government Board notice with satisfaction Dr. Frankland's statement that the supply from the Thames and Lea during that year was of better quality than in any previous year since the system of periodical analysis was begun in 1868. This result is mainly attributed to increased capacity of the companies' storage reservoirs, and greater efficiency of their filter-beds.

[2] Report to Water Companies for 1883. The distinguished chemists responsible for these reports add that this excess in the average proportion of organic matter in Thames-derived water is entirely due to the effect of winter floods, and that, comparing the results for the eight months, March to October, 1883, the proportion of organic matter in Loch Katrine water was somewhat greater than the proportion in Thames water.

sentiment must always be reckoned with so long as the drinking water of London "is derived from rivers into which is poured the sewage of a great part of the large population in the basins of the Thames and Lea, and also the surface-drainage from the highly-cultivated, and therefore highly-manured, land of those basins."[1]

Constant supply. Something must now be said about methods of supply. We have seen,[2] so lately as the year 1820, how scanty a service was given by the companies, who contented themselves sometimes with a supply for two or three hours a day, on four days a week, and made an extra charge for high pressure. Competition by new companies led to improved and more frequent services, but even in the year 1867, with some trifling exceptions, water was turned on for only a short time in each day; on Sundays no supply whatever was received by the larger part of the Metropolis; and no effect had been given to the intentions of Parliament that a constant supply should be afforded.[3]

General legislation to secure constant service. In 1847, the general Waterworks Clauses Act[4] had provided for a constant supply to the top story of every house, within the area of each special Act, but all Metropolitan companies were exempt from this provision. In 1852, however, the same condition was imposed upon them,[5] after a requisition from four-fifths of the owners or occupiers of houses on a district main, unless the company could show that one-fifth of the houses on such district main were not fitted with proper apparatus.

Its failure. Elaborate provisions were added in order to carry out this enactment, but the Committee of 1867 found that it had "failed to secure for the inhabitants the advantage which they ought to have long since enjoyed, of a well-regulated supply of water for domestic purposes." They strongly de-

---

[1] Sir F. Bramwell and Mr. Easton, in their Paper, cited *ante*, pp. 165-6.
[2] *Ante*, pp. 136–7.
[3] Report of Commons' Committee, 1867, on East London Water Bills,

&c., p. 16.
[4] 10 & 11 Vict. c. 17. See Vol. I., p. 250 *et seq.*
[5] By Metropolis Water Act, 1852 (15 & 16 Vict. c. 84) ; *ante*, p. 157.

precated the use of cisterns as " probably a more fertile cause of impurity than any pollution of the river."   In the public Act of 1847, cisterns were not made obligatory if a constant supply were given; in the Metropolitan Act of 1852, they were made peremptory conditions of such a supply.   Im- pressed with the injury to health caused by cisterns, the Committee recommended an amendment of the Act of 1852, so that, with a constant service, water might be drawn direct from the pipes in each house throughout London, and at any hour.   As experiments had shown that where intermittent had been changed to constant service without alteration of house-fittings, there was " an enormous waste of water," fresh arrangements to prevent such waste were suggested.   In 1869, the Royal Commissioners also urged that earnest and prompt efforts should be made to introduce constant service throughout the Metropolis.

Recommendations of Committee of 1867 and Royal Commission, 1869.

After inquiry, in 1871, before a Committee in the House of Commons,[1] Parliament legislated in the spirit of these recommendations, and an Act passed amending that of 1852, and making " further provision for the due supply of water to the Metropolis."[2]   One section required every company to furnish " sufficient pure and wholesome water for domestic use " on Sundays as on other days.   A constant supply was to be given by every company upon application by a Metro- politan authority, or upon their own motion; but, to pre- vent waste, provision was made for proper fittings and for regulations binding on consumers.   Power was given to the Board of Trade to interpose in certain cases.   With a view to a regular examination of the quality of water, the Board was also authorised to appoint " a Water Examiner, being a competent and impartial person," whose duty it was to ascertain whether every company had complied with section 4 of the Act of 1852, requiring that all water supplied for domestic use should be effectually filtered.[3]   It

Metropolis Water Act, 1871.

Water Examiner.

[1] Special Report from Select Committee on Metropolis Water (No. 2)
Bill; 381 of Session 1871.

[2] 34 & 35 Vict. c. 113.
[3] " The process of filtration may
be said to be both chemical and me-

was further provided that annual accounts should be furnished to the Board of Trade and to local authorities by each company, and that these accounts should be audited twice a year by an official auditor.[1]

Progress made in constant service.

Under the provisions of this Act, regulations as to house fittings adapted to a constant service have been made, and confirmed by the Board of Trade, and all the companies are, by degrees, substituting, voluntarily, a constant for an intermittent supply. From the Water Examiner's report for September, 1885, we find that 306,142 houses then received a constant supply, out of a total of 698,744 houses served by the Metropolitan companies, so that considerable progress has been made in carrying out the new system. Other information of great value is contained in the monthly and annual reports made by the Official Examiner pursuant to the Act. For example, in August, 1885, out of an average daily supply

Water Examiner's

chanical, especially in the case of large filter-beds, for a process of chemical decomposition goes on simultaneously with the merely mechanical process of straining. Decaying organic substances poured with water into a filter-bed are not merely arrested, but are rapidly decomposed and resolved into their elementary constituents, which again are promptly recombined in other forms. This chemical change is scientifically explained by the theory that every particle of sand is closely enveloped in a film of condensed air, and that the particles of organic matter, being thus brought into close contact with a body of oxygen, undergo rapid decomposition. It is well known that all solid bodies attract about them an atmospheric film, and therefore, as a bed of sand and gravel is an agglomeration of minute stones, each with its coating of compressed air (or, in other words, compressed oxygen and nitrogen), the water filtering through the interstices has to pass through a con-

contrated body of oxygen capable of rapidly decomposing it and forming other compounds. Consequently, if we take a dead leaf, for example, we can see that it would be resolved to some extent into carbon, nitrogen, and hydrogen, which, recombining with the oxygen, form carbonic acid gas, ammonia, and water. As the result of this chemical process, the polluting vegetable matter will have actually vanished; and though the filter-bed has really abstracted it from the percolating water, the bed itself will show no trace of it." (London Water Supply, by Col. Sir Francis Bolton, C.E., Water Examiner under the Act of 1871. This useful volume was published in connection with the International Health Exhibition, 1884.)

[1] By sect. 47, "the landed estate, houses, or property of the New River Company not directly used for or connected with their water supply," were excepted from this audit, as well as from the general operation of the Act. (See *post*, p. 192.)

of 167,771,000 gallons, about fifty-eight parts of the whole hundred came from the Thames, and from chalk springs in the Thames valley. From the river Lea and chalk springs in the Lea valley, came about thirty parts of the whole. Ten chalk wells in northern London yielded about five parts; ten chalk wells in South London about seven parts. Companies drawing water from the Thames are restricted to 110,000,000 gallons daily. Together, the companies possess subsiding and storage reservoirs for unfiltered water capable of holding 1,290,100,000 gallons, and covered reservoirs holding 160,000,000 gallons of filtered water.[1] Besides reporting upon the appearance of the water before and after filtration, and upon the condition of samples taken daily, the Official Examiner furnishes in each month a careful analysis of the water supplied by each company.[2] Other analyses are also made for the companies by analysts of their own appointment, and serve as correctives, if necessary, of the official report.[3]

The extinction of fires, a subject intimately connected with the water supply of London, has been repeatedly considered by Parliament. In 1844 inquiry was made into this subject by a Committee of the House of Commons, to whom was referred a Bill "for the better prevention of damage by fire in the Metropolis." This Bill was amended by the Committee, but did not become law.[4] A Select Committee of the same House sat in 1862, and made an elaborate report, with

Margin notes:
Report, August, 1885.

Fires in the metropolis.

Commons' Committees, 1844–67.

---

[1] Pp. 8, 9. "During the winter months the water in the Thames and Lea is frequently very turbid, and when in that condition is extremely difficult to deal with. The solid impurities in suspension are only practically got rid of by long subsidence previous to filtration, as they chiefly consist of clay, marl, and chalk in a very finely divided state; but the companies, being generally provided with sufficient storage reservoirs, are nearly always enabled to allow the turbid water to flow by, and only take in water when the rivers are at their best." (Sir Francis Bolton on London Water Supply, p. 20.)

[2] This analysis has been regularly made by Professor Frankland since the year 1865.

[3] See analyses prepared for and at the joint expense of the water companies, by Dr. Bernays and Dr. Tidy, addressed to the Official Water Examiner, and appended to his Reports.

[4] Bill 320 of 1844.

plans.[1] In 1865 the task of extinguishing fires was entrusted to the Metropolitan Board of Works;[2] provision was made for the maintenance of a fire brigade; the insurance companies' stations and plant were transferred to the Board; and certain duties as to fire-plugs were thrown upon the water companies.[3] There had always, however, been a want of water at high pressure, and in sufficient quantities, for this purpose. Such a want, and the necessity of further means for fire extinction, led to renewed inquiry in 1867.[4] In the same Session, the Committee who reported on the East London Water Bills received complaints from the Metropolitan Board, that, with an intermittent supply, full pressure could not be obtained at any spot until every receptacle for water served by the main was filled, and the supply to them thus arrested. A constant service, with proper hydrants, the Committee pointed out, would enable the fire brigade, with some unavoidable exceptions, to throw water direct from the mains, without aid from any engine, in sufficient quantity to arrest most fires at their first outbreak.[5] The Royal Commission in 1869 also urged that abundant water should be provided for general public purposes, such as watering and cleansing, public fountains, and fire extinction.[6]

Committee of 1876-7.

In 1876-7, a Committee presided over by Sir H. Selwin-Ibbetson again fully investigated this question. It was

[1] Fires in the Metropolis; Report of Committee, No. 221 of 1862.

[2] By 28 & 29 Vict. c. 90.

[3] See also 34 & 35 Vict. c. 113, s. 34.

[4] Fire Protection; Report of Commons' Committee, with plans and index; 471 and 471-I. of Session, 1867.

[5] Committee on East London Water Bills, &c.; Report, p. 22.

[6] "None of the companies are under any statutory obligation to provide water sufficient for the extinction of fires; all that is required of them being to allow the gratuitous use of their water for this purpose, and to grant certain special facilities. . . . The Metropolitan Board can require the companies to provide fire-plugs at the Board's expense; but, as a matter of fact, the companies provide them gratuitously. The value of constant supply for the purpose of fire extinction has been said with truth to be of even greater moment than its convenience to ordinary consumers." (Sir Francis Bolton's "London Water Supply," pp. 24-5.)

stated in evidence before them that property in London was insured for 540,000,000*l.*, while estimates of uninsured property varied, Captain Shaw being of opinion that two-thirds of the property in London were uninsured. If so, this property must reach a total value of about 1,600,000,000*l.* Sir F. Bramwell complained that nothing had then been done by London water companies beyond giving a supply of water at the street level, to be picked up by engines and pumped upon fires; and his opinion, given in evidence, was that, whether a service was constant or intermittent, it would be a waste of money to put hydrants upon mains in which there was no greater pressure than forty feet above the pavement.[1] Captain Shaw told the Committee that, at a large fire, he required 2,000 gallons of water a minute, to be played upon the flames through fourteen hose, each 200 feet long, and each conveying 150 gallons per minute. He added that, in many instances, this moderate quantity could not be obtained.[2]

About 80,000*l.* a year was available in the year 1875 for the protection of London from fire. Of this sum, 48,000*l.* arose from a half-penny rate levied by the Metropolitan Board, 20,000*l.* from a contribution by insurance offices, at the rate of 35*l.* for each million insured, 10,000*l.* from the Government, and the rest from miscellaneous sources.[3]

Annual cost of London Fire Brigade.

[1] This was the pressure which, under their special Act, the East London Company were then bound to maintain.

[2] "It is not surprising that the pipes of the companies, which have been laid with a due regard to economy of capital, large enough merely to supply the needs of the houses (those needs being at the average rate of a pint and a quarter per minute per house, or 227 gallons per house per day) should be inadequate, in many instances, to bring to the scene of a fire two thousand gallons per minute, even when delivered at the level of the street for the service of a fire-engine." (Paper by Sir F. Bramwell and Mr. Easton, 1877.) "Before Manchester had a constant supply, with high pressure, 21 per cent. of the entire property attacked by fire was destroyed. With a constant service the per-centage of property destroyed was reduced from 21 to 6 per cent." (Mr. Fawcett, in House of Commons; Hansard, August 13, 1879.)

[3] In the Paper already cited, the proportionate expenditure for fire

Recommen-
dations of
Committee,
1877.

Sir H. Selwin-Ibbetson's Committee recommended that the Metropolitan Board's rating power for fire purposes should be doubled, and that hydrants should be fitted to mains and services wherever there was constant service. The latter recommendation has been carried out by the Board concurrently with the extension of a constant supply by the water companies.[1] Through this joint action, in September, 1885, out of 3,085 miles of mains in the Metropolis, 1,126 were constantly charged, and there were 8,157 street hydrants.[2]

Proposed
transfer of
London water
supply to
public body.

Before 1877, as we have seen, a long line of Committees and Commissions had recommended a transfer of the water supply of London to a public authority. More effectual means of extinguishing fires formed the chief ground for this recommendation in 1877. In 1869, the Royal Commissioners made a similar recommendation upon broader grounds.[3] They were of opinion that constant service could not be effectually carried out in London so long as water was supplied by private companies;[4] and they could point to many provincial towns, a number since then largely in-

extinction per thousand of the population is stated as follows:—London, 22l. 17s.; Paris, 50l. 6s.; New York, 233l. 14s.; Chicago, 202l.

[1] The alteration of house-fittings, made necessary by a change from intermittent to constant service, imposes an enormous burden upon consumers. Sir F. Bramwell and Mr. Easton estimated the ultimate cost of this alteration at 3,600,000l. The Metropolitan Board have not exercised the power, given them in 1871 (*ante*, p. 171), to require from the water companies a constant supply, because they allege that the regulations to which consumers are subjected, as a condition of constant supply, are unnecessarily expensive and harassing to owners and occupiers of houses. (Sir James McGarel-Hogg, House of Commons, August 6, 1883; 282

Hansard, 1624.) These regulations were opposed both by the Metropolitan Board and the Corporation of London, but were approved by the Board of Trade.

[2] Report of Water Examiner, p. 9.

[3] Report, p. 122.

[4] It is only fair to note the considerable progress made by the companies since 1869 in extending constant supply. The number of houses receiving a constant supply on December 31, 1883, was 35,383 in excess of the number so supplied on the last day of 1882. In 1884 there was a similar increase of 41,125; and, as already stated, of 698,744 houses returned by the London companies in September, 1885, 306,142 had constant service.

creased,[1] which had returned to ancient practice by placing their water supply under municipal control.

These Commissioners had also considered the incidence of rates for water, and were of opinion that existing methods in London should be altered. They found that, in Manchester, the corporation were authorized to levy two water rates. One, of threepence in the pound, was a public general rate on all rateable property, irrespective of supply, inasmuch as all property benefits alike from street-watering and cleansing, sewer-flushing, public fountains, and fire-extinction. The other rate, of ninepence in the pound, was a charge for water actually supplied. By such a system, which is also adopted at Glasgow and other places, a juster apportionment appears to be effected between the public and private interests served by a water supply than by one uniform domestic rate. Accordingly, the Commissioners recommended similar rates in London; but as no trading company could be permitted to levy or expend these compulsory rates, a responsible public body should be created, with powers to purchase and extend existing undertakings. In their opinion this plan offered "the only feasible means" of securing not only constant service, but " a compulsory supply to the poor." They believed it would also tend to economy and an improved quality of water, with better provision for fire-extinction, and for other public objects.

Incidence of water rates.

As the chief local authority in London, the Metropolitan Board of Works tried, but with signal want of success, to carry out a policy which had been so often suggested. Early in the Session of 1878 they brought forward two Bills. One, based upon a dual plan already described,[2] sought authority to provide a new high-pressure service of pure water for drinking and cooking, and for extinction of fires, not interfering with existing supplies for ordinary household purposes. Wells and pumping stations were proposed at Dereham, Bucks; at Hayes, Middlesex; Epsom, Surrey; Kes-

Metropolis Water (New Works) Bill, 1878.

---

[1] *Ante*, Vol. I., p. 254.   [2] *Ante*, pp. 165–6.

ton and Eynsford in Kent; and Grays Thurrock, Essex; with
reservoirs at Great Stanmore, Banstead and Chelsfield. There
was to be constant service, with a pressure which would force
jets of water from hydrants to a height of not less than 100
feet above the street level. In addition, or as an alternative
to these powers, the Board promoted another Bill, enabling
them to purchase the undertakings of the eight existing
companies, and to supply London with water.

Metropolis Water (Purchase) Bill, 1878.

These measures were read a first time in the House of
Commons, but went no further. A debate on the second
reading was adjourned,[1] but was not afterwards resumed, as
both Bills were withdrawn. Strong objection was taken,
on the companies' behalf, to attempts to depreciate the
value of their undertakings by a competitive scheme, and
then purchase them at this depreciated value. It was alleged
that the dual scheme would be uneconomical, would disturb
the streets by a double system of mains and pipes, require a second set of fittings in each house, and, after all,
would not ensure a sufficient supply of drinking water, while
it would deprive the Kent Company of their sources. A
further objection to the proposed new authority was that the
Board's jurisdiction extended only over 120 square miles,
while the water companies served an area of 520 square
miles; so that the Board were seeking to purchase waterworks
occupying an area four times as extensive as their own, and
in no way represented by them.[2]

Bills withdrawn after debate.

Although the Board's two Bills were not considered in
Committee of either House, a sum of nearly 16,000*l.* was
nevertheless incurred in preliminary and incidental expenses.
Had these Bills passed, the costs' clause in each would
have authorized payment of all expenses of promotion. As
it was, these expenses were disallowed by the auditor, because they had been incurred without proper authority.
In order to relieve individual members from liability, a
relief Act was necessary, enabling the Board to defray

Costs surcharged on Board.

Metropolitan Board of Works In-

[1] Hansard, March 12, 1878.   [2] Speech of Mr. Samuda, ib.

these expenses.[1] This statute was passed with difficulty, demnity Act, 1879. although there could be no doubt that, as the recital set forth, legislation had been sought and costs incurred by the Board "in good faith, and in the belief that they were acting within their legal powers."

In view of this failure by the Metropolitan Board of Mr. Fawcett's motion, August, 1879. Works, Mr. Fawcett, late in the Session of 1879, moved a resolution calling upon the Government, without further delay, to deal with the water supply of London. An interesting debate followed.[2] Mr. Fawcett admitted that the weight of evidence as to the quality of river water supplied in London was against any hasty condemnation of existing sources, and that any change in these sources would enormously increase the cost of supply, and the difficulty of any transfer to a public body. But he urged strong reasons for improved methods of supply. An intermittent system, which involved the storage of water in dirty and exposed cisterns in poor people's houses, would hopelessly spoil the purest spring water that ever flowed from a mountain side. He quoted evidence to show how frequently, owing to this cause, water drank by poor persons in London was contaminated and unwholesome. An intermittent system was also wasteful and costly. In Manchester and other manufacturing towns the average consumption of water was no more than sixteen gallons daily a head, while the average daily consumption in London was thirty-two gallons, so that about one-half of the water supply in London was wasted. Parliament, he said, had conferred no exclusive monopoly on either water or gas companies.[3] If, therefore, these companies were unreason-

[1] 42 & 43 Vict. c. 68. A schedule contains details, according to which counsel received 1,045*l.*; engineers, 6,425*l.*; parliamentary agents, 1,378*l.*; chemists, 1,714*l.*; and advertisements cost 1,159*l.*

[2] Hansard, House of Commons, August 13, 1879.

[3] No additional proof on this point is necessary beyond that repeatedly cited in these pages. Two statutes were, however, quoted in debate, the Sewers Act of 1846, and the Metropolis Local Management Act, 1856, which respectively authorized the Commissioners of Sewers and Metropolitan Board to sink wells and supply water for street watering, and other public purposes.

able, a great public reform might, without any breach of faith, be carried out in spite of them.

Undertaking by Govern-ment to deal with question.

Mr. Fawcett suggested a public Water Commission to manage the water supply of London. Mr. Sclater Booth, then President of the Local Government Board, again pointed out that the London water companies supplied an area extending far beyond the Metropolitan district, so that unification of these companies could hardly be combined with any management of the water supply by a purely Metropolitan authority.[1] The Home Secretary, Mr. Cross, thought that a mere amalgamation of companies would be an ineffectual reform, but undertook to consider the whole question in the recess,[2] and upon this assurance the motion was withdrawn.

Metropolis Waterworks Purchase Bill, 1880.

In fulfilment of this pledge, Mr. Cross, early in the Session of 1880, introduced a Bill to purchase the eight water undertakings. He was averse from compelling the companies to surrender their statutory powers. On the faith of these powers, a large amount of capital had been subscribed, much of it being held by trustees. For Parliament to take over these powers by compulsion would be a strong step, for which there were few precedents, and which would be so violently opposed that it would probably end in failure. Nor did the Home Secretary approve of a Parliamentary transfer, leaving terms to be settled by arbitration. There had been some unpleasant experiences of the danger and uncertainty of such a mode of settlement. The only other course, then, was to agree upon price and conditions of transfer, subject to ratification by Parliament. Acting upon these lines, negotiations had been entered into, and provisional arrangements

[1] In nearly every case in which a gas or water supply has been taken over by municipal authorities, the same distinction has existed between municipal areas and areas of supply; but Committees have seldom found a difficulty in providing fairly for any conflict of interests.

[2] In order to discourage speculative dealings, the Home Secretary announced that, if any transfer were effected, the price of water stock would be reckoned as it stood on June 30, 1879, and no account would be taken of subsequent variations in price.

made with each company.   Mr. E. J. Smith, a professional surveyor and valuer of great experience and ability, was the intermediary.   No purchase-money was to be paid.   The plan was to constitute a water trust of twelve members,[1] in part nominated and in part elected, for the future management of the London water supply.   Each company was to receive a nominal capital, consisting of ordinary stock, bearing interest from July 1, 1880, and of deferred stock, on which interest would begin to run at subsequent periods. Existing dividends would thus be converted into immediate annuities; estimates of growing profits, based upon the increase in past years, would be represented by deferred annuities, beginning when these profits might be expected to accrue.   In each case the capital converted into water stock was to bear interest at three and a-half per cent., and stockholders would have had the double security of (1) all property belonging to the trust, with all their water rents and revenue; and (2) the consolidated rates levied respectively by the Metropolitan Board and City Sewers Commission.   The amount of ordinary stock was 22,098,700*l.*; of deferred stock, the last of which would have been created in the year 1892, 6,851,300*l.*; together, 28,950,000*l.*

Plan of purchase.

A sinking fund was part of the scheme.   In addition, it would have been necessary to provide for existing obligations of the companies: 3,061,500*l.* preference and debenture capital, and a mortgage and bond debt of 223,055*l.*; the annual interest on these two heads of charge amounting to 141,720*l.*   Mr. Smith calculated that this yearly interest, together with the annuities, present and deferred, would be covered by a growing income from water after the transfer.   Adding these charges to the total annuities, the

---

[1] There were to be three paid members: the chairman, receiving 2,000*l.* a year; and two vice-chairmen, one for finance and one for works, with 1,800*l.* each.   The Government were to appoint two of these paid members.   The extra-metropolitan districts were to return two members, though in 1880 the water companies only derived a revenue of 120,000*l.* a year from these districts.

annual payments would have been finally 1,240,673*l*., and the total capital value would have stood at 33,018,836*l*.

Such was the price proposed to be paid by water consumers in London for the Metropolitan water undertakings. The plan was ingenious, and had the merit of simplicity and ease.[1] It was at once, however, attacked, as Sir George Grey's proposal in 1851 had been attacked, because its terms were unduly favourable to the companies. Their shares had, indeed, gone up by leaps and bounds during the negotiations; and though this enhancement in no way affected the proposed terms of transfer, it showed how good a bargain was thought to be in store for water shareholders. For them undoubtedly it was a good bargain. But, looking to the yearly increment of value, earned and unearned, which each company was then, and still is, able to show, the bargain was defended as, on the whole, a good one for water consumers also.[2]

Before the Bill could be considered by a hybrid Committee,

Unfavourable reception of scheme.

---

[1] In its scheme of finance it closely followed the precedent set when the Birmingham Water Company's undertaking was transferred to the municipality in 1875. Mr. E. J. Smith told the Committee of 1880, that if he had arranged for the same terms as were paid at Birmingham, the London Companies would have received from four and a-half to six millions more than he had consented to give. But, according to Ald. Avery, the Corporation of Birmingham gave 25¼ years' purchase of the actual net earnings of the water company in 1875, their last year of working, and only 24½ years' purchase of the net earnings of 1876, the first year after the transfer to the municipality; whereas Mr. Smith had agreed to pay to the London Companies from 40 to 45 years' purchase. It appears, however, that the Birmingham Water Company's dividends were limited to seven and eight per cent. (Commons' Committee of 1880; App. to Report, p. 292.)

[2] In introducing the Bill, Mr. Cross mentioned that for many years previously the net incomes of the respective companies showed an average annual increase of 35,000*l*.; that, in 1879, about 19,000 new houses were built in London, and about sixty miles of new streets, all swelling the water revenue. As years go on, he added, the price of taking these undertakings compulsorily will increase. "If you had bought them ten years ago you would have saved enormously. If you defer buying them for five or ten years, you will have to pay more than now." (251 Hansard, p. 232; March 2, 1880.) In 1884, the increase of houses in London was 20,214.

as its framers intended, a dissolution in 1880 brought about a change of Ministry. The scheme was then foredoomed. A Select Committee was appointed [1] "to inquire and report as to the expediency of acquiring on behalf of the inhabitants of London the undertakings of the existing Metropolitan water companies, and also to examine and report whether certain agreements, or any of them, already entered into provisionally for the purchase of those undertakings, would furnish a satisfactory basis for such an acquisition." Before this Committee the water companies were heard by counsel, along with the Corporation of London and Metropolitan Board. These two bodies were of opinion that the terms contained in the provisional agreements did not furnish a satisfactory basis of purchase; and in this opinion the Committee concurred, chiefly because they thought an excessive sum would be paid for future increment of profits. This estimated increment was based " on the assumption that all items of receipt would grow at a greater rate in the future than in the past; that the number and value of houses and the rate of water rentals would perpetually augment; but that, on the other hand, the growth of capital expenditure which has hitherto been required in order to earn an increased income, would sink almost to nothing, and might be discarded from calculation." In the Committee's view this did not appear to be a sound basis of a financial estimate for the future.[2]

Like most of their predecessors, the Committee of 1880

margin notes: Committee of 1880. — Hostile report. — Public control of water

---

[1] Sir William Harcourt, who had succeeded Mr. (now Sir Richard) Cross as Home Secretary, was Chairman. The Committee consisted of eighteen members, and included Sir James McGarel-Hogg, Mr. Chamberlain, Sir Richard Cross, Mr. Sclater-Booth, Mr. Hubbard, and Mr. Pemberton.

[2] Report, p. 4. Mr. Smith, who was examined for eight days before the Committee, based his calculations of value on three considerations: that competition was practically impossible; that in quantity the water now furnished by the companies was adequate, and would remain adequate under a system of constant supply, for the next ten or fifteen years; and that in quality the water was satisfactory.

price, coincided with the opinions of the Corporation and
Metropolitan Board, that the price arranged for was " greatly
beyond the estimated value of the property."

Back divi-
dends.

It will be remembered that the Waterworks Clauses Act,
1847, imposed a limit upon the dividends of water companies.[1]
But the Metropolitan companies asserted before the Committee a right practically to escape from any such limit, by
their power of making up back dividends,[2] bringing up to a
ten per cent. level any dividends which had fallen short of that
maximum in previous years. This right was conceded in the
preliminary negotiations, and was represented by a considerable sum in the terms of agreement.[3] We have seen that
the early career of the Metropolitan companies was not
prosperous. Their counsel contended that their right to
make up past deficiencies of income went back to the origin
of each company during all these years of penury. According to Mr. Smith's evidence, the possible amount of these
back dividends was nearly twenty millions; and the New
River Company alone made out a possible claim of fifteen
millions. Such pretensions seem to have aroused much
indignation in the Committee. " Without," they say, " pro-
nouncing an opinion on the legal point, your Committee
must observe, that if the contention of the companies is well-
founded, the population of the Metropolis and its suburbs,
amounting to four millions of people, would be left at the

---

[1] 10 & 11 Vict. c. 17 ; *ante*, Vol. I.
p. 250.

[2] See 10 & 11 Vict. c. 17, s. 75,
on which is founded this claim to
make up deficiencies in past dividends.

[3] The whole sum allowed in the
agreements as back dividends was
1,302,000*l*., distributed among the
Kent, Southwark & Vauxhall, West
Middlesex and Grand Junction Companies. The New River Company was
dealt with on a different footing. To
the Chelsea, Lambeth, and East London Companies nothing was allowed
on this account. See Min. of Proceedings, 18. See also Sir John
Lambert's Paper on the statutory
rights of the respective companies
under general legislation, and by
virtue of their special Acts, to maximum and back dividends (App.
pp. 229–33); and remarks by Mr.
Stoneham, auditor under the Metropolitan Water Act, 1871, in his
Report to the Local Government
Board for 1883–4. (App. to Board's
Report for that year, pp. 158–9.)

mercy of certain trading companies, armed with the power of raising the price of one of the first necessities of life to an extent, practically, without any limit; a situation from which the companies seem to consider there is no escape, except in the purchase of their undertakings at such a price as they may be willing to accept. If that were the only remedy, the consequences to consumers of improvident legislation in the past would be indeed intolerable. But Parliament is not unequal to redress such mischief to the public interests. The manner in which the gas companies have been dealt with by Parliament may be referred to in illustration of the methods by which a remedy for such a state of things may be effectually provided."[1]

An amendment was proposed in the Committee by Sir Richard Cross, to the following effect:—" Your Committee feel very strongly that every year's delay in acquiring the undertakings of the existing companies will necessarily, owing to the rapid increase in the growth of the Metropolis, greatly affect the price to be paid for them. It is, therefore, with great regret that they feel bound to come to the conclusion that, at this period of the Session, no sufficient opportunity can be afforded to the Corporation of London and the Metropolitan Board of Works, representing the water consumers on the one hand, and to the water companies on the other, of agreeing upon such modifications of the agreements, or of some of them, as would have secured, with the assistance of your Committee, an immediate and satisfactory solution of the question." This amendment was negatived by six votes to four;[2] and the same fate attended another amendment:—" Your Committee are of opinion that if the Bill of the late Government had been before them, the terms embodied in it might, with the consent of the water

Views of minority in Committee.

---

[1] Report, p. 5.

[2] Sir James McGarel-Hogg, Mr. Alderman Lawrence, Mr. Brand, Mr. Firth, Mr. Thorold Rogers, and Mr. John Holmes, against Sir Richard Cross, Mr. Pemberton, Sir Gabriel Goldney, and Mr. Sclater-Booth.

companies, have been so modified as to form an acceptable basis of purchase; but, that Bill having been allowed to drop, it would be impossible to deal with the companies under these agreements."

Proper basis for assessment of water rents.

An important incident in the history of the Metropolitan water supply occurred in the year 1883. By special Acts regulating the rates of water companies, as well as by the Waterworks Clauses Act, 1847,[1] the charge for water supplied for domestic purposes is to be based upon the annual value of premises. There is no definition of "annual value" in the Acts just mentioned, and, in practice, companies based their assessment of a water rate, not upon "rateable value," but upon the "gross value" of premises, as interpreted by the Valuation (Metropolis) Act, 1869.[2]

"Annual value," whether meaning rateable or gross value.

A case arose in which this basis of assessment was challenged by the lessee of a house supplied by the Grand Junction Waterworks Company. He paid no rent but a ground-rent; and under this company's special Act, passed in 1826, they were bound to supply water at certain rates, payable, where the actual rent could not be ascertained, according to the "annual value upon which the assessment to the poor's rate is computed." A later Act of the company, passed in 1852, omitted any reference to the poor's rate assessment, and based the assessment for water rates simply on annual value. The question was whether, no actual rent being paid in the disputed case, "annual value" meant gross value; or rateable value, allowing deductions for usual outgoings. A police magistrate, to whom this question

Dobbs v. Grand Junction Waterworks Company.

---

[1] 10 & 11 Vict. c. 17, s. 68.

[2] 32 & 33 Vict. c. 67, s. 4 of which says:—"The term 'gross value' means the annual rent which a tenant might reasonably be expected, taking one year with another, to pay for an hereditament, if the tenant undertook to pay all usual tenant's rates and taxes, and tithe commutation rent-charge, if any, and if the landlord undertook to bear the cost of the repairs and insurance, and the other expenses, if any, necessary to maintain the hereditament in a state to command that rent. The term 'rateable value' means the gross value after deducting therefrom the probable annual average cost of the repairs, insurance, and other expenses as aforesaid."

was referred under the Waterworks Clauses Act, 1847,[1] decided in favour of the company, that the proper assessment was upon gross value. His decision was reversed by the Queen's Bench Division. The Court of Appeal again reversed that judgment, going back to the police magistrate's finding. Finally, the case was taken to the House of Lords,[2] which reversed the decision in the Court of Appeal, holding that the words "annual value" had the same meaning in both the Company's Acts, and meant "net annual value," as defined in the Parochial Assessments Act, 1836.[3] It appears that the New River Company estimated the probable reduction in their water rental, owing to this decision, at 12,000l. yearly; the East London Company's estimate was 6,000l.; and the Kent Company, 3,000l.[4]

Decision by House of Lords.

In the Session of 1885, all doubts as to the proper basis of assessment were set at rest by legislation. When introduced as a public measure into the House of Commons, the Bill, described as one "to declare and explain sect. 68 of the Waterworks Clauses Act, 1847," applied to every water company in the kingdom. It was afterwards limited to the Metropolis. In the view of the Examiners, it thus became a private or at least a hybrid Bill, but the House of Lords

Water Rate Definition Act, 1885.

---

[1] 10 & 11 Vict. c. 17, s. 68, which gives jurisdiction to magistrates in certain disputes between companies and consumers.

[2] Dobbs v. Grand Junction Waterworks Company, 9 App. Cas. 49.

[3] 6 & 7 Will. IV. c. 96, s. 1, which says that the net annual value of houses is "the rent at which they might reasonably be expected to let from year to year free of all usual tenant's rates and taxes and tithe commutation rent-charge, if any, and deducting therefrom the probable average annual cost of the repairs, insurance, and other expenses, if any, necessary to maintain them in a state to command such rent."

[4] See Report to Local Government Board, for 1883-4, by Mr. Stoneham, auditor under Metropolis Water Act, 1871; App. pp. 158-9. In his report for 1884-5, Mr. Stoneham says that, from their net water rental, this judgment has considerably diminished the annual increment of income which would otherwise have accrued to the East London, New River, Grand Junction, and Southwark and Vauxhall Companies: but the Chelsea and West Middlesex Companies have largely increased their income by a recent revision of charges.

refused to receive petitions from Metropolitan water companies praying to be heard against it by counsel, and referred the Bill to a public Committee.[1]   The House afterwards ordered that a representative of the eight companies, not being a counsel, should be heard before the Committee,[2] but the Bill was reported without amendment, and received the Royal assent on July 31.[3]   After setting forth the provision in the Act of 1847, that water rates should be payable according to the annual value of any tenements supplied, the Act provides that " annual value " in the recited provision shall, within the Metropolitan area, mean " the rateable value as settled from time to time by the local authority as duly constituted."

Before this Bill left the Commons an attempt was made to modify, by its means, another rating power possessed by the Metropolitan water companies, which has often given rise to unfavourable comment.   Mr. Fawcett brought this power prominently under notice in 1879, when he urged the Government to deal with the water supply of London.

Mr. Goschen's Valuation Act, 1869.

In 1869, an Act passed which provided for the re-valuation of property in the Metropolis every five years for rating purposes.   It had no reference to the water companies, but was simply meant to adjust more equitably from time to time the burdens on property for poor relief and other public objects, according to the altered value of such property at each quinquennial period.   Indirectly, however, without intending to do so, Parliament by this Act enabled the water companies to advance their rates in proportion to the increased value at which houses, after re-valuation, may appear on the rate-books.   The Committee of 1880 showed that this

[1] Lords' Minutes, July 6, 1885, on Waterworks Clauses Act (1847) Amendment Bill.

[2] Mr. John Hollams accordingly addressed the Committee for the Companies, July 16, and Mr. W. F. Dewey, Vestry Clerk of Islington, in support of the Bill.   In the debate on the second reading (July 6, 1885), Lord Bramwell said this Bill would take away from the London water companies one-fifth or one-sixth of their incomes.

[3] 48 & 49 Vict. c. 34.

claim to revise and increase water rents, taking advantage of an official re-valuation for wholly different purposes, was wholly irrespective of any increase in quantity or improvement in quality of the water supplied. An amendment was moved to the Bill of 1885, which would have prevented the London water companies in future from taking advantage of these periodical valuations for raising their water rates, unless premises had become of greater value by structural alterations. This amendment was defeated.[1]

The practical grievance thus suffered by water consumers in London was also one of the questions dealt with in a Bill to regulate the water supply of London, promoted by the Corporation of London in 1884. Like its two immediate predecessors, this Bill was a failure. Its objects were comprehensive. They embraced a supply of water by measure, and a stringent regulation of companies as to charges, dividends, issue of new capital, and other matters. A supply by meter, it was contended, would be a fairer mode of charging for water than one based upon the rateable value[2] of premises, and, therefore, quite irrespective of consumption. The Bill would have given to a consumer the option of being charged either by measure, at the rate of sixpence per gallon, or upon rateable value, making the poor-rate valuation conclusive for purposes of water-rates. There was to be a minimum charge for water if consumed by measure, with a small charge for meterage. Further, the Bill provided for auction clauses governing the raising of any fresh capital, as in the case of gas companies.

This proposal to substitute meter rates for the existing

Metropolis Water Bill, 1884.

Proposed supply by meter.

Opposition in House of Commons.

---

[1] Hansard, May 1, 1885; amendment of Mr. Firth.

[2] It was stated by the Recorder, in moving the second reading, that when the charge for water was first assessed on the present system, the rateable value of property in London was about 4l. per head of the whole population, whereas in 1884, it was 7l. per head, with a constant tendency to still further increase. Thus there was a possible enhancement of rating to the extent of 75 per cent. without necessarily any larger supply or improved quality of water.

assessment was treated by the water companies as a measure of confiscation. Their calculations, it was said, only differed as to whether they would be totally ruined, or would simply lose one-half of their income.[1] Under a meter system, the poor would stint their use of water for personal and house-hold purposes; there would be an insufficient flow of water for flushing and cleansing drains and sewers; and an addi-tional supply for this purpose must, therefore, be provided out of public rates. There was an attempt in the Bill to meet at least one of these arguments. The Corporation recognised "that sanitary requirements demanded that water should be used without stint, and that it is necessary that the wealthier consumers should, by paying an enhanced price, cheapen the cost of water to their poorer neighbours, and encourage them to use it freely." This proposal, however, in its turn was denounced as socialistic.[2] As to the rate of sixpence per gallon, it was described as absolutely unre-munerative to the companies; while the plan of making the poor-rate valuation a conclusive basis for water rates would be a breach of arrangements made by Parliament, would place the companies wholly in the hands of parochial authorities, and bind them to accept, as final, assessments in making which they had no voice.[3]

New River
Company's
estate.

Another provision in the Bill was also strongly repre-hended in debate. It was a clause pointing chiefly to the New River Company, and declaring that any net rents and profits derived by a company from landed estate, houses,

[1] Speech of Mr. Coope against second reading of Bill, March 11, 1884; 285 Hansard, 1205.

[2] Speech of Lord Randolph Church-ill, ib. p. 1223.

[3] Speech of Sir Henry Holland; ib. pp. 1213–4. Colonel Makins said, if the Bill passed, the com-panies "would be unable to pay a dividend on their ordinary stock, or upon their preference shares, or upon their borrowed capital, though there would be an immense augmentation of their working expenses." (Ib. p. 1216.) But Colonel Makins, from his experience as chairman of a gas company, favoured further regula-tion of the water companies, with powers to amalgamate, and with auction clauses on the raising of any fresh capital.

or property, although not now directly used for, or connected with, their water supply, should be carried to the credit of the undertaking, and form part of profits, for the purpose of computing the prescribed rate of dividend. It was stated in debate that in a few years, when existing leases fell in, the estate of the New River Company would produce 50,000*l.* per annum. It was further pointed out that this estate was specially excepted from the operation of the Metropolis Water Act, 1871, and the official auditor was not empowered to investigate any accounts of the New River Company, except those directly connected with their water supply.[1] Therefore, the Corporation of London, it was contended, who ought to be rigid defenders of the rights of property, were asking Parliament to "confiscate, without compensation," property which Parliament only a few years back had agreed to treat as private property.[2]

A formidable opposition was aroused by these proposals to interfere with private interests. It was in vain that the Government, represented by the Home Secretary, Sir William Harcourt, supported the Bill. Sir William had acted as Chairman of the Committee of 1880. He was now told by Sir Richard Cross that he had then missed a splendid opportunity of placing the London water supply on a better footing. But the ex-Home Secretary refused his sanction to a Bill upon these lines, regarding its main principle as one of "absolute confiscation."[3] Another member said, if passed, "it would inflict a deadly blow upon joint-stock enterprise."

Defeat of Bill.

---

[1] *Ante*, p. 172, n.

[2] 285 Hansard, 1225. In 1885, the House of Commons ordered a Return to be made (quoted *post*, pp. 194–8), giving, among other details, "the amount of bonuses or other payments made to shareholders, excluding dividends, but including, in the case of the New River Company, any payments in respect of the landed estate, houses, or property of that company not directly used for or connected with their water supply." The New River Company "declined to furnish this information, on the ground that the estate and houses in question are private property." (House of Commons' Return, 136, Sess. 1885, p. 6.)

[3] 285 Hansard, 1230.

These views found acceptance on both sides of the House, and the second reading was defeated by a majority of 45, 197 votes against 152.[1]

Increase in houses supplied and in water rentals, 1872-83. Some valuable information bearing on the position of the London water companies was laid before the House of Commons in 1885. It appears from this Return[2] that in 1872 the number of houses or other buildings supplied by the eight Metropolitan water companies was 497,736, yielding a rental of 948,277*l.*; in 1883 the number of houses and buildings had increased to 659,249, and the water rental to 1,505,057*l.*, showing an increase, varying from 46 per cent. on the revenue of the Chelsea Company, to 87 per cent. on that of the Lambeth Company, or an average of more than 58 per cent. increase upon the water revenue of all the companies. It will be seen that, during the period covered by this Return, the increase in houses was only 32 per cent., against an increase of 58 per cent. in water rentals. An **Increase of average water rental per house.** average rental per house of 2*l.* 5*s.* 8*d.* in 1883 has, therefore, to be set against one of 1*l.* 18*s.* 1*d.* in 1872. This increased rental per house is attributed by the companies to the fact that houses newly built, or rebuilt, are generally of a better class and larger than houses previously existing; that, in many cases, owing to works of public or private improvement, two or three houses have been converted into one; and that thus, while houses in densely-populated parts of London have diminished in number, they have increased in rateable value commensurately with their increase in size.[3]

Diminished supply of water per house, 1872-83. It appears by another table that this increased rental per house, from whatever cause arising, has not been accompanied by any larger supply of water. On the contrary, if the annual summaries published by the Registrar

---

[1] After the division, a motion was made that the vote of Mr. Coope, one of the tellers, be disallowed, he being director of a water company, and therefore personally interested in the question. This motion was rejected by a majority of 255 to 36.

[2] No. 136, Sess. 1885.

[3] Ib. p. 4.

General's authority can be trusted, the average quantity of water supplied daily to each house, for domestic purposes, by six of the eight companies, was less in the year 1883 than it was in 1872.[1]

From 1872 to 1883, the aggregate amount of dividends received by the shareholders of the eight companies was 8,501,486*l.*, on a share capital which grew from 7,955,578*l.* in 1872 to 10,344,313*l.* in 1883.[2] The rate per cent. divided by each company was higher in 1883 than in 1872,[3] al-

Water dividends, 1872-83.

Share capital issued at par.

---

[1] Ib. Tabular statement, p. 4, showing that, in 1872, the Chelsea Company supplied 252 gallons, and in 1883, 246 per house; East London, 160 and 205; Grand Junction, 279 and 238; Kent, 135 and 134; Lambeth, 185 and 173; New River, 166 and 167; Southwark & Vauxhall, 171 and 168; West Middlesex, 178 and 161. It will be seen that the New River Company supply one gallon more, and the East London forty-five gallons more than in 1872. Probably this excess in East London is explained in the following passage, taken from Colonel Sir Francis Bolton's Report for March, 1885 (p. 12):—"The East London Company report that the waste of water consequent upon the bad state of the fittings in the new constant supply districts, is enormous. This wilful waste has caused numerous complaints from the higher parts of the district, and notwithstanding the fact that the engine power is greater than ever, the open ends of the pipes in the lower district, running full force by day and night, prevents the higher parts from being reached." It should be added that the East London Company supply a population of 1,130,000, a larger, and no doubt on the whole poorer, population than that served by any other company.

Their constant supply is also more extended than that of any other company; for, out of a total of 150,673 separate services in September, 1885, 130,350 were constant. It is well ascertained that, with proper fittings, kept in proper order, there is less waste with a constant than with an intermittent service. It is equally clear that, without proper fittings and vigilant supervision, constant service means constant waste, and drain upon the sources of supply. The Lambeth Company now employ a superintendent and twenty-two water-waste inspectors exclusively to inspect fittings in their constant supply districts with a view to check waste.

[2] Thus in twelve years the dividends amounted to more than the whole share capital in 1872.

[3] The following were the dividends actually paid (see p. 5 of Return):— Chelsea, in first half-year of 1872, 6*l.* per cent., and in last half-year of 1883, 7*l.* 5*s.*; East London, at the same periods, 6*l.* and 7*l.* 10*s.*; Grand Junction, 8*l.* and 8*l.* 10*s.*; Kent, 6*l.* 2*s.* and 10*l.* 10*s.*; Lambeth, 6*l.* and 7*l.* 10*s.*; New River, 7*l.* 8*s.* 9*d.* and 11*l.* 18*s.* 8*d.*; Southwark and Vauxhall, 5*l.* 10*s.* and 7*l.* 10*s.* and 8*l.* 10*s.*; West Middlesex, 9*l.* 16*s.* 7*d.* and 10*l.*

though " by far the greater part of the new capital created was issued to the shareholders or their nominees at par, an arrangement by which the dividend-bearing capital was increased to a greater extent than would have been neces- sary if it had been raised in the open market."[1] There- fore, in calculating the gains of shareholders we must reckon not only the dividends they received but their profits from share and loan capital taken by them at par under their statutory powers,[2] though under auction clauses such capital would in each case have commanded a considerable premium. During the period in question the total amount of share capital issued by the eight companies, and taken up by share- holders or their nominees, was 2,202,433*l*.;[3] and of loan capital, 715,117*l*.[4]

Shareholders' gains from par issues of ordinary capital;

How valuable is this privilege of taking up capital at par may be seen by other tables,[5] which show that while, in 1872, the share capital of the eight companies was 7,955,578*l*., and in 1883, 10,344,313*l*., an increase of thirty per cent., the estimated value of this share capital on December 31, 1871, was 12,330,830*l*., and on December 31, 1883, 24,795,531*l*., an increase of over 101 per cent. It follows that the gains of water shareholders during 1872-83, in addition to their dividends, and in addition, also, to the increment upon their capital already issued, amounted to over one hundred per cent. upon the amount of all new issues received by them at par.

and from taking up loan capital.

They derived a similar advantage, though less in amount, by taking up loan capital. In 1872 the eight companies had an outstanding loan capital of 2,285,293*l*., the estimated

---

[1] Return, p. 4.

[2] By the incorporation in their private Acts of the Companies Clauses Act, 1863, ss. 17-19. See *ante*, Vol. I., p. 130 *et seq.*

[3] By comparing this amount with the total issue during 1872-83 (Re-

turn, p. 6), it will be seen that only 186,302*l*. was taken up by outsiders.

[4] The Return of 1885 states (p. 5) that the East London were the only company whose shareholders did not take up share capital at par.

[5] Ib. pp. 6-7.

value of which was 2,144,266*l*. In December, 1883, the amount of their loan capital was 2,714,036*l*.,[1] and its estimated value on December, 31, 1883, was 3,050,952*l*. During this period the amount of loan capital increased by 18·8 per cent., while its average value increased by 42·3 per cent.[2] Water shareholders, therefore, who took up the 715,117*l*. of loan capital before mentioned, found this investment enhanced by the substantial sum of 300,400*l*.[3]

It may be well to give, in conclusion, the amount of share and loan capital of the eight companies at September or December, 1884: — Chelsea, 1,150,700*l*.; East London, 2,089,700*l*.; Grand Junction, 1,335,000*l*.; Kent, 741,250*l*.; Lambeth, 1,537,977*l*.; New River, 3,349,958*l*.; Southwark and Vauxhall, 1,864,459*l*.; West Middlesex, 1,154,541*l*. These amounts are exclusive of the following sums received as premiums on shares, debenture stock, &c.:—East London, 82,062*l*.; Grand Junction, 53,748*l*.; Kent, 16,630*l*.; Lambeth, 6,061*l*.; New River, 26,714*l*.; Southwark and Vauxhall, 4,505*l*.; West Middlesex, 17,570*l*.[4]

Total share and loan capital of companies, December, 1884.

[1] During 1872–83, a portion of the loan capital of the eight companies was converted into share capital, and a further portion was raised by terminable bonds, now paid off.

[2] These estimates of the value of share and loan capital were furnished by the Committee of the Stock Exchange, upon a basis explained in the Return of 1885, p. 3.

[3] These details account, in part, for the prices here mentioned :—"At the Auction Mart, this day, Messrs. Edwin Fox & Bousfield sold parts of a freehold King's share in the New River at the rate of from 87,000*l*. to 90,000*l*. per share ; also several new 100*l*. fully-paid shares in the same water company at an average of 355*l*. 10*s*. per share" (*The Times*, City Article, July 8, 1885). Reasons have been given (*ante*, p. 69) for discrediting the popular belief that Sir Hugh Middleton only applied for help to James I. after seeking it in vain from the Corporation of London. However this may be, the Corporation must afterwards have had opportunities of acquiring the thirty-six King's shares before these came into private hands. Had they done so, how splendid an inheritance would to-day have fallen, and justly, to the community whose growth has led to these great gains ! And the whole of this vast wealth in land, houses, and annual income might have been available for public objects if the Corporation had made use of their powers under the Act of 1606.

[4] House of Commons' Return, 231, Sess. 1885.

Dividends,
1884.

In their Report for 1884-5,[1] the Local Government Board remark that, during 1884, the New River Company paid a dividend of nearly twelve per cent., the West Middlesex between ten and eleven, the Kent ten per cent., and that no company paid less than seven and a quarter per cent.

[1] Page 124.

CHAPTER XI.

LOCAL AUTHORITIES:— BOROUGHS, BEFORE AND AFTER THE
CONQUEST: BURGHAL CUSTOMS IN DOMESDAY: CHARTERS:
INCORPORATION—BY IMPLICATION OR PRESCRIPTION AND
BY EXPRESS GRANT: BOROUGHS AFTER 1688: POLITICAL
ABUSES ARISING UNDER CHARTERS: MUNICIPAL CORPO-
RATIONS IN 1835: MUNICIPAL REFORM ACT: EARLY
EXAMPLES OF LOCAL GOVERNMENT: BUILDING ASSIZE IN
LONDON: FIRES: ACT FOR GOOD ORDER IN LONDON,
A.D. 1285: TAVERNS: WATCH AND WARD: CLEANSING
OF STREETS: VILLEINS TAKING REFUGE IN TOWNS.

FEW branches of social history are more attractive than those *Early rise of urban communities.* which concern the early growth of urban communities in England, and their gradually-acquired powers of local taxation and self-government. We can do no more here than indicate their humble origin, and some of the steps by which they have attained their present prodigious development.

Population naturally gathered in any spot exceptionally convenient for trade, as on a river bank; at points on the coast whence shipment was easy to Ireland, the Low Countries, France, and Spain; or, again, at inland centres where wool, the great English staple, was collected, distributed, or worked into fabrics, and where rude native manufactures, with those afterwards introduced by Flemish and other immigrants, could be carried on to advantage. A castle held for the *Manors and demesnes.* King, or a stronghold belonging to some other feudal lord, was often the nucleus of such a population, who received protection, and in return did homage, paid dues, rendered services, and were subject to the usual incidents of vassalage in the manor or demesne.[1]   Even in Saxon times, large numbers of these manors, including any urban communities which had then grown up, were held by the King, and by his bishops, abbots, or secular lords, yielding a large proportion of their respective revenues.[2]   Out of the usual manorial courts, or engrafted upon them, grew a separate

Burghal organization.

jurisdiction from that of the sheriff, and a burghal organization adapted to the wants of a population closely collected, and possessing common interests. These burghers were sometimes authorized to elect a chief representative, corresponding in position with a modern mayor, though under a different title. Customs, too, arose which were gradually recognized as having the force of law.

Boroughs during the Saxon period.

Boroughs must have risen to some importance during the Saxon period, for they are frequently mentioned in Domesday, along with the "burgesses" who resided there. These burgesses were free inhabitants, householders[3] paying scot

[1] Stubbs's Select English Charters, 41. "Their internal condition was but that of any manor in the country : the reeve and his companions— the leet jury as it was afterwards called—being the magistracy. . . . The towns so administered were liable to be called on for talliage at the will of the lord, and the townsmen were in every respect, except wealth and closeness of organization, in the same condition as the villeins of an ordinary demesne." This description by the Bishop of Chester omits mention of the law-worthy townsmen, the liberi homines, who, before and after the Conquest, formed part of the population, though probably at first less numerous than the servi, or villeins. The charter granted to London by William the Conqueror refers to and confirms an earlier allowance of "law-worthiness" by Edward the Confessor (*post*, p. 204).

[2] The ancient demesne of the

Crown, recorded in Domesday, consisted of 1,422 manors, almost all of which were previously held by Edward the Confessor, Harold, Earl Godwin, Ghida (mother of Harold), Goda (sister of King Edward), Guert, Tosti, Stigand, Algar Earl of Mercia, Earl Edwin, Earl Morcar, Edric or Editha (the Confessor's Queen). Liberal grants of Saxon nobles' lands were also made by the Conqueror to his followers. The Earl of Moretaine, his half-brother, held 793 manors ; Alan, Earl of Bretagne, who commanded the rear-guard at the battle of Hastings, 442 ; Odo, Bishop of Bayeux, 439 ; the Bishop of Contance (who was also a soldier), 280 ; and so in proportion among soldiers of inferior rank. (Sir Henry Ellis's Introduction to Domesday, 225-8.)

[3] But all householders were not burgesses. Peers, ecclesiastics, minors, women, villeins, and persons of

and bearing lot,[1] distinguished, on the one hand, from "foreigners" and "strangers," such as traders who had business in the borough, or guests there; and, on the other hand, from "servi" or villeins.[2] They were presented, sworn and enrolled at the folk-mote, afterwards known in boroughs as the burgh-mote or court leet. Here they were bound by oaths and pledges to keep the King's peace and obey the law, a householder being held responsible for the due regulation of his house, and the conduct of his guests and inmates. Here also every burgess performed his public duties, and gave his voice in regulating the local government. He was not law-worthy unless he submitted to the jurisdiction of the borough, and publicly undertook to abide by the law. This obligation he was required to enter into at the age of twelve years, subject to punishment for his default.[3] Boundaries were fixed to the separate municipal jurisdiction. Merchant guilds and their members were exempt. It appears, also, from Domesday that, as a rule, the lord's castle was not included within these limits.

After the Conquest the main principles of the Saxon law regulating boroughs seem to have been preserved. Scot was paid and lot was borne; freemen still gave pledges, owned allegiance, and swore to keep the King's peace in their court leet; watch and ward in boroughs were enforced as of old; goods must be sold only in the presence of witnesses, another ancient provision to which great importance was attached at a time when prices were closely watched in the interest of

Boroughs after the Conquest.

bad character, were excluded from the privileges and duties of burgess-ship. (Merewether and Stephens, Hist. of Boroughs, Int. 13.)

[1] "Scot" (Saxon, *sceat*) signifies a customary contribution laid upon all subjects according to ability. The term "scot and lot" is sometimes used collectively in this sense, but "lot" denotes liability to perform, in due rotation, all public personal duties imposed on a free burgess, as to take part in watch and ward.

[2] There were numerous methods by which villeins could acquire freedom: one was a service for seven years. Again, according to Glanville, who wrote in the year 1180, all bondmen who remained without claim for a year and a day in any borough became free (*post*, pp. 252-4).

[3] Merewether and Stephens, Int. 5—11.

consumers. All boroughs were exempt from the sheriff's jurisdiction; they were "quit of writs of shires and hundreds," and minor pleas were disposed of in their courts. In Domesday are recorded the "customs" of several towns. Some of these customs may be mentioned here, as, besides any dues and services payable to the King or feudal lord, they show the powers and resources then possessed by burghal authorities, the small beginnings of those local laws and rates which have since been so enormously extended by private legislation.

Burghal customs in Domesday.

Dover. Dover,[1] which was given to the Bishop of Bayeux, had its guildhall, and supplied the King with twenty ships for fifteen days once in every year, each vessel having twenty-one persons on board, because he had granted to the townspeople sac and soc.[2] This and other customs prevailed before the Conquest.[3] At Lewes, if the King sent a force to keep the sea, twenty shillings were collected of every burgess, which were paid to those who manned the vessels. In the nature of market dues were certain payments to the bailiff: a penny by the buyer and another by the seller of each horse; for an ox, a halfpenny; for a man, fourpence. For bloodshed a fine of seven shillings and fourpence was levied; for adultery, eight shillings and fourpence on each of the parties; and, as in Kent, the man became the property of the King, and the woman of the Archbishop.

Lewes.

---

[1] The summary which follows is compiled from materials gathered by Sir Henry Ellis, in his General Introduction to Domesday, I. p. 190 et seq.

[2] *Saca* (mentioned in the laws of Edward the Confessor) was the power and privilege of hearing and determining causes and disputes, levying forfeitures and fines, executing laws, and administering justice within certain limits. *Soca* was the territory or precinct in which these privileges were exercised. (Ellis, I. 273–4.) Soke also signifies franchise, liberty, or jurisdiction.

[3] The account of Dover in Domesday says:—"Omnes hæ consuetudines erant ibi quando Willielmus Rex in Angliam venit." So under Wallingford, "Modo sunt in ipso burgo consuetudines omnes ut ante fuerunt"; sufficient proof, if any were necessary, of immunities and privileges acquired, whether under charters or through natural growth, by these and other English boroughs before the Conquest. Of Saxon charters, two, of which there is fair though not conclusive evidence, are by King Athelstan to Beverley, and by Edward the Confessor to the Cinque Ports.

Taunton belonged to the Bishop of Winchester. Oxford, in lieu of toll, gable, and all other customary rents, paid to Edward the Confessor twenty pounds in money and six sextaries[1] of honey.

Hereford was the King's demesne. The tenants did personal service, under the sheriff's direction, reaping three days and hay-gathering one day. One person from each house was bound to aid the King when he hunted. Every man whose wife brewed paid tenpence. Six smiths paid every one a penny for his forge. In Cambridge the burgesses were bound to find ploughs and carts. At Shrewsbury, if any burgess's house was burnt, either by negligence or accident, he forfeited forty shillings to the King and two shillings each to his two nearest neighbours. A widow entertaining a husband paid twenty shillings to the King; a maid, ten shillings. At Chester there were similar forfeitures in the case of fires. Any man or woman giving false measure, or brewing adulterated beer, forfeited four shillings, or was placed in the dung chair,[2] and paid four shillings to the bailiff. For repairing the city wall and bridge, one labourer must be supplied to the bailiff for every hide of land in the county. The King and Earl of Chester shared some of the fines and forfeitures. The bishop also had his customs. Thus, if any freeman worked on a holiday, the bishop received eight shillings as a fine; for a villein or a maidservant, four shillings. If a trader came into the city with a pack, and opened it, between the ninth hour on Saturday and Monday, or on any festival, without licence from the bishop's officer, he forfeited four shillings. Rents were paid to the King or lord in money, and also in honey and corn. London, York, Winchester, and Exeter had peculiar immunities and privileges. At Canterbury the burgesses held of the King thirty-three acres of land in their guild.[3]

Oxford.

Hereford.

Cambridge and Shrewsbury.

Chester.

Episcopal customs at Chester.

Anglo-Saxon guilds.

[1] A measure of four gallons.

[2] Cathedra stercoris. This afterwards became the cucking stool, used for scolds, who might be " presented" at the court leet as common nuisances.

[3] The clergy of Canterbury also had their guild. Elsewhere, in

The charter granted by William I. to London, when conciliation was deemed politic after the battle of Hastings, was as follows :—

Charter of
William I. to
London.

"Wiłłm kýnᵹ ᵹɲet Wiłłm biſceop ꝼ ᵹoſꝼɲeᵹð poɲtiꝼeꝼan, ꝼ ealle þa buɲhƿaɲu binnan lonðone ꝼɲenciſce ꝼ enᵹliſce ꝼɲeonðlice. ꝼ ic kýðe eoƿ þ ic pýlle þ ᵹet beon eallɲa þæɲa laᵹa peoɲðe þe ᵹýt ƿæɲan on eaðƿeɲðeſ ðæᵹe kýnᵹeſ. ꝼ ic pýlle

"William, king, greets William, bishop, and Gosfrith, portreeve,[1] and all the burghers[2] within London, French and English, friendly. And I make known to you my will that ye be all lawworthy that were in king Edward's days.[3] And I will

Domesday and contemporary records, these Anglo-Saxon guilds are frequently mentioned. "They seem, on the whole, to have been friendly associations, made for mutual aid and contribution, to meet the pecuniary exigencies which were perpetually arising from burials, legal exactions, penal mulcts, and other payments or compensations." (Sharon Turner's Hist. of Manners of Anglo-Saxons.) The subsequent connection of the trade guilds with municipalities in London and other cities opens too wide a subject for treatment here. Our Norman kings watched their growth with some jealousy. In the year 1179, Henry II. caused the burgesses of Totnes to be fined five marks for setting up a guild without authority, and in the same reign the aldermen of certain "adulterine" guilds in London, the gold workers, bochers, guild of Holywell, and others, paid fines for similar offences. (1 Madox, Exch. 562.) Sometimes they proved troublesome constituents of a municipality, from the *imperium in imperio* they set up. Thus, in 1482, the commons of Exeter complained to Parliament of a tailors' guild, which had been constituted by letters patent of Edward IV., but many of whose members were "of such evil disposition and unpeaceable" that the Mayor could not properly guide or rule the city, "according to his oath, duty, and charge." Upon this representation the letters patent were revoked. (6 Rot. Parl. pp. 219–20.)

[1] In the time of Athelstan, who reigned within twenty-four years after King Alfred, the bishops (appointed by the Archbishop of Canterbury) and reeves were the chief magistrates in London. This special legal jurisdiction, preserved at the Conquest, has always been considered by the citizens one of their most valuable immunities. It was expressly secured to them by a law of Edward the Confessor and by the earliest of their charters (one of Henry I.) which refer to any of their privileges in detail. The same charter confirms another highly-prized civic privilege, that of freely electing their own magistrates.

[2] Literally, burgh-men; from burb, and war or wara, Scandinavian for man.

[3] That is, the citizens were to enjoy the privileges of freemen in courts of justice; for, by Saxon as well as feudal law, none but freemen were entitled to the privileges of trial according to any recognized judicial

þæt ælc cýlb beo hif ꞃæðeꞃ
ýꞃꞃnume æꝼꞇeꞃ hif ꞃæðeꞃ
bæȝe. ꞇ ıc nelle ȝeþolıan þ
ænıȝ man eop ænıȝ ꝥꞃanȝ
beoðe. ȝob eop ȝehealðe."

that each child be his father's
heir after his father's days.[1]
And I will not suffer that any
man do you any wrong. God
keep you."

From this short and simple assurance of good-will, and Chartered boroughs. confirmation of existing rights,[2] there is a long step to the elaborate provisions of similar instruments in more modern times. Under Norman rule, most of the chief towns belonged to the Crown, and were called boroughs, or boroughs of ancient demesne. To these communities several grants were made by Henry I., confirming local customs and franchises, and occasionally extending powers of local self-government. As towns became more populous, and their inhabitants increased in wealth and influence, charters were frequently granted for political reasons, that favour and support might be won from townspeople by Sovereigns who wished to stand well with them. Then, and in later times, Royal favour the necessities of kings and nobles were in some respects the opportunities of English townsfolk. During the troubled

form, either in civil or criminal suits. (Norton's Commentaries on History and Chartered Franchises of London [Butterworth, 1829], p. 333, and authorities there cited.)

[1] Villeins, or strict tenants in demesne, belonged, themselves, their families, and effects, to the lord of the soil, like the rest of the stock or cattle upon it, and had no heritable rights. Among free tenants heirship was a general common-law right in Saxon times. As to land, all the sons shared alike, though, under the Normans, this rule of descent soon gave way to primogeniture, with few exceptions. As to personalty, the custom of London only allowed a bequest of one-third; another third going to the widow, as her dower; the remainder to the children in equal shares by right of inheritance. (Ib.

335-6.) This custom was abolished by statute in 1725 (11 Geo. I. c. 18.)

[2] For these we must look back to the original establishment of the common law by Alfred; and if any further proof were wanting that he was the true founder of the municipal laws and privileges of London, we shall trace it in the identity of many of them with the provisions of that ancient Saxon code. (Norton's Commentaries, 22.) The Dombok, which embodied this code, is said to have been long preserved among the City records, and the Mirror of Justices, a legal work written in the reign of Edward II. by Horne, City Chamberlain, A.D. 1311, seems to have been compiled from this work. (Ib. 23, quoting Edinburgh Review, XXXIV. 187.)

reign of King John, more charters were granted to boroughs than during the same space of time in any other period of our history.[1] Richard III. tried to gain their favour by liberal concessions. In 1484 he reduced the fee-farm rent of Winchester by 20l. annually out of a total of 100 marks, owing to its decay from wars and plague;[2] reduced or abolished the fee-farm rents of Beverley, Cambridge, Gloucester, Huntingdon, Newcastle, Northampton, Oxford, Shrewsbury, and York; granted a charter of manumission to nineteen bondmen of the King's manor of Framlingham; and made grants to Dartmouth, Dover, Newcastle, Plymouth, Sandwich, Yarmouth, and Youghal for fortifying their ports or improving their havens.[3]

Charters commuting feudal dues for fixed annual sum.

Charters were still oftener conferred as bargains with the Crown or other feudal lord in return for fresh money payments or services to be rendered by a community. In these cases a desire to be relieved from the annoyance of collecting dues, and to possess a certain instead of a fluctuating income, led to Royal or baronial charters commuting all dues payable within the borough for a fixed annual sum, no doubt of larger average amount than that previously paid.

This in itself was no small advantage, but another step towards free self-government was necessary. After the Conquest, the Crown and other feudal lords had generally asserted the right to appoint each burghal chief, or reserved a veto over any choice made by the burgesses. Burgh or port-reeves, whose titles followed those of shire-reeves (sheriffs) in counties, then sometimes became stewards, bailiffs, or mayors, who, in the interest of those to whom they owed their appointments, assessed and collected feudal dues with unsparing rigour. Unjust exactions, too, were easy when modes

---

[1] Merewether and Stephens, Int. p. 4.

[2] A petition from the city of Winchester to Henry VI., in the year 1450, enumerates seventeen churches and 997 "householdes," which had fallen down there, chiefly within the eighty years preceding.

[3] See Patent Rolls, 1 & 2 Richard III., among those quoted in Annals of England, 265-6.

of assessment and amounts to be levied were alike arbitrary and unsettled.[1] The new bargains entered into with the Plantagenets and their nobles gave to growing municipalities an unfettered choice of chief magistrates. It was then a simple process, free from the harshness and uncertainty of old methods, for the borough-reeve or port-reeve, high bailiff, alderman, or other chief authority, to re-apportion among the townspeople the fixed dues to be paid in each year. This burgage-rent, as it was called, implied emancipation from villein services,[2] and marks an important era in the rise of municipal liberties.

While many privileges, however, were thus conferred upon townspeople, their municipal life was still incomplete. Ecclesiastical bodies had long enjoyed the right of holding and transmitting lands by perpetual succession. But this was a right which successive monarchs were chary of enlarging, for reasons mentioned in a previous chapter,[3] namely, the withdrawal of such property from its fair share of national burdens. Even eleemosynary foundations were long denied this privilege, which appears to have been first conferred by Henry V., A.D. 1416, upon a fraternity or hospital at Bristol.[4]

Boroughs not at first incorporated.

It was not until the middle of the next reign, A.D. 1439, that a municipality was incorporated. Before that year, neither in the Saxon charters nor in those granted under Norman rule is there a trace of any municipal corporation.[5] As such a body could only then be created by Royal prerogative, the numerous charters granted to their boroughs by the great barons were of course silent on this subject. But the Crown in its early grants did no more than the barons did; it bestowed rights and privileges on the burgesses for the time being. There was no specific

First municipal incorporation, A.D. 1439.

---

[1] " Misera est servitus ubi jus est vagum et incertum," was a maxim which might well apply to these levies.

[2] Stubbs's Select English Charters, 41.

[3] *Ante*, Vol. I. pp. 457–8.

[4] In the Rolls of Parliament the spelling of this city varies, thus— Brissteut, Bristowe, Bristut, Bristuyt, Bristwit, Bristyt, Brustut, Brustuyt.

[5] Merewether and Stephens, Int. 10, 11.

incorporation in the modern sense, with power to hold lands by perpetual succession, have a common seal, and sue and be sued in the corporate name.

Kingston-upon-Hull-incorporated by charter, A.D. 1439.

Kingston-upon-Hull is generally mentioned as the first town thus favoured.[1] Probably it owed this much-coveted boon to the dynastic quarrels of the period, and a wish by Henry VI. to secure in his interest a place of great strength, commanding the waterway into Yorkshire and other counties. But Hull was incorporated by charter as an act of Royal grace. Plymouth in the same year was incorporated by statute,

Plymouth.

and is a more interesting as well as an earlier example, for its claims to this new municipal status were considered by Parliament in the year 1411.[2] In that year, the inhabi-

Petition to Parliament for incorporation, A.D. 1411.

tants petitioned,[3] setting forth that their town and port, with the vessels sheltering there, had often in time of war been destroyed by the King's enemies, and might easily again meet the same fate, as there were no walls or defensive fortress. They therefore prayed his Majesty to allow the appointment of a mayor, having jurisdiction within certain limits to be defined, for the better government of their town, and that they, their heirs and successors, might become a body corporate, able to purchase lands for life or in fee without royal licence (q'ils, lour heirs, & lour successours, soient un Corps corporat, pur purchacer franc ten' a terme de vie, ou en fee, sanz licence roial). Further, they asked

Anchorage and dues on merchandise, &c.

that every foreign vessel using the port, for the next hun- dred years, should pay anchorage dues, and other tolls on merchandise exported or imported, to be applied by the cor- poration in fortifying their town. This prayer was not refused, but the petitioners were told to confer with lords who had franchises in their town, and, if they could agree, so to report in the next Parliament, when his Majesty would consider what was best to be done.

[1] Merewether and Stephens, Int. 33 ; 2 ib. 860-9.
[2] It is then described as the towns of Sutton Priour and Sutton Vau- tort, "otherwise called Plymmouth."
[3] 3 Rot. Parl. 662-3.

It will be seen that incorporation and town dues were *Public objects of incorporation.* justified on national grounds, that funds might be provided for resisting invaders and protecting a great port and its shipping.   But by creating a new municipality, with new rights to burgesses and a separate jurisdiction, existing feudal interests within the municipal bounds would be swept away, unless specially safeguarded.   In this instance there would have been an interference with certain franchises belonging respectively to the priors of Plympton and Bath and the Abbot of Bokland.   According to modern practice, any questions at issue between these great ecclesiastics and their feudatories would have been fought out in the committee rooms.   In 1411 the promoters were told, that before ap- *Interference with private rights.* proaching Parliament they had better prepare a matured scheme, based upon private arrangements with any persons whose interests were affected.   Such arrangements appear to have been difficult, and were, at any rate, long delayed, for it was not until 1439 that Plymouth again came before Parliament.   That the subject of its renewed petition was *Statutory authority to Lords of Council and chief justices to frame scheme of incorporation.* thought to demand grave deliberation is clear from a short Act passed early in the session authorizing the Lords of the Council, with the two chief justices, to settle the petition, and insert such provisions as they deemed necessary, not only, it may be assumed, between the parties, but for the protection of the public.   This Act runs as follows :—

"The king willeth and ordaineth by the advice and assent of the lords spiritual and temporal, and the commons of this his noble realm, in this present Parliament assembled, that as touching the corporation of the town of Plymouth, especified in a petition put up to the king in this Parliament, by the commons of this land, and the residue of the matter contained in the same petition, the lords of the king's council, calling to them the king's two chief judges of both his benches, have power by authority of this Parliament to set such provision therein as shall seem to them necessary and behoveful in this party."[1]

---

[1] 5 Rot. Parl., p. 9.

Incorporating statute.

Accordingly, later in the records of this Parliament of 1439, we find a long and elaborate scheme of incorporation, preserving the form of petition, as was then the custom, and setting forth in technical language, and with all necessary provisoes, the terms agreed upon for such feudal rights

Frequent destruction of town through want of fortifications.

as were to be ousted.[1] In this petition, or Bill, which is afterwards perfected as a statute by royal assent, the men of Plymouth again complain that, through its want of walls, their town has frequently been burnt and destroyed, their cattle and goods have been carried off as spoil, and many inhabitants taken into captivity, and there miserably detained (diris carceribus miserabiliter mancipati) until ransomed. They therefore ask his Majesty, with assent of Parliament, to allow them to enclose and fortify their town, so that they may be better able to resist attack, and may dwell in greater security. Then they pray for incorporation as the Mayor

Incorporation of mayor and commonalty, with perpetual succession.

and Commonalty of the borough of Plymouth, with perpetual succession, power to hold land, have a common seal, and sue and be sued as a corporation. Next are set out the boundaries of the borough, which is to be held from the Crown at a rent of 40l. The corporation may enclose the town with walls, place towers at intervals, and crenelate and strengthen these walls and towers by

Election of mayor.

battlements.[2] William Ketrich, one of the more worthy and discreet townsmen[3] (unus probiorum et magis discretorum hominum), had been already nominated by the Crown as first mayor; and the King is asked graciously to allow, by authority of Parliament, an annual election by the burgesses

Office vacated, and new election made, upon death or delinquency.

of some fit and discreet person from among their number to the same office. To any person so elected, a successor may be appointed, not only if he dies, but if he governs badly.

---

[1] 5 Rot. Parl., 18—21; 18 Hen. VI. The original is in Latin.

[2] Kernellare et batellare.

[3] So an Act of the Scotch Parliament, in 1487 (c. 108), declared that officers in boroughs should be chosen from "the best and worthiest indwellers of the town, and not by partiality or mastership."

Whosoever is chosen as mayor, before taking office, must Oath of mayor. take oath in the guildhall, before the commonalty, and also before the Prior of Plympton, or his steward, to rule and govern the borough well, faithfully, and impartially (ad Burgum bene, fideliter ac indifferenter regend' et gubernand'), and to observe the articles[1] and pay the rents agreed upon and specified in the Act. From time to time Burgesses. the mayor and commonalty are authorized to elect burgesses. Three messuages belonging to the Prior and convent of Reservation of rights to Prior of Plympton. Plympton, together with the island of St. Nicholas, are excluded from municipal franchises and jurisdiction, and made for ever free from any local taxes, dues, or payments borne by the inhabitants; the Prior's rights over his church are likewise excepted. Felons may, however, be followed and lodged in gaol if they seek refuge within these places. In like manner, members of the convent, with their servants and tenants, are for ever free to buy and sell goods, chattels, provisions, and merchandise within the borough, exempt from tolls or dues.[2]

Other clauses exempt the Prior and convent from any Distraint upon lands and chattels of burgesses as well as corporation. burghal jurisdiction, and require the corporation to pay them 41*l*. yearly. Heavy penalties are imposed for breach of any of these conditions, and upon default there may be distraint for the stipulated rental upon the lands and chattels not only of the corporation, but of every burgess. It seems that Feudal rights of Abbot of Bokland. the Abbot of Bokland, in the county of Devon, had feudal rights within the limits assigned to the new municipality. They accordingly ask for an assignment of these rights, and that once a month a Court may be held in Guildhall before the mayor, who shall there exercise such jurisdiction[3] as the

---

[1] Appunctuamenta vel appunctamenta; agreements (facta) brought to a point, i. e., made clear by embodiment in articles or points (puncta).

[2] These exemptions are wide enough:—"Sine aliquo tolneto, custuma, pycagio, panagio, portagio, muragio, stallagio, ac quibuscumque aliis oneribus, exactionibus, impositionibus et demandis."

[3] "Omnes defectus, excessus, transgressiones, articuli, visus Francipleg'," were to be cognizable.

Abbot of Bokland and his predecessors exercised, with like powers of presentment, amendment, and punishment.

Royal assent with provisoes.

This petition, which is interesting as the creation of a new municipality by statute, besides being the first example of municipal incorporation by the same authority, ends with a reservation of all rights and jurisdictions belonging to the Crown. The royal assent which follows is in English. His Majesty wills, "that it be as it is desired by this petition," but, as was not then uncommon,[1] he adds a proviso, excluding from its operation the manor of Trematon, the burgh of Saltash, the water of Tamar, and all "possessions, franchises, liberties, waters, fishings, rents, services, courts, jurisdictions, offices, inheritances, forfeits, escheats, or any other issues, profits, or commodities," held for life by Sir John Cornwall, Lord of Faunhope, "the reversion thereof to the king belonging."[2]

Grants of incorporation to boroughs after 1439.

Grants of incorporation were expressly given by Henry VI., after 1439, to Ipswich, Southampton, Coventry, Northampton, Woodstock, Canterbury, Nottingham, and Tenterden. They did not, however, become general, for Norwich, Bristol, and the Cinque Ports received charters without incorporation from Edward IV., who, however, conferred this privilege on the community of Romney Marsh, together with Rochester, Stamford, Ludlow, Grantham, Wenlock, Bewdley, and

Prescription.

Kingston-upon-Thames. About the same period it began to be contended, on the part of boroughs which had not been expressly incorporated, that this right must be presumed from the circumstances of their creation, and must have been conferred by some grant beyond legal memory.

Words of incorporation implied.

In the year 1466 it was held by the Court of Common Pleas that words of incorporation might be implied in a grant:—"If the King gave land in fee-farm to the good men of the town of Dale, the corporation was good; and so

---

[1] *Ante*, Vol. I., pp. 304–10.

[2] See also 5 Rot. Parl. 555–61 (A.D. 1464). An Act was then passed which, the Prior of Plympton concurring, relieved the corporation from several charges imposed in 1439, as the borough had since fallen into poverty and decay, and could not pay or bear these charges.

likewise where it was given to the burgesses, citizens, and commonalty."[1] In this way attempts were made to escape from the consequences of non-incorporation without the necessity of surrendering old and obtaining new charters, doubtless a costly process, and, in some cases, perhaps, not free from danger. We shall see that, in a later reign, the absence of this right of perpetual succession was made a pretext for proceedings, which, though prompted by party, and designed to narrow the constituencies electing members to Parliament, were not without a colour of law.

It is probable, though far from certain, that in the early history of boroughs, important business was sanctioned, if not initiated, by the whole body of burgesses. If so, practical difficulties would naturally occur in transacting business, and would suggest the appointment of a select body, dissolved when the special work committed to them was concluded, but gradually becoming permanent. In some boroughs common councils seem to have been formed out of fragments of the leet juries; in others, they were probably what their name imports, counsellors called in to advise the alderman or bailiff and his colleagues of the Court leet,[2] who acted as municipal administrators and as magistrates. About the reign of Richard II. new and important powers, those exercised by "justices of the peace and of labourers," were entrusted to the municipal magistracy, with a considerable enlargement of their civil and criminal jurisdiction. In the same reign it became usual to appoint them justices of the peace by charter.[2]

Governing body in boroughs.

Municipal magistracy, circa 1377.

When, after the Reformation, the House of Commons grew bolder and more independent, holding the nation's purse-strings tightly, the Crown tried to obtain an ascendancy in that body by issuing writs to many decayed boroughs, in

Boroughs after the Reformation.

[1] Merewether and Stephens, Int. 37-8.

[2] General and Special Reports of Municipal Corporation Commission-ers, 1835; collected and published by A. E. Cockburn, one of the Commissioners (afterwards Lord Chief Justice), i. 12.

Political
influence
exerted by
Crown.

which Court influence was paramount, calling upon them to return members. This stretch of Royal prerogative was last resorted to by Queen Elizabeth in the case of Newark. The House of Commons then inquired into the grounds upon which some of these places sent members to Westminster, and the Crown did not think fit further to insist on its prerogative. A majority of the existing municipal charters were created between the reign of Henry VIII. and the Revolution. Almost all the councils named in these charters were constituted by self-election,[1] and the general aim appears to have been to take away power from the community, and create a governing class independent of the burgesses, who were less easily subjected to Court influence. With this view some charters of the period contained clauses by which the right of electing members of Parliament was expressly limited to the select bodies which they created.[2] Control over local government followed the same limitation.

Growing exclusiveness of governing body.

A similar tendency towards exclusiveness showed itself in many boroughs besides those which had been newly summoned or restored to representation. Privileges and jurisdictions properly belonging to the whole borough were monopolized by the select body, and in practice became merged in them. Disputes arose as to the burgesses who were entitled to vote for members. To secure the domination of the Court, or of some powerful patron, these disputes were generally settled in the narrowest sense, and in a large number of cases select bodies, whether duly incorporated or not, followed the teaching of the new charters, and assumed the sole right of returning members to Parliament. After

Members of
Parliament
returned by
some corporations independently of
burgesses.

---

[1] Curious Acts passed by the Scottish Parliament in 1469 and 1474, prescribed that, at the annual elections in the Royal burghs, the old council should choose the new; that both acting together should choose the officers; and that four persons from the old council should be appointed to the new body.

[2] Non-residents had begun to be admitted by governing bodies to the freedom of towns in the reign of Elizabeth. At this time, also, in many boroughs the honorary office of high steward was created, which linked them with the aristocracy and Crown.

the Restoration, a statute passed[1] as a scourge to such boroughs as had offended the Court by their independence. Stimulated by the success of the *quo warranto* against the Corporation of London,[2] Charles II. sent his agents into all parts of the kingdom, threatening similar proceedings, unless existing charters were surrendered, but promising new grants from the Crown upon such surrender.

Quo warranto informations under Charles II.

This policy was to a large extent successful; the rights of burgesses, which stood upon a different footing from the rights of corporations, were given up by many of these bodies, or else seized; and in the re-grants, clauses were inserted, giving to these corporations the whole power of returning members of Parliament, and enabling the Crown to remove or nominate the principal corporate officers. Several charters were surrendered, and others were brought in from the West of England by Lord Bath, just before the death of Charles II. James II. followed the same course, but tried, when too late, to avert public indignation by his Proclamation of October 1688, which annulled all the surrenders then made, and revived the ancient charters.[3]

Surrender of charters and re-grants by Crown.

[1] 13 Car. II. c. 1 (A.D. 1661), "an Act for the well-governing and regulating of corporations."

[2] This information *quo warranto* against the Corporation of London called upon them to show by what authority they claimed to be a body corporate. London claimed to be a corporation by prescription, existing before the time of legal memory, and therefore relating back to 1189, the first year of the reign of Richard I. It could produce no actual evidence of incorporation, and therefore to that extent the judgment against it was according to law. But it was the most ancient exclusive jurisdiction in the kingdom; and all the immunities and authority connected with that jurisdiction, and with its character as a borough, were its undoubted right, and stood upon

as secure ground as the Crown, or any title under the law. The same may be said of all the other boroughs. Merewether and Stephens, Int. 53. By 2 Will. & Mary, c. 8, the judgment of the Court of King's Bench upon the *quo warranto* against the Corporation of London, in Trinity Term, 35 Chas. II., and all other judgments against the rights of the city, were declared void.

[3] Merewether and Stephens, Int. 54. In the claim of rights presented to William & Mary, April 11, 1689, a special grievance is that the Stuarts subverted the rights of Royal burghs in Scotland by "imposing on them not only magistrates, but also town councils and clerks, contrary to their liberties and express charters." Under the ancient constitution of these burghs, and express words in

Rights of burgesses further limited under William III.

Through his advisers, William III. continued the efforts of the Stuart kings to strengthen governing bodies in boroughs at the expense of the burgesses generally; and more was done during his reign to confirm the monopoly of local government by corporations, and to poison the sources of Parliamentary representation in boroughs, than at any other period.[1]

Charters after the Revolution.

In succeeding reigns, the number of charters granted to boroughs by the Crown was small. Queen Anne allowed six, of which only three, to Wareham, Salisbury, and Bristol, were charters of incorporation. George I. granted two, to Henley-upon-Thames and Tiverton, the latter being required owing to a not unfrequent occurrence, the accidental dissolution of the ancient corporation. George II. gave seven, but these were for comparatively unimportant powers. During his reign of fifty-nine years, George III. granted thirteen charters, though only seven towns were newly incorporated, namely, Bath, Carmarthen, Helston, Northampton, Bodmin, Lancaster, and Lampeter. It may be added that the charters of George III. recognized popular rights as little as those granted in the worst period of municipal history.[2]

their charters, magistrates and common councils were elected annually by the free suffrage of burgesses.

[1] Merewether and Stephens, Int. p. 54. In the reigns of Elizabeth and the Stuarts, Courts of law upheld the principles advocated by the Crown; their decisions "supported usage, maintained select bodies, sanctioned non-residents, confirmed numerous bye-laws not in accordance with the charters, or with each other, but giving a different constitution to every different borough, and, as the greatest and worst innovation of all, gave the stamp of judicial authority to the doctrine of the arbitrary admission of burgesses by corporations." Under Queen Anne and her immediate successors these abuses "were fully maintained. Freemen were substituted for burgesses, and the latter name was applied to burgage-tenants, freeholders, 'pot-wallers,' and inhabitants without any other qualification." The unrestrained admission of freemen as burgesses placed all the municipal privileges and jurisdiction in the power of whatever party, commanding a majority in the select body, could secure the admission of their friends. "Hence, in some places a sufficient number of non-resident honorary freemen were admitted to overawe or neutralise the votes of the real burgesses," so that the large powers and exclusive jurisdiction confided to boroughs became "not the means of local government, as they were intended to be, but the tools of party violence and private intrigue." (Ib., pp. 58—60.)

[2] General Report of Municipal Corporations Commission, 1835. p. 13.

From these causes most of the chartered municipalities had long ceased to command public confidence; and after the reform of Parliament in 1832, Commissioners were appointed to inquire into the constitution, privileges, powers, revenue, and expenditure of each corporation. These Commissioners found great defects and abuses. Most of the early charters were granted to the burgesses generally, very few designating a select body. Usually, however, charters were silent as to any general right to a municipal franchise; and custom, or disuse and oblivion where this general right formerly existed, had practically established a restricted constitution. In other cases governing authorities had limited their own number, with a view to enhance their privileges, and also limited the right of freedom, citizenship, or burgess-ship to a much smaller class than that which formerly possessed it. In a great majority of those towns in which there was a large body of freemen, they had been deprived of all share whatever in electing governing bodies, though they retained a right to elect members of Parliament.[1]

Commissioners of 1835.

Close corporations.

General body of townspeople excluded from municipal rights.

In some boroughs, as at Kingston-upon-Hull and Pontefract, the mayor, portreeve, bailiff, steward, or other head of the corporation, together with the aldermen, or persons filling an analogous position, constituted the whole council. Occasionally, the recorder was made, by charter, a member of the common council, and there were other *ex officio* members, as the bailiffs at Carlisle; the sheriff at Newcastle; the coroners and chamberlains at Scarborough; the sheriffs, coroners, and chamberlains at Lincoln; the sheriffs, and all who had served the office of sheriff, at York. In the majority of instances, members of the common council were self-elected, or were nominated by the aldermen. In some cases they were nominated by the mayor. The election was generally for life. Residence was sometimes a necessary qualification, but was often not insisted on. In London, Norwich, and some other

Town councils.

Ex officio members.

---

[1] General Report of Municipal Corporations Commission, 1835, pp. 13-15.

places, aldermen were elected by the freemen, but in most cities and boroughs they filled up vacancies in their own body from the other division of the common council.[1]

Corporate officers.
High steward.

Many corporations elected a corporate high steward, usually a peer. This office probably originated in a wish that the town should secure protection at Court in cases of difficulty or danger to its privileges. Many parliamentary boroughs enjoyed the advantage of a "patron," who was commonly also high steward, but sometimes was the recorder. His services were peculiar. There were many instances in which revenue in parliamentary boroughs did not meet municipal expenditure : a patron was expected to supply this deficiency.

Patron.

Purchase of right to nominate members.

Before the Reform Act of 1832, some municipalities defrayed their expenses from this source. In return, a patron nominated the members of Parliament,[2] giving the usual inducements to electors, if there were any. When the Reform Act took away the consideration for these pecuniary aids, they were withheld by patrons, who also called in any debts due to them. At New Radnor and at Westbury, in 1835, all corporate revenue was collected by the patron's agent, and applied towards these repayments.

[1] General Report of Municipal Corporations Commission, 1835, pp. 15 –17.

[2] Ib., p. 26. Many instances are given. At Launceston, since 1812, the patron, who was the Duke of Northumberland, besides private advances to members of the corporation, had expended 18,000*l.* in paying debit balances in the corporate accounts; but when the Reform Act placed the borough in Schedule B., "the corporation did not know where to obtain" any such balance. At Bodmin, the patrons after 1800 were successively Lord Camelford, Lord de Dunstanville, and Lord Hertford. When Lord Hertford became patron, the securities for money advanced to the corporation by his predecessors were transferred to him; and "it was understood that he was to come in on the usual terms, that is, 'do all the services he could to the place, and recommend the members.' Private as well as public loans were also exacted. Several members of the corporation became indebted to the patron in sums amounting in the whole to 2,000*l.* No interest was ever paid on these loans. Two or three members of the corporation, having fallen into distressed circumstances, received small annuities from the patron. In consideration of these services, the corporation returned any candidates nominated by the patron; and no one was admitted into the corporation unless supposed to be friendly to the patron's interest." (Ib., pp. 3, 4.)

A Recorder, sometimes called a Steward, was elected in Recorder.
most cases by the common council; in others, by the aldermen; more rarely, by the general body of burgesses or freemen. Occasionally, the consent of the Crown was requisite to his appointment. That he should be learned in the law was provided by most of the charters in which a recorder was named. According to practice, this condition was satisfied Peers as recorders.
if a peer of the realm were elected, he being a judge by the constitution of Parliament.[1] Sometimes, notwithstanding such a provision in the charter, patrons were made recorders, or other persons chosen, who were neither peers nor lawyers. In most of these cases, either there were no real functions to be exercised, or the recorder appointed a deputy. Bailiffs Bailiffs.
were chosen annually. They seem to have been originally receivers or managers for the Crown, or other feudal lord of the borough, and had at first no duties in connection with the corporate body.

In almost all the principal boroughs municipal magistrates Magistrates.
were chosen by the common council, usually from among the aldermen. In many cases all the aldermen were magistrates. Their criminal jurisdiction formerly extended, in many cases, Criminal jurisdiction in 1835.
to capital offences. In 1835 this jurisdiction had been generally abandoned, and serious offences were sent to the county sessions or assizes. At Salisbury, Southampton and Chichester, capital offences were still tried, although, when capital punishment was expected to follow conviction, arrangements were made to prevent a trial before corporate authorities solely. But at Berwick-upon-Tweed, Bristol, Canterbury, Exeter, Rochester, and some other places, the corporations still exercised their chartered privileges of trying and exe-

[1] Municipal Corporations Commission, 1835; General Report, p. 18. As examples, at Penryn, in 1835, the recorder was Lord de Dunstanville; his predecessor was Lord Mount Edgcumbe. At Penzance and at Truro the recorder was Lord Falmouth, and both offices had generally been held by some member of his family. At Launceston the Duke of Northumberland was both patron and recorder: at Liskeard, Lord St. Germans.

Civil Courts.

cuting criminals for capital offences.[1]   In a large majority of
the boroughs in England and Wales there were local civil
Courts, with a jurisdiction, the nature of which varied, though
it never extended beyond the limits of the borough.   These
Courts generally had their origin in particular charters, but
occasionally existed by prescription.   In some, actions real,
personal, and mixed might be brought.   In practice, suits
were seldom instituted except to recover debts.   Such actions
might often be brought for an unlimited amount, but were
subject to a power of removal.   In some of the large
boroughs corporate officers tried the ordinary kinds of
actions which occur at assizes.   These borough Courts, or
as they were usually termed, Courts of Record, resembled, in
their general constitution, the superior Courts of common
law.   When created by charter, the proceedings were analogous to those in the superior Courts at Westminster.   They
seldom, however, possessed any rules regulating procedure;
their practice, therefore, was very ill-defined.[2]

Gaols in
boroughs.

In nearly all boroughs possessing criminal jurisdiction,
there were gaols superintended by the corporation or municipal magistrates.   Sometimes the gaol expenses were defrayed
by the corporation, or out of a borough rate, or even out of
the poor rate.   There was rarely any proper classification of
prisoners.   In some large towns the gaols were in a very discreditable condition; in many small boroughs they were
totally unfit for the confinement of human beings.   Frequently,
they were mere dungeons under the town hall, with no proper
supply of air and light, and no possibility of setting prisoners
to work, or of separating criminals from debtors, so that creditors who had obtained executions were often unwilling to
consign their debtors to such dens, and in one town it was said
that the same feeling hindered the prosecution of prisoners.[3]
Poor debtors occasionally received a small allowance from
the corporation whilst in confinement.   In a great number

Police.

[1] Municipal Corporations Commission, 1835; General Report, p. 21.
[2] Ib., p. 22.   [3] Ib., pp. 23-4.

of towns there were no watchmen or police officers of any kind, except the constables, who were unsalaried officers. In some towns, the relief of the poor rested with the corporation. In others, it was vested in a distinct corporate body. At St. Ives, and a few other boroughs, the aldermen, who were the ancient select vestry,[1] had the management of the poor. In many instances, this duty was regulated by local Acts.

Poor relief.

This general summary will suggest many of the defects which, in 1835, disfigured most municipal bodies in England and Wales. The men were no doubt often better than the system, and there were exceptions to the rule of mal-administration and jobbery; but, however tempered in administration, both the system and its working, as a whole, were indefensible.[2] Corporations, the Commissioners said, "look upon themselves, and are considered by the inhabitants, as separate and exclusive bodies: they have powers and privileges within the towns and cities from which they are named, but in most places all identity of interest between them and the inhabitants has disappeared." This was the case even where the corporation included a large body of inhabitant freemen. But local privileges were often conferred on non-resident freemen, excluding the inhabitants. Only freemen were entitled to take part in municipal affairs, though in most corporate towns they were "a small number, compared with the respectable inhabitants interested in their municipal

No identity of interest between corporations and communities.

---

[1] Municipal Corporations Commission, 1835; General Report, pp. 34-6.

[2] "Despite their narrow constitution, there were some corporations which performed their functions worthily. Maintaining a mediæval dignity and splendour, their rule was graced by public virtue, courtesy, and refinement. Nobles shared their councils and festivities; the first men of the county were associated with townsmen; and while ruling without responsibility, they retained the willing allegiance of the people by traditions of public service, by acts of munificence and charity, and by the respect due to their eminent station. But the greater number of corporations were of a lower type. Neglecting their proper functions ... they grasped all patronage, lay and ecclesiastical, for their relatives, friends, and political partisans; and wasted the corporate funds in greasy feasts and vulgar revelry. Many were absolutely insolvent. Charities were despoiled, public trusts neglected and misapplied, jobbery and corruption in every form were fostered." (Sir Erskine May's (Lord Farnborough) Const. Hist. III. 281.)

government, and possessing every qualification, except a legal one, to take part in it."[1]

It will be gathered that the chief cause of this municipal degradation was a corrupt political influence which had gradually overshadowed nearly every Parliamentary borough, and a consequent perversion of municipal privileges to political objects. The Commissioners found that, in boroughs which returned no members to Parliament, the corporations, even when strictly self-elected, were those which had most faithfully discharged the duties of local government, and acquired the confidence and goodwill of their fellow townsmen. Elsewhere, rewards for political service, in money and appointments, obtained by governing bodies, brought them to view the Parliamentary franchise as the main, if not the sole, object of their being. That they kept their numbers as low as possible is explained by this motive, rather than by a desire to monopolize municipal authority. Hence, the Commissioners remarked, a large number of corporations had been kept up solely as political engines, and the towns to which they belonged derived no benefit, but often much injury, from their existence. "To maintain the political ascendancy of a party, or the political influence of a family," was their one end; and this object was "systematically pursued in the admission of freemen, resident or non-resident; in the selection of municipal functionaries for the council and magistracy; in the appointment of subordinate officers and the local police; in the administration of charities entrusted to municipal authorities; in the expenditure of corporate revenues, and management of corporate property."

[1] Municipal Corporations Commission, 1835; General Report, pp. 26-7. In sixteen corporate towns, of which a table is given, the population was 659,431, and the number of freemen (resident and non-resident) was 34,697. In Ipswich, the resident freemen formed about one fifty-fifth part of the population. Of these, more than one-third were not rated; many were excused from paying rates; about one-ninth of the whole were paupers. More than eleven-twelfths of all the property assessed belonged to persons who were excluded from the corporation.

Admission into a corporation was commonly sought, mainly with a view to profit from the Parliamentary franchise. Political influence was secured by a rigid exclusion of all political opponents from the governing body, and this ascendancy was easily maintained, as town councils were usually self-elected, and held their offices for life. After the Corporation and Test Acts were repealed, and Catholic disabilities removed, Dissenters or Catholics, however numerous, wealthy or fit, were rarely admitted. Yet these councils, strictly confined to one political party, appointed magistrates, civil and criminal judges, superintendents of police, with all other superior and subordinate officials concerned in the municipal government and administration. Holding their offices for life, members of these close corporations had no due feeling of responsibility towards their fellow citizens.[1] As close corporations, their affairs were managed with strict secrecy, sometimes enforced by oaths administered to the councillors. The inhabitants, who were subject to the corporate authority, were often imperfectly informed as to its nature and extent. They were ignorant whether this authority derived its sanction from prescription, from charter, or from bye-laws, and could only obtain this knowledge by the troublesome and costly process of a *mandamus* or *quo warranto*.[2]

Town councils self-elected for life.

Their party character.

Party spirit, which dominated the town councils, extended to the magistrates, who were chosen by these bodies, generally from among the aldermen. Hence, even when decisions were not unjust, a strong suspicion of injustice was excited;

Administration of justice in boroughs.

[1] Municipal Corporations Commission, 1835; General Report, pp. 28-30. One striking exception to these abuses is noted by the Commission (p. 30):— "The common councilmen of the city of London," they observe, " are annually elected by a numerous constituency, yet changes seldom happen among them. The important requisites of experience in the functionary, and the power of control in the electors, are there effectually united, and produce that efficiency and confidence which are wanting in most other corporate towns. The history of the common council of London is that of a body which has watched vigilantly over the interests of its constituents, and for a long series of years has studied to improve the corporate institutions with great earnestness, unremitting caution, and scrupulous justice."

[2] Ib., p. 30.

The magistrates.

local tribunals did not command respect; and corporate magistrates were often regarded by their fellow townsmen with positive distrust and dislike. They were sometimes taken from a class not competent to discharge judicial functions, thus occasioning grave defects in the administration of justice. At East Retford, the Commissioners were told by a witness, who had been clerk to the magistrates, that one of these gentlemen used to converse familiarly with culprits brought before him, sometimes endeavouring to impress them with a belief that he was performing an unwilling office. On one occasion he saw this magistrate fighting with a prisoner and struggling with him on the floor. At Malmesbury, magistrates were often unable to read or write. Even when corporate magistrates belonged to a superior class, they soon, being chosen from the senior aldermen only, became incapable, through age and infirmities, of performing the duties of their office, while a mistaken notion of dignity kept them from resigning it.[1]

Juries in borough Courts.

Juries for the borough Courts were often taken exclusively from the freemen, and, besides being of an inferior class, were so tainted with party feeling that their verdicts were untrustworthy. Instances of this nature, at Northampton and elsewhere, are quoted in the Report. At Carmarthen, verdicts are said to have been frequently given against justice, from party bias. The population of the town was 10,000, but the jurors were chosen from a small body of 178 burgesses. At Haverfordwest, where none but burgesses could be jurors, there were only 141 burgesses, not fifty of whom were fit to serve. Juries there had been openly reprimanded by judges and magistrates for improper acquittals of burgesses upon criminal prosecutions, but the practice was not checked, and, according to the general opinion, "it

Civil jurisdiction.

was impossible to convict a burgess."[2] Similar defects prevailed in the administration of civil justice. If the Recorder did not attend, as frequently happened, the town-clerk be-

[1] Municipal Corporations Commission; General Report, p. 33.

[2] Ib., pp. 33, 34.

came the real judge, owing to incompetent magistrates. Yet these civil Courts possessed an unlimited power of imprisonment, which in some cases was made the means of great oppression.

There was glaring mismanagement of corporate property. Some corporations had been in the habit of letting their lands by private contract to members of their own body, upon a rent and at fines wholly disproportionate to value, and frequently for long terms of years.[1] Others had alienated in fee much of their property for inadequate considerations. In large towns such malversations were less common, but the Commissioners note even there a careless and extravagant administration of municipal funds, and an exclusive distribution of patronage among friends and political partisans. In some towns these funds were spent in bribery and other illegal practices during Parliamentary contests. During an election in 1826, the Corporation of Leicester spent 10,000*l*. to secure the return of a political partisan, and mortgaged some of their property in discharge of liabilities thus incurred. At Barnstaple and Liverpool corporate funds were wasted in defending from threatened disfranchisement a body of freemen who had been guilty of bribery. In numerous instances members of a governing body received pecuniary allowances from the patron of the borough. There was a strongly-rooted opinion, sometimes openly avowed and defended, that corporate property was held in trust for the benefit of corporate bodies only, and not of communities. Charitable trusts administered by these corporations were mismanaged and misappropriated to a considerable extent. At Winchester the management of local charities was taken from the corporation in consequence of notorious malversation. At Norwich, Leicester, Coventry,

Mismanagement and malversation of corporate property.

Specific trusts and patronage.

---

[1] General Report of Municipal Corporations Commission, pp. 38-9. At Berwick-on-Tweed, where the freemen managed the corporate property, and possessed commons worth about 6,000*l*. a year, they borrowed money expressly for the purpose of dividing it among themselves.

Northampton and Ipswich, pensioners were placed on charitable foundations in return for their votes at elections. A provision intended for the poor was, therefore, by some corporate authorities, made a source of corrupt influence.[1]

**Measure of
thorough
reform
suggested by
Commis-
sioners.**

These facts, amply confirmed in details by inquiries held in each borough, led the Commissioners to report " that there prevails among the inhabitants of a great majority of the incorporated towns a general, and, in our opinion, a just dissatisfaction with their municipal institutions ; a distrust of self-elected municipal councils, whose powers are subject to no popular control, and whose acts and proceedings, being secret, are unchecked by the influence of public opinion ; a distrust of the municipal magistracy, tainting with suspicion the local administration of justice, and often accompanied by contempt of the persons by whom the law is administered ; a discontent under the burdens of local taxation, while revenues that ought to be applied to the public advantage are diverted from their legitimate use, and are sometimes wastefully bestowed for the benefit of individuals, sometimes squandered for purposes injurious to the character and morals of the people." For these reasons the Commissioners were of opinion, " that the existing municipal corporations of England and Wales neither possess nor deserve public confidence or respect, and that a thorough reform must be effected before they can become, what they ought to be, useful and efficient instruments of local government."[2]   From this Report sprang a necessary complement to Parliamentary reform, the Municipal Reform Act of 1835,[3] which enlarged the basis of local representation,

---

[1] General Report of Municipal Corporations Commission, pp. 40-1.

[2] Ib., p. 42.

[3] 5 & 6 Will. IV. c. 76. The corporation of London, always a representative body, and, as we have seen, very favourably mentioned by the Commissioners, were exempted from the operation of this Act. In 1882 the Act of 1835 was repealed, together with, in whole or in part, sixty-nine scheduled statutes affecting municipal boroughs dealt with by the present Act. For the existing municipal code of England and Wales, thus consolidated and amended, the Municipal Corporations Act, 1882 (45 & 46 Vict. c. 50), must now be consulted.

and put an end to most of the abuses exposed by the Commissioners.

This sketch of chartered municipalities, until their reconstitution in 1835, outstrips the general narrative, but was necessary to explain what would otherwise have hardly been intelligible, namely, the passing of local Acts, which did not recognize these corporations, but created bodies of trustees or commissioners for many purposes of municipal government. Sometimes, indeed, members of the common council had, by statute, a share in these functions, and a few were named commissioners *ex officio*. But there could be no better proof of popular distrust than the fact that, as a body, they were deliberately ignored when Parliament made better provision for lighting, watching, paving, and cleansing in the towns they were supposed to govern. By their charters, corporations or governing bodies were generally empowered to make byelaws, and, in some instances, to tax the inhabitants for municipal purposes. Many corporations derived considerable revenues from land or other property,[1] from tolls of markets and fairs, from town dues on imports or exports, from quay dues, anchorage, and other sources. They should, therefore, have been natural guardians of the interests of the whole community in all matters pertaining to local government. But by their prolonged neglect of those duties, their exclusiveness, and political demoralization, they were left with hardly any duties to perform, and only nominally responsible for health and good order in their towns.

It has been already stated that, in 1835, there were in many boroughs no watchmen or police, except unsalaried constables, sworn in to keep the peace, but having their own affairs to look after, and seldom, therefore, available when wanted. In some boroughs a general Act, passed in 1830,[2] was adopted, enabling parishes to levy rates for lighting and watching. Hence there was a divided authority, which caused much con-

Marginal notes: Local Improvement Acts constituting Commissioners.

Police.

[1] Some corporations held their estates on condition of repairing bridges or other works.

[2] 11 Geo. IV. c. 27.

fusion. For example: every quarter of the town of Bath was, for police and other purposes, under the care of a separate Board, except one district, which was left totally unprotected. In other boroughs, where the corporation employed an insufficient force of police, and other police were authorized by local Acts, great jealousy often existed between the two bodies. In Bristol, as the Commissioners of 1835 reported, a notoriously ineffective police could not be improved, chiefly because the inhabitants distrusted their corporation. At Hull, in consequence of disputes between the governing body and inhabitants concerning corporate tolls and duties, only seven persons attended to suppress a riot, out of a thousand who had been sworn in as special constables; and on another occasion none attended. At Coventry, serious riots and disturbances frequently occurred, and the police, being usually selected from one political party, were often active in fomenting them.[1] In some instances the separate and conflicting authority of the Commissioners under local Acts was avowedly used as a check and counter-balance to the political influence of the corporation. At Leeds, in 1835, no persons were elected Commissioners of Police under these local Acts whose political principles were not opposed to those of the corporation. In some towns, as the corporation failed to provide any well-organized system, watchmen were paid by public subscriptions.[2]

Conflicting jurisdiction over paving, &c.

There was a similar failure by corporate bodies to make proper provision for paving, lighting, and sewerage; and the Commissioners who, in their default, received authority from Parliament to act, exercised a conflicting jurisdiction, which often led

Market tolls and town dues.

to needless expense and inconvenience. Well-grounded complaints were also made that, for tolls taken by corporations at markets and fairs, and for town dues, no proper equivalent was rendered, while, as the persons who paid them

---

[1] General Report of Municipal Corporations Commission, p. 36.

[2] Ib., pp. 36-7.

were not represented in the governing body, they had no power to prevent this neglect. Freemen were exempted from some of these oppressive charges, and merchants, therefore, paid fines for admission to the freedom where they could do so. In Liverpool and other towns, corporations refused to sacrifice revenue by allowing these admissions, and non-free-men were unfairly handicapped in competition with free merchants. *Exemptions enjoyed by freemen.*

We may now go back to some examples of medieval regula-tions, ordinances, or byelaws, as they would now be called, which were made and issued by municipal bodies under the general powers of local government vested in them, or in virtue of specific powers conferred by charter. London is naturally the fountain-head for such information. There the authority exercised by mayor, aldermen and council was exceptional, and was occasionally reinforced by royal man-date, edict or statute. But, as far as their powers extended, and as local circumstances required, corporations in other cities and large towns would naturally frame their codes upon that of the capital. In London, this civic authority can be traced in copious records of the middle ages. Erring on the side of over-regulation, it was not confined to the preserva-tion of order, of public health, comfort and decency, but attempted to regulate trade, and even wages, with a harsh-ness, and sometimes a barbarity, which were in keeping with the rough customs of those days. The elaborate powers thus enforced, in London and elsewhere, for what were then understood to be necessary purposes of good government, offer a curious contrast to the powers now exercised by the same corporate bodies, under modern statutes.[1] *Local ordi-nances in the middle ages.*

A series of ordinances known as Fitz-Alwyne's Assize, to regulate building in the city, was issued in the year 1189, *Building in London regulated, 1 Richard I.*

[1] The chief civic ordinances of London will be found in the Rolls' series of publications. For the sum-mary which follows, necessarily con-fined to a few out of a multitude of ordinances, I must again acknow-ledge my indebtedness to these sources, and to Mr. Riley's expla-nations.

during the first year's office of Henry Fitz-Alwyne, first mayor of London.[1] These ordinances form a complete code, and, considering their early date, are remarkable for their fulness and precision. They recite the necessity of preventing disputes between neighbours as to buildings. Another

Inflammable
materials of
ancient
houses.

object may also have been the prevention of fires. Up to that period the great majority of London houses were built wholly of wood, thatched with straw, reed or stubble. Hence a great fire in King Stephen's reign, beginning at London Bridge, destroyed St. Paul's Cathedral, and burnt all the houses as far as St. Clement Danes.[2] Houses somewhat more substantial took their place. By the Assize of 1189, party walls were to be of free-stone, three feet thick and sixteen feet high. At this period houses in London consisted of only one story above the ground floor.[3] Contrary to the

Ancient
lights.

modern presumption in law, the Assize declared that ancient lights might be obstructed, unless the owner could show some written agreement to the contrary.[4] Glass was only used by rich citizens; windows were generally openings, protected by iron bars, and closed at night by wooden shutters.[5] Chimneys are not mentioned in the Assize. If they existed

---

[1] Henricus, filius Elwyni, as he is described. This Assize has been termed the first English Building Act in existence. Though no doubt binding on the citizens, it does not appear to have had any statutory authority, and does not even recite any allowance by the Crown. The earliest copy of this Assize is contained in Liber de Antiquis Legibus, among the muniments in Guildhall.

[2] See Latin Mem. inserted in the Assize, probably written by John Carpenter, who was town-clerk A.D. 1436.

[3] Riley's Int. to Liber Albus, 31. It was not until early in the fourteenth century that houses of two or three stories are mentioned. Each

of these stories, with the cellar beneath, occasionally formed different freeholds, and caused such disputes that Edward II. interfered, by mandate, directing each owner to keep his own part in due repair. The upper stories in houses of this description were entered by stairs on the outside. (Ib.)

[4] See ordinances "de obscuratione fenestrarum"; 1 Liber Albus, 324.

[5] Ib., Int. 33. In the reign of Henry III. (1216-72), glass is enumerated among the regular imports, probably from Flanders. Glaziers (verrers) are mentioned as an ancient mystery, in the time of Edward III.

at all in 1189, they were to be rarely found; in most houses the smoke found its way out of doors and windows.[1]

If this Assize had been intended to prevent fires, we might have expected a peremptory prohibition of inflammable materials for roofs. No such rule, however, was made, though, a century and a half later, the civic authorities repeatedly ordered that houses should be roofed only with lead, tiles,[2] or stone. As further precautions, when houses had increased in height, it was ordered that certain occupiers should keep one or two ladders as fire escapes, and, in the height of summer, should provide, in front of their houses, a barrel or large earthen vessel full of water. For a more speedy removal of burning houses, each ward was enjoined to provide a strong iron crook, with a wooden handle, two chains, and two strong cords. These were to be left with the beadle of the ward, who was also to keep a good, loudly-sounding horn, for a fire-alarm.[3]

Means of preventing fires in middle ages.

A second building Assize was passed in 1212, owing to a fire less extensive than that in Stephen's reign, but far more calamitous. On the night of July 12, in that year, a fire broke out in Southwark which destroyed the great church of St. Mary. Many people gathered on London Bridge to view the scene. By a fatal mischance, embers, borne by wind, set fire to some wooden buildings on the city end of the bridge, and the flames rapidly extended to similar buildings on the Southwark side. Hemmed in by fire, with no means of escape except by plunging into the tide below, a thousand people, men, women, and children, are said to have

Great fire in London and Southwark, A.D. 1212.

[1] But in the year 1300 there was a civic ordinance that chimneys should be faced with tiles or plaster, on pain of being pulled down.

[2] Bricks are not mentioned in this Assize, or, indeed, in any other English work of so early a date, but there is reason for believing that tiles in 1189, like the Roman tiles, were used as thin bricks. Tilers, as well as carpenters, masons, plasterers and daubers, were the artizans employed in building, temp. Edward I. Daubers filled up the timber framework of house gables with mud-clay mixed with straw. Int. to Liber Albus, 35-6.

[3] Ib. Int. 34.

perished.[1]   The fire raged for ten days.   Summoned then to meet in Guildhall, by the venerable Mayor who had given his name to the Assize of 1189, the citizens approved a new code, expressly designed to make any new houses less likely to take fire or spread it.   In Cheap and other important thorough-fares, wooden houses still existed.   Their owners were ordered to take certain precautions, or, upon view by the mayor, sheriffs and reputable men in the ward, these houses would be pulled down.   All dwellings then covered with rushes or reeds were to be duly plastered within eight days, or they, too, would be levelled.   Every person building a new house was to take care, " as he loved himself and his family," not to roof it with reeds, rushes, stubble or straw, but only with tiles, shingles, boards or lead.   Cookshops, brewhouses and bakehouses were to be plastered and whitewashed both within and without ; at night no brewer must brew, or baker heat his oven; and for fuel, no reeds, straw or stubble must be used, but wood alone. [2]

It was not until 1666 that, by express legislation, new buildings in the city of London were made of prescribed materials.   An Act then passed,[3] which set forth how " the city of London, being the Imperial seat of his Majesty's kingdom, and renowned for trade and commerce throughout the world, by reason of a most dreadful fire lately happening therein, was for the most part thereof burnt down and de-stroyed within the compass of a few days, and now lies buried in its own ruins." [4]   " For the speedy restoration

Marginal notes:
Wooden houses and thatched roofs.

Legislation after the fire of 1666.

---

[1] Matthew Paris relates this inci-dent.   According to some histo-rians, 3,000 people lost their lives.

[2] Liber Custumarum, Int. 31-3. The use of coal in London was pro-bably then unknown, but came into common use, temp. Edward II. Charcoal, prepared in the suburbs, is frequently mentioned.

[3] 18 & 19 Charles II. c. 8.

[4] That the citizens of London " for all time to come may retain the me-morial of so sad a desolation, and reflect seriously upon their manifold iniquities, which are the unhappy causes of such judgments," it was enacted, by sect. 26, " that the second day of September (unless the same happen to be Sunday, and, if so, then the next day following) be yearly for ever hereafter observed as a day of public fasting and humiliation within the said city and liberties thereof, to implore the mercies of Almighty God

thereof, and for the better regularity, uniformity and gracefulness of such new buildings as shall be erected for habitations, and to the end that great and outrageous fires (through the blessing of Almighty God, so far as human providence, with submission to the Divine pleasure, can foresee) may be reasonably prevented for the time to come, by the matter and form of such buildings," it was provided that all future houses should be built as directed by the Act. There were elaborate provisions to carry out this and other objects, such as the widening of thoroughfares[1] and the adjustment of disputed boundaries; and as brick was "not only more comely and durable, but also more safe against future perils of fire," it was enacted that, with certain exceptions, the outsides of all buildings should be of brick or stone, or brick and stone together. Of the churches formerly standing, not more than thirty-nine were to be rebuilt.[2]

In the year 1675, great part of the town of Northampton having been burnt down, a similar statute was passed,[3] constituting a Court of Record for the settlement of differences between landlord and tenant, and also for ordering the mode of reconstruction. One provision was that all new houses should be covered with lead, slates or tiles. Again, in 1677, after a fire which destroyed great part of Southwark, Commissioners were appointed by statute,[4] armed with large powers for speedily determining similar differences.

Fires at Northampton, A.D. 1675, and Southwark in 1677.

There was no mention of kennels in Fitz-Alwyne's Assize, but they probably existed, for there were precise directions

Street regulations.

---

upon the said city, and to make devout prayers and supplication unto Him to divert the like calamity for the time to come." Sect. 27 further enacts, that "the better to preserve the memory of this dreadful visitation, a column or pillar of brass or stone be erected," on or near to the place where the fire began, with an inscription prepared by the Court of Aldermen. This was the origin of Pope's "tall bully."

[1] Before 1666, the city streets were much more numerous and narrower than they afterwards became; alleys, courts, and by-paths abounded in every direction. A fire would take hold of houses on both sides of these narrow ways.

[2] Sect. 29. But by 22 Charles II. c. 11, s. 55, this number was enlarged to fifty-one.

[3] 27 Charles II. c. 1.

[4] 29 Charles II. c. 4.

as to the gutters which carried water from house-roofs, and as to any easements thereby acquired.[1] Each householder was enjoined to keep clean the space in front of his dwelling. Rakers, or scavengers,[2] were appointed to cleanse the roadways, and were paid by the ward authorities.[3] In the reign of Edward I., citizens were allowed to keep swine "within their houses," but no pigsties were to encroach upon the streets. If a pig strayed in a public way, any person might catch it, kill it, and either keep the carcase or return it to the owner for a stated sum. So great, however, was the nuisance from these animals, sent out probably to feed upon street garbage, that four men were "chosen and sworn to take and kill all swine found wandering within the city walls, to whomsoever they might belong," excepting the rector of the hospital of St. Antony, patron saint of swine; and he was required to take oath (temp. Edward II.) "that he will not avow any swine found at large in the city, nor will he hang any bells around their necks, but only around those pigs which have been given in pure alms."[4] Stray dogs were similarly dealt with, always excepting well-bred dogs (chiens gentilz).

Regulations as to foot-paths were stringently enforced. Each householder was expected to pave the foot-way in front of his house, keeping it neither higher nor lower than his

Pigs kept in city.

Paving of foot and roadway.

[1] "De aqua stillante et stillicidiis"; Liber Albus, 331. Kennels for carrying off sewage and rain water are mentioned in city bye-laws about a century and a half later. An Act of 1662 (22 Chas. II. c. 11, s. 8) provided that in London water should be carried from the tops of houses by pipes. The cascade from open gutters on the roofs had previously been a sore nuisance to pedestrians in rainy weather.

[2] The original business of the city "scavagers" was to attend at hythes and quays to take city dues upon the scavage, or unlading and exposure of imported goods. These officials are mentioned in the Assize as also em-

ployed to see that when houses were constructed due precautions were taken against fire; and, further, to see that pavements were kept clean and in proper repair. (Liber Albus, Int. 41.)

[3] An ordinance of about the year 1300 is as follows:—"Item, qils eient rakyers suffisauntz pur nettere les Gardes de diverses ordurez; et ordeignent lez conestables, ore le bedelle, de luy eydere, coillere soun salarie dez gentz de la Garde." (Ib. 335.)

[4] Ib., Int. 41-2. St. Antony's Hospital was situate in Threadneedle Street. St. Antony's pigs were distinguished by bells round their necks.

neighbour's. Aldermen were required (temp. Edward I.) to choose at each wardmote four men resident in the ward, "to preserve, lower and raise the pavements; to remove all nuisances, and take distresses, or else fourpence, from those who placed them there; the same being removed at their cost." Roadways appear to have been paved by the municipality out of a toll or tax called "pavage," and levied upon horses and vehicles. This toll is supposed to have been collected at the city gates and barriers. Remembering the greater value of money in those days, the following ordinance (temp. Edward III.) shows that it must have been a heavy tax:— "A cart, on entering the city or going forth, shall pay for **Pavage toll.** pavage one penny; a laden horse, one farthing; a cart that brings sand and potters' clay, three pence per week; carts with corn and flour from Stratford, three pence per week; carts with firewood on sale, one farthing; with charcoal, one penny. But carts and horses of great persons and others, which bring victuals or other goods for their use and for consumption in their houses, shall pay nothing." There was an ordinance (temp. Edward I.) that wheels of carts bringing wood, sand or stone, should not have iron bands; in other cases, the size of these bands (*ferramenta*) was strictly regulated, to prevent roadways from being unduly worn. Public safety was consulted by an order that carts were to **Furious driving.** be driven no faster when unladen than when laden.[1]

Visors and masks were not allowed to be worn in streets. **Order observed in streets after curfew.** After curfew, rung at eight each evening from several church steeples, no person was to carry sword, buckler, or any other arms, excepting "great lords or men of substance, and such of their household as go before them with lights." Persons found abroad at night, and unable to give a satisfactory account of themselves, were carried to a prison called the Tun, at Cornhill. Each city gate was **City gates.** watched at night by a serjeant-at-arms, who occupied chambers over the gateway, and was assisted by watchmen.

---

[1] At this period carriages for personal use were unknown; they only came into use after 1580, when the Earl of Arundel set the fashion.

During the day two armed men kept each gate. It was their duty to see that no leper entered the city, and that pavage toll and other city dues were paid upon carts and produce. Sometimes these tolls appear to have been farmed; there is a lease of Aldgate, supposed to be for this purpose, **Begging.** to Geoffrey Chaucer. Lazars, or diseased beggars, were forbidden to solicit alms within the city, and no one able to subsist by labour was allowed to beg there. Lepers had a common deputy (*attourne*) who went round every parish **Common women.** church on Sundays to collect alms on their behalf. Women of ill-fame were under strict supervision. None were allowed to dwell within the city, but had a certain walk assigned to them there, and fixed places of residence at Southwark. If they were found in the streets after curfew, they were lodged in the Tun. Their dress was regulated by royal proclamation. From the City Letter Books it appears that, in the fourteenth century, most of these women were Flemings.[1]

Markets. In the reign of Richard II., and earlier, stands were let near the city gates and at other convenient places for various purposes of trade. Of these stalls, some were appropriated to fishmongers on fish days, and to butchers on flesh days. Sellers of bread, cheese, poultry, and market produce were allowed to stand in specified portions of certain streets, or on broad pavements. In order to keep up the market tolls and prevent forestalling, no one could go outside the city **Regulation of wages and trade.** to buy corn, cattle, bread or other goods. There were minute and vexatious ordinances regulating wages and trade. As the Great Plague of 1348-51 had caused a scarcity of labour, it was enacted that every workman and labourer, as well as "the servants of substantial people," should charge no more than before, and that workmen and labourers who would not work should be arrested and imprisoned. In the same reign, that of Edward III., royal writs directed that working saddlers, skinners, and tanners, should be chastised if they made excessive charges.[2] When a brewer, or

---

[1] Int. to Liber Albus, 50-2.   [2] Ib. 54-5.

brewess,[1] finished a brewing, the ale-conner must be sent Brewing and ale-conners. for. He tasted the ale, and if he found it not equal to the assize, he set it at a lower price than was fixed for ale of good quality, and this price must not be exceeded. His decision, however, must be confirmed by the Alderman of the ward, who also impressed with his seal the gallon, pottle, Deficient measures. and quart measures of each brewer and taverner, so that customers might not be defrauded. Faulty measures were publicly burnt, and persons were pilloried for using such as were unstamped, or for thickening the bottom with pitch.

In like manner no wine could be sold until it had been Wine. examined and gauged; and in the reign of Edward III. four vintners were chosen to assess prices. Under the first Plantagenets, a wine-fleet, consisting of "hulks and keels," freighted with produce from the banks of the Moselle, and with general merchandize, arrived in the Thames every year, and was subject to minute regulations. Masters of these vessels were bound to arrange them in due order, and raise their ensigns; the crews singing, if they wished, their "kiriele," or song of praise and thanksgiving,[2] "according to the old law." No part of the cargo could be sold until one of the sheriffs and the King's chamberlain had boarded each vessel, and selected such produce as they thought fit for royal use, including precious stones, gold or silver plate, and tapestry, the price of which was assessed by lawful merchants of London, and credit given until a fortnight's end. If foreign merchants came ashore, they must "take hostel" within prescribed limits, were forbidden to buy woolfels, lamb-skins, fresh leather, and unwrought wool, and were subject to a most irksome supervision, with varying dues.[3]

---

[1] Sometimes brewster, as a market-woman was called a huckster, and a woman-baker a bakester (hence the surname Baxter). In these times brewing was chiefly in the hands of women, and Fleet-street was tenanted almost wholly by brewes- ses, or ale-wives, and makers of felt caps. Int. to Liber Albus, 54-5.

[2] Probably originating in the "Kyrie eleison" of the Litany; hence, too, the Christmas "carol."

[3] Liber Cust. Int. 36 et seq.

Bakers.
Bakers were closely looked after. Prices were fixed; loaves were to be of a given size or weight.[1] Every baker within the city walls was bound, under penalties, to keep a seal, and impress it on all his loaves. From time to time the Aldermen inspected these seals, and kept counterparts, with a view to trace and punish offenders in case of default. Servants of substantial people had a legal right to be present when the baker kneaded his dough. According to a statute of Edward I., all bread must be sold in open market. Bells were rung
Forestalling.
when the sale of corn might begin. So, to prevent forestalling, no fish could be bought till a vessel was moored. Care was taken that "good people" should have an opportunity of supplying themselves before the fishmongers, who were under penalties not to buy fresh fish till after mass sung (probably at sunrise) at the chapel on London Bridge, and not to buy salt fish till after prime was rung at St. Paul's (six o'clock a.m.). There were similar restrictions on the sale of other articles of food.

Weaving.
Weaving was carried on within the city, and a large wool and cloth market was held there. The weavers were probably descendants of the Flemings brought over by Henry I. They received charters from that King and from Henry II.,
Low status of weavers in London.
paying a certain annual ferm or rent to the Crown. For some reason, perhaps on account of their foreign origin, they were despised as a class by their fellow citizens. In other towns, the local laws or usages of which appear to have been copied from those of London, it would seem that, during the twelfth and thirteenth centuries, weavers had a status little superior to that of "not law-worthy" serfs of Anglo-

---

[1] Int. to Liber Albus, 66–7. In the Assisa Panis, among the records at Guildhall, there is a pen-and-ink sketch (date about 1320) representing a baker drawn on a hurdle, with the deficient loaf hanging from his neck. Another baker was pilloried for putting a piece of iron into his bread to make up the weight. By a civic enactment (temp. Edward II.) sheriffs were ordered to take no fines from bakers or brewesses, but to put them in the pillory. For a third offence a baker was drawn on a hurdle to the pillory, his oven was pulled down, and he could never afterwards carry on his trade in the city.

Saxon times.[1] At Winchester, no weaver or fuller could go *Weavers at Winchester.* beyond the city precincts for purposes of trade, and might only sell his cloth within the city. If any weaver or fuller, "for enriching himself," went beyond the gates, the substantial men might take back his chattels into the city and deal with them as forfeited. Cloth might be seized if sold by a weaver to any trader not being a citizen, and the weaver was liable to forfeiture of all his goods. No freeman could be accused by a weaver or fuller, nor were such persons allowed to bear witness against a freeman. If a weaver became so rich that he could leave his craft, he was bound solemnly to forswear it, and remove all looms from his house. He might then be admitted to the freedom.[2]

At Marlborough, similar regulations prevailed. A weaver *At Marlborough, Oxford, and Beverley.* might work for no one except substantial men of the town, nor could he possess any property of his own to the value of one penny beyond what pertained to the art of making cloth. He was, however, allowed to have five ells of cloth for his own use. Before adopting any other trade he was bound to remove all looms from the house. At Oxford he was not allowed to weave or full without leave from the substantial citizens. A weaver's widow must marry none but a weaver, if she wished to follow the same craft. At Beverley, a place famed for its textures during the middle ages, usages no less arbitrary prevailed. In London, during the reign of Edward I., the status of these poor handicraftsmen seems to have improved.

In more modern times, municipal bodies continued to *Jurisdiction over woollen manufacture at Leeds by Corporation, A.D. 1626.* exercise jurisdiction over this and other trades, for in a charter granted by Charles I. to the Corporation of Leeds in 1626 we find that, "for the better government of the inhabitants of the borough, and especially the workers and labourers for making woollen cloths,"[3] the Corporation were

---

[1] Lib. Cust. Int. 60-1. "Not lawworthy," *i. e.*, debarred from the privileges of freemen in courts of justice.

[2] Ib. 62.

[3] English wool was reckoned the

allowed to create "all reasonable guilds within the borough
and the liberties and precincts thereof," with power "to
distinguish and divide them into separate fraternities, societies, and mysteries," so that no such fraternity or guild
should make "any statutes, laws, jurisdictions, institutions,
or constitutions," to bind any burgess or inhabitant, unless
they had licence given by the Corporation under their common seal. This charter, abrogated during the Commonwealth,
was renewed and confirmed by Charles II. in 1661.

Statute *circa*
1285, pro-
viding for
good order in
London.

From charters, and local bye-laws made under them, often,
no doubt, in excess of corporate powers, we now pass to a few
early instances of local laws possessing statutory force.   Here,
too, we must begin with London.   Among the statutes of uncertain date is one passed *circa* 1285, containing no reference
to the authority of Parliament.   It is in the not unusual form
of Articles,[1] "which our lord the King doth command to
be kept in his City of London for better maintaining his
peace."   It recites that many disorders arise and murders
and robberies are done in the city by night.   Therefore it
orders that no one be so hardy as to be found in the streets
after curfew tolled at St. Martin's le Grand, unless he be
a great lord (grand seigneur) or other person of good

best in Europe, and was largely exported to Flanders and other countries when its export was allowed.
In the year 1340 (14 Edw. III), the
Commons in Parliament voted thirty
thousand packs of wool towards the
cost of a war with France.   Each
pack was then valued at 4*l.*, equal
to more than 40*l.* of present money.
At that time Norfolk was the chief
centre of the worsted and woollen
industries, through the settlement
there of Flemish weavers.   It was
then the richest county in England,
and was adjudged able to contribute
2,206 packs, or the equivalent in
money.   Next came Kent, with
1,274 packs; Lincoln, 1,265 ; Yorkshire, 1,157.   The City of London

paid 503 packs.   This wool, when
collected at the seaports of London,
Lynn, Boston, Hull, and a few other
places in which the staple of wool
existed, was shipped by the King's
officers to Antwerp and Bruges,
where it fetched high prices. (2
Baines's Hist. of Yorkshire, 537-8.)

[1] 13 Edw. I., Stat. Civitatis Lond.;
I. Stat. of the Realm, p. 102.   The
original is in Norman-French.   See
also Liber Albus (Riley's translation), pp. 245-6.   Edward I., upon
some dispute with the city, made
these Articles, and willed that no
franchise or ancient usage should
hold good which conflicted with
them.

repute (prodome[1] de bone conyssaunce) having warrants to go from one place to another, and furnished with a lantern. Offenders are to be taken before the Warden, Mayor and Aldermen, and punished as the custom is. There is a further recital that evil-doers going about by night "do commonly resort and have their meetings, and hold their evil talk in taverns more than elsewhere, and there do shelter themselves, lying in wait and watching their time to do mischief." It is therefore ordered that after curfew no one do keep a tavern open for sale of wine or ale. Any taverner found offending is to forfeit for the first offence forty pence, with increasing penalties up to his fifth offence, when a delinquent "may be forejudged of his trade for ever" (seit forsjugge del mestier pour tutz jourz). *Taverns: early closing of.*

This is a very early, if not the first, specimen of what would now be called a Police Act. It is not confined to early closing clauses; there is a fierce provision against fools who delight in evil doing (fous qui sei delitent a mal fere), and who learn to fence with sword and buckler, being thereby more encouraged to commit their follies. The statute therefore declares "that none shall hold school for or teach the art of fencing with buckler," under penalty of imprisonment for forty days.[2] Then follow provisions to secure a stricter punishment for offences. As evil-doers within the city are often delivered too easily, whereby they are "encouraged in often transgressing against the peace," no man arrested for certain offences is henceforth to be set free by a sheriff, or any officer under him, without an award by Mayor and Aldermen. *Fencing schools.* *Better punishment of offenders against the peace.*

There is a further recital that "divers persons do resort unto the city, some from parts beyond sea, others of this land, and do there seek shelter and refuge, by reason of *Outlaws and refugees of bad character harboured in city.*

---

[1] Prudhomme.

[2] In other European capitals at this period fencing schools seem to have led to frequent brawls, and similar enactments against them were common.

banishment out of their own country, or who for great offence or other misdeed have fled from their own country; and of these some do become brokers, hostelers, and innkeepers, as though they were good and lawful men of the City's franchise; and some nothing do but run up and down through the streets, more by night than by day, and are well attired in clothing and array, and have their food of delicate meats and costly; though neither do they use any craft or merchandize, nor have they lands or tenements out of which to live, nor any friend to vouch for them; and through such persons many perils do

Innkeeping confined to freemen.

often happen in the City." It is therefore provided that no alien or other person shall keep inn or hostel in the City unless he be a freeman admitted before the Warden or Mayor and Aldermen as a good man and true (bon home e leal), with good testimony from the parts whence he comes,

Sworn brokers.

and able to find sureties. There are also to be no brokers in the City except those admitted and sworn before the Warden or Mayor and Aldermen. Thus the existing jurisdiction to this effect has lasted six hundred years. Vested interests were not much considered in those days, for the statute declares:—" All that are innkeepers, hostelers, and brokers in the City contrary to the forms aforesaid, from one month after the day when these Articles shall be read and published in the City, shall forego the same, and withdraw themselves that they do so no more." Imprisonment and other penalties are prescribed for disobedience.

Act of 1552-3 limiting number of taverns in specified towns.

Nearly three hundred years later, we find Parliament restricting the numbers of taverns in specified towns. In 1552-3, an Act was passed "for avoiding many inconveniences, much evil rule, and common resort of mis-ruled persons using and frequenting many taverns of late newly set up in very great numbers in back lanes, corners, and suspicious places within the City of London, and in divers other towns and villages in this realm."[1] Among other regula-

[1] 7 Edw. VI. c. 5.

tions accordingly made are these :—Tavern-keeping[1] is forbidden except in cities and towns, and there only by licence from local authorities, under their common seal; such licence to be continued or withdrawn at their pleasure; and in non-corporate towns by licence from justices at petty sessions. In Gravesend, Sittingbourne, Bagshot,[2] and in other cities, towns, and places not specially excepted, the corporation and justices must only appoint two retail wine-sellers or taverners. In the City of London there may be forty; in York, eight; in Bristol, six. Four apiece are allotted to Kingston-upon-Hull, Exeter, Gloucester, Canterbury, Cambridge, and Newcastle. Three only are allowed to Hereford, Worcester, Southampton, Westminster, Lincoln, Shrewsbury, Salisbury, Ipswich, Winchester, Oxford, and Colchester.

Local option as to taverns.

Local option was thus introduced, with restrictions to a maximum number of taverns where local authorities sanctioned any. In this statute, too, there are provisions against retailing wine in private houses. No one must have in his house for his private use more than ten gallons of wine unless he be worth a hundred marks a year; and severe penalties are levied upon any person retailing wine in his private house "by any colour, craft, engine, or means." Exceptions as to the quantity of wine to be kept in private houses are made in favour of merchants importing it for their own use; high sheriffs, mayors, and bailiffs, during their year of charge; and persons living in towns fortified and kept for the wars. Justices of the peace are to inquire into offences and levy penalties; prosecutions are limited to one year; and there is a clause saving the jurisdiction of the Universities at Oxford and Cambridge.

Provision against private retailing.

All "fit and able" citizens and burgesses were expected to render service as guardians of public order. Such a liability still remains at common law upon any summons to assist a constable or prevent a breach of the peace. But this common

Liability to watch and ward.

[1] A tavern was for sale of wine: this Act did not apply to ale-houses.

[2] Why these places are specially mentioned does not appear.

liability resting upon bystanders, or upon townspeople sworn as special constables in case of apprehended disturbance, differs greatly from the constant service, by day and by night, which good men and true in cities and boroughs were bound of old to render under direction from the Alderman of each ward.   It will be not without interest to see, from examples in London, what were the incidents of this duty, performed without payment as an essential function of good citizenship, but gradually superseded by the old and incapable watchmen of more modern times, and afterwards by the efficient force of police which we owe to Sir Robert Peel.

Night watches. In the reign of Edward I., it was ordered that Aldermen and householders in London should keep watch on horseback at night, each Alderman maintaining three horses for this purpose. According to its size, each ward furnished a certain number of men, who "must be strong, and with good arms, well able to defend themselves." At night the watches and waits[1] were "set." Watchmen were sworn and charged well and lawfully to keep ward, without favour to any one,[2] or corruption, through either gift or affinity ; to arrest and attach those who go about by night and act in breach of the peace, and to present the same before the Warden or Mayor. Towards their sustenance hostelers and housekeepers in the ward were to make contribution. Watchmen who failed in their duty, or showed favour unto any one who for his offence ought to have been attached and arrested, might be punished by imprisonment at the discretion of the Warden and Aldermen. Arms required for keeping watch[3] were provided by

---

[1] Sometimes minstrels or musicians paraded the streets and sounded the watch.

[2] *Dogberry :* "This is the end of the charge :—you, constable, are to present the Prince's own person : if you meet the Prince in the night you may stay him." *Verges :* "Nay, by'r Lady, that I think a' cannot." *Dogberry :* " Five shillings to one on't, with any man that knows the statues, he may stay him."—Much Ado Abont Nothing, Act 3, Scene 3.

[3] In later times bills were used. So *Dogberry :* "Why, you speak like an ancient and most quiet watchman ; for I cannot see how sleeping should offend : Only have a care that your bills be not stolen."

the wards. If any felon took sanctuary in a church, householders in the ward were required to keep watch upon
him, until he had abjured the realm.[1] If any such misdoer
escaped, those persons who ought to have kept watch were
held answerable to the King in the sum of one hundred
shillings.[2]

In 1312 (6th Edward II.), we find substituted service
allowed. An inquisition was ordered to assess all persons
possessing " in goods and merchandizes to the value of fifty
shillings and more." Each of those persons was to find, at
his own expense, " one strong man, well and fittingly armed,
that so at every gate there may be in the day-time sixteen,
or at least twelve, strong men and well armed to keep ward;
and twelve or eight by night." They were to see that no
men-at-arms entered the city, mounted on great horses
(chargers), and with arms, unless they brought a certain
warranty, or royal message. To each gate there was assigned
one serjeant, a discreet man, whose quaint instructions from
Mayor, Aldermen and Commonalty were these :—

" We do command you, on the King's behalf, strictly
enjoining you, on peril of forfeiting as much as you may
forfeit, that you, together with two men of the watch, well
and fittingly armed, be at all hours of the day ready at the
gate, within or without, down below, to make answer to such
persons as shall come on great horses, or with arms, to enter
the city ; and that you set a guard over above the gate, upon
the leads thereof, to look out afar, that so you may be the
better warned when any men-at-arms approach the gate.
And if any do approach in manner aforesaid, then let the
chain be drawn up without, and answer be given in this
wise :—' Lordings, the King has given charge to us that no
person shall enter his city by force of arms, if he have not
special warranty from him. Wherefore, sirs, we pray you
that you will not take this amiss; but as for you who are
upon palfreys, and you who come without bringing great
horses or arms, you may enter, as being peaceful folk.' And
if they will not thereupon turn about, then let the portcullis

---

[1] Making oath before the coroner   [2] Articles of 1285.
to quit it.

be quickly lifted by those of your people above; that so those other persons may in no way enter."[1]

Guard of gates strengthened in perilous times.

This is a picturesque mediæval scene. Afterwards, says the City chronicle,[2] "it befel that the Earls of Lancaster, Hereford, Warwick, and Arundel, against whom the King and his people, for certain reasons, had conceived no slight indignation, drew nigh to the city, with a great multitude of barons, knights, and others, both horse and foot, and arrived at Ware." Strict injunctions were then given to the Mayor, Aldermen, and Commonalty, by Edward II. and his Council, that they must keep more diligent and stronger ward at the city gates. During this time of peril, therefore, it was agreed that "at every gate there were to be sixteen men, strong and befittingly armed, those who watch by day coming early, at sunrise; those who watch by night coming at sunset."

Precautions during revels and jousts;

It was not only in time of peril that extraordinary precautions were taken. Feasting and revelry led to brawls, and in 1390 each Alderman was charged "for safe keeping and maintenance of the King's peace, and for saving the honour of this city," to provide "sufficient watch" in his ward, "by persons able for defence, well arrayed, every night while the revels and jousts, now approaching, shall be continued; and this in such manner that by your default no danger or disgrace shall befall the city."[3] Again, in 1405,[4] each Alderman is enjoined to keep in his ward "good and sufficient watch of folks, properly armed and arrayed, during this solemn feast of Christmas, passing through all the streets and lanes according to wont." No persons were to go about "with visors or false faces, on the pain that awaits the same;" and on every night, and during the feast, outside

and at Christmas-tide.

[1] Riley's Memorials of London Life, 102-3.

[2] A translation from the City Letter Book of the year 1312. The original is in Norman-French, continued in Latin.

[3] Mem. of London Life, 522; City Letter Book, 14 Rich. II. These jousts are described by Froissart.

[4] Ib. 561; 7 Hen. IV.

every house in the high streets and lanes, a lantern was to be hung, "with a lighted candle therein, the same to burn so long as it may last."[1]

A ceremony to which great importance was attached was the setting of the watch on the eves of the nativity of St. John, June 24, and of St. Peter and St. Paul, June 29. At these periods, owing to the heat and drought, fires were frequent, and a custom grew of marshalling the watch with peculiar care and formality. In 1378, each Alderman was warned, for the city's honour, to attend on these evenings, with the good men of his ward, "arrayed in red and white, parti-coloured over your armour." Thus equipped, the Aldermen with their followers met in Smithfield, and thence passed through the city in assigned order; first, men of certain wards lighting the way with cressets, or grated fire-pans on poles; others bearing white lances, powdered with red stars; and men of other wards with lances all red, white lances "environed, that is to say, wreathed, with red," black lances, powdered with white stars, and lances all white. These must have been imposing spectacles,[2] but sometimes they had another design, as when, in the year 1386, the Aldermen were ordered to come, on the same eves, "arrayed in red, and your household and other good people, such as shall seem to you to desire the city's honour and profit, arrayed in white with a band of red, at nine of the clock at the latest, in St. Paul's churchyard, with two cressets at least, or more if you may; to go with us through the city in manner as was done last year, or in better manner if you may; and this the more especially, because of the wars at present existing, and for view and report of strangers."[3]

In 1591, by direction of the Lords of the Council, watch-

Marginal notes:

Setting the watch.

Watch set in numbers and array, "for view and report of strangers."

Seizure of flesh by

---

[1] City Letter Book, 1 Rich. II.; Mem. 419-20.

[2] Rembrandt's picture commonly known as "The Night Watch" suggests a similar scene. Henry VIII. forbade these spectacles on the ground of their cost.

[3] City Letter Book, 9 Rich. II.; Memorials, 488. The original is in Norman-French.

watch during
Lent, 1591.

Complaint of
inefficient
watch, 1661.

men were appointed, during Lent, to seize all flesh brought
in for the supply of persons not licensed to eat it at this
season.   There is a letter from Mr. Secretary Nicholas to the
Lord Mayor, in 1661, complaining that the number of men
set in the night watches was too small, and the men themselves too feeble, to prevent disorder, and also that they
quitted their watch before daybreak,[1] leaving thieves to their
villainies without control.   There was a direction upon this
letter, that the number of watchmen should be increased, and
only fit and able men employed.[2]   It is clear that at this
period the unpaid watch was an institution in its decline, and
Shakespeare no doubt faithfully depicts its inefficiency as well
as its humours.

Statute of
Winchester,
A. D. 1285, as
to watch in
towns.

In the year 1285, the Statute of Winchester[3] ordained,
"for the more surety of the country," that "in great towns,
being walled," the gates should be closed from sunset until
sunrise, and in every city, six men be kept at every gate; in
every borough twelve men; in every town, six or four, according to the number of inhabitants, "watching the town
continually all night."   If any stranger passed, he was to be
arrested till morning, when, if no cause of suspicion arose,
he might go quit: otherwise he was to be delivered to the
sheriff.   If strangers would not obey the arrest, hue and cry
must be raised upon them, and such as kept the watch were
to "follow them with all the town, and from town to town,
until they be taken."

Paid watch-
men in Lon-
don, A.D. 1737.

This general liability of watch and ward remained, as we
have seen, during the middle ages.   In the eighteenth century it was, in some cases, replaced by a paid watch, generally
very inefficient.   The first Act by which this liability was
removed was one passed in 1737, for better night-watching
in London.   This statute[4] recited the importance of a well-

---

[1] *Watchman :* "Well, masters, we
hear our charge ; let us go sit here
upon the church-bench till two, and
then all to bed." — "Much Ado

About Nothing," Act 3, Scene 3.
[2] Remembrancia, 395, 650.
[3] 13 Edw. I. c. 4.
[4] 10 Geo. II. c. 22.

ordered and regulated night-watch, for which no laws then in force adequately provided. The Corporation of London were therefore authorised to appoint watchmen and "bedels." In each ward the Alderman was to choose "honest and able-bodied men" for this work, and set their bounds and duties. A constable in every precinct was to supervise the watchmen, whose business it was "to apprehend all night-walkers, male-factors, rogues, vagabonds, and all disorderly persons, whom they shall find disturbing the public peace, or shall have just cause to suspect of any evil designs." Rates were to be assessed on houses for payment of expenses, and no persons so rated were liable to watch and ward under the Statute of Winchester, or any amending Acts.

This statute was followed by others modelled upon its provisions in whole or in part, and applying to provincial towns. In 1748, for example, an Act[1] "for keeping and maintaining a nightly watch" at Liverpool, among other objects, exempted persons paying rates for this purpose from any liability under the Statute of Winchester, or any subsequent statute relating thereto, "except in cases of public calamities or disturbances." But the sub-bailiffs and assistant constables were still bound to attend by turns every night, to keep watch and ward within the town, and "use their best endeavours to prevent, as well all mischiefs happening by fire, as all murders, bur-glaries, and other outrageous disorders." They were, there-fore, to "arrest and apprehend all night-walkers, malefactors, and suspected persons who shall be found wandering and misbehaving themselves." To these sub-bailiffs or assistant constables was delivered a transcript of all orders regulat-ing the watch, and at convenient times in every night they were to go about their respective wards or stations, and take notice whether the new staff of watchmen, sixty in number, were performing their duties.[2] There seem to have

Watch and ward abolished at Liverpool, A.D. 1748.

---

[1] 21 Geo. II. c. 24 (see *post*, 463).

[2] As an example of the jealous care taken to prevent an increase of poor-rates, this Act of 1748 provides

been no paid watchmen at night in Liverpool before their appointment under this Act.[1]

Street cleansing and disposal of refuse.

Besides the liability of householders to cleanse the footway in front of their houses, we have seen that a staff of public scavengers was maintained in each ward in London,[2] and probably in other towns. Refuse was removed from the city by these street-sweepers or "rakyers" in carts and horses provided for that purpose,[3] and was probably used as manure in the outskirts. Another mode of disposing of refuse was by placing it on board "dung-boats," which cast it into the tidal water lower down the river. It was ordered, in 1375, "that no one shall, by night or by day, privily or openly, throw rubbish, dung, or any manner of filth or other thing into the water of Thames,[4] or into the fosses of the city, or any other place. . . But let every one keep the streets clean according to this ordinance. And let no one cause any water or other thing to be thrown from the windows, by night or by day, within the franchise of the city; but let them bring the same down to the ground below and put it into the kennel there; on pain of imprisonment and of paying two shillings every time."[5] This order seems to conflict with one of the year 1357—that any person before whose door filth or nuisances were found should pay a fine of two shillings.[6]

Bathing near the Tower forbidden.

Notwithstanding the efforts of the Corporation, both streets and river-banks must have been in a state which left much

that no persons employed as watchmen shall gain a settlement thereby, nor is the payment of rates under the Act to confer a like privilege.

[1] See now 3 & 4 Will. IV. c. 90, 2 & 3 Vict. c. 93, 3 & 4 Vict. c. 88, and numerous amending Acts, which established a uniform police force in boroughs and counties.

[2] *Ante,* p. 234.

[3] "Ordered, that no man belonging to the sheriffs' serjeants, assigned to take cartage, shall take any one of the carts or horses that are provided for carrying dung and filth out of the City, on pain of imprisonment and of losing his office." (Letter Book of Corporation, A.D. 1357; Mem. 299.)

[4] *Ante,* p. 46.

[5] Letter Book of Corporation, 49 Edw. III.; Mem. 389.

[6] Letter Book, 31 Edw. III.; Mem. 299.

to be desired. A fierce proclamation by Edward III., in 1350, addressed to the sheriffs, commands them immediately to make known that no person must " dare or presume to bathe in the fosses of our Tower of London," or in the Thames opposite to the Tower, " on pain of forfeiture of life and limb."[1] Again, in 1357, his Majesty thus admonishes the Mayor and Sheriffs :—

Edward III.
enjoins
greater clean-
liness,
A.D. 1357.

" Considering how that the streets and lanes, and other places in our City of London, and the suburbs thereof, in the times of our forefathers and our own, were wont to be cleansed from dung, lay-stalls and other filth, and were wont heretofore to be protected from the corruption arising there-from, from which no little favour did accrue unto the city and those dwelling therein : And whereas now, when passing along the water of Thames, we have beheld dung, and lay-stalls and other filth accumulated in divers places in the city upon the river-bank, and have also perceived the fumes and other abominable stenches arising therefrom, from the corruption of which, if tolerated, great peril as well to persons dwelling within the city as to nobles and others passing along the river will, it is feared, ensue unless indeed some fitting remedy be provided : Therefore we, wishing to take due precaution against such perils, and to preserve the honour and decency of the city, in so far as we may, do command you that you cause as well the banks of the river as the streets and lanes of the city and suburbs thereof, to be cleansed of filth without delay, and the same when cleansed so to be kept ; and in the city and suburbs public proclamation to be made, and it on our behalf strictly to be forbidden, that any one shall, on pain of heavy for-feiture unto us, place or cause to be placed dung or other filth to be accumulated in the same. And if any persons, after proclamation and prohibition so made, you shall find doing to the contrary hereof, then you are to cause them to be so chastised and punished, that such penalty and chastise-ment may cause fear and dread unto others of perpetrating the like. And this, as you would preserve yourselves safe and would avoid our heavy indignation, you are in no wise to omit."[2]

[1] Letter Book, 24 Edw. III.; Mem. 260.

[2] The original, in Latin, is in the Civic Records, 31 Edw. III.; Mem. 295.

Complaints of borough franchises, A.D. 1330.

A petition in Parliament in 1330 shows that sometimes the franchises granted to boroughs were deemed a public injury. In that year the Commons complained that many towns had received from the King and his ancestors grants which were injurious to the Crown, contrary to the general law (par qey la ley ne peut estre servie), and hurtful to the people. In answer to this complaint, those who were aggrieved were told to seek their remedy at law, and if they could obtain no remedy, the King would provide one.[1]

Defence of Southampton a local burden, A.D. 1376.

On the other hand, we find certain towns petitioning for a removal of exceptional burdens. In the Parliament of 1376, Southampton complained to Edward III. of heavy charges for fortifications, which were driving away the inhabitants. These, therefore, sought relief from the payment of two years' farm-rent then due, and further asked that he would command soldiers to defend their town, as they were unable to do so against the enemy then expected.[2]

Borough boundaries, A.D. 1376.

At this period, as might be expected, the separate jurisdictions retained within many boroughs often led to dispute, and there is a petition, in the year 1376, from inhabitants of cities and boroughs, that hamlets lying within their walls, but exempt from municipal authority, shall contribute to all local charges, inasmuch as from their situation they necessarily share the advantage of such charges. Another prayer is, that Mayors and bailiffs may be authorized to arrest offenders within these separate jurisdictions, the existence of which was a source, no doubt, of much inconvenience, and encouragement to offenders.[3]

Villeins freed by residence in municipal boroughs.

Much natural sympathy was felt by burghers for villeins who sought refuge among them, hoping to become free men by immunity within a walled town for a year and a day.[4] During this period villeins might be pursued and reclaimed by their feudal lords, acting through their reeves or attorneys; and there were prohibitions, enforced by fines, against the

---

[1] 2 Rot. Parl. 37; 4 Edw. III.
[2] 2 Rot. Parl. 346; 50 Edw. III.
[3] 2 Rot. Parl. 351.
[4] *Ante*, p. 201 (n.).

harbouring of fugitives.   London was naturally a place of
resort for these poor people, for there they were most likely
to escape from recognition during the prescribed period.

A singular absence of Saxon Christian names in London
after the beginning of the thirteenth century has been accounted for by these attempts of native bondmen and villeins
to avoid identification, so that they might not be carried
back to servitude.[1]   There is a pathetic record, in 1288, of a
claim preferred before one of the city courts, by attorneys of
the Earl of Cornwall, to several men and children "as being
bondmen born (*natiri*), of whom the claimants were seised
until one month before the day of St. Michael," when "they
ran away from their lands."[2]   Of this process the end is not
recorded.

Good-will in contributing to the liberty of these fugitives
was clearly not wanting among townspeople.   In a petition
to Parliament A.D. 1391, various feudal lords complain that
if they or their officers enter a franchised city or borough in
order to seize their villeins according to law and custom, the
burghers prevent such seizure by force (si les ditz seigneurs,
ou ascun de lour ministres, viegnent dedeinz les ditz citees
et burghs issint enfranchises, pur seiser ou prendre les ditz
villeins pur eux justicer selonc la ley et custume de la terre,
les gentz des citees et burghs ne les voillent suffrer, einz les
distourbont forciblement).   Moreover, if a villein be taken
by his lord, the citizens or burghers set up their franchise,
and will not allow him to be removed, to the lord's serious
damage.   These petitioners therefore pray his Majesty to
give directions in Parliament that existing feudal rights
over the persons of fugitive villeins may be peacefully exercised in all cities and boroughs, notwithstanding any franchises, customs, and usages to the contrary.[3]   But it did not
answer the King's purpose at this period to offend the Com-

Marginal notes:

Feudal claim to villeins in London, A.D. 1288.

Feudal rights of villeinage hindered by burghers.

[1] Riley's "Memorials of London Life," Int. 39.

[2] Ib. 23; Letter Books of Corporation, 16 Edw. I.

[3] 3 Rot. Parl. 296; 15 Richard II.

mons; and Richard II. negatived this petition, or Bill, in the usual form—"Le roy s'advisera." Cities and boroughs were, therefore, valuable places of refuge, and during the middle ages must have yielded some glimmer of hope to wretched serfs, who were otherwise bound to the soil with little prospect of relief.[1] This right of a fugitive serf to freedom if he had been unreclaimed for a year and a day within the walls of a free borough was a Saxon custom, and, in the ancient work "De Antiquis Legibus," among the records of the City of London, is mentioned as existing long before the Conquest.

---

[1] Men of Kent were exempt from villeinage, "a most glorious and valuable birthright" at a period when so many Englishmen were in a state of hereditary bondage. (Robinson on Gavelkind, 351, quoting 30 Edw. I.; Fitzh. Villenage, 46.) In a writ of Niefe, or neife (from *nativa*, as being born on the estate), whereby a lord claimed his bondwoman, the defendant pleaded that she was free, and the jury found that her father was born in Kent, whereupon, without further inquiry, the Court gave judgment that she was free, for that there were no born villeins in Kent. Again, in the Year-books (7 Hen. VI. 33), it is said that, according to the custom of Kent, every one born within the county shall be free, although his father was a villein, and Martin, J., answers that this is by Parliament, and a statute made for the purpose.

CHAPTER XII.

LOCAL AUTHORITIES (CONTINUED) :—PAVAGE AND IMPROVE-
MENT ACTS, A.D. 1301—1662: CALAIS: LONDON AND
WESTMINSTER IMPROVEMENT ACT, 1662: REBUILDING
DECAYED TOWNS, A.D. 1540: TWO PENNIES SCOTS ACTS:
EARLY SANITARY LEGISLATION: COMMISSIONS OF SEWERS:
SANITARY STATE OF TOWNS, 1800-47: PARLIAMENTARY
COMMITTEES AND ROYAL COMMISSIONS: LOCAL RATING,
1845: CHARGE FOR PERMANENT WORKS: SANITARY AD-
MINISTRATION IN THE METROPOLIS, 1845-7.

IN London, as we have seen, householders in the time of
Edward I. were required to pave footways in front of their
houses, while roadways were made and repaired by the
municipality out of a pavage toll levied upon horses and
vehicles at the city barriers.[1] Some early statutes, however,
impose upon householders the duty of paving both street and
footway; while in other cases municipalities are charged to
mend the main thoroughfares.

Of pavage, the earliest statutory mention occurs in the
year 1301, when burgesses of Huntingdon obtained permission from Edward I. to levy this toll for five years. In 1306
they asked that it should be continued for another three
years, as their city could not otherwise be completely paved
(ad plenum pavata). This request was also granted.[2] In 1304,
Guy, Earl of Warwick, petitioned for leave to levy duties for
repairing walls and roads (muragium et pavagium) in the
city of Warwick for as long a period as the King in Parliament was pleased to grant. Edward I. assented to this
petition or bill, and fixed the term at seven years.[3]

Pavage in towns, A.D. 1301 et seq.

1 *Ante*, pp. 234-5.
2 1 Rot. Parl. 193; 35 Edw. I.
3 Ib. 163; 33 Edw. I.

Road between
Temple Bar
and West-
minster,
A.D. 1314.

A petition presented in Parliament in 1314 complained of defective pavement in the roadway between Temple Bar and Westminster Palace (entre la barre du Novel Temple de Londres tant qu'a la porte du palais de notre Seigneur le Roi a Westminster). This pavement was in such bad condition that both rich and poor, on horse or on foot, suffered great inconvenience in passing to and fro, and in bad weather their business was often hindered by holes or pits in the roadway (sont sovent en mauveis temps desturbez de lor busoignes suivre por profoundesce del dit chemin). The King and his Council were prayed to order, for the common good, that the pavement should be properly repaired. Two commissioners were accordingly appointed to inspect this roadway, with power to require that all persons owning tenements or rents between the points mentioned should pave in front of their respective premises (ad distringendum omnes illos qui tenementa seu redditus habent inter Barram predictam et predictum Palatium, ad paviandum quilibet videlicet coram tenemento suo, pro rata porcionis cujuslibet tenementi et redditus predictorum). Letters were also sent to the mayor and aldermen of London, the sheriffs of Middlesex, and bailiffs of Westminster, desiring them to assist the commissioners in carrying out these instructions.[1]

Cambridge
University
complain of
foul ways,
A.D. 1320-30.

Complaint was made in Parliament by the University of Cambridge in 1320 that the burgesses did not cleanse their town or pave in front of their dwellings, and that money derived from pavage was applied to other uses.[2] Ineffectual remedy was provided on this occasion, for in 1330 we find the chancellor and masters of the University laying before Parliament three serious grievances : first, that wine was sold dearer in Cambridge than in London or Oxford ; secondly, that the town was still in a most filthy state and that the mayor and council could not be constrained to cleanse it ; next, that streets were ill-kept and broken up, although

---

[1] 1 Rot. Parl. 302 ; 8 Edw. II.   [2] Ib. 381 ; 14 Edw. II.

by royal grant the University had been promised that they should always be properly paved. The petitioners, therefore, begged that the mayor and bailiffs should be made to require each tenant to level and repair the pavement in front of his house and maintain it in good order thereafter. As to the two first grievances, Edward III. answered that nothing could be done at present (nihil potest fieri ad presens), but a writ was directed to issue with a view to carry out the terms of the University charter as to local paving.[1]

In the fifteenth century we come to more elaborate paving **Northampton Paving Act, A.D. 1430-1.** Acts than have hitherto been recorded, such as that proposed for Northampton in 1430-1.[2] The mayor and commonalty of that town petitioned the Commons (les tresages communes) to pray his Majesty to ordain and grant, with their assent, and that of the Lords Spiritual and Temporal, as follows:— That the mayor and commonalty of Northampton and their successors for ever may compel every person, whatever his condition, seised of any house or tenement abutting upon any highway or street in that town, to pave anew, and thereafter to repair when necessary, from the front of such house or tenement into the middle of the channel[3] of the road or street and for the full width of the tenement. (Purra loialment compeller et constreiner chescun persone, de quel astate ou condition q'il soit, seisi d'ascuny mees[4] ou tenement en son demesne come de fraunk tenement, buttant sur ascun hault chemyn, ou ru du dit ville, pur novelment paver, et apres tout temps bussonable repaveler; c'est assavoir, du le frount de tiel mees ou tenement, jusqes al my del chanell du tiel chemyn ou rue, et en laydur de l'une corner du tiel mees ou tenement, jusqes a l'autre corner du mesme le mees.) Upon default there was to be a view and inquest by good and loyal townsmen, and offenders were to be summoned to pave or

[1] 2 Rot Parl. 48; 4 Edw. III.

[2] 4 Rot. Parl. 373; 9 Hen. VI.

[3] The channel, or gutter, as in old French towns, then usually ran down the middle of the street.

[4] Mees, otherwise mese, or mease (maison), has its modern equivalent in messuage, a house and appurtenances.

repair. If any work so ordered were not done within three months after summons, the mayor might distrain for the cost, or, upon notice to any tenant, might receive his rent and therewith execute the work.

Restrictions introduced in Royal assent, Henry VI.

Such was the form of Bill presented. It would have applied to every street in Northampton, but after consideration in Parliament its operation was restricted to certain specified thoroughfares. These conditions were imported into the Royal assent:—"Soit fait come il est desire as to the following highways : from North Gate to St. Thomas's Bridge, and from West Gate to East Gate; and also as to the following streets : Berward Street, St. Gelys Street, Swynwil Street, Kingwel Street, St. Mary Street, St. Martin Street, the Market Place." As the Market Place was doubtless an open space, no owner there was compelled to pave or repair beyond a distance of thirty feet in front of his house or tenement; the remaining space was to be kept in order at the common cost.[1] It is clear that these important restrictions, which form part of the Act, must have been the result of evidence brought from Northampton, or of local knowledge obtained in some other way; but in this and similar instances there is no record of any investigation by committees, or local inquiry.[2]

Bill for paving Gloucester rejected, A.D. 1455.

Later in the same reign an unsuccessful application for a similar Act was made by the bailiffs and commonalty of Gloucester.[3] In their petition, which is in English, the streets of Gloucester are represented as " greatly broken, feebly paved, and full perilous for the King's liege people to ride and to go upon, insomuch that divers of the King's people have been greatly hurt oftentimes, and in great peril of their lives, as well men of great worship as other mean persons." Moreover, the bailiffs and commonalty " be in great poverty, by reason of costs and charges which they have borne and yet do daily for the town, and have no lands,

[1] 4 Rot. Parl. 374.

[2] There would probably be a writ

ad quod damnum (see *post*, p. 281–2, n.).

[3] 5 Rot. Parl. 338 ; 33 Hen. VI.

tenements, rents, nor other yearly returns incoming, where-
out they may make and maintain their pavement." They
therefore ask for power to warn by proclamation every person within the town and suburbs seised of any burgage,
mees,[1] land or tenement, to make sufficient pavement in front
of it, extending into the middle of the street. Upon default
within a year after proclamation so made, the bailiffs ask
that they may do this work at the cost of owners, levying a
distress and refunding any surplus. Persons with rent-charges
are to contribute in proportion to the yearly value of such
charges. Some objection must have been raised to the grant
of these general powers, for the answer is, "Le roy s'advisera." Parliament or the King's advisers appear to have
been of opinion at this period that it was only necessary to
pave a few of the most frequented streets in any town.

Fifteen years afterwards, a Bill with an almost identical
preamble, promoted by the bailiffs and stewards of Gloucester, met with greater favour.[2] It was, however, limited
to the pavement of four main thoroughfares, owners in
which were, upon reasonable warning, to pave in front
of their premises as far as the middle of the street. All
previous paving Bills or Acts had imposed this burden
upon owners, limiting distress to the property liable. This
Gloucester Act went a step further. It authorized the
local authorities to serve notices upon either landlords or
tenants, and to levy upon the goods and chattels of tenants
if their landlords were in default. There was a proviso
that "if any other person's goods than his that ought to
make such pavement, or to contribute to the same, be distrained," the tenant might keep back his rent till he was
reimbursed, or might bring his action for debt before the
bailiffs of Gloucester, who were to have jurisdiction in any
such action "as they have in any action of debt by their old
authority and franchise."

A similar Act, passed in 1477, for paving the principal

Gloucester Paving Act, A.D. 1472-3. Exclusive liability of owners.

On default, distraint upon tenants, with power to them to retain amount out of rent.

Canterbury Paving Act, A.D. 1477.

[1] *Ante*, p. 257, note.   [2] 6 Rot. Parl. p. 49; 12 & 13 Edw. IV.

streets of Canterbury, deserves notice if only for its quaint recitals in praise of that city.[1] "Forasmuch," the mayor and commonalty set forth, as Canterbury "is one of the eldest cities of this realm, and therein is the principal see of the spiritual estate of the same realm, which city is also most in sight of all strangers from parts beyond the sea resorting into this realm and departing out of the same; and because of the glorious saints that there lie shrined, is greatly named through Christendom, unto which city is also great repair of much people, as well of estates as others, in way of pilgrimage to visit the said saints. And it is so that the city is oftentimes full foul, noyous (noxious) and uneasy, as well to all its inhabitants as to all other persons resorting thereunto, whereof oftentimes is spoken much disworship in divers places, as well beyond the sea as on this side the sea, which cannot be remedied in any wise but if the city be paved; whereunto most part of the inhabitants having burgages, houses, or tenements be right well-willed and agreeable, so that there might authority be had to compel other such persons as have burgages, houses, lands or tenements therein, to be contributory to do the same."

Restriction to leading thoroughfares.

There is then an elaborate description of leading thoroughfares to which the Act shall apply, " into which streets and places commonly is more resort, as well of strangers as of others, than to any other street or place within the city." Reasonable notice of necessary pavements and repairs is to be given to owners liable. If they make default, the mayor, sheriff, and city chamberlains may levy upon the goods and chattels of occupiers, who may deduct from their rent the amount so levied, or recover it by action of debt,

"Waging their law," by defendants sued for debt.

the defendants in which are not to be " admitted in any wise to wage their law."[2] This petition or Bill concludes,

---

[1] 6 Rot. Parl. 177–9; 17 Edw. IV.

[2] *Vadiatio legis*, so called because in an action for debt, upon the defendant's plea of *nil debet*, declaring also his readiness " to wage his law," he was bound in sureties to do so on a day fixed by the judges, when the defendant attended with eleven neighbours (*compurgatores*), and repeated the following formula:— "Hear this, ye justices, that I, A. B., do not owe to C. D. the sum of, &c.,

" And they shall pray to God for you !" It received statutory effect without qualification.

In the same Session similar Acts were passed, upon petitions similarly worded, for paving the towns of Taunton,[1] Cirencester, and Southampton.[2] In all these cases, however, taking warning by the precedent of Gloucester, power was only asked to pave the principal streets, and not the whole town, so that the recognized policy of Parliament was to keep remote streets unpaved, rather than throw a burden upon owners of poor property, in front of which there was, perhaps, little traffic. In the Taunton statute is a proviso, which appears by no means justified, " that this Act extend not, nor be prejudicial unto William, Bishop[3] of Winchester, nor unto his successors, of nor for any burgages, messuages or tenements, in the said town of Taunton pertaining to his bishopric."

There is an interesting variation in the Cirencester petition, which is from " inhabitants and residents " who are " not corporate, nor can by the common law of this kingdom be compelled to make or repair the pavement." They, therefore, ask that all owners of messuages, shops, or tenements, resident in the town, shall meet early on Michaelmas day, and choose two conservators of pavement, who shall have like powers to those given to local authorities in other Paving Acts. In all these instances, again, pavage is imposed on owners, not on occupiers, though, to facilitate collection, it is, in some cases, charged primarily on the latter.

---

nor any penny thereof, in manner and form as the said C. D. hath declared against me." Then his compurgators swore that they believed he was speaking the truth, and the plaintiff was barred for ever. Such a plea was only allowed upon a simple contract debt, not vouched by deed or record. The reason for it was, that a defendant might have paid his debt privately, or before witnesses who were dead, and therefore the law would rather accept his oath than suffer him to be charged upon the plaintiff's bare allegation. This plea was last used in 1824. (2 B. & C. 538.) It was abolished by 3 & 4 Will. IV. c. 42, s. 13.

[1] 6 Rot. Parl. 179 ; 17 Edw. IV., A.D. 1477.

[2] Ib. 180.

[3] In the original, " Busshopp."

Bristol
Paving Act,
A.D. 1487.

A more recent Paving Act, passed in 1487 for the benefit of Bristol,[1] contains some changes deserving notice. According to the preamble, Bristol was then "an ancient merchant town and port, reputed and taken in great fame and worship amongst other honorable cities and towns within this realm, to which town and port hath ever been, and daily is, great resort and coming, as well of merchants, strangers and others, from divers and many parts beyond the sea, as of men of worship and merchants from all parts of this realm of England. And it is so that the paving in the streets and suburbs is much decayed, broken, and hollowed and pitted, by water falling out of gutters, by riding and carriage, to great hurt and disease of the King's liege people, and other strangers going, riding or carrying therein, and also great uncleanness of the same. Wherefore, as the mayor, bailiffs, sheriffs and commonalty have no authority, custom or laws to compel the inhabitants, or persons having any messuage, tenement, ground or rent within the town or suburbs, to make or repair pavement, or contribute towards making such pavement," the petitioners pray for like powers to those given in previous statutes. They are allowed these powers, and in case any messuages are ruinous and decayed, and there are no occupiers upon whom distraint can be made, may also make the necessary pavement, and enter into possession, receiving rents and profits until the cost is defrayed. This Paving Act is not limited to any specified streets. On the other hand, it is only to be in force for seven years.

Calais is the subject of several statutes passed at Westminster for its better government, after its capture by Edward III. in 1347.[2]

Calais Improvement
Act, A.D. 1376.

In the year 1376, the burgesses petition his Majesty in

---

[1] Called Bristowe. 6 Rot. Parl. 390-1; 3 Hen. VII.

[2] Great efforts were made to Anglicise the town by a partial removal of the French population, and by gifts of their land and houses to English settlers, who received a three years' exemption from tolls.

Parliament for various powers.[1] They in fact promote what would now be called a general Improvement Bill, which recites that means are necessary to restore prosperity to their town and district, much impoverished by war. First they ask his Majesty to re-grant them the staple of wool, and of other smaller merchandize coming from England, Ireland, and Wales. This monopoly is defended because not only it will bring business, but will also make the town safer from assault, inasmuch as when the whole staple was at Calais, and the garrison issued forth, upon any adventure, the mayor kept watch in the town, the merchants and their followers aiding him with their swords, bills, and bows, and doing this service without pay. (Qar quant l'entiere estaple fuist a Calais, et le capitayn fist aucun chivalchie, le meir fist gaite deinz la ville ove e gleyves et ove e archiers des marchauntz et lour servantz, qui ne pristrent nulles gages du Roy.) *Better defence of town.*

Each item, or clause, of this Bill receives a separate answer from the King. The first request is conceded. Calais, excluding all other parts beyond the sea, is fixed for the staple of wool, skins or leather, and woolfels, and also for lead, tin, worsted, cheese, butter, feathers, garlic, saltpetre, and onions (Ceo lour soit grauntez ; c'est assavoir que le dit estaple y soit tenuz, et null part aillours es parties de outre myer, si bien des leynes, quirs, et pealx lanutz, come de plumbe, esteym,[2] draps appelles worstedes, furmage, bure, plume, gaul, selperie et suire). *Staple of wool, &c.*

Under an old charter received from Mahaut, Count d'Artois, certain franchises and privileges were conferred upon the burgesses of Calais. They now pray that these privileges may be confirmed, except that the law relating to lands and tenements may follow the common law of England, and saving also any franchises granted to merchants of *Ancient franchises withheld.*

[1] 2 Rot. Parl. 358-9; 50 Edw. III.
[2] Kelham's Norman dictionary gives the following variants:—Esteyme, estainte, estagne, estank, estonbz, esteigne.

the staple.   On this point the petitioners are not gratified:
"le roy s' advisera."   They next ask that, in place of the
bailiff and other civic officers appointed under their charter,
they may have a mayor and twelve aldermen, elected as in
the city of London, the mayor and each alderman maintaining six men to safeguard the city.   This clause receives
Election of mayor and aldermen.   a lengthened answer.   His Majesty allows the burgesses
a free election of mayor and aldermen, who must, however,
be Englishmen.   They are required to defray all manner
of charges within the city, such as paving, repairs of common gutters and public fountains, and cleansing (come de
reparation du pavment, et des communes gutteres et fon-
taignes, et nettement de la ville; et touz autres charges a
faires en y celle).

Local rates, &c. allowed in aid of paving and cleansing.   In aid of these charges, the municipality are allowed an
assize on bread, wine, and ale.   They are also to receive
pickage;[1] stallage from butchers, drapers and mercers, and
other market tolls; with any profits, such as fees and fines,
arising in the court held by the mayor and aldermen.   The
latter are relieved from all duties of keeping watch within
the city, except those which they are bound to discharge as
householders; and the mayor is allowed to hold Court with
a limited jurisdiction.   (Et y ait le mair poair de cognoistre
en tous quereles, et de faire justice a chescun qui se y vorra
plaindre de choses qui a luy appartiennent.)

Liberty to devise lands, as in London.   Another request is that burgesses may devise their lands
and tenements within the city to English people as freely as
is done in the City of London.   This request is at once
granted.   (Il plest bien au Roi que ceo lour soit grantee.)
Burghers to import goods from England duty free.   Then the burgesses ask leave, for themselves and their servants, to buy freely, throughout England, all manner of mer-
chandise and provisions, for consumption in Calais, exempt

---

[1] Pickage (*picagium*, Low Lat.) from *piquer*, i.e. *effodere*, was money paid to a lord of the manor for breaking ground to set up booths, stalls, or stands at fairs.

from toll and customs, except articles included in the staple. This privilege, they say, was granted by English sovereigns to the good people of Calais, even when it belonged to France, in the time of King Richard, King John, and King Henry of England. (Laquele fraunchise fuist grante as bonz gentz de la dite ville qant ele estoit Franceoys, el temps del roy Richard, le roy John, et le roy Henry, jadis roys d'Engleterre.) A favourable answer is also given to this prayer, saving always the customs and duties on wool and other staple merchandise.

Common pasture is then requested by the burgesses for their cattle on downs between Calais and Wale on one side, and Calais and Sandegate on the other; and his Majesty replies that he will inform himself what damage may come to him and others if this concession be made. Another petition is that, as many houses within the city have come into the King's hands, they may not be given by him, either in fee, for life, or otherwise, freed from their liability to rates for watching; otherwise charges of this kind borne by citizens will be much increased, and the safety of Calais endangered. This request is readily granted. (Le roy le voet bien.) *Common pasture.* *Houses granted by King to bear their quota of watch-rate.*

A further clause in the Bill proposes that every burgess be admitted to his rights within a year and a day after taking the oaths, and that for greater safety of the city, no stranger be admitted by any means. To this request the King assents, saving his right, if he pleases, to except a stranger-merchant from the rule. Next, the King is prayed to grant a commission to the governor and treasurer of Calais enabling them to let to Englishmen, at small rentals, lands, tenements, and vacant grounds belonging to the King within the walls. In this way, it is hoped, many houses now destroyed may be rebuilt and inhabited, to the city's manifest benefit. His majesty is pleased to grant this prayer. (Il pleist au roy qu'ainsi soit fait.) *Admission of burgesses.* *Power to let vacant land for building.*

A request, which one might have supposed would be as readily granted, is put off in wonted form, " Le roy ent *Royal protections.*

s 2

se advisera." It is that no Royal protection shall thenceforth be given which will hinder creditors from enforcing payments due from merchant to merchant or soldier to townsman, for goods bought. It is clear that these protections were sometimes used for purposes which were unjust, if not fraudulent; and the rejection of this prayer looks as though English monarchs were aware of the abuse, and continued it as a cheap and easy method of rewarding zealous partisans, or perhaps of eking out inadequate pay for military service.

Burgesses to be sued in Calais in local causes. There is another reasonable prayer, that no burgess shall be taken beyond the liberty of Calais by the King's writ or otherwise, on plea of debt, action on lands and tenements, or any other pretext. This request is granted, as to causes arising within the town, if the King be not a party to them. **Jurisdiction of Court of mayor and aldermen.** A still more important provision is that no plea affecting lands or tenements, nor any cause, civil or criminal, shall be adjudged in any court in Calais except by the mayor or aldermen, according to the laws and privileges granted to them by the King, always excepting privileges of the staple. This provision is also assented to, saving to the governor his jurisdiction, and saving also that if any dispute arises between a soldier and a burgess, it shall be pleaded and adjudged before the governor as well as the mayor. **Power to make bye-laws.** Lastly, the mayor, aldermen, and burgesses ask for power to make such bye-laws as they think fit for the good government of their city, by night and by day, and that these bye-laws, made for the common good, shall be allowed full effect. (Item, que les mair, aldermans et burgeois aient poiar de fair ordenances que bons soient pur le bone governement de les gentz liges et autres deinz la ville, si bien par neot come par jour deinz la dite ville; et que celles ordenances q'ils ferront pur la commune profit soient tenus pur fermes et estables.) But the royal answer is equivocal: inquiry will be made whether this prayer can be granted without injury. (Ent ferra enquiz quele domage y purrount avenir.) So this interesting Bill comes to an end, in part receiving statutory effect, and in part modified or rejected by the terms of the King's answer.

In 1533-4, a then recent Act, establishing commissions of sewers, was extended to Calais.[1] The maintenance of its harbour had been previously provided for.[2] That its beacons and fortifications should be kept up,[3] and provision made and renewed for watch and ward against surprise,[4] was matter of course. Better provision was made in the year 1548 for maintenance of its streets, lanes, and ways, which, as the statute recites,[5] were " very foul, ruinous and noisome, and full of pits and slowes (sloughs), very dangerous for all passing through them, for lacke of good paving." For amendment and reformation it was accordingly enacted that from and after the feast of St. Michael the Archangel, 1551, a respite which gave the townspeople ample grace, all owners of land and houses in Calais should pave with paving stone the ground in front of their property and up to the channel running in the middle of the causeway. But the mayor and aldermen were to pave the four high streets, " which they have used to pave and of right ought to do." When paved, owners were to repair at all times afterwards, as often as need required, under penalty of forfeiting eightpence for his Majesty's use for every square yard of pavement. Default was to be presumed on presentment by verdict of twelve men, or by three sufficient witnesses before the mayor and aldermen, who were empowered to levy fines. If they themselves made default, they in turn might be fined by the Lord Deputy of Calais.

Calais Paving Act, A.D. 1548.

This liability was again confined to owners solely, the Act providing that if lessees or occupiers paved, they should " abate and retain in his or their own hands as much of the rent due to the lessors as they can duly prove to have

In absence of agreement, owners liable.

---

[1] 23 Hen VIII. c. 5.
[2] 10 Hen. VI. c. 5.
[3] 21 Rich. II. c. 18.
[4] 11 Hen. VII. c. 16.
[5] 2 & 3 Edw. VI. c. 38.

expended on the same paving; and the lessor, for so much as the same doth amount unto, to have no action of re-entry for non-payment of the same, except it be otherwise agreed between them." Thus, for the first time, we find a statutory recognition of the owner's right to shift the burden of pavage to his tenant by express agreement between them. Another section was directed against houses roofed with reed or thatch "to the great danger of fire, which God defend." Owners were, therefore, ordered before 1552, to replace this covering with a whole roof of tiles or slates, under penalties of 10*l.* for default.

Provision against fire.

A Chichester Paving Act, passed in 1575-6, adopts the same principle of requiring each owner to pave in front of his property.[1] This statute recites that the Corporation of Chichester have paved at the common charge some part of that city, namely, the market places and other ways of greatest resort, to the inhabitants' "great pleasure and ease." Other streets in the city, however, are ill-kept and noisome; and although the mayor and corporation are very willing to pave these, they "find the charge and burden thereof so great" that they cannot do so without help from owners. Within two months after notice, therefore, every owner must pave in front of his property with good paving stones, and keep the same in repair under penalties for every square yard not paved or repaired; default herein to be proved by the oaths of twelve honest and substantial men. As in other cases, tenants and lessees may deduct from their rent any outlay on pavage.

Chichester Paving Act, 1575-6.

An Act in 1662, for paving and keeping clean streets in London and Westminster, and for other purposes, is the first to lodge with local authorities a power to execute all works of paving, instead of leaving these to be done by each owner or householder.[2] This statute appoints commissioners, with power to make "vaults, sewers, and new pavements," and remove "encroachments, by sheds, stalls

General Improvement Act, London and Westminster, A.D. 1662.

[1] 18 Eliz. c. 19.   [2] 14 Car. II. c. 2.

balks, shops, posts or walls" projecting into streets.   Certain
streets are mentioned as needing immediate repair, including
one " in St. James's Fields, commonly called the Pall Mall."
Inhabitants of these streets are required to pay "according to their several interests and estates," and in such
proportions as the commissioners shall fix, after the rate of
sixteenpence for every square yard in front of their dwelling-
houses or lands.   The Lord Mayor is also authorized to receive subscriptions towards the cost of widening certain narrow
lanes in the city, then too narrow for coaches.   Various
sections direct, for the first time, a licensing of hackney
carriages.   No persons may presume to drive or let hackney
coaches unless so licensed; horses to be used for such coaches
must not be under fourteen hands high; and the number
licensed must not exceed four hundred.   Regulations still
in force are met with in this enactment.   For example, every
coach is to be distinguished by a figure or otherwise, "to the
end that they be known on complaint made of them."   Special
care must be taken by the commissioners "not to license
any person that useth any other trade or occupation; and in
the first place to license all such persons as have been ancient
coach owners, or such coachmen as have suffered for their
service or affections to his late Majesty, or his Majesty
that now is."

Licensing of hackney coaches.

Rates of hire are fixed at ten shillings for a day of twelve
hours; eighteenpence for the first hour, and one shilling for
every hour afterwards.   To and from several places the fares
are specified; amongst others one shilling from the Inns of
Court, or thereabouts, to any part of St. James's or city of
Westminster; so that the legal cab fare from the Temple to
Westminster Hall remains now what it was two centuries
and a quarter ago.   For every coach a high licence duty is
charged, called a " yearly rent of 5*l.*," which may be paid
in quarterly instalments.   There are regulations for rakers or
scavengers and their carts.   Householders must no longer
throw their coal ashes and filth into streets, but under penalty

Rates of coach hire in 1662.

Scavengers.

of five shillings, must wait for the scavengers, who are bound to give warning of their approach " by bell, horn, clapper, or otherwise," making " distinct and loud noise." With certain exceptions, all streets are to be thenceforth sufficiently repaired and maintained at the cost of house-holders. **Street lighting.** From Michaelmas to Lady Day every householder is to " hang out candles or lights in lanterns or otherwise in some parts of his house next the street to enlighten the same for passengers, from such time as it shall grow dark until nine o'clock in the evening."[1] This statute contains thirty-one sections, and is by far the most elaborate Improvement Act passed up to 1662.

Parts of many ancient towns suffered decay in times of pestilence, and during the Wars of the Roses. Persons of moderate fortunes, allied to the nobility, resided there, at least during part of the year, but the alternate success and downfall of York and Lancaster led in many cases to the abandonment and ruin of numerous town houses maintained by this class in provincial capitals.[2]

Rebuilding parts of Some remarkable statutes were called for in 1540 through

[1] The city streets were first lighted at nights by public lanterns, under the Lord Mayor's direction, in the reign of Henry V. Late in the 17th century a company appear to have leased from the Corporation the right to light the streets by some newly-invented lamps, each householder being assessed towards the expenses. (*Post*, p. 390.)

[2] *Ante*, Vol. I., pp. 29, 30. According to a vague but probably not exaggerated estimate, twelve princes of the blood, two hundred other nobles, and a hundred thousand English knights and gentry perished during the Wars of the Roses. No chronicler then thought it necessary to record the loss of any men who were not of noble or gentle blood ; but in this contest it was probably less, proportionately, than that of the higher class, who fought with all the fierceness of personal rivalry. " Kill the nobles, and spare the commons," was the maxim and practice of both Edward and Margaret. (Annals of England, 246.) Throughout England the Lancastrian nobles and gentry were impoverished by a wholesale confiscation of their estates under Edward IV. Philip de Comines asserts that he saw the Duke of Exeter (brother-in-law of Edward) begging in the streets. The widow of De Vere, Earl of Oxford, and sister of the Earl of Warwick, supported herself by her skill in needlework, but, in consideration of her " great poverty," received a pension of 100*l.* a year. (Patent Rolls, 21 Edw. IV. ; 1 Rich. III.)

this cause, and the powerlessness of local authorities to abate a serious nuisance. These statutes set forth that many once "beautiful houses of habitation" had "fallen down decayed, and at this day remain unre-edified, and do lie as desolate and vacant grounds, many of them nigh or adjoining the high streets, replenished with much uncleanness and filth, with pits, cellars and vaults lying open and uncovered, to the great peril of inhabitants passing by; and some houses be feeble and very like to fall down, and dangerous to pass by, to the great impoverishing and hindrance" of those cities and towns.[1]

To set right this evil, it was enacted (with a saving of rights of minors and others) that if owners of these decayed houses did not rebuild them within three years, the lords, of whom they were holden, might enter and do so two years afterwards. In their default persons having rent-charges might rebuild within one year; and, them failing, mayors and corporations were allowed a period of three years to execute the like work. How they were to be repaid or secured does not appear. The cities and towns specified are York, Lincoln, Canterbury, Coventry, Bath, Chichester, Salisbury, Winchester, Bristol, Scarborough, Hereford, Colchester, Rochester, Portsmouth, Poole, Lyme, Faversham, Worcester, Stafford, Buckingham, Pontefract, Grantham, Exeter, Ipswich, Southampton, Great Yarmouth, Oxford, Great Wycombe, Guildford, Stratford, Hull, Newcastle-upon-Tyne, Beverley, Bedford, Leicester, and Berwick. In another statute of the same session,[2] like powers are given in twenty-two other towns, mostly in the west of England, among others Sherburne, Dorchester, Weymouth, Plymouth, Plympton, Barnstaple, Tavistock, Dartmouth, Launceston, Liskeard, Lostwithiel, Bodmin, Truro, Helston, Bridgewater, Taunton, Ilchester, Maldon, and Warwick. In subsequent years similar Acts[3] were passed for the same purpose, and

Municipalities empowered to execute works.

Enumerated towns.

---

[1] 32 Hen. VIII. c. 18.
[2] 32 Hen. VIII. c. 19.
[3] 33 Hen. VIII. c. 36; 35 Hen. VIII. c. 4.

applied to Stamford, Great Grimsby, Derby, Cambridge, Dunwich, Liverpool, the Cinque Port towns with their members, Lewes, Carmarthen, Brecknock, and other places.

Another series of local Acts of much later date, known as Two Pennies Scots Acts, conferred upon local authorities in Scotland powers to levy duties on beer, in addition to public duties, during a limited period for specified local objects.[1]

Edinburgh enjoyed this privilege under a Scotch Act passed in 1693; and all revenue derived from this source was continued to the municipality in 1716.[2] The duty thus conceded was two pennies Scots, or the sixth part of a penny sterling, on every pint of ale and beer vended or sold within the city or liberties; and the reasons for this concession are set forth

in a preamble to the Act of 1716:—" Edinburgh, by being the metropolis and seat of the government of Scotland, was subject to all the vicissitudes and changes of the State, and particularly has ever since the Reformation been remarkably zealous in supporting and defending the Protestant interest, and thereby involved in great debts above what the common revenue of the city could discharge."

Then it is recited that King William and Queen Mary, with consent of Parliament, by an Act of the Scotch Parliament in 1693, granted to the magistrates and town council for public use and behoof the duty before mentioned, but excepting all ale and beer brewed in the country by heritors, and brought into the city for their own consumption, together with all ale and beer consumed at the Palace of Holyrood and the Castle. It is further recited that since the Union there has been a gradual decrease of revenue in Edinburgh, which is much in debt, in part occasioned by the late rebellion; and there are several necessary public works which ought to be carried on, including a proper provision for the poor, " who are now become very numerous." The duty on beer is then continued, but the municipality is not to receive

---

[1] *Ante*, I., p. 8.   [2] 3 Geo. I. c. 5.

or spend it. This business is entrusted to two Lords of Session, one baron of the Exchequer, and two heritors elected by each of the shires of Edinburgh—Linlithgow, and Haddington; and any moneys accruing, or loans raised on security of the duty, are to be applied towards renewing the water-pipes and helping the conduits which carry water to the town; enlarging the harbour and deepening the channel of Leith; building a new quay at Leith; 300*l.* annually towards employing and maintaining the poor of Edinburgh and adjacent counties; 100*l.* as a salary to a Professor of Law in the University of Edinburgh; for rebuilding the city walls, and causewaying the highways leading to the city; for building two new churches and settling stipends upon the ministers; and in aid of the city's ordinary revenue.

Application of duty.

Glasgow, a staunch supporter of the Hanoverian succession, received like privileges in statutes of 1693, 1705 and 1714. The last[1] contains a most effusive preamble. "The preserving and encouraging of cities eminent by their situation and usefulness in trade and manufactures," it declares, "has been at all times and in all kingdoms and states the care of the Legislature, more especially in Great Britain." Glasgow is "a place distinguished for these advantages, but yet more considerable for its loyalty and zeal for the Reformed religion, constitution, and liberty of the people, whereof on all proper occasions it has given undeniable proofs, more particularly by furnishing, at the charge of the inhabitants, considerable numbers of men well-armed and disciplined, not only for defence of their city, but even for the support and defence of the Government in other places since the Revolution, on divers very remarkable occasions, and lately in a most cordial and cheerful manner, in opposition to the unjustifiable rebellion begun and carried on by a Popish Pretender to the crown and dominions of his most excellent Majesty."

Glasgow.

Its loyalty and Protestant zeal recited.

[1] 1 Geo. I. c. 44.

Cost of defending Glasgow during Jacobite rising.

The yearly revenues or common good ·of the city are then declared to be "scarce sufficient for the annual necessary charge of the government of so great, populous, and useful a place, much less for payment of the debts of the corporation, which have lately been greatly increased by very considerable sums laid out for furnishing a battalion of foot to serve at Stirling, and for putting the city into a posture of defence against the above-mentioned rebels and traitors." King William and Queen Mary, and Queen Anne (it is further recited), and the Estates of the Parliament of Scotland, did, "in consideration of signal loyalty at the Revolution," grant to the corporation, in 1693 and 1705, a duty on ale and beer, to continue for sixteen years, towards enabling them to pay their debts, beautify their city, and improve trade therein. As the city's necessities are now even greater than before, this duty is continued till the year 1738, "to the end that other cities, seeing that just encouragement is provided as a reward of duty and loyalty, while the merit of laudable service is fresh in memory, may be excited by the example of Glasgow to adhere steadfastly and cheerfully to his Majesty's royal person and to the succession as by law established." This beer duty was afterwards extended to Port Glasgow.[1]

Reward for adhering to the Hanoverian succession.

Dumfries.

A similar duty upon ale and beer was, in 1716, given to Dumfries, whose municipality, according to the preamble of its Act,[2] " during the time of the late rebellion exerted themselves 'in a distinguishing manner to defend their town, and out of their hearty affections to the present establishment have been at great charge and expence in fortifying their town, providing arms and ammunition, and upon other occasions, for the public service, whereby Dumfries is at this time greatly in debt." Any money arising from the duty was to be devoted towards making a convenient harbour,

---

[1] 9 Geo. II. c. 31; and see 28 Geo. II. c. 29; 15 Geo. III. c. 60; and 39 Geo. III. c. 39.

[2] 3 Geo. I. c. 6. See also 10 Geo. II. c. 7; 2 Geo. III. c. 55; 27 Geo. III. c. 57.

paying off municipal debts, building a new church, and providing for ministers.

Among other Scotch towns which, at a later period, obtained the same privilege, may be mentioned Dundee,[1] Bruntisland[2] (*sic*), Dunbar,[3] Inverness,[4] Montrose,[5] Dysart,[6] with Kirkcaldy, Alloa, and Aberbrothock. In some of these cases provision, as in Edinburgh, is fitly made for applying a portion of the revenue thus raised on ale and beer to an improvement in the local water supply. These Two Pennies Scots Bills continued to be passed down to a comparatively recent period. One for Kirkcaldy became law in 1812; another for Dalkeith in 1825.

Other towns.

Here is an example of a petition in Parliament, being in fact a local statute, which received the Royal assent in 1542-3, at the request and for the benefit of the municipality and inhabitants of Poole,[7] relieving them from the feudal obligation to carry their corn four miles, to be ground at the lord's mill, and also enabling the corporation to provide a water supply :—

Corn-mill and water-conduit at Poole.

"To the King, our sovereign lord, in most humble wise shewen unto your most excellent Highness, your poor daily orators and true and faithful subjects, the mayor, burgesses, and inhabitants of your town and port of Poole, in your county of Dorset: That where your said orators and their predecessors always heretofore time out of mind have been compelled and driven, of very necessity, to carry and re-carry all manner of corn provided for the sustentation of their poor households, unto certain mills, being four miles distant at the least from your said town and port, to grind, to the great loss, trouble and unquietness of your said orators : for remedy whereof, and for the more ease, quietness and com-

[1] By an Act of 1707, renewed by 4 Geo. II. c. 11; 20 Geo. II. c. 17; 16 Geo. III. c. 16; 42 Geo. III. c. 27.

[2] By 6 Geo. I. renewed by 20 Geo. II. c. 26.

[3] 5 Geo. I. c. 16.

[4] 5 Geo. I. c. 17.

[5] 6 Geo. I. c. 8.

[6] 26 Geo. II. c. 44.

[7] 34 & 35 Hen. VIII. c. 25; 3 Stat. of Realm, 925. It is entitled "an Act for the edification of a windmill and a conduct (*sic*) at the King's Majesty's town of Poole."

modity of your said orators, and for the more and better
safeguard of your town and port, Be it enacted, ordained and
established by your Highness, with the consent of the Lords
spiritual and temporal, and of the Commons in this your
present high court of Parliament assembled, and by authority of the same, that it shall be lawful to your said orators
and to their successors, at their liberty and pleasure, to erect,
make, frame and set up, at, in and upon your waste ground
and common within the said town called Baiter, in a place there
most requisite and convenient, at their proper costs and charges,
one good and sufficient windmill, to serve the said town and
Land to be taken. port, and the burgesses and inhabitants of the same, and to take
and have one hundred foot of assise square of the said waste
ground for a convenient hill to be made to set one windmill
Conduit to be made. upon. And a like liberty and licence of one conduicte head
at a certain place called Totnam, in the King's waste ground
without the said town of Poole, taking and having sixteen
foot of assise square of the same ground, for the situation
of the same conduit head, for the conveying of fresh water
for the serving of the same town; and to have also like
free liberty to dig and draw in, by, through, and upon all
places and ways thereunto most meet and convenient, with
free course and recourse into and from the same at all times
hereafter for ever; yielding and paying therefor yearly
unto your Highness, your heirs and successors, one peppercorn if it be asked, for all exactions, services and demands;
and your said orators shall, according to their most bounden
duties, continually pray to God for the prosperous preservation of your most noble and royal Majesty long in felicity
to reign and endure."

This is the whole statute.

Early sanitary legislation. From the municipal records of London which have been
cited, it appears that as early as the twelfth century efforts
were made to ensure cleanliness in streets and preserve
the Thames from pollution. No doubt, in other cities and
towns, similar attempts were made. How ineffectual they
proved is shown by the plagues which swept over this and
other countries in the middle ages, and seem to have been
chiefly owing to an utter neglect of sanitary precautions.

Common law remedies: Apart from municipal regulations or manorial bye-laws[1]

---

[1] The court-rolls of Stratford-on-Avon show that, in 1552, Shake-speare's father was fined for de-positing filth in a public street, in

one remedy against nuisances endangering health, as against Presentments of nuisances at courts leet. bad roads and bridges,[1] or scolding women, was by presentment in the sheriff's tourn or court leet. This ancient local jurisdiction was useful in its day, and survived far into the nineteenth century.[2] Such presentments, however, must always have involved an invidious duty, and the difficulty of ensuring evidence in recent times generally caused a failure of justice. In most places this jurisdiction had fallen into disuse even before the year 1800, and as courts leet usually met only once a year, they could afford no speedy or effectual means for a removal of nuisances.[3]

Another common law remedy, procedure by indictment, was Indictment. far too expensive and uncertain a process to be adopted by private individuals, save in very exceptional cases. In a few local Acts, local authorities[4] were authorized to pay the costs of such prosecutions out of the rates, but this power does not seem to have been exercised.[5]

There is ample evidence to show how ineffectual were these

---

violation of the bye-laws of the manor, and again in 1558 for not keeping his gutter clean.

[1] *Ante*, p. 5.

[2] In 1801, eleven owners of factories at Manchester were respectively "presented" by the court leet jury, and fined 100*l.* for not consuming their own smoke; but the fines were respited to allow time for alterations. In 1840, before the Public Health Act provided a statutory remedy, presentments were also made at Manchester and other places against nuisances hurtful to health; and at Ashton-under-Lyne leet juries exercised their jurisdiction vigorously against such nuisances, amercing owners who did not provide proper conveniences for houses, and fixing the number which were deemed necessary.

[3] In spite of its shortcomings, a tribunal which survived for over a thousand years deserves to be mentioned with respect. The Statute of Westminster (13 Edw. I. c. 13) ordered that all presentments in a tourn or leet should be by twelve persons at least; but if the number were not made up by persons residing within a manor, the steward might compel strangers travelling within the jurisdiction to be sworn. If the jury refused to present defaults of which they were informed, the steward might fine them. No notice need be given to offenders in the case of presentments for nuisances, as all residents were supposed to attend the court. (Com. Dig.)

[4] As at Manchester, Salford, Leeds, and Rochdale.

[5] Royal Commission of 1844-5 on the State of Large Towns, Second Report, p. 42.

proceedings at common law, nor were they effectually reinforced by statute. In Parliament, as early as the year
1290, certain Carmelite friars in London, along with the
Bishop of Salisbury and other persons, complained that their
services were hindered through stench arising in some neighbouring premises, and that deaths had been caused by this
nuisance :—" Prior et fratres de Carmelo in London' qui ita
. . . de fetore. . . . propinqui, quod durare non possunt,
nec divinum officium ministrare, et occasione multi dictorum
fratrum mortui sunt, petunt quod Rex velit precipere dictum
fetorem removeri, et fratres predicatores petunt illud ; et
Episcopus Sarum et omnes vicini propinqui petunt illud idem."[1]
In the 35th of Edw. III., upon petition from prelates, peers,
and other inhabitants, an Act or ordinance was passed in
Parliament against the slaughter of cattle in the City of
London, but it seems to have been little regarded, and, nine
years afterwards, a Royal proclamation was issued to the
mayor, recorder, aldermen, and sheriffs, commanding them to
enforce the law, and ordering that no butcher should slaughter
cattle within the walls, or throw offal into the Thames,
under pain of forfeiting the carcase, and of imprisonment.[2]

In 1379-80, however, the nuisance is the subject of a
petition in Parliament from inhabitants of Smithfield and
Holborn, who complain of the horrible smells and mortal
abominations (grantz et horribles puours et abhominations
morteles) arising from blood and offal thrown into ditches near
Holborn-bridge from a slaughter-house near the church of
St. Nicholas, Newgate. This source of infection, they declare, has caused both sickness and death ; and they pray
that the butchers shall be required to slaughter at Knightsbridge, or that in default the penalties already enacted be put
in force against them—namely, forfeiture of all carcases and
imprisonment for a year. In his answer, Richard II. refers

Complaint by
Carmelites of
nuisance,
A.D. 1290.

Act or ordi-
nance, A.D.
1362, against
slaughter-
houses in
London.

Complaints
that law was
not enforced,
A.D. 1379-80.

[1] 1 Rot. Parl. 61 ; 18 Edw. 1. To
this petition, which is imperfect,
there is no recorded answer.

[2] Rot. claus. 44 Edw. III. ; 2 Rot.
Parl. 460.

to the ordinance of 1362, and the proclamation of 1371, and directs that they be put into execution, and that fresh writs to this effect be sent to the mayor and sheriffs.

These writs appear to have been no more effectual than the ordinance and proclamation which had preceded them. In the year 1388, therefore, Parliament passed a general Act against "nuisances which cause corruption of the air near cities and great towns."[1] This Act denounced the practice of casting refuse of slaughtered animals and other garbage into "ditches, rivers and waters," and otherwise exposing this offensive matter nigh unto populous places, "so that the air there is greatly corrupt and infect, and many maladies and other intolerable diseases do daily happen." Proclamation was, therefore, to be made in the city of London, and other places, that all persons who had caused these nuisances should remove them by a stated day, under a penalty of twenty pounds; and mayors and bailiffs were directed to carry out this proclamation upon the like pain. If they failed so to do, any person aggrieved might complain to the Chancellor, and was entitled to a writ calling upon any offender "to come into the Chancery, there to show why the said penalty should not be levied of him." Thenceforth no persons, "of what condition soever they be," were to commit these nuisances, under pain of being "called by writ before the Chancellor at his suit that will complain;" and if found guilty they were to be punished at the Chancellor's discretion.

For a time this statute appears to have been effectual. Perhaps the dread of being dragged into Chancery may have had a wholesome influence. At any rate we find, in 1392-3, complaints made in Parliament by citizens of London that existing restrictions on the slaughter of animals had raised the price of meat; and upon their intercession, an ordinance

Margin notes: General Act against nuisances, A.D. 1388.

Penalties levied and punishments inflicted in Chancery.

Law relaxed in London, A.D. 1392-3.

---

[1] 12 Rich. II. c. 13; 2 Stat. of Realm, 59. The Sanitary Commission of 1871 say that this may be considered as the first sanitary law in our statute book. It is the first general Act, but was based upon the local ordinance of 1362.

passed, allowing slaughter-houses to be opened on the river bank, but stipulating that all offal should be cut into small pieces and thrown into the Thames at high water.[1] With this encouragement the nuisance grew as bad as ever in London, for a century later [2] Parliament passed an Act founded

Slaughter-
houses in
London,
A.D. 1488-9.

on a petition which begins in this wise:—" To our liege lord the King, and his Lords spiritual and temporal, and to his Commons in this present Parliament assembled, most humbly beseech your abundant grace your poor subjects and orators, parishioners of St. Faith's and St. Gregory's in London next adjoining unto the cathedral church of Powlys " (Paul's). These humble petitioners set forth that a great concourse of people resorting to St. Paul's are greatly annoyed by corrupt airs engendered in these parishes through the slaughter of beasts and the scalding of swine in the butchery of St. Nicholas Fleshamles (flesh shambles), " whose corruption by violence of unclean and putrified waters is borne down through the said parishes and compasseth two parts of the palace where the King's most royal person is wont to abide when he cometh to the cathedral church for any act there to be done, to the jeopardous abiding of his most noble person . . . . complaint whereof at divers and many seasons, almost by the space of sixteen years continually, as well by the canons and petty canons of the cathedral church, landlords there, as also by many others of the King's subjects of right honest behaviour, unto divers mayors and aldermen of the city of London hath been made, and no remedy had nor found."

His Majesty is therefore prayed to provide for the safety of his person, and also to succour his suppliants, considering

Extra-mural
slaughtering
elsewhere in
Christendom.

that in few noble cities and towns, or none within Christendom, as travelling men bear witness, is a common slaughterhouse of beasts kept within the walls, lest sickness destroy the people. To these prayers the King and Parliament give

---

[1] 3 Rot. Parl. 306 ; 16 Rich. II. ; *ante*, pp. 46–7.

[2] 4 Hen. VII. c. 3, A.D. 1488–9 ; *ante*, Vol. I. p. 29.

ear, and enact "that no butcher nor his servant slay no manner of beast within the said house called the scalding-house, or within the walls of London" on pain of forfeiting one shilling for every ox, and eightpence for every cow or other beast ; and the same law is to be observed "in every city, burgh and town walled within this realm, and in the town of Cambridge ; the towns of Berwick and Carlisle only except."[1]

Special and general law against slaughtering in walled towns.

From very early periods of English history the Crown issued commissions by virtue of its prerogative, or, in later times, under statute, chiefly with a view to prevent damage from incursions of the sea or from river floods and rainfall.[2] The laws and customs of Romney Marsh appear to have been taken as models for general imitation. These laws, resting on customs of much more ancient date, were drawn up by a learned judge, Henry of Bathe, acting under special commission from Henry III., in order to settle the respective liabilities of tenants of the marsh for repairs and maintenance of banks and dikes. After inspecting the works, and summoning the tenants to appear before him, this learned judge ordained and deposed that which, in his view, was "meet to appease strife" among the tenants.[3]

Commissions of Sewers.

Laws and customs of Romney Marsh, A.D. 1225.

Clearly the sole aim of this code was to discharge land water, and prevent inroads from the sea. Such also was the chief object of a commission issued by Henry IV. in the year 1402, upon a petition from the municipality of Kingston-upon-Hull. This commission, however, is remarkable for its attempt to provide a supply of fresh water, as well as to relieve the town from floods.[4] It recites the need of protect-

Commission for preventing floods at Hull, A.D. 1402 ;

[1] Although long before obsolete, these Acts of 1388 and 1488-9 remained on the statute-book until the year 1856, when they were repealed by 19 & 20 Vict. c. 64.

[2] *Ante*, Vol. I. pp. 10-13. In 1307 a commission of sewers was directed to the mayor and sheriffs of London, commanding them to cleanse the river Fleet (Woolrych's Law of Sewers, 2nd ed. p. 2).

[3] 9 Hen. III.

[4] This commission, and a report made in compliance with it, are given in App. A. It appears to have been one of the ancient writs *ad quod damnum*, issued, when permanent works were necessary for the benefit

ing the townspeople against inundations from the Humber,
" which is an arm of the sea."   Considering, therefore, that
Kingston-upon-Hull is a Royal borough held from the King
" at a fee-farm of sixty and ten pounds per annum," and
is " the key of the country there adjacent, and of the whole
county of York," his Majesty assigns to certain " chosen and
faithful " persons the duty of considering how best to provide
and for pro- against floods.   These persons are also to devise means for
viding sweet ensuring supplies of sweet water, which now can only be had
water. " by boats, and that at sumptuous cost, whereby the poor
inhabitants in large numbers every year during the summer
time, of necessity, on account of the scarcity and dearness of
water of this kind, depart from the town, and renounce and
avoid it," to its manifest injury, " and in process of time to
its final destruction, unless a suitable and speedy remedy be
speedily applied."   But the text of this commission, and the
return made in compliance with it, do not appear to support
the assumption [1] that any provision for drainage was contemplated, except that of surface and flood waters.   " Sweet
water was to be provided " as well by sewer courses as other

of any locality, with a view to ascertain what private injury, if any,
they would cause, and how they
should be carried out, so as to
cause the least possible damage to
private persons.   Sometimes these
commissions were issued for the formation of new roads or the better
maintenance of those already existing, *e. g.*, a writ (12 Edw. II.) " to
inquire whether the causeway and
bridges in the way called Longford,
between Bletchley and Newport, in
the county of Salop, are so broken
as to be dangerous, and if any certain persons are bound to repair
them, and if they be not, whether it
will be to the prejudice of the King
or others if he grant a pontage for
repairs."   Commissioners were also
appointed (Patent Roll, 10 Edw. III.)
to survey the walls, ditches, sewers,

bridges, &c., on the sea-coast in
Leveryngham, Nenton, and Wis-
beach, county Cambridge (except the
field called Rummere), and to inquire
by whose default they had become
ruinous, and to distrain persons
holding lands, tenements, fisheries,
&c., there to repair them.   Other
examples are cited by the Commissioners on the State of Large Towns
in 1843-5, Second Report, p. 8, n.   In
the Record Office is a collection of
inquisitions *ad quod damnum*, formerly preserved in the Tower, from
1 Edw. II. (A.D. 1307) to the end of
Henry V.'s reign (1422), and from 1
Rich. III. (A.D. 1483) to the end of
the reign of Will. III. (A.D. 1702).

[1] Royal Commission on State of
Large Towns, 1843-5 ; Second Report, p. 8.

methods; and certain new dikes were to serve this purpose, with sufficient dams for warding off salt water.[1]

Writs for previous local inquiry and survey before the issue of sewer commissions appear to have been discontinued upon the passing, in 1427, of a general Act to regulate these commissions.[2] In this and four amending statutes,[3] great damage caused by encroachments of the sea, or by occasional river floods, was set forth as the object of legislation. Neither here nor in the Act of 1531, the fountain-head of subsequent legislation on this subject, is there any evidence to show that sewers were thought of as useful for the discharge of offensive matter, or for any sanitary end, except such as would be incidentally served by draining off storm or river water which might otherwise become stagnant and noisome.

Sewers Acts, Hen. VI.

By the celebrated Statute of Sewers, passed in 1531,[4] previous legislation is consolidated and strengthened to accomplish the same object. It recites "the great damages and losses which have happened by the influx of waters upon marsh grounds and other low places, heretofore through politic wisdom won and made profitable, for the great commonwealth of this realm, as also by occasion of land waters, and other outrageous springs, in and upon meadows, pastures, and other low grounds adjoining to rivers, floods, and other watercourses; and over that, by and through mills, mill-drains, weirs, fish-garths, kedels, gores, gotes, flood-gates, locks, and

Statute of Sewers, A.D. 1531.

Obstacles to free flow of streams.

---

[1] In the reign of Richard II. there were serious apprehensions that the port of Kingston-on-Hull would be destroyed by inroads of the sea (see the judgment pronounced against Michael de la Pole, Earl of Suffolk, A.D. 1386, 3 Rot. Parl. 220). Half a century afterwards the river Hull had shifted so far from the town that the same apprehensions existed. With a view to prevent so great a calamity, Henry VI. granted his licence to the mayor and commonalty of Hull to purchase lands worth 100l. a year for the reparation and protection of their port. (Frost's Early History of Hull, p. 35.)

[2] 6 Hen. VI. c. 5.

[3] 8 Hen. VI. c. 3; 18 Hen. VI. c. 10; 23 Hen. VI. c. 8; 12 Edw. IV. c. 6; 4 Hen. VII. c. 1.

[4] 23 Hen. VIII. c. 5. The statute seems to have been an experiment; its operation was limited to twenty years, but it was made perpetual by 3 & 4 Edw. VI. c. 8.

other impediments in and upon the same rivers and other watercourses, to the inestimable damage of the common-wealth of this realm, which daily is likely more and more to increase, unless speedy redress and remedy be in this behalf shortly provided." It enacts that Commissions of Sewers shall be created in all parts of the realm from time to time "where and when need shall require." They are directed to proceed " by such ways and means, and in such manner and form " as to them " shall seem most convenient to be ordained and done;" to reform, repair, and amend the said walls, ditches, banks, gutters, sewers, gotes, calcies, bridges, streams; and to cleanse and purge the trenches, sewers, and ditches in all places needful. Further they are to reform, amend, prostrate, and overthrow all such mills, streams, ponds, locks, fish-garths, hebbing-wears, and other impediments and annoyances as shall be found, by inquisition or by their survey and discre-tions, to be excessive or hurtful; and also to " depute and assign diligent, faithful and true keepers, bailiffs, surveyors, collectors, expenditors, and other ministers and officers, for the safety, conservation, separation, reformation, and making of the premises."

Appointment of Commis-sioners. Before 1531, these Commissioners of Sewers were named directly by the Crown, which also defined their limits of juris-diction. Under the statute of 1531, all Commissioners were to be nominated by the Lord Chancellor, the two Chief Justices, and the Lord Treasurer. They must be "sub-stantial and indifferent "[1] persons qualified—(1) by possess-ing lands to the clear yearly value of forty marks; or (2) by residence and freedom in any city, borough or town corpo-rate, with moveable substance of a clear annual value of one hundred pounds; or (3) by being " learned in the laws of this realm," and " admitted in one of the four principal Inns of Court for an utter barrister." The Commissioners were entrusted with powers to levy rates, were to sit as a Court of

---

[1] Impartial.

Record, and might proceed by jury, or upon their own view, exercising, at their discretion, within the limits defined in their commission, the large powers already mentioned. Their statutory pay was four shillings on each day they "took pains in executing" their commission.[1]

Although offensive matter must have found its way into these open sewers near any large towns, and required from time to time such cleansing as the Act provided, no sewerage in its modern sense was contemplated by this legislation. It was, indeed, a penal offence to discharge offensive matter into the sewers, and so continued until the beginning of the present century.[2] These sewers were regarded as channels for surface water only, and were either natural streams, whose channels were kept free for outfall, or new watercourses,[3] made to carry off any excessive rainfall from fields, roads, or streets. About eighty rural districts, comprising large tracts of country, were drained under the authority of the Act of Henry VIII. In London and its suburbs north of the Thames there were six commissions—for the districts of the City;[4] Westminster, first constituted in

Margin notes: Early sewers intended only for carrying off surface water. — Rural sewer districts. — Metropolitan Sewer Commissions.

---

[1] In 1531, 4s. a day would equal about 24s. of our money. A list of salaries (apart from fees) received by some judges and Crown officers at the close of the reign of Henry VIII. may be compared with this payment:—Chief Justice of King's Bench, 154l.; Chief Justice of Common Pleas, 130l.; Chief Baron, 133l.; Puisne Judges, 100l.; Chancellor of Exchequer, 26l. 13s. 4d.; Chamberlain of Exchequer, 52l. 3s. 4d; Chamberlain of King's Household, 20l.; French Secretary, 40l.; Chief Surgeon, 26l. 13s. 4d.; Under Clerk of Parliament, 5l.; Solicitor-General, 10l.; Constable of the Tower, 100l. (Sanitary Commission (Metropolis), 1847; Min. of Ev. 38.)

[2] Royal Commission on Metropolitan Sewage, 1884, p. xi.

[3] For a long period it was doubted whether Commissioners could make new sewers, or had jurisdiction over such as had been constructed since their appointment. In 1605, a local Act (3 James I. c. 14) gave a jurisdiction to the City Commissioners over "ditches, banks, gutters, sewers, causeways, bridges, streams and watercourses" within two miles of the city. See also 2 Will. & Mary, sess. 2, c. 8.

[4] The powers of the City Commissioners of Sewers extend within the city to paving, lighting, and cleansing, as well as sewerage. In what are called the Liberties, these powers are confined to sewerage and drainage. Besides the powers given by the general law as to sewers, several local Acts confer special authority on

the year 1659; Holborn and Finsbury, in 1683; the Tower Hamlets in 1686; St. Katharine; Poplar and Blackwall. South of the Thames there was a separate commission for Greenwich, and one for parts of the metropolis in Surrey and Kent, the earliest of which bears date so far back as the year 1295.[1]

While this statutory provision was in force against floods from sea, rivers, or storm water, offensive house refuse was either collected by public rakers or scavengers, as already described, or accumulated in cesspools, which were emptied from time to time, or overflowed into the open kennels. As population increased in London and other towns, the **Act for London and Westminster, A.D. 1662.** latter nuisance became serious.[2] A local Act, of the year 1662, applying to London and Westminster,[3] set forth the

the Commissioners (11 Geo. III. c. 29; 33 Geo. III. c. 75; 4 Geo. IV. c. 114; and others of recent date).

[1] These commissions were originally of limited duration. Under 3 & 4 Edw. VI. they were to hold good for five years; and by 13 Eliz. c. 9, for ten years. An Act of 1660 (12 Car. II. c. 6), "for the present nominating of Commissioners of Sewers," repeats in its recitals explanations given in older Acts, namely, that some speedy remedy was needed against great damage which had "arisen in many parts of this realm by inundations of water."

[2] By a well-known statute in 1592–3, of like tenor to a Royal proclamation issued some years previously, one of Queen Elizabeth's Parliaments tried to prevent any further increase of population and buildings, as well as overcrowding, in London. It recited "the great mischiefs and inconveniences that daily grow and increase by reason of the pestering of houses with divers families, harbouring of

inmates, and converting of great houses into several tenements, erecting of new buildings within the cities of London and Westminster, and other places near thereunto adjoining, whereby great infection of sickness and dearth of victuals and fuel hath grown and ensued, and many idle, vagrant and wicked persons have harboured themselves there, and divers remote places of the realm have been disappointed of workmen and dispeopled." It was therefore provided that no new buildings for habitation should be erected in the cities of London or Westminster, or within three miles thereof, unless "fit for the dwelling of such a person as heretofore hath been assessed for the subsidy to her Majesty at 5l. in goods or 3l. in lands." There was a further provision that no existing houses should be divided into several dwellings, and that no new inmates should be taken as lodgers, under penalties for disobedience. (35 Eliz. c. 6.)

[3] 14 Car. II. c. 2; *ante,* pp. 268–70.

multitude of houses lately built within the weekly Bills of Mortality,[1] from which cause, and the stopping and filling of ditches and sewers, through want of timely reparation, the common ways had become so miry and foul as to be noisome and dangerous. This Act accordingly provided for the appointment of Commissioners, who were authorized to make any new vault or sewer, to cut into any drain or sewer already made, to alter, enlarge, amend, or scour any old vaults, sinks, or common sewers, and remove all kinds of nuisances. Householders were forbidden[2] not only to deposit any dust, dirt, or refuse before their houses in any street, but to throw such refuse "into any common or public sink, vault, watercourse, or common sewer," or into any private vault or sink belonging to their neighbours.

Underground sewers.

Prohibition to cast refuse into sewers.

In the Act of 1666,[3] to regulate the rebuilding of London after the great fire, persons nominated by the Corporation were to design and set out "the numbers and places for all common sewers, drains, and vaults," as well as the order and manner of paving and pitching streets and lanes. They also might enlarge, cleanse, and scour any old vaults or common sewers, and defray expenses by imposing a reasonable tax

Sewers, drains, and vaults in Act of 1666 for rebuilding London.

---

[1] Bills of mortality were commenced in London towards the end of Queen Elizabeth's reign, A.D. 1592. "It was part of the general measures of her able government, by which abstracts of burials, baptisms, and marriages were directed to be compiled in each parish." Searchers, who were ancient matrons sworn to their office, were appointed to view the bodies of all that died before they were suffered to be buried, and to certify (on information received from any surgeon employed or from friends of the deceased) of what probable disease each individual died. Their statements were reported to the parish clerk, and it was the clergyman's duty to make a weekly return. Deaths by plague and other diseases were published in the London Bills so early as 1603. Even these imperfect reports were of great value. (Registrar - General's Report for 1866; App. by Dr. Farr.) Returns were made to the Bills of Mortality from 148 city and suburban parishes. In 1836, by 6 & 7 Will. IV. c. 86, the registration of births, deaths, and marriages was amended and enforced, and a Registrar-General appointed, whose duty it should be to submit to Parliament an annual abstract of sanitary and statistical information based on the registers.

[2] 14 Car. II. c. 2, s. 16.

[3] 18 & 19 Car. II. c. 8.

upon all houses in proportion to the benefit they would receive.

Fouling of underground courses for rainfall.

From these statutes it is clear that, in the metropolis in 1662-6, the increase of houses, and consequent discharge of rainfall from roofs, had led, for public convenience, to the construction of underground courses for rain water; while provisions for cleansing and scouring, as well as recitals about the foulness of roadways, also show that these vaults, with the open sewers and water-courses provided for similar purposes, were polluted in spite of all prohibitions to the contrary.[1] While, therefore, according to ancient usage, sewers were only intended to carry off rainfall and prevent floods, a growing population in large cities made it gradually expedient, and even essential, that they should be turned to account as carriers of liquid refuse. This view is borne out by a passage in the life of Lord Guildford, Keeper of the Great Seal under Charles II. and James II. :—

Drain for house sewage made by Lord Guildford, circa 1680.

"His lordship procured to be done another good work which exceedingly improved the dwellings in all Chancery Lane, from Jackanapes Alley down to Fleet Street. He found in a house a small well in the cellar into which all the drainage of the house was received, and when it was full a pump went to work to clear it into the open kennel of the street. But during this pumping the stench was intolerable, and offended not only his lordship, but all the houses in the street, and also passengers that passed to and fro in it. Other houses there which had cellars were obnoxious to the same inconveniences. His lordship proposed to them to join in the charge of making a drain or sewer all along the street, deep enough to discharge into the grand common sewer in Fleet Street.[2] The inhabitants would not join,

---

[1] In contemporary writings "common sewer" was already synonymous with a receptacle for all that was vile. Thus Milton—

"As one who long in populous city pent,
Where houses thick and sewers annoy the air."

Paradise Lost, Book IX.

So, an Act of 1771, "for better paving, cleansing and enlightening the City of London," declares that, for want of proper sewers, drains or vaults, several streets are "frequently annoyed, the houses and buildings therein weakened and rendered of less use, and the health of his Majesty's subjects greatly affected" (11 Geo. III. c. 29).

[2] This sewer, no doubt, ran into

alleging danger to their houses, and other frivolous matters; and thereupon his lordship applied to the Commissioners of Sewers[1] and obtained a decree, by virtue of which it was done whether they would or no, and the charge paid by a contribution levied upon them; and then they thanked his lordship as for a singular good done them. Which is an instance showing that the common people will be averse to their own interest till it is forced upon them, and then be thankful for it."[2]

A Keeper of the Great Seal, suffering personally from an intolerable nuisance, would not find it difficult to set in motion Commissioners of his own nomination. But in other parts of London, and in provincial centres, there was not likely to be similar diligence. So lately as the year 1844, the Commissioners' power to construct new sewers was still disputed in Westminster and the Tower Hamlets; and at Greenwich, in 1847, any rates made were employed solely for keeping up the river banks, preventing the irruption of tidal waters, and providing for surface drainage. In the eighteenth century local Acts in other metropolitan divisions gave the Commissioners increased powers over surface drainage, but bye-laws under these local statutes were framed with this object only, having no reference to house drainage or sewerage.[3] Improvement Acts obtained by Liverpool, Bristol,

Limited view of Sewer Commissioners' functions, 1844-7.

___

the Fleet river, which from a navigable stream had gradually become so offensive that in 1732 it was covered over below Holborn, and used as a common sewer, under statutory powers (5 & 6 Geo. II. c. 22. See also 29 Geo. II. c. 86, s. 24). At about the same period the Ranelagh and King's Scholars' Pond sewers, with other important arterial drains in the Metropolis, were also closed in. (Royal Commission on Metropolitan Sewage, 1884; Report, p. xi.)

[1] These may have been the Commissioners appointed under the Act of 1662, with power to make sewers. A paper written by Sir Christopher

Wren, in 1678, and still preserved in MS., proposed some important improvements in " y⁰ new sewers " and "y⁰ back waters in St. Margarett's, Westminster." See Sir Joseph Bazalgette's Paper on Main Drainage of London, Proc. Inst. C. E., vol. 24, 1864-5.

[2] Life of Lord Guildford, by Dudley North, quoted by Sanitary Commission (Metropolis), 1847, Rep. p. 47.

[3] Royal Commission on State of Large Towns, 1843-5; First Report, p. 9. Sanitary Commission (Metropolis), 1847; Ev. of C. Smith, clerk to Greenwich Sewers Commission, 180.

Chester, Shrewsbury, and other towns contained no provisions whatever for drainage; their sanitary clauses were limited to street cleansing.

Removal of refuse from streets and houses in London;

These clauses seem to be founded on the Metropolitan Act of 1662,[1] which required public rakers or scavengers to make daily rounds, giving notice of their approach, and provided with "carts, dung-pots, or other fitting carriages," to remove all refuse brought to them by householders. So in the Liverpool Improvement Act of 1748,[2] after recitals that " it would tend greatly to the safety, preservation, and benefit " of the inhabitants that their streets " should be kept clean, and properly lighted in the night-time, and an able watch kept therein," provision was made for the annual election by inhabitants paying poor-rates of eighteen Commissioners, who, joined with the mayor, recorder, and justices, were to put this portion of the Act into execution.[3] These Commissioners might appoint watchmen, keepers and lighters of street lamps, and scavengers, rakers, and street cleansers. All occupiers under penalties were bound to sweep and cleanse before their respective houses, buildings, and walls twice in every week at least, " or oftener if occasion be," between the hours of two and five in the afternoon, "to the end that dirt and soil in the streets, lanes, and public places, may be heaped ready for the scavengers to carry away." No coal-ashes, wood-ashes, rubbish, tubs, or other annoyances, were to remain in any public place longer than twelve hours, but all refuse was to be kept by householders "in their respective houses, backsides, or yards," until the appointed scavenger came by with his cart, wheelbarrow, or other

and in Liverpool.

---

[1] 14 Car. II. c. 2, s. 20; *ante*, p. 270.

[2] 21 Geo. II. c. 24.

[3] It is worth noting, in proof of the distrust of municipal corporations, that while they were required to keep in repair a new church, they were ignored in these provisions for the better government of the town, save by the *ex officio* appointment of the mayor, recorder, and justices. But as the Commissioners were not incorporated by the Act, it was necessary to vest in the mayor, bailiffs, and burgesses the property in the new street lamps.

vehicle, to which they were bound to carry and deliver such refuse. Scavengers were required to come round twice a week, or oftener if occasion required, notifying their approach " by bell, horn, or clapper, or otherwise by a loud voice or cry." This Act remained in force until 1842.[1]

Between the years 1800 and 1845 nearly four hundred Improvement Acts were obtained for various purposes of local government and some sanitary purposes in 208 towns in England and Wales.[2] We shall presently see how inadequate was all this legislation to preserve health among large communities. To remedy some of the most glaring defects in local Acts affecting the metropolis a general statute, in the year 1817,[3] enabled the numerous paving Boards then constituted to contribute from the rates towards repairs or construction of sewers, but no use appears to have been made of this provision. In many populous provincial towns where no special legislation was in force, roads and streets could only be cleansed by recourse to a general Highway Act of 1814,[4] under which highway surveyors might require occupiers of adjoining land to scour and cleanse main sewers and drains, or pay the expense of doing so. This power, however, applied only, or mainly, to surface waters which it was necessary to convey from roads with a view to their better maintenance. A later public Act to the same effect was the Turnpike Act of 1823,[5] which provided road drains for the drainage of adjacent houses, and empowered justices, on an application by turnpike trustees, to apportion costs of maintenance between these trusts and inhabitants using their drains. No populous town or district, however,

Marginal notes:
Local Improvement Acts, 1800–45.

Highway Act, 1814.

Turnpike Act, 1823.

---

[1] Repealed by 5 & 6 Vict. c. 106.

[2] Supplement to Second Report of Commissioners on State of Large Towns, 1845, pp. 106–8. A schedule to the Municipal Corporations Act of 1835 sets out nearly 200 Acts then in force conferring special powers in the boroughs regulated by it.

[3] 57 Geo. III. c. 29.

[4] 54 Geo. III. c. 109.

[5] 3 Geo. IV. c. 126, s. 115.

seems to have adopted this provision, its operation being necessarily limited to roads or streets controlled by turnpike trustees.

Highway Act, 1835.

A later measure, more frequently resorted to for drainage purposes, was the Highway Act of 1835.[1] This public statute was in force in many places of considerable population, and generally afforded the only means for draining the suburbs even of the largest towns. Its execution was entrusted to the parish vestry, through surveyors appointed by them. The powers contained in this Act, again, were evidently intended only to provide means for carrying off surface water from streets and roads. But drains made under its provisions were frequently used as the sole mode of carrying off refuse from houses in some large towns, and still more frequently in suburban districts. The use of these drains for a purpose for which they were not originally intended, and were not constructed, was a cause of serious annoyance, felt in all parts of any town through which they passed. Nor could surveyors be compelled to carry out their powers of scouring, cleansing, and keeping open ditches, gutters, drains, or water-courses. In many instances, indeed, surveyors, who were only appointed for a year, neglected this important duty, and magistrates could not, under the Highway Act, compel them to remove any nuisance so arising.[2]

Up to this period, we may gather, no great sanitary progress had been made in London or other towns, since the municipal regulations of the thirteenth and fourteenth centuries, for preserving cleanliness in the City.[3] Covered sewers had, indeed, replaced open kennels in the leading thoroughfares. But down to the year 1840, few houses were drained into these sewers. In some large towns, indeed, all

House drainage in 1840-4.

---

[1] 5 & 6 Will. IV. c. 50, s. 67.

[2] Second Report of Commissioners of 1843–5 on State of Large Towns,

pp. 10, 11.

[3] *Ante*, pp. 234, 250–1.

entrance into sewers by house-drains, or drains from closets or cesspools, was prohibited at this period, as under the old statutes which have been quoted. In other places, including parts of the metropolis, permission to connect house-drains with main sewers was "commonly deemed the concession of a privilege, subject to regulations and separate proceedings, with attendant expenses, tending to restrict the use of sewers for these most important purposes, or to confine this advantage to the wealthy."[1]

One reason for this apparent exclusiveness may be found in an invention introduced about the year 1810, but for some time confined to houses of rich people. This was the water-closet, which, for its proper working, required a connection with the main sewers, but might strain their capacity if connections were allowed too freely. Other obstacles to its general use were the cost of fittings and want of an efficient water supply.[2] Until the outbreak of cholera in 1831-2, however, the want of house drainage, and other sanitary defects, attracted little attention. Proofs then accumulated that dirt and bad drainage in and around the houses of the poor were a source of danger to all classes.

Reports made to the Poor Law Commissioners in 1838-9, upon causes of disease throughout London, led to a general inquiry extending over Great Britain; and, in 1839, the Registrar General's first report showed how excessive a death rate prevailed in all towns, and to how large an extent disease and mortality might be avoided. Something was thus done to educate the public mind, and establish the necessity for sanitary precautions. But con-

Water-closets, introduction of.

Reports of Poor Law Commissioners and Registrar-General, 1838-9.

[1] Royal Commission on State of Large Towns, 1843-5; First Report, p. 9.

[2] Royal Commission on Metropolitan Sewage, 1884, p. xi. : — "Its adoption was at first slow, but its advantages in promoting domestic cleanliness became gradually appreciated, and after 1830 its progress became rapid and remarkable. Water-closets were originally made to discharge into cesspools, but this large addition to their contents rendered it necessary to introduce overflow drains running from the cesspools into the street sewers."

viction came slowly, and Parliament itself had still much to learn.

Mr. Slaney's
Committee,
1840.

Mr. Slaney, an early labourer in this field, induced the House of Commons, in 1840, to appoint a Committee upon the Health of Towns. Their inquiries disclosed grievous sanitary evils. Dense masses of people had at this period been brought together by the rapid growth of trade and

Increased
population of
large towns
since 1800.

manufactures. Between 1801 and 1831, the whole population of Great Britain increased at the rate of about 47 per cent., but Manchester during the same thirty years grew at the rate of 109 per cent.; Glasgow, 108 per cent.; Liverpool, 100 per cent.; Leeds, 99; and Birmingham, 73 per cent. "Most melancholy and appalling," said the Committee, was the effect upon health and morals among the poor caused by overcrowding,[1] a want of restrictions upon buildings, and of proper drainage and cleansing. In populous districts throughout Great Britain the most obvious precautions to preserve health had been neglected. Fevers and other disorders of a contagious and fatal nature prevailed, in consequence, to an alarming extent, causing not only wide-spread misery by death, but permanent weakness and prostration among survivors, and thereby swelling the poor rate in all large communities.[2]

Cellar dwell-
ings and
courts.

In Liverpool there were upwards of 7,800 inhabited cellars, occupied by upwards of 39,000 persons, one-fifth of all the working classes employed in that town; a large proportion of these cellars were "dark, damp, confined, ill-ventilated, and dirty," proper drainage and ventilation being, in fact, impracticable. In the same town there were about 2,400 close courts, rows of small houses placed back to back, so as

---

[1] In Liverpool, in 1840-1, there were 100,000 inhabitants to the square mile; in Birmingham there were no more than 33,000; in Manchester, 83,000. Out of a thousand deaths in country districts, 202 persons reached the age of seventy years; in Liver-

pool only ninety persons in a thousand. (App. to Second Report of Commissioners on State of Large Towns, 1843-5, p. 295.)

[2] Commons' Committee on Health of Towns, 1840; Report, p. 6.

to exclude the possibility of thorough ventilation. These courts were built up at the sides and end, had only one entrance, frequently under a narrow archway, and contained a population of 68,345 working men with their families.[1] Most of these courts had no underground sewers; no attention was paid to cleansing; there was no inspection of any kind; surface gutters were often almost choked with filth; and in some courts the stench was such "as to render it almost impossible to remain for any time in them." In Manchester 15,000 persons, nearly twelve per cent. of the working population, lived in cellars; in Salford, 3,300.[2] Manchester had no building Act. "New cottages, with or without cellars, huddled together, row behind row," were springing up, with streets unpaved and badly sewered, yet no one could interfere. Manchester, also, had "no public park or other ground where the population could walk and breathe fresh air."

Upon these conditions in Liverpool, the Committee comment as follows:—"It is painful to contemplate, in the midst of what appears an opulent, spirited, and flourishing community, such a multitude of our poorer fellow subjects, the instruments by whose hands these riches were created, condemned, for no fault of their own, to evils so justly complained of, and placed in situations where it is almost impracticable for them to preserve health or decency of deportment, or to keep themselves and their children from moral and physical contamination. To require them to be

Liverpool in 1840.

[1] These figures are taken from a report made to the town council by their surveyors in 1841.

[2] Report of Mr. Slaney's Committee, p. 8, quoting account given by Statistical Society of Manchester and Mr. Cobden's evidence. According to the Royal Commissioners of 1843-5 (Second Report, p. 60), the number of inhabitants in cellars at Manchester was then computed at 18,000. There and elsewhere these dwellings were often totally unfit for the residence of human beings. In a range of cellars in Clitheroe, the beds were found raised on bricks to keep them out of the water. Before 1845 local Acts had been passed prohibiting the use of cellars as dwellings in Liverpool, Leeds, and London, unless they were constructed with due regard to health.

clean, sober, cheerful, contented under such circumstances would be a vain and unreasonable expectation. There is no building Act to enforce that the dwellings of these workmen shall be properly constructed; no drainage Act to enforce that they shall be efficiently drained; no general or local regulations to enforce the commonest provisions for cleanliness and comfort." [1] Independent of these physical evils, the Committee express a strong opinion that dirt, damp, and discomfort in poor habitations have "a most pernicious and powerful effect on the moral feelings, induce habits of recklessness, and disregard of cleanliness and all proper pride in personal appearance; thereby take away a strong and useful stimulus to industry and exertion;" and by a want of home comforts, and the gloomy prospect around them, drive both men and women "to dram-drinking, the fertile parent of innumerable ills." [2]

Glasgow.

In Glasgow the sanitary condition of the humbler classes was even worse than in its sister port on the Mersey. An intelligent witness, who had every means of knowledge, told the Committee of 1840 "that penury, dirt, misery, drunkenness, disease, and crime culminate in Glasgow to a pitch unparalleled in Great Britain;" and again, "I did not believe, until I visited the wynds of Glasgow, that so large an amount of filth, crime, misery, and disease existed in one spot in any civilized country."

London.

London was in no better condition than provincial towns. The "abodes of multitudes of the working classes" in Bethnal

---

[1] Report, p. 9.

[2] Ib. p. 14. "With these facts before us," the Committee add, "it is not surprising that the number of reckless and worthless characters should be considerable in Liverpool, viz., one in forty-five of the whole population." The cost of those living on the public, and by other than honest means, was, in 1838, calculated annually at no less than 700,000l. (Report of Royal Commissioners on Constabulary Force, 1838.) Parliamentary Returns are quoted showing an increased consumption of spirits in Great Britain and Ireland from 9,200,000 gallons in 1817, to 29,200,000 in 1837. The number of criminal commitments in England and Wales rose from 4,600 in 1805 to 22,000 in 1838.

Green, Whitechapel, portions of Wapping, Ratcliff Highway, the parish of Stepney, and other districts in East
London, were in "a miserably neglected condition." They
were no better in parts of the Holborn Union, of St. Olave's,
St. George's, Southwark, Lambeth, Bermondsey, Walworth,
Peckham, and Vauxhall. A high sanitary authority who
had personally inspected some of these districts declared that
it was "utterly impossible for any description to convey to
the mind an adequate conception of the filthy and poisonous
state in which large portions of all these districts constantly
remain."[1] Some insanitary conditions prevailing in East
London and other densely-populated metropolitan districts
are thus summarized by the Committee: "1. Houses and
courts and alleys without privies, without covered drains, and
with only open surface gutters, so ill-made that the fluid in
many places was stagnant. 2. Large open ditches containing
stagnant liquid filth. 3. Houses dirty beyond description, as
if never washed or swept, and extremely crowded with inhabitants. 'Heaps of refuse and rubbish, vegetable and
animal remains, at the bottom of close courts and in corners.'"

Some details, which "can scarcely be read without shud-
dering," are given of the results of this gross sanitary neglect
upon public health. In Glasgow, in 1839, the number of
persons who died was 10,270, at the rate of one in $24\frac{6}{10}$ to
the whole population; of this number 2,180 died of typhus
fever. In the same city there had been a rapidly increasing
rate of mortality, which, in 1821 was one in 39 of the population; in 1831, one in 30; in 1835, one in 29; in 1838, one
in 26. Again, it was shown that the mortality among
children in Glasgow under ten years of age had risen from
one in 75 in 1821 to one in 48 in 1839.[2] Fever, it was stated,

Effect upon public health in Glasgow.

[1] Dr. Southwood Smith's Report
on the Prevalence of Fever in Twenty
Metropolitan Unions during the year
1838; App. to Report of Committee
of 1840.

[2] Report, p. 13. It also appeared
that two-thirds of the children between three and twelve received no
instruction whatever. (Ib. n.)

had been gradually increasing, and its victims constituted within a fraction of 55 out of every hundred patients treated in the Glasgow hospitals, this increase, too, coinciding with a period of great commercial prosperity. "Our mortality bill in 1837," a Glasgow physician wrote, "exhibits a rate of mortality inferring an intensity of misery and suffering unequalled in Britain and not surpassed in any town I am acquainted with in Europe."[1]

Rate of mortality in Liverpool and London.

In Liverpool, in 1839, the rate of mortality was one in 33⅓; and the proportion of cases of fever occurring among the inhabitants of cellars was reckoned at about 35 per cent. more than it ought to be, relatively to the whole population. London showed even greater misery arising from neglect of sanitary measures. In the year 1838 twenty metropolitan unions yielded nearly 14,000 cases of fever; above 9,000 occurred in only seven of these unions, namely, Whitechapel, Lambeth, Stepney, St. George the Martyr, Bethnal Green, Holborn, and St. George-in-the-East, which again furnished 4,002 cases of typhus out of 5,692.[2] The seven unions specified, comprising the most populous and the poorest population in London, were described as "pre-eminently malarious districts," constantly ravaged by fever; and returns quoted by the Committee showed that while, in the year 1838, one-fifth of the whole pauper population of the metropolis were attacked by fever, the proportion in Bethnal Green was one-third, in Whitechapel nearly one-half, and in St. George-the-Martyr, the number was 1,276 out of 1,467.[3] Whitechapel showed an annual mortality of four per cent., while that of Hackney and Camberwell was less than two per cent.[4]

Cellar dwellings and small

At this period cellar dwellings and small houses in the

---

[1] "Vital Statistics," by Dr. Cowan, quoted at p. 13 of Report.

[2] Dr. Southwood Smith's Report on the Prevalence of Fever in Twenty Metropolitan Unions during the year 1838, printed in App. to Report of Committee of 1840.

[3] Report of Committee, p. 7.

[4] Ib. p. 5.

close courts just described, all built as cheaply as possible, and entirely destitute of sanitary appliances, were a rapidly increasing class of property. It was also a very profitable and tempting investment, and while, in its effect upon public health, it caused great expenditure to the community, it contributed but little to public burdens.[1] Thus, Mr. Slaney's Committee were told that in the parish of Liverpool 16,800 houses were assessed under 12*l.* a year, and of this number only 900 contributed to the rates, the amount they paid being 700*l.* on a levy of 10,000*l.*[2] Nearly 15-16ths of this property paid no rates. Some years previously attempts had been made to compel the owners to pay poor-rates, but they "annoyed each succeeding vestry so much" that this attempt failed.[3]

Among other measures, this Committee recommended legislative provision for effectual drainage and better regulation of buildings, and the appointment of local boards of health and inspectors of nuisances. But although their report, and the evidence it furnished of defects in both local and general statutes, produced for a time some impression, it led to no sanitary reforms. In 1840-1 a step was taken to improve public health in another direction by means of Acts[4] prohibiting the production of small-pox by inoculation or other means, empowering guardians to contract for the vaccination of all poor persons, and directing that the expenses should be paid out of poor-rates, but that gratuitous vaccination should not be considered parochial relief. A report to the Poor Law Board by Mr. Chadwick in 1842 again described, with great force, the unhealthy, deplorable homes of the labouring classes, the beneficial effects of sanitary

Marginal notes:
houses a remunerative investment.

Vaccination Acts, 1840-1.

Mr. Chadwick's report, 1842.

---

[1] Report of Committee of 1840, p. 9.

[2] Dr. W. H. Duncan, a physician residing in Liverpool, Ev. p. 145; and of this 700*l.* a great portion was paid by the Reform and Conservative Associations for political purposes.

[3] Ib. According to Dr. Duncan, 124,000 of the working classes lived in unhealthy cellars or in the neglected and miserable courts which have been mentioned.

[4] 3 & 4 Vict. c. 29; 4 & 5 Vict. c. 32.

measures in raising the standard of health and chances of life, the feebleness of local and general legislation, and the principles on which it should be amended. Impressed by this renewed and vigorous exposure of existing evils, Sir James Graham, then Home Secretary, brought the subject before the Cabinet,[1] and in 1843 Sir Robert Peel issued a Royal Commission, again to investigate the causes of disease in populous districts.[2] By means of assistant commissioners, local inquiries were instituted into the condition of fifty large towns throughout Great Britain, but no amendment could be reported since the same investigation by Mr. Slaney's Committee.

Royal Commission, 1843-5.

It has been stated that, up to the year 1845, nearly 400 local Improvement Acts had been passed since the century began, applying to 208 towns in England and Wales. But these local Acts were sadly defective for sanitary purposes. Many of them contained no provisions whatever for the drainage either of streets or houses. When there were such provisions they did not contemplate or provide for any previous survey of the whole area to be drained, an essential preliminary to efficient and economical drainage; they afforded no guarantee for a proper consideration of the separate works which should be comprised within this area; nor did they ensure the appointment of duly qualified officers to construct and superintend these works. Several local Acts conferred no jurisdiction beyond the public highways, giving local authorities no powers to drain or cleanse courts, alleys, and closes inhabited by poor persons. In some important towns, which had obtained no special legislation, the drainage, usually most imperfect, was carried out under general powers already

Defects in local Improvement Acts, 1800-45.

[1] Royal Sanitary Commission, 1871; Report, p. 5.

[2] The Royal Commissioners were the Duke of Buccleuch, chairman; the Earl of Lincoln; Mr. R. H. Slaney; Mr. George Graham; Sir H. T. de la Beche; Dr. Lyon Playfair; Dr. D. B. Reid; Professor Owen; Capt. Denison, R. E.; Mr. T. Ranald Martin; Mr. James Smith, of Deanston; Mr. Robert Stephenson; and Mr. William Cubitt.

quoted in the Highway Act of 1835.[1] In many towns even such special powers as did exist were neglected by local authorities, and in most cases were but partially exercised.[2]

After detailed evidence and careful inquiry in the fifty selected towns, the Royal Commissioners declared that in scarcely one instance could the drainage or sewerage be pronounced complete and good, while in seven it was indifferent, and in forty-two decidedly bad in districts inhabited by the poorer classes.[3] It was necessary to receive with discrimination local evidence on these questions, for drainage was often pronounced "good" when only the principal streets had main drains or sewers, while houses in those streets were imperfectly provided with house or branch drains, and the most crowded portions of a town, those most densely

General results of inquiry, 1843-5.

---

[1] Sheffield depended for its drainage on the Highway Act. The Inspector of Highways stated in 1843 (App. to Second Report of Commissioners, pp. 342-6):—"There are in reality no legal powers in force to regulate the drainage of towns like Sheffield, and the general Highway Act contains many defects. . . . The highway funds are extensively wasted and mismanaged. . . . My predecessor, who was employed many years, could neither read nor write. He recommended and overlooked the making of common sewers, and at the same time contracted to do the work himself, without level, plan, specification, or written agreement, and of course without any regard to the dimensions required in the localities. Within the last eight years several miles of such sewers have required to be entirely reconstructed. . . . No books of the expense of roads and works were kept, and the annual cost of maintaining a certain length of any kind of road was so little known that the last surveyors, before the passing of the present

Highway Act, rendered the public liable to repair, for a consideration of 100l., a line of three roads which have cost annually, since that time, an average sum of 241l." At this period sewers and roads were under the management of different surveyors. "My jurisdiction is confined to the township of Sheffield. There is a separate Board in Ecclesall Bierlow. I believe there are some few sewers there, but the officers confess they know nothing about them. If there are any sewers in the other townships, namely, Brightside Bierlow, Attercliffe-cum-Durnall, Nether Hallam, and Upper Hallam, the respective authorities do not know it. . . . The private streets and lanes were generally in a filthy and abominable state, until a few months since, when I induced the Board of Guardians to employ a large number of able-bodied paupers in removing the refuse, and it has not yet had time to accumulate again."

[2] First Report of Commissioners, 1843-5, p. 9.

[3] Ib. p. 10; App. p. 6.

inhabited by the poorer classes, were "utterly neglected, and had no drainage, the refuse being allowed to accumulate and decompose in open channels and pools, or to run into open and stagnant ditches in the immediate vicinity of houses."[1]

Badly con- structed drains and sewers.

House drains were frequently made on erroneous prin- ciples, and were no better than elongated cesspools. Main sewers and drains were often so constructed that decomposing refuse accumulated in them, and offensive smells escaped into streets and houses. Even properly constructed drains conferred little benefit, through the want of a water supply sufficiently abundant to flush them. Hence there arose a natural prejudice against all drainage, and an increased opposition to local Improvement Bills, or general measures of sanitary reform.

Water supply in 1845.

The comparative inutility of sewerage without a copious service of water will be better understood when it is added that, in the great majority of towns and districts from which the Royal Commissioners had evidence, water mains were only carried through the principal streets. There was then no statute regulating water supply,[2] and few special Acts contemplated a service to houses in poor districts. Through- out a large proportion of these districts water could only be obtained from stand-pipes, common tanks, or wells. In some instances poor people were obliged to fetch water from considerable distances, at much inconvenience and labour. In many towns they were dependent on collections of rain water, or on water taken from adjacent streams or pumped from springs, frequently liable to pollution.[3] The water supply could only be "deemed in any comprehensive sense good" in six out of the fifty towns visited; in thirteen towns it was indifferent; and in thirty-one of such deficient quantity and inferior purity as to be bad. But while abundant water was essential to good drainage, it would only lead to increased

[1] First Report of Royal Commis- sion, 1843–5, p. 10; App. p. 6.
[2] The Waterworks Clauses Act was passed in 1847.
[3] First Report of Royal Commis- sion, 1843–5, p. 11.

damp, heighten the causes of disease, and add to dilapidations of premises in districts imperfectly drained.[1]   Thus these two essential conditions of public health were interdependent and almost inseparable.

As in 1840, the drainage was found most deficient in towns which had advanced within a brief period from the condition of villages, chiefly seats of pottery and iron manufactures in Staffordshire, and mining districts in South Wales, Monmouthshire, and the north of England. Among places of this class, Merthyr Tydvil, which in 1844 contained 37,000 inhabitants, is cited by the Royal Commissioners as a lamentable instance of the total absence of all drainage. Increasing suburbs of large towns outside municipal boundaries, or beyond the jurisdiction created by local Acts, showed similar neglect. Even within the jurisdictions created by these Acts, paving, lighting, watching, and the regulation of street traffic, were the objects chiefly provided for, rather than health. At Bath, Commissioners under a local Act[2] had power to construct new sewers, and alter and repair old ones, in a district extending over about a fourth or fifth part of that city; no similar power was vested in any body for the remaining districts.[3] In Gloucester, although three local Acts were in force, none of them applied to sewerage or drainage, which was in a most neglected condition.[4]

For reasons mentioned in the preceding chapter,[5] powers under local Improvement Acts were formerly vested, not in the close and corrupt municipal corporations, but in bodies of Commissioners, elected by ratepayers or authorized to

Side notes: General want, in 1845, of legislative provision for drainage. Merthyr Tydvil. Bath. Gloucester. Constitution of local authorities in 1845.

[1] Ib. 11; and Ev. of Mr. Quick, engineer of Southwark Water Company, p. 393. In March, 1844, within this company's district, there were about 5,000 tenements, containing 30,000 people, who took no water whatever from any company, but depended on pumps or rainfall. About 2,000 persons were supplied from 250 common stand-pipes. (Ib.)

[2] 6 Geo. IV. c. 74.

[3] Town clerk of Bath; App., Second Report of Commissioners, 1843–5.

[4] Ib.; Replies of Mayor and Committee of Inhabitants.

[5] *Ante*, p. 227.

nominate their successors. By the Municipal Corporations Act, 1835, these Improvement Commissioners in any town were enabled to transfer their powers to the municipal body.[1] Down to 1845, however, such transfers were extremely rare, Manchester and Newcastle-under-Lyme affording almost the only exceptions. At Swansea, after these functions had been handed over to the municipality under the Act of 1835, a local statute, in 1844, vested them in the corporation jointly with twelve Commissioners appointed for life.[2] In only a few instances were original powers under local Improvement Acts confided to town councils, a signal instance of the distrust caused by generations during which municipal institutions had been abused for political objects. This distrust only gradually gave way upon proofs of general efficiency and honesty in local administration under reformed municipalities.

Conflicting jurisdictions.

Liverpool.

In various towns the Commissioners found flagrant examples of conflicting jurisdictions, causing great confusion and inefficiency. At Liverpool the following bodies existed: —1. Commissioners for the general sewerage and paving of the town and the townships of Everton and Kirkdale,[3] whose powers were confined to sewerage of streets, and did not extend to courts and alleys or to house drainage. 2. A Committee of the Town Council, acting under an Act of 1842,[4] and appointed exclusively for the paving and sewering of courts. 3. Another set of Commissioners for Toxteth Park, an extra-parochial district, but part of the borough.[5] These independent authorities had to a large extent a concurrent jurisdiction, which could hardly be exercised without clashing. There were also two competing water companies, both giving a deficient supply, so that the Commissioners of Sewers obtained powers in 1843[6] to provide water for the extinction of fires and watering of streets.

[1] 5 & 6 Will. IV. c. 76, s. 75.

[2] 7 & 8 Vict. c. 102.

[3] Acting under 2 Geo. IV. c. 15; 5 & 6 Vict. c. 26.

[4] 5 & 6 Vict. c. 44.

[5] 5 & 6 Vict. c. 105 ; 5 & 6 Vict. c. 104; 6 & 7 Vict. c. 105.

[6] 6 & 7 Vict. c. 75; *post*, p. 473.

In like manner, at Birmingham, several distinct bodies of Commissioners exercised jurisdiction under various local statutes. There were also four distinct boards of surveyors. The parish of Edgbaston had no local Act. Among the local authorities within the borough there was "no co-operation or uniformity of proceedings as to paving, lighting, or cleansing." In Manchester, the townships were under distinct jurisdictions. Only four—Manchester, Chorlton, Ardwick, and Hulme—had local Acts.[1] Powers conferred by two of these Acts (for Chorlton and Ardwick) had been transferred to the Town Council by virtue of the Municipal Corporations Act; but although these districts were governed by one body, they were still under different local laws, while the other townships remained under the general law, although they stood equally in need of special legislation.[2]

Another cause of inefficient sanitary administration was the limited area administered by local authorities for drainage purposes, comprising only a part of their natural and proper drainage area. Thus Manchester, in 1845, was subdivided into jurisdictions, partly municipal and partly parochial, utterly inconsistent with any natural limits for drainage; the authorities acting within these limits had no powers whatever over the river, which was dammed up for mill power; and the sewage accumulating there gave off an effluvium to which much of the prevailing fever was attributed. Owing to these dams, low-lying parts of Manchester were at times overflowed, and effectual drainage of the worst districts, inhabited by the poorest population, was in this way prevented.[3]

Similar causes were in operation at Bradford and Halifax.

Margin notes: Conflicting jurisdictions. Birmingham. Manchester. Limited areas for drainage. Manchester. Leeds and other towns.

[1] 11 Geo. IV. c. 47; 2 & 3 Will. IV. c. 90; 6 Geo. IV. c. 5; 5 Geo. IV. c. 95.

[2] Royal Commission of 1843-5 on State of Large Towns; Second Report, p. 22.

[3] Ib.; App., Report on Towns in Lancashire.

At Leeds, the river Aire, which naturally had a strong and regular current, was dammed up in several places for mill power, and for purposes of water communication. These dams acted as a series of catch-pits for sewage from a population of 120,000. In this case, also, authorities controlling town drainage had no jurisdiction over the natural outfalls, and rights had grown up which the town could only redeem by purchase. From Nottingham, Norwich, Leicester, and Coventry came complaints that extended areas for outfalls were necessary for an effectual removal and application of refuse.[1]

No power to drain unoccupied land;

Through a serious blot in most local Acts at this period, stagnant pools and ditches were allowed in the suburbs, and often in the more crowded parts of large towns. Improvement Commissioners were rarely authorized to make sewers through ground not built upon, which thus became a nuisance as well as a source of disease to the neighbourhood.[2] Elsewhere the Commissioners' powers were sometimes limited to streets in which a certain portion, generally one-half, of the **or unfinished streets.** houses was built. Houses in unfinished streets might therefore stand for years unconnected with a public sewer; and, meanwhile, occupiers were compelled to adopt very objectionable modes of drainage. Moreover, instead of preceding the buildings, sewers and drains were made when houses were finished, so that expense was increased, occupiers suffered unnecessary inconvenience, and there was a like unnecessary interference with public traffic. Tenants were also aggrieved by this delay, because they were called upon to pay for an outlay of which they could only recover a portion, if any, while from the new works their landlords reaped a permanent benefit.

Neglected state of courts and alleys.

Deplorable as was the insanitary condition of streets, it

[1] Royal Commission of 1843-5 on State of Large Towns; Second Report, p. 18.
[2] Ib. pp. 24-5. At Leeds, by 5 & 6 Vict. c. 104, s. 256, and at Southampton, by 7 & 8 Vict. c. 75, s. 269, the local authorities possessed the necessary powers in these cases.

sank into insignificance when compared with the state of courts and alleys not commonly considered thoroughfares. No change for the better seems to have occurred in this respect since 1840. The parish of Birmingham alone contained above two thousand courts in 1844, and their population exceeded 50,000; the adjoining parish of Aston also had many. A description of these courts and alleys is common to most towns where they existed at this period:— "The atmosphere, which is necessarily close and confined, is often further deteriorated by the presence of open privies, close to which there are often one or more pigsties, tubs full of hogswash, and heaps of offensive manure. These courts are frequently unpaved, and the open channel for dirty water ill-defined, so that stagnant puddles form there."[1] Local Acts which gave powers for making sewers generally authorized their formation in "streets, lanes, ways, passages, and places." These words were construed as not applying to courts unless they were thoroughfares. Although this class of property was almost always rated under local Acts, it was, by a strange interpretation, held to be private property, not entitled to any share of the improvements towards which it contributed.[2] In the number and unpaved condition of its courts Liverpool had still, as in 1840, an unhappy preeminence, surpassing all other towns, bad as many of them were. "Thousands of houses and hundreds of courts" in Liverpool were again, in 1844, reported to be "without a single drain of any description." These places were subject to no local regulation whatever until the year 1842. Even then an Act applying to these courts[3] did not require the Health Committee to make, or authorize them to compel the owners to make, any but surface drains.

Courts in Liverpool, 1844.

The earliest local Act compelling house owners to drain

Earliest local Act compel-

---

[1] Royal Commission of 1843-5 on State of Large Towns; Second Report, p. 37, and App. (Report on Birmingham, and Replies from Norwich).

[2] Ib.; Second Report, p. 26.

[3] 5 & 6 Vict. c. 44.

ling house drainage.

into sewers is one obtained by the Corporation of Leeds in 1842;[1] an example followed in 1844 by Rochdale, Southampton, and Manchester.[2] All these Acts forbade the building of any house until a proper drain was made to a sewer if one were situated within ten yards; if not, to some cesspool within the same distance. Under these Acts, a great sanitary advance upon then existing legislation, owners of property in any "street" (defined as including courts) might also be required "to pave, flag, level, sewer and drain it." In sanctioning this system of compulsory house and street drainage, Parliament had become persuaded that the cheapest and most effectual mode of removing offensive matter from the interior of dwellings was by underground channels. But until a copious supply of water was available for securing the efficient action of house drains and sewers, local authorities had to enforce this system discreetly.

Local rating in 1845.

An important part of local legislation, the system of rating, was responsible, in 1845, for many shortcomings in local administration. Rating clauses for drainage, paving, cleansing, and, not unfrequently, lighting and watching, contained "almost every possible variety of provision" for exempting different descriptions of property from liability to

Exemptions.

Agricultural land.

local burthens.[3] Lands in cultivation and market gardens were so exempted, on the plea that they derived little benefit from what were, primarily, urban improvements. At North Shields, however, these lands were assessed,[4] upon a principle afterwards adopted in public as well as private legislation, at rates one-third less in proportion than those applicable to

Public buildings.

urban property. Public buildings, places of worship, and schools were frequently exempted, although they derived benefit from drainage in common with all other descriptions of house property. There were differences in local legisla-

---

[1] 5 & 6 Vict. c. 104.
[2] 7 & 8 Vict. cc. 104, 75, 40.
[3] Royal Commission of 1843–5 on

State of Large Towns; Second Report, p. 29.
[4] By 9 Geo. IV. c. 37, s. 74.

tion on this and other rating questions which could not be justified by local circumstances. For example, at Sunderland public buildings were exempted, but in the neighbouring town of North Shields they were partially assessed.[1]

Powers were sometimes vested in Improvement Commissioners, sometimes in justices, to excuse from local improvement rates, as from poor-rates, on grounds of poverty. Frequently there was an absolute exemption for all houses under a certain rent. In a few cases a graduated scale of rating was adopted, increasing with the amount of annual rent. In Salford these two principles were combined. Houses let at rents under 6*l.* were exempted; those between 6*l.* and 7*l.* were rated upon one-third of the annual rent; those under 9*l.* at one-half; under 10*l.* at two-thirds.[2] In Manchester, though virtually the same town, and, up to 1830, subject to the same body of Improvement Commissioners, the limit for exemption was 4*l.* 10*s.*, and instead of a graduated scale, the Commissioners were authorized to remit rates on the ground of poverty, or to compound with landlords at not less than one-half of the full rates charged.[3] These inconsistent provisions were contained in Acts passed during the same Session of 1830. Similar differences were enforced by three Acts which, in 1845, governed the different districts of Birmingham. They all contained graduated scales for rating, but no two of them agreed in the proportions to be charged according to different rentals.[4] Anticipating a later inquiry, and an attempt to make local legislation more uniform, the Commissioners of 1843-5 call attention to these and other inconsistencies, and remark that, allowing for local peculiarities, "there are

Poverty a ground for exemption.

Graduated scale of rating.

Power to compound with landlords.

Inconsistent provisions in local Acts.

---

[1] 9 Geo. IV. c. 37, s. 75.

[2] 11 Geo. IV. & 1 Will. IV. c. 8, s. 162.

[3] 11 Geo. IV. & 1 Will. IV. c. 47,

ss. 107, 114.

[4] One of these Acts was passed in 1791 (31 Geo. III. c. 17); another in 1829 (9 Geo. IV. c. 54).

certain principles of rating which justice demands should be uniformly established, and which no local circumstances ought to vary."[1]

In 1838, a Committee of the House of Commons inquired into the expediency of granting relief from rates on the ground of poverty. This inquiry was renewed by the Poor Law Commissioners in 1843.[2] The Royal Commissioners of 1843-5, after considering the unconditional exemptions, in whole or in part, then allowed under local Acts, agreed with both authorities that these exemptions ought not to continue. Although occupiers of small houses benefited

greatly by better drainage and other local improvements, landlords benefited still more: their property was permanently increased in value, and their risk of losses diminished, because poor tenants, enjoying better health in healthier houses, were able to pay rent more regularly than before.[3] Tenants were also charged higher rents owing to the immunity of small houses from rating. Thus, directly or indirectly, landlords were the chief gainers, and were tempted to construct houses which none would occupy except persons entitled by poverty to these exemptions. In fact, the amount from which tenants were relieved was paid to landlords as rent, instead of to the public purse as rates; increased burdens were, therefore, necessarily thrown upon other occupiers.[4]

As in other instances previously noticed, local Acts paved the way for public legislation on this question. A Derby Improvement Act, of 1825, made the landlord liable for rates on inferior descriptions of pro-

---

[1] Second Report, p. 29.

[2] Report on Local Taxation, 1843, p. 94.

[3] Royal Commissioners of 1843-5; Second Report, p. 30. One witness, an owner of small tenements in London, when asked, "What are the chief causes of loss of rent?" replied—"Three out of five of these losses occur through the sickness of tenants, who are working men. . . . I find that rent is best paid in healthy houses."

[4] Ib. p. 30.

perty.[1] A Hull Improvement Act, of 1840,[2] and Acts for Southampton and Swansea, in 1844,[3] adopted the same principle, though these Acts gave the Improvement Commissioners somewhat inconsistent powers " to reduce or remit the payment of any rate on account of the poverty of any owner or occupier, or any persons liable." The Royal Commissioners recommended that landlords of houses should be rated for drainage and other local improvements when houses were let in separate apartments, or when rents were collected more frequently than once a quarter, or when the yearly rent was less than 10*l*., a reasonable deduction being allowed from the gross rate as an equivalent for losses incurred in collecting the rents of such property.[4] A composition to owners paying poor rates had been allowed by public legislation since 1819.[5] Hence that puzzle of later years, the compound householder.

When sewerage and drainage began to be recognized as essential parts of local administration, most local Acts authorized the payment for main sewers out of a general rate, levied upon the whole district, while street drains were constructed at the expense of owners, and afterwards controlled by the public body. If owners made default, local authorities might do the work, and at once levy for expenses either on owners or occupiers. An occupier who paid was entitled to retain the money from his rent, and could not be required to pay more than was due as rent. *Mode of charging for permanent works.*

Levy upon owners or occupiers.

No provision was made for distributing over a series of years the cost of sewers, drains, or paving. The existing machinery by which local authorities can raise money for permanent works, extinguishing debt by annual payments in specified periods, is so easy, and now appears so obvious, that *Lump payments.*

---

[1] 6 Geo. IV. c. 132. The limit there fixed was 20*l*.; but in local Acts which adopted the same principle after the Reform Act, the limit was fixed at 10*l*.

[2] 3 & 4 Vict. c. 76, s. 50.
[3] 7 & 8 Vict. c. 75; 7 & 8 Vict. c. 102.
[4] Report, p. 30.
[5] 59 Geo. III. c. 12, s. 19.

we can hardly appreciate the hindrance to good government, even so lately as 1845, from the want of such powers. Levied in one collection, as the general practice then was, these expenses often entirely absorbed the immediate rents or profits of absolute owners, while owners of short terms, who might derive little benefit from the works, had still greater cause of complaint. That charges for permanent improvements should be borne, in part, by the next generation was not only a bare act of justice to existing ratepayers, but was essential to the success of any general system of sewerage. As it was, uniform evidence was given that this immediate charge upon owners or occupiers was "the great obstacle to an extensive voluntary adoption of improvements and to works of admitted necessity."[1]

Time for repayment.

In a few instances time might be allowed for repayment, but, with one exception,[2] this period never exceeded three years. At Manchester the Town Council generally allowed twelve months. They had no authority to do more. But these expenses frequently exceeded the whole yearly rent of premises, and therefore pressed with great harshness upon persons solely dependent upon such property, and without power to mortgage it, as, for example, artisans who borrowed money from building clubs to erect houses, the interest on which absorbed the whole rent.[3]

Nuisances prevailing in 1845.

Some flagrant nuisances are noticed by the Royal Commissioners as existing in most large towns through apathy and neglect among local authorities or from a want of any effectual legal remedy. "Collections of dung, frequently kept for sale, pig-sties in the most densely-populated situations, noxious matters from manufactories, and, above all,

---

[1] First Report of Royal Commissioners, 1843–5, pp. 10–12. In App., p. 161, an instance is given of a lady in Manchester, who had a life interest in premises which were sewered and paved by the local authority, at a charge to her of nearly two years' rental; she died before the two years ended.

[2] At Rochdale, by 7 & 8 Vict. c. 104, which defined no time for repayment.

[3] Second Report, p. 32.

the animal refuse almost invariably found in the neighbourhood of slaughter-houses, all contribute in their several
degrees to increase atmospheric impurity, and lower the
physical condition of the population." In Sunderland there **Dung-heaps.**
were no fewer than 182 public middensteads, receptacles
for filth of all kinds, generally situated in close, narrow
streets and lanes inhabited by the poorer classes, and in some
cases placed " in the basement floor of a dwelling-house, the
upper parts of which are occupied as bed-rooms."[1]

Slaughter-houses were nuisances as rife in 1845 as they **Slaughter-**
had been five centuries before. Sometimes they were even **houses.**
found below dwelling-houses, the smell in which was insuf-
ferable, while the inhabitants looked pale and sickly, and
diarrhœa frequently prevailed, although absent from courts
contiguous. In the township of Manchester alone there were
seventy-seven slaughter-houses, all without regulations, and
an impression prevailed among some of the neighbours " that
these smells were very healthy."[2] In scarcely one instance,
either in the metropolis or in provincial cities and towns,
were there any regulations or supervision for removal of
animal refuse, proper ventilation or efficient cleansing of
shambles or slaughter-houses. On the contrary, they were
found to be, almost without exception, noisome centres,
deteriorating the sanitary condition, generally of poor and
dense neighbourhoods, and constituting a general nuisance.[3]

Next to slaughter-houses ranked the nuisance arising from **Pig-sties.**
pigs, often kept in the most thickly populated districts. In
the year 1843 there were 1,680 pig-sties within the parish of
Birmingham alone.[4] At Sunderland such spots were most

---

[1] Royal Commission of 1843–5
(Replies by Committee of Inhabitants of Sunderland); Second Report,
p. 40, and App.

[2] Ib., Report on Towns in Lancashire, by Dr. Lyon Playfair; App.
pp. 17, 18.

[3] Ib.; Second Report, pp. 40, 41.

[4] Ib. p. 41; Report on Birmingham, by R. A. Slaney, App. p. 2.
Pig-sties in Edgbaston and Aston,
within the borough, brought up the
total number to 2,359, with 3,375
pigs. These were sties " accessible
to the police." Presumably, therefore, there were others.

visited by cholera in 1831. These and other crying sanitary evils might have been cured but for the supineness of local authorities. A clause in the Municipal Reform Act[1] empowered town councils to frame bye-laws, subject to sanction by the Home Secretary, for the suppression of nuisances not made an offence by any local Act. Bye-laws in several towns had been so framed and sanctioned, and town councils there had ample powers to suppress these nuisances, which, however, remained without remedy. It was time, indeed, these nuisances should be absolutely forbidden in large towns.

Power to frame bye-laws against nuisances.

Early in the present century special provisions were introduced into some local Acts requiring owners of furnaces "to use the best practicable means of preventing or counteracting the annoyance from smoke." Finding smoke an increasing evil, the Commissioners in 1845 recommended that, after a period of grace, these provisions in local Acts should be made general, and that local authorities should be authorized to proceed against owners of any factory from which noxious fumes proceeded. No statutory provision had at this time been made for the regulation of lodging houses in any part of England and Wales, but in some Scotch towns such powers had been exercised with great advantage under a local Act passed in 1840.[2] Commissioners of Police for the burgh of Calton, a suburb of Glasgow, licensed all lodging houses, and might issue regulations for their proper management, limit the number of persons accommodated in each house, and enforce due attention to cleanliness. Above all, they might require that immediate notice should be given of any case of fever or other disease, in order that the nature of the complaint might be ascertained, and the lodger treated, or, if necessary, removed. The inspection and regulation of lodging houses is now enforced by public statute,[3] but the

Prevention of smoke and noxious fumes.

Common lodging-houses.

Notification of infectious diseases.

[1] 5 & 6 Will. IV. c. 76, s. 90.   [3] 38 & 39 Vict. c. 55, ss. 76—89.
[2] 3 Vict. c. 28, ss. 20, 21.

notification of infectious diseases has only in recent years
obtained general recognition in local Acts.   This early precedent, therefore, due to the intelligent foresight of local
administrators in Scotland, deserves honourable mention.

Sanitary administration in the metropolis at this period was
in some respects worse than in provincial towns.[1]   In the latter,
with a few exceptions, the duties of sewering, paving, and
cleansing, that is, the union of surface cleansing and underground drainage, were combined under one management,
although there were often separate jurisdictions within one
municipal area.   In the metropolis, however, these duties
were managed by distinct bodies, except within the City and
in a narrow district administered by commissioners under
a local Act for draining and paving Regent Street and
Regent's Park.[2]   The separate jurisdictions of commissioners
of sewers throughout the metropolis have already been
described.   Even in 1845 the power of these commissioners in
Westminster and the Tower Hamlets to construct new sewers
was disputed.   Other metropolitan districts had set at rest
this question by obtaining local Acts, but these did not contemplate a proper combination of house and main drainage.
The Commissioners could not compel owners to connect their
houses with street sewers, and, indeed, as we have seen,
generally discouraged such connections.   Owing to these
causes the surveyor of one district stated that not more than
one-third of the houses there communicated with the sewers;
and elsewhere very few houses had been drained even into
sewers lately built.   Throughout the whole metropolis old
drains and cesspools frequently remained below the levels of

Sanitary administration in the metropolis, 1845.

House drainage.

---

[1] The rate of mortality in some
poor districts of London equalled or
exceeded that of the worst and most
neglected provincial towns.   In St.
Andrew's, Holborn, there were 3·5
deaths per cent.; Whitechapel, 3·3;
and St. Luke's, City Road, 3·2.   In
Liverpool the annual mortality was
3·5; in Manchester, 3·2; in Bristol,
3·1 per cent.   (Royal Commission of
1843-5; Second Report, pp. 68-9.)

[2] 5 Geo. IV. c. 100, amended by
6 Geo. IV. c. 38; 9 Geo. IV. c. 64;
2 & 3 Will. IV. c. 56.   Like much
other legislation relating even to
districts in the metropolis, these
were public Acts.

sewers, becoming a fruitful source of disease; and there was no power to prevent new cesspools from being sunk below these levels.[1] If house owners wished to connect drains with a main sewer, they were charged with a proportion of the expense of the sewer, according to house frontage. This charge affected different descriptions of property very unequally, especially houses at street corners.[2]

Sub-divisions in metropolis for paving and cleansing.

Outside the City and Regent Street and Regent's Park, paving and cleansing were managed, in 1845, by no fewer than eighty-four separate bodies of commissioners, at whose instance at least 129 Acts of Parliament had been passed since 1800. Many of these districts were of very limited extent, having been formed generally, under separate local Acts, in connection with the boundaries of particular properties. The parish of St. Pancras alone contained sixteen different districts, their limits coinciding with no parochial or other boundary, and only to be ascertained by diligent inquiry. Scarcely two local Acts agreed in the method of appointing commissioners, their qualifications, the definitions of offences, or the penalties prescribed. There were no powers to combine with adjoining authorities for common objects. The excessive multiplication of establishments and officials was obvious. District surveyors, commissioners of sewers, and commissioners of paving throughout these numerous isolated jurisdictions, all for the most part acted independently of each other. Gas and water companies, having powers to break up thoroughfares, had, up to the year 1835, exercised these powers in the same thoroughfares, and added to the existing confusion. District surveyors inspected the construction of house drains, but had no power over the main sewers into which these drains were run. Commissioners of paving, responsible for the surface-drainage of streets, had little or

---

[1] Royal Commission of 1843–5; Second Report, p. 70.

[2] The hardship caused by requiring immediate payment for such work was partly remedied in 1844 by 7 & 8 Vict. c. 84, s. 51, which also required proper drains to be made previous to the erection of any new house.

no control over the sewers which received surface water. In some districts, the gratings and gully-shoots belonged to the commissioners for paving; in others, to the commissioners of sewers.

This jumble of authorities and jurisdictions was no better in 1847, when a Royal Commission made special inquiry into this subject. Twenty parishes were then under supervision by the Westminster Court of Sewers. There were in these parishes twenty-five separate boards charged with street paving and cleansing.[1] Some sewers belonged to private owners. When a person desired to lay a drain from his house to the sewer, he had to obtain permission from any private owner who might be concerned and from the Court of Sewers; he must also pay for this privilege, and obtain leave from a paving board to open the ground. He had still to reckon with a gas or water company if he interfered with their pipes; and the delay, inconvenience, and expense often practically hindered these connections. The Westminster Court was overburdened with business. It had no plans of the district for the guidance of its professional advisers, so that they recommended a suspension of all sewerage works of magnitude for a year or more, until plans could be completed; without them it was impossible that any trustworthy estimates of new sewers could be furnished.[2]

Payment for any such works was demanded at once; in

Sewers and drainage in Westminster, 1847.

Plans.

System of paying for

---

[1] Metropolitan Sanitary Commission, 1847; Min. of Ev. p. 30. The "fifteen to twenty paving boards" of St. Pancras consisted of nearly a thousand commissioners. (Ib. p. 32.) One of these boards alone spent about 1,000l. a year upon management, exclusive of works. Sewer-rates and other rates were separately collected, so that the waste in every way from want of consolidation was enormous. In 1770 the necessity of consolidating all commissions for sewerage and paving in London was pointed out in a petition to Lord Bathurst, then Chancellor. At this period an Act had passed for uniting these bodies in the City, and had been found a measure of great convenience.

[2] Metropolitan Sanitary Commission, 1847; Ev. of Mr. Hertslet, chief clerk to the Westminster Court of Sewers, p. 29.

sewerage
works in
London.

London, as in provincial towns, there were at this time no means of spreading the charge over a period of years. The result was a heavy and also an unequal pressure upon property, for district A was provided with sewers out of funds raised in districts B and C, which remained without any such provision. Thus, in 1847, owners of property in courts and alleys in St. Clement Danes' had to pay for branch and main sewers required in Marylebone, while their own premises were undrained.[1] Another objection was to the mode of constituting courts of sewers. It was alleged that many of the substantial as well as "indifferent" men who were to be Commissioners under the statute of Henry VIII. were not substantial, and too often were not "indifferent." Appointment was obtained by nomination. Men of high station attended irregularly or not at all. Business, therefore, fell into the hands of a few members, and those not the most competent or trustworthy. In an Act regulating the Commissioners' proceedings there was a clause prohibiting them from acting or voting when interested, but it was sometimes set at defiance, as no penalty attached.[2]

Constitution
of sewer
commissions.

Local govern-
ment in
metropolis,
1855.

Even so lately as 1855, the number of local Acts in force within the metropolis was ·about two hundred and fifty, administered by no fewer than three hundred different bodies, consisting, it was estimated, of more than ten thousand vestrymen, Commissioners, trustees, or other members.[3] Many of these bodies were self-elected, or appointed for life; the multiplication of officials and the cost of establishments were enormous; and in most cases the ratepayers exercised little or no real control. Owing to divided jurisdictions, paving, lighting, and other public works, were almost universally ill-done. In Westminster, the boundaries of these jurisdictions were in the middle of streets, so that each

[1] Metropolitan Sanitary Commission, 1847; Ev. of Mr. Hertslet, p. 31.
[2] Ib. p. 34.

[3] 137 Hansard, 711-12; Speech of Sir Benjamin Hall on introducing Metropolis Local Management Bill, March 16, 1855.

side was governed by different bodies. In one great thoroughfare the paving was done by one authority, the lighting and watering on either side rested with two other authorities; and these three bodies had frequent differences and quarrels, so that the street was watered in the morning on one side, in the evening on the other.[1]

Such were the defects in local government, and especially in sanitary law or administration, which, notwithstanding manifold warnings, continued, in the first half of the nineteenth century, to encourage pestilence, swell mortality, and harbour disease in every large centre of population throughout the kingdom. They were grievous defects, all the more deplorable because they mainly concerned the health and well-being of the poor. In our next Chapter we shall see a welcome awakening to these evils, and many and strenuous efforts by Parliament to promote public health by general legislation. More remarkable still, it will be seen, have been the efforts everywhere made in the same direction by local authorities, interweaving this general legislation with special Acts of their own for better local government, and developing a public spirit and an intelligence of which there had as yet been little trace, but which were only commensurate with the rapid growth of wealth and population in their several jurisdictions during the later half of this century.

Evils awaiting amendment.

[1] 137 Hansard, 707.

CHAPTER XIII.

LOCAL AUTHORITIES (CONTINUED) :—GENERAL LEGISLATION
SUPPLEMENTING LOCAL STATUTES: PUBLIC HEALTH,
SANITARY, AND LOCAL GOVERNMENT ACTS, 1848-75:
LOCAL LEGISLATION IN LONDON: SEWERS COMMISSIONS:
METROPOLIS LOCAL MANAGEMENT ACT, 1855: MAIN
DRAINAGE: EMBANKMENTS OF THE THAMES: STREET IM-
PROVEMENTS: JURISDICTION AND FINANCIAL POWERS OF
METROPOLITAN BOARD: PRINCIPLES OF CENTRALIZATION
AND LOCAL AUTHORITY RECONCILED IN ACT OF 1855:
FUTURE LOCAL GOVERNMENT IN METROPOLIS.

General legis-
lation for
sanitary and
other pur-
poses after
1845.

IN their Second Report the Duke of Buccleuch's Commission
made a series of recommendations which produced a wholesome effect upon public opinion, and led to abundant legislation.   It will be necessary to notice briefly some of the
numerous public measures by which Parliament, after 1845,
tried to strengthen the hands of local authorities for sanitary
and other purposes, to supplement local Acts, and to regulate
local government.   Side by side with these measures, numerous local Acts were passed containing provisions suited
to special wants and circumstances.   Thus the laws now
administered by municipal and other authorities must be
looked for in public as well as in local statutes dating from
this period.

Nuisances
Removal and
Diseases Pre-
vention Act,
1846.

By a general Act in 1846[1] a summary jurisdiction for the
removal of nuisances was given to magistrates, on the information of Town Councils, Commissioners under local Acts,

---

[1] 9 & 10 Vict. c. 96.

or Boards of Guardians. This was the first of a series of statutes passed for similar objects, and by enabling guardians to act in removing nuisances, it may be said to have first extended sanitary legislation to rural districts.[1]   In 1847 various provisions for improved local government were consolidated in the Towns Improvement Clauses Act[2] and the Towns Police Clauses Act.[3]   Similar provisions, for the regulation of streets and buildings, the consumption of smoke, and many other objects, had been found by experience to be useful and necessary in many populous places, and were repeated, as " model clauses," in most private Improvement Acts. This repetition now became unnecessary. Henceforth the two consolidating statutes, or parts of them, might be incorporated, by reference, in local Acts, which thus became shorter and also more uniform. Unless so incorporated these general measures did not apply to any community.

Towns Improvement and Police Clauses Acts, 1847.

A great and comprehensive measure, which has been called the groundwork of our sanitary legislation,[4] was passed in the following session. This was the first Public Health Act.[5] It did not apply to the metropolis, and elsewhere was permissive, only coming into force upon petitions from a certain proportion of ratepayers, unless the Registrar-General's returns showed a larger proportion than twenty-three to 1,000 in the mortality of any district. In either case the General Board of Health, who were created by this Act,[6] might bring it into force by provisional Order. Like other

Public Health Act, 1848.

---

[1] Royal Sanitary Commission, 1871 ; Report, p. 7.

[2] 10 & 11 Vict. c. 34. An Act of 1833 (3 & 4 Will. IV. c. 90) empowered local authorities to rate inhabitants for the public lighting of towns. This power, by insuring a certain demand for gas for public lighting, increased the number of gasworks in small towns, and tended greatly to public convenience.

[3] 10 & 11 Vict. c. 89.

[4] Royal Sanitary Commission, 1871 ; Report, p. 7.

[5] 11 & 12 Vict. c. 63.

[6] This Board consisted of a President (who received 2,000l. a year) and two other persons appointed by the Crown. In 1858, after several reconstitutions, the Board ceased to exist, its functions being transferred in part to the Privy Council, in part to the Home Office, and afterwards to the Local Government Board.

public statutes which have been mentioned, this first Public
Health Act was founded to a large extent upon provisions
in local Acts obtained by metropolitan Commissioners of
Sewers and by authorities in a few large towns.   In municipal
boroughs town councils were made local boards of health; in
other districts owners and ratepayers elected these boards.
They might construct and control sewers and drains, all public
sewers being vested in them; they could regulate closets,
slaughter-houses, offensive trades, and common lodging-
houses; remove nuisances; supervise the laying-out of streets
and building of houses; provide burial-grounds and places of
recreation; supply public baths with water; and appoint, along
with other officers, a medical inspector, whose special care was
the public health.

Outbreaks of cholera, 1848-9, and 1853-4.

The main defect of this legislation was its permissive
character; there was also a want of zeal and intelligence in
administering it.   A second outbreak of cholera in 1848-9
did much to hasten sanitary measures, especially when the
medical officers who had been appointed easily traced its
most fatal ravages to crowded alleys, impure air, and polluted
water.   In 1853-4 cholera visited us again, but with abated
virulence, except in localities still notorious for insanitary
conditions.   These new proofs of danger from neglect and
benefit from precautions already taken induced Parliament,

Nuisance Removal Act, 1855.

in 1855, to confer enlarged powers upon local boards of
health.[1]   They were authorized to appoint sanitary inspectors,
who, among other salutary powers, might examine and seize
unwholesome food, provide against overcrowding, and more

Diseases Prevention Act, 1855.

effectually abate nuisances.   In the same session a new
Diseases Prevention Act[2] enabled the Privy Council to issue
Orders during the prevalence of any " formidable epidemic,
endemic, or contagious " disease.   While these Orders were
in force the Board of Health might make regulations for the
speedy interment of the dead, house-to-house visitation, and

[1] 18 & 19 Vict. c. 121; a consolidation and extension of Nuisance

Removal Acts previously passed.
[2] 18 & 19 Vict. c. 116.

the dispensing of medicines; but they were not to interfere with the functions of local authorities, under local or general Acts, in cleansing streets, disinfecting houses, and removing nuisances.

In 1858, a Local Government Act[1] took effect in all places where the Public Health Act, 1848, was in force at the time of its passing; and the two Acts were construed together as one statute. This new legislation amended the constitution and powers of local boards in towns and populous districts. Without any provisional Order, or even any sanction by the central authority, it might be put in force, wholly or partially, by simple resolutions, passed in municipal boroughs by town councils; in districts under Improvement Commissioners, by these Commissioners; and in all other places having defined boundaries, by owners and ratepayers. In other places not having defined boundaries the provisions of these two statutes might be adopted with the Home Secretary's approval. Extended powers of police and municipal government, as well as for carrying out sanitary works, were given in urban districts. The machinery of provisional Orders was also largely extended; and for the first time local boards were authorized to take land compulsorily, by means of these Orders, subject to confirmation by Parliament.[2] Through the same process, local Acts might be amended or altered, and areas re-arranged.

Local Government Act, 1858.

In 1861, local bodies constituted under local Acts were enabled to adopt portions of the Acts of 1848 and 1858, although they were not so constituted for sanitary purposes. To local boards whose authority was thus derived from local statutes, these and other general Acts were extended, unless their provisions were opposed to, or restrictive of, any provisions locally in force, when the latter were to prevail. It was also declared that whenever the general Acts and a local Act contained provisions for effecting the same or a similar

Local Government Act Amendment Acts, 1861-3.

---

[1] 21 & 22 Vict. c. 98.   [2] Ib. s. 75.

object, but in different modes, the local board of health might proceed at its discretion either under the general Acts or the local Act.[1] Local boards were at the same time authorized to exercise compulsory powers, outside their own districts, in making outfall sewers. Two years afterwards, Parliament restricted the voluntary adoption of the Act of 1858 in places having less than three thousand inhabitants, unless with the Home Secretary's approval.[2] Two Sewage Utilization Acts, of 1865 and 1867, applied to Scotland and Ireland as well as England. The first of these statutes[3] enabled town councils, Improvement Commissioners, vestries, and other local bodies to dispose of sewage in their districts, applying it to agricultural purposes, or in such other ways as to avoid nuisance. As sewer authorities, they were entrusted with large powers for these objects, and to prevent the pollution of streams. The Act also tried to make rural authorities efficient guardians of public health; it may, indeed, be said to have introduced into rural districts " the first real instalment of active sanitary powers."[4] By the Act of 1867,[5] further facilities were given for carrying sewage outside local boundaries. Land might be purchased, and districts and boards might unite, for purposes of this nature.

Sewage Utilization Acts, 1865-7.

Sanitary Acts, 1866-70.

All these public statutes were intended to promote better local government, and to improve public health by means of voluntary local effort. We now come to a series of statutes, specially devoted to sanitary objects, but recognizing that local bodies could not always be trusted, and must in certain cases be compelled to discharge essential duties. By the Sanitary Act, 1866,[6] some previous legislation was amended, and sewer authorities, including vestries, obtained extended powers to make and use sewers and supply water. A larger definition was again given to nuisances, such as

---

[1] 24 & 25 Vict. c. 61, s. 29.
[2] 26 & 27 Vict. c. 17.
[3] 28 & 29 Vict. c. 75.

[4] Royal Sanitary Commission, 1871; Report, p. 10.
[5] 30 & 31 Vict. c. 113.
[6] 29 & 30 Vict. c. 90.

overcrowded houses, unhealthy workshops, and smoke. New duties were imposed on nuisance authorities, who were called upon to provide means for disinfection, and mortuaries. In case of default by a nuisance authority, proceedings might be taken by the chief officer of police under the Home Secretary's direction. The Privy Council might also compel two or more boards of guardians to act together in executing the Diseases Prevention Act. Above all, in the event of serious default by sanitary authorities, the Home Secretary might call upon them to do their duty, and, upon continued default, might carry out any necessary work at the expense of the district.[1] A second Sanitary Act, passed in 1868,[2] amongst other useful provisions, gave to vestries, as sanitary authorities, many powers similar to those of guardians as nuisance authorities. Another of these statutes, in 1870, was chiefly intended to facilitate, with proper safeguards, the removal to hospitals or elsewhere of persons suffering from infectious disease.[3]

This prolific legislation by no means exhausted the list of sanitary measures. Many subsidiary Acts bore witness to the same wholesome anxiety now awakened in Parliament and the country. A Royal Commission in 1843 had disclosed the scandalous condition of overcrowded graveyards in towns and a serious injury to public health arising from this cause. It was not, however, till 1853 that Parliament passed a general Act,[4] the first of a long series, which provided for the discontinuance of burials in towns, the appointment of burial boards, and the acquisition of ground for extra-mural interment. Between the years 1844 and 1867, no fewer than twenty general Acts added to the stringency or extended the application of the Factory Acts, limiting the hours of labour

Burials in towns.

Factory Acts, 1844–67.

---

[1] 29 & 30 Vict. c. 90, s. 49. Practical effect was given to this provision by the Sanitary Loans Act, 1869, which enabled the Public Works Loan Commissioners, upon the Home Secretary's certificate, to advance money for sanitary works executed by his orders, on such default, charging local rates with its repayment (32 & 33 Vict. c. 100).

[2] 31 & 32 Vict. c. 115.

[3] 33 & 34 Vict. c. 53.

[4] 16 & 17 Vict. c. 134. London obtained legislation on this subject in 1850 and 1852.

of young people, or enforcing cleanliness and ventilation in factories.[1] A Bakehouse Regulation Act in 1863,[2] and a Workshop Regulation Act in 1867,[3] belong to the same category of measures.

Workshops and bake-houses.

Town councils were enabled in 1846-8 to construct baths and wash-houses;[4] and, in other places than towns, vestries might provide these means of cleanliness upon a resolution passed by a two-thirds vote, and approval by a Secretary of State. Besides provisions in the Public Health Act, 1848, requiring local boards to register and inspect common lodging-houses, see to their cleansing and ventilation, and fix the number of lodgers,[5] special Acts in 1851-3 compelled keepers of these houses to give immediate notice of any infectious disease to local authorities.[6] With a view to provide better accommodation of this nature for the labouring poor, local boards of health, town councils, and Improvement Commissioners were, in 1851, empowered to construct lodging-houses and raise loans for this purpose.[7] Nor were these advantages limited to urban districts possessing the means of local government just mentioned, for, with the Home Secretary's consent, the Act might be adopted in a parish or in united parishes having a population of 10,000.

Baths and wash-houses.

Common Lodging-houses Acts, 1851-3.

Labouring Classes' Lodging Houses Act, 1851.

To the period under review also belongs the first Artisans and Labourers' Dwellings Act, which, in 1868, upon a report by householders that any premises were dangerous to health and unfit for habitation, made it incumbent on local autho-

Artisans and Labourers' Dwellings Act, 1868.

---

[1] Legislation on this subject began in 1802 (42 Geo. III. c. 73). Other early Acts are 59 Geo. III. c. 66; 60 Geo. III. c. 5; 6 Geo. IV. c. 63; 10 Geo. IV. cc. 51, 63; and 1 & 2 Will. IV. c. 39. The Extension Act of 1867 (30 & 31 Vict. c. 103) embraced within the definition of Factory almost every description of manufacturing premises.

[2] 26 & 27 Vict. c. 40.

[3] 30 & 31 Vict. c. 146.

[4] 9 & 10 Vict. c. 74; 10 & 11 Vict. c. 61.

[5] 11 & 12 Vict. c. 63, s. 66.

[6] 14 & 15 Vict. c. 28; 16 & 17 Vict. c. 41. Compulsory notification of infectious disease is now being steadily extended under local Acts, and in January, 1886, was required in more than forty cities and towns in England and Wales.

[7] 14 & 15 Vict. c. 34.

rities, in all towns in the United Kingdom having more than 10,000 inhabitants, to force an owner of such premises to remedy defects, or undertake the remedy themselves, at his expense.[1] The Vaccination Acts were consolidated in 1867, *Vaccination Act, 1867.* boards of guardians being charged with specific duties and payment of fees incurred in executing the law.[2] Adultera- *Adulteration of Food Act, 1860.* tion was dealt with for the first time in 1860, when courts of quarter sessions in counties, and town councils in boroughs having separate courts of quarter sessions, were authorized to appoint analysts, from whom any purchaser of food or drink might, for a small payment, procure an analysis; penalties were also provided for adulteration. It was hoped by this legislation to protect consumers, especially the poor, against frauds from which they suffered in health as well as in pocket.

This summary of general legislation[3] shows that during the quarter of a century preceding 1871 Parliament could not be reproached for want of industry or good intentions. It seemed, indeed, to have acted upon the maxim, attributed at a later date to Lord Beaconsfield, "Sanitas sanitatum, omnia sanitas." The statute-book now teemed with measures relating to public health. Scotland and Ireland shared in this legislation. Local authorities within the same period had not been idle. It was reckoned that in 1871 there were *Extended local govern-ment in 1871.* upwards of seven hundred districts, urban and semi-rural, which, through town councils, improvement commissioners, or elected boards, exercised powers under the Public Health and Local Government Acts above enumerated. A few towns were still governed under local Improvement Acts alone. But local authorities in these towns, as well as all boards of guardians and vestries in rural and other districts, respectively possessed the powers conferred by the Nuisance

[1] 31 & 32 Vict. c. 130.

[2] 30 & 31 Vict. c. 84, amended in 1871 by 34 & 35 Vict. c. 98.

[3] It is based upon a valuable his-tory of sanitary laws given by the Royal Sanitary Commission, 1871 (Rep., pp. 4—14), which should be referred to for fuller details.

Removal, Sanitary and Sewage Utilization Acts.[1] Parliament, therefore, had done all that could fairly be expected of it. It had furnished local authorities with the means of meeting many of their difficulties. Henceforth, improved sanitary conditions throughout the country depended mainly upon them.

Royal Sanitary Commission, 1871.

Unfortunately, the Royal Commission over which Mr. Adderley presided[2] were obliged to report that, in many cases, the duties which Parliament had assigned to local authorities were not discharged by them, and that they frequently tolerated insanitary conditions, resulting in a large amount of preventible sickness and mortality. Considerable numbers of people, both in town and country, were "habitually drinking polluted water." In many places accumulations of filth were "widely vitiating the air." Numbers of the working classes were "debilitated, and thrown into sickness and poverty," by a tainted atmosphere and unhealthy dwellings." Overcrowding remained, as a quarter of a century previously, "the cause of much physical as well as moral evil;" and the close connection between physical and moral pollution was once more urged.[3]

Causes of neglect by local authorities.

Inertness and neglect were chiefly found in small towns and rural or semi-rural districts. Many causes contributed to this neglect. The fact that the Public Health Act of 1848 and the Local Government Acts only took effect upon voluntary adoption by ratepayers or their representatives, accounted of itself for the very partial adoption of sanitary remedies. Other causes were, the confusion of areas and of autho-

---

[1] Royal Sanitary Commission, 1871; Report, p. 11.

[2] This Commission was first appointed in 1868; it was re-constituted in April, 1869, and reported evidence at the end of that year; its second Report, containing a mass of valuable information, with the conclusions of the Commissioners, bears no date, but was printed early in 1871 [C. 281]. It bears the following signatures :—C. B. Adderley, Rom-

ney, Ducie, Robert Montagu, Russell Gurney, Stephen Cave, Thomas Watson, C. B. Ewart (Lieut.-Col. R. E.), J. R. McClean, Samuel Whitbread, John T. Hibbert, Evan M. Richards, George Clive, Francis S. Powell, Benjamin Shaw, James Paget, Henry W. Acland, R. Christison, William Stokes, John Lambert, Francis T. Bircham.

[3] Royal Sanitary Commission, 1871; Report, p. 15.

rities, as well as difficulties in interpreting the intricate and undigested mass of law which had by this time grown up. Thus doubts often arose, among various bodies, as to which of them possessed certain responsibilities or powers; and litigation, the stoppage of contemplated works, and, still oftener, inaction, were not uncommon consequences. Boards of guardians, again, seldom seemed aware that they were responsible for the removal of nuisances in country places; vestries were equally unconscious; nor was the central administration in London able to rouse these bodies to a proper execution of their important sanitary duties.[1]

This report was not encouraging. With some slackening of speed, however, Parliament continued, in 1871, its efforts to improve sanitary legislation and local government. The Royal Commissioners had pointed out several defects in the central authority, chief among which were its want of concentration, for local administration was then controlled by the local government department of the Home Office, the health department of the Privy Council, and the Board of Trade. This divided jurisdiction caused delay and confusion; the Commissioners therefore advised that it should be centred in one minister and one department, who should control all laws concerning both public health and relief of the poor.[2] No time was lost in carrying out this recommendation by an

Want of concentration in central authority.

---

[1] Royal Sanitary Commission, 1871; Report, p. 21. "So large a discretion must of necessity be left to local authorities as to details, that in practice much will always depend on the energy and wisdom of those who compose such authorities. Moreover, there are limits to the power of any central authority to remedy the evils produced by local inefficiency. It may control, stimulate, and in some cases supplement, the efforts of local bodies, but it cannot be a substitute for them." (Ib. 71.)

[2] "There should be one recognized and sufficiently powerful minister, not to centralize administration, but, on the contrary, to set local life in motion: a real motive power, and an authority to be referred to for guidance and assistance by all the sanitary authorities for local government throughout the country. Great is the vis inertiæ to be overcome; the repugnance to self-taxation; the practical distrust of science; and the number of persons interested in offending against sanitary laws, even among the local authorities who are to enforce them." (Report, p. 31.)

Constitution of Local Government Board, 1871. Act of 1871, constituting a Local Government Board, and vesting in it certain functions of the Home Secretary and Privy Council, concerning public health and local government, together with the powers of the Poor Law Board.[1] In the same Session another statute facilitated gifts of land for public parks, exempting such gifts from the Mortmain Act, but providing that they must be made twelve months before the donor's death and must be duly enrolled.[2]

Gifts of land for public parks.

Public Health Act, 1872. Another Public Health Act for England, beyond the metropolis, was the feature of 1872.[3] The Royal Commissioners had recommended "that there should be one local authority for all public health purposes in every place, so that no area should be without such an authority, or have more than one." They also recommended that, instead of allowing localities to adopt, wholly or partly, or to ignore, the provisions of existing general Acts, no option should be left to local authorities, and that sanitary laws should be applicable everywhere. Upon these lines the new statute proceeded, dividing England into urban and rural sanitary districts; the sanitary authorities in the former being town councils, improvement commissioners, or local boards, and in the latter boards of guardians. In order that these authorities in populous places might not be crippled for want of funds, it was now provided[4] that the limit of rating under local Acts should not apply to expenses for sanitary purposes; and the Public Works Loan Commissioners were authorized to lend money to sanitary authorities on the security of their rates, for periods of thirty or fifty years, at three and a-half per cent. interest.

Sanitary Laws Amendment Act, 1874. An Act to amend and extend the sanitary laws[5] provided, in 1874, that orders against a defaulting sanitary authority might be enforced by mandamus. It imposed upon all urban authorities the duty of cleansing streets, conveniences,

---

[1] 34 & 35 Vict. c. 70. In 1872 a Local Government Board was constituted in Ireland by 35 & 36 Vict. c. 69.

[2] 34 & 35 Vict. c. 13.
[3] 35 & 36 Vict. c. 79.
[4] Sect. 43.
[5] 37 & 38 Vict. c. 93.

and ashpits, with penalties for neglect.   In order to clear up doubts as to the effect of provisions of 1872 for concentrating sanitary powers in some urban districts, it was also declared that all such " powers, rights, duties, capacities, liabilities, and obligations " belonging to any body constituted by a local Act in an urban district, were transferred and became attached to the urban sanitary authority.

Hitherto Parliament had not grappled with the chief work suggested by the Royal Commissioners in 1871, namely, to rid the statute book of the numerous and complicated Acts which encumbered it relating to public health, and include the whole in one comprehensive measure.   This great work was successfully accomplished by the Public Health Act, 1875, which still remains the governing code on sanitary subjects and local government for England and Wales, excluding the Metropolis.[1]   It was little more than a consolidating Act, embodying in its provisions, 343 in number,[2] some forty-seven statutes, which were now wholly or partially repealed.   The new statute came into force in urban districts concurrently with any local Acts, unless it was opposed to or restrictive of their provisions; and it made the law as uniform, simple and clear as could reasonably be expected on a range of subjects so difficult and far-reaching.   Among subsequent statutes which may be noted is one passed in 1881, consolidating two similar Acts of 1863, 1874, and further regulating the discharge of noxious vapours from alkali and similar works. It has not, however, succeeded in removing this nuisance.[3]

Public Health Act, 1875.

Alkali, &c. Works Regulation Act, 1881.

---

[1] 38 & 39 Vict. c. 55.   A separate Act was passed on the same model for Ireland in 1878 (41 & 42 Vict. c. 52, amended by 42 & 43 Vict. c. 57).   In Scotland the governing statute is a Public Health Act of 1867 (30 & 31 Vict. c. 101).

[2] With thirty pages of schedules.

[3] 44 & 45 Vict c. 37.   At the end of 1884 about a thousand alkali works were registered under this Act.   Notwithstanding the improved means now adopted for preventing the discharge of noxious vapours from these works, it is calculated that about a thousand tons of alkali waste are daily deposited in the neighbourhood of Widnes alone.   At this rate of output, a single year's accumulation would cover the whole of St. James's Park, sixty acres in area, to a depth of between three and four feet.   This enormous mass of material, when oxidised by the wind and the rain, gives off sulphuretted hydrogen in large quantities, destroying vegeta-

Amended powers of rating.

It will be remembered that much of the unwillingness to carry out local improvements arose from a want of power to defer any part of the payment for these improvements. By special Acts at this period many communities had cured this blot in general legislation. The Public Health Act, 1848, following in their track, enabled local authorities to raise money on loan for permanent works and spread the repayment over a series of years.[1] Every local body administering this statute, and the corresponding Act of 1858, had power to make a general district rate, private improvement rates, and a water supply rate, and to raise money by mortgage of the general rates.

Private improvement rates.

When private premises were improved by permanent works not properly chargeable on the general district rate, private improvement rates might be assessed on occupiers of any premises so "improved." The amount of these rates was to be such as would suffice to discharge the cost of any improvement, together with interest, spread over such period, not exceeding thirty years, as the local authority might determine. Hence the hardship and injustice of enforcing a lump payment were avoided. In the event of premises being unoccupied, private improvement rates became a charge upon owners. An occupier holding at rack rent was entitled to deduct from his rent three-fourths of the amount paid by him; or might make an equitable deduction based upon any other terms of holding.[2] General district rates were to be levied on all descriptions of property assessed for the relief of the poor, and fell entirely on occupiers.

Local Improvement Acts after 1840.

From this series of public measures we may now turn to the private legislation with which they are so closely connected. It is not possible to take more than a rapid survey of the numerous Acts for sanitary and other purposes which

---

tion for several miles around. Hitherto it has not been found possible at these works to extract from the fumes discharged the sulphur, which is their most noxious and at the same time their most valuable constituent. (Report of Local Government Board for 1884–5, pp. 120–1.)

[1] 11 & 12 Vict. c. 63, ss. 107 *et seq.*, repealed by 21 & 22 Vict. c. 98, s. 57. See now 38 & 39 Vict. c. 55, ss. 233–244.

[2] 11 & 12 Vict. c. 63, ss. 90, 91. See now Public Health Act, 1875, ss. 213–215.

Parliament passed at the instance of local authorities during the present century, but especially since the public inquiries mentioned in the last chapter. Between the years 1801 and 1865 the statute-book contains about 470 Improvement Acts relating to various districts of the Metropolis alone.[1] Soon after the year 1840, most large communities elsewhere also began to seek special legislation. The changes and improvements which have by these means been made in local administration will be best appreciated by following them in a few specific instances.

It will be remembered that the Metropolis was mentioned by successive Committees and Commissions as a conspicuous example of inefficient sewerage and house drainage, paving and cleansing, due in great measure to a multiplicity of co-ordinate and often conflicting authorities. In 1848 a first step was taken towards better government, by consolidating seven of the eight Metropolitan Commissions of Sewers into one general Board, having jurisdiction over any places in Middlesex, Surrey, Essex and Kent "not more than twelve miles distant in a straight line from St. Paul's Cathedral."[2] It was enacted that every house should be provided with proper conveniences and drained into the main sewers. The new Board were to carry out these provisions and effectually drain the area assigned to them. They and their successors[3] began zealously to improve house drainage, abolish cesspools, and make communications between houses and main sewers. After six of these Commissions had been appointed, partly nominated by the government, partly elected, it was felt, even by themselves, that their administration had not proved successful.[4] In 1855, therefore, a

Consolidation of Metropolitan Sewer Commissions, 1848.

---

[1] Lords' Index to Local and Personal Acts.

[2] 11 & 12 Vict. c. 112. The City Commission of Sewers was left untouched.

[3] A Royal Warrant issued under the Act of 1848 appointed twelve Commissioners, to whom were added five ex officio representatives from the City of London. All were unpaid; they were to hold office for two years.

[4] Though charged with control over a large area, and possessing large powers of rating, they had, up to 1854, attempted only one large work, a sewer in Victoria Street,

Metropolis
Local
Management
Act, 1855.

new Act was passed " for the better local management of the Metropolis."[1] This Act, which became operative on January 1st, 1856, superseded the old vestries and numerous other local authorities, substituting for them thirty-six vestries or Boards, each charged with the entire control of local drainage and sewerage, and other works within its district, while a corporate body, the Metropolitan Board of Works, regulated streets and buildings, superintended all great municipal undertakings, and, in particular, were made responsible for main sewerage. The local bodies were directly elected by ratepayers, and then nominated representatives on the central Board.[2]

John Martin's
plan, 1834,
for embank-
ing the
Thames and
intercepting
London
sewage.

A work of extreme costliness and difficulty, the interception of sewage from the Thames, had long been deemed essential on sanitary grounds. It originated in the fertile brain of a well-known painter, John Martin, who, in 1834, proposed to embank both sides of the river, with a tunnel in each embankment to intercept the sewage and convey it to distant points near the sea. This plan attracted attention, and was examined by a Committee. An embankment of the Thames had previously been more than once suggested. As a whole, however, Martin's plan was a bold and original conception, anticipating, in principle, both the works ultimately executed, but too far in advance of the time.[3] Similar schemes were afterwards proposed, particularly one in 1845, by Mr. Wicksteed, C.E., whose intercepting sewers would have discharged their contents at Barking Creek and Greenwich Marshes, after deodorization by chemical means.[4]

which, after costing a large sum, fell into ruins. (Royal Commission on Metropolitan Sewage Discharge, 1882–4 ; First Rep. p. 15.)

[1] 18 & 19 Vict. c. 120.

[2] In 1885 the number of local bodies represented on the Board was increased to thirty-eight, and the number of members to sixty, including the chairman, a paid officer, who is not a representative member (48 & 49 Vict. c. 33). The City of London sends three representatives to the Board ; the vestries and district boards send two or one.

[3] Royal Commission on Metropolitan Sewage Discharge, 1882–4 ; First Rep. 12. Among the members of the Committee who investigated John Martin's scheme were the Earl of Euston, Col. Sir Frederick Trench, M.P., and General Sir Patrick Ross.

[4] Ib. 12.

Before 1855, the necessity of preserving the Thames from Urgency of interception, 1848—55. pollution had grown to be urgent. By the abolition of cesspools after 1848, and the connection of every house drain with a main sewer, one nuisance was abated but another took its place. The Thames became foul, and, in hot weather, noxious. Large deposits of offensive matter on the low, flat, river-banks were left dry at low water; and the more effective the house drainage, the more alarming grew this new source of injury to health.[1] Even in 1849 the consolidated Commission of Sewers had instructed their consulting engineer to prepare a plan for lines of sewers converging into large tanks, or "sumps," whose contents might, by pumping, be conveyed away for agricultural purposes. There was a rival plan of interception, based upon a discharge into the Thames below London. As the Commissioners could not agree they invited competition, but were still more perplexed when a hundred and sixteen plans were sent in.[2] They then resigned.

Their successors included some eminent engineers, including Sir John Burgoyne, Mr. Robert Stephenson, Mr. Rendel, and Capt. Vetch, R.E.; and in 1850, setting aside all the fruits of competition, they instructed Mr. Frank Forster to submit a Mr. Frank Forster's plan of 1850. scheme. Following old lines, he designed on each side of the river intercepting sewers, with pumping stations, and outlets for discharge, on the south bank, in Woolwich Marshes, and, on the north, near Galleon's Reach. But the Commissioners had no money with which to carry out these works, and were superseded before they could initiate legislation. In 1853, a

---

[1] The Royal Commission on Metropolitan Sewage Discharge, 1882–4, had evidence that, in 1848, there were some 200,000 cesspools in the populous districts of the Metropolis, containing an aggregate capacity of about five and a quarter million cubic feet. These collections of pestiferous matter were gradually pumped into the Thames; and water-closets were compulsorily substituted. (First Report, p. 15.)

[2] " Some of these had much merit, particularly one by Messrs. Maclean & Stileman, who, adopting the principle of interception, carried the outfalls to the sea, and made use of the sewage for reclaiming waste lands on the Essex coast." (Ib.; First Report, p. 16.)

Great London Drainage Bill, 1853.

"Separate" system of drainage, 1854.

private company promoted a "Great London Drainage" Bill, which, after prolonged discussion and enquiry, was rejected by a Committee of the House of Commons. In 1854, a plan was brought forward for entirely remodelling the drainage of London, by separating sewage from rainfall, and providing independent channels for the removal of each. This project was approved by the General Board of Health, and also by the Home Secretary. It was opposed, however, by the Sewers' Commission, who resigned upon finding themselves at variance with the Government upon this question.

Eight years had now passed since the first scheme for diverting sewage from the Thames had been prepared for the Consolidated Board. After endless discussions, and great waste of ingenuity, however, nothing had been done. By the Act of 1855, constituting the Metropolitan Board, Parliament imposed upon this new governing body the duty of completing, before December 31st, 1860, "such sewers and works as they may think necessary for preventing all or any part of the sewage within the Metropolis from flowing or passing into the river Thames in or near the Metropolis."[1] But no plan was to be carried into effect until it had been approved by the Government.

Duty of interception imposed on Metropolitan Board, 1855.

Plan of 1856.

In 1856 Mr. (afterwards Sir Joseph) Bazalgette, engineer to the Metropolitan Board, prepared an intercepting scheme for the southern, and also, in concert with Mr. Haywood, engineer of the City Sewers Commission, for the northern side of London, with outfalls at Plumstead Marshes and Barking Creek. Sir Benjamin Hall, then First Commissioner of Works, objected that these outfalls, being not only near to, but actually within the Metropolis, would contravene the Act of 1855. Considering, therefore, that the scheme was "entirely at variance with the intentions of Parliament," in providing by this Act for the purification of the Thames, he sent back the Board's plan. Later in 1856,

Vetoed by the Government.

[1] 18 & 19 Vict. c. 120, s. 135.

an amended proposal by the Board, with outfalls two or three miles lower down the river, was also rejected. These outfalls were just outside the Metropolitan boundary, but the First Commissioner of Works was of opinion that the sewage would flow back into the Metropolitan area.

Other plans had been considered by the Metropolitan Board for outfalls below Gravesend; but as such an extension would cost between one and two millions sterling, and would mainly benefit persons residing on the river-banks outside the Metropolis, the Board intimated that they could only undertake this extension if the additional outlay were provided by the Government. Meanwhile, Captain Burstal, afterwards secretary to the Thames Conservancy Board, who, at Sir Benjamin Hall's request, had made a series of experiments on tidal flow in the Thames, reported that Erith Reach, fifteen miles below London Bridge, and Rainham Creek, nearly opposite, were the nearest points at which sewage could be discharged without danger of its return into the Metropolis. For a time the Metropolitan Board adopted this recommendation, and sent in a third plan thus amended. Sir Benjamin Hall, however, determined to submit the whole subject of Metropolitan drainage to independent advisers,[1] who, in 1857, reported that, in their opinion, the plans of the Metropolitan Board did not provide for the removal of a sufficient quantity of sewage or of storm-water; and that Erith Reach was not a proper point of outfall because of its liability to shoal, and because, also, the sewage would flow back within the Metropolis. They suggested Sea Reach, fifteen miles lower down.

Proposed extension of outfalls.

Government Referees, 1857.

As Sir Benjamin Hall declined to ask Parliament for any contribution towards the additional cost of executing this work, the Metropolitan Board refused to undertake it, on the ground that such a burden could not be justly imposed upon the ratepayers. They then, in November, 1857, requested

[1] Captain Douglas Galton, R.E., Mr. James Simpson, C.E., and Mr. Thomas Blackwell, C.E.

their engineer, Mr. Bazalgette, with whom were associated Mr. Thomas Hawksley, C.E., and Mr. G. P. Bidder, C.E., to consider once more the best means of carrying out the main drainage of London. Accordingly, in April, 1858, these gentlemen reported that the works proposed by the Government Referees would be of " a magnitude and character wholly unexampled," of " enormous and uncertain cost," and unnecessary for preserving the Thames from pollution. As points of outfall they suggested, on the north side, Barking Creek, on the south side, Crossness Point ; the former about two miles, the latter but three and a-quarter miles from Woolwich ; " both situated in low and dreary marshes, where neither the works nor the sewage can give reasonable cause of offence to any one."

Much controversy followed upon the merits of these rival plans. Meanwhile the Thames became more offensive, and strong language was used in both Houses of Parliament.[1] At length, on June 29, 1858, the Metropolitan Board adopted in its main features the scheme proposed by their engineers.

They also complained of hindrance in carrying out intercepting works, through interference and opposition by the Government, and asked to be relieved from this check in the Act of 1855. A change of Ministry had brought about a change of policy, and, in July, 1858, Mr. Disraeli, then Chancellor of the Exchequer, brought in a Bill giving the desired relief, on the ground that, as the Metropolitan ratepayers paid for the work, they had a right to construct it as they pleased.

This proposal met with determined opposition. Upon works assumed to be of national importance, a veto by the

---

[1] " Members are unable to remain in the Library and Committee-rooms owing to the stench " (Mr. Brady, June 11, 1858). " By a perverse ingenuity one of our noblest rivers has been changed into a cesspool " (Mr. Mangles, June 15). " The Thames is one vast sewer, which will surely spread disease and death around " (Mr. Palk, June 17). Its " vile state " and " pestilential condition " were subjects of indignant comment on June 18. (See also discussion in House of Lords, June 25.)

Government, it was urged, should always be retained.[1] But the prolonged deadlock had become a national scandal, nor was there any sufficient answer to the argument that, no national subvention being asked for, the Metropolitan ratepayers should not be compelled to carry out a costly plan, pronounced by eminent engineers to be unnecessary for securing the object which Parliament desired. It was also pointed out with much force in debate, that, as the principle of interception would be adopted, the point of outfall now chosen might easily be extended hereafter, if necessary.

Notwithstanding, therefore, the late period at which it was introduced, the Bill became law on August 2, 1858.[2] Instead of subjecting any works of interception to previous approval by the Government, it was now enacted that "the Metropolitan Board shall cause to be commenced, as soon as may be after the passing of this Act, and to be carried out and completed with all convenient speed, according to such plan as to them may seem proper, the necessary sewers and works for improving the main drainage of the Metropolis, and for preventing, as far as may be practicable, the sewage of the Metropolis from passing into the Thames within the Metropolis." Borrowing powers were given to the amount of three millions; the time for executing the works was extended till December 31, 1863, and the Board were made liable to indictment if they caused any nuisance.

Metropolis Management Amendment Act, 1858.

After the passing of this Act the works were at once commenced, and were "opened" by the Prince of Wales in April, 1865. Although they were not then wholly finished, the Thames had become much purer through the gradual diversion of sewage. On the north side the low-level sewer was delayed by the Thames Embankment, of which it formed a structural part. It was not until the year 1875 that this

Completion of works, 1875.

[1] The Royal Commissioners of 1882–4 (First Report, p. 28) think it is "remarkable that the Legislature should have withdrawn all control over the construction of gigantic works of this kind, which were certain to have influences of a wide national character."

[2] 21 & 22 Vict. c. 104.

colossal undertaking was pronounced complete.[1] But in dealing with such works, adapted for a vast and rapidly increasing population, and tested by conditions often changing and sometimes unforeseen, "completion" is a relative term. As the Government Referees of 1857 predicted, the outlets for storm water were found insufficient. Since the year 1879, therefore, large extensions of the main drainage system have been made, and in 1885-6 were still in progress, in order to prevent floods in low-lying districts.[2] Exclusive of relief

Extensions
since 1879.

[1] On the north side there are three great lines of interception:—1. A high-level sewer beginning at Hampstead and Highgate, passing by Hackney and Stratford, crossing over the Lea by Bow, and thence to Barking Creek. This and the next conduit act entirely by gravitation. 2. A middle-level sewer, beginning at Kensal Green, passing through Oxford Street, Clerkenwell and Bethnal Green, and joining the high level sewer near Bow. 3. A low-level sewer which begins at Chiswick and passes through Chelsea. At Pimlico its contents are pumped into another conduit lying slightly higher, which runs along the Thames Embankment to the Tower, then strikes off to the north-east through Stepney to Abbey Mills, near Stratford, where the contents are again pumped up to the level of the high and middle-level sewers. From this point the whole of the northern drainage flows through the same outfall sewer to the Thames. This outfall sewer is formed of three parallel conduits, which can be made to communicate when necessary to equalise the flow. On the south side of the Thames there are two great lines of interception. 1. A high level gravitating sewer which begins at Balham, and passes through Clapham, Brixton, Camberwell, New Cross, Greenwich, Woolwich and Plumstead Marshes to Crossness. 2. A low-level sewer beginning at Putney, and passing through Wandsworth, Battersea, and Vauxhall, with a pumping station near Nine Elms, delivering the sewage brought to that point by the river Effra. At Deptford the contents are pumped into the outfall sewer, and flow down to Crossness. On both banks the outfall sewers communicate with covered reservoirs, from which the sewage is discharged into the Thames at certain times of the tide.

[2] Report of Metropolitan Board of Works for 1885, p. 2. When the rainfall is so great as to exceed the discharging capacity of the intercepting conduits, there is no alternative but to allow the superfluous quantity to be discharged directly into the river, at the old points of discharge within the Metropolis. Suitable arrangements are made for this purpose. The sizes of the intercepting sewers being graduated to take the calculated quantity, a long weir is formed at the points of interception of each of the original sewers ; and when the rain exceeds the calculated quantity, the surplus contents of the sewer flow over this weir, and follow the former course down the original sewer, from the mouth of which the fluid escapes directly into the river. There are

works and extensions, the main drainage of London cost about 4,600,000*l.*; including these works, the total expenditure will be brought up to 6,250,000*l.*[1]

Even then "finis" will probably remain long unwritten in the history of these works. Before the outfalls discharged their full complement, there were complaints of nuisance. In 1868, a memorial addressed to the Home Secretary by inhabitants of Barking alleged that shoals impeding navigation were forming, and the river had become dangerous to health in every populous town below London. An inquiry was held before Mr. (afterwards Sir) Robert Rawlinson, chief-engineering Inspector to the Local Government Board, who found no sufficient proof of these allegations.[2] Again, in 1870, the Thames Conservancy Board, alarmed by the formation of offensive mud-banks near the outfalls, promoted a Bill, one of the objects of which was to prevent any discharge of sewage into the river without previous deodorization. In Committee this Bill was opposed by the Metropolitan Board, and, as a compromise, passed without reference to deodorization; it obliged the Metropolitan Board to "keep the Thames free from such banks or other obstructions as may have arisen or may arise from the flow of sewage from their outfalls." Differences as to the origin of any banks or obstructions were to be determined by arbitration.[3]

Complaints of nuisances from outfalls, 1868–70.

Thames Navigation Act, 1870.

forty-eight of these storm or relief outlets within the Metropolitan area: thirty-five on the north, and thirteen on the south side. They are generally of large size, capable of delivering large discharges when they come into action. For the prompt relief of certain low-lying districts, the storm discharge is aided by steam power. On the banks of the Effra at Nine Elms there is a pumping station of 200-horse power for lifting the storm-waters into the river when they are penned up by the tide. There is another at the Falcon brook of the same power. It is obvious that the fluid discharged from these storm-outlets does not consist merely of rain water, but must contain a mixture of sewage. (Royal Commission on Metropolitan Sewage Discharge, 1882–4; First Report, p. 11.)

[1] Ib. p. 11. In the accounts of the Metropolitan Board the cost of main drainage and main sewers up to December 31, 1885, is set down at 6,243,699*l.*

[2] Parl. Paper, No. 7 of 1870.

[3] 33 & 34 Vict. c. 149, ss. 20, 21.

Such differences, in fact, arose. Chemical analyses of the mud, and an examination of the river bed, convinced some experts employed by the Conservators that offensive accretions, accounted for by the discharge of sewage, had formed near the outfalls. These statements, made in 1878, were challenged by the Metropolitan Board. An arbitration followed, extending from November, 1879, to March, 1880. The arbitrators were of opinion that three banks, to which their inquiry was specially directed, had arisen from suspended matter in the tidal water; that this suspended matter was derived from various sources, but only a small proportion of it came from the Metropolitan sewers. As the three banks, therefore, had not arisen from "the flow of sewage," the arbitrators held that the Metropolitan Board could not be called upon, under the Act of 1870, to contribute any portion of the expense of removing these banks.

Arbitration, 1879-80, between Thames Conservancy and Metropolitan Board.

Relieved from this difficulty, the Board were soon confronted with another. In the year 1882 complaints were made to the Home Secretary by the Corporation, as sanitary authority of the port of London, and by inhabitants and local authorities of Erith, that the river was polluted by Metropolitan sewage so as to be offensive and even injurious to health.

Royal Commission, 1882-84.

A Royal Commission, over which Lord Bramwell presided,[1] was therefore appointed to inquire (1) whether any evil effects resulted from the system of sewage-discharge into the Thames, and (2) in that case, what remedies could be applied. After hearing counsel and ample evidence, during the latter half of 1882 and a great part of the year following, the Commissioners made their first report in January, 1884, confined to the first branch of inquiry. In their opinion, the main

---

[1] The other members of this important Commission were Sir John Coode, C.E.; Sir Peter Benson Maxwell; Colonel Ewart, R.E.; Dr. Williamson, Professor of Chemistry at University College; Dr. De Chaumont, F.R.S.; Dr. Thomas Stevenson; and Mr. James Abernethy, C.E. Dr. Pole, F.R.S., acted as secretary. The narrative in the text is based on their first report. (Parl. Paper, C. 3842.)

drainage works of the Metropolitan Board were "executed in a highly creditable manner," and had been " of great benefit to the metropolis."[1] One weak point in the system was, they thought, the storm overflows, which allowed an occasional discharge into the river within the metropolis of considerable quantities of offensive matter; but these had hitherto caused no serious damage or offence.[2]

Greater objection was taken to the flow of sewage from the outfalls in its crude state, without any attempt to render it less offensive by separating the solids or otherwise, a practice "at variance with the original intention, and with the understanding in Parliament when the Act of 1858 was passed." It appeared to the Commissioners that a discharge from the main outfalls might be traced in dry seasons almost as high as Teddington, and "oscillated for a long period before getting finally out to sea," although partially purified by oxidation, and by animal and vegetable organisms. Above Greenwich and below Greenhithe the river did not afford ground for serious complaint; within these limits the effects of sewage were more or less apparent at all times. In hot and dry weather there was serious nuisance, to a considerable distance both below and above

Objection to discharge of crude sewage.

State of the Thames near the outfalls.

---

[1] "The discharge of the sewage into the river within the heart of London had become intolerable, and its interception has exercised a powerful influence in improving the general health of the metropolis. For the system has not only removed an offensive and deleterious element from the most populous part of London, but has also promoted general salubrity by improving the drainage of the entire metropolitan area. And even granting some evils may be caused, as we think is the case, by the present mode of discharge, yet these are not of a nature to be compared with those that have been removed by the main drainage scheme." (P. 41.)

[2] "Mr. Phillips, formerly surveyor of the metropolitan sewers, states that there are now in the metropolis hundreds of miles of sewers, called deposit sewers, in which the sewage does not flow at the velocity ($2\frac{1}{2}$ feet per second) necessary to prevent sewage matter from depositing. In these and many other sewers large accumulations take place in dry weather; when sudden heavy rains occur, as in thunderstorms, great masses of filthy material are washed out, and, as the intercepting sewers are gorged by the sudden rain, find their way by the storm outfalls directly into the urban reaches of the river." (P. 42.)

the outfalls, from foulness of the water and offensive smells.
Fish had disappeared from the Thames for a distance of
some fifteen miles below the outfalls, and for a considerable
distance above them. " For these reasons the river is not,
at times, in the state in which such an important highway
to a great capital, carrying so large a traffic, ought to be; "
and the Commissioners declared that these evils and dangers
were likely to increase with the increase of population in the
districts drained.

Second
Report of
Royal
Commission,
1884.
Before their second and final report, dated November, 1884,
the Commissioners took evidence upon proposals to remove
the outfalls lower down the river, or to the sea ; the expediency
of separating sewage from rainfall ; the utilization of metropolitan sewage, with the prospect of doing so at a profit ;
and various methods of treating sewage, and obtaining
a pure effluent, as by broad irrigation, filtration through
land, and deposit or precipitation. They now expressed a
stronger opinion of the evils resulting from the outpour of
sewage into the Thames, especially in a crude state, a system
" neither necessary nor justifiable." Some process of deposi-
tion or precipitation, to separate solid from liquid sewage,
might be applied at the existing outfalls, the solid matter,
or sludge, being used to raise low-lying lands, or burnt or
dug into land, or carried away to sea. Even then the liquid
residue " would not be sufficiently free from noxious matters
to allow of its discharge at the present outfalls as a permanent measure. It would require further purification, and
this, according to the present state of knowledge, can only be
done effectually by its application to land." Intermittent
filtration was pronounced the best method of applying liquid
sewage; and sufficient land, of a quality suitable for this
purpose, existed near the northern outfall. When so purified, any effluent might run into the river. If suitable land
could not be procured near the existing outfalls, any liquid
residue should be conveyed lower down the river. The main
conduit might then, " if thought desirable, be made of suffi-

cient capacity to include a general extension of the drainage to all the districts around London, as recommended by Sir Joseph Bazalgette and Mr. Baldwin Latham. In new drainage works the sewage should be, as far as possible, separated from the rainfall."

In this stage the disposal of London sewage remains, far removed from finality. During an unusually hot and dry summer in 1884, there were renewed complaints as to the state of the river.[1] The Metropolitan Board subsequently caused the sewage at the outfalls to be deodorized, and set up apparatus and machinery at Crossness to manufacture the chemicals required for this purpose.[2] A larger question is a possible utilization of the sewage. Several projects of this nature have been tried and failed. The first, in 1846, was sanctioned by Parliament upon solicitation by a private company,[3] who hoped to make profits by emptying some of the principal London sewers and selling their contents for

Deodorization.

Plans for utilizing metropolitan sewage.

---

[1] See Commons' Paper, No. 323 of 1884. Mr. J. Thornhill Harrison, inspector of the Local Government Board, in a report upon the outfalls (dated August, 1884) writes :—" It is probably no exaggeration to say that at the present time there is a month's sewage from the metropolis oscillating between Greenhithe and Teddington. It is evident that the foul water from below Deptford must, during spring tides, reach as high, or even higher, than Putney Bridge. The water during high spring tides is polluted even up to Richmond, and leaves a foul deposit on the banks of the river and on the towing-path. The Thames in its present condition can only be compared to a huge sewage tank, which for many months has not been cleaned out."

[2] Report of Metropolitan Board for 1885, pp. 4—9, which describes certain methods of precipitation and further purification recommended by four eminent chemists as obviating the necessity for earth filtration. The discharge from the Metropolitan outfall sewers averages nearly a hundred and sixty million gallons daily ; the daily deposit, after precipitation, amounts to 3,000 tons, which, when pressed, is reduced to 850 tons daily. The Board state that it is impracticable to use this enormous quantity as the Royal Commissioners suggested, for raising the level of low-lying lands, nor can it be burnt without creating a nuisance, except at a prohibitory cost. There remains the suggestion that the sludge should be carried to sea, and the Board, in 1886, adopted a recommendation of their Committee that a suitable vessel should be constructed for this purpose.

[3] 9 & 10 Vict. c. 398, " an Act to incorporate a company by the name of 'The Metropolitan Sewage Manure Company.'"

manure. This speculation came to nothing. In discussing
the Bill of 1858, Mr. Robert Stephenson said he "believed
that sewage matter would eventually be made useful for
agricultural purposes; he therefore thought it impolitic to
enter then into any larger expenditure than could be helped,
if even it were found necessary to carry the sewers down to
Sea Reach hereafter."[1] Two years afterwards, and again in
1864, the Metropolitan Board endeavoured to enlist private
enterprise in so applying the sewage. Committees of the
House of Commons, in 1862 and 1864, encouraged a belief that
sewage might be sold for use as manure; and Parliament
gave to municipalities additional powers, already noticed,[2] for
effecting this object. The Metropolitan Board hoped that the
projectors whose co-operation they invited would profit, and
that at the same time the burthens of metropolitan tax-payers
might be lightened.

Metropolis
Sewerage,
and Essex
Reclamation
Act, 1865.

In answer to this appeal, private capitalists offered to
form, under statute, a company with a capital of two millions, who were to take the dry-weather flow from the
northern outfall by a conduit some forty or fifty miles long,
discharging it at the Maplin Sands on the Essex coast,
and applying it to the reclamation and irrigation of a large
tract of land there. This offer was accepted by the Board,
and embodied in a Bill, which became law after some opposition.[3] Meanwhile, in order to satisfy doubts expressed as
to the merits of their scheme by Baron Liebig and other
scientific men, the company established at Barking, in 1866,
a large sewage farm, supplied directly from the northern
outfall, and reported the results of this experiment as
satisfactory. But their principal scheme was never carried
out. Under their Act the main conduit to the Maplin Sands

[1] 151 Hansard, p. 1937.
[2] *Ante*, p. 324.
[3] 28 & 29 Vict. c. 121, "an Act
for reclaiming from the sea certain
lands on and near the eastern and
south-eastern coast of Essex; for

making conduits from the North
London main discharging sewers to
the coast of Essex; for utilizing the
sewage of North London; and for
other purposes."

was to be finished in four years. In 1866, upon their application, Parliament extended the time for completing it to 1876. In 1871, however, little having been done towards its construction, the Metropolitan Board promoted a Bill to set aside the arrangement, while the company introduced another Bill for leave to modify their plans. Both measures were rejected by the House of Commons, and no more was heard of this undertaking.[1]

Another experiment, made in 1872-3 at Crossness, with the Board's permission, by a Native Guano Company, was equally fruitless. Works were constructed at the company's expense, a large quantity of solid manure was produced, and there appeared to be no offensive smell or nuisance in preparing it, or from the effluent water. But the Metropolitan Board saw no "hope of profit to the ratepayers" from the adoption of this process, and on this ground seem to have abandoned it, compelling the company to remove their works and plant. Alluding to previous efforts by the Board to utilize sewage, Mr. Rawlinson said they had "evidently fettered themselves throughout with striving to obtain what they consider the full value of the sewage, when this ought to have been a secondary consideration, prevention of pollution to the Thames being the first consideration."[2] As their second Report shows, the Royal Commissioners in 1884 took, substantially, the same view, being of opinion that the solid portions of the sewage should no longer find their way into the river, and that the liquid should be purified, or carried further down, irrespective of any profit to the ratepayers. These results have yet to be attained. While, however, much remains to be done, it is due to the chief governing body in the metropolis to place on record in these pages some detailed account of a sanitary work of unique

Native Guano Company.

---

[1] Royal Commission on Metropolitan Sewage Discharge; First Report, p. 31.

[2] Report on Discharge of Metropolitan Sewage from the Barking Outfall, November, 1869 (Parliamentary Paper, No. 7 of 1870).

·importance,[1] accomplished by them in the face of unexampled difficulties.

Embankment of the Thames.

Specified in Act for rebuilding London, 1666.

Another improvement of the same period, and carried out by the same authority, was a revival of many schemes for embanking the Thames. The earliest of these projects was one recommended by Sir Christopher Wren, and prescribed by statute in 1666 after the great fire, that a quay forty feet in breadth should be made from the Tower to the Temple.[2] This provision was neglected, and much of the land built upon which should have been left vacant. Again,

In Act of 1767.

in 1767, a coal duty of sixpence was continued on condition that the Corporation of the City of London, among other works, should embank the north side of the Thames between Paul's Wharf and Milford Lane in the Strand.[3] Only 7,500l. was directed to be applied to this embankment, which was also subject to special hindrances by riverside owners. The work, therefore, was very imperfect, and left the Thames between these points practically unchanged. In

Plan of 1825.

the year 1825, on a petition from the Duke of Devonshire, Lord Darnley, and other persons, the House of Commons allowed a bill to be introduced " for building a quay and terrace carriage-road on the northern shore of the river Thames, from Craven Street, in the Strand, to Blackfriars Bridge." Upon a division, the Ayes were 85, the Noes 45. Mr. Trench, Mr. Baring, and Viscount Palmerston were sponsors for the Bill,[4] which was strongly opposed by the Duke of Norfolk, as an owner of river frontage, and was

Plan of Corporation of London in 1840.

dropped after a struggle upon Standing Orders. A more ambitious scheme was framed by the Corporation in 1840, namely, an embankment on both shores of the Thames between London Bridge and Vauxhall, with provision for deepening the river-bed. A Committee of the House of

---

[1] In 1885–6 there were 250 miles of main and intercepting sewers under the Board's control.

[2] 19 Chas. II. c. 3, s. 35 ; 22 Chas. II. c. 11 ; repealed by 1 Geo. IV.

c. 40.

[3] 7 Geo. III. c. 37. Paul's is called " Powell's " wharf throughout this Act.

[4] 80 C. J. 199 ; March 15, 1825.

Commons was appointed to consider this proposal,[1] but, like the last, it met with so much opposition from owners of wharves and other vested interests that it was not proceeded with.[2] When Battersea Park was laid out as a Royal park, the Commissioners of Woods of that day were authorized, in 1846, to make a roadway along the foreshore between Battersea and Vauxhall Bridges,[3] as well as a suspension bridge across the river near Chelsea Hospital.[4] This was the first Thames embankment.

Embankment between Battersea and Vauxhall.

A public Bill, enabling the Commissioners of Woods "to form a terrace and embankment, with convenient landing-places for the public," on the Middlesex shore, between Westminster and Blackfriars Bridges, was discussed in the year 1844, but withdrawn.[5] In 1858 the Metropolitan Board took up this plan at the instance of Mr. Bidder, Mr. Hawksley, and Mr. Bazalgette. Their report to the Board in 1858 showed that the offensive state of the river was due chiefly to deposits on filthy mud-banks, laid bare at low water. By confining the current within a narrowed channel this cause of mischief would be removed. At the same time a noble thoroughfare might be won from the river. After public inquiries,[6] an embankment between Westminster and Blackfriars Bridges was begun by the Board under Parliamentary powers in 1862.[7] In 1863 similar authority was given to the Board to embank part of the southern side of the river, between Vauxhall and Westminster Bridges;[8] and in 1868 Parliament also sanctioned an embankment and road between Chelsea Hospital and Battersea Bridge.[9] These works, admirably executed, at no excessive cost,[10] have done

Plan of Commissioners of Woods, 1844.

Victoria, Albert, and Chelsea embankments.

---

[1] 95 C. J. 230; March 30, 1840.

[2] The report of this Committee, with plans, is given in Commons' Paper 554 of 1840.

[3] 9 & 10 Vict. c. 38.

[4] 9 & 10 Vict. c. 39.

[5] 99 C. J. 565. The Earl of Lincoln, afterwards Duke of Newcastle, was then first Commissioner of Woods.

[6] See Parly. Paper [2872] of 1861; and report from Select Committee of Commons on Thames Embankment Bill, 344 of 1862.

[7] 25 & 26 Vict. c. 93.

[8] 26 & 27 Vict. c. 75; 27 & 28 Vict. c. 135.

[9] 31 & 32 Vict. c. 135.

[10] According to the Board's accounts of 1885 (p. 186), the exact

more than any works of any time in London to rid Englishmen of the reproach that their capital was the most sordid
and ugliest in Europe.

Noble waterway as it is, and essential to the life and
greatness of London, the Thames has thus been to local
authorities on its banks the source of exceptional duties,
obligations, and outlay.   Nor have these yet been all
recounted.   Old statutes to restrain the "outeragiousness"

**Prevention of
Floods Act,
1879.**
of the Thames[1] had their counterpart in 1879, when Parliament empowered the Metropolitan Board to see that owners
on the river-side, by raising wharf-walls and banks, prevented those tidal overflows which had previously been the
cause of great suffering to poor persons on low-lying lands.[2]

**Bridges freed
from toll.**
Again, by various Acts, the Board were required to free
from toll various bridges over the Thames within the metropolis, and thereafter to maintain and repair these bridges.[3]
Under other Acts the Board have built new, or altered and
improved existing, bridges.[4]   At the end of 1885 their outlay
upon bridges and Woolwich ferry was 1,972,500*l.*

**Communica-
tion across
the Thames
below London
Bridge.**
An obligation to provide improved means of communication across the Thames below London Bridge has also been
recognized by the Board.   For some years their plans with
this object were not approved by Parliament.   In 1879 they
applied, without success, for power to construct a high-level
bridge, of one span, with a spiral approach on the south
shore, about half a mile below London Bridge.   In 1884,
their proposal to construct a tunnel under the Thames from
Nightingale Lane to Dockhead was also rejected, and they
Steam ferries. then withdrew a concurrent proposal to establish two steam

cost was 2,156,855*l.*   Fifty-two acres
of land were reclaimed; the embankments are three miles and a half in
length.

[1] *Ante,* Vol. I., p. 12.
[2] 42 & 43 Vict. c. 198.
[3] 32 & 33 Vict. c. 19, amended by
37 & 38 Vict. c. 21; 40 & 41 Vict.
c. 99.   The first of these Acts provides for freeing from toll Kew and

other bridges over the Thames and
Lea, beyond the metropolitan limits,
but within the area over which the
London coal and wine duties are
levied.   Westminster Bridge is maintained by the State.

[4] 44 & 45 Vict. c. 192 (Putney,
Battersea, Vauxhall, and Deptford
Creek Bridges); 46 & 47 Vict. c. 177
(Hammersmith).

ferries, one between Greenwich and the Isle of Dogs, and another between Woolwich and North Woolwich. In the session of 1885 the latter of these steam ferries, free to all traffic, to convey vehicles as well as foot-passengers, and to be worked by the Board if they think fit, was at length sanctioned by Parliament,[1] together with another project by the Corporation of London for a low-level swing bridge near the Tower.[2]

Before 1855 no local authority existed in the metropolis New streets. with power or means to make new arterial communications. This duty is now performed by the Metropolitan Board. The thoroughfares they have opened, by virtue of special Acts, include Queen Victoria Street, from Blackfriars to the Mansion House, a continuation of the Victoria Embankment;[3] a communication between Oxford Street and Bethnal Green;[4] Northumberland Avenue, giving a direct approach from Charing Cross to the Victoria Embankment, for which purpose Parliament empowered the Board to buy Northumberland House and grounds from the Duke of Northumberland;[5] streets from Tottenham Court Road to Charing Cross, and from New Oxford Street to Piccadilly Circus;[6] and by arrangement with the Metropolitan and District Railway Companies, a street between Eastcheap and Fenchurch Street in connection with the Inner Circle Railway.[7] Excluding the cost of Embankments, the Board have spent upon street improvements, carried out under special Acts, the sum of 11,537,000*l.* This expenditure applies only to communications of general utility. But the Board also contribute Local street improvements. towards the cost of approved local street improvements made by any constituent body, and, since 1856, the amount of such contributions has been nearly 800,000*l.*[8]

---

[1] 48 & 49 Vict. c. 167, s. 14 *et seq.*

[2] 48 & 49 Vict. c. 195.

[3] 26 & 27 Vict. c. 45, which authorized a loan of a million for this purpose.

[4] 35 & 36 Vict. c. 163, which authorized a loan of 2,500,000*l.* for this and other street improvements.

[5] 36 & 37 Vict. c. 100. The cost of this improvement has been 711,000*l.* (Accounts of 1884).

[6] 40 & 41 Vict. c. 235.

[7] See, among other Acts relating to this arrangement, 42 & 43 Vict. c. 201 ; *ante*, Vol. I. p. 153.

[8] Accounts of 1885, p. 186.

Commons, parks, and open spaces.

A series of Acts, dating from 1857, gave the Board power to acquire, lay out, and maintain various open spaces in and near the metropolis.[1] On January 1, 1886, twenty-nine commons, parks, and open spaces,[2] containing more than nineteen hundred acres, were under the Board's control. In acquiring these places for health and recreation, the Board have spent more than half a million.[3] Other statutes authorize the Board or any vestry or district board to acquire and hold open spaces, such as gardens in squares and disused burial grounds, for the public benefit.[4]

Metropolitan Open Spaces Acts, 1877–81.

Artizans and

Under the Artizans and Labourers' Dwellings Improve-

---

[1] 20 & 21 Vict. c. 150 (Finsbury Park); 27 Vict. c. 4 (Southwark Park); 29 & 30 Vict. c. 122; 40 & 41 Vict. c. 71; 34 & 35 Vict. cc. 57, 63, 77, and 81 (Blackheath, Shepherd's Bush, Hampstead Heath, and Wandsworth Common); 35 & 36 Vict. c. 43, and 44 & 45 Vict. c. 148 (Hackney Commons); 36 & 37 Vict. c. 66 (Tooting Beck Common); 37 Vict. c. 10 (Leicester Square); 40 & 41 Vict. c. 201 (Clapham Common); 41 & 42 Vict. c. 145 (Plumstead Common); 42 & 43 Vict. c. 160 (Wormwood Scrubs); 44 Vict. c. 18 (Brook Green, Eel Brook Common, and Parson's Green); 47 Vict. c. 2 (Streatham Common); 48 & 49 Vict. c. 167 (Dulwich Park).

[2] Chief among these are Blackheath, containing 267 acres; Hampstead Heath, 240; Clapham Common, 220; Wormwood Scrubs, 193; Tooting Beck Common, 144; and Finsbury Park, 115.

[3] Victoria Park, at Hackney (300 acres), Battersea Park (250 acres), and Kennington Park, formed before the constitution of the Metropolitan Board, are maintained by the State; but, in 1872, the Board purchased for 20,450l. additional land, which was added to Victoria Park, and is, with the rest, managed by the Commissioners of Works (35 & 36 Vict.

c. 53). A park at West Ham (77) and Epping Forest (5,529 acres) were acquired for public use by the Corporation of London. When to this list are added the Royal parks, —St. James's (83 acres), the Green Park (71 acres), Hyde Park (700 acres), Kensington Gardens, Regent's Park and Primrose Hill (400 acres), with Greenwich, Richmond, and Bushey Parks, Kew Gardens, Hampton Court Gardens, Wimbledon, Putney, Mortlake, and Barnes Commons in Surrey, Hayes Common in Kent, Hadley Common near Barnet, and other smaller commons more or less accessible, London cannot be said to be ill supplied with open spaces.

[4] 40 & 41 Vict. c. 35; 44 & 45 Vict. c. 34. See also the Gardens in Towns Protection Act, 1863 (26 Vict. c. 13), which enables the Board to deal with gardens or ornamental grounds in the metropolis, set apart for the use of inhabitants, and not kept in proper order. By an Act of 1884, no buildings can in future be erected upon any disused burial ground, except for the purpose of enlarging a church, chapel, meeting-house, or other place of worship. The Act does not, however, apply to any burial ground sold under special statutory powers (47 & 48 Vict. c. 72).

ment Acts, the Board, at the end of 1885, had spent Labourers'
Dwellings,
1876–83. nearly 1,400,000*l.* upon schemes confirmed by Parliament for the improvement of unhealthy areas.   Various special Acts regulating metropolitan gas companies impose upon Gas and water. the Board the duty of testing, by examiners appointed for this purpose, the purity, illuminating power, and pressure of all gas supplied within the metropolis, outside the City. In like manner they are constituted the metropolitan authority, excluding the City, under an Act of 1871,[1] which provides for a constant supply of water by the London water companies.   The Board also exercise a veto under the Tram- Tramways and railways. ways Act, 1870 ; and all recent statutes authorizing railways through the metropolis provide that plans of any bridges shall be submitted to them for the purpose of ascertaining that these bridges will be of sufficient strength and proper construction, and that there will be due width and headway under them for road traffic.

By a public statute of 1774, churchwardens and overseers Fire brigade. in each parish were bound to keep a fire engine.[2]   Through- out London, fire engines were also maintained by the insur- ance companies.   In 1865, these engines were transferred to the Metropolitan Board, and Parliament imposed on them the duty of protecting life and property in case of fire.[3] The obelisk popularly known as Cleopatra's Needle was Monuments. placed under their care in 1878,[4] together with other monu- ments on the Embankment.   They regulate slaughter- Slaughter-
houses and
offensive
trades. houses and other premises on which offensive businesses are carried on.[5]   They supervise the lines of streets, regulate width, name new streets, alter existing names, re- number houses, control the erection of buildings, and have Control over buildings.

---

[1] 34 & 35 Vict. c. 113.

[2] 14 Geo. III. c. 78.

[3] 28 & 29 Vict. c. 90 ; *ante*, pp. 173–6.   The Board are authorized to apply one-halfpenny of their consoli- dated rate towards the maintenance of a fire brigade.   In 1885, the amount raised by the halfpenny rate

was 73,177*l.*   In addition the Trea- sury contributed 10,000*l.*, and the fire insurance companies, 25,420*l.*, or 35*l.* per million of the gross amounts insured.

[4] 41 & 42 Vict. c. 29.

[5] 37 & 38 Vict. c. 67.

large powers over dangerous structures and houses so dilapidated as to be unfit for occupation. For supervising buildings, the Board are authorized to appoint surveyors,[1] and have, for these purposes, divided the metropolis into seventy districts, each superintended by a surveyor. Lastly, though

Theatres and music halls.

this enumeration of duties leaves much untold, no new theatre or music hall exceeding certain dimensions must be opened without a certificate from the Board that it satisfies their regulations made to guard against fire. This authority was given by Parliament in furtherance of public safety, by an Act of 1878.[2] Over theatres and music halls then in use the Board have a limited jurisdiction when it appears to them that, owing to structural defects, there is special danger from fire. They can also, with the same object, regulate the opening and closing of means of exit from these places.[3]

Financial powers.

In financial powers and position the Metropolitan Board stand at the head of British local authorities, and their annual budget and debt exceed those of many minor European States.[4] At the end of the year 1885, the total sum raised and applied by them since their creation in 1856 was more than thirty-five millions and a quarter, and their net liability, after allowing for debt redeemed, and deducting assets,[5] stood at close upon seventeen millions. In 1869 they set an example

Loans Act, 1869.

which has been widely imitated, by obtaining statutory

---

[1] Metropolitan Building Act, 1855 (18 & 19 Vict. c. 122).

[2] 41 & 42 Vict. c. 32.

[3] Various Powers Act, 1882 (45 Vict. c. 56), s. 45.

[4] The favourable terms on which they can now raise money are shown by the fact that in May, 1884, for an issue of three per cent. stock of 1,900,000*l.*, tenders were received covering 7,616,000*l.*, and the average accepted price was 100*l.* 9*s.* But in 1869 a three-and-a-half per cent. loan of 2,500,000*l.* could only be floated at an average price of 94*l.* 14*s.* 10*d.* per 100*l.* stock. Since

the creation of the Board their rates have more than trebled, and this upon a rateable value two and a-half times greater than in 1856. In that year the rate levied was 2·09*d.*; in 1857, it was 1·86*d.* In 1885 the rate was 7·34*d.*; in 1886, 6·89*d.* The rateable annual value of the Metropolis, in 1856, was 11,283,000*l.*: in 1886, it had risen to 30,709,000*l.*

[5] These assets included 7,347,000*l.* outstanding loans advanced by the Board to other local authorities; and 2,091,000*l.*, estimated value of surplus land and property.

powers[1] to create consolidated stock or annuities, charged indifferently on all their property and securities, and to be redeemed within sixty years. To meet this charge, and for all other purposes, they were to levy but one rate, called the Metropolitan Consolidated rate. Before any borrowing powers could be exercised, however, the sanction of the Treasury was made requisite. By this and subsequent Acts,[2] the Board were enabled to lend money with the same sanction, for permanent works, to subordinate local authorities in the metropolis, as well as to the School Board. In 1871 Parliament placed the Board's consolidated stock on the same footing as public securities for purposes of investment by trustees,[3] and thereby added considerably to its market value. In 1885 Parliament allowed the Board, with the consent of the Treasury, under certain conditions, to raise money required for temporary purposes by means of bills, somewhat in the form of Treasury bills. These "Metropolitan bills" are charged on the consolidated rate, with a condition for repayment in not less than three or more than twelve months after date.[4]

Money raised by "Metropolitan bills."

A Money Bill is now passed in every session, empowering the Board to borrow the money which will be required for various purposes during the succeeding year. Under these Acts, "the control of the Treasury over the Board's financial arrangements is wide-reaching and constant,[5] and by the

Annual Money Act.

Control of Treasury.

---

[1] 32 & 33 Vict. c. 102.

[2] See, as examples, 34 & 35 Vict. c. 47, and 38 & 39 Vict. c. 65. An Act of 1870 (33 & 34 Vict. c. 24), enabled the Board to compound for the stamp duty chargeable on transfers of stock by a payment to the Inland Revenue Commissioners of 7s. 6d. for every hundred pounds of stock issued. This payment was raised to 12s. 6d. by the Inland Revenue Act, 1880.

[3] 34 & 35 Vict. c. 47, s. 13:—"A trustee, executor, or other person empowered to invest money in public stocks or funds, or other government securities, may, unless forbidden by

the will or other instrument under which he acts, whether prior in date to this Act or not, invest the same in consolidated stock."

[4] 48 & 49 Vict. c. 50, ss. 19, 20.

[5] A recent instance may be cited. In 1883 the Board's expenditure on their fire brigade exceeded by 7,222l., and in 1884 by 10,854l., the statutory limit of income produced by the half-penny rate. The Government auditor refused to pass these accounts; and it was necessary, in 1884 and 1885, to insert a clause in the Board's annual money bills ratifying this extra expenditure. (See 48 & 49 Vict. c. 50, s. 18.) A Bill was promoted by the

Treasury auditor the Board are called to account for every item of expenditure, however trifling, which does not in his judgment appear to have been properly incurred." [1]

In tracing some portion of the duties discharged by the Board we may well wonder that only thirty years ago the metropolis was without any central authority, and that its local government so long remained the bewildering chaos described in the last chapter. Responsibility by one governing body for great arterial works, with effective control over all questions affecting the general well-being, were essential

Future local government in London.

reforms in 1855, too long delayed. But it would be easy to carry this centralizing influence too far, and, in the name of local self-government, to lose many of the safeguards without which local self-government throughout London would become a fiction. The Act of 1855 was carefully framed with a view

Principles of centralization and local authority reconciled in 1855.

to reconcile these opposing principles. Enough has been said of the chief governing body then constituted. Parliament, however, attached hardly less importance to the necessity of leaving each district in full possession of purely local functions. With this object thirty-six vestries and district boards (now thirty-nine) were created, care being taken that, in all matters not affecting the metropolis as a whole, these bodies should have substantial power, and not be mere puppets moved by a central authority. For example, they were to plan, construct, and pay for local sewers. It is true that these sewers must first be approved by the Metropolitan Board, but only to ascertain whether they would harmonize with the general system of drainage. In like manner, these local bodies were to be sole judges as to the expediency of making local improvements. They might ask for a contribution from the central Board, who then considered whether the improvement would be of such general benefit as to justify them in bearing a part of the cost. For paving footways, maintaining streets and roads, lighting, cleansing, and other usual municipal functions, the

---

Board, in 1884, and again, but ineffectually, in 1885-6, to obtain increased funds for the maintenance of

their fire brigade.

[1] Report of Metropolitan Board for 1884, p. 27.

vestries and local boards were made solely responsible.   They still possess this independent jurisdiction, levy rates, control expenditure, are recognized as local authorities in the Tramways and other general statutes, and, in short, exercise, without undue subordination to the central Board, all necessary powers of self-government.

Thus, by the legislation of 1855, Parliament recognized that analogies drawn from ordinary municipal institutions were misleading, and that London was too unwieldy to be governed as one municipality, with minor bodies possessing no practical power over expenditure and having hardly any initiative.   These considerations now apply much more strongly than in 1855.   The metropolis is more than ever a " province of houses."   It has become a congeries of cities, whose inhabitants are utterly ignorant of local wants and conditions elsewhere than in their own immediate surroundings. For all purposes of purely local government, Plumstead and St. Pancras, Bethnal Green and Marylebone, Clerkenwell and Chelsea, Greenwich and Shoreditch, have no community of interest, and might almost as well be associated with Liverpool or Bradford.[1]   It would seem indispensable, therefore, to the practical enjoyment of self-government by London, that, in any new scheme of this nature, each metropolitan district should continue, as now, independent of any central body upon all questions save those involving common interests.

Minor authorities should be independent on local questions.

[1] Many people born and bred in London know far more of provincial towns than of outlying metropolitan districts represented on the Board. Here is the full list :—City of London; St. Marylebone; St. Pancras; Lambeth; St. George, Hanover Square; Islington; Shoreditch; Paddington; Bethnal Green; Newington; Camberwell; St. James, Westminster; Clerkenwell; Chelsea; Kensington; St. Luke, Middlesex; St. George the Martyr, Southwark; Bermondsey; St. George-in-the-East; St. Martin-in-the-Fields; Mile End; Woolwich; Rotherhithe and St. Olave; Hampstead; Whitechapel; Westminster; Greenwich; Wandsworth; Hackney; St. Giles-in-the-Fields; Holborn; Strand; Fulham; Hammersmith; Limehouse; Poplar; St. Saviour's, Southwark; Plumstead; and Lewisham.

CHAPTER XIV.

CORPORATION OF THE CITY OF LONDON: COAL DUTIES: CITY
ORPHANS: ORPHANS' RELIEF ACT, A.D. 1694: CITY AND
METROPOLITAN IMPROVEMENTS CHARGED ON COAL AND
WINE DUTIES: WORK OF CORPORATION: CHARITABLE AND
PATRIOTIC GRANTS: EDUCATION: THE ROYAL HOSPITALS:
THE IRISH SOCIETY: CORN DUTIES: OPEN SPACES AROUND
LONDON: EPPING FOREST: EXCEPTIONAL POSITION OF
CORPORATION: EFFECT OF SANITARY IMPROVEMENTS UPON
MORTALITY IN METROPOLIS.

Corporation
of the City of
London.

ON the same principle by which, in other parts of the
metropolis, local bodies were entrusted, in 1855, with full
powers of self-government, the Corporation of the City of
London retained their ancient privileges and jurisdiction.
They could recall a municipal, though not perhaps a corporate, history more ancient by far than that of English parliaments, and indissolubly connected with the history of the
English people. For eight hundred years, in the true municipal spirit, they had tenaciously asserted and preserved their
privileges and charters,[1] and so helped to keep alive muni-

---

[1] "The citizens of London were
permitted by virtue of this charter (of
William the Conqueror) to hold their
lands in a manner scarcely less free
than in the days of Edward the
Confessor. The galling incidents
of aids, relief, wardship, marriage,
livery, and so forth, which were incident to even the best form of feudal

tenure, were unknown in London.
. . . . So, too, the free right of
transmitting property to a successor
was to be found under the Norman
kings in London alone. The good
old customs were preserved nearly
intact: the privilege of electing their
own magistrates . . . the right of
suing and being sued in their own

cipal freedom in England at times when it was all but overborne by royal prerogative. Upon critical occasions of State,
taking a wider view of their position and functions, they had
rendered many and signal services in the cause of public
liberty. They could point to an unstained record of administration within their own boundaries, even in the darkest
days of municipal corruption; throughout the shameful period
of close corporations elsewhere, their elections had always
been ruled by the popular voice.[1] From the earliest, also, to
the latest of these many centuries, they had worthily represented a wealthy and generous nation by splendid hospitalities
towards royal and distinguished visitors, by abundant charity,
bestowed at home and abroad, and by civic honours and gifts,
always of high esteem, to Englishmen who in peace or in
war deserved well of their country. Parliament, in 1855,
was not minded to break with these proud traditions and
needlessly confuse or obliterate an ancient and memorable
landmark.[2] The Corporation, therefore, were left to govern
the City as they had governed it for so many centuries,
but were made, like other local bodies, subordinate to the
Metropolitan Board on questions affecting the whole Metropolis.[3]

It may be well here to sketch the outlines of a constitution Governing
so venerable, and in essentials still unchanged.[4] The govern- bodies of the
ing bodies of the City are three : the Courts of Aldermen, of City.

---

hustings court; the right of trial by
jury .... The position of London
was a most enviable one, enshrining
as it did all the freedom and independence of the laws of Alfred the
Great and Edward the Confessor,
amid the bondage of an enslaved
nation." (Firth's "Municipal London," pp. 3–5.)

[1] See the testimony borne by the
Royal Commissioners on Municipal
Corporations in 1830, quoted *ante*,
p. 223, *n*.

[2] Lord Palmerston was Prime

Minister in 1855; the Metropolis
Local Management Bill was intro-
duced by Sir Benjamin Hall, then
President of the Board of Health.

[3] The Corporation are represented
by three members on the Board.

[4] "It is to London that we should
look if we want to see most clear,
best recorded, and most active the
principles which appear in the foundation of English corporations."—
Archbishop Benson on Municipalities (Address at Birmingham, Nov.
30, 1885).

Court of
Aldermen.

Common Council, and of Common Hall. The Court of Aldermen consists of the Lord Mayor and twenty-five Aldermen, of whom one-half form a quorum. Its functions are both judicial and executive. In its judicial capacity it is a Court of Record, and decides disputes respecting the validity of certain civic elections in the City and wards. This Court also appoints the Recorder and some other officers; admits brokers to the privilege of carrying on business within the City;[1] and adjudicates upon complaints of misconduct against various functionaries. In its executive capacity it possesses certain powers of ordering payments out of the City's cash, superintends the police, and exercises powers under several Acts of Parliament.[2] Aldermen act as magistrates for the City, and are appointed for life.

Court of
Common
Council.

The Court of Common Council consists of the Lord Mayor, the Aldermen, and 206 Common Councillors, of whom the Lord Mayor, or his *locum tenens*, at least two other Aldermen, and a sufficient number of Councillors to make up forty members (the quorum required in the House of Commons), constitute a Court. Since 1867, both Aldermen and Councillors have been elected by occupiers, who need not be freemen.[3] Anciently, the franchise was exercised by liverymen, and afterwards by freemen, both being very numerous. As comparatively few of the existing voters reside within the City, it follows that the Corporation represent no small part of the wealth and influence of the capital beyond City limits.[4] The Common Council controls expenditure, appoints officers, and discharges the most important duties of the Corporation; it alters City customs and regulations without any

[1] *Ante*, p. 242.

[2] Com. Committee on Metropolis Local Taxation, 1867; Third Report, pp. 6, 7.

[3] 30 Vict. c. 1; see also 12 & 13 Vict. c. 94, and 11 Geo. I. c. 18.

[4] This was one of the reasons assigned by the Epping Forest Commissioners, in 1877 (p. 16 of their final Report), for making the Corporation Conservators of the Forest: —"The Corporation is more representative than the mere area of its jurisdiction would imply, inasmuch as there is an annual election of Councillors, and the electors reside in all parts of the Metropolis, and beyond."

intervention by the State, and embodies its decisions in "Acts" like those passed in Parliament.   Its business, however, in- Committees. cluding the management of the corporate estates, is chiefly transacted by committees,[1] which act under references made by the Court, and report upon all subjects so referred to them.   These bodies correspond with the Grand Committees formerly appointed by the House of Commons, and lately revived there.   Standing orders and resolutions carefully guard against any undue exercise of power by these dele- gations,[2] the Court reserving to itself the control of expen- diture and all important business, while it obtains from its committees a thorough examination of all details, with reports generally well considered, and seldom set aside.

Like each House of Parliament, the Court prints its Standing Orders. Standing Orders every year.   These orders regulate its pro- ceedings, and also provide as far as possible that members shall not misuse their powers.   Neither directly nor in- directly must any member be concerned in any contract, work, or employment paid for by the Corporation.   No member, nor the son of any member, is allowed to be a can- didate for an office to which the Court appoints.[3]   Precautions

---

[1] The chief committees are seventeen : — City Lands, Bridge House Estates, Gresham, Coal and Corn and Finance, General Purposes, Markets, Library, Police, City of London School, Offices and Clerks, Improvement, Orphan School, Law and City Courts, Gas and Water, Local Government and Taxation, Port of London Sanitary, and Me- tage in Grain.   Of these the Police Committee is the largest; it consists of more than eighty members, in- cluding all the Aldermen, their de- puties, and twenty-nine commoners. Next in number is the Markets Committee, with twelve Aldermen and fifty-eight commoners.   Most of the other committees consist of six Aldermen and twenty-nine com-

moners.

[2] For instance, a committee in- structed to watch and report upon a Bill in Parliament, can undertake no active proceedings for or against it without express authority from the Court.   For any outlay exceeding a hundred guineas the Court must be first consulted and its assent ob- tained.   No committee can entertain any proposal affecting the City's cash or estates, unless referred to them by the Court, or can alter the conditions of any contract or engagement en- tered into with the Corporation, but must report the circumstances and their opinion for sanction by the Court.

[3] To prevent evasion of this order by a member's resignation for the

are also taken that no members pecuniarily interested, as shareholders or otherwise, in an undertaking shall vote upon any question affecting it; and if the Corporation are opposing this undertaking in Parliament, such members must not sit on any committee charged with the opposition. A member must not sit or vote in any committee when a matter is discussed in which he has a personal interest. The same rule applies in the Commission of Sewers, and it is specially provided there that no shareholder or officer in any lighting company shall vote upon any question affecting the lighting of the city, or take part in the discussion. Lastly, for the purposes of any statutory description, the style of the Corporation is set forth as " The Mayor, Aldermen, and Commons of the City of London in Common Council assembled."

Style of Corporation.

Court of Common Hall.
The Court of Common Hall appears to be lineally descended from the ancient folk-mote of the citizens which met at Paul's Cross, and there deliberated upon affairs generally affecting the City. This Court consists of the Lord Mayor, or his deputy, four Aldermen at least, and such liverymen of the City companies as are freemen. Its jurisdiction is now confined to the choice of Lord Mayor, Sheriffs, Chamberlain, and a few other officers. In each year the liverymen, summoned by the masters and wardens of their respective companies, choose two Aldermen, one of whom, generally the first nominated, is then selected to be Lord Mayor by the Court of Aldermen.

Wards.
For certain purposes of local government the City is also divided into wards, each of which elects an allotted number of Councillors annually, with one Alderman. This Alderman and the Councillors are the governing body of the ward.

Commission of Sewers.
The Commission of Sewers is appointed by the Corporation and consists of the Lord Mayor, the Recorder, Common

purposes of appointment, it is provided that he must have ceased to be a member for three months before appointment, unless the office has become vacant since his membership.

Serjeant, six Aldermen, and 83 Councillors. It attends to drainage, with the paving, cleansing, lighting and improvement of streets, abates nuisances, and controls all sanitary matters. It is a Corporation in itself and possesses rating powers under several local Acts.[1]

It has been stated that the ancient local institutions which have thus survived always rested on a popular basis. They were accompanied also by special methods for uniting and consolidating the community. From the Anglo-Saxons was *Frank-pledge.* handed down the system of frank-pledge, by which men became liable, as sureties, for each other's good conduct. A later bond of association was the freedom of the City. Freemen enjoyed peculiar advantages which strengthened *Freemen.* their common tie of allegiance to the City. Still closer *Liverymen.* relations were established by the livery companies, a mediæval reproduction of the Anglo-Saxon and Norman guilds. Under the Plantagenets, adults carrying on any trade or handicraft within the City were, in practice, forced into membership of one of these companies. All three expedients seem to have been devised to knit together the citizens by common objects and with common interests. This policy the livery companies, closely connected with the Corporation, supplemented by regulations to promote the prosperity of their respective callings, by restrictions intended to maintain a trading monopoly, and by encouraging and practising a free-handed hospitality in furtherance of harmony and good-fellowship. As most citizens were both freemen and liverymen, it follows that, for the election of the civic Parliament, a constituency composed, whether of freemen solely, or of liverymen being freemen, was sure to be a wide and popular one.

That the citizens preserved their ancient institutions so *Military spirit and resources of London.* successfully amid the despotism and anarchy of so many centuries was due, in part, to the necessities of the Crown,

---

[1] See 11 Geo. III. c. 29; 33 Geo.   12 Vict. c. 163; 38 & 39 Vict. c. 4.
III. c. 75; 4 Geo. IV. c. 114; 11 &

but also, in no small degree, to their own spirit and determination. They had often to humble themselves, and suffered many exactions; but when occasion served they boldly asserted their rights. From very early times they could set in array the best-equipped troops in the kingdom. In the year 1000, towards the end of Ethelred's reign, they beat back the attacks of Sweyn, and his victorious army of Danes, obliging him to abandon the siege of London. Fitz-Stephen, secretary to Thomas à Becket, whose description of London has been cited, declares that in the reign of Henry II. the City could muster sixty thousand foot and twenty thousand horse. This is clearly an extravagant estimate. King Stephen, however, owed his success against the partisans of Matilda to an army chiefly composed of Londoners. A charter given to the City by Edward II. recites the military services of the citizens in besieging Leeds castle, Kent, and grants that such military service shall not be drawn into a precedent.[1] It is related of an Alderman Philpot, in the reign of Richard II., that at his own private expense he fitted out a fleet of vessels containing a thousand men, and took or destroyed some piratical vessels which had long infested the coast, and had made numerous captures.[2] Cade, like Wat Tyler, was admitted within the gates; but Cade's followers, who had broken their promises of good behaviour, were afterwards shut out, when, after a short raid in Kent, they sought to re-enter, and the citizens defended London Bridge against them so successfully, that they were discouraged and dispersed. The fortifications of the City were strong and well-guarded. In the Wars of Succession they were twice subjected to furious assaults by Lancastrian armies: one under Lord Scales, who, having possession of the Tower, vainly plied the City with ordnance for several days; and

[1] Because it was a condition of burgage tenure that citizens were bound only to defend their own walls.

[2] In the assessment of the famous poll-tax, which during this reign caused Wat Tyler's rebellion, the Lord Mayor ranked as an earl, and the Aldermen as barons.

again by Falconbridge, who, at the head of seventeen thousand men, attempted to storm the walls in two places at the same time, but was repulsed by the citizens with great slaughter.[1] Queen Elizabeth directed the Lord Mayor to maintain a standing body of citizens, well instructed in military discipline, and on news of the Spanish invasion demanded from the City fifteen thousand men with thirty-eight ships. Charles I. required twenty good ships, well manned and furnished;[2] and the City train-bands afterwards did good service on the side of Parliament when the citizens were driven into arms against their king.

Some notice will now be given of various sources of revenue possessed by the Corporation, in addition to their large estates, and of the work done by means of this revenue. Along with many ancient municipalities in England, the Corporation, under charter or by prescription, received various dues and tolls to ease their charges of administration. From time immemorial, in order that trade might be centred within their walls, it was their privilege to prohibit the holding of any market within seven miles of the City. This ancient privilege was confirmed, in 1327, by Edward III. The Corporation, therefore, have always derived a large revenue from market tolls. They also had chartered as well as statutory rights of scavage, baillage, package, and portage.[3] A considerable revenue accrued to

Monopoly of markets within the city.

Scavage, metage, and other chartered rights.

[1] Norton's Commentaries on History and Chartered Franchises of City of London (Butterworths, 1829), p. 167, quoting Fabian and Hall's Chron., A.D. 1460.

[2] *Post*, p. 367.

[3] Granted or confirmed by charter of Edward IV., and ratified by 5 Hen. VIII. c. 16. These rights were bought by the Treasury, in 1833, for 162,000*l.*, and abolished, as being hindrances to trade. (See 3 & 4 Will. IV. c. 66.) Scavage was a search or survey of customable goods, to note their quality or quantity; Baillage, a toll on delivery or unlading. Before the charter of Edward IV. these tolls had been enjoyed by the citizens time out of mind. Package was a survey of merchandize packed for export or imported. A monopoly of portage was given by a charter of Charles I., which provided that no porters not appointed by the citizens should intrude into this employment. See *post*, in Chap. "Docks in the Thames," the opposition by City porters to the London Docks, as an interference with their chartered rights.

them from a compulsory metage of coal, wine, grain, salt, and fruit. Besides these privileges, shared in less measure by other favoured communities, the Corporation, for nearly two centuries and a quarter, have possessed an exceptional source of local revenue, for they have been allowed, under statute, to raise money for various City or Metropolitan improvements, by indirect taxation in the nature of octroi duties.

After the great fire of 1666, a duty on sea-borne coals was granted by Parliament to the Mayor and Commonalty, and their successors, in order that they might accomplish the public works specified in the Act then passed for rebuilding the City.[1] This duty, to continue until 1677, was one shilling per chaldron or ton, according to the description of coal. The proceeds were to be applied by the Corporation, first, in satisfying persons whose land was taken under the Act, "for enlarging the streets and narrow passages within the City, with a view to guard against future fires, and also to afford greater accommodation for traffic;" secondly, in paying for land taken for making wharfs or quays on the north bank of the Thames, "and upon each side of the sewer called by the name or names of Bridewell Dock, Fleet Ditch, and Turnmill Brook," and also for building "such prisons within the City as were necessary for the safe custody and imprisonment of felons and other malefactors."[2] Four years afterwards it was found that this coal duty was insufficient, and that "far greater sums of money" were required to defray the cost of enlarging streets, making market places, and other public works. For further enabling the Corporation, therefore, to complete these works, the tax on coals was increased to three shillings per chaldron or ton, to continue until 1687.[3] This tax was altogether independent of the Corporation's ancient metage of fourpence per chaldron.

We come now to a series of statutes under which St. Paul's Cathedral and many churches in and outside the City were

---

[1] 18 & 19 Chas. II. c. 8, s. 34.   [2] 22 Chas. II. c. 11, s. 33.

[3] Ib. s. 37.

rebuilt or built by means of coal duties. During the *churches rebuilt out of coal tax.* Commonwealth, the cathedral designed by Inigo Jones had suffered wofully, both in its fabric and in the loss of funds devoted to its completion.[1] At the Restoration, Parliament naturally desired to make good this spoliation, and a local tax contributed by inhabitants of London seemed a fitting means for reconstructing the cathedral church of London. It was enacted, in 1666, that various City parishes *Act of 1666.* should be consolidated, and that thirty-nine City churches, and no more, should be rebuilt from the proceeds of the coal duty then authorized.[2] Sites and materials of any churches not rebuilt, together with the churchyards, were vested in the Lord Mayor and Aldermen, who were allowed to use the land for widening streets. Any lands not so used were to be sold, if the Archbishop of Canterbury and Bishop of London gave consent, and the proceeds employed in rebuilding other churches. In 1670 it was found that the number of City parishes could not be conveniently reduced below fifty-one, and the churches to be rebuilt were *Act of 1670.* therefore increased to that number.[3] The Act of 1670 provided that, during seven years, three-fourths of the additional duty of two shillings should be employed in rebuilding or repairing these churches.[4] From 1677 until the Act expired, ten years afterwards, a moiety of the whole duty was made applicable to the same object. This money was to be laid out as directed by the Archbishop of Canterbury, the Bishop of London, and the Lord Mayor for the time being,

---

[1] Dean Milman, in his "Annals of St. Paul's," says that one of the first acts of the Parliament was to seize and appropriate to other uses a sum of more than 17,000*l.* remaining out of a national subscription for repairing the cathedral, and deposited in the Chamber of the City of London. The scaffolding erected around the tower was assigned to Colonel Jephson's regiment for arrears of pay. On striking this scaffolding, part of the south transept with its roof came down. The noble portico of Inigo Jones was let out for mean shops, to sempstresses and hucksters; the body of the church became a cavalry barrack and stable. Of Paul's cross, with its famous pulpit, not a vestige was left.

[2] 18 & 19 Chas. II. c. 8, s. 29.

[3] 22 Chas. II. c. 11, s. 55.

[4] Sect. 34.

who might appropriate one-fourth towards building or repairing St. Paul's.[1] The whole duty was to be paid into the Chamber of London, and the Corporation were allowed to retain ten shillings per cent. for their "trouble, hazard and incident charges" in collecting it.[2] The Act contained usual powers for raising loans secured by the duty.

Act of 1685 "for rebuilding, finishing, and adorning" St. Paul's. In 1685, two years before the three shilling coal duty would have expired, it was renewed by Parliament for the express purpose of "rebuilding, finishing, and adorning" St. Paul's.[3] Wren's inspiration had produced a general desire to complete the splendid pile then rising. Accordingly, an Act for this purpose passed through both Houses without opposition. It recited that, under the two statutes of Charles II., "a small part of the imposition upon coals imported in or near the City of London was given towards rebuilding the cathedral church of St. Paul's, wholly ruined by the dreadful fire of London." But this revenue, although, with other supplies, carefully expended, had fallen "so far short of finishing a fabric of so large dimensions that, without further encouragement by a supply from the public, the work in a little time must be left imperfect and useless, and consequently all the former expense totally lost, to the dishonour of our established religion and reproach of the City." In order, therefore, to enable the Archbishop, Bishop, and Lord Mayor to finish so "great and pious" an undertaking, **Coal-duty renewed, but reduced by one-half.** a duty of eighteenpence per chaldron or ton was laid upon all sorts of coals brought into the port of London. This duty, one half of that imposed in 1670, was to continue from 1687 until 1700. Like the larger duty, it was independent of the Corporation's ancient metage of fourpence per chaldron, and was expressly stated to be in addition to "all other impositions and duties." It was to be collected by the City coal meters, and administered by the three great functionaries who had already acted in this trust. Inasmuch as four out of the

[1] 22 Charles II. c. 11, s. 36.   [3] 1 James II. c. 15.
[2] Ib. s. 35.

fifty-one parish churches remained unbuilt, and the towers One-fifth to go towards parish churches. of some others were left imperfect, the Act provided that one-fifth of the duty might be appropriated to this work. When the churches were finished, the cathedral was to have the whole revenue.[1]

As even this aid proved insufficient, recourse was again had Act of 1696-7. to Parliament in 1696-7, when the duty was renewed in a modified form, and a share given to Westminster Abbey and St. Thomas's, Southwark. A recital in the Act[2] then passed explains that "not only the moneys hitherto received from the duty, but several great sums of money advanced upon credit (a considerable part whereof is now owing), and all other supplies, have been carefully expended, whereby the works are far advanced, and yet, by reason of the extraordinary expense of shipping in time of war and dearness of materials, the money hitherto provided hath proved defective, and unless some further provision be made for completing the works, that which is already done will be greatly damaged, if not wholly lost; and in case the same shall be completed, it will be necessary that some other things be done, both for the convenience and ornament of the cathedral."

After the year 1700, the duty was by this Act reduced Duty renewed, but reduced to one shilling. from eighteenpence to one shilling per chaldron or ton, to continue until 1716. Then the Act recited that "the collegiate church of St. Peter in Westminster, being of ancient Westminster Abbey to share in coal duty. and royal foundation, is now in great decay, and in case the same be not speedily repaired, will become wholly ruinous." To prevent this disaster, one-sixth of all moneys produced under the Act was to be paid over to the Chancellor of the Exchequer, the Lord Chief Justice, and the Dean of Westminster, and laid out by them in repairing the Abbey.[3] The Also St. Thomas's Church, Southwark. parish church of St. Thomas, in Southwark, was also " so much decayed that of necessity it must be rebuilt." This charge properly devolved on the governors of St. Thomas's

[1] 1 James II. c. 15, s. 12. [3] Ib. s. 3.
[2] 8 & 9 Will. III. c. 14.

Hospital, but they had recently rebuilt the hospital, and could not apply more money in building without trenching upon "revenue now laid out for the cure of sick and wounded seamen and soldiers, which in great numbers, together with other poor people, are every year sent thither for help and relief." A sum of three thousand pounds, therefore, was to be contributed, out of the new coal duty, towards repairing St. Thomas's Church.[1]

Two shilling duty imposed bv Act of 1702.

Subject to these deductions, a shilling duty appears to have been insufficient to provide for current expenditure upon the cathedral. In the next reign, therefore, Parliament doubled the tax.[2] It was not to take immediate effect, but to begin in 1708 and continue till 1716, the term granted by the preceding statute, " over and besides all other impositions and duties." All the increased tax was to be applied for the benefit of the cathedral, a part in removing certain houses on the north side lying so near as to expose it to danger from fire. As an encouragement to Parliament and taxpayers, the Act also declared that the cathedral was "now so far advanced that it may in a few years be perfected if vigorously carried on."

One-half of Wren's salary suspended till completion of St. Paul's.

In order, no doubt, to expedite the rebuilding, one-half the " surveyor-general's " salary had been suspended by the Act of 1696-7 until the works were completed.[3] In the words of the Act, this provision was "for the encouragement" of the surveyor-general, so that he might proceed " with the utmost diligence and expedition." It is not easy to see how such a withholding of salary could have had any other effect than that of discouraging an architect who was doing his best and anxious that his work should be solid and enduring. Wren, as might be expected, bitterly resented this provision, as it clearly imputed that he was delaying the work for his own emolument. He therefore petitioned the House of Commons, in 1711,[4] and they inserted in a Bill then before

---

[1] 8 & 9 Will. III. c. 14, s. 6.
[2] 1 Anne, st. 2, c. 12.
[3] 8 & 9 Will. III. c. 14, s. 7.
[4] 16 Com. Journ. 678; May 25,

them a declaration that the cathedral, so far as concerned the surveyor-general, was finished.[1] The suspended salary was therefore ordered to be paid; all other standing salaries were to cease after December 25, 1711.

Here, therefore, closes the statutory history of St. Paul's and its obligations to the coal duty. This duty, however, had proved so valuable and easy a source of revenue that it was kept alive for similar ecclesiastical objects. We have seen that, besides the cathedral, fifty-one City churches had been rebuilt by its means. Queen Anne had at heart the erection of an equal number of new churches in and around London. The statute of 1711 was meant to furnish all necessary funds. It begins, "Most gracious Sovereign,— We, your Majesty's most dutiful and loyal subjects, the Commons of Great Britain in Parliament assembled, being zealous to provide such supplies as may enable your Majesty to pursue your pious and gracious intentions to increase the number of churches in or near the populous cities of London and Westminster, or the suburbs thereof, for the better in-

Fifty New Churches Act, 1711.

1711. In this petition Sir Christopher Wren "humbly conceives" that Parliament in 1696–7 "did apprehend that the building and everything belonging to it was wholly under his management, and so in his power to protract it as surveyor thereof; that the same is now completed except the iron fence, some ornaments undetermined, and some other matters which some of the commissioners of the work have so interposed in that his measures for completing the same are wholly overruled, and thereby neither paid the salary due to him, nor suffered to perfect the work that is made the condition of it, though he believes he could finish the same by Christmas next." Wren's differences with the commissioners, their interference with his design, and the mortification to which he was ex-

posed in completing his noble work and monument, are well known.

[1] 9 Anne, c. 22 (c. 17 in Stat. of Realm), s. 9. The first stone was laid June 21, 1675, in pursuance of a Royal warrant setting forth "that a portion of the duty on coal, which by Act of Parliament is appointed and set apart for rebuilding the cathedral church of St. Paul in our capital City of London, doth at present amount to a considerable sum, which, though not proportionate to the greatness of the work, is, notwithstanding, sufficient to begin the same." Divine service was first performed on December 2, 1697, the day of thanksgiving for the peace of Ryswick. The last stone in the lantern of the cupola was laid in 1710. The whole cost was something under three-quarters of a million.

struction of all persons inhabiting the several parishes wherein the same shall be built in the true Christian religion as it is now professed in the Church of England, and established by the laws of this realm, do most humbly present to your Majesty the several impositions, rates, and duties hereinafter mentioned." The coal duty for the benefit of St. Paul's had been continued till 1716. It was now renewed from 1716 for eight years, and increased to three shillings per chaldron or ton, again "over and besides all other impositions and duties." The money was to be paid into the Exchequer, and applied in building in or near the cities of London and Westminster, or their suburbs, "fifty new churches of stone and other proper materials, with towers or steeples to each of them." Sites were to be bought, together with houses for ministers.

Westminster Abbey and Greenwich Hospital. Out of the revenue, four thousand pounds a year were to be applied in repairing Westminster Abbey and its chapels; and six thousand pounds a year in finishing Greenwich Hospital.[1]

Act of 1712. An Act of the subsequent year[2] enlarges the time appointed for proceedings by the Commissioners under the original Act, and elaborates a scheme regulating the division of parishes and other details. One of the fifty churches was to be built in East Greenwich, and a sanitary provision, in advance of the time, declared that no persons should be buried in the new churches. This Act also appropriated certain sums for rebuilding the parish church of St. Mary Woolnoth, in the City. In 1714, under George I., a new use was found for

One year's coal duty applied for maintenance of ministers of new churches, A.D. 1714. the coal duty. It was continued for one year from September, 1724, at the rate of three shillings per chaldron or ton, in order that "a due maintenance may be provided and settled for the ministers" of the fifty new churches, "for the honour of the Church of England, and the advancement of our holy religion."[3]

Produce of duty up to 1718. It appears that the duties granted by the Acts of Anne produced up to the year 1718, including money borrowed

[1] 9 Anne, c. 22, s. 2.　　　　　Realm).

[2] 10 Anne, c. 11 (c. 20 in Stat. of　　[3] 1 Geo. I. st. 2, c. 23.

upon this security, a sum of more than 161,000*l*., which had been applied as the Acts directed. The cost of sites and of building, however, greatly exceeded this amount, so that in the year 1718 "a great debt" was owing "to workmen and others," and it was clear that the whole produce of this coal duty during the remaining term for which it was continued would be insufficient, and probably "leave a great debt for work and materials unprovided for."[1] With a view, therefore, to carry out the "pious and gracious intentions" of George I., Parliament, in 1718, renewed the three shilling coal duty from 1725—the end of the statutory term then in force—until 1751. Upon the security of the duty so extended, the Act directed that a sum of 360,000*l*. should be raised by loan, and 500,000*l*. by lottery.[2] Any overplus from this local tax was, most unjustly, placed at the disposal of Parliament for public objects.[3]

<small>Duty renewed, 1718.</small>

Tiring of these frequent renewals, Parliament, in 1719, made this duty permanent.[4] It was the subject of legislation again in 1726, when, acting upon the power just mentioned, Parliament voted 370,000*l*., to be raised by loan or exchequer bills, and "charged on the surplus moneys of the duties on coals and culm, granted by 5 Geo. I. for a term of years, and since made perpetual."[5] A sentence in the preamble removes any doubt as to the public purposes contemplated by the Act of 1726 :—"We, your Majesty's most dutiful and loyal subjects, the Commons of Great Britain, in Parliament assembled, taking into our serious consideration the great expense and charges your Majesty must necessarily be at for the defence of this realm, and maintaining the important town and fortress of Gibraltar, now actually besieged by the forces of the King of Spain; for preserving the trade and navigation of this kingdom, and maintaining and preserving a just balance of power and peace in Europe; and being

<small>Made perpetual, 1719.</small>

<small>Applied to public objects, 1726.</small>

---

[1] Recitals to 5 Geo. I. c. 9.
[2] Ib. ss. 13–41.
[3] Ib. s. 42.
[4] By 6 Geo. I. c. 4, s. 1.
[5] 13 Geo. I. c. 21.

desirous to raise the necessary supplies which we have cheerfully granted to your Majesty for these purposes in the
easiest manner we are able, for the benefit of your subjects,
have freely and voluntarily given and granted . . . the sum
of 370,000*l.*" This sum was appropriated for the service of
Advance by
Bank of Eng-
land in 1727,
on security of
coal duties.
the year 1727.[1]   A further use of the same duties was made
in that year, when the Bank of England advanced 1,750,000*l.*
for the public service, in return for an annuity of 70,000*l.*,
charged upon the proceeds of these local coal duties, which
at the same time were freed from all former incumbrances
by means of this advance.[2]   If the duties did not produce
sufficient funds to satisfy the annuity, any half-yearly deficiency was to be made up from the sinking fund.[3]

Repeal of
duties in
1787.
It was not until the year 1787 that a general statute[4] repealed
these duties on coal.   Their original object had meanwhile
been lost sight of, and they appear to have been continuously
applied for national objects, notwithstanding the fact that
they were contributed solely by the metropolitan district, and
had been imposed for City and metropolitan purposes.   So
unwarrantable a diversion of local taxation for general uses
during at least a quarter of a century deserves to be remembered in favour of City and metropolitan ratepayers.

This coal-tax, mainly intended for the benefit of St. Paul's
and metropolitan churches, had continued during parts of
seven reigns.   It is now necessary to go back to concurrent
legislation which increased this local tax for another object,
by allowing the City an addition to its metage on coals
City orphans:
their custody
by Lord
Mayor and
Aldermen.
under very peculiar circumstances.   A feudal right of great
antiquity exercised by the Lord Mayor and Aldermen, and
confirmed by a charter of Richard II., was the custody of
orphan children and their property.[5]   By ancient usage,

---

[1] 13 Geo. I. c. 21, s. 20.

[2] 1 Geo. II. st. 2, c. 8.

[3] Ib. s. 9.

[4] 27 Geo. III., an Act which abolished duties upon goods brought
coastwise, from port to port.   There
was a special saving of "the duties

of package, scavage, baillage, or
portage, or any other duties payable" to the Corporation (sect. 1).

[5] This jurisdiction was perhaps of
some advantage, but must certainly
have been subject to many abuses,
during the rude times in which it

citizens of London were not allowed to dispose by will of more than one-third of their personal estate;[1] their executors or administrators were required to pay into the City Chamber the shares of any orphans, who were thus supposed to gain protection from fraud and loss.[2] Until these compulsory payments were abolished in 1694,[3] large sums were received by the Corporation, and employed as they thought fit before distribution. In 1626, when Charles I. required the citizens, upon their allegiance, "to set forth twenty of the best ships in the Thames, fully furnished and victualled for three months, for the defence of the realm," the Corporation were "forced to disburse large sums of orphans' money out of the Chamber." Nor do they appear to have always recovered it, as the

Use of orphans' funds in equipping ships, A.D. 1626.

was exercised. In the City records of 1610 is an entry setting forth the dismissal from office of Francis Morgan, son and deputy to the judge of the Sheriff's Court, "for enticing and taking away from the house of Sir Thomas Cambell, knight, then Lord Mayor, one of the daughters and orphans of Myles Hubbard, and grandchild of Sir Thomas, and marrying her without the licence and consent of the Court of Aldermen." By his example, it is added, "one Thomas Harrys, of mean friends and estate, being an apprentice of Sir Thomas Cambell, did steal, carry away, and marry another of the daughters." (Remembrancia, 292, n.; and see other instances of this jurisdiction, Ib. pp. 307–20.) According to City custom, infant orphans marrying without consent forfeited their portions. Edmund Waller, the poet, so married, in 1631, Annie Banks, a City ward, her portion being 8,000l. This offence was brought before the Lords of the Council, and the lady was placed in the Lord Mayor's custody. But Charles I. wrote to the Lord Mayor and Aldermen, "stating that,

having pardoned Waller and other defendants to the information before the Star Chamber, he expected the City would show a like clemency, and required that such sums of the lady's portion as were in their hands might be paid to Waller." The Lord Mayor and Aldermen complied accordingly, contenting themselves with levying a fine of 500 marks, to be deducted from her portion in the chamberlain's hands. Waller appeared before the Aldermen, and showed that he had settled a jointure of 1,000l. a year upon his wife, and had also empowered her to dispose of 2,000l. of her portion. (Ib. p. 320.)

[1] This limitation upon a citizen's power of bequest was repealed by 11 Geo. I. c. 18.

[2] Norton's Commentaries p. 509. There was a Court of Record, called the Court of Orphans, in which the Common Serjeant tried questions concerning the persons and property of these wards. Executors do not seem to have been bound to pay orphans' money into the Chamber if they could give proper security against embezzlement or misapplication.

[3] 5 & 6 W. & M. c. 10; *post*, p. 390.

citizens refused to pay their quota, " and vexed and molested the constables and officers with suits at common law, who in defence were forced to plead long pleas, which were very chargeable and troublesome both to them and the City."[1]

Investment by Corporation.

Even this forced use of the orphans' funds proved to be better than investment. The Corporation were in the habit of allowing interest at the rate of four per cent. upon all moneys belonging to orphans lodged in the Chamber. Large sums were deposited with them on these terms, and were then re-invested by the Corporation, usually, no doubt, at a profit. Loans to the Stuart kings were one mode of employing this and other money.[2] After the Restoration, still larger amounts belonging to the orphans appear to have been placed in the Royal Exchequer, bearing interest. Bankers, goldsmiths, and merchants having spare funds adopted a like practice, feeling a like security. They did not, however, allow for the utter degradation of the Court of Charles II. The closing of the Exchequer in 1672[3] brought upon the

[1] Letter-book of Corporation, circa 1630 ; Remembrancia, pp. 466-7. The City had previously refused a loan of 100,000*l.*, which Charles I. requested. This forced equipment of vessels by inhabitants of ports, for defence of the realm, was followed in 1631-7 by the attempts to levy ship money, in further aid of a fleet, without authority from Parliament. In 1634, to the King's claim for ship money, the Common Council, relying on the City charters, returned no satisfactory answer ; but, by threats of confiscation, and the imprisonment of the Lord Mayor, Sheriffs, and four Aldermen, the City was brought to terms. London struck a notable blow for liberty during this stormy reign, when the Lord Mayor, Aldermen, Common Councillors, and leading citizens petitioned the King to summon a Parliament and redress the grievances of ship money, mono-

polies, imprisonment of citizens, constant dismissal of Parliaments, and acts of the Star Chamber from which the people suffered ; grievances, as they believed, contrary to the law of England. The King promised to summon a Parliament, whereupon the City set out twenty-eight different grievances, and petitioned the House of Lords for the impeachment of Strafford. (Firth's "Municipal London," p. 17.)

[2] A book in the City archives, bearing the date of 1627, shows that a sum of about 267,000*l.* had been lent to James I. and Charles I. from the Chamber. (Com. Committee on Metropolis Local Taxation, 1867: evid. of Mr. Scott, City Chamberlain, p. 23.)

[3] "The Court of Exchequer was closed for one year. By this iniquitous act a sum of about 1,300,000*l.* was placed at the disposal of the

Corporation a loss which they set at 747,000*l.* Their finances had borne heavy strains under the Commonwealth and in the disaster of 1666. They were now unable to pay either the interest or principal of their debts. Many orphans thus lost their whole means of support.

For several years, in the disorders that marked the latter portion of the King's reign, the Corporation remained insolvent, and the orphans without remedy. At length, after the death of Charles II., Parliament intervened. In 1685 we find the Earl of Midleton and Lord Preston obtaining leave from the House of Commons to bring in a bill "for relief of widows and orphans of the City of London" by means of an additional duty on coals.[1] It was read a second time by a narrow majority of 137 to 128.[2] No time was lost in pressing it forward, though this division did not promise favourably. A numerous Committee was appointed to consider its provisions, with "power to inquire into the amount of the debts due to the widows and orphans"; how "these moneys received into the Chamber were from time to time applied; and what estate, revenue and fund the City hath for satisfaction of these debts." The Committee were also instructed to inquire "what of these debts have been assigned or sold to any person whatsoever, and for what consideration;" and they were to prepare a clause "appropriating the moneys to be raised to the payment of the widows and orphans only, so that no part thereof be diverted."[3] On the same day there was a debate "concerning the taking away a certain custom used in London of enforcing the payment of orphans' money into the Chamber." Here the record ceases, for troublous times arose. Finding

Marginal notes:
Bill for relief of City orphans, 1685.

Committee of House of Commons.

Ministers; but the benefit was dearly purchased with the loss of popularity and reputation. Many of the bankers who had placed their money in the Exchequer failed; a general check was given to commercial credit, and a number of annuitants, widows and orphans, were reduced to a state of the lowest distress." (Lingard's History, bk. 12, p. 239.)

[1] 9 Com. Journ. 746.
[2] Ib. 748; June 25, 1685.
[3] Ib. 754.

the deliberations of the House of Commons inconvenient, James II. interrupted them by frequent adjournments and prorogations; and redress of either private or public wrongs became hopeless.

Relief Bill of 1689. After the Revolution, another Bill to relieve the orphans was, in 1689, laid before the House of Commons.[1] The Corporation appear to have proposed a sale of some of their lands in satisfaction of their debts, and Sir Peter Rich, the City Chamberlain, was required to furnish particulars of the value of these lands and how far they would satisfy debts.[2] Ultimately the House passed several resolutions,[3] founded upon a report by a Committee on the Bill.

Mode of liquidating debt suggested by House of Commons. They determined that towards payment of the civic debts to the orphans there should be appropriated, (1) a duty of twopence per chaldron on all coals brought into the port of London; (2) twopence out of the City coal metage of fourpence per chaldron; (3) the City's ancient duty of water bailage; (4) an additional penny per quarter upon the City's metage of corn; (5) one-half the revenue from hackney coaches; (6) the City's profits from tronage, or weighing at the King's beam, with any like profits from the office of outropers;[4] (7) sixpence per chaldron to be taken off the duty levied on coals towards rebuilding St. Paul's, in return for which the statutory term for the remainder of this duty was to be enlarged.

New Bill based upon resolutions. A Committee was appointed to prepare a Bill upon these lines, to be substituted for the measure already introduced. The House also directed that other provisions should be inserted, taking away the City's "power to compel orphans'

---

[1] 10 Com. Journ. 104; April 26, 1689.

[2] Ib. 131, 136.

[3] Ib. 208-9; July 6, 1689.

[4] Common cryers, whose duties, according to a charter of 1638 (14 Chas. I.), embraced the selling of household stuff, apparel, and other personal effects, including even the leases of houses, by public outcry, in open places in the City and its liberties. Norton (p. 520) derives the term outroper, or outrouper, from the breaking-up (*ruptum*) of stock. It was also the business of this officer to summon meetings of the Common Council, and call for order during their deliberations.

estates to be brought into the Chamber of London," securing a right application of all moneys set apart for the orphans' relief, "that it might not be in the power of any person whatsoever to divert the same to any other use," and enacting that purchasers of orphans' estates should be allowed no more than four per cent. upon their purchase-money, the residue of income reverting to the use of orphan vendors.[1] From this proposal virtually to set aside sales, and other suggested clauses, it is clear that the House of Commons at this period was strongly moved on behalf of the orphans who had been so greatly wronged by the Crown through the Corporation.

Such a Bill as that proposed was sure to meet with strong opposition. The London coal meters saw in it an interference with their receipts from offices which, as they declared, they held for life, and had purchased of several Lord Mayors for valuable consideration, with power to alienate. They also reminded Parliament "that, time out of mind, the duty of fourpence per chaldron for metage of sea coals, and eightpence per ton for weighing of Scotch coals, was granted to the City, whereof part was constantly paid to the Lord Mayor to bear part of the great charge of government."[2] There was a petition from the Royal African Company of Merchants, on behalf of themselves and other trading bodies, praying for exemption from any new rates and duties, and from the provisions relating to tronage and the office of outroper.[3] Complaint was also made by the hackney coachmen. A more remarkable ground of objection was advanced by "very many artizans and others concerned in the public works of St. Paul's and the parochial churches of London." They told the House of Commons that a sum of over 23,000*l.* was due to them "for work done upon credit of the Act allowing one shilling and sixpence per chaldron towards the expense" of rebuilding these churches. As they had contracted no part of the debt due by the City to the orphans, they prayed the

Opposition to Bill of 1689. Coal meters.

Exemptions sought by merchants.

Artizans employed in rebuilding St. Paul's.

[1] 10 Com. Journ. 209.   [3] Ib. 241.
[2] Ib. 235.

House before allowing any deduction from this statutory duty to "compassionate the wives and children of poor artizans and labourers," and first provide that the amount due to them should be paid.[1]

Bill dropped, but re-introduced, 1690.

Owing probably to difficulties interposed by these and other petitioners, the Bill of 1689 did not go beyond a second reading. It was, indeed, considered in Committee of the whole House, but the chairman reported that they "had not time to go through with the same."[2] In the second Session of this year the measure was re-introduced, and again discussed in Committee of the whole House. Nothing, however, was settled before the prorogation at the end of January, 1690. Another Session passed with many recorded resolutions that the subject should be considered,[3] but more pressing business always intervened.

Attempted legislation in House of Lords, 1690.

Meanwhile the House of Lords endeavoured to redress the wrong done to the orphans, and, in 1690, sanctioned the first reading of a Bill for " erecting a judicature" to relieve them. This Bill was referred to a Committee of thirty-three peers, including six bishops, with instructions to hear the Lord Mayor and Aldermen, and provide " that all contracts for compositions with any of the orphans be made void."[4] Two judges, Mr. Justice Ventrice and Mr. Baron Nevill, were appointed to attend this Committee,[5] which reported, through Lord Halifax, that they thought it would " do little good to set up a judicature," and that "inquiry might be of more use at present." Agreeing with this recommendation, the House ordered two other judges to attend the Committee, so that the Bill might be re-drawn as suggested. It was afterwards sent down to the Commons,[6] its title now being " for erecting a Court of Inquiry, in order to the relief of the dis-

[1] 10 Com. Journ. 235. An account annexed to this petition gives the particulars of these large arrears, due to masons, plumbers, plasterers, and smiths.

[2] Ib. 240; July 26, 1689.

[3] Ib. 363–94; April, 1690.

[4] 14 Lords' Journ. 561; Nov. 21, 1690.

[5] Ib. 576.

[6] Ib. 592; December 16, 1690.

tressed orphans of the City of London." In December and January, 1690-1, two messages were sent to the Commons putting them in mind of the Bill.[1] They, however, thought it unsatisfactory or inadequate, for they negatived the second reading, though by a narrow majority—68 votes to 52.[2]

In the next Session the Bill was again considered by the House of Lords and referred to a numerous Committee, who ordered the Lord Mayor and Aldermen to appear before them. The Lord Mayor and Aldermen, however, demurred to this jurisdiction, and, upon their petition, were allowed to be heard by counsel at the bar, together with counsel for the orphans, before further proceedings on the Bill.[3] Afterwards, the Committee were directed to name Commissioners to inquire, and the Bill as amended was then sent to the Lower House.[4] Here, however, after another reminder from the Lords,[5] it met with the same reception as the previous measure, being finally defeated, after two divisions, by 116 to 68 votes.[6]

Lords' Bill of 1691, for inquiry.

Rejected by Commons, 1692.

In justification of the Commons for this continued refusal to co-operate with the other House of Parliament, it may be mentioned that they were at this time engaged in considering a more practical measure. In November, 1691, the Lord Mayor, Aldermen, and Common Council had petitioned for leave to promote a Bill, alleging, "that by the many losses of the City, in and since the reign of Charles I., their debts to the orphans amount to a greater sum than they are able to pay, without assistance from Parliament; that, after many considerations of the best ways of satisfying these debts, as far as possible, without destroying the government of the City, the petitioners have agreed in Common Council that eight thousand pounds per annum shall be charged upon the lands

Petition to House of Commons by Corporation, 1691.

---

[1] 14 Lords' Journ. 604-14.

[2] 10 Com. Journ. 533; January 2, 1691.

[3] 14 Lords' Journ. 651; Nov. 18, 1691.

[4] 15 Lords' Journ. 56; February 1, 1692.

[5] Ib. 74.

[6] 10 Com. Journ. 682; Feb. 20, 1692.

and all other the estate belonging to the City, towards paying the orphans four per cent. per annum ; and humbly imploring the compassion and assistance of this House in their necessities, towards raising and settling a sufficient fund for an annual payment to be made, in lieu of the said debts, or such other provision for the same as the House shall think fit."[1]

Plan of settlement adopted by House of Commons, 1692.

This proposal was carefully considered in Committee of the whole House, and, in February, 1692, resolutions were agreed upon [2] for a fund towards satisfying the civic debts. These resolutions, as amended by the House, charged the City revenues with an annual payment of 8,000*l*., laid a duty of twopence per ton on coal, four shillings a tun on wine, to be paid by all freemen, and further appropriated the ancient duties of water bailage and tronage, with certain increased fees to be paid by apprentices on being bound, and by freemen on admission, together with fines from aldermen, sheriffs, councillors, and liverymen. It was also proposed, as before, that " the benefit to arise by licensing of six hundred hackney coaches in and about the City of London after the rate of five pounds per annum apiece," should be paid into the fund ; but this resolution was negatived. A Bill founded upon these resolutions was ordered to be prepared by the Attorney and Solicitor-Generals, Sir Edward Seymour, Mr. Finch, Sir Richard Temple, and other members, but dropped soon after it was presented.[3]

Petition by Corporation, November, 1692.

In November, 1692, the Corporation again petitioned the House of Commons, substantially as before, acknowledging their indebtedness but pleading inability to meet it without help. Owing to "the general troubles in and after the reign of Charles I., the dreadful conflagration, and the late *quo warranto*," the Corporation stated, "their debts due to

---

[1] 10 Com. Journ. 562-3 ; November 27, 1691.

[2] Ib. 669-70 ; February 13, 1692.

[3] Ib. ; Feb. 18, 1692. On Feb. 24, "the Lord Chief Baron of the Exchequer declared to both Houses that it was his Majesty's pleasure that they should adjourn themselves until the 12th day of April next." Parliament did not meet for the despatch of business until Nov. 4, 1692.

the orphans amounted to a sum vastly greater than they were able to pay." They had again agreed, in Common Council, to charge eight thousand pounds per annum upon the City estate and revenues towards paying the orphans the sum of four pounds per cent. per annum. But since "so vast a debt cannot be satisfied by all the estate or powers of the City, nor the government of the City supported without some further provision," they once more prayed assistance from the House in raising and settling a fund sufficient to secure to the orphans an annual payment in lieu of the debts due to them from the City.[1] The orphans also solicited redress. "By the supreme power of the City to force their money into the Chamber of London," they declared, "many of them are brought to great misery." Being sensible of their necessities, the Lord Mayor and Aldermen had ordered that all improvements in the corporate revenues, above what was necessary to support the government of the City, "should be applied to their relief, and the discoverers of such improvements rewarded proportionably: that such discoveries had been made," and it could be shown, "that the City hath enough to pay their debts and support their government also." The petitioners therefore prayed for inquiry, asking that any surplus civic revenue might be applied for their benefit.[2]

Orphans' petition.

Before considering either petition, the House of Commons directed the Lord Mayor and Aldermen to produce "a true state" of their revenues, of all offices in their disposal, and of their charges for government.[3] In this return[4] the gross revenue of the City was set down at only 11,658*l.*, including 3,480*l.* from rents, and 3,100*l.* market tolls. Various ancient sources of revenue were alleged to be, "by reason of the late troubles and revolutions of government," in such

State of corporate finances, A.D. 1692.

[1] 10 Com. Journ. 702 : November 17, 1692.
[2] Ib. 788-9 ; Jan. 25, 1693.
[3] Ib. 713.
[4] Given *in extenso* in 10 Com. Journ. 796-800.

a state that they yielded nothing. Upon this income there were charges amounting to 5,289*l.*;[1] cost of "pavements and amendments of ways and sewers belonging to the City" was estimated, *communibus annis*, at 420*l.*; miscellaneous fees and salaries and wages to City officers and servants, 3,526*l.*[2] Thus the whole outlay was about 9,250*l.* A stringent report was presented by a Committee of the House of Commons to whom the petitions from orphans and other creditors were referred. They recommended that ten thousand pounds a year should be allowed out of the whole revenue of the City for " necessary charges of government and of the magistracy "; and that any surplus "in possession and reversion, with all improvements, and other contingencies in lands, disposition of offices, or otherwise, be applied towards raising a fund of perpetual interest of four pounds per cent. to satisfy the debts" due to the orphans. Towards the same fund, every Alderman was to pay five pounds a year, every Common Councilman forty shillings, and every liveryman twenty shillings; and some minor sources of revenue were added, including a yearly payment of four pounds " by every unfree and foreign merchant, trading beyond the seas, who do inhabit the City of London or within ten miles thereof." After debate, the House directed Sir Edward Seymour, Sir Thomas Clarges,

Resolutions of Commons' Committee, 1793.

[1] One item of expenditure is "otters' heads brought into the Chamber, to prevent the destruction of fish, at 6*s.* 8*d.* per head, estimated, *communibus annis*, at 3*l.*"

[2] Some of these items are worth record : Retaining fees of eighteen guineas were paid to the Attorney and Solicitor-General every Christmas " to be standing counsel for the City." " Wine to the keeper of his Majesty's closet, annually, 30*l.*" Every Lord Mayor received an ancient fee of 80*l.* out of the Chamber, besides other fees, including one of 100*l.* as clerk of the markets. Anciently, it is stated, he and his under officers received all the profits from the markets. The Recorder's salary was 80*l.*; his deputy received 40*l.*; the Chamberlain, 50*l.* of salary, with fees amounting to 33*l.* 10*s.*; the Common Serjeant, 40*l.*; the Town Clerk, 23*l.* 6*s.* 8*d.* in salary, "and for writing the Repertory, 4*l.*"; the Remembrancer, 50*l.*; the City Solicitor, 26*l.* 13*s.* 4*d.* The Remembrancer's and Solicitor's bills were computed at 500*l.* a year.

Sir Christopher Musgrave, Sir John Parsons, Mr. Harcourt, and the members for the City of London, or any three of them, to prepare a Bill founded upon these resolutions.[1]

This Bill affected the Corporation so prejudicially that they petitioned against it after the second reading. While "thankfully acknowledging the care of the House towards the orphans," they complained that the Bill would divest the City of its revenues, and take away many ancient and necessary jurisdictions, without answering the ends proposed. The House of Commons appear to have been of opinion that a settlement had been too long delayed, for a motion that the Corporation should be heard by counsel was strongly opposed, and only carried by 99 votes to 84.[2] When they had been heard, a motion that counsel for the orphans should also be heard was carried, after another narrow division, by 101 to 96 votes.[3] Afterwards the House considered the measure on two or three occasions in Committee, but no further progress was made before the prorogation on March 14. *Bill of 1693.*

When the House re-assembled in November, 1693, the Corporation renewed their former prayer to the House of Commons for aid. Their insolvency they now attributed to "the general and national troubles after the reign of Charles I.; their former payments of great sums for interest to the orphans; the Great Fire of London; the late illegal *quo warranto* brought against them; and other great losses. They alleged that they had "used their utmost endeavours to raise moneys, and from time to time had paid the same, towards the relief of the orphans; but all the powers and estate of the City cannot satisfy their debts."[4] As more than two months passed and nothing was done, the orphans in their turn once more prayed for relief. For many years, they said, they had "laboured under the greatest calamities, their fortunes being swallowed up, under a colour of *Petitions of Corporation and orphans, 1693-4.*

---

[1] 10 Com. Journ. 818; Feb. 17, 1693.

[2] Ib. 836.

[3] Ib. 839.

[4] 11 Com. Journ. 14; November 30, 1693.

protection and guardianship, by the City." They were now "without hopes of redress unless this House will take their condition into compassion, being a multitude without counsel, without friends, or almost the least support."[1]

Legislation
of 1694.

At length, after a wearisome delay of ten years, there seemed a prospect of legislation. The Corporation of London cannot be fairly charged with contributing to this delay. Year after year they had petitioned for a Bill, proposing considerable charges upon the City estate to satisfy the orphans' just claims, though they resisted charges which would have disabled them from an effective performance of their duties, and asked Parliament to help them in making good losses, many of which were due to unavoidable misfortune or to illegal acts done by the Crown. On February 17, 1694, Colonel Goldwell reported a series of resolutions to which the Committee of the whole House had come.[2] They were of opinion that, towards satisfying the debts due to the orphans, all the City revenues should be subject to an annual rent-charge of 8,000*l.*, "for raising a perpetual fund of interest;" that 2,000*l.* a year should also be raised by a charge upon the personal estates of the citizens; that, out of the profits of a lease of twenty-one years granted to the patentees of certain convex lights supplied within the City, the Corporation should set aside 600*l.* a year; that an additional metage duty of fourpence per chaldron should be laid upon coals within the port of London, and another duty of sixpence per chaldron, to continue for fifty years, but only commencing after the termination of the duty then levied for the building of St. Paul's; that an additional duty of four shillings per tun should be levied on wines imported into London; and that towards the same fund should be appropriated the profits upon the City aqueducts, fees of half-a-crown from apprentices and five shillings from freemen.

Bill intro-
duced in

Before proceeding with a Bill founded upon these reso-

---

[1] 11 Com. Journ. 91 ; February 12, 1694.   [2] Ib. 98–9.

lutions, the House ordered the members for the City to present a list of debts owing to the orphans, and also of debts due upon bond to other creditors who had paid money into the Chamber. Sir John Fleet accordingly produced this return,[1] which was referred to a Committee. Against an additional tax on wine certain wine-merchants petitioned, alleging that wine already paid a greater duty than any commodity, and praying that an equal duty might be laid upon other merchandize. An unusual entry[2] follows the notice of this prayer: "Resolved, that the said petition be rejected." When the Bill came before the House it seems to have been much discussed, but the entries in the Journals are so imperfect that it is not always possible to understand the purport of amendments moved.[3] There were three divisions, but finally the Bill as amended was ordered to be engrossed, and it passed on March 12th. In the Lords no time was wasted. The wine-merchants were heard "by one counsel" before the Committee of the whole House upon the Bill; so also were certain persons claiming antagonistic interests in the convex lights.[4] But the Lords were not convinced that any case had been made out for protective clauses, and did not give the lower House another chance of delaying the Bill. They therefore passed it without amendment.

This Act[5] recited that the Mayor, Commonalty, and citizens "have been and are answerable for and chargeable with all moneys of the orphans of the City, but by reason of sundry accidents and public calamities," the Corporation were then "indebted to the orphans and other creditors[6] for principal money and interest in a much

Marginal notes:

House of Commons.

Recitals to Act of 1694.

---

[1] 11 Com. Journ. 115.

[2] Ib. 107.

[3] Ib. 122; March 8, 1694.

[4] 15 Lords' Journ. 396.

[5] 5 & 6 W. & M. c. 10.

[6] 10 Com. Journ. 817-18. The City Chamberlain, in his evidence before the Committee on Metropolis Local Taxation (p. 23), says that the 747,000*l.* lost by the Corporation in the Exchequer belonged entirely to the City orphans and their representatives, the "other creditors" mentioned in recitals to 5 & 6 W. & M. being not general creditors, but creditors under the custom of

Chief cause of
civic losses
not specified
in Act of
1694.

greater sum than they are able to satisfy and pay unless some assistance be given them." It is remarkable that neither the civic petitions nor these recitals mention the main cause of the Corporation's losses. The explanation offered is a reluctance to place upon record in Parliament any reflection upon Charles II. or his advisers. But papers preserved in the Record Office show that, after the closing of the Exchequer in 1672, acknowledgments were issued by the Crown for balances then due, and a list is preserved of "loans made to King Charles II. by several bankers, and payable at the Exchequer." No debt due to the Corporation appears in this list, nor was any grant afterwards made to them under the great seal as to other creditors. According to City authorities, however, a list of bankers' liabilities would not necessarily include a debt due to the Chamberlain. The books of the Corporation at this period to the debit of the Crown are missing. They are supposed to have been abstracted by one Alderman Rich, who, in 1684, was appointed Chamberlain by Charles II. in contravention of the City charters, and remained in office till 1692.[1] Failing any specific evidence from City records, the presumption is that the Corporation's losses were due to various causes set forth in their own petitions, and not exclusively to the closing of the Exchequer.[2]

orphanage. This statement is not borne out by the Journals of the House of Commons. From these it appears that various petitioners who had lent money to the Chamber of London, secured by bonds under their common seal, complained that they could not recover principal or interest, and prayed the House that, "their circumstances being so near to the City orphans," they might be treated in the Bill upon the same footing. (10 Com. Journ. 746, 835, 838; 11 ib. 35, 40, 98, 99, 109.) All these petitions were referred to the Committees of 1692–4, who recommended "that an equal consideration shall be had" of their case "as of the orphans of the City of London." Apart from this report, sects. 13 et seq. are conclusive that the Act applied to other creditors than the orphans.

[1] Com. Committee on Metropolis Local Taxation, 1867; evid. of Mr. Scott, pp. 23–5.

[2] Norton, who was a common pleader of the City, in his Commentaries already cited, gives an explanation bearing out the view above taken:—"In the troublesome times which attended and followed the great Rebellion, the City finances, which suffered by plunder and ex-

However this may be, the Act of 1694 gave to the City Coal and wine duties imposed. as help or compensation in its troubles a grant of coal and wine duties, supplementing payments out of its own resources. The debt of 747,000*l.*[1] was converted into a perpetual annuity, at the rate of four per cent. For payment of the interest, 29,800*l.*, a fund was created from sources suggested by the Committee on the Bill, namely, a perpetual duty of fourpence a ton, added to the City's existing metage on coals; a temporary duty of sixpence a ton on coals to begin in 1700 and continue for fifty years; a perpetual duty of four shillings per tun on wine;[2] an assessment of two thousand pounds annually on the personal estates of the citizens, unlimited as to time; a perpetual charge of eight thousand pounds a year on the City estates, excepting those of the five Royal hospitals, with a further charge of six thousand pounds after fifty years, when the sixpenny coal duty was to cease; a tax of five shillings upon each admission as a freeman, and of two and sixpence upon each apprenticeship to a freeman; a charge upon the proceeds of the City aqueducts, excepting water supplied to hospitals, halls, prisons, and public conduits, and of a twenty-one years' lease for

tortion in common with the rest of the nation, fell into much confusion and decay; and the distress of the City Chamber was not a little aggravated by the fire of London, in which immense property belonging to the City was consumed, and much more expended in restoring the Metropolis in a manner far surpassing in splendour its ancient condition. The arbitrary acts of Charles II., in borrowing great sums of the City, shutting up the Exchequer, and finally seizing on the City charter, completed the ruin of the Chamber; and when the liberties were restored at the Revolution, the City purse had not only been emptied by the public robbers, who usurped the chartered rights of the citizens, but a heavy debt of no less a sum than 750,000*l.* had accumulated, on the responsibility of the Corporation, due to the City orphans and other persons, who were, by the ruin which had thus involved the City, reduced to a state of utter destitution." He refers to reports of the House of Commons on the Orphans' Fund, 1812 and 1823; and Journals of Proceedings in the Common Council, 1818 and 1820.

[1] This amount, however, is nowhere specified in the Act.

[2] Four shillings per tun Winchester measure, or 4*s.* 9½*d.* on a tun of imperial measure. This is equal to something less than one halfpenny on a dozen quarts.

Compulsory payment into Chamber by orphans abolished.

600*l.* a year granted for permission to set up "convex lights" for public lighting within the City. No person was thenceforth to be compelled to pay money into the City Chamber, so that similar risk of future losses was avoided.[1] Lastly, that relief to the orphans should not be given by halves, any transfers of debts which they had made in their days of poverty, for small consideration, were made redeemable within three years; and all bonds and agreements made by them with agents or solicitors, depending upon the recovery of their debts, were declared absolutely void, these agents and solicitors being paid for their services what the Corporation "judge may be reasonable." If they demanded or received from the orphans more money than was so adjudged to them by the Corporation, they were to forfeit treble the amount.[2]

Act of 1694 unjust in principle.

This Act of 1694 is memorable for the charge brought against Sir John Trevor, then Speaker of the House of Commons, that he accepted a thousand guineas from the City after the Act passed. No doubt it relieved the Corporation from serious financial embarrassment. Assuming, however, that the funds it replaced, or any portion of them, were confiscated for private or public uses by Charles II.,[3] this legislation can be regarded as no act of grace or favour, and was, in fact, wholly inequitable. The State was responsible for a debt so incurred. But instead of a public vote, restoring money which the Crown had misappropriated, the citizens were taxed for this purpose directly and indirectly. They had been robbed, and Parliament allowed them to make good any deficit out of their own pockets! Still greater injustice was dealt to inhabitants of the Metropolis outside the City, who were no more bound to bear any part of this burden than the people of Cumberland or Corn-

[1] 5 & 6 W. & M. c. 10, s. 17.
[2] Ib. ss. 21, 22.
[3] Mr. Firth, no fanatical admirer of the Corporation, thinks (p. 184, n.) that they proved their case before the Committee of 1867 as to the Orphans' Fund and closing of the Exchequer, "so far as could be fairly expected in the absence of documents indisputably showing it."

wall. The Corporation had no unfair ends to serve in pro- Motives of
Corporation.
moting an Act so framed. That they should be overjoyed
at the prospect of being lifted out of insolvency, and able
to meet just claims, was natural and laudable. It does
not appear that they had any other motive when they substituted a "gratuity" for the Speaker's usual fees upon
the Orphans' Relief Bill.[1] For the evil example he thus set, Expulsion of
the Speaker,
Sir John
Trevor,
A.D. 1695.
Sir John Trevor was rightly expelled from the House. But
there is no proof that he exercised, or could have exercised,
any undue influence in forwarding the Bill, which, as we
have seen, passed only after much consideration and enquiry.[2]

It appears that the arrangement effected by this statute Coal duties
continued by
Acts of
1748–67.
was so unfavourable to the Corporation that, in 1713, their
original debt had increased by a sum of 90,000*l.*[3] Neither
Parliament nor the Corporation supposed, in 1694, that the
fund then created would do more than pay interest yearly
upon the debt. For more than half a century this expectation was justified. In 1748 another Act was passed,[4]
which, after reciting that the City rents had fallen and the

---

[1] At this period, the salaries of the chief officials in both Houses were supplemented by regular fees on private or *quasi*-private Bills (see *post*, Chapter on Fees), a vicious system, no doubt mainly responsible for this shameful passage in Parliamentary annals.

[2] The enquiry set on foot by the House of Commons will be found reported in 11 Com. Journ. 269 *et seq.* (March 12, 1695). Mr. Hungerford, Chairman of the Grand Committee on the Bill, who had received twenty guineas from the Corporation "for his pains and services," was also expelled (Ib. 283). The East India Company and other promoters of Bills were at the same time accused of similar practices. Sir John Trevor was a cousin of Judge Jeffreys, and became Master of the Rolls as well as Speaker of the House of Commons under James II., in 1685, retaining both positions after the Revolution. William III. employed him to do the work of corruption then thought indispensable in Parliament. Apart from this uncleanly business, his antecedents made him many enemies there, but some even of them must have felt for his bitter humiliation when he was called upon, as mouthpiece of the House, to put the question which declared his own shame (11 Com. Journ. 271). His offence, though adjudged "a high crime and misdemeanour" by the House of Commons, was not followed by any address to the Crown to remove him from judicial office, and he died in harness, at the Rolls, twenty-two years after he was expelled from Parliament.

[3] Norton's Commentaries, p. 511.

[4] 21 Geo. II. c. 29.

Corporation were still unable to meet their obligations, reduced to 2,000*l.* a year the second annual charge of 6,000*l.* which they should then have paid. Their total direct payment was thus raised from 8,000*l.* to 10,000*l.* a year. At the same time the coal tax of sixpence, instead of lapsing in 1750, as the Act of 1694 directed, was continued for thirty-five years; any surplus income to be applied in redeeming capital of debt. In 1767, the sixpenny duty was further continued until 1813,[1] the Corporation's annual payment was raised from 10,000*l.* to 11,500*l.*, and the fund charged with the cost of various Metropolitan as well as City improvements, a recognition for the first time that other contributories to this fund were entitled to share its benefits with the City.[2]

Orphans' fund appropriated for London Bridge approaches, 1829.

There was another continuance Act in 1804,[3] in order to make further improvements, and in 1807[4] an additional coal duty of one penny per ton was created, principally for the establishment of a free market for the sale of coals brought into the port of London. A substantial change occurred in 1829, when the Orphans' fund became the London Bridge approaches fund, and was charged with a million pounds for these approaches, to be paid out of the fourpenny and sixpenny coal duties.[5] In the year following the City agreed that its annual contribution of 11,500*l.*, with the wine duty and other sources of revenue specified in 1694, should be applied to the same objects.[6]

Coal duties reduced, 1831.

Select Committees were appointed by both Houses of Parliament in 1831, upon the London coal duties, and the result of their enquiries was a statute[7] which reduced taxation, substituted weight for measurement in all dealings,

---

[1] By 7 Geo. III. c. 37.

[2] Among these improvements were the completion of the first Blackfriars Bridge, the building of Sessions Houses for Middlesex and Westminster, rebuilding Newgate, repairing the Royal Exchange, and improving the approaches from the Strand to Temple Bar.

[3] 44 Geo. III. c. 27.

[4] 47 Geo. III. c. 68.

[5] 10 Geo. IV. c. 136; the duty of sixpence was continued for twenty-one years.

[6] 11 Geo. IV. c. 64.

[7] 1 & 2 Will. IV. c. 76.

and superseded the chaldron by the ton as the standard of weight.   Before 1831, the local taxes levied on coal in London were the City metage of fourpence, the orphans' duties of sixpence and fourpence, and the additional penny imposed in 1807, making, altogether, fifteenpence.   By this Act of 1831 the penny duty was continued, the orphans' duties were reduced from tenpence to eightpence, and the City metage of fourpence per chaldron, which was subject to certain deductions, was commuted to a duty of fourpence per ton, or four-fifths of a chaldron, without deduction, to be levied on all coal brought into London both by land and sea.   Thus there was established, under statute, an aggregate tax of thirteenpence per ton, made up of three distinct items.   All coal brought within an area described by a radius of twenty miles around the General Post Office was subjected to these duties in the year 1845.[1]

City metage on coal commuted.

We have seen that, during a considerable portion of the period under review, local duties on coal in London have been levied simultaneously, under different statutes, for entirely different local objects.   In the aggregate these taxes were, at times, considerable.   But coal also bore a general customs duty, which made the burden upon London consumers still more onerous.   A customs duty on all sea-borne coal was first granted to William III. in 1693-4, at the rate of five shillings a ton, for carrying on the war against France.[2]   An Act of the following Session continued this duty until May, 1696.[3]   In 1697-8 it was re-imposed for a term of five years.[4]   With some intermission and modifications coals continued subject to customs duties, both when carried coastwise and exported,

Customs duty on coal, 1694-1845.

---

[1] 8 & 9 Vict. c. 100. A drawback is allowed by 14 & 15 Vict. c. 146, on all coal reconveyed outside this radius.   Before 1845 clauses were generally inserted in private Railway Acts to protect the rights of the Government and Corporation, defining certain points at which coal duties should be collected.   These provisions were repealed by 8 & 9 Vict. c. 101, and 14 Vict. c. 146.

[2] 6 & 7 Will. III. c. 18.

[3] 7 & 8 Will. III. c. 31.

[4] 9 Will. III. c. 13.

until the year 1831. The coastwise duties on coal for home consumption were then repealed.[1] The export duty on coals, then four shillings a ton, did not cease till 1845.[2] During the great war both duties were very high. In 1819 the tax on coals exported to foreign countries was, if in British-built ships, 7s. 9d. per ton, and in ships not British built, 12s.[3] There were differential rates in favour of British colonies and the United States. Coals brought coastwise in 1819 paid a reduced customs duty, deducting drawback of 3s. 6d. a ton.

Liquidation of debt to orphans, 1834.

Although portions of the fund constituted in 1694 were diverted from their original destination, the main object of that fund, the extinction of debt due to City orphans, was not forgotten. This debt would have been liquidated in 1782 if no public improvements had been paid for out of it. From 1782, therefore, until 1834, when the debt was paid off, the rent-charges of 11,500l. a year, and other charges upon City revenue, may be " considered as having been appropriated for the sole object of accomplishing public works."[4] As these works were not confined to their own boundaries, the Corporation are fairly entitled to take credit for such an application of their direct contributions, and also for devoting to similar objects, before and since 1834, the proceeds of a tax belonging to them by prescriptive right.[5]

Appropriation of coal

Parliament had for so long a period allowed the expenses

---

[1] 1 & 2 Will. IV. c. 16.

[2] 8 & 9 Vict. c. 7.

[3] 59 Geo. III. c. 52, sched. Table C.

[4] Com. Committee on City Orphans' Fund, 1829. See, also, previous enquiries by Commons' Committees, in 1812 and 1823; the City Chamberlain's evidence on this subject before Commons' Committee on coal duties, 1853; Corporation Inquiry Commission, 1854; Metropolitan Improvement Commission, 1859; Thames Embankment Committee, 1860; and Metropolis Local Taxation Committee, 1867 (pp. 16 et seq.).

[5] Mr. Scott reckons that, from 1782 to 1860, the City applied for metropolitan improvements 2,106,000l., out of which, for coal metage, they received 1,767,000l., so that they spent for these purposes about 340,000l. more than they received. The metage duty they considered their own property, by prescriptive right, but they felt "a moral claim upon them to expend it for metropolitan improvements." (Com. Committee on Metropolis Local Taxation, 1867, pp. 17-19.) A list of these improvements is given in the Committee's Report, p. 74, App. 11.

of City and metropolitan improvements to be defrayed, in and wine duties, 1845-63. part, out of indirect taxation, that it was easily induced to continue this system.[1] For some years the expenditure of the ninepenny duty,[2] as well as of their prescriptive metage, was left to the Corporation.   In 1845, the penny duty on coal was applied towards the formation of Victoria and Battersea Parks, amongst other purposes, and the proceeds were paid to the Commissioners of Woods and Forests.[3] Two years afterwards the Corporation charged their metage of four-pence with the cost of opening Cannon Street, and other City improvements.   In 1861, the duties on coal and wine were continued for ten years, and Parliament directed that the proceeds, excepting the City coal metage, should be credited to a "Thames Embankment and Metropolis Improvement Fund," the Corporation retaining, for City improvements, their fourpenny metage.[4] This tax was charged in 1863 with the cost of the Holborn Valley viaduct.[5]

The latest, but probably not the last, of these statutes was Continuance Act, 1868. passed in 1868,[6] when all the coal and wine duties were continued until 1889, in which year they are to be applied by a joint Committee of the Corporation and Metropolitan Board in freeing from toll Kew, Kingston, Hampton Court, Kew and other bridges to be freed, 1889. Walton and Staines bridges over the Thames, and Chingford and Tottenham Mills bridges over the Lea. This specific appropriation was meant to benefit inhabitants of outer London who pay these duties, but are beyond the Metropolitan limits, and have therefore derived little direct benefit from improvements hitherto effected out of the fund. Commencing with the first Blackfriars Bridge in 1767, down to the Holborn Viaduct and Thames Embankment, the duties on coals and wine have contributed by far the largest share to public improvements in the Metropolis. So great is the

---

[1] 1 & 2 Vict. c. 101; 3 & 4 Vict. c. 131.

[2] That is, the penny duty created in 1807, and the eightpence to which the orphans' duties were reduced in

1831.

[3] 8 & 9 Vict. c. 101.

[4] 24 & 25 Vict. c. 42.

[5] 26 & 27 Vict. c. 46.

[6] 31 & 32 Vict. c. 17.

increase and so heavy the pressure of rates there, that, if the
ninepenny coal duty ceases, many most desirable improvements must in future remain unexecuted;[1] nor is this indirect
taxation a serious grievance to consumers generally. As to
the remaining fourpence per ton, which has been since 1831
a statutory tax, their prescriptive metage will revert to the
Corporation in the event of this tax not being renewed in
1889. With a view to such a contingency, the rights of the
Corporation have been effectually guarded by saving clauses
in all Acts passed on this subject since 1831.[2]

A summary of the chief work done by the Corporation
during the last century and a quarter, without imposing any
rates, yields a record of which any public body may be proud.
Their chartered and prescriptive rights and valuable estates[3]
have given them large resources, which have been applied, on
the whole, wisely, and to objects of acknowledged utility.
From about the year 1760 to the close of 1885 they spent
nearly ten millions on various City and Metropolitan improvements, undertaken by them under the authority of Parliament,
or in virtue of their corporate powers.[4] Towards these and
other improvements they contributed, from the year 1792 to
1861, the rent-charges of 11,500*l.* a year, originally appropriated, as we have seen, to a totally different object. This
payment ceased in 1861, but amounted, during the period
mentioned, to a sum of over 900,000*l.*[5] Further, from 1845
to 1861, they contributed annually out of their own funds
20,000*l.*, or 310,000*l.*, towards City improvements; and since
1861, under the Act of that Session, they have applied to the

*City metage
on coal re-
vives if statu-
tory duty
lapses.*

*City and
Metropolitan
improvements
carried out by
Corporation.*

*Produce of
City coal
metage,
1862-84.*

---

[1] In 1886, the net income received
from coal and wine duties by the
Metropolitan Board was 300,000*l.*

[2] Report of Coal, Corn and Finance Committee of Common Council, presented November 1, 1877.
The proceeds of the coal duty of
fourpence, after deducting draw-
backs, was, in 1884, about 115,000*l.*

[3] In 1885 the corporate income

from rents and quit rents was
136,000*l.*

[4] The authority for the particulars
which follow is an official hand-book
for 1886-7, a volume annually printed
by the Guildhall Library Committee.

[5] According to the House of Commons' Committee of 1829 (*ante,* p.
394), the date from which this contribution should be calculated is 1782.

same purposes the net produce of their fourpenny coal duty, which produced during 1862-85 a sum of 2,435,000*l.* In aid of purely local objects of this nature, such as setting back houses and widening City streets and thoroughfares, they have also voted 186,000*l.* out of the City's cash. Together these payments amount to more than 3,840,000*l.*[1]

Under modern legislation passed to provide better dwellings for the labouring poor, the Corporation have erected three blocks of buildings, in central situations,[2] at a cost of 105,000*l.* This sum has provided more than a thousand rooms for three hundred and sixty families, and is exclusive of the expenditure by the City Commissioners of Sewers on similar objects charged upon the rates.

Dwellings for labouring poor.

As owners of property, administering large estates, it was the duty of the Corporation to remember the poor and needy in their midst. Fortunately they have had the will as well

Charitable purposes.

---

[1] Among the more prominent works carried out by the Corporation have been the building, &c. of the first Blackfriars-bridge (1760–1812), which cost 230,000*l.*; freeing London-bridge from tolls (1767), 30,000*l.*; repairing Royal Exchange (1768), 10,000*l.*; rebuilding Newgate and Sessions-house (1769-85), 90,000*l.*; improving approach to Temple-bar from Strand (1795–1811), 246,000*l.*; building Debtors' prison for London and Middlesex (1812-20), 95,000*l.*; providing site for General Post Office (1815-24), 80,000*l.*; rebuilding London-bridge (1824-33), exclusive of contribution from Treasury, 483,000*l.*; approaches to London-bridge (1824-46), 1,021,000*l.*; Farringdon-street, and removal of Fleet-market (1825-31), 250,000*l.*; enlarging site of Royal Exchange (1839-44), 228,000*l.*; erection of Royal Exchange (1839-44) (City's moiety), 85,000*l.*; building New Coal-market, and widening Thames-street and St. Mary-at-hill (1847-51), 111,000*l.*; Clerkenwell new street (1851), 88,000*l.*; Holloway House of Correction (1850-1), 92,700*l.*; New Metropolitan Cattle-market, Copenhagen-fields (1852-77), 504,000*l.*; New Cannon-street and other street improvements (1850-62), 540,000*l.*; Holborn Valley viaduct (1861-84), 1,571,000*l.*; rebuilding Blackfriars-bridge (1863), 401,000*l.*; Pauper Lunatic Asylum (1862-85), 94,000*l.*; Central Meat, Poultry and Provision Markets, and approaches (1862-84), 1,412,000*l.*; New Central Fish-market (1873-82), 380,000*l.*; New Foreign Cattle Market, Deptford (1870-83), 331,000*l.*; enlarging Billingsgate-market (1872-80), 272,000*l.*; New Leadenhall-market (1880-85), 222,000*l.*; purchase of Southwark-bridge, &c. (1866), 218,000*l.*

[2] Farringdon-road, Metropolitan Market, and Holborn Viaduct.

as the power to look beyond their own confines, and have materially helped to make our Metropolis renowned, all the world over, no less for its wealth than for its boundless charity. From the year 1781 to the close of 1885, rather more than a century, they have given for charitable purposes, not including education, nearly 267,000*l*. Beginning at home, London almshouses have had 67,000*l*. But of 70,000*l*. granted to asylums, dispensaries, hospitals, infirmaries and benevolent institutions, nearly all has gone outside the City. Places of worship received 8,000*l*. Many of these, again, were beyond civic jurisdiction. St. Paul's had less than 1,500*l*., including the cost of its tenor bell in 1879. A catholic spirit was shown by donations to Wesleyan and Baptist chapels and a pulpit given to the City Temple.

Patriotic grants almost supply an epitome of our great wars. We begin with bounties of 2,500*l*. to seamen in 1787-93.[1] A sum of 500*l*. is voted, in the year 1793, to sustain British commerce by encouraging captures of French privateers; and a like amount is given to British troops serving on the Continent. Officers, seamen and soldiers wounded, with the widows and orphans of those killed, in the fleets under Admiral Howe in 1794, Admiral Jervis and Viscount Duncan in 1797, and Lord Nelson in 1798, are not forgotten. There is similar provision in 1800-1 for sufferers in the ill-starred expedition to Walcheren, the battle of Copenhagen, and the campaign in Egypt. Towards the voluntary contributions raised for national defence in 1798, ten thousand pounds are given. A patriotic fund at Lloyd's receives two thousand five hundred pounds in 1805. British prisoners in France are kept in needful remembrance in 1811. Sharing the universal gratitude and enthusiasm felt for those who fought and fell at Waterloo, the Cor-

Marginal notes: Almshouses, hospitals, &c. / Churches and chapels. / Patriotic grants.

---

[1] At this period, London watermen, then very numerous and a chartered and privileged body, supplied, by volunteering and impressment, a considerable proportion of sailors for the Royal navy. See their petition to Parliament (*post*, pp. 631-2) against the London Docks, which, as they thought, would destroy their means of living.

poration pass a specific vote of two thousand pounds for the relief of sufferers in that crowning victory. A long interval separates the French from the Russian war, but another generation of citizens is then found animated by the same spirit, and two thousand pounds are given to the patriotic fund of 1854. Next comes the Indian mutiny, and, still later, the disaster of Isandula, when practical sympathy is again shown to all widows and orphans. No public body could have identified itself more completely with the loyalty and patriotism of the nation in the trials and triumphs which marked these hundred years.

The same spirit has been shown in the honours bestowed on distinguished Englishmen, civil and military, during the same period. From very early times the Corporation of the City of London have been accustomed to receive from the Crown prompt news of most events of national interest. City records contain a letter from the Black Prince to the Mayor, Aldermen and Commonalty, informing them of his victory at Poitiers, and describing the battle.[1] This selection of the municipality as representatives of the whole people naturally led to reciprocal courtesies, such as banquets and receptions; or illustrious guests were made freemen, the highest honour which a city can bestow, with a sword or gold box to hold and hand down in commemoration. Going no farther back than the last century, a long line of British worthies have been thus distinguished:—Chatham, Pitt,[2] Earl Grey, Peel, Palmerston, Brougham, Cobden, Russell and Beaconsfield,[3] among statesmen; Rodney, Hood, Howe, Duncan, St. Vincent, Collingwood, Hardy, Broke and Nelson,[4] among our naval heroes; among our soldiers, Abercrombie, Cornwallis, Auchmuty, Wellington[5] and his

Honours to distinguished men.

[1] Riley's Mem. 285.

[2] The City monument to the Earl of Chatham cost 3,200*l.*; that to his still more illustrious son, 4,000*l.*

[3] These, and other names more lately added to the roll, show that the Corporation rise above party in their distribution of honours.

[4] Nelson received a gold box enclosing the freedom in 1797; a sword in 1799: the monument erected to him by the City cost 4,400*l.*

[5] The Great Duke's City honours were a sword in 1812, a gold box in

lieutenants, and in later times Gough, Hardinge, Sale, Outram, Havelock, Pollock, John Lawrence and Lord Clyde.

Other honours.

To this list may be added a few well-known names belonging to widely different classes: the Cossack chief, Count Hetman Platoff, Field Marshal Blucher, Prince Schwartzenberg and Count Barclay de Tolly, reminiscences of 1814 and the visit of the Allied Sovereigns; Clarkson, Jenner and Peabody, philanthropists; Rowland Hill, Joseph Hume, Livingstone, President Grant and Garibaldi. These and other men form a cosmopolitan group. In honouring them, again, the Corporation were in thorough harmony with their fellow countrymen. They were not less so in their munificent wedding present of a diamond necklace and earrings to the Princess of Wales in 1863, and the plate they gave to the Duke and Duchess of Edinburgh twelve years later.[1]

Relief of distress abroad.

In relieving distress abroad the Corporation have also been faithful and generous exponents of national feeling. Suffering Portuguese obtained a thousand pounds in 1811, Russians twice that sum during the invasion of 1812, Germans a substantial grant in 1814. Like relief was forthcoming for Spaniards and Greeks in 1823, for Spanish and Italian refugees and distressed Hanoverians in 1825, for Spanish refugees again in 1828, and Polish refugees in 1836. Succour was given to sufferers from earthquakes at Agram, Chio, Ischia, Peru and Ecuador; from famine in Asia Minor and India; from cholera in Egypt; from floods in France and Hungary; from fire at Hamburgh, Constantinople and Chicago; from outrages on Bulgarians by Turks and on Jews in Russia. In quarrels not our own, the National Society for aid to sick and wounded French and Germans received a thousand pounds in 1870; distressed inhabitants of Paris after the siege, two thousand pounds. Of grants to aid the

1813, a bust in 1815; 500*l.* was voted towards a statue in 1838, and his monument in 1854–6 cost the Corporation nearly 5,000*l.*

[1] These gifts were worthy of the City: the former cost 10,000*l.*; the latter 3,150*l.*

poor and suffering at home and in our colonies, the record is too long for quotation.

Under private Acts the Corporation have established two schools. One of these, the City of London School, was first founded by John Carpenter, town clerk of the City A.D. 1419,[1] who left to the Mayor, Aldermen, and Commons, certain estates, charged with a yearly payment of 19*l.* 10*s.* towards the education and clothing of four sons of freemen. These estates having greatly increased in value, the Corporation resolved to discharge their trust by creating a day school of the first grade. They obtained statutory powers for this purpose in 1834,[2] charging the City estates with nine hundred pounds a year, and building a large school in the heart of the City, on the site of an old market in Honey-lane. This school the Corporation were bound to maintain in perpetuity, providing for the instruction of boys in " religious and virtuous education, in the higher branches of literature, and in other useful learning." In 1881 it was resolved to transfer the school to a more convenient and conspicuous site belonging to the City upon the Victoria Embankment at Blackfriars. Up to 1886 the school had cost nearly 63,000*l.*, exclusive of 42,000*l.* paid under the Act of 1834 in respect of Carpenter's bequests. The handsome new building on the Embankment cost over 96,000*l.*; the valuable site on which it stands about 105,000*l.*, less the estimated value of the old site. The Corporation have, therefore, devoted to this institution in money, or money's worth, more than 264,000*l.*, and are rewarded by a successful City school, educating seven or eight hundred boys, under nearly forty masters, and possessing from various endowments and benefactions twenty-two exhibitions, tenable at the school, and twenty-five at the Universities, besides many valuable prizes given annually. The Common Council make regulations and appoint the head and second masters. A special committee appoint other masters, and are practically responsible for management.

Education.

John Carpenter.

City of London School.

[1] He was a Member of Parliament, and friend and executor of Richard Whittington.

[2] 4 & 5 Will. IV. c. 35.

Another civic school now regulated by private statute is that for freemen's orphans. Its origin may be traced to special legislation, which, in the year 1662,[1] incorporated the Lord Mayor as president, and the Aldermen and fifty-two citizens chosen by the Common Council as governors, to relieve the City poor, empowering them to hold lands for that purpose, whether purchased, given or devised, not exceeding three thousand pounds in annual value. In 1830, Parliament directed that the proceeds from these "charity estates of the London workhouse," as they were then called, should be spent, partly in "putting out and placing forth poor freemen's children of the City of London to trades and employments;" partly in maintaining, educating and apprenticing poor and destitute children.[2] It was felt by the citizens and private benefactors who formed this incorporated body, that wider benefits might be conferred by means of their trust if the Corporation would supplement its funds and undertake its control. In 1850, a scheme was accordingly approved by Parliament, and embodied in an Act,[3] under which the Corporation bound themselves to provide a site for a new building, and maintain the school for ever "for the maintenance and the religious and virtuous education of orphans of freemen." This school, too, is managed by a special committee of the Common Council. Between 1851-81, the building of this school, with additions, cost nearly 25,000l.; and since its establishment up to the close of 1885, annual grants amounting to 125,000l. were also made from corporate funds for its support.

These two institutions, along with the more ancient schools founded and managed by the City companies,[4] have done

[1] 14 Chas. II. c. 12, s. 4.

[2] 10 Geo. IV. c. 43; "an Act for enabling the President and Governors of the London Workhouse to sell or grant leases of the workhouse and other hereditaments vested in them, and to purchase other estates for the education and apprenticing of poor children."

[3] 13 & 14 Vict. c. 10. The school is situated in Shepherd's-lane, Stockwell.

[4] St. Paul's School (Mercers' Company), now removed to Hammersmith; Merchant Taylors' School, on site of Charterhouse; Tonbridge School (Skinners' Company); schools of the Grocers', at Hackney; the

splendid educational service, not confined to the City of London or the children of citizens. But the Corporation have also given freely to other schools throughout the whole Metropolis, especially to ragged and industrial schools, and those intended for the very poor. In its day the British and Foreign School Society received valuable help. Since Board schools provided elementary education at the public expense, there has been less need for these grants. Between 1881-6, however, the Corporation gave 11,000*l.* towards technical education. In 1876 they founded a School of Music, with a principal and numerous professors. This institution, which is managed by a committee of thirty-six Aldermen and Councillors, cost 23,000*l.* up to 1886. Towards the Royal College of Music the Corporation have also voted 3,000*l.* For educational purposes up to 1886, and mainly within the last half century, they have applied altogether 474,000*l.*[1]

Guildhall School of Music.

A trust for education left by Sir Thomas Gresham is administered jointly by the Common Council and the Mercers' Company, of which he was a member. This famous citizen, diplomatist as well as financier, gave large sums towards building London's first Exchange, which was opened by Queen Elizabeth in 1570. By his will, which was confirmed by statute in 1580-1,[2] he devised property to found a college, served by seven celibate professors, who were to lecture there, in Latin and in English, upon divinity, astronomy, geometry, law, physic, rhetoric and music. In 1641, the joint trustees obtained letters patent authorizing them to hold this property in perpetuity. They have had twice to rebuild the

Gresham College.

Brewers', Trinity Square; the Haberdashers', at Hatcham; and the Stationers' Companies.

[1] Two votes in 1883, of 1,000*l.* towards the International Fisheries, and 5,000*l.* for the Health Exhibitions, have a certain connection with these objects, but are not included in the above total. In 1886, the Corporation guaranteed 10,000*l.*

towards the Colonial and Indian Exhibition.

[2] 23 Eliz. c. 29; an Act "for establishing an agreement between Sir Henry Nevill and Dame Anne Gresham, for better performing the last will of Sir Thomas Gresham, Knight, deceased, and for payment of his debts."

Exchange: in 1666, and again in 1838, through its destruction by fire. This outlay has trenched considerably upon their revenue. Gresham's own house, in Bishopsgate-street, was the original college. It was sold to the Government for an excise office in 1767. By an Act providing for this sale,[1] the professors were relieved from restrictions of residence and celibacy, and their salaries increased to 100*l.* a year. A handsome college has since been built in Gresham-street, but the occasional lectures delivered there are practically useless for any educational purpose. A "Committee on Gresham affairs," composed of the Lord Mayor, two Aldermen and nine commoners, manages what is called "the City side" of this trust. There is a corresponding committee on the "Mercers' side."

The Royal hospitals. Another City endowment of great renown, mainly devoted to education, should properly be treated among these institutions, but is generally classed among the Royal hospitals. These will be mentioned in the order of their foundation. They are five in number, all under the control of the Corporation, and regulated by an Act of 1781.[2] Most of these hospitals have their origin in the dissolution of the monasteries. Henry VIII. recognized the Corporation as legitimate successors of the clergy in administering endowments for relieving sick and indigent persons, and promoting education in and around the City. By letters patent, dated **St. Bartholomew's, founded 28 Hen. VIII.** 1539,[3] he made over to the Mayor and Commonalty the lands and tenements belonging to St. Bartholomew's Hospital,[4] constituting them masters, governors and keepers, whereupon they endowed it with five hundred marks a year, while the **St. Thomas's.** King added an equal amount. In 1553, the Corporation, with a ready sanction from Edward VI., bought the estates belonging to St. Thomas's Hospital, Southwark; and two noble

---

[1] 8 Geo. III. c. 32.

[2] 22 Geo. III. c. 77.

[3] These letters patent are confirmed by the first charter of 14 Charles I.

[4] Originally part of a priory for black canons, founded in 1102 by Rahere, jester to Henry I., and repaired by a legacy from Richard Whittington, in 1423.

institutions thus arose in northern and southern London for the treatment of sick poor, combined with the study and advancement of surgery and medicine. Largely added means now enable them to fulfil this beneficent mission over a wider area, with a corresponding increase of usefulness; and their good government and high efficiency have rarely been questioned. St. Bartholomew's continues on its old site, though its advantages are no longer confined, as the letters patent of 1539 express, to "poor of West Smithfield."[1] St. Thomas's, removed from Southwark, where it was side by side with another ancient hospital, and rebuilt upon a prominent site opposite the Houses of Parliament, is an example of a City trust administered wholly for the benefit of a population beyond the City.[2]

An ancient palace, near the well of St. Bride, Blackfriars, **Bridewell.** once possessed by Wolsey, and rebuilt, in 1553, by Henry VIII. for the reception of Charles V., was granted to the Corporation by Edward VI., as one of the Royal hospitals. It was burnt in 1666, and rose again as a house for the detention and correction of vagrants, refractory apprentices, and disorderly persons. A new Bridewell prison was built in 1829, but was pulled down in 1864; its site is now covered with warehouses and offices. The increased revenue from the Bridewell estates is applied, under a scheme sanctioned by the Charity Commissioners in 1860, towards the maintenance of two industrial schools: one at Witley, Surrey, for boys; the other at St. George's-fields, for girls. Bridewell affairs are now managed by a Committee of the Corporation[3]

---

[1] The governors of St. Bartholomew's derive various powers of leasing, &c. from 6 Geo. IV. c. 51; 14 & 15 Vict. c. 3.

[2] See 6 Geo. IV. c. 46; 13 & 14 Vict. c. 7 (leasing powers); and 25 & 26 Vict. c. 4, enabling the Corporation, as Governors of the Possessions, Revenues and Goods of St. Thomas's Hospital, to convey the site of the present Hospital to the Charing Cross Railway Company, and to acquire a new site.

[3] See 6 Geo. IV. c. 49, conferring leasing powers on "the Mayor, Commonalty and Citizens of the City of

Bethlehem.

along with those of a more celebrated charity, Bethlehem Hospital, founded by Henry VIII. Bethlehem, by corruption Bedlam, was anciently the hospital of St. Mary of Bethlehem, established in 1246 by a citizen, one Simon Fitzmary, who had been Sheriff of London. It stood originally in Bishopsgate Without, and, when the religious houses were suppressed, was granted to the Corporation, who have since used it as a hospital for the insane. In 1674 it was rebuilt in Moorfields, the Corporation granting land there for "a new hospital-house capable of receiving one hundred and twenty lunatics and distracted persons, with officers and servants to attend them."[1] In 1810, under statutory powers then obtained, the site at Moorfields was revested in the Corporation, who in lieu of it were authorized to grant nearly twelve acres of land in St. George's-fields, where at least two hundred patients could be treated, and their cure "accelerated by exercise in the open air."[2] By this transfer the hospital acquired an open site, with spacious grounds, and a dome reproducing in miniature that of St. Paul's. Bedlam is the saddest word in our language, and suggests the most painful memories.[3] For skilful and humane treatment, with the most approved methods and appliances, it is now a model asylum.[4]

Christ's Hospital.

Christ's Hospital, better known as the Bluecoat School,

London, Governors of the Possessions, Revenues and Goods of the Hospital of King Edward VI., called Bridewell."

[1] Recital to 50 Geo. III. c. 198.

[2] 50 Geo. III. c. 198. Eight acres were devoted to the grounds and building; the surplus land was applied in augmenting the revenues of the hospital (sects. 4, 5).

[3] Until the latter part of the seventeenth century male patients here were shown like wild beasts in cages at so much per head, for the benefit of warders, or to raise funds for their own support. Harmless patients were, with the same object, sent out to beg, with badges on their arms, and were known as "Tom-a-Bedlams." Even in the Vagrant Act of 1744, which first provided for the safe custody of lunatics, justices were authorized to chain them (17 Geo. II. c. 5, s. 20).

[4] An Act of 1871 authorized the governors to establish at Witley a convalescent hospital in connexion with, and as part of, Bethlehem (34 & 35 Vict. c. 122).

had the same Royal founder, Edward VI. At the citizens' request, he assigned to them lands belonging to a suppressed house, the Greyfriars' Monastery, for the support and education of orphans and foundlings. Since then the foundation has been enriched by many benefactions, and, besides the governors appointed under statute by the Corporation, any person contributing 500*l*. may become a governor, with a right of nominating a child for admission. Under these altered conditions, the class of children now admitted is not always that originally intended to be beneficiaries. Besides the school in Newgate-street, where some eight hundred boys are fed, clothed and instructed, a branch was established at Hertford, in 1683, for boys of tender age, and also for girls, altogether about four hundred. The hospital in Newgate-street was destroyed in the fire of 1666, and has been twice rebuilt.[1]

During the last century serious differences arose between the Mayor, Commonalty, and citizens, as "Governors of the Possessions, Revenues and Goods" of the five Royal hospitals, and the presidents, treasurers, and acting governors, touching their respective rights and powers in the management of the hospitals and estates. A practice had gradually arisen of choosing as governors benefactors who were not necessarily members of the Corporation, or even citizens. Hence the differences which made legislation desirable. Articles of agreement were therefore drawn up in 1782, and embodied in an Act of that Session, defining these respective rights, and regulating the government of the five hospitals.[2] The Act declared that great benefit had been

Government of the Royal hospitals.

Settled by Act of 1782.

[1] See 35 Geo. III. c. 104 (enlargement of schools at London and Hertford); 6 Geo. IV. c. 48; 6 & 7 Will. IV. c. 24; and 14 & 15 Vict. c. 2 (leasing powers); 46 Geo. III. c. 22, to "regulate the charities of John West and Frances his wife," relating to Christ's Hospital.

[2] 22 Geo. III. c. 77. An interesting narrative is given in the recitals to this Act of the method of appointing governors, under the charter or letters patent of Henry VIII. and Edward VI., from the year 1557 downwards. It appears that at first all the hospitals were treated as one body, and a comptroller, a surveyorgeneral, being Aldermen, with three

derived by these institutions from the donations of persons outside the Corporation, who had been elected as governors, and their right to a share in the management was recognized.

Corporate governors.

Under an " ordinance " made in the year 1557, " by the Mayor, Commonalty, and citizens of London, Governors of the Possessions, Revenues and Goods of the Royal Hospitals," the Lord Mayor for the time being is head of all the hospitals. The general practice, however, has been to preserve the Royal character of these foundations by connecting with them some member of the reigning family as President.[1] By virtue of their office all the Aldermen are governors of all the hospitals. Under the Act of 1782, the Court of Common Council also appoints twelve governors to each. These appointments are apportioned among the wards by rotation or otherwise, under regulations made by the Council, so that there may be a fair distribution. By the same statute, the corporate style is to be used in all actions or suits brought by or against the hospitals, and their seal restored to the City Chamber, together with all leases and deeds affect-

London almshouses.

ing them.[2] In elections to the London almshouses, orders of the Common Council provide for a rotation of wards, settled by ballot, so that this patronage also may be fairly apportioned. The inmates of these almshouses are decayed freemen, their widows and daughters.

Plantation of Ulster, 1609.

Another function of quite a different character, and possessing great historical interest, has descended to the Corporation. Through frequent rebellions Ulster had become depopulated early in the seventeenth century, and half a million acres were forfeited to the Crown. James I. and

other Aldermen, a treasurer, and eight citizens, were made governors. After 1564, a president, treasurer, and other governors were chosen for each hospital.

[1] In 1886 the Prince of Wales was President of St. Bartholomew's; the Duke of Cambridge, of Christ's; the Duke of Connaught, of St. Thomas's. Alderman Sir J. C. Lawrence was President of Bridewell and Bethlehem.

[2] 22 Geo. III. c. 77, articles 2 and 3.

his advisers, but especially the Earl of Salisbury, then Lord High Treasurer, thought that the best way of securing the loyalty of this province was by colonizing it with English and Scotch Protestants. Accordingly, in 1608, an order of the Privy Council declared that "the greatest part of six counties," Armagh, Tyrone, Coleraine, Donegal, Fermanagh, and Cavan, "being escheated and come to the Crown, his Majesty, of his princely bounty, not respecting his own profit, but the public peace and welfare of Ireland, by the civil plantation of these unreformed and waste countries, is graciously pleased to distribute these lands to such of his subjects, as well of Great Britain as of Ireland, as being of merit and ability shall seek the same, with a mind not only to benefit themselves, but to do service to the Crown and commonwealth." Suitable conditions were imposed against alienation, and to ensure residence and colonization.

Forfeiture of land in Ireland.

Upon an appeal to them, in 1609, the Corporation consented to engage in this work, but first sent four "wise, grave and discreet citizens" to view the escheated land. It was a great national work, and the Corporation, acting on this occasion solely for national interests, undertook it with what was quaintly described as "flagrant zeal."[1] Articles of agreement were therefore signed securing to the Mayor and Commonalty a large tract, comprising the city of Derry, with the town of Coleraine; and the Common Council ordained that, for the purpose of conducting the plantation, a Society should be constituted, consisting of a governor, a deputy-governor, and twenty-four assistants. Of these, the governor and four assistants were to be Aldermen, and the rest commoners, one-half of them elected by the Council annually; the Recorder was an ex officio member. In March, 1613, a charter was granted to this Society, who were to build houses in Derry and Coleraine, "with convenient fortifications," cultivate the land, promote industry, and spread

The Irish Society.

---

[1] Recitals in charter granted by James I. to the town of Coleraine.

true religion. Enlisting the wealth and patriotism of the livery companies, the Society raised 60,000*l.* by assessment among them, and otherwise did much to make the plantation successful. In order to attract subscribers and colonists, the citizens were reminded that, during the reign of Henry II., Dublin, then desolate, was populated by the city of Bristol, "whose posterity doth continue there unto this day." This plantation, undertaken without any charge to the King, "to the perpetual commendation of Bristol, was not the least cause of civilizing and securing that part of the country;" and the advantages of a new plantation in Ulster were set forth in a statement as sanguine and as glowing as any modern prospectus.[1]

Colonization of Dublin by Bristol under Henry II.

Division of land between Irish Society and livery companies.

As the twelve great livery companies of London had contributed equally towards the first outlay, all lands granted to the Irish Society were divided for apportionment into thirteen lots. The first lot, including Derry and Coleraine, and contiguous lands, with all woods, ferries, and fisheries, was reserved to the Society; the other lots were apportioned among the companies in perpetuity.[2] James I. had this settlement

Desire of James I. to

[1] Concise View of the Origin, Constitution, and Proceedings of the Irish Society, 1822 (privately printed by authority), pp. 17—21. The country was described, no doubt truthfully, as well-watered, with a navigable river, a good harbour, a city (Derry) easily made impregnable, plentiful salmon and sea fishing, land fit for all sorts of husbandry, and the breeding of sheep and cattle, hemp and flax of natural growth, linen stuff more fine and plentiful than anywhere in the kingdom, building materials abounding; and (a final touch, well worthy of the last new "company limited"), "there be also some good store of pearls upon this coast, especially within the river of Lough Foyle." As to the fishing, indeed, there was no

exaggeration; "a very long salmon could be procured for 4*d.*, 6*d.* or 8*d.*" There is an entry in the society's records for January 23, 1721, that their salmon "could only be sold for 12*l.* a ton, Irish currency." (An Irish pound was equivalent to 1*l.* 1*s.* 8*d.* The currency of Great Britain and Ireland was assimilated in 1825 by 6 Geo. IV. c. 79.) Next year "the charges attending the fishery of Lough Foyle exceeded the value of the fish taken;" in 1723, "the quantity of salmon produced was 97½ tons, which the society sold at 15*l.* per ton;" in 1724, the fishing was let at 16*l.* 15*s.* a ton, and produced 138 tons.

[2] The twelve companies, in their established order of precedence, were:—Mercers, Grocers, Drapers,

specially at heart. In 1615, believing that the City was slow or negligent in performing its agreement, he desired Sir Arthur Chichester, then Lord Deputy of Ireland, to make strict inquiry, and in his own hand added:—" My Lord, in this service I expect zeal and uprightness from you, and that you will spare no flesh, English nor Scottish ; for no private man's worth is able to counterbalance the particular safety of a kingdom, which this plantation, being well accomplished, will procure." There was a difficulty at first in providing settlers as well as funds ; but the City, on the whole, did its part faithfully. We read of a conspiracy, in 1615, to surprise and destroy Derry and Coleraine. Arms, ammunition, and warlike stores, were at once sent over by the twelve companies ; and, besides the fortifications already constructed at Derry, the Court of Common Council proposed a keep or citadel at Coleraine.[1] Again, during the rebellion of 1641, the City of London sent four ships to Derry, with all kinds of provisions, clothing, and accoutrements for several companies of foot, and abundance of provisions. Each of the twelve livery companies also sent two pieces of ordnance, besides twenty pieces which the Society had provided some years before. With this timely succour the besieged were able to hold their own, and protect the Protestants who had flocked to Derry for refuge. Eight years afterwards Derry was once more successfully defended, this time against the Royal forces, and on behalf of Parliament.

Meanwhile, in 1634, Charles I. had revoked the Society's charter with no reasonable justification, sequestrated the whole county of Derry, and caused all rents there to be levied for his use. Charles II., beginning his reign with fair promises, gave a fresh charter in 1662, confirmed the grant of James I., and, in compliment to the citizens,

perfect settlement.

Munitions of war supplied by City of London, 1615–41.

Revocation and renewal of Society's charter, 1634–62.

Fishmongers, Goldsmiths, Skinners, Merchant Taylors, Haberdashers, Salters, Ironmongers, Vintners, and Clothworkers. Some of the minor companies were also contributories.

A licence was granted by the Crown to the twelve companies to hold the land in mortmain. Some of them have since sold their Irish property.
[1] Concise View, &c., p. 43.

prefixed to Derry the name of London. Henceforth, the new plantation acquired a new interest in the English capital. This interest became absorbing when, after the Revolution had been peacefully accomplished in England, Catholic Ireland welcomed in James II. a monarch of kindred faith, and Londonderry became a city of refuge to fugitive Protestants throughout Ulster, the sole place which held out for William III. It was as though the citizens of London, who had done so much for the Protestant cause at home, were maintaining it almost single-handed, through their kinsmen and settlers, in the sister island. On the other side, the importance of reducing this Protestant stronghold was duly recognized, and James, with the French generals who had sailed with him from Brest, led his troops to the walls in person.

James II. welcomed in Ireland after the Revolution.

The story of the siege which followed is one of the most spirit-stirring in English history. A fitter or finer subject for poet or painter it would be hard to find. No one can read unmoved of the daring and devotion shown by an undisciplined garrison,[1] who, exhorted as well as commanded

Siege of Londonderry, 1689.

[1] They made their sallies in a manner unauthorized by military rules. Any officer that could be spared engaged in the adventure; any soldiers who pleased followed his standard. "A garrison we had," said Governor Walker, "composed of a number of poor people frightened from their homes, and who seemed more fit to hide themselves than to face an enemy. When we considered that we had no persons of any experience in war among us, and those very persons that were sent to assist us had so little confidence in the place that they no sooner saw it but they thought fit to leave it; that we had but few horse to sally out with, and no forage; no engineers to instruct us in our works; no fireworks; not so much as a hand-grenade to annoy the enemy; not a gun well-mounted in the whole town ... it was obvious enough what a dangerous undertaking we had ventured upon. But the resolution and courage of our people, and the necessity we were under, and the great confidence and dependence among us on God Almighty, that He would take care of us and preserve us, made us overlook all these difficulties." Besides Governor Walker, eighteen other clergymen of the Established Church, with seven Nonconformist ministers, cheerfully shared the labours and dangers of the siege. In turn, every day they collected the people in the cathedral church, and by the fervour of their devotions, and those strains of eloquence which their circumstances inspired, ani-

by the heroic clergyman, Governor Walker, when deserted by officers who should have led them, and contending against faint-hearted counsels and open treachery, rejected all promises, were undaunted by the most barbarous threats, and, though gaunt with famine and reduced almost to despair, beat back, after a hundred and five weary days, all the forces which could be brought against them.[1] Their stubborn zeal for the Protestant faith, and their sufferings until

mated and influenced their hearers.— Leland's Hist. of Ireland.

[1] An English fleet of thirty sail, with troops, arms, ammunition, and provisions, entered the harbour, but sailed away, Kirke, its commander, thinking that he could not force a passage. Every day the garrison was lessened by disease, and the wretched survivors more and more enfeebled by fatigue and hunger. Yet when numbers of them were scarcely able to support their arms, they threatened death to any one who talked of yielding. Marshal Rosen, in command of the besiegers, enraged at the obstinacy of the townsmen, declared that if they did not surrender by a given day, all Protestants in the surrounding country should be given up to plunder, and driven under their walls to perish. At the time appointed a confused multitude was seen hurrying towards the walls, consisting of thousands of miserable Protestants, of all ages and conditions, infirm, old, young, women, infants, goaded on by the soldiers. After three days of horror, during which many of these people perished, the survivors were released. Meanwhile, within the town, the flesh of horses, dogs and vermin, hides, tallow and other nauseous substances, were purchased at extravagant prices, and eagerly devoured. Still the languid and ghastly crowd listened to the exhortations of Walker. Still he assured them from the pulpit that the Almighty would grant them deliverance. While their minds were yet warm with his harangue, delivered with all the eagerness of a man inspired, they discovered three ships in the lake making their way to the town. Kirke, who had abandoned them from the 13th day of June to the 28th July, at length thought fit, in their extreme distress, to attempt to relieve them. Two ships laden with provisions, and convoyed by the Dartmouth frigate, advanced in view both of the garrison and the besiegers. The enemy, from their batteries, thundered furiously on the ships, the frigate returning their fire with spirit. The foremost merchantman, the Mountjoy, struck against the boom and broke it, but, rebounding, ran aground. Shouts of joy burst from the enemy, who prepared to board her; on the crowded walls the garrison stood in silent despair. But her consort made her way through the breach; and with a rapidly-rising tide, the Mountjoy floated and also passed safely, though her brave captain was killed by a cannon shot. The town was relieved, and the enemy retired. Of a garrison of 7,500 men, 4,300 only remained to be witnesses of this deliverance; and of these more than one thousand were incapable of service.—Abridged from Leland's History.

the boom across their river was broken and tardy relief came, contributed materially at this critical time to uphold the cause of religious liberty and confirm the Revolution. We need not wonder that their descendants cherish proudly the memory of this great exploit.[1] That the same gallant spirit still lives among them we may well believe; that it may never again be tested in civil strife we must all eagerly desire. Whatever may happen in our own day, it is clear that the policy of James I. in planting Ulster, and the effective help given by the City of London in carrying out his plans, were abundantly justified.

Honours conferred on Walker. William III. wrote with his own hand a handsome letter to Walker and his co-governor, Michelborne, for their "resolute and unparalleled defence." Upon Walker's visit to England after the siege, the Irish Society, whose special champion he had been, by defending their chartered property and rights, directed several of their members to wait upon this famous member of the church militant and thank him for his services. Mr. Walker afterwards attended the Society, and, in consequence of his representations that "most of the houses in Derry were demolished by the enemy during the late siege," the Lord Mayor called a Common Council, and money was contributed by the citizens and the livery companies for distribution among the sufferers.[2] In November, 1689, the House of Commons, upon his petition, voted 10,000*l.* towards the relief of orphans and widows left after the siege. The Speaker also thanked him, in the name of the House, for "the extraordinary service you have done to their Majesties, and to England and Ireland, in defence of

---

[1] Lord Macaulay follows his vivid narrative of the siege (Hist. IV. 237–50, ed. of 1863) by regretting that the animosities of Londonderry's brave champions have descended with their glory. But, he says, the annual celebration of this great deliverance indicates "a sentiment which belongs to the higher and purer part of human nature, and adds to the strength of States. A people which takes no pride in the noble achievements of remote ancestors will never achieve anything worthy to be remembered with pride by remote descendants."

[2] Concise View, &c., pp. 74, 75.

Londonderry, and especially in that you undertook it when those to whose care it was committed did shamefully, if not perfidiously, desert that place." Dr. Walker, as modest as he was brave, replied, " Sir,—As for the service I have done, it is very little, and does not deserve this favour you have done me. I shall give the thanks of the House to those concerned with me, as you desire, and dare assure you that both they and I will continue faithful to the service of King William and Queen Mary to the end of our lives."[1]

Owing to disputes with the Bishop of Derry respecting the ownership of certain lands, fisheries, and tithes of fisheries, an Act was passed in 1704, putting an end to litigation which had begun, and quieting all differences between the see and Society.[2] This statute met the Bishop's claims by a perpetual rent-charge of 250*l.* per annum, settled upon him and his successors by the " Governor and Assistants of the new Plantation in Ulster."

Act of 1704 quieting differences with Bishop of Derry.

The income arising to the Irish Society from the town lands, ferries, and fisheries retained by them had always been applied for public purposes beneficial to the plantation, such as the endowment of schools, the support of the city and corporation of Londonderry, the building of churches, chapels, town-halls, gaols, quays, bridges, fortifications, and other public works, and relief of the poor, any surplus being divided among the livery companies in proportion to their original contributions. In 1832 the Skinners' Company filed a bill against the Corporation and the Society, alleging breaches of trust on account of extravagant expendi-

Application of income.

---

[1] 10 Com. Journ. 290; 19th Nov. 1689. Walker, the hero of Derry (which Lundy, the previous governor, would have surrendered to King James), was born of Yorkshire parents in Tyrone, educated in the University of Glasgow, and afterwards became rector of Donoughmore, not many miles from Londonderry. During the Revolution, he raised a regiment in the Protestant cause, and proceeded to Derry on hearing that James II. intended to besiege it. Created D.D. by the University of Oxford, he was afterwards appointed Bishop of Derry; but, resolving to serve another campaign before entering upon his bishopric, he was killed at the battle of the Boyne.

[2] 3 & 4 Anne, c. 1.

ture by them, and alleging that they were, in fact, no more than trustees for the companies.   Upon appeal, affirming a judgment of Lord Langdale, Master of the Rolls, the House of Lords in 1845 decided (1) that the Irish Society, by their charter, were constituted trustees for permanent public purposes independent of the livery companies, and had a discretion in applying funds arising from the property which they retained for those purposes; (2) that, although they were accountable to the Crown for any neglect of their duty as trustees, and also to the City of London for misconduct in managing the property, they were not accountable to the companies.[1]

In its preamble, the charter given to the Society by James I. sets forth:—"And whereas the province of Ulster, in our realm of Ireland, for many years now past, has grossly erred from the true religion of Christ and divine grace, and hath abounded with superstition, insomuch that for a long time it hath not only been harassed, torn, and wasted by private and domestic broils, but also by foreign arms, we, deeply and heartily commiserating the wretched state of the said province, have esteemed it to be a work worthy of a Christian prince, and of our Royal functions, to stir up and recall the same province from superstition, rebellion, calamity, and poverty, which heretofore have horribly raged therein, to religion,

obedience, strength, and prosperity."   Lord Lyndhurst, Lord Chancellor in 1845, quoted these words to show the objects for which the charter was granted.   He held that these great public objects were by no means performed and completed, as the Skinners' Company had contended.   The Irish Society, he said, "have a constant superintendence and control over the Corporation of Londonderry, for their consent is required to any bye-laws that may be enacted.   They have to provide for the Protestant religion and Protestant establishment in that district.   That is not a temporary, but a permanent object.   They have also to superintend and take care of

[1] 12 Clark and Finnelly, House of Lords Cases, 425–90.

that which is closely and intimately connected with religion, namely, the education of the inhabitants of the district. They have also to perform other public duties of great importance connected with the district: duties, as it appears to me, from the very nature and character of them, of a permanent description. It appears to me, therefore, that there is no foundation whatever for the argument which has been urged, that their authority as public officers has long since expired, and they have no public duties at present to discharge."[1] Lord Cottenham and Lord Campbell concurred in this decision.

Since the status of the Irish Society, as trustees for public objects of a permanent character, was definitively settled by this carefully-considered decision, their history has been uneventful. Their Governor and Court of Assistants, consisting of six Aldermen, the Recorder, and nineteen commoners, are still, as directed by the charter of 1613, elected annually by the Common Council in February.

Annual election of Governor and Assistants by Common Council.

We now come to a memorable struggle, and to legislation by means of which the Corporation have acquired for the people of London in perpetuity privileges of the highest value. Some account has elsewhere been given of the gradual enclosing of commons, and the modern policy of Parliament upon this question.[2] But a desire to preserve open spaces around London from spoliation is by no means of modern origin. A statute of 1592-3,[3] in a provision which seems to have been overlooked, was emphatic in its assertion of public rights over metropolitan commons, and ignored altogether any private property in them. This statute recited that "divers commons, waste grounds, and great fields near adjoining" to the cities of London and Westminster, "which have been heretofore used for training and mustering of soldiers, and for recreation, comfort and health of the

Open spaces in and near London.

Enclosure of commons, &c., within three miles of London forbidden by Act of 1592-3.

---

[1] Ib. pp. 485-6.
[2] Introduction, Vol. I. 13-27.
[3] 35 Eliz. c. 6, s. 4, one of several statutes in this and the succeeding

reign, which had for their main object the prevention of new buildings in London and the resort there of immigrants from rural districts.

people inhabiting the said cities and places, and for the use
and exercise of archery, have of late years been enclosed and
converted into severalties, and to other private uses;" and it
proceeded to enact "that it shall not be lawful to any person
or persons to enclose or take in any part of the commons or
waste grounds situate, lying or being within three miles of
any of the gates of the City of London, nor to sever or divide
by any hedge, ditch, pale or otherwise any of the said fields"
within the same radius, "to the let or hindrance of the training or mustering of soldiers, or of walking for recreation,
comfort and health of her Majesty's people, or of the laudable
exercise of shooting, where there hath been usual exercise
of shooting, and marks have been there set." Continuing
penalties were imposed for breach of this enactment.

Here is an early and remarkable proof of foresight shown
in Parliament to preserve open spaces not only for State
objects, as training-grounds for soldiers and for practice in
archery, but as places for public "recreation, comfort and
health." Unfortunately, Parliament relaxed its care for
this laudable object, and wrongful enclosures went on with
little check both within and outside the limits prescribed in
1592-3. A signal instance occurred in the ancient forest
of Waltham, which for many centuries was a Royal hunting-
ground. This forest, once of great extent, had, by grants
or encroachments, dwindled in the eighteenth century from
sixty thousand to less than ten thousand acres, and even this
area was in course of rapid appropriation by lords of manors,
or persons claiming under them, who defied the rights both
of Crown and commoners.[1] It was clear that little would
soon be left of a tract of ancient woodland which, though
within easy distance of East London, was as wild and
picturesque as any in England. Such a pleasure resort, long
popular, under the name of Epping Forest, with inhabitants

Royal forest of Waltham.

[1] A Report by the Land Revenue
Commissioners in 1793 shows that
the Forest then consisted of about
9,000 acres. In 1850, the unenclosed acreage was reduced to 7,000.

of the densest and poorest parts of the Metropolis, was worth a struggle. Local efforts were accordingly made, and in the year 1848 a Committee of the House of Commons, which inquired into the management of Crown woods and forests, though reporting generally in favour of disafforestation, strongly recommended that as much of Epping Forest as possible should be preserved for public use.

Under a public Act of 1849,[1] Royal Commissioners, chief of whom was Lord Portman, investigated questions of rights, claims, and boundaries in Waltham and the New Forest, with a view to check encroachments and unlawful enclosures derogating from forestal rights of the Crown. These rights, although no longer in themselves of much pecuniary value, neither forest being any longer used or available as hunting-grounds, were priceless as means of preventing enclosure and keeping Epping Forest open for public resort. The Commissioners accordingly recommended that all such rights should be strenuously defended, and no injustice, they pointed out, could thereby arise to private proprietors, whose land had been taken, under the original grants, with full knowledge of the existence of Crown rights, at a price adjusted upon this basis. *Forestal rights of Crown.*

It might reasonably have been expected that a report founded upon these reasons, and enforced by public feeling in London, would have had some weight with Governments and public departments. The subsequent history of this question, a singularly suggestive one, will show how far this expectation was fulfilled. Between 1854 and 1863 the Commissioners of Woods and Forests sold for a paltry sum of 18,600l., less than five pounds an acre, Crown rights extending over four thousand out of the seven thousand acres to which Epping Forest was then reduced. It was high time then for Parliament to intervene; and it did intervene, irrespective of party. In February, 1863, an address to the *Sale of Crown rights by Commissioners of Woods and Forests.*

[1] 12 & 13 Vict. c. 81.

Crown was carried against the Government, by 113 to 73 votes, praying her Majesty to sell no more Crown rights over land within fifteen miles of the Metropolis.[1] In 1865, another Committee of the House of Commons recommended that further encroachment in Epping Forest should be prevented. In 1870, however, Mr. Lowe, then Chancellor of the Exchequer in Mr. Gladstone's Administration, was of opinion that it would be unjust to individuals to enforce hunting rights of the Crown for objects differing from those

for which they were originally destined. So discouraging was the prospect, that in this Session Mr. Fawcett moved another Address to her Majesty; and, as feeling in the House of Commons set strongly in its favour, Mr. Gladstone accepted it, with an amendment which left her Majesty to " take such measures as in her judgment she may deem most expedient in order that Epping Forest may be preserved as an open space" for public recreation and enjoyment.[2]

In August, 1870, Mr. Lowe told the House of Commons what measures were proposed to fulfil its wishes. An arrangement, he said, had been come to, and embodied in a Bill, between the Government, representing the public, the lords of manors, and commoners. There remained still unenclosed three thousand acres of Epping Forest. Of this area, the lords of manors were willing to give for public use and enjoyment one thousand acres, which he proposed to vest in three Commissioners, with power to sell four hundred acres. Out of the proceeds compensation would be given to commoners, and their rights extinguished. The remaining six hundred acres would be set apart for the public, in addition to any portion of the four hundred acres which the Metropolitan Board might think fit to purchase under a power to that effect reserved to them in the Bill. On its side

[1] 169 Hansard, p. 318. Mr. Peacocke, Conservative member for an Essex constituency (Maldon) moved the Address, which was opposed by Mr. Gladstone, then Chancellor of the Exchequer.

[2] 199 Hansard, 246.

the Crown would surrender its forestal rights. This arrangement appeared to the Government a fair and reasonable one, securing for the public advantages which the Government had no power of asserting in any other way.[1]

The House of Commons was hardly less dissatisfied and indignant than were the inhabitants of London on hearing of this proposal, and the Bill which was to have embodied it perished still-born. In 1871, Mr. Cowper-Temple gave voice to public feeling. He pointed out that the Ministerial scheme was really one for surrendering 2,400 acres, to be sold or appropriated by lords of manors; and he moved " that it is expedient that measures be adopted, in accordance with the Address of 1870, for preserving as an open space, accessible to her Majesty's subjects, for purposes of health and recreation, those parts of Epping Forest which have not been enclosed with the assent of the Crown, or by legal authority." His motion was strenuously opposed by Mr. Lowe and Mr. Gladstone, but was carried on a division by 197 votes to 96.[2] *Mr. Cowper-Temple's motion, 1871.*

This crushing condemnation of the Ministerial scheme was followed by legislation which was thought more likely to preserve the Forest, but fell far short of its object. East London, even after an earnest support from Parliament, was, in fact, as yet but at the threshold of success, which was only assured by years of continued struggle. An inquiry under statute into the best mode of preserving the Forest was recommended by the Government, and adopted by Parliament. Four Commissioners named in the Act[3] were made a body corporate, with a common seal, and empowered to call evidence and prepare and settle within two years a scheme for disafforesting Epping Forest and preserving and managing the waste lands. Their powers were enlarged in the following Session,[4] when further enclosures *Epping Forest Act, 1871.* *Commissioners.* *Amendment Acts, 1872–76.*

---

[1] 203 Hansard, 1272-3.
[2] 205 Hansard, pp. 1852-71.
[3] 34 & 35 Vict. c. 93. The Commissioners were Mr. Charles Wood,

Mr. J. W. Perry Watlington, Mr. H. F. Barclay, and Mr. John Locke.
[4] 35 & 36 Vict. c. 95.

were prohibited and all litigation stayed, except a pending suit brought on public grounds by the City Commission of Sewers.   In 1873, the time allowed for making a final report was extended for a further period of two years,[1] again in 1875[2] until the following Session, and in 1876 for a like period.[3]

Naturally, many and powerful vested interests were aroused by these proceedings, and it became clear that, without equally powerful and wealthy backing, the popular claim must fail.   Such a champion was found in the City of London.   By ancient usage, as well as by property, the Corporation had some connection with Epping Forest.   They claimed, and in old times had long exercised, a right to hunt there.   Through the Commission of Sewers, they were also commoners by ownership and partial occupation of a farm called Aldersbrook, within the Forest, and possessed a technical right to intervene.   A suit was therefore brought by them, in 1871, to restrain lords of manors from further enclosure and to throw open lands illegally enclosed.   This suit, long and bitterly contested for three years, could only have been carried on by a wealthy body.   The costs were enormous.   First, the lords of manors demurred to the rights of common and pasture claimed by the Corporation, and appealed from Sir George Jessel's decision in favour of the Corporation, but it was affirmed by the Lords Justices.[4]   A mass of evidence was produced on both sides as to the use and extent of these rights of common.   At length, in August, 1874, after arguments lasting twenty-three days, the Master of the Rolls held that the Corporation had established their case, and that the defendants by their enclosures had " taken other persons' property without their consent, and appropriated it to their own use."   As the decree asked for by the Corporation excepted " lands which on August 14, 1871, were actually covered with buildings, or enclosed and used as

Marginal notes:

Commissioners of Sewers v. Glasse (suit brought in 1871).

Demurrer overruled by Sir G. Jessel, M.R., and, on appeal, by Lords Justices, March, 1872.

Final decision of Master of Rolls, August, 1874.

---

[1] 36 & 37 Vict. c. 5.   [3] 39 & 40 Vict. c. 3.
[2] 38 & 39 Vict. c. 6.   [4] L. R., 7 Ch. App. 457.

gardens belonging to or curtilages of buildings," and also " lands actually enclosed on or before August 14, 1851," Sir George Jessel said that lords of manors would still " retain considerable portions of property which they had illegally acquired." But with these exceptions, the defendants were restrained " from permitting or suffering to be or to remain enclosed or built upon any of the waste lands of Epping Forest."[1] No appeal was brought from this decree.

Meanwhile, the Commissioners appointed by Parliament in 1871 did not make their final report until 1877. Throughout these six years' proceedings the Corporation again appeared in defence of public interests. They had asked for permission, under the Act of 1871, to lay a scheme before the Commissioners and provide a fund for preserving and maintaining the Forest, but the Government refused.[2] In their final report, however, the Commissioners testified to the great " energy, labour, and ability " which the Corporation brought to bear upon the complicated questions of fact and of law involved in this protracted investigation. They had " made use of their rights of common as a means whereby to work out a great public good, and had freely and without grudging borne great and necessary expense." The decision given in their favour in 1874 had indeed proved of the highest value; it furnished a basis for a settlement which could not have been reached by statute alone. Much, however, remained to be done, and the Corporation applied themselves vigorously to complete the good work they had begun. By purchase from several lords of manors they acquired upwards of three thousand acres of the Forest, for a sum of eighty thousand pounds. They also agreed to bear the whole expense of preserving and managing the Forest, so that it was unnecessary to provide for this expense by rate. The

Final Report of Epping Forest Commissioners, March, 1877.

[1] L. R., 19 Eq. Cases, 134–65. The form of decree was not settled till November 24, 1874. As nominal plaintiffs, the Commissioners of Sewers were indemnified by the Corporation, who were the real plaintiffs in the suit.

[2] See speech of Mr. Ayrton, then First Commissioner of Works, 208 Hansard, 1192.

Commissioners therefore agreed that the Corporation should be made Conservators of the Forest, and Parliament adopted this suggestion.[1]

One of the Commissioners'. recommendations, if adopted, would have left untouched many enclosures made since 1851, notwithstanding the decree declaring them illegal, subject only to an inadequate rent-charge paid to the Conservators. Continued watchfulness was necessary to prevent this part of the scheme from being carried out. Fortunately, Lord Beaconsfield's Government accepted the responsibility of disregarding it, and introduced a Bill which was accepted as a final settlement of a long controversy.[2] By this measure all existing forestal rights of the Crown were surrendered; rights of pasture and of mast were preserved under conditions; compensation was given for other rights, such as cutting trees for fuel, and digging gravel, which would have interfered with amenities in the Forest. On the one hand, the Commissioners' scheme, allowing enclosures made since 1851 to remain, would not have preserved an adequate open space for public recreation and enjoyment. On the other hand, there might have been some hardship in the position of persons who had bought enclosed land for full value, in the belief that they had a good title, who had afterwards built upon this land, but who would have been subject to ejectment from their whole property, pursuant to the decree of 1874. While, therefore, it was

---

[1] 41 & 42 Vict. c. 213. As regards the fitness of the Corporation to perform the duties of Conservators, the Commissioners add:—"We have only to point to its ancient renown and its distinguished usefulness, and to the ability with which it discharges onerous and important duties devolving upon it through the many vast interests committed to its charge by Parliament, or belonging to it by charter or prescription" (p. 7 of final report).

[2] Sir Henry Selwin-Ibbetson, Under-Secretary for the Home Department, had charge of the Bill. It was a private Bill, but was considered by a special Committee of five members. Mr. Shaw-Lefevre expressed his satisfaction that the Government had brought in this measure, and hoped "it would permanently secure to the public this great open Forest, and put an end to one of the most gigantic systems of land robbery there had ever been in this country."

provided that all enclosures should be thrown open, except such as on August 14, 1871, were actually covered with buildings, or occupied as curtilages and gardens, compensation was given for land so restored to the Forest. These and other questions were left for decision by an arbitrator, who received full powers to settle all differences with as little delay and expense as possible.[1]

Under this Act of 1878 the Corporation, as Conservators *The Corporation as Conservators.* of the Forest, were bound at all times to keep it unenclosed and unbuilt upon as an open space for public recreation and enjoyment, to preserve its natural aspect, and protect its ancient earthworks, remains and boundaries, its timber, shrubs and underwood. A Royal lodge, named after Queen Elizabeth, who is supposed to have visited it, was also vested in the Conservators, to be maintained as an object of antiquarian interest. Sir Arthur (afterwards Lord) Hobhouse was appointed arbitrator to determine all questions of title and of compensation arising under the Act, and his awards were final. By an Act of 1880,[2] the arbitrator's powers *Epping Forest Act, 1880.* were extended for a further period of two years, and the Conservators were enabled, with his consent, to exchange portions of the Forest for other lands.

The Act of 1878 recited that the Corporation "have made great exertions to preserve the Forest as an open space for public recreation and enjoyment, and for that purpose have purchased and hold a large proportion of waste lands, and have expended large sums of money, as well in those purchases as in prosecuting the suit" before the Master of the Rolls and in appearing before the Commissioners. In order to defray the great costs of these proceedings, *City metage of grain.* and promote similar objects, the Corporation had already, under Parliamentary sanction, applied one of their acknowledged and valuable sources of revenue. From time out of mind they had possessed and exercised a right to a compulsory

---

[1] Recitals to 41 & 42 Vict. c. 213.   [2] 43 & 44 Vict. c. 130.

metage or measuring of grain, and other articles of consumption, brought into the port of London. This prescriptive franchise, originally conferred with a view to ascertain the amount of Royal customs and other dues, as well as to prevent fraudulent sales, was expressly confirmed by a charter of James I., and by the great Inspeximus charter of Charles II. As grain was now sold by weight instead of measure, a metage duty became difficult of adjustment, and caused disputes. With advantage to trade, therefore, the City dues on grain were, in 1872, commuted into a fixed duty chargeable by weight, to continue for thirty years, and the Corporation agreed to hold this duty " for the preservation of open spaces in the neighbourhood of London, not within the Metropolis as defined by the 'Metropolis Management Act, 1855.'"[1] For the purpose of preserving any open space to which the Act applied, the Corporation were allowed to borrow on the security of this duty, and of their estates and revenues, any sum not exceeding 99,000*l.*[2]

Commuted into fixed duty by weight, 1872.

A statutory obligation was thus taken upon themselves by the Corporation in 1872 to apply this ancient source of civic revenue in preserving open spaces outside the Metropolis, beyond the jurisdiction of the Metropolitan Board. No more beneficial object could have been first chosen than the defence of Epping Forest from encroachment. When the Corporation intervened, they found three thousand acres enclosed, and of this area succeeded in restoring to the public 2,500 acres. But even when the final victory seemed won by the crowning Act of 1878, much remained to be done. Before the arbitration under that Act began, the Corporation had purchased 3,554 acres. Under some of the arbitrator's orders, there was a further purchase of 1,842 acres. By judicious exchanges 134 acres were gained. The arbitration

Statutory obligation to apply grain duty for preserving open spaces.

Area acquired by Corporation.

[1] 36 & 36 Vict. c. 100, s. 5, which fixed this duty at the nominal rate of three-sixteenths of a penny per cwt., to continue until the year 1902, under the name of the City of London grain duty. The full duty is allowed as a drawback upon all grain exported or carried coastwise without breaking bulk.

[2] Ib., s. 9.

alone lasted nearly four years.[1]   At the end of a contest Length of contest.
of eleven years, the Corporation could point to a total area of
5,530 acres[2] secured by their means for public recreation and
enjoyment, a picturesque tract of woodland scenery extend- Results.
ing from the confines of the Metropolis for a distance of
thirteen miles.   When this grand popular inheritance is
contrasted with the miserable six hundred acres offered by
the Government of 1874, inhabitants of East London have
indeed reason to be grateful to those who fought their battle so
long and so resolutely, not counting the cost, but persevering
under much discouragement until they had achieved a splendid
success.   To this narrative may be added the Duke of Con- Epping Forest dedi-
naught's appointment as Ranger, and the Queen's visit on cated to public use by Queen
May 6th, 1882, when her Majesty "dedicated this beautiful Victoria, 1882.
Forest to the enjoyment of her people for ever."

Concurrently with the Epping Forest Act, 1878, the City of Lon-
Corporation promoted, and Parliament sanctioned, another don Grain Duties Act,
measure enabling them to act generally for like objects within 1878.
a specified area.   They were authorized to acquire, by purchase, gift or devise, any common, commonable land or open
space outside the limits in which the Metropolitan Board
have jurisdiction, but within twenty-five miles of the nearest
City boundary.[3]   All such lands may be held by the Corpo- Open spaces may be
ration in mortmain; and persons interested in these lands bought and held by
may devise them to the Corporation, notwithstanding any Corporation
statute or rule of law to the contrary.   They must be main- outside Metropolis.
tained "as open spaces for ever."[4]   The Corporation are
bound to keep these spaces unenclosed and unbuilt upon, for
public recreation and enjoyment; they must not alienate;
they are to resist and abate all encroachments, and, as far as
possible, to preserve the natural aspect of such commons,

[1] Besides sittings in chambers, the arbitrator held 114 public sittings. He paid many visits to the Forest, and, indeed, resided there for a time.

[2] Of this area, 5,347 acres form the Forest proper; Wanstead Park, with its famous heronry pond and perch pond, the largest ornamental waters in East London, consists of 182 acres.

[3] 41 & 42 Vict. c. 127.

[4] Ib., s. 5.

with a public spirit befitting the capital of a great empire. We have seen that for some centuries, by means of aqueducts and public fountains, they supplied the City with water, and were almost the first of English municipalities to obtain statutory powers for supplementing this supply.[1]

Mistaken policy in surrendering supply of water.

It was a blunder in policy to surrender these powers, and leave the water supply to private speculators. But the Corporation acted according to their lights at this period, and must not be condemned if they saw immediate difficulties and outlay which they were not prepared to meet, and did not foresee the monopoly they were helping to create, or the remote advantages, public and private, they were sacrificing. We must remember that Parliament itself has only in recent years been converted to the policy of giving to local authorities a control over water and light.

In its proper place an account has been given of the Corporation's unsuccessful attempt to undo, by private legislation, evils caused by the existing water monopoly in London.[2] On other occasions they have been forward in

Attempt by Corporation to establish system of fire insurance in London.

seeking to promote civic interests. After the Great Fire, in 1666, a calamity which destroyed much corporate property and brought ruin on many citizens, they tried to establish a system of fire insurance,[3] and thus gave a wholesome stimulus to prudence and forethought within their jurisdiction. When,

Their scheme of dock accommodation,

at the close of the eighteenth century, increased accommodation was required for shipping, they were ready, as Conservators of the Thames, to improve its navigation and establish docks, and their plan was the first which Parliament sanctioned for that purpose.[4] Long before the Metropolitan Board

and to embank the Thames.

was constituted, they promoted a Bill to embank the Thames.[5]

Zeal to main-

It is due to the Corporation to remember that, in these and other public objects treated in this Chapter, they have generally been alive to the wants of their age. Jealous of

---

[1] *Ante*, pp. 48 *et seq.*

[2] *Ante*, p. 191; Metropolis Water Bill, 1884.

[3] *Post*, chapter on Marine, Fire,

and Life Insurance, pp. 591-3.

[4] *Post*, chapter on Docks in the Thames, pp. 632, 642, 646-50.

[5] *Ante*, pp. 318, 349.

their privileges they have been from the earliest times, whether against Crown or Parliament. This jealousy, however, has arisen not necessarily from selfish motives, but from legitimate pride in their ancient independence, and a wish to hand down their rights and franchises unimpaired,[1] save by modifications which were called for by social changes or new conditions of trade. It was in this spirit that the City itself proposed, in the private legislation which has been noticed, readjustments of its chartered rights to duties on coal and corn, proposing also, in view of the existing incidence of these duties, to apply a considerable proportion of the revenue they produced to public objects outside the City. It was in this spirit that the Court of Aldermen, in 1870, relinquished their ancient statutory jurisdiction over brokers in the City of London,[2] and, in 1884, abolished all brokers' fees,[3] surrendering a yearly revenue of eight thousand pounds which accrued to the City from this source. It was in this spirit, too, that the Corporation have preferred to keep in their own hands the City police,[4]

---

[1] In this connection we must not forget how many other municipalities throughout this kingdom borrowed their municipal rights and privileges from London. See pp. 15—17 of Int. to Calendar of City Letters, circa 1350-70, by Dr. Reginald Sharpe, Records' clerk at Guildhall, a volume published in 1885 by order of the Corporation. A learned German antiquary there quoted (Dr. Charles Gross) shows that the laws and customs of no fewer than twenty-seven English municipalities were based upon those enjoyed by the citizens of London. Oxford, Exeter, and Gloucester, among other cities, had charters conferring substantially the same privileges; and the archives of Guildhall in the fourteenth century record occasional enquiries from these places for information and guidance upon civic customs. London was therefore, both directly and indirectly, the parent of English municipalities, and specially bound to guard their interests with its own against encroachment.

[2] 33 & 34 Vict. c. 60. This jurisdiction, first conferred in 1285, had lasted nearly six hundred years. Ante, p. 242.

[3] 47 Vict. c. 3; London Brokers' Relief Act, 1884, which came into effect after September 29, 1886.

[4] The City police force is regulated by the Corporation under the provisions of 2 & 3 Vict. c. 94, and, by general assent, is a body of the highest efficiency. In 1863, owing to enormous crowds at the entry of the Princess Alexandra, and an alleged break-down in City police arrangements, Sir George Grey, then Home Secretary, introduced a Bill to amalgamate the city and metropoli-

Fondness of
City in all
times for
feasts and
spectacles.

rather than share the State subvention received by other municipalities, as a condition of State control.

One charge against the citizens must be admitted. They are fond of good cheer, and spend much money in feasting, and in banquets to illustrious visitors. But a wealthy Corporation, representing the nation in its hospitalities, may be forgiven for profuseness rather than for parsimony. Moreover, lavish hospitality, and a taste for magnificent spectacles, are in keeping with early and unvarying tradition among London citizens. Lord Mayor's show is now the sole survival of those costly pageants and rejoicings which mediæval chroniclers describe in such glowing colours.[1] In feasting, the citizens of London still inherit "the defects of the qualities" of their predecessors.[2]

---

tan forces. (118 Com. Journ. 173.) This was generally felt to be an unworthy return for the great expenditure and loyal devotion shown by the Corporation in their welcome to the Princess. The Bill failed on Standing Orders. (*Ib.* 211.)

[1] Not to mention the entry of Richard I., after his captivity, we are told that when Edward I. returned from the Holy Land, the walls of houses were hung with silks and tapestries; conduits ran with rich wines; and wealthy citizens threw gold and silver among the people. After the battle of Poitiers, John, King of France, with his illustrious captor, the Black Prince, were conducted through the City in a procession; there were costly pageants, with tapestries, plate, silks, and warlike accoutrements. Henry V. was received with great magnificence after his French campaigns, and tapestries representing his exploits hung from the houses. Anne Boleyn's public entry into the City before her coronation surpassed, it is said, all other spectacles. When Henry VIII. went to see the City watch mustered on Midsummer eve, two thousand foot and horse marched in several divisions, with spears and arms, and attended by bands of musicians, pages, and dancers. (Norton, pp. 178–81.) Cf. accounts of the decorations at London Bridge and other places, and of the brilliant festivities and memorable progress through the City of Princess Alexandra, March 7, 1863, before her marriage with the Prince of Wales. (105 An. Register, 36 *et seq.*)

[2] One convivial member of the Clothworkers' Company left them 20,000*l.*, the interest of which was to be spent annually "in making themselves comfortable." Similar bequests for promoting harmony and good-fellowship were not uncommon.

CHAPTER XIV.

LOCAL AUTHORITIES (*continued*):—EFFECT OF SANITARY IM-
PROVEMENTS UPON MORTALITY : PRIVATE LEGISLATION
RELATING TO GLASGOW : THEATRES ESTABLISHED BY LOCAL
ACTS : MUNICIPAL IMPROVEMENTS IN EDINBURGH, DUNDEE,
GREENOCK, ABERDEEN, LIVERPOOL, MANCHESTER, BIRMING-
HAM, LEEDS, BRADFORD : ENLARGEMENT OF MUNICIPAL
FUNCTIONS BY PARLIAMENT : INFLUENCE OF PUBLIC LEGIS-
LATION ON LOCAL EXPENDITURE : LOCAL REVENUE AND
DEBT : CORPORATION STOCKS : ANNUAL INCREMENT IN RATE-
ABLE VALUE : OPERATION OF SINKING FUNDS : REPRODUC-
TIVE OUTLAY—GAS, WATER, MARKETS, &C. : EXISTING
CHECKS UPON LOCAL EXPENDITURE : NEED FOR CONTINUED
IMPERIAL CONTROL.

THE record given in the last chapter of sanitary and street *Effect of sanitary im-provements upon mor-tality in London.*
improvements effected throughout the Metropolis in recent
years would not be complete without some attempt to sum-
marise their effect on public health. Upon this question
a veteran sanitary reformer, who has largely contributed to
enlighten public opinion and expedite legislation, tells us
clearly what remains to be done and what has been done to
check disease :—[1]

. "In the whole metropolis we estimate that upwards of
20,000 lives are still yearly sacrificed; and in the whole of
the United Kingdom upwards of 100,000 fall victims to
gross causes which are preventible. Sir James Paget, in his
address as President of the Health section of the International Exhibition, showed from the experiences of friendly
societies that the insurable charges of excessive sickness, loss
of work, and premature mortality, bearing upon the wage
classes were not less than 24,000,000*l.* per annum—that is to
say, about three times the amount of poor rates. We know

---

[1] Mr. Edwin Chadwick, C.B. ; Letter in *The Times*, December 12, 1885.

that by competent sanitary administration, by efficient sanitary works, these charges are largely reducible, at a considerably less expense." Still, much has been done.

"In the metropolis of the reign of Elizabeth, that is, in 'Old London,' the death-rate was upwards of forty in a thousand. Of the whole metropolis within this year of the reign of Her Majesty Queen Victoria, almost entirely by the reduction of the deaths effected by sanitation, we have recently had it touch upon sixteen and fifteen and even thirteen in a thousand. In my sanitary report of 1842, I estimated that by sanitation the duration of life and working ability of the wage classes might be prolonged by ten years. In the model dwellings, where the death-rate is reduced to fifteen in a thousand, the extension of the duration of life from infancy by ten years is in the course of accomplishment. Captain Douglas Galton, in his presidential address at the Sanitary Congress held at Newcastle, gives *data* for the declaration that each head of the 11,000 families occupying the model dwellings in the metropolis receives as a present on his admission to them a grant of ten years more of life, and that the present value of ten years of increased wages would be nearly two and a-half times the cost of the property occupied. At the time of the report of 1842 the mean duration of life in the metropolis was—to all born men, women, and children —twenty-nine years. Professor Corfield estimates that it has now, for the whole of the metropolis, advanced to thirty-eight years."

Provincial municipalities.

We may now turn with advantage to a few provincial centres, and see what improvements have been made by municipalities during the last quarter of a century, chiefly through private legislation. These examples are fair types of progress made in smaller towns, possessing smaller means, within a still shorter period.

Glasgow in 1865.

Glasgow, in population the second city in the empire, was especially condemned for its insanitary conditions by the Reports of 1840-5.[1] These conditions remained without any serious attempts to remedy them, except by voluntary means, until the year 1866. Overcrowding and excessive mortality, with their inevitable accompaniments, pauperism, intemperance and crime, had meanwhile in-

[1] *Ante*, pp. 296, 297-8.

creased.[1] Narrow lanes or closes ran, "like so many rents or fissures" from each side of the Gallowgate, Saltmarket, Trongate, and other thoroughfares: houses of three and four stories were built so close that "women could either shake hands or scold each other from the opposite windows." In many of these lanes and closes there lived five, six, and even seven hundred people: in one case, thirty-eight families, comprising nearly three hundred persons, occupied tenements having one common stair.[2] In the centre of Glasgow, about eighty-eight acres contained a population of 51,300, packed together at the average rate of 583 persons to the acre.

These crying evils were at length confronted by the Town Council, who, in 1866, obtained statutory powers[3] to clear forty of the most crowded of these areas, upon some portions of which the population was housed at the rate of a thousand per acre, or 640,000 to the square mile; plague spots and fever dens, in which the death-rate in 1865 was 52·21, afterwards rising to seventy per thousand.[4] In its preamble, the Act of 1866 recited that portions of the city were so built, and houses so densely inhabited, as to be highly injurious, morally and physically; that many thoroughfares were narrow, circuitous, and inconvenient, and it would be of public advantage if various houses

Glasgow Improvements Act, 1866.

[1] Glasgow was subjected to exceptional difficulties, sanitary and social, in housing the poorer classes, owing to its exceptionally rapid increase of population. In 1801, the population was only 77,000; in 1821, 147,000; in 1841, 255,000; in 1861, 395,000; in 1881, 487,000. In 1885, it was estimated at 510,000. These figures do not include the suburbs beyond municipal limits. Municipal Glasgow covers an area of nine and a-half square miles; with the outlying districts its area is about twenty-four square miles, containing a total estimated population of 750,000.

[2] Description by Sir James Watson, Lord Provost of Glasgow, in 1860.

[3] 29 Vict. c. 85.

[4] Paper read in 1874 before Social Science Congress by Mr. James Morrison, Chairman of Committee of Glasgow Improvement Trust. Mr. Morrison quotes from the Registrar-General's report:—"Any deaths exceeding seventeen in a thousand annually are unnatural deaths. If the people were shot, drowned, poisoned by strychnine, their deaths would not be more natural than the deaths wrought clandestinely by disease in excess of the quota of natural deaths."

and buildings were taken down, and those portions of the city reconstructed; that new streets should be made, and existing streets altered, widened, and diverted; and that new dwellings should be provided for the labouring classes who would be displaced by this reconstruction.

Improvement Trust.

For the purpose of carrying into effect these radical changes an Improvement Trust was created, consisting of the Lord Provost, Magistrates, and Council.[1] Compulsory powers of purchase were given by Parliament over the property scheduled,[2] the area of which was eighty acres, and its value

Extent of scheme.

more than 1,500,000l. This improvement scheme, the largest ever sanctioned by Parliament, although no larger than was imperatively necessary, involved the purchase and demolition of 10,000 houses, which no structural alterations, however extensive, could make healthy residences. It was also requisite gradually to remove the population, forming of themselves a considerable town, so that they might be accommodated in more wholesome abodes; to open out these unwholesome districts, cut forty new streets through the centre, and re-sell surplus lands for the erection of improved buildings. To prevent wholesale ejectment, the Act

Provision against wholesale displacement of labouring classes.

prohibited the displacement of any number of the labouring classes exceeding 500 within any period of six months, unless the sheriff certified that other and suitable accommodation had been provided for them in the city or its immediate neighbourhood.[3] Due notice was also to be given of any intention to take down houses of this class.

Cost of scheme and taxation under it.

According to the original estimate upon which the Act was based, these improvements were to cost 1,250,000l., covered by an authorized tax of sixpence per pound on rental for five years, and threepence for ten years. In 1880, however, Parliament increased the borrowing powers of the Trust to 1,500,000l., spreading the assessment over a longer period

Glasgow Improvements Amendment Act, 1880.

---

[1] 29 Vict. c. 85, s. 3.

[2] These powers were limited for five years, but were renewed for a similar period in 1871 (34 & 35 Vict. c. 74).

[3] 29 Vict. c. 85, ss. 28, 29.

and at a smaller rate than had been originally contemplated, so that the burden should not fall too heavily on existing ratepayers.[1]

The assessment actually levied was sixpence for the first year, fourpence for four years, threepence for two years, and twopence for six years; and Parliament, in 1880, allowed the continuance of this last assessment until the works sanctioned in 1866 were completed and the whole debt due by the Trust extinguished by means of a sinking fund. In 1880, the Trust had expended upon these improvements the sum of 1,869,000*l.*, less about 380,000*l.* received for property resold. At that date the trustees still held a large amount of property purchased for the same purposes, which they wished to realise gradually. Time was therefore given to them to continue their work until this property could be advantageously disposed of. *Assessment for improvements.*

Up to May 31, 1885, the gross cost of property acquired by the Trust was 1,924,000*l.* Towards this sum the ratepayers had contributed in yearly assessments since 1866, 471,000*l.* Deducting amounts already received for land and feu duties, and estimated value of property in hand, it is reckoned that the total cost of this great improvement scheme, "from first to last," will be 523,000*l.* In return for this outlay, the ratepayers have obtained a public park, the Alexandra, which cost 40,000*l.*; seven model lodging-houses, which cost 87,000*l.*; nearly 93,000 square yards of land applied in forming twenty-seven new streets and widening twenty-four existing streets; improved sanitary conditions and conveniences caused by more open spaces; with new sewers and other works, which cost 101,000*l.*[2] *Cost of improvement, 1885.* *Advantages obtained.*

Considering the results obtained, this improvement has been very cheaply effected. Fortunately, the construction of

---

[1] 43 & 44 Vict. (sess. 2), c. 11. The assessment for these city improvements was in addition to a rate of twopence in the pound for general sanitary purposes, so that the ratepayers contributed about 40,000*l.* a year towards these objects.

[2] Balance-sheet of Glasgow Improvement Trust, 1884-5, App. No. 3.

Economical procedure of trustees.

the City Union Railway concurrently with these operations enabled the trustees to sell to advantage a considerable portion of surplus land. But they could not have presented so favourable a balance-sheet if they had not acted with great deliberation and caution. Although their first Act was obtained in 1866, four years passed before any extensive improvements began,[1] as the trustees found that, if they proceeded with reconstruction before acquiring the greater part of the property, any compensation claimed was based upon an improved value which they had themselves created. Again, a commercial depression which began in 1879 at once reduced the demand for building land, and they therefore continued to hold this land instead of forcing it upon the market at a sacrifice. Although armed with compulsory powers, the trustees adopted the policy of purchase by private negotiation wherever this course was practicable. Up to August, 1874, out of more than a thousand tenements bought, at a cost of nearly a million and a quarter, only sixty-four cases went to arbitration, and many of these arbitrations were formal, being necessary for the protection of trustees or agents, in the absence of beneficiaries, or from some other unavoidable cause.[2]

Effect of clearances.

These clearances have changed the face of ancient Glasgow, and have not only improved health,[3] but diminished crime by driving the criminal classes from their haunts, and enabling the police to exercise greater control and supervision over them.[4] In Glasgow as well as in Edinburgh and

Local legislation of 1866

---

[1] Meanwhile considerable sums were spent in abating nuisances by temporary remedies.

[2] Bailie Morrison's Paper (1874) on measures taken under the Act of 1866, p. 12.

[3] In the four years 1881–4 the mean death-rate in Glasgow was 26·5 per thousand. In some parts of Glasgow the condition of the houses in 1885 was still "very bad;" and in 1881 nearly 36,000 families,

or about 25 per cent. of the population, were reported to be living in single rooms. (Royal Commission on Housing of Working Classes, 1885, Vol. V., pp. 49, 53, 54.)

[4] Morrison, pp. 14, 15. "Districts through which you may now walk during daylight with perfect safety and confidence were formerly the scene of many murders, robberies, and assaults of the most aggravated character. The intricate net-work

other towns which followed the example of Glasgow, opinion and Artisans' Dwellings Acts contrasted. seems to be in favour of procedure under local Acts like that of 1866 for the clearance of insanitary areas rather than under the Artizans and Labourers' Dwellings Acts of 1875, inasmuch as these Acts are heavily handicapped by the provision that artisans' dwellings must be provided by municipalities upon the same areas, whereas such accommodation, it is found, is amply supplied by private enterprise.[1] It will be understood that no obligation to reconstruct dwellings for the poor people displaced was imposed upon local authorities in Scotland under private Improvement Acts, though they received permissive power to do so.[2]

Although this power to provide dwelling-houses for the Model lodging-houses. working classes has not been exercised in Glasgow, seven public lodging-houses (six for males and one for females) have been built by the Improvement Trustees, at a cost of 87,000l., chiefly for sanitary reasons, owing to overcrowding in low private houses of this class, and the propagation of disease from these centres. In these lodging-houses, which are frequented by a "loose floating population" averaging about two thousand nightly, a few pence are charged per night for bed and the use of cooking ranges. Great attention is here paid to cleanliness and ventilation, and all persons who appear to be suffering from disease are at once removed to the hospitals. Besides diminishing the liability to disease,

---

of houses then existing, now partially broken up, consisted of miles of alleys or closes, on an average not more than three or four feet wide, with lofty dark tenements on each side, forming a series of communicating fortresses, from which the criminal classes sallied with comparative impunity at night, having at hand facilities of escape and refuge. In 1867 the crimes reported to the police rose to the highest point ever attained, were of a more serious nature than at any previous time in the history of Glasgow, and were rapidly increasing."

[1] Royal Commission on Housing of Working Classes, 1885, Vol. V. See evidence of Sir W. Collins and Bailie Morrison, pp. 49, 53, 57. See also as to Edinburgh, evidence of Mr. Knox Crawford, p. 23.

[2] Glasgow Improvements Act, 1866, s. 23, which gives the trustees power to build houses for the working classes, and either to let or sell them.

and the cost of treating it, the net return from these lodging-houses has year by year increased, and in 1884-5 amounted to nearly five and a half per cent. upon the original cost.[1]

Glasgow Police Act, 1866.

An elaborate Act, containing more than four hundred sections, also passed in 1866, consolidated existing provisions relating to police and sanitary matters in Glasgow, and vested their management and control in the Board of Police.[2]

Police Board.

This Board, though created a body corporate, with a common seal and perpetual succession, was substantially a Committee of the Corporation, consisting of the Lord Provost and Magistrates, the Dean of Guild, the Deacon convener of the Trades' house, and twenty-two other members of the Town Council.[3] All the public streets and sewers were vested in this Board for purposes of maintenance and repair, and they were authorized to buy land, but only by agreement, for widening, or otherwise improving streets.

Further street improvements authorized in 1873.

In 1873, owing to increased population and trade, many thoroughfares, outside the areas marked for clearance in 1866, were found " so narrow and circuitous as to be inconvenient and dangerous." Compulsory powers were therefore given to the Board to acquire land for these and other sanitary improvements, and, in addition to previous loans, they were authorized to borrow 250,000*l.*[4]

Accommodation for labouring classes displaced.

The work of demolition and reconstruction under this Act was carried out by the Police Board on the same lines as those followed by the Improvement Trust. No obligation was imposed upon them to provide accommodation for persons displaced, but, as in 1866, they were not to eject " within any period of six months any number of the

---

[1] Exclusive of sums written off for depreciation. See Report and Balance-sheet of City Improvement Trust for year ending May 31, 1885. One of these blocks, in Drygate, returned nearly seven per cent.

[2] 29 & 30 Vict. c. 273. This statute contained a more or less complete code, classified under no fewer

than thirty-three different heads of municipal government. .

[3] In 1872 there was a slight change in the constitution of the Board, the number of elected members of the Council being increased from eighteen to twenty-two. (35 & 36 Vict. c. 41.)

[4] 36 & 37 Vict. c. 38.

labouring classes exceeding five hundred without a certificate from the Sheriff of Lanarkshire that other and suitable accommodation has been provided, or exists within the city or in its immediate neighbourhood." They were also required to give two months' public notice of their intention to "take, in any parish, fifteen houses or more occupied, either wholly or partially, by persons belonging to the labouring classes as tenants or lodgers."[1] In 1877 a change occurred in the view of Parliament upon this question; and an Act authorizing further street improvements required the Board, before displacing any persons belonging to the labouring classes, "to procure sufficient accommodation" for them elsewhere, "unless the Board and such persons otherwise agree." Any difference as to the sufficiency of such accommodation was left for decision by the Sheriff of Lanarkshire.[2]

The separation, more nominal than real, between municipal and police functions, did not long continue. It was terminated by a Provisional Order, confirmed in 1877,[3] which united in the Magistrates and Council the municipal and police government, and transferred to them all the powers of the Police Board, to be exercised by them under the title of Police Commissioners. There was a provision, however, that the accounts of the Corporation, as substitutes for the Board of Police, should be kept distinct from those of the Corporation, and of the other trusts under their administration. Owing to the structural changes which had been made since 1870, and the displacement of population, Parliament

Municipal and police functions reunited, 1877.

Police Commissioners.

Removal of parish churches

[1] 36 & 37 Vict. c. 38, ss. 22, 23.
[2] 40 & 41 Vict. c. 167, s. 23. According to local evidence, no practical hardship has been caused to working men by their enforced change of abode, as the Corporation tramways afford cheap and easy access to and from out-districts of Glasgow by workmen's cars. These cars and suburban railways appear to be largely used by workpeople living in the city to go to and from their work outside the city. In Glasgow, however, as elsewhere, considerable numbers of workpeople, for convenience in marketing and social reasons, prefer town to suburban life.
[3] 40 & 41 Vict. c. 128.

owing to
displacement
of population,
1879.

in 1879 authorized a re-arrangement of parochial divisions, as well as a removal of such parish churches belonging to the Corporation as might with advantage be placed elsewhere.[1] These removals, and the choice of new sites, were subject to approval by the Presbytery of Glasgow, and the Kirk Sessions of parishes. From the proceeds of old materials and sites, new churches were built in situations " as conducive as possible to the interests of the community of the city."[2]

Baths and
washhouses.

In five districts of Glasgow the Corporation have erected, at an expense of nearly 100,000*l.*, baths and wash-houses, which were first provided under the Glasgow Police Act, 1866.[3] As they were found of great public utility, the Police Commissioners made considerable additions to them, pursuant to further powers granted in 1879.[4] The wash-houses are largely used by poor women, who, for a very moderate charge,

---

[1] 42 & 43 Vict. c. 123. Corporate rights over parish churches in Scotch burghs originated soon after the Reformation. The parish churches throughout Scotland appear to have fallen into general decay about that period, and many churches, as well as religious houses, were entirely destroyed. An Act was, therefore, passed in 1563 " anent the re-paralling and upholding of paroche kirkes, and of kirke zairdes of the samin for burial of the dead." An Order of Council, made under authority of this Act, threw the chief burden upon parishioners, " according to their substance." This order was ratified by a statute of 1572, which complained that nothing had been done through the sloth and unwillingness of parishioners, who refused to choose persons to tax their neighbours. In compliance with more imperative directions, these statutes were gradually enforced, and embody the existing law of Scotland for upholding and rebuild-

ing parish churches. The whole expense now falls, not upon parishioners at large, but upon the heritors, or proprietors of real property. In a town the expense is borne by the community of the borough, out of the common good, or by feuars and proprietors of houses, according to the real rents of their properties (Dunlop on Parochial Law (Scotland), Third Edition, 1841). See also the Two Pennies Scots Acts (*ante*, pp. 272–5), which, in Edinburgh and other towns, applied a part of the municipal revenue from a local beer duty towards church building and ministers' stipends.

[2] 42 & 43 Vict. c. 123, s. 9.

[3] 29 & 30 Vict. c. 273, s. 387. Sect. 388 provides that " the number of baths for the use of the working classes, in any building provided by the Commissioners, shall not be less than twice the number of all the other baths of higher classes."

[4] 42 & 43 Vict. c. 123.

are saved the discomfort of washing clothes in their one living room at home.[1] The Corporation also cleanse, free of charge, in wash-houses connected with their fever hospitals, all clothing taken from houses where there have been infectious diseases.

Until the close of the last century, live cattle in Glasgow *Markets.* appear to have been exposed and sold without restraint in the public streets. These sales were prohibited, with certain exceptions, in 1799, when the Corporation were authorized to construct a market-place and levy duties on cattle sold there.[2] In 1820 sales in the streets were still further restricted, and the market tolls increased.[3] Since then the Town Council have added largely to the market accommodation, not only for cattle and horses, but for raw hides and ordinary market produce.[4] Long before English municipalities undertook a *Slaughter-houses.* control over slaughter-houses, these places were built and owned by the community in Glasgow; and we find powers taken in an Act of 1806 to remove the public slaughter-houses and rebuild them in a more convenient situation.[5] They were held and used by the corporation of fleshers, but the Magistrates and Council were required to take the new buildings "under their care and management, in so far as concerns keeping the same sweet, clean, and in good order."[6] This accommodation, also, has been largely extended and improved by local legislation of modern date.[7]

---

[1] "In every country town [in Italy] a large washing cistern is always provided by the authorities for public use; and at all hours of the day the picturesque figures of the peasant women . . . . may be seen gathered around it, their heads protected from the sun by their folded *tovaglie*, their skirts knotted up behind, their waists embraced by stiff, red bodices. Work is always enlivened with song, and when their clothes are washed, the basket is lifted to the head, and home they march, stalwart and majestic, like Roman caryatides."— "Roba di Roma," by W. W. Story; 7th ed., 34.

[2] 39 & 40 Geo. III. c. 88.

[3] 1 Geo. IV. c. 88.

[4] See, amongst others, Market Acts passed in 1826 (6 Geo. IV. c. 107), in 1845 (8 & 9 Vict. c. 29), in 1850 (13 & 14 Vict. c. 101), in 1865 (28 & 29 Vict. c. 63), and in 1884 (47 & 48 Vict. c. 25).

[5] 46 Geo. III. c. 74, ss. 1, 25–9.

[6] Ib., s. 28.

[7] See 47 Vict. c. 25, and Acts there recited.

Public parks and open spaces.

Before the year 1859, the Corporation had acquired lands which were afterwards formed into Kelvingrove Park and Queen's Park. By an Act of that Session[1] they were authorized to levy for these purposes an annual assessment not exceeding twopence per pound on heritages exceeding four pounds in annual rental. These parks have since been considerably enlarged. The Alexandra Park, acquired under the Improvement Act of 1866,[2] has already been mentioned. Glasgow Green, a fine open space situated on the north bank of the river, was laid out under powers obtained by the Corporation in 1878.[3] At the same time they were allowed to take over, lay out and maintain disused burial grounds and other open spaces "in a manner conducive to public health and comfort, and the amenity of the City." The public parks occupy a total area of about five hundred acres. The Royal Botanic Gardens of Glasgow, an institution incorporated by Royal Charter in 1818, have also been transferred to the City under the Act of 1878.

Art galleries, museums, libraries.

Art galleries, with collections chiefly due to private munificence, have been vested in the Corporation since 1859.[4] The mansion of Kelvingrove, in the park of that name, has since been opened as an industrial museum, with additional buildings fitted for collections of natural history and scientific objects.[5] Donations and bequests from wealthy citizens have been encouraged by the sight of public buildings, suited for the display of such objects, and by the knowledge that they will be properly cared for and appreciated. A public library, founded by a citizen who left 80,000*l.* for this purpose, is also managed by the Corporation.

Water supply.

Private companies, 1806-55.

Through its municipality, Glasgow enjoys a water supply of which any city may be proud. The statutory history of this supply is not a long one. A private company, called the Glasgow Water Company, was incorporated in 1806 for

[1] 22 Vict. c. 17.

[2] 29 Vict. c. 85, s. 24.

[3] Glasgow Public Parks Act, 1878

(41 & 42 Vict. c. 60).

[4] 22 Vict. c. 17.

[5] 41 & 42 Vict. c. 60.

providing the City and suburbs with water from the Clyde, near Dalmarnock Bridge.[1] Another private undertaking, the Cranstonhill Waterworks, sprang into existence two years subsequently, also deriving water from the Clyde,[2] but was absorbed by the older company in 1837.[3] In 1846 this company obtained powers to increase its service with water taken from Loch Lubnaig, in the county of Perth,[4] but the works so authorized were never executed. In the same year another company was incorporated,[5] called "the Gorbals Gravitation Water Company," to serve the barony of Gorbals and other places from the Brockburn, near Barrhead, and other sources. Glasgow soon found its supply deficient both in quantity and purity. A strong feeling arose that a more abundant supply should be procured, and the business of furnishing it vested in the Corporation. In 1855, there- *Glasgow Corporation Waterworks Act, 1855.* fore, an Act was obtained[6] transferring to the Corporation, as Water Commissioners, the undertakings of the Glasgow Water Company and the Gorbals Gravitation Water Company, and authorizing them to substitute for existing sources water from Loch Katrine. For this purpose they were authorized to borrow 700,000*l.*

Loch Katrine is thirty-four miles from Glasgow. With *Loch Katrine as source of supply.* Lochs Vennacher and Drunkie, which are also laid under contribution, it presents a splendid source of pure water, covering more than four thousand acres. Glasgow owes much to a situation which commands natural reservoirs so capacious and so near. But this advantage was not won *Works.* without great labour and skill.[7] It was necessary to con-

---

[1] 46 Geo. III. c. 136, amended by 59 Geo. III. c. 67.

[2] 48 Geo. III. c. 44, amended by 52 Geo. III. c. 52, and 59 Geo. III. c. 117.

[3] 1 & 2 Vict. c. 86.

[4] 9 & 10 Vict. c. 21.

[5] 9 & 10 Vict. c. 347; 13 & 14 Vict. c. 92; 16 & 17 Vict. c. 97.

[6] 18 & 19 Vict. c. 118. A public water rate of one penny was imposed on all property within the City, in addition to a domestic water rate charged on houses actually supplied. The Commissioners were also bound to give a gratuitous supply from 32 stand-pipes or fountains.

[7] The engineer was Mr. J. F. Bateman.

struct seventy tunnels, some mined, others built, one of them six hundred feet below the surface. Twenty-seven aqueducts of iron or masonry carry the water over rivers and ravines to reservoirs at Milngavie, eight miles from Glasgow, whence the water is distributed throughout the City. It was not until 1859 that these great works were completed, and Queen Victoria, in October of that year, opened the aqueduct which brings the water from Loch Katrine for use by the citizens. This inestimable boon, an abundant and wholesome service of water, has largely contributed to public health and comfort. An incidental advantage secured by the difference of levels is a pressure of seventy feet above the highest point in Glasgow. This pressure is also used in various warehouses and works for hydraulic lifts.

Extension of works and borrowing powers, 1859–85.

For the task of completing works so formidable, we cannot wonder that the estimates of 1855 proved insufficient. On two occasions, in 1859-60,[1] the borrowing powers of the Water Commissioners were increased to 1,250,000l. for completing and extending the works. In 1865, the operation of the sinking fund contemplated by the original Act was postponed for a period of five years.[2] In 1866, the Water Commissioners were authorized to construct what are called the River Supply Works, in order to take water from the Clyde for trade and manufacturing purposes. For the construction of these works an additional sum of 150,000l. was raised.[3] Owing to a further increase of trade and population, an increased service for domestic purposes became necessary in 1877. Works were therefore authorized[4] which would

[1] 22 Vict. c. 9 ; 23 & 24 Vict. c. 33.

[2] 28 Vict. c. 69, which also authorized the construction of a bridge for carrying the aqueduct from Loch Katrine over the river Endrick.

[3] 29 & 30 Vict. c. 328. The time for constructing the works authorized by this Act was extended in 1873, and part of the works allowed to be abandoned (36 & 37 Vict. c. 36). Again, in 1879, a further extension of time was allowed for the completion of the River Supply Works (42 & 43 Vict. c. 40).

[4] 40 & 41 Vict. c. 165.

enable the Commissioners to bring into the City from Loch Katrine the whole fifty million gallons a day contemplated by the Act of 1855. At the same time their borrowing powers were increased to a total sum of 1,850,000*l.*[1] An additional service reservoir and other works were authorized in 1882,[2] and the Commissioners' borrowing powers brought up to 2,000,000*l.*[3] Increasing population, however, demanded a still further supply. New works were therefore sanctioned in 1885,[4] consisting of a second and larger aqueduct from Loch Katrine, together with dams or embankments, for the purpose of enlarging Loch Katrine and an adjoining loch called Loch Arklet, and raising the level of the water in these lochs. The Commissioners were bound not to withdraw in all more than a hundred and ten million gallons a day from Loch Katrine, unless they introduced into that loch water from other sources ;[5] but this quantity is exclusive of the water obtainable from Loch Arklet, which will be about ten million gallons a day. By the Act of 1885 the total outlay sanctioned on waterworks in Glasgow was brought up to three millions of money.[6]

Glasgow is lit as well as provided with water by its representative body. A private company, called the Glasgow Gas Light Company, was incorporated in 1817, by an Act[7] which recited that "inflammable air, coke, oil, tar, pitch, asphaltum, ammoniacal liquor, and essential oil" might be procured from coal; that " inflammable air, being conveyed by means of pipes, might be safely and beneficially used for public and private lighting," while the coke would serve as fuel, and the

Lighting in Glasgow.

---

[1] 40 & 41 Vict. c. 165, s. 5.

[2] 45 & 46 Vict. c. 87.

[3] Ib., s. 16. Sect. 17 enables the Commissioners to borrow from a bank on cash account, " according to the usage of bankers in Scotland," and assign the rates as security for such advances.

[4] 48 & 49 Vict. c. 136.

[5] Ib., s. 17.

[6] Ib., s. 40.

[7] 57 Geo. III. c. 41. Sect. 49 is noteworthy for expressly disclaiming the creation of any monopoly. It reserves the rights which the local authority and any private persons then possessed, or thereafter might acquire, of lighting streets or houses with gas or in any other manner.

other products mentioned might be "used and applied in various other ways with great advantage." Another gas-light company, the City and Suburban, was constituted in 1843.[1] Both companies subsequently obtained powers to increase their capital and extend their area of supply. In 1869, these undertakings were transferred to the municipality.[2] Their joint capital was 415,000*l*., shareholders being entitled to maximum dividends of ten per cent. upon 300,000*l*., and of seven and a half per cent. upon the remainder. The terms of purchase were that the shareholders should receive perpetual annuities of nine per cent. and six and three-quarters per cent. respectively upon these two stocks, secured, if the gas revenue were deficient, by a sixpenny " gas guarantee rate."[3] These annuities together amounted to nearly 35,000*l*. per annum. The Corporation, as Gas Commissioners, also took upon themselves a mortgage debt of about 120,000*l*. The purchase has proved highly remunerative, and no rate has been necessary. An Act of 1873[4] authorized the Commissioners, by agreement with the annuitants, to issue to them in substitution for the gas annuities a capital sum of consolidated stock, with a fixed interest of four per cent., sufficient to yield an annual return equal to these annuities.

In 1882, the standard of the gas supplied for illuminating purposes was reduced from twenty-five to twenty candles. The Commissioners were also authorized to supply non-illuminating gas, regulated by no standard, for heating, motive, and other than illuminating purposes, and to construct short railways for the carriage of coal from the Caledonian system to their Dalmarnock gas-works.[5] From their predecessors in title they have acquired wide districts of supply outside the city.

An extensive system of tramways, largely under municipal control, exists in Glasgow, and connects it not only with the

[Side notes:]
Glasgow Corporation Gas Act, 1869.

Consolidated Gas Stock, 1873.

Non-illuminating gas.

Tramways.

---

[1] 6 & 7 Vict. c. 58.
[2] 32 & 33 Vict. c. 58.
[3] Ib., ss. 10, 11, 42.
[4] 36 & 37 Vict. c. 148.
[5] 45 & 46 Vict. c. 190.

suburbs, but with adjacent burghs. A company was incorporated in 1870 to provide this accommodation.[1] To guard against monopoly in a matter so closely affecting traffic, street repairs, and public convenience generally, the Corporation took power to substitute themselves for the company within six months after the Act passed. They exercised this power; and under a similar provision in an Act of 1871 took over certain tramways from the Vale of Clyde Company, which had been authorized to make tramways from Glasgow to Paisley, Johnstone, and Govan, as well as from Port Glasgow to Greenock and Gourock.[2] Parts of tramways were in the same way acquired by the Corporation from a company constituted in 1872 to construct tramways from Glasgow to Bothwell and Hamilton, with a branch to Motherwell and Wishaw.[3] Money powers, and powers to construct additional tramways in the city and suburbs, were obtained by the Corporation in 1872[4] and 1875.[5]

Acquired by Corporation, 1870-5.

As this accommodation proved still insufficient, authority was obtained in 1879 to make other tramways in the city and suburbs.[6] In 1885, there was a further extension.[7] This system of municipal tramways in and around Glasgow is now twenty-five miles in length, constructed by means of loans amounting to half a million,[8] and leased to a company, who work under regulations imposed by the lessors.[9] These tramways, by the cheap, easy, and frequent access they

Accommodation given by tramways in Glasgow.

[1] 33 & 34 Vict. c. 175.
[2] 34 & 35 Vict. c. 108.
[3] 35 & 36 Vict. c. 198.
[4] 35 & 36 Vict. c. 121.
[5] 38 & 39 Vict. c. 123.
[6] 42 & 43 Vict. c. 122.
[7] 48 & 49 Vict. c. 156.
[8] Ib., s. 41.
[9] Under their original lease, lasting for twenty-three years from July, 1871, the company pay interest to which the Corporation are liable for capital cost, together with a sinking fund of three per cent. per annum, and a yearly rental of 150*l.* per mile of tramway. A later agreement of 1879 provides that upon all new lines the company shall pay four and a half per cent. interest on cost of construction, and the same yearly rental of 150*l.* upon lines within the municipal boundaries. (Burdett's Official Intelligence of Stock Exchange, 1886, p. 1003.) Since 1882, this company have not divided less than ten per cent. The estimated

afford to every suburb of Glasgow, have been of signal convenience to the whole population, as a supplement to local railway facilities. They were, indeed, almost indispensable adjuncts to any large scheme of street improvements, for in no other way could the displaced artizan and labouring population have been enabled to live in healthier dwellings and purer air in the suburbs, and at the same time follow their work in the city, without fatigue and at trifling expense.

Boundaries. A struggle which began some centuries ago, when boroughs began to grow in size and importance,[1] still continues. In every Session corporate towns ask Parliament to include within their municipal boundaries suburbs which have sprung up, containing a population employed in these towns, and enjoying many advantages provided by the municipality, but making no contribution to municipal rates. Glasgow has made repeated attempts to annex these suburbs. Sometimes these attempts have failed, but Parliament extended the municipal boundaries in 1846,[2] and again in 1872,[3] the city having since 1846 "greatly increased in extent and population, and spread beyond the boundaries and limits then fixed." In 1878, there was a further enlargement of the municipal area.[4] Continued growth justified an application to Parliament with a similar object in 1886.

New municipal buildings. A convincing proof of pride in their great city was given by the municipality in 1878. At that time their annual income had risen to nearly a million sterling, and was increasing every year. But the various bodies and trusts into which the Corporation were divided, the Police Commissioners, Water Commissioners, Gas Commissioners, Improvement Trustees, Market Commissioners, and Parks Commissioners, were meanly housed in buildings separated

---

number of passengers conveyed in the year 1884-5 was close upon forty-two millions. (Commons' Return 317 of 1885.)

[1] *Ante*, p. 252.
[2] 9 & 10 Vict. c. 289.
[3] 35 & 36 Vict. c. 41.
[4] 41 & 42 Vict. c. 100.

from those in which the municipal business was transacted. To prevent this inconvenience and delay, it was determined, with general assent, to concentrate the offices of the Corporation and their various trusts in buildings more worthy of the City, and occupying a central position. These buildings, erected under Parliamentary sanction,[1] have cost above a quarter of a million.

This concentration of offices perhaps suggested, a few years later, a consolidation of municipal finance. Instead of the system under which the Corporation, as the general municipal authority, and their four delegated bodies, the Gas, Water, Markets and Police Commissioners, raised money separately, the Corporation were enabled[2] to borrow all money required from time to time by these Commissioners, and lend it to them. For this purpose Corporation stock was created, redeemable in 1914, with the usual sinking fund. The total borrowing powers of the Corporation amounted in 1885 to over eight millions, but were only exercised to the extent of about six millions and a quarter, and were reduced by sinking funds to about five millions.[3] Through the operation of the sinking funds, even allowing meanwhile for considerable additions to debt, the City will, early in the next century, possess a princely revenue from its markets, gas, water, and tramway undertakings, which will add to the common good, and should effect large reductions of charges and rates. Up to 1886 its average net revenue from water was about 35,000*l.* a year, which must be applied to sinking fund or in lowering rates. From gas there is an average profit of nearly 17,000*l.* a year.[4]

To Glasgow, lastly, belongs the credit of having led the way by local legislation to public measures for reforming

Municipal finance.

Corporation stock.

Operation of sinking funds.

Juvenile offenders.

[1] Glasgow Municipal Buildings Act, 1878 (41 Vict. c. 79).
[2] 46 & 47 Vict. c. 106.
[3] Burdett's Official Intelligence, 1886, Table A. p. 54, where the City expenditure is stated to have been, for remunerative works, 3,449,000*l.* ; for unremunerative works, 2,844,000*l.* The gross annual rental of Glasgow was then 3,395,000*l.*
[4] Ib., Table C., p. 57.

juvenile offenders. As early as the year 1841, a Board of Commissioners was constituted for this object by a local statute.[1] A society had some years previously built "houses of refuge," in which juvenile offenders of both sexes were "supported, instructed, and usefully employed, for the purpose of reclaiming them from their errors and vicious habits." These houses were found very useful in preventing crime, but as voluntary contributions proved insufficient, Parliament sanctioned the incorporation of Commissioners, in whom property already existing might vest, and who might acquire and hold other property, sue and be sued, and exercise full powers for the same purpose. At first, thirty of these Commissioners were appointed by the Corporation of Glasgow, and five by each of the Town Councils of three adjacent burghs, Calton, Anderston, and Gorbals. Inmates were admitted on their own request, signified in the presence of the Sheriff of Lanarkshire, or a magistrate for Glasgow, and were detained under proper control for a specified period, being maintained, instructed, and sometimes remunerated for their work. Offenders under trial might also pray to be admitted previous to conviction, consenting to enter a house of refuge instead of abiding trial and sentence; and judges, sheriffs, or magistrates were authorized thereupon to discharge the proceedings, giving a warrant to the Board to receive and detain such offenders for a specified period. Expenses were defrayed by a maximum assessment, upon occupiers of premises exceeding twelve pounds, of one penny in the pound of yearly rateable value.

In 1866 the construction of the Board was altered, and made to consist of three *ex officio* members—the Sheriff of Lanarkshire, the Lord Provost and Dean of Guild, with twenty-seven members elected yearly by the Town Council.[2] Meanwhile, under public legislation, beginning in 1866,[3]

Side notes:
"Houses of refuge."

Amendment Acts, 1866-70.

---

[1] 4 & 5 Vict. c. 36.
[2] 29 & 30 Vict. c. 66.
[3] 29 & 30 Vict. cc. 117, 118, s. 8;

followed by 37 & 38 Vict. c. 47; 40 & 41 Vict. c. 53, s. 67; 41 & 42 Vict. c. 40.

various reformatory and industrial schools were established Reformatory and industrial schools. in Glasgow and the neighbourhood for similar objects; and in 1870[1] they were made to share in the assessment authorized by private legislation in 1841. A change was made in 1877 in the proportions in which the assessment was divided between the houses of refuge and the public reformatories and industrial schools.[2] In the following Session all previous New administration, 1878. Acts were repealed,[3] and a new Board of Commissioners was incorporated, consisting of the Lord Provost, the senior bailie, and nine persons elected by the Corporation, as "Commissioners for the prevention and repression of juvenile delinquency in the City of Glasgow." They levy the assessment, and pay it to a Board of Directors, who were at the same time incorporated for carrying the Act into execution, as "Directors of houses of refuge and reformatory and industrial schools in the City of Glasgow." The two houses of refuge for youths and girls, with the Protestant reformatory schools connected with them, and all property belonging to the Commissioners of 1866, including two industrial schools for boys and girls, were transferred to the Directors, who were empowered to establish and maintain, out of the assessment, additional houses of refuge, with Protestant reformatory and industrial schools.

By this Act,[4] day industrial schools are also authorized, in Day industrial schools. which is received, and detained during certain hours of the day, "any child between five and thirteen years of age who is not being provided with elementary education, or is found habitually wandering, or not under proper control, and who is brought with his parent by summons" by the School Board before the magistrates, provided they think such detention expedient. Parental responsibility is recognised, for the Court may order a parent to pay any sum not exceeding two shillings a week towards the child's industrial training, education, and meals. Public money for the same

---

[1] 33 & 34 Vict. c. 42.   [3] 41 & 42 Vict. c. 121.
[2] 40 & 41 Vict. c. 62.   [4] Ib., s. 30.

purpose is also contributed at the rate of a shilling per head.
If a parent is unable to pay, his contribution must be paid
by the parochial board, provided they are satisfied of his
inability. To these useful day schools children may be
admitted upon the parent's application, and undertaking to
contribute not less than one shilling per week, which is
supplemented by public money to half the amount. Out of
the local assessment, there are capitation grants to Roman
Catholic reformatory and industrial schools, and grants to
the training ship stationed in the Clyde. Payments are
also made to "feeding schools." These philanthropic efforts
by the City to repress crime at its source, and train up
young people to habits of industry, fitly close a record of
municipal work in every way worthy of the Second City in
the Empire.

Number of local Acts, 1880-86.
Of local legislation, it will be seen, Glasgow has had a
full share. Since the year 1800, about two hundred and fifty
Acts have been passed relating to roads, City improvements,
the Clyde, and other local subjects, exclusive of railways.
One of these statutes enabled his Majesty, in 1803, "to grant
Theatre established at Glasgow by statute, 1803.
letters patent for establishing a theatre" in Glasgow.[1] This
Act recited that a licensed play-house " would be of convenience to the City and to persons resorting there." To explain
this curious statute, it will be necessary to refer briefly to
legislation which had previously made all theatrical perform-
Players classed as rogues and vagabonds, A.D. 1713.
ances out of London irregular. A statute of Queen Anne[2]
included in the category of " rogues, vagabonds, sturdy beggars and vagrants," all " fencers, bearwards, common players
of interludes, minstrels, jugglers; all persons pretending to be
gipsies, or wandering in the habit or form of counterfeit
Egyptians, or pretending to have skill in physiognomy,
palmistry or like crafty science, or pretending to tell fortunes or like fantastical imaginations, or using any subtle

[1] 43 Geo. III. c. 142.
[2] 12 Anne, st. 2, c. 23. This was
also a consolidation Act; the first
Vagrant Act of 1530-1 (22 Hen.
VIII. c. 12), was less wide in its
definition.

craft or unlawful games or plays." Such persons might be taken before a justice, ordered to be whipped, and then passed on and punished in each county in like manner until delivered at their place of settlement.[1]

This statute was explained and amended in the year 1737,[2] when Parliament distinctly enacted that every person who should "for hire, gain or reward, act, represent or perform, or cause to be acted, represented or performed, any interlude, tragedy, comedy, opera, play, farce or other entertainment of the stage, or any part or parts therein," such person having no legal settlement in the town where he was performing, and not being authorized by Royal letters patent, or by licence from the Lord Chamberlain, should be deemed a rogue and vagabond within the meaning of the Act of 1713, and be liable to all penalties and punishments thereby incurred by rogues and vagabonds "found wandering, begging, and misordering themselves."[3] Performances, even by virtue of letters patent or a Lord Chamberlain's licence, were forbidden "in any part of Great Britain, except in the City of Westminster, and within the liberties thereof, and in such places where his Majesty, his heirs or successors, shall in their Royal persons reside, and during such residence only." Thus, as far as public statutes could provide, the provinces were effectually cut off from the pleasures of the drama, and

Vagrant Act of 1713 made to include players, 1737.

Plays for reward forbidden, except at Westminster, or other place of Royal residence.

---

[1] Offenders were to be whipped, as appointed in the Act of 1530-1, after being stripped from the middle upwards. This statute to punish beggars and vagabonds, then largely increasing in number through "idleness, mother and root of all vices," authorized county justices to licence impotent persons to beg within certain limits. Among other offenders specified are "scholars of the Universities of Oxford and Cambridge that go about begging, not being authorized under the seal of the said Universities;" and all "shipmen pretending losses of their ships and goods by the sea." On repetition of his offence, a prisoner was "to be scourged for two days, and the third day to be put upon the pillory from nine of the clock to eleven before noon, and to have one of his ears cut off." On a third offence he was again whipped and pilloried, and his other ear was cut off. See also 39 Eliz. c. 4, s. 3.

[2] 10 Geo. II. c. 28.

[3] Tumbling was not a stage entertainment within the meaning of this statute.

poor strolling players were at the mercy of any officials who chose to enforce this harsh law.

Exemptions by private Acts.

Edinburgh was the first city to gain, by a local statute in 1767, exemption from this arbitrary public enactment.[1] Bath and Norwich were similarly favoured next year;[2] York and Kingston-upon-Hull, in 1769;[3] Liverpool, in 1771;[4] Manchester, in 1775;[5] Chester and Bristol two or three years afterwards.[6] Then an interval of eight years followed, in which the provincial drama obtained no further privileges. But Margate and Newcastle pleaded to Parliament for them successfully in 1786-7.[7] Under the Glasgow Act of 1803, Royal letters patent might be granted for a theatre or playhouse in that city or neighbourhood, with such privileges and subject to such restrictions and regulations for orderly management as to his Majesty seemed fit. It was also provided that the theatre and its management should be under control and inspection by the Lord Provost, bailies, Dean of Guild, and Deacon Convener of the City trades, and by the sheriff depute of Lanarkshire.[8] Birmingham obtained a similar Act in 1807.[9] This narrative will explain in part the stigma attached to strolling players in the last and even early in the present century. By public legislation, in 1788,[10] magistrates at quarter sessions might license theatres in country towns, but only for sixty days at a time, and under restrictions. Players were only relieved from inclusion within the Vagrant Acts by a general statute of 1825.[11]

Edinburgh Improvement Act, 1867.

The good example set by Glasgow in 1866 was followed by Edinburgh in 1867, when an Improvement Act was passed,[12] which constituted the Corporation trustees for making clearances of unhealthy dwellings on twenty-one densely

[1] 7 Geo. III. c. 27, s. 19.
[2] 8 Geo. III. cc. 10, 28.
[3] 9 Geo. III. sess. 2, c. 17.
[4] 11 Geo. III. c. 16.
[5] 15 Geo. III. c. 47.
[6] 17 Geo. III. c. 14 ; 18 Geo. III. c. 8.
[7] 26 Geo. III. c. 29 ; 27 Geo. III. c. 50.
[8] 43 Geo. III. c. 142, ss. 1, 2.
[9] 47 Geo. III. sess. 2, c. 44.
[10] 28 Geo. III. c. 30.
[11] 5 Geo. IV. c. 83.
[12] 30 & 31 Vict. c. 44.

populated areas. Under this Act new streets have been constructed, existing streets, wynds and closes widened and improved, and houses inhabited by more than 14,000 persons removed. The maximum assessment for purposes of this trust, which comes to an end in 1887, was fourpence in the pound. After deducting receipts for land re-sold, ground-rents and other sources of income, the net outlay upon these improvements is estimated at 300,000*l*., allowing nothing for land given up to the Corporation for streets.[1]

In Dundee the worst districts in the old and most densely Dundee. populated parts of the town were cleared of houses, and new streets made, under statutory powers obtained in 1871,[2] which also enabled the Police Commissioners to control the erection of new houses, and require proper sanitary arrangements. Since this Act was passed, the Commissioners have sanctioned 176 new streets, in aggregate length fourteen and a-half miles; unhealthy dwellings have been removed, drainage has been greatly improved, and the death-rate has decreased from over 27 per thousand in 1870-2, to an average under 20 in 1885-6. In their Act of 1871 the Commissioners were authorized to construct dwellings for the population displaced, but private enterprise supplied this want, and the power was not exercised. Overcrowding, and confined, badly-ventilated dwellings are still too numerous,[3] and their ill-

[1] Royal Commission on Housing of Working Classes, 1885, Vol. V.; evidence of Mr. Knox Crawford, p. 23.

[2] Dundee Police and Improvement Act, 1871 (34 & 35 Vict. c. 153). See now Dundee Police and Improvement Consolidation Act, 1882 (45 & 46 Vict. c. 185).

[3] The close connection between drink and overcrowded, wretched dwellings, is illustrated by the following question and answer:—Mr. Goschen: "A London witness told us he had never known a teetotaller to be found in one of the worst slums?" Sir William Collins (Lord Provost of Glasgow, 1877-80): "I was a Sabbath-school teacher in the worst portion of Glasgow for a number of years . . . . and our experience was that, as soon as we had reclaimed people from drunkenness, they left the locality and went to better houses. Of course they had then the money to pay for them."— Royal Commission on Housing of Working Classes, 1885, Vol. V., p. 47.

effects are shown by the medical officer's report that, during 1882-3, seventy-four per cent. of the total cases of zymotic disease, and seventy-eight per cent. of deaths from the same cause, occurred in dwellings consisting of one or two rooms. By adding the number of deaths from measles, then an epidemic, the percentage of deaths in these dwellings was raised to 89·94.[1] According to the census of 1881, out of a population of 142,000, 22,800 persons lived in single rooms and 73,190 in dwellings with two rooms.

Sanitary powers of Police Commissioners, Dundee.

Local legislation gives the Dundee Police Commissioners power to restrict to four storeys the height of all dwelling-houses to be occupied separately in flats, unless in streets over fifty feet wide, when an additional storey is allowed.[2] For purposes of ventilation a minimum space, in proportion to height, must also be left open in the rear of houses.[3] The municipality took into its hands the gas supply in 1868,[4] and the water supply in the following Session.[5] Both undertakings were purchased from private companies, and have since been largely extended and improved under various statutes. They are vested in Commissioners, who are virtually the Town Council. No profit is made from water or gas: the assessments are adjusted to meet working expenses, interest, and sinking fund; any surplus goes in reduction of charges. The acquisition of gasworks has been very beneficial; the rate per 1,000 feet has been reduced from upwards of 6s. to 3s. The Corporation have constructed tramways,[6] which, as in other towns, are of great use in conveying working men to and from their dwellings in the suburbs.

Gas and water in Dundee.

Greenock.

Greenock was the first burgh to adopt the Artizans' Dwellings (Scotland) Act, 1875. An improvement scheme was sanctioned in 1877,[7] and about three acres were cleared of

---

[1] Royal Commission on Housing of Working Classes, 1885, Vol. V., p. 85 ; evidence of Mr. Gentle.

[2] 45 & 46 Vict. c. 185, s. 109.

[3] Ib., s. 130. See, for similar conditions, sects. 56 et seq. Aberdeen Corporation Act, 1881 (44 & 45 Vict. c. 73).

[4] 31 & 32 Vict. c. 94.

[5] 32 & 33 Vict. c. 46.

[6] 35 & 36 Vict. c. 191.

[7] Provisional Order, confirmed by 40 & 41 Vict. c. 102.

houses, a district with a population of 2,300, whose mortality ranged from forty up to sixty per thousand on an average of ten years.   The property cost much more than was esti- Excessive compensation for houses under Artizans' Dwellings Acts. mated, chiefly through large compensations given under arbitration for twenty-one licensed houses, but also through excessive sums awarded for insanitary dwellings, based on their actual yield in rent, without any deduction for the amount required to make these dwellings healthy and habit- able.   Thus, owners who spent hardly anything upon repairs, who allowed overcrowding, and whose houses were a source of danger to public health, received a handsome " premium for their misdeeds," and for their benefit the town has been heavily burdened for many years to come.   In Greenock, as in other places, the result has been to deter local authori- ties from undertaking improvement schemes.[1]   Through the sanitary clauses of a local Police Act,[2] and the clearance begun in 1878, there has been a marked improvement in public health.   Lodging-houses are now regulated, over- crowding and cleanliness are strictly enforced, and efficient measures taken for the isolation of infectious disease.

In Aberdeen, to prevent overcrowding among the fisher- Dwelling-houses built and sold by Corporation of Aberdeen. men who live in one part of the City, the Corporation built thirty-eight houses, and afterwards sold them on easy terms, chiefly to the occupants, who first paid a fourth of the purchase-money, and were then allowed to repay the rest by instalments over periods of seven, ten and twelve years, with four and a half per cent. interest.   There appears to have Payment by instalments. been no difficulty in obtaining payment of the instalments and interest; in fact, after the first instalment very little more was paid than the former rent.[3]   In 1884, a Provisional Order[4] under the Artizans' Dwellings Acts enabled the Corporation to

[1] Royal Commission of 1885, Vol. V.; evidence of Mr. A. T. Turnbull, pp. 69, 71.

[2] 40 & 41 Vict. c. 193.

[3] Royal Commission of 1885, Vol. V.; evidence of Dr. Simpson, medical officer of health for Aberdeen.

[4] Confirmed by 47 & 48 Vict. c. 108.

Power to close insanitary dwellings.

clear a space of an acre and three-quarters occupied by insanitary dwellings.   An Act previously obtained by the municipality in 1881, contains valuable powers for sanitary purposes, including a strong clause enabling the Corporation to close insanitary dwellings summarily, without appeal, on a certificate from their medical officer of health, surveyor or sanitary inspector.[1]   In 1881-5 more than fifty houses were closed under this provision.   Still, in 1885, one-seventh of the population of Aberdeen lived in single rooms, and five thousand in narrow courts, so that while the mortality of the whole City steadily decreased to about twenty per thousand, it stood at over thirty per thousand in these closes.   In the area marked for clearance in 1884, the death-rate was fifty per thousand.[2]

Liverpool.

On the banks of the Mersey, as of the Clyde, a rapid expansion of commerce, and an equally rapid increase of population, led, as we have seen,[3] to sanitary evils, all the more deplorable because they chiefly affected the poor, and coincided with a vast increase of national and local wealth. Liverpool, like Glasgow, but in a still greater degree, suffered from density as well as numbers.[4]   Hence the old cellar dwellings, which were condemned in every report of the early sanitary reformers, and contributed so largely to swell the death-rate.   Another evil of that period, it may be remembered, arose from needless divisions of authority and want of powers to abate nuisances.   A third

[1] 44 & 45 Vict. c. 73, s. 72. Any person afterwards letting the premises, or even occupying them, is liable to daily penalties. If satisfied that the house has been made habitable the Town Council may revoke their order. Other provisions in this Act, securing the height and ventilation of rooms, with open spaces behind dwelling-houses, and restricting the height of houses, are worth attention.

[2] Royal Commission on Housing of Working Classes, 1885, Vol. V.; evidence of Dr. Simpson, pp. 63, 66.

[3] *Ante*, pp. 294 *et seq.*

[4] Even in 1885, within the municipal bounds, the number of inhabitants per acre exceeded that in any town in the United Kingdom. There were then in Liverpool 111·3 persons per acre; Glasgow, 86·1 ; Manchester, 78·6. See Tables, *post*, p. 504.

hindrance to effective local government was the multiplicity of local Acts. No fewer than sixty of these Acts were in force in 1846, filling several large volumes, and so complicated and contradictory on many points that "no inhabitant except a lawyer, and no lawyer without great trouble," could find out what the law really was.[1]

In this Session of 1846, the Corporation obtained, for the first time, what was then considered a complete sanitary code in an Act[2] which put an end to the Commissioners for paving and sewering, repealed various statutes more or less confusing, consolidated jurisdictions, and placed in the hands of the Town Council all existing powers, along with the new powers then granted. This Act rightly set forth the expediency of having but "one management" and uniform local laws throughout the whole borough, with a view to prevent nuisances, improve health and comfort, and diminish disease and mortality among the inhabitants.[3]

Liverpool Sanitary Act, 1846.

Such a reform was, indeed, urgently needed. The Act of 1846 prescribed a convenient width for new streets, required the Council to cleanse the town and make sewers, compelled house-owners to drain into sewers, allowed time to owners to repay expenses of paving and draining, prohibited the use of cellars in courts as separate dwellings, imposed penalties on persons who let certain underground rooms for dwellings, secured in new houses proper space for ventilation, empowered the Council to appoint an inspector of nuisances and a medical officer of health to inquire into the local causes of fever and other disorders, and provided for the regulation and inspection of lodging-houses and slaughter-houses, and the consumption of smoke in factories and steam-vessels. In pursuance of powers previously obtained by the Commissioners,

General objects of Act.

Power to Council to supply water

---

[1] Commons' Committee on Private Bills, 1846; evidence of Mr. Rushton, stipendiary magistrate of Liverpool, pp. 1–3, who says that the inhabitants acquired a painful and expensive knowledge of the law by penal informations, of which, in 1845, nearly eleven thousand were issued under local Acts and bye-laws.

[2] 9 & 10 Vict. c. 127. It contained 231 sections.

[3] Ib., preamble.

for public
purposes.

the Council were also authorized to sink wells, lay down pipes, and provide water throughout the borough, but only for public purposes, such as street watering, the extinction of fires, a gratuitous service by means of public cisterns, and a supply of "any public baths or washhouses that may be established for the use of the poorer classes."[1] Adequate rating powers were also given to the Council.

Street im-
provements,
1786.

Street improvements under local statutes in Liverpool date from 1786, when the Corporation were authorized to purchase and pull down a considerable extent of property for widening and improving certain thoroughfares, narrow and inconvenient in themselves, and "very much obstructed by projections of shop windows, and sheds, and other annoyances," to the great prejudice of traffic and hindrance of business.[2] There is a

Lighting.

curious provision that as the buildings which would be erected in a new street leading to Derby Square would probably be "wholesale and retail shops for goods, wares and merchandizes of very considerable value," the Corporation should, at their own expense, for better security, fix on the door of every house a lamp, which the house-owner should maintain and keep "well and sufficiently lighted in every

Obstructions.

night of the year from sun-setting to sun-rising."[3] No timber, bricks, tubs or other articles were to be laid in any street; no casks must be hooped, cleansed or scalded there, nor timber hewed, nor horses shod or fed. Bonfires and fireworks in streets were also forbidden. No one must ride or drive upon the footway. Swine or cattle found wandering within the town might be impounded. All projecting signs were to be taken down within three months. Spouts and gutters were no longer to project from roofs. Projecting

Power to
Corporation
to take down
ruinous
buildings.

steps and cellar doors might be removed after notice; and the Corporation were authorized to take down all buildings presented as nuisances at quarter sessions, when "from litigated titles, or through the obstinacy or poverty of the

---

[1] 9 & 10 Vict. c. 127, ss. 136 *et seq.*

[2] 26 Geo. III. c. 12.

[3] Ib., s. 20.

owners," such buildings were in so ruinous a condition that passers-by were in danger from falling materials.[1] Three-quarters of a century later, the Corporation were able to quote this statutory power as a valuable precedent for further remedial legislation.[2] Provision was made in 1786 for public markets and slaughter-houses. The abolition of watch and ward in Liverpool in the year 1748, and substitution of paid watchmen, has already been mentioned.[3]

Further powers to improve and widen streets were not again conferred on the Corporation until the year 1820. It was necessary to provide in this Act that no wind-mills should be erected within fifty yards of any street or road.[4] Since then more than twenty Improvement Acts have been sanctioned for these and like purposes, ending with one of 1885.[5] A local statute to which some historical interest attaches, was obtained by the Corporation in 1864,[6] and contains the germ both of the Glasgow Act, two years later, and the subsequent Artizans' Dwellings Acts of 1868 and 1875. This statute recited very fully the powers over ruinous and dangerous structures first given to the Corporation in 1786, and continued in an amended form in 1820 and 1842. It set forth that these provisions had been enforced with great public advantage. Equal benefit had arisen from the appointment of a medical officer of health, sanctioned in 1846, and his periodical reports upon the sanitary condition of the borough, upon local causes tending to produce contagious disease, and the best mode of checking such disease. Then there was a further recital, that "there are in the borough a great number of houses situated in, or" near "courts and alleys, which houses, by reason of defects in the construction thereof, or of the want of ventilation or

Liverpool Sanitary Amendment Act, 1864.

Recitals.

---

[1] Ib., ss. 31-39.

[2] Cf. statutes passed in the reigns of Henry VIII. and Elizabeth, giving to municipalities large powers over ruinous structures in default of repairs by owners. (*Ante*, Vol. I.,

30 ; II., 270-2.)

[3] *Ante*, p. 249.

[4] 1 Geo. IV. c. 13, s. 20.

[5] 48 & 49 Vict. c. 95.

[6] 27 & 28 Vict. c. 73.

of proper conveniences, or from other causes, are unfit for human habitation, and fevers and other diseases are constantly generated there, causing death or loss of health not only in the courts and alleys, but also in other parts of the borough: and it is expedient that provision be made for remedy thereof."

Houses unfit for habitation or injurious to health.

It was then enacted that on a representation by four or more householders, living in or near to any court or alley, that disease existed in premises there, the medical officer of health should inspect these premises.[1] The absence of any such representation, however, did not excuse him from inspecting courts, alleys or insanitary premises. If he found them unfit for habitation or injurious to health, he was, in either case, bound to report them. His report was to be made in duplicate, one copy being delivered to the Town Clerk, the other to the Clerk of the Peace, for consideration by the grand jury at the next general or quarter sessions. If they "presented" the premises, a copy of the presentment was to be communicated to the Council, who were required forthwith to direct their borough engineer to report upon the necessary works. These must then be executed by the owner, or, if he failed to do so, by the Corporation; or the owner might require the Corporation to purchase the premises, the price being assessed by a jury in case of difference. If the presentment involved total demolition and not improvement, the owner was bound to take down the premises. If he did nothing, the Corporation might remove them, paying compensation: and an owner might either part with the site or elect to retain it, but he could not then rebuild without the Council's consent.[2] If dissatisfied with a presentment, he might appeal to the next Quarter Sessions,

Presentment at quarter sessions.

---

[1] 27 & 28 Vict. c. 73, s. 5. Upon a similar representation made by four or more householders under the Act of 1842 (5 & 6 Vict. c. 44), the Corporation might pull down dangerous structures. This machinery was adapted to insanitary premises causing danger to public health.

[2] 27 & 28 Vict. c. 73, s. 23.

and again to the Court of Queen's Bench. Any land or premises so acquired by the Corporation was to form part of their corporate estate, or might be dedicated for public use, as part of a highway or other public place. For purposes of the Act they might impose a general rate not exceeding one penny in the pound.

A valuable amendment made in this Act in 1882 dispenses with any intervention by Quarter Sessions in cases where the Town Council find that they can acquire by agreement insanitary property upon which the medical officer has reported; nor need any copy of his report be delivered to the Clerk of the Peace unless the Council specially direct.[1] If, however, any such property has to be taken by compulsory purchase, the procedure must be by presentment under the Act of 1864, and compensation assessed under the Lands Clauses Acts. *Liverpool Improvement Act, 1882.*

Before introducing his Artizans' Dwellings Bill in 1875, the Home Secretary (Mr. Cross, afterwards Sir Richard A. Cross) visited Liverpool, Glasgow and Edinburgh, to see what had been done in those cities under the local Acts which have been noticed. He found that in Liverpool five presentments had been made by grand juries, and 503 houses demolished, and 392 courts improved by the Corporation, at a cost of about 87,000l.[2] But the Liverpool Act, like the public statute of 1868, applied to single houses and small groups of insanitary dwellings. The Home Secretary's Bill of 1875 was adapted to the clearance of large areas, by means of an improvement scheme, proposed by the local authority and submitted for confirmation by Parliament. The preamble, drawn up by the Home Secretary himself, sets forth similar objects to those contemplated in the local Acts just mentioned, and rests the necessity of interference on sanitary and moral grounds, avoiding any recognition of socialist principles.[3] It must not be forgotten, however, that the merit of initiating *Artizans' and Labourers' Dwellings Act, 1875.*

---

[1] 45 & 46 Vict. c. 55, ss. 78—80.

[2] 222 Hansard, 103.

[3] 38 & 39 Vict. c. 36 (England and Ireland); c. 49 (Scotland).

this public legislation belongs to English and Scotch municipalities.[1]

Local museums and libraries.

Mr. Ewart, whose name should be remembered with gratitude by all social reformers, carried through Parliament as
early as 1845 a public Act authorizing local authorities, in
towns containing a population of over ten thousand persons,
to establish and maintain out of the rates museums of art and
science.[2] In 1850 he also proposed, and succeeded in carrying, a similar Act for the establishment of free libraries, as
well as museums, in any municipal borough; but a veto upon
its adoption was given to ratepayers.[3] Under the Act of
1845 the Corporation of Liverpool bought the Botanic
Garden and Herbarium. In 1852 they obtained a special
Act,[4] under which they established one of the most successful

Derby Museum.

free libraries in the Kingdom, connecting it with a museum
and gallery of arts, and providing fitly for a large and
valuable collection of stuffed birds and animals, with other
specimens illustrative of natural history, presented to the
city by the thirteenth Earl of Derby. This Act empowered
the Corporation to levy a maximum rate of one penny in the
pound for the maintenance of buildings, to receive gifts, and

[1] In a valuable report upon the effect of the various public and local statutes, drawn up in November, 1883, for the information of the Committee on Insanitary Property and Artizans' Dwellings, the Town Clerk of Liverpool points out "that the public statutes do not authorize private negotiations at an early stage, and that, before their provisions can be put into force, publicity is obliged to be given to the fact that it will probably be incumbent upon the local authority to purchase specified premises. The disadvantage of there being no sufficiently adequate power to acquire premises by private treaty was removed, so far as Liverpool is concerned, by the Liverpool Improvement Act, 1882. There is no public statute, and, so far as the Town Clerk is aware, there is no local or private one, giving so wide a discretion to the local authority, and affording such facilities for the purchase of property at a reasonable price, without incurring considerable preliminary expenses and much delay, as the Liverpool Acts of 1864 and 1882."

[2] 8 & 9 Vict. c. 43. The rate applicable for this purpose was not to exceed a halfpenny in the pound. A small entrance fee might be charged to defray the expense of curators and maintenance.

[3] 13 & 14 Vict. c. 65, which repealed the Act of 1845.

[4] 15 & 16 Vict. c. 3.

purchase "books, maps, plans, pictures, drawings, engravings, sculptures, specimens of art or science, or other articles which they might deem suitable and proper" for exhibition. They could also provide lecture-rooms and establish lectures on subjects of art or science.

In this, as in all other like cases, the existence of municipal libraries and museums, free to the public and appreciated by them, led to munificent gifts by other inhabitants. Larger accommodation soon became necessary, and Sir William Brown defrayed the whole cost of a new and handsome range of buildings, at a cost of 40,000*l.* Mr. Joseph Mayer *Mayer Museum and* contributed a valuable museum of antiquities and objects of art. *Walker Art Gallery.* Sir Andrew Walker gave to the town an art gallery which *Gallery.* cost nearly 50,000*l.* A domed and circular reading-room, *Picton Reading-room.* which will accommodate three hundred readers, and a lecture-room, which holds 1,500 persons, were built by the Corporation in 1880 at a cost of 25,000*l.* The reference library, containing a valuable collection of county works, and two lending libraries, are largely used.

Under the authority of various statutes, Sefton Park, con- *Public parks.* taining four hundred acres, with four smaller parks, have been laid out by the Corporation since 1865 at a cost of more than 400,000*l.* An Improvement Act of 1865[1] enabled the Corporation to charge a rate of fivepence in the pound for public parks, &c.; this was raised to sixpence in 1871.[2] Their borrowing powers for these objects were also increased to 575,000*l.* St. George's Hall, in which the Law Courts are situated, is *St. George's Hall.* one of the most imposing municipal buildings in the Kingdom; it was built by the Corporation and first used in 1854, though not fully completed until some years later. From an early period the Corporation of Liverpool have possessed large landed property, and in 1885 derived from this source, apart from rates, a revenue of more than 80,000*l.*

In Liverpool, as at a much earlier date in London, the *Water supply.*

---

[1] 28 & 29 Vict. c. 20, s. 23.   [2] 34 & 35 Vict. c. 184, s. 68.

necessity of obtaining for the inhabitants a proper supply
of water was recognized by the Corporation. Both cities,
too, after statutory powers had been thus obtained, allowed
this duty to fall into the hands of private speculators.
In Liverpool, however, the municipality, though too late,
were sagacious enough to foresee the danger to public
interests which might arise from a private monopoly, and
vigorously, but ineffectually, opposed its creation by Parliament. The supply of water to Liverpool, therefore, so
far as it depends on private legislation, has a history of
exceptional interest. It begins in 1786, when, in a general
Improvement Act already mentioned,[1] that the town and
shipping might be "more plentifully and expeditiously
supplied with fresh and wholesome water, and for the purpose
of the more easy extinguishing of any accidents by fire (*sic*)
to buildings and shipping," the Council received compulsory
powers to dig for and collect springs or fountains in neighbouring land. They might also make and erect "dams,
damheads, ponds, cisterns, reservoirs, engines, buildings, or
any other device or devices whatsoever, for raising water and
conducting the same into the town for the use and benefit of
the inhabitants." Further, as a proper complement to these
powers, the Corporation might lay all necessary pipes, mains
and troughs, and break open highways for this purpose.[2]
The charge for supplying private houses was to be settled by
agreement; for extinguishing fires, water might be used by
any person without charge.

Thirteen years after these powers were granted, no water
whatever had been brought to the town. A Bill was therefore promoted in 1799 by a company, which proposed to
supply Liverpool with water from springs at Bootle. The
Corporation petitioned the House of Commons against this
Bill, alleging, not that they had actually provided water, but
that they were "fully enabled" to provide it; had purchased

*Power to
Corporation
to provide
water, 1786.*

*Bill of 1799,
promoted by
private com-
pany.*

*Opposition by
Town Council.*

---

[1] 26 Geo. III. c. 12.   [2] Ib., ss. 26 *et seq.*

one spring, and "had in contemplation the perfecting of contracts for other springs within the town, which had been offered for this intended public supply." The petitioners, therefore, complained that the Bill would prejudice their rights and interests and be "inconvenient to the inhabitants." They also alleged that the springs at Bootle would not yield sufficient water to serve the town.[1]

Upon this petition the House made the usual order that the Corporation should be heard by counsel, along with counsel for the Bill. Meanwhile, two petitions from merchants and others, and directors of the Phœnix Fire Office, were presented in favour of the Bill. Public opinion in Liverpool seems to have been divided, for certain "merchants, tradesmen and others," referring to the Act of 1786, represented to the House that the Council "have made great progress in executing the improvements thereby directed, in a manner very beneficial and advantageous to the inhabitants, and have also been engaged in the performance of divers other great works for the good of the town; and that from the magnitude of these works, and the great sums of money required for the execution thereof, the Council have not yet been able to carry into effect the powers given by the Act for supplying the town with water; but the petitioners are informed that they have purchased a spring of water, have declined offers from other persons for supplying the town, and will without delay take all proper steps for carrying the same into effect; that the Common Council have executed the several other purposes of the Act, and have also made many other works for the accommodation and advantage of the town, in a manner so highly creditable to themselves and beneficial to the inhabitants, that the petitioners are convinced the town will be supplied with water, under their control and management, much better and more advantageously to the inhabitants than could be done by the individuals proposed to be incorporated

Other petitions.

---

[1] 54 Com. Journ. 429; April 15, 1799.

by the Bill, whose chief object can only be private emolument, whereas that of the Common Council can only be the accommodation and advantage of the inhabitants."[1]

Committee on Bill.

This petition against the Bill, like that of the Corporation, was presented before the second reading, and the House was ready to hear counsel at the bar for and against it at that stage, according to then existing practice. Some understanding between the parties must have been come to, for the Corporation withdrew their objections to the second reading. Pending its consideration in Committee, churchwardens and overseers of the poor in the parish of Liverpool, on their own behalf and that of other inhabitants, urged against the Bill that "from time immemorial the town and shipping there, have been and still are supplied with good water from several wells within the parish, the owners or occupiers of which have been rated to the relief of the poor, and for other parochial purposes." A clause in the Bill exempted the proposed water company and their works from rating.[2] The petitioners therefore complained that this exemption would prejudicially affect the parochial revenue. The House accordingly allowed them to be heard by counsel before the Committee, together with the Corporation.[3]

Proposed exemption of Water Company from local rates.

Mr. Stanley was Chairman of the Committee, who reported in favour of the Bill, influenced no doubt by the fact that the Corporation had for so many years left the town to its ancient stock of water in private wells until awakened to a keener sense of municipal duty by private enterprise. As opposition was not renewed in the House of Lords, the Bill, with some modifications, soon became law,[4] and the works then authorized were extended by subsequent legislation.[5] Meanwhile, the Town Council had not allowed their powers to lapse, and used them concurrently with those of

Liverpool Waterworks Company's Act, 1799.

---

[1] 54 Com. Journ. 435.

[2] See *post*, pp. 555–60, as to exemptions from rating.

[3] 54 Com. Journ. 480.

[4] 39 Geo. III. c. 36.

[5] 50 Geo. III. c. 165; 53 Geo. III. c. 122.

the private company. But they had not sufficient command of funds to embark in the business of water supply, or thought it better to entrust this business to private hands. They, therefore, after 1799, "opened a subscription" for the necessary capital. In other words, they established a second company, with shares of 200*l.* each, and thus raised, chiefly from inhabitants of Liverpool, a sum of close upon 100,000*l.* With this capital the company bought springs, made reservoirs, provided engines and machinery, and in the year 1822 had laid fifty-three miles of mains, through which they then supplied "with the purest spring water upwards of thirteen thousand families and a numerous shipping."[1]

"Subscription" opened by Corporation.

Nominally the Town Council of Liverpool were still responsible for these works, but seem to have lost all substantial control over them. The subscribers, who carried on the undertaking, had not been incorporated, and in 1822 found it necessary to go to Parliament for statutory powers, seeking also indemnity and confirmation for what they had already done.[2] There were several petitions against this Bill in the House of Commons, from the Corporation, the old Waterworks company, inhabitants, and representatives of private interests. Neither the Corporation nor the company persisted in their opposition before the Committee, but counsel were heard there on behalf of other dissentients, and the Bill was recommitted with a view to further amendments.[3] It passed without opposition in the Upper House, and repealed so much of the Act of 1786 as enabled the Corporation to supply water, transferred these powers, with extensions, to the subscribers, and incorporated them as the Liverpool Corporation Waterworks Company.[4]

Water Bill, 1822.

Liverpool Corporation Waterworks Company.

Thus, while their old connection was preserved in name, the municipality lost their statutory rights, and only succeeded in securing competitors to the company established

---

[1] Preamble to 3 Geo. IV. c. 77.
[2] See their petition for Bill, 77 Com. Journ. 43; February 21, 1822.
[3] Ib., 241, 303. Mr. Canning was one of the Committee.
[4] 3 Geo. IV. c. 77.

Concessions to
municipality.

in 1799. They retained, however, under the Act, a share in
managing the new company, by a provision allowing them to
nominate three members of the Council as directors.[1] Another
concession to the Council was, that they should receive five
per cent. upon all net profits made by the company exceeding
five per cent. per annum. This "interest and percentage"
was to be paid to "the Mayor, bailiffs, and burgesses, and
their successors," as lords of the manor of Liverpool, for
allowing the company "to dig for and collect springs of
water, break up certain highways and streets, lay down main
and other pipes, and construct works within the manor."[2]
Public interests were also protected by a limitation of rates
and a provision giving to justices a summary jurisdiction in
the event of complaints by private consumers.[3] Shareholders
were allowed a curious privilege: in respect of each of the
four hundred shares into which the undertaking was divided,
they might nominate one house to be served with water for
domestic consumption, free of charge.[4]

**Extension to
Toxteth Park
and Harring-
ton, 1827.**

In 1827, this company's district was extended to "the
township of Toxteth Park, including the town or village of
Harrington," which "was immediately contiguous to Liverpool, and had become very populous." As the inhabitants
were in great want of water, a supply by the company
"would much tend to their comfort and accommodation."[5]
The company's name at the same time became "The
Liverpool and Harrington Waterworks Company;" and a
percentage upon surplus profits arising in the new district
was reserved to the Corporation, as in 1822. The municipality, however, were soon to discover that, when their
control over the supply of water was once relinquished, it was
not easy to recover even a small share of their former powers.
In 1843, the commissioners for paving and sewering applied to
Parliament for permission to provide for street watering and

**Restriction
upon water
powers of**

[1] 3 Geo. IV. c. 77, s. 8.   [4] Ib., s. 51.
[2] Ib., s. 52.   [5] 7 & 8 Geo. IV. c. 36; preamble.
[3] Ib., ss. 36, 39.

the extinction of fires.[1] At this period fires in warehouses Liverpool Commissioners, 1843.
in Liverpool were so frequent and alarming, and occasioned
such serious losses of life and property, that special legislation
was resorted to in order to secure an improved construction
of warehouses and other buildings, restrict the storage of
dangerous goods, and enforce other precautions against fire.[2]
The commissioners asked leave to sink wells, take water from
the Mersey or the docks, make reservoirs, lay pipes, and construct all necessary works for an efficient service. Their Bill,
however, was jealously watched in Parliament by the two water
companies, upon whose opposition clauses were introduced
declaring that the commissioners should sink no wells within
the borough, or the townships of Toxteth Park, or Bootle, or
within a mile and a quarter of the Liverpool and Harrington
Waterworks; and, further, that they should apply no water Supply for domestic consumption forbidden.
to be obtained from any wells "in any other manner than
for the purpose of extinguishing fires, watering streets, or for
other public purposes."[3] In the interests of the companies
Parliament even put an end to a statutory right of digging
wells and pumping water conferred upon the commissioners
in 1830.[4]

Power to raise further capital was given to the Liverpool
and Harrington Company in 1846,[5] when the right of
shareholders to nominate houses for a free service of water
was abolished, together with the Town Council's percentage.[6]
By the same Act, the company were required to sell their
works to the Corporation, who, in the next Session, obtained Liverpool Corporation Waterworks Act, 1847.
leave to buy both the water undertakings.[7] At this time, the

---

[1] *Ante*, p. 304. As an instance of
the division of authority then existing in Liverpool, it may be mentioned that the fire police was then
managed by the Corporation, who
levied a halfpenny fire police rate.
(5 & 6 Vict. c. 106.)

[2] 6 & 7 Vict. c. 109, an elaborate
statute of 124 sections, vesting large

powers in the Town Council, who
were to form a "Committee for the
preservation of property from fire."

[3] 6 & 7 Vict. c. 75, ss. 5-8.

[4] 11 Geo. IV. & 1 Will. IV.
c. 15.

[5] 9 & 10 Vict. c. 35.

[6] Ib., s. 17.

[7] 10 & 11 Vict. c. 261.

supply was intermittent and inadequate. Population and trade were rapidly increasing, and the Corporation felt that abundant and wholesome water should be provided not only for the present but for any future population.[1] In 1847, new sources yielding additional water were, therefore, obtained. Fresh powers were given by Parliament to the Corporation in 1850 and 1852;[2] in 1856 they purchased[3] the Chorley water undertaking, belonging to a small company established under statute ten years before,[4] whose works were contiguous to those of Liverpool, and had given rise to conflicting claims. Additional reservoirs and other works were sanctioned by Parliament in 1860 and 1862;[5] again in 1866, for taking water from the river Roddlesworth, and in 1871.[6] But the water obtained from this and older sources was still inadequate to meet the wants of an ever-growing population. In 1880, therefore, the Corporation broke entirely new ground, and obtained Parliamentary sanction for a bold plan to impound and use water from the rivers Vyrnwy, Marchnant, and Afon Cowny, in the county of Montgomery, with their tributary streams, at an estimated cost of 3,250,000*l.*[7] Among the works embraced in this plan is a masonry embankment across the valley of the river Vyrnwy. The reservoir to be thereby formed will be 1,115 acres in extent, and is calculated to hold 12,000 million gallons. The village of Llanwddyn will be submerged by this work. A new burial ground has already been opened, and the Corporation will have to build a new church. The new reservoir will be connected with existing reservoirs at Prescot by an aqueduct sixty-seven miles in length, consisting of three tunnels (the Hirnant Tunnel, two and a quarter miles, and the Cynynion and Llanfordd Tunnels, each about one mile long) and a triple line of pipes, which will cross the river Mersey (about two miles

Chorley Waterworks purchased, 1856.

Liverpool Corporation Waterworks Act, 1880.

[1] 10 & 11 Vict. c. 261, preamble.
[2] 13 & 14 Vict. c. 80; 15 & 16 Vict. c. 47.
[3] 19 & 20 Vict. c. 5.
[4] 9 & 10 Vict. c. 287; 14 & 15 Vict. c. 77.
[5] 23 & 24 Vict. c. 12; 25 & 26 Vict. c. 107.
[6] 29 & 30 Vict. c. 126; 34 & 35 Vict. c. 184.
[7] 43 & 44 Vict. c. 143.

above Runcorn), the river Weaver, and numerous railways and canals.

Liverpool is lit with gas by a private company, although the duty of public lighting was imposed upon the Corporation by local statutes in 1748[1] and 1786.[2] Fearing the growth of a similar monopoly in electric lighting, the Corporation, for the purpose of experiment, obtained powers in 1879 to manufacture and supply electric light, but not for profit, and only for lighting streets and other places of public resort.[3] These powers expired in 1884, and have not since been renewed.

By various special Acts and Provisional Orders,[4] the Corporation have acquired and constructed a tramway system extending over sixty miles. These tramways are leased to a company, and are not only of great convenience in expediting traffic but a considerable source of profit. In addition to the railway tunnel under the Mersey, now open and connecting Liverpool with Birkenhead,[5] a company was incorporated in 1880, with a share and loan capital of 665,000*l*., to make a subway for passengers and carriages between the same points.[6] In 1885, the subway not having then been begun, the time for completing the company's works was extended until 1894.[7] There is a special restriction against the use of rails in this subway, so that it may not compete with the tunnel.[8]

Until 1857 the great docks at Liverpool were administered by the Corporation, who acted as statutory trustees for this purpose,[9] deriving no revenue from the docks, but applying any surplus towards improvements and extensions, or in reducing dues. In 1851, merchants and shipowners paying dock rates were admitted to a share in the management.[10] The Dock Committee, as it was called, then consisted of

Margin notes: Lighting. Liverpool (Corporation) Electric Lighting Act, 1879. Tramways. Railway tunnel and subway under the Mersey. Liverpool Docks.

[1] 21 Geo. II. c. 24, *ante*, p. 290.

[2] *Ante*, p. 462.

[3] 42 & 43 Vict. c. 213, s. 3, *ante*, Vol. I., p. 233.

[4] See Liverpool Tramways (Purchase) Act, 1872, the first, and Liverpool Corporation Tramways Extensions Order, 1884, tho last, of these numerous enactments.

[5] *Ante*, Vol. I., p. 201.

[6] 43 & 44 Vict. c. 152.

[7] 48 & 49 Vict. c. 37, s. 4.

[8] Ib., s. 5.

[9] 61 Geo. III. c. 143.

[10] 14 & 15 Vict. c. 64.

twenty-four members, one-half nominated by the Town Council, and one-half by dock ratepayers. In 1855 the Birkenhead
Docks were transferred to the Corporation of Liverpool[1] for
a sum of 1,143,000*l.* Two years afterwards the whole of
this property, with the rights and powers of the Corporation,
were vested in a new body, called "The Mersey Docks and
Harbour Board."[2] Included in this transfer was the great
landing-stage for sea-going and river steamers, constructed by
the Corporation in front of Prince's Dock,[3] and the Observatory, also erected by them. A statutory obligation rested
on the Corporation to contribute towards the maintenance and
repair of a sea-wall, called the Wallasey Embankment, and
towards the conservancy of the Mersey. These liabilities were
assumed by the new Board, who also undertook the control
of pilotage and harbour lights, the maintenance of lifeboats,
buoys, landmarks and telegraphs within the port, and other
duties relating to the safety and convenience of shipping.
From very ancient times the Corporation had levied town
dues on all goods imported or exported, not being the property of freemen of Liverpool, or of resident freemen of
London, Bristol, Waterford, or Wexford. They had also
levied anchorage dues on all vessels entering the port, both
dues being carried to the credit of the borough fund. In
consideration of the transfer to them of these dues, together
with the landing-stage and Observatory, the new Board
agreed to pay the Corporation 1,500,000*l.* With this statute
ended a connection between the municipality and the docks,
which had lasted nearly a hundred and fifty years.[4]

As in most other large boroughs, Liverpool now has its
Corporation stock, which, created in 1880, was a much-
needed financial reform. At that period the Corporation
had borrowed under various Acts 4,216,000*l.*, "charged upon

Marginal notes:
Birkenhead Docks.

Mersey Docks and Harbour Board.

Town and anchorage dues.

Liverpool Corporation Loans Act, 1880.

---

[1] 18 & 19 Vict. c. 171.

[2] 20 & 21 Vict. c. 162.

[3] As now rebuilt, after being
partially consumed by fire in 1874,
this remarkable structure is two-
fifths of a mile long and eighty feet
broad.

[4] 8 Anne, c. 12 (c. 8 in Stat. of
Realm). See *ante*, Vol. I., p. 8.

different securities, with different priorities, at different rates of interest, subject to different conditions, and repayable at different times."[1] Unity and simplicity were consulted by converting these loans into capital stock, and raising in like manner all future loans, charged indifferently upon the corporate property, rates and revenues, with provision for payment of interest and redemption of debt out of one fund. Since 1880, outlay upon new waterworks has added largely to municipal liabilities. In 1886 the total amount of money which had been borrowed by the Corporation was 7,500,000*l.* They had then redeemed 630,000*l.* of this amount by means of their sinking fund. In 1885, the net annual value of property in Liverpool rated to the poor was 3,381,501*l.*

By a royal charter dated May 11, 1880, her Majesty declared that Liverpool should thenceforth be styled a City, and its body corporate the Mayor, Aldermen and Citizens. The see of Liverpool was created in the same year, under the Bishoprics Act, 1878;[2] an endowment fund amounting to 100,000*l.* had been subscribed for this object. By Order in Council the parish church of St. Peter was assigned to the bishopric as a cathedral church. As this church is small and ill-adapted for such a use, a committee of inhabitants was formed to consider the best available site for a new cathedral, and choice was made of the church and churchyard of St. John, erected in 1762-7 upon lands granted by the Corporation. Under an Act of 1885[3] this cathedral committee were incorporated, with power to receive subscriptions and erect a cathedral. Provision was also made for the foundation of a dean and chapter by means of an endowment fund, also voluntarily subscribed.[4]

Liverpool has ever been noted for its public spirit and patriotism. Proof of this feeling was afforded in 1798, when its defence against invasion was recognized as a municipal duty. The Corporation then represented to Parliament " the

Liverpool created a city, 1880.

See and Cathedral.

Floating batteries and other defences, by municipality, authorized, 1798.

---

[1] 43 & 44 Vict. c. 207 ; preamble.   [3] 48 & 49 Vict. c. 51.
[2] 41 & 42 Vict. c. 68 (public).   [4] Ib., ss. 20—27.

critical situation of the nation at large, under apprehensions of danger from an inveterate enemy, who threatens daily to invade our coasts, and the particular mischief and injury to which the town and port of Liverpool, its docks and shipping, will be exposed if these should become objects of attack." They therefore sought for power "to provide suitable and adequate floating batteries and other works, with gunboats, to be stationed at the mouth of the harbour and upon the coast, in addition to the military force upon land, under such regulations as the House shall deem proper, in order to resist and repel attack."[1] Parliament sanctioned this plan of municipal defence, ordering, as the Corporation suggested, that the cost should be met, as to one moiety, by a rate upon the inhabitants; as to the other moiety, by a voluntary contribution from municipal funds, and another contribution of equal amount from the dock trust, then also a municipal body, to be raised by a tonnage rate on vessels.[2]

Manchester.

Treated as one with Salford, 1765–92.

Manchester was only freed by statute in 1758 from an obligation to grind corn and grain at the manorial water mills.[3] It was not incorporated until 1838, was made a city in 1853, and obtained charters for its university in 1880-3. Until a period comparatively recent the contiguous borough of Salford shared its local legislation. Thus, in 1765, Commissioners were incorporated " for cleansing and lighting the streets, lanes, and passages " of both towns, "and for providing fire-engines and firemen, and preventing annoyances" there.[4] A similar Act, in 1792, extended the jurisdiction of these Commissioners to watching and general purposes, among

---

[1] 53 Com. Journ. 620-1; May 23, 1798.

[2] 38 Geo. III. c. 72, "an Act for the better security and defence of the town and port of Liverpool." Sir Erskine May (Lord Farnborough) does not seem to have been aware of this statute. It adds peculiar force to his remark (Const. Hist. III. 296), that "the local administration of Liverpool resembles that of a maritime State." He adds:—"In the order and wise government of large populations by local authority rests the general security of the realm. And this authority is everywhere based upon representation and responsibility."

[3] 32 Geo. II. c. 61.

[4] 5 Geo. III. c. 81.

which were " widening and rendering more commodious " several streets, lanes, and passages.[1]

Early street improvements were made in Manchester, in 1776, by a public subscription of 10,000*l.* For the proper expenditure of this sum special commissioners were appointed by name, a long list, headed by Sir Thomas Egerton and Dr. Samuel Peploe, together with every person who should, within twelve months, subscribe the sum of twenty pounds. In an Act which gave them the necessary powers,[2] Manchester is described as " not only very large and populous, but much resorted to by strangers," and the principal mart for various manufactures, but with narrow and inconvenient streets around the Exchange, where merchants and manufacturers resort on market days.

Street improvements by subscription, 1776.

To the Corporation in 1843 were transferred all powers and property of the old Improvement Commissioners,[3] whose rule in Salford had ended in 1828.[4] The new governing body in Manchester soon became honourably distinguished for attention to sanitary measures. In 1844 they obtained two Acts for the good government and police regulation of their borough, and its general improvement.[5] Of these Acts the former was among the earliest which dealt with general police and sanitary matters ; the Public Health Act of 1848 was based, to a large extent, upon its provisions.[6] Again, in 1845, " for the purpose of promoting the health of the inhabitants," the Corporation were authorized to take compulsorily a large extent of scheduled property.[7] This, again, is one of the earliest instances of compulsory powers acquired by a municipality to demolish property for distinctly sanitary purposes. By agreement, also, they might purchase other property, in order to secure such sanitary improvements as from time to time they deemed necessary. Local legislation was

Sanitary improvements.

[1] 32 Geo. III. c. 69.
[2] 16 Geo. III. c. 63.
[3] 6 & 7 Vict. c. 17.
[4] 9 Geo. IV. c. 117.
[5] 7 & 8 Vict. cc. 40, 41.

[6] Royal Sanitary Commission of 1869, first Report ; evidence of Mr. (afterwards Sir) Joseph Heron, town clerk of Manchester, p. 130.
[7] 8 & 9 Vict. c. 141.

made simpler and more intelligible by a consolidation Act in 1851.[1] Since that date some fifteen statutes have passed enlarging the Corporation's powers for street improvements, and sanitary and police purposes. These powers are now very comprehensive and effectual.

Manchester and Salford Waterworks Company, 1809.

In the last century Manchester was supplied with water from works and reservoirs belonging to the lord of the manor, and having an intake from the river Medlock at Holt Town. In 1809, when the population of Manchester and Salford together was under 100,000, these "ancient" waterworks and reservoirs, as they were then described, required additions and improvements, which could only be effectually carried out by joint enterprise. With the consent of Sir Oswald Mosley, then lord of the manor, a company was therefore incorporated to supply both towns.[2] By several subsequent Acts their powers were extended. So inadequate, however, was the quantity, that for some years prior to 1847 the company were in the habit of bringing water from the Peak Forest and Macclesfield canals for distribution. These canals belonged to the Manchester, Sheffield and Lincolnshire Railway Company, which in 1847 obtained powers to construct reservoirs and works for impounding flood water, storing and purifying it. After supplying their canals, they might sell the surplus for domestic consumption and use in trade.[3] In the same Session,

Corporation waterworks, 1847.

the Corporation of Manchester were authorized to acquire the water company's undertaking and construct new waterworks.[4]

Frequent enlargements of these works became necessary, owing to increasing demand; in the course of thirty years nine Acts were passed for this object.[5] A watershed in the

Existing Works.

Longdendale District of about thirty square miles is now laid under contribution; the water is stored in a series of sixteen reservoirs, one of which, at Woodhead, eighteen

[1] 14 & 15 Vict. c. 119.
[2] 49 Geo. III. c. 192.
[3] 10 & 11 Vict. c. 279.
[4] 10 & 11 Vict. c. 203.
[5] 11 & 12 Vict. c. 101; 17 Vict. c. 38; 21 & 22 Vict. c. 87; 23 Vict. c. 93; 26 & 27 Vict. c. 68; 28 & 29 Vict. c. 145; 30 Vict. c. 36; 32 & 33 Vict. c. 117; 38 & 39 Vict. c. 161. Some of these Acts comprised general objects.

miles from Manchester, has an area of 135 acres, is 71
feet deep, and holds 1,181 million gallons. The height of
this reservoir above Ordnance datum is about 800 feet. In
extent and capacity it is surpassed by the Torside reservoir,
which has an area of 165 acres, is 84 feet deep, and holds
1,474 million gallons. The sixteen reservoirs occupy altogether 855 acres, and store nearly 6,000 million gallons.
But for this great supply there is as great a demand.
About 14 million gallons per day are sent down the river
for compensation to mills; upwards of 20 million gallons per
day are consumed. Besides the population of Manchester,
that of Salford and of twenty-seven townships beyond the
limits of the City relies wholly upon the City works. In
addition, the Corporation supply in bulk the whole of the
water distributed to eleven townships by the North Cheshire
Water Company, and to two townships by the Tyldesley
Local Board, and also afford a partial supply to the Stockport
District Waterworks Company and the Hyde Corporation,
who together supply twenty-eight townships. It will thus be
seen that the Corporation directly or indirectly supply wholly
fifty townships (nine being in the City), and partially twenty-
eight townships; in all seventy-eight townships, with a population of about a million. There is little wonder that, in
1877, the Corporation, apprehensive of continued dependence
upon the Longdendale gathering ground merely, and looking
at the continual growth of population, endeavoured to secure
other sources. After strenuous opposition during two sessions, a
great plan was sanctioned by Parliament in 1879 for bringing   Lake Thirl-
water into Manchester from Lake Thirlmere, in Cumberland,   mere scheme,
a distance of about a hundred miles, with power, and in cer-   1879.
tain events an obligation,[1] to supply towns and places on the

[1] 42 & 43 Vict. c. 36. Parliament
insisted in both Sessions upon clauses
enabling communities along the
route of pipes to obtain the Thirlmere water, under suitable conditions. A valuable precedent was
thus established against a monopoly
by municipalities or companies in
any gathering-ground, to the prejudice of inhabitants equally or better entitled, from their geographical
position, to a supply from the same
sources.

way. The estimated cost of the Thirlmere Works was about three and a half millions, and the works are now in progress.[1] An immediate supply of ten million gallons, and an ultimate supply of fifty million gallons, daily, will be obtained from Thirlmere. Within the City a public water rate of three-pence in the pound upon the poor rate assessment is paid by owners, and a domestic water rate of ninepence in the pound by occupiers. Outside the City five per cent. upon the annual rackrent or value is charged for water. In each case there is a minimum charge.

Charges for water.

Lighting.

No statutory powers have been possessed by any private company for lighting Manchester, although upon the first use of gas for this purpose it was supplied, as in other towns, without Parliamentary sanction. Public lighting was attended to, under the Acts of 1765 and 1792, by the old Police and Improvement Commissioners, who first used gas for street lighting in 1807. In 1825, an Act "for better lighting with gas the town of Manchester" set forth the expediency of enabling these Commissioners to provide gas, not only for public lamps, but for private consumption.[2] Accordingly, they received authority to elect thirty directors, who were to

Improvement Commissioners authorized to supply gas, 1825.

---

[1] Hackneyed though the theme is, one cannot help turning from these modern exploits of engineers to the still greater waterworks of imperial Rome. Fourteen aqueducts (some authors say twenty) supplied Rome with water. Of these, the Anio Novus was sixty miles long, and was borne for fourteen miles upon arches, some of which were 109 feet high. Another almost equally colossal work, the Claudian aqueduct (commenced by Caligula in the year 36 A. D.; finished by Claudius, 50 A.D) was more than forty-six miles long, was carried on equally lofty arches for ten miles, and, according to Pliny, cost no less a sum than 350 million sesterces, equivalent to nearly 3,000,000*l*. Another noble work, the Aqua Marcia, drew its supply from the mountains near Subiaco, and at the end of its long course, the water was carried into Rome upon an arched aqueduct nine miles long. Of Marcus Agrippa, who enlarged and enriched this work, we read that in his edileship he created 700 wells, 500 fountains, and 130 reservoirs, adorning them magnificently with 300 statues of marble or bronze, and 400 marble columns. Of all the great aqueducts which drew their supplies from the "heart of the purple mountains," only four remain; the rest may be tracked by long lines of ruined arches stretching across the Campagna. In these aqueducts the water flowed through channels of brick or stone lined with cement, and covered with an arched coping. At intervals were constructed settling reservoirs (*piscinæ*), in which any sediment might be deposited; near the city was a vast reservoir (*castellum*); the water then flowed into other smaller reservoirs, whence it was distributed throughout Rome by pipes. (See Story's "Roba di Roma," Chap. "Fountains and Aqueducts.")

[2] 5 Geo. IV. c. 133.

establish gas works and supply gas. As in most early gas Acts, no rates were fixed; these were left to be settled by agreement. That a monopoly was not contemplated is clear by a provision that no Commissioner acting as a director should be a shareholder in any gas company. The Corporation, which took over the gas works from the Commissioners, have greatly extended them, and in 1886 supplied, wholly or in part, twenty-three townships outside the City. In 1885, a net profit of 26,000*l.* was derived by the Corporation from their manufacture of gas, after providing for depreciation of works, interest, sinking fund, and cost of street lighting. These profits are applied in or towards local improvements.

For two centuries the Chetham library has been open in Manchester as a free library; it contains about forty thousand volumes, with many rare manuscripts. Manchester is also well supplied with other means of gratuitous reading and study. Sir John Potter, three times mayor, promoted in 1851 a public subscription, by means of which a building was bought and furnished with books, and then handed over to the municipality, who have since maintained and extended it. There are now a central library, and a reference library with over seventy thousand volumes. Six lending libraries in different districts give great facilities to readers, and all are open on Sundays. In the reference library copies of local Acts may be inspected. An art gallery was established by the Corporation under a special Act in 1882,[1] and already contains a collection, acquired by purchase and gift, worthy of a community whose taste for art has for many years been steadily cultivated. A Town Hall, which the Corporation were authorized to build in 1866,[2] and first occupied nine years afterwards, is an architectural ornament of which the citizens may be justly proud.[3] It has a tower over 280 feet high, with a carillon and twenty-one bells, the largest weighing eight tons, and the whole thirty-four tons; these, with the great clock, alone cost 7,000*l.* In the building are 314 rooms,

Free libraries.

Art gallery.

Town Hall.

---

[1] 45 & 46 Vict. c. 203.
[2] 29 Vict. c. 29.

[3] The architect was Mr. Alfred Waterhouse, R.A.

with some admirable mural paintings. The hall is a hundred feet long by fifty wide, with an organ which has forty-three stops and three thousand pipes. For civic receptions there is a suite of state apartments three hundred feet long; and the Mayor for the time being uses a service of plate, consisting of seventy-four pieces and weighing over ten thousand ounces, presented by the citizens, the result of a voluntary subscription which reached 7,000*l.* The Town Hall cost altogether about 1,045,000*l.*, including interest on capital during construction.

Municipal boundaries. Manchester is one of those rapidly-increasing communities which found itself cramped within its old municipal limits. According to the census of 1881, a population of 341,414 was contained within an area of 4,293 acres, while the neighbouring borough of Salford, with half the population, had 5,170 acres. By an Act of 1885,[1] an adjoining township, Harpurhey, and two Local Board districts, Bradford and Rusholme, were brought within the City bounds, adding 1,634 acres, and **Parks and cemeteries.** making the new municipal area 5,927 acres.[2] In area, the five public parks of Manchester do not show to advantage; they contain together no more than 131 acres. In the Queen's Park there is a museum. Some open spaces and recreation grounds have also been laid out and are maintained by the Corporation. Special legislation has enabled them to **Markets.** provide two cemeteries of 138 acres.[3] Ample market accommodation has also been provided by the Council, who purchased the manorial rights and properties in 1846 from the **Baths and washhouses.** then lord of the manor for 200,000*l.*;[4] they have established baths and washhouses in four districts of the City, and have **Tramways.** constructed a tramway system under several Provisional Orders made since 1875.[5]

Finance. Manchester was one of the first provincial cities to consolidate its debt. Authority to issue Corporation stock was given

---

[1] 48 & 49 Vict. c. 126.

[2] The municipal and parliamentary boundaries are not even now coterminous; the latter embraces 6,358 acres.

[3] 20 & 21 Vict. c. 117; 35 & 36 Vict. c. 31.

[4] 9 & 10 Vict. c. 219; 10 Vict. c. 14; 28 Vict. c. 90.

[5] 38 & 39 Vict. c. 167; 41 & 42 Vict. c. 163; 44 & 45 Vict. c. 105.

in 1872.[1] All issues of authorized stock have, as their security, the City rate, which is the only rate now levied for municipal purposes, and the waterworks, gas works, and all other property belonging to the Corporation, the estimated value of which is over 8,000,000*l.* Commercial depression somewhat reduced the net rateable value of the borough from 1881 to 1884; in the year 1886 it amounted to 2,400,000*l.*, compared with 830,000*l.* in 1841. In 1885 the City had a total debt of 6,819,810*l.*, of which 3,193,377*l.* was contracted for waterworks, 812,312*l.* for gas, and 2,814,191*l.* for town hall, improvement, and general municipal purposes.

Salford, divided from Manchester by the narrow boundary Salford. of the Irwell, was, as we have seen, long subject to the same local government. In 1828 Parliament dissolved this partnership, and repealed the old Acts of 1765 and 1792, which associated the two towns.[2] Although, therefore, not more easily distinguished from Manchester than are many metropolitan districts from each other, Salford now has its own municipality and separate government. It was incorporated in 1844. Since then drainage from time to time has been greatly improved; streets have been opened out, and other means adopted for promoting health.[3] The gas works belong to the Corporation; water is supplied in bulk from Manchester. Four public parks, besides Kersal Moor, are maintained by the municipality. In Peel Park there are a museum and art gallery, with a public library, which has three branches and reading rooms in other parts of Salford. The Corporation have also provided public baths, markets, cemeteries, and tramways.[4]

[1] 35 & 36 Vict. c. 31; 38 & 39 Vict. c. 161.

[2] 9 Geo. IV. c. 117, *ante*, p. 478. Soon after 1792, the Manchester and Salford Commissioners divided, forming two distinct bodies, and thenceforth continued to meet separately. As this separation was unauthorised, the Act of 1828 confirmed all proceedings of both bodies, and incorporated each, with separate jurisdiction.

[3] 25 & 26 Vict. c. 205; 33 & 34 Vict. c. 129; 34 & 35 Vict. c. 110; 45 & 46 Vict. c. 97.

[4] 38 & 39 Vict. c. 101; 48 & 49 Vict. c. 102.

Birmingham.　　　Birmingham, as we have seen,[1] shared with other large towns the disease and mortality due to bad drainage, over-crowding, and defective legislation, and possessed, even in larger measure than was common early in the century, that strange medley of jurisdictions by which harmonious and efficient local government was rendered impossible.[2] Its

Early Improvement Acts.

earliest improvement Acts, administered by various bodies of Commissioners, date from 1769 and 1773.[3] Cleansing, lighting, the laying open of streets, the regulation of police, were the chief objects of these statutes, which were amended or repealed in 1790, in 1801, and again in 1812 and 1828.[4] When the town was incorporated in 1838, there were thirteen Boards of

Improvement Act, 1851.

Commissioners, and it was not until 1851 that local adminis-tration was centred in the Council by a statute which trans-ferred to them the powers and property of these Commissioners, at the same time providing for better drainage, paving, and other objects.[5] This and subsequent amending Acts have

---

[1] *Ante*, p. 307.

[2] *Ante*, pp. 305, 309. That police supervision in the district was imper-fect may be gathered from a local re-cord that, in 1835, three bulls were baited for four days at Hockley. As to streets, "there was not one, says Hutton, but was ill-constructed, so ill that, in his own rude simile (quite appropriate to his time), the houses 'crowded before each other like men at a dog-fight.' They were almost without public light, and quite with-out public water. Police were not, nor public library, nor gallery, nor bath, nor park. They were poisoned with graveyards and slaughter-houses, and soaked with sewage. All rates were high, and the death-rate highest."—Archbishop Benson, Ad-dress to Birmingham and Midland Institute on Municipalities, No-vember 30, 1885. Following Mr. Bunce, a local historian, Dr. Ben-son has pointed out how a mediæval

guild, the Guild of the Holy Cross, did what it could, until its suppres-sion in 1547, to supply the want of efficient municipal organization in Birmingham. It mended the roads, then often "foul and dangerous"; it maintained, and perhaps built, two bridges across the Rea; it pro-vided a bellman to convene public meetings. Among other good works, less distinctly civic, it found deserv-ing poor in food and coals, nursed the sick in their houses, endowed clergymen, and provided an organist. In other communities these guilds, which must be distinguished from the later trade guilds, probably un-dertook the same kind of useful and charitable offices.

[3] 9 Geo. III. c. 83; 13 Geo. III. c. 36.

[4] 31 Geo. III. c. 17; 41 Geo. III. c. 39; 52 Geo. III. c. 113; 9 Geo. IV. c. 54.

[5] 14 & 15 Vict. c. 93, amended by

given the Corporation large sanitary and police powers. A scheme under the Artisans' and Labourers' Dwellings Act was sanctioned in a Provisional Order of 1876.[1] The Act of 1851 is remarkable for a provision which embodies, to some extent, the principle afterwards adopted in a general Act of 1872, identified with the name of Mr. Leeman; it declared that no application should be made to Parliament by the Town Council for further powers until after public notice and approval by the ratepayers in a meeting convened for the purpose. Provision was also made for a poll, if demanded.

Borough Funds Act, 1872, anticipated.

A company, incorporated in 1826,[2] supplied water to Birmingham from the River Tame and Hawthorn Brook, near Salford Bridge. Notwithstanding the existence of this private undertaking, the Town Council, by a section in their Improvement Act of 1851, were authorized to supply water both for public purposes and for private use.[3] With this object they were further empowered to contract with the company for "pure and wholesome water," and after twelve months' notice might purchase the undertaking by agreement, or upon terms to be settled by arbitration under the Lands Clauses Consolidation Act.[4] But these provisions were insufficient to enable the Corporation to raise the necessary funds. Nearly a quarter of a century passed, therefore, before they asked Parliament to sanction this purchase. Meanwhile the company were allowed on several occasions to raise further capital, extend their limits, and construct new works.[5] Prudently distrusting the doubtful results of arbitration, the Corporation came to Parliament, in 1875, with an agreement already entered into, and a price fixed. The transfer of the waterworks, so arranged, was sanctioned, with safeguards suggested by local authorities in outlying

Birmingham Waterworks Company, 1826.

Birmingham Corporation Water Act, 1875.

24 & 25 Vict. c. 206, and by Provisional Orders of 1876 (39 & 40 Vict. cc. 200–2).

[1] 39 & 40 Vict. c. 235.
[2] 7 Geo. IV. c. 109.
[3] 14 & 15 Vict. c. 93, s. 109.

[4] Ib.; they might raise 250,000*l.* and mortgage the waterworks for this purpose.
[5] 17 & 18 Vict. c. 37; 18 & 19 Vict. c. 34; 29 & 30 Vict. c. 83; 33 & 34 Vict. c. 128.

districts within the company's area of supply. Thus, for water outside the borough the Corporation were to charge the same rate as for water provided under like circumstances within the borough; and some neighbouring local boards might require a supply of water in bulk, whereupon all powers of the Corporation within these districts would cease.[1]

In the same Session of 1875 the gasworks were also successfully transferred to the municipality. There were then

Gas companies incorporated, 1819 and 1826.

two companies in Birmingham. The Birmingham Gaslight and Coke Company, incorporated in 1819,[2] abstained from coming again before Parliament until 1855.[3] Meanwhile, in 1825,[4] the Birmingham and Staffordshire Gaslight Company were allowed to compete within part of the same district. Twenty years subsequently, in an Act giving fresh powers to this company, they were authorized to sell their undertaking to the Corporation or Improvement Commissioners, who were respectively enabled to buy it.[5] As neither body availed itself of this authority for thirty years, the company obtained fresh powers in 1858 and 1864.[6] An agreement for purchase, settled with both gas companies by the Corporation before

Birmingham Corporation Gas Act, 1875.

their application to Parliament, was scheduled to the Act of 1875.[7] With two exceptions, districts outside the borough, but within the area of gas supply, were protected, as in the water transfer, against higher prices than those charged under like circumstances to borough ratepayers; and sanitary authorities outside the borough were enabled to buy such portions of either gas undertaking as were within their districts.

Purchase of outlying gasworks by sanitary authorities.

Four of these sanitary authorities—Oldbury, Smethwick, Tipton, and West Bromwich—exercised, under separate statutes, in 1876,[8] the power thus reserved to them. A protracted arbitration was held to settle terms of purchase, and the question afterwards came before the Queen's Bench

---

[1] 38 & 39 Vict. c. 188.
[2] 59 Geo. III. c. 68.
[3] 18 & 19 Vict. c. 48.
[4] 6 Geo. IV. c. 79.
[5] 8 & 9 Vict. c. 66.

[6] 21 & 22 Vict. c. 1; 27 & 28 Vict. c. 239.
[7] 38 & 39 Vict. c. 178.
[8] 39 & 40 Vict. cc. 191, 178, 148, 149. See also 42 & 43 Vict. c. 392.

Division and Court of Appeal. The Corporation claimed to re-sell to each outlying authority at an enhanced value, but were held, substantially, to have purchased as trustees for these authorities, to whom any accruing advantage enured. Again, in 1879, Northfield and Yardley, the two excepted districts just mentioned, prevailed upon Parliament, notwithstanding strenuous opposition by Birmingham, to relieve them from the statutory arrangement of 1875, and place them on the same footing as other outlying districts supplied with gas.[1] Notwithstanding these adverse decisions, the policy of purchase by the Birmingham Corporation, involving for the water and gas works a cost of about three millions, has been amply justified by increasing revenue and good service. A market-hall, one of the largest in the kingdom, cost nearly 70,000*l.* Nine parks and pleasure grounds, with an area of 218 acres, are maintained by the Corporation.[2] The Town-hall, famous for the important political meetings held there, gives standing room to 5,000 persons. New municipal buildings, "a municipal palace,"[3] have been erected at a cost of 200,000*l.* In 1854, the Council were authorized to grant a site for the buildings of the Birmingham and Midland Institute.[4] They have established baths[5] and wash-

(Marginal notes:) Birmingham Gas (Northfield and Yardley) Act, 1879.

Market-hall, parks, Town-hall, municipal buildings.

Free libraries,

---

[1] 42 & 43 Vict. c. 130.

[2] 17 & 18 Vict. c. 113; Provisional Order confirmed by 39 & 40 Vict. c. 202.

[3] Archbishop Benson, Address, p. 24.

[4] 17 & 18 Vict. c. 91.

[5] Story, in the pleasant volume already quoted, somewhat disturbs our complacency in this modern revival by British municipalities. The hot and cold baths of Caracalla accommodated 1,600 persons. At each end was a large hall, adorned with statues, its pavements and roof inlaid with rich mosaics. These halls were probably devoted to gladiatorial exercises, recitations of poets, lectures by philosophers and rhetoricians.

Outside the central building was an open space, surrounded by porticoes and gardens, and containing a gymnasium, stadium, arena, and theatre, where games, sports, plays, and races were held. This enclosure was nearly a mile in circuit. Still larger were the baths of Diocletian, which covered an area of 150,000 square yards, and held 3,200 bathers at a time. There were also the baths of Agrippa, Constantine, Nero, and Severus, and those of Titus on the Esquiline. Here the people lounged and bathed, looked upon the games, betted on gladiators, struggled in the gymnasium, or listened to recitations by poets and rhetoricians. The price of a bath was only a quadrant, the smallest coin in

art gallery,
industrial
museum.
houses; a fire brigade; hospitals for infectious diseases; tram-ways, leased to private companies and connected with the suburbs and adjoining towns; and free libraries, consisting of a central reference and lending library, with four lending libraries and reading-rooms in other parts of the town. An art gallery and industrial museum, and a museum of natural history at Aston Hall, also belong to the Corporation. A municipal school of art, with seven branches, has lately been established, and students of both sexes are encouraged by prizes, free admissions, and scholarships, to qualify themselves for employment in the local trades. At Birmingham, as elsewhere, private munificence, awakened by a more vigorous municipal life, has done much for higher culture as well as for charity.

Finance.
In 1880, the Corporation consolidated their loan debt, and obtained power to issue stock.[1] Up to 1885, the total amount raised by them was 8,250,000l., reduced by the sinking fund to 7,182,000l. From gas their net profit in 1885 was nearly 45,000l., the largest made by any municipality; the water supply left a small deficit. In 1886, the assessable value of Consolidation
of local law. Birmingham was about 1,750,000l. A work of great labour and utility was accomplished in 1883, when existing local statutes were repealed and embodied in the Birmingham Corporation Consolidation Act.[2]

Leeds.
Leeds is one of the boroughs in which municipal abuses, already described,[3] led to an entire withdrawal of public confidence from the Corporation, and the practical government Improvement
Acts, 1755-90
and 1809. of the town by statutory commissioners. Incorporated by Charles I.,[4] it seems to have remained without any attempt

use; children under a certain age paid nothing. After the Emperors built their thermæ no charge was ever made. —"Roba di Roma," pp. 467-70.

[1] 43 & 44 Vict. c. 178.
[2] 46 & 47 Vict. c. 70; *post*, pp. 535-6.
[3] *Ante*, pp. 217 et seq.
[4] Dr. Whitaker, in his "Loidis and Elmete" (1816), says that,

though incorporated, Leeds "by a singular felicity escaped the inconvenient privilege of sending members to Parliament." To the "absence of those periodical seasons of popular frenzy which accompany general elections," he attributes "that comparative sobriety and restraint" enjoyed by the inhabit-

at street or sanitary regulation until 1755, when an Act passed "for enlightening streets and lanes and regulating pavements," within certain specified limits.[1] In 1790 these limits were extended and commissioners incorporated, among other objects, "for more effectually lighting and cleansing streets," and "removing and preventing nuisances, annoyances, encroachments, and obstructions."[2] The nuisances set forth in this Act are chiefly projecting signs, sign-irons, sign-posts and boards, water spouts, and hindrances to traffic. Public scavengers for cleansing streets were to be provided by the commissioners, but there is no mention of drains, sewers or sewerage, either in this Act or in a later statute, of 1809,[3] by which it was amended and the commissioners' powers enlarged.

A "police and nightly watch" was established in 1815.[4] **Night-watch, 1815.** Justices of the peace were entrusted with this and other powers. They were to appoint, at any special sessions, such number of able-bodied men as they thought necessary, "to be employed as watchmen or patroles within the town and one mile of the bars thereof." Justices were also authorized to make and levy a watch rate,[5] local taxation without even the semblance of representation. A saving clause preserved all existing rights and powers of the Corporation; otherwise this body, and the commissioners, were ignored. In 1824 **Lighting and cleansing, 1824.** the Corporation were treated with equal contempt in an

ants when his history was written. This rev. historian also thought it "certainly a creditable circumstance" that the theatre at Leeds had been shut up for four years; and he was doubtful about the library founded by Dr. Priestley, thinking that indiscriminate reading produced "under a semblance of study a pleasing dissipation of thought," and that, unless the books were carefully selected, they might, by their rapid circulation, through the medium of such institutions, "corrupt all principles, moral, political, and religious, with a facility and to an extent unattainable by any other means."

[1] 28 Geo. II. c. 41.

[2] 30 Geo. III. c. 68.

[3] 49 Geo. III. c. 122. This statute prohibited the slaughter of cattle except in specified shambles (sect. 28), limited the hours for emptying cesspools (sect. 26), and empowered the Commissioners to order the removal of any offensive "hog-stye, swine-cote, necessary-house, dunghill, or midden" (sect. 29).

[4] 55 Geo. III. c. 42.

[5] Ib., s. 16.

elaborate statute of 130 clauses for lighting, cleansing, and improving the town.[1] Under this statute the borough justices, with thirteen elected commissioners, formed the governing body. Certain property was scheduled for purposes of street improvement; and other property might be purchased for further improvements, but only after consent given by three-fourths of the ratepayers in parish vestry assembled.

Neglect of drainage.

Although this Act empowered the commissioners to remove slaughter-houses and other nuisances, if offensive,[2] it resembled the legislation of 1790, in containing not a single provision for drainage or sewerage. Rainfall from houses was, however, to be conducted by pipes " underneath the foot pavement into the common channel when practicable," so as " not to fall upon or incommode " passers-by. With a rapidly increasing population, densely crowded in some districts of the town, its sanitary condition during this period was deplorable. A local historian records an alarming

Epidemic of 1801-2.

epidemic fever in 1801-2, when " whole streets were infected nearly house by house, and in one court of crowded population typhus raged for four months successively." He goes on to congratulate the authorities that, in 1814, "thirty different streets produced no more than sixty patients of typhus and scarlatina conjointly."[3] It was not until 1842 that the Cor-

Improvement Act, 1842.

poration, by this time freely chosen, relieved also from the ill-favour into which their predecessors had fallen, superseded the old commissioners, and took into their own hands the whole local government, under Parliamentary authority.[4] Under this Act the Corporation might enforce proper sewerage and drainage, and regulate the width of streets. Thatched houses were forbidden;[5] cellars were not to be occupied as dwellings without a window and fireplace; there was also a restriction upon houses in close alleys. Among other measures of police, was one inflicting penalties on keepers or

[1] 5 Geo. IV. c. 124.
[2] Ib., s. 78.
[3] Whitaker's " Loidis and El-
mote," p. 85.
[4] 5 & 6 Vict. c. 104.
[5] Ib., s. 176.

managers of "any house, room, pit, or other place for the purpose of fighting or baiting lions, bears, badgers, cocks, dogs, or other animals."

This Act of 1842, containing nearly four hundred clauses, was one of the most comprehensive and complete which had then been obtained by local authorities, and scheduled a large extent of property for improvements. Since 1842 Sanitary legislation the corporate powers for sanitary, police, and general 1842–77. purposes have been extended and strengthened by nine statutes.[1] One of these, passed in 1870, enabled the Corporation, upon the report of their officer of health, to improve or remove houses which prevented proper ventilation in courts, or were in themselves unfit for habitation. They might also prohibit the occupation as a dwelling-house of any building under the rateable value of 20l. until the drainage had been made and completed, or until their officer had certified that it was fit for habitation.[2] Several rows of houses were improved or demolished under this Act of 1870, but as the compulsory powers of purchase then given expired three years afterwards, they were renewed in 1877.[3] At the same time the Corporation were allowed to erect suitable dwellings for families displaced by street improvements or by regulations against overcrowding.[4] Under the powers afforded by these Acts the Corporation have diminished the rate of mortality, widened and improved the chief thoroughfares, and done much to kindle local pride in a well-ordered town.

Except in certain small outlying districts, which are being Sewerage. dealt with, the whole borough is now well sewered and drained. The total length of sewers is about 260 miles; their total cost has been 518,000l. The outfall is at Knostrop,

---

[1] 11 & 12 Vict. c. 102; 19 & 20 Vict. c. 115; 29 & 30 Vict. cc. 151 and 157; 32 & 33 Vict. c. 11; 33 & 34 Vict. c. 93; 35 & 36 Vict. c. 97; 40 & 41 Vict. c. 178; 42 Vict. c. 23.
[2] 33 & 34 Vict. c. 93, s. 33.
[3] 40 & 41 Vict. c. 178.
[4] Ib., Preamble, and s. 25.

about $2\frac{1}{4}$ miles from the Town Hall, where the Corporation have constructed extensive works for treating and purifying sewage.

Water supply. Water supply in Leeds has a curious history. It was first undertaken by a few individuals, then transferred to a public body, again handed over to private speculators, and finally bought up by the municipality. Before 1790, an insufficient and irregular service of water was provided from Pitfall Mill by some adventurers acting without statutory powers.

Undertaken by Commissioners, 1790. Thirteen Improvement Commissioners were incorporated in 1790, as Leeds Waterworks Commissioners, with power to buy the existing works, provide sufficient water from the river Aire, and distribute it through pipes.[1] The owners of Pitfall Mill works were willing to sell on very moderate terms—an indemnity from the obligations of their lease, and the investment for their use of " a sum of money sufficient to produce an annual income of 150*l.* in the four per cent. consolidated Bank annuities."[2]

Exemptions from water rates. By this statute of 1790 persons occupying houses under 58*s.* of annual rent or value were exempted from water rates. For gratuitous use by poor persons the Commissioners were bound to place cisterns and cocks at convenient distances in public streets.[3]

Act of 1809. An amending Act of 1809 enlarged the previous exemption, applying it to persons occupying houses of 4*l.* annual value.[4] This statute contained one of the earliest provisions against waste, by imposing penalties on persons failing to provide proper cisterns, with balls and stop-cocks.[5] Down to the year 1837 Leeds continued to derive water from the Aire, but the Commissioners could not provide a sufficient quantity, and the water had become impure and unfit for domestic use.

Transfer of waterworks to company, 1837. As they were not inclined to incur the risk and outlay of erecting new works, served from fresh

[1] 30 Geo. III. c. 68, Preamble.
[2] Ib., s. 11.
[3] Ib., s. 26.
[4] 49 Geo. III. c. 122, s. 6.
[5] Ib., s. 7.

sources, they transferred their works, in 1837, to a private company, receiving no consideration whatever on behalf of the town, and stipulating only that the new proprietors should take over all their obligations.[1]

The only material opposition to the Bill effecting this transfer came from Lord Cardigan, Lord Mexborough, and millowners whose interests were prejudiced by a new scheme of supply.[2] After 1837, therefore, the Leeds Waterworks Company enjoyed a monopoly, and gave an improved service of water from streams near Eccup and Allwoodley. Their subscribed capital was 91,500l., all of which was to be raised before they could exercise compulsory powers. Although the Corporation did not oppose the transfer, they required the promoters to insert clauses restricting profits to six per cent., and enabling the town to buy their undertaking, in whole or in part, after the lapse of twelve years, paying the amount subscribed by the proprietors, with such further sum, if any, as would make up their dividends to six per cent. from the period of subscription.[3] These safeguards showed great foresight on the part of the Council, and prevented the growth of any injurious monopoly. Ten years afterwards this Act was repealed, and the company re-incorporated, the Town Council being authorized to appoint half the directors.[4] This provision was declared to be "for securing publicity to the company's proceedings, and a due attention to the interests of the inhabitants." Profits were restricted and dividends limited as in 1837; accounts were to be audited and published as the Town Council might direct; and their powers to purchase the company's works were re-enacted and confirmed.

Limit upon company's profits.

Power of purchase reserved to Town Council.

Act of 1847.

In 1852 Leeds had outgrown its supply from the sources which had hitherto served it, and Parliament sanctioned a

Transfer to Corporation, 1852.

---

[1] 7 Will. IV. & 1 Vict. c. 83, s. 2.

[2] 92 Com. Journ. 257.

[3] 7 Will. IV. & 1 Vict. c. 83, s. 167.

[4] 10 & 11 Vict. c. 262, ss. 22, 23.

scheme for taking water from the river Wharfe.[1] At the same time the company's undertaking was transferred to the Corporation upon terms already stated. Extensions of existing works were sanctioned in 1856 and 1862,[2] but in 1867 Leeds again required both purer water and a larger supply. The Corporation were therefore authorized to take water by gravitation from the river Washburn, a tributary of the Wharfe.[3] Their area of supply was extended in 1874;[4] and to meet the continually increasing demand, new reservoirs, filter-beds, and other works were sanctioned in 1877.[5] There was a profit of 7,600*l.* upon the water supply in 1885.[6] Upon their waterworks undertaking the Corporation have expended 1,534,000*l.*, reduced by 116,000*l.* through the operation of the sinking fund. Considering the wide area of supply, the frequent changes of source, and the new works due to rapid increases of population, this is a moderate expenditure, largely owing to the municipal control so prudently acquired over the water undertaking in 1837.

In 1818 a Leeds Gaslight Company was incorporated,[7] and in 1824 another company to supply gas made from oil.[8] There was no distinction of limits; both undertakings were authorized to light the town and neighbourhood. But in

Supply from Washburn, 1867.

Leeds Gaslight and Oil Gaslight Companies, 1818–24.

---

[1] 15 & 16 Vict. c. 102.

[2] 19 & 20 Vict. c. 80; 25 & 26 Vict. c. 52.

[3] 30 & 31 Vict. c. 141.

[4] 37 & 38 Vict. c. 34.

[5] 40 & 41 Vict. c. 178.

[6] Prior to the Act of 1877—under which the Corporation were compelled to set apart and appropriate annually from rates and rents forming the security for their loans a sum of 1 per cent. on the aggregate amount of their borrowed moneys as a sinking fund for repayment of those moneys—they had made large profits on their waterworks undertaking, all of which had been paid every year into the borough fund. Since the sinking fund provisions came into operation, although the Corporation have continued to make a profit, it has been entirely absorbed in meeting the annual contribution to the sinking fund. In the year 1885, as stated in the text, the profit on the water sales, excluding that contribution, was 7,600*l.*

[7] 58 Geo. III. c. 56.

[8] 5 Geo. IV. c. 110.

order to disarm opposition the new company debarred themselves from making gas from coal, while their older rivals agreed not to make gas from oil. This statutory bargain proved fatal to the last comers. Like other adventures of a similar kind elsewhere,[1] the attempt to compete against coal-gas with oil-gas proved an entire failure, and in 1833 the oil-gas company were dissolved, and their property was vested in trustees, and sold for the benefit of creditors and shareholders.[2] Two years afterwards, in spite of strenuous opposition from the existing company,[3] a Leeds New Gas Company were incorporated, again with no restriction of limits, for better lighting the town and neighbourhood.[4] By various statutes these two bodies extended their capital and powers until the year 1870, when they agreed to sell their respective undertakings to the Corporation.[5] For each 100*l.* of stock and shares, each company received 140*l.* The total purchase money, including outstanding loans taken over by the Corporation, and some perpetual debenture stock, was about 808,000*l.* Since 1870 the works and supply have been greatly extended,[6] and the gas outlay amounted in 1885 to about 1,025,000*l.*, reduced to less than 900,000*l.* by the operation of the sinking fund. There was a profit of 5,300*l.* upon the supply of gas in 1885.[7]

Leeds New Gas Company, 1835.

Leeds Corporation Gas Act, 1870.

Under the Public Libraries Act reference and lending libraries, the latter of which now has twenty-five branches, were founded by the municipality in 1868. Roundhay Park,

Public libraries and parks.

---

[1] *Ante*, Vol. I., p. 214.

[2] 3 & 4 Will. IV. c. 21. This Act is not among the local and personal statutes for 1833, but will be found in the collection of private Acts.

[3] 90 Com. Journ. 338.

[4] 5 & 6 Will. IV. c. 86.

[5] 33 & 34 Vict. c. 56.

[6] See Leeds Improvement Act, 1877 (40 & 41 Vict. c. 178).

[7] The remarks just made upon the operation of the sinking fund as to water apply equally to gas. The profit on the gas undertaking in 1885 was 5,300*l.* (on a turn-over of nearly 211,000*l.*), but this profit was entirely absorbed and converted into a deficit of 3,193*l.* by sinking fund requirements. In considering these figures it must also be borne in mind that, although the Corporation have power to charge at the rate of 3*s.* 9*d.* per 1,000 cubic feet of gas, they are only charging 1*s.* 10*d.*, their policy being to supply consumers at as near cost price as practicable.

including two lakes of thirty-three and five acres respectively,[1] Woodhouse Moor, situated on high ground near the town, Holbeck and Hunslet Moors, Woodhouse Ridge, and other lands, have been laid out for public recreation and enjoyment under special legislation.[2] By similar authority, cattle and other markets have been acquired and enlarged at a cost of nearly 290,000*l.* A noble Town Hall, 250 feet long, 200 wide, with a tower 225 feet high, was opened by Queen Victoria in 1858, and, with municipal offices of more recent erection, cost about 240,000*l.* Consolidated stock was issued by the municipality under an Act of 1877.[3] In 1886 the corporate debt of the town was 4,243,000*l.*, its rateable value 1,177,000*l.*

Markets and municipal buildings.

Finance.

Manorial customs.

A charter of privileges granted by Maurice Paganel, lord of the manor, to his burgesses of Leeds, in the reign of King John, required that they should bake their victuals in the lord's oven (*commune furnum*), according to the custom. This custom continued for several centuries;[4] the obligation to grind corn, grain, and malt at the lord's water-mills[5] continued until 1839, when, to end the litigation and ill-blood occasioned by attempts to enforce this "soke, suit, and service," all claims in respect of it were extinguished, upon a payment of 13,000*l.*, which was raised by "a soke rate" assessed upon inhabitants[6] through trustees chosen by them. The Corporation took no direct part in this negotiation, which was completed by statute,[7] though the trustees were required to send yearly accounts to the town clerk

---

[1] Roundhay Park has a total area of 774 acres, 300 of which have been set apart for public use. The remaining area is reserved for building sites.

[2] See Leeds Corporation Act, 1879 (42 & 43 Vict. c. 23), and earlier Acts there cited.

[3] Leeds Improvement Act (40 & 41 Vict. c. 178 ; Part IX.).

[4] Whitaker, 11.

[5] The toll or mulcture paid to the mill-owners or farmers was one sixteenth part of all corn or grain and one thirty-second part of all malt.

[6] Inhabitants of those parts of the manor which had belonged to the Knights Templars or Hospitallers and Knights of St. John of Jerusalem claimed exemption from the custom, and were freed from assessment.

[7] 2 & 3 Vict. c. 17.

for public inspection. Thus, in 1839, and not before, the inhabitants of Leeds were at liberty " to grind their corn, grain, and malt at any mill" they might choose, to build mills " at their free will and pleasure," and to buy for sale, or their own consumption, flour wherever ground.

Bradford is a conspicuous example of municipal energy, **Bradford.** reflecting the enterprise and energy of a population which has increased in half a century from about 43,000 to nearly five times that number.[1] Like other towns it suffered from lax administration at a time when economy was thought of greater moment than public health and convenience. Its first Improvement Act was obtained in 1803, when, according to the preamble, its streets, lanes, entries, causeways, and foot-paths were in many parts "incommodious and unsafe for pas-sengers," very ill-paved, not lighted, insufficiently cleansed and watched, and subject to various " nuisances, annoyances, and obstructions." Commissioners were therefore appointed with powers to amend these defects and establish a nightly watch.[2] Bradford was incorporated in 1847, and the duties of these Commissioners then devolved on the Council, but further powers of local government were obtained in 1850, when the Act of **Bradford** 1803 was repealed.[3] By a series of statutes dating from this **Improvement Act, 1850.** period down to 1885,[4] works of drainage, sewage purification, street improvement and reconstruction, have been vigorously carried out, a large extent of insanitary property has been cleared away by the Corporation under compulsory powers, sanitary precautions have been enforced, and the result has been a striking diminution in the death-rate, which used sometimes to be thirty per thousand, but in 1885 was only 17·7 per thousand.

In 1873 and 1881 the municipal limits were extended ; they **Markets, parks, libraries, &c.**

[1] According to the Registrar-General's returns, the estimated population in the middle of 1885 was 214,431, giving 19·9 persons to an acre within the municipal limits.

[2] 43 Geo. III. c. 90.

[3] 13 & 14 Vict. c. 79.

[4] 48 & 49 Vict. c. 124.

now include 10,776 acres.[1]   All market rights at Bradford
formerly belonged exclusively to the lord of the manor, who,
as at Leeds, also claimed that grain and malt should be
ground in his mills, or pay toll if ground elsewhere.   In
1866 the Corporation bought up these market rights for a
term of a thousand years at an annual rental of 5,000*l*.[2]
They also extinguished the soke, put an end to the sale of
cattle and horses in the streets, and built spacious markets, with new slaughter-houses, placed under proper supervision.   ·There are now in Bradford public baths and wash-
houses; five parks, occupying a total area of 219 acres,
including Peel, Lister, and Bowling Parks, from fifty to
sixty acres each; a free library for reference and circulation,
with seven branches; an art gallery and museum; and a fine
Town Hall, opened in 1873, which cost 125,000*l*.   Buildings erected with excellent taste by the municipality, their
construction of broad thoroughfares in the business-centres,
the good frontages thus afforded, and the spirit and
growing wealth shown in the architecture of factories,
shops, and warehouses, have transformed Bradford from
the unsavoury picture drawn of it in 1803, into one of
the handsomest and healthiest manufacturing towns in the
kingdom.

Bradford
Waterworks
Company,
1790.

Before the year 1790 Richard Sclater and four other persons provided Bradford with water from a spring belonging
to them in the township of North Bierley.   They obtained
statutory powers in 1790, and were incorporated as the
Bradford Waterworks Company.[3]   These powers, incomplete
as they were, sufficed until 1842, when an Act was obtained
which, in bulk at any rate, made amends for past shortcomings, and incorporated a new company under the old
name, to afford "a sufficient and constant" service instead
of the very inadequate service then given.[4]   This company

---

[1] 36 & 37 Vict. c. 167; Bradford
Water and Improvement Act (44 &
45 Vict. c. 122).

[2] 29 & 30 Vict. c. 222.

[3] 30 Geo. III. c. 63.

[4] 5 & 6 Vict. c. 6; it contained
362 sections, besides schedules.

were authorized to buy the old works for the modest sum of 4,000*l.*; their dividends were limited to ten per cent., all excess profits going in reduction of rates. In 1854, after having once increased their capital,[1] the company were dissolved, but re-incorporated with new powers and extended limits.[2] By agreement, however, come to in the same Session, their undertaking was sold to the Corporation, and Parliament confirmed this transfer.[3] The amount of purchase-money, including the company's liabilities, was 200,000*l.*; the new works then contemplated cost 240,000*l.* A public water rate was sanctioned[4] in addition to charges for supply. Increasing population and manufacturing wants have rendered necessary frequent applications to Parliament for power to appropriate new and distant sources, construct new reservoirs and other works, extend the limits of water supply, and borrow further money. No fewer than eleven Acts for these purposes have been sanctioned since 1854.[5] Water is now taken from streams in the Worth Valley beyond Haworth, and from Wharfedale beyond Bolton Abbey. Besides the borough, twenty-eight townships outside it are supplied by the municipality. About 2,100,000*l.* has been sunk in necessary works, and interest on this sum, with the charge of a sinking fund, more than swallows up the municipal income from water, leaving an average annual deficit of about 5,000*l.*

Limitation of dividends.

Bradford Corporation Waterworks Act, 1854.

A transfer of gas-works to the Corporation, which was effected in 1871, has proved highly remunerative, and far more than recoups them for unavoidable losses upon their water undertaking. A gaslight company, established in Bradford, under statute, in 1823,[6] obtained in 1845 further

Gas.

---

[1] 12 & 13 Vict. c. 20.

[2] 17 & 18 Vict. c. 124.

[3] 17 & 18 Vict. c. 129.

[4] Ib., s. 38. This rate is three-pence in the pound.

[5] 18 & 19 Vict. c. 152; 21 & 22 Vict. c. 76; 25 & 26 Vict. c. 18; 29 & 30 Vict. c. 222; 31 & 32 Vict. c. 140; 32 & 33 Vict. c. 135; 36 & 37 Vict. c. 167; 38 & 39 Vict. c. 80; 41 & 42 Vict. c. 133; 44 & 45 Vict. c. 122; 48 & 49 Vict. c. 124. Some of these Acts were for general improvement as well as for water purposes.

[6] 3 Geo. IV. c. 6.

powers, with some modification of those previously existing.[1]   When the Corporation sought to acquire the gasworks this company resisted.   Alternative proposals were
accordingly submitted to Parliament by the municipality in
1871 : a Bill for a compulsory transfer, and, failing success,
another Bill enabling them to establish competing works.
The company then gave way, obtaining liberal terms, and the
Corporation acquired a property which yields them an annual
profit of about 19,000*l*., although they have reduced the price
of gas from three shillings to half-a-crown per thousand feet.

Finance.   Naturally these benefits have not been secured for the
town without a large aggregate outlay.   Street improvements
alone have cost about 1,250,000*l*.; the water undertaking,
2,250,000*l*.; gas, 530,000*l*.; markets, 160,000*l*.   The total
debt of Bradford, at the end of 1885, was 4,222,343*l*., and is
being steadily reduced by means of a sinking fund, which
clears off 40,500*l*. per annum.   In 1886, the rateable value
of Bradford was 952,470*l*.

Development
of municipal
spirit in Great
Britain.
            These examples may suffice.   Almost every other town
can produce records of similar improvements, made by means
of local legislation, and through the increased energy and
intelligence of its governing body, in the latter half of this
century.   During this period, it will be seen, public health
has gained by sewerage, drainage, and other sanitary measures ;[2] public comfort and convenience have been promoted
by better lighting, a purer and more abundant water supply,
and wider thoroughfares, as well as by markets, baths, and
wash-houses ; provision has also been made for public
recreation and enjoyment by parks, libraries, art galleries,
and museums.   This recognition by municipalities that
they do not exist for purposes of bare utility alone is
a striking feature of modern municipal life.   It has been
accompanied in the examples we have traced, and in
other boroughs, by new town halls and offices some-

[1] 8 & 9 Vict. c. 12.
[2] In App. B. some striking figures

on this point are supplied from
Merthyr Tydfil.

times rivalling in their architecture those of the Italian Republics and the Low Countries. Side by side with this growth of municipal spirit, and no less striking, is the increased civic pride which has been awakened among all classes of townspeople, so that the poor have acquiesced, on the whole cheerfully, in rates imposed for civic objects, while the rich have contributed generous gifts of parks, libraries, pictures, or even whole galleries, and have erected private buildings which ornament every town.[1] Heavy municipal rates, which yield no immediate return, form no small sacrifice by townspeople of the artisan and lower middle-class in order to secure municipal efficiency. Such a feeling can only be expected when there is a town worth the sacrifice. Under good local government such towns have arisen, and if we could recall their narrow, foul streets and sordid dwellings, at the beginning of this century, the contrast with their present condition would hardly be less great than with the clay-walled, thatch-roofed shops and hovels which existed five hundred years before.

Although much remains to be done, the sanitary work performed by municipalities under public and local legislation has amply fulfilled the expectations of sanitary reformers and of Parliament. We must not, it is true, exaggerate the influence of this work. While with better drainage, restrictions upon over-crowding, street-cleansing, and other measures enforced by local authorities, mortality has largely diminished, greater sobriety and better food, compulsory vaccination, increased surgical and medical skill, and more hospitals and dispensaries, have contributed in no small measure to the same result. Even with this neces-

Effect of local sanitary measures upon public health.

---

[1] Cf. Archbishop Benson's allusion to Florence and the free Italian cities, ruled by the votes of thousands of citizens who were "yet free from the insane idea that every man is worthy of every office," and who were also "animated by a universal readiness and zeal to subordinate every individual self to the community, and to place their whole pride in regulating, strengthening, and adorning their city." (Address on "Municipalities," p. 6.)

sary reservation, the figures which follow are eloquent; they show the smaller death-rate of 1885 as compared with that of 1865, in eight English and four Scotch towns, notwithstanding a denser population in all but one.[1]

Towns.	Year.	Population (estimated at middle of year.)	Acreage.	Density per Acre.	Death rate per thousand.
London .... {	1865	3,015,494	78,052[2]	40·	24·44
	1885	4,083,928	78,052	54·2	19·7 [3]
Liverpool .. {	1865	476,368	5,210	91·22	36·42
	1885	579,724	5,210	111·3	23·8
Manchester.. {	1865	354,930	4,292	82·29	33·01
	1885	337,342	4,292[4]	78·6	26·5
Salford .... {	1865	110,883	5,208	21·15	29·32
	1885	204,075	5,208	39·5	21·1
Birmingham. {	1865	327,842	8,420	38·7	24·53
	1885	427,769	8,420	50·9	19·3
Leeds ...... {	1865	224,025	21,572	10·8	30·95
	1885	333,139	21,572	15·4	19·9
Bristol...... {	1865	161,809	4,632[5]	33·8	23·52
	1885	218,169	4,632·	47·1	19·7
Hull ...... {	1865	103,747	3,621[6]	28·19	27·27
	1885	186,292	7,901[6]	23·5	17·2
Edinburgh.. {	1865	174,180	..	41·670	28·10
	1885	250,616	..	42·427	18·2
Glasgow .... {	1865	423,723	..	85·690	32·89
	1885	519,965	..	86·187	25·8
Dundee .... {	1865	96,607	..	28·347	31·0
	1885	152,838	..	44·847	20·1
Aberdeen .. {	1865	74,716	..	12·858	26·5
	1885	113,212	..	19·482	17·9

Sanitary outlay, whether remunerative.   Sewers and drains, the opening out of wider thoroughfares, the clearance of insanitary property, are generally classed as unremunerative works, yet their economical results in prolonging human life, averting disease, and sustaining health and vitality among our bread-winners, entitle these works to the highest place of merit in all municipal balance-sheets.

[1] For the greater part of these figures I am indebted to the courtesy of the Registrar-Generals for England and Scotland.

[2] Or 122 square miles, including 2,718 acres of tidal water, and 1,600 miles' length of streets.

[3] In London the year 1885 was remarkable for a marriage rate and a death rate which were the lowest on record, while the birth rate was the lowest since 1850.

[4] Since increased; see p. 484.

[5] Part of the Downs, though vested in the Corporation for all purposes of police, is often incorrectly included in the municipal boundary.

[6] The southern boundary of Hull extends to the middle of the Humber, but this water-space is not here included.

Disease, and the depression and lowered vitality which spring from unwholesome surroundings, lead by many paths to pauperism, and sometimes to vice and crime. Although, therefore, the results of sanitary expenditure are indirect and unseen, they are not the less certain, and have often been calculated with more or less precision.[1] They are, no doubt, reflected in the decreasing inmates of our workhouses; nor can we doubt that they have a deterring influence upon crime. The following table contrasts the mortality in twenty-eight English cities or towns in 1885 with their average mortality during the preceding ten years, 1875-84.[2]

Cities and Boroughs.	Population (estimated to middle of 1885.)	Persons to an Acre.	Average death rate per thousand, 1875-84.	Death rate in 1885.
London	4,083,928	54·2	21·8	19·7
Brighton	114,672	45·6	19·9	17·1
Portsmouth	134,659	31·2	19·7	19·7
Norwich	91,215	12·2	21·8	20·3
Plymouth	76,045	51·8	22·2	22·3
Bristol	218,169	47·1	21·3	19·7
Wolverhampton .	79,185	23·3	23·0	20·2
Birmingham	427,769	50·9	22·5	19·3
Leicester	136,147	42·5	22·8	19·8
Nottingham	211,424	21·2	22·5	19·9
Derby [3]	89,691	26·0	18·4	18·1
Birkenhead [3]	93,093	24·2	19·9	19·5
Liverpool	579,724	111·3	27·0	23·8
Bolton [3]	110,085	45·8	22·9	20·8
Manchester	337,342	78·6	28·0	26·5
Salford	204,075	39·5	25·8	21·1
Oldham	126,390	26·7	24·8	22·0
Blackburn [3]	112,574	16·1	24·6	21·8
Preston [3]	100,406	27·0	26·8	27·1
Huddersfield [3] ..	87,327	8·3	21·1	20·1
Halifax [3]	77,378	20·5	21·3	19·7
Bradford	214,431	19·9	22·6	17·7
Leeds	333,139	15·4	23·8	19·9
Sheffield	305,716	15·6	23·5	20·7
Hull	186,292	23·5	23·2	17·2
Sunderland	125,327	41·3	23·5	23·8
Newcastle	153,209	28·5	23·8	26·1
Cardiff [3]	97,034	13·2	21·5	25·7

[1] *Ante*, pp. 433-4; see also App. B.
[2] Compiled from the Registrar-General's Annual Summary for 1885, pp. 12, 16.

[3] As the death rates prior to 1882 are not available for these towns, the mean rate for the three years 1882-4 is here given.

In an early portion of this work reference was made to the checks upon local expenditure imposed by Parliament in local Acts.[1] Besides the strict appropriation of money powers to specific objects, and the proof of estimates for such objects required by Committees, the consent of the Local Government

Board is sometimes necessary before money can be borrowed under local Acts, and is always necessary in the exercise of powers given to local authorities for sanitary or other objects by public Acts. Rural sanitary authorities obtain this sanction chiefly for works of sewerage, sewage disposal and water supply. Urban sanitary authorities borrow money with the same sanction for more numerous purposes, among which are the construction, widening, paving, flagging and channelling of streets, the erection of offices, public baths and wash-houses, bridges, gas-works, public libraries, markets, hospitals, mortuaries, sea defences, the provision of pleasure-grounds, cemeteries, slaughter-houses, ferry boats, steam road-rollers, fire-engines and appliances, manure depôts, and works for the removal of night-soil and destruction of refuse.[2]

The Local Government Board require specific details as to the manner in which it is proposed to expend loans, and are careful in satisfying themselves, first, that the works they are asked to sanction are expedient; and, secondly, that the estimates are not excessive.[3] Thus a check is imposed in the joint interests of ratepayers and of lenders, for both must be benefited by guarantees that money shall not be spent at all unless it is wanted, and that, when borrowed, it shall be

spent thriftily. With a view to obtain information on these points, and afford all persons interested an opportunity of being heard, the Local Government Board, on receiving applications from sanitary authorities for leave to borrow, cause a local inquiry to be held by one of their engineering inspectors, after public notice in the district.[4] Before sanc-

---

[1] Vol. I. p. 266.

[2] Report of Local Government Board for 1884-5, p. 59.

[3] Ib.

[4] In the year 1884, there were 453 local inquiries by officers of the Board, the majority relating to applications for leave to borrow money under the

tioning such loans, the Board further require information as to the arrangements made by sanitary authorities for the due discharge of their debts, if any, under the Sanitary Acts and Public Health Act, 1875. Powers of borrowing conferred by these enactments are subject to certain conditions, one of the most important of which is that annual provision shall be made for repaying each loan within a prescribed term, either by instalments or by means of a sinking fund. In some cases the Board have found these conditions disregarded, and their interference has brought about a more strict compliance by local authorities with their statutory obligations.[1]

Compulsory provision for repayment of loans.

With this explanation of the control exercised by the responsible department, we may now show to what extent local authorities have raised money in order to perform the sanitary and other duties imposed upon them by Parliament. The loans sanctioned by the General Board of Health under the Public Health Act, 1848, up to September 1, 1858, when the first Local Government Act came into force, were only three millions. Under the latter Act, and the Sewage Utilization Act, 1865, the Home Secretary, up to August, 1871, sanctioned loans amounting to 7,363,000*l.* Since the Local Government Board were constituted in 1871, they have allowed loans, up to the end of 1884, amounting to more than thirty-one millions and a half, of which no less than 26,600,000*l.* has been spent upon sanitary improvements in urban districts.[2] From 1848, therefore, up to January 1, 1885, nearly forty-two millions sterling have been spent by local authorities, under departmental sanction, chiefly for sanitary improvements in their respective districts.

Amount of loans to local authorities sanctioned by departments.

A much larger amount has been borrowed by governing

Borrowing powers not

Public Health Act, 1875, the Public Health (Interments) Acts, 1879, the Public Libraries Acts, the Baths and Wash-houses Acts, or under Local Acts. (Report for 1884-5, p. 87.)

[1] Ib., p. 59.

[2] Ib., pp. 55-6. Sanitary improvements in rural districts during 1871-84 absorbed 2,029,000*l.* of these loans. Between 1875-84 the loans sanctioned under the Artizans and Labourers' Dwellings Act, 1875, were 2,083,000*l.*; and to joint boards, 891,000*l.* for sewerage and sewage disposal, provision of hospitals, &c.

subject to departmental sanction.

bodies during the same period under local Acts without departmental sanction. In the thirteen years covering 1872—84, little more than one-third of this period, the specific loans allowed by local Acts, not subject to control by the Local Government Board, amounted to 40,515,000*l.* This amount, however, does not include numerous cases in which borrowing powers for unascertained amounts have been given by Parliament, when specific estimates could not be supplied.[1] Among the chief objects included in these local Acts have been the purchase of gas and water undertakings by local authorities, street improvements, sewers, municipal buildings, markets and abattoirs, and docks.[2] During each Session these and other private Bills promoted by local authorities are examined by the Local Government Board, whose reports are submitted for the information of Committees. Attention is thus effectually called in Parliament to any provisions which in the view of this department injuriously affect public interests.

Returns by local bodies under Local Loans Act, 1875.

Repayment of corporation stock.

Public Works Loans Acts, 1875-83.

Another valuable security to ratepayers and creditors is the duty assigned to the Local Government Board of examining into repayments of loans by local authorities,[3] who are required to make annual returns to the Board for this purpose. In cases in which municipal corporations issue consolidated stock, these returns relate to funds set aside by them to pay dividends on the stock and its ultimate redemption. Upon the Board's recommendation the Public Works Loan Commissioners make advances at a reduced rate of interest to urban and rural sanitary authorities[4] for sanitary works of primary importance, such as water supply, sewerage and sewage disposal, and hospitals.[5] Under provisions of the Public Works Loans Acts,[6] the Local

---

[1] Report of Local Government Board for 1884-5, p. 60.

[2] As in Bristol Dock Act (Purchase by Corporation), 1884, King's Lynn Dock Act (Subscription by Corporation), 1884.

[3] 38 & 39 Vict. c. 83, s. 16.

[4] Public Health Act, 1875, s. 243.

[5] Report of Local Government Board, 1884-5, p. 63.

[6] 38 & 39 Vict. c. 89, and subsequent Acts down to 1883 (46 & 47 Vict. c. 42).

Government Board also investigate all payments made by local authorities out of loans advanced by the Public Works Loan Commissioners on the security of rates, and may enforce the proper application of these loans.[1]

As Parliament, before 1875, had imposed many duties upon local authorities, and especially by the Public Health Act of that year, it was thought right to aid them in raising money for approved objects. In the same Session, therefore, facilities were granted to them for raising loans by means of debentures, debenture stock, and annuity certificates.[2] But the success of the Metropolitan Board, in 1869, in raising money by a direct appeal to capitalists, encouraged local authorities in other parts of the kingdom to try the same experiment. By this time investors had greater experience of the security offered to them by local rates: and a scarcity of equally solid investments led to the rapid popularity of the new municipal stocks. First in this field were the Corporations of Birmingham,[3] Liverpool, and Nottingham, in 1880. In the following Session similar Acts were obtained by Birkenhead, Hull, the Lancashire County Justices, Reading, Stalybridge, and Swansea. In 1882, Blackburn, Bolton, Derby, the Essex County Justices, Halifax, Huddersfield, Macclesfield, Newcastle, Rotherham, Tynemouth, and Wolverhampton, were added to the list; in 1883, Burnley, Glasgow, Heywood, Longton, Portsmouth, Preston, and Sheffield; in 1884, Croydon, Leicester, and Rochdale; and in 1885, Eastbourne, Rathmines and Rathgar (suburban townships of Dublin), Southampton, Southport, Sunderland, and Worcester. Thirty-six local authorities, therefore, are now able to exercise their statutory borrowing powers by the

Local Loans Act, 1875.

Corporation stocks.

---

[1] 38 & 39 Vict. c. 89, s. 36; 41 & 42 Vict. c. 18, s. 4.

[2] 38 & 39 Vict. c. 83. See also 43 & 44 Vict. c. 20, ss. 53, 55; 44 & 45 Vict. c. 12, ss. 45-6, as to stamp duty; and Amendment Act of 1885 (48 & 49 Vict. c. 30), as to discharge of loans by sinking funds.

[3] Birmingham obtained its powers under Provisional Order, confirmed by 43 & 44 Vict. c. 178, but this example has not been followed.

creation and issue of redeemable or irredeemable stock, charged indifferently upon their whole revenues.

Redemption, and returns to Local Government Board.

Each special Act by which these powers are conferred necessarily varies according to local circumstances in the borough or district concerned. Periods for redemption also vary according to the nature of the works to be paid for.[1] Stringent powers are given to the Local Government Board. An annual return must be made to them, giving an abstract of accounts relating to the stock and the fund for paying interest and principal; and in case of wilful default not only a Corporation but their town clerk are liable to fines. On failure to comply with any requisition relating to payment, application, or investment, the Local Government Board may enforce an order by mandamus.[2]

Revenue of local authorities.

It will now be of interest to show the existing revenue of local authorities. Including loans, this revenue in England and Wales amounted in 1883-4 to 51,121,000l.; in 1877-8 it was 50,507,000l.[3] These figures refer to poor-law and

---

[1] S. O. 173 A. of House of Commons, passed in 1882, provides that the maximum limit allowed for repayment shall be sixty years.

[2] A general Act has been suggested regulating the issue of corporation stock (Burdett's Official Intelligence, Stock Exchange, 1886, p. 53) on the model of the Colonial Stock Act, 1877, which governs the issue of inscribed stock by colonies. Such a statute would diminish the length of these private Acts but would not supersede them. Meanwhile, uniformity is secured in practice by the model Bill published every year by the House of Lords under the direction of its Chairman of Committees. This Bill contains clauses of general application which must be adopted by local authorities asking for these powers.

[3] Treasury subventions, included in these receipts, amounted to 2,488,000l. These grants were made—to poor law authorities, 671,000l. for salaries of medical officers and other medical expenses, salaries of teachers, maintenance of pauper lunatics in asylums, and registrars of births and deaths; to county authorities, 591,000l. for pay and clothing of police, lunatic paupers chargeable to counties, criminal prosecutions, conveyance and maintenance of prisoners, and judges' lodgings; to Municipal Corporations, 431,000l. for the same purposes, excepting judges' lodgings; to urban sanitary authorities, 93,600l., for salaries of medical officers of health, inspectors of nuisances and main roads; to rural and port sanitary authorities, 45,500l., for salaries of medical officers of health and inspectors of nuisances; to the Metro-

county authorities, school boards, highway boards, and the metropolis. Excluding the metropolis, and limiting our view to Municipal Corporations, Town Councils acting as urban sanitary authorities, urban sanitary authorities other than Town Councils, joint boards, rural and port sanitary authorities and burial boards, we find their receipts in 1883-4 were 20,474,317*l.*, which includes 3,896,000*l.* for loans, 8,500,000*l.* for rates, and 5,384,000*l.* for water and gas supply.[1] Between 1875 and 1883, local rates had risen 27·5 per cent., an increase chiefly due to increased rates levied by urban sanitary authorities, school boards, the metropolitan vestries, and Board of Works. Between the years 1874 and 1883, local rates levied in the metropolis show an increase of 2,030,000*l.*, or 52 per cent.; those levied in urban districts outside the metropolis, 2,276,000*l.*, or 49·3 per cent.[2]

Allowing for repayments by sinking funds or other means, the amount of outstanding loans owing by all descriptions of local authorities at the end of the year 1883-4 was 164,879,000*l.* In 1875 it was only 92,820,000*l.* During the nine years 1875-83 the loans raised were 116,664,000*l.*;[3] the increase of debt was 66,322,000*l.*, or 71·5 per cent., while

Debt of local authorities.

politan Board, 10,000*l.* towards the fire brigade; to the Metropolitan Police Commissioners, 615,000*l.*, for salaries of the Commissioner, Receiver, and two Assistant Commissioners, and a contribution towards police rates calculated on the rental assessed; and to highway authorities in rural districts, 124,000*l.* for main roads. The grants to school boards are not reckoned in this account.

[1] Commons' Paper 161 of 1886, p. 10.

[2] Report of Local Government Board for 1884-5, p. 136. This increased revenue from rates is no doubt generally due to increased burdens imposed, but is also ex-

plained by an increased rateable value of property. In 1873 the rateable value of property assessed to poor's rate in England and Wales was 112,392,000*l.*; in 1883, it was 143,222,000*l.*, an increase of 27·4 per cent. How greatly railways have swollen the revenue of local authorities may be gathered from a recent statement that during the fourteen years 1871-84, a sum of nearly twenty millions was paid by railway companies in local and parochial rates. (Mr. Grierson, General Manager of Great Western Railway; *The Times*, May 6, 1886.)

[3] What proportion of this sum went in paying off and renewing old loans does not appear.

in the same period our national debt decreased by 14,490,000*l.*[1]
During the two years 1883-4, however, the amount of loans
raised fell off considerably, and there is good ground for the
belief that, in provincial boroughs and urban sanitary districts, the necessity for borrowing will continue to diminish.
In 1883-4, the outstanding loans debited to this class of local
authorities outside London was 83,533,000*l.*, rather more
than half the total of local loans in England and Wales,
including the metropolis.[2]

Checks upon
governing
bodies in
promoting or
opposing
Bills.

    Alarm is often expressed at this rapid increase of local
liabilities.　There is no good reason, however, to apprehend
that, with the departmental supervision which has been
explained, and the strict control exercised by Parliament
over local Bills, expenditure and loans by municipal and
other authorities are now sanctioned for inadequate objects.

Municipal
Corporations
(Borough
Funds) Act.

On the contrary, in each case pressing necessity must be
proved before Committees, and since 1872 governing bodies
have been unable to apply the funds at their disposal, either
in promoting or opposing Bills, without express approval
by owners and ratepayers, to be signified at a public meeting
convened for this purpose.[3]　Ratepayers are not usually
favourable to unremunerative or unnecessary outlay likely to
add to existing burdens.　Parliament at the same time
enacted that no expense shall be incurred by governing
bodies in promoting or opposing Bills without ample notice

[1] Local Government Board Report,
1883-4, pp. 138-9.　As might be expected, increased indebtedness goes
hand in hand with increased rates.
Between 1877 and 1883 the loans of
urban sanitary authorities had risen
75·9 per cent.; those of the Metropolitan Board (excluding advances
to minor authorities), 55·6 per cent.;
those of school boards nearly 135
per cent.　The aggregate increase
in the outstanding loans of these
authorities during the six years was

more than 85 per cent. of the total
increase in local indebtedness.

[2] See Commons' Return relating to
Local Taxes (161 of 1886), p. 11.　In
the 83,533,000*l.* are included the
loans of Municipal Corporations,
Town Councils acting as urban sanitary authorities, urban sanitary authorities other than Town Councils,
joint boards, rural and port sanitary
authorities, and burial boards.

[3] 35 & 36 Vict. c. 91, s. 4.　*Post*,
pp. 546 *et seq.*

to each member, an absolute majority of their whole number, and a confirmation of this vote by a similar majority at a second meeting after the Bill has been lodged. Lastly, the approval of the Local Government Board, or the Home Secretary, must be obtained, and if they are not satisfied they may order a local inquiry upon the application of any rate-payer.[1]

So far as local expenditure depends upon the promotion of private Bills, these safeguards seem to be ample. But other conditions should be taken into account. One is the natural increment in rateable value, which in urban districts far exceeds the increase already noted throughout England and Wales.[2] Rates continued upon their present footing must therefore yield, on an average of years, a growing revenue.

Annual increment in rateable value.

Again, the operation of sinking funds, or other machinery for repayment of loans, must always be kept in view. This repayment proceeds very rapidly, and of late years Parliament has taken care to hasten it. A Standing Order of the House of Commons, passed in 1882, lays down the rule that sixty years shall be the outside term allowed for extinction of loans.[3] This period, however, is usually given only when money is borrowed for objects of permanent utility, such

Operation of Sinking Funds, &c.

---

[1] Ib., ss. 5, 7. Before giving their consent the Local Government Board require a written statement of the grounds of a proposed promotion or opposition, and a statutory declaration proving compliance with the conditions of the Act of 1872.

[2] The valuation of 1883 showed a decrease in rateable value in thirteen counties (Bucks, Somerset, Oxford, Cambridge, York, North and East Riding, Salop, Hereford, Wilts, Norfolk, Rutland, Suffolk and Huntingdon), due to the depreciated rental of agricultural land. (Local Government Board, Rep. 1844-5,

p. 140.)

[3] In 1869 the Corporation of Sligo were allowed 100 years to pay off a loan for waterworks and other purposes; but the Lords' Committee in granting this term said it was a very exceptional case. (32 & 33 Vict. c. 147, s. 170.) Since 1882, the Corporations of Stockton and Middlesbrough were allowed ninety years to repay loans for works to prevent pollution in the river Tees. (Stockton and Middlesbrough Waterworks Act, 47 & 48 Vict. c. 203.) *Post*, pp. 537-8.

as the purchase of gas[1] or water undertakings,[2] when benefit will clearly accrue to more than one generation of ratepayers. Even in cases of permanent works, such as sewerage and street improvements, the maximum term allowed, in 1884, was only forty years.[3] For repaying the costs of completing a town-hall, with sessions courts and police courts, thirty years were considered sufficient; for furnishing these municipal buildings, seven years.[4] Twenty years are usually allowed for paying off costs of private Acts. Under this system local authorities are compelled to set aside in each year large sums towards extinguishing loans. In 1882-3, out of an expenditure of 43,508,000*l.*,[5] they applied 10,456,000*l.*, or nearly a fourth part, towards interest and repayment of principal.[6] This sum is two millions and a-half more than the total loans for 1883-4; and it appears that, during the eight years ending 1882-3, the average annual amortisation of debt amounted to about 4,692,000*l.*[7]

The growth of population, especially in urban districts, and new demands of civilization, must always render necessary from time to time new expenditure by governing bodies upon sewerage and other works for the health and convenience of each community. But in most large towns the heaviest works of this nature, the great trunk sewers and their subsidiary drains, have now been completed,[8] and the

Reproductive outlay by governing bodies.

outlay upon them is in course of repayment. In recent years a very large proportion of the annual loans raised by local authorities has been for reproductive undertakings, such as tramways, but chiefly for gas and waterworks, which

---

[1] Coventry Corporation (Gas Purchase) Act, 1884.

[2] Northampton, Windsor, and Kingston - upon - Hull Corporations Water Acts, 1884.

[3] Chester Improvement, York Extension and Improvement, and Ventnor Local Board Acts, 1884.

[4] Birkenhead Act, 1884.

[5] Other than the expenditure out of loans.

[6] Report of Local Government Board for 1884-5, p. 132; App. 233.

[7] Com. Return, 290, Session 1885.

[8] In some large towns, however, the pail and midden systems have been adopted; in others, one system of sewerage is being replaced by another, to prevent a continued pollution of streams.

have been transferred to them by Parliament from private hands with general approval. This large outlay will not recur. In another part of this book it is shown that, up to 1883, between forty-one and forty-two millions have been borrowed by local authorities for these three objects.[1] Other like purposes are markets, cemeteries,[2] and docks owned by Municipal Corporations, or in which they are shareholders under statutory powers. From their gas supply, in 1883, local authorities derived an income of 3,217,000*l.*; from water, 1,932,000*l.*[3] As a rule, besides conferring many indirect advantages, both undertakings, especially the supply of gas, are remunerative; they tend to reduce public burdens by the surplus income they yield, and represent valuable properties, entitled to rank as available assets against local debt, to an amount far exceeding their prime cost.

Assets of local authorities.

Before criticising in a hostile sense the growth of local rates and local indebtedness, we must also remember how considerably they have been swollen under the influence of modern legislation. Since the first Public Health Act, in 1848, Parliament, as we have seen, in a long series of measures has enlarged the powers of local authorities, has invited them to spend money in exercising these powers, and sometimes has insisted that they should spend it. By indignant reports from Committees and Commissions, by debates

Influence of public legislation upon local debt.

---

[1] Vol. I., p. 263. In 1884, out of loans amounting to 3,059,800*l.* to be raised by local authorities under private Acts, 1,077,500*l.* was for waterworks, 218,000*l.* for gasworks, and 1,075,000*l.* for purchase of docks, or subscriptions towards them—altogether 2,370,500*l.*

[2] At p. 51, Mr. Burdett (Official Intelligence, Stock Exchange, 1886), summarises the accounts of forty-four municipal corporations, which, in 1885, had spent 12,092,000*l.* on gas, 25,439,000*l.* on water, 5,300,000*l.* on markets, fairs, and ferries, and 745,000*l.* on cemeteries; a total of 43,578,000*l.* Upon gas Birmingham made a profit of 44,934*l.*; Manchester, 43,579*l.*; Nottingham, 21,485*l.*; Bradford, 19,101*l.*; Glasgow, 16,863*l.* Eighteen Corporations derived profits from the supply of water, Glasgow heading the list with 36,329*l.* Thirteen Corporations show an apparent loss from this source. Markets and fairs generally prove remunerative; cemeteries are generally unprofitable under corporate management.

[3] Report of Local Government Board for 1884-5, App. 233.

in both Houses, by pressure from enlightened public opinion, governing bodies were urged to drain, cleanse, and purify · their respective districts; abundant facilities were offered to them in public statutes for raising the necessary funds; and they were, and indeed still are, sometimes reproached for not more readily availing themselves of these facilities. To guard against possible supineness, a statutory obligation was imposed upon them to carry out sanitary improvements, and a public department was charged with the duty of enforcing it if they made default. Even now hardly a year passes without complaints from ratepayers to the Local Government Board of insufficient water supply or defective drainage. In these cases the Board have been armed by Parliament with means[1] for constraining local bodies to do what is needful, and, as a last resort, may go to the High Court of Justice for a mandamus requiring compliance with their order.[2] If adequate cause cannot be shown to the contrary, a local authority must then execute the necessary works, and raise money for that purpose.

Defaulting authorities.

Nor has Parliament been content with enforcing measures intended to promote health by means of efficient sewerage. It expects governing bodies to prevent the pollution of rivers, to utilise sewage, to cleanse, pave, and light streets, and maintain an efficient police, to clear unhealthy areas, and replace insanitary dwellings by suitable abodes for artisans and labourers, to remove house-refuse, open out and improve thoroughfares, and in some cases provide wholesome water, along with markets, baths and wash-houses, mortuaries, cemeteries, and even public libraries, public museums, and public parks. It is hardly fair or consistent first to urge, or even force, upon local authorities, by general legislation, new duties and new expenditure, and then

New duties devolving on governing bodies.

[1] Public Health Act, 1875, s. 299. By s. 141, and by the Public Health (Interments) Act, 1879, the Board can also require a local authority to provide a cemetery.

[2] See case of Cheshunt Local Board, in Local Government Board Report for 1884-5, pp. 79-83, where proceedings against other defaulting authorities are mentioned.

complain of the inevitable result in increased rates and debt.

Most well-wishers to municipal institutions will regret the party spirit which of late has generally ruled in local elections. During the latter part of Queen Victoria's reign, local self-government has been so extended by public, but especially by private, legislation, that there is more need than ever that the best men should take part in it, irrespective of party.[1] But will the best men long undergo the trouble, turmoil, and cost of frequent party contests from a simple wish to serve their town in offices which gratify only a moderate ambition, though they involve no small sacrifice of time and convenience? Municipal administration and finance lie outside the domain of politics; and there is ground for alarm lest party spirit should degrade these functions, and lower the status of men willing to undertake them under party conditions. Here, then, is another reason why local legislation should remain subject to Imperial control, and to searching and public inquiry before Committees in Parliament, as a guarantee against the jobbery and extravagances which have arisen under local and party rule in kindred institutions elsewhere, and for which there are fresh temptations and opportunities now that so many local authorities have become large traders.

Party spirit in local elections.

In many aspects local government involves that branch of private legislation which is of by far the greatest moment to the nation. Local laws and administration, indeed, concern a community more directly and intimately than most Imperial measures. There is ground, therefore, for signal satisfaction when we find what rapid, and at the same time solid, progress has been made in local government throughout the kingdom. Local self-government is essentially an English institution. But we have seen it degenerate in our own

Municipal administration substantially pure in Great Britain.

---

[1] "The system of self-government, of which the English nation is so justly proud, can hardly be applied with success to any subject, unless the governing bodies comprise a fair proportion of enlightened and well-informed minds." (Royal Sanitary Commission, 1871; Rep., p. 71.)

stock, and become a by-word for corruption, open, shameless, and apparently incurable.[1]   Happily, a wide basis of election in British municipalities has hitherto brought with it no such scandals.   On the contrary, we have seen, in a retrospect of less than forty years, the growth of a municipal administration not only more vigorous and intelligent, but much more honest than that which marked an era of close corporations and restricted constituencies.   When that era closed, in 1835, there still remained among governing bodies a parsimony and prejudice which delayed sanitary and other essential improvements; and it became necessary for Parliament to apply a strong stimulus, and even provide machinery for compelling some of these authorities to perform an obvious duty.   We have shown, in part, how different is the view now taken by governing bodies, and how much they have done, according to their means, for public health and comfort in the metropolis, and in other large communities.

Increased intelligence and spirit among local bodies.

That there are some laggards, and that much sanitary work yet remains everywhere undone, has been more than once admitted; but a striking contrast may be drawn between the inefficiency and ignorance of 1840 and that knowledge of shortcomings and general willingness to amend them

---

[1] "While from 1860 to 1880 the value of property in New York City increased from $576,631,700 to $1,098,387,775, an increase of 100 per cent., the municipal expenses increased from $9,758,507 to $33,254,779, an increase of 340 per cent.; the per capita tax increased from $11.17 to $27.71; the per capita cost of public instruction increased from $11 to $22; that of charities from $20 to $33; and the per capita cost of governing this city is, excepting war debt, over ten times the per capita cost of the government of the United States.   It is, therefore, not surprising that the Council for Municipal Reform have estimated that $160,000,000 have been stolen and wasted in the expenditures of the city during the last twenty years." (Article on the Government of New York; *Harper's Weekly*, January 12, 1884.)   In 1881 a Senate Committee, appointed to investigate the condition of the municipal government of New York, reported:—" It is badly regulated, badly administered, exorbitantly and inexcusably expensive, and in its various parts substantially irresponsible . . . . The city offices are filled with adherents of political organizations, who make it their primary duty to attend to the interests of their political masters."

which now prevail. Another point to be noted is that new duties and responsibilities have been undertaken by local authorities, with infinite advantage to their constituents. By sanctioning the transfer to these bodies of so many gas and water undertakings, Parliament has done something to redeem its error in not providing for such a transfer upon equitable terms in the original Acts creating these monopolies. It must, however, be remembered in fairness that, although Parliament was advised to make this provision by one of its own Committees,[1] it was seldom, if ever, asked to do so by local authorities themselves, who were too timid to try costly experiments, and would not, indeed, have been allowed to try any, for they had not then acquired public confidence by efficient and conscientious administration. It might have been premature, therefore, in a majority of instances, to make municipalities traders on a large scale. This system has been of gradual growth in Parliament, founded, like many Imperial measures, upon continued examples of successful working under private Acts, rather than upon what seemed in 1845-6 only a plausible theory. Such a policy caused an enormous increase of expense when municipalities afterwards came to acquire gas and water undertakings. Its advantages were that it was no leap in the dark, and, though slow, was sure. Any risks had been run by private speculators, who were well entitled to a substantial gain upon their ventures, though not to a perpetual monopoly.

Beneficial control of gas and water supply.

Policy of Parliament on this question.

We have seen how every step in this successful enlargement of municipal functions has been taken under strict supervision by Parliament. With a local debt so enormous, and sixty or seventy millions of corporate stock floated by virtue of special Acts, it seems now more than ever necessary, on financial grounds alone, that this close supervision should not be relaxed. Elsewhere reasons have been given for asserting that these securities would not so readily have

Danger of surrendering Imperial control.

---

[1] By Mr. Hume's Committee on Private Bills in 1846, adopting recommendations of Royal Commission of 1845; *ante*, Vol. I., p. 253.

obtained the confidence of investors but for their conviction
"that Parliament, by its control of private legislation, could
and would prevent any reckless outlay of municipal funds,
and ensure, as far as statutory provisions can do so, the
specific application, for legitimate purposes, of all moneys
borrowed."[1] It is very doubtful whether, if Parliament gave
over this control to County Boards or other tribunals, either
with or without ostensible guarantees, investors would feel
equal confidence in the grant of new powers to local authorities, or in the proper appropriation of any money they
might raise; and if capitalists were distrustful, economy in
procedure, if any, would be dearly bought by new difficulties of borrowing and by the increased interest which
would be expected from a more doubtful security.

[1] *Ante*, Vol. I., pp. 266, 266*.

CHAPTER XV.

LOCAL AUTHORITIES (*concluded*): CONSOLIDATION ACTS, 1845-7:
MUNICIPAL LAW, OFTEN INTRICATE AND CONFLICTING:
FREQUENT VARIATION FROM GENERAL LAW: ATTEMPT TO
BRING THEM INTO GREATER HARMONY: CONSOLIDATION OF
LOCAL ACTS: COMMONS' COMMITTEES ON POLICE AND SANI-
TARY REGULATIONS, 1882-6: BOROUGH FUNDS ACT, 1872:
APPLICATION OF GAS AND WATER REVENUE: METROPO-
LITAN WATER ACTS, 1886—SINKING FUND IN INTEREST
OF COMMUNITY: STREET IMPROVEMENTS—DISPOSAL OF
SUPERFLUOUS LAND: EXEMPTIONS FROM LOCAL RATING:
NUMBER OF LOCAL AUTHORITIES.

ELEVEN Consolidation Acts, passed in 1845-7, apply to private companies as well as to local authorities, and may be conveniently treated under the same head. *(margin: Consolidation Acts.)*

A consolidation statute, the first of its kind, passed in 1801,[1] recites that, "in order to diminish the expense attending the passing of Acts of Inclosure, it is expedient that certain clauses usually contained in such Acts should be comprised in one law." This precedent, however, appears to have been forgotten, for when the promotion of other private under-takings under statute became frequent, a question revived, which led to much difference of opinion, and is still some-times debated: Should a private Act be self-contained or speak by reference? Before the year 1845 each private Act comprised within itself all provisions governing the particular undertaking. This system had some manifest advantages. Each Act, though lengthy, was an intelligible whole: it was *(margin: First Consolidation Act, 1801 (Inclosure). Private legislation before the Consolidation Acts, 1845.)*

---

[1] 41 Geo. III. c. 109.

unnecessary to go outside its provisions to some general statute in order to find out the law regulating each community or undertaking. On the other hand, though the common form clauses, and those inserted in compliance with Standing Orders by Parliament, purported to be in substance alike, no adequate means existed for ensuring absolute uniformity in these provisions, and the result was, that local authorities and companies, which ought to have been subject to the same rules, sometimes escaped from restrictions which were essential in public interests.

Conflict of statutes.

These varied provisions led to a considerable increase of litigation; and as sections relating to similar objects often differed in different Acts, a decision upon one Act seldom determined the proper construction of any other. Sometimes special provisions were inserted relating to the devolution of property and other matters, already provided for by the common law, which was abrogated for no sufficient reason; and the new remedies and incidents affecting real estate were often imperfect, again causing frequent litigation. These inconveniences arose to a large extent upon railway Acts, but also applied to Improvement Bills promoted by municipal corporations and other local bodies.[1]

Commons' Committee, 1838.

It was obviously necessary to render private bill legislation more uniform, and with this object a Committee of the House of Commons on Private Business, in the year 1838, suggested that drafts of general bills should be prepared, which, if sanctioned by Parliament, might be incorporated by reference in each private Act, thus relieving promoters from an obligation to adopt Standing Order clauses, and securing, beyond possibility of mistake, that companies incorporated by statute for the same class of objects should be subject to the same general code. Another incidental advantage contemplated was to free Committees from a considerable burden of work as well as from a risk of overlooking new

---

[1] Second Report of House of Commons' Committee on Private Business (1839); evidence of Mr. John Tyrrell, conveyancer.

and objectionable provisions, owing to the extreme length of most bills. Recognising the necessity of these general Acts, the Treasury, prompted by Mr. Poulett Thompson, who, as President of the Board of Trade, had presided over the Committee of 1838, employed two draftsmen to prepare the necessary measures.[1] The result was a series of bills containing provisions common to enclosures, railways, canals, docks, harbours, bridges, cemeteries, town improvements, police and gas and water works. These common clauses, essential to good government in every urban community, and the proper working of every newly-incorporated company, instead of being considered in turn by each Committee upon each Bill of the same class, were to be enacted by Parliament in an authoritative form, after careful consideration; and Committees, no longer responsible for seeing that bills contained every usual provision, expressed in proper form, would be able to give their undivided attention to the special circumstances of each measure.

Experimental Bills drafted.

Some communications which passed between the Committee of 1839 and Lord Shaftesbury, then Chairman of Committees in the House of Lords, were not encouraging. The Government, however, were induced to take up this work by an earnest recommendation from the Committee, and Mr. Tyrrell, a conveyancer and draftsman of great experience, who had served upon the Real Property Commission, was engaged by the Board of Trade to revise the Consolidation Bills then prepared. Six years, however, passed before they became law. In 1845, Parliament adopted three of these measures. Their object sufficiently appears in a preamble to the Companies Clauses Consolidation Act,[2] first of the series, which recites that "it is expedient to comprise in one general Act sundry provisions relating to the

Legislation of 1845.

Companies Clauses Act.

---

[1] Mr. Symonds, with Mr. Booth, who at this time prepared the breviates, and was afterwards Speaker's Counsel, were the draftsmen employed. See Appendix to Second Report of Commons' Committee on Private Business (1839), p. 23 *et seq.*

[2] 8 Vict. c. 16.

constitution and management of joint stock companies, usually introduced into Acts of Parliament authorizing the execution of undertakings of a public nature by such companies, and that as well for the purpose of avoiding the necessity of repeating such provisions in each of the several Acts relating to such undertakings as for ensuring greater uniformity in the provisions themselves." This Act provides an elaborate machinery chiefly governing the relations of shareholders *inter se*,[1] and, unless its provisions are expressly varied or excepted by the special Act, it applies to every joint stock company incorporated by Parliament to carry on any undertaking. In the same Session an Act containing a similar code was passed for Scotland, with such changes in its machinery as were made necessary by differences between Scotch and English law.

Lands Clauses Acts. In 1845, also, another statute was passed[2] " for consolidating in one Act certain provisions usually inserted in Acts authorizing the taking of lands for undertakings of a public nature." Where public bodies or private promoters propose to construct works, there are few cases in which they can obtain possession of all the necessary land by agreement. They must, therefore, ask Parliament for powers to acquire **Common form clauses.** such land by compulsory process. In all these cases methods of procedure and of assessing compensation should obviously agree, and not be left for settlement by common form clauses in each Bill. These clauses purported to be substantially the same, but sometimes, through accident or intention, small differences were introduced which caused endless disputes, and inflicted considerable hardship on owners who were dispossessed. That litigation has been ended by the Lands Clauses Act, cannot, unfortunately, be said. Probably no modern statute has brought so much grist to the legal mill. It has called into existence almost a literature of its own in treatises and commentaries written upon its provisions, and in every

---

[1] *Ante*, Vol. I. p. 103.   [2] 8 Vict. c. 18.

populous district it has enriched a numerous band of surveyors, land-valuers, and arbitrators.

This very important statute[1] refers, first, to purchases by promoters of lands which their special Act has authorized them to take by agreement. Without express power, corporations and many individuals would be unable to convey some land required by promoters. The Act, therefore, provides that parties under disability may lawfully sell and convey. But it is any purchase and taking of lands "otherwise than by agreement," as the Act mildly puts it, which necessitates its fighting clauses. Promoters cannot exercise compulsory powers until their whole capital is subscribed.[2] Disputes as to compensation are settled by two justices if the amount claimed does not exceed 50*l*.; if above that amount, by arbitration or a jury, at the claimant's option.[3] Procedure in these cases is prescribed in elaborate provisions. If the claimant's interest is a limited one, the Act points out how to apply any compensation which may be awarded. Promoters may also be required to take the whole of "any house or other building or manufactory," if they touch any part of the premises.[4] Much litigation has

Lands taken by agreement or compulsorily.

[1] Amended by the Lands Clauses Consolidation Act Amendment Act, 1860, and the Lands Clauses Consolidation Act, 1869, which are usually cited together as the Lands Clauses Consolidation Acts. Some Consolidation Acts are not applicable to private undertakings authorized by statute, unless these Acts are incorporated with the special Act. But the Lands Clauses Consolidation Act, 1845, applies in its entirety (s. 1) to every undertaking thereafter authorized to take land, so far as its provisions are applicable, and unless they are expressly varied or excepted by the special Act.

[2] 8 Vict. c. 18, s. 16. In practice, however, this condition is not always insisted upon by landowners when they are otherwise satisfied as to a company's solvency.

[3] Ib., ss. 22, 23.

[4] Ib., s. 92. Long before the passing of the Lands Clauses Consolidation Act, it was a condition upon the grant of statutory powers to take lands, &c., that the whole property should be taken, though only a part might be required. See Act of 1795, empowering the Governors of Christ's Hospital to enlarge their site. (35 Geo. III. c. 104, s. 6.) This provision is, in fact, of still older date. It often entailed upon promoters an outlay out of all proportion to the objects sought, and greatly exceeding the estimates, rendering necessary applications to Parliament for fresh capital. (See recitals to 42 Geo.

Portions only of property to be taken in certain cases.

arisen upon the extent of property covered by these words in particular cases; and private Acts of modern date usually amend this general law, by allowing promoters to take portions only of houses, buildings, or manufactories, "provided that, in the judgment of the jury, arbitrators, or other authority who are determining the compensation, such portions can be severed without material injury to the rest of the property."[1]　Another modern innovation in private Acts is a power to promoters to agree for the purchase of easements only.[2]

Railways Clauses Consolidation Act, 1845.

A sufficient sketch has already appeared of the third Act passed in 1845, consolidating "provisions usually inserted in Acts authorizing the making of railways."[3]　This legislation for a time exhausted the energies of Parliament in its work of consolidation.　Nothing, however, had been done to abridge length or ensure uniformity in Bills of local authorities, unless they took land for any civic object.　In 1846, another Committee upon Private Business, of which Mr. Hume was chairman, drew attention to this want of uniformity, and, as one method of producing greater harmony in local legislation, suggested public general Acts upon the model of those of

Consolidation Acts of 1847.

1845.　This suggestion was adopted in 1847, when eight similar statutes became law.

Markets and Fairs Clauses Act, 1847.

First among these was a statute containing provisions usually inserted in Acts for constructing or regulating markets and fairs.　Each consolidation statute passed in

III. c. 49, enabling the Corporation of the City of London to raise further money for improving navigation in the Thames by a cut through the Isle of Dogs.)

[1] See, among many other instances, Chester Improvement Act, 1884, s. 92. Relief from the operation of s. 92 in the public Act seems to have been first allowed in what are known as the underpinning clauses of the Underground Railway Acts. These lines would have cost a prohibitory sum for construction if the promoters had been compelled to purchase all property interfered with. They were therefore freed from this obligation upon undertaking properly to strengthen the foundations of buildings.

[2] Chester Improvement Act, 1884, s. 88.

[3] *Ante*, Vol. I., pp. 102-4. 8 Vict. c. 20. This statute may be incorporated, either wholly or partially, by reference in the special Act.

1845, whether incorporated in special Acts or not, applies to all undertakings of the same nature subsequently authorized, but the markets and fairs statute, and its seven sister Acts, must be expressly incorporated, in whole or in part, to affect any undertaking. Local authorities, however, in certain cases obtain the advantages of parts of two of these statutes through their incorporation in the Public Health Act, 1875.[1] In the statute under notice, what was in 1847 supposed to be a complete code was furnished for use by local authorities, enabling them to prohibit sales elsewhere than in authorized markets, or in dwelling-houses and shops, to inflict penalties for the sale of unwholesome meat or provisions, to provide weighing machines, take stallages, rents and tolls, and make bye-laws. In modern practice, special Acts relating to markets are much fuller and contain more ample powers for regulating markets and keeping order there.

Next among the Consolidation Acts of 1847 applicable to local authorities was one embodying all provisions usually enacted when commissioners or trustees are constituted for improvement or other public purposes.[2] This statute prescribed the qualifications and disqualifications of all such public bodies, provided for their election by ratepayers, regulated their meetings and other proceedings, explained how accounts should be kept, contracts entered into, and mortgages and deeds executed by them, and laid down rules as to their liabilities, legal proceedings taken by or against them, the appointment, duties, and responsibility of their officials, and the making of bye-laws. *Commissioners Clauses Act.*

Another statute contained provisions usually inserted in Acts authorizing local authorities or private undertakers to make or improve harbours, docks and piers.[3] It declared that no works on the foreshore should be begun without authority from the Admiralty; that, before taking any harbour, dock or pier rates, the promoters should, under penalties for failure, *Harbours, Docks and Piers Clauses Act.*

---

[1] 38 & 39 Vict. c. 55, which incorporates parts of the Towns Police and Towns Improvement Clauses Acts.

[2] 10 Vict. c. 16.

[3] 10 Vict. c. 27.

"provide and always thereafter maintain in good repair an efficient and well-appointed lifeboat, a Manby's mortar, and a sufficient supply of Carte's rockets," or such other mortar or rockets as the Admiralty should specify, "with all necessary tackle, and a competent crew," and other workers to assist vessels in distress; that they should also keep a tide gauge and barometer, and communicate to the Admiralty daily results, with an account of wind and weather. This Act also empowered promoters to construct warehouses and other incidental works, provided for the levy and recovery of rates, the appointment of harbour, dock, and pier masters, and their duties, and regulated the discharge of vessels and removal of goods, and the placing of buoys, lighthouses, and beacons.

Towns Improvement Clauses Act. Provisions generally inserted in special Acts for paving, draining, cleansing, lighting, and improving towns were collected in another public statute.[1] Some portions, at least, of this statute are incorporated by reference in most local Improvement Acts, but such incorporation, as with other consolidation statutes of 1847, is optional. Chief among the provisions of this important public Act are those which relate to the mode of making and maintaining public sewers, the enforcement of house-drainage, and proper necessaries, street-paving, the naming of streets and numbering of houses, improving lines of streets and removing obstructions, dealing with ruinous or dangerous buildings, street cleansing, the prevention of nuisances, precautions to be taken in constructing houses so as to prevent or check fire, and ventilation. Cellars are forbidden as habitations, unless they fulfil certain conditions; lodging-houses are put under regulation and inspection; local authorities may contract for public lighting or water supply, put up public clocks, and, with the ratepayers' approval, provide slaughter-houses, baths, wash-houses, and pleasure-grounds. In cases where owners are bound to execute improvements, the Act points out how expenses may

---

[1] 10 & 11 Vict. c. 34.

be recovered, allows time for repayment, and regulates the levy of rates for sewers and other purposes.

Special Acts for making cemeteries had become numerous in 1847. They were promoted by local authorities as well as private companies, and certain provisions, common to all these undertakings, were therefore embodied in a Consolidation Act.[1] When a special Act prescribed no limit of distance, the public Act, if incorporated, allowed no part of a cemetery to be constructed nearer to any dwelling-house than two hundred yards without consent from the owner, lessee and occupier. Remedies were given for nuisances arising from the cemetery; for offences committed there penalties were imposed. Specific regulations were made as to burials in consecrated and unconsecrated ground, monumental inscriptions, and payments of fees to incumbents of parishes.

Cemeteries Clauses Act.

Last among the eight consolidation statutes of 1847 to be mentioned here[2] is the Towns Police Clauses Act,[3] which contains provisions usually found in special Acts for regulating the police of towns and populous districts. This is a statute of special interest to local authorities, but some of its sections are defective, and it is rarely incorporated except in parts. Among other matters of police, it relates to the appointment, powers, duties and privileges of constables, obstructions and nuisances in the streets,[4] fires, places of public resort, hackney carriages, and public bathing, and generally is meant to arm governing bodies with powers of keeping good order within their respective limits.

Towns Police Clauses Act.

The effect of three of these consolidation statutes alone, the Lands, Companies, and Railways Clauses Acts, when included by reference in an average railway bill, was to

Effect of consolidation statutes upon private Acts.

---

[1] 10 & 11 Vict. c. 65.

[2] The Gasworks Clauses Act (10 Vict. c. 15), and Waterworks Clauses Act (10 Vict. c. 17), have been treated *ante*, Vol. I., pp. 221, 250.

[3] 10 & 11 Vict. c. 89. As already stated, parts of this Act are incorporated in the Public Health Act, 1875, and therefore apply to all urban communities.

[4] Sect. 28 contains a long list of offences under this head.

reduce its bulk from a hundred pages to ten.[1] In addition to other advantages arising from this brevity, Committees could more easily and quickly direct their attention to what was special in each Bill. Lord Chancellor
Cranworth stated, in 1853, that the number of folio pages
saved, since 1845, in printing railway Acts alone had been,
upon a single copy of each Act, no fewer than 116,000 ; and
as each Bill was printed several times in its course through
Parliament, and the Bills that passed did not perhaps represent one-half of those introduced and printed, but not passed,
the economy was beyond calculation. Lord Cranworth
added, that whoever devised the Consolidation Acts had been
a public benefactor.[2] In 1856, Sir Fitzroy Kelly estimated
that, since 1845, the consolidation statutes had been applied
to more than three thousand private Acts, saving some 130,000
pages of print, or, reckoning the reprinting of bills, " at least
a million pages."[3] This advantage has continued to our
day, with the result not only of relieving statutes of an
enormous mass of print, but of securing far greater precision
and uniformity in local Acts than were possible under the
former system, however carefully it might be watched by
private individuals, or by public departments.

Municipal
law intricate
and conflict-
ing.

Mr. Hume's Committee of 1846 complained that public
interests were occasionally prejudiced by provisions in Acts
obtained by local authorities, " some varying or interfering
with the general statute or common law of the country ;
some, though ordinary in their nature, yet of a perplexing
and needless diversity in form ; and finally, some so contradictory and mutually discordant as to render their enforcement impossible, and to make the law doubtful and embar-
rassing even to those who are professionally versed in it."[4]

[1] Com. Committee, 1846, on Private Business; evidence of Mr. Booth,
Speaker's counsel, p. 62.

[2] Hansard, House of Lords' Debates, Aug. 18, 1853.

[3] Letter of Sir Fitzroy Kelly to

Lord Brougham on Consolidation of
Statute Law, 1856.

[4] Com. Committee on Private
Bills, 1846; Report, p. 4. Incidentally, the Committee mention
that, since the Union with Ireland

These evils, the Committee hoped, would be mitigated by Remedies suggested and adopted. Consolidation Acts, and also by general sanitary measures applicable to all urban and rural communities. Parliament carried out both these recommendations, by the measures of 1847, which have just been noticed, and, in the following Session, by the first Public Health Act. Local legislation, however, though far more effective and better administered than it was before 1847-8, has outgrown both these classes of public Acts, and has now become by no means uniform among different communities. With some exceptions, also, the laws of each town have to be sought in many enactments, and these not always easy to reconcile.

In theory, it might not unreasonably be expected that, as Apparent want of an urban code of general application. the wants of urban populations must in all essential respects be the same, Parliament would hold in its hand a code applicable to all such communities, amending this code from time to time as necessity arose, but refusing to pass exceptional legislation at the instance of local authorities, save when works were to be executed, and funds to be raised for such works, proposals which must be special in their nature. A stranger, it might be supposed, going from one town to another, should surely find the same municipal laws in each, though the rates levied must of necessity differ in amount, and local circumstances sometimes require different treatment. In practice, it has been found that uniformity in local government has been established neither by the general measures suggested in 1846, nor by the consolidation statutes, much as the latter have done in this direction. One reason is, that Parliament will not take the trouble to amend these general measures from time to time, and so keep pace with local wants. Thus local authorities are obliged to apply for special powers, rendered necessary by new social conditions.

Local laws in the same town are also often difficult to trace Numerous

to the end of 1845, 9,200 local and   and only 5,300 public statutes.
personal Bills had passed into law,

local Acts in same town.

and to understand, owing to the number of Acts obtained at different periods, frequently relating to the same class of subjects, and in part amended or repealed by subsequent Acts. In 1835, when the Municipal Reform Act was passed, local Acts then existing and applicable to corporate towns, in England and Wales alone, numbered more than seven hundred. Mention has been made of Liverpool, which in 1846 was under sixty local Acts, puzzling even to lawyers, but enforced in one year by nearly eleven thousand penal informations.[1] Consolidated jurisdictions, and amending Acts promoted by municipalities, have now got rid of much of this tangled legislation in large towns.

Modern Improvement Bills.

But a considerable part of the work of Committees in Parliament still consists in a consideration of Improvement Bills, containing provisions engrafted upon those of previous Acts applying to the same community, and either varying or in excess of those which Parliament has embodied in its general public Acts. Local circumstances, and the changes which a growth of population brings about, make such applications to Parliament inevitable. It is inevitable, too, that if Parliament does not keep abreast of public wants in its general sanitary and police legislation, local communities should try to supplement proved omissions and defects in the general law by means of private legislation. Nor is such legislation without its advantages, for we may again point out that much of our public law has been based upon statutes passed at the instance of particular bodies or communities, and the proof of their public utility afforded by local experience. Even the Consolidation Acts themselves, which now fill so large a part in private legislation, are only a collection of the best and most frequently recurring sections found in local Acts, often obtained after long and costly struggles by individual towns, before the principle involved in those sections was generally accepted.[2]

[1] *Ante*, p. 461, text and note.

[2] The first public Naturalization Act of 1709, the first public Inclosure Act of 1801, the Public Health Acts, and other general statutes are also founded largely upon provisions repeated in private Acts.

We may now consider the difficulties encountered by a Difficulty of mastering municipal law in any town. ratepayer in any city or town anxious to understand the municipal law under which he is governed.   First, he must study the Municipal Corporations Act,[1] which regulates the election of the Town Council, their powers and duties.   He must then look carefully at the Public Health Act of 1875 for a mass of law on sanitary and other subjects, applying to all urban or rural communities.   This statute, unfortunately, is not complete in itself, for it incorporates by reference parts of other statutes, which must be searched for and digested. Here, however, an enquiring ratepayer is on common ground with the inhabitants of similar places, and shares with them the benefits and defects of this general legislation, that is— and the reservation is important—so far as it is not varied by provisions in special Acts.   After having mastered this very considerable body of law, a student's difficulties may be said to begin.   He next has the task of ascertaining what general statutes, such as the Public Libraries Act or the Baths and Washhouses Acts, have been adopted by the local authority, and what parts of the Consolidation Acts have been incorporated in his local Acts.   As this incorporation is by reference only, he must go again to the public statute book for his information, which he will find scattered over many volumes, the fruit of many Sessions.   Long before reaching this stage he will probably have found that the local Acts affecting his own community are still more numerous and scattered, the earlier in part repealed, and when unrepealed often involving great difficulties in reconciling their provisions with those of later enactments.

To the body of local and general enactments just indicated, Local administration of general Acts. may be added the numberless general statutes which regulate poor-law relief and rating, highways[2] and elementary educa-

---

[1] The Act of 1835 was repealed and amended by the Municipal Corporations Act, 1882.

[2] Speaking of poor-law and high-way legislation, Mr. Goschen said: "There is no labyrinth so intricate as the chaos of our local laws." (Speech delivered at Hitchin, 1882.)

**Gas, Water,
Cemetery,
Harbour and
Dock Acts.**

tion; together with the local Acts (often very numerous)
obtained by gas and water authorities, cemetery companies,
harbour or dock boards, when any such exist, and the public
Acts which they again incorporate, but do not reproduce.
Such a collection would form a library in itself, and no inconsiderable one.   Probably of the many rate-supported
public libraries in large towns, not one contains a complete
series of the special and general statutes which would enable
a diligent ratepayer to obtain exact knowledge of the
municipal law to which he is subject within the municipal
boundary.   We may assume with reasonable certainty that,
even if these dry volumes were accessible, it would still remain true, as in 1846, that no one except a lawyer, and sometimes no lawyer without great trouble, could tell what the
law really was.[1]

**Attempted
consolidation
of Railway
Acts.**

A partial remedy for this confusion in local law is the further .
consolidation of local Acts.   In the case of railway companies
consolidation has not been found practicable, though the
number of Acts affecting every large railway company in
this country makes the study of its position and its relations to other companies a task of great intricacy and diffi-

---

It will be seen that this criticism has even a wider application.

[1] According to an American writer in *Harper's Magazine* (Sept. 1883) the same complications have arisen in New York, eliciting from the Chief Judge of that State in 1875 a judicial statement that it was "clearly unsafe for any one to speak confi-
dently of the exact condition of the law in respect to public improve-
ments in the cities of New York and Brooklyn. The enactments with re-
ference thereto have been modified, superseded, and repealed so often and to such an extent that it is dif-
ficult to ascertain what statutes are in force at any particular time." With a view to put an end to this confusion, the State Legislature ap-
pointed a Commission, whose labours resulted in "An Act to consolidate the special and local laws affecting public interests in the City of New York." This Act occupies a large octavo volume "of over 700 pages, and contains about 2,150 sections," a body of legislation about as large as the entire civil code of France. "And this," continues the writer, "is the law relative to a single city, not to mention legislation which emanates from the local authority itself, such as City ordinances, which are enacted by the Board of Aldermen, or sanitary ordinances by the Board of Health."

culty. In earlier days of railway enterprise, many Members of Parliament wished to compel railway companies to repeal and consolidate their Acts on coming for fresh powers. This task was attempted by the Great Eastern (then the Eastern Counties) Railway Company in 1861, when about two hundred Acts were repealed and consolidated. In 1854, the Manchester, Sheffield, and Lincolnshire Railway Company repealed and consolidated more than a hundred Railway and Canal Acts which they had obtained, or the interests created by which they had acquired by purchase. The Stockton and Darlington Company, now the North Eastern, performed a similar work. But it was found that the repeal of old and apparently obsolete Acts raised doubts, and called forth opposition from parties whose interests were protected by those Acts; and repeal and consolidation, however desirable on many grounds, did not become general.

Less difficulty has been experienced in consolidating municipal law. For example, the Corporation of Birmingham, in 1883, obtained an Act, already mentioned,[1] which consolidated with some amendments no fewer than twenty local statutes and Orders relating to the borough. These repealed Acts extended over a period of more than thirty years, and contained in the whole nearly one thousand sections. The Consolidation Act[2] reduced this number of sections to less than three hundred. Three Orders of 1880-1-2, relating to the issue of Corporation Stock, an Order under the Artizans' Dwellings Act, and one authorizing the formation of a Drainage District Board, were excluded from the Act as not dealing with suitable subjects for consolidation. The Public Health and Municipal Corporations Acts, with various Consolidation Acts in whole or in part, must still also be referred to. With these exceptions, however, the whole local law of Birmingham, including that relating to the supply of gas and water, is now contained in this one Act of 1883. Such a work reflects infinite credit on the municipality. It is due to

Birmingham Corporation (Consolidation) Act, 1883.

---

[1] *Ante*, p. 490.   [2] 46 & 47 Vict. c. 70.

every community that their local law should not only be, as far as possible, simplified and condensed, but made generally accessible. With this view the Corporation of Birmingham have published their Consolidation Act in a handy volume, including appendices, which give the Acts or parts of Acts incorporated with it,[1] and those incorporated in part with the Public Health Act.[2] Inhabitants of Birmingham, therefore, possess a short, simple, clearly-arranged municipal code, which, on ordinary subjects of reference, is complete. This consolidation, with the book which has so greatly increased its usefulness to the community,[3] are models for

Importance of municipal legislation and administration.

imitation elsewhere. To the municipalities which, at Birmingham and elsewhere, initiated, carried, and now administer these local Acts, whether consolidated or not, hearty praise is due. Such measures are of the highest importance to each community, affecting their health and comfort, and entering into most concerns of their daily life far more intimately and directly than the bulk of Imperial legislation. It is a work undertaken on behalf of no mean cities ; a work undervalued only by those who have had little occasion to study it; it supplies, too, a thoroughly English discipline, and useful training and practical experience, for the equipment of men otherwise qualified to take a larger part in public affairs.

Police and sanitary legislation, 1882-6.

In 1882, the want of harmony in municipal legislation, on which Mr. Hume's Committee had commented so strongly more than thirty-five years previously, was again noticed in the House of Commons, and its attention was directed [4] to several Bills promoted by municipalities containing sanitary and

---

[1] Lands Clauses Consolidation Acts, 1847, 1860, 1869 ; Markets and Fairs Clauses Act, 1847 ; Gasworks Clauses Acts, 1847 and 1871 ; Waterworks Clauses Acts, 1847 and 1863 ; and parts of Towns Improvement Clauses Act, 1847.

[2] Parts of Towns Improvement Clauses and Towns Police Clauses Acts, 1847.

[3] The editors of this volume are Mr. Edward Orford Smith, Solicitor, Town Clerk of Birmingham, and Mr. Charles Albert Carter, Assistant Solicitor, who supply useful notes of reference and a general index.

[4] By Mr. Hopwood, March 7, 1882; 267 Hansard, 320.

police regulations which extended, and in some cases were at variance with, the general law, and trenched upon individual rights and liberties, contrary to the intention and, in substance though not in form, without the knowledge of Parliament. After debate, these Bills, eight in number, were referred to a hybrid Committee of seven members, instructed to hear evidence and counsel, and deal with these measures as an ordinary Private Bill Committee would, but, in addition, to report specially their reasons for sanctioning any powers varying the general law.[1] The Bills in question were accordingly considered with great minuteness by the Committee, who made important changes, even in clauses which were unopposed, and repeated a recommendation made by several of their predecessors, "that some steps should be taken by the House to secure more uniform and stringent supervision of unopposed clauses in private Bills."[2]

The effect of this unusual, but not uncalled for, intervention by Parliament may be shortly described. Questions of finance, though not specially included in the order of reference, necessarily came under notice. There were many local precedents to the contrary, but the Committee in no case permitted repayments of loans to be extended beyond the period of sixty years, which is the maximum period sanctioned by the Public Health Act, and for moneys borrowed by the Metropolitan Board of Works.[3] In several instances, also, they required that, as in the case of moneys borrowed under the Public Health Act, local authorities should obtain

Repayment of loans by local authorities.

---

[1] Com. Journ., March 13 and 14, 1882. Mr. Sclater-Booth, formerly President of the Local Government Board, was Chairman of the Committee.

[2] Report of Committee on Police and Sanitary Regulations, 1882, p. 3.

[3] *Ante*, p. 513, n. As instances of undue periods for repayment of loans by local authorities, Mr. Sclater-Booth quoted, in 1877, the following cases: — Acts of 1875: Birmingham Gas, 85 years: Birmingham Water, 90 years; Rochdale Improvement (Waterworks), 100 years. Acts of 1876:—Leicester (Works for Prevention of Floods), 80 years; Stockton and Middlesbrough Water, 90 years; Halifax (Water and Gas), 100 and 110 years; Huddersfield Waterworks and Improvement, 100 years. (Speech introducing Local Budget, 233 Hansard, 1723.)

Notification of infectious diseases.

the sanction of the Local Government Board before raising loans for purposes contemplated in Bills. As to sanitary regulations, the Committee found that the notification of infectious diseases had been dealt with by local Acts in twenty-three urban districts,[1] and that the Local Government Board had allowed similar legislation, in excess of the general law, in several Provisional Order Bills.[2] The Committee, therefore, recommended that, in any future amendment of the Public Health Act, similar powers should be extended to all urban authorities.

New powers to prevent the spread of infectious diseases.

New provisions proposed with a view to prevent the spread of infectious diseases were regarded with less favour by the Committee, though these also were supported by precedents in local Acts; few of them therefore were sanctioned. For example, some corporations sought powers to close schools during the prevalence of infectious diseases: these powers

Hours of employment of children.

were not granted. To correct an evil of another kind, the Committee allowed a string of clauses limiting the hours of labour of children under school age in casual employment, chiefly that of selling newspapers in the streets at night. Provisions framed for this object already exist, substantially, in a Scotch general Act,[3] but have no force in England,

Police regulations.

except when they have been embodied in local statutes. Of proposals for new police regulations, the Committee rejected many which were in excess of the general law, but approved, *inter alia*, of clauses regulating street music, street betting, bicycles, and sales of coal in small quantities, as well as for preventing obstructions on footways, annoyances caused by affixing or delivering objectionable advertisements, and stray dogs. Such provisions in local Acts had worked satisfactorily in other towns, though not contained in general codes. A large number of clauses proposed to give powers which may be obtained by means of bye-laws under general Acts: these clauses were struck out.

[1] Commons Paper, 164 (1882).
[2] See Manchester Provisional Order Act, 1881 (44 Vict. c. 66, Art. 8).
[3] Education (Scotland) Act, 1878 (41 & 42 Vict. c. 78, s. 6).

As the Committee of 1882 point out, the growth and development of private Bill legislation are abundantly shown by these applications and precedents cited in support of them. It must be admitted, they add, that Parliament has encouraged amendments in the general law for the advantage of particular localities. "Experience thus gained has served, and may serve again, to lay the foundation of useful public Acts of general application." On the other hand, the Committee refer to anomalies which Parliament has sanctioned without full knowledge.[1] They recommend, as a practical remedy, that the Towns Police Clauses Act should be amended, so as to meet present requirements. But this suggestion, as well as that of an amended Public Health Act, was not adopted. Parliament was unable to afford time to keep abreast with the growing wants of urban populations by general legislation. Municipal bodies representing such communities had accordingly no other resource than still to seek for exceptional legislation.

Policy of allowing local variations from general law.

As an easy method of preventing further variance between municipal and public law, the House of Commons adopted, in 1882, a new Standing Order,[2] requiring Committees on any Bill promoted by local authorities to report specially how they have dealt with powers asked for upon police and sanitary matters which differ from the general law, and also with powers to issue bye-laws which may already be obtained under general Acts. Committees were also instructed in no case to allow a longer term than sixty years for repaying loans, "or any period disproportionate to the duration of the works to be executed, or other objects of the loan."[3] Any borrowing powers sought for were in like manner to be scrutinized, with a view to ascertain whether

New Standing Order of Commons, 1882.

---

[1] Report of Committee, pp. 1—6.

[2] Com. S. O. of 1886, 173 A.

[3] *Ante*, p. 513. See Commons' debate on this S. O., August 8 and 11, 1882 (273 Hansard, 1130-5, and 1498—1506), and complaints made on behalf of local authorities as to the injustice of a hard-and-fast line fixing a maximum period for repayment of loans, no matter under what special circumstances contracted. But a sinking fund of one per cent. will pay off a debt in sixty years.

they did not already exist under public Acts. Lastly, in order to secure proper attention to reports upon Bills from the Local Government Board or Home Office, the Committee were required to inform the House in what manner they had dealt with recommendations in these reports.

Commons' Committee on Police and Sanitary Regulations, 1884.

In 1883, the Select Committee on Police and Sanitary Regulations did not sit, but were re-appointed in the Session following, and reported to the House of Commons that they had amended Bills of municipal and other local authorities upon two main principles which they believed to be accepted by the House, "first, that no local powers should be given which are in excess of the general law, unless strong local reasons exist for such powers; secondly, that no statutory enactments should be permitted for purposes which can be effected by bye-laws."[1] In providing for repayments of loans for works, the Committee of 1884 curtailed the periods demanded in all Bills referred to them, permitting in no case a longer period than sixty years, and in most instances imposing a much shorter period. They acted on "the general principle that, for works which are not permanent, only short terms should be given for repayment, seeing that such expenditure can only be expected to benefit the existing generation, while, for works that are of a more durable character, it is reasonable that the charge should be spread over a longer succession of ratepayers."[2]

New Consolidation Act recommended.

After repeating the recommendation of their predecessors that there should now be a new general Act amending and consolidating the laws relating to police and sanitary regulations, the Committee "strongly advised" that, pending such a measure, "care should be taken in succeeding Sessions to control the attempts which local bodies not unnaturally make to arm themselves with powers which the general law has not yet sanctioned."[3] In 1885,

Committee of 1885.

the Committee, being re-appointed, acted upon this view in a

[1] Report of Committee, p. 3.　　[3] Special Report, p. 4
[2] Ib., p. 4.

typical case. The Public Health Act, 1875, declares that
new streets or roads shall be sewered, paved, flagged, kerbed,
and channelled at the expense of private owners, the work
being in certain cases performed by local authorities, and the
cost afterwards apportioned among these owners.[1] But the
Act provides no funds with which local authorities can discharge this duty. If, therefore, they advance the money,
they must raise it irregularly and without legal powers.
The Corporation of Bury asked for authority to borrow
20,000*l.* in advance for purposes of this expenditure, but
the Committee refused to sanction any such loans in advance,
on the ground that, however necessary and desirable such a
provision might be, the want of it was common to every
other urban authority, and that Parliament must therefore be
asked to amend the general law.[2]

Private improvement expenses.

A Bill of 1886 to amend the Public Health Acts on this
subject was considered by a Select Committee in the lower
House, and approved by the Local Government Board, but
was withdrawn a day or two before the dissolution of Parliament, owing to the insertion of a clause giving, as the Government contended, undue exemptions in favour of railway
companies.[3] This Bill would have authorized sanitary authorities to spread over a period of twenty years repayment of
sums due-from owners for private improvement expenses, and,
if the Local Government Board assented, to borrow money
"for the purpose of temporarily providing for expenses of
private street works."[4] But this would obviously at the best
have been piecemeal legislation, leaving other defects in
police and sanitary regulations still unamended. While,
therefore, Parliament Session after Session disregards the
recommendations of its Committees to pass public measures,
and at the same time through the same Committees prevents
private legislation of admitted necessity, it really inflicts
serious injury upon those "rapidly-growing communities,"

Private Improvement Expenses Bill, 1886.

Injustice to communities through denial of private and delay of public legislation.

---

[1] 38 & 39 Vict. c. 55, s. 150.

[2] Bury Improvement Bill, 1885;
Minutes of Committee, pp. 79, 94.

[3] See Lords' Debates, Hansard,
June 22, 1886.

[4] Public Health Acts (Private Improvement Expenses) Amendment
Bill, 1886.

to whom the Committee of 1884 referred, " whose wants are every year pressed upon Parliament." Their neighbours, before the first appointment of this annual Committee, may have succeeded in obtaining statutory powers which experience has shown to be necessary, yet they are debarred from the benefit of similar powers because a Committee of one House thinks, not that they are unnecessary, but that they should be made of general application. Uniformity in local legislation is much to be desired, but local communities may long suffer from defective provisions affecting their health and general well-being if they are told that they must wait till Parliament has leisure to pass some general measure of relief to everybody.

Two principles of extreme importance to gas and water consumers and also to local authorities have recently been adopted by Parliamentary Committees. Until the year 1885, no limit of profits was imposed upon public bodies supplying gas; they were generally at liberty to apply surplus revenue from this source at their discretion, in reduction of rates or otherwise, Parliament assuming that the interests of consumers were substantially the interests of rate-payers and would not be neglected by a representative body. But in an Act of 1885,[1] transferring a private gas undertaking to the Corporations of Stalybridge and Mossley, a standard price is fixed in each borough, with a higher charge for extra-municipal limits. In any year during which gas is supplied by either Corporation below the standard price, they may carry to the credit of their rates, or may otherwise apply for the public benefit, one-third of the difference between actual revenue and that which would have accrued from the standard charge, the remaining two-thirds being carried forward in aid of gas revenue for the following year. If in any year the charge is above the standard price, no portion of any gas revenue must be applied in aid of rates or for public purposes. When the balance carried forward to the credit of gas revenue from all sources exceeds in any

Application of gas revenue by local authorities.

Standard price and sliding scale in Corporation Gas Act, 1885.

[1] 48 & 49 Vict. c. 148.

year a specified sum, the charge for gas must be reduced by each Corporation so as to bring the next balance to this sum. These provisions go far to secure from municipalities equal justice both to their own ratepayers and to consumers in out-districts, which are not represented, directly or indirectly, by the authority supplying gas.

A stronger case occurred in 1886. The Corporation of Oldham promoted a Bill, among other objects, to obtain further capital for gas purposes. Some districts beyond the municipal boundary, but within the area of gas-supply, complained that they had long been charged gas-rates exceeding those paid in Oldham itself, and that the profits thus made were spent for the benefit of Oldham exclusively.[1] One of these districts had some years previously promoted a Bill to free itself from Oldham, but was told by the Committee to wait until the proper time, *i.e.*, until Oldham itself came to Parliament for further gas powers. Accordingly, in 1886, after much discussion, the out-districts were protected by very special clauses, repealing the differential charges in all cases beyond the borough, and limiting the rate of profits to be made within it, so that these districts now enjoy a double protection. The Corporation were required to accept these clauses as a condition of retaining the supply of the out-districts.[2]

Oldham Corporation Act, 1886.

A condition still more material in the public interest has been imposed by a Parliamentary Committee upon metropolitan water companies. Since the provisional agreements for purchase, acquiesced in by these companies,[3] Parliament has allowed them to raise fresh capital for necessary works, but has tried to prevent such issues from being used to enhance the price of their undertakings upon any future purchase by the public. With this view, in the Lambeth case of 1883, Parliament required that new capital should be

Metropolitan water companies.

---

[1] Some judicial *dicta* quoted in the course of this case have from time to time thrown doubt upon the right of public bodies to make profits out of their gas or water supply, without specific powers to do so, but the question of principle has never been expressly decided.

[2]. 49 & 50 Vict. c. 117, ss. 30-1.

[3] *Ante*, pp. 180 *et seq.*

issued as a four per cent. debenture stock, not convertible at any time into share capital.[1] In 1886 Parliament went a step further. The Lambeth, East London, and Southwark and Vauxhall Companies promoted Bills to authorize new works and issue fresh capital in the form of debenture stock. The Corporation of the City of London opposed these Bills on behalf of consumers generally, and a hybrid Committee of the House of Commons insisted on the creation by each company of a sinking fund, formed out of annual profits, by a certain percentage upon the amount of the new debenture stock. Of this sinking fund the City Chamberlain is appointed trustee, and it is to be applied in " purchasing and extinguishing " the company's share capital, or otherwise as Parliament may determine. After consideration, the three companies took their Bills subject to this condition.[2] Thus, if these undertakings are transferred to a public body, Parliament has not only guarded against higher terms of purchase, based upon an increase of capital, but has made each company help forward its own dissolution by setting aside annually funds with which to extinguish its liabilities.

Sinking fund under Metropolitan Water Acts, 1886.

Public trust managed by City Chamberlain.

For this result water consumers throughout the metropolis are mainly indebted to the Corporation of the City of London, who intervened when no other public opponents of these water Bills appeared. The circumstances under which the Metropolitan Board of Works did not petition in the House of Commons deserve record. Elsewhere we have noticed[3] the

City Corporation left to defend interests of metropolitan water consumers generally.

Position of Metropolitan Board.

---

[1] 46 Vict. c. 28, s. 8.

[2] 49 & 50 Vict. c. 71 (Lambeth), c. 82 (East London), c. 85 (Southwark and Vauxhall). The following clause is inserted in all these Acts :—
" From and after the expiration of three years from the issue from time to time of any debenture stock under the powers of this Act, there shall be carried to a sinking fund in each year such percentage on the amount of such debenture stock as shall be equal to the excess of the average percentage of the dividend or interest paid for that year on all the capital of the company, whether share capital or borrowed, above the interest, together with an additional one per cent. per annum added thereto for management on such debenture stock ; such sinking fund to be held and applied by the Chamberlain of the City of London as trustee for the purpose of purchasing and extinguishing the share capital of the company, or for such other purposes as Parliament may from time to time determine."

[3] *Ante,* pp. 178-9.

Board's escape in 1879, under a statute of indemnity, from surcharge for costs for promoting water Bills. This lesson was a painful one, and doubts were felt whether the Board were authorized by their Act of 1855 to charge the rates even with the costs of opposing water Bills promoted by the companies.[1] Such a state of the law, reducing to utter helplessness the chief metropolitan local authority, when grave interests of their constituents were threatened in Parliament, was felt to be intolerable. It was the Board's obvious duty to remove this disability if possible. They accordingly promoted a short Bill early in 1886, expressly enabling them to charge the rates for the purpose of opposing water Bills in Parliament.[2] This measure was defeated in the House of Commons by a majority of 130 to 76, mainly on the ground that, pending the creation of a municipality in London, it was not well to arm a moribund Board with new powers.[3] Meanwhile, therefore, the interests of ratepayers were to suffer, and London was to be forced into reform by disabling her chief representative body![4] On this occasion, if the Corporation had not possessed the means with which to petition, and the public spirit to do so, the principle of a public sinking fund would not have been conceded; a principle not only most valuable in its application to these water companies, but likely to be followed as a precedent in other cases.

Metropolitan Board of Works (Water Supply) Bill, 1886.

During the discussion on this measure, some of its opponents appear to have contended that the Metropolitan Board should not be exempt from a rule laid down by Parliament in 1872 —that no expense in promoting Bills must be charged upon

Municipal Corporations (Borough Funds) Act, 1872.

---

[1] See Metropolis Management Act, 1855, s. 144, which vaguely authorizes the Board to defray the expenses of applications to Parliament for "further powers for the purpose of any work for the improvement of the metropolis or public benefit of the inhabitants thereof."

[2] Bill 34, Session 1886. When introduced, the Bill enabled the Board to promote as well as oppose water Bills, but to meet objections raised by the Government, the Bill was afterwards limited to opposition.

[3] See Commons' debate, March 5, 1886; 303 Hansard, pp. 81-7.

[4] Fifty-six Irish Home Rule members were among the majority who refused any efficient control over the water supply of London to the governing body of London.

rates unless expressly sanctioned by ratepayers. The public statute enforcing this rule[1] itself declares that it shall apply neither to Ireland nor to the metropolis. In the latter case, indeed, its machinery would be impracticable. Scotland is not mentioned in the Act, but from the outset its provisions were recognized as unsuitable there also. It has, however, exercised a material influence upon attempts at private legislation affecting local authorities elsewhere, and the circumstances which led to it are worth relating.

Right of municipal corporations to appear in Parliament under Act of 1835.

The Municipal Corporations Act of 1835 directed that borough funds should be applied in defraying certain expenses, and others "necessarily incurred in carrying into effect the provisions of this Act," and that the surplus should be then spent "for the public benefit of the inhabitants and the improvement of the borough."[2] Until the year 1870 it was generally supposed that these words enabled Town Councils, out of their borough fund or rate, to promote or oppose Bills in Parliament which affected the interests of their constituents. Such a right was undoubted if they were defending any corporate property, which, for example, was scheduled in a railway or other private Bill. But when expenses were incurred in promoting Bills, or in opposing them, on public grounds alone, judicial decisions established that municipal corporations having no property out of which to defray these costs could not charge them on the borough fund, and that a personal liability therefore attached to members of governing bodies for any such outlay.

Corporation of Sheffield

The principal case governed by these decisions was that of

---

[1] 35 & 36 Vict. c. 91.

[2] 5 & 6 Will. IV. c. 76, s. 92, which created a "borough fund," consisting of the annual rents and proceeds of all corporate property, together with all fines and penalties levied under the Act. The expenses specifically charged upon this fund include the payment of interest on existing debts, salaries of Recorder, Town Clerk, Treasurer, and other officers; prosecution, maintenance, and punishment of offenders; expenses of maintaining corporate buildings, payment of constables, and election expenses. Any deficiency in the fund was to be made up by a borough rate, and as a majority of boroughs have little or no corporate property, such a rate is usually necessary. (See now 45 & 46 Vict. c. 50, ss. 139 et seq.)

the Corporation of Sheffield.   In 1870, this body, which had *and the Sheffield Gas and Water Companies.* for several years previously desired to acquire the local gas and water undertakings, promoted unsuccessfully three Bills, two for compulsory purchase, and an alternative Bill, enabling them to manufacture and sell gas in competition with the existing company.   On the application of ratepayers, who .were directors of the water company, an injunction was granted by the Court of Chancery restraining the Corporation from expending any portion of the rates in promoting these Bills, and the costs therefore fell upon individual councillors. In 1869, the Sheffield Water Company, becoming liable to give water under constant pressure, made regulations for preventing waste.   These regulations were subject to approval by two justices, before whom the Corporation appeared to protect the interests of consumers.   Owing to this opposition, the proposed regulations were greatly modified in the consumers' favour.   The Corporation also incurred expenditure in preparing to oppose a Bill promoted by the company in 1870, under which a constant service of water would have been deferred for five years, and onerous regulations imposed on consumers.   This Bill was withdrawn by the company on March 16, 1870.   The costs of both oppositions were paid out of the borough fund; but on an application for a writ of *certiorari* by ratepayers,[1] who again were directors of the water company, the Court of Queen's Bench, though reluctantly, quashed the orders upon which these payments were made, on the ground that they were not "expenses necessarily incurred in carrying into effect the provisions" of the Act of 1835, and could not come within the clause enabling town councils to apply any surplus of their borough funds "for the public benefit of the inhabitants," as in Sheffield there was no surplus.[2]   Thus a fresh liability was cast upon individual members of the Corporation.

[1] This remedy to ratepayers in case of misapplication of a borough fund was provided by 7 Will. IV. & 1 Vict. c. 78, s. 44.

[2] L. R., 6 Q. B. 652.   Lord Chief Justice Cockburn, in the course of his decision, said:—"I very much regret the conclusion at which I am forced to arrive, as I believe that the Corporation were actuated by a laud-

Bills intro-
duced by
Mr. Leeman,
1871-2.

If the law thus formulated had been left without change, its effect would clearly have been to paralyze local self-government in many matters of vital importance to urban communities, and especially to leave them at the mercy of private companies enjoying a monopoly for the supply of gas and water. Numerous petitions were promptly presented to Parliament in this sense, urging that the law as laid down would seriously cripple local authorities in their care of local interests. The decision of the Court of Queen's Bench was given on June 10, 1871, and a Bill founded upon it by Mr. Leeman, "to authorize the application of funds of municipal corporations and other governing bodies in certain cases," came before the House of Commons for a second reading on June 30. It met with strenuous opposition from the companies, who alleged that its object was really to enable governing bodies to acquire private undertakings compulsorily at the public expense. In principle, however, the Bill commanded general assent.[1] It was considered by a Select Committee, but did not become law until 1872, after inquiry before a second Committee.[2]

able desire to protect the true interests of the borough, and prevent the water company from frustrating a very important sanitary provision, namely, that they shall afford a constant supply. I wish I could protect the Corporation against expenses which must now fall upon individual members; but we cannot strain the words of the statute."

[1] Mr. Bruce, Home Secretary in 1871, said:—"The recent decision of the Court of Queen's Bench makes municipal councils utterly powerless for the purpose of either promoting or protecting the interests of their constituents." On the same occasion, Sir Roundell Palmer (afterwards Lord Selborne), alluding to the Sheffield case, said:—"Whatever may be thought of the powers of corporations to promote Bills affecting the

borough, and whatever may be thought of the safeguards which should be imposed in the interests of ratepayers generally, the common sense of all mankind must perceive that the governing body of a borough, the municipal council freely elected by the ratepayers, ought, in the interests of the borough, to have power to watch, and, if necessary, to oppose, Bills introduced into Parliament with reference to markets, tramways, slaughter-houses, gasworks, waterworks, or other such subjects. If they are not to do this, who is to do it? What functions can be more proper for them to exercise than these?" (Debate on Second Reading of Borough Funds Bill, MS. Report.)

[2] Among other modifications, a retrospective clause was struck out

As originally introduced, the Bill was much more favour- Provisions of
Act of 1872. able to governing bodies than the measure as passed. It authorizes them to apply borough funds, or other moneys under their control, in defraying costs, charges, and expenses incurred in promoting or opposing Bills, or in prosecuting or defending any legal proceedings, affecting the interests of inhabitants. Parliament, however, imposed many conditions designed to secure departmental control, prevent hasty proceedings by the governing body, and obtain the special sanction of owners and ratepayers. Their consent must be obtained at a Consent of
owners and
ratepayers. public meeting, at which a poll may be demanded.[1] This is a cumbrous and expensive method, and proposals have more than once been made to omit it,[2] especially as any ratepayer can question the expediency of proceedings under the Act by lodging objections with the Local Government Board or Home Secretary, who may then order a local inquiry.

Another proviso was introduced forbidding governing bodies Proviso in Act
protecting
gas and water
companies. to promote Bills for the establishment of gas or water works to compete with any existing gas or water company established under statute.[3] The vested interests which were thus effectually protected against competition had asserted themselves before this period. For example, a local board could not construct waterworks under the Public Health Act, 1848, if any waterworks company within their district were able and willing to supply water upon terms prescribed by that Act.[4] The same protection was continued to water companies in public Acts of 1858 and 1875.[5] Unfortunately, while imposing these restrictions, Parliament took no notice

which enabled the Home Secretary to allow the payment of costs incurred by governing bodies in the belief that they might be legally paid out of rates.

[1] 35 & 36 Vict. c. 91, s. 4 ; and Local Government Act, 1858 (21 & 22 Vict. c. 98, ss. 12, 13). *Ante*, pp. 512–13.

[2] See proposed Amendment Bill (No. 80, of 1885).

[3] 35 & 36 Vict. c. 91, s. 2.

[4] 11 & 12 Vict. c. 63, s. 75.

[5] See Local Government Act, 1858, s. 53, and Public Health Act, 1875, s. 52, which is the existing law.

of recommendations made by the Royal Commissioners in 1844-5, that, as a condition upon the establishment of new water companies, local authorities should be enabled to purchase their works after the lapse of a certain number of years, on specified terms and after a rate of interest to be fixed in the incorporating Act.[1] Until the year 1870, and again in 1882, this principle was not adopted in general legislation.[2] After past warnings, it is not likely to be again lost sight of.

Tramways Act, 1870; Electric Lighting Act, 1882.

Modern recitals in conformity with Borough Funds Act.

In conformity with this Act of 1872, a modern Improvement Bill now recites that the works for which borrowing powers are sought are " permanent works within the meaning " of the Public Health Act, 1875 ;[3] that the requisite notices have been given ; that an absolute majority of the council or local board at an ordinary and afterwards at a special meeting have approved of the Bill, and resolved that the expense of promoting it shall be defrayed out of the borough fund or rates ; and that owners and ratepayers summoned in the manner specified in Schedule III. of the Public Health Act, 1875,[4] have likewise consented.

Street improvements: superfluous lands.

A question of considerable importance to local authorities arises upon Bills enabling them to acquire property for street and other improvements. Before 1845, Parliament always bound promoters to take as nearly as possible the area wanted for their undertaking, and if superfluous land were left after its completion, adjoining owners were allowed rights of pre-emption, unless the land were situate within a town, or were land built upon or used for building purposes. This policy

[1] Royal Commission on the Health of Towns, Second Report, p. 54 ; *ante*, Vol. I., pp. 253-4.

[2] *Ante*, Vol. I., pp. 189, 236-47. The Tramways Act, 1870, has worked freely notwithstanding this condition ; it was too rigidly applied in the Electric Lighting Act, 1882.

[3] " Money shall not be borrowed except for permanent works, including under this expression any works

of which the cost ought, in the opinion of the Local Government Board, to be spread over a term of years." (Sect. 234 (1).)

[4] Under sect. 313 of the Public Health Act, 1875, Schedule III. of that Act takes the place of sects. 12—15 of the repealed Local Government Act, 1858, as to meetings of owners and ratepayers.

was continued in the Lands Clauses Act of 1845. If rights of pre-emption were not exercised, then promoters were required to sell superfluous lands within ten years after the time limited for completion of their works, and apply any purchase-money to the purposes of their special Act. In default of such sales, the land vested in adjoining owners, in proportion to the extent of their holdings.[1]

The effect of this rigorous policy was to discourage, and sometimes altogether to prevent, the opening out of new streets by local authorities, inasmuch as they could only acquire or retain the exact quantity of land necessary for laying out a street, while the frontages, with their greatly-improved value, remained the property of private owners. Hence ratepayers bore the whole burden, while, apart from any advantages to public traffic, private owners reaped the whole advantage of such improvements. Influenced by this obvious injustice, Parliament gradually relaxed its rule in favour of public bodies, recognizing that they were carrying out public works for public objects, and not for purposes of speculation or private advantage.[2] Cases arising under statutory powers already granted have also been liberally construed by judges in favour of local authorities. In one of these cases, decided upon appeal by the House of Lords in 1866,[3] Lord Cranworth, then Lord Chancellor, distinguishes between legislation obtained by private companies and by public bodies undertaking local improvements:— *Effect of rule upon local authorities.* *Galloway r. Mayor, &c. of London, 1866.*

" When local authorities have made a new or widened an old street, they will necessarily have incurred a very great expense for which they can get no return. The new or improved street is dedicated to the public, and, unlike a railway, *Outlay upon street improvements unremunerative.*

---

[1] 8 Vict. c. 18, ss. 127–9.

[2] A similar exception has, though rarely, been made in favour of companies. See 31 & 32 Vict. c. 108, s. 15, which gives the Metropolitan District Railway Company power to hold certain superfluous lands adjoining their railway without restriction as to time.

[3] Galloway v. Mayor and Commonalty of London, L. R., 1 H. L. 45.

yields no profit to those by whom it has been made. In
order to meet this difficulty, and enable corporations to
reimburse themselves, the course has been to authorize them
to take compulsorily not only the buildings actually necessary
for forming the streets or other projected improvements, but
also other neighbouring lands and buildings, the value of
which, and the proper mode of dealing with which, the legislature considers to be connected with and dependent upon
the projected improvements. . . ." The object of the
sections in the Act under review, his Lordship added, was

Outlay of local authorities, how, in part, reimbursed.

plain. "It was anticipated that the projected improvements
would be likely so to add to the value of property in the
neighbourhood, that by enabling those at whose cost the
improvements had been made to appropriate to themselves,
at their old value, the houses and lands adjoining the improvements, and then to sell them at their increased value,
they might be able wholly or partially to reimburse themselves
the outlay they had made." [1]

Metropolitan Street Improvements Bill, 1877.

More recently, in 1877, this question came before Parliament upon a Bill promoted by the Metropolitan Board for
making, among other improvements, a new street from
Trafalgar Square to Tottenham Court Road. In drafting
their Bill, the Board inserted provisions enabling them,
following the decision just quoted, to acquire ground not
only for making the street but for forming frontages which,

Lord Salisbury's case.

when leased or sold, would reduce its cost to the ratepayers. A petitioning owner, however, asked that the Board
should be restrained from taking more of his land than
was actually required for the surface of the street. As the
Board alleged, the result would have been that they would
have had to pay this owner the full value of his ground,
with ten per cent for compulsory sale; that they must then
have fully compensated all persons holding under him whose
leasehold and trade interests were affected; afterwards they
would have been called upon to re-sell to the owner, for what
would have been only a nominal sum, all property not
required for the street; and he would then have been in

---

[1] Galloway v. Mayor and Com-   46.   Cf. proceedings of Glasgow
monalty of London, L. R., 1 H. L.   Improvement Trust, *ante*, pp. 435-41.

possession of valuable street frontages created by the new thoroughfare, the ratepayers being thus deprived of any means of partially recouping themselves, by a sale of these frontages, for their immense outlay in making the improvement.[1]

A House of Commons' Committee refused to put the Board under this restriction; a Committee in the other House inserted it. Considering the large additional sum which the street would cost, the precedent established, and the injury thereby inflicted upon public interests, the Board thought that they would not be justified in making the new street under such a condition. They resolved rather to abandon this portion of their Bill. Here, however, the House of Commons intervened, and passed without a division Mr. Fawcett's motion to disagree with the Lords' amendments.[2] The usual Committee was then appointed to draw up reasons for submission to the Lords. Chief among these reasons were the serious losses which such a clause would inflict upon ratepayers; the absence of exceptional circumstances affecting Lord Salisbury, so that the same clause must in justice be conceded to other owners; and the fact that such a clause "is inconsistent with the powers which are as a rule conceded to applicants for authority to make street improvements, which powers cannot be dispensed with if such improvements are to be made."[3] Upon consideration of these reasons the Lords gave way, and the Bill passed, allowing the Metropolitan Board usual powers to lease and sell lands not required for the street.[4]

Intended abandonment of part of Bill.

Disagreement by Commons with Lords' amendments.

---

[1] Report of Metropolitan Board for 1877, p. 34.

[2] 236 Hansard, pp. 212, 448-59. In the Chelsea Embankment Act, 1868, a similar clause protecting Lord Cadogan was inserted by the Upper House, and accepted by the Metropolitan Board. Some other precedents of the same nature were quoted by Mr. (afterwards Sir R.)

Gorst during the debate. It is fair to add, also, that exceptional circumstances were alleged, justifying the restriction introduced in Committee by the Upper House. (See Mr. Gorst's Speech, Ib.)

[3] 132 Com. Journ., p. 417.

[4] 40 & 41 Vict. c. 235. An unpassed Bill of 1886 proposed a material extension of the principle thus recog-

Investments
by trustees in
Corporation
stocks.

An example of the elasticity which prevails under the
existing system of private legislation is afforded in the provisions which from time to time have regulated investments
by trustees in Corporation stocks. When the Metropolitan
Board obtained their first Act to issue consolidated stock,
they asked that trustees should be authorized to invest in it,
unless expressly prohibited from doing so. Parliament, however, distrusted the stability of this new security, and struck
out the enabling clause. After a short experience, Parliament changed its mind, and, in 1871, allowed Metropolitan Stock to be bought by all trustees who were "empowered to invest money in public stocks or funds or other
Government securities." [1] This privilege has hitherto been
refused to all other local authorities issuing consolidated
stock, although some of their issues are probably not inferior
in solidity and security to those of the Metropolitan Board.
Some concession, however, has gradually been obtained from
Parliament.

Local Loans
Act, 1875, and
subsequent
private legis-
lation.

In 1875 trust funds were allowed to be invested in nominal
debentures or debenture stock issued by local authorities
under the Local Loans Act of that year, if, by the will or
other instrument, these funds could be invested in railway
debentures or debenture stock.[2] In 1880, trustees having
this power were enabled to invest in the various consolidated

nized by Parliament as to street improvements. Its object was to enable
not only local authorities but public
companies and other promoters of
works of public utility, who acquire
from Parliament powers of compulsory purchase, to show, if they could,
on any inquiry for assessing compensation, that this compensation ought
to be reduced because other adjoining land belonging to the same owner
would increase in value if the proposed works were carried out. This
law, it was stated, exists in the
United States and in some European
countries. (See Bill, No. 145 of

1886.)

[1] *Ante*, p. 355. In connection with
the attempted purchase by Mr. (now
Viscount) Cross, in 1880, of the metropolitan water undertakings (*ante*, pp.
180-88), a return to the House of Commons (353 of 1885) should be carefully
studied. It shows, from the subsequent revenue of the companies, that
the purchasing authority, and therefore the water consumers, would
have gained largely had the provisional agreements made with the
companies been carried out by the
Bill of 1880.

[2] 38 & 39 Vict. c. 83, s. 27.

stocks then authorized, subject to a restriction on holding stock certificates to bearer and coupons.[1] To this enabling power a proviso was added in 1881, that " where two or more persons are successively interested in the trust funds, no such investment shall be made at a price exceeding the redemption value of the stock."[2] There was no uniformity in the special legislation of 1882 on this subject.[3] But Parliament relaxed to some extent its restriction, and allowed investments in some of these municipal securities by trustees if they were " authorized to invest money in the mortgages, debentures, or debenture stock of any railway or other company."[4] No advance was made upon this legislation in 1885, so that local authorities elsewhere have not quite the advantages conceded to the Metropolitan Board, and their consolidated stock is not equally open to investment by trustees.

Some attention must now be given to those partial or entire exemptions from rating, which were formerly allowed by local enactments. At the end of the last century, when the profits of private enterprise were doubtful, several canals obtained a statutory exemption from rating in whole or in part. For example, the rates, tolls, and duties, authorized

Exemptions from local rating.

---

[1] Nottingham Corporation Loans Act, 1880, s. 10; Liverpool Corporation Loans Act, 1880, s. 9; Birmingham Provisional Order (43 & 44 Vict. c. 178).

[2] Birkenhead Corporation Act, 1881, s. 266, but this proviso did not appear in other similar Acts of the same Session.

[3] Cf. s. 283 of Blackburn Improvement Act, 1882, s. 133 of Bolton Act, and s. 44 of Essex County Loans Act.

[4] Bolton Improvement Act, s. 133; Derby Corporation Act, s. 106. In the model Bill for 1886 the clause stands in this form:—" (1) Trustees or other persons for the time being authorized to invest money in the mortgages, debentures, or debenture stock of any railway or other company, shall, unless the contrary is provided by the instrument authorizing the investment, have the same power of investing that money in corporation stock (other than stock for the time being represented by a stock certificate to bearer) as they have of investing it in the mortgages, debentures, or debenture stock aforesaid. (2) Provided that where two or more persons are successively interested in trust money, no investment thereof shall be made in corporation redeemable stock at a price exceeding the redemption value of the stock."

was opposed by ratepayers as an injustice.[1] At Leeds, a local Act, passed so lately as 1825, freed "the engine for supplying the town and neighbourhood with water from any rates and assessments."[2] For many years, too, the mains and pipes of water companies were not rated for the relief of the poor. Thus, it was only in 1831 that, in Lambeth, these underground works were so rated, nearly fifty years after the company's incorporation.[3]

Three-fourths exemption from rating under Public Health Acts.

Another class of exemptions was recognized in 1833, when an Act relating to watching and lighting[4] provided that houses, buildings, and property, other than land, should be rated for these purposes three times higher than land. The same principle was afterwards laid down in the Public Health and Local Government Acts. It was admitted that, especially in urban districts, certain classes of agricultural land, together with railways and canals, would derive comparatively little benefit from the sanitary objects and local improvements to which rates levied under these Acts were appropriated. Accordingly, in the first Public Health Act of 1848,[5] and in the Local Government Act, 1858,[6] partial exemptions were made in favour of these classes of property, and were continued in the existing Public Health Act, 1875. Tithes, tithe commutation rent-charges, land used only as arable, meadow or pasture, or as woodlands, market-gardens or nursery grounds, land covered with water, or used only as a canal or towing-path, or as a railway constructed under statutory powers, were, by the Act of 1875, to be assessed in the proportion of one fourth part of their net annual value.[7]

Incidence of general district rates and borough rates.

This partial relief from assessment applies only to general district rates levied for objects defined in the Act of 1875 as

[1] *Ante,* p. 470.
[2] 5 Geo. IV. c. 124, s. 127.
[3] Paper on Centenary of Lambeth Waterworks Company (July 4, 1885), p. 21.
[4] 3 & 4 Will. IV. c. 90, s. 33.
[5] 11 & 12 Vict. c. 63, s. 88.
[6] 21 & 22 Vict. c. 98, s. 55.

[7] 38 & 39 Vict. c. 55, s. 211. In some cases, especially in Scotland, where the length of mains to be laid, for the accommodation of sparsely populated districts, is excessive, gas and water undertakings have obtained for their underground works the benefit of this one-fourth rating.

sanitary objects; it does not extend to a city or borough
rate which is levied under the Municipal Corporations Act,
1882,[1] for general municipal objects. In practice, when private
Bills are promoted by local bodies, to sanction new objects of
expenditure, frequent disputes occur, chiefly with railway
companies, who seek to charge this new expenditure upon
the district rates, when their three-fourths exemption would
arise, instead of on the borough rate, when they would be
liable to a full assessment. In some cases, when borough
boundaries have been extended so as to include railways,
attempts have been made by companies to apply their three-
fourths exemption even to the city or borough rate.[2] Corporations have occasionally consented to make this concession,
the amount at issue being small, or in order to avoid a contest.[3] In other cases in which improvements of a sanitary
nature have been charged to borough rates, Parliament has,
upon any increased rating which might accrue from these improvements, allowed to railway companies their three-fourths
exemption.[4] Speaking generally, however, where Corporations
have been resolute and prepared to contest the point against
powerful railway interests, they have hitherto been able to
protect from exemptions their borough as distinguished from
their general improvement rate. The reason no doubt is
that, while, from a sanitary point of view, railways may be
regarded as mere birds of passage through a locality, few
ratepayers have so immediate or so large an interest in the

---

[1] 45 & 46 Vict. c. 50. A schedule defines the objects to which a
borough fund or rate is applicable.

[2] Worcester Extension Act, 1885,
in which an opposing railway company succeeded in fixing their assessment at one-fourth for the borough
rate as well as the general district
rate (s. 22).

[3] By arrangement ~ a Middlesbrough Corporation, in their Extension Act, 1866, allowed the railway company a three-fourths exemp-

tion from borough rate on all their
property in the added part of the
borough. See also Stafford Extension Act, 1876; Over Darwen Extension Act, 1879; Hartlepool Extension Act, 1883, in which the corporation agreed to charge their costs
of promotion upon the general district rate instead of the borough rate.

[4] Hartlepool Headland, &c. Act,
1885, s. 39; Jarrow Improvement
Act, 1878, s. 52; Jarrow Improvement Act, 1884, s. 73.

general welfare and activity of a town as the railway whose system it feeds.

Exceptional rating at Pontefract. In some towns special circumstances have led to exceptional rating. For example, at Pontefract, before 1875, sanitary and municipal expenses were alike charged upon the borough rate; and when the borough boundaries were extended in that year, railway companies, whose property was thereby included, were allowed, by arrangement, a three-fourths exemption covering the whole rate.[1] Since 1881, the Corporation have had power to levy a general district rate as well as a borough rate, but the settlement of 1875 was not disturbed.

General result of cases. Allowing for these arranged cases, and cases in which exceptional views have been taken by Committees under special circumstances, it is fairly accurate to say that, on this oft-fought question, the general practice of private Bill Committees has been to abide as nearly as possible by the general law, and to allow an exemption of three-fourths only upon sanitary expenses, whether charged to general district or borough rates.

General law as to railway exemption in Scotland. In Scotland the General Police and Improvement Act[2] provides that railways shall be assessed for local rates at one-fourth their annual value, excepting stations, and buildings, which are assessed to the same extent as other lands and buildings. The general law of Scotland therefore appears to make no distinction between municipal and sanitary rates, and is therefore more favourable to railway property than the English public statutes which have been quoted.

Number of local authorities in England. Lastly, from a Parliamentary Return for 1884 the following particulars are compiled as to the number in each class of local authorities in England there specified. These consist of 15,574 poor law authorities, comprising boards of guardians of 647 unions and separate parishes, and the overseers of 14,927 poor law parishes; 63 county and 244 municipal authorities;[3] 995 urban, 576 rural, and 40

---

[1] Pontefract Borough Extension Act, 1875, s. 82.

[2] 25 & 26 Vict. c. 101, s. 90.

[3] According to a Commons' Re-

port sanitary authorities; 192 lighting and watching commissioners; 52 commissioners of sewers, and 165 drainage and embankment authorities; 6,471 highway boards; 190 turnpike trusts; 737 burial boards; 202 church boards; 2,017 school boards; 43 vestries and district boards for metropolitan management, with the Metropolitan Board, the Metropolitan Police Commissioners, and the Municipality of London; 12 commissioners for baths and washhouses; 16 market and fair, 36 bridge and ferry, 65 harbour authorities; and 21 Trinity Houses (pilotage). Here, then, in England alone are 27,710 local authorities, of twenty-four different classes, exercising jurisdiction, levying annual rates in 1881-2 amounting to nearly twenty-eight millions, with a total revenue of 42,800,000*l.* and raising within the year loans to the amount of 15,350,000*l.*[1]

turn (260-1) of later date (July, 1885), there were then in England and Wales 255 municipal boroughs, of which 13 had been incorporated since 1881.

[1] Commons' Return 123 of 1884, abstracted by Local Government Board from accounts of local authorities in England during 1881-2.

CHAPTER XVI.

MARINE, LIFE AND FIRE INSURANCE: EARLY USE OF MARINE
INSURANCES: THE HANSE MERCHANTS AND LOMBARDS:
STATUTE CONCERNING INSURANCES AMONG MERCHANTS,
A.D. 1601: LOSSES AMONG UNDERWRITERS, A.D. 1693:
LONDON AND ROYAL EXCHANGE ASSURANCE CORPORA-
TIONS, 1720: RESTRAINTS UPON INSURANCES BY PARLIA-
MENT, 1752: MONOPOLY OF 1720 REPEALED, 1824:
STATUTORY INCORPORATION OF LLOYD'S, 1871: FIRE IN-
SURANCE: CHURCH BRIEFS: MUNICIPAL INSURANCE IN
LONDON: COMPETITION BETWEEN COMPANIES, 1683:
COMMON LAW LIABILITY FOR FIRES; RISE OF LIFE IN-
SURANCE: MERCERS' COMPANY'S SCHEME: INSOLVENT
SOCIETIES: GAMBLING POLICIES: PLAN OF PAROCHIAL
LIFE ANNUITIES, 1773: STATE ANNUITIES AND IN-
SURANCE.

Early use of marine insurance.

MARINE insurance, at all events in its simpler forms, was practised among the Romans, probably copied by them from maritime nations whose commerce was of still earlier date.[1]

Bottomry bonds.

An edict of Justinian (A.D. 533) allowed a return of twelve per cent. upon bottomry bonds (*fœnus nauticum*), as an advance of money involving special risks, while the ordinary rate of interest was not to exceed six per cent. An interval of eight centuries occurs before we find reference again made

---

[1] An insurance of slaves existed among the ancient Greeks. We read that Antigenes of Rhodes, in consideration of a yearly contribution of eight drachmas for each slave that was in the army, undertook to make good the value of the slave if he ran away. (Art. "Servus," Smith's Dict. of Ant. 2nd ed. 1035.)

to any provision against nautical risks. The first revival of commerce during the middle ages leaves no trace of insurance. It is mentioned neither in the laws of Oleron nor the "Consolato del Mare," maritime codes supposed to have been drawn up during the twelfth and thirteenth centuries. These were southern codes, mainly for use by traders in the Mediterranean States. In the laws of Wisby, made about the beginning of the fourteenth century, bottomry is briefly noticed. Wisby, a Baltic town situate in the isle of Gothland, and now utterly decayed, was then a rich and prominent member of the great Hanseatic League. Subsequent ordinances passed by this league at Lubeck, Bruges, and elsewhere treat fully of bottomry, and regulate its practice, with a view to prevent those frauds, "and even wicked crimes,"[1] by which in all ages the acknowledged benefits of marine insurance have unhappily been abused.

Laws of Wisby.

Hanseatic League.

In the middle ages, and subsequently, persons of condition voyaging by sea in the Mediterranean often took out policies under which insurers guaranteed to pay a sum sufficient to ransom them if they were taken by corsairs. Agents in seaport towns frequented by pirates, whether Christians or Turks, were intermediaries under this system.[2]

Personal insurances against capture by pirates.

---

[1] Recessus civitatum Hanseaticarum. See, in an early "Recessus" of Lubeck, a chapter on bottomry (bödemerey), quoted in Martin's History of Lloyd's, 1870, p. 5. As one method of checking frauds, the Marine Code of Barcelona, A.D. 1435, limited insurances on foreign vessels freighted there to one-half, and on native vessels to three-fourths their value. The word insurance, understood and clearly described in the modern sense, first occurs in an old historical work, the Chronicles of Flanders, which says that, on the request of inhabitants of Bruges, the Count of Flanders, in the year 1310, permitted the establishment there of a Chamber of Assurance, by means of which merchants, on paying a stipulated percentage, could insure their goods from sea-risks, and enacted laws and regulations which both assurers and assured were bound to observe. At this time Bruges was the centre of an immense commerce, and might fitly be chosen for the home of such an institution. The statement in these Chronicles, however, is not free from doubt. (Ib., pp. 6, 7.)

[2] In the "Guidon de la Mer," a French work of authority, supposed to have been published at the end of the sixteenth century, this form of insurance is described. Seamen or other travellers too poor to insure

First marine insurances in England.

In England the earliest insurances of ships and goods were made by Hanseatic merchants, who, from the reign of Edward the Confessor to that of Elizabeth, a period of more than five centuries, by purchase or through policy, enjoyed special privileges in London and other ports, and monopolized almost the entire commerce of this country in staple commodities.[1] Their great warehouses and dwellings, rigidly secluded by walls and gates, for safety of property and secrecy of trade, were built on the river-side, at a site now occupied by the Cannon Street railway station. This was Gilhalda Teutonicorum, the German Guildhall, otherwise the Stapelhof or staple-house and yard, by corruption familiarly known as the Steel-yard.[2]

The Steelyard merchants.

As English commerce developed, there arose a corresponding jealousy of these aliens' privileges. Queen Elizabeth and her advisers, chiefly at the instance of Sir Thomas Gresham, then acting as Royal agent in Flanders, first laid heavy duties on all imports and exports of Hanse merchants, and

against captivity were either left to languish in servitude or released by charitable donations and bequests, and by "God's pence," contributed by merchants and others in boxes placed outside the door of each greffier, or insurance registrar, and in other public places of resort. (Martin, pp. 41-4.)

[1] As far back as the time of Ethelred II. (A.D. 979—1016) "the Emperor's men," as these German merchants were then and long after called, coming with many ships to Billingsgate, were held "worthy of good laws," in return for certain tolls and gifts to the royal exchequer. They were free of many imposts and burthens resting upon native industry; they paid fixed customs duties, instead of being subjected to numberless vexatious tolls and extortions placed in the way of general commerce; they had

liberty to ship their goods in whatever bottom they liked; they were under a separate jurisdiction, and were governed by their own self-elected rulers. In nearly every respect these members of the Hanseatic League in England formed a state within a state. (Ib., pp. 8, 9.)

[2] Ib., pp. 1, 2. The Steelyard merchants lived like inmates of a monastery, in separate cells, built only for single men, and ate in common. No inmate was allowed to marry, nor even to hold intercourse with or visit any person of the other sex, and a breach of this rule, however slight, was followed by immediate expulsion, if not by severe penalties. At a fixed hour in the evening the gates were closed against all comers. The community was governed by a master, or alderman, two assessors, and nine common councilmen, annually chosen on New Year's Eve. (Ib., p. 8.)

when retaliating imposts on English traders were levied Expulsion of the Hanse merchants, 1597. by the League, and severer measures threatened, Elizabeth, in 1578, abolished all exclusive privileges possessed by the Hanse merchants, and in 1597 expelled them from the kingdom. The Lombards, who settled here in the thirteenth The Lombards as marine insurers. century, to avoid internecine strife at home, combined marine insurance with their trade of lending money at interest, acting as the Pope's agents by sales of "pardons,"[1] and remittances of ecclesiastical revenues to Rome. Their wealth and enterprise gave them great advantages ; they were Royal bankers and money-lenders, receiving protection and encouragement in return ; they farmed the customs in some towns, or had these assigned to them as security for Crown debts. Profiting by their teaching and that of their rivals of the Steelyard, English merchants in the fifteenth and sixteenth centuries began to hold their own in commerce, and there are records of insurances effected by Sir Thomas Gresham in 1560 upon cargoes of gunpowder and armour shipped by him from the Low Countries to England.

In 1601, four years after the Hanse traders were expelled, First statute concerning assurances among merchants, A.D. 1601. an Act was passed " concerning matters of assurance among merchants,"[2] founded upon the practice among German insurers, and intended to furnish an easy method for settling differences arising in this business. In its recitals, full according to custom, at a period when the reasons for legislation could nowhere else be so conveniently published, the practice of marine insurance, even in England, is referred to as of high antiquity :—

" Whereas it ever hath been the policy of this realm by all Policy of State to encourage merchant ventures. good means to comfort and encourage the merchant, thereby to advance and increase the general wealth of the realm, her Majesty's customs, and strength of shipping, which considera-

---

[1] Stow calls them "the Pope's merchants," and says they "had good markets here for their wafer cakes, sanctified at Rome, their par-dons, &c."

[2] 43 Eliz. c. 12. It is given in its original quaint spelling 4 Stat. Realm, 978–9.

tion is now the more requisite because trade and traffic is not at this present so open as at other times it hath been :

"And whereas it hath been time out of mind an usage amongst merchants, both of this realm and of foreign nations, when they make any great adventure (specially into remote parts) to give some consideration of money to other persons (who commonly are in no small number) to have from them assurance made of their goods, merchandizes, ships, and things adventured, or some part thereof, at such rates and in such sort as the parties assurers and the parties assured can agree, which course of assurance is commonly termed a policy[1] of assurance, by means of which policies of assurance it cometh to pass upon the loss or perishing of any ship there followeth not the undoing of any man, but the loss lighteth rather easily upon many than heavily upon few, and rather upon them that adventure not than those that do adventure, whereby all merchants, especially the younger sort, are allured to venture more willingly and more freely :[2]

"And whereas heretofore such assurers have used to stand so justly and precisely upon their credits that few or no controversies have risen thereupon, and if any have grown the same have from time to time been ended and ordered by certain grave and discreet merchants, appointed by the Lord Mayor of the City of London, as men by reason of their experience fittest to understand and speedily to decide those causes, until of late years divers persons have withdrawn themselves from that arbitrary course,[3] and have sought to draw the parties assured to seek their moneys of every several assurer, by suits commenced in her Majesty's courts, to their great charges and delays."

From the operative clauses which follow, we learn that at this period there was in the City of London an office or chamber for the registry of marine insurance policies. The statute proceeded to constitute a special Commission to hear and determine insurance causes. This Commission, re-

newed yearly, consisted of the Judge of the Court of Ad-

---

[1] From the Italian polizza, a promise. Italian merchants practised insurance at an early date, and Martin (p. 27) quotes evidence of policies current between London and Venice and Pisa, A.D. 1400—1512.

[2] Cf. Lord Keeper Bacon's speech on opening Queen Elizabeth's first Parliament :—"Doth not the wise merchant, in every adventure of danger, give part to have the rest assured?"—1 Parl. Hist., 641.

[3] Mode of arbitration.

miralty, the Recorder of London, two doctors of civil law, two common lawyers, and eight "grave and discreet merchants," who were empowered to proceed "in a brief and summary course," and "without formalities of pleading." In its constitution and jurisdiction, this Court seems to have been founded on the insurance laws of the Hanseatic League.[1] Its numerous members made the new tribunal unwieldy; a still stronger objection probably was the appeal allowed from its decrees to Chancery. Its powers, too, were defective, and suitors were delayed in obtaining remedies, as the Commissioners could not enforce their orders against ships or goods. New powers were given to them in 1662,[2] and the number of members was reduced, but the Courts of common law did not favour a tribunal composed in part of laymen, and did much by their decisions to curtail its jurisdiction.[3]

As may be supposed, the earliest English insurers did not confine their attention to this branch of business only, but were merchants and bankers, who "underwrote" lives as well as ships. As commerce expanded, and marine insurance became more common, it was also carried on at the coffee houses set up in London during the reign of Charles II., and frequented by merchants and captains of vessels.[4] Here sales of ships and cargo were made "by candle," freights were arranged, commercial news was sought, and business transacted. There were also marine insurance offices in the Royal Exchange. Among the underwriters were men of insufficient means, through whose failure insurers sometimes could not recover in case of loss. These failures were especially

Underwriting at coffee-houses.

Failures of underwriters.

---

[1] Martin, p. 14.
[2] 14 Chas. II. c. 23.
[3] Both 43 Eliz. and 14 Chas. II. were repealed by the Statute Law Revision Act, 1863.
[4] Lloyd's coffee-house, then in Tower Street, afterwards removed to Lombard Street, is first mentioned in 1868. Soon after 1770, the underwriters and brokers, united under the name of Lloyd's, removed to Pope's Head Alley, and, in a few years, to their present quarters in the Royal Exchange. (Martin, pp. 59, 120.)

numerous during the war with France in 1693, among persons
who had insured vessels against capture.

A Bill was therefore promoted in the House of Commons,
apparently without much justification, to enable these " merchant insurers the better to satisfy their creditors."[1] It
was opposed by sundry merchants of London, creditors
for large sums, whose petition was referred to a Committee on the Bill. This Committee consisted of thirty-
seven nominated members, with Sir Samuel Barnardiston at
their head, to whom were added " all members who are
merchants, and all that serve for seaports."[2] Among the

defaulters who thus sought relief was Daniel Foe, merchant,[3]
who represented " that having sustained divers losses by insurances since the war with France, and having met and
proposed to his creditors a means for their satisfaction, some
few of them will not come into those proposals ; " therefore he
asked that his name might be inserted in the Bill.[4] The Commons passed this measure, but it was summarily rejected by
the Upper House before commitment.[5]

These failures among underwriters were cited, a few years
afterwards, as reasons for establishing one or more companies, whose joint capital would save insurers from loss.
In 1718-19, some previous applications having been made in
vain, Lord Onslow and others petitioned his Majesty in
Council to grant them a charter enabling them to insure
ships and merchandize at sea ; and Lord Chetwynd headed
another party of merchants in praying for a similar privilege. These petitions were referred, in the usual course, to

---

[1] 11 Com. Journ. 25, A.D. 1693.

[2] Ib. 38.

[3] This was the well-known author
of Robinson Crusoe, who signed his
name indifferently Foe and Defoe.
He failed as a city merchant in 1692,
for 17,000l. His biographers do not
notice his losses as a marine insurer.
Although he did not obtain the sta-

tutory relief for which he petitioned,
his creditors accepted a composition ;
and, to his honour, he afterwards
paid them in full. These experiences led him to write upon defects
in the bankruptcy laws.

[4] 11 Com. Journ. p. 87.

[5] 15 Lords' Journ. 390 ; March
10, 1693.

the Attorney-General, Sir Nicholas Lechmere, for his report, and he heard counsel in his chambers for and against the grant.[1] Lower rates, additional security, and more effectual means of recovering sums assured were reasons urged in favour of chartered companies. On the other side, underwriters in London and Bristol declared that such companies were not required, and would lead to monopoly, and other evils. They also urged the advantages of competition, the benefits arising from individual supervision in such a business, and the probability that chartered bodies would be more ready to contest claims than individuals were, because "corporations have no sense of shame."

Lord Onslow, who had been Speaker of the House of Commons in 1708,[2] was one of the chief supporters of this project. Against him no charge was brought, but so many scandals were rife affecting persons in high places during the speculative mania of this period, that the House of Commons appointed a Committee to examine into "subscriptions for fisheries, insurances, annuities for lives, and all other projects carried on by subscriptions in and about the cities of London and Westminster." Before this Committee the Solicitor-General, Sir William Thompson, charged Sir Nicholas Lechmere with receiving large sums of money, "contrary to his duty as Attorney-General," from some of the persons who had solicited charters.[3] Sir William Thompson informed the Committee "that there were public biddings for charters, as if at an auction, in the Attorney-General's chambers, between some of the persons concerned;" and to encourage offers from these persons, the Attorney-General's chief clerk told them "that the other side had

Marginal note: Charges of corruption against Attorney-General Lechmere, A.D. 1720.

---

[1] The proceedings at the Attorney-General's chambers began at six o'clock in the evening and lasted till ten or eleven. An account of these proceedings, and of fees paid to the Attorney-General, and to counsel, is given in 19 Com. Journ. 306.

[2] Uncle of the more celebrated Speaker Onslow, who acted in that capacity from 1727 to 1761, and was then created Viscount Cranley.

[3] 19 Com. Journ. 305.

given handsomely." After hearing evidence, the Committee pronounced these charges "malicious, false, scandalous, and utterly groundless," further declaring " that the Right Honourable Nicholas Lechmere, Esquire, has discharged his trust in the matters referred to him by his Majesty in Council with honour and integrity." [1]

Offer by companies to make good deficit in civil list.

Both projects would undoubtedly have been rejected but for the anxiety of George I. to supply certain arrears in his civil list, which had been left unprovided for in 1720. Probably the noblemen interested in the two companies received a hint that necessities of State might prove their opportunity. They accordingly offered to meet the deficit by a payment of no less than 600,000*l.* in return for charters, with statutory sanction.[2] As they were able to offer satisfactory evidence of solvency, their proposal was accepted, and Mr. Aislabie, Chancellor of the Exchequer,[3] brought to the House of Commons the following Royal message :—

Royal message.

" His Majesty having received several petitions from great numbers of the most eminent merchants of the City of London, humbly praying he would be graciously pleased to grant them his letters patent for erecting corporations to insure ships and merchandize, and the said merchants having offered to advance and pay a considerable sum of money for his Majesty's use in case they may obtain letters patent accordingly; his Majesty being of opinion that erecting two such corporations, exclusive only of all other corporations and societies for assuring of ships and merchandize, under proper restrictions and regulations, may be of great advantage and security to the trade and commerce of the kingdom, is willing and desirous to be strengthened by the advice and assistance of this House in a matter of this nature and importance. He, therefore, hopes for their ready concurrence to secure and confirm the privileges his Majesty shall grant to such corporations, and to enable him to discharge the debts

---

[1] 19 Com. Journ. 310. Throughout this record the two projects are described, one as " commonly called Lord Onslow's," the other as " Lord Chetwynd's insurance."

[2] 7 Parl. Hist. 648; 6 Geo. I. 1720.

[3] Afterwards expelled from the House with other members for his share in the South Sea scheme.

of his civil government without burdening his people with any new aid or supply."[1]

Leave was immediately asked to introduce a Bill "enabling his Majesty to grant letters of incorporation to the uses and purposes mentioned in his Majesty's most gracious message." This motion was carried, but not without protest from a respectable minority, the voting being 186 to 72.[2] Two days afterwards an ineffectual attempt was made to procure for the House some information respecting civil list deficiencies, by an address for an account of debts owing, and "of the arrears of civil list funds to pay the same." This motion was negatived by 146 votes to 47.[3] The House next resolved to reply to the Royal message. They acknowledged it as "an instance of so much condescension as deserves the highest returns of duty and thankfulness." "It is a great satisfaction to your Commons," they added, "to see the honour and dignity of the Crown supported under the difficulties which the necessity of your Majesty's affairs may have occasioned, without laying the burden of any new aid or supply upon your people;" and they assured the Crown of their resolve "to render effectual your Majesty's gracious intentions for the ease, security, and welfare of your trading subjects."[4]

After consideration, the House resolved to authorize in one Bill the two charters recommended by his Majesty, with general safeguards "to restrain the extravagant and unwarrantable practice of raising money, by voluntary subscriptions, for carrying on projects dangerous to the trade and subjects of this kingdom."[5] On May 31, the measure was passed in this form by 123 to 22 votes, and the House of Lords sanctioned it without amendment.[6] In its preamble, this Act[7]

Bill introduced.

Reply to King's message.

Act of 1720.

---

[1] 19 Com. Journ. 355-6, May 4, 1720; 7 Parl. Hist. 648.

[2] 19 Com. Journ. 356.

[3] Ib. 357.

[4] Ib. 358.

[5] Ib. 361.

[6] 21 Lords' Journ. 350; June 7, 1720.

[7] 6 Geo. I. c. 18.

set forth the expediency of constituting two companies, for reasons already cited—the failure of private insurers, and consequent "ruin and impoverishment of many merchants and traders, discouragement of adventures at sea, and great diminution in the trade, wealth, strength, and public revenues of this kingdom." His Majesty was authorized to grant charters of incorporation to the two companies, excluding all other companies or associations for marine insurance, but saving the rights of private underwriters. These special privileges might be revoked upon three months' notice, but any consideration money paid by the companies was, in this event, to be returned to them. After thirty years the Act might be repealed without this repayment if the privileges conferred were found "hurtful or inconvenient to the public;" and all such privileges were then to "remain suppressed for ever."

Monopoly given against all other marine insurance companies.

Grant of charters, June, 1720.

In June, 1720, a fortnight after this Act received the Royal assent, charters were granted to the Royal Exchange Assurance Corporation, Lord Chetwynd's venture, and the London Assurance Corporation, with which Lord Onslow was associated. In order, it would appear, to raise more easily the stipulated 600,000*l*., which was to be paid into the Exchequer by instalments, each corporation, acting in concert, formed an affiliated body for "the insurance of houses and goods from fire." These companies were incorporated by charter in April, 1721, under the same names as the parent corporations, but with distinct objects and organizations, and without any monopoly of fire insurance business; and they undertook to contribute one-half of the 600,000*l*. But evil days soon came upon all speculations planned, whether legitimately or corruptly, at this period. A special misfortune happened to the London Assurance Corporation. It underwrote a fleet of twelve Jamaica merchantmen, all of which were lost in October, 1720, and its 10*l*. stock, which had risen to 160*l*, became almost worthless.[1] Its companions in adversity were as little able to meet the instalments still due to the Exchequer.

In these straits an appeal, *ad misericordiam*, to the King and Parliament was resolved on. Accordingly, in July, 1721, the parent companies, again acting in concert, petitioned Parliament for relief. They stated that each had paid 111,250*l.* and had given security for 38,750*l.*, part of the 300,000*l.* "which they were obliged to advance, without interest, for the use of his Majesty's civil government." They added that they were desirous, and had attempted, to raise the remainder, but without success; and it was "utterly impossible for them to make any further payment." At the same time his Majesty informed the House of Commons that he had no objection to the relief prayed for by the two companies if the House thought it of public advantage. In both Houses the influence of Lord Onslow and Lord Chetwynd was considerable. Another cause which contributed materially to leniency in Parliament was the general collapse of public credit, and grave disasters occurring to individuals through the bursting of the South Sea bubble. A relief clause was therefore inserted in a public Act,[2] relating to civil list liabilities; it declared that his Majesty, "in tender consideration of the great difficulties which the corporations do severally labour under," was graciously pleased to remit all further payments on account of the moiety of 600,000*l.* unpaid or unsecured.[3]

During the latter part of the last century heavy losses were suffered by English underwriters from captures by French and Spanish privateers and men-of-war. In 1780, the combined navies of France and Spain fell in with the outward-bound East and West India fleets, and took fifty-

Margin notes:
Petition to Parliament for relief.

Relief Act, 1721.

---

[1] Martin, 101, quoting Malachi Postlethwayt, a contemporary writer. In July, 1720, South Sea stock was at a premium of a thousand per cent.: the bubble burst in September.

[2] 7 Geo. I. c. 27.

[3] The recitals to this Act specify the dates of the four charters to the parent and affiliated corporations, and the obligations undertaken by the latter.

five of them, the convoy, consisting of three British men-of-
war, the Ramilies of 74 guns, and two frigates, making their
escape. Another great blow was the seizure of all British
ships in Russian ports by the Emperor Paul in 1799. On
the whole the history of Lloyd's, even at these trying periods,
is a very honourable one. Considering the enormous losses,
the number of failures was inconsiderable,[1] owing, no doubt,
in part, to the method of dividing risks.

Throughout the great wars of the eighteenth century
underwriters at Lloyd's impartially insured foreign merchantmen against captures by British cruisers, upon a sufficient consideration. By some persons this practice was
thought unpatriotic, and in 1740 a Bill, brought into the
House of Commons, after debate, " to prevent some inconveniences arising from marine insurances," proposed to "restrain
the making of insurances upon any ships or effects belonging
to any foreign kingdom, or the subjects thereof, trading to or
from the East Indies; and also to restrain all insurances on
any ships or effects of the subjects of any prince or State not
in amity with the Crown of Great Britain.[2] The London
Assurance Corporation petitioned against this measure, setting
forth their charter, and the considerable sums they had paid
for it, and taking a business-like view which the House
adopted. "We conceive," they said, "the business of
assurances to be advantageous to the country which assures ;
and as assurances on foreign ships and goods may be made
in many other countries, as well as in this kingdom, we are
apprehensive that the restraints proposed by the Bill may
prejudice the interest of this nation, and even prevent
assurances on some branches of trade now lawfully carried on
by British subjects." Although the Government appear to
have supported this Bill,[3] a motion in Committee for ad-

Margin note: Bill of 1740, to restrain insurance.

---

[1] See evidence of Mr. Julius An-
gerstein, Chairman of Committee of
Lloyd's, 1790-6, before Committee
of House of Commons in 1810. (Martin, 178-82.)

[2] 23 Com. Journ. 700.

[3] The Solicitor-General "backed"
the Bill, and the Secretary for War
was a teller in support of it.

journing its consideration was carried against them, and the measure dropped.

Twelve years afterwards, Parliament, without much deliberation, and, so far as is recorded, without debate, did impose on underwriters one of the restraints contained in the dropped Bill of 1740. This new legislation was intended to strengthen the monopoly of the East India Company. It was based upon a statute of 1723, prohibiting British subjects from " subscribing or being concerned in encouraging or promoting any subscription for an East India Company in the Austrian Netherlands, and for better securing the lawful trade of his Majesty's subjects to and from the East Indies."[1] Advancing a step further in this attempt to discourage all rivalry by foreign traders with our East India Company, Parliament now enacted[2] that after May 1, 1752, no insurances should be made within the British dominions, or money lent on bottomry, upon foreign ships or goods bound to or from the East Indies. This Act was to be in force, as a piece of experimental legislation, for seven years only. But its effect in transferring insurance business to other capitals led to its unqualified repeal in 1758.[3]

British underwriters forbidden to insure foreign vessels trading to East Indies,

by statute of 1752,

repealed in 1758.

Another public measure regulating the business of underwriters may here be shortly noticed. Marine insurances effected without any insurable interest became so common and led to such abuses that, in 1746, Parliament interfered and declared all policies by way of gaming or wagering to be illegal.[4] Insurances, interest or no interest, the Act recited, had been found by experience " productive of many pernicious practices, whereby great numbers of ships, with their cargoes, have either been fraudulently lost, destroyed, or taken by the enemy in time of war," so that " under pretence of assuring risks on shipping and fair trade, the institution and laudable design of making assurances hath been perverted, and that which was intended for encouragement

Wager policies prohibited, 1746.

---

[1] 9 Geo. I. c. 26.
[2] 25 Geo. II. c. 26.
[3] 31 Geo. II. c. 27.
[4] 19 Geo. II. c. 37.

of trade and navigation has, in many instances, become hurtful and destructive to the same."

Globe Insur-
ance Com-
pany, 1806.

Meanwhile, various attempts had been made to put an end to the monopoly given in 1720 to the London and Royal Exchange Corporations, a monopoly extended, in 1801, by Acts enabling them, owing to increased trade on canals and rivers, to "insure vessels from the risks of inland navigation,"[1] business which was not covered by their original charters. Among other rivals, the Globe Fire and Life Insurance Company, which obtained a private Act in 1799,[2] sought in 1806[3] for a charter enabling them to add marine insurance to their other branches of business. They repre-

Increase of
British ship-
ping 1720-
1806.

sented "that, since 1720, the shipping, British and foreign, entered inwards at the several ports of Great Britain, on the annual average of the years 1803-5, has been quintupled, and that, on an average of five years, to January 5, 1805, the annual exports from Great Britain have also been quintupled in official value; that foreigners have been accustomed to effect marine insurances in this country to a considerable amount, but, in order to provide new means of effecting marine insurances, which increased trade appears to require, a great number of companies have been established, within a recent period, in the British East Indies, Hamburg, America, and elsewhere." This competition, the petitioners urged, would be most effectually met if Parliament allowed a new company in London, since "it hath ever been deemed a wise policy to encourage the insurance of foreign property, as a means of bringing wealth into this kingdom, and increasing revenue."[4] Their capital was to be not more than 2,000,000l., of which one-half would be invested in Bank annuities to satisfy claims. As a

---

[1] 41 Geo. III. cc. 57, 58.

[2] 39 Geo. III. c. 83. This Act only enabled his Majesty to grant a charter, but hitherto it had been refused, and the company carried on their fire and life business under the general law. *Post*, p. 617.

[3] There is no trace in the House of Commons' Journals of the earlier applications mentioned in Martin's History.

[4] 61 Com. Journ. 390.

bribe for the privilege they asked, the company, following the precedent of 1720, offered to pay 100,000*l.* into the
Exchequer as consideration money.[1]

After debate, a Bill to incorporate this company " for insurance of ships, goods, and merchandize at sea, and for
lending money on bottomry, and for other purposes therein
mentioned," was read a first time. Numerous petitions
against the Bill were at once presented from the two marine
insurance corporations, and various fire and life offices.
All these petitions were referred to a Committee upon the
Bill, with instructions to hear counsel for and against it,
but the Session closed before this Committee reported, and
although the company were again before Parliament in
1807,[2] their application to engage in marine insurance was
not then repeated.

Proceedings in House of Commons, 1806.

Fearing that private insurers would suffer, members of
Lloyd's were keen opponents of this attempt to throw their
business open to public companies. In 1810, their influence was also used against a similar attempt by a body
of merchants and shipowners who told the House of
Commons that the two chartered corporations did not
then insure " more than three parts in one hundred of the
ships, goods, and merchandize," which were insured in Great
Britain. In order to prevent the diversion of this business
to foreign countries, they proposed a new company, with a
capital of 5,000,000*l.*[3] In the same Session the Globe Company also returned to the charge, setting forth the increased
foreign and colonial insurance business which might be
looked for in London if the Act of 1720 were repealed, or if
they were allowed, like the two chartered corporations, to take
risks at sea and on inland navigation. For this purpose they
proposed to form a new association, and stated that they had
already raised a capital of over 1,600,000*l.*, which they were

Proceedings in House of Commons, 1810.

---

[1] 61 Com. Journ. 390.   [2] 65 Com. Journ. 56.
[3] *Post*, p. 617.

willing should be secured as Parliament might direct, to answer obligations; they were also willing to raise an additional sum of 1,000,000*l.* within three months after incorporation.[1]

That the monopoly granted in 1720 was a restraint on commerce could not be denied. Members of Lloyd's declared that it had injuriously affected their general rights as insurers, a statement which could not be impeached, because the Act of 1720 not only prohibited any other company from effecting marine insurances, but any two or more individuals from underwriting on a joint account. This argument was unanswerable against any new monopoly in favour of a single company. It pointed, however, to a repeal of the Act, and Lloyd's as a body somewhat inconsistently opposed this repeal, believing that it would flood the City with business rivals, each possessing enormous capital, so that individuals who had hitherto made marine insurance their sole business would be ruined. In order, if possible, to quiet these opposite views, the House of Commons, after strenuous opposition, appointed a select Committee to inquire into the operation of the Act of 1720,[2] and consider petitions for its repeal. The Committee accordingly sat, and examined thirty-six witnesses, reporting, in April, 1810, in favour of abolishing the monopoly of the two chartered companies, but " saving their charters and their powers and privileges in all other respects."[3] A Bill was accordingly introduced to carry these resolutions into effect,[4] but was soon abandoned. At this period, therefore, the influence of Lloyd's was paramount.

---

[1] 65 Com. Journ. 54.

[2] Ib. 108. The motion for this Committee was made by Mr. Manning, then member for the City of London, and father of Cardinal Manning, and was opposed by a prominent member of Lloyd's, Mr. Joseph Marryatt, father of the well-known novelist. (See a sketch of Mr. Marryatt's speech, Martin, 234 –41.) Both these members served on the Committee, with Mr. Alexander Baring, Sir W. Curtis, Mr. Huskisson, and Mr. Brougham.

[3] 65 Com. Journ. 300.

[4] Ib. 395.

As the statute of 1720 did not apply to Ireland, a marine insurance company was established there in or before 1813. To avoid legal difficulties, this company obtained an Act in 1813,[1] enabling the secretary to sue and be sued in its name. As the law stood, no such association could be formed in England or Scotland, yet the Act of 1813 recited that the Dublin undertaking had been of great public benefit and that " a considerable revenue is derived to his Majesty therefrom." This anomaly continued some years longer. It was not, in fact, until 1824, more than a century after the two chartered companies were constituted, that their monopoly was successfully assaulted in Parliament.

Dublin Marine Insurance Company, 1813.

Nathan Meyer Rothschild, acting on behalf of a new company, the Alliance, prompted this attack. The Alliance was established, with a nominal capital of five millions, for fire and life insurance,[2] in which there was no monopoly; but the directors desired also to effect marine insurance. A proposal to repeal existing restrictions was, as before, opposed by Lloyd's, on the old ground that, so far from creating new competition, it would give rise to new monopolies.[3] Every step taken on behalf of the new company was therefore resisted. After a debate protracted until past midnight, Mr. Fowell Buxton and Dr. Lushington, supported by Lord Liverpool's Government, were allowed to bring in a Bill

Alliance Insurance Company, 1824.

[1] 53 Geo. III. c. 211.

[2] A Stock Exchange tradition, related by Mr. Martin, is that Nathan Rothschild was one day leaning against his favourite pillar in the Royal Exchange (long known as the Rothschild pillar), when his cousin by marriage, Mr. Benjamin Gompertz, a distinguished mathematician and actuary, came to him and complained that he had been rejected for the vacant office of actuary in a large insurance company, although admittedly the best candidate, the directors declaring that they would have no Jew. " Not take you because of your religion ?" Rothschild replied ; " then I will make a bigger office for you than any of them." This suddenly formed design was soon matured, and Mr. Gompertz became first actuary of the Alliance.

[3] Speech in House of Commons of Mr. Ald. Thompson, who insisted that at Lloyd's, with its thousand underwriters, there was already as effectual a competition as existed among corn merchants and produce brokers in Mark Lane and Mincing Lane.

repealing so much of the Act of 1720 as restrained any corporations, societies, or partnerships from effecting marine insurances and lending money on bottomry.[1] Both the chartered bodies at once petitioned, asking to be heard by counsel, and were supported in similar petitions by underwriters and insurance brokers in London. No strong sympathies among the mercantile community seem to have been enlisted on either side. Shipowners and traders at Newcastle wished to repeal the existing monopoly; in Hull they wished to preserve it. These were the only petitions outside the underwriting interest.

Bill to repeal 6 Geo. I. in part.

Before the Bill was read a second time, counsel were heard against it at the bar of the House of Commons on behalf of all interests. A motion to commit the Bill was next carried by fifty-one to thirty-three votes.[2] At this stage, the London and Royal Exchange Corporations interposed with fresh petitions, asking that their counsel might be once more heard "against certain parts" of the Bill. An order was made that they might appear at the bar in Committee of the whole House. This concession was not deemed sufficient, and a motion to refer the Bill to a select Committee was only defeated by twenty-nine to twenty-five votes. Objection was raised to the numbers declared by the tellers, because certain members who voted in the majority were personally interested in the Bill, being concerned in the Alliance Company. It was decided, however, that they were not so interested as to preclude their voting to repeal a public Act.[3] Then, after lively debate and a further division of thirty-three to twenty-two votes, the House went into Committee, and considered clauses.

Further debate and divisions.

Upon the next stage, that the Committee's report be received, the contest was renewed with equal spirit, although few members took part in it. An amendment to postpone the Bill for six months was lost by fifty-five to

---

[1] 79 Com. Journ. 378–9.   [2] Ib. 431.   [3] Ib. 455.

thirty-one votes.[1]   Upon request, the House ordered that counsel should be heard at the bar against the third reading, if petitioners thought fit.   On June 14-15, came a final struggle, when the third reading was carried by fifty-nine to fifteen votes.   It was then long after midnight, but a wearied House was informed that petitioners' counsel were again in attendance, to continue their arguments against the measure, and motion was made that "they be now called in."   It is easy to imagine the cries of impatience and disgust with which such a proposal, at such a time, would be met.   A prompt amendment that the House should adjourn was negatived by fifty-eight to ten votes; a motion to hear counsel was also negatived; and the Bill passed, in a sitting protracted until half-past two a.m.[2]

In the Upper House Lord Chancellor Eldon tried, in Lord Liverpool's words, "to smother the Bill" by restrictive clauses, but withdrew them upon a personal appeal made to him by the Prime Minister.   The Bill, therefore, passed without amendment;[3] it saved all rights and privileges of the two chartered corporations, except by allowing "other corporations and bodies politic, and persons acting in society or partnerships," to engage in marine insurance.   Henceforth this business became open to companies as it had always been to private individuals.   The Alliance Marine Insurance Company was accordingly formed, and in 1825 obtained an Act enabling it to sue and be sued in the chairman's name, or that of any other member of the company.[4]   In a schedule its deed of association is set out, but the Act expressly provides that no validity shall thereby be given to any provisions in the deed not capable of being enforced in law; and nothing in the Act is to be construed as incorporating the company, or relieving any of its members from obligations to which they are liable by law.[5]   A few marine

Repealing Act, 1824.

Alliance Act, 1825.

New companies.

---

[1] Ib. 482-3.
[2] Ib. 494.
[3] 5 Geo. IV. c. 114.

[4] 6 Geo. IV. c. 202.
[5] Ib. s. 12.

insurance companies in London and the out-ports obtained similar privileges in succeeding reigns,[1] but association has done less than was expected in fostering this species of enterprise, and members of Lloyd's have suffered little from the rivalry which was to have ruined all private insurers. Last among the statutes passed upon this subject was one of 1871, which repealed a provision in the Act of 1720, restricting persons from being at the same time members of both the chartered corporations.[2]

Act of 1871 relating to London and Royal Exchange Corporations.

Incorporation of Lloyd's, 1871.

Up to 1871, "Lloyd's," the headquarters of marine insurance in Great Britain, or indeed the world, was only held together by a deed of association dated 1811, and by regulations made from time to time under this deed. This constitution of a society so important was felt to be imperfect. It also occasionally led to difficulties in law, and in management. In 1871, therefore, an Act of incorporation was obtained.[3] It recites that there has "long existed in the Royal Exchange, in the City of London, an establishment, or society, formerly held at Lloyd's coffee-house, for effecting marine insurance, and generally known as Lloyd's." The functions of the newly-incorporated body are then defined as (1) the business of marine insurance carried on by members of the society; (2) protection of interests of members in respect of shipping, cargoes, and freight by, among other means, the investigation of frauds, and punishment of persons concerned in them; (3) collection, publication, and diffusion of intelligence and information as to shipping. An elaborate machinery of government is provided, and any other kindred institution may hereafter be incorporated with the society, if an agreement to this effect be recommended by the Board of Trade, and confirmed by Order in Council.

---

[1] Liverpool Marine Insurance (2 & 3 Will. IV. c. 1); Ocean Insurance (4 & 5 Will. IV. c. 9); Neptune (4 & 5 Vict. c. 93); Forth Marine Insurance (5 & 6 Vict. c. 99); Glasgow (6 & 7 Vict. c. 107).

[2] 34 & 35 Vict. c. 16.

[3] Ib. c. 21.

In this private Act, which authorizes the society to apply its funds in the recovery of " property wrecked, sunk, lost or abandoned . . . in, on, or beneath the sea, or on the shore, at home and abroad," an old and romantic tale of the sea is revived. On October 9, 1799, the 32-gun frigate *Lutine*, conveying a large quantity of gold and silver coin and bullion, of unascertained amount,[1] was despatched from Yarmouth Roads to the Texel, and was lost off the Zuyder Zee on the same night. Of her crew and passengers only one passenger was rescued, and he died from exhaustion before reaching home. England was then at war with Holland, which claimed both frigate and treasure as lawful prize. For years more or less successful attempts were made by Dutch fishermen and others to recover portions of this precious freight. In 1800-1, gold and silver bars, and gold and silver coin, worth more than 55,000*l.* were dredged up, of which the salvors were allowed one-third. Storms, shifting sands, and new channels from time to time concealed the wreck, but between 1814-22, an enterprising Dutchman, M. Eschauzier, made new attempts, with powerful dredgers and a diving-bell, to reap this harvest of the sea. Although aided, however, by a public grant from the Dutch Government, his venture proved a total failure.

As the treasure thus lost had been insured at Lloyd's, the underwriters there laid claim to it, and, after some negotiation, Mr. Canning, then Foreign Secretary, induced the King of the Netherlands, in 1823, to cede to George IV., on behalf of Lloyd's, the half-share which, in 1814, had been reserved to the Dutch Crown under agreement with the then salvors. Thirty-five years passed before any further efforts were made to visit the wreck. Then, in 1857, an arrange-

Loss of H.M.S. Lutine, A.D. 1799.

Attempted salvage.

Treasure claimed by Lloyd's.

[1] A conjectural estimate, founded upon the numbers impressed on gold and silver bars recovered, makes the total value about 1,175,000*l.* If this estimate be anywhere near the truth, it is curious that contemporary records notice so lightly so great a loss in treasure. Calculations made by Capt. H. M. Hozier, now Secretary of Lloyd's, tend to the much more probable conclusion that only 140,000*l.* worth of treasure was on board the *Lutine*.

ment was made with Lloyd's by representatives of the old salvors, and, as a portion of the shifting sands under which the *Lutine* had been so long buried was swept away by north-easterly gales, work was renewed with success. In 1857-9, treasure worth 39,203*l.* was recovered. Fierce gales then re-closed the channel of the "Iron Gate," through which the wreck had been approached. Salvage operations were carried on in 1860-1, and 4,920*l.* recovered. They were renewed in 1886, but with small success.

Statutory
application
of treasure
salved from
Lutine.

At this point the Act of 1871 takes up the narrative. Already Lloyd's hold possession of the moiety of treasure recovered in 1857-61. This money, with accretions of interest, amounting, in 1871, to 25,000*l.*, really belonged to representatives of individual underwriters, who, in 1799, made good the heavy losses arising from the wreck. But the Act recites that, according to the mode of business at Lloyd's, "the names of those who underwrite a particular policy cannot, when a considerable time has elapsed, be traced with certainty, if at all, especially as to policies effected before 1838, when the society's books and papers were lost in the fire which destroyed the Royal Exchange." Parliament was therefore asked to sanction, and did sanction, an application to general uses of the 25,000*l.* already salved from the *Lutine,* and of any further gains from this source, as well as the unclaimed residue of any sums derived from wrecks or freight hereafter salved by Lloyd's. The society were empowered to aid in or undertake the recovery of property wrecked before or after the Act passed, and particularly in further efforts to salve from the *Lutine.* Any money so yielded, with the fund in hand, is to be "applied for purposes connected with shipping or marine insurance," according to a scheme confirmed by Order in Council.[1] If, therefore, the sea and sand off the Isle of Vlieland at any time yield further spoils, and the treasure carried in the *Lutine* has not been exaggerated, Lloyd's may one day from this source obtain large sums to be disposed of for public objects speci-

[1] 34 & 35 Vict. c. 21, s. 35.

fied in their Act of incorporation.[1]   Hitherto a few Orders in
Council have authorized the expenditure of small portions of
the money in hand for the punishment of frauds connected
with marine insurance, and for other objects of general benefit to the shipping, mercantile and underwriting community.

Of other objects specified in the incorporating statute, by
far the most important is the collection and issue of shipping
news. Almost from the earliest times in the history of Lloyd's
this intelligence has been obtained and published at great
expense for the information and guidance of members. *Shipping news at Lloyd's.*

Lloyd's List, a daily record of shipping movements and
intelligence, first established as " Lloyd's News" in 1696,
was compelled to suspend its publication in 1697 for breach
of privilege in mentioning inaccurately an unimportant petition then before the House of Lords, and was revived in ·
1726.   Through their correspondents in all parts of the
world, London underwriters then, as long afterwards, often
obtained earlier information than the Government could
procure.   Thus, it is recorded, that " Mr. Baker, master of
Lloyd's coffee-house in Lombard Street, waited on Sir Robert
Walpole with the news of Admiral Vernon's taking Porto-
bello.   This was the first announcement received thereof,
and, proving true, Sir Robert was pleased to order him a
handsome present."[2]   Each entry in Lloyd's List is now
carefully indexed from day to day under the ship's name,
arranged in alphabetical order in huge volumes, so that the
last news of each vessel can be at once ascertained. *Lloyd's List.*

In order further to utilize these records, the information
collected at Lloyd's from all parts of the world, both by tele-
grams and letters, is. digested and compiled weekly in Lloyd's *Lloyd's Weekly Shipping Index.*

---

[1] Striking mementos of the *Lutine*
stand in the library at Lloyd's : the
ship's bell, weighing eighty pounds,
recovered from the wreck, and impressed with the royal arms of
France ; and her broken rudder,
converted into a table and carved
chair, after having been submerged
for sixty years.   Each object bears
an inscription recording this memorable wreck.   The *Lutine* was originally a French frigate launched in
1785, and afterwards captured by
Admiral Duncan.

[2] Gentleman's Mag., March 11,
1740 ; Martin, 108.

Weekly Shipping Index, which is issued every Friday, and contains precise details of all casualties, arrivals and sailings of vessels, as well as intelligence concerning ports, harbours, and other facts of commercial interest. A confidential Index is published quarterly for the use of underwriters only, and gives secret information concerning all matters which may assist them in carrying on their business of marine insurance. The committee of Lloyd's also publish a book termed "Hints to Captains," which is issued gratuitously to officers of the mercantile marine, together with a book which shows the distinctive flags of all steamship lines.

Confidential
Index for
Underwriters.

"Hints to
Captains."

Lloyd's
Registry of
Shipping.

Lloyd's Registry of Shipping, giving the age, burthen, state of repair, and general condition of all British vessels proposed for insurance, dates from about the year 1730. Surveys and classification of vessels by Lloyd's began towards the close of the eighteenth century, and from time to time were extended and improved. In 1834, "Lloyd's Register of British and Foreign Shipping" was established upon a new basis. The laborious and responsible task of preparing, renewing, and authenticating the ever-changing information contained in this publication is performed by a small army of surveyors at home and abroad, under a committee of revision and management, consisting of merchants and shipowners as well as underwriters. Although an offshoot of Lloyd's, the Register therefore has a wider basis; its managing committee is elected in the chief outports and in London; and impartiality is thus secured in dealing with varied and sometimes conflicting interests.

Lloyd's
Captains'
Register.

Another part of an underwriter's equipment is a Captains' Register. Besides a vessel's age and comparative seaworthiness, and the voyage she is undertaking, her commander's antecedents and qualifications are important elements for consideration. The Captains' Register is a succinct but sufficiently complete biographical dictionary of every certificated commander in the British mercantile navy, numbering about 25,000, and corrected to the latest date.

Lloyd's have for some years distributed among all underwriting associations over the world shipping intelligence, and have also, on payment, granted to certain newspapers the privilege of publishing portions of this intelligence. In 1886, the committee promoted a Bill to extend their powers. The preamble recited that, since 1871, Lloyd's Society, "by means of their stations at home and abroad, and by their officers and servants, are enabled to obtain intelligence and information of various kinds not strictly connected with shipping," but of great public utility. Authority was therefore sought to collect, publish, and distribute this news, and for that purpose to establish signal stations, with telegraph and telephone wires, at any points on the coast, with a proper staff of officers. The Bill was brought into the House of Lords, but was withdrawn,[1] as the Board of Trade undertook to bring in a public Bill giving these and other facilities for extending and improving Lloyd's signal stations.

Lloyd's Bill, 1886.

Insurance against fire has no early origin, unless we go back to the Anglo-Saxon guilds, whose common fund was used, amongst other objects of self-help, to secure members against losses from this cause. A later method of providing relief for sufferers from fire, and other calamities, was by briefs, or royal letters, licences authorizing collections in parish churches. These licences were granted by the Lord Chancellor, upon an Order in Council, made on adequate proof of loss and of good faith by applicants. One of these briefs, drawn up in 1653, the first year of Cromwell's Protectorate, sets forth a petition from the mayor and inhabitants of Marlborough, backed by certificates from magistrates of Wiltshire, testifying "that upon Thursday, April 28, 1653, the Lord, whose judgments are unsearchable, and His ways past finding out, in His overruling providence disposing, a fearful and most violent fire broke out at the lower end of the said town, which in the space of three or four hours burnt and destroyed all the considerable parts and body thereof,

Fire insurance practically effected in Anglo-Saxon guilds.

Briefs authorizing charitable collections.

Great fire at Marlborough, 1653.

---

[1] House of Lords' Min., March 22, 1886.

with one of the churches and the market-house, to the number of 224 houses . . . to the utter undoing of the greater part of the said inhabitants, they not having anything for their future livelihood, and withal to supply the urgent necessities of their languishing families. The sense of this weighing deeply and seriously on the hearts of the Council, with tenderest bowels commiserating the much-to-be lamented condition of the distressed inhabitants, they have thought themselves bound, both in conscience and duty . . . to recommend the same to the charity and benevolence of well-disposed persons, and upon this extraordinary occasion to appoint, as they do hereby, a collection to be made in the cities of London and Westminster, and in all other cities, counties, boroughs, and other principal places within England and Wales . . . for relief of the inhabitants, and for re-edifying the town, which is exceedingly necessary, and of great importance for commerce and trade; not doubting that a business of this nature (so Christian, and of such concernment to so many ruined and desolate families) will find ready acceptance with all those who have anything of bowels of compassion in them, and that they will be easily provoked to such a cheerful and liberal contribution as shall be answerable to so great a loss."[1]

Funds collected under briefs.

A committee of London aldermen and other persons was appointed in this brief to receive sums collected and manage the distribution; and they were to sit in Saddlers' Hall. There was also a particular recommendation of this object to the Lord Mayor, Aldermen, and Common Council, so that the Lord Mayor was recognized then, as now, as a source and centre of charity. Traces of similar collections by Royal order may be found in many ancient church registers. These briefs furnished frequent opportunities for fraud. They were sometimes counterfeited; more frequently the money was diverted and embezzled. To guard against malpractices

Act to prevent abuses, 1705.

[1] The full text of this brief is given in Walford's Insurance Cyclopædia, III. 313.

an Act was passed in 1705[1] "for better collecting charity money on briefs by letters patent, and preventing abuses in relation to such charities." This Act recited many inconveniences and frauds greatly troubling and prejudicing all proper objects, and discouraging charity. It was therefore provided that all money thus collected should be paid to trustees, that briefs should be printed in limited numbers by the King's printers only, and each copy authenticated by endorsement of one trustee or more. These Royal letters were to be sent not only to churches, but "to the respective teachers and preachers of every separate congregation, and to any person who hath taught or preached in any meeting of the people called Quakers." All such persons, and ministers of churches, were to read the brief on some Sunday within two months after its receipt, "immediately before the sermon, preaching, or teaching." On each brief, when returned, the amount collected was to be marked. A register of all sums so collected was also to be kept in each parish, and provision was made for inquiries by a Master in Chancery into alleged frauds. An evil practice had grown up of " farming and purchasing " for a sum down the money that might be collected on briefs, "to the very great hindrance and discouragement of almsgiving." This practice was prohibited under a penalty of 500*l.*[2]

Notwithstanding this legislation, briefs continued a means of fraud, and in 1716 there was a proposal in the House of Commons to amend the Act of Anne, with a view to make it more effectual. The Bill introduced with this object was referred to a Committee, but did not go farther.[3] Church briefs, as they came to be called, were in use until the year 1828. From the statute abolishing them[4] we learn that there was then an official called "the undertaker of briefs," who held an unnamed sum, consisting of balances left which had not been required for objects of collection. These

Act to abolish Church briefs, 1828.

---

[1] 4 & 5 Anne, c. 25 (in Stat. Realm; c. 14 in the common printed editions).

[2] 4 & 5 Anne, c. 25, s. 11.

[3] 18 Com. Journ. 425, 466.

[4] 9 Geo. IV. c. 42, s. 1.

balances were transferred by the same Act to a society incorporated "for promoting the enlargement, building, and repair of churches and chapels."[1] Vested interests had arisen, and compensation was provided, upon the abolition of his office, to a "clerk of the briefs," who held this appointment under letters patent, not only for his own life, but for his son's.[2]

First proposals for fire insurance, 1635-8. Proposals for fire insurance in England are first recorded in 1635-8, when Charles I. was prayed to grant letters patent to William Ryley and Edward Mabb for a term of forty-one years, empowering these petitioners to carry out a scheme in London and Westminster. In return for an assessment at the rate of 1s. per annum for every house rented at 20l., they offered, if it were destroyed by fire, to rebuild or set it "in as good or better state, as it was before." A sum of 5,000l. was to be deposited in the Chamber of London as security for the fulfilment of this and other conditions.

Precautions to be used against fire. "There shall also be kept," the petitioners promised, "a continual watch in all parts of the city and suburbs all night, that if any fire shall break forth it may presently be espied. And engines shall be made and kept in every ward thereof to be ready at hand for the quenching of the same, and the watch brought speedily to the fire, and those several watchers in every ward shall speedily repair themselves to assist where the fire shall be. Reserves of water shall be made in convenient places for sudden use. From hence will arise great profit, comfort, and safety to the inhabitants and to their landlords, for many times a poor man's house is burnt, being all his livelihood, and he not able to build it again, and so utterly undone, whereupon divers briefs are granted, which by this means will be prevented. And if any house be on fire, terror thereof causes neighbours adjacent to cast their goods into the street, whereby they are exposed to great loss, which (by the plan proposed) shall be guarded by the watch, or, by God's blessing and this extraordinary care, may be much prevented. Besides, the continual watch which shall

---

[1] 9 Geo. IV. c. 42, s. 13.　　　　[2] Ib. s. 14.

be going through all the streets and lanes will hinder ill-disposed persons from breaking into houses and warehouses, and also prevent many murders and other harms which befall many in the night time." Another inducement to his Majesty to grant letters patent was the offer of "200*l.* per annum towards rebuilding the steeple of St. Paul's Church until finished." [1]

A favourable report upon this scheme was made by the Attorney-General, to whom it was referred, on condition "that no man be pressed to come in to subscribe, but every man left to his voluntary choice." In October, 1638, Charles I. granted letters patent, under the limitations suggested, and "Mr. Attorney-General is forthwith to prepare a Bill for his Majesty's signature accordingly, for which this shall be his warrant." Probably the petitioners were unable to raise the money they undertook to lodge as security, for we hear no more of their plan.

Scheme approved on a voluntary basis.

Private persons first began the business of fire as of marine and life insurance. A Dr. Barbon, said to be descended from Praise-God Barebones of the Commonwealth period, is credited with originating a practice of underwriting fire risks, in 1667. There is no doubt that the Great Fire of 1666 stimulated projectors, whose attention had already been directed to this business. In London, the Corporation were looked to as the proper authorities to organize and conduct fire insurance. They had already, in 1660, been asked by Charles II. to aid in launching a plan framed by "several persons of quality and eminent citizens," but had replied that such an enterprise should be conducted by the municipality. [2] In 1669, Mr. Benjamin Delaune submitted a scheme to the

Underwriting fire risks, 1667.

Insurance by municipality in London.

---

[1] Walford's Cycl., III. 439–40. Probably the steeple was to have been used as a watch-tower in case of fire.

[2] *Ib.* 440–1. In Hamburg and some other places, it is supposed that fire insurance was then in the hands of municipalities, a fact which would explain the Corporation's desire to control this business. Fire insurance by the State was adopted during the eighteenth century in Saxony, Silesia, Brunswick, Norway, Hanover, and Wurtemburg.

Common Council, who considered it, and thanked its author, but did not see their way to adopt it. Mr. Newbold, a member of the Corporation, afterwards made similar proposals in 1674-9.

During this interval the city had been reconstructed with substantial brick buildings, protected by party walls; it was reckoned that 12,000 such houses had been erected. As the Corporation hung back, private speculators busied themselves in framing a scheme. Fearing to be forestalled, the Corporation, in 1681, appointed a Committee, which suggested that this business should be undertaken in the Chamber of London, which would be able to "give security to the full satisfaction" of owners and occupiers. Instructed to prepare a definite plan, the Committee did so, after "daily meetings and serious consultations," and were of opinion that it would be not only of benefit to citizen-insurers but would "also be certain to raise a good revenue to the Chamber." At a subsequent meeting of the Common Council, in 1681, they agreed to undertake the business and instructed another Committee to consider how a guarantee fund might be provided. Such a fund was accordingly constituted, consisting of lands and ground-rents belonging to the City, worth 100,000*l.* at least, together with all premiums received. Brick houses and buildings were to be insured for terms of years at the rate of three and nine-pence per cent.; timber structures at double rates.[1]

Civic plan of 1681.

Attacks on Corporation.

This civic plan caused great dissatisfaction among private projectors, who complained that the Corporation had appropriated their invention, intending to reap the fruits of their skill and ingenuity. Mr. Samuel Vincent, Dr. Nicholas Barbon, and other persons associated to form the first fire insurance company, were vigorous controversialists, and attacked the Corporation's scheme in broadsides and other

[1] Walford, Cycl., III., 446–51. Insurances were only effected at first upon houses and buildings; stock-in-trade and household furniture were not insured until 1704.

publications, upon details as well as on general grounds. "Those citizens who manage the revenue of the City are but stewards for the rest, and if they (through rashness and want of knowledge) venture the public revenue of the City on a project that brings loss, they prejudice the whole body of citizens; for if this revenue be wasted, then the charge of government must be supported by taxes. And it is very probable that there is no great overplus of revenue belonging to the City, more than is necessary to defray the charge of the government, the trust of the orphans, and repairs of public places; for if there were, why is money borrowed at interest?"

This conjecture, thrown out at random in 1681, was truer than even its authors supposed. It may be remembered that, at this period, the Corporation were practically insolvent, and, somewhat later, had to plead to Parliament for help to enable them to pay debts due upon their bonds to City orphans and other creditors.[1] If, it was argued, the Corporation cannot repay moneys deposited in their chamber and secured by their bonds under the City seal, how can they satisfy claims after a great loss by fire? There was no answer to this reasoning; insurers, too, held back; and on November 13, 1682, the Corporation determined to relinquish this business, instructing their chamberlain to repay all premiums and obtain a surrender of existing policies.[2]

Insolvency of Corporation; their plan of insurance abandoned, 1682.

Municipal fire insurance in London, therefore, collapsed through the jealousy of private competitors and the unfortunate condition of civic finance, which would have effectually prevented Parliament from authorizing the Corporation to act as insurers. By this time a company was established "at the back of the Royal Exchange," but was not long allowed exclusive possession of the field. A rival "Friendly

Competition between companies, 1683.

---

[1] *Ante*, pp. 376 *et seq.*

[2] Strype says curtly, and no doubt truly, the project "would not take, perhaps, because at this time the City's credit was low." According to Walford (III. 455), a few policies were issued in 1683, and the business was finally relinquished only after a mandamus granted by the Court of King's Bench to restrain the Corporation.

Society," projected by Mr. Spelman and others in 1683, had some success in attracting customers. Feeling the stress of this competition, the original company, consisting of Vincent and his partners, and known as "the Fire Office," appealed to the Privy Council for protection in 1686-7, on the ground that they had invented this new business, had conveyed to trustees 60,000*l.* in ground-rents as security for losses, and had, during six years, paid for such losses 20,000*l.* To encourage them in a good undertaking so begun, they humbly prayed his Majesty to grant them an exclusive privilege of insuring from fire all houses within the Bills of Mortality for a term of thirty-one years.

Both companies were now ordered to appear before the Council. After reference to the Attorney and Solicitor-Generals, and much consideration, their Lordships were of opinion that Spelman and his partners, carrying on the Friendly Society, gave the greatest "benefit and satisfaction to the public," by their method of insuring.[1] A grant of letters patent was therefore ordered to them, but they were required to "present a proposal in writing whereby Vincent and his partners may be preserved from ruin." Vincent petitioned against this adverse decision, and in January, 1688, letters patent were granted to both companies, coupled with the absurd condition that they were to carry on business, alternately, three months at a time.[2]

---

[1] Vincent's method was reimbursement of losses from an already subscribed fund. In Spelman's society, each subscriber paid his quota to rebuild a house when burnt. Thus, in the London Gazette of July 6, 1685, the following notice appears :—"There having happened a fire on the 24th of last month by which several houses of the Friendly Society were burned to the value of 965*l.*, these are to give notice to all persons of the said society that they are desired to pay at the office in Falcon Court, in Fleet Street, their several proportions of the said loss, which comes to five shillings and one penny for every 100*l.* insured, before August 12 next." This was really a system of underwriting, as in marine insurance, applied on a much smaller scale to fire policies.

[2] Walford gives the text of these accommodating, impracticable Orders in Council (III. 458-9). They provided that a clause should be inserted in the letters patent, reserving power to his Majesty to appoint a reward

How the two companies solved this problem is not recorded. New rivals entered the field before the century closed, calling themselves "Amicable Contributors," now the Hand-in-Hand, the oldest existing fire office, and only survivor of all the companies started in the seventeenth century. Many schemes of fire insurance were floated during the speculative mania which culminated in 1720. It is unnecessary to do more than refer to these and subsequent proposals which involved no legislation. The Royal Exchange and London Corporations, chartered in 1721, have already been mentioned.[1] Fire insurance was generally carried on under the general law, requiring no special Acts. The earliest private statutes relating exclusively to this branch of insurance appear to be two which were obtained in 1796 by the Royal Exchange and London Corporations. Their charters had authorized them to insure houses and goods " in England and Wales, or the town of Berwick-upon-Tweed, or within the kingdom of Ireland, or within any other of the King's dominions beyond the seas." Their new statutes enabled them to insure in like manner " in all parts and places whatever."[2]

Since 1800, private Acts have been obtained by more than sixty fire insurance companies, chiefly to relieve them from certain difficulties which unincorporated bodies formerly had in carrying on legal proceedings or prosecuting in case of fraud. Powers were given to each company under these Acts to sue and be sued in the name of their chairman, secretary, or some other officer. This special legislation is only of technical interest.

By the common law, persons whose houses were burnt had ground of action against a neighbour in whose house the fire

---

to be paid by the grantees " to the gunners and others belonging to the Office of the Ordnance who shall from time to time assist in extinguishing fires."

[1] *Ante*, pp. 568-73.

[2] 36 Geo. III. cc. 26, 27. There was no opposition to these Bills, but a Committee in the House of Commons took formal evidence in their favour. (51 Com. Journ. 141.)

originated; and negligence was assumed, though liability might be barred by proof of unavoidable accident. In 1697, one Pemberton, at Westminster, was sued for this cause, and the plaintiff recovered 350*l.* In order to prevent similar actions by other persons whose houses had also been burnt in this fire, Pemberton engaged that if they would stay their actions he would procure King's briefs authorizing charitable collections for their relief. This attempted fraud was brought under notice in Parliament, and led subsequently to the statute of Anne regulating all issues of briefs and collections made under them. Recovery of damages in case of fires was suspended, experimentally, in 1707 by a statute directing that "no action, suit, or process whatsoever shall be maintained or prosecuted against any person in whose house or chamber any fire shall accidentally begin, nor shall any recompense be made by such person for any damage suffered or occasioned thereby, any law, usage, or custom to the contrary notwithstanding."[1]

Suspended by Act of 1707.

This indemnity was only to continue for three years, but was made perpetual in 1711,[2] and in 1774.[3] Although, too, it was originally contained in a local Act limited to the metropolis, it has been held, as re-enacted, to be of general application. Under the Metropolitan Buildings Act, 1855,[4] and Metropolitan Fire Brigade Act, 1865,[5] the same indemnity is preserved. But in London and elsewhere it applies to fires which are the result of chance or are incapable of being traced to any cause, and not to fires which, although accidental, are occasioned by negligence or want of reasonable care.[6] To this extent, therefore, the old common law liability still attaches to a person through whose default, or that of his servants, a fire is caused on his premises and damages

Made perpetual, 1711.

---

[1] 6 Anne, c. 31, s. 7.

[2] 10 Anne, c. 14.

[3] 14 Geo. III. c. 78, s. 86, which added to the words "house or chamber" the words "stable, barn, or other building."

[4] 18 & 19 Vict. c. 122, s. 109.

[5] 28 & 29 Vict. c. 90, s. 34.

[6] Chitty's Stat. II. (ed. 1880), p. 1142.

his neighbour's property.[1] In 1834 Viscount Canterbury tried to enforce this liability against the Crown, by petition of right, alleging that through negligence of its servants in the Palace of Westminster by overheating stoves with the old wooden exchequer tallies, the Houses of Parliament were burnt, and damage was done to petitioner's property when Speaker of the House of Commons. His claim, however, was rejected, the Court holding that the principle on which private employers are made responsible for servants' negligence did not apply to the Crown.[2]

Lord Canterbury's case, 1834.

The statute of 1707, "to prevent mischiefs by fire," followed by one with similar objects in the next Session,[3] applied only to the cities of London and Westminster. To this area, comprised in the Bills of Mortality, the first insurance companies also confined their operations. A duty was cast upon all metropolitan churchwardens in 1707 to provide means for extinguishing fires, and each parish was to maintain a fire-engine with proper appliances. There was a recital that several fire offices employed, and gave coats and badges to, watermen who helped in extinguishing fires, and were always ready at call, being "provided with various sorts of poles, hooks, hatchets, and several other instruments and things."[4] It was further recited that these watermen, through habit and skill, ventured much further and gave greater help at fires than other persons not used to this dangerous work. The Act, therefore, exempted all such watermen, in number not exceeding thirty in each office, from impressment for service at sea, or as marines or soldiers. This privilege of freedom from impressment was continued in later Acts applying to the metropolis.[5]

Fire Prevention Acts of 1707-11 (London and Westminster).

Firemen employed by insurance offices relieved from impressment.

---

[1] Fisher's Dig. "Fire," III. 1781. To this summary it may be added that, in the metropolis, by 28 & 29 Vict. c. 90, s. 23, and under the Towns Police Clauses Act, 1847, fire in a chimney is made a public offence, and punished by penalty.

[2] Lord Canterbury v. Attorney-General, 1 Phill. 306.

[3] 7 Anne, c. 17.

[4] 6 Anne, c. 31, s. 3.

[5] 12 Geo. III. c. 73; 14 Geo. III. c. 78.

Punishment
of careless
servants.

As fires often happened through carelessness of servants, the Act of 1707 provided that, upon conviction for this offence they should pay 100*l.*, which the churchwardens of the parish were to distribute amongst any sufferers. In default of payment, servants were to be imprisoned, with hard labour, for twelve months in some workhouse or house of correction.[1] Later Acts in 1772-4 increased the period of imprisonment to eighteen months.[2] This statutory treatment of carelessness as a criminal offence in the metropolis was abolished in 1865.[3] As it was found that insurance money, to be applied as insurers thought fit, often led to wilful incendiarism by "evil-minded persons, whereby the lives and fortunes of many families" were lost or endangered, Parliament, in 1772, required insurance offices to see that this money, when paid, should be laid out only in rebuilding or reinstating the property insured.[4]

Application
of money
insured.

Stamp and
percentage
duties.

In 1694, a stamp duty of sixpence was levied upon fire and other policies of insurance.[5] A heavier impost at the rate of eighteen-pence per cent. on each 100*l.* insured was added in 1782, during the administration of Lord North. This tax on prudence, as it came to be called, was increased to two shillings in 1797, and to three shillings in 1816. In 1864 it was partially remitted, and was abolished in 1869.

Provision for
burial by
Anglo-Saxon
guilds.

Insurance of a sum at death, commonly known as life insurance, took practical shape in England at a somewhat earlier date than insurance against risks of fire. For its most ancient form we must again go back to the Anglo-Saxon guilds which, among other kinds of material aid, provided for the decent burial of members:—"When any member shall die, he shall be carried by the whole society to whatever place of burial he shall have chosen; and whoever shall not come to assist in bearing him shall forfeit a sextarium of

---

[1] 6 Anne, c. 31, s. 4.
[2] 12 Geo. III. c. 73; 14 Geo. III. c. 78, s. 84.
[3] 28 & 29 Vict. c. 90, s. 34.
[4] 12 Geo. III. c. 73.
[5] 5 Will. & M. c. 21.

honey, the society making up the rest of the expense, and furnishing each his quota towards the funeral entertainment."[1]

Private capitalists at first engaged in life insurance, and the grant of life annuities, as in marine insurance. Thus, a case is reported[2] in 1649, in which the Court of King's Bench was asked to prohibit an action begun in the Court of Insurance to recover money due on a policy upon the life of a merchant-captain. This policy, which held good only during his voyage to the West Indies, was effected by two persons who had become his bail on a suit in the Court of Admiralty. In 1690, another case is recorded of a life policy subscribed by individuals;[3] and down even to the middle of the eighteenth century, many similar policies existed, this business being chiefly carried on by private underwriters.[4]

Towards the end of the seventeenth century, companies began to be established for annuity business and the payment of sums at death. At first there was a prejudice against this traffic on religious grounds. Defoe, in his Essay on Projects, published in 1697, decries life insurance, which the Puritans thought an attempt to avert the decrees of Providence. Halley, astronomer royal, drew up, in 1693, the first recorded tables showing the probable duration of life. But there existed long afterwards a general ignorance as to sound methods of life insurance in all its forms. Dr. Assheton, an ingenious and benevolent clergyman, Vicar of Beckenham, Kent, was among the first to advocate the substitution of corporate for individual insurance, on account of losses repeatedly sustained through the failure or death of individual underwriters. He drew up a scheme of annuities, therefore, upon a permanent instead of a precarious system,

[1] Rule of Cambridge Guild.

[2] Denoir *or* Bendir *v.* Oyle, Style, 166, 172.

[3] Whittingham *v.* Thornburgh, 2 Vernon, 206.

[4] Ross *v.* Bradshaw, 1 Bls. 312. This was one of the reasons assigned in 1761 by the law officers for advising the Crown to refuse a charter to the Equitable Society. *Post*, pp. 614-15.

as a means of providing safely for widows and orphans, especially of clergymen. After submitting this plan in vain, first to the Corporation of the Clergy, and afterwards to the Bank of England, it was taken up, in 1698, unfortunately for themselves, by one of the City Companies, the Mercers', who were then in financial difficulties and hoped to gain substantial profits from this source. In 1699-1700, this example was followed by a "Society of Assurance for Widows and Orphans;" and in 1706, through the influence of the Bishop of Oxford and other gentlemen, Queen Anne granted a charter to "The Amicable Society for a Perpetual Insurance Office."

Loans raised by life annuities. In these and other examples a favourite form of assurance was the payment of a sum by a husband in return for an annuity to his widow, if she survived him. No difference appears to have been made as to the amount of these capital sums, whether the annuitant in expectancy was seventy or thirty years old. So, in the insurance of sums upon death, **Ignorance and recklessness of projectors.** companies established early in the eighteenth century took no pains to ascertain by medical evidence whether members were in good health and of sound constitution. Still more extraordinary is the fact that in the Amicable Society, which at first distributed a varying sum among the representatives of deceased members, annual premiums were identical in amount, irrespective of the age, from twelve to forty-five, at which members were admitted.[1] This ignorance and imprudence among projectors led to the frequent collapse of companies. In other cases fraudulent associations were established, holding out expectations which, as the projectors must have known, they could never fulfil.

Insolvent companies. Unfortunately the track of every form of life insurance in England, from the earliest down even to very recent times, may be said to be strewn with wreck and ruin. Continued

---

[1] For more than a century all members continued to pay the same rates; but under a new charter obtained in 1807, the society began to rate members "according to age and other circumstances."

failures by societies and companies to fulfil their obligations have caused incalculable suffering, chiefly among the most deserving classes of our population, those who have tried to help themselves. Among the working classes these failures have not only brought misery into tens of thousands of homes, but have tended more than any other cause, except intemperance, to discourage thrift, by frequent examples of long years of small savings sacrificed and self-denial borne in vain. A record of this grievous disappointment and suffering among the poorer classes is not to be found in private statutes. But Parliament has sometimes legislated in cases affecting insurers among the middle classes. It was first called upon to intervene on behalf of annuitants under the Mercers' Company's scheme of 1698. This little-known incident in the history of a company now rich and above reproach deserves a fuller description than it has yet received.[1]

When Dr. Assheton induced the Mercers' Company to take up his scheme, they were already in straitened means, through the forced loans levied upon them during the civil war, but especially through their outlay in rebuilding the Royal Exchange, as joint trustees with the Corporation under Sir Thomas Gresham's will. They hoped, in 1698, to retrieve their position, and, at the same time, perform a service of public utility, by affording to married clergymen and others an easy and sure method of providing for their families. Accordingly, the Company invited payments of not less than 300*l.* from each subscriber, who was to be in "good and perfect health" and under sixty years of age, and they offered in return at his death to pay his widow an annuity of thirty per cent. upon this principal. Seafaring men and soldiers were excluded from subscribing; if a subscriber were

Annuity scheme of Mercers' Company, 1698—1745.

---

[1] Herbert, in his History of the City Companies (I. 237-9), dismisses this annuity scheme very curtly; a more detailed account will be found in Report of City of London Livery Companies Commission, 1884; II. 13—15.

killed in a duel, or committed suicide, or were executed, his payments were returned. At first, as money rolled in and there were few outgoings, the plan seemed profitable. In 1713, however, when claims had become numerous, the wardens were directed to be careful in admitting subscribers over fifty years old. In 1714, the principal sums received were more than 67,000*l.* Annuities were then reduced to twenty-five per cent. upon future subscriptions; in 1723 there was a further reduction to twenty per cent.; and in 1740 to fifteen per cent. Meanwhile, subscribers above fifty years of age had been excluded. But these precautions came too late, and in 1745, when 74,000*l.* more had been paid in annuities than had been received in subscriptions, the Company stopped payment.

Dr. Shaw's petition to House of Commons, 1746.

Parliament first had cognizance of these proceedings in 1746, when Peter Shaw, a physician, with other creditors of the Company, subscribers for annuities and annuitants, petitioned the House of Commons. They alleged that the Company had " fraudulently established [1] and kept on foot this annuity scheme; but that, instead of making a capital of the subscription money, and improving the same (which would have been more than a sufficient fund for the annuities), they applied great part thereof to the discharge of their debts, without the consent or privity of the subscribers or annuitants; and by such misapplication, or by some other mismanagement," totally exhausted the funds subscribed.[2]

Debts of company, 1745.

In 1745 the Company were " indebted, upon bond, 84,700*l.*, and for arrears of interest, annuities and charities, charity-money misapplied, and otherwise, upwards of 26,300*l.*: in all, above 111,000*l.* Their annuities then payable amounted to above 8,000*l.* per annum; those in expectancy to above 12,000*l.* per annum; and the income of their estates (clear of taxes and benefactions charged thereon) fell short of

---

[1] Meaning probably that the Company acted in excess of their legal powers.

[2] 25 Com. Journ. 258; Jan. 26, 1746.

5,000l. per annum." Under these melancholy circumstances, the petitioners continued, "they and their fellow-sufferers, above six hundred in number, many of whom are aged, infirm, and friendless widows, that have no other support (or married women who, in case of their becoming widows, have no other provision), are without any prospect of relief but from the equity, wisdom, and power of Parliament. As the frauds and mismanagement complained of have been transacted under sanction of a charter from the Crown; as the mischievous effects thereof are of an extensive and public nature, affecting not only so large a number of individuals, but, in their consequences, the honour and credit of a whole trading nation, the petitioners presume to hope the same will not be thought unworthy of attention and redress from the supreme authority."[1]

Appeal of sufferers to House of Commons.

To this petition the House gave prompt attention. They referred it to a numerous Committee, including all members for the City, and all gentlemen of the long robe; on two occasions they added new members; and they at once acceded to a request which the Committee instructed their chairman (Lord Strange) to make, that, "apprehending that the matters to them referred are of the greatest concern, and in their consequences likely to affect several persons of character and reputation," they might examine any witnesses they thought fit, "in the most solemn manner."[2] Power to call for persons, papers, and records had already been given to the Committee.

Proceedings in House, 1746–7.

Another petition soon came before the House from governors of a charity for the relief of poor widows and children of clergymen, a corporation constituted by letters patent of Charles II., in 1678. This charity had been "so much encouraged by many pious and well-disposed persons" that for several years it had distributed "5l. a year each to seven hundred widows of poor" clergymen, and had "put

Corporation of the Clergy.

---

[1] Ib., 259.   [2] Ib., 269; Feb. 3, 1746.

out many of their children yearly to useful trades;" but the objects of this charity had always been far more numerous than could be provided for out of annual revenues and casual benefactions. As a great number of the Mercers' Company's annuitants were clergymen's widows, likely to be left destitute through the Company's mismanagement, the governors prayed to be heard on behalf of these widows.[1]

Corporation of Huntingdon.

Of two petitions of a different class subsequently received, one, from the Corporation and inhabitants of Huntingdon, alleged that, under the will of Richard Fishbourne, in 1625, the Mercers' Company had received 2,000l., with which, as directed, they had purchased lands, namely, the manor of Charlgrave, Beds, in trust to apply the yearly income of 100l. for ever to good and charitable uses within the borough of Huntingdon. Until the year 1745, 60l. had been applied to maintain a lecturer there, and 40l. for apprenticing poor children, but since then default had been made, and petitioners asked that no claims of the Company's annuitants, or of bond or judgment creditors, should affect their security, but that the trust attaching to Charlgrave should be established and performed.[2]

Wakefield.

From Wakefield, Yorkshire, the vicar, lecturer, and principal inhabitants, alleged that, in 1642, Elizabeth, Viscountess Camden, bequeathed 3,100l. to the Company, upon trust to purchase two church livings in the counties of York, Lincoln, or bishopric of Durham, and appoint two "preaching ministers" thereto. In 1645, the Company fulfilled their trust by nominating a lecturer at Wakefield, and a second at Grantham, but since 1745 had refused to pay their stipends "on pretence that the whole legacy of 3,100l., not having been laid out in any purchase, was exhausted and sunk."[3]

Answer of Mercers' Company.

In reply, the "Wardens and Commonalty of the Mystery of Mercers" did not deny these defaults, but explained the causes of their embarrassments. "Under their present unhappy

---

[1] 25 Com. Journ. 289–90.   [3] Ib. 305.
[2] Ib. 305.

circumstances," they said, they "desired to give their respective creditors all the aid, and do them all the justice in their power." They were therefore advised to inform the House that they lent to his Majesty King Charles I., and to the Parliament and City of London, in the troublesome times of that reign, several sums, amounting to 10,000*l.* and upwards; and "by the great expense of rebuilding the Royal Exchange after it was destroyed by the fire of London," Sir Thomas Gresham's charities and endowments had become indebted to the Company in the sum of 100,000*l.* and upwards. They therefore asked to be heard before the Committee to prove these allegations, and make out a claim to relief from Parliament.[1]

Their losses and outlay.

It was not until nearly four months after Dr. Shaw's petition that the Committee reported upon the whole case submitted to them, and then a motion that their report should be considered was defeated by adjournment, which delayed it until after a prorogation.[2] In the next session of 1747-8, the Company were first in the field as petitioners. They repeated the story of their losses by loans to Charles I., the Commonwealth, and City of London; and of the moiety contributed by them, as devisees in trust under Gresham's will, towards rebuilding the Royal Exchange. This work was more costly than it would otherwise have been, as Charles II. desired that the Exchange might be "rebuilt in a more magnificent manner." Through these causes the Company "not only expended several large sums which had been given them for charitable purposes, but also contracted a considerable debt."

Case reconsidered, 1747-8.

Then the petitioners described the scheme of annuities into which they had been led by Dr. Assheton in 1698; a scheme "which Dr. Assheton represented would be of public utility and great advantage to the Company, and which they

Annuity scheme described.

---

[1] Petition of Mercers' Company, Ib. 310, March 5, 1747.

[2] 25 Com. Journ. 393; May 22, 1747. There was a division; thirty-one members voting for delay, and fourteen for immediate consideration.

accepted in hopes they should thereby discharge their debts and replace the charitable donations which they had expended." They acknowledged that they had not only applied subscriptions towards paying annuities, liquidating debts, and supporting charities, but had even spent for the same purposes further sums afterwards given or left to them for charity, and had also been obliged to borrow largely to meet current obligations.

Failure of scheme.

Notwithstanding all their efforts, "this undertaking, while well intended, had proved so detrimental by forty years' experience, that at Michaelmas, 1745, they owed 100,000*l.* to the charities and other creditors; the annuities then due amounted to 7,620*l.* a-year; annuities in expectancy to upwards of 10,000*l.* a-year; while the whole income of their estates was only 4,100*l.* a-year, consisting chiefly in houses in or about London, liable to great repairs and daily falling in their rents." Then the petitioners declared that their outlay under Gresham's Trust so far exceeded income, that the trust was indebted to them, for principal and interest, 140,000*l.* Under these circumstances, the Company prayed Parliament for help in satisfying their liabilities, pointing to the relief which, under similar circumstances, had been given to the Corporation of London by a grant of coal duties. They hoped that the House would aid them, if only out of compassion to their annuitants, "who are for the most part the widows of clergymen, and many of whom, the petitioners fear, are in a starving condition."[1]

Gresham's Trust.

Company appeal for aid in discharging liabilities.

Inquiry by Committee, 1747–8.

Forced loans, 1640–3.

A Committee, to whom this petition was referred, took evidence and examined records in proof of the Company's statements. It was shown that a sum of 3,250*l.*, advanced to Charles I. in October, 1640, was part of a forced loan of 50,000*l.* which the City was required to raise through the Corporation, to "supply his Majesty's present and important occasions, upon the security of ten lords that have

---

[1] 25 Com. Journ. 524–5; February 16, 1747.

offered themselves to be bound for the same." This money could not be contributed except by using benefactions; but the Company then ordered that, in case of any loss, these benefactions should be reimbursed by their members, and levied on them by poll.[1]   Another forced contribution of 6,500*l.*, raised by the Company in 1642, upon an ordinance by Parliament, through precept from the Lord Mayor, was "towards the relief and preservation of Ireland, and speedy supply of the great and urgent necessities of this kingdom." A third sum of 3,250*l.* was lent to the Corporation in August, 1643, part of 50,000*l.* "to be employed for the safety and defence of this city."   All these sums were to bear interest at eight per cent., but only small portions of either capital or interest had been paid.[2]

In proof of their outlay in rebuilding the Royal Exchange, 1666-7, and of the King's interest in this work, an entry was produced from the Company's records: "Be it remembered that the King's Majesty, King Charles II., came to the Royal Exchange on October 23, 1667, and there fixed the first pillar, at the re-edifying thereof, which is that standing on the west side the north entrance.   He was entertained by the City and Company with a chine of beef, grand dish of fowl, gammons of bacon, dried tongues, anchovies, caviare, &c., and plenty of several sorts of wine.   He gave 20*l.* in gold to the workmen.   The entertainment was in a shed, built and adorned on purpose, upon the Scotch walk.   Also his Royal Highness James, Duke of York, fixed the pillar on the east side that entrance, on the last day of October, 1667, and was entertained by the City and Company in that place.   His Highness Prince Rupert fixed the pillar on the

Margin notes: Rebuilding of Royal Exchange, 1666-7. Pillars fixed by Chas. II.; the Duke of York; and Prince Rupert.

---

[1] Entry in original Repertory of Mercers' Company, produced by Mr. Crump, their clerk; 25 Com. Journ. 540.

[2] Ib. 540-1. Referring to these forced loans, Herbert (I. 239) says that "the City itself had been obliged to borrow from the Companies in order to satisfy the rapacity of the parties who alternately swayed the government."

east side the south entrance, on November 18, 1667, and was entertained by the City and Company in the same place."[1] The total expense of rebuilding the Royal Exchange amounted to 58,962*l*., of which the Company's moiety was 29,481*l*.[2]

At this period the Corporation of the City of London were before Parliament, in view of the approaching expiration, in 1750, of the "orphans' duty" of sixpence per chaldron on coals, authorized in 1694,[3] and were asking for a renewal of this duty. Their petition, along with the report upon the Mercers' petition, was referred in the House of Commons to a Committee, who recommended that the orphans' duty should be continued for an additional term of thirty-five years, subject to a yearly contribution of 3,000*l*. to the Mercers' Company towards meeting annuities contracted by them.[4] This recommendation was adopted by the House, who ordered a Bill to be founded upon it, to relieve, by these means, the Company's annuitants and creditors. Before its committal the wardens and commonalty were ordered to produce detailed accounts connected with St. Paul's School, and specifying all their bond and simple contract debts owing at Michaelmas, 1745. At this stage Dr. Shaw again approached the House, setting forth that, upon security of the Company's common seal, he had entrusted them with 3,500*l*., at a time when they must have known they were insolvent. As the House now appeared to think that the widows were "proper objects of public compassion," he claimed special consideration for the time and trouble he had spent in bringing their case under notice, especially as he had "refused several very advantageous offers, made to him for his private benefit, to induce him to give up the interest of his fellow-

Marginal notes:

Report of Committee.

Subvention of 3,000*l*. yearly from orphans' coal duty towards satisfying Mercers' annuities.

---

[1] Gresham Repertory of Mercers' Company ; 25 Com. Journ. 542.

[2] Much curious information is contained in the Papers published by the House of Commons relating to this inquiry. (25 Com. Journ. 539–59.) They contain a copy of Sir Thomas Gresham's will, and of benefactions to the Mercers' Company. The Committee appear to have been satisfied with the vouchers laid before them, and so reported to the House.

[3] *Ante*, pp. 389–92.

[4] 25 Com. Journ. 569.

sufferers."[1]   Dr. Shaw appears to have been heard at the bar when the House was in Committee.[2]   His petition was afterwards referred to the Committee on the Bill, which passed on May 6, 1748, after repeated consideration and amendment, was agreed to by the Lords without alteration, and received the Royal assent on May 13th.

For the timely help thus afforded by Parliament two private statutes of 1748 must be consulted.   That passed "for further relief of the orphans and other creditors of the City of London" continued the coal duty of sixpence, subject to a contribution of 3,000l. to be paid to the Wardens and Commonalty of the Mystery of Mercers, and applied by them towards paying annuities and other debts, "in such manner as by any Act of Parliament is or shall be directed."[3]

Orphans' Further Relief Act, 1748.

Another Act of the same session[4] recited a deed of trust which the Mercers' Company executed in 1699.   By this deed most of their estates in the City of London, along with their moiety of "all that great fabric and place called the Royal Exchange," and all their estates in Londonderry, were settled in trust to satisfy, first, all charitable gifts charged upon any of their property; secondly, all annuities. Subsequent recitals stated that the clear annual income yielded by these settled estates was only 4,150l., while annuities due when the Act passed amounted to 7,500l. yearly, and arrears owing to annuitants, 9,628l.   Then the distressed condition of these annuitants was set forth, and stress laid on the Company's "public losses and misfortunes."   Through the burning of the Royal Exchange in 1666, and other causes, it is said, "they have long laboured under great difficulties, and have taken up and borrowed great sums of money upon bonds, and are otherwise become indebted in a much greater sum than they are able to pay and satisfy."

Act for Relief of Mercers' Company's Annuitants, 1748.

Company's liabilities.

[1] Ib. 639.

[2] Ib. 643.

[3] 21 Geo. II. c. 29, s. 1.

[4] 21 Geo. II. c. 32.

Strangely enough, no mention is made of loss incurred through the grant of annuities by the Company upon erroneous data. Throughout, it is assumed that their misfortunes occurred from other causes. In its operative parts, the Act provided that the 3,000*l*. yearly payable to the Company from the coal duty should be applied in meeting annuities and in paying off arrears with interest. When any surplus arose, it was to be applied in paying off " such other creditors as shall be deemed proper objects of relief, and in such manner as shall be directed by any future Act or Acts of Parliament."[1] Accounts were to be kept, for inspection by annuitants and other creditors, and annuitants were to hold a public meeting once a year in Mercers' Hall to elect auditors. Parliament was also to be supplied with a statement of receipts and disbursements. In order to relieve annuitants from any forced assignments of their interest, made upon ruinous terms when in distress, all such assignments were declared redeemable on return of any principal money *bond fide* paid. Lastly, the Company were strictly restrained from receiving further subscriptions for annuities, and Dr. Shaw's exertions were acknowledged by a provision authorizing the Court of Exchequer to order him a just and reasonable sum on account of his expenses. By their direction he afterwards received 600*l*. from the Company.[2]

In the interest of annuitants, trustees of the Company's settled estates had been empowered to let their London property on building and repairing leases for twenty-one years, and estates in Londonderry for terms not exceeding sixty-one years, or for three lives. These leasing powers were explained and amended in 1751,[3] and a mistake in this amending Act was rectified in the following Session.[4] Nothing had been done by the Act of 1748, except for the relief of

Marginal notes:

Application of the 3,000*l*. a year from coal duty.

Accounts and audit.

Assignments declared redeemable.

Further annuities by Company prohibited.

Acts of 1751–2.

---

[1] 21 Geo. II. c. 32, s. 4.
[2] See Company's accounts, printed in 1764. (29 Com. Journ. 813.)
[3] 24 Geo. II. c. 14.
[4] 25 Geo. II. c. 7.

annuitants. In 1764, therefore, the Company again peti- Company's petition of 1764. tioned, acknowledging, "with the greatest thankfulness, the bounty of Parliament," and alleging that by means of the 3,000*l.* a year allotted to them from the orphans' coal duty, together with the rents and profits of their settled estates, they had been enabled not only to meet current annuities, but discharge all arrears with interest. They also had in hand from the orphans' fund a surplus of 4,600*l.*, applicable, according to the Act of 1748, towards satisfying such other creditors as Parliament might deem proper objects of relief. As the Company were still "indebted in very considerable sums of money for charities, or money legacies, bond debts, and simple contract debts," and had no other means of meeting these obligations than the surplus from their settled estates, "which is very insufficient to discharge the same," they again prayed Parliament to intervene.[1]

A numerous Committee, including "all the merchants of Committee of 1764. the House," was appointed to consider this petition, and ascertained that the Company had received 37,500*l.* from the coal duty up to October, 1763. There were then 127 widows Company's liabilities, 1764. in receipt of annuities amounting to 4,432*l.*, and 113 annui- tants in expectancy entitled to annuities of 3,847*l.* 10*s.* in return for payments of capital amounting to only 18,683*l.* Besides unpaid benefactions, the Company also owed to 103 bondholders principal sums of 84,600*l.*, and 62,087*l.* for arrears of interest.[2] To tradesmen, workmen, and other per- sons, they owed, on November 8, 1745, "the time they stopped payment," 515*l.*[3] Upon this Committee's report a Act of 1764, for relief of Company's bond and other creditors. Bill was introduced, and, after consideration by a second Committee, passed without opposition, authorizing the Com- pany to apply their statutory share of the coal duty, and all

[1] 29 Com. Journ. 724; Jan. 23, 1764.

[2] Like the Corporation of London, the Mercers' Company, with other City Companies, received money on loan, upon the security of their common seal. They acted, in fact, as bankers for deposits. Upon the sums received from bondholders, the Com- pany allowed four per cent.

[3] All these accounts are given 29 Com. Journ. 801–24.

their surplus rents and profits after meeting annuities, towards paying, first, any money owing on account of charities and legacies; secondly, simple contract debts; and, thirdly, the annual interest upon bonded debts, with the principal money and arrears of interest.[1]

Annual lottery.

Under this Act, old bonds were extinguished by money raised upon a new issue, which was paid off through an annual lottery, drawn in Mercers' Hall. Meanwhile, bondholders were restrained from suing for their principal as long as interest was regularly paid. By means of this statutory arrangement of their affairs, by the substantial grant of 3,000*l.* a year from local taxation, and by carefully nursing their estates, the Mercers' Company, at the end of the eighteenth century, were gradually enabled to retrieve their broken fortunes, and discharge all liabilities.[2]

Widows' Pension Society, 1761-75.

A "Laudable Society for the Benefit of Widows," founded in 1761 on equally unsound principles, applied to Parliament in 1775, stating that annuities were being paid much greater in amount than the annual payments of subscribers, and asking for a private Act to reduce annuities or increase subscriptions, so as to save the society from ruin.[3] In this case the House of Commons declined to interfere, and left the unfortunate members to settle their affairs as they best could.

Albert Life Assurance Company.

In more recent times this old story of disappointment and disaster has often been repeated, and in two cases, occurring almost simultaneously, Parliament was compelled to interpose. A company known as the Albert, and established in 1839, became insolvent thirty years afterwards, and was ordered to be wound up. At various times it had purchased the assets and business of nine other companies, giving them a general indemnity against all claims on policies, annuities, and endowments; and these nine companies represented, by a similar process of absorption, ten other like associations. So complicated were the questions, so hopeless was the con-

[1] 4 Geo. III. c. 50.
[2] City of London Livery Commission, 1884; II. 15.
[3] 35 Com. Journ. 158, 212.

fusion, thus arising, that it was necessary to supersede the ordinary course of liquidation. All other proceedings, there- Albert Arbi-
fore, were stayed, and, in 1871, Lord Cairns was appointed tration Acts,
1871–4.
statutory arbitrator, with full powers to arrange, compromise, and finally settle the affairs of all these companies. No appeal was allowed against his awards : his jurisdiction was extended to India and all other parts of her Majesty's dominions ; and in exercising it he might act " not only in accordance with the legal or equitable rights of the parties as recognized in courts of law or equity, but upon such terms and in such manner in all respects as he, in his absolute and unfettered discretion, may think most fit, equitable, and expedient, and as fully and effectually as could be done by Act of Parliament."[1]

Such wide powers had never yet been entrusted under private legislation to any judge, and would only have been conferred in this instance upon one of high position. In 1872 similar powers were given to another ex-Lord Chancellor, Lord Westbury, to adjust the rights of parties in a case still more complicated and disastrous.[2] The Euro- European
pean Society, established by deed of settlement in 1854, Life Assur-
ance Society.
acquired the assets and business of seventeen other companies, which had, in like manner, previously absorbed twenty-seven similar undertakings. Forty-five independent Arbitration
companies, with their members, representing 22,155 sepa- Acts, 1872–
3–5.
rate claims, and current policies and annuities valued at 1,810,755*l.*,[3] were therefore concerned in this arbitration. Unfortunately, both Lord Westbury and his successor, Lord Romilly, died before their task was completed, and, as they had differed upon certain questions, it became necessary to provide for an appeal in order to reconcile their decisions. Under an Act passed in 1875[4] for this purpose, Sir Francis

---

[1] 34 & 35 Vict. c. 31, s. 11. See also 37 & 38 Vict. c. 58, and *ante*, I. 142, n.

[2] 35 & 36 Vict. c. 145 ; 36 & 37 Vict. c. 9.

[3] Final award of Sir Francis Reilly, Sept. 2, 1879, p. 69.

[4] 38 & 39 Vict. c. 157.

Reilly was appointed arbitrator, but it was not until September, 1879, that this almost unexampled litigation closed. It had then cost 214,124*l.*;[1] another striking example of a truth elsewhere illustrated in this work,[2] that if great interests are at stake and funds are not wanting, litigation, whatever its name, and before whatever tribunal, always will be costly.

These old and new Arrangement Acts, and the many similar failures they represent, will explain the slow progress of associated life insurance during the eighteenth century. Warned by experience, and by many bubble creations based on life insurance during the South Sea period, Parliament did not favour this enterprise, and its influence was seen in a like refusal of charters by the Crown. The London and Royal Exchange Corporations, who for a consideration had been authorized, in 1720-1, to engage in fire and life as well as marine insurance, naturally disliked competition, and were joined in their opposition to new Acts or charters by the Amicable Society, who, through exceptional influence, obtained chartered rights in 1706. This society's system of disregarding age in their premiums, and excluding from membership persons over forty-five years old,[3] led to an application in 1757, on behalf of an Equitable Society, for a

charter enabling them to work upon juster principles. After long delays, counsel for the three existing corporations being heard by the law officers against this application, it was finally refused in 1761. Various reasons for refusal were assigned in a long report to the Privy Council, signed by the Attorney-General, C. Pratt (afterwards Earl Camden, Lord Chancellor), and Solicitor General, C. Yorke (also afterwards Lord Chancellor).[4] One reason was the

---

[1] Final Award, p. 75. The items are, expenses in Court of Chancery, 32,827*l.* ; in Parliament (three Acts), 7,629*l.*; arbitration, 173,668*l.*
Ante, I., 260-2, n.

[2] *Ante*, 600.

[4] Second son of Lord Chancellor Hardwicke. He held the great seal only three days, in 1770, dying before his patent of peerage, as Lord Mor-

absence of any sufficient capital fund. Another was the company's new system of basing premiums upon the bills of mortality in London and the Breslau tables, "whereby the chance of mortality is attempted to be reduced to a certain standard: a mere speculation never yet tried in practice, and consequently subject, like all other experiments, to various chances." So the company were punished for their prudence in acting upon the best data they could procure. Referring to the three existing charters as wholly exceptional, the law officers proceeded :—

"The Crown has very wisely been always cautious of incorporating traders, because such bodies will either grow too great, and by overwhelming individuals become monopolies; or else, by failing, will involve thousands in the ruin attendant upon a corporate bankruptcy. As trade seldom requires the aid of such combinations, but thrives better when left open to the free speculation of private men, such measures are only expedient where trade is impracticable upon any other than a joint stock, as was thought to be the case in the East India, South Sea, Hudson's Bay, Herring Fishery, and some other companies erected upon that principle; but there does not appear to be any such necessity in the present case, because the business of insuring lives is carried on, not only by" the companies already mentioned, "but such policies are duly underwritten by numbers of private persons." *General reasons against incorporation.*

On these and other very insufficient grounds, as they now appear, the Attorney and Solicitor General declared that they could not advise the Crown to trench upon rights given to the three existing companies " on the bare request of any set of men, without a clearer and more certain prospect of public good." But they suggested that the projectors might carry out their scheme of insurance, without a charter, under the ordinary law. This suggestion was adopted, a deed of settlement was framed, and the Equitable Institution of to-day arose upon this foundation.[1] *Equitable Company established under deed of settlement.*

den, was completed, and before he was either installed at Westminster Hall or had sat in the Court of Chancery. (Campbell's Lives of Lord Chancellors, V. 366—431.)

[1] It was not the first of its name. See Walford's Cycl., II. 568.

Parliament afterwards rejected several applications for a statutory incorporation of life insurance companies. Ineffectual efforts, for example, to obtain an incorporating Act were made in 1785 by the British Assurance Society, established in 1773, and " held at the Queen's Arms Tavern, Newgate Street, London,"[1] although a Bill was passed by the Commons. A similar fate befell, in 1789, the Royal Exchange Fire and Life Assurance Company itself, which petitioned Parliament setting forth its incorporation by letters patent in 1721, and asking that a Bill might be introduced to enlarge its powers, and enable it to grant or purchase annuities upon lives.[2] A Committee, over which Lord Westcote presided, was appointed to consider this petition, and reported that the company's stock was then 500,000*l.*, a sum declared to be more than sufficient to satisfy losses by fire and life policies.[3] One witness, Mr. John Lubbock, banker, said that a public office for granting or purchasing life annuities, under due restrictions, would be a public benefit, because its rates would be more equitable, and its security better, than those of private individuals. A stockbroker, Mr. Richard Twopenny, gave evidence to the same effect, adding that " very little of this business had for some years past been done by respectable persons in or about Lloyd's Coffee-house, or the Bank, or Royal Exchange." Upon this evidence, and a favourable report from the Committee, an enabling Bill was brought in. This Bill was passed, but dropped in the Lords. In the same session, the Westminster Society sought authority to grant life annuities, and insure lives and survivorships.[4] Their Bill was strongly opposed by the Amicable Society, who were heard by counsel against it.[5] A vigorous debate then arose, and was renewed after adjournment. At further stages there was fresh opposition, and though the Bill at last passed the Commons, it failed in the Upper House.

Side notes:
British Assurance.

Royal Exchange Company's Bill, 1789.

Alleged decay of life insurance business by underwriters, 1789.

Westminster Society.

[1] 40 Com. Journ. 610, 1115.
[2] 44 Com. Journ. 226.
[3] Ib., 324 : evid. of Mr. James

Booth, accountant of the society.
[4] 44 Com. Journ. 153.
[5] Ib., 240, 278.

A departure from these precedents, more apparent than real, occurred in 1799.   An Act then passed, although opposed by the Amicable and London Assurance Societies, "for enabling his Majesty to incorporate by charter a company to be called the Globe Insurance Company, for insurance of lives, and against loss or damage by fire."[1]   This statute followed those of 1720 relating to the London and Royal Exchange Corporations: it did not incorporate, but only authorized incorporation by royal charter.   Upon application for a charter, there was the usual reference to the law officers, Sir John Mitford and Sir William Grant, whose opinion was adverse to any grant, unless under further statutory restrictions, and the Committee of Privy Council rejected a fresh petition in 1802, notwithstanding a favourable report from the Attorney and Solicitor General.   In 1803 the company began business as a proprietary fire and life office, but renewed their application for a charter and were supported by the influence of Messrs. Glyn, bankers.   So strong was the jealousy and so strenuous the opposition of existing insurance societies, both chartered and proprietary, that this attempt proved again unsuccessful, and was never repeated.[2]   In 1807 the company obtained the usual statutory power of suing and being sued in the name of one of their officers.[3]   Another private statute in 1858 enabled them to alter and amend some provisions in their deed of settlement.[4] Their statutory history as an independent company closed in 1864, when, by amalgamation with another body, they became the Liverpool and London and Globe Insurance Company.[5]

Owing chiefly to this discouragement of combinations for insurance by Parliament, only eight life offices, including the

Globe Fire and Life Insurance Society.

---

[1] 39 Geo. III. c. 33; 54 Com. Journ. 595 *et seq.*

[2] Their attempt to obtain powers for marine insurance is described *ante,* pp. 576-8.

[3] 47 Geo. III. (sess. 1) c. 30, amended and explained by 47 Geo. III. (sess. 2) c. 87, and 49 Geo. III. c. 123.

[4] 21 & 22 Vict. c. 60.

[5] 27 & 28 Vict. c. 116.

Private Acts to 1886.

three chartered bodies, were in existence in 1800. Afterwards their growth under the general law became rapid, and there have been passed, up to 1886, nearly 150 private statutes relating to more than a hundred life assurance companies. Of these Acts, some provide for amalgamation; others amend or enlarge existing powers; but most of those obtained prior to 1844 give facilities for suing and being sued. This prolific source of private legislation wholly ceased in 1844, on the passing of a general statute incorporating all existing and future joint-stock companies upon registration and compliance with other conditions.[1]

Insurances of smuggled goods, 1692.

Gambling, deeply-rooted in all nations at all ages, found in insurance an easy means of gratification. Smuggling was made simple and safe by insuring the delivery of goods liable to customs duties, so that, in 1692, Parliament imposed severe penalties upon both insurers of these goods and insured.[2]

Wagering policies, 1708.

It also became necessary, in 1708, to prohibit policies of assurance executed by way of wager "upon several contingencies relating to the present war and other matters of government," and to punish not only the principals, but all brokers and agents concerned in these practices.[3] This Act by its general terms left many loop-holes, and remained in practice a dead letter. Wagering policies were

New legislation, 1774.

again prohibited in 1774, together with all insurances of lives in which insurers had no interest. For many years previously these policies had led to discreditable gambling. During the rebellion of 1745, heavy insurances were opened upon the lives of the Pretender, of Lord Lovat, and other Jacobite leaders, against the chances that they would lose their heads. Kings and statesmen, British and foreign, any

[1] 7 & 8 Vict. c. 110; and see Companies Acts, 1862–79. Among some instances of later private statutes, passed for the same object, is one of 1877 (40 & 41 Vict. c. 49), relating to the Clergy Mutual Assurance Society, which was established as a Friendly Society in 1829, under 10 Geo. IV. c. 56, for the benefit of clergymen, their families and connections.

[2] 4 Will. & Mary, c. 15, s. 11.

[3] 7 Anne, c. 16.

men or women of note, reported as ill, Admiral Byng during his trial, were counters with which underwriters and their customers played, cynically indifferent to any result save that which affected their own interests.   In like manner policies were opened upon Mr. Wilkes's life for one year, upon the prospects of his return to Parliament, of war with France or Spain, of the length of the siege of Gibraltar, or upon such events as the result of the Duchess of Kingston's trial. Sham insurances were sometimes opened upon property supposed to be situated in towns then besieged; and one ambassador is said to have taken advantage of this practice by insuring 30,000*l.* on Minorca, in the war of 1755, with advices at the same time in his pocket that Minorca was taken.   The Act of 1774 declared that " no insurance shall be made on the life of any person, or on any event whatsoever, where the person on whose account such policy shall be made shall have no interest, or by way of gaming or wagering; and that every such insurance shall be null and void."[1] Other precautions were taken that policies should be issued in good faith; and it was provided that no greater amount should be recovered upon any policy than the amount of interest in any life or event.

Two remarkable decisions were given soon after the passing of this Act.   In one case a broker had received several premiums of thirty-five guineas, promising to return a hundred for each on condition that the Chevalier d'Eon should prove to be a woman.   Chief Justice Mansfield decided that these policies were contrary to the spirit of the Act, and void as being " by way of gaming or wagering."   Again, in 1803, a firm of coachmakers, to whom the great minister, William Pitt, owed 1,000*l.*, insured his life for seven years for 500*l.*   During this term Pitt died insolvent, but as his debts were discharged by the nation, the insurance company refused to pay on the ground that all insurable

Judicial decisions under Act of 1774.

[1] 14 Geo. III. c. 48. Cf. 19 Geo. II. c. 37, prohibiting similar gambling by means of marine insurances (*ante,* pp. 575-6).

interest of Pitt's creditors in his life ended with the payment of his debts. This view was upheld by Lord Ellenborough.

Life annuities by parochial authorities.

Efforts were made by legislation in 1773, and again in 1789, to establish a system of parochial insurance. This system was first suggested by Mr. Baron Masères, who, impressed with the necessity of encouraging labourers and artizans to provide for old age, wrote a pamphlet to advocate what he described as a " plain and easy method" to secure this end.[1] In every parish he proposed that churchwardens and overseers should be not only authorized, but compelled, to grant deferred life annuities upon request, in return for small payments made at a purchaser's convenience. These annuities were to be met out of the poor's rate, so that all rated lands and other property would be charged as security for them. No annuity depending on one life could exceed 20*l.*, and, to avoid intricacy and multiplicity of accounts, no less than 5*l.* could be invested at one time in purchasing an annuity. A parochial register of all payments was to be kept ; and this register-book would be good evidence of any purchaser's right to his annuity. All principal money would be invested in the purchase of Three per Cent. Bank Annuities (then considerably under par), and held by churchwardens and overseers for the time being, the interest being re-invested, so as to form a fund to satisfy annuities as they fell due.

Objections to scheme.

This proposal naturally met with objections that land and other rateable property would bear new and unknown burdens, as it would be liable, under the scheme, to make good any deficiency. Mr. Baron Masères endeavoured to show that, with proper management, no deficiency could arise, and

[1] Proposal for Establishing Life Annuities in Parishes for the Benefit of the Industrious Poor: London, 1772. Francis Masères, an English gentleman of French extraction, after having for some years filled the office of Attorney-General in Canada, returned to England, and was appointed Cursitor Baron of the Exchequer, serving occasionally as Deputy Recorder of London. He published many works upon mathematics and political history, and died in 1824 at the age of 93.

that ratepayers generally would gain relief from high poor's rates, "since many of the poor who must otherwise, in their old age, come to be a burthen upon the parish, would now be maintained, in part at least, by annuities paid to them out of a fund of their own raising." The House of Commons, in 1772-3, favoured this plan, and at once permitted Mr. Dowdeswell[1] to bring in a Bill "for the better support of poor persons in certain circumstances, by enabling parishes to grant them annuities for life upon purchase, and under certain restrictions." Besides Mr. Dowdeswell, Mr. Burke, Sir George Savill, Lord John Cavendish, and Mr. Dunning were among the members ordered to prepare and bring in this measure.[2]

Reception in House of Commons, 1772-3.

Mr. Dowdeswell was sanguine enough to expect that labouring men, both in town and country, would gladly take advantage of the Bill. Their payments, he said, would be regulated according to tables annexed to the Act, and accumulate at compound interest in the Three per Cents. Annuities would begin after contributories had reached their fiftieth year. Women as well as men might purchase annuities. Churchwardens and overseers would be authorized to receive legacies and charitable contributions in aid of the annuity fund.[3] And Mr. Dowdeswell insisted that not only would labouring poor be enabled to provide for old age, but that the prospect of future comfort would render them more sober, industrious, and thrifty. The Bill passed its second reading without opposition, and, after much consideration and amendment in Committee of the whole House, clauses were added extending its provisions to the numerous corporations

Speech in introducing Bill.

---

[1] The Rt. Hon. W. Dowdeswell, who figures prominently in the debates at this period. He was Chancellor of the Exchequer, 1765-6, when he resigned.

[2] 34 Com. Journ. 33; December 11, 1772.

[3] "It is common for people who have been successful in trade to leave money for relief of the poor of their parish. And how can they leave it with a greater prospect of serving mankind than to such a fund?" Dowdeswell, 17 Parl. Hist. 642.

then constituted by private legislation in towns and country districts for the care and management of the poor.[1]

Debate on third reading. Upon its third reading it was sharply debated. Opponents objected that its effect, if any, would be a bad one. It would encourage idleness, be serviceable only to drones, and bring country people acquainted with the funds, with Exchange Alley, and brokers (the worst people they could possibly know); it would place great temptation in the way of parish officers, their attorneys and agents; and, as labouring men might sell their expectant annuities, they might still come upon the rates, which would have to make good these annuities, and so be doubly charged.[2] Notwithstanding these arguments, and others less forcible, the Bill was carried by sixty-two to thirty-four votes.[3]

Bill rejected in Lords. In the Upper House it was ordered to be printed, and its second reading postponed for ten days, so that the Lords might be summoned.[4] On the appointed day, after an unrecorded debate, the measure was rejected,[5] chiefly, it is said, upon the opposition of Lord Camden, who represented that land would fall in value if charged with any deficiency in poor's rates to make good annuities. A similar measure was drafted in 1789, with tables computed by Dr. Price, but does not seem to have come before either House of Parliament.[6]

State annuities, 1808. A brief record may follow of a system of annuities adopted by the Government in 1808,[7] in order to extinguish

[1] 34 Com. Journ. 152; February 24, 1773.

[2] 17 Parl. Hist. 791–3.

[3] 34 Com. Journ. 171; March 5, 1773. The tellers for the Bill were Sir Charles Bunbury and Mr. Whitworth; against, Mr. John Calvert and Mr. Nicholson Calvert.

[4] 33 Lords' Journ. 552.

[5] Ib., 577; March 25, 1773. A copy of this Bill, together with the tables computed for it, will be found in Masères' Doctrine of Life Annuities.

[6] Baily on Life Annuities (London, 1810), p. 473. Dr. Price's Tables to this Bill are inserted in his Obs. on Reversionary Payments, II. 473.

[7] 48 Geo. III. c. 142, which contains elaborate tables of rates; it was amended by 49 & 50 Geo. III. c. 64; 52 Geo. III. c. 129; 56 Geo. III.

debt, and, at the same time, afford to thrifty members of the middle classes a safe means of providing for old age. Mr. Perceval was the minister responsible for this legislation. But the Treasury and their advisers fell into the same errors which had ruined so many private societies, and the result was a series of financial misadventures. An initial blunder was their adoption, as a basis for sales of annuities on nominated lives, Dr. Price's tables of mortality, on which various life assurance companies founded their premiums. Speculators soon discovered that money might be made by buying Government annuities on selected lives. In vain were successive Chancellors of the Exchequer informed that the State was suffering a loss which varied from fifteen to nearly twenty-five per cent.[1] At length a Finance Committee appointed by the House of Commons, on Mr. Peel's motion in 1828, put an end to any more bad bargains of this nature. It was, indeed, time to abandon this business. Mr. Finlaison, who was employed by the Government to compile new tables for their guidance, reported, after much delay, that the State was losing about 8,000l. a week by continuing it, and that, taking a period of sixty years, the amount of debt which would be redeemed by grants of annuities was 32,000,000l. less than would be redeemed by means of the ordinary sinking fund.

An Act was soon passed[2] repealing all Acts authorizing the National Debt Commissioners to grant life annuities. Parliament, however, still favoured this method of reducing debt and encouraging providence. Mr. Goulburn was therefore allowed to pass a new measure, based on new tables, enabling the Commissioners to sell annuities for life, and for terms of years.[3] Another flaw was then found in the rates

Repealing Act of 1828.

New annuity tables.

---

c. 53; 57 Geo. III. c. 26; 3 Geo. IV. cc. 9, 61; 5 Geo. IV. c. 11; 7 Geo. IV. c. 39.

[1] Mr. Finlaison and other actuaries called the attention of the Government to the unsoundness of their system in 1819. Annual Register for 1828, p. 71; 19 Hansard, 50.

[2] 9 Geo. IV. c. 16.

[3] 10 Geo. IV. c. 24; amended by 2 & 3 Will. IV. c. 59.

on which these annuities were granted. By the practice of assurance offices at this period, a man's expectation of life when ninety years old was computed at a year and a quarter. But this average was much below the duration of life in nonagenarians specially chosen. Speculators accordingly employed agents who searched all over the kingdom for hale old men of ninety, whose lives were insured for large sums at the Government rate, and who afterwards, if poor, received medical aid and creature comforts with a view to prolong life. For each 100*l*. paid, a nonagenarian was entitled to an annuity of 62*l*., the first payment commencing three months after purchase; so that if he lived a year and a quarter, the whole purchase-money was recovered. Upon the lives thus nominated, the State again, for a short time, sustained heavy losses. These continued until 1830, when Mr. Goulburn availed himself of a provision which allowed the Commissioners to refuse grants of annuities found to be unfavourable to the State.[1]

Fresh losses incurred by State.

Post Office annuities and insurance.

A system of State insurance on a small scale was revived in 1864,[2] when the Post Office was authorized to grant annuities and insure lives under certain restrictions as to amount. This system has proved less popular than was expected; the contracts existing on December 31, 1885, were only for 9,496 immediate annuities, 810 deferred annuities, and 5,155 life insurances.[3]

---

[1] 10 Geo. IV. c. 24. Francis's Annals, &c. of Life Assurance, pp. 199—212.

[2] 27 & 28 Vict. c. 43.

[3] Postmaster-General's Report, 1886, p. 8.

CHAPTER XVII.

DOCKS IN THE THAMES :—STATUTES AGAINST EVASION OF CUS-
TOMS: ORIGIN OF LEGAL AND SUFFERANCE WHARFS:
WANT OF ACCOMMODATION FOR SHIPPING, 1762-1800:
MERCHANTS' BILL OF 1796: COMPETING SCHEME OF COR-
PORATION OF LONDON: INQUIRIES IN HOUSE OF COMMONS:
INCREASED COMMERCE OF PORT: RIVAL BILLS, 1797-9:
PORT OF LONDON AND WEST INDIA DOCKS ACT, 1799:
LONDON DOCKS, 1800: EAST INDIA DOCKS, 1803:
ST. KATHERINE'S, 1826: AMALGAMATION OF EAST AND
WEST INDIA COMPANIES, 1838: SURREY COMMERCIAL,
VICTORIA, MILLWALL, DAGENHAM, TILBURY, &C.

FOR more than three centuries the loading and unloading
of vessels at all our chief ports have depended upon regulations imposed by the Crown for collecting revenue.
To prevent evasions of duties an Act in 1558-9[1] declared *Act of 1558-9,*
that all goods, except fish, should be laden and dis- *against evasion of*
charged in the daytime, and at open wharfs, where cus- *customs.*
toms' officers[2] were in attendance. Customs and subsidies
on merchandise (this statute recited) were an ancient revenue
annexed to the imperial crown, and in and since the reign of
Edward III. " amounted to great and notable sums of money,
till of late years many greedy and covetous persons, respecting more their private gain and commodity than their duty
and allegiance, or the common profit of the realm," had *Frauds upon*
succeeded in conveying their goods into and out of England *revenue.*

---

[1] 1 Eliz. c. 11.   [2] In old Acts these officers are
called " customers."

without payment, by loading or discharging them in creeks or places where there was no customer, or by negligence or corruption of officers. By these or "divers other fraudulent, undue and subtle practices and devices," the revenue was much diminished, and greater burdens than would otherwise be necessary were imposed upon her Majesty's loyal and loving subjects. It was therefore enacted that no goods, wares, or merchandise whatsoever, fish and salt excepted, should be laden or discharged into or from any ship, vessel, crayer,[1] lighter, or bottom (being not in a leak or wreck), **Legal quays appointed.** except during the daytime, and upon such open places, quays, or wharfs as the Crown should appoint in London, Southampton, Bristol, West Chester,[2] and Newcastle. A similar restriction applied to all other ports, creeks, havens, or roads, Hull only excepted, unless a customer, controller and searcher had resided there for ten years.[3] In each case the penalty for disobedience was forfeiture of all goods, or their value.

Stat. of Eliz. amended by 14 Chas. II. Another statute "for preventing frauds and regulating abuses in his Majesty's customs" enabled the Crown, in 1662, to appoint further "places, ports, members, and creeks for discharge and shipment of goods."[4] "Sea-coal, stone, and bestials "[5] were now specified as articles of free export as well as fish. Early during the next century, it was found that, owing to a great increase of trade, the legal quays and wharfs, appointed in pursuance of these Acts, were of insufficient extent, and that great delays were therefore occasioned

---

[1] Johnson gives Old Fr. craier, Low Lat. crayera, a small war vessel with one mast. Shakespeare (Cymb.) uses this word—
" Who ever yet could sound thy bottom? find
The ooze, to shew what coast thy sluggish crare
Might easiest harbour on?"
[2] Chester.
[3] In Queen Elizabeth's reign the customs were farmed and only produced 14,000l. yearly, a sum afterwards increased to 50,000l. In 1613 they produced 110,000l. From the farmers they were transferred to the management of a Board of Commissioners so lately as 1671.—De Hamel's Int. to Customs Consolidation Act, 1853.
[4] 14 Charles II. c. 11.
[5] Fr. bestiaux, cattle.

in the despatch and landing of merchandise. After repeated Royal Com- complaints by merchants and traders, Commissioners were missions, 1762-5. appointed in 1762 with a view to provide further facilities. They fixed certain open places on the sides of Tower Ditch, but their proceedings were quashed as irregular in 1763. Another Commission, in 1765, specified various quays in the precincts of St. Katherine's beyond the Tower, and declared it lawful, as heretofore, "to unship and lay on land deal boards, balks, and all sorts of masts and great timber," at any place between Westminster and Limehouse Dock, on payment of duties, and on receiving sufferance or permission from the customs' authorities. In addition, also, to the legal quays, these authorities were enabled "to give suffer- Sufferance wharfs. ance or permission for landing or shipping any goods, wares, and merchandise at any other place or places, or in any other manner, than at those hereinbefore assigned and appointed to be further lawful places, keys, and wharfs." But persons enjoying these privileges were bound to perform all conditions attached to them.

An ever-growing trade soon made these new facilities Want of wholly inadequate. In 1795, the legal quays were not of further accommoda- greater extent than they had been in the year 1666, and tion, 1795. contained in length only about 1,500 feet.[1] They stretched, with some breaks of continuity, from the western extremity of Tower Ditch to London Bridge, and here warehouses and other buildings were erected, in such situations as to leave only three thousand square yards of uncovered wharf space. Within this confined area, a business exceeding in magnitude that of any port in the world was principally confined. It was not uncommon to see these wharfs, the warehouses being full, "encumbered with piles of costly goods, exposed to every risk of weather and plunderage; while two or three lighters, filled with like valuable articles,

[1] Statement by Committee of London Merchants, July 14, 1795.

were attending undischarged upon each."[1] It was not safe for the largest and deepest laden ships to come higher up the river than Deptford. The greater number did not moor within one mile and a half of the nearest legal quays, and few or none could be laid alongside the wharfs. Hence, numerous lighters were necessary; and, owing to the limited space of the legal quays, it was impossible to discharge them without lengthened detentions. At any time, this state of things was "a scandal to the port," accumulating intolerable charges and losses, and greatly increasing the cost of goods to consumers. But in time of war, when ships under convoy arrived in fleets, the scandal was still greater. Commissioners of Customs granted some relief by appointing sufferance wharfs. But these wharfs were not calculated for such business, and could not be used without much risk and expense. Even, however, with their aid, several ships which arrived in the Thames early in September, 1793, were, after three months interval, and every possible exertion on their part, undischarged in December.[2]

Some indifferent sort of dock and quay accommodation appears to have existed in the seventeenth century above London Bridge, probably for small vessels engaged in inland trade. A second statute for rebuilding the City, after the fire of 1666, provided in 1670, "that for the better benefit and accommodation of trade and for other great conveniences, there shall be left a continued tract of ground all along from London Bridge to the Temple, of the breadth of forty feet of assize from the north side of the Thames, to be converted to a key, or public and open wharf."[3] This open space was still to be subject to private rights of ownership, but the Act declared that any person might load or unload goods there on

Margin notes:

Lighterage.

Detention of vessels.

Quays between London Bridge and Temple, 1670.

---

[1] Report of Committee of West India merchants on the landing and delivery of sugar at the legal quays, December 20, 1793; Richard Neave, chairman; James Allen, secretary.

[2] Ib.

[3] 22 Chas. II. c. 11, s. 38.

payment of rates according to a scale fixed by his Majesty with the advice of his Privy Council.[1]

For further convenience to trade the same statute enacted that "the channel of Bridewell Dock from the Thames to Holborn Bridge shall be sunk to a sufficient level whereby to make it navigable." In breadth this channel and the wharfs on each side were not to be less than 100 or more than 120 feet, and the lines and levels were to be set out by the Lord Mayor and Aldermen within a given time, subject to his Majesty's approval.[2] All costs were to be defrayed by the Corporation out of the coal duty,[3] and they were to charge reasonable rates for use of the navigation and quays. This channel was accordingly made and levelled pursuant to the Act,[4] but in 1732 that part of it lying between Fleet Bridge (at the end of Fleet Street) and Holborn Bridge was found by experience to be of no benefit to trade; the navigation was disused and choked by mud; and it had been for several years previously "a grievous and dangerous nuisance."[5] An Act of 1732, therefore, enabled the Corporation to fill up that part of the channel lying between these two bridges, and vested the fee simple of the ground in them "to such uses and purposes as they and their successors shall think proper and convenient for the benefit and advantage of the City."[6]

> Bridewell "Dock:" navigable channel from Thames to Holborn Bridge.

At Rotherhithe there was a Greenland Dock, which, in 1789, was stated by the Board of Customs to be intended for landing cargoes from the Greenland or Southern whale fisheries. This dock was capable of holding ships of 1,500 tons when unloaded, but in 1799 no vessels were suffered to

> Greenland Dock.

---

[1] Ib. s. 40.

[2] Ib. s. 41.

[3] Ib. s. 42.

[4] See, in Guildhall library, "Rates for Wharfage and Cranage, to be taken and paid at the Wharfs and Keys of the new Channel or Cut of Bridewell Dock and Fleet Channel, from the River Thames to Holborn Bridge": London, 1676.

[5] Recitals to 6 Geo. II. c. 22.

[6] Ib. s. 2; and see 29 Geo. II. c. 86 (an Act of 1755 for building Blackfriars Bridge), s. 24.

London out-
stripped by
outports.

use it except such as were leaky.[1] Under these circumstances,
it was a natural subject of surprise and concern to London
merchants and shipowners, that, while at this period some
outports[2] had improved navigation or constructed commodious docks, with warehouses and other commercial facilities, "the metropolis of Great Britain alone had, in these
material respects, remained torpid; its improvements checked
or suspended, and its abuses gradually gaining head."[3] In
various parts of the Thames there were dry docks for repairs
of shipping, but of wet docks the port of London, at the end
of the eighteenth century, possessed not one.

Plans.

With a view to supply this want, various plans were suggested and keenly discussed.[4] Among them was one on a
large scale, prepared by the Corporation of London for docks
in the Isle of Dogs. First in the field, however, was a scheme

Merchants'
petition for
Bill, 1796.

for docks at Wapping, promoted by a committee of merchants, with Mr. John Rennie as their engineer. After
making necessary surveys, and giving the usual notices, these
promoters petitioned the House of Commons for a Bill early
in 1796.[5] Their petition was referred to a Committee, which
heard evidence, and in which all members who chose to attend

Evidence.

had "voices." The chief witness was Mr. Robert Milligan,
a West India merchant. He was cross-examined with a view

---

[1] Greenland Dock still forms part of the Surrey Commercial Dock Company's system. *Post*, p. 659.

[2] In Liverpool the corporation obtained statutory powers to build a wet dock in 1709 (8 Anne, c. 12, *ante*, I. 8); in Hull, the corporation assisted in forming a dock company, and were authorized to subscribe in 1774 (14 Geo. III. c. 56); the municipality of Glasgow obtained an Act to improve the navigation of the Clyde in 1758 (32 Geo. II. c. 62), but had been conspicuous in their attempts to provide better facilities for shipping nearly a century before.

[3] Report of Committee of West India Merchants, December, 1793.

[4] Among the dock literature of the period in the Guildhall library are pamphlets "On Wet Docks, Quays, and Warehouses in the port of London, and Hints respecting Trade," 1793; "Reasons in favour of the London Docks," 1794; "Porto-Bello; or a Plan for Improvement of the Port and City of London," 1798; while the voice of vested interests and prejudice was raised in "The Story of Tom Cole : with old Father Thames's Malediction on the Wapping Docks," 1796.

[5] 51 Com. Journ. 297-8.

to show that existing wharfs and quays would answer all purposes if improved.[1] This proposition he totally denied, and dwelt on the enormous plundering [2] which occurred because many West India and other ships homeward-bound drew so much water that they were obliged to discharge their cargoes into lighters at Deptford. Upon the Committee's report, the House ordered "that leave be given to bring in a Bill for making wet docks, basins, cuts, and other works," with "a navigable canal from Blackwall to the said docks in Wapping." Mr. Manning [3] was chairman of this Committee.

On February 18, 1796, the Bill was read a first time. Opposition to Bill. Vested interests in great numbers at once made themselves heard. The "rulers, auditors, comptrollers, and assistants of Watermen, lightermen, and wherry-men. the Society or Company of Watermen, Wherrymen, and Lightermen, upon the River Thames between Gravesend and Windsor" petitioned [4] under their common seal, setting forth that their company consisted of more than 10,000 persons, many of them having numerous families, who were wholly maintained by navigating boats and vessels, and that they would be deprived of their means of subsistence if the Bill passed. Under a local Act [5] a certain number of watermen Relief of poor out of Sunday fares.

---

[1] Ib. 401.

[2] Gangs of plunderers preyed upon the valuable contents both of ships and lighters. Sometimes these men were in league with the ships' officers and crew, sometimes with customs' officers. They were known as "river pirates," "night plunderers," "light and heavy horsemen," "game lightermen," "mud - larks," "scuffle-hunters," and "copemen," or receivers of stolen property. (See an account of these gangs in Smiles's Life of Rennie, pp. 299-302, ed. of 1874.) At the close of last century the value of property thus stolen was estimated at 500,000l. a-year. The Bumboat Act, so called because it was directed against thefts by itinerant

dealers who sold liquor, tobacco, and other articles from bumboats, was passed in 1761 (2 Geo. III. c. 28), to put down this system of organized plunder; but the penalties imposed were often paid by a club of these thieves, who subscribed for the purpose. In 1800 the Thames police were established (39 & 40 Geo. III. c. 87), but so long as valuable goods were landed on open wharfs or in lighters, all attempts to protect them effectually were in vain.

[3] Ante, p. 578, n.

[4] 51 Com. Journ. 424; February 22, 1796. Ante, p. 398.

[5] The petition refers to 1 James I. c. 16, but the statute in question is 11 Will. III. c. 21, ss. 13, 16.

might ply upon the Thames between Vauxhall and Limehouse on Sundays, and their surplus earnings were applied
to the use of poor aged, decayed, and maimed watermen
and their widows. From these funds more than five hundred
aged and necessitous persons were annually relieved. Of
these Sunday earnings by watermen, the greater part arose
from carrying seamen on board vessels lying in the Thames,
but such earnings would be wholly lost if the Bill became
law. More than three hundred apprentices were bound to
watermen in each year, and nearly four thousand Thames
watermen and lightermen were then serving as impressed
sailors or volunteers in the royal navy.[1] One of the best
nurseries for seamen would therefore be destroyed by this
scheme for docks. A similar petition was presented by watermen and wherrymen plying between Gravesend and Windsor.[2]

Corporation of London. Other opposing petitioners were the Corporation of London,
who said that their rights and privileges as Conservators of
the Thames would be invaded, and "the trade and commerce of the port of London, where it has flourished for a
great length of time, to the great advantage of the city, and
the kingdom in general, would, in a very material degree, be
removed to a new site, out of their control and care."[3] They
also complained that this removal would produce "most ruinous
and distressing consequences to divers incorporated societies
and companies, as well as to great numbers of individuals, the
value of whose property, or the profits of whose labour and
industry, in a great measure depend on the trade and commerce of the city and port of London being continued to
Civic plan of docks. be carried on within civic limits and jurisdiction." They
declared that, " ever careful of the rights and welfare of their
fellow-citizens," they had formed a plan for giving increased

---

[1] By 4 & 5 Anne, c. 6, s. 20, the
Admiralty, upon notice to the Company, could order watermen to serve
in the fleet. See, also, as to impressment of London watermen, 2 & 3

Ph. & M. c. 16, s. 6; and 11
Will. III. c. 21, s. 2.

[2] 51 Com. Journ. 484.

[3] Ib. 431.

accommodation to vessels, without creating a new corporation or expensive establishments, and without imposing fresh burdens on trade; and they pledged themselves to carry out this plan if sanctioned by Parliament.

Wardens and assistants of the Fellowship of Carmen, or free carmen, as they were called, stated [1] that from time immemorial they had acted under the control and regulation of the magistrates of London, with respect to price and conditions, so as to prevent imposition upon merchants and traders. They also paid nearly 400*l.* a year to Christ's Hospital for licences which gave them an exclusive privilege of working carts for hire within the city.[2] If docks were constructed outside the city, any man might carry on this trade there, and material injury and distress, if not total ruin, must follow to fellowship carmen and their families.

Fellowship of Carmen.

Inhabitants of St. Olave's, Southwark, were greatly alarmed [3] at a Bill which would remove trade from its ancient and accustomed channels. From time immemorial many of the principal sufferance wharfs had been established in this parish. These wharfs, with the warehouses belonging to them, were rated in the parish books at more than 6,000*l.* per annum, contributing upwards of 800*l.* a year to the maintenance of the poor, and to other public rates in still larger proportion. The parish was overburdened with poor, and a measure which would so greatly lessen its rates, and remove its trade, would prove an irreparable injury. Owners, lessees, and occupiers of sufferance wharfs, on both sides of the river, joined in representing that there was no need for docks, as every existing inconvenience arose entirely from a want of due regulations, and might be easily remedied. They prayed the House, therefore, to sanction no measure which would injure men who had " embarked very considerable fortunes, and employed the labour and industry of their lives," in raising and maintaining sufferance wharfs and

St. Olave's, Southwark.

Owners, &c., of sufferance wharfs.

---

[1] 51 Com. Journ. 439.   [2] *Post*, p. 653, n.   [3] 51 Com. Journ. 447.

Magdalen
College.

St. John's,
Southwark.

warehouses.   Magdalen College, which owned some of these
wharfs, presented a separate petition.

Governors and directors of the poor, and ratepayers in the
parish of St. John, Southwark, took high ground.[1] They
were "greatly alarmed" at "a mischievous project, tending
to create exclusive privileges, and restrict the liberty of
trading, with an arbitrary exaction and levy on tonnage that
would necessarily raise the prices of every article of merchandise to consumers." These petitioners were specially prejudiced, because their parish comprised a line of wharfs nearly
three thousand feet long, opposite to the Custom House and
Tower, "in the very heart and seat of commerce, with depth
of water convenient for ships of great tonnage to lay and unload."   During the last sixty years, they said, large sums had
been invested in sufferance wharfs and warehouses here, together with granaries and storehouses for corn and flour.
Fully "four in five of the housekeepers" in this parish consisted of lightermen, warehousemen, watermen, persons using
the sea, and others engaged in wharfs and warehouses.   If
these persons lost their employment, or removed, as they probably would, when docks were built at Wapping, poor rates
would be largely increased.   Already four shillings in the
pound were found an insufficient levy, and a private Act had
been necessary, enabling the petitioners to borrow considerable sums by way of life annuities, to pay off debts contracted
on behalf of the poor.   Under another private Act, the
petitioners, joined with the neighbouring parish of St. Olave,
had spent large sums in widening and improving the approaches to London Bridge, borrowing for this purpose by
means of life annuities secured upon the rates.   More than
two-fifths of these rates were paid by occupiers of waterside
premises, and if their trade were removed to other sites, ratepayers would be impoverished, annuitants would lose their
security, and the whole community would suffer.

[1] 51 Com. Journ. 464-5.

On similar grounds the Bill was opposed by governors St. Mary, Bermondsey. and directors of the poor, with ratepayers, in St. Mary, Bermondsey.[1] They also detected in the Bill exclusive privileges, which would tend to destroy competition, and amount to a monopoly in favour of the dock proprietors. Much capital had been invested, along nearly four thousand feet of quayage, and also in providing sufferance wharfs, giving ample accommodation to trade. Under a private Act, the petitioners, whose parish was greatly burdened with poor, had erected a workhouse, which now had three hundred inmates, with many out-paupers; the poor rates were three and sixpence in the pound, but inadequate; and for paving, lighting, and cleansing, there was a further annual rate of two shillings and three pence. They also had borrowed money for all these purposes, by way of life annuities, and saw no prospect of keeping up these annuities if so serious an injury was inflicted upon trade within their parish. An almost identical case was pre- St. Mary's, sented [2] by parishioners of St. Mary's, Rotherhithe, which Rotherhithe. extended for nearly two miles along the south bank of the Thames, and afforded convenient wharfage.

Master lightermen represented that they had upwards of Master twenty thousand tons of craft engaged in shipping and land- lightermen. ing merchandise from ships in the river; six hundred persons helped to navigate these craft. The petitioners were " under the greatest anxiety and fear" of losing their employment if any docks were made, and thousands of lightermen and watermen would be thrown out of work. To the same effect spoke " the registrar and rulers of the Society of Ticket Ticket Porters,"[3] who numbered about two thousand, and alleged porters. that, from time immemorial, they had been authorized by the Corporation to unlade and house, and in like manner to ship off, all goods entering the port from " British plantations, America, the East country, and other places." It seems that,

---

[1] 51 Com. Journ. 472.   [2] Ib. 481-2.   [3] Ib. 453.

upon their admission as ticket porters, these men entered into bonds, each with two sureties, for a due performance of their duty under a penalty of 100*l.*, so that a merchant was secured against any loss to goods under their care. If docks were built, and trade shifted beyond the City bounds, these petitioners foresaw " great injury and distress, if not total ruin to themselves and their families."

Masters of the tackle houses. Similar complaints of injury and possible ruin were made by " the masters of the tackle houses of the twelve superior companies of the City of London."[1] These petitioners held appointments for life from the Corporation on the nomination of their several companies. Under these appointments they enjoyed a monopoly of tackle portage[2] within the port. Accordingly, a considerable proportion of all imports and exports from legal wharfs must be landed and shipped under their care and custody, they being responsible for accidents, damages, and losses, by theft or otherwise, while goods were in their charge. They contended that, with certain practicable improvements, and under proper regulations, the existing legal quays would afford every necessary accommodation even for the increased trade of London.

Owners of legal quays. Owners and occupiers of legal quays were, of course, urgent[3] in representing the ruin which would be brought upon them. They had expended capital in improving accommodation, " in confidence that Parliament would at all times protect" interests which had arisen by virtue of Royal Commissions, acting under statute; and they suggested that further accommodation might be given without annihilating the ancient trade of these quays. Other opponents in the same interest were Balliol College; the Cordwainers' Company, owners of Smart's quay, near Billingsgate; and the Fishmongers' Company, owners of Porter's quay, near the Custom House. Inhabitants of Aldersgate and

Balliol College; Cordwainers' and Fishmongers' Companies.

---

[1] 51 Com. Journ. 464; March 3, 1796.

[2] Loading and landing goods from

wharf to hold, or hold to wharf, by tackle or cranage.

[3] 51 Com. Journ. 480-3.

Queenhithe separately alleged injury to their respective Aldersgate
and Queen-
hithe Wards. wards by reductions of rates, through depreciation of property. They implored the House of Commons[1] "to discountenance all unnecessary innovations, and protect the citizens and their extensive property from the baneful consequences which must ensue on removing the seat of commerce" from civic jurisdiction. The Corporation of London, "natural guardians and protectors of the port," were willing to make all necessary alterations and improvements, and this "without oppressing individuals, invading ancient rights, impoverishing valuable property, or loading the port with great and perpetual expense," for the private emolument of individuals.

Inhabitants of Dowgate Ward complained of similar injury, Dowgate
Ward. though their language was more reserved. From the parishes of St. Paul, Shadwell, St. Ann, Limehouse, and the hamlets Shadwell,
Limehouse,
Ratcliff, and
Poplar. of Ratcliff and Poplar came a joint petition, setting forth not only diversion of trade, but structural changes and consequent obstruction of traffic, for the proposed canal was to be cut through Ratcliff Highway and other roads, and stoppages at the various drawbridges would be a great injury and an intolerable nuisance. Billingsgate Ward joined its Billingsgate
Ward. voice to the general chorus of lamentation, predicting "the most melancholy consequences" if docks were made. Vintry Vintry Ward. Ward "could not help feeling the greatest alarm and apprehension" at a measure which would divert trade "into new and untried channels, destroy the hopes and expectations of men who had spent years of industry in establishing their" business, and "deprive a number of honest, laborious citizens of chartered and inalienable rights." Local injury was alleged to water-side premises in the ward, but these petitioners took broader ground, doubting whether "from a national point of view" wet docks should be made

[1] 51 Com. Journ. 487.

at all, as tending "to supersede the necessity of employing working lightermen, a hardy and gallant set of men, who form one of our principal nurseries for seamen."

Candlewick Ward. Candlewick Ward denounced the "baneful and destructive consequences" of a measure which would load the trade of London with "an unnecessary and perpetual burden" for **Southwark.** private emolument. Inhabitants of Southwark spoke for the industrious poor as well as for owners of waterside premises in that borough against a measure fraught with mischief, big with evils; "an unprecedented attempt to monopolize and divert" trade from its ancient channels.[1]

Vintners' Company and wine tackle porters. "The master, wardens, freemen, and commonalty of the Mystery of Vintners" were owners of Hammond's quay, part of Botolph's Wharf, which, since 1563, had been appointed a legal wharf. Here were employed fifty wine tackle porters belonging to the Company. If docks were made, these men and their families would be ruined; and as the Company's quay would be idle, and other estates belonging to them on the Thames would become of little value, they would no longer be able to assist in keeping up " the honour and dignity of the Corporation of the City of London." **Tower Ward.** Inhabitants of Tower Ward reminded the House that they contributed a large quota towards the general land-tax, but if trade were removed they could no longer support this burden; and they loudly denounced proposals which were founded on monopoly, would annihilate the privileges and destroy the property of citizens, and bring ruin on innumerable families. It was not proposed to indemnify sufferers, and even if evils existed through a want of docks, " it would still be a momentous question whether the abolition of the old port, with all its concomitant devastation, should take place in favour of this new speculative plan," especially as the Corporation had pledged themselves to provide all

---

[1] 51 Com. Journ. 518; March 16, 1796.

fitting accommodation for trade, without any desire to profit thereby, and "without injuring the chartered rights or hazarding the long-established welfare and dignity of this metropolis."[1]

Another ground of opposition to the scheme was its inter-ference with sewers. The Tower Hamlets Commission of Sewers therefore joined the array against it, alleging that it would stop up outlets for great bodies of water now dis-charged into the river, and would thereby probably cause some pestilential disease. The Corporation of Hertford alleged injury to the ancient navigation of the Lea, which would be crossed by the proposed canal between Bromley and Limehouse, thus interfering with the carriage of malt, flour, and timber, from Hertford and its neighbourhood to the Thames, and the return carriage of coal and other goods. To the same effect was a representation from Trustees for the River Lea Navigation. About thirty years previously this navigation had been much improved, at great expense, under authority from Parliament, and with money borrowed on security of tolls. A navigable canal from Blackwall to docks at Wapping would intersect and cross the Lea navigation from Bromley to Limehouse, and thereby would interrupt navigation, and diminish tolls.

Injury to private owners led to several petitions, as from proprietors of the Hermitage Iron and Brass Foundry, which furnished to ships of war numbers of guns and quan-tities of naval stores. The proposed docks would cut through and destroy this foundry, an injury for which no adequate compensation could be given. These petitioners, with others in the same category, asked that no part of their premises should be taken for the docks.

One indefensible part of the Bill was a proposal to charge compulsory rates on every vessel, exceeding forty-five tons

Marginal notes: Tower Hamlets Commission of Sewers. Corporation of Hertford. Trustees of Lea Naviga-tion. Hermitage Gun Foundry.

[1] 51 Com. Journ. 487-8.

in burden, trading coastwise between the port of London and any part of Great Britain, even though these vessels did not use the proposed docks. If they did use the docks or enter the canal, further rates were to be paid. To this proposal there was naturally a stout opposition from shipowners. One petition from owners and freighters at Thorne, in the Humber, alleged that they would have no occasion to enter the docks, and set forth the hardship they would suffer from forced dues which would confer upon them no advantage. These petitioners were "perfectly satisfied with the present state and navigation of the Thames, and the conveniences for landing and shipping goods there."[1] Similar petitions came from Gainsborough and other places.

Owners of coasting vessels.

These numerous predictions of evil are amusing when contrasted with the results of to-day. They also give a suggestive picture of the numerous interests then supposed to be injuriously affected by the construction of wet docks in the Thames. Some plan of this kind was clearly essential to commerce, but the greater number of these opponents would have objected to any plan. In the city there was a natural leaning towards the Corporation's scheme, which promised greater accommodation to trade, and would also have placed the docks of London, like those of Liverpool and other places, in municipal hands, with a guarantee therefore against high dividends and oppressive rates, which were possible under a speculative company.

General view of opponents.

While formidable opposition was aroused from vested interests, the Bill was not without strong support. Among other petitioners in its favour were "the Governor and Company of Merchants trading into the Levant Seas;" insurers of the city of London; the Royal Exchange Assurance Corporation; West India planters and merchants; "the fellowship of English merchants for the discovery of new Trades,

Petitions supporting Bill.

---

[1] 51 Com. Journ. 476.

commonly known by the name of the Russia Company;" the Court of Directors of the united company of merchants trading to the East Indies; merchants of London trading to North America; owners and masters of ships; pilots engaged in piloting vessels into and from the port of London; merchants, traders, and shipowners of Maldon; merchants and others of Scarborough; shipowners of Aberdeen, and others.

So strong an agitation on both sides had seldom been known in Parliament upon any private measure, and could not be without its effect in Parliament. Accordingly, the Bill embodying the merchants' scheme was postponed until March 16, when it should have come on for a second reading. There was then an attempt to defeat it by further delay for four months. After considerable discussion, the House resolved to put it off for three weeks, and meanwhile appoint another Committee " to inquire into the best mode of providing sufficient accommodation for the increased trade and shipping of the port of London." This Committee included thirty-six members specially named, including Mr. Pitt, Mr. Fox, Mr. Sheridan, Lord Arden, the Earl of Mornington, the Chancellor of the Exchequer (Mr. Addington), the Lord Mayor of London, Alderman Lushington, with all members who serve for the City of London, for Middlesex, and twenty-six other counties, and for the Cinque ports, " all the knights for shires, gentlemen of the long robe, and merchants in the House;" a substantial, not to say an unwieldy tribunal, significant of the importance attached to this question. It was, in fact, little short of a Committee of the whole House, for all who chose to attend it were " to have voices."[1]

Second Committee of 1796.

Eight plans were submitted to this Committee. " Recesses or docks clear from the river channel," formed the basis of nearly all, including those of the merchants and the Corpo-

Plans of 1796.

[1] 51 Com. Journ. 520–1 ; March 16, 1796.

The mer-
chants' plan:
Docks at
Wapping.

ration of London.   For the merchants' plan the estimate was
993,000*l.*; it contemplated the purchase of land at Wapping,
for docks to contain three hundred and fifty ships, and a
smaller dock to receive lighters.   There were to be two
entrances for shipping: one communicating directly with
the Thames at Bell Dock; the other by a canal, navigable
for ships of three hundred and fifty tons, running eastward
two miles and three-quarters, communicating with the river
at Blackwall, between Parry's Dock and the river Lea.
Exclusive of docks, this canal would have occupied forty
acres.

Plan of the
Corporation
of London:
Docks in the
Isle of Dogs.

Accommodation on a far greater scale was planned by
the Corporation: a dock of over a hundred acres in the
Isle of Dogs, stretching from the reach at Limehouse to
that near Parry's Dock, and communicating with the river
at each end; with another dock at Rotherhithe of equal
dimensions, appropriated to colliers.   These two docks would
have held more than eight hundred vessels.   At the same
time existing legal quays, 1,500 feet long, by 50 feet
deep, would have had their frontage indented and extended to 4,150 feet by 60 feet of depth.   Spacious warehouses, and avenues opened "to facilitate conveyance to
every part of the metropolis," were another feature of this
scheme, the estimated cost of which was 1,109,000*l.*   The
Committee of 1796 pronounced it to be " worthy of the magnificent and commercial spirit of the Corporation," but the
Trinity House objected that much of the dock accommodation it would afford was too remote for the convenience of
trade.   They also objected to encroachments on the Thames,
and interference with navigation, which would be caused by
the projecting quays.   For these and other reasons the Trinity
House and Commissioners of Customs [1] preferred the smaller

---

[1] Trade at this period was not
much furthered by the constitution
of this department.   In 1792 the
first Earl of Liverpool was Collector
inwards; the Duke of Manchester
was Collector outwards; the Duke
of Newcastle, and afterwards Lord
Guildford, was Comptroller inwards

scheme put forward by the merchants, and specially reported that a cut from Blackwall to docks at Wapping would greatly benefit trade by freeing ships from risks in passing through crowded parts of the river.

Abundant evidence was given to the Committee of increased commerce, and of losses sustained by traders through inadequate accommodation.   In the year 1700 the value *Increased* of imports brought into London was 4,875,000*l*., and of *trade in port of London, 1700-90.* exports, 5,387,000*l*.   Seventy years afterwards trade in the port had nearly doubled, the imports rising in value to 8,889,000*l*.; exports to 9,267,000*l*.   In 1790 the imports were 12,275,000*l*.; the exports did not show their usual proportionate increase, being only 10,716,000*l*.[1]   In the year *Shipping.* 1702 the number of ships entered inwards, foreign and British inclusive, was 1,335, with a tonnage of 157,035.   In 1751 the number was 1,682, with a tonnage of 234,639; in 1794 they numbered 3,663, tonnage 620,845.   This return did not include the coasting trade, which had nearly doubled

and outwards.   Lord Stowell was surveyor of subsidies and petty customs.   These noblemen, holding patent offices, performed no official duties, but exercised the right of appointing deputies and clerks.   Both principals and deputies were remunerated by fees; the former by "patent" fees, the latter by what were called "fees of usage."   Deputies and clerks also received fees for "despatch."   Throughout the whole department the same system prevailed.   Officers received nominal salaries; their chief income was derived from fees, constantly varying in amount, and forming a continual source of dispute and complaint with merchants.   Although repeatedly denounced by various commissions of inquiry, and by a Committee on finance in 1797, this system was only abolished in 1812 by 51 Geo. III.

c. 71, which put an end to all patent offices and fees, and established fixed salaries, granting compensation allowances to the patent officers. Letter addressed to Mr. Goulburn, by a late Chairman of Board of Customs (quoted in De Hamel's Introduction to Customs Consolidation Act, 1853).

[1] Report of Inspector-General of Customs, App. D. to Report of Commons' Committee, 1796.   But these estimates of values were based upon an ancient scale of prices drawn up in 1696, and still adhered to a century afterwards.   In his oral evidence before the Committee, the Inspector-General stated that the value of imports and re-exports of foreign articles, at actual and current prices, was double that reported in the official document.

Tonnage.

since 1750. In dimensions, ships engaged in foreign trade had doubled during the eighteenth century; coasting vessels also showed a considerably increased tonnage.[1]

Over-crowd-
ing of river.

The whole number of ships which entered the port of London in 1794 was 13,949.[2] Of these, 775 were frequently stationed in tiers, in that part of the river termed the Pool. Only from seventeen to eighteen hundred vessels could be properly accommodated at moorings, even including the inconvenient and circuitous course of the Thames round the Isle

Colliers.

of Dogs. Of this number, nearly four hundred colliers were

Timber-laden
ships.

sometimes in the river at one time. There were also about five hundred timber-laden vessels which arrived during the summer months, and discharged their cargoes in the river, each cargo occupying a large surface of water. These cargoes remained there for measurement by revenue officers, and afterwards for sale, as merchants preferred to sell timber

West
Indiamen.

alongside their vessels. All the West Indiamen, which in 1794 numbered 433, arrived in the Thames between May and October.

Barges,
lighters, &c.

Besides foreign-bound and coasting vessels, the river was blocked by more than three thousand five hundred small craft used in loading and unloading, such as barges, lighters, punts,[3] lugger boats, sloops, cutters, and hoys. This great mass of small vessels, taking up stations or moorings in the tideway, and often used as warehouses for coals and other goods until sale, added to the obstruction. At times the river was so full that between the Tower and Limehouse "even a wherry sometimes was scarce able to pass with safety between the tiers, much less a vessel." At such times, much

---

[1] The Committee of 1796 note, as a remarkable fact (p. 2), "that many ships in the West Indian and other trades have reached to four and even five hundred tons, requiring an adequate space for navigation, and relative depth of water for their draught. Ships in the East Indian trade have increased to a yet greater degree in dimensions and tonnage."

[2] Of these, 10,286 were "coasters;" of the rest, 1,444 were foreign, and 2,219 British.

[3] A word denoting, in 1796, not small boats, but craft of twenty tons apiece. This was then the minimum tonnage of punts; the maximum was seventy-one tons.

damage was done to each other by vessels in trying to pass up and down. In a gale of wind, or when there was much drifting ice, if one or two vessels broke loose, they generally fouled several others, and perhaps drove a whole tier adrift. The risk from fire of vessels so overcrowded was also considerable.[1] Ships often ran foul of and damaged each other. Fouling. For days together they were hindered from moving up or down. Opportunities of winds and convoys were continually lost by outward-bound vessels. At the same time, the river Silting. was losing depth in many parts. Ships forming the inside tiers grounded at low water, gathering silt and forming shoals. Other ships ballasting in the Pool shed the ballast while lading it. After rain-storms, it was noticed that the London sewers discharged into the river hundreds of tons of soil, which the ballast lighters were supposed to clear away, but did not.

In their report, the Committee clearly explained the injury Report of to trade caused by deficient accommodation. They also ex- Committee. plained the several plans laid before them, and gave an abstract of the evidence, with maps and a mass of information in appendices. No definite opinion, however, was expressed in favour of any one scheme; the Committee simply laid these materials before the House, "in order that they may be better and more fully enabled to decide on the premises." Their report, which bore date May 13, left no time for legislation, even had there been unanimity in favour of the Merchants' Bill, instead of a most determined opposition. The Session ended abruptly on May 19, 1796, when his Majesty acquainted both Houses with his intention to summon a new Parliament. As a concession to the promoters of the Question Merchants' Bill, the House of Commons resolved that, if they postponed till 1796-7. thought fit to renew their application next Session, "for the specific purposes stated in their petition, and no other," general notices of this application would be treated as sufficient,

---

[1] Evidence of Mr. Spence, Admiralty Surveyor, before Committee of 1796.

without a renewal of notices to individuals. A motion also passed for a reconsideration then of the whole question.[1]

In the new Parliament the merchants were again early in the field, renewing their petition to the House of Commons for a Bill, and stating that they were prepared with plans and estimates of works, and had raised a subscription for carrying them into effect.[2] This was the signal for a fresh contest. Strenuous opposition to these Wapping Docks came from the old quarters. The Corporation of London urged once more that their own scheme might be carried out without incorporating a new body or prejudice to existing interests. They added, that they sought from it no emolument or advantage whatever, having no other wish than to " accommodate, promote, and increase " trade.[3]

Three weeks afterwards, the Corporation asked leave to bring in a Bill embodying their plan. They proposed, as before, to make wet docks in the Isle of Dogs instead of at Wapping, to widen existing legal quays, purchase mooring chains between London Bridge and the King's moorings at Deptford, appoint harbour masters, who should regulate the navigation and mooring of vessels, and make and maintain a navigable cut or passage, sufficient for sea vessels, across the Isle of Dogs, between Blackwall and Limehouse hole, so as to straighten the river channel there and obviate the circuitous course of vessels. Lastly, the Corporation showed that they were " conservators of the Thames, and natural and legal guardians of trade and commerce in the City and Port of London, by whose predecessors that trade and commerce had been managed for a long series of years, to the great benefit of the City and parts adjacent, and of the public ; " they were also " willing and desirous to take on themselves the care, management and superintendence " of the works they proposed to execute.[4]

---

[1] 51 Com. Journ. 765, 783.

[2] 52 Com. Journ. 143 ; November 30, 1796.

[3] Ib. 219 ; December 20, 1796.

[4] Ib. 269-70 ; February 14, 1797.

That there were precedents and good reasons for entrusting the control of docks and navigation to a municipal and non-speculative body, specially interested in the prosperity of local trade, has already appeared. Formal evidence, there- **Port of London Bill, 1797.** fore, having been taken in proof of the Corporation's state- ments, four members, Aldermen Anderson, Curtis, Lushing- ton, and Combe, were nominated to introduce a Bill.[1] Like its rival, it did not escape attack from private and public bodies, and the tactics of 1796 were repeated, both measures being delayed, by adjournments and other proceedings, until the prorogation. Resolutions were then passed to facilitate their reintroduction in the next Session.[2]

When the Session opened in November, the merchants again **Proceedings in House of Commons, 1797-8.** appeared, but, at its close, in June 1798, they had not been able even to secure the second reading of their Bill, though, as before, they received facilities for renewing their appli- cation if they thought fit.[3] The Corporation submitted a modified scheme. They still proposed to straighten the river-channel across the Isle of Dogs, and to regulate moor- ings, with other provisions suggested by them in 1797. But a friendly arrangement had meanwhile been come to with certain West India planters, merchants, and shipowners, who now for the first time petitioned, offering to undertake the construction of docks in the Isle of Dogs, as a complement to the civic scheme for improving navigation there. They explained that the Corporation's cut or canal would pass very near to the site proposed for their docks, and the two plans, if carried out together, would tend greatly to faci- litate trade and free the river from obstruction.[4] Both these plans were covered by one Bill, the City relinquishing its attempt to become the dock authority and confining itself to duties more obviously in keeping with its ancient jurisdic- tion as conservator of the Thames. But the Bill did not

---

[1] Ib. 301.

[2] Ib. 738 ; July 14, 1797.

[3] 53 Ib. 679 ; June 18, 1798.

[4] Ib. 312-3 ; February 23, 1798.

secure a second reading in 1798; and legislation was again postponed.

In 1799, the East India Company, the Russia Company of merchants, and other trading bodies, implored the House to delay no longer, though they did not suggest any particular scheme.[1] This appeal was followed by fresh Committees and investigations. The merchants' Bill, now specifically called the London Docks Bill, came before a Committee over which Mr. Manning presided, in February 1799. This Committee was ordered to sit notwithstanding any adjournments of the House, and heard counsel and evidence for the Bill, as well as on behalf of numerous petitioners against it. A similar course was taken with the City Bill; Sir John W. Anderson was Chairman of this Committee. In order that the House might follow their proceedings, both Committees were ordered to report, from time to time, the minutes of evidence taken by them. On May 7, both Committees reported in favour of both Bills, with some amendments.[2] But before these reports had been received, the House, tired of waiting for them, had referred the whole subject to a third Committee, who were directed to consider all previous reports made in previous Sessions, with the minutes of evidence of 1799, and any new plans since submitted to Parliament.[3]

As experience had shown that little could be expected from investigations by bodies practically unlimited in number into a subject so hotly contested, the new Committee was composed of only fourteen members, including Mr. Pitt (Chancellor of the Exchequer), Lord Hawkesbury, Mr. Nicholas Vansittart, and Mr. Wilberforce; five to be a quorum. Lord Hawkesbury acted as chairman. Besides the merchants' and City plans, a third scheme, devised by Mr. R. Dodd, engineer, and favoured by a considerable section of merchants and traders in London and South-

[1] 54 Com. Journ. 148; January 24, 1799.

[2] Ib. 517–18.

[3] Ib. 498; May 1, 1799.

wark, proposed so to reconstruct London Bridge as to enable ships of 500 tons to lie between it and Blackfriars Bridge, at a range of quays on each bank of the river, with a frontage of 8,000 feet.[1] Against this scheme the Committee promptly decided, as they thought it could never be an efficient substitute for wet docks, owing to the security thus afforded to shipping at every season of the year, and the convenience of loading and unloading.   By the London Dock scheme the Committee were favourably impressed, because this site was near the centre of trade, the Custom House, and warehouses already existing.   On the other hand, docks in the Isle of Dogs, being lower down the river, would be better adapted for large ships, which would avoid a circuitous passage, and much danger and delay.   The Committee thought that docks ought to be constructed in both situations.   Considering, however, how important it was that something should be done without further loss of time, they "unanimously resolved, most earnestly and decidedly," to recommend the House to pass the Corporation's Bill.   Further, the Committee expressed well-founded regret, that " though this subject has now been under consideration for several years, no measure should yet have been taken for remedying evils so universally felt and acknowledged."[2]

Agreeing with the Committee in this resolution, and stung, perhaps, by their concluding reproof, the House at last proceeded energetically, considered the London Port Bill, as it was now called, in Committee of the whole House, and disregarded the new petitions which poured in against it. Under the influence of this new-born zeal, the Bill passed

Marginal notes:
First Report, in favour of City Bill.

Port of London and West India Docks Act, 1799.

---

[1] 54 Com. Journ. 501; Second Report of Lord Hawkesbury's Committee, 1799.

[2] This report, dated June 1, 1799, will be found, with numerous Appendices, in 54 Com. Journ. 570–87. The Corporation of the Trinity House had, on May 23, after considering the amended plans of the City and merchants, resolved that docks both in the Isle of Dogs and at Wapping were "absolutely necessary;" and four days afterwards recommended that the former, with the new cut, should be first constructed.

on June 28, was agreed to by the Lords on July 11, and next day received the Royal assent.   This Act,[1] promoted jointly by the Corporation and West India merchants, first authorized the Common Council to make a navigable channel across the Isle of Dogs, to build piers at Blackwall and Limehouse Hole for facilitating entrance into the canal, and to make all incidental works.   They were also authorized to improve legal quays, lay down mooring chains, appoint harbour-masters, and undertake other duties with a view to improve navigation.   Then came a clause[2] reciting the necessity of wet docks, for West India shipping, in the Isle of Dogs, and forming certain specified subscribers into a company, to be called the West India Dock Company, for the purpose of making these docks.

This company were authorized to pay five per cent. as interest or dividends upon their subscribed capital until their works were completed, and afterwards dividends not exceed-ing ten per cent.[3] Of the directors, four were to be Alder-men and four Common Councilmen;[4] and if the Corporation subscribed to the company's stock they might appoint repre-sentatives to vote at general meetings.   " Commissioners for compensation " were to decide upon claims, including loss or injury suffered by owners and occupiers of legal and suffer-ance wharfs, as well as by porters and other persons employed there; but no such claims could be made until three years after the docks had been opened. The Corporation were to buy up necessary land in trust for the company.[5] Ton-nage rates in respect of the canal were to be paid, with some exceptions, by all vessels using the port, in addition to transit rates.[6] Lastly, money to defray its cost might be lent by the Treasury, upon the security of these rates.

Meanwhile, the London Docks Bill, as that of the mer-chants was now called, had, in July, 1799, been again post-

Side notes: City Canal. | West India Dock Company. | Interest during construction of works. | Corporation to be represented at Board. | Tonnage and transit rates. | London Docks Bill, 1800.

[1] 39 Geo. III. c. 69.
[2] Ib. s. 31.
[3] Ib. s. 42.
[4] Ib. s. 48.
[5] Ib. s. 74.
[6] Ib. ss. 134-6.

poned for another Session, the usual relaxation of Standing Orders as to notices being made in its favour.[1] In February, 1800, the Bill was re-introduced. It was opposed by the Corporation as conservators of the river, and also as guardians of trade, on account of a proposal "to lay a further and general impost upon the whole commercial tonnage which enters the port of London, except coasting vessels." The Corporation also urged that new docks were now unnecessary, as those sanctioned last year at their instance, in conjunction with the West India merchants, were "in great forwardness." Should it, however, be found hereafter that further accommodation was still wanting, the Corporation stated that they were ready to provide it. Meanwhile they begged the House to discourage speculations no longer based on any legitimate commercial wants, and certain to increase charges, depreciate the value of wharfs and other waterside property, and prejudice their ancient corporate rights."[2]

Opposed by Corporation.

Upon these issues, and upon more local and technical questions raised in other petitions, the Bill was contested. The Corporation might have been heard by counsel at the bar against the second reading, but declined to avail themselves of this opportunity.[3] With other petitioners, however, they appeared by counsel before a Committee to which the Bill was referred.[4] This Committee, of which Mr. Manning again acted as Chairman, met on March 5, and reported two months afterwards in favour of the measure, but omitting the obnoxious provision imposing a general tonnage rate on vessels.[5] Their report was more than once considered and discussed by the House in detail, and the Bill underwent many amendments.[6] It was discussed again after a third

Proceedings in Committee.

---

[1] 54 Com. Journ. 729; July 11, 1799.

[2] 55 Com. Journ. 252-3; March 3, 1800.

[3] Ib. 264.

[4] The House ordered that " all have voices who come" to this Committee (Ib. 265).

[5] Ib. 463; May 5, 1800.

[6] Ib. 544.

.... were .... in Com-
....

... . of
... ... measures as
... . and for
.... This Committee
.... Their
....
. ... should be
.. .. and not less than
.... high-water mark," so
.. . . of the tide, for
... . depth of the river
... . London and Blackfriars
.....," ... ... that .. shoals
.... Bridge should be re-
....., ... from the
.... with wharfs and warehouses
......, ..."

.... was .... the House, the
.... years of patience
... . which received
... . As in the Act of 1799,
.... vas .. ..[4] Maximum
.... be paid and a reserve fund
.. .. and .... After a suffi-
...., the company were re-

---

[1] .. ..

[2] Mr. N... .. Vansittart was chairman .. .. Hawkesbury, though .. .. . member, ... up.. the London Docks B.. ...

[3] This report is dated July 23, ..., and is printed with the Committee's resolutions in 55 Com. Journ. 791. An Act to rebuild London Bridge was not passed until 1823

[4] Geo. IV. c. 5... Mr. Rennie was engineer both for the London Docks and the new bridge, but did not live to construct the latter. Its site was some thirty yards west of the old bridge, and new approaches on both sides were necessary.

[4] 39 & 40 Geo. III. c. 47.

[5] Ib. s. 6.

quired to lower their rates of tonnage.[1] Their capital was fixed at 1,200,000*l.*, with borrowing powers of 300,000*l.*[2] A provision in the Act of 1799, now reproduced, bound them to make " just and liberal compensation, by purchase or by employment or otherwise," for loss or injury suffered by owners and occupiers of legal and sufferance wharfs and warehouses, by owners of lighters and other craft, tackle-house porters, ticket porters, free carmen, and other persons employed there, and by the governors of Christ's Hospital, on account of car-roons[3] or licences for using free carts within the City and liberties.[4]

In 1801, although no special legislation was proposed, a General Committee was once more appointed to consider fur-ther measures for making the port more commodious. Some of the old members of this Committee served again ; it included Mr. Abbot, Lord Hawkesbury, Mr. Pitt, Mr. Vansittart, Mr. Nicholas Vansittart, and Mr. Wilberforce. Later in the Session the Chancellor of the Exchequer was added. Plans were considered for docks and warehouses in other parts of the river, including the southern bank at Southwark and Rotherhithe, where the land was below the level of high water, and for the most part was marsh and morass.[5]

General Committee, 1801.

In 1802 the Corporation found that the cost of making their canal through the Isle of Dogs was greater than had been estimated, not because the works were heavier, but, as they alleged, on account of the legal obligation imposed upon them and other promoters to buy the whole of certain properties, though only part was actually wanted for their undertaking.[6] A further advance to complete the canal was accordingly sanctioned from the consolidated fund, secured,

City canal.

---

[1] Ib. s. 8.

[2] Ib. s. 22.

[3] Carroon or carroom. Ducange gives *Carrœum*, Med. Lat., Vectigal quod ex carris percipiebatur, and refers to its use in A.D. 1229. This revenue, and a control over carmen, were given by the City to Christ's Hospital in 1582. (Index to Remembrancia, p. 56, n.)

[4] 39 & 40 Geo. III. c. 47, s. 109.

[5] 56 Com. Journ. 502.

[6] See petition of Corporation, 57 Com. Journ. 120.

Repeated ad-
vances from
consolidated
fund.

as before, upon the tonnage duties authorized in 1799.[1]   It
was a work which had been pronounced by experts, and by
Parliament, a most useful aid to navigation in the Thames;
but its cost was out of all proportion to its utility.   New
loans from the consolidated fund became necessary, and
obtained legislative sanction, on four occasions after 1802.[2]
Even in 1807 the canal, with its flood-gates and other appliances, was not completed.[3]   Seven statutes record the
history of this ill-fated enterprise.   All keep a prudent
silence upon the total amount advanced towards it from the
public purse.   A recital of "large sums" so applied is the
utmost admission we can extract.

Sale of canal
to West India
Dock Com-
pany, 1829.

At length, in 1829, as the canal was no longer required
for navigation, the Government and Corporation agreed to
sell it to the West India Dock Company, whose works it
adjoined.   At that time none of the advances made by the
Treasury had been repaid; the tonnage rates on which these
loans were secured had been found insufficient to do more
than meet interest and expenses.   To end as quickly as possible a bad business, Parliament allowed the Treasury to
sacrifice, after 1829, all claim for interest; the tonnage rates,
for a term of twenty-one years,[4] were devoted towards repayment of principal; and the canal was handed over to the
dock company, freed from all obligation to maintain it as a
channel for vessels.[5]   Here, therefore, after thirty years, the
Corporation closed their statutory connection with the dock
and kindred enterprises of the century.

West India
Dock Acts,
1802–31.

Neither of the authorized dock companies found it possible

[1] 42 Geo. III. c. 49.

[2] 43 Geo. III. c. 124; 44 Geo. III.
c. 2; 45 Geo. III. c. 63; and 47
Geo. III. sess. 2, c. 31.

[3] The Act of 1807 authorizes advances of further sums from the consolidated fund "to be applied in
completing the canal," and "for
effecting other improvements in the
port of London."   The improvement, and purchase by the Treasury,
of legal quays between the Tower
and London Bridge formed part of
the scheme of these and some public
Acts at this period.

[4] Existing provisions for the collection of these tonnage dues were
repealed in 1849 by 12 & 13 Vict.
c. 90 (Pub.), ss. 41–2.

[5] 10 Geo. IV. c. 130.

to finish their works within the five years allowed them by their respective Acts.   The West India Company were allowed extensions of time to raise further capital in 1802 and 1804, on account of " the increased magnitude and extent " of their docks, and a " great advance in prices of materials and labour." [1]   Their import dock was opened in September, 1802 ; an export dock was a somewhat later development.   In 1829 the City canal, after purchase, became their " south dock," and for this and other extensions they were allowed to raise additional capital.[2]   Their previous Acts were repealed and consolidated in 1831, when the company were " further established and incorporated." [3]

Up to 1829, the London Dock Company could point to fifteen private statutes, averaging more than one in every two years, granting them further time to complete works, enabling them to raise fresh capital, extend their docks, and exercise further powers.[4]   As they demolished many houses for their works, and therefore seriously interfered with the business of the Shadwell Water Company, they bound themselves by their original Act to buy this undertaking, which had been established under statute in 1691.[5]   Their short career as suppliers of water has been traced elsewhere.[6]   In 1807, they added to their waterworks, by purchase, those of a company which supplied Stratford and adjacent parishes under an Act of 1743.[7]   For some years they continued to discharge this double duty of selling water and providing docks, but in 1808 transferred their waterworks to the East London Company.[8]   Their fourteen previous Acts were repealed by a consolidating Act of 1829, which for the first time incorporated the company.[9]   Their

London Dock Acts, 1804-29.

London Dock Company as suppliers of water.

---

[1] 42 Geo. III. c. 113; 44 Geo. III. c. 7.

[2] 10 Geo. IV. c. 67.

[3] 1 & 2 Will. IV. c. 52.

[4] 39 & 40 Geo. III. c. 47; 44 Geo. III. cc. 2, 100 ; 45 Geo. III. c. 58 ; 46 Geo. III. c. 59 ; 47 Geo. III. sess. 2, c. 5 ; 49 Geo. III. c. 156 ; 50 Geo. III. c. 151 ; 51 Geo. III. c. 49 ; 52 Geo. III.

c. 114 ; 54 Geo. III. c. 40 ; 55 Geo. III. c. 3 ; 58 Geo. III. c. 62 ; 4 Geo. IV. c. 124 ; 9 Geo. IV. c. 116.

[5] 3 & 4 W. & M. c. 37.

[6] *Ante*, Water Supply of London, pp. 110–11.

[7] 21 Geo. II. c. 47.

[8] 48 Geo. III. c. 8.

[9] 9 Geo. IV. c. 116, s. 2.

capital stock then amounted to 3,238,000*l.*, with 300,000*l.* borrowed upon the security of their rates from the Globe Insurance Company.

Compensation to vested interests.

Vested interests, which had struggled so hard against the construction of any docks, continued for some time to assert themselves. Wide compensation clauses, as we have seen, were inserted in the Acts of 1799-1800. Another example occurred in 1805, when the fellowship of carmen petitioned the House of Commons, alleging that their claim to compensation under these Acts was illusory. They therefore prayed for a Bill to repeal these compensation clauses, and provide that they might

Claim to monopoly of cartage from London Docks.

"enjoy the like exclusive right and privilege of working carts for hire from the new docks as they enjoy from the legal quays and sufferance wharfs." Their petition was opposed by the London Dock Company, by other carmen in Middlesex, and by sugar refiners, who declared that adequate compensation had been provided for the carmen if they suffered loss, and that the monopoly asked for would be injurious to trade. This reasonable view was adopted by the House, and although a Bill founded upon the carmen's petition was introduced, it did not pass a second reading.[1]

Vintners' Company,

An attempt made in the same Session by the "Master, Wardens, Freemen and Commonalty of the Mystery of Vintners" was more successful. They had been left out of the compensation clauses in the London Docks Act, but, as this Company were again in Parliament in 1805, they asked for a clause giving them the same claim, in case of loss from the new docks, as had been allowed to other interests. Powerful influence must have been used on their behalf, for on May 7,

Royal message in favour of.

"Mr. Chancellor of the Exchequer, by his Majesty's command, acquainted the House that his Majesty, having been informed of the contents of this petition, recommends it to the consideration of the House."[2] This recommendation

---

[1] 60 Com. Journ. 366; June 11, 1805.　　　[2] Ib. 246.

was equivalent to a command. Accordingly the Committee on the Bill were instructed to provide for compensation to the Vintners' Company if the docks diminished their income or caused any injury to their rights and interests.[1]

Having followed so far the statutory career of the two oldest dock companies, it is now necessary to go back to the year 1803, which saw a rival proprietary armed by Parliament with similar powers. A much smoother path was trodden by the East India and China merchants and shipowners when they sought to construct docks. In their petition to the House of Commons, they alleged that ships employed by the East India Company were larger than all other merchantmen, being nearly equal in size to ships of the line, while their cargoes, especially those homeward bound, were always extremely valuable. As a site for docks they proposed Blackwall, a point lower down the river than had been chosen by either of the other companies, and they were fortified by the approval of the East India Company's directors.[2] This petition was referred to a Committee consisting of Sir Francis Baring, Sir T. T. Metcalfe, with other members, and a Bill was afterwards introduced without opposition either from the vested interests who had appeared in 1799 and 1800, or from existing dock companies.

East India Docks, 1803.

Mr. Pitcher, a shipbuilder of Northfleet, complained of injury to his interests as owner of extensive premises which, with great labour and expense, had been fitted for building and repairing vessels of war, as well as large merchantmen. A subsequent petition from merchants and shipbuilders prayed for compensation similar to that given to other interests in the London and West India Dock Acts. Like the Vintners'

Shipbuilders' opposition.

[1] 45 Geo. III. c. 58, s. 4.

[2] 58 Com. Journ. 364; April 29, 1803. Four directors of the East India Company, Mr. John Roberts, Mr. Stephen Williams, Mr. Joseph Cotton, and Mr. William Thornton, were appointed on the dock company's first board, with Sir William Curtis, Bt., Mr. John Atkins, Mr. Henry Bonham, Mr. Abel Chapman, Mr. Joseph Huddart, Mr. Richard Lewin, jun., Mr. W. Wells, jun., Mr. Robert Wigram, and Mr. John Woolmore (43 Geo. III. c. 126, s. 16).

Company, these petitioners were able to command Royal influence, and "Mr. Chancellor of the Exchequer, by his Majesty's command, acquainted the House that his Majesty, having been informed of the purport of this petition, recommends it to their consideration."[1]　In accordance with this intimation, the Act of 1803, sanctioning the construction of docks to accommodate East India shipping at Blackwall,[2] declared that if Mr. Pitcher "should receive any actual loss or injury by reason of the trouble and expense of conveying ships and vessels to and from his yard for the purpose of repairs, or by any other means, or if any of the owners, proprietors, or occupiers of any other of the docks, slips, and dockyards in the port of London should be injured," and this property "should become less valuable; or if by reason thereof any person or persons interested in the trade carried on at such docks, slips, or dockyards, or any of them, should sustain actual loss or damage, just and liberal compensation or satisfaction, by purchase or employment," should be assessed by the commissioners for compensations appointed under previous Dock Acts.[3]

Compensation clauses.

By an Act of 1806,[4] the company's powers were enlarged, and their capital increased.　Compensation in case of injury was also directed to be made to owners of lighters and craft, to the governors of Christ's Hospital on account of car-roons, and to lightermen, tackle-house porters, ticket porters, and free carmen.[5]　As trade to places within the limits of the East India Company's charter had been thrown open to private enterprise in 1813,[6] under certain limitations, it became necessary in the following year to accommodate private ships engaged in this trade.　Powers to this effect were accordingly given by Parliament.[7]　Nearly a quarter of a century passed without further legislation.　Changes in trade

East India Dock Acts, 1806–35.

[1] 58 Com. Journ. 550; June 27, 1803.
[2] 43 Geo. III. c. 126.
[3] Ib. s. 87.
[4] 46 Geo. III. c. 113.
[5] Ib. s. 40.
[6] 53 Geo. III. c. 155.
[7] 54 Geo. III. c. 228.

then made it necessary to relax previous statutes which required all vessels with cargoes from the East Indies and China to unload in the Company's docks, and allowed no other vessel to use these docks, unless the East India Company's directors and the Treasury consented. In 1829, therefore, these restrictions were removed, and the dock company were authorized to provide additional accommodation. At the same time, their Acts were consolidated and amended, and all previous legislation affecting them repealed.[1] It had been usual to convey from their docks to the East India Company's warehouses, in "covered carts, waggons, and caravans," all merchandise belonging to the Company or consigned for sale at the India House. But in 1835 the East India Company had no longer any shipping or trade, and the dock company were therefore authorized to purchase their old warehouses, or to build new ones.[2]

On the southern bank of the river private enterprise, after 1800, soon supplied the wants of trade there. A Greenland dock at Rotherhithe has already been mentioned,[3] and seems to have been the oldest on the Thames below London Bridge. It was owned by a private company, which, without statutory powers, had constructed two other docks, called the Commercial Docks, strictly used for timber vessels. These three docks occupied about sixteen acres. In 1810, the company wished to buy forty acres, then open fields, adjacent to their property, for conversion into additional docks and timber yards. As their works would interfere with roads and involve another entrance into the Thames, it was necessary to promote a Bill for these purposes.[4]

In the same Session a competing scheme was promoted by individual merchants and shipowners, and a second Bill introduced, also for docks at Rotherhithe, to be called the

Docks on the southern bank.

Commercial Docks.

Rotherhithe Docks.

---

[1] 9 Geo. IV. c. 95.
[2] 5 & 6 Will. IV. c. 44, s. 20.
[3] *Ante,* p. 629.

[4] 65 Com. Journ. 60; Feb. 8, 1810.

South London Union.[1]   The two Bills were considered
concurrently, but by different Committees. Both were
opposed, chiefly by the same petitioners—wharfingers, landowners, shipbuilders at Rotherhithe and Deptford, the
Thames Archway Company, whose tunnel under the river
near this point had been sanctioned in 1805,[2] commissioners
of roads and sewers, porters of Billingsgate, directors of the
London Dock Company, and the Corporation of London.
The Rotherhithe Bill was only read a second time by a
majority of 27 to 23 votes.[3]   It was afterwards referred to a
Committee, but a petition was then presented to the House,
alleging a misrepresentation of material facts by the promoters in their evidence showing compliance with Standing
Orders, especially in stating that certain owners and occupiers
had assented to the scheme, whereas they were really opposed
to it.[4]   This petition was referred to a Committee, which
reported that Standing Orders had not been complied with.[5]

Promoters'
petition for
indulgence.

In reply, the promoters admitted an unintentional deviation
from "the strict letter" of Standing Orders, but represented
that their undertaking was of great public importance, "it
being intended to receive 700 ships out of the river, and to
lay up in ordinary, when required, not less than one hundred
of his Majesty's ships of war." They added that they had
already spent considerable sums in forwarding their plan, and
that the complaint as to breach of Standing Orders came from
the Commercial Dock Company, whose rival Bill proposed to
take the same land, and who admitted their motive to be a
wish to prevent the construction of competing docks.[6]   The
House of Commons would not, however, relax its rules, and
the Bill therefore dropped.

Commercial
Docks Bill,
1810.

Meanwhile the Commercial Docks Bill was not without its
difficulties.   Fifteen opponents appeared against it in Com-

---

[1] 65 Com. Journ. 56; Feb. 8,
1810.
[2] 45 Geo. III. c. 117; *ante*, Vol. 1,
pp. 194-5.

[3] 65 Com. Journ. 205.
[4] Ib. 277; April 11, 1810.
[5] Ib. 306; April 18, 1810.
[6] Ib., 324-5.

mittee, and counsel were heard on behalf of nine. It was necessary to enlarge on three occasions the time within which the Committee was bound to make its report. At length, on June 1, a report in favour of the Bill with amendments was presented. On a third reading the House showed itself less inclined to recognise vested interests than it had been ten years previously, for it rejected by forty-eight votes to five an attempt to procure compensation for wharfingers and other persons.[1] The Bill was agreed to by the Lords with some amendments, and received the Royal assent on June 20.

This Act[2] authorized the promoters to extend and improve their existing docks in order to facilitate the discharge of timber-laden vessels, and remove one great impediment to navigation. The docks were only to be used by vessels laden with timber, or chiefly so laden, provided that the rest of their cargoes consisted of "hemp, flax, pitch, tar, tallow, or fish, or ships laden with fish-oil, blubber and whale fins, or any other goods, wares and merchandises usually delivered afloat by river sufferance."[3] The Corporation of London confined their opposition to points affecting river conservancy. Clauses therefore provided that new entrances into the Thames should only be made with their consent, and that a nominal sum should be paid to them annually as an acknowledgment for leave to cut into the river.[4] Like their predecessors, the company were not incorporated, but received power to sue and be sued in the name of their treasurer. They had already subscribed 130,000*l.*, and were

Provisions of Act.

---

[1] 65 Com. Journ. 463; June 6, 1810. Sir Charles Price, Chairman of the Committee, and Mr. Huskisson, were tellers for the Bill. 'In the same Session a measure was promoted by wharfingers, lightermen, and others, to explain and amend those sections in the Acts of 1799 and 1800 which purported to award them compensation in case of in-jury; but the second reading was negatived. Ib. 295; April 17, 1810.

[2] 50 Geo. III. c. 207.

[3] Ib. s. 3.

[4] Ib. ss. 20, 24. A similar acknowledgment is provided for in the London water companies' Acts. *Ante*, pp. 93, 108. Other clauses saved the civic rights of metage and porterage.

allowed to raise an equal amount. In the next Session, and again in 1817, further capital powers were obtained.[1]

Two attempts were made in 1811 to make docks at Bermondsey and Rotherhithe. Bills, however, for these objects, though introduced, were not read a second time. But rivals to the Commercial grew up in a company which had been constituted in 1801 for making a canal from the Thames at Rotherhithe to Mitcham, with basins, docks, quays, and other conveniences for inland shipping.[2] In 1855, and again in 1860, this company were authorized to extend their dock system, the primary importance of which was shown by a change of name in 1855 to the Grand Surrey Docks and Canal

Company.[3] Another early dock in Rotherhithe was the East Country Dock, adjoining the Greenland. This dock, like the Commercial, was begun without statutory powers, "for the convenience of trade to the East country, and the reception of such articles of merchandise as are usually imported in East country ships."[4] In 1811, this dock being still unfinished, the subscribers obtained from Parliament power to complete it, and raise fresh capital as a joint stock company.[5]

A vigorous effort in 1824 to procure authority for making new docks near St. Saviour's Dock, in the parishes of St. John, Southwark, and St. Mary Magdalen, Bermondsey, met with determined opposition from vested interests both on the north and south banks.[6] A Committee, to which the promoters' Bill was referred, were strongly impressed with the advantage of new docks in relieving the crowded state of the river, and reducing, by competition, the high dock dues which, it was then stated,

---

[1] 51 Geo. III. c. 66; 57 Geo. III. c. 62.

[2] 41 Geo. III. c. 31. Further powers were obtained by 47 Geo. III. sess. 2, c. 80; 48 Geo. III. c. 99; 51 Geo. III. c. 170.

[3] 18 & 19 Vict. c. 134; 23 & 24 Vict. c. 74.

[4] Preamble to Act of 1811. British East country ships are, of course, meant.

[5] 51 Geo. III. c. 171; 6 Geo. IV. c. 64.

[6] 79 Com. Journ. 190 et seq.

had driven much trade from the port. On June 1, however, the House of Commons was informed that the promoters had withdrawn their Bill, through "unexampled length" in the examination of witnesses by opponents, and because other adverse petitions had still to be heard, "for the investigation of which, if pursued with the same spirit of procrastination which has marked the conduct of preceding petitioners, neither the residue of this Session, nor the whole length of any known Session, would afford time."[1] In 1825, the promoters renewed their application with success, after another prolonged contest, but they do not appear to have made use of their statutory powers.[2]

To this record may be added an Act passed in 1837 for making wet docks and other works at Rotherhithe and Deptford,[3] but these powers were not exercised. At the beginning of Queen Victoria's reign, therefore, only three separate dock systems existed on the southern bank. {Grand Collie Docks.}

Meanwhile, amid many more exciting topics, Parliament found time to give some attention to the old dock companies. Under the Acts sanctioning both the West India and London Docks, annual accounts from each company were laid before Parliament. In 1810, attention was called to an alleged breach by the West India Company of the clause which restricted their dividends to ten per cent., and directed that any surplus profits should be applied in reducing charges. {Dividends of West India Company, 1810.} Their accounts when presented were therefore referred to a Committee, consisting of the Attorney and Solicitor-General, Mr. Huskisson, and several other members,[4] who reported[5] that the docks had been completed, the estimate having been exceeded by only 26,800*l.*; while a rapid increase of profits left a balance of 53,000*l.* applicable to purposes specified in the Act. Thus, the Committee proceeded, a work of great public benefit had been accomplished by private enterprise, {Report of Commons' Committee, 1810.}

---

[1] Ib. 445; June 1, 1824; Report of Committee by Mr. Holme Sumner, Chairman.

[2] 6 Geo. IV. c. 118.

[3] 7 Will. IV. & 1 Vict. c. 123.

[4] 65 Com. Journ. 128.

[5] Ib., App. 721; March 22, 1810.

and the company's affairs had been conducted "with much industry, skill and correctness." But they had evaded the intention and letter of their Act by first paying property tax on their whole profits, without deducting any proportion from dividends, so that stock-holders had really received eleven per cent. instead of ten per cent., as the Act directed. Moreover, "while their income was thus exempted from the tax belonging to it," their surplus income, applicable to reduction of rates, had been charged not only with its own share of property tax, but with that properly chargeable on stock-holders.[1] Upon this report, after some opposition, the following resolution was passed:—"That, in the opinion of this House, the West India Dock Company, in dividing a clear ten per cent. on their capital, without deducting therefrom a due proportion of the property tax previously paid on the whole of their profits, have therein exceeded, by such amount of the property tax, the extreme rate of interest which they were empowered to divide by 39 Geo. III. c. 69."[2]

Resolution of House.

St. Katharine's.

More than twenty years passed before further accommodation was proposed on the north bank of the Thames. St. Katharine's docks, near the Tower, were not authorized until after a struggle protracted throughout two Sessions. It began in 1824, when, in a petition to the House of Commons, certain merchants represented "that the utility of commercial docks, with suitable vaults and warehouses surrounded by walls, whether considered as producing security to property, accommodation and facilities to trade and shipping, or economy in the collection of revenue, is, after an experience of upwards of twenty years, indisputably established." The petitioners wished to construct a dock between the Tower and London Docks, appropriated to goods from all parts of the world.[3] They added, that they desired no exclusive privileges or immunities, nor to interfere with those of existing

Petition of merchants, 1824.

[1] This is a question which still arises under similar statutory limitations upon dividends.

[2] 65 Com. Journ. 345; May 8, 1810.

[3] At this period the West and East India Docks were specifically appropriated by their respective Acts to the produce of those countries.

companies, " but in the legitimate employment of mercantile capital sought no other advantages than those which necessarily attached to a spirit of honourable rivalry, through the . means of general competition."

At this period a wholesome stimulus had been given to commerce, pursuant to recommendations of a Committee of the House of Commons, by the removal of various restrictions upon the landing and bonding of goods, with a view to give full effect to a public Act of 1823, permitting imported goods to be secured more freely in bonded warehouses, without payment of duty.[1] Certain imported goods were first permitted to be landed and left in bonded warehouses free of duty in 1803.[2] The public Act of 1823 extended this permission, " for the general encouragement and increase of commerce," to " all goods and merchandize whatsoever imported to any part of the United Kingdom." This removal of what had hitherto been galling and injurious restrictions upon trade,[3] was urged by the petitioners as a reason why new docks would be of public utility.[4]

Bonded warehouses.

It was probably no more than a coincidence that, in the same Session of 1824, Mr. Samuel Brown, R.N., proposed to build " a bridge of suspension," connecting the two banks of the river at St. Katharine's, and of sufficient height to admit sea-going ships under it at high water and spring tides without striking or lowering their masts or in any degree impeding navigation.[5] This project was strongly opposed, and the Bill

Suspension bridge proposed at St. Katharine's, 1824

[1] 4 Geo. IV. c. 24.

[2] 43 Geo. III. c. 132.

[3] Without a system of bonding in warehouses, England could not have become the chief market of the world. Formerly, if duty was not paid when goods arrived, consignees had to enter into bonds to provide security for the amount. Merchants were therefore often obliged to sell immediately upon importation, when possibly the market was glutted.— Lloyd's General Report for 1881,

Int. p. 18.

[4] 79 Com. Journ. 64. For further legislation to this effect in 1853 and 1876, see *post*, pp. 674-5.

[5] 79 Com. Journ. 45. Mr. Brown pointed to his success in building a similar bridge over the Tweed " of great extent and magnitude, which has been in constant use for the passage of carriages, carts, waggons, horses, cattle, foot passengers, and all ordinary traffic," since its opening on July 19, 1820. The Hunger-

embodying it did not pass a second reading.[1] During an interval of more than sixty years, almost every variety of project was broached for connecting the opposite shores of the river at or near this point, by means of high level and low level bridges, swing bridges, subways for foot passengers alone, and subways for general traffic, with and without hydraulic lifts; but none of these plans could reconcile the conflicting interests of road and river. It was reserved for the Corporation of London, in 1886, to give another proof of public spirit by beginning here, at their own expense, and without entailing any additional public burdens, the construction of a bascule, or lifting bridge, yielding priority when occasion requires to river traffic, and supplying a new link of communication vitally important to East London.[2]

Tower bridge of Corporation, 1886.

Like the older docks, St. Katharine's was strenuously opposed by watermen, wharfingers, "fellowship porters," and many other interests. The chief opponents were the London and Commercial Dock Companies, whose respective undertakings, situated on opposite sides of the Thames, would, they alleged, be injured by any new competition. These and other petitioners were heard by counsel. The same tactics of delay which in the same Session had been fatal to the South London project, were employed here. In Committee the proceedings were protracted until June, when the House directed that minutes of evidence should be laid before it. Mr. Grenfell, Chairman of the Committee, presented them on June 21, but Parliament was prorogued four days afterwards.

Opposition in House of Commons, 1824.

ford Suspension Bridge, sanctioned in 1836 (6 & 7 Will. IV. c. 133), was not opened till 1845; it was removed to Clifton in 1864.

[1] 79 Com. Journ. 190, 247, 329.

[2] *Ante*, p. 351. Recognizing the great value of this civic work to the teeming population of London below bridge, the Prince and Princess of Wales laid the memorial stone, with great ceremony, June 21, 1886. The cost of the Tower Bridge, 750,000*l.*, will be defrayed from surplus rents of estates which the Corporation have possessed for centuries, and which were partly bestowed by generous citizens, and partly derived from gifts made at the chapel of St. Thomas-à-Beckett, on London Bridge, for repairs of that bridge. From the proceeds of these estates, London and Blackfriars bridges have been rebuilt, and Southwark Bridge freed from toll, without any expense to the ratepayers. (See Recorder's Address to Prince of Wales, June 21, 1886.)

On February 4, 1825, early in the next Session, the Bill passes, 1825. merchants renewed their application. Many petitions from outports were now presented in favour of their Bill. As before, the London Docks Company were its chief opponents; they were heard by counsel in Committee, and after the preamble had been passed, urged the House to recommit the Bill, with a view to its amendment. On a division, the Committee's decision was upheld by 91 to 20 votes.[1] The Bill was passed on April 22, was approved by the Lords without amendment, and received the Royal assent June 10. It recited the expediency of placing new docks Provisions of Act. " as near as may be to the City of London," and also of establishing them " on the principle of free competition in trade, and without any exclusive privileges or immunities."[2] The promoters were required to subscribe the whole cost of their works, estimated at 1,352,000*l.*, before using any statutory powers.[3] During construction interest upon capital might be paid at the rate of five per cent.[4]

Apart from the rivalry of other dock companies, this Act Appropriation of St. Katharine's Hospital. excited much interest and opposition, for it appropriated, compulsorily, an entire parish, the precinct of St. Katharine, about eleven acres in extent, and containing, in 1821, 2,624 inhabitants, a number reduced in the census of 1831 to 72. The Act also required the removal, from a site which it had occupied for nearly seven centuries, of an ecclesiastical corporation, unique in English history, and supposed to be of higher antiquity than any other corporation now existing. Founded about 1148 by Queen Matilda, and re-established by Queen Eleanor in 1273, " The Royal Hospital and Free Chapel of St. Katharine near the Tower " was independent, as a Royal Peculiar, of any diocesan control whatever; it owed no allegiance to the Bishop of London or Archbishop of Canterbury; it had its own Ecclesiastical Court, and granted probate of wills and marriage licences within its limits; it ranked in privileges and dignity with Westminster Abbey and St.

---

[1] 80 Com. Journ. 257.   [3] Ib. s. 2.

[2] Geo. IV. c. 105.   [4] Ib. s. 14.

George's, Windsor. More remarkable still, it retained, and had possessed from its earliest foundation, female members equal in status and voting power to the clerical members or canons. By another rule of this body, its patronage was vested, not in the King or Prime Minister, but in the Queen Consort for the time being. To obliterate an entire parish was an easy undertaking compared with the disturbance and re-settlement of a foundation such as this. Still, if the docks

Removal of Hospital.

were to be made, it was inevitable that the Royal Hospital of St. Katharine, with its chapter-room and burial-ground, should disappear from its old site. Fortunately, at that time, the Regent's Park was in process of formation, and to a new site granted by the Crown there the Hospital was transferred, receiving 163,000*l.* as compensation from the Dock Company, and being clothed by the Act of 1825, as far as practicable, with all its ancient attributes.

Collier Dock (Isle of Dogs), 1825.

Parliament was evidently inclined, in 1825, to disregard hostile dock interests and sanction any substantial schemes offering additional accommodation. With this view, besides the St. Katharine's and South London undertakings, it authorized in the Isle of Dogs new docks especially designed for colliers and the coal trade.[1] In vain the West India Dock Company headed a formidable opposition to this project. That it was never carried out was probably due to the clause inserted in all Dock Acts of 1825, that the whole cost, estimated in this case at 600,000*l.*, should be subscribed before the Act was put into force.[2]

Amalgamation of companies:

Dock companies on the Thames, no less than water and gas companies, have obeyed that law of life which seems to govern associated enterprises, prescribing, first, active competition: then agreement and amalgamation. In 1838, the

East and West India;

East and West India undertakings were allowed to set this example,[3] notwithstanding many complaints of the monopoly

---

[1] 6 Geo. IV. c. 119.

[2] Ib. s. 2.

[3] 1 & 2 Vict. c. 9, which, while sanctioning their amalgamation, also amended the several Acts relating to the two companies. See also 37 & 38 Vict. c. 59, a statute with like objects.

which would surely follow. In 1851, the Commercial Company obtained powers to buy and enlarge the East Country Dock, adjoining their system, to construct new entrances to the Thames, and a tramway connecting their undertaking with the Brighton Railway.[1] Again, in 1864, a powerful combination was formed by the union of the Commercial and Grand Surrey Companies,[2] under the title of the Surrey Commercial Dock Company. This amalgamation left only one incorporated dock company on the south bank.

Commercial, East Country, and Surrey Canal.

A new undertaking, below the East India Docks, was sanctioned in 1850 by an incorporation of the Victoria Dock Company,[3] who received powers three years afterwards,[4] and again in 1857, to extend their works by a new cut eastwards.[5] This company fell into pecuniary difficulties, and the Victoria Docks were managed by lessors. Advantage was taken of this position in 1864 to combine the interests of three dock companies, the London, St. Katharine's, and Victoria, by the amalgamation of the two first, and the transfer to them of the Victoria Dock undertaking.[6] Since 1829, the London Dock Company had obtained three additional Acts extending their powers,[7] and their capital, in stock and loans, amounted to nearly five millions. Since 1826, the St. Katharine's Company had obtained four grants of new powers,[8] and their capital, in stock and loans, was 2,652,000*l.* Of their authorized capital of 1,599,000*l.*, the Victoria Company had raised in stock and debentures 1,029,000*l.* As this company had been unable to carry out their eastern extension, authority to do so was given, in 1875, to the London and St. Katharine's Dock Company, as the amalgamated undertakings were now called.[9]

Victoria Dock, 1850.

London and St. Katharine's Dock Act, 1864.

---

[1] 14 & 15 Vict. c. 43. See also 22 Vict. c. 30 ; and 23 & 24 Vict. c. 39.

[2] 27 Vict. c. 31.

[3] 13 & 14 Vict. c. 51.

[4] 16 & 17 Vict. c. 131.

[5] 20 & 21 Vict. c. 83. The time for completing these works was extended by 22 Vict. c. 29.

[6] Sanctioned by 27 & 28 Vict. c. 178.

[7] 16 & 17 Vict. c. 106; 19 & 20 Vict. c. 1 ; 21 & 22 Vict. c. 35.

[8] 10 Geo. IV. c. 1; 11 Geo. IV. & 1 Will. IV. c. 13 ; 2 & 3 Will. IV. c. 49 ; 6 & 7 Will. IV. c. 31.

[9] 38 & 39 Vict. c. 153.

Deep water docks.

While these amalgamations were in progress, increased size in ocean steamers, and a desire to attract them to the Thames from ports like Southampton, led to proposals for dock accommodation lower down the Thames, connected by railway with trading centres in London. The first plan of this kind, in 1855, ended in failure. A company was then incorporated[1] to make docks at Dagenham, a point on the Essex coast between Woolwich and Erith. A hundred and fifty years previously, Dagenham had been a subject of private legislation, through a great irruption of the Thames, which occurred in 1703, when five thousand acres were laid under water.[2] It was proposed in 1855 to use part of this area for dock purposes. Further time for the construction of works was obtained in 1862,[3] and in 1866 power was given to enlarge the docks and provide abattoirs with other conveniences[4] for the landing of foreign cattle. In 1870, however, the company being then in liquidation, an Act passed to facilitate the sale of their undertaking.[5]

Dagenham Dock Company, 1855–70.

Proposed Alfred Docks, 1880.

Unsuccessful application was made to Parliament in 1880 for leave to construct a tidal basin and docks, to be called the Alfred Docks, embracing the greater portion of Dagenham Gulf. This site was also adopted in 1881 by the Thames Deep Water Dock Company, who obtained powers to construct a large deep-water dock at Dagenham, capable of accommodating the largest class of steam and other vessels.[6] These powers have not been exercised, for before the new company could raise its capital, existing interests took alarm, and proposed to establish docks still nearer the mouth of the Thames.

Tilbury Docks, 1882.

In 1882 the East and West India Dock Company, impressed with the necessity of saving time and avoiding risk in the transit of large steamers and other vessels up the tideway, projected docks at Tilbury, opposite Gravesend, and

[1] 18 & 19 Vict. c. 162.
[2] *Ante*, Vol. I. p. 13; 13 Anne, c. 20. Capt. Penny received 25,000*l.* from Parliament for partial success in closing the breach, and draining

off the water.
[3] 25 & 26 Vict. c. 213.
[4] 29 & 30 Vict. c. 46.
[5] 33 & 34 Vict. c. 162.
[6] 44 & 45 Vict. c. 198.

thirteen miles and a half lower down the river than Dagenham, so that the largest class of steam vessels might arrive and depart at all times of the tide.   This Bill was opposed, on the ground of competition, by the Thames Deep Water Dock Company, who alleged that docks at Tilbury were intended to intercept vessels which would otherwise use their Dagenham docks.   An old contest was also revived, under somewhat altered conditions, by an opposition from owners, lessees, and occupiers of legal quays and sufferance wharfs, and also from lightermen and barge owners.   These petitioners complained that they would be subjected to an unfair competition, as the dock promoters and the London, Tilbury and Southend Railway Company proposed to carry from Tilbury to London, at exceptional rates, goods which would otherwise come to docks higher up the river, and be conveyed by the petitioners.[1]   This opposition was unsuccessful, and docks at Tilbury, constructed under statutory powers,[2] at a cost of about three millions, were opened in 1886.   Here are to be found powerful hydraulic machinery, and the most modern appliances for facilitating the berthing of vessels and transhipment of goods, irrespective of tidal conditions.

A dock undertaking in the Isle of Dogs, south of the West India Dock, had a similar origin to that of the Surrey Canal. In 1864, there was a revival of the old scheme for a canal across the Isle of Dogs, sanctioned in 1799, carried out by the Corporation, and afterwards abandoned under circumstances already described.   A "Millwall Canal Company" was therefore incorporated, with power to make and maintain a canal having entrances from Limehouse Reach and Blackwall Reach, with basins and other works, and also to appropriate adjoining land for wharfs, shipbuilding, and other purposes requiring water passage.[3]   Additional capital was authorized in 1866.[4]   In 1870, the business carried on had

Millwall Canal Company.

Millwall Dock Company, 1870.

---

[1] Locus Standi Reports of Clifford & Rickards, III. pp. 138–42.

[2] 45 & 46 Vict. c. 90 (East and West India Dock Extension).

[3] 27 & 28 Vict. c. 255 (Millwall Canal, Wharfs, and Graving Docks Act).

[4] 29 & 30 Vict. c. 323.

grown to be practically that of a dock company. The company's name was changed accordingly; and they were enabled to build new warehouses, make tramways along their quays,[1] and construct and work a Millwall extension of the London and Blackwall Railway. Further capital powers were given to the company in 1879 and 1882.[2]

Regent's Canal. Another canal company, designed to connect western and eastern London, and based largely upon dock development on Thames' side, has not, like the two similar undertakings which have been mentioned, expanded into docks there. Soon after the West India and London docks were authorized, **Project of 1803.** Parliament was asked, in 1803, to sanction an extension of the Grand Junction Canal from Paddington to communicate with the London Docks at Shadwell. Such a work, it was said, would largely diminish the cost of carting heavy goods through London, and the need for draught horses, " whereby much land now applied in the growth of provender for them may be more beneficially used in the culture of food for mankind."[3] This plan was referred to a Committee, who do not seem to have reported upon it.

Regent's Canal Company, 1812. It was only in the year 1812 that this project took statutory shape,[4] and the Regent's Canal was made, not connected with the London Docks, as was originally proposed, but having a basin and an entrance to the Thames, half-way between the London and West India Docks, and close by the river entrance to Limehouse Cut. In order to enable them to complete their works, the company obtained advances of 200,000l. from the Consolidated fund.[5] A basin which they had been authorized to make at Limehouse was converted from a barge to a ship basin after 1819.[6] In 1821 the company were helped by another advance of 100,000l. from the Consolidated fund, secured upon their undertaking.[7] They

---

[1] 33 & 34 Vict. c. 20 (Millwall Dock Act, 1870).

[2] 42 & 43 Vict. c. 67 ; 45 & 46 Vict. c. 36.

[3] Petition of promoters, 58 Com. Journ. 161.

[4] 52 Geo. III. c. 195, amended by 53 Geo. III. c. 32; 56 Geo. III. c. 85.

[5] Under public Acts, 57 Geo. III. cc. 34, 124.

[6] 59 Geo. III. c. 66.

[7] 1 & 2 Geo. IV. c. 43.

were enabled to enlarge a reservoir on the river Brent in 1851,[1] purchase the Hertford Union Canal in 1855,[2] and improve their Limehouse basin and make a new entrance from the Thames, with wharfs and other works at Limehouse in 1865.[3]

A new chapter in the history of this undertaking began in 1875, when a canal and dock company were incorporated to buy it, further enlarge the basin at Limehouse and Ratcliffe, give more direct and convenient communication with the Thames, and make a railway communicating with the Great Eastern line.[4] This new company failed in finding the purchase-money, and in 1877 their plan of fresh dock accommodation was abandoned, and the company dissolved.[5] To this project there succeeded a still greater one in 1882, when a Regent's Canal, City and Docks Railway Company were incorporated, with a share and loan capital of nearly 10,500,000*l.*, and were authorized to buy up the canal, and construct, chiefly on surplus land along its bank, a new metropolitan railway from the Great Western line at Paddington to the Royal Albert Dock of the London and St. Katharine's Company, with a spur line to Barbican, in the City, connecting the Great Northern and Midland systems with the same points.[6] Stringent clauses were inserted in this Act to secure the maintenance of the canal as a competitive route and the interests of all canal traffic. In the following Session the canal was constituted a separate undertaking, with a separate capital;[7] and to facilitate the raising of money for the contemplated railway, Parliament deviated from its Standing Orders in 1885, and allowed the company to pay interest on capital during construction.[8] In making this concession Parliament really reverted to its former practice when sanctioning the earlier docks.[9]

Among other projects which received legislative sanction, but have not been carried out, was one for docks, wharfs and warehouses in West London, at Battersea. A company incorporated for this object obtained three Acts in 1863 and

Marginal notes:
Regent's Canal and Dock Company, 1875.

Abandonment Act, 1877.

Regent's Canal, City and Docks Railway Company.

Interest on capital during construction.

West London Company, 1863-5.

---

[1] 14 & 15 Vict. c. 32. [4] 38 & 39 Vict. c. 206. [7] 46 & 47 Vict. c. 212.
[2] 18 & 19 Vict. c. 95. [5] 40 & 41 Vict. c. 205. [9] 48 & 49 Vict. c. 138.
[3] 28 & 29 Vict. c. 365. [6] 45 & 46 Vict. c. 262. [9] *Ante*, pp. 650, 652.

Greenwich
and South
Eastern
Docks,
1859-67.

Victoria and
Albert Docks,
1884.

Customs'
Regulations,
1853-76.

subsequent Sessions. They restricted their works in 1865 to wharfs and warehouses.[1] Powers were granted in 1859 for the construction of what were to have been called the Greenwich and South Eastern Docks.[2] These powers expired, were revived in 1867,[3] but again lapsed.

In 1884 the London and St. Katharine's Company were enabled to make a new entrance to their Royal Albert Dock at Galleon's Reach.[4] This dock gives accommodation to the largest steamers, and extends, with its companion dock, the Victoria, and their connecting links, to a distance of three miles.

Mention has been made of the great impetus given to commerce and to dock enterprise by the establishment of bonded warehouses.[5] In 1850 a Committee of the House of Commons inquired into the constitution and management of the Customs. Owing to their report, made two years afterwards, trade received new facilities in 1853. Chief among these was the option of giving general covering bonds on removals of warehoused goods instead of separate bonds in each case. Formerly, the attendance of principal and surety was essential on these occasions; a merchant could not remove a bale of tobacco or a bag of currants from London to Liverpool without taking his surety to the Long Room, and together executing there the required obligation. The removal of this harassing and needless form, a source of enormous delay, gave such an impetus to business, that in 1876, when an amending Act was required, 70,000 general bonds were issued annually: and the solicitor to the Customs, writing in 1877 of the public convenience resulting from this change of system, pointed out that there would then have been necessary under the old system of more than 1,400,000 attendances of principals and sureties.[6]

---

[1] 26 & 27 Vict. c. 228; 27 & 28 Vict. c. 238; 28 & 29 Vict. c. 372.

[2] 22 & 23 Vict. c. 20.

[3] 30 & 31 Vict. c. 80.

[4] 47 & 48 Vict. c. 15.

[5] *Ante*, p. 665.

[6] De Hamel's Introduction to Customs' Consolidation Acts, 1853 and

1876 (16 & 17 Vict. c. 107, and 39 & 40 Vict. c. 36). In the former of these statutes, a work of immense labour, Mr. Felix De Hamel, then solicitor to the Customs, first consolidated into a single Act, by direction of the Treasury, the voluminous and intricate Customs' laws, which had

Several recent statutes have given to the dock companies increased capital and other powers.[1] Their systems are now connected, more or less directly, by the North London and Great Eastern lines, with all the railways north of the river, as well as with those on its southern bank, by the East London line, passing through the old Thames Tunnel. Goods may, therefore, be despatched with little, if any, transhipment to the most distant parts of Great Britain. In the heart of the City vast "up-town warehouses" are provided by the two great amalgamated companies, and bonded goods are sent there in padlocked waggons, that they may be within easy reach of dealers and consumers. No want of accommodation now exists, nor, in spite of amalgamation, which has reduced the number of dock companies on the Thames to four, is there any reasonable complaint of excessive charges or absence of wholesome competition. That all these great works on the Thames should have been created under legislative authority within the century is a striking proof of private enterprise, tardily begun, but carried on with unflagging spirit, and a resolve even in times of depression to meet by fresh outlay at new sites the altered conditions of trade.[2]

long been the despair of all concerned in administering them. At the same time many of their provisions were amended and simplified. Lord Penzance, then counsel for the Crown in Customs' cases, described this statute as "replacing the old cumbrous procedure by a simple and expeditious system;" and the Board of Customs informed the Treasury in 1877 that by its operation during twenty years nearly half-a-million sterling was saved to the country in the legal department of the Customs alone. Its chief merit, however, was the facility it afforded for the despatch of business, and it therefore eminently deserves notice in any record of an enterprise so closely connected with the Customs as the docks of London. The further consolidation of Customs' laws in 1876 was also the work of Mr. De Hamel.

[1] London and St. Katharine, 41 & 42 Vict. c. 22; and 45 & 46 Vict. c. 2; East and West India, 42 & 43 Vict. c. 169; 46 & 47 Vict. c. 39; 48 & 49 Vict. c. 25.

[2] Perhaps the most striking of these changes is illustrated by a report of a House of Commons' Committee in 1604 (1 Com. Journ. 218), from which it appears that trade was then so centred in London that the Customs produced there 110,000l. a year; and at all other ports in the realm only 17,000l.

CHAPTER XVIII.

PROVISIONAL ORDERS AND CERTIFICATES; AND ORDERS IN COUNCIL.

Provisional Order system. To various departments of the Government important duties have from time to time been assigned by statute, not only in watching, and reporting to Parliament upon, the plans of promoters, but in examining and sanctioning these plans, subject to veto by the Legislature. This "Provisional Order system," as it is called, though confined to projects relatively small and unimportant, has during the last twenty‑years reached a remarkable development. By its means, an attempt has been honestly made to render private legislation less costly, as well as to lighten the work and economize the time of Parliament; and no fewer than eight departments in England, two in Scotland, and three in Ireland, acting independently of each other, now make and issue these quasi-statutory Orders. The system has some warm advocates, but many persons who are conversant with its practical working, and have watched its gradual growth, object with equal warmth to its centralizing influences, and other shortcomings. A history of private legislation would be incomplete if it did not take account of this new system, and, while doing justice to the labours of these different departments, try also to discover whether experience had revealed any defects in the nature or administration of the system itself.

As the term implies, a department has no inherent authority of its own to legislate, and can only give "provisional" effect to any scheme, Parliament reserving in each case the

right to review and amend or reject the scheme, even after
its sanction by the department. This sanction, however,
gives great advantage to any proposals, by local bodies
or companies, embodied in a Provisional Order, and it is
right, therefore, that private interests prejudicially affected
by these proposals should be adequately protected by opportunities of appeal to the Legislature. In order to afford such **Provisional**
protection, Provisional Orders granted during the year are **Order
Confirmation**
grouped in schedules to Bills which come before the two **Bills.**
Houses for confirmation; and until a confirmation Bill has
passed no Order contained in it has any force. After a first
reading the confirming Bill goes before the Examiners, who
see that each scheme complies with Standing Orders, which
resemble but are not identical with those applicable to
private Bills.

Every Order is, theoretically, a private Bill, with a
preamble and clauses, though it is not brought in upon the
usual petition from its promoters. Some, however, of the
Provisional Orders, and notably those issued by the Board
of Trade as to gas, water, piers and harbours, pilotage
and tramways, cannot be said to afford, in their preambles,
any clear or definite information of the circumstances in
which the Orders had their origin. In the event of opposition
to any Order in a group, the confirming Bill is referred to a
select committee, and thereupon the opposed Order is treated
as a private Bill;[1] the preamble must be proved by evidence;
and the promoters, though relieved from the payment of
House fees, are liable to all other costs of procedure in Parliament, besides the expenses already incurred in carrying
the Order through the department.

Some detailed description may with advantage be given
of the jurisdiction thus exercised by public departments, and
of its growth and extent. The Inclosure Commissioners[2] **Powers of
Inclosure**

---

[1] Com. S. O. (1887), 72, 151.

[2] Now the Land Commissioners.
The Settled Land Act, 1882, provides

that "the Commissioners now bearing
the three several styles of the Inclosure Commissioners for England

Commissioners.

were the first body to whom these functions were entrusted. By numerous Acts, dating from that which in 1845 constituted the Commissioners,[1] they were authorized, after public inquiries held in the locality, to make Provisional Orders for

Inclosure and regulation of commons.

the inclosure and regulation of commons. From 1845 down to the end of the Session 1869, no fewer than 958 Provisional Orders of this nature were granted by the Commissioners, and 842 of these were confirmed by Parliament without opposition. From 1869 till the passing of the Commons Act, 1876,[2] 33 Orders were granted, but none were confirmed, owing to the growing jealousy felt in Parliament as to inclosures, and pending legislation. From 1876 till October, 1882, 33 Orders were granted for regulating or inclosing commons, of which 30 were confirmed by Parliament. The House of Commons now watches with close attention all these proposals, and appoints a Select Committee in each Session to consider every report made by the Land Commissioners certifying the expediency of any scheme for inclosing or regulating a common, before a Bill can be introduced to confirm it.[3] Metropolitan commons were the subject of 15 Orders for regulation between 1866[4] and 1885, comprising

and Wales, and the Copyhold Commissioners, and the Tithe Commissioners for England and Wales, shall, by virtue of this Act, become and shall be styled the Land Commissioners for England" (45 & 46 Vict. c. 38, s. 48).

[1] 8 & 9 Vict. c. 118. There are fourteen later Acts, ending with one passed in 1878 (41 & 42 Vict. c. 56). They are usually cited as the Inclosure Acts, 1845 to 1878.

[2] 39 & 40 Vict. c. 56. As to the policy and extent of earlier inclosures, see Vol. I. pp. 13-28.

[3] The importance of the Commissioners' duties may be gathered from the following, among other, schemes of regulation and inclosure autho-

rized by Parliament under the Commons Act, 1876, and in progress in 1885:—*Regulation:* Ashdown Forest, Sussex, 6,000 acres; East Stainmore Common (part of), Westmoreland, 6,383 acres. *Inclosure:* East Stainmore Common (part of), Westmoreland, 4,075 acres; Llanfair Hills, Salop, 1,634 acres; Hildersham common fields and pastures, Cambridge, 1,174 acres; Llanbyther Common, Carmarthen, 1,891 acres. —(Report of Land Commission for 1885.)

[4] The first Metropolitan Commons Act passed in 1866 (29 & 30 Vict. c. 70); and see 31 & 32 Vict. c. 89, and 41 & 42 Vict. c. 71.

an area of 1,738 acres. Besides their jurisdiction over commons, the Inclosure Commissioners were also, in 1861, authorized to order provisionally the compulsory acquisition of lands by Commissioners of Sewers,[1] and the constitution of drainage districts with elected boards of management.[2] They have granted 22 Provisional Orders under the powers last mentioned.[3]

Drainage districts.

In conformity with the oldest precedents of legislative interference in the interests of salmon fisheries,[4] the Home Secretary can, by Provisional Orders in England and Wales, authorize fishery conservators to acquire and remove by compulsory purchase weirs and other artificial obstructions in rivers.[5] He may also confirm improvement schemes under the Artizans and Labourers' Dwellings Improvement Act, 1875, a jurisdiction, however, confined to the City of London and Metropolis.[6] Between 1875 and August, 1882, 18 Orders of this nature were issued from the Home Office and confirmed by Parliament. The Home Secretary

Powers of Home Secretary:

over weirs:

under Artizans and Labourers' Dwellings Acts.

Explosives.

---

[1] 24 & 25 Vict. c. 133, Part I.

[2] Ib. Part II.

[3] The authority for this and subsequent statements as to the use made of the Provisional Order system is Commons' Return, 99 (Session 1883). This Return is unfortunately silent as to any alterations made in any opposed Order by Committees, short of its rejection; nor can it, of course, show how far a Parliamentary decision in one case modified the action of the department in subsequent cases; but it gives valuable information as far as it goes.

[4] *Ante*, Vol. I. pp. 3, 4.

[5] 36 & 37 Vict. c. 71, s. 49.

[6] 38 & 39 Vict. c. 36, s. 6; 42 & 43 Vict. c. 63; and 45 & 46 Vict. c. 54, Part I.; see *post*, p. 690 *et seq.* Mr. Shaw Lefevre, when First Commissioner of Works, stated that in eleven schemes promoted by the Metropolitan Board before 1882, affecting districts inhabited by 4,500 families, the loss to ratepayers on the purchase and re-sale of property taken under these Acts was 1,250,000*l.*, or nearly 300*l.* for each family; and that the houses rebuilt on this property had been peopled, not by the persons dispossessed, but by a superior class of persons. This heavy outlay and loss arose chiefly from the enormous compensation obtained by owners of the miserable dwellings swept away. The Act of 1882 limited this compensation to some extent, and relieved local authorities from onerous obligations (ss. 3, 4). If these provisions had been inserted in the earlier Acts, it is estimated that the ratepayers' loss would have been 400,000*l.* instead of 1,200,000*l.* (Speech at Reading, "The Times," Nov. 16, 1883.)

may repeal or alter local Acts or charters relating to the

Secretary for
Scotland.

manufacture and storage of explosives.[1]　In Scotland his authority was superseded in 1885 by that of the Secretary for Scotland,[2] who is also Vice-President of the Scotch Educational Department, and now exercises in Scotland all powers hitherto vested in the Home Secretary, Privy Council, Local Government Board, and Treasury.　This new minister issues Provisional Orders applying the General Police and Improvement (Scotland) Act, 1862.[3]　Under the Public Health (Scotland) Act, 1867, and the Public Parks (Scotland) Act, 1878, he may also authorize the acquisition of lands, both by agreement and compulsorily, for the purposes of these Acts.[4]　The Secretary for Scotland also issues Provisional Orders for confirming improvement schemes under the Artizans and Labourers' Dwellings Improvement (Scotland) Act, 1875, in Royal and Parliamentary burghs containing a population of over 25,000 according to the last census;[5] and for bringing into force the Roads and Bridges (Scotland) Act, 1878.[6]　Before 1885, the jurisdiction of the Home Office under these Acts was generally exercised after a local inquiry in open court.

Powers of
Board of
Trade:
Electric
lighting.

Important powers in the grant of Provisional Orders have been conferred upon the Board of Trade.　In 1882, the Electric Lighting Act provided for the issue by the Board of licences and Provisional Orders authorizing the supply of electricity, a new jurisdiction, which was at first largely resorted to by promoters.[7]

---

[1] 38 & 39 Vict. c. 17, s. 103.

[2] 48 & 49 Vict. c. 61, s. 5. This section transfers to the Secretary for Scotland all powers to issue Provisional Orders relating to Scotland previously possessed by departments in England.

[3] 25 & 26 Vict. c. 101, ss. 79—83.

[4] 30 & 31 Vict. c. 101, s. 90, and 41 & 42 Vict. c. 8, ss. 6, 8—10. See as to alteration of boundaries of special drainage and water supply districts in Scotland, 42 & 43 Vict. c. 15, and 45 Vict. c. 11.

[5] 38 & 39 Vict. c. 49; 43 Vict. c. 2.

[6] 41 & 42 Vict. c. 51, ss. 9, 10.

[7] 45 & 46 Vict. c. 56, ss. 3, 4. In 1883, upon 106 applications for Provisional Orders, the fees charged by the Board to promoters amounted to the substantial sum of 5,400l.,

Under the General Pier and Harbour Acts, 1861 and 1862,[1] the Board may provide for the construction, improvement, management and maintenance of piers and harbours throughout the United Kingdom, except portions of the rivers Thames, Mersey, Clyde, Wear, Humber and Tyne. An Order is made after such inquiries as the Board of Trade may think expedient.[2] The Board avail themselves of advice from their staff, and, when occasion requires, from coastguard officers in districts in which the proposed piers or harbours are situated. Promoters under the Piers and Harbours Acts are required to pay a fee of 35*l.* to the Board of Trade towards the expense of settling the Provisional Order. The Board consider objections founded on alleged injury to public interests (as that the proposed work will injure a public harbour, or that tolls are imposed on ships which will derive no benefit from them), and decline to proceed with any Order to which valid objections of this nature are made. They will only attempt to settle questions arising out of competition or opposing local interests if the parties are willing to abide by their decision.[3] When promoters and opponents cannot come to terms, the Board will not order a local inquiry or anticipate the decision of Parliamentary Committees.[4] From 1861 up to the end of the Session, 1882, 260 Orders were granted relating to piers and harbours; 225 were confirmed by Parliament without opposition; of 35 petitioned against and referred to Select Committees, 25 were afterwards confirmed.[5]

A Public Works Loans Act, 1882, enables the Board, upon certain conditions, by Provisional Order, to authorize urban sanitary authorities to charge any fund or rate under

Piers and harbours.

excluding the costs of local inquiries. (Com. Paper, 237 of 1883.) In 1884 there were only four applications for Orders. In Vol. I. pp. 236-47, this jurisdiction of the Board of Trade is fully treated.

[1] 24 & 25 Vict. c. 45; 25 Vict. c. 19.

[2] 24 & 25 Vict. c. 45, s. 15.

[3] See *post,* p. 711.

[4] Board of Trade Regulations, 1880.

[5] Commons' Paper, 99 (Session 1883), pp. 4, 12.

their control for the purpose of aiding harbour authorities in raising loans for the construction of harbours, piers, or other works within the meaning of the Act of 1861.[1]

Pilotage.

Under the Merchant Shipping Act Amendment Act, 1862, the Board of Trade may by Provisional Orders transfer pilotage jurisdiction; constitute new pilotage authorities, and provide schemes of management; and amend local

Sea fisheries.

pilotage regulations within the United Kingdom.[2] A series of Acts relating to Sea Fisheries also enables the Board, in England and Scotland, to grant Provisional Orders creating exclusive fisheries of oysters and mussels, regulating these fisheries, and restricting or prohibiting beam and other trawling where it is injurious to clam or bait beds.[3] In these cases a public inquiry is held, before an Inspector appointed for the purpose, in some convenient place in the neighbourhood of the sea shore to which the proposed Order relates. Orders made under these Acts applying to a limited area of sea, or amending a previous Order without extending the area, may be submitted for confirmation to Her Majesty in Council, if unopposed, and on such confirmation have full operation as though they had received statutory sanction. They may also at any time be revoked, either wholly or partially, by Her Majesty in Council on a representation from the Board of Trade.[4]

Gas and water works.

A Gas and Water Works Facilities Act, 1870, and an Amending Act of 1873, apply to the United Kingdom, excepting the Metropolis. Provisional Orders may, under these Acts, be granted by the Board of Trade authorizing the construction, maintenance and continuance of gas or water works, the raising of additional capital by gas and

[1] 45 & 46 Vict. c. 62, s. 7; and see Report of Local Government Board, 1882-3, p. 77.

[2] 25 & 26 Vict. c. 63, ss. 39, 40.

[3] 29 & 30 Vict. c. 85, repealed and re-enacted by 31 & 32 Vict. c. 45, Part III.; 32 & 33 Vict. c. 31; 38 & 39 Vict. c. 15; 40 & 41 Vict. c. 42, s. 7; and 44 Vict. c. 11.

[4] See the two statutes last quoted (Oyster, Crab and Lobster Fisheries Act, 1877, s. 7, and Fisheries (Clam and Bait Beds) Act, 1881, ss. 4, 5); and 47 & 48 Vict. cc. 26, 27.

water companies, and the confirmation of agreements entered into by these companies for a joint supply of gas or water, or for an amalgamation of the companies.[1] Between 1870-82, 197 Orders were granted under this Act.

Another important branch of the same jurisdiction is *Tramways.* derived by the Board of Trade from the Tramways Act, 1870, which allows the Board to sanction, by Provisional Order, the construction of tramways in England and Wales.[2] A condition precedent, however, is the assent of local and road authorities controlling districts which comprise two-thirds in length of the proposed tramway.[3] Under this Act, 175 Provisional Orders were issued up to the end of 1882; 56 were opposed and referred to Select Committees, and 11 were rejected. Before granting a Provisional Order *Local inquiries.* under the Gas and Water Facilities or Tramway Acts, the Board of Trade may, if they think fit, direct a public inquiry in the locality by one of their inspecting engineer officers, but this inquiry is not essential unless the consent of local or road authorities is to be dispensed with.[4]

Provisional certificates are also granted by the Board of *Provisional certificates:* Trade and resemble Provisional Orders in their effect, but are simpler in form, for if the scheme they embody be unopposed, they do not then require any express sanction from Parliament. These certificates came into use under two Acts of 1864; one for facilitating the construction of railways;[5] the other[6] for enabling railway companies to make agreements,

---

[1] 33 & 34 Vict. c. 70; amended by 36 & 37 Vict. c. 89. The latter Act is repealed in part by 46 & 47 Vict. c. 39.

[2] 33 & 34 Vict. c. 78. In 1885 this jurisdiction over tramways in Scotland was transferred from the Board of Trade to the Secretary for Scotland.

[3] Ib. s. 5. As to tramway legislation, see Vol. I. pp. 185-94.

[4] Com. Paper, 99 (Sess. 1883).

[5] Railways Construction Facilities Act, 1864 (27 & 28 Vict. c. 121),

amended by 33 & 34 Vict. c. 19.

[6] Railway Companies Powers Act, 1864 (27 & 28 Vict. c. 120), extended by 31 & 32 Vict. c. 119, s. 38, and amended by 33 & 34 Vict. c. 19. The two Acts of 1864 owe their origin to Mr. Booth, whose important services in various public appointments have been already mentioned. When Secretary to the Board of Trade, he suggested the provisions of both Acts to the

inter se, and do other acts which would, in the ordinary course of procedure, have required the promotion of a private Bill. The former of these Acts (when all the landowners and parties beneficially interested assent), enables the Board of Trade to sanction by its certificate the making of branch and other lines of railway, the deviation of existing railways and of railways in course of construction, together with the execution of new works connected with existing railways. By virtue of the latter Act and of Acts extending and amending it, the Board of Trade by certificate can give validity to working agreements between railway companies, extend the time for their sale of superfluous lands, authorize them to raise additional capital, and regulate the procedure at general meetings of companies, the right of voting by shareholders, the appointment, number, rotation, powers and liabilities of directors, and the appointment and duties of auditors.

When an application under either Act is unopposed, a draft certificate settled by the Board of Trade is laid upon the tables of both Houses of Parliament. At the expiration of six weeks, if neither House resolves otherwise, the certificate is issued and published in the " Gazette," in accordance with the draft, and has the same effect as a special Act of Parliament.[1] If there was opposition from a railway or canal com-

[margin note: For branch and other railways;]

[margin note: For general powers to railway companies.]

[margin note: Procedure on certificates.]

Commons' Committee of 1858 on Private Bills, six years before they became law. (Min. of Evidence, pp. 139, 143—145.)

[1] Against a certificate granted by the Board of Trade in 1873 under the Railways Construction Facilities Act, 1864, a landowner (Lord Falmouth) petitioned on the ground that his consent had been given conditionally to the sale of his land, and that certain powers in the certificate virtually set aside an agreement on the strength of which that consent was obtained. The Board of Trade having made their certificate thought themselves precluded from with-

drawing it ; but the House of Lords resolved that the certificate ought not to be made, and referred it to a Committee before whom the applicants for the certificate were then promoting two bills for like objects. This Committee varied the certificate, consolidating its provisions with those of the two bills in one enactment. (See Cornwall Minerals Railways Regulation Act, 1873; 36 & 37 Vict. c. 162. See also Cornwall Minerals Railways Bill; Petition of Lord Falmouth, 2 Clifford & Rickards's Reports in Court of Referees, p. 3.)

pany affected by the certificate, the Board of Trade, until 1870, were unable to proceed further with it, and the parties were then left to proceed in Parliament by Bill and opposing petitions in the ordinary course. In 1870 the practice under these Acts was further amended;[1] and now, if the application is opposed by a railway or canal company, the Board of Trade are not stopped from proceeding further, but may settle a provisional certificate, which is introduced into Parliament as the schedule to a confirming Bill, and if petitioned against is referred to a Select Committee, as in the case of an opposed Provisional Order.[2]

This jurisdiction by the Board of Trade over railways is usefully exercised when no public or private objection can be raised to the proposals of companies; and generally in each Session a few provisional certificates are laid before Parliament.[3] Applications under the Railway Companies Powers Act, 1864, are usually made by small companies for authority to raise new share and loan capital. In these cases the Board of Trade require proof that shareholders have approved of the application in the same manner as would be required under Standing Orders of Parliament in the case of a Bill. Draft certificates to construct short lines of railway under the Facilities Act are only given upon proof that promoters have already contracted to purchase the necessary lands, and have complied with the general rules respecting deposit and notice, as well as with all provisions of the Act. If application is made by an already incorporated company, the Board also require proof of consent by shareholders. No local inquiry is prescribed by the Railway Facilities Act, though such an inquiry is held where the Board think one desirable. Only sixteen draft certificates were granted between 1864 and 1882. In one of these cases the House of Lords resolved that the

Proofs required before grant of certificates.

---

[1] By 33 & 34 Vict. c. 19.

[2] Commons' Paper, 501 (Session 1871).

[3] Commons' Papers, 231 (Session 1883); 251 (Session 1882); and 296 (Session 1881).

certificate ought not to be made.   In two cases, owing to opposition by a railway company, provisional certificates were issued by the Board and Bills introduced to confirm them. Under the Railway Companies Powers Act and amending statutes, 69 draft certificates were issued by the Board between 1864 and 1882; all of these were confirmed by Parliament without opposition.

Education Department.

Sites for schools and school board offices.

In 1870 the Education Department were enabled to issue Provisional Orders authorizing school boards in England and Wales to acquire sites otherwise than by agreement for elementary schools[1] and for offices.[2]   Similar powers were afterwards conferred on the Education Department for Scotland.[3]   In these cases a local inquiry is held, though not always an open inquiry, by some person appointed by the department.   From 1870 to October, 1882, 59 Orders were issued authorizing school boards to take sites for schools by compulsory purchase.   All these were confirmed by Parliament, though not always in the mode sanctioned by the department;[4] 52 were confirmed without opposition.

Endowed schools.

The necessity for private Bills to amend the trusts of endowed schools is avoided by powers enabling the Committee of Council to submit to Parliament provisional schemes.[5] Similar powers are exercised by the Committee of Council for continuing, abolishing, or adjusting rights claimed by existing local authorities on a petition for a municipal

Police and Improvement (Scotland) Act.

charter.[6]   In 1862 the Privy Council were authorized to apply the provisions of the General Police and Improvement Act (Scotland) in certain cases, by Order in Council,[7] but this power has not been exercised.

In 1871 Parliament concentrated in a new department

[1] 33 & 34 Vict. c. 75, s. 20 ; 36 & 37 Vict. c. 86, s. 15.

[2] 39 & 40 Vict. c. 79, s. 42.

[3] 41 & 42 Vict. c. 78, s. 31.

[4] But this, as already mentioned, is not shown in the return, e. g. an Order authorizing the West Ham (Essex) School Board to put in force the Lands Clauses Acts was amended in 1882 by a Committee in the House of Lords, upon a landowner's opposition (45 & 46 Vict. c. 102).

[5] 32 & 33 Vict. c. 56, continued by 46 & 47 Vict. c. 40.

[6] 40 & 41 Vict. c. 69.

[7] 25 & 26 Vict. c. 101, ss. 80—82.

the supervision of laws relating to public health, poor relief, and local administration. To this new department, the Local Government Board, were transferred all the functions of the Poor Law Board, together with certain powers up to that time exercised by the Privy Council and Home Secretary, under a variety of Acts relating to registration of births, deaths, and marriages, baths and washhouses, recreation grounds, artizans and labourers' dwellings, vaccination, public health and local government.[1] The Board consists of the President, who is specially responsible for the discharge of these functions, and the following *ex officio* and unpaid members:—The President of the Council; all the principal Secretaries of State; the Lord Privy Seal; and the Chancellor of the Exchequer for the time being.[2] By subsequent Acts, further powers were also transferred to the new department from the Board of Trade relating to the working of the Alkali and Metropolis Water Acts;[3] from the Home Office as to highways, turnpike roads and trusts, and bridges in England and Wales,[4] and as to money borrowed under the Baths and Washhouses Acts[5]; and from the Treasury concerning sanitary purposes.[6]

Constitution of Local Government Board.

From time to time the Local Government Board have received statutory powers of an important character for the direction and control of private legislation by means of Provisional Orders. Dealing first with the work inherited from the Poor Law Board, whose authority in this respect dates from 1867, Provisional Orders may be granted by the Local Government Board in England and Wales wholly or partially repealing or altering any local Act relating to poor relief, or the making and levying of poor rates;[7] and re-

Powers to grant Provisional Orders.

Relief of the poor.

---

[1] 34 & 35 Vict. c. 70.

[2] Ib. s. 3. In practice these *ex officio* members never assemble, and are never consulted upon the work of the department, which is transacted by the President for the time being, and his subordinates.

[3] 35 & 36 Vict. c. 79, s. 35.

[4] Ib. s. 36.

[5] Ib. c. 76, s. 34.

[6] Ib. s. 34. See also Public Health Act, 1875 (38 & 39 Vict. c. 55, s. 343, and sch. 5, part 3), which keeps alive these Transfer Acts of 1872.

[7] 30 & 31 Vict. c. 106, s. 2; amended by 31 & 32 Vict. c. 122, s. 3, and 42 & 43 Vict. c. 54, s. 9.

Division of parishes.

adjusting, or dividing, large parishes or parishes which are separated from one another, or intermixed with other parishes.[1] In compliance with the respective Acts, local inquiries are made in these cases by an Inspector.

Formation of new parishes.

These powers of the Board for dividing and readjusting parishes having been found beneficial, Parliament in 1876 went a step in advance and authorized the Board to constitute by Provisional Orders separate parishes out of divided parishes or parts of several such parishes: to unite parts of a divided parish, or of several divided parishes, with each other, and amalgamate the parts so united with an adjoining parish: and to amalgamate any part of a divided parish, or parts of several divided parishes, with an adjoining parish or parishes.[2] A local and public inquiry is held in these cases by an inspector of the Board, after due notice given.

Public health and local government.

By far the most important branch of jurisdiction exercised by the Local Government Board in the grant of Provisional Orders is that relating to sanitary and kindred subjects. Their chief powers are derived from the Public Health Act, 1875,[3] which enables them to issue Provisional Orders, usually, though not invariably, on the application of local authorities, for the following objects:—

Repeal, &c. of local Acts and Provisional Orders.

For repealing and altering (a) any local Acts relating to the same subject-matters as the principal Act, but excluding River Conservancy Acts;[4] and (b) any Provisional Orders confirmed by Parliament and made in pursuance of any of the Sanitary Acts or of the Public Health Act, 1875.

Compulsory purchase of land.

For enabling sanitary authorities to put in force the compulsory clauses of the Lands Clauses Consolidation Acts for purposes of the Public Health Act, 1875.[5]

Alteration of areas and union of districts.

For the alteration of areas and the union of districts, by (a) extending or diminishing local government districts; (b) constituting local government districts, or dissolving them, and merging them in rural sanitary districts; (c) dissolving

---

[1] 30 & 31 Vict. c. 106, s. 3.

[2] 39 & 40 Vict. c. 61 ; 42 & 43 Vict. c. 54 ; 45 & 46 Vict. c. 58.

[3] 38 & 39 Vict. c. 55, ss. 297, 298.

[4] Ib. s. 303.

[5] Ib. ss. 176, 316.

special drainage districts in which loans have been raised for the execution of works; (d) dissolving Improvement Act districts comprised within or having areas co-extensive with boroughs;[1] and (e) forming united districts with a view to procure a common supply of water, to carry into effect a system of sewerage for the use of such districts, or for any other purposes of the Public Health Act, 1875.[2]

For permanently constituting a sanitary authority in any port, or a joint board exercising such authority over two or more ports.[3]

Port sanitary authorities.

For altering the mode of defraying the expenses of urban authorities in certain cases.[4]

Expenses of urban authorities.

For removing exemptions from assessment to general district rates, when such exemptions arise under any local Acts.[5]

Exemptions under local Acts.

For settling doubts and differences and adjusting accounts arising out of any transfer of powers under the Public Health Act, 1875, or under any Provisional Order issued pursuant to the Act.[6]

Settling differences upon transfer of powers.

For dissolving main sewerage or joint sewerage districts constituted under the Sanitary Acts.[7]

Joint sewerage districts.

For dividing districts into wards for the purpose of electing local boards; also for abolishing wards or altering their boundaries, and determining from time to time the proportion of members to be elected by each ward.[8]

Boundaries, &c. of wards.

For authorizing the supply of gas and water by urban sanitary authorities in districts where there is no company or person with statutory authority to supply gas, or where there is no company or person able and willing to supply water; and for revoking, amending, extending, or varying any Orders confirmed by Parliament which give such authority.[9]

Gas and water supply by urban authorities.

---

[1] 38 & 39 Vict. c. 55, ss. 270—275.
[2] Ib. ss. 279—281.
[3] Ib. ss. 287—290.
[4] Ib. s. 208.
[5] Ib. s. 211.
[6] Ib. s. 304.
[7] Ib. s. 323.

[8] Ib. sch. 2, part 1.
[9] Ib. ss. 51—53, as to water supply; and as to gas, s. 161, which sanctions the grant of Provisional Orders under the Gas and Water Works Facilities Act, 1870 (33 & 34 Vict. c. 70), and the Amendment Act of 1873 (36 & 37

**Procedure,
and Orders
issued.**

In all these cases a public inquiry is held in the locality; in the last-mentioned it is conducted by an inspector acting as commissioner.[1] From 1848 until 1882, the total number of Orders issued under the Sanitary Acts by the Local Government Board, and the departments to whose jurisdiction they succeeded, was 1,205, including 503 issued under the Public Health Act, 1875. Of the 1,205 Orders, 1,114 were confirmed by Parliament without opposition; 84 were referred to Select Committees on adverse petitions; 71 of these were afterwards confirmed by Parliament with or without amendment; 13 were withdrawn or rejected. Of the Orders granted under the Public Health Act, 1875, 19 were amended by Select Committees; 12 were considered and not altered; Parliament refused to confirm five, and one fell through, as both the sanitary authority promoting, and the petitioners opposing it, objected to the frame of the Order itself.

**Artizans'
and labourers
dwellings.**

The desire of Parliament to provide easy methods for improving artizans' and labourers' dwellings has found expression in various statutes passed with this object, and dating from 1868.[2] The Home Secretary's power to grant Pro-

---

Vict. c. 89). A somewhat singular case arising under these Acts occurred in 1877. The Westhoughton Local Board desired to promote a bill authorizing them to supply water within their district. The Local Government Board were of opinion that this object might be accomplished by the cheaper process of a Provisional Order. The Order was accordingly drafted and introduced by the Board into a confirming bill, but on opposing petitions from the Duke of Bridgewater's trustees and several other owners, a Committee of the House of Lords decided that the Local Government Board had acted *ultra vires* in giving compulsory powers for the taking of waters and water rights; and the Order was rejected. (Local

Government Board's Provisional Orders Confirmation (District of Westhoughton) Bill, 1877; minutes of House of Lords' Committee.) A local inquiry had been held by the Local Government Board in this case. Next year the Westhoughton Local Board proceeded by bill, which obtained the Royal Assent (Westhoughton Local Board Act, 1878). It was necessary to provide in this Act for payment of the costs incurred by the Westhoughton Board in relation to the Provisional Order. (41 & 42 Vict. c. 62, s. 30, and recitals in preamble.)

[1] 36 & 37 Vict. c. 89, s. 13.

[2] Artizans and Labourers' Dwellings Acts were passed in 1868 (31 & 32 Vict. c. 130); in 1879 (42 & 43

visional Orders under the Act of 1875 has already been noticed.[1] A like authority is given by that Act to the Local Government Board. Such authority, however, is limited. Provisional Orders can only be granted by the board to urban sanitary authorities in England whose districts, according to the last published census, contain a population of 25,000 and upwards.[2] In these districts the Board may sanction schemes for improving unhealthy areas, subject to the ratification of Parliament. They may also modify such schemes after confirmation under certain conditions without any confirming Act, after laying such modifications before both Houses for consideration and objection. But there must be a Provisional Order confirmed by Parliament in cases where the modified scheme (a) requires a larger public expenditure than that previously sanctioned ; (b) involves a compulsory taking of property; or (c), without consent of owner and occupier, injuriously affects other property not so affected in the original scheme.[3] In case any scheme is subjected in Parliament to an opposition which Committees may think unjustifiable, they are authorized to award costs more readily than is possible under the general Act relating to costs on Private Bills.[4] A public inquiry is held by an Inspector of the Board, after due notice, before any Provisional Orders are granted. From 1876 to 1882 only eleven Orders had

Award of costs by Parliamentary Committees.

Vict. c. 64); and in 1882 (45 & 46 Vict. c. 54, Part 2). To prevent confusion, these Acts and Part 2 of the Act of 1882 are now cited as the Artizans' Dwellings Acts, 1868 to 1882. See also the Labourers (Ireland) Act, 1883 (46 & 47 Vict. c. 60). To be distinguished from these Acts are the Artizans and Labourers' Dwellings Improvement Acts, dealt with in the text, the first of which became law in 1875 (38 & 39 Vict. c. 36). It is amended by 42 & 43 Vict. c. 63 ; and 45 & 46 Vict. c. 54, Part 1. See now Housing of Working Classes Act, 1885 (48 & 49

Vict. c. 72).

[1] *Ante*, p. 679.

[2] 38 & 39 Vict. c. 36, ss. 2, 6. The Whitehaven Improvement Act, 1876 (39 & 40 Vict. c. 105, s. 42); the Jarrow Improvement Act, 1878 (41 & 42 Vict. c. 120, s. 53); and Over Darwen Improvement Act, 1879 (42 & 43 Vict. c. 202, s. 91), repeal this limitation and make the statute applicable in their respective urban sanitary districts, though at the date of these Acts the population in each district was under 25,000.

[3] 38 & 39 Vict. c. 36, s. 12.

[4] Ib. s. 7.

been issued; all were confirmed by Parliament, three after inquiry and alteration.

Roads.

On application by a county authority in England and Wales as to any road within their jurisdiction, the Local Government Board were authorized in 1878 to cause such road to be inspected and order that it shall cease to be a main road and become an ordinary highway.[1] Up to 1882, fourteen such Orders had been issued, all confirmed by Parliament without opposition. An earlier jurisdiction relating to turnpike roads in England was given to the Home Office in 1851 by an Act "to facilitate arrangements for the relief of

Turnpike trusts.

turnpike trusts, and to make certain provisions respecting exemptions from tolls."[2] This jurisdiction was in 1872 transferred to the Local Government Board.[3] On the application and certificate of trustees, the Board make Provisional Orders reducing the rate of interest paid on the trust's mortgage debt and extinguishing arrears of interest. From 1851 to 1882, 197 Provisional Orders were issued giving relief of this nature to turnpike trusts; and 195 were confirmed by Parliament.

The Alkali Acts.

Certain powers and duties of the Board of Trade under the Alkali Act, 1863, were transferred to the Local Government Board in 1872.[3] In 1880 the Alkali Acts of 1863, 1868 and 1874 were repealed and re-enacted with amendments in a consolidated statute. Under its provisions the Local Government Board by Provisional Order may require the owner of salt works or cement works to adopt the best practicable means for preventing the discharge from furnaces or chimneys, of sulphurous or muriatic acid gases, or for rendering these gases harmless or inoffensive when discharged.[4] A condition precedent to the issue of an Order is that the Board, after inquiry by an inspector, are satisfied that the means they propose for effecting this im-

[1] 41 & 42 Vict. c. 77, ss. 16, 34.

[2] 14 & 15 Vict. c. 38, extended by 23 & 24 Vict. c. 73, s. 3, and 24 & 25 Vict. c. 46, s. 2.

[3] By 35 & 36 Vict. c. 79, s. 36; and see 38 & 39 Vict. c. 55, s. 343, sched. 5, part 3.

[4] *Ante*, p. 331, n.

provement can be adopted by the owner of works at a reasonable expense.[1]

By the Charitable Trusts Act, 1853,[2] the Charity Commissioners for England and Wales were authorized to approve and certify, provisionally, new schemes affecting the revenues or management of particular charities. The Commissioners' reports are laid before Parliament; and all schemes approved by them are included in a confirmation bill, which, after receiving the Royal Assent, is deemed a Public General Act.[3] From 1853 to the end of 1882, only 23 schemes were approved by the Commissioners, and Parliament confirmed them all.

Exceptional powers of taking land compulsorily have been conferred upon the Post Office by an Act of 1881, in order to meet the exigencies of the public service.[4] The Act applies to the United Kingdom and, incorporating the Lands Clauses Acts, provides that, three months before application to Parliament for any compulsory purchase, the Postmaster-General shall serve notices on every owner, lessee and occupier of land proposed to be taken, inquiring whether they assent or dissent. Answers must be sent to the Treasury, who are to institute a local inquiry into any objections which may be raised to the purchase. If satisfied after such inquiry that the land should be taken, the Treasury may submit a Bill to Parliament authorizing the purchase. This Bill is to be deemed in all respects a public Bill, but if a petition is presented, it may be referred to a Select Committee before which petitioners are allowed to appear and oppose as in the case of private Bills. The period limited for compulsory purchase is three years.[5]

In 1860, ten years before the passing of the English Tramways Act, the Lord Lieutenant was authorized to sanction by Order in Council the construction of tram-

Marginal notes:
Charity Commissioners.

Sites for post offices.

Tramways in Ireland.

---

[1] 44 & 45 Vict. c. 37, s. 10.
[2] 16 & 17 Vict. c. 137, ss. 54—59.
[3] Ib. s. 60.
[4] Post Office Land Act, 1881 (44 & 45 Vict. c. 20).
[5] Ib. s. 3.

694 ORDERS IN COUNCIL

Tramways (Ireland) Act, 1860.

ways in Ireland, with a view to improve and cheapen communication there.[1] The Act of 1860 mainly contemplated the making of tramways along highways in rural districts, "for the conveyance of passengers, produce, minerals, merchandize and other goods." Competition with railways was prevented by restraining the use of other than animal power,[2] and by a proviso that no tramway should be made under the Act to unite places between which statutory powers for making a railway were in force.[3] The standard gauge, like that for Irish railways, was fixed at 5 feet 3 inches,[4] whereas in England the standard gauge for tramways and railways is 4 feet 8½ inches, though a narrower tramway gauge is in practice frequently sanctioned in order to meet the exigencies of narrow urban thoroughfares.

Amending Acts.

The procedure under the Act of 1860 was meant to save expense in promoting private Bills, but was itself both cumbersome and costly. An amending Act was therefore passed in the following session[5] for further facilitating applications by tramway promoters. In 1871, another Act, known as Lord Cairns's Act,[6] sanctioned the adoption of steam or other mechanical power on these tramways, certain conditions being imposed to secure public safety. A maximum speed of six miles an hour was one of these conditions.[7] A statute of 1876[8] made easier the application of preceding Acts to tramways in the county and city of Dublin. In 1881, changes were made in the prescribed tolls, in the interests of promoters; and the maximum speed of tramway locomotives was raised to ten miles an hour.[9] Promoters were also relieved from the necessity of obtaining a confirming Act in certain cases; nor were they any longer required to construct tramways on a level with public roads, provided

---

[1] 23 & 24 Vict. c. 152.
[2] Ib. s. 24.
[3] Ib. s. 1.
[4] Ib. s. 24.
[5] 24 & 25 Vict. c. 102.
[6] 34 & 35 Vict. c. 114.
[7] Ib. ss. 3, 4.
[8] 39 & 40 Vict. c. 65.
[9] 44 & 45 Vict. c. 17, ss. 4, 5.

they obtained permission from the Lord Lieutenant and grand jury, and left a clear roadway of 18 feet between their tramway and the opposite footpath or roadside boundary.[1]

In 1883 Parliament showed their continued anxiety to extend tramway communication in Ireland by establishing in its favour a system of baronial and other local guarantees, and by again removing restrictions on private enterprise in this direction.[2] Statutory powers for making a railway between two places are now no longer a bar to tramways for connecting those places; the authorized railway must be either constructed or in actual course of construction; or the railway company clothed with such powers must satisfy the Lord Lieutenant in Council that they intend " forthwith to proceed in good faith to construct " their line.[3] Orders in Council sanctioning tramway deviations, extensions or abandonments, or extending the time for completion, were formerly inoperative until confirmed by Parliament;[4] they now take effect when made, and do not require such confirmation.[5]

Tramways, &c. (Ireland) Act, 1883.

A system of baronial guarantees in favour of railways already existed in Ireland. By the Act of 1883 this system was applied to tramways, and guarantees may now be given to these undertakings in certain cases by Order in Council. Grand juries, if satisfied that a proposed tramway would be of public utility, are authorized to make a presentment guaranteeing for a limited period dividends on the company's paid-up capital not exceeding 5l. per cent. They may also charge a barony with the payment of such sums as may be required for completing, working or maintaining a tramway. Municipal corporations and town commissioners are authorized to charge local rates in like manner.[6] They will receive State help in this effort to extend tramway com-

Baronial guarantees.

---

[1] 44 & 45 Vict. c. 17, ss. 6, 7.
[2] 46 & 47 Vict. c. 43, amended by 47 & 48 Vict. c. 28.
[3] 46 & 47 Vict. c. 43, s. 23, sub-s. (1).

[4] Under ss. 26 and 27 of the Act of 1860.
[5] 46 & 47 Vict. c. 43, s. 23, sub-s. (2).
[6] Ib. ss. 1—9.

Contribution by Treasury.

munication. So long as the tramway is maintained in working order and carries traffic, the Treasury may, out of any moneys provided by Parliament, contribute one-half of the sum paid by local authorities as guaranteed dividend; but this contribution is not to be more than two per cent. on the company's paid-up capital, and the aggregate sum so paid by the Treasury must not exceed 40,000*l.* a year.[1]

New facilities to tramway promoters.

Every Order in Council which sanctions a baronial or other guarantee may also authorize tramway promoters to take by compulsion lands which they were formerly precluded from taking except by consent.[2] The Board of Trade may from time to time by Order authorize tramway locomotives to be driven at a speed of twelve miles an hour elsewhere than through any town or village; and so long as a tramway locomotive is being driven at a greater distance than thirty feet from the centre of any public road, no restrictions as to speed now apply.[3] Lastly, light railways, as well as tramways, are included in the benefits of the Act.[4]

Local inquiries.

The procedure under the Irish Tramway Acts may now be shortly stated. A local inquiry is held before an officer of the Public Works Commissioners as to engineering merits. Grand juries hold a similar inquiry into engineering, financial and other questions, having before them a report from the Board of Works, and also hearing any owner, lessee or occupier who alleges that his property will be injuriously affected by the tramway; any railway company opposing it on the ground of competition or of interference with their

---

[1] 46 & 47 Vict. c. 43, s. 9.

[2] Ib. sub-s. (5).

[3] Ib. sub-s. (6).

[4] Ib. s. 25. By the Regulation of Railways Act, 1868 (31 & 32 Vict. c. 119, part 5, ss. 27—29), "a light railway" is defined as one upon the rails of which no greater weight than eight tons can be brought by any one pair of wheels in any locomotive or vehicle, and the rate of speed must not exceed 25 miles an hour. In a circular letter to local authorities (dated November 2, 1883), the Lord Lieutenant stated that, in carrying out the Act, these restrictions would be maintained, and preference given, on the ground of their cheaper construction, to light railways of a 3-feet gauge, which is the gauge of all steam tramways and narrow gauge railways in Ireland.

rails or works; and inhabitants objecting to the scheme. If a grand jury approve, and there is no appeal against such approval, the Order in Council takes immediate effect. If a petition of appeal be proceeded with, statutory sanction must be given to the scheme, and until 1885 it was supposed that petitioners could then appear against it in Parliament.

In 1885, this course was taken upon a Provisional Order for the Cork, Coachford and Blarney Light Railway, which was promoted under the Tramway (Ireland) Acts. The proposed line had been considered and approved by Grand Juries of the county and city of Cork; the measure had then, being opposed, gone before the Irish Privy Council, which also passed it after hearing counsel on each side. It was afterwards included in a Provisional Order Confirmation Bill, and, as it was still opposed, the Order was, according to practice, treated as a private Bill. A Lords' Committee rejected it on its merits. Objection, however, was taken that under sect. 14 of the Act of 1860, which is incorporated in the Act of 1883, the Confirmation Bill should have been " treated in all respects as a public Bill," the intention of Parliament being that all disputed cases should be tried locally, and withdrawn from the ordinary jurisdiction of Parliament over Private Bills. Upon debate in the Lords this view prevailed, the decision of the Committee was set aside, and the Bill referred as a public Bill to a Committee of the whole House.[1] It was afterwards withdrawn in the Commons.[2]

Cork and Blarney Light Railway, 1885.

Orders in Council confirming presentments by a grand jury or other local authority under the Act of 1883 can only be made if sanctioned by the Treasury.[3] They must contain provisions that tramways shall be completed, maintained in good order and condition, and efficiently worked; and also that, upon default herein by the company, the guarantors shall further contribute any sums necessary for these pur-

Sanction of Treasury.

---

[1] 299 Hansard, 383-91: speeches of Earl Spencer and Lord Fitzgerald.

[2] Hansard, July 16, 22; August 7, 1885.

[3] 46 & 47 Vict. c. 43, s. 3.

poses.[1] As onerous obligations may thus be imposed upon ratepayers, any twenty persons collectively liable to pay one-eighth or upwards of the county cess in any barony specified in a presentment may appeal against it to the Lord Lieutenant.[2]

Appeal against presentment. This right of appeal is in addition to corresponding rights conferred by earlier Tramway Acts, and secures the control of Parliament, subject to the decision of 1885.

Tramways as feeders to railways. Besides rates in aid from baronies and local authorities, and help from the Treasury, railway companies may, under the Act of 1883, encourage tramways as feeders to their undertakings; and the Lord Lieutenant in Council may, by Provisional Order, authorize a railway company to contribute towards a tramway made under the Act. Orders in Council sanctioning these contributions will take effect without confirmation by Parliament unless an adverse petition to the Lord Lieutenant is presented and proceeded with.[3]

Grant of Provisional Orders by Board of Trade in Ireland. We have seen that the Board of Trade can provide by Provisional Orders, in Ireland as well as England, for improving piers and harbours,[4] and allowing urban sanitary authorities to charge their rates for this purpose;[5] for constituting new pilotage authorities; constructing gas and water works; making branch and other railways; sanctioning agreements between railway companies, and other analogous objects.[6] Two other departments in Ireland possess like powers for promoting sanitary works and drainage of land.

By Chief Secretary. In 1871, the Chief Secretary for Ireland was allowed to give, by Provisional Order, considerable powers to local authorities for acquiring lands, forming new districts, and other objects relating to local government.[7] In 1872, the English precedent of the previous session was followed, and **Local Government Board (Ireland).** a Local Government Board constituted for Ireland, in which were vested certain functions previously belonging to the

[1] 46 & 47 Vict. c. 43, s. 10.
[2] Ib. s. 2.
[3] Ib. s. 11.
[4] In Carrickfergus, Holywood, Bray, Kilcubbin, Ardglass, Carlingford, Wexford, and other places, piers or harbours have been constructed under these Orders.
[5] 45 & 46 Vict. c. 62, s. 7.
[6] *Ante*, pp. 681 *et seq.*
[7] 34 & 35 Vict. c. 109.

Lord Lieutenant, Privy Council and Chief Secretary, concerning public health and local government, together with the powers and duties of the Irish Poor Law Commissioners.[1] The Board consists of the Chief Secretary, who is President, and the Under Secretary to the Lord Lieutenant, both unpaid; together with a Vice-President and two Commissioners.[2] In 1874 was passed the first Public Health Act for Ireland.[3] It was wholly repealed by the Public Health (Ireland) Act, 1878, which also repealed, in whole or in part, most of the sanitary Acts then in force,[4] and, following the lines of the English statute of 1875, contains the sanitary code now operative in Ireland for provisional order as well as for other purposes. It was amended in 1883 by a short Act which enables sanitary authorities to deal more effectually with outbreaks of infectious and other diseases.[5]

Public Health (Ireland) Act, 1878.

Amendment Act, 1883.

By Orders under the Public Health Act, 1878, the Local Government Board may grant to Irish sanitary authorities increased borrowing powers[6] and compulsory powers of purchasing land,[7] may repeal or amend local Acts, or extend or vary the area in which they take effect,[8] transfer to town councils or urban sanitary authorities the jurisdiction of grand juries over roads, bridges, footpaths and public works,[9] authorize a higher maximum of rating for certain purposes,[10] settle

Powers of Irish sanitary authorities.

---

[1] 35 & 36 Vict. c. 69.

[2] Ib. s. 3. In the year 1874, a Committee of the House of Lords, feeling doubtful whether a Provisional Order issued by the Irish Local Government Board was within their powers, adjourned the case, and required the principal members of the department to attend and explain the circumstances under which the Order had been made. Sir Alfred Power, Vice-President, Major Robinson, C.B., and other officials, accordingly attended the Committee and gave evidence. The Order was ultimately confirmed; but on the recommendation of the Committee a new stand-

ing order was adopted by the House of Lords, requiring that, in all applications by municipal authorities, a certificate under seal from the Irish Local Government Board should be produced. (Lords' S. O. 635.)

[3] 37 & 38 Vict. c. 93.

[4] 41 & 42 Vict. c. 52, ss. 214, 215, and Sched. A.

[5] 46 & 47 Vict. c. 59. See also Amendment Act of 1884 (47 & 48 Vict. c. 77).

[6] 41 & 42 Vict. c. 52, s. 237.

[7] Ib. ss. 203, 278.

[8] Ib. s. 205.

[9] Ib. s. 206.

[10] Ib. ss. 227, 228.

differences between local authorities arising from transfers of powers or property,[1] alter or unite areas of sanitary districts,[2] for securing a common water supply or carrying into effect a joint system of sewerage,[3] transfer burial grounds from one board to another,[4] and sanction gas undertakings by local authorities.[5] From 1871 to 1882 the number of Provisional Orders granted in Ireland under the Public Health and Local Government Acts was 91.

Artizans and Labourers' Dwellings, Ireland.

For sanctioning the clearance of unhealthy areas in order to improve artizans and labourers' dwellings, the Local Government Board in Ireland received, in 1875, the same power of issuing Provisional Orders as was given to the board in England; in both countries the Act applied to urban sanitary districts containing, according to the last published census, a population of 25,000 and upwards.[6] The Artizans' Dwellings Acts, 1868 to 1882,[7] applied to Ireland, and made the Local Government Board there, as in England, the sanctioning authority for improvements effected by local authorities under the Acts. These improvements are not carried out under Provisional Orders. An Act of 1883, however, " to better the condition of labourers in Ireland,"[8] and applicable exclusively to that country,[9] gives to the Board large powers in this respect.

Labourers' (Ireland) Act, 1883.

Rural sanitary authorities may, under this Act, upon a representation to them by twelve ratepayers, adopt an improvement scheme within any portion of their district where the existing house accommodation for agricultural labourers and their families is deficient or unfit for human habitation, owing to sanitary defects. Under this improvement scheme, other and sufficient dwellings are to be erected in lieu of or

---

[1] 41 & 42 Vict. c. 52, s. 277.

[2] Ib. s. 7.

[3] Ib. ss. 12—14.

[4] Ib. s. 207.

[5] Ib. s. 80, subject, as in England, to the provisions of the Gas and Water Works Facilities Acts; and see as to water supply, ss. 61, 62.

[6] 38 & 39 Vict. c. 36, ss. 1, 31, amended by 42 & 43 Vict. c. 63, and 45 & 46 Vict. c. 54, Part 1.

[7] *Ante*, p. 691, note.

[8] Labourers' (Ireland) Act, 1883 (46 & 47 Vict. c. 60).

[9] Ib. s. 2.

in addition to existing dwellings. The twelve persons joining in any representation must be rated within the area
on which the cost of a scheme will fall.[1] All dwellings
must have requisite approaches and proper sanitary arrangements; to each must be allotted a plot or garden not exceeding half a statute acre; but in each case lands are to
be selected with due regard to the general situation and convenience of an owner's property, so as to diminish its value
as little as possible.[2]

Of the improvement scheme, when framed by the rural
sanitary authority, public notices must be given, and personal
notice served on owners whose lands are to be taken compulsorily. On formal proof to this effect, the Local Government
Board, if they think fit to proceed with the case, are to direct
a local inquiry, and may then make a Provisional Order sanctioning the scheme, with any necessary amendments. If
opposed, such Order had no validity until confirmed by Parliament in a public Act. But in 1885 this restriction was
removed.[3] A Provisional Order now becomes absolute
under the Act unless land be taken otherwise than by
consent; or unless within a month there is an adverse
petition from twelve ratepayers in the district liable to be
assessed for purposes of a scheme.[4] In either case the
Lord Lieutenant in Council, after hearing a petition, may
confirm or disallow a Provisional Order; and any Order so
confirmed, as well as any not requiring such confirmation,
has the same effect as if confirmed by Parliament.[5] On
failure by a sanitary authority to complete within two years
a scheme sanctioned by Provisional Order, the land must
be reconveyed to the original owner, at his option, at the
price paid for it, and "in a condition at least as suitable
for agricultural or grazing purposes" as it was when originally taken from him.[6]

Improvement schemes under.

---

[1] 46 & 47 Vict. c. 60, s. 4.
[2] Ib. s. 6.
[3] 48 & 49 Vict. c. 77, s. 12.
[4] Ib. sub-s. (2).
[5] Ib. sub-s. (4).
[6] 46 & 47 Vict. c. 60, s. 15.

Water supply in rural districts.

Powers are also given to the Local Government Board in Ireland to sanction by Provisional Order a compulsory taking, by rural sanitary authorities, of lands within their district for purposes of the Act, and also the purchase of water rights within or beyond their district in order to furnish it with a proper water supply. An owner may, at his option, when his land has been compulsorily taken, put an end to the purchase and Provisional Order, if sanitary authorities fail to pay the purchase-money in certain events.[1] Rates to be levied for purposes of the Act must not exceed in any one year one shilling in the pound.[2] The Treasury may sanction advances by the Board of Works in Ireland to assist sanitary authorities in giving effect to the Act,[3] which, as a piece of experimental legislation, is limited in duration to seven years.[4] The powers under this statute were extended and amended in 1883 and 1886.[5]

Treasury advances.

Drainage and improvement of land, Ireland.

Lastly, by a series of Acts dating from 1842 and 1863, the Board of Works in Ireland perform the same functions as the Land Commissioners in England, and may sanction by Provisional Order the formation of districts with a view to better drainage and improvement of lands, the constitution of drainage boards, and grants of loans by the Public Works Commissioners for these purposes.[6] Up to August, 1882, twenty-six Orders had been granted and confirmed by Parliament under these Acts. In 1880 drainage boards obtained increased powers to construct works outside the limits of their districts in certain cases. A Provisional Order must be obtained for these works when they are sought to be made in another drainage district without consent, or when lands are taken compulsorily.[7]

[1] 46 & 47 Vict. c. 60, s. 16.
[2] Ib. s. 17.
[3] Ib. s. 18.
[4] 48 & 49 Vict. c. 77, s. 26.
[5] 48 & 49 Vict. c. 77; 49 & 50 Vict. c. 59.
[6] 26 & 27 Vict. c. 88. There are ten subsequent Acts dealing with the same subject. These are now cited as the Drainage and Improvement of Land (Ireland) Acts, 1863 to 1880.
[7] 43 & 44 Vict. c. 27, s. 2.

In this sketch of the Provisional Order system some details have been given of its working under particular statutes. The general result is that, from its first introduction down to 1882, the various departments which administer the system issued 3,554 Provisional Orders or certificates, of which 3,142 were confirmed by Parliament without opposition.[1] There is no information as to the number of cases in which Orders have been applied for and, after inquiry, refused by Departments. Total number granted.

Some insight into the working of the system is given in a letter addressed to Lord Beaconsfield by Sir Thomas Nelson, when Chairman of the Lower Thames Valley Joint Sewerage Board, and privately printed in 1884.[2] From this source and other authentic records, an instructive history may be traced. It begins with attempts made by local authorities in the Lower Thames Valley to dispose of sewage without incurring the statutory penalties prescribed in 1867 for polluting the Thames.[3] Upon application by these authorities many local inquiries were held, by the Local Government Board and their predecessors, with a view to enable each district, under a Provisional Order, to acquire land on which to deal with its own sewage. Every such application, however, was rejected by the department, and the costs of these inquiries fell upon the ratepayers. At this period the Local Government Board viewed with disfavour separate action by separate authorities, and, here as elsewhere, leant towards combinations of districts formed by Provisional Order for united systems of sewerage or other objects.[4] This policy Lower Thames Valley Drainage Board. Applications for Provisional Orders, 1869—77.

[1] Commons' Return, 99 (1883), p. 17.

[2] "An Incredible Story," 3rd edition, 1884.

[3] 30 & 31 Vict. c. 101 (Thames Conservancy Act).

[4] Darenth Valley Joint Sewerage Board (Provisional Order), 1878 (41 & 42 Vict. c. 211); Godalming Joint Drainage Board (Provisional Order), 1882 (45 & 46 Vict. c. 170); Districts of Haslingden, Ramsbottom, and Rawtenstall, 1883 (46 & 47 Vict. c. 225). A Provisional Order by the Local Government Board for a combination of districts in Yorkshire (Cartworth, &c.), was rejected by the House of Lords in 1879.

Joint Sewer-
age Board
created by
Provisional
Order, 1877.

prevailed in 1877, when an Order was issued, and confirmed by Parliament, for the formation of a Lower Thames Valley Main Sewerage Board, representing and exercising rating powers over nine urban and ten rural sanitary districts, some of which were brought in against their will.[1]

In 1878, after an unavailing effort to find an outlet through the metropolitan sewers, the Joint Board, as it was called, invited competition for plans, and chose one based on a system of broad irrigation at Molesey. The Board was advised that, as water rights affecting the rivers Ember and Mole would be interfered with, it would be necessary, following the Westhoughton decision,[2] to proceed by Bill, and

Attempted
legislation by
Bill, 1879.

not by Provisional Order. The House of Commons, however, rejected the second reading of a Bill then promoted,[3] and by an information subsequently filed in the Chancery Division of the High Court, the Board was prevented from defraying the costs of this Bill out of the rates. It was, therefore, obliged, in 1881, to ask for statutory powers to pay the costs. Parliament assented, after some demur, in

Indemnity
Act of 1882.

1882, when the rates were used for this purpose.[4]

Scheme of
1880.

Under these circumstances the ill-starred Board was advised, in 1880, to ask the Local Government Board for a Provisional Order, authorizing, substantially, the Molesey scheme, but leaving out all water rights, which the Board could not legally sanction. A local inquiry followed, and lasted forty-five days.[5] The scheme was bitterly opposed by landowners, inhabitants residing around the proposed sewage farm, and water companies. It was finally rejected by the

[1] 40 & 41 Vict. c. 229. An amended Order was confirmed in 1878 (41 & 42 Vict. c. 162). The Local Government Board included Twickenham in its Order of 1877, but Twickenham vigorously opposed inclusion, and was released by Parliament. *Post*, p. 706.

[2] *Ante*, p. 690, n.

[3] 244 Hansard, 375-401, March 7, 1879. The second reading was defeated by 168 to 146 votes.

[4] 45 & 46 Vict. c. 46 (Authorization of Expenses Act).

[5] Sir Thomas Nelson states that the inspector "examined eighty witnesses, and heard fifteen counsel and six solicitors against the scheme."

Local Government Board, with a "recommendation to adopt a scheme of Sir Joseph Bazalgette, which the Local Government Board had refused to sanction a few years back. But the hardest fate of all was, that the absence of power to take water rights was made one of the reasons for not granting the application."[1] This inquiry alone cost the ratepayers of the united district about 20,000*l.*[2] But it has been estimated that the total outlay of the earlier local authorities and of the Board during the twenty years' struggle up to 1880, was more than 50,000*l.*, with an equal expenditure by opponents.[3]

Expenditure up to 1880.

But the story told by Sir Thomas Nelson was incomplete. After a fruitless attempt to carry out plans devised by Mr. Hawksley, C.E., the Joint Board again, in 1884, applied for a Provisional Order to buy land at Mortlake on which to treat the sewage by chemical precipitation. There was another local inquiry, which was opened at Kingston by an inspector of the Local Government Board, was at once adjourned to London, and lasted fifteen days. During this inquiry local authorities, constituents of the Board, and landowners strongly opposed the scheme. Very large preliminary costs were thus incurred by all parties. But the real contest began when the Provisional Order, after its sanction by the Local Government Board, came before Parliament. A Committee of the House of Commons occupied ten days in hearing evidence, much of which had been already heard by the inspector. They then stopped the case and rejected the Order.

Renewed inquiry in 1884.

Provisional Order rejected by House of Commons, 1884.

In a special report to the House of Commons, the Committee of 1884[4] declared that in their opinion the continuance

Special report of Committee.

---

[1] "An Incredible Story," p. 23.

[2] Ib., p. 23.

[3] Speech by Mr. Michael, Q.C., for the Joint Board, in 1884. See Min'. of Commons' Committee, June 25, 1884, on Local Government Provisional Orders (No. 3) Bill.

[4] It was a hybrid Committee; four members were nominated by the House, and three added by the Committee of Selection. Mr. Giles was Chairman.

of the Joint Board was "not only unnecessary" but hindered the constituent authorities from "successfully purifying the sewage of their respective districts." They were strengthened in this opinion by evidence that Twickenham, which was left out of the united district by Parliament in 1877, had since purified its own sewage, and that neighbouring districts not included in the united district had been equally successful. The Committee were satisfied that each constituent authority would in like manner "be able to treat its sewage more speedily and with greater efficiency and economy than the Joint Board." They therefore recommended that Parliament should give facilities for the separation of these constituent authorities from the Joint Board, and their formation into groups for the treatment and disposal of sewage.

Advantages of decentralization.

Among incidental advantages to be derived from this decentralization, the Committee were satisfied that the oxidizing power of the Thames water on the purified effluent would be most effective when this effluent was delivered at several points in the river. Disposal of the compressed sludge for agricultural purposes would also be easier if it were produced at several sewage works. Experts laid much stress on the necessity of carrying off the sewage as rapidly as possible, so as to reach the purifying works in a fresh instead of a putrid condition. This consideration, said the Committee, suggests the expediency of a system of short sewers and a treatment of sewage by the same authority that produces it. Again, "if each sanitary authority were responsible for the purification of its own sewage, the difficult question of a limitation of the quantity of sewage per house per day to be delivered to the purifying authority would be avoided." On the other hand, it was desirable not unnecessarily to multiply the number of purification works; and the Committee believed that "a satisfactory solution of the problem would not be reached until the whole system of drains from the dwelling-house to the Thames in each district was under the control of the same authority." Lastly, the Committee suggested that, in any new system of treatment, the chemically purified effluent should, if possible, be filtered through earth, a process not provided for in the Joint Board's scheme.[1]

The Joint Board was originally allowed three years to perform the duty of wholly diverting or purifying the sewage. This period was extended from time to time;[2] and a second Provisional Order, sanctioned by the Local Government Board, in 1884, further extended this period, as well as the period protecting constituent local authorities on the Board from proceedings for penalties under the Thames Conservancy Acts. This second Provisional Order, though unopposed, was rejected by the Committee of 1884, who believed "that under this pressure the various districts would more readily find the means of executing the necessary works for the disposal of their sewage." *Second Provisional Order of 1884 also rejected.*

With a view to carry out, in part, the policy recommended by this Committee, the Local Government Board, in 1885, granted a fresh Provisional Order, releasing one of the constituent bodies from its long and useless association with the Joint Board. Parliament, however, adopted a much more radical remedy: it put an end to the system of combination favoured by the Local Government Board in 1877, disregarded the Provisional Order, and passed an Act dissolving the Joint Board, and giving facilities to the various local bodies which composed it to form new united districts by mutual agreement.[3] Richmond availed itself of these facilities in 1886. But all the costly proceedings which have been described under the Provisional Order system, devised to insure simplicity and economy in procedure, ended in nothing; the work of providing proper sewerage for the Lower Thames Valley was obstructed and delayed for more than ten years; and in 1886 the local authorities had to begin afresh. *Provisional Order, 1885, not confirmed.* *Joint Board dissolved, 1885.*

[1] Report of Select Committee, p. 4; Commons' Paper, 272 of 1884.

[2] By Provisional Order of 1880, confirmed by 43 & 44 Vict. c. 178;
and Order of 1883 (46 & 47 Vict. c. 89).

[3] 48 & 49 Vict. c. 112.

The full extent to which private Bill legislation is superseded by the statutory powers of Government Departments
cannot be known without information as to those unopposed
Orders which, under the Acts authorizing them, do not become
" Provisional," but have the force of statutes without express
Orders not sanction by Parliament. For example, under the Act of
requiring 1876[1] the Local Government Board may reconstitute divided
Parlia-
mentary parishes by Orders which are Provisional only when objected
sanction. to by one-tenth of the ratepayers in number and rateable
value, and otherwise take effect without any confirming
Act.   During 1882-3, no fewer than 120 Orders affecting
the areas of parishes were issued by the Board, only five of
which were objected to and became Provisional.[2] In 18 cases
during this period Orders in like manner took effect for adjusting the interests of the several unions, parishes or districts
affected by these alterations of areas.[3] Again, the Public
Health Act, 1875, enables the Board, upon the application of
rural sanitary authorities, to give them certain powers otherwise confined to urban districts.[4] During 1882-3, Orders to
this effect were issued in 48 cases; the total number issued
up to that period was 444.[5]

Private Acts As each confirming Bill may, and usually does, include
and Provi- several Orders, the table and titles of the statutes give no
sional Orders
in 1883-85. clue to the relative number of Provisional Orders and of
Private Acts passed in each Session. The following list
shows the proportion between the two systems for the three
years 1883-5.   It will be seen that in those years the
number of Local and Private Acts was 180, 203, and 160
respectively; of Provisional Orders, 241, 176, and 146. The
69 Electric Lighting Orders made the Session of 1883 an

[1] 39 & 40 Vict. c. 61, s. 2, amended
by 42 & 43 Vict. c. 54, and 45 & 46
Vict. c. 58.
[2] Annual Report of Local Government Board, 1882-3, pp. 45, 46, 58.
[3] Ib. p. 60.
[4] Sect. 276.

[5] Annual Report of Local Government Board, 1882-3, pp. 88, 89;
and see p. 102, as to Orders suspending
the operation of the Rivers Pollution
Prevention Act, 1876, s. 3, respecting the discharge of sewage into
streams.

exceptional one. Omitting these from the record, the growth of the new system is still very striking; in numbers, though by no means in importance, it now approaches closely to the year's legislation by private Acts:—

	1883.	1884.	1885.
No. of Local and Private Acts...................	180	203	160
„ Quasi-Public	4	4	1
„ Acts confirming Provisional Orders	53	61	46
Total......................	237	268	207

No. of Provisional Orders included in Confirming Acts:—	1883.	1884.	1885.
Under Artizans, &c. Dwellings Acts	4	1	2
„ Electric Lighting Act	69	4	—
„ Elementary Education Acts	6	2	6
„ Gas and Water Facilities Acts	17	17	17
„ Highways and Locomotives Acts	1	1	—
„ Inclosure Acts	1	2	3
„ Land Drainage Acts (England and Ireland)..	8	2	3
„ Labourers (Ireland) Act	—	34	18
„ Piers and Harbours Acts	8	11	8
„ Poor Law and Divided Parishes Acts [1]	25	15	8
„ Public Health Act, 1875	67	56	52
„ Public Health, &c. Acts (Ireland)	8	7	11
„ Public Health Act (Scotland)	1	1	2
„ Sea Fisheries Acts	3	1	1
„ Tramways Acts (England and Ireland)	23	20	14
„ Miscellaneous	—	2	1
Total......................	241	176	146

A marked distinction between the systems remains to be noticed. From the description given it will be seen that legislation by Provisional Order differs from legislation by private Bill in various respects, but in none more widely than in the constitution of the tribunal itself. The House of Commons has laboured to perfect -a system under which the Committee upon each Bill shall be absolutely impartial as between contending parties, the views and even the constitution of the Committee being unknown till it is struck upon the eve of its assembling. Provisional Orders, on the contrary, owe their shape and sanction to permanent departments of the State, with the constitution and opinions of which promoters can always

The two systems distinguished.

[1] The number of confirming Acts is only given; each provides for from twelve to twenty-five separate parishes.

familiarise themselves; and the Orders themselves cannot fail to bear the impress of the department's views, which have frequently been revealed in official correspondence already, and are sometimes successive stages in the development of a policy which the department is seeking to introduce. Much may be urged in favour of either course, but it is obvious that the systems themselves are radically different, and hence that it is not correct to speak of Provisional Orders as an easy and inexpensive substitute for private Bills, following in other respects the same beaten track.

Position of departments considered. The departments which grant Provisional Orders stand, indeed, in one sense in the shoes of Parliamentary Committees; in another, they may be said to occupy a different and almost an inconsistent attitude towards the legislative proposals of the year. Thus, when private Bills are promoted, departments contribute, through the medium of reports, facts and opinions based upon their knowledge or experience, for the information and guidance of Parliament and its Committees; and Committees, with the evidence and arguments before them, submitted by promoters and opponents, decide whether and how far it is expedient to act upon these reports. On the other hand, when Provisional Orders are sought, the department is itself legislating upon questions which, from official proceedings elsewhere, are probably not new to it, as to which it may even have been called upon to take a line already in correspondence, at deputations, in reports to Parliament, or otherwise, so that to the decision of these questions it comes, if not committed by some previous action, at any rate with its mind more or less made up. Where a department administers as well as judges, this result is to some extent inevitable. Indeed, it is commonly, though erroneously, supposed that a Provisional Order, once made, becomes "a Government measure," and that petitioners, whatever the merits of their case, will be at a disadvantage in opposing the confirmation of the order in Parliament. But this view, however natural, has not been intentionally favoured by Parliament, for in most of the General Acts authorizing Provisional Orders, Parliament has been careful to insert and retain,[1] by way of safeguard and control, a special clause declaring that, when a confirming Bill is before Parliament, petitioners may appear and oppose it as though it were a private Bill.

When so many departments are entrusted with the duty of making and issuing Provisional Orders, it is not surprising that, in different offices, different and even inconsistent rules prevail. Thus, as we have seen, the Board of Trade will only attempt to settle disputed questions affecting local interests if the parties are willing to abide by their decision.[2] But the Local Government Board apparently undertakes to decide not only where the parties, or some of them, are unwilling to accept its decision but even in the face of strong remonstrance from a district.[3]

Conflicting rules in different departments.

Various suggestions have from time to time been offered with a view of securing that, while a scheme remains in the hands of the department, local inquiries, although conducted by permanent Government officials, shall not lose their character of independence, and run the risk of becoming

Independent local inquiries.

---

[1] In the Session of 1871, the usual provision—("In case of a petition, Bill confirming Provisional Order to be referred to Select Committee")—was omitted from "The Local Government (Ireland) Act" of that year (34 & 35 Vict. c. 109), during its passage through the House of Commons. Attention having been called to this omission in the House of Lords, the section (8) was, after discussion, reinstated without a division; and the House of Commons, when the Bill was returned to it, acquiesced in the amendment.

[2] *Ante*, p. 681.

[3] The following passages occur in the cross-examination of a Local Government Board Inspector upon a Provisional Order (Marsden), for the amalgamation of two Local Board districts, before a Lords' Committee in 1882:—

"*Q.* Can you tell me why, if those were both voluntary acts of the two districts, the Local Government Board should interfere?—*A.* We had an application in this case for a Provisional Order from the Marsden-in-Almondbury Local Board. *Q.* From one of the two Local Boards? —*A.* Yes. *Q.* And you had an equally strong representation against the proposal from the other of them? —*A.* Yes. *Q.* Then what the Local Government Board is proposing to do is to side with one of the Local Boards against the other?—*A.* Yes. *Q.* And compulsorily to transfer the district of the one to the other?—*A.* Quite so."—Minutes of Evidence, July 24, 1882.

merely stages in a centralised and bureaucratic system, echoing back, as it were, through an inspector's report, opinions entertained at head quarters in London. This danger is one that may easily be exaggerated; at the same time, it is not altogether imaginary.[1] One possible safeguard consists in requiring from each department a strict account of the exercise of its powers, and the grounds on which its decisions rest, so that Parliament may have materials for giving its own judgment in case of appeal, and for interfering, if need be, whenever it may think right to do so. For reasons about to be stated, this security for prompt intervention, or indeed for any intervention, by Parliament, can hardly be said to exist at present.

Return of 1883 as to Provisional Orders and certificates.

An illustration will be found in the Return of 1883, "relating to Provisional Orders and Certificates," particulars from which have been freely cited in the foregoing pages.[2] These particulars, furnished from official records, and supplied under direction from Parliament, cannot be treated otherwise than as work upon which peculiar care and scrupulous attention have been bestowed by the departments, with the object of avoiding error, and of giving to Parliament a full account of their stewardship. In the absence of anything to raise a doubt, such information should be accepted on all hands as authoritative. It is disappointing, therefore, to find that in some points the Return is not only inaccurate, but misleading. Materials can only exist, very partially, outside the departments themselves for checking

[1] Upon the hearing (June 20, 1882), before a Commons' Committee, of the Marsden Provisional Order, one inspector gave the following evidence:—" Q. In the case of these Provisional Orders, is there any actual hearing by the Local Government Board itself, as distinct from the inspectors?—A. The inspector reports, and his report goes through the department. Q. But there is no opportunity, I understand, for individuals who may consider themselves aggrieved, to be heard by the Local Government Board, in the same way as they are now being heard by this Committee?—A. It is not the practice of the Board, or of the President, to sit and hold these inquiries himself. The inspectors are deputed to hold these inquiries, and on their report and the evidence he decides." (See Printed Minutes of Evidence, p. 65.)

[2] No later Return on this subject has been published.

such a Return, and Parliament is obliged to take the information very much upon trust, having deprived itself by its
own act of immediate knowledge and control in the matter.
But testing the Return by such side lights as are available,
and taking, by way of example, one of the most important
departments, that of "The Lord Lieutenant of Ireland in
Council," in its dealings with tramways, there is enough
in the circumstances to call for explanation, and excite mis-
givings about the record as a whole.

Thus, a Return of "the several Acts of Parliament em- Incomplete-
ness of details
as to Irish
Tramway
Orders.
powering the Lord Lieutenant in Council to grant Provisional
Orders and Certificates," correctly enumerates the Tramways
(Ireland) Acts, 1860, 1861, 1871 and 1881, and summarises
their provisions, but omits "The Tramways (Ireland) Acts
Amendment (Dublin) Act, 1876," 39 & 40 Vict. c. 65,
although, by sect. 7, that Act is to be read as one with all
the other Tramway Acts, and by sect. 5, "doubts concerning
the validity" of an Order "by the Lord Lieutenant in
Council, made at the Council Chamber in Dublin, and bearing
date the 11th day of March, 1867," are recited and cured by
express provisions in the same Act. The "Return showing the number of Provisional Orders, Orders, Certificates,
. . granted under each Act" is even less satisfactory. A
head-note purports to give "the number of Orders, &c., from
the commencement of each Act to August 10, 1882," but
mentions only one Order as having been granted by the Lord
Lieutenant in Council throughout this period, under the Acts
of 1860 and 1861, making no mention of any Orders granted
under the Acts of 1871, 1876 or 1881, or of those Acts themselves. As far, therefore, as the Return is concerned, the
working of the Irish Tramway code, consisting of no fewer
than five public Acts, and extending over a period of twenty
years, is exhibited, with one solitary exception, as a blank.
Meanwhile, another Government Department, that of the
Public Works Commissioners (Ireland), charged with the duty
of holding preliminary inquiries, under the same Tramway

Acts, show in their yearly reports to Parliament that during this very interval of twenty years their engineering inspectors held no less than forty-four inquiries in all.[1]

The Public Works Commissioners' Reports are also very meagre, for though they specify the inquiries held, they do not in any case state the nature of the report made or whether a Provisional Order was ultimately issued.   Doubtless some of the applications were reported against, some were competing schemes, and some were dropped, to re-appear later in an amended form.   But among those which succeeded, and were ultimately carried out, are such well-known and conspicuous instances as the Steam Tramway to the King's Bridge (Dublin) and the Electric Tramway near the Giant's Causeway, which the Lord Lieutenant opened in state.   There were also the Belfast Tramways, authorized by the Lord Lieutenant in Council, 22nd December, 1871, the Cork Tramways, authorized by two Orders of 19th October, 1871, and 31st May, 1872, and the Warrenpoint and Rosstrevor, authorized in 1875.   As in all these cases, whether successful or not, formal steps must have been taken, official correspondence carried on, and presumably some fees paid, it is difficult to conceive how they can have been entirely overlooked by a Government department.

These particulars refer to one only out of several departments granting Provisional Orders, whose labours are supposed to be set forth in this Return.   An exposure of error in the case of the Lord Lieutenant in Council is rendered possible by the fact that two departments are set in motion by the machinery of the General Act.   Had the powers been vested in a single department it might not have been possible to check the statements in this Return.   But the error itself, and the character of the information withheld, show that if Parliamentary control over Provisional Order legislation is to be as real as it undoubtedly is over private Bill legislation, some

[1] These were held, one in 1867; one in 1871; six in 1872; three in 1873; three in 1874; one in 1875; one in 1877; one in 1878; five in 1879; four in 1880; seven in 1881; seven in 1882; and four in 1882-3.

further check is wanted than Returns supplied by departments years after the Provisional Orders themselves have been made and forgotten.

The distinction between the two systems will become clear if it is remembered that an error or irregularity detected in proceedings before a Committee of either House of Parliament can be, and usually is, reported the same afternoon to the House itself by the Chairman of the Committee, at a time when the facts are fresh in everybody's mind, when all necessary parties are upon the spot, and a remedy can be promptly applied. It is otherwise outside the walls of Parliament, where a similar error or irregularity if detected may have to wait weeks, months, or even years before an opportunity arrives for calling attention to the facts and securing, however tardily, the attention and interference of the Legislature.[1]

Means of correcting errors under private Bill and Provisional Order systems.

[1] Some of the more salient objections to the jurisdiction of Government departments in connection with Provisional Orders have been thus summed up by an expert:—"The Local Government Board, in discharging its ordinary functions, plays the following parts: First, it prescribes, recommends, or sanctions a certain course to be taken by local authorities. If statutory powers are applied for, conformably with this advice or sanction, it deputes one of its inspectors to hold a local inquiry, and report as he deems expedient. On his report a draft Provisional Order is framed by the department, acting upon its own discretion. To this order all objections must be made in writing, as no machinery exists at the department for hearing parties *vivâ voce*. Then, with any amendments the Board thinks proper to introduce, the Provisional Order is launched. If all parties accept it as 'a Government measure,' well and good. If not, and the confirming Bill is opposed in Parliament, we then see the same inspector, who has conducted the local inquiry, and who is really responsible for the Order, appearing before the Committee and giving evidence in its favour. By this evidence, or by official reports, the Board always finds means to exercise its influence on the side of promoters and against opponents. This blending of administrative and judicial functions would appear in a strange light, if one could conceive the judges of some division—say the Queen's Bench—first recommending people to go to law upon certain lines, then sitting to administer justice indifferently between them, and then, if their decree failed to give satisfaction, proceeding to assist in arguing the case in person before the Court of Appeal."

CHAPTER XIX.

FEES ON PRIVATE BILLS: FORMERLY PAID, WITH OTHER
EMOLUMENTS, TO OFFICERS OF BOTH HOUSES: FREQUENT
INQUIRIES BY COMMITTEES, SEVENTEENTH CENTURY:
NATURALIZATION BILLS: ATTEMPTS TO AVOID PAYMENT:
QUASI-PUBLIC BILLS, FEES CHARGED ON: SINGLE AND
DOUBLE BILLS: COMPLAINTS OF CUMULATIVE FEES:
LORDS COMMITTEE OF 1827: AMENDED RULES AS TO
MULTIPLIED FEES: EXHIBITS: SALARIES APPOINTED IN
LIEU OF FEES: REGULATED BY STATUTES, 1790—1864:
AD VALOREM RATES: OTHER HOUSE AND COMMITTEE
FEES: CHANGES IN SCALE SINCE 1800: REVISION IN
HOUSE OF LORDS: REVENUE DERIVED FROM FEES IN
BOTH HOUSES: PAID TO CONSOLIDATED FUND.

Early pay-
ment of fees
in Parlia-
ment.

FEES were paid in each House of Parliament, both by promoters and opponents of private Bills, in the earliest times of
which we have Parliamentary record. This practice may
have been brought from the Courts at Westminster by the
clerks in Chancery, who, in 1363, were assigned to receive
petitions.[1] As these petitions, and proceedings upon them,
often raised questions of a judicial as well as a legislative
character, it was not unreasonable to require from suitors
some contribution toward the expense of maintaining any
additional staff which their business made necessary in
Parliament. Fees paid by litigants invoking the appellate jurisdiction of the Lords would also naturally lead
to similar payments from petitioners in that House, whose
prayers for relief could only be settled by private statute.

---

[1] 2 Rot. Parl. 275; *ante*, I. 272.

It must be understood that the two Houses have always fixed their own scales of fees, varying from each other both in incidence and amount.   It will also be seen that a practice, just in itself, was continually abused by excessive charges, and a vicious system of using fees to supplement salaries, even among the highest officials.

In the ancient treatise, "Modus tenendi Parliamenti," which, though not entitled to the antiquity sometimes claimed for it as dating from the Conquest, is found in manuscripts of the fourteenth century, and is shown by contemporary writs and records to be a fairly credible account of the state of Parliament under Edward II.,[1] a penny per ten lines is stated to be the authorized charge made by clerks in Parliament for transcripts of Parliamentary records :—" Clerici parliamenti non negabunt cuiquam transcriptum processus sui, sed liberabunt illud cuilibet qui hoc petierit, et capient semper pro decem lineis unum denarium, nisi forte facta fide de impotentia, in quo casu nihil capient."[2]   And then there is a sentence, meant probably as a guide to the length of each line in making this charge : that the Parliament rolls shall be ten thumbs in breadth : " Rotuli de parliamento continebunt in latitudine decem pollices."

Charge for transcript of records in Parliament, temp. inc.

In the Royal letters patent, by which the office of under clerk of the Parliaments used to be granted, the salary was ten pounds of lawful money of Great Britain, payable half-yearly at the Exchequer, " together with all other rewards, dues, rights, profits, commodities, advantages and endowments whatsoever to the said office, after what manner soever, or however, now or heretofore, anciently appertaining, incident, accustomed, incumbent, or belonging."[3]   These

Clerk of the House of Commons.

---

[1] Stubbs's Select English Charters, 492.

[2] In judicial proceedings in the House of Lords poverty has always been recognized as a ground for the remission of fees.

[3] Hatsell (II. 266-7) says these

letters patent had probably been copied, one from another, ever since the separation of the two Houses (supposed to have occurred in 1332). He cites the opinion of Speaker Onslow, and of several antiquarians, that upon this separation the under

rewards and emoluments included other customary payments besides those arising from private Bills, which were then comparatively few in number; though Bills which could only by a strained construction be deemed to belong to the class of private measures were made liable to fees. Some of these customary payments to officials in each House may now be mentioned.

Fees on proxies were paid by peers to the Gentleman and Yeoman Ushers.[1] Black Rod's fees, and those of the Serjeant-at-Arms, appear, however, to have been chiefly derived from delinquents in custody for contempt or other **Fees to clerk of Parliaments, 1597.** cause. To the clerk of the Parliaments were paid fees on the first admission of peers. In Queen Elizabeth's reign an Archbishop or a Marquis paid 6*l.* 13*s.* 4*d.*; an Earl, 4*l.* 10*s.*; a Bishop or Baron, 2*l.* For every proxy or licence to be **On admissions of peers and on private Bills.** absent, a peer paid 30*s.* At the same date the clerk received a moderate fee of one shilling on each reading of a private Bill; for engrossing each Bill, he also received for the first skin, 33*s.* 4*d.*, and for every other skin, 6*s.* 8*d.*[2]

Contributions assessed from peers for clerk and assistants, In 1626, the Lords ordered " that every Earl shall give to the clerk 40*s.*, every Viscount 30*s.*, and every Bishop and Baron 20*s.*, as well they that were absent by proxy as they that are present, in respect of his pains in this and former Parliaments. And it is further ordered that every Lord of Parliament, as well they that are absent by proxy as they that are present, shall pay the clerk's two men 10*s.* between **and Black Rod.** them also, in respect of their pains. And also each Lord is to give unto the gentleman usher of the Black Rod in like manner as to the clerk."[3] This levy in aid of the officials was made on the last day of the Session.

Committal to Fleet for In 1625, a deputy serjeant-at-arms of the Lords was com-

clerk went with the Commons, and has accordingly from that time, in his appointment, and in several public instruments, been styled, ' Under Clerk of the Parliaments, attending

upon the Commons.' "

[1] 1 Lords' Journ. 431.

[2] 2 Ib. 225 ; February 8, 1597.

[3] 3 Ib. 682 ; June 15, 1626.

mitted to Fleet prison, during the pleasure of the House, for taking undue fees, 1625. taking undue fees from a prisoner in custody for contempt.[1] On a report from the Committee of Privileges in the following Session, all the officers were ordered to "set down what fees they claim due unto them" for consideration by a Grand Committee.[2] In 1628, a Sub-committee for Privileges was Committees of 1628–40. again deputed "to examine what fees are due to all the officers of this House, and to disburse the money in the poor man's box."[3] Again, in 1640, upon order by the House, the Grand Committee of Privileges appointed a Sub-committee to examine into "the roll of all the officers' ancient fees in this House." The Grand Committee approved and presented to the House a list of fees reported by their Sub-committee, including the Lord Keeper's fees, which were "to be due and payable in the same manner as they have been accustomed to his predecessors." Upon hearing this report, presented by the Earl of Warwick, "and the roll of fees being read openly before the Lords Spiritual and Temporal, in the High Court of Parliament assembled, it was agreed and ordered by all their lordships that the said fees, entered upon the said roll, are hereby confirmed, and shall be accordingly paid."[4] Included in this roll were, no doubt, the fees usually paid in appeals.

Members of the Lower House receiving leave of absence Other fees in House of Commons. paid, before quitting the House, a fee of 6s. 8d. to the clerk.[5] Members in custody for non-attendance, and defaulters at calls of the House, also paid fees to the clerk and serjeant.[6] Delinquents taken into custody by order of the House contributed to the same fund. In 1610, Sir Henry Poole reported the allowance agreed on by the Committee for messengers—20s. to the serjeant for summons for every man; 1s. a mile coming and going for the messengers."

[1] 3 Lords' Journ. 514.
[2] Ib. 572.
[3] Ib. 878.
[4] 4 Ib. 77.
[5] 1 Com. Journ. 351, 1029.
[6] 8 Ib. 343; 9 ib. 210, 218.

Assessment
on members
for benefit of
officers.

"After much dispute" these charges were allowed.[1] The mileage rate here sanctioned continued to be charged till 1864, when it was reduced to 6d. Occasional subscriptions were made among members for the benefit of officers, as in the Upper House, and these do not appear to have been voluntary, for in 1641, it was resolved "that every Knight shall pay 20s., and every burgess shall pay 10s., to be disposed of, by order of this House, among such officers as they shall think fit, for a reward for their several great pains." These moneys were to be paid in by the following Monday; members who had not then paid were to forfeit double; and Sir Robert Pye and Mr. Glyn were appointed treasurers to give account to the House what moneys they had received, and from whom.[2] A Committee was afterwards nominated to consider the distribution of this money among the officers and servants, as well as such other persons as had done service.[3]

Fees on
Ordinances in
House of
Lords during
the Long
Parliament.

During the Long Parliament, after the final rupture with Charles I., the Lords who still met at Westminster ordered, "that no private Ordinance do pass this House until the parties that are concerned therein do first pay such fees for the same unto the clerk as hath usually been paid upon the passing of private Bills; and all members of this House that do present any Ordinances wherein the advantage or benefit of any private persons is concerned are desired to acquaint such persons herewith, and appoint them first to pay such ancient and accustomed fees as aforesaid to the clerk."[4] Three months afterwards, a Sub-committee of Privileges reported upon the same subject, and the House ordered that the same fees shall be paid to the Speaker and officers, upon each private Ordinance, as upon a private Bill."[5]

[1] 2 Com. Journ. 428; May 14, 1610.

[2] Ib. 186; June 24, 1641.

[3] Ib. 196.

[4] 7 Lords' Journ. 124; January 4, 1644-5. The House of Commons had passed similar resolutions on December 31, 1644.

[5] Ib. 319; April 14, 1645.

In the Commons' Journals the first mention of fees occurs in 1604, upon a Bill to "establish certain lands, called assart lands, in the possessors and owners thereof."[1] This would now be regarded as a general measure, but counsel for the possessors (Mr. Serjeant Nicholls) was heard at the bar. There is an entry, "No counsel for the King, but Sir Francis Bacon, of the King's counsel, and a member of the House (thereby holding the place of a judge), after the other counsel retired, stood up to speak," representing no doubt the King's interest. Then follows another entry, "It was a long time not well understood by Mr. Speaker or any other, who preferred and followed this Bill. At length it was discovered that one Haynes paid fees to Mr. Speaker's servant. This Haynes was said to be servant to Sir Thomas Leighton. Sir Thomas himself was thereupon consulted withal, and writ his mind in a letter to Mr. Speaker," which was read in the House as follows :—

Assart Lands Bill, 1604.

Speaker's fees on Bill.

"Mr. SPEAKER,—Whereas I am informed that one Henry Haynes, my servant, doth follow a Bill in the Parliament concerning Assart lands, and that he hath been with you about it : true it is that he holdeth under me certain Assart lands, whereof I have a grant, among other things, from the late Queen's Majesty, under the Great Seal of England : Wherefore I do disclaim in the prosecution of the same, as done without my privity or allowance ; for that I conceive the same will rather prejudice my estate therein than any way amend or confirm the same. And I further assure you, upon my knowledge, if this Bill should take place it will be the utter overthrow of his Majesty's game, in all or most of his Majesty's forests and chases within this realm, besides the infinite loss which thereby will ensue to his Majesty and his successors. The consideration whereof I leave unto your wisdom. And so, with my very hearty commendations, I rest, this 28th day of April, 1604,

Promotion of Bill disclaimed.

"Your very loving friend,
"THO. LEIGHTON."

1 Com. Journ. 197. Assart, assert, or essert lands (med. Lat., assartum or exartum), are lands within Royal forests, stubbed and made fit for tillage without the King's licence. The Bill appears to have been intended to quiet titles to lands of this nature claimed by the Crown.

Notwithstanding this disclaimer the Bill passed the Commons, though it was stopped in the Upper House.[1] The Speaker, whose fees are thus mentioned in the Journals, only received an allowance from the Civil List of five pounds a day, and naturally took care that private Bills did not

Highway Bill, 1607.

escape from all usual payments.[2] An example of his vigilance occurred in 1607, when, after much delay in a Bill for repairing highways in Sussex, Surrey and Kent, a member moved that "it might have some expedition, since this Session was not like to be long." Mr. Speaker answered "that the Bill was long and of much labour to the clerk; that it was followed and pressed as a public Bill, but was indeed, by all former precedents, to be accounted and taken as a private Bill, being only for three shires; yet no fees were paid for it to the officers, nor any man took care to answer them." Thereupon the House ordered "that the ordinary duties should be performed, or else there should be no further proceeding in the Bill."[3]

Cumulative fees on Bills.

Officers in the House of Commons were the first to devise a system of charging more than one fee upon the same Bill.

---

[1] James I. strongly resented the passing of this measure. It is mentioned by the Commons in the Apology touching their privileges, which they drew up in 1604.

[2] Sir Edward Seymour, who was Speaker of the House of Commons, 1673–8, gave the fees on private Bills to the poor of his parish (St. Giles). Proud of his descent from a Protector of the realm, he bore himself with corresponding pride as first commoner. A message being brought that the King (Charles II.) was on the throne, and desired the presence of the Commons to hear the prorogation of Parliament, Sir Edward refused to stir until the Bill of Supply had been returned, according to precedent; and, upon a second warning that his Majesty was waiting, declared that he would be torn by wild horses rather than quit the chair. The Bill was brought; and Sir Edward, with the Commons, then obeyed the summons. It was he who, passing through Westminster Hall, directed the Mace to take Serjeant Pemberton into custody, because "though I was near him, he paid me no respect, or very slightly"; who treated William III. with the airs of an equal; and when dismissed from his place of Comptroller of the Household by Queen Anne, sent word that he should return his staff by the common crier. Townsend's History of the House of Commons, pp. 29, 30.

[3] 1 Com. Journ. 388; June 27, 1607.

This practice is authorized in a table of fees appointed to be taken by the clerk in 1649, and giving him 2*l.* for every person taking benefit under any private Act or proviso. Under like circumstances, every corporation, town, company, society, shire or place paid a double fee of 4*l.* Smaller fees were fixed for copying, engrossing, and other services. The under-clerks were to receive 10*s.* for each Bill. To the Serjeant-at-Arms, besides 4*s.* for every knight of the shire and 2*s.* for every burgess, each person or interest affected by a private Bill must pay 1*l.*, and half that sum to " the Serjeant's men." At this period fees were also extracted by the Serjeant and his men from parties represented by counsel opposing a Bill.[1] This charge, and the system of cumulative fees, were not introduced into the Upper House until a much later period.[2]

Committees in the Commons, as in the Upper House, were frequent during the seventeenth century, to consider the fees demanded by their officers, not always upon private Bills. Thus the Serjeant's allowance for summonses was investigated in 1610.[3] A Committee sat in 1661 " to consider what fees were anciently due to the several clerks and officers of this House, and how they were paid, and how for the future they may receive a recompense suitable to their pains and attendance;" while another Committee was directed to consider all fees demanded by the Serjeant-at-Arms, and report upon his just dues.[4] This functionary came in for a good deal of complaint in executing orders of the House. Andrew Marvel charged him, in 1660, with demanding excessive fees for the arrest and custody of John Milton. On this occasion, after debate, it was referred to the Committee for Privileges to determine what fees were proper.[5]

Inquiries by House of Commons, 17th century.

Excessive fees demanded by Serjeant-at-Arms.

---

[1] 6 Com. Journ. 287; Aug. 30, 1649.

[2] Inquiry was ordered by their lordships in 1690 into complaints that fees were demanded by some officers of the House from petitioners and respondents "for counsel coming to the bar in causes." 14 Lords' Journ. 587.

[3] 2 Com. Journ. 146.

[4] 8 Ib. 309, 343.

[5] 8 Ib. 209; December 17, 1660. The Committee was directed "to

Renewed
complaints,
1689-99.

Renewed complaints of the Serjeant-at-Arms for taking excessive fees were made in 1689, and new inquiry was made as to the fees which were properly due to him[1] and other officers. At length, in 1694, a carefully compiled table of fees was drawn up, with a view to prevent disputes. They do not appear to have given satisfaction, for in 1695-6 this table was investigated by three Committees, to whom a petition from the Serjeant-at-Arms was referred.[2] Again, in 1699, there was a Committee "to inspect and settle fees taken by officers and servants of the House, and examine their salaries or allowances." In the two following Sessions there was a like inquiry.[3]

Complaints
by officials of
insufficient
remunera-
tion.

In their turn the clerks and other officials sometimes complained of insufficient remuneration. This troublesome topic came before both Houses in 1709, when addresses were agreed to[4] praying Queen Anne to give to the officers "some recompense and encouragement," on account of great losses which they had already suffered and would continue to suffer from the General Naturalization Bill, and from a recent Standing Order concerning private Bills. In the House of Commons the officers thus specified were "the clerk, Serjeant-at-Arms, clerk Assistant, and other clerks, officers and servants." The Queen's reply to the address was, that she would take these losses into consideration, and give such recompense and encouragement as she should think proper.[5]

Printing
private Bills.

The recent Standing Order referred to was that passed in

---

call Mr. Milton and the Serjeant before them, and determine what is fit." This was the arrest and prosecution ordered for Milton's defence, "Pro populo Anglicano," and his answer to the Icon Basilike. It was during this debate that Sir Heneage Finch, afterwards Lord Chancellor Nottingham, said that Milton had been Foreign Secretary to Cromwell, and deserved hanging.

[1] In 1751, the House of Commons resolved that the Serjeant-at-Arms was entitled to take from every person brought to the bar, to be reprimanded by Mr. Speaker, a fee of 5*l.*, or 3*l.* 6*s.* 8*d.* for taking such person into custody; 1*l.* for each day of custody, 6*s.* 8*d.* for the messenger; and 6*s.* 8*d.* for bringing a delinquent to the bar. 28 Com. Journ. 290.

[2] 11 Ib. 288, 367, 584.

[3] 13 Ib. 160, 280, 357, 679.

[4] 16 Ib. April 12, 1709.

[5] Ib. April 20, 1709.

the previous year, " That all private Bills brought into this House be printed, and presented to the House before the first reading of such Bills."[1]   Probably the printing of private Bills put an end to charges made for manuscript copies.   From Naturalization Bills officials in both Houses had always derived considerable fees.   Generally these Bills were special, but sometimes they included several persons, each of whom was bound to pay.   Attempts by any of these persons to evade payment were sternly dealt with. Thus, in 1625, a warrant was issued in the Commons against a delinquent " to answer his contempt to the House in not paying fees for his Bill to the Speaker, Serjeant, &c."   This matter appears to have been brought before the House as a question of privilege.[2]   Again, in December 1661, the House was informed that divers persons whose names were inserted in a Naturalization Bill had refused to pay fees, whereupon it was ordered that " Mr. Speaker do send for such persons, and all other persons who shall at any time refuse to pay their fees ; and if payment be not thereupon made, to report to the House, that such course may be taken as shall be thought fitting for the enforcing thereof."   The course taken in this and other instances was to strike out of the Bill the names of defaulters, and further order them to attend and answer for their default.[3]

It will be seen, therefore, that there was reasonable cause for complaint in 1709, by officials in both Houses, as a general Naturalization Act would remove the necessity for private Bills in many cases.   The Act in question was one for naturalizing foreign Protestants.[4]   It recited that " the increase of people is a means of advancing the wealth and strength of a nation," and that " many strangers of the Protestant or reformed religion, out of a due consideration of the

Marginal notes: Naturalization. — Attempted evasion of fees. — Naturalization Act, 1709.

---

[1] Ib. December 20, 1708.
[2] 1 Ib. 808 ; July 11, 1625.
[3] As an exceptional grace, leave was given in 1698 to pass a Naturalization Bill gratuitously in consideration of public services rendered by the person to be naturalized.
[4] 7 Anne, c. 5.

happy constitution of the government of this realm, would be induced to transport themselves and their estates into this kingdom if they might be made partakers of the advantages and privileges" of natural-born subjects. It was, therefore, enacted that all persons taking the oaths and subscribing a declaration should be deemed natural-born subjects; but they were first to receive the Sacrament.

Inquiry by Lords' Committee, 1725.

Hitherto, all inquiries into fees by the Upper House appear to have been far from thorough. But in 1725, searching investigation was made into the officers' claims by a Committee of fifty-four peers, over which Lord Delaware presided. The clerks and officers were then examined upon oath,[1] and "produced an old roll of fees which they said was their guide in most things; but when any business happened that was not mentioned in this roll, they took such fees as they 'apprehended' their predecessors had done." The "old roll" was drawn up in 1640 and signed by Lord Warwick, the report of whose Committee has been mentioned. Some doubt, however, was thrown in 1725 upon the authority of this roll as evidence of ancient fees, and erasures were found with alterations of sums to greater amounts, plainly shown by " different handwriting and fresher ink." As several fees claimed and received by the officers were " unreasonable and excessive, the Committee conceived no further regard ought to be had to the roll," and in lieu of it drew up a new table.

New table of fees in Lords, 1725.

This table gave 5s. to the clerk assistant for writing and entering each proxy, and conceded considerable payments "from every Peer, being newly created, on his first coming to Parliament, or on his being advanced to any higher dignity." These payments were divided in specified proportions among Black Rod, the clerk of the Parliaments,

First admission of peers.

clerk assistant, Yeoman Usher, and door-keepers. Under this scale Archbishops and Dukes paid 17l., and other Lords of Parliament in proportion, the Bishops of London, Durham

[1] 22 Lords' Journ. 606 ; February 24, 1725.

and Winchester paying 9*l.* 10*s.*, while other Bishops escaped
with 6*l.* But the Committee were of opinion that these fees
ought not to be paid by any Peer whose peerage came to him by
descent, or to whom any higher honour should descend ; and
no Bishop should pay on translation, unless to an Arch-
bishopric, or to London, Durham, and Winchester. Upon
commitment to the custody of Black Rod, an Archbishop or
Duke was to pay 20*l.*, and so in proportion ; and for every
day of custody each Peer was mulcted in 6*l.* 13*s.* 4*d.* Considerable fees were also awarded to the clerk of the Parliaments, clerk assistant, Gentleman Usher, and Yeoman Usher,
when any delinquent was committed to close custody by the
House.[1] If any person so committed escaped, the Gentleman Usher or Serjeant-at-Arms was not only to lose his own
fees, but to pay those of other officials.

For every order made on a petition to bring in a private
Bill, the clerk of the Parliaments received 10*s.*, the clerk
assistant, 4*s.* 6*d.* ; and the reading clerk, 2*s.* For each
witness sworn, the clerk assistant and Yeoman Usher
received 1*s.* A certificate of his being sworn, for the satisfaction of the judges, pursuant to Standing Orders, cost
6*s.* 8*d.* On each private Bill, the Lord Chancellor, or
Speaker, received 10*l.* ; clerk of the Parliaments, 5*l.* ; Black
Rod, 5*l.* ; clerk assistant, 2*l.* ; Yeoman Usher, 1*l.* ; reading
clerk, 2*l.* ; four door-keepers, 2*l.* These fees were to be
paid before the second reading ; and if a Bill concerned
divers persons, " as for settling an award between lord and
tenants and the like, or for a turnpike to mend any highway,
they are to pay as for a double Bill." No more than a
double fee could be asked for on any private Bill, but every
person in a naturalization Bill was to pay as for a single
Bill.

Committee fees were settled thus : clerk assistant, for
entering the names of the Lords' Committees, and giving a

Scale appointed for private Bills, 1725.

Committee fees.

---

[1] 22 Lords' Journ. 627–9 ; March 22, 1725.

Engrossing. copy thereof if desired, 10*s.* ; clerk attending the Committee, 2*l.* : Yeoman Usher, 1*l.*; door-keepers, 2*l.* For engrossing a private Bill, the clerk assistant could charge for the first skin, 13*s.* 4*d.* ; for every other skin, 10*s.* ; but the Committee were of opinion that forty lines at least ought to be written on every such skin.

To the clerk of the Parliaments for certifying of a private Bill, upon a writ of certiorari out of Chancery, or any other matter of record, for the first skin, 1*l.* 6*s.* 8*d.* ; every other skin, 13*s.* 4*d.* Half these fees were given to the clerk

Fees on Appeals. assistant. Again, all the officials received considerable fees upon appeals. Then the Committee concluded their report with an opinion that no other fees ought to be allowed to clerks or other officers, and that " if they should demand, take, or receive any higher fee or other gratuity, they ought to incur the displeasure of this House." Approving of this report, the House ordered that the list of fees contained in it should be " printed and affixed on the doors, and hung up in the offices." [1]

Gradual addition to fees. Gradually the officers seem to have enlarged on their own authority the table thus settled. In 1732, the House was informed that, no fee being specified for administering the oaths of allegiance and supremacy to persons, with a view to naturalization, their solicitors refused to pay to the clerk assistant and Black Rod the fees demanded and taken in the Commons. This new charge was authorized.[2] A later

On employment of counsel. attempt in 1739 was equally successful. It will be seen that the table of 1725 allowed no fees to officers when counsel were employed upon private Bills, although such fees, after dispute in 1690, were charged when counsel appeared at the bar on appeal. In 1739, Black Rod, Sir Charles Dalton, complained that Sir John Dinely, who was promoting a divorce Bill, had refused to pay any bar fees when employing counsel.[3] A Committee of Peers decided " that the

[1] 22 Lords' Journ. 629.   [2] 25 Ib., 411.
[3] 24 Ib., 207.

same fees should be taken by officers of the House upon the hearing of counsel for and against any Bill, as are directed by the table of fees upon the hearing of appeals."[1]

In 1756, the officers of the House of Lords were once more successful in increasing their fees on private Bills. They had chafed under a restriction which, in 1725, had prohibited them from charging more than a double fee on any Bill, except in cases of naturalization. They therefore procured a reference of this matter to a Committee, who accepted a series of resolutions which, five years previously, had been adopted by the other House,[2] and which largely increased the Lords' scale of fees. These resolutions declared that every Bill concerning " a county or counties, a corporation or corporations, or body or bodies of people," should be deemed a double Bill; that every enacting clause " for a particular interest or benefit," should " pay fees as for a private Bill," whether inserted in a public or private measure; and that fees should be paid " for every distinct provision made in any Bill, for the particular interest of any person or persons, or of any county or counties, corporation or corporations, or body or bodies of people, or relating to a distinct interest, estate, or matter: provided that, in Bills containing distinct provisions for more than three bodies of people, no more than a single fee should be paid for each body."[3]

These rules were adopted by the House, and must have added considerably to all official incomes depending upon private Bill fees. How wide, and at the same time how rigid, a construction was placed upon these rules, was shown

Restriction on double fees removed, 1756.

Bills relating to the poor.

---

[1] Ib., 413–14; June 8, 1739.

[2] Hatsell says that these resolutions were drawn up by Mr. Dyson, then clerk of the House of Commons. He was afterwards cofferer to his Majesty's household and member of the Privy Council. Hatsell dedicates his Precedents to Mr. Dyson, and describes him as a man of "universal knowledge" upon all subjects relating to the history of Parliament.

[3] 28 Lords' Journ. 520; March 11, 1756.

in 1765. A public Bill then came before the Lords, "for the better relief and employment of the poor in that part of Great Britain called England."   A motion was made that all similar Bills should be "deemed of a public nature, and pass without paying any fees," but after debate this motion was negatived.[1]   Yet in 1699 and 1700, the Lower House had ordered that all Bills relating to the poor should be taken as public Bills, and passed without fees.[2]

One object of the resolutions which the House of Commons passed in 1751 was to distinguish more clearly, for fee-paying purposes, between public and private Bills. Officials whose incomes depended mainly on fees were naturally ingenious in expedients for enlarging them.   Hence arose frequent disputes with promoters: disputes which were encouraged by vagueness in the existing rules, drawn up in the year 1700, and fixed by Order of the House in 1731.[3] Measures which would undoubtedly now be classed as of a public character had therefore been gradually made to pay toll.   Hatsell[4] gives many curious examples, occurring between the years 1730-47, of Bills on which, as he puts it, "private persons and corporations had paid fees for the benefit they derived from those Bills, whether in their nature public or private:"—

Quasi-public measures subjected to fees, 1730-47.

Examples.   Bills for encouraging trade in the sugar colonies; for regulating pilots; for recovering debts in the plantations; for preventing the exportation of hats out of the plantations; to secure the trade of the East Indies; to encourage the growth of coffee in the plantations; for free importation and exportation of diamonds; to secure the trade of the sugar colonies; to encourage the engraving of historical prints, &c.; for vesting printed copies of books in the authors or purchasers; to make more effectual the laws for recovery of ecclesiastical dues from Quakers; for relief of shipwrecked mariners; for continuing additional duties on stamped vellum, &c.; for encouraging the consumption of raw silk and mohair

---

[1] 31 Lords' Journ. 146; April 22, 1765.

[2] S. O., H. C., March 7, 1699:

February 25, 1700.

[3] 26 Com. Journ. 277-8.

[4] Precedents, II. 268-9.

yarn; to prevent frauds in gold and silver wares; for regulating the cheese trade; for collecting at Genoa money for relief of shipwrecked mariners; to regulate the importation of Smyrna raisins; to obviate doubts relating to tanned leather; for liberty to carry sugars from the colonies to foreign parts in British ships; for opening a trade to and from Persia through Russia; relating to insurance on ships; to prevent the counterfeiting of gold and silver lace; for laying an additional duty on foreign cambrics imported; for making provision for widows and children of clergy of the Church of Scotland; to prevent brewers' servants from stealing barrels; for allowing additional bounties on the exportation of British and Irish linens; for regulating pawnbrokers; for securing the duties on foreign-made sail-cloth; for support of maimed seamen; to empower distillers to retail spirits.[1]

But the resolutions of 1751, as might have been foreseen, failed in applying any clear distinction between public and private measures from the officials' standpoint. In 1781, a Bill was brought in by representatives of Hull, Lancaster, and Liverpool, ports then interested in the Greenland fisheries, to increase the statutory bounties allowed to vessels employed in those fisheries. Application being made for fees upon this Bill in the House of Commons, the members responsible for it made answer that, though it contemplated the interest of particular bodies of merchants, yet it was of general application, and merchants in any seaport might take advantage of its provisions, so that it could not properly be subjected to fees. The merchants, however, were obliged to pay. After a similar dispute in 1788, fees were also exacted upon a Bill for consolidating into one Act laws relating to the export of wool. This was a still harder case.[2]

Even more intolerable was the spoliation practised under

Failure of resolutions of 1751.

Bill for increasing bounties to Greenland fishing-vessels.

Cumulative fees.

---

[1] The way for exacting fees upon Bills of this character in the House of Commons had been paved by a Standing Order of February 15, 1700, dividing private Bills into three classes; the third comprised measures which, though not strictly of a local or personal character, affected some special trade or interest.

[2] Hatsell's admission is conclusive. "This," he says (II. p. 271), "was certainly a very general law, as the purport and intent of it were only to prevent more effectually the illicit exportation of wool."

cover of the rule which, if different interests were concerned in a Bill, and powers of levying rates were sought for different objects, allowed two or more sets of fees.[1]   Thus, in 1744-5, a Westminster Bridge Act paid double fees, "because it contained a grant of public money, and further powers to the Commissioners."   The system, however, did not stop with double fees, but multiplied them almost indefinitely; and promoters complained bitterly of charges not only excessive in amount, but so arbitrary and uncertain that it was very difficult to ascertain under what circumstances they would be levied.

It was hoped that complaints would cease with a clearer definition of this system, contained in the resolutions of 1751.   This hope was unfulfilled.   On the contrary, towards the end of the century, new classes of Bills came into existence which suffered peculiarly from these exactions.

Excessive fees charged on Inclosure Bills. Inclosure Bills, often affecting many interests, must have yielded a rich harvest.[2]   In fourteen years, from 1786 to 1799 inclusive, the House of Commons alone received in fees upon these Bills, 707 in number, the sum of 59,867*l*.[3]   On an average of fourteen years, Bills of Inclosure in the two Houses yielded fees reckoned at 8,552*l*. per annum.   As a basis of charge, they were classed, in the year 1799, in seven divisions, as single, double, three-single, two-double, five-single, three-double, or four-double Bills.   Single fees were taken on Bills which concerned an individual only.   Double

[1] An attempt to explain this practice is made in 26 Com. Journ. 278 ; June 4, 1751, signed J. Dyson, Cl. Dom. Com.

[2] See Vol. I., pp. 14—28. In App. B., Vol. I., is a table giving the number of Inclosure Acts passed between the years 1719—1845, with much other information.

[3] Report of Commons' Committee on Inclosure Bills, 1800; App. No. 9. The fees included Bill and small

fees, 21,768*l*. ; Committee, 10,468*l*. ; housekeeper and messenger, 2,436*l*. ; engrossing, 25,193*l*. Besides the stated fees here summarized, the doorkeeper usually received a guinea for distributing printed Bills; the engrossing clerks two guineas for expedition and for alterations on third reading; and other small gratuities were paid to inferior officers of both Houses.

fees were charged where a body of people were interested. Three single fees were levied on Bills which concerned a body of people and an individual, with distinct interests. Two double fees were charged when there were two bodies of people with distinct interests, and so throughout the remainder of this highly artificial classification.[1] A fee-clerk in the House of Commons formed his opinion of the fees which each Bill should pay, according to its preamble and provisions. From his decision there was an appeal to the Speaker.

Upon four later Inclosure Acts mentioned in 1827,[2] House, Committee, and engrossment fees alone were as follow:—West Ardsley (Session 1826), 183*l.*; Christchurch and Milton (Session 1825), 167*l.*; Aberford (Session 1826), 194*l.*; Cley Inclosure and Embankment (Session 1821), 508*l.* When the charges of solicitors and agents and expenses of opposition were added, even considerable tracts of land were often insufficient to bear the cost of an Act and of partition; and instances are numerous in which that cost was barely paid by the sale of all the land inclosed.[3]

Value of land inclosed swallowed up by costs of Act.

Drainage and navigation Bills formed another class which was grievously burdened by multiplied fees. Upon the Nene Outfall Bill of 1827, the fees in both Houses amounted to 2,000*l.* This and other flagrant instances led, in 1827, to strong complaints from Lord Hardwicke, and other proprietors in the Bedford Level. A Committee of Peers then appointed found that, under the rule which multiplied fees according to the number of interests affected, twenty sets of fees were claimed upon the Nene Bill, though, at a conference between the agents and Speaker in the House of Commons, it was subsequently settled that only fifteen should be paid.[4]

Drainage and navigation Bills.

Nene Outfall.

Lords Committee of 1827.

[1] Commons' Committee on Inclosure Bills, 1800; Evidence of Mr. John Dorington, Assistant Clerk of Fees, House of Commons.

[2] Lords' Committee on Private Bill Fees, 1827, pp. 105–8.

[3] Wingrove Cooke on Inclosures, Preface, p. 8.

[4] Lords' Committee of 1827 on Private Bill Fees; App. p. 178.

Bedford Level.

On the Bedford Level Drainage Bill of 1827, fourteen sets of fees were charged.[1] Upon the original Bedford Level Act[2] of 1663, the fees amounted to no more than 180*l.*, though it contained provisions for drainage, navigation, and the appointment of commissioners of sewers.[3]

Ely drainage.

In 1810, the Ely Drainage Bill paid no fewer than thirty-two sets of fees.[4] There seemed, therefore, to be good ground for supposing that appetite had grown in eating, and that the system of multiplied fees on the same Bill had developed with practice.

Turnpike Bills.

Drainage Bills did not alone suffer. In turnpike Bills, when there happened to be more than one application of toll, each was supposed to be a distinct interest, and a fee was paid on each. For example, if, besides tolls applicable to the repair of roads, another toll was charged for watering roads, a separate Bill fee was demanded, carrying with it a

Improvement Bills.

number of small fees and gratuities. On Improvement Bills, too, the burden was occasionally heavy, if they comprised

Estate Bills.

many distinct objects, as such Bills frequently did. If estate Bills contained a power to lease for ninety-nine years, they were charged as double Bills; if they contained a clause enabling parties to borrow money on mortgage to pay the cost of promotion, this again involved another set of fees. In both Houses the fees in 1827, though not identical, were assessed on the same system; and by arrangement between the officials, Bills paid on the same scale in the second as in the first House.[5]

Littleport and Downham Drainage.

A case often cited, in 1827, was that of the Littleport and Downham Drainage Bill. In 1799-1800, it became law, at an expense, for fees in both Houses, of 197*l.* In 1810, it was found convenient to subdivide the one district originally

[1] Lords' Committee of 1827; Minutes of Evidence, p. 6.

[2] 15 Chas. II. c. 17, which refers to an earlier drainage, "according to a law of sewers made at King's Lynn in 1630."

[3] Lords' Committee of 1827; Min. of Evidence, p. 7.

[4] Ib. p. 53; Evidence of Mr. Dorington, Assistant Clerk of Fees, House of Commons.

[5] Ib. pp. 10, 14.

created into several districts, managed by different bodies of commissioners. The Bill thus became subject to separate sets of fees, in proportion to the number of distinct managements and interests, and the sums charged on account of officers of the two Houses, though at this date no longer actually received by most of them, were as follow:—"House of Commons—Speaker, 160*l.*; clerk, 243*l.*; clerk assistant, 35*l.*; Serjeant, 48*l.*; Fee-clerk, 16*l.*; Speaker's secretary, 16*l.*; door-keepers, 8*l.* House of Lords—Lord Chancellor, 320*l.*; clerk of Parliaments, 160*l.*; Black Rod (including bar fee), 161*l.*; clerk assistant, 64*l.*; reading clerk, 64*l.*; Yeoman Usher (including bar fee and fee on swearing witnesses), 49*l.*; eight door-keepers (including bar fee and Committee fee), 103*l.*" The charges for both Houses came to 1,448*l.*[1]

In spite of this evidence, and the experience of 1751, the only change recommended in 1827 was that more explicit rules should be drafted, so that promoters might ascertain the probable expenses of Bills before submitting them to Parliament. This change was adopted by both Houses. The amended rules were long, but seem by no means easy to understand. One of them was as follows: "Every Bill containing separate objects or provisions, not essentially connected with each other, or which shall be executed by different bodies of persons, shall pay fees for each object, provision, or body." A revised table of fees was prepared in 1829-30;[2] but although fees to officials now happily disappeared, the scandalous abuse of multiplied charges upon one Bill still continued.

Another charge of which promoters often complained, that for exhibits, was also left untouched. Notices served upon landowners, or required to be posted on church doors, and proved on Standing Orders, were treated as exhibits, and a fee of 2*s.* was charged for each. A large revenue in both

Marginal notes:

Inadequate change in 1827.

Revised scale of 1829–30.

Exhibits.

---

[1] Lords' Committee of 1827; Appendix, p. 110.

[2] 85 Com. Journ. 653-5; July 22, 1830.

Houses was derived from this source, for these notices, especially when a great railway scheme was pending, numbered many hundreds, sometimes even many thousands. The nature and incidence of the charge may be gathered from some evidence given in 1827 upon a drainage Bill, solicited two Sessions previously. This Bill was thrown out for non-compliance with Standing Orders. It was therefore only considered before a Committee on the petition. A single form of notice was alone necessary; that was an "exhibit," charged with a fee of 2s. Thirteen witnesses were required to prove the service and publication of this notice. The agent was willing to pay for thirteen exhibits. But there were 125 church doors on which the notice was placed; and as it was affixed there on three different Sundays, the fee-clerks multiplied 125 by three, and charged 2s. each on 375 exhibits.[1] Exhibit fees were abolished in 1847, and *ad valorem* rates, according to the capital to be raised by promoters, were regarded as a substitute for these fees.

More than a century before the period now reached, Parliament had recognized the inexpediency of leaving its higher functionaries to depend upon a precarious income, extracted from suitors or promoters of Bills. Only by slow degrees, however, was the system abolished. First to move was the House of Commons, at whose instance an Act passed in 1790, "for the better support of the dignity of the Speaker." It provided that the Treasury should " direct from time to time a sum to be issued at the Exchequer which, together with the fees and allowance of 5l. per day, may amount to the clear yearly sum of 6,000l."[2] A quarterly account was to be rendered by the Speaker's Secretary; if the fees and allowance from the Civil List exceeded 1,500l., such excess was credited to the next quarter; any deficiency was made good from the Consolidated Fund. From 1790,

Act of 1790 as to salary and fees of Mr. Speaker.

---

[1] Lords' Committee on Private Bill Fees, 1827; Ev. pp. 85-6.

[2] 30 Geo. III. c. 10.

therefore, Mr. Speaker's emoluments from all sources became a minimum of 6,000l. a year, but he retained his interest in fees on private Bills, which were still paid to his account, and he was entitled to any excess which they produced over his statutory income.

In the year 1800, a first step was taken to substitute salaries for fees. An Act of that year[1] recited letters patent,[2] granting to Mr. John Hatsell the office of clerk of the House of Commons, with an annuity of 10l., and customary fees and emoluments; to Mr. John Ley,[3] the same office after Mr. Hatsell's death; and to Mr. Edward Coleman,[4] the office of Serjeant-at-Arms attending the House of Commons, with a salary and fees. Commissioners were appointed who, at the expiration of these letters patent, which conferred life appointments, should receive the fees and emoluments, and in lieu thereof pay to the clerk a salary of 3,000l. on first taking office, and 3,500l. after holding such office for five years; to the clerk assistant, 1,500l., and, after five years, 2,000l.; to the Serjeant-at-Arms, 2,300l., of which 300l. was for payment of a deputy.

Act of 1800 for regulating certain offices in House of Commons.

Salaries substituted for fees to clerk, clerk assistants, and serjeant.

Fees and emoluments belonging to these offices must have averaged considerably more than the statutory salaries assigned to them, for the Commissioners were directed to apply any balance remaining in their hands "towards making a more certain and regular provision for the support of such officers in the departments of the Speaker, clerk, and Serjeant-at-Arms, as may from casual circumstances appear to require the same, and for affording relief to such persons belonging to, or who may have belonged to, these two departments, and who may have been disabled by age or infirmity from the discharge of their respective duties." A copy of the Commissioners' proposals was to be laid before Parliament

Application of fees.

---

[1] 39 & 40 Geo. III. c. 92.

[2] Dated June 3, 1768. Mr. Hatsell was in 1800 still acting as clerk.

[3] Dated July 4, 1797.

[4] Dated November 16, 1776.

in each Session, and was to take effect unless the House otherwise ordered. If a balance still remained, it was to be at the disposal of the House of Commons, who might apply it towards providing a remuneration for the Chairman of Ways and Means.

Act of 1812. This Act was found defective, and repealed in 1812.[1] It appears that, notwithstanding the efforts of the House of Commons twelve years before to substitute salaries for the fees paid to their three chief officers, Mr. Clementson, whom the Prince Regent had appointed Serjeant-at-Arms in 1811, was held to have acquired a vested interest in these fees.[2] Forced to recognize this interest, the Act directed that fees belonging to the Serjeant-at-Arms should be paid to the Commissioners after Mr. Clementson ceased to serve. Another restriction was imposed on this official's income. He had long held the post of housekeeper in addition to his own, drawing the salary, fees, and emoluments of both offices. As Parliament in 1800 had overlooked this fact, the Act of 1812 directed that, after existing interests lapsed, these two appointments should be consolidated, and both sets of fees handed over to the Commissioners. Any surplus remaining in their hands after remunerating the Chairman of Ways and Means was to be paid to the Consolidated Fund. The Deputy Serjeant was to receive 800l. in lieu of all other allowances, fees, and emoluments. As incidents of office which were significant of the period, it may be noted that, after the letters patent to Mr. Hatsell and Mr. Ley expired, the Act directed that "no clerk of the House of Commons should exercise the said office by deputy," and further, that offices under the Serjeant-at-Arms which had been accustomed to be sold should continue to be sold, and the proceeds paid over to the Commissioners.[3]

New Serjeant-at-Arms excepted from Act of 1800.

Housekeeper.

Surplus fees.

Deputy Serjeant.

Sale of offices.

[1] By 52 Geo. III. c. 11.
[2] We may be quite sure, therefore, that Mr. Clementson, in the teeth of the Act of 1800, chose the better income.
[3] 52 Geo. III. c. 11, ss. 14, 15.

In 1832 further progress was made in substituting salaries for fees by an Act,[1] which appropriated to the fee fund of the House of Commons the fees payable to the Speaker, and provided, in lieu of them and of his allowance of 5*l.* a day from the Civil List, a fixed salary of 6,000*l.* charged on the Consolidated Fund, free from all taxes. A subsequent statute, in 1834,[2] reduced the Speaker's salary to 5,000*l.*, and fixed that of the clerk at 2,000*l.*; clerk assistant, 1,500*l.*; second clerk assistant, 1,000*l.*[3]; Serjeant-at-Arms, 1,500*l.*; deputy Serjeant, 800*l.*; Speaker's secretary, 500*l.* At the same time the offices of principal Committee clerks and of clerks of engrossments, then held as sinecure offices, were abolished. In lieu of fees and perquisites the Speaker's secretary was granted a salary of 500*l.*, and his fees with those of the Committee and engrossing clerks were transferred to the Commissioners already mentioned. In all these cases existing interests received compensation.

Patent offices, like that of clerk of the Parliaments, were often disposed of long before any vacancy. For example, in 1783, during the lifetime of Mr. Ashley Cowper, who then held this post, George III. appointed as his successor Mr. Samuel Strutt, after whom, by the same letters patent, it was given to Mr. George Rose. Again, in 1795, Mr. Rose then being clerk, his Majesty granted the office to Sir George Rose, upon his father's death or resignation. All these appointments were for life, with a right to nominate all clerks at the table, and to serve by deputy. In 1824, it was provided by statute[4] that service by future clerks of Parliament should be rendered in person, and their patronage vested in the Lord Chancellor. Saving existing interests, the House of Lords also annexed fixed salaries to the offices

---

This statutory permission to the Serjeant-at-Arms to sell offices in his gift was repealed in 1825 (6 Geo. IV. c. 123, s. 3).

[1] 2 & 3 Will. IV. c. 105.

[2] 4 & 5 Will. IV. c. 70.

[3] In 1856 the provisions of this Act fixing the salary of the second Clerk Assistant were repealed (19 Vict. c. 1).

[4] 5 Geo. IV. c. 82.

of clerk of the Parliaments and his assistants. Fees belonging to these offices were then collected and carried to a general fund for defraying salaries and superannuation allowances.[1] How lucrative a post was enjoyed by the clerk of the Parliaments will be seen from the fact that, in 1829-30, Sir George Rose received 7,184*l*., of which only 40*l*. was salary; the remainder arose from fees.[2] At the same time, the clerk assistant received 4,000*l*., with an allowance of 500*l*. from the Treasury in lieu of an official house; additional clerk assistant, 2,500*l*.; reading clerk, 1,800*l*.; his assistant, 1,200*l*.; clerk of the journals, 1,391*l*.; copying clerk, 1,172*l*.[3] These salaries were regulated and fixed by the House of Lords, upon reports from Committees of 1824-7, and were paid from the fee fund, any deficiency being made good by the Treasury upon an address to the Crown.[4] In 1848 the retiring clerk assistant received a pension of 2,000*l*. a year charged on this fund.[5]

An account of the Lord Chancellor's income, in 1831-2, shows a total of 17,731*l*. derived as follows:—Salary at the Exchequer, after deductions, 4,829*l*.; secretary of bankrupts, 4,250*l*.; purse-bearer, for fees in bankruptcy, &c., 2,127*l*.; secretary of fines, 693*l*.; clerk of the Crown, 309*l*.; clerk of letters patent, 305*l*.; clerk of the hanaper, 1,125*l*.; fees at House of Lords, 4,089*l*. There were deductions of 3,025*l*., including 2,500*l*. paid to the Vice-Chancellor, leaving a net income of 14,706*l*.[6] All these fees were abolished in 1832, when a fixed salary of 10,000*l*. was substituted,[7] exclusive of the Lord Chancellor's income from the House of Lords. Upon an average taken during the previous five years, his emoluments there as Speaker, chiefly derived from private Bills,

Marginal notes:
Income of clerk of the Parliaments, 1829-30.

Assistant Clerks.

Lord Chancellor's fees, 1831-2.

---

[1] 56 Lords' Journ. 368, 441-2; June 19, 1824.

[2] Lords' Paper, 165, Sess. 1832. Sir George Rose was also allowed an unfurnished house in Old Palace Yard.

[3] Lords' Paper, 165, Sess. 1832,

p. 2.

[4] Ib.; and Lords' Committee of 1827 on office of Clerk of Parliaments; Rep. p. 2.

[5] Lords' Journ. Feb. 29, 1848.

[6] Lords' Paper, 257, Sess. 1832.

[7] 2 & 3 Will. IV. c. 122, s. 5.

were found, in 1832, to be 4,256*l.* per annum. A fixed
salary of 4,000*l.* was substituted by the House for this
income, the fees being paid into the general fee fund, as
under the arrangement of 1824.[1] Down to 1851, the Lord
Chancellor enjoyed this combined income of 14,000*l.* It
was then reduced to 10,000*l.*, including any payment made
to him from the fee fund, as Speaker of the Upper House.[2]

During ten years ending January 5, 1812, the Gentleman
Usher of the Black Rod received fees, upon the scale settled
in 1725, varying from 1,350*l.* to 3,381*l.* yearly. Within the
same period there was paid to him nearly 6,000*l.*, arising from
sales of offices. The total receipts were 32,573*l.*[3] In 1829-
30, Black Rod's income was 2,965*l.*, of which 344*l.* came
from salary, 2,621*l.* from fees on private Bills, judicial proceedings, and introductions of Peers upon creation.[4]

Black Rod's
income,
1803-12.

Down to the year 1821 the following officials in the House
of Commons continued to depend for their emoluments upon
fees:—clerk of the Committee of Privileges; the four out-
door clerks and their deputies, Speaker's secretary, officers
of the Engrossing Office and Private Bill Office, the door-
keepers, and others. A Select Committee of the House of
Commons which sat in 1821 were of opinion that fees
should not generally be reduced; nor were they " prepared
to recommend an entire abolition of individual emolument
from fees, which obviously tend to stimulate the exertions of
those persons during a period of accumulated business."[5] The
four out-door clerks were supposed to be in constant attendance on Committees, but never in fact attended, and their
offices in 1821 had become sinecures. Several officers of the
House received fees until the year 1836, when Mr. Hume
carried resolutions, founded upon the recommendations of

Fees of officers
in House of
Commons,
1821.

---

[1] 64 Lords' Journ. 436 ; August 8,
1832.

[2] 14 & 15 Vict. c. 83, s. 17.

[3] Lords' Paper, 95, Sess. 1812. In
these ten years the Yeoman Usher's

income amounted to 8,908*l.*

[4] Lords' Paper, 165, Sess. 1832.

[5] Report of Select Committee of
1821 on Private Bills.

various Select Committees on which he had served, and the practice was finally discontinued.[1]

Paymaster of House of Commons.

Further statutory provision was made in 1846[2] for collecting fees on private Bills, and a "Paymaster of the House of Commons" was appointed to receive them from the Commissioners, and pay to the various officers their salaries, allowances, and superannuations, with the expenses of the House.

Fees carried to Consolidated Fund, 1849.

But this system was abandoned in 1849,[3] when the whole proceeds of fees in the House of Commons were carried to the Consolidated Fund, and all charges and salaries (except that of the Speaker), after 1849, were paid by annual

Salaries, &c., paid by annual votes.

votes.[4] In 1869, the House of Lords also surrendered its fees to the Exchequer, on condition that its salaries and charges should be defrayed by an annual vote in the Lower House. All the fees are now paid in one office to the fee-clerk of the House of Commons, instead of being charged and collected there, as they used to be, by nine officers, in a great measure for their own benefit.

Changes in scale in House of Lords, 1824.

The scale of fees agreed to by the House of Lords in 1725 appears to have remained without alteration for a hundred years. It was then revised upon the report of a Select Committee in 1824. Though in some items higher, the fees were then generally less in their total amount than those

In House of Commons, 1847.

charged by the Commons.[5] In that House two tables of fees were in use until the year 1847: one regulating House fees, drawn up in 1731; the other, for the Committee and Private Bill Offices, in 1830. These fees consisted

---

[1] 31 Hansard, 214. These resolutions chiefly referred to gratuities paid by members. It is amusing now to note Hatsell's opinion in 1796 upon the probable effect of this reform:—"It has been sometimes proposed to take away the fees of the Speaker, clerk, &c., and to substitute in their place a salary from the public. The immediate consequence of this operation would be, that the overflowing of private applications, which

at present very much interrupt public business, would overwhelm everything else, and it would be impossible for the Speaker, or the officers under him, any longer to attend to any part of their public duty."—Precedents, II. 272.

[2] 9 & 10 Vict. c. 77.

[3] 12 & 13 Vict. c. 72.

[4] Ib. ss. 4, 5.

[5] Report of Lords' Committee of 1827 on Fees upon Private Bills.

of a great variety of small items, still charged on a system so complicated as not to be easily understood either by the parties who paid or the clerk who collected them.[1] On the second reading of each Bill there were eight different charges, imposed originally for the benefit of various officers, from the Speaker to the doorkeepers.[2] Fees were collected under the heads of House, Committee, Private Bill offices, housekeepers, messengers, and copying, inspection, and engrossing fees. House fees were for business transacted in the House itself, upon various stages of a Bill there. Even forty years ago abuses died hard. An old grievance still flourished in 1847. Notwithstanding continued complaints by promoters, multiplied sets of House fees were still charged, pursuant to the resolutions of 1751, upon Bills involving more than one object or interest.[3] No blame could now be attributed to officers; no vested interests were concerned in maintaining this antiquated, arbitrary, and oppressive system; the House adhered to it because it was a lucrative source of revenue, or from sheer indifference to complaint. An appeal was occasionally made to the Speaker in disputed cases, and, happily, he was no longer a judge in his own cause; but the system itself was wholly wrong and indefensible. A detailed statement shows that out of 30,681*l.* paid upon Bills which received the Royal assent in 1844, 6,906*l.* was for House fees; 11,159*l.*, Committee fees; 10,439*l.*, engrossing; 1,884*l.*, Private Bill office; and 291*l.*, doorkeepers.[4]

Incidence of fees charged in House of Commons.

On an urgent recommendation from a Committee appointed in 1847, the House of Commons requested its Speaker to

New scale of 1847.

---

[1] Second Report of Commons' Committee (1847) on Private Bills, p. 1.

[2] Ib.; Third Report, evidence of Mr. Dorington, fee clerk, p. 43.

[3] On Improvement Bills the fees were usually very large, owing to the numerous objects which they included. Mr. A. Grahame, Parliamentary agent, stated to a Com-

mittee in 1847, that he recollected a Bill on which he paid nine sets of fees. (Page 120 of evidence.) Another Parliamentary agent, Mr. G. Pritt, mentioned a Bill on which he had paid sixteen sets. (Ib. p. 71.)

[4] Third Report of Commons' Committee on Private Bills, 1847, p. 47.

cause a new table of fees to be prepared.[1] Accordingly several tables and resolutions as to fees of February 22, 1731, June 19, 1746, June 13, 1751, July 2, 1801, April 4, 1803, May 18, 1813, July 4, 1822, February 16, 1829, and July 22, 1830, were cancelled. A comparatively few large fees were now substituted for a multitude of small items, and were charged on the principal stages of a Bill, with a progressive increase in amount in proportion to proposed capital. The old system of double and treble, and many more sets of fees, upon the same Bill, by which promoters had so long been harassed, was discontinued. Engrossing being now abolished, an equivalent fee was imposed on third readings, in lieu of the old and heavy charge for this service. The year 1844 was taken by the Speaker as a fair average year on which to base a new scale. In 1844 the total amount of fees received in the House of Commons on private Bills was 40,963*l.*; on the 159 private Acts which passed, the fees were 30,681*l.* The scale of 1847 was arranged so as to produce, with a corresponding quantity of business, the same proportionate income.

New scale of 1852.

Only five years passed before further changes were made. A new table of fees, based on that of 1847, was settled by order of the House of Commons, in June, 1852. It provided for a minimum payment of 5*l.* on the petition, and 15*l.* for each of four stages, first, second, and third reading, and report; these fees to be increased according to the money raised or expended under a Bill, in conformity with the following scale :—

Ad valorem charges.

"If the sum be 50,000*l.* and under 100,000*l.*, twice the amount of such fees.

,,	100,000*l.*	,,	200,000*l.*,	three times	,,
,,	200,000*l.*	,,	300,000*l.*,	four times	,,
,,	300,000*l.*	,,	400,000*l.*,	five times	,,
,,	400,000*l.*	,,	500,000*l.*,	six times	,,
,,	500,000*l.*	,,	750,000*l.*,	seven times	,,
,,	750,000*l.*	,,	1,000,000*l.*,	eight times	,,
,,	1,000,000*l.*	,,	1,500,000*l.*,	nine times	,,
,,	1,500,000*l.*	,,	2,000,000*l.*,	ten times	,,

"And at the same rate of increase for every additional 500,000*l.* up to

[1] Com. Journ. May 14, 1847.

five millions, and further at the like rate of increase for every additional million beyond five millions."

This was the same differential scale as was sanctioned in 1847, and it pressed heavily upon railway and other Bills under which large capital was to be raised for the construction of works. These Bills, if the capital was over 1,500,000*l*. and under 2,000,000*l*., paid 650*l*. on their five stages in the House of Commons, besides Committee fees and fees for depositing plans, petitions, and documents in the Private Bill Office. On a capital of 4,500,000*l*., the five stages cost 975*l*.

In the Upper as well as the Lower House, when officers were paid by salaries, no vested interests stood in the way of a revision and substantial reduction of fees on private Bills. Sir John Shaw-Lefevre, clerk of the Parliaments, was then able to propose a much simpler scale, the effect of which was to reduce very considerably the charge upon Bills embracing objects more or less of a public character, and increase the charge on schemes of trading companies. It was stated in 1858 that, as the result of this reduction, the total amount of fees did not pay establishment expenses, though they more than defrayed the cost of that part of the establishment which dealt with private Bills.[1] *Reductions in House of Lords.*

In 1862 a Commons' Committee on Standing Orders' revision were "strongly of opinion that a reduction in some of the fees of the House, and other charges paid in respect of private Bills, may be made and should take effect as early as possible." This recommendation was repeated in 1863 by a Select Committee on private business, who showed that *Commons' inquiries of 1862-3.*

---

[1] Lords' Committee on Private Bills, 1858; evidence of Sir J. Shaw-Lefevre, p. 137. A Parliamentary agent, examined in 1858, stated that, upon the last forty unopposed Bills passed by his firm the average amount of fees charged by both Houses for each Bill was 199*l*. On the same number of opposed Bills, the average fees were 403*l*. Of House fees, the maximum amount paid on any single opposed Bill was 1,344*l*. According to this witness, the expense of carrying a Bill through Parliament had been considerably reduced since 1845, and the course of procedure rendered much more certain and uniform. Ib., evidence of Mr. C. E. Thomas, pp. 91—2.

the revenue from fees in both Houses was greater than the cost of carrying on this business, and suggested that *ad valorem* charges should be abandoned. The Committee made this suggestion, because the trouble and expense incurred by Parliament in private Bill legislation did not depend upon the amount of capital raised; and because, though great works and correspondingly large capital might lead to protracted contests, daily fees charged in Committee were the legitimate source from which any additional cost should be defrayed. They also recommended generally "that the scale of fees payable upon proceedings connected with private legislation should be revised so as to meet, but not exceed, the expenses thrown upon the House by private business."

The suggestion that differential rates should be abandoned was not adopted; but in 1864, the reduced scale now in force was made a Standing Order.[1] Initial fees of 5*l.* and 15*l.*, charged upon the petition, first, second and third readings and report, now rise in conformity with the following moderate scale, according to the money to be raised or expended under any Bill:—

If the sum be 100,000*l.* and under 500,000*l.* twice the amount of such fees.
　　　　　" 　　500,000*l.* 　　" 　1,000,000*l.* three times 　　　　"
　　　　　" 　1,000,000*l.* and above 　　　　four times 　　　　"

The maximum charge upon a Bill in respect of the five specified stages is now, therefore, 260*l.*, as compared with the unlimited sliding scale previously in force; while Bills authorizing works, with capital powers below 100,000*l.*, only pay the minimum rates.

Acting on the report of the Standing Orders' Committee in 1862, the Speaker directed the clerk of fees to submit a more equitable distribution of other House and Committee charges. One change recommended in this report was that, instead of charging promoters a fee of 10*l.* a day if they appear in Committee by counsel, and 5*l.* if they

Marginal notes:

Suggested abandonment of *ad valorem* scale.

Reductions of 1864: existing rate of *ad valorem* charges.

Fees on employment of counsel in Commons.

---

[1] Com. Journ. July 27, 1864.

appear by agents, a uniform charge of 5l. should be made in both cases; and that, instead of 5l. and 3l. in like cases, petitioners should pay 3l. each day, whether they appear by counsel or agents.[1] Promoters, however, continue to pay a double charge for each day's appearance by counsel. This distinction, which does not seem easily justified, has been abolished in the case of opponents of a private Bill, who now pay 2l. a day, whether they employ counsel or agents.[2] These heavy fines upon the employment of counsel and agents were first imposed in 1847. They are based upon the old, but much smaller, fees imposed for the benefit of officers in each House, but especially of the Serjeant-at-Arms, who was entitled to ten shillings " for every counsel pleading at bar or before any Committee." No charge was then made if agents were employed, for they were formerly themselves officers of Parliament. A daily charge for Committees is said to be in conformity with the ancient usage of Parliament.[3] If counsel are heard at the bar, a proceeding now very rare, each party employing them pays 10l.

Fees now charged by the House of Lords differ materially in arrangement and amount from those in the other House, and contain more numerous items. For first readings, equivalent in the Commons to petitions for leave to introduce Bills, there is a charge of five guineas. The heaviest fee is on second readings; and here a distinction is drawn between personal and local Bills in favour of the former. Included in this class are estate and patent Bills, each of which pays 81l.; on disabilities, removal, divorce, naturalization and name Bills, the fee for a second reading is reduced to 27l. No fees are charged upon two other kinds of personal Bills— those for indemnity or restoration of rights or dignities.

Existing scale in House of Lords.

Personal Bills.

---

[1] Commons' Committee on Private Bill Business, 1863; Appendix, p. 342.

[2] Commons' Table of Fees, 1887.

[3] Third Report of Commons' Committee on Private Bills, 1847; evidence of Mr. Dorington, fee clerk, p. 46.

Local Bills in House of Lords.

On the second reading of local Bills, those relating to charitable, literary, or scientific purposes, promoted for no private profit or advantage, pay 27*l.* Bills restricted to gas or water supply pay on an *ad valorem* scale, according to capital, from 54*l.* to 135*l.* On other Bills the fees begin at 81*l.*, and rise to a like maximum. Committee fees vary, as in the Commons, according to the employment of counsel or agents,

Committee fees.

Counsel and agents.

but are less in total amount than those in that House. The effect, however, in discouraging the employment of counsel is the same. An order, costing one guinea, has to be obtained, giving leave for counsel to appear before a Committee. On each day of such appearance, what is called a bar fee of 3*l.* 10*s.* is charged both to promoters and opponents. On the first day this fee is supplemented by a charge of 4*l.* 4*s.* for " attendance ; " and opponents pay, in addition, 3*l.* 1*s.* as a " Committee fee." For the first day's hearing, therefore, promoters represented by counsel pay 7*l.* 14*s.* ; for every subsequent day, 3*l.* 10*s.* ; that is, the bar fee alone. Opponents employing counsel pay, on the first day, 10*l.* 15*s.* ; on the second day, 3*l.* 10*s.* ; and for every subsequent day till the inquiry closes, 4*l.* 10*s.* If they employ an agent, they pay fees of 3*l.* 1*s.* on the first and second day ; for every subsequent day, 1*l.* Promoters pay nothing beyond the ordinary Committee fees if they employ agents. Here, again, personal pay on a lower scale than local Bills. On a third reading, Bills containing not more than twenty pages of print pay

Provisional Order Confirmation Bills.

10*l.* ; others, 15*l.* As in the Commons, no fees are charged to promoters of Provisional Orders ; the confirmation Bill is treated as a public Bill. Petitioners against Provisional Orders pay the same fees as those charged to petitioners against local Bills.[1]

Amount of fees in House of Lords, 1812-26.

No continuous record, even in recent times, has been published by either House of the revenue derived from fees on private Bills. During the fifteen years from 1812 to 1826

---

[1] Scale of Fees, House of Lords, 1887.

inclusive, the amount of these fees in the House of Lords was as follows :—1812, 17,932*l.*; 1813, 18,839*l.*; 1814, 19,193*l.*; 1815, 15,023*l.*; 1816, 11,015*l.*; 1817, 9,172*l.*; 1818, 10,429*l.*; 1819, 10,362*l.*; 1820, 11,403*l.*; 1821, 12,955*l.*; 1822, 12,409*l.*; 1823, 12,199*l.*; 1824, 15,828*l.*; 1825, 21,090*l.*; 1826, 14,727*l.* Total, 217,576*l.*[1] Of this total, the fees received from Inclosure and Drainage Bills were 47,743*l.*; Road and Railway Bills, 66,489*l.*; Navigation, Harbour, Dock, Bridge, &c., Bills, 16,323*l.*; Gas and other Bills, 52,406*l.*; Estate Bills, 29,338*l.*; Divorce Bills, 1,373*l.*; Naturalization, Restoration and Name Bills, 2,693*l.* As to Road Bills, a resolution of the House of Commons in 1829, pursuant to a recom- Road Bills. mendation from one of its Committees two years previously,[2] directs that fees incurred upon renewals of Turnpike Acts shall be paid by the Treasury. The fees in both Houses upon each bill for amending or continuing Turnpike Road Acts then averaged about 200*l.*

In 1881 the total fees on 210 private Bills in the Upper Proceeds in House of House was 28,555*l.*, of which 24,891*l.* was paid by promoters, Lords, and 3,653*l.* by opponents. England contributed 20,587*l.*, 1881-2. Scotland 4,662*l.*, and Ireland 3,335*l.* of this amount. In 1882, a Session of greater business activity, 261 private Bills came before the Lords, and brought 40,878*l.* in fees. Promoters paid 35,260*l.* of this sum. Opponents, indeed, contribute a comparatively small proportion of fees in either House. Nor is the whole amount received on Scotch and Irish Bills considerable. In the Lords, it was 4,971*l.* and 1,958*l.* respectively in 1882.[3]

---

[1] Lords' Committee of 1827 on Private Bill Fees, App. p. 102.

[2] Committee on Turnpike Trusts Renewal Bills, 1827. A similar recommendation was made by a Committee on private Bill fees, in 1821.

[3] Lords' Paper 2, Sess. 1884. In the Session of 1871, Mr. D. C. Heron, who strongly advocated the transfer of Irish private Bill business to Ire- land, proposed to establish a separate tribunal for that country. Finding, however, that the fees annually payable on Irish Bills would be inadequate to support the new tribunal, and that a balance must be contributed out of general taxation, the motion was allowed to drop, and was not renewed in a subsequent Session. (204 Hansard, 257 ; 207 ib., 1539.)

Revenue in
House of
Commons,
1837-46.

In the House of Commons the revenue from fees has always been much more considerable than in the Upper House, as more Bills originate there, and some go no farther. In 1837 this revenue amounted to 52,101*l.*; 1838, 22,412*l.*; 1839, 28,326*l.*; 1840, 29,917*l.*; 1841, 24,618*l.*; 1842, 23,028*l.*; 1843, 23,758*l.*; 1844, 40,963*l.*; 1845, 105,412*l.*; 1846, 201,643*l.*[1] Periods of depression and revival in trade leave their trace in these figures. The railway mania accounts for the enormous yield of 1846. Upon the transfer, in 1845, of the Commons' fees on private Bills to the Consolidated Fund, there was a sum to the credit of the fee fund amounting to 220,000*l.*, which the Chancellor of the Exchequer found an acceptable windfall and appropriated to the public.[2]

Windfall for
Exchequer,
1845.

Revenue,
1853-63.

Notwithstanding reductions in the scale, the produce of subsequent years in the House of Commons was large. It was 75,566*l.* in 1853; 61,251*l.* in 1854; 42,865*l.* in 1855; 31,057*l.* in 1856; 44,943*l.* in 1857; 41,101*l.* in 1858; 42,706*l.* in 1859; 57,094*l.* in 1860; 76,533*l.* in 1861; 68,369*l.* in 1862;[3] and 66,614*l.* in 1863.[4] Of these totals, payments by opponents varied from twelve to twenty-one per cent.[3] During ten years, 1853—62, the total fees received at the House of Commons amounted to 541,489*l.* In this period, salaries and charges in the House of Commons amounted to 591,605*l.*[5] The fee fund, therefore, covered, within about 5,000*l.* a year, the whole establishment expenses of the House, including salaries of Speaker, Serjeant-at-Arms, and clerks at the table, although the larger part of the staff properly formed a public charge, as it served for the despatch of public business.[6] In 1863, the estimate voted

Fees and
establishment
charges.

[1] Commons' Committee on Private Bills, 1847; Third Report, evidence of Mr. Dorington, fee clerk, p. 46.

[2] Commons' Committee on Standing Orders Revision, 1862; evidence of Mr. Jones, clerk of the Fees, p. 81.

[3] Com. Return 500, Sess. 1862.

[4] Ib. 184, Sess. 1864.

[5] Including those voted in the annual estimates and those charged on the Consolidated Fund. Commons' Return 500 (1862).

[6] Com. Committee on Private Bill Legislation, 1863, App. p. 346.

for the House of Commons' establishment was 50,785*l.*, with 7,700*l.* paid to the Speaker, Chairman of Ways and Means, and Serjeant-at-Arms, making 58,485*l.* The fees paid into the Consolidated Fund defrayed the whole of this expense, and left a balance of 8,129*l.*[1]

In later years, owing to reductions, and in large measure, also, to the increased number of Provisional Orders[2] in lieu of private Bills, there has been a considerable decrease in the yield of fees. In 1869, they amounted in the House of Commons to only 23,377*l.*, in 1870 to 25,219*l.*; but these were years of exceptional depression, when the number of local and personal Acts passed was only 160 and 167 respectively. In 1872, 313 Bills yielded 38,112*l.*; in 1873, 347 Bills, 44,420*l.*; in 1874, 305 Bills, 33,021*l.*; in 1875, 273 Bills, 32,306*l.*; in 1876, 276 Bills, 32,145*l.*; in 1877, 285 Bills, 32,209*l.*; in 1878, 272 Bills, 32,500*l.*; in 1879, 247 Bills, 30,223*l.*; in 1880, 225 Bills, 27,857*l.*; in 1881, 245 Bills, 31,567*l.*; in 1882, 349 Bills, 45,795*l.* The total in these eleven years thus received by the Lower House was 380,160*l.*[3] No corresponding figures are available relating to the House of Lords, but it will be seen that, in relinquishing its private legislation, Parliament would abandon a considerable and legitimate source of revenue. And as the establishment charges of the House would still have to be met, the deficit must be made good out of annual revenue; in other words, by shifting to the shoulders of taxpayers a burden at present voluntarily borne by suitors for private Bills and their opponents.

Later proceeds of fees.

[1] Com. Return 184, Sess. 1864.
[2] Provisional Order Confirmation Bills are free from fees (*ante*, p. 748), and are even printed at the public expense.
[3] Com. Return 355, Sess. 1883.

CHAPTER XX.

STANDING ORDERS: SESSIONAL ORDERS AND RESOLUTIONS:
HOURS FOR PRIVATE BILLS: POSTPONEMENT TO PUBLIC
BUSINESS: MEMBERS PERSONALLY INTERESTED: PRESSURE
USED BY PEERS ON LOWER HOUSE: NOTICES: PLANS:
PETITIONS FOR BILLS: REFERENCE TO JUDGES: ESTATE
AND DIVORCE BILLS: LOCAL BILLS: ESTIMATES: SUB-
SCRIPTION CONTRACTS: DEPOSITS AND PENALTIES: PAYING
INTEREST OUT OF CAPITAL: EXCLUSIVE JURISDICTION OF
COMMONS OVER BILLS IMPOSING CHARGES: DISTRIBUTION
OF PRIVATE BUSINESS BETWEEN THE TWO HOUSES.

Standing
Orders.

EACH House of Parliament has its Standing Orders for the
regulation of public business and debate, as well as of
proceedings relating to private Bills. These Orders have
sometimes differed materially, and in complying with them
promoters have therefore been subjected to needless difficulty.
Although still not identical, the conditions of procedure in
each House are now substantially alike, save at one stage of
an opposed Bill. In 1864, the Commons framed, under their
Standing Orders, a new procedure, by creating a special Court
for determining whether petitioners against a Bill have any
locus standi.[1] The House of Lords adhered to its old system,
leaving its Committees to decide, as before, upon all questions
which involve the right of petitioners to a hearing.

Sessional
Orders.

Sessional Orders are agreed to at the beginning of every
Session, and fix the last days for presenting petitions, reading

---

[1] *Post,* p. 805 *et seq.*

Bills a first time, and receiving reports on such Bills.   These Orders are distinguished from Standing Orders by being only in force for the Session in which they are adopted, whereas Standing Orders remain in force until suspended or repealed by vote of the House.   As procedure in private *Resolutions.* business has often been enlarged or restrained by resolutions, it is necessary to take note of them here, although they do not necessarily come under the head of either Standing or Sessional Orders.

Orders of the Upper House appear to have been first *Lords' Orders* printed in 1642, when the Earl of Lincoln, Lord Wharton, *first printed* Lord North, and Lord Robartes were directed to "send for *1642.* what printers they think fit, to consider of a print that the orders and declarations set forth by this House shall be printed in."[1]   There is a report from the Committee of Privileges in 1664 that, as the old roll of Standing Orders was worn out, they had caused a new roll to be engrossed for use, and the other laid up among the records of Parliament.[2] These orders refer chiefly, if not exclusively, to public matters.   It appears to have been only in 1707 that Standing Orders relating to private Bills were ordered to be printed at the beginning of every Session, "to the end all persons concerned may take notice thereof."[3]

One of the earliest collections of Standing Orders in the *Study of* House of Commons bears no date, but appears to have been *Parliamen-* printed about the year 1745.[4]   In somewhat sarcastic lan- *and forms* guage, which we should expect to be used by some person *recommended.* who had suffered from a stringent application of these rules, we are told :—"And this is a known truth, that men

---

[1] 5 Lords' Journ. 214 ; July 16, 1642. The orders and declarations here referred to were no doubt chiefly those made "for the safety of the kingdom."

[2] 11 Lords' Journ. 597 ; April 20, 1664.

[3] 18 Ib. 336 ; Nov. 7, 1707.

[4] In the library of the House of Commons there is a copy, which, with other official documents, the author had an opportunity of consulting, for the purposes of this work, by the courtesy of the Speaker, the Right Hon. Arthur W. Peel.

of very slender parts, by rendering themselves thorough masters of the forms of the House, have made themselves considerable, and fancied themselves to be more so; and by the mere dint of calling to order, and quoting journals and precedents, have sometimes defeated arguments they could not answer, and triumphed over talents and abilities that infinitely transcended their own; which is all that need be said to recommend a study hitherto, perhaps, too much neglected."

Rules affecting private business. Careful study of all rules affecting private Bills has always been equally necessary by petitioners for or against these Bills, or by persons acting on their behalf. During three centuries, at least, orders made by the two Houses have prescribed, more or less in detail, procedure upon private legislation. As private business has increased, so has the necessity for more elaborate rules, and almost every Session has seen some change or addition. It is only possible, therefore, to notice here a few of the more striking developments which have occurred in this code and in the practice depending upon it. In other parts of this work many Standing Orders are mentioned which deal with subjects there treated.

Early hours for private business. A manuscript volume in the library of the House of Commons, written about the year 1680,[1] mentions the early hours at which private business used to be taken. In 1572, the House of Commons departed from its usual custom of sitting only in the forenoons,[2] and ordered sittings "at afternoons from three of the clock till six"; but only to proceed in private Bills, "and not to go to the question of any such Bill if it concern any town or shire, unless the Knights of such shire or the burgess of such town shall then be present."[3]

---

[1] Observations, Rules, and Orders collected by Ambrose Kelly, clerk to the Committees of the House of Commons, on "such matters as are necessary and fit for every member of that House (to know) touching their proceedings." This volume deals chiefly with public business.

[2] Eight a.m. appears to have been a usual time for meeting, and the day's record in the journals showed by a *post meridiem* what business was done after noon.

[3] 1 Com. Journ. 101.

In the first Parliament of James I., however, it was ordered that the House should meet at seven a.m., and that the time until nine o'clock should be spent in the reading of private Bills. No Committee was to sit after eight o'clock, when the House was sitting, without special order.[1] During the next reigns the House usually met at eight a.m., and private Bills and business were proceeded with " until nine o'clock, in such order as the House shall think fit; the debate of such of them as shall not be despatched at the hour of nine shall be adjourned till the next day."[2] Public Bills were appointed to be taken between nine and twelve o'clock, and " if any man shall move the members of the House contrary to that, he shall incur the censure of the House."[3]

Gradually a later hour for taking Private Bills was appointed. In 1691, it was ordered that no such Bills be proceeded upon after ten o'clock.[4] In the year following this time was enlarged, and six years afterwards we find an order " that no private Bill be read a third time before eleven o'clock."[5]

Change to later hours.

When great affairs of State were pending, the House of Commons often postponed private business. In 1621, the petition for grievances being then under consideration, it was ordered, " all public business shall be preferred, and no private till the public done." There was a protest from Sir Samuel Sandys that some public Bills were of a private, and other private Bills of a public nature, but it was not heeded.[6] Postponements of private business in the seventeenth century for a week or for longer periods, are frequently recorded.[7] Sometimes, as in 1642, the postponement was " till a certain future day." [8] A month before its dissolution in 1659-60, the House of Commons resolved, " that no private business be

Private postponed to public business.

---

[1] Order of May 2, 1624.
[2] Resolution, December 7, 1660.
[3] Order of July 26, 1641.
[4] Order of November 24, 1691.
[5] April 6, 1698.

[6] 1 Com. Journ. 623.
[7] 2 Ib. 498; 3 Ib. 472; 6 Ib. 138, 349.
[8] 5 Ib. 530; 6 Ib. 28, 178, 269 *et seq.*

admitted during the sitting of this Parliament." [1] After
the Restoration, a Royal message in 1661 urged the House
to pass the Bill of Indemnity, "and that you will, for
the present, lay aside all private business, that so, betaking
yourselves only to the public, you may be ready to adjourn
by the middle of the next month." On receiving this message,
the House at once complied with its terms, and " ordered
that no more private Bills be brought in, nor any new
private business be taken into consideration but such as is
already depending; and that to be speeded; except a Bill
for some of the inhabitants of the town of Plymouth, which
Mr. Samuel Trelawney hath leave to bring in." [2]

Special appointments of private business. Another form, used in 1690, was to order that no private
business should be taken after ten o'clock "until the Bills for
their Majesties' supplies be finished"; [3] or, as in 1656-7, to
order that it should be taken only on one day a week, either
by Committees or in the House itself. [4] An order frequently
met with in and after 1624 is that no more Bills should be
brought in during the Session, [5] or until " such as be depending be finished." [6] On the other hand, particular days were
set apart for receiving and hearing petitions or Bills; or for
considering private business only; and in 1621 the House
of Commons appointed a meeting " every Saturday in the
afternoon," for these affairs. [7]

In dealing with private interests it was above all things
necessary that members should be clean-handed. The Upper
House recognized no necessity for orders on this head.
But from a resolution passed by the Commons in 1692,
members must sometimes have yielded to small tempta-
Treating of members, 1692. tions:—" Resolved that no member of this House do presume to accept of any entertainment at any public-house,
for the carrying-on any matter under the consideration of

---

[1] 7 Com. Journ. 849.
[2] 8 Ib. 278; June 22, 1661.
[3] 10 Ib. 529.
[4] 7 Ib. 478.
[5] 1 Ib. 702 et seq.; 10 Ib. 131; 11 Ib. 501.
[6] 10 Ib. 385, 474; 11 Ib. 252.
[7] 1 Ib. 596 et seq.

the House, upon pain of incurring the censure of this House."[1] Again, in 1695, it was resolved, "that the offer Bribery. of any money, or other advantage, to any member of Parliament for the promoting of any matter whatsoever depending, or to be transacted, in Parliament, is a high crime and misdemeanour, and tends to the subversion of the English constitution."[2] It will be remembered that, in 1695, Sir John Trevor, Speaker of the House of Commons, and Mr. Hungerford, Chairman of a Committee on a private Bill, were expelled for accepting "gratifications" from the promoters.[3] The period was one of great corruption in Parliament.

It may be assumed that no members personally interested in a Bill were knowingly appointed upon any Committee, for upon proceedings in the House of Commons itself care was taken to secure impartiality. In 1604, before committing the Duke of Somerset's estate Bill, it was "moved that Mr. Seymour, a member of the House, and a party, might go forth during the debate, which was conceived to be agreeable with former precedent in like cases, and was so ordered ; and Mr. Seymour went presently forth by the door." This motion was made by "Mr. Kyrton, servant and officer to the Earl of Hertford," who was another party to the Bill ; whereupon Mr. Seymour's friends in the House moved "that all my Lord of Hertford's officers might go forth also." This resolution was "not urged nor assented" to by the House, because these members were not themselves parties to the Bill.[4]

Exclusion from debate of members personally interested.

A similar question arose in 1664 upon a "Bill for settling differences between the towns of Great and Little Yarmouth touching the lading and unlading of herrings, and other commodities." A Committee reported to the Commons that

Bill to settle differences between Great and Little Yarmouth.

[1] 10 Ib. 769.
[2] 11 Ib. 331.
[3] *Ante*, p. 391.
[4] This I take to be the meaning of an entry in the margin of Com. Journ. (I. 237). The presence, and

sure influence, of these nominees of peers are suggestive. In another notice of the same debate (Ib. 990) is the quaint entry, "Moved also that my Lord of Hartford's officers go forth ; but winked at."

they had "examined and heard the claims and interest of
both towns, and upon due and serious consideration of the
whole matter had, with some amendments, agreed the Bill."
Upon motion then made that the Bill and amendments be
engrossed, there was a division, with eighty-one yeas against
eighty noes. Sir Robert Paston, who voted with the yeas,
had presented this Bill, with his petition annexed. His vote
was therefore objected to. "Sir Robert, to avoid engaging
the House in a debate, freely offered to withdraw, and that
no advantage should be had by his being told with the yeas;
and the voices being then equal, Mr. Speaker declared himself with the yeas."[1] But the practice is now well established that personal interest disqualifies a member from
voting upon a private Bill, though the degree of interest
which involves disqualification may be disputable.[2]

Pressure by
peers.

While, by resolution and practice, care was taken to secure
impartiality, the Commons were not able, in early times,
to guard against personal pressure brought to bear upon
the House by powerful peers, in addition to the influence
and voting power they commanded there by servants and
other nominees who were returned as burgesses or knights at
their bidding. Sometimes peers who promoted Bills came

Duke of
Norfolk per-
sonally re-
quests the
Commons to
pass his Bill,
A.D. 1553.

into the Lower House to make suit for their passing. There
was much opposition in 1553 to a measure reversing the
Duke of Norfolk's attainder, as interests in his lands had
meanwhile been created and would be injured by the Bill.
Thereupon, "the Duke of Norfolk came into the House, and
made request that the House would pass his Bill, showing
that, for the causes betwixt him and the patentees, he would
abide the order of certain Lords and others to whom the
matter was compromitted; and if the arbiters did not agree,
then the Queen to make a final end, as it should please her
Highness."[3]

[1] 8 Com. Journ. 594; February 4,
1664-5.
[2] See division on Metropolis Water

Bill, 1884; *ante*, p. 194, n.
[3] 1 Com. Journ. 32; December 4,
1553.

Similar questions arose in 1554, upon the Bill to revive and restore the Bishopric of Durham, as Edward VI. had granted to Sir Francis Jebson and other persons patents for some of the episcopal lands. This Bill had been rejected by the Commons in 1553.[1] But in the next Session "the Bishop of Durham came into the House and declared his whole cause, forcing (*sic*) his Bill, and his trouble by the Duke of Northumberland, and required the House to consider the Bill."[2] Next day, after arguments, "the House did divide, and the number that said yea to the Bill were 201 persons, and against but 120, so the Bill passed with yea."[3]

So, in the same Session, Lord Willoughby, "making suit to come into this House, required the House to favour" a Bill assuring certain lands to him, after the Duchess of Suffolk and her husband. This Bill was much debated, counsel were heard at the bar for the Duchess, a Committee was appointed, and at its last stage, on the last day of the Session, the measure was rejected by 120 votes to 73.[4] In Queen Mary's reign the peers of her faith used peremptory language. The Commons' Journal notes another visit, in 1555, from the Duke of Norfolk, who, "with four Serjeants-at-Law, came to this House, and required his Bill to be furthered, and declared the special points of his Bill, and then departed out. Whereupon, Mr. S. Petre, with three other members, were sent to him to show him that the House would consider the case."[5] In 1628, more civil language was used by a peer:—"The Lord of Devonshire desireth that all that are unsatisfied with his Bill will, at the Committee this afternoon, declare their objections; wherein he hopeth to satisfy them; for he would be loth to offer anything to the House which shall be thought un-

Marginal notes:
Bishop of Durham's Bill, 1554.

Lord Willoughby.

Duke of Norfolk, A.D. 1555.

Earl of Devon, A.D. 1628.

[1] 1 Com. Journ. 32.
[2] Ib. 34; April 18, 1554. The Bishop was Cuthbert Tunstall, the last Catholic who filled this rich see. Bishops of Durham were princes palatine,
drawing enormous revenues and exercising royal powers within their see.
[3] Ib.; April 19, 1554.
[4] Ib. 41; January 16, 1554–5.
[5] Ib. 44; November 18, 1555.

C.P.—VOL. II.　　　　　　3 C

fitting."[1] Occasionally, peers returned thanks to the Commons, through Mr. Speaker, for their "favour and readiness" in passing private Bills.[2] Lord Arundell further promised "that both by example and otherwise he would strive to merit of the Commonwealth."[3]

Necessity of notices on private Bills.

When public legislation is proposed, the whole community has notice through its representatives. Private legislation, asked for in the interests of particular bodies or persons, stands in a different category, and unless some restrictions were put upon promoters, private interests might often be prejudiced by provisions never heard of until they had received statutory authority. But before private Bills were printed, or newspapers existed, notice was far more essential than it is now, and it was also given with far greater difficulty. Before the year 1705 there was no obligation upon promoters to print private Bills. In that year the Commons ordered all such Bills to be printed before the first reading ;[4] an order renewed in following Sessions.[5] In 1722 it was made a Standing Order, with an addition that no private Bill be read before printed copies had been delivered to members.[6] A similar rule was made by the Upper House in the same Session.[7] This condition ensured a certain publicity, but other steps to prevent surprise or injustice to individuals had long before been necessary.

Order that private Bills be printed, 1705.

London fishmongers, 1511.

In the Lords' Journals the first mention of notice occurs upon the consideration of a Bill of 1511, attempting to regulate the price of salt and fresh fish in London, and the status of retailers there :—" Memorandum.—It is agreed by the Lords that stock fishmongers and fishmongers be warned to be here, upon Thursday next, by nine of the clock."[8] We are not told how this warning was given, whether orally to indiv-

---

[1] 1 Com. Journ. 906; May 29, 1628.
[2] Lord Southampton, in 1604; 1 Com. Journ. 183.
[3] Ib. 915; June 18, 1628.
[4] 15 Ib. 18; November 12, 1705.
[5] Ib. 212 ; December 12, 170. 16 Ib. 50; December 20, 1703. Ib. 229 ; November 30, 1709.
[6] 20 Ib. 161; March 5, 1722.
[7] 18 Lords' Journ. 20.
[8] 1 Ib. 12.

duals or by letter to the Fishmongers' Company. There was less difficulty in dealing with personal Bills, such as those affecting estates, which for at least two centuries continued the chief source of private business in Parliament. In both Houses, but especially in the Lords, Committees were enjoined by frequent orders to require strict proof of assents to the provisions of these Bills by all persons mentioned in them.

Mr. Speaker sometimes gave notice to parties by direction of the Commons, as in the year 1562-3, when the Journals contain this entry :—"For that it is said that T. Elrington hath interest in the iron mill in the town of Shere, in Surrey, whereof the Bill is to put down the same : it is resolved that Mr. Speaker shall direct his letter to him in the name of the House, to come and shew, if he will, for saving his estate therein."[1] Two similar instances are recorded in 1604.[2] One of these occurred upon a Bill to confirm the lands of Henry Butler, on the marriage of his son William, and this was Mr. Speaker's letter to the father :— *Notice by Mr. Speaker.*

Butler's Estate Bill, 1604.

"After my hearty commendations : Whereas a Bill preferred concerning the assurance of some of your lands, upon the marriage of your son, William Butler, hath received a second reading, and a commitment in the Commons' House of Parliament : the Committees have made a report that they conceive it just that notice be given unto you before any further proceeding : Which the House hath accordingly ordered and commanded me, their Speaker, to do ; requiring your answer, immediately upon the receipt hereof, that there may be a due and speedy proceeding of the Bill, if you so like it. And so I bid you farewell. From Boswell-house this 7th of May, 1604.
"Your loving friend,
"EDWARD PHELIPS, Speaker.
"To my very loving friend, Henry Butler, Esq., at Rawcliffe, in Lancashire. Delivered to Mr. William Butler, his son, to be conveyed accordingly."

Several orders were made by the Commons in 1700, to *Orders of 1700-5.*

[1] 1 Com. Journ. 63.   [2] Ib. 202, 203.

3 c 2

secure that Bills should not pass without notice to parties interested. In reporting every private Bill, the chairman was directed to state whether its allegations had been examined, and also to acquaint the House whether the parties concerned had given their consents. A week's public notice in the lobby of the sittings of each Committee was also directed, with a three days' interval between the several readings of all private Bills.[1] In 1705 the Lords went further, and ordered that in future "all parties concerned in the consequences of any private Bill" should sign the petition for leave to introduce it.[2]

Local Bills.
Much greater difficulty used to be experienced in securing proper publicity for local Bills, by which, though no person was named, a whole community might be more or less affected.

Order of 1572.
As some guarantee for a proper representation of interests, the Commons ordered in 1572 "that no private Bill, if it concerns any shire or town, shall go to the question unless the knights of such shire, or the burgesses of such town, be then present."[3] The object was praiseworthy, but, if literally observed, this rule must have enabled any local member, by mere absence and without active opposition, to stop the progress of any local measure. As, however, the Commons asserted their exclusive jurisdiction in initiating Bills which imposed any charge, it devolved especially upon them to see that such Bills did not slip through Parliament without proper notice and discussion.

Lindsey Level Drainage Bill, 1675.
A first attempt to give formal notice upon something like the modern system was made in 1675 upon a Bill for draining Lindsey Level, Lincolnshire. This Bill was committed on November 20, and appointed to be heard at the bar on the first Wednesday after Christmas. During this interval, the House ordered that a written summons be delivered to

[1] 13 Com. Journ. 333; Feb. 15, 1700-1. They were made Standing Orders in 1722-3. 20 Ib. 161.

[2] 18 Lords' Journ. 105.

[3] 1 Com. Journ. 101; *ante*, p. 754.

clergymen in twenty-eight specified parishes, towns, and villages, "to be by them published in their several churches, after divine service," and also affixed to the church doors. The same summons was also to be left with high constables in the several hundreds affected. Lords, owners, and commoners were to take this as a sufficient notice of the proposed hearing at bar.[1] Similar methods of summons must then have been usual, for in 1678 a Bill for erecting a new parochial church in St. Martin's-in-the-fields was recommitted, because "there was no summons sent forth to the parties concerned therein." Notices were therefore ordered to be affixed at the church doors, and read in church, informing owners, occupiers, and other parishioners of the time and place appointed for the next meeting of the Committee, so that "such of them as think themselves concerned may then and there attend, and be heard to the Bill."[2]

Church of St. Martin's-in-the-fields Bill, 1678.

Precise orders for notice were first made in 1707, upon applications for Irish Estate Bills. All promoters of these Bills were then required "from henceforth to give public notice of their intention, by affixing printed papers, setting forth their pretensions, in each of the four Courts of Justice in Dublin, during the whole term which shall precede the Session of Parliament, as also in the chief assize town in each county where the lands happen to lie, for one month at least before the Bill be brought in. Resolved, that there be thirty days at least between the first and second reading of every such private Bill."[3]

Irish Estate Bills, 1707.

Drainage of lands, requiring united efforts with special legislation, and improvements in navigation, were followed soon after the middle of the eighteenth century by canals, inclosures, and roads.[4] The want of regular system in securing publicity for these local Bills came then to be keenly felt. They interfered with rights of ownership and occupa-

Canal, Drainage, Navigation and Inclosure Bills.

[1] 9 Com. Journ. 381.
[2] Ib. 490.
[3] 15 Ib. 530; A.D. 1707.

[4] *Ante,* Vol. I. pp. 10, 13—27, 33—42.

tion extending over wide districts, and it is probable that much hardship and injustice were often occasioned by private statutes of this nature, the full effect of which only became known when it was too late to oppose and hopeless to repeal them. These evils induced the House of Commons, in 1774, to draw up orders requiring that notices of intended inclosure, drainage, and improvement Bills be posted on church doors, and proclaimed in open Court at Quarter Sessions.[1] Turnpike road Bills, besides being notified at Quarter Sessions, were to be announced by advertisements in newspapers.

Specific applications to owners, &c. affected.

These general notices were still deemed insufficient. Promoters of canal Bills were therefore required, in 1774, to make specific application to each owner, lessee, and occupier whose property would be taken or interfered with, informing them of the intended Bill, and asking them whether they assented, dissented, or were neuter. Lists were also to be presented to Parliament along with each petition for a Bill showing the results of this application. The earliest order relating to railways or tramroads was one passed by the Commons in 1799.[2] These tramways were then mere feeders to canals.[3] The House, therefore, subjected them to the same orders as applied to canals and navigations.[4]

Railways or tramroads.

Deposit of plans.

While this system of notice was gradually built up, Parliament soon saw an equal necessity for giving to persons affected by proposed works early opportunities of ascertaining the exact nature and position of these works. In 1774 the House of Commons ordered that promoters of canal and navigation bills should lodge with their petition for a Bill plans showing the line through which their works would be carried.[5] As just complaints were made of inconveniences and expense to which persons affected by these works were

[1] 34 Com. Journ. 609, 676.
[2] 54 Ib. 664, 689.
[3] *Ante*, Vol. I. p. 43.
[4] All the entries in the Commons' Journals of 1799 describe these new projects as "dram" roads, and will be found so indexed; an amusing proof of the small consideration then paid to the invention which was to produce a revolution in inland transit.
[5] 34 Com. Journ. 609, 676.

subjected by an examination of plans at Westminster, Parliament, in 1813, called upon promoters of most local Bills to deposit plans, books of reference, and sections with clerks of the peace, parish clerks and other official persons throughout any district traversed by works.[1]

In substance this is the system which now exists, though, after prolonged experience, and inquiries by innumerable Standing Order Committees, it has been frequently modified in detail, especially in its application to railways. Until the year 1824, Standing Orders limited the period for giving notices and depositing plans to the months of August and September, so that sometimes before one Session closed it was necessary for promoters to begin a new campaign for the Session following. In 1824 the time was extended to October and November,[2] and is now further extended to the latter month.

Period for giving notices.

Twenty years later an end was put to a fertile source of expense in fulfilling these conditions. Standing Orders required that, accompanying the notice to each individual, there should be sent a schedule showing how the line of the proposed work, as delineated upon the plan and section, would affect his property. It was difficult to correct these schedules and prepare them in time; even when correct they were frequently misleading. On an average each schedule cost about 15s. It was reckoned that there were 8,000 landowners' notices for the Midland Railway Company's extension into London in 1863, so that the expense of these schedules alone was 6,000l.[3] A Committee of the House of Commons, in 1863, recommended that, in lieu of schedules,

Schedule to owners, &c. showing effect of works.

[1] 69 Ib. 873-5. By 7 Will. IV. & 1 Vict. c. 83, clerks of the peace, town clerks, parish clerks, and other persons were required to take charge of documents deposited with them under Standing Orders.

[2] Com. Journ. June 22, 1824.

[3] Commons' Committee on Private Bill Legislation, 1863; evidence of Mr. Coates, p. 161. The London and York Railway, projected in 1845, passed through 300 parishes, and the cost for notices was enormous.

there should be sent with each notice a tracing of the deposited plans and sections coloured so as to distinguish the particular property. Even this was a troublesome process, which gave little specific information. Ultimately Standing Orders were altered so as to require that a schedule should be annexed to such notice describing the property affected, and simply giving its number on the plans. As notices indicate the nearest place where plans are deposited and may be inspected, it is easy for each owner, lessee, or occupier to see how his property will be interfered with under any Bill.

Existing system.   Under the system now in operation, plans and sections of all proposed works which involve the taking of property are deposited on or before November 30th, accompanied by a book of reference, with clerks of the peace in each county where the property is situated. Copies of the plans and sections relating to any parish are also lodged for public inspection with the parish clerk, town clerk, or clerk of the union, as the case may be, and in these plans each property is designated by a number corresponding with that in each schedule.[1]

"Books of reference" contain the names of owners, lessees, and occupiers of all lands and houses in the line of the proposed work, or within the limits of deviation as defined on the plan, and shortly describe these lands and houses.[2] The owner, lessee, or occupier is asked whether he assents or dissents; his answer may be filled in and returned to the promoters' solicitor on a postcard, which is enclosed in the notice, and is printed, stamped, and addressed. Such is the cheap and easy method of notices as now developed. It contrasts advantageously with the cumbrous system which existed in 1825, when no written notices of any Bills were sent, but promoters had to wait upon each landowner, explain

[1] Standing Orders, House of Commons, 1887, Nos. 24—31.
[2] Ib. No. 46.

their plans in person or by deputy, take his decision, and prove it, if necessary, on Standing Orders.[1]

Another preliminary condition, the origin of which has been traced, is that requiring the publication of notices in the London, Edinburgh, or Dublin *Gazette*, and in local newspapers, setting forth the objects of each Bill, the course of a railway, or nature of any works contemplated, with other information intended to place on their guard all persons whose interests may be affected. Before the year 1847, Standing Orders required these notices to be published very unreasonably, so that, if a new branch railway were proposed, the company had to publish notices in every county in which the works of its main line and other branches were situated. Again, every amending Bill or Bill for additional capital promoted by a railway company was required to be advertised in every county in which any part of the company's existing or authorized works were situated. Under these rules the London and North Western Company, before constructing their Lime Street Station at Liverpool, were obliged to publish notices in nine counties, while in the case of a line which passed through three counties only, and was intended to complete a communication between Manchester and Southampton, the promoters were obliged to advertise it in the newspapers of seventeen counties, as well as in the London *Gazette*. A Committee of the House of Commons, which sat in 1847, struck by the unnecessary outlay thus caused to promoters, recommended that promoters of any new works should only be called upon to give notice of their intended application once in the *Gazette* and three times in a newspaper of the county in which such works were to be constructed.[2] This Committee's recommendations were not entirely adopted, but Standing Orders as to advertisements have been materially relaxed with

Gazette notices.

---

[1] Commons' Committee on Private Business, 1863; evidence of Mr. G. P. Bidder, C.E., who said that he had done this himself when a young man.

[2] Third report, p. 5.

Notices on
church doors
abolished,
1847.
Petitions for
Bills.

a view to save expense.　Notices affixed to church doors were also dispensed with in 1847.

In both Houses the ancient rule was that private Bills should originate in petitions, and instances before given show that a petition really furnished the text of a Bill.　All petitioners were therefore enjoined to prepare accurate statements.　In 1685 the Commons ordered " that for the future no private Bill be brought into this House but upon a petition first presented, truly stating the case, at the peril of the parties preferring the same ; and that such petitions shall be signed by the parties who are suitors for such Bill."[1]　This resolution was only a revival of the ancient rule, but it was a rule which required to be frequently enforced.　With a view to facilitate progress, or perhaps to avoid fees, members of both Houses sometimes introduced private Bills by motion. In 1699, therefore, the Lords made a fresh order that in future no private Bill should be introduced " until the House be informed of the matters therein contained, by petition." In 1858 this rule was modified[2] so as to except local Bills, which are therefore brought in and read a first time without petition.　All estate, divorce, naturalization, name, and other personal Bills remain subject to the rule.[3]　In the House of Commons all private Bills whatever must still be brought in upon petition, to which a printed copy of the proposed Bill is annexed.[4]

References to
judges.

It is probable that, when private Bills were chiefly of a personal character, they were always first referred by the Lords to the judges, who were summoned to attend that House as assistants, and had their allotted places there. An order passed in 1705 appears to continue an ancient usage by directing that petitions for private Bills " shall be referred to two judges who are forthwith to summon before them all parties concerned in the Bill; and after hearing

---

[1] 9 Com. Journ. 719.

[2] Lords' Journ. July 30, 1858.

[3] Lords' Standing Orders, Nos.

149, 150 (1887).

[4] Commons' Standing Order, No. 193 (1887).

them and perusing the Bill, are to report to the House the state of the case, and their opinion thereupon, under their hands, and are to sign the said Bill."[1]

Here, then, was a judicial investigation, and a judicial opinion communicated to the Lords upon each Bill, after hearing evidence; and it was provided in 1706, with a view to make this inquiry more conclusive, that all witnesses examined by English judges should be first sworn at the bar of the House. This order was made owing to information that, upon referring petitions for private Bills to the judges, "there arises some difficulty as to the examination upon oath of persons produced to prove the facts."[2] By swearing witnesses at the bar, the House asserted its jurisdiction, and no witness could be examined unless a certificate that he had been so sworn was produced from the clerk of the Parliaments. If the Bill referred to Scotland or Ireland, the judges there, in order to save expense, received statutory power in 1801 to administer oaths.[3]

Witnesses examined before judges first sworn at bar.

In 1843, the order was so modified as to take away from the judges the task of hearing evidence. They were simply, after perusing the petition and Bill, "without requiring any proof of the allegations therein contained," to report to the House their opinion "whether, presuming the allegations contained in the preamble to be proved," it was "reasonable that such Bill do pass into a law, and whether the provisions thereof are proper for carrying its purposes into effect, and what alterations or amendments, if any, are necessary in the same."[4] This order was still general in its terms, and included all private Bills without distinction. In practice, however, it applied only to estate Bills; and a later order now makes this clear by specifying the petitions for such Bills as those upon which the judges are to report. A report is only needed when the Bill has not been first

Judges not to hear evidence, 1843.

[1] 18 Lords' Journ. 105; February 16, 1705.
[2] Lords' Journ. Dec. 18, 1706.
[3] 41 Geo. III. c. 105.
[4] 75 Lords' Journ. 736; Feb. 20, 1843.

approved by the Chancery Division of the High Court. Similar provision is made for the examination of Scotch and Irish estate Bills by judges of the Courts of Session and High Court of Justice in Ireland respectively; and no estate Bill can be read a first time until delivery of the judges' report to the Chairman of Committees.[1]

Petitions against Bills to be specific. Amongst other improvements made in Standing Orders in the year 1824, two may be mentioned here. Before that time petitioners against private Bills were allowed to appear upon general allegations, which placed promoters at a disadvantage, as they were unable to ascertain on what specific ground opponents would rely to defeat a measure. In 1824, a new Standing Order directed that petitioners must distinctly specify their grounds of objection, and shall only be heard on grounds so stated. This is the existing practice. On the other hand, opponents were at a disadvantage in not knowing, until they came into Committee, what alterations, if any, promoters intended to propose in a Bill **"Filled-up" Bills.** as deposited. A salutary rule added to Standing Orders in 1824, and still observed, provides that what is called a filled-up Bill, that is, one containing the latest manuscript amendments of promoters, signed by their agent, shall be deposited at the Private Bill Office before the Committee meet, and copies shall be furnished to opposing petitioners in time to allow them to consider the effect of these amendments.

Estates. For reasons already given,[2] personal Bills, once so numerous, are now rare. The rules relating to them, therefore, are now of little practical importance. Estate Bills, like all other measures of this class, have, with few exceptions, always originated in the Lords, and were the subject of very carefully framed orders in 1705.[3] These rules, and the modifications they have undergone, are of too technical a

[1] Lords' Standing Orders, Nos. 153-6 (1887). Each Bill is referred to two judges.
[2] *Ante*, Vol. I. 378, 384.
[3] 18 Lords' Journ. 105.

nature to be followed here. Their general object has been,
while facilitating dealings with property which were shown
to be beneficial to the parties, properly to secure the rights
and interests of all concerned, especially of married women,
children, and persons entitled in remainder. Naturalization   Naturaliza-
Bills were subjects of many orders. Besides those already   tion.
mentioned in their place,[1] the Commons ordered, in 1624, a
proviso to be inserted in all these Bills " that if the person
naturalized be convicted of colouring any stranger's goods,[2]
he shall lose the benefit of his Act."[3]

Although since 1857 divorces of English marriages have   Divorce.
become a judicial instead of a legislative proceeding,[4] Standing Orders still provide for Bills of this nature in Irish and
other cases. There is nothing, indeed, in these orders, or in
the Act of 1857, to prevent a husband or wife of English
domicile from applying to Parliament for a divorce under
circumstances not provided for by the Act,[5] as in the case of
desertion, of incurable insanity on either side, or a husband's
adultery with aggravations stopping short of legal cruelty.
It would, however, be hard to repel arguments founded upon
the absence of any such remedy in the general law, and the
expediency of seeking to amend that law instead of asking
for a *privilegium.* No applications for private divorce Acts
have been made since 1857 by married persons domiciled in
England. But a private Act obtained by an Irish lady in   Westropp's
1886[6] is of importance in showing that Parliament has   Divorce Act,
relaxed its old and strict rule against allowing divorce to   1886.
injured wives, unless in most exceptional cases.[7] According

---

[1] *Ante,* pp. 378-85.

[2] Assume colourable ownership.

[3] 1 Com. Journ. 695, 780.

[4] See Chapter on Divorce, *ante,*
Vol. I. pp. 387 *et seq.,* where some
of the old orders on this subject are
treated.

[5] See remarks of Attorney-General
(Sir Richard Bethell) in House of

Commons ; Hansard, August 14,
1857.

[6] Westropp's Divorce Act, 1886.

[7] Only in four previous cases had
Divorce Acts been passed on an application by women :—Mrs. Addison,
in 1801, and Mrs. Turton, in 1830,
obtained divorces on the ground of
incestuous adultery ; Mrs. Battersby,

to former precedents, the cruelty and adultery proved in 1886 would have been wholly ineffectual to procure a private divorce Act.   But in this instance the House of Lords exercised its old jurisdiction in the spirit of the legislation of 1857.

Some descriptions of obsolete local Bills, formerly regulated by Standing Orders, may now be shortly mentioned. Early in this century it was necessary to provide for the promotion of Bills, which then became numerous, to establish Courts of Conscience and other Courts for the recovery of small debts.   Occasionally these Courts may have been of local convenience, but they were sometimes also sought for personal objects.   Each Act, when applicable to a country district, included several parishes. Standing Orders prescribed that these parishes should consent to the promotion of any Bill, but this consent was often obtained by some professional person who desired to be appointed clerk under the Act.   A considerable sum was spent by him out of his own pocket in canvassing and in promoting the Bill, and though no costs could be allowed except by consent of magistrates in Quarter Sessions, they always were allowed in practice.   There was thus little or no check, and as costs were made by the Act a first charge upon the suitors' fund, the promoter, besides his emoluments of office, recovered all his outlay.[1]

Small Debt Courts.

It was calculated, in 1832, that no fewer than sixty of these local Acts had passed, fifty during the reigns of George III. and George IV.   Some provisions crept into them which were very harsh in their effect upon small debtors.   The House of Commons, therefore, adopted a Standing Order that all Bills for constituting these Courts

Debtors protected against undue imprisonment.

in 1840, for adultery coupled with cruelty and bigamy ; and Mrs. Hale, in 1850, also for adultery with bigamy.   See a record of these and several unsuccessful applications by wives, *ante*, Vol. I. pp. 414 *et seq.*

[1] Commons' Committee on Private Bills, 1846; Evidence of Mr. G Elliott, Police Magistrate, p. 81. *ante*, Vol. I. p. 266*.

should provide " that no person be committed to prison for more than twenty days where the debt does not exceed 20s.; nor for more than forty days where the debt does not exceed 60s.; nor for more than eighty days where the debt does not exceed 80s.; nor for more than 100 days where the debt does not exceed 100s. And that every person so committed shall be discharged at the expiration of these respective periods, without paying any fees to any gaoler or turnkey." This was then deemed a merciful enactment. Another Standing Order is significant of the class of persons some- times appointed to act as judges, or commissioners, of these Courts. It declared that every Bill should contain a clause " that no person be capable of acting as commissioner, unless he be a householder within the county, district, city, liberty, or place for which he shall act, and be possessed of a real estate of the annual value of 20l., or of a personal estate of the value of 500l."

In like manner the House of Commons took steps to guard against abuses in the numerous local Bills formerly promoted for maintaining, lodging, or employing the poor.[1] With this view, all Chairmen of Committees were directed to report specifically that these Bills contained no clause varying the general law of poor law settlement, or giving the power of corporal punishment.

Poor Relief Bills.

Bills for compounding debts due to the Crown are met with in the last century, and somewhat later. These debts were generally incurred by infringements of the revenue laws. Standing Orders made in 1713 required that peti- tions for these Bills should be accompanied by certificates from the revenue department to which the debt was owing, setting forth the amount of the debt and any prosecutions instituted for its recovery.[2] Satisfactory evidence was also necessary to show how much of his debt a petitioner and his sureties were able to pay. A Bill of this nature could

Bills for com- pounding Crown debts.

---

[1] *Ante*, Vol. I. pp. 266*, 266**.   [2] 17 Com. Journ. 300.

only originate in the Commons, in Committee of the whole House,[1] and if they reported in its favour it was afterwards treated as a public Bill.

Estimates and subscriptions.

Long before the introduction of railways, or even of tram-roads, Parliament called upon promoters to furnish a signed estimate of the cost of works, so that it might be challenged by opponents if they thought fit to do so. With a view also to discourage merely speculative undertakings, promoters were required to prove their good faith and command of money by giving a list of subscribers, and the amount of their promised subscriptions. These precautions were found necessary in 1774, on account of the many bubble canal projects then brought forward.[2] On the recommendation of a Committee in that year, the House of Commons ordered that "when any petition is presented for making a navigable canal, or for making or improving the navigation of a river, or for making a turnpike road, or for raising any further sum of money for these purposes, there be annexed to the petition an estimate of the expenses of such undertaking, together with an account of the money subscribed for carrying the said work into execution, and the names of the subscribers, with the amounts respectively subscribed by them."[3]

Clause compelling subscribers to make good their subscriptions.

As a mere list of subscriptions might be worthless, unless coupled with an effective guarantee, these orders were supplemented by another directing Committees to see that each Bill contained a clause compelling all nominal subscribers to pay the sums for which they were set down.[4] This was the origin of a system which, with some modifications, lasted for three quarters of a century, and in recent times chiefly operated in restraint of railway undertakings. Subscription contracts were first required by the House of Lords in 1813. A stringent order then passed forbids the third reading of any Bills for works to supply water, improve navigations, make railways, tram-roads, tunnels, archways, bridges, ferries,

Subscription contracts, House of Lords, 1813.

[1] 15 Com. Journ. 367; A.D. 1707.   [3] 34 Com. Journ. 609, 676.
[2] *Ante*, Vol. I. pp. 33 *et seq.*   [4] Ib.

docks, piers, ports or harbours, or of any Bills to enlarge works for these purposes, " unless four-fifths of the probable expense of the proposed work shall have been subscribed by persons under a contract binding the subscribers, their heirs, executors, and administrators, to pay the money so subscribed within a limited time, nor unless there shall be contained in such Bill a provision that the whole of the probable expense of such work shall be subscribed in like manner " before the powers given by the Bill were enforced.[1]

In the Commons, proof upon these points was necessary before the Committee on petitions, that is, before the Bill itself was considered in Committee. At times Parliament varied its conditions as to the amount of previously subscribed capital. Three-fourths were at one time insisted on. No such contract also was valid unless entered into before the close of the previous Session, and one tenth part of the subscribed sum must have been invested in the joint names of the clerk of the House of Commons and of two promoters. When the House had decided upon the Bill, this amount was repaid to promoters or to persons named by them. In later practice, it commonly happened that subscription lists fell far short of estimated expenses, and some Committees then were satisfied if promoters could show good reason for believing that any deficiency would be made good.[2] *Varying conditions in practice.*

An odd feature in the old practice was that persons whose names were attached to a subscription list were not allowed to give evidence in favour of a projected Bill.[3] This restriction naturally kept out of the list names of persons chiefly interested in the Bill, and substituted their nominees, who might or might not be responsible persons.

On consideration of the London and York Railway Bill, by a Committee of the House of Commons in 1845, it appeared that the capital originally contemplated and sub- *London and York Railway Bill, 1845.*

---

[1] 49 Lords' Journ. pp. 539, 580. 1825.
[2] Practical Instructions, by a Parliamentary Agent, p. 15; London,
[3] Ib. p. 16.

scribed for under the contract deed was 5,000,000*l*., whereas the capital proposed to be authorized by the Bill was 6,500,000*l*. Objection was taken by counsel for a competing scheme because, (1) it was not within the power of the Committee to authorize this additional capital; (2) even if the Committee had this power, the alteration would render the contract deed null and void; (3) as the company could not, under these circumstances, enforce any claim against subscribers, the railway could not be constructed even were the Committee to pass preamble. In reply it was contended that the question thus raised was not within the province of a Committee on a Bill, *i. e.*, that this objection should have been taken on Standing Orders. The Committee, however, resolved that it was within their province to decide the question; and, further, that it was competent for them " to authorize the London and York Railway Company to raise the sum proposed as their capital under the provisions of the Bill, three-fourths of that amount having been subscribed."[1]

Subscription contracts illusory. Estimates of expense are still required by Standing Orders.[2] Repeated inquiries into the *bona fides* of subscription contracts proved that they were liable to gross abuses, and were valueless as a test of solvency. During the railway mania the subscribers were often men of straw, who laughed at any attempt to enforce the contract they had entered into.[3] It was in vain that Committees were directed by Standing Orders to " make special inquiry into the *bonâ fide* character " of subscription contracts, and the sufficiency of subscribers.[4] Although, therefore, not immediately abolished, this system was supplemented by another form of guarantees imposed on promoters.

An explanation of these guarantees will not be clear without reference to a classification of private Bills first adopted

---

[1] Supp. to Commons' Votes, 1845, p. 1436.
[2] Commons' Standing Order, No. 56, Sess. 1887.
[3] *Ante*, Vol. I. pp. 91-2.
[4] Commons' Standing Order, No. 125, Sess. 1852; 107 Com. Journ. 345; 108 Ib. 780.

in 1837. That these Bills might be more readily dealt with, they were then divided by Standing Orders of the Commons into three classes.[1] Fresh arrangements in 1842 and 1847 reduced them to two classes.[2] Bills of the first class are for the most part those promoted by local authorities, for ordinary purposes of local government. Bills of the second class are those which propose to make, maintain, vary, extend, or enlarge any aqueduct, archway, bridge, canal, cut, dock, drainage (when the cut exceeds eleven feet width at the bottom), embankment for reclaiming land from the sea or any tidal river, ferry (where any work is to be executed), harbour, navigation, pier, port, railway, reservoir, sewer, street, subway to be used for the conveyance of passengers, animals, or goods, in carriages or trucks drawn or propelled on rails, tunnel, turnpike or other public carriage road, waterworks.[3]

Classification of private Bills under Standing Orders.

In 1842, besides a subscription contract guaranteeing three-fourths of the estimated expense of new works, the House of Commons ordered that, before a petition was presented for any Bill of the second class, one tenth part of the amount subscribed should be deposited with the Court of Chancery in England or Ireland, or with the Court of Exchequer in Scotland, according to the country in which the work was proposed to be executed.[4] Upon the passing of the Bill, or its withdrawal or rejection, deposits were returned under regulations specified in an Act of 1838 " to provide for the custody of certain moneys paid in pursuance of the Standing Orders of either House of Parliament by subscribers to works or undertakings to be effected under the authority of Parliament."[5]

Deposits.

Repayment of deposits.

1 & 2 Vict. c. 117.

If a Bill did not pass, an important condition was imposed by this Act upon the return of the deposit. Promoters were then required to obtain a certificate from the Chairman of

Conditions upon repayment of deposits.

---

[1] 92 Com. Journ. 638.
[2] 96 Ib. 602 ; 102 Ib. 880.
[3] Commons' Standing Orders of 1887, No. 1.
[4] 97 Com. Journ. 561.
[5] 1 & 2 Vict. c. 117, s. 4.

Committees in the House of Lords, or from the Speaker in the other House, that their petition or Bill had been "rejected, or not allowed to proceed, or withdrawn, by some proceeding in one or other House of Parliament." This provision obviously had for its object to check the introduction of speculative or immature schemes for railways, withdrawn before consideration by Parliament, but never meant to be pressed, and probably projected in the hope that they would be bought up by some existing company with which

9 & 10 Vict. c. 20.

they were meant to interfere. Substantially the same provisions were contained in an Act of 1846[1] which repealed and re-enacted with amendments the previous Act, but required a certificate from the Chairman of Lords' Committees or the Speaker in every case where deposits were transferred out of Court to the persons entitled to them. This Act is still in force.

Injury to landowners.

A serious flaw was the absence of every check upon promoters of railways which were sanctioned but not made. Owing to this defect, both statutes proved wholly ineffectual as guarantees of legitimate enterprise. It will be remembered that the speculative mania of 1846 was followed by a disastrous collapse, leading to the abandonment, under a general Act passed in 1850, of more than 3,500 miles of railway which had been sanctioned by Parliament,[2] while other schemes, sanctioned for the construction of 2,000 miles, at a cost of over forty millions, were abandoned without any statutory authority.[3] In some cases an abandonment of unfinished works caused serious injury to landowners;[4]

[1] 9 & 10 Vict. c. 20, s. 5.
[2] *Ante*, Vol. I. p. 89.
[3] Ib., quoting Fourth Report of Mr. Cardwell's Committee of 1852-3, p. 6.
[4] Brighton Railway Company's Bill, 1868 (Abandonment of Ouse Valley line); Petitions of R. J. Streatfield and H. King. 1 Clifford & Stephens's Locus Standi Rep. 18. In this case a residential estate was seriously disfigured by half-finished works upon the line to be abandoned. Under the general law the landowner had a right to pre-emption, but it was alleged that the cost of restoring the land to its original condition would far exceed its value.

and when promoters had once so drawn out their deposits, as they always did when their Bills became law, no fund was left to satisfy any claims whatever.

With a view to prevent this hardship, and also put an end, *New rule as to railway deposits, 1853.* as far as possible, to the levy of black-mail upon existing companies, Mr. Cardwell, in 1853, proposed a new Standing Order, applicable only to railway Bills, and providing for a suspension of dividends and forfeiture of deposits. The Committee upon Railway and Canal Amalgamation, over which Mr. Cardwell presided, was at this time pursuing its inquiries, and the resolution then come to by the House of Commons was recommended by him upon the authority of that Committee.[1] By this resolution, which became a Stand- *Penalties for non-comple-tion of autho-rized railway.* ing Order in August, 1853,[2] Committees were instructed to insert in any Bill promoted by existing railway companies a clause providing that after the expiration of a specified period, not exceeding five years in the case of a new line, and three years if the time for completing it were extended, all *Suspension of dividends.* dividends upon the ordinary and unguaranteed capital should be suspended until the line was completed and opened for public traffic.

If the Bill were promoted by a new company, a clause was *Locking-up of deposit.* to be inserted requiring that the deposit of one tenth part of

---

[1] "Your Committee strongly recommend that in future no mere adventurers shall be permitted to obtain the sanction of Parliament to Bills embodying schemes which they have no intention of carrying into effect, but purpose using as a means of extorting advantage from the *bonâ fide* undertakers of railway enterprise in the district." (Fifth Report, p. 15.) Mr. Cardwell spoke to the same effect in the House of Commons (April 18, 1853) upon "a class of Bills, generally called 'fighting Bills,' projected by persons who had no intention of completing them, by speculative solicitors and engineers who sought to obtain the sanction of Parliament to a Bill, and then put it up to auction among companies already in existence. The Committee were determined to put a stop to those Bills, in case the parties refused to give any evidence of the sincerity of their purpose for the prosecution of their proposed lines." (125 Hansard, 1202-3.) And the plan adopted was the Standing Order summarized in the text.

[2] 108 Com. Journ. 780. See also Report from Committee on Standing Orders Revision, 1852-3.

three-fourths of the estimated cost should not be repaid to
the parties unless in two events—(1) the opening of the line
for public traffic; (2) proof to the satisfaction of the Board
of Trade that the company had paid up one-half of their
authorized share capital, and had expended for the purposes
Forfeiture of deposit. of the Act a sum equal to such moiety. If the period fixed
in the Act for completion of the railway expired before either
of these conditions was satisfied, the amount of deposit was
Deposit released upon bond of double the amount. to be forfeited, and carried to the Consolidated Fund. At
any time, however, after the passing of the Act, the amount
of deposit might be released upon execution by the company of a bond, with sureties approved by the Solicitor to
the Treasury, for payment of twice the amount of deposit
upon non-performance of one of the conditions already mentioned.

Reduction in amount of deposits. In 1844, the amount of deposit was reduced to one
twentieth part of the amount subscribed[1] for all other than
railway Bills, which were still left subject to the deposit of
one-tenth.[2] In 1858, when subscription contracts were abolished, there was a further change, and it was provided that
the amount of deposit should be "in the case of a railway
Bill a sum not less than eight per cent. on the amount of the
estimate of expense, and in the case of all other Bills a sum
not less than four per cent. on the amount of such estimate."
In 1868, the amount of deposit on railway, tramway,
and subway Bills was reduced to five per cent.; on all other
Bills to four per cent. This change brought the Orders of
the two Houses into harmony. The same deposit is still
required, but only as before from new companies, or from
existing companies which have no line opened for public
traffic or have paid no dividend on their ordinary share capital
during the previous year.[3] Bonds are no longer called for.

No case occurred in which the dividends of an established

---

[1] Commons' Standing Orders, 1844; 97 Com. Journ. 315.

[2] Commons' Standing Order, No.

46, Sess. 1845.

[3] Standing Order, No. 57, Sess. 1887.

company were suspended by virtue of this Standing Order Application to suspend dividends. clause. On one occasion, however, the Court of Chancery intervened upon an application from landowners interested in the construction by the South Wales Railway Company of a branch to the Pembroke Docks. In this case an injunction was granted against further payments of dividends by the company, who had allowed their statutory powers for making this branch to expire. The injunction was afterwards suspended so as to give the company an opportunity of applying to Parliament to revive their powers, and the necessary Act was obtained.[1]

In practice the system adopted by Parliament for enforcing the construction of new lines operated somewhat unequally, as existing companies, when they put forward block lines, or lines with an aggressive object, avoided any risk of suspended dividends by an indirect promotion of such lines, subscribing towards them, or guaranteeing a certain percentage upon the subscribed and borrowed capital. As they were not technical promoters of the Bill, they thus escaped the Standing Order. A new process was therefore adopted in 1864, under Standing Orders still in use by both Houses. Existing railway, tramway, or subway companies Penalties of 50l. daily instead of suspended dividends. which make default in completing and opening for traffic an addition to their authorized system must bind themselves in their special Acts to pay a penalty of 50l. for every day of such default, until these accumulated penalties amount to five per cent. upon the estimated cost of the works. If the Deposit from new company impounded. promoting company are a non-dividend-paying company, or are newly incorporated, their deposit of five per cent. upon the estimated outlay is impounded as security for completion of the line, and may be applied in compensating any land-

---

[1] And in 1855 Parliament required the London and South Western Railway Company, under penalty of a suspension of dividends, to apply for in the next Session, and in good faith promote, a Bill for a line which the company had pledged themselves to make. (May, 757; 18 & 19 Vict. c. 188, ss. 62-9.)

owners or other persons "whose property may have been interfered with, or otherwise rendered less valuable, by the commencement, construction, or abandonment" of the railway or tramway. Should any surplus then remain, it is forfeited to the Crown and paid into the Consolidated Fund. On the other hand, if the line is completed and opened for traffic, the fund in Court is released from the lien attaching to it, and, upon a certificate from the Board of Trade, is repaid to the company. A similar certificate declaring that part of the line is opened will release a *pro ratâ* proportion of the deposit.[1]

Loan capital of railway companies restricted, 1836.

In further restraint of the promotion of speculative undertakings, the House of Commons, in 1836, ordered that no railway company should raise, by loan or mortgage, a larger sum than one-third of their share capital, and this only when one-half the share capital was paid up.

Deposits not to be paid out of capital.

In 1847, the House also ordered that a clause should be inserted in every railway Bill prohibiting companies from paying deposits out of capital already authorized.[2]

Interest not to be paid on calls during construction of works.

With the same object, in the same Session, a clause was made obligatory in every railway Bill prohibiting the payment of interest on calls during the construction of works. These orders remain on the roll of both Houses, but recently, after much inquiry and debate, the condition against payment of interest has been relaxed in special cases, and the Commons have made material modifications in their order on this subject.

Such interest formerly allowed.

In the last century there was a common provision in canal Acts not only allowing but requiring a company, during the progress of their works, to pay to shareholders interest upon the amount of their subscriptions at the rate of five per cent., unless a majority of proprietors at any general meeting should determine that no interest, or a lower rate, should be paid.[3] The earliest dock Acts mentioned in a previous

---

[1] Commons' Standing Order, No. 158, Sess. 1887.

[2] 102 Com. Journ. 890.

[3] Aberdare Canal Act, 1793 (33 Geo. III. c. 95, s. 36).

chapter contained similar provisions.[1] In some of the early railway Acts payment of interest out of capital was also authorized.[2] No restraint was put upon promoters in this respect until the lamentable results of railway speculation in 1845 led to the Order of 1847. This order was often evaded both by old and new companies, by means of various expedients, especially by arrangements with contractors employed to construct the line.[3] It was a provision which, although contained in the Companies Act, 1862,[4] was not compulsory upon a registered company if they expressly excluded its operation; and there was the further anomaly that a registered tramway company, after thus escaping from the general law, might obtain through the Board of Trade a provisional Order in which, if confirmed, Parliament would practically sanction a proceeding forbidden by its Standing Orders in a private Act.[5]

A Committee of the House of Commons appointed in 1882 to consider this restriction upon promoters reported that, although it was in accordance with sound principle, and a protection to investors, it might be safely relaxed in special cases, subject to certain conditions. This recommendation was adopted, after debate, by the House of Commons, which allowed its order to be varied, if a Committee on a Bill thought fit, provided that interest during construction did not exceed five per cent. per annum and was continued in no case longer than the time limited for completion of the railway. Among other conditions, ample notice must be given to investors, and there must be a certificate by the Board of Trade showing that at least two-thirds of the authorized share capital has been subscribed.[6]

Modification of Standing Order by Commons, 1882.

[1] *Ante*, pp. 650, 652, 667.

[2] Commons' Committee on Standing Order 167, Sess. 1882; Ev. of Mr. Rees, Parliamentary agent, who cites (pp. 9, 10) several railway Acts containing this provision, including the South Eastern Railway Act, 1839.

[3] An injunction was obtained on this ground against the Hull and Barnsley Railway Company.

[4] Following Companies Clauses Consolidation Act, 1845, s. 121.

[5] Commons' Committee of 1882; Rep. p. 3.

[6] Commons' Standing Order 167, Sess. 1887.

Similar changes by Lords.

In 1886 similar changes were made by the Lords, so that the practice of the two Houses upon this point is no longer conflicting.[1] In two instances since 1852, both Houses concurred in allowing payment of interest out of capital. These cases were exceptional only in the large amount of capital proposed to be raised.[2] In principle no valid reason can be assigned why, if relaxed in one Bill, the restriction should not be relaxed in all.

Wharncliffe meetings.

In order to prevent directors of companies from promoting Bills without the knowledge or sanction of shareholders, the House of Lords framed, in 1846, a series of Orders, under which "Wharncliffe" meetings, as they were afterwards termed,[3] must be held, to consider each Bill so promoted. In 1846, a certificate recording the shareholders' approval of the Bill was required before a third reading.[4] Proof must now be given of this approval before the Bill is introduced into the second House. This obviously necessary condition was not insisted on by the Commons until 1858.[5]

Privilege of initiating Bills.

Each House has, at various times, asserted its privilege to initiate legislation upon certain classes of Bills. Personal Bills of a quasi-judicial character, such as those relating to divorce, naturalization, estates, or restitution, were always claimed by the Lords.[6] On their side, the Commons jealously main-

Rights of Commons over local Bills levying rates.

tained the constitutional principle that all Bills authorizing taxation must begin with them, and they extended this principle for some centuries even to private Bills imposing tolls for services rendered or rates by local authorities.

Westminster Paving Bill, 1661.

An instance of this nature occurred in 1661, upon a Bill

[1] Lords' Standing Order 128, Sess. 1887.

[2] Regent's Canal City and Docks Railway Act, 1885 (48 & 49 Vict. c. 138); Manchester Ship Canal Act, 1886 (49 & 50 Vict. c. 111), amending original Act (48 & 49 Vict. c. 188).

[3] They derived their name from a peer who took great interest in private business, and was mainly responsible for their present shape.

[4] 78 Lords' Journ. 319.

[5] 113 Com. Journ. 348. Standing Order 64 (Sess. 1887).

[6] But restitution and naturalization Bills must first be sanctioned by the Crown.

sent from the Lords, for paving and repairing streets and highways in Westminster and parts adjacent. Observing that this Bill " was to alter the course of law in part, and lay a charge upon the people, and conceiving that it is a privilege inherent to this House that Bills of that nature ought to be first considered here," the House of Commons "ordered, that the said Bill be laid aside, and the Lords be acquainted therewith, and with the reasons inducing this House thereunto : and the Lords are to be desired for that cause not to suffer any mention of the said Bill to remain in the Journals of their House. And the Lords are further to be acquainted that this House, finding the matter of their Bill to be very useful, and of public concernment, have ordered a Bill of the like nature to be prepared and brought in to-morrow morning."[1] At a conference the Lords were acquainted with this decision, accepted it, and passed the substituted Bill of the Commons.

Acting upon this case, the House of Commons, in 1753, Ashburnham
Estate Bill, even laid aside an estate Bill promoted by surviving trustees 1753. and executors of John, late Earl of Ashburnham, which seems to have infringed in some way the principle asserted in 1661.[2] A new Bill was accordingly introduced there, and passed the other House. As the number of local Bills increased, great inconvenience arose from this indiscriminate maintenance of their privilege by the Commons. No canal Inconvenience
of rule. or railway Bill imposing tolls could originate in the Upper House. In years of pressure, the result was almost a deadlock in legislation. Opposed Bills came before the Lords at so late a period of the Session that all were hurried and some laid aside. Delays and unnecessary expense to suitors were not the only evils, for as the rule applied even to alterations of

---

[1] 8 Com. Journ. 311 ; July 24, 1661.

[2] 26 Com. Journ. 757–8 ; April 11, 1753. The entries of 1661 (quoted in the text) were cited as precedents on this occasion. Hatsell (iii. pp. 126 –7) mentions an estate Bill of the Duke of Bedford laid aside by the Commons for similar reasons.

toll charges, Lords' Committees often had to choose between permitting an injury to individual toll-payers, and causing the loss of a Bill admitted to be of public utility.[1]

Commons' Committee on Railway Bills, 1845. Under such a system as that just described it was impossible that proper consideration could be given to the 248 railway Bills which, during the Session of 1845, were promoted in Parliament. Even before this period the same inconvenience had been felt; and numbers of Bills for the levy of tolls and rates were "brought up Session after Session," when, if they had been allowed to begin in the House of Lords, they might **Proposal to leave tolls in blank.** have passed in a single Session.[2] It was proposed that tolls should be left in blank by the Lords, but the obvious objection to this course was that the merits of a railway Bill, especially when there were competing lines, sometimes turned mainly upon questions of rates and fares. For this great blot in private legislation, Lord Redesdale, in 1845, suggested the natural remedy that the Commons should waive a privilege which had ceased to be important or expedient, save in Supply, and that at the beginning of each Session all private Bills should be apportioned equally between the two Houses.[3]

Resolutions of 1846. So grievous was the loss caused to individual projectors by this rule through the repeated postponement or rejection of their schemes, and so irresistible also was the evidence of public injury through railway Bills passed too hurriedly to ensure a proper regard for either private or public interests, that, in 1846, the Commons resolved to waive their privileges upon any bills brought from the Upper House fixing or regulating rates or tolls.[4] With a view also to "afford early and increased means of employment in Ireland," the Commons at the same time resolved that it was "expedient to

---

[1] Committee on Railway Bills, 1845; Evidence of Earl of Shaftesbury and Lord Redesdale, pp. 9, 10.

[2] Committee on Railway Bills, 1845; Evidence of Earl of Shaftesbury and Lord Redesdale, p. 10.

[3] Ib.

[4] 101 Com. Journ. 83; Feb. 6, 1846.

give facilities for the early consideration of Irish railway Bills " by allowing these Bills to commence in the House of Lords.[1]

These resolutions only held good for the Session in which they were passed, and when railway extensions revived after the panic, the same evil was experienced. Mr. Cardwell's Committee in 1852-3 recommended that a large portion of private business should begin in the Lords. It was not, however, until 1858 that the Commons consented to forego their privileges, and by a resolution, which afterwards was made a Standing Order, allowed the Lords first to consider Bills of this character if they only imposed tolls and charges not in the nature of a tax, but for services performed, or if they referred to "rates assessed and levied by local authorities for local purposes."[2] With the same object of ensuring a more equal distribution of business between the two Houses, another Standing Order directed the Chairman of Ways and Means to confer, at the commencement of each Session, with the Chairman of Committees in the Lords " for the purpose of determining in which House of Parliament the respective private Bills should be first considered."[3]

Privilege waived by Commons, 1858, in certain cases.

---

[1] 101 Com. Journ. 83; Feb. 6, 1846.

[2] 113 Com. Journ. 348; see now Commons' Standing Order 226, Sess. 1887. This order has been held to extend to turnpike, harbour, drainage, and similar Bills, but does not extend to clauses in an improvement Bill imposing a tax upon all insurance companies having policies within a borough. (May's Parliamentary Practice, 9th ed. 1883, pp. 758-9)

[3] Standing Order 79, 1887.

CHAPTER XXI.

PRIVATE BILL OFFICE: COMMITTEES ON PETITIONS: EXAMINERS:
STANDING ORDERS COMMITTEE: COMMITTEE OF SELECTION:
STANDING COMMITTEE ON RAILWAY AND CANAL BILLS:
CHAIRMAN OF COMMITTEES IN LORDS: CHAIRMAN OF WAYS
AND MEANS: SPEAKER'S COUNSEL: BREVIATES: COURT OF
REFEREES: LOCUS STANDI OF PETITIONERS: TAXATION OF
COSTS.

Private business, as regulated by Standing Orders.

STANDING Orders not only prescribe conditions under which promoters shall prepare and frame their Bills, but lay down general rules for administering this business in each House. Like other parts of the system, the administration thus regulated has been of gradual growth; but the amendments and improvements which will now be sketched were made exclusively during the present century.

Until the year 1813, there was no separate machinery in either House for transacting private, as distinguished from public, business. The House of Lords, indeed, still retains its old system, in name though not in substance; its Standing Orders provide that all private business shall be transacted through the clerk of the Parliaments. An increasing pressure of this business in the Commons, however, led them in the year 1810 to appoint a Committee "to consider of providing more effectually for the accuracy and regularity of proceedings upon private Bills." This Committee suggested "that a book, called 'The Private Bill Register,' be kept in a room called 'The Private Bill Office.'" In this book were to be entered various particulars, such as the names of Parliamentary agents in town, and of

Private business in Lords still transacted at Parliament Office.

Commons' Committee, 1810;

Recommendations.

"agents in the country, soliciting the Bill;" a brief record of each day's proceedings in the House or in any Committee to which the Bill or petition was referred; with the day and hour on which any Committee was appointed to sit. This book was to be open for public inspection daily in the new office.[1] In the year 1813, this recommendation was embodied in Standing Orders substantially resembling those still in force.[2]

Private Bill Office established, 1813.

Committees on petitions were appointed by the Lords from the earliest times. An instance has been given in which this House, in the year 1399, referred petitions to Committees instead of to the usual Triers.[3] These petitions were mainly for relief in pending causes, but presumably included relief by private legislation. No special notice of the work performed by Lords' Committees on Petitions occurs before the year 1621, when they were directed " to report to the House what answers were fit to be made."[4] In the same Session the House instructed attendants to advise with the Committee, and named three serjeants-at-law and Mr. Attorney for this duty, with such of the judges as their Lordships pleased to call to them.[5] After 1621, frequent reference is made to these tribunals of first instance. In 1624 they were authorized " to reject any petition which the major part of the Committee will agree to be rejected ";[6] but they were required to report their reasons.[7] As their duties became more onerous, they were instructed, in 1626, to divide themselves into several parts; five peers together to have power to perform their business.[8]

Committees on petitions in House of Lords.

Sub-Committees, 1626.

Ordinary suitors were as troublesome as they had been nearly four centuries previously,[9] and the Committee were therefore ordered, in 1640, to reject all petitions which were

Ordinary suitors referred to Courts of Law or Chancery.

[1] Select Committee on Private Bills, 1810; Report, p. 1.

[2] 69 Com. Journ. 873. See now Commons' Standing Orders 227 *et seq.*, Sess. 1887.

[3] *Ante*, Vol. I., pp. 278–9.

[4] 3 Lords' Journ. 141.

[5] Ib. 179.

[6] Ib. 296.

[7] Ib. 505.

[8] Ib. 630.

[9] *Ante*, Vol. I., p. 281.

proper to be relieved at common law or equity, but to retain such as were fit for their Lordships' consideration, and were "without remedy in any other place than in Parliament."[1]

Practice in Commons. Lord Derby's case, 1656.

Committees on petitions for Bills in the Lower House are mentioned in the year 1614.[2] This procedure is also recorded in 1656, upon a petition from Charles, Earl of Derby, which was referred to a numerous Committee, with an instruction that, if they found "the matter of fact to be as alleged," they should then "bring in a Bill, as is desired."[3] At the same sitting some other petitions were similarly treated. Thirteen years passed before another Committee was appointed upon a petition. They were then instructed "to send for persons, papers, and records; to examine the matter of the petition (from Magdalen College, Cambridge); and certify their opinions therein to the House, whether it be fit to bring in a Bill on the petitioners' behalf."[4] No similar reference can be traced until 1691, when a Committee was directed to examine and consider a petition for an estate Bill, and "report the matter specially to the House."[5] As the Committee were of opinion that "a Bill such as the petitioner desired was just and reasonable," leave was given to bring it in.[6] A few more instances occur in this and succeeding years, but the practice did not become common until the eighteenth century.

Magdalen College, Cambridge, 1669.

Cripps's estate, 1691.

As their Standing Orders regulating private Bills increased, both Houses appear to have made use of Committees on petitions to ascertain not only whether there was a *primâ facie* case for a Bill, but also whether promoters had complied with these Orders. This tribunal still, however, inquired into

---

[1] 3 Lords' Journ. 155, 254, 263, 455.

[2] 1 Com. Journ. 481, 490.

[3] 7 Ib. 472; December 22, 1656. Chief Justice Glyn served upon this Committee along with the Earl of Salisbury and Lord Broghill, Colonel Ireland, General Disbrow (*sic*), and many other officers. A petition from Lord Salisbury for payment of a debt due from Parliament was then under consideration by a Committee. (Ib. 466.)

[4] 9 Com. Journ. 102; Nov. 4, 1669.

[5] 10 Ib. 592.

[6] Ib. 614.

cases governed by no Orders. Thus, upon Lady Ferrers's petition, in 1758, for a Bill of separation and maintenance, a Lords' Committee heard evidence at great length before leave was given to bring in the Bill.[1] There are frequent instances of similar Committees on petitions for canal, inclosure, and dock Bills in the eighteenth and early in the following century. Some of these inquiries have been mentioned in previous chapters. The preliminary inquiry into merits, like other preliminary inquiries afterwards instituted under other conditions,[2] largely increased expenses in contested cases without reducing either in length or in outlay the subsequent investigation by Committees upon Bills.

Gradually, therefore, Committees upon petitions, with their Sub-Committees, restricted their inquiries. In the Commons, a Standing Order was passed excluding adverse evidence upon merits before those Committees, and providing that this portion of the promoters' case should be *ex parte*. But Committees on petitions were large and fluctuating bodies, possessing no competent knowledge of Standing Orders, and ill able to apply a code of technical rules. They were also liable to local and other influences which were often brought to bear when feeling was aroused among their constituents for or against a local measure. As constituted by the House, partly by nomination and partly from a "Speaker's list,"[3] they were an unwieldy body consisting of about 120 members. A Committee, almost as numerous, exercised similar functions in the Upper House; and the same proofs had to be repeated before that tribunal at a later period of the Session. *Defects of Committees on Petitions.*

Under this system the old practice was as follows:—A petition to introduce a Bill was immediately referred to one of these Committees,[4] but members seldom attended unless *Old practice before Committees on Petitions.*

---

[1] 29 Lords' Journ. 271-5; *ante,* Vol. I., pp. 437 *et seq.*

[2] *Post,* pp. 890-7.

[3] *Post,* pp. 828 *et seq.*

[4] Except petitions for Inclosure Bills not authorizing the drainage of lands and the levy of rates for works. In such cases proof of compliance with Standing Orders was given before the Committee on the Bill.—

the Bill was strongly opposed. On the day appointed for its meeting the Committee was constituted by the clerk, who chose from the list the names of any five members mentioned who happened to be present. It often happened that the only member present was the member who had charge of the Bill, but as it was necessary to show that the petition had been considered by a quorum, the clerk usually set down the names of four other members taken from the list, whether they attended or not.[1] The member charged with the Bill was then generally elected Chairman. The Committee's functions resembled those of a grand jury. They inquired, first, whether Standing Orders had or had not been complied with; and, secondly, the promoters were bound to make out such a *primâ facie* case of expediency as would justify the Committee in recommending the introduction of the Bill. Although under the Standing Order just mentioned no opposing petitioners could appear at this stage, the rule was sometimes evaded by hostile members, who were supplied with a brief by opponents, and availed themselves of their right to ask any questions and call for any evidence which would damage the Bill.[2]

Extent of Committee's inquiry.

Decisions by these Committees upon the technical questions submitted to them were final, subject to an appeal to the whole House, which had not heard the evidence, and was a still less competent tribunal. In 1824 this evil was in part corrected by the constitution of a Standing Orders' Committee,[3] consisting of twenty-one members, to be appointed

Standing Orders' Committee constituted, 1824.

Sherwood on Private Business in House of Commons; London, 1829, p. 5.

[1] Sherwood, p. 6. In 1828 a member complained to the House that his name had been entered by the Committee clerk as if he had been present at a Committee, which had reported a compliance with Standing Orders, whereas he had determined upon opposing the Bill on the ground that Standing Orders had not been complied with. The Speaker thereupon issued an order that no names should be entered by the Committee clerk unless the members were really present. It is clear that this rule, however necessary, acted as a serious hindrance to business. (Ib. *n.*)

[2] Ib. p. 8, *n.*

[3] 79 Com. Journ. 71

at the commencement of each Session. A similar tribunal
was created in the Upper House. If the Committee on a
petition reported favourably, a Bill might be introduced
without further objection. It was otherwise if the Committee found that Standing Orders had not been observed.
Their report then went before the Standing Orders' Committee, with a statement of the facts upon which they based
their decision, and of any special circumstances connected
with the case.[1] Promoters were then allowed to petition and
allege reasons for dispensing with Orders which they had,
perhaps, accidentally broken, or the breach of which involved
no substantial irregularity. From an adverse decision by the
Committee on Standing Orders promoters might still appeal
to the House, and there are instances in which this appeal
succeeded.[2]

Petitions to dispense with Standing Orders.

An abuse which tended to prolong contests and create
expense was the attempt often successfully made by opponents to raise Standing Order objections before Committees on Bills. Opponents used to hold back their case
on technical grounds until the Committee stage, when great
cost must have been incurred upon the Bill, and incurred,
perhaps, in vain. With a view to check this practice, the
House of Commons adopted, in 1825, an Order (known as
Mr. Stuart Wortley's), providing that no petitions "referring
solely" to non-compliance with Standing Orders should be
received after a first reading. But through the difficulty
often experienced by opponents in raising these objections at
earlier stages of the Bill, they were still sometimes raised,
directly or indirectly, in Committee, and influenced the
decision.[3]

Standing Order objec-tions before Committee on opposed Bills.

Although the appointment of a Standing Orders' Committee was a beneficial reform, the Committees on Petitions
were still left with all their defects of constitution and pro-

---

[1] Commons Standing Order 5, Sess. 1837.
[2] Liverpool Dock Bill, February 25, 1828; London Bridge Approaches Bill, March 14, 1834.
[3] Sherwood, 57.

Commons'
Committee on
Petitions,
1837.

cedure. In 1837 the House of Commons, endeavouring to amend some of these defects, appointed a new Committee on Petitions,[1] of which Mr. C. Shaw-Lefevre was Chairman. This Committee was strictly of a judicial character; its functions were limited to questions arising upon Standing Orders; and it consisted of forty-two members, who had power to form themselves into Sub-Committees for greater despatch of business. The Committee, however, met occasionally in a body to discuss and settle points of procedure. Greater uniformity of decision and more consistent practice were thus secured than had been known in these Committees at any former period. So far there was a distinct improvement in practice, but private business was still greatly delayed and cost increased by the faulty arrangements for hearing Standing Orders cases at this time.[2]

Appointment
of Examiners.

No Committees could be struck until Parliament met. An obvious remedy for delay was to begin private business earlier. This plan occurred to a Commons' Committee in 1846. They were of opinion that inquiries upon Standing Orders might be safely delegated to officers of Parliament; that one such inquiry on the part of both Houses should be substituted for a separate investigation by each House; and that this inquiry should open before Parliament met, so that, when there had been no breach of Standing Orders, Bills might be at once brought in. This recommendation was

Business of
1847.

adopted by the House of Commons.[3] In 1847, two Examiners replaced the Committees on petitions, and, beginning their duties in the middle of January, disposed, in less than eight weeks, of 487 petitions, of which ninety-five were opposed on Standing Orders. It was calculated that the business thus dealt with by the two Examiners,[4] sitting separately,

[1] 92 Com. Journ. 636; 97 Ib. 561.
[2] Letter of the Speaker (Mr. C. S. Lefevre), in Fifth Report of Mr. Cardwell's Committee, 1853; Appendix, pp. 251-2.

[3] 101 Com. Journ. 1266; 107 Ib. 342.
[4] The examiners first appointed were Mr. Samuel Smith and Mr. Erskine May.

would have occupied four Committees, sitting during the usual hours, nearly double that time. The results gained were a great saving of labour to members,[1] and an estimated saving of at least 100,000*l.* to suitors, while private business in the House of Commons was advanced about two months, as compared with previous Sessions.[2] These advantages are still secured, and inquiries into Standing Orders are now usually concluded in the Commons at about the period when sub-committees on petitions used to begin their labours.

In 1855, after ample experience of the new system in the Commons, the House of Lords agreed to appoint the same examiners. At first they were not authorized to report upon Bills which were opposed, leaving these to be dealt with by the Standing Orders' Committee. In 1858, however, a Committee of the House of Lords, presided over by Lord Stanley of Alderley, recommended that the examiners should report upon all Bills; that their decision should be final upon matters of fact; and that the Standing Orders' Committee should consider and determine all memorials praying that Standing Orders should be dispensed with. This was the system in the Commons, and the House of Lords adopted it. For the purposes of this preliminary inquiry the two Houses now work practically in concert, and two examiners, one appointed by the Speaker, the other by the Chairman of Lords' Committees, act concurrently on behalf of both Houses, but make separate reports to each House. The appeal, however, is not to a joint tribunal. Each House still asserts its own appellate jurisdiction, and exercises, through its Committee on Standing Orders, the right of deciding upon

New system adopted by House of Lords, 1855.

Appeal to Standing Orders Committee in each House.

---

[1] In 1846 six sub-committees sat to inquire into compliance with Standing Orders. Hundreds of witnesses were in attendance for this purpose in each important case. Upon one Bill alone four hundred witnesses were called to prove Standing Orders, at an expense estimated at 10,000*l.*, including delays, for promoters had sometimes to wait for weeks with their witnesses before their turn came.—Commons' Committee on Private Bills, 1846; Evidence of Mr. St. George Burke, pp. 104, 105; Mr. Creed, Committee clerk, p. 132.

[2] Commons' Committee of 1847 on Private Bills; Third Report, p. 4.

memorials by promoters to dispense with Standing Orders.[1] Considering the great cost incurred in preparing Bills, and the purely technical nature of many objections upon Standing Orders, a right of appeal from any finding of the examiners is obviously expedient.[2]

Committee of Selection, 1840.

Some useful suggestions for improving the transaction of private business were made by a Committee of the House of Commons in 1840. One was the appointment of a Committee of Selection which should nominate Committees on Bills, instead of leaving this duty to the House. This change, made during the same Session,[3] with subsequent modifications,[4] has tended to secure better tribunals than were before appointed. At first the jurisdiction of this body extended over all Bills, which were divided by them into groups to be submitted to the same Committee. In 1853, however, a new tribunal was appointed in the hope of securing special experience and more uniform decisions upon railway and canal Bills. The unsatisfactory results of departmental reports, founded upon preliminary inquiries, led Mr. Cardwell's Committee, in 1853, to the conclusion that consistency in dealing with railway and canal Bills could not be secured by laying down any general rules for the guidance of Committees, or by zeal and ability in any tribunal acting upon less than Parliamentary authority.[5] They therefore communicated through their chairman with

Committees on Railway and Canal Bills.

---

[1] The House of Lords appoints a Standing Orders Committee of forty members; the Chairman of Committees presides *ex officio*. Eleven members constitute a similar Committee in the other House.

[2] In 1878, as a condition of passing the Manchester Corporation Waterworks (Thirlmere) Bill, the House of Commons compelled the promoters to supply water to towns along the route, and waived the objection that this power was not covered by the notice. The House of Lords, however, held that of so large a power express notice was required, and the Bill accordingly failed for that Session. (*Ante*, pp. 481-2.) Sometimes the Standing Orders' Committee put promoters upon terms (*e.g.*, by striking out clauses which go beyond their notices), as a condition of dispensing with Standing Orders and allowing the Bill to proceed (Manchester Ship Canal Bill, 1883).

[3] 95 Com. Journ. 85.

[4] 101 Ib. 1263; 169 Ib. 410.

[5] Fifth Report, p. 14.

the Speaker,[1] suggesting "a Committee of a character more permanent than has heretofore been the practice, which might take a more comprehensive view of all schemes submitted to Parliament in every Session," and receive assistance from the Railway Department. This Committee was to "make provision for facilitating the passing of unopposed Bills, and for the investigation of contested Bills; divide the whole country into districts, upon the plan of territorial arrangement; collectively decide all questions of principle and questions in the decision of which more than one district might be interested; and so direct the investigation of schemes within the respective districts as to secure for the public within reach of them the utmost advantage which might be derived from a judicious combination of new lines with those which already exist."[2]

In reply, the Speaker formulated a plan, to be tried at the commencement of 1854. The Committee of Selection was to be authorized to appoint a Committee on railway and canal Bills, consisting of forty members, divided into eight sub-committees of five members each, naming eight chairmen, of whom one should preside over the whole Committee whenever they met, to lay down rules for the conduct of business, or to settle points of practice. To a Committee so chosen, all opposed Bills should be referred; while unopposed Bills were dealt with in the usual method.[3] In substance this plan was adopted; the Committee was constituted of not less than twenty-four or more than forty members; and to them was given the appointment of all Committees, and the task of grouping all railway and canal Bills.[4]

This system still exists. A Committee of Selection is appointed in each Session by the Lords; but they have not

General Committee on Railway and Canal Bills. Chairman's panel.

---

[1] The Rt. Hon. C. Shaw-Lefevre.

[2] Mr. Cardwell's letter to Speaker. Fifth Report of Committee of 1853; Appendix, 251.

[3] Ib. 252.

[4] 108 Com. Journ. 770; 109 Ib. 410. The Commons' Committee of Selection now consists of eight members, including the Chairman of the Committee on Standing Orders, who presides *ex officio*. (Commons' Standing Order 98, Sess. 1887.)

followed the Lower House in appointing a general Committee on railway and canal Bills. Private Bills in the Lords are grouped by the Chairman of Committees.

Chairman of Committees, House of Lords.

In each House the Chairman of Committees, better known in the Commons as Chairman of Ways and Means, exercises an important control over private business. Unopposed Bills go before him; he also examines each Bill after its introduction, to see that it contains no provisions repugnant to the rules and practice of Parliament. By long usage, which dates back at least to the time of Lord Shaftesbury, who filled this office from 1814 to 1851[1], peculiar authority is vested in the Chairman of Lords' Committees. He reads every private Bill, no matter in which House it may be first taken, and at once states his objections to inadequate recitals of material facts, and to proposals which seem against precedent, or are not likely to receive sanction. These objections are sometimes removed by explanation, or met by amendments; and, if a Bill begins in the Commons, promoters save time and expense by thus providing against alterations in the second House. This close supervision is also of public advantage, as some guarantee for uniformity of legislation. If in either House substantial amendments are made, a copy of the "filled-up" Bill is usually laid before the Chairman of Committees, for his information and approval.[2]

In the House of Commons, between the first and second readings, private Bills were formerly examined by clerks in the Private Bill Office. But these clerks were not competent to discharge such a duty, and in practice did not attempt to discharge it.[3] In theory, the Chairman of Ways and Means

Chairman of Ways and Means.

was expected to supervise, generally, both opposed and unopposed Bills, but his duties in the House itself have always been so onerous that he has never been able to devote to

---

[1] Succeeding Lord Walsingham.

[2] Joint Committee of 1876 on Parliamentary Agency; Evidence of Mr. Warner, counsel to Lord Redesdale, pp. 41–2.

[3] Commons' Committee on Private Business, 1838; Evidence of Mr. E. Johnson, principal clerk in Private Bill Office, p. 25.

private business the time and attention bestowed upon it in the corresponding office of the other House. In 1840, a Commons' Committee on private business recommended in vain that he should have legal assistance, but the House adopted their suggestion that he should act as chairman upon every unopposed measure, along with two or more members interested in the Bill; with power to report his opinion that it should be treated as an opposed measure. In 1850, the Chairman of Ways and Means again pleaded for the services of a competent legal assistant: he might then, he said, hope to render equal service with that given by Lord Shaftesbury, and hold a position of equal authority.[1]

Recognizing the need for further help in his department, the House of Commons agreed, in 1851, that, in examining and watching private Bills through their various stages, the Chairman of Ways and Means should be assisted by the counsel to Mr. Speaker. This officer, besides advising the Speaker on any legal questions coming before him, had previously acted as examiner of recognizances in election petitions, and also prepared the breviates of private Bills. He only gave occasional aid to the Chairman of Ways and Means in supervising Bills.[2] It was thought that, if relieved from the duty of examining recognizances, and preparing breviates, he would be able to render more useful service by "perusing private Bills on behalf of the public," communicating with agents, and seeing that no greater powers than were necessary were granted to promoters, and that those powers were guarded with due restrictions.[3]

Speaker's counsel.

According to a later authority the duties of Speaker's counsel are to see that private Bills contain nothing incon-

---

[1] Commons' Committee on Private Business, 1850-1; Evidence of Mr. Bernal, p. 31.

[2] Ib. p. 8; Evidence of Mr. Booth, who acted as Speaker's counsel up to 1850.

[3] Ib. pp. 10, 12, 13. See also Commons' Committee on Local Acts (Preliminary Inquiries), 1850; Second Report, p. 5. This Committee suggested that the Speaker's counsel should endeavour to promote uniformity of practice by frequent communication with Chairmen of Committees on opposed Bills.

sistent with Standing Orders, or with certain established rules and principles acted upon by Committees, or anything that may conflict with general legislation or prejudicially affect private interests.[1] He does not inquire into the merits of a Bill or engineering details. Apart from this supervision, the check established by Consolidation Acts and the intervention of public departments, it struck acute observers, in 1865, that before Private Bill Committees "the public have no friend" whose special business it is to protect them, especially in the case of unopposed Bills. When a Bill is opposed, opponents "put themselves in the shoes of the public," and allege all the public objections which occur to them. When promoters can satisfy individual opponents, Parliament, save for the checks mentioned, which are sometimes imperfect, knows nothing of public objections to a Bill: whatever is unnoticed by officials, or unopposed, is assumed to be unobjectionable.[2]

Public interests sometimes not effectually cared for.

Breviates,

It was formerly one of the Speaker's duties to state the effect and objects of every Bill before the Commons, from an abstract or breviate, supplied to him for the purpose. This practice was probably introduced to save time, as a substitute for that reading of the whole measure which seems to have been the ancient method in times when Bills were short. Traces of the old form still survive in the motions put "That this Bill be read a first time," and so at each successive stage.

Ancient use of, in Commons.

According to D'Ewes,[3] the system of presenting breviates with every Bill was introduced at a very early period, when business began to be conducted with regularity. These breviates, however, were often merely an abstract of the marginal notes, when such notes began to be used, and gave little information as to the effect of a measure, and none as to its bearing upon the existing law.[4] Owing to this want of clear information there were complaints that many Bills were

[1] Commons' Committee of 1865 on Court of Referees; Evidence of Mr. G. K. Rickards, p. 113.
[2] See questions of Lord Robert Cecil and Mr. Lowe, Ib. pp. 114-15.

[3] He compiled Journals of the Parliaments of Elizabeth.
[4] Todd on Practice and Privileges of Parliament, note to p. 208.

passed by the House in ignorance that they established monopolies, or otherwise injuriously affected public and local interests.

An order of 1661 in the Lords directed that private Bills were not to be read until a brief was made. In 1689 "brevials" were to be made of all Bills.[1] Breviates, or briefs, are first mentioned in the Commons' Journals in 1606, when Committees were directed, if they amended any Bill referred to them, to amend the brief annexed, and make it agree with the Bill.[2] During the Commonwealth it was ordered "that no Ordinance shall be brought in but with a brief unto it; and that the party that brings in the Ordinance shall bring in the brief; and Mr. Speaker open the Ordinance."[3] There must have been frequent evasions of this rule, for we find it repeated more peremptorily in 1651:— "Resolved, and the Parliament doth declare, that no Act ought to be presented to this House without a brief thereof given to Mr. Speaker; and that Mr. Speaker ought not to open any Bill, nor command the same to be read, unless a brief thereof be first delivered to him; and that this order be from henceforth duly and exactly observed accordingly."[4]

Breviates mentioned in Commons 1606.

It may be gathered from this entry that breviates were handed in by a member responsible for the Bill. At a later date breviates of private Bills were drawn up by agents for promoters, under Standing Orders, and clerks in the Private Bill Office were expected to compare each breviate with the Bill, and see that the effect of its chief provisions was sufficiently indicated. At the foot of each breviate, the examining clerk stated whether it was or was not prepared in due form. The form of breviate was such as the Speaker from time to time directed.[5] During the Speakership of Mr. Abbot[6] he required that a breviate should set forth the principal provisions and be divided into classes of clauses,

Practice as to breviates in private Bills.

---

[1] 11 L. J. 335; 14 Ib. 410.
[2] 1 Com. Journ. 346.
[3] 3 Ib. 299, A.D. 1643.
[4] 6 Com. Journ. 570.

[5] Commons' Standing Order No. 16, Sess. 1832.
[6] He served from 1802 to 1817, when he was created Lord Colchester.

but not made too lengthy.[1] When a Bill passed a second reading, the breviate was sent into the engrossing office, and afterwards to the House of Lords.

New rules of 1838.
Although care was thus taken to inform the House of the effect of pending legislation, complaints were made that local Bills imposing burdensome tolls, penalties, and obligations, and deviating from general legislation, were often passed in ignorance. After inquiry, the House of Commons came to the conclusion that breviates of private Bills should be prepared by one of its own officers, and further time given to consider them. It accordingly resolved that no private Bill should be read a second time until six days after a breviate thereof had been laid on the table and printed. This breviate was to "contain a statement of the objects" of a Bill, with " a summary of its proposed enactments," and in what respects it would vary the general law.[2] In order to carry out these resolutions, the Speaker was authorized to appoint an officer of legal experience to prepare the breviate on private Bills.[3]

Practice after 1838.
Private Bills were not at this period printed until they had passed the Committee on petitions. After being printed promoters sent their Bill to the Speaker's counsel, accompanying it with a meagre summary prepared by themselves, in conformity with the old system. Having obtained the official breviate in manuscript, promoters caused it to be printed, and before the second reading were required to deposit in the Vote Office 660 copies of this breviate, for distribution among members with the votes. As no Bills could be read a second time until six days after the printed breviate had been placed on the table, and as the preparation of the official breviate often took a week or more, there were bitter complaints of delay in the conduct of private business. Fresh

[1] Commons' Committee on Private Business, 1838 ; Evidence of Mr. E. Johnson, p. 25.
[2] Com. Journ., January 23, 1838.
[3] He appointed Mr. Booth, who then acted as Speaker's counsel, and whose name has so often occurred in these pages. Mr. Booth, afterwards joint secretary at the Board of Trade, was a public servant of great experience and ability.

delay also occurred when amendments of substantial importance were made in Committee, for then another official breviate was necessary, showing the effect of these changes.[1] Unless specially applied for, private Bills are not supplied to members, as public Bills and Parliamentary Papers are supplied. Thus, breviates furnished materials which generally came before members in no other form; and, assuming that any attention was paid to them, they were presumably useful records of proposed legislation.

Excellent in theory as the revised system may have been, and carefully as breviates were now prepared, the House of Commons, after experience of the practical results, did not think it a system worth preserving. Changes, too, occurred meanwhile in the form of Bills. The experiment of 1838 was made at a time when private Bills were of enormous size, containing clauses common to all measures of the same class. It was then difficult for members to ascertain the provisions which were special to a particular measure, and breviates therefore had much justification. But the Consolidation Acts of 1845 and 1847 took away these common clauses from private Bills, and so reduced their bulk that a railway Bill, which, before 1845, occupied something like 100 folio pages, was afterwards contained in about ten pages.[2] This wholesale abridgment greatly facilitated reference. On the other hand, besides causing intolerable delay, two sets of breviates on each Bill caused no inconsiderable expense,[3] which varied from 15l. to 20l., so that, according to the number of Bills introduced, the total annual cost rose from about 5,000l. to an estimated sum, in 1846, of 15,000l.

Failure of experiment.

Cost of breviates.

[1] Commons' Committee on Private Business, 1838; Evidence of Mr. St. George Burke, p. 2.

[2] Without the Consolidation Acts, it has been said, private legislation in 1846 would have come to a deadlock. (Commons' Committee on Private Bill Legislation, 1863; Evidence of Mr. Booth, p. 4; *ante,* pp. 521 *et seq.*)

[3] Commons' Committee on Private Business, 1838; Evidence of Mr. J. P. Hayward, parliamentary agent, p. 15.

Breviates
abolished,
1851.

A still stronger objection was the fact that summaries received little attention, unless members were specially interested in the subject, and then they consulted the Bill itself, now reduced to reasonable dimensions. In 1847 the Speaker[1] pronounced against breviates, and repeated this opinion in 1851. He had expected advantages from them, and they were of some benefit before the era of Consolidation Acts; but he frankly owned that latterly they had been perfectly useless, only causing needless outlay to promoters.[2] In conformity with this and other evidence, a Committee reported that the value of the system was not commensurate with its expense, and breviates were accordingly discontinued.[3]

Suggested
revival of
breviates on
public Bills,
1875.

It may be noted here that, in 1875, a Committee appointed "to consider whether any and what means can be adopted to improve the manner and language of current legislation," recommended the revival of breviates upon public Bills, to explain their object, and show how previous legislation will be affected.[4]

Petitions
against Bills.

The common right of petitioning Parliament in favour of or against any pending measure extends to private as well as public Bills. As, however, the jurisdiction exercised by Parliament over private Bills is quasi-judicial as well as legislative, it follows that though all persons or corporations may petition, all have not necessarily a right to be heard. Petitioners in favour of a private Bill are not in practice allowed to appear upon their petitions, for they may, if promoters think fit, be called as witnesses on behalf of a Bill, in which capacity they may state their reasons for supporting it, and the value of their evidence may then be tested by cross-examination. On the other hand, complaints of opposing petitioners that a Bill will injure them if passed into law may be groundless, or without adequate grounds, even on the face

---

[1] The Rt. Hon. Charles Shaw-Lefevre. The change had been made during Mr. Abercromby's Speakership.

[2] Commons' Committee on Private Business, 1851; Evidence, p. 6.

[3] Commons' Committee on Local Acts, 1850–1; Second Report, p. 3.

[4] Report, p. 6.

of their petition. How and at what stage of a Bill should this issue be raised?

Before the year 1864 the practice of the two Houses was uniform on this point. When an opposed Bill came to be heard in Committee, counsel for promoters, at the end of his speech, or when opposing counsel rose to cross-examine the first witness, took objection to the petitioners' *locus standi.* This proceeding was in the nature of a demurrer, and the objection was based upon the petitioners' own statements, as showing no injury from the Bill, or no sufficient injury entitling them to be heard. Sometimes objections rested upon informality in a petition, such as the want of adequate authority on the part of signatories professing to represent public bodies, or the absence of sufficiently specific allegations. No previous notice was necessary of an intention to raise objections, and it happened not infrequently that petitioners who had prepared an elaborate case, and brought witnesses at great expense from distant parts of the kingdom, did so only to be dismissed at the outset, without having an opportunity even of opening their case.

Practice of Parliament before 1864.

In 1864, the House of Commons came to the conclusion, after inquiry,[1] that its procedure in this respect might be amended. One reason for amending it was the needless expense incurred by petitioners, whose right to be heard should, it was thought, be determined at an earlier stage of a Bill. Still stronger grounds for change were found in the time occupied before Committees in discussing *locus standi* questions, and the uncertainty of decisions then given upon more or less technical points by fluctuating bodies suddenly called upon to deal with each case as it arose. "Although," it was said, "decisions are continually being given upon points of the greatest consequence to the public, no rule, no law is created. A judicial decision is of value to litigants, but is of still greater value to the rest of the community, who steer

Change of procedure by Commons, 1864.

[1] Commons' Committee on Standing Orders, 1864.

their course by it, and are thus enabled to avoid litigation. Such a result, however, has not been attained by the action of our Committees. One does not know what another has done or is doing. No record is kept; although a point may have arisen twenty times before, it is treated as a case of first impression; and the same question is often decided by different Committees in diametrically opposite ways. . . . . If a judicial and permanent element be introduced into the Committees, their judgments will be reported and gathered together, and will form precedents which will guide future decisions." [1]

Establishment of Court of Referees, 1864.

Concurring in this view, the House of Commons agreed to establish a tribunal, called the Court of Referees, who should, at an early stage of each opposed Bill, determine the right to a hearing of all petitioners whose *locus standi* was disputed.

Duties first assigned to referees.

For some time after the constitution of this Court, which first met in 1865, it also undertook a preliminary investigation into engineering details and estimates whenever promoters proposed to construct works. In the case of waterworks Bills, it was bound to investigate sources of supply, actual and proposed, quality of water, and provision for storage reservoirs. Gas Bills were subjected to inquiry as to quality, quantity, price, amount of pressure, cost of production, and modes of testing purity and illuminating power. So comprehensive, in fact, was this preliminary examination by the referees that difficulty was at times experienced in determining the exact border line between their labours and those of Committees, who, later on, inquired into merits and policy. Under Standing Orders of 1865, the referees were authorized to examine the whole subject-matter of any Bill, if promoters and opponents agreed that all questions at issue should be referred to the new tribunal. Such agree-

---

[1] 175 Hansard; speech of Mr. Lowe, pp. 1563-4. Such a body of precedents now exists, and forms a continuous record of decisions upon the *locus standi* of petitions in the House of Commons from 1867. (See *post*, pp. 809, 810, *n*.)

ment, however, was hardly to be expected, and this complete jurisdiction was rarely exercised.[1]

As first constituted, the Court consisted of the Chairman of Ways and Means, three paid referees appointed by the Speaker, and any members of Parliament who consented to serve without payment. One or more tribunals might, if necessary, be formed; over the first the Chairman of Ways and Means presided, the rule being that the chairman of any second Court should also be a member of the House. Petitioners against private Bills, upon any of the points to which the referees' jurisdiction extended, endorsed upon their petitions a statement of the grounds on which they desired to be heard. Promoters, in their turn, were required to lodge with the Court, and to serve upon petitioners, notice of the grounds on which they intended to object to the *locus standi*. Every report made by the referees to the House, upon engineering or financial details, was communicated to the Committee upon the Bill, who accepted this report as a record of facts, and rejected further evidence upon any points covered by it. If the referees reported that the engineering was bad or the estimate insufficient, no further proceedings were taken upon a measure unless the House ordered otherwise.[2]

The expediency of continuing this wide range of inquiry by referees was a good deal discussed by the House of Commons, who, in 1865, appointed a Select Committee to consider whether the system had worked satisfactorily. On the somewhat uncertain basis of a comparison of the average time occupied by opposed private Bills in portions of the three Sessions, 1863-5, this Committee were of opinion that members had been spared considerable labour in transacting private business, which was one material object in establishing the new Court. They also thought that, on the whole,

Margin notes: Constitution of Court. Early practice. Committee of 1865.

[1] Practice of Court of Referees on Private Bills, by Frederick Clifford and Pembroke S. Stephens, Q.C., 1870, pp. 2, 3.
[2] Ib. pp. 3, 4.

member; the two other paid referees also sit when not serving upon Committees. Procedure is regulated by Standing Orders,[1] which empower Committees on Bills to refer questions to the referees,[2] and lay down certain general conditions regulating the admission of petitioners, including shareholders, railway companies, chambers of commerce or agriculture, traders and freighters, and municipal and other local authorities.[3] There is often no little difficulty in applying these rules to the special circumstances of each case, and in deciding upon points not covered by Standing Orders.[4] When facts pertinent to the issue are in dispute the referees hear evidence, and have a statutory power to administer oaths;[5] but they always decline to go into merits, except so far as is necessary to enable them to understand a case.

It will be seen that to the referees is given a power of excluding petitioners in Parliament, not merely from relief, but even from the opportunity of urging, before the Committee who consider a Bill, reasons why they should receive relief. This is a very grave power; it depends frequently upon the

Referee Courts, sat as Chairman of Railway Committees for 57 days in 1860; 42 days in 1861; 56 days in 1862; 41 days in 1863; and 48 days in 1864. Mr. Hassard, another able and assiduous Chairman of Committees, presided over a Court of Referees, and served as Chairman of Railway Committees for 48 days in 1861; 47 in 1862; 51 in 1863; and 54 in 1864. (Com. Committee on Referees, 1865, Ev. p. 1.) Lord Stanley in 1862 acted for sixty-five days as Chairman of Railway Committees. The great services also rendered by Mr. Wilson Patten (afterwards Lord Winmarleigh) must not be forgotten. To him the establishment of the Court of Referees was mainly due, and, excepting one year, when he held office under the Crown, he served on the Standing Orders Committee for forty years; during

a large portion of this time he was Chairman of the Committee. Such a record of unobtrusive but most useful work in Parliament is probably unparalleled. It must be understood that the services of all these members were unpaid.

[1] Commons' Standing Orders 87—90, Sess. 1887.

[2] Ib. 90; this power is very rarely exercised.

[3] Ib. 130—135.

[4] As this is not a work on Practice, reference must be made to the Reports for the principles established by current decisions. An excellent summary of these principles, taken from the Reports by Clifford and Stephens and Clifford and Rickards, is given by Lord Farnborough (Sir Erskine May) in his Parliamentary Practice, 9th ed., pp. 815 *et seq.*

[5] 30 & 31 Vict. c. 136.

discretion of the tribunal ;[1] and in case of accident or mis-apprehension it may inflict a serious injustice upon individuals. To deny them the right of appeal from an adverse decision would be an added injustice, all the more keenly felt, perhaps, because a majority of the judges deciding their case upon this Parliamentary tribunal may not themselves be members of Parliament.[2]

Such an appeal is provided by the Lords, who retain their own jurisdiction upon questions of *locus standi*, and exercise it in the old form. A Committee of this House, which sat in 1858 to inquire into private Bill procedure, recommended "that questions of *locus standi* be referred to a Committee appointed for the consideration of such questions." The Lords, however, have not acted upon this recommendation; each Committee upon an opposed Bill decides upon the petitioners' right to appear, and sometimes differs in opinion from the fixed tribunal in the Commons. Nor does the House of Lords attempt to fetter the discretion of its Committees by rules, except in declaring that shareholders dissenting at a Wharncliffe meeting shall be heard against a Bill.[3]

Practical appeal in Lords from decision in Commons.

A constitutional question of some interest affecting the referees was decided in 1876. Complaint was made in the House of Commons that referees serving on Committees claimed under the Standing Orders a right to vote; that their claim had been allowed; and that local Bills had thus been defeated.[4] A strong Committee was thereupon appointed,

Right of referees to vote in Committees.

---

[1] Commons' Standing Orders 130, 134, leave the *locus standi* of local authorities and inhabitants and of petitioners complaining of competition entirely to the referees' discretion, which is also very often exercised in considering the degree of injury entitling petitioners to appear against a Bill.

[2] The Court is constituted if a single member be present (in the chair) with two paid referees.

[3] Lords' Standing Order 105, Sess. 1887. See also the more recent Standing Order 105A, which allows a Committee, if they think fit, to hear a Chamber of Commerce or Agriculture, "sufficiently representing a trade or business," to be heard against new railway rates and fares. This power of petitioning is much more restricted than that given by a corresponding Order (133A) in the Commons, which extends to rates and fares already authorized.

[4] 227 Hansard, 486; February 18, 1876.

consisting of twenty-one members, to inquire and report " as to the legality and expediency of allowing the referees the same power of voting on a Private Bill Committee as a member of Parliament regularly elected by a constituency." After hearing evidence this Committee were unanimously of opinion that referees serving upon a Private Bill Committee were assessors only, and that it was " inconsistent with ancient Parliamentary usage, and opposed to constitutional principle," to give them a right of voting.[1]   In accordance with this view Committees on private Bills were instructed that referees should in future take part in all their proceedings, but should not vote.[2]

Power of Committees to award costs. So lately as the year 1865, though Election Committees could give costs at their discretion, Committees on private Bills had no power of doing so, however frivolous and vexatious the petition, or however unjustifiable the conduct of promoters.   In 1865, Committees in both Houses received a statutory power to award costs, but only if they are unanimously of opinion that a petitioner has been " unreasonably or vexatiously subjected to expense in defending his rights," or, on the other hand, that promoters " have been vexatiously subjected to expense " by a petitioner's opposition.[3]   In the former case Committees may award to a petitioner all or a part of his costs ; in the latter, such portion of the costs of promotion as they may think fit.   They must report their decision to the House, and the costs awarded must be taxed. An exception is made in favour of a " landowner who *bond fide* at his own sole risk and charge opposes a Bill which proposes to take any portion of his property."[4]   Such a petitioner is not liable to costs.   Committees, however, rarely exercise their power of giving costs against either petitioners or promoters.   When Committees award costs against promoters, reporting " preamble not proved," such costs are

[1] Commons' Committee on Referees, 1876 ; Report, p. 4.
[2] 131 Com. Journ. 120 ; 228 Hansard, 614–18.
[3] 28 Vict. c. 27.
[4] Ib. s. 2.

to be paid out of the preliminary deposit required under Standing Orders.[1]

By an Act passed in 1867,[2] the Court of Referees was authorized to award costs "in the same manner as Committees on private Bills." But as this authority was limited to cases in which the referees were "empowered to inquire into the whole subject-matter" of any Bill,[3] and as this jurisdiction was afterwards abolished, it follows that this Court no longer possesses power to give costs in any cases whatever.

Costs in Court of Referees.

A general statute, passed in 1871,[4] repealing an Act of the previous Session, extended the power of awarding costs to Committees on Bills confirming Provisional Orders. In some more recent Acts, however, dating from 1875, and authorizing the issue of Provisional Orders by various Departments, special provision was made for costs, with a view to discourage unnecessary opposition and expense. Committees in these cases are required to "take into consideration the circumstances" under which the Bill was opposed, and "whether such opposition was or was not justified"; in awarding costs they need not be unanimous, as they must be upon ordinary private Bills; and no protection, as in that case, is given to opposing landowners.[5] Provisional certificates are not mentioned in the Act of 1871 above mentioned. Select Committees, to whom are referred Bills for confirming provisional certificates, cannot, therefore, award costs unless specially empowered to do so by the statutes which authorize departments to grant certificates.

Costs on Provisional Order Confirmation Bills.

A scale regulating the charges of Parliamentary agents

Scale of charges of

---

[1] Ib. s. 8.

[2] 30 & 31 Vict. c. 136.

[3] Ib. s. 3.

[4] 34 Vict. c. 3. In part repealed; see 34 & 35 Vict. c. 83, s. 2; 46 & 47 Vict. c. 49.

[5] See Artizans and Labourers' Dwellings Improvement Acts for England, Ireland, and Scotland (38 & 39 Vict. c. 36, s. 7, and c. 49, s. 7); Public Parks (Scotland) Act, 1878 (41 Vict. c. 8, s. 9); Roads and Bridges (Scotland) Act, 1878 (41 & 42 Vict. c. 51, s. 10, which omits any express provision that the Committee need not be unanimous); and Labourers (Ireland) Act, 1883 (46 & 47 Vict. c. 60, s. 9).

Parliamentary agents.
was first drawn up about the year 1827 by the authority of Lord Devon, applying to Bills in the Upper House.[1] In the Commons a scale was settled in 1845, at an informal meeting attended by Mr. Palk, Lord Shaftesbury's counsel, by Mr. Booth, the Speaker's counsel, and the principal Parliamentary agents, Mr. Aglionby, a member of the House, acting as chairman. This scale did not include the bills of solicitors engaged in Parliamentary practice, or those of Scotch agents.[2] At the instance of a Committee in 1847,[3] a more complete scale was drawn up under the Speaker's authority.[4]

Taxation of costs.
The first statute providing for the taxation of costs in the House of Commons was passed in 1825;[5] and a similar Act relating to the House of Lords in the following Session.[6] By the Act of 1825 the Speaker could only refer Bills for taxation upon an application from a promoter; nor was there any power of taxing the costs of opponents. The Speaker could refer a bill of costs to any person. On the retirement of Mr. Rose, who used to discharge this duty, no officer of the House possessed the necessary experience to continue it, and from 1841 to 1845 there was practically no taxation. The Speaker then arranged with the Lord Chancellor that bills of costs should be referred to Mr. Follett, a taxing master in the Court of Chancery, but his other duties soon prevented him from carrying on this work.[7]

Costs Act, 1847 (House of Commons).
In furtherance of recommendations made by the Select Committee of 1846-7, an Act was passed "for the more effectual taxation of costs on private Bills in the House of Commons." This statute authorized the Speaker to appoint

---

[1] Commons' Committee of 1847 on Private Bills; Evidence of Mr. R. B. Follett, pp. 3, 11, 12.

[2] Ib. Evidence of Mr. Lefroy, Speaker's Secretary, p. 2.

[3] Ib. Third Rep., pp. 11, 12.

[4] See 10 & 11 Vict. c. 69, s. 4, enabling the Speaker from time to

time to prepare a list of charges to be made by agents, solicitors, and others.

[5] 6 Geo. IV. c. 123.

[6] 7 & 8 Geo. IV. c. 64.

[7] Commons' Committee of 1847 on Private Bills; Evidence of Mr. Lefroy, p. 2.

a taxing officer who might tax the costs on the application of either party,[1] with power to examine witnesses on oath, call for books and papers, and charge fixed fees for this service.[2]

In 1849 a similar Act was passed, applying to private Bills in the Lords, and giving equal powers to a taxing officer appointed by the clerk of the Parliaments.[3] Other provisions extend the power of taxation in both Houses, and require taxing officers in Parliament and in other Courts to assist each other in settling mixed bills of costs.[4] The object is to secure a settlement, upon the usual and proper scale, of Parliamentary charges which may happen to be mixed up in an ordinary bill of law costs. Upon a requisition from any one of the principal Secretaries of State, or the President of the Local Government Board, the taxing officers deal with Bills promoted or opposed by local authorities under the Borough Funds Act.[5] Estate Bills have always been taxed in the Court of Chancery. The taxing officers in each House have co-ordinate jurisdiction.

It must be understood that comparatively few bills of Parliamentary costs are taxed. This ordeal is necessary only on measures over which public departments have a statutory control, or when clients ask for taxation, or when agents or solicitors require legal process to compel payment from clients. The taxing officer of the Commons stated in 1851 that he taxed Bills in the previous Session to the amount of 200,000l.; that, since his appointment three years before, bills of costs for more than 500,000l., including disbursements, had been submitted to him for taxation.[6] In the Lords, the taxing officer stated in 1876 that "not one bill out of twenty" came before him.[7]

Costs Act, 1849 (House of Lords).

Extent of taxation.

---

[1] 10 & 11 Vict. c. 69, s. 4.
[2] Ib. ss. 3—8.
[3] 12 & 13 Vict. c. 78.
[4] Ib. ss. 10—13.
[5] 35 & 36 Vict. c. 91, s. 6.

[6] Commons' Committee on Private Business, 1851; Evidence of Mr. Erskine May, pp. 27-9.
[7] Joint Committee of 1876 on Parliamentary Agency, p. 27.

CHAPTER XXII.

PROCEEDINGS ON OPPOSED BILLS:—HEARING BY SELECT COM-
MITTEES: ATTENDED IN LORDS BY JUDGES AND SERJEANTS:
NOTICE OF MEETING OF COMMITTEES: TIME AND PLACE OF
MEETING: ABUSE OF POWERS BY COMMITTEES: PROCEED-
INGS VOID AFTER HOUSE AT PRAYERS: CONSTITUTION OF
COMMITTEES: NOMINATED BY HOUSE: VOICES: SPEAKER'S
LISTS IN COMMONS: CHANGES IN NUMBER OF MEMBERS:
CHOICE OF CHAIRMAN: CHAIRMEN'S PANEL: COURT AND
COMMITTEES OF APPEAL.

Three stages for hearing opposed Bills. WHEN Committees on petitions for Bills reported favourably, and the Bills were introduced, opposing petitioners,
according to old practice, might be heard at the bar, in
Committee of the whole House, or before Select Committees.
Both Houses used their discretion in fixing the stage for
hearing, and varied it according to convenience or the circumstances of each case. With other points of procedure,
however, this will be more conveniently treated in the next
chapter, along with the employment of counsel in Parliament.
Here the system of constituting Committees on private
Bills will be mainly considered.

Lords' Com-mittees not always peers. References of these Bills to Committees by either House
are among the earliest entries in the Journals, and no doubt
are of still more ancient date. But members of Committees

in the Lords were not always peers. In 1511 a private Bill was referred by this House to Serjeants-at-law, who appear to have reported that a new Bill was necessary.[1] In the same Session five peers were appointed to consider a Bill for abolishing the corporation of stock-fishmongers and investigate complaints against this body.[2] Two commoners, John Fyneux and Robert Reed, were named on the Committee. No description of them is given, and no reason for nominating them.

At this period, and down to the present century, the Judges, who were "assistants," and the Serjeants, who, with the Masters in Chancery, were "attendants," in the House of Lords, were frequently appointed to Committees on private Bills, no doubt to advise the peers upon legal points. King's counsel ordered "to attend on the woolsacks" were "never to be covered" while the House was sitting, whereas the Judges so attending might be covered on receiving leave from the House, conveyed through the Lord Chancellor.[3] In Committees neither Judges nor counsel were allowed to sit or be covered, "unless it be out of favour for infirmity."[4] Judges also acted as assistants to Committees on public Bills. On December 6, 1641, a Bill "for the relief of captives taken by the Turkish and Moorish pirates, and to prevent the taking of others in time to come," was referred to a Committee of eighteen prelates and peers, with Justice Reeves, Justice Foster, and Justice Malett as assistants.[5]

Assisted by Judges and Serjeants.

Judges attending and advising Committees on public Bills.

As early as 1640-2 we find directions given by the House of Commons for due notice of the sittings of Committees.

Notice of Committees.

---

[1] After notice of second reading, the entry is—" hodie billa concernens Johannem Heyron liberata servientibus ad legem." (1 Lords' Journ. 12.)

[2] Ib.

[3] Lords' Journ. June 9, 1660.

[4] Ib. June 28, 1715. It is recorded of Chief Justice Popham, who often attended Committees, that, "though he was Chief Justice, Privy Councillor, and infirm, yet he would hardly ever be persuaded to sit down, saying it was his duty to stand and attend, and desired the Lords to keep those forms which were their due."

[5] 4 Lords' Journ. 463.

All chairmen were "required to set up notes at the door of the times and places when the several Committees do meet."[1] Similar directions were given by the House in 1657 and 1660, the duty being then delegated to the clerk, "that persons may take notice when they sit."[2] In 1699 Committees were ordered not to sit "without a week's public notice thereof set up in the lobby."[3]

Time of meeting.

The early hours kept by ancient Parliaments extended to their Committees. In 1648 it was ordered that no Committee of the House of Commons should sit in the morning after nine o'clock, and the House was "enjoined to meet every day at nine a.m."[4] A different method was adopted in 1694, when it was ordered "that no Committee sit in the morning without special leave of the House."[5] Even then no Committee authorized to sit in a morning was to do so after ten o'clock.[6] In 1699 Committees were directed not to meet at any time "until two hours after the rising of the House."[7] But this rule was abandoned in favour of the old practice, by which Committees met before the House sat. A rule of 1620 enjoins Commons' Committees not to sit on Saturday afternoons.[8]

Place of meeting.

Accommodation seems to have been wanting in the House of Commons for the meetings of Committees. They used to deliberate in the Star Chamber, the Treasurer's Chamber, the Chequer Chamber, using rooms commonly appropriated for other purposes. In default of space when these rooms were occupied, the Committees between the years 1571 and 1580 were frequently appointed to meet in the Temple Church.[9] Another place of meeting was at the Savoy. The Guildhall was frequently used for Commons' Com-

---

[1] 2 Com. Journ. 67, A.D. 1640. Ib. 549; April 30, 1642.

[2] Ib. January 21, 1657; May 26, 1660.

[3] 13 Ib. 6.

[4] Com. Journ. February 12, 1648.

[5] Ib. November 19, 1694. Revived February 9, 1697, and November 29, 1710.

[6] Ib. February 18, 1697.

[7] Ib. April 19, 1699.

[8] 1 Ib. 513.

[9] Ib. 85 et seq.

mittees upon Bills relating to trade or affecting the City, as the Free Grammar School at Tonbridge; a Bill introduced in 1572 " against injuries offered by Corporations in the City of London to divers foreign artificers"; a Bill " touching the making of woollen cloths"; and another "for cutting and working tanned leather."[1] In 1604, and for many years afterwards, the Middle Temple hall, then just rebuilt, was frequently appointed for inquiries by Committees of the House.[2] The Inner Temple, Lincoln's Inn, and Goldsmiths' halls were also used for the same purpose. Besides occasional want of accommodation, there was another reason why Committees had these distant places of meeting. Inconvenience arose from the attendance of strangers at Committees within the precincts of the House. It was therefore ordered in 1650 " that such Committees of the House who shall have occasion to call any other persons to attend them upon any Bill, or other business to them referred, do from henceforth forbear to sit in any of the rooms within the doors of the Parliament-House, called the Speaker's Chamber, but that they sit in such other place as they shall think fit."[3]

During the Commonwealth, or perhaps earlier, a practice appears to have grown up, by which Committees took upon themselves to issue directions and impose conditions which derogated from the authority of Parliament. In the year 1641, one Theophilus Man petitioned the House of Commons, setting forth that a Committee, over which Mr. King presided, had passed a resolution, signed by the chairman, directing the petitioner not to take any fees in his office as searcher until further orders. Thereupon the House declared " that no Committee ought by vote to determine the right and property of the subject, without first acquainting the House therewith."[4] Some days afterwards there was further debate upon this question, and it was resolved " that no vote passed at a Committee of this House, and not reported or confirmed by the House, shall be any rule or direction in any court of

Abuse of powers by Committees.

---

[1] 1 Com. Journ. 97, 106-7.　　[3] Com. Journ. Dec. 20, 1650.
[2] Ib. 154-5.　　　　　　　　　[4] Ib. July 28, 1641.

justice in Westminster Hall, to ground any proceedings upon."[1] Some authority, however, must then have attached to orders of Committees, for in 1651 the House of Commons resolved, "that every order made by any Committee of Parliament shall from henceforth be signed by so many at the least of the members of that Committee as are of the quorum of that Committee."[2]

As a means of making a House, it was usual for the Serjeant-at-Arms to go into each Committee Room, with the Mace on his shoulder, whereupon all members were bound to proceed at once to the House, because private must always give way to public business. Repeated directions to this effect were given to Committees; when the Serjeant came to any Committee and announced that the House had met, the chairman must "immediately come away."[3] A special order from the House was declared necessary for any breach of this "constant rule."[4] To prevent infractions, which seem to have been frequent, the House declared, in 1699, that "what Committees shall do after the sitting of the House be void."[5] This order was repeated in 1701 and 1707,[6] and was extant in 1846. Committees in the Lower House are now warned by a doorkeeper when "Mr. Speaker is at prayers," but their proceedings afterwards are no longer deemed invalid if merely prolonged for a few minutes. When the sitting

is continued, permission is obtained from the House. A point often and hotly discussed, was whether the chairman of a Committee might put the question for adjournment after receiving the Serjeant's message, and before the Speaker was actually in his place. This difficulty was generally avoided by settling the question of adjournment early in the sitting. If it were not so disposed of, the Committee, not having appointed a day for their next meeting, ceased to exist, unless revived by order of the House, and the Bill might be lost.

Sometimes the question of adjournment was vexatiously

---

[1] Com. Journ. August 6, 1641.
[2] Ib. May 1, 1651.
[3] 2 Ib. 191; A.D. 1642.
[4] 11 Ib. 126; A.D. 1693.
[5] 13 Ib. 231; A.D. 1699.
[6] Ib. 714; 15 Ib. 448.

delayed with a view to get rid of a Bill.[1] Other equally objectionable methods were occasionally resorted to by Committees for shelving Bills, or relieving themselves from the obligation of hearing evidence and reporting to the House. A motion was occasionally made that the Committee do adjourn *sine die*, or for three months, probably after the prorogation; or that the chairman do leave the chair, thus putting a stop to further proceedings on a Bill.[2] In these days both Houses would deal very summarily with Committees which thus failed to discharge the duty entrusted to them. The House of Commons has repeatedly ordered into the custody of the Serjeant-at-Arms members who, without adequate explanation, have failed to attend the meetings of Committees on which they were appointed.

Before the constitution of Committees on private Bills was settled by Standing Orders, both Houses appointed all these Committees, naming such members as were supposed to be best able to deal with the subject. In 1580 a Bill in the Commons for repairing Dover Haven was " committed unto all the Privy Council being of this House."[3] An estate Bill in 1604 was committed " to all Knights of the Bath members of this House."[4] An obvious method of ensuring local knowledge was to nominate local members. An instance of this nature, in 1604, was a Bill for draining fens in Ely, Huntingdon, and other counties, which was committed to a

---

[1] Sherwood, 52 (published in 1825).

[2] Ib. 72-3, where this practice is spoken of as " most objectionable and dangerous," and, again, as " alike unbecoming and unparliamentary." In 1825, notice being taken that the Committee on the Berks and Hants Canal Bill had adjourned for a month, the House ordered that the Committee should meet and proceed forthwith. In the same Session a Select Committee reported strongly upon the improper conduct of Committees in seeking to defeat private Bills by striking out essential clauses, or adjourning to a distant day and thereby avoiding any report to the House. Although perhaps checked, this impropriety was not ended, for, in 1836, " the House being informed (March 23) that the Committee on the Trinity (North Leith) Harbour and Docks Bill had adjourned till the 16th day of May next : Ordered, that the Committee do meet to-morrow, and proceed on the said Bill."—Com. Journ. p. 195.

[3] 1 Com. Journ. 131.

[4] Ib. 184.

number of members for these counties and their boroughs.[1]
" All the lawyers of the House " were added to a Committee
in 1628.[2] This addition was afterwards frequent, but was
sometimes varied by a limitation to Privy Councillors, King's
counsel,[3] or serjeants-at-law.[4]

" Bill for
Mr. Hatton,"
1575.

In one instance which occurred in 1575, a person named in
a private Bill was allowed to serve on the Committee. This
member, a Mr. John Spencer, " so resolved the residue of the
Committee that, upon the report thereof made to the House
by Mr. Treasurer, it was presently ordered the Bill should be
engrossed."[5]

Holditch's
Relief Bill,
1606.

Parties to a Bill were allowed to nominate a
Committee in 1606. This was a remarkable case. The Bill
was one " to relieve John Holditch, gentleman, disinherited
by the extraordinary amending of the errors of a fine." In
the Lords, where the Bill originated, the Committee, upon
advice given by some judges who were consulted, wrote to
the tenants of the estate of which Mr. Holditch had been
deprived, requesting them " to yield him some composition "
(compensation) " as they formerly promised, but afterwards
did go from the same." The tenants' answer was unsatisfactory, " some of them very coldly offering some composition; others absolutely refusing to compound at all."[6]
Upon this special report, the House appears to have requested
the Lord Chancellor's attention to the case, and afterwards

[1] 1 Com. Journ. 207. Sir Oliver
Cromwell, the future Lord Protector's uncle, served on this Committee. It may be remembered that,
thirty years afterwards, Cromwell's
opposition to the interference of
Royal Commissioners in draining the
Bedford Level procured him the local
title, " Lord of the Fens."

[2] 1 Com. Journ. 897.

[3] Ib. 291.

[4] Ib. 237, 991.

[5] Ib. 105. It is only described
in the Journals as " a Bill for Mr.
Hatton." The statute book easily
explains the general readiness in
passing it, for it was to " assure

certain lands and tenements unto
Christopher Hatton, Esq., gentleman of the Queen's Privy Chamber,
and Captain of her Majesty's Guard."
(18 Eliz. c. 29.) Hatton was the
comely but graceless student of the
Inner Temple who danced himself
into Elizabeth's favour, and in 1587
was appointed Lord Chancellor, to the
intense disgust and indignation of the
bar, so that " the sullen serjeants "
at first refused to plead before him,
as being " one not thoroughly bred
to the laws." (Camp. Lives, II.
147.) He died in 1591, neglected
for a later favourite.

[6] 2 Lords' Journ. 423; May 8, 1666.

passed the Bill without alteration. In the Lower House, upon the second reading, Holditch was heard at the bar, an entry in the Journals stating "he could get no counsel," doubtless through poverty. For the tenants, Mr. Whitelock, of the Temple, appeared. Two letters were read which had been addressed to the tenants by judges of the Court of Common Pleas, and a third letter from the Lords' Committee, probably informing the House of the steps taken by them. Then follows an entry : " The matter being opened, it was moved to be compromitted to certain gentlemen of the House on both parts. The parties at the bar made choice of certain Committees, Mr. Holditch of Sir Roger Wilbraham, Sir Thomas Mounson, and Sir John Scott; the tenants chose Sir H. Poole, Sir Valentine Knightley, and Sir Anthony Cope."[1] These arbitrators, as they are afterwards called in the Journals, met, but could do nothing, as only one of the tenants interested was present. Upon report to this effect by Sir H. Poole, the Bill was read a third time. Then Holditch, for reasons not assigned, petitioned " that the Bill might sleep." The House " much disputed whether it should go to question or sleep," and upon a division decided, by 133 votes to 74, that the question, " that this Bill now pass," should not be put. A curt entry, " the Bill to sleep," concludes this singular example of attempt at private legislation.

[margin note: Committee chosen by parties to Bill.]

[margin note: Bill allowed to "sleep."]

Sometimes, instead of appointing a Committee, the Lords did not hesitate to attempt informally the reconciliation of promoters and opponents. Thus, in 1624, a dispute between Sir Urian Leigh and his brother Edward was referred to " my Lord Bishop of Chester and Sir James Whitelocke, chief justice there, to end it if they can, or else to certify their opinion thereof," in the following Session.[2] In the same year a Bill was promoted by John Edwards to reverse a decree obtained against him by his father. A Committee, of

[margin note: Peers deputed to attempt reconciliation of parties.]

---

[1] 1 Com. Journ. 311-12 ; May 23, 1606.

[2] 3 Lords' Journ. 413.

which the Bishop of Bangor was chairman, reported that in their opinion "right was in the son, equity in the father." Thereupon the Lords requested the Bishop, with three judges, Mr. Baron Bromley, Mr. Justice Hutton, and Mr. Justice Chamberlaine, "finally to end the same if they can ; or else to certify their opinion at the next Session."[1]

Exemptions from service on Committees.

Bishops, it has been seen, used to sit on Private Bill Committees, and so lately as 1846 Bishop Wilberforce alludes to his service on an Irish Railway Bill.[2] By courtesy and custom, the Bishops are now relieved from this duty. In the Lower House the same relief is extended to practising barristers, and also to all members over sixty years of age who choose to take advantage of this exemption.

" Voices" in Committees of House of Commons.

A practice of giving " voices " to all members who chose to attend Committees, appears to have become common in the Lower House, circa 1621. In that Session a public Bill, supported by Sir Edward Coke, to prohibit the export of wool, yarn, and fuller's earth, was committed to eleven nominated members, with an instruction " all that will come to have voices."[3] During the same Session this matter was discussed, and some difference of opinion expressed. In appointing a Committee upon Recusants, Sir Thomas Hobby moved a general order that when voices were thus given to members "they should be Committees as well as those nominated," meaning, probably, that they should be not only able to vote, but to examine witnesses and take part in all proceedings. An opposite view, taken by Sir George Moore, was that all members attending should be at liberty " to inform the Committee," but that votes should be confined to nominated members ; and, he added, "this is the ancient and best course," from which we may infer that the practice of giving voices

---

[1] 3 Lords' Journ. 414, 463; May 28, 1624; July 9, 1625. For later instances to reconcile differences, see proceedings upon Lady Anglesea's Separation Bill, 1700; and Lady Ferrers's case, ante, Vol. I. pp. 433, 437.

[2] Life by Canon Ashwell, vol. i. p. 361.

[3] 1 Com. Journ. 597; A.D. 1621.

to members indiscriminately was then a modern innovation. However, the opinion of the House was in favour of general voices.

Dr. Gooch said this practice was a remedy against the exclusion of "those who sit far off from the chair," clearly a protest (often still made) against limiting the nomination of Committees to a few official or prominent members. Sir Peter Haman pointed this remark, by declaring that, upon a recent Committee for regulating Courts of Justice, if only nominated members could have voted, "officers of the Courts would have overborne it." It was thereupon ordered generally, that when upon appointments of Committees all members attending them were allowed voices, "they in that case, if they came, are Committees, as well as those nominated."[1] In 1641, it was ordered "that all that will come shall have voice at all public Bills."[2]

Reasons for giving "voices" to all comers.

Order of 1621.

At this period the practice does not appear to have been settled in Committees on private business. Sir J. Savile, therefore, in 1624, called attention to a Committee on a private Bill then pending, as to "the poor tenants of Gooteland Manor," upon which Committee "all are to have voice, contrary to order in a private Bill." Without disturbing the constitution of this Committee, the House "ordered, upon question, for a general rule hereafter, that in private Bills there shall not be that general clause for all that will come to have voice."[3] Upon other Bills, nominated members came to be treated as having no precedence over other members. It was therefore resolved, in 1627, "those that are Committees shall have place given them that they may the better discharge the service committed to their trust."[4]

Practice as to private Bills.

---

[1] 1 Com. Journ. 616–17; May 11, 1621. But, in 1624, a motion to give voices to all members attending the Committee of Privileges was rejected by the House, as being against precedent in the case of this Committee. (Ib. 671.)

[2] 2 Ib. 156.
[3] 1 Ib. 771.
[4] 2 Ib. April 25, 1627. Another rule, adopted in 1641, to prevent irregular attendance, was "that the doors shall be locked at the Committee, and the keys brought up,

This practice of "voices," or open Committees, was soon extended to private Bills. In the Lords many instances occur early in the eighteenth century. "All lords that come" were to be of a Committee in 1701;[1] were to have votes, in 1707;[2] and "voices," in 1719.[3] These orders were varied in 1735, when "all lords present this day, and not" of a Committee, were added to it;[4] and, again, in 1757, all lords who had been present that Session were appointed.[5]

After 1800, open Committees are too numerous to need mention, and continued until the year 1837. The general practice was to commit an opposed Bill to certain peers nominated by the House, with the addition of all peers who had been present during the Session, or were present that day.[6] There was an old rule of 1714, that any peer might attend and speak, but "must not vote; as also he shall give place to all that are of the Committee, though of lower degree, and shall sit behind them."[7] This rule, however, had fallen into disuse in Committees on private Bills. The

peer who moved the second reading almost invariably presided,[8] so that the peer presumably most interested in passing the Bill acted as chief judge in deciding its fate. Nor was this the only evil, for, as the order that all lords might attend was inoperative to secure attendance, the Committee was generally constituted by the same peer "getting as many peers as he could to attend;" while, if there was an active opposition, the same influence was used upon the other side. Then the Committees met at different hours,

---

that no man may go out without leave."

[1] Lords' Journ. March 20, 1701; December 11, 1704.

[2] Ib. January 26, 1707.

[3] Ib. February 8, 1719.

[4] Lord Pembroke's Estate Bill, February 26, 1735.

[5] Molyneux Estate Bill, March 14, 1757; Inclosure Bill, March 30, 1759; Tancred's Charity Bill, March 1, 1762.

[6] 67 Lords' Journ. 186; June 5, 1835. Commons' Committee on Private Business, 1838; Ev. of Mr. H. S. Smith, Lords' Committee Clerk, p. 22.

[7] Lords' Journ. June 10, 1714.

[8] Commons' Committee on Private Business, 1838; Ev. of Duke of Richmond, p. 46.

some of them at noon, others at two o'clock, and adjourned *Short* frequently after a very short sitting.   The same peers seldom *sittings.* listened to the whole evidence ; sometimes different chairmen acted on different days; peers came to vote upon the pre- amble "who had not listened to a single syllable of the evi- dence"; and there was "canvassing both by letter and personal *Canvassing.* application,"[1] though "not to the same extent, or with the same indecency," as in the Commons.[2] Agents, indeed, some- times thought it hopeless to proceed with Bills which were strongly opposed by influential peers, because the latter were able to command a much larger body of friends in the Com- mittee than the promoters could have brought there.[3]

As deep dissatisfaction prevailed, both in and out of *Change of* doors, at the miscarriage of justice which often occurred *system in* *1837.* under this system, or want of system, a Select Committee was appointed in 1837, upon whose recommendation the House of Lords made important changes in their Standing Orders.[4] It was then provided that each Committee on an *Committees* opposed private Bill (not being an estate Bill), should *of five* *selected* consist of five peers chosen, with the chairman, by a Com- *members.* mittee of Selection,[5] and bound to attend the proceedings throughout the whole Committee.   No other peers could take any part in the proceedings, and peers were exempted from service on any private Bill in which they were interested. All Committees were required to meet at 11 A.M. and adjourn at four. From their first appointment the Committee of Selection chose for service on an opposed Bill peers having no interest in its subject-matter, " and, indeed, as little knowledge as possible of the locality, or even of the county;" and "these peers were to act as a jury bound to give their decision according to the evidence brought before

[1] Ib. 46, 51.

[2] Ib. ; Ev. of Mr. J. Richardson, Parliamentary Agent, p. 36.

[3] Ib. ; Ev. of Mr. St. George Burke, p. 7.

[4] Lords' Journ. July 6, 1837.

[5] The five peers who formed the first Committee of Selection were the Earl of Shaftesbury (Chairman of Committees), the Duke of Richmond, the Earl of Devon, Viscount Falk- land, and Lord Redesdale.

them, and not from any knowledge they might possess *aliunde.*"[1] This great improvement in the conduct of private business, made, far in advance of the Commons, by the House supposed to be least open to influences from without,

Impartial and thorough investigation secured.

at once secured an investigation more impartial and more thorough than that which it replaced, and satisfied both promoters and opponents. Substantially, the same system remains in force.[2] Unfortunately, the Lower House did not for several years follow the example thus set them, though repeated inquiries directed by that House led to strong evidence in its favour.

Speaker's lists.

In describing the progress of local Bills through the Commons, frequent reference has been made to Committees which, besides nominated members, consisted of numerous representatives of neighbouring counties and towns, and therefore presumably interested in these Bills. This addition to a Committee was made, not by the House, but according to a list prepared by the Speaker, and the locality immediately affected by each Bill. The system was adopted towards the close of the eighteenth century, as a modification of open Committees. It did not, however, supersede them, for they were still occasionally appointed, upon motion to

Voices in 1820–3.

that effect. Thus, in 1820, out of twenty-one Bills contested in Committee, "voices" were ordered in four cases; in 1821, with the same number of opposed Bills, "voices" were ordered in twelve; in 1822 and 1823, out of thirty-five and forty-seven opposed Bills "voices" were ordered in eight and seventeen, respectively.

Inquiry of 1825.

With the railway projects, which began to excite such keen interest and opposition in 1824,[3] this abuse grew, and "voices" were admitted in forty contests of that Session. In 1825, therefore, the House of Commons directed an inquiry into "the constitution of Committees on private Bills." No

[1] Commons' Committee of 1838 on Private Business; Ev. of Duke of Richmond, p. 47.

[2] See Lords' Standing Orders, 95 —101; Sess. 1887.

[3] *Ante*, Vol. I. p. 50.

outside testimony can be more emphatic than that borne by this Committee to the vicious system then existing. They refer as an "admitted evil" to complaints that the only regular attendants in protracted and expensive proceedings were "members whose constituents were locally interested in the results; or, in some cases, members who have themselves had an individual interest" in Bills; while not unfrequently clauses and reports were virtually settled by other members who flocked in merely for the division.

At this period, the nominated and list members made up a formidable array on any Bill which excited public feeling or attacked vested interests in a given district; and the number of members varied according to the local position of any town or area affected. According to the lists of members for counties and divisions of counties, made under the Speaker's direction for this purpose about the year 1800, above two hundred members were at liberty to attend some Committees, while others were open to no more than sixty or seventy. If the friends of a projected canal, or a road passing through two or three counties, found that their Bill was likely to be supported by a majority of local members, they were satisfied with the constitution of the Committee. But the same discovery led invariably to a motion in the House by their opponents, "that all who come shall have voices," thus "augmenting tenfold" the evil in question.[1]

Constitution of Commons' Committees in 1825.

Acting upon the recommendation of this Committee, the House of Commons determined in future to abolish "open" inquiries into private Bills. But, though the Committee of 1825 recognized the evil of retaining on these inquiries members directly or indirectly interested in the issue, they were too timid, or too much attached to precedent, to do more than suggest a limitation of number. Their object was to preserve some security for adequate attendance and local knowledge: and they thought this object could hardly

Open Committees abolished, 1825.

[1] Commons' Committee of 1825 on the Constitution of Private Bill Committees, p. 2.

be ensured without a committal of each contested Bill to sixty local members, and an equal number of members taken indiscriminately from other parts of the United Kingdom, a total number considerably larger than that of the Grand Committees, which were revived in the Session of 1833. A further suggestion was that promoters and petitioners should be allowed to strike out fifteen members on either side, "which would then leave ninety at liberty to serve;" a number which the Committee did not consider too large, having regard to the necessary absence of some members, and the unavoidable avocations of others.[1]

In 1826, the House of Commons made some small changes in conformity with this report,[2] but the system remained without substantial amendment. Twelve years afterwards, fresh inquiry was instituted, with as little avail as before.

Committees in 1838.

According to the procedure of 1838, Committees on opposed Bills then consisted of about 120 members. Half of these members were taken from the Speaker's lists, and included all representatives of the county, and of places within that county, in which projected works were to be executed, together with members for adjoining counties, and for certain boroughs within those counties. These members were placed above a line, and to them were added, below the line, an equal number of other members, whose names were taken by chance, and who were supposed to be impartial. When a railway passed through several counties, members for these counties and their boroughs were always added to the Bill. This was an addition of members all of whom were locally interested.[3]

The presence of so large a number of members, or rather their right to be present, naturally occasioned great interruption to actual business, and was incompatible with an im-

Unwieldiness. partial decision upon the evidence. Committees were so

---

[1] Commons' Committee of 1825 on the Constitution of Private Bill Committees, p. 4.

[2] Com. Journ. April 19, 1826.

[3] Commons' Committee on Private Business, 1838; Ev. p. 3.

numerous as to be to a great degree irresponsible. Relying on the relative strength of promoters and opponents on particular occasions, objections were often taken and propositions made which would never have been raised before any judicial tribunal.[1] Agents and solicitors in charge of a Bill were "in constant alarm if their case was much opposed, lest they should be tripped up in any proceeding when they had not a majority of their friends in the room." Canvassing was resorted to generally by the local *Canvassing.* solicitors or by deputations of promoters, who came to town for the purpose. Sometimes paid canvassers were employed to go round to the houses of members and request their attendance. These persons made canvassing a regular business, and professed to be able to influence the attendance and votes of certain members. Even graver scandals were sometimes talked of.[2] When a division was expected, a whip was made, and issues, especially upon competing railway Bills, were decided "by the number of friends on one side or the other" rather than by merits. A vain *Voting with-* attempt was made to bring public opinion to bear by print- *out hearing.* ing in official records the names of members attending and voting in railway Committees; but members still had "no scruple in coming down to vote without having heard a word of the evidence."[3]

The large number of members attending a Committee, *Delays in* and the questions put by them to elicit opinions or facts *Committee.* favouring the side they happened to take, tended to prolong inquiry and add to its cost. Delay was still a favourite weapon with opponents, who were able to use it with signal effect, owing to the size of each Committee. All the principal railway Bills, including those for the Liverpool and Manchester, London and Birmingham, and Great Western lines,

[1] Ib.; Ev. of Mr. J. Richardson, Parliamentary Agent, p. 36.

[2] Ib.; Ev. of Mr. J. E. Dorington, clerk of the Fees, p. 40; Mr. J. R. Hayward and Mr. J. Richardson,

Parliamentary Agents, pp. 17, 19, 21, and 35.

[3] Ib.; Ev. of Mr. St. George Burke, p. 3.

were defeated, chiefly by delay, upon their first promotion in Parliament. The Liverpool and Manchester Bill occupied a Commons' Committee for thirty-eight days, although only thirty-seven witnesses were examined; the preamble was passed in Committee by thirty-seven to thirty-six votes, but the Bill failed upon clauses. The Great Western Bill was fifty-seven days in Committee in the Commons, and its Parliamentary agent was amazed and disgusted at the vast body of evidence given there " having nothing to do with the question."[1] Including expenses of surveys, the Great Western Railway Company spent 40,000l. during the Session in which their Bill was rejected.[2]

Liverpool and Manchester railway, 1825.

Great Western railway, 1834.

Naturally list Committees were not maintained without what then appeared to be valid grounds. They were defended because local members were the most competent judges of benefits to arise from measures affecting their own districts, and also had exceptional opportunities of settling compromises and making friendly arrangements, which were often effected on behalf of poor constituents who could not otherwise have afforded to engage in a Parliamentary contest.[3] If local members were excluded from Committees they might be compelled by their constituents to bring on discussions and propose clauses in the House itself. Not only would valuable time be occupied with these controversies, but the evil of canvassing would be much greater than it was in Committees, and influential members would have much greater chances of success in carrying or defeating a private Bill.[4] Another objection raised by experienced

Defence of list Committees.

[1] Commons' Committee on Private Business, 1838; Ev. of Mr. St. George Burke, p. 4.

[2] It passed the Commons, but was thrown out on the second reading in the House of Lords, " in mercy to the promoters," as it could not have been carried through Committee at that late period of the Session, owing to delays in the Commons. The London and Birmingham Bill, under

the canvassing system, was thrown out in the Lords' Committee by nineteen votes to twelve; exactly the same Bill passed in the following Session without opposition. (Ib. pp. 6, 2..

[3] Commons' Committee on Private Business, 1838; Ev. of Lord Granville Somerset, p. 56; Mr. J. C. Talbot, p. 57.

[4] Ib.; Ev. of Mr. J. C. Dington, p. 41.

counsel was that, under the new system in the Lords, Committees were rather inclined to "jump at conclusions;" that there was now and then "a little pressure of ennui;" and that the hearing was not so "patient and deliberate" as in tribunals having substantial local representation.[1] A broader ground of opposition to tribunals composed of only five members was that, as Committees now decided the principle of each Bill, they really discharged the functions of the House itself, and ought, therefore, adequately to represent the House.

Argument that Committees should adequately represent the House.

These arguments prevailed with a majority of the Committee of 1838, who rejected resolutions which declared the business of Committees on Private Bills to be "of so judicial a character," and one so frequently involving decisions upon rights and pecuniary interests of vast importance and amount, that it was expedient to assimilate these Committees "as much as possible in their functions and practice to a judicial tribunal."[2] To the plea that valuable information was afforded to Committees by the presence of local members, it was answered that this benefit was "more than counterbalanced by the local interest, influence and prejudice necessarily attending it," and that any such information would be of greater weight and value if given by a member in the character of a witness. Every witness admitted that members voted without hearing the evidence or arguments; there was proof, also, of "a system of canvassing, alike harassing to members and prejudicial to the ends of justice." Besides the "great inconvenience, expense and delay" arising from a tribunal so constituted, the rejected resolutions declared that it was "impossible to secure a strictly judicial decision where so many of the judges represented parties deeply interested in the result;" and that personal responsibility ought to be increased by reducing the numbers of Committees and securing continuous attendance.

Reforms rejected by Committee of 1838.

[1] Ib.; Ev. of Mr. J. C. Talbot, p. 58.

[2] Ib. App. The resolutions were proposed by Mr. Greene and Mr. Shaw Lefevre.

Although the reform thus proposed was supported by ample evidence that the five-member system worked satisfactorily in the Lords, while the constitution of Private Bill Committees in the Commons was "universally complained of," the timid counsels of 1838 were followed in succeeding years. In 1839 the Committee of the previous Session were re-appointed. They did not think it necessary to hear further evidence, but, with the Speaker's aid, again discussed the proposal for excluding local members from Committees. Fully recognizing once more existing abuses, the Committee still shrunk from recommending the only remedy which would completely remove them. Thus, a motion to exclude members representing local interests "from the Committees in which such interests are concerned," was rejected by a small majority, among whom were Sir Robert Peel, Sir James Graham, Lord Stanley and Mr. Ellice.[1] Certain changes were, however, suggested, and adopted by the House,[2] with a view to reduce the number of members on Committees, enforce more regular attendance, and combine a "due representation of local interests," with securities for the presence of impartial members. By these changes the Speaker, in preparing the usual Sessional lists, was authorized to reduce considerably the number of names "above the line," that is, of members locally interested in each Bill. As a corrective, however, to this reduction, any member omitted from the list was allowed to serve on a Committee upon making a declaration that his constituents were locally interested. No members were appointed who did not, on application, express their willingness to serve; if they assented they were required to sign a declaration that they would "never vote on any question which may arise without having duly heard and attended to the evidence relating thereto."[3]

Committee of 1839.

Changes adopted in 1839.

[1] Commons' Committee on Private Business, 1839; Min. of Proceedings, p. 3.

[2] Resolutions of House of Commons, March 11 and April 22, 1839.

[3] Ib. April 22, 1839.

By far the most important change made in 1839 was the Committee of
Selection. appointment of a Committee of Selection. A similar body had, two years previously, been nominated by the peers. It was the business of this new Committee in the Commons[1] to receive applications from members not upon the Speaker's list, and to satisfy themselves that the constituents of such members were locally interested in a Bill. They also had the more material duty of adding impartial members to each Committee in such proportions as they saw fit. Each member so chosen, besides making the usual declarations that he was willing to serve, and would not vote without having heard the evidence, was called on to declare that his constituents had no local interest, and that he had no personal interest in the Bill.[2]

As these selected members were the only unprejudiced Provision for
quorum of
selected
members. members of the Committee, care was taken that a quorum of their number should always be present. On each Committee upon opposed Bills there were five selected members; three of them were a quorum, without whose attendance no Committee was allowed to proceed. On each unopposed Bill one unprejudiced member was placed, with a like veto upon the transaction of business in his absence. Owing to practical difficulties in procuring the attendance of members on unopposed Bills, a member of the Committee of Selection generally served in that capacity.[3] On opposed Bills regular attendance was also rare, owing to the absence, first, of compulsion, and, secondly, of responsibility, as the Speaker's list, though considerably reduced, still nominally engaged the services of a large proportion of members. Thus, on one Nominal
service on
Committees
under
Speaker's
lists. day during the Session of 1838, no fewer than 360 members were supposed to be employed on private Bill Committees,

---

[1] The first chairman was Mr. J. G. B. Estcourt, afterwards Home Secretary, and better known as Mr. Sotheron-Estcourt.

[2] This is the basis of the declaration now made by members appointed to Committees on Private Bills. (Com. Standing Order 118, Sess. 1887.)

[3] Commons' Committee on Private Business, 1839, Second Report; Ev. of Mr. Estcourt, p. 5.

although no more than sixty actually attended. As the remaining 300 were not available for service, the Committee of Selection were a good deal hampered in their choice. Fresh experience obtained in 1839 led to renewed evidence in favour of discontinuing Speaker's lists, and selecting all members of Committees, but the Committee of 1839 again declined to recommend this change, even though local interests, as before, would have been represented.[1]

Inquiry of 1840.

In 1840 the Select Committee, which had sat in two previous Sessions, were re-appointed, and upon their recommendation some changes were made in practice, but these changes were described by competent witnesses as "a step towards improvement rather than an improvement." In vain they pointed to the plan which for two Sessions had been successful in the Lords.[2] New as well as old arguments were brought forward against an abolition of Speaker's lists. A member in the House of Commons, it was said, had duties towards his constituents which did not devolve upon peers. It was his business to interpose for the protection of constituents who could not afford to lodge petitions, employ agents, or summon witnesses. An exclusion of local influence from Committees would, therefore, tend to "the oppression of the lower classes."[3] Local members, from knowledge of the parties and personal communication with constituents, often brought opponents together, acted as mediators and umpires, and so materially shortened the proceedings of Committees. Such members paid close attention to a Bill which concerned their constituents, and from their better acquaintance with the subject, formed a sounder judgment than members wholly selected and indifferent.[4]

Arguments for Speaker's lists, 1840.

[1] Commons' Committee on Private Business, 1839, Second Report; Ev. of Mr. Estcourt, p. 8.

[2] Commons' Committee on Private Business, 1840, First Report; Ev. of Mr. J. R. Hayward, Mr. J. R. Hall, Mr. Pritt, Mr. St. George Burke, Parliamentary Agents; and Mr. H. Stone Smith, clerk to Committees, House of Lords, pp. 1, 13, 19, 22, 24, 26.

[3] Ib.; Min. of Ev. p. 2.

[4] Ib. p. 42.

Of the Parliamentary agents examined in 1840, only one supported the system of Speaker's lists. Even he was driven to admit that, under that system, "votes had been perceptibly swayed by political bias, and in other instances by motives of private friendship." As a compromise, he suggested that local influence should be excluded when Bills were opposed upon preamble, and should be confined to opposition upon clauses.[1] Other experts concurred in their approval of changes which in the Lords had substituted something like a judicial for a partisan tribunal, and rigidly excluded local or personal bias. As to the intervention by members on behalf of constituents, the answer was, that it was almost necessarily based upon *ex parte* statements, made probably by a political party, or by individuals, to whom a member chiefly owed his election, and that it by no means therefore tended to an equal administration of justice. Evidence, the value and good faith of which might be openly tested, was, with reason, again declared to be the only legitimate mode of influencing Committees. As it was, local members generally entered Committees with a strong bias on their minds in favour of a Bill, or against it, and acted throughout an inquiry rather as advocates than as judges, sometimes taking advantage of their position to defeat a measure by delay, and lending their help to bad cases which would never be brought before an impartial tribunal.[2]

Compromise suggested.

Case for excluding local members.

In aid of these arguments, the Stone and Rugby Railway Bill, hotly contested in 1839, was cited as "a battle principally fought for delay."[3] First, the Committee on the petition for this Bill sat for twenty-two days, and had to consider and deal with 452 specific allegations of non-compliance with Standing Orders.[4] Then came the Committee on the Bill, which, at its first meeting, was attended by

Stone and Rugby Railway Bill, 1839.

---

[1] Ib.; Ev. of Mr. Robert Chalmers, p. 42.

[2] Ib.; Min. of Ev. pp. 2, 5, 6.

[3] Ib. pp. 6, 12.

[4] The line was opposed by competing companies, including the London and Birmingham, Grand Junction, Midland Counties Railway, and Grand Trunk Canal Companies, with several landowners.

thirty-eight members, and sat for sixty-one days. Manchester was anxious that the railway should be made. The members for Manchester therefore attended to support it; many other members claimed places on the Committee upon the recognized plea that their constituents were interested in the Bill. To those who watched, on either side, the constitution of the Committee, its judgment was, therefore, a foregone conclusion. Its opinions were so notorious that, at its first meeting, the agents "had lists of the probable votes on the last day;" and, excepting the selected members, they were "not wrong in one vote." Opponents "were beaten before they went into Committee." They were therefore driven to delay the Bill by numerous divisions and other familiar methods. As members had a greater latitude in examination than counsel or agents, these tactics so protracted the proceedings that, though the preamble passed by a large majority, the promoters had to drop their Bill. In the next Session[1] it was reintroduced and defeated. The Trent Valley Railway Bill of 1840 occupied sixty-three days in Committee, besides twenty-two days before a sub-committee on petitions. Parliament was prorogued before the Committee reported.

Voting without hearing.

Notwithstanding the declaration which members were now required to make, it was found that they still frequently voted without hearing the whole of the evidence. There were different constructions of the rule, and in practice it was applied with considerable elasticity. As the list system left members free to serve upon several Committees sitting at the same time, it was impossible for them in all cases to give continuous service. In 1838 and 1839 the private business was not large, but it is on record that in previous Sessions as many as forty Committees were sitting simultaneously. On some occasions there were not sufficient rooms to be found, either in the temporary buildings then in use, or in the house in Great George-street, which served as an annexe;

[1] Commons' Committee on Private Business, 1840, First Report; Min. of Ev. pp. 10, 26-7.

and Committees sat in the Law Courts, or in the coffee-house then standing in New Palace Yard. Members were sometimes appointed to Committees seven or eight of which met on the same day, and gave this fact as a reason for not remaining long in any one Committee.[1]

In spite of weighty evidence against Speaker's lists, and continued satisfaction expressed by suitors and practitioners with the disinterested tribunals of the Lords, the Committee of 1840 again declined to recommend this change. They admitted that inequitable decisions, reiterated complaints by suitors, and undisguised canvassing of members occurred under the existing system, to "the discredit of Committees and the disparagement of their proceedings;" they admitted also that the changes introduced by a Committee of Selection had done no more than abate practices which had excited "general reprobation;" but they remained of opinion that, without further experience, Committees on opposed Bills should not be converted into "purely judicial bodies."[2] A smaller number of members drawn from the Speaker's list was the only change suggested and adopted;[3] the essential reform initiated by the Lords was again postponed in the other House of Parliament.

Recommendations of Committee in 1840.

By the modifications which came into force in 1841, Committees were only formed from the Speaker's list of a county or division affected by a Bill, together with members nominated by the Committee of Selection, and all members who alleged that their constituents were interested. This privilege was often abused, and, especially on railway Bills, members interested in a very remote degree obtained leave to serve. For example, the members for Brighton applied to serve upon a Greenwich Railway Bill.[4] This practice was checked in 1841 by a rule ensuring greater publicity when

Modifications of 1841

[1] Ib. pp. 40-1.
[2] Commons' Committee on Private Business, 1840; Second Report, p. 3.
[3] 95 Com. Journ. 533; July 17, 1840.
[4] Greenwich Railway Bill, 1840; Commons' Committee on Severn Navigation Bill, 1841, pp. 5, 6.

such requests were made, and providing that members locally interested should only be added to a Committee by special leave of the House. Committees were in practice, therefore, generally constituted by selected members, and from the Speaker's list of members for one county only.

Speaker's lists, 1841. This rule, however, often worked inequitably, especially when railways or canals affected many conflicting interests, and ran through several counties. Under the old lists, Bills relating to these undertakings would have been sent before Committees composed of members from the counties affected, so that there was some safeguard against an undue preponderance of one class of interests. No such safeguard existed in Committees constituted from the modified lists of Mr. Speaker.

Severn Navigation Bill, 1841. So strong was the feeling in some cases against the operation of these lists, that, in 1841, petitions were presented, praying that the Severn Navigation Bill might be referred to a Committee solely nominated by the House of Commons. There was a special inquiry into the point raised by these petitions. It appeared that, in practice, a county list was not necessarily confined to members for and within that county, but, at the Speaker's discretion, was drawn up so as to represent also, as fairly as possible, adjoining districts connected with the county by geographical position or common interest. Thus, the Worcestershire list comprised members for the two divisions of Worcester, East Gloucester, South Warwick, South Stafford, South Salop, Hereford, together with borough members for Droitwich, Evesham, Dudley, Worcester, Kidderminster, and Bewdley. Petitioners urged that Worcester interests would dominate a Committee so constituted, and that, as the Bill affected the trade of various other districts, the tribunal should either be wholly unprejudiced or composed of other local members. After hearing evidence, however, a Select Committee decided that the Bill should not be exempted from the usual rules.

Although members appointed from the Speaker's list were not called upon to disclaim any personal interest, their votes were sometimes challenged on this ground.   Thus, in 1844, a Committee on the Middle Level Drainage and Navigation Bill asked the House to decide " whether a member having property within the limits of an Improvement Bill, which property may be affected by the passing of the Bill, has such an interest as disqualifies him from voting on preamble or clauses."   This appeal was answered by a resolution that the rule governing votes given in the House by members interested in the subject under discussion " applies likewise to any vote of a member so interested in a Committee." [1]

It was not until the great pressure of railway business in 1844 that the House of Commons took a first step towards the appointment of more judicial tribunals.   In that Session, besides other private business, no fewer than 248 railway Bills were laid before Parliament.[2]   So enormous a task naturally appalled the House of Commons; the old plan of constituting Committees would obviously have broken down under such pressure.   On Mr. Gladstone's motion, a Select Committee was therefore appointed early in the Session to inquire into the best mode of constituting Committees on railway Bills and arranging their work.   This Committee recommended, with other reforms, that competing Bills should be referred to the same tribunal, and that Committees on opposed railway Bills should be nominated by the Committee of Selection, and consist of five members, each of whom should declare that his constituents had no local interest, and that he himself had no personal interest for or against any Bill or project referred to him.   Three members were to be the quorum, and each member absenting himself was to be reported to the House.[3]

Personal interest of members.

Middle Level Drainage Bill, 1844.

New tribunal on railway Bills, 1844.

---

[1] 99 Com. Journ. p. 447.
[2] Commons' Committee on Railway Bills, 1845, Second Report; Ev. of Mr. Samuel Laing, of the Board of Trade (Railway Department) p. 13; App. p. 22.
[3] Commons' Committee on Railway Bills, 1844; First Report, pp. 3,

Attempts to
retain local
representation
on railway
Committees,
1844.

At last, then, the principle of an impartial tribunal was accepted, although limited to the Session, and to railway Bills. Even with these limitations the old practice did not pass away without a struggle in the Committee, and afterwards in the House of Commons. It was proposed in the Committee that members locally interested should still be added by the Committee of Selection, with a proviso that they should not exceed in number the selected members. This proposal only obtained one supporter, while twelve voted for a thorough reform. In the House itself the change of opinion was no less marked. Little favour was shown to an amendment that members whose constituents were locally interested in any competing lines should be permitted to sit on Committees, but not to vote. Mr. Gladstone upon this occasion said that, notwithstanding the new rule, a member not nominated upon a Committee might still attend it and make any statement he chose. The Speaker, however, declared that members not so nominated would have no right whatever to address a Committee, or put questions to witnesses, or interfere in any way with the proceedings.[1]

The new tribunal was found so satisfactory that no attempt was made to revive the old system. It might have been supposed that the experience thus gained in dealing with railway Bills would soon have led to the establishment of similar Committees for all private Bills. More than ten years passed, however, before local representation ceased on Committees: a striking example of tenacity in adhering to an antiquated system.

Speaker's lists
abolished,
1847.

In 1847 the House of Commons abolished Speaker's lists as a basis for the constitution of Committees, but retained the principle of local representation, directing the

4. Among the members of this Committee were Lord Granville Somerset (Chairman), Viscount Howick, Sir George Grey, Mr. Gladstone, Lord Harry Vane, Mr. Estcourt, Mr. Greene, and Mr. Pakington.

[1] Hansard, March 8, 1844.

Committee of Selection to appoint as members of each Committee on an opposed Bill (not being a railway, canal, or divorce Bill) a certain number of representatives from the county, division, or borough to which a Bill related.[1] In 1850, a Committee recommended that these local members should not be entitled to vote, but merely to assist in the deliberations of Committees.[2] This compromise was ignored by the House, and it was not until 1855 that the constitution of all Committees on private Bills was assimilated, and local representation disappeared from these tribunals.[3]

Local representation abolished 1855.

Eight was the ancient quorum for a Select Committee in the Commons. It was more than once ordered, A.D. 1604, "that if eight of any Committee do assemble, they may proceed to a resolution in any business;"[4] and again, in 1640, the House declared "that eight is a full number for a Committee."[5] This rule prevailed for 220 years. In 1824 the number sufficient to constitute a Committee on an opposed Bill was reduced to five.[6] The House afterwards directed that this quorum should be made up of three selected members and two appointed from the Speaker's list. In 1845 the quorum was three, a limit which still remains.[7] In the Lords' Committees all the members must attend, except by leave of the House, or, if the House is not sitting, by consent of the parties; but the number of peers must in no case be less than four.[8]

Quorum.

In both Houses, when Committees were limited to impartial members, the full number was fixed at five. In the Upper House each Committee still consists of five peers. For ten years the Commons adhered to the same number. In the Session of 1864, however, more than 500 Bills came before that House, and the strain upon its time and attention

Numbers.

---

[1] 102 Com. Journ. 880.

[2] Commons' Committee on Local Acts; Second Report, p. 4.

[3] 110 Com. Journ. 388. The motion to exclude local members was carried by eighty to fifty-seven votes.

[4] 1 Com. Journ. 169, 944.

[5] 2 Ib. 17.

[6] 79 Ib. 535 ; June 22, 1824.

[7] Commons' Standing Order 119, Sess. 1887. On unopposed Bills the quorum is two. (Ib. 137.)

[8] Lords' Standing Orders 100–1.

was severe. Two important railway Bills were also delayed so long in Committee that they could not be read a second time in the Upper House within the period limited by Standing Orders there, and the promoters' labour and expense were wasted. In order to shorten the time devoted to private legislation, Lord Stanley proposed, in 1863, in a Committee on private business, that each opposed Bill should be referred to three instead of five members. It was then felt that the unavoidable absence of a single member would stop further proceedings, and that Committees of three would be too small a body to command public confidence, or deal satisfactorily with the vast interests before them.[1] After the experience of 1864, the Committee on Standing Orders became converts to Lord Stanley's view. Their recommendation, however, was rejected in the Commons by a majority of seven votes, and that House substituted four members for five,[2] a change which came into operation in 1865.

Lord Stanley's plan of three-member Committees.

Committees of four, 1865.

By old custom in both Houses, as we have seen, the peer or member who introduced a Bill was generally chosen to preside over the Committee which considered it. He was therefore naturally an active partisan in its favour, and was indeed appointed on that ground.[3] In order to avoid the stigma of partiality, he was reluctant to check evidence hostile to a Bill. While, however, outwardly impartial, competent observers who watched the proceedings of Committees "never found that the evidence or arguments of counsel shook his opinion."[4]

Chairman of Committee.

An improvement in this system was made in 1840, at the instance of a Committee, by limiting the choice of chairman to a selected member, who had no local or personal interests in the Bill.[5] Instead, therefore, of a partisan, a chairman of

Restriction in Commons to selected members, 1840.

---

[1] 176 Hansard, 1456 (Speech of Colonel Wilson-Patten).

[2] 176 Hansard, 2011–12; the numbers against Committees of three were 74 to 67; for Committees of four, 98 to 50 (July 25, 1864). See also *ante*, p. 808, n.

[3] *Ante*, p. 826.

[4] Ib.; Ev. of Mr. R. Chalmers, Committee clerk, p. 29.

[5] Commons' Committee on Private Business, 1840, First Report; Min. of Ev. p. 17.

Committees in the House of Commons, after 1840, was always Procedure in choosing Chairman. free from bias, though still chosen by the members indiscriminately. The general course of procedure was that, at the first meeting of a Committee, the room was cleared of strangers, the door locked, and a choice made. If, after being once locked, the door was inadvertently opened before a chairman's appointment, or before he had taken the chair, and fresh members entered, the whole proceeding was vitiated; the new-comers had a right to sign the declarations and qualify themselves to serve; and the door must be again locked with a view to a fresh appointment.[1]

With a view to greater uniformity of decision, and the Chairman's panel. better guidance of tribunals on private Bills, it was suggested in 1840 that the chairmen upon all opposed Bills in the Commons should be chosen from a Standing Committee appointed early in every Session.[2] This body, it was proposed, should consist of members taken for their experience in private business, who would command the special confidence of suitors, and be a guarantee for a satisfactory investigation. This suggestion was, in part, adopted in 1847, on the recommendation of a Committee over which Mr. Hume presided.[3] Chairmen were then appointed by the Committee of Selection; in 1853, the general Committee on railway and canal Bills, then first created, were directed to appoint, from among their own body, the chairmen on all opposed Bills of this class.[4] Committees on private Bills in the Lords continued to choose their own chairmen down to the year 1859. In accordance with a recommendation made by a body of peers then appointed to inquire into private legislation, the chairman of each Committee was, after that Session, appointed by the Committee of Selection. In both Houses this deliberate choice of a chair-

[1] See case of Birkenhead Docks Bill, 1845; Frere's Practice of Private Bill Committees, 1846, pp. 24-5.

[2] Commons' Committee on Private Business, 1840, First Report; Ev.

of Mr. St. George Burke, p. 30.

[3] Commons' Committee on Private Bills, 1847; Third Report, p. 7.

[4] This order of 1853 was amended in 1854. (109 Com. Journ. 410.)

man, instead of the former haphazard selection, has proved of great advantage in the consideration of all opposed Bills.

Powers of chairman in Lords.

In the Lords, following the practice of the House itself, the chairman of a Committee has no second or casting vote, and the general rule prevails—*semper præsumitur pro negante.* On a private Bill of 1606, however, an exceptional course was taken.

Throckmorton's Estate Bill, 1606.

This was a Bill " to settle the manor of Rye, in the counties of Gloucester and Worcester, upon William Throckmorton and his heirs, according to a feoffment thereof made by Charles, late Earl of Devonshire." It was referred to a Committee of nineteen peers and bishops, who were attended by two judges, Mr. Justice Williams and Mr. Justice Yelverton, with Mr. Serjeant Crooke. Some days afterwards the chairman reported that the Committee were divided in opinion, "nine of one side and nine of the other, and therefore left the further proceeding on the Bill to the House." Promoters and petitioners had already been heard by counsel before the Committee.[1] The House ordered that they should be reheard at the bar, and afterwards passed the Bill.[2]

Rule as to chairman's vote in Commons' Committees.

According to ancient practice the chairman of a Committee in the House of Commons did not vote unless the numbers were equal. In 1836, the House was informed of a departure from this practice. The chairman of a Committee on a private Bill had, upon a division, first claimed the privilege to vote as a member of the Committee, and afterwards, the voices being equal, had given a casting vote as chairman. This claim, the House was further informed, had of late years been made and allowed in other Committees. It was therefore declared by the House "that, according to the established rules of Parliament, the chairman of a Select Committee can only vote when there is an equality of voices."[3]

Change of rule in railway cases, 1845.

When Committees were limited in number, and chairmen ceased to be partisans, the effect of this rule was to

---

[1] 2 Lords' Journ. 433. The Committee met at eight a.m.

[2] Ib. 440; May 23, 1606.

[3] 91 Com. Journ. 214.

deprive generally of any voting power the most experienced member. In 1845, therefore, a special resolution was agreed to, giving to the chairman of Committees on railway groups or Bills a right to vote with his fellow-members, and a second, or casting vote, if the numbers were equal.[1] This right was extended, in 1850, to the chairmen of all Committees on private Bills, and still continues.[2]

When complaint was made of the proceedings in Committee on a private Bill in the Commons, the remedy was an appeal to the House for a Committee of Appeal. This ground was taken in 1836, in opposition to a motion by Mr. Hume impugning the conduct of a Committee on the South-West Durham Railway Bill.[3] Under Standing Orders this Court of appeal, like other Committees of the time, was unwieldy in numbers and absurdly constituted.[4] It consisted of all the knights of shires, all the members for cities, as though their position made their competence as judges indisputable, and in addition such other members as might be named, so that the whole number might be at least two hundred.

Recognizing that so large a body was an unsuitable tribunal, Standing Orders provided that complaints from the parties might be referred to a Committee chosen by ballot from this body. They were to have before them a report upon the Bill, together with minutes and evidence taken before what may be called the Court below. This appellate tribunal was to be chosen with considerable formality. On a day appointed, at half-past four o'clock, the doors of the House were to be locked, and the clerk was to draw seven names from a glass containing slips of paper with the names of the two hundred members of the full Court. These seven members, if they were present and had not

Court of appeal in Commons.

Constitution.

Committee of Appeals.

---

[1] 100 Ib. 426; May 9, 1845.

[2] Commons' Standing Order 125, Sess. 1887.

[3] 34 Hansard, 779-80. For special reasons the Committee on this Bill was ordered to re-assemble, although the old practice was not disputed.

[4] Commons' Standing Orders, 24—29, Sess. 1837.

voted in the Committee upon the Bill, constituted the appellate tribunal. They were directed to meet at eleven o'clock on the day following, and continue their sittings *de die in diem* until they made their report. With a view to shorten their proceedings, only one counsel or agent was allowed to be heard for any one party, and it was strictly ordered that no member of the Committee should absent himself without leave of the House, and that the Committee should only be constituted by the attendance of all their members, except those specially excused.[1] There is little wonder that suitors rarely sought to put into motion a machinery so cumbrous, or that the House declined to exercise it. Only in one case was an Appeal Committee ever granted.[2] Probably both petitioners and promoters were satisfied with the substantial right of going before the second House or of renewing their application for a Bill in the next Session. The disuse of this appellate jurisdiction may also have been due to a rule laid down in Standing Orders that petitioners for appeal must first enter into a bond, with sureties, for payment of all costs and expenses of parties opposing their petition in case the Committee reported that such petition was frivolous and vexatious. In this rule may be traced the germ of the Costs Act. Committees of Appeal dropped out of existence in 1839. There was no such tribunal in the Lords.

Cumbrous machinery, little used.

A private Bill Committee has not, like a Committee on public matters, power to send for persons, papers, and records. If the attendance of an unwilling witness is desired, a Speaker's warrant must be obtained through the Committee. If a member of the House declines to give evidence, the only course for a Committee to adopt is to report the fact to the House in order that they may adopt such measures as

Power to summon witnesses.

[1] Resolutions regulating the appointment of Committees of Appeal will be found in 82 Com. Journ. 41, 178; 87 Ib. 20, 26.

[2] Commons' Committee on Private Business, 1838; Ev. of Mr. St. George Burke, pp. 10, 11. Ib. 1840 · Ev. of Mr. Pritt, p. 19.

they may think fit.[1] In 1731 Sir Archibald Grant, a member, was committed to the custody of the Serjeant-at-Arms, in order to secure his attendance before a Committee; and the Serjeant was directed to "bring him from time to time to attend the said Committee, in order to his being examined as often as the said Committee shall think fit to require the same."[2]

For greater publicity, as well as to secure that decisions of Committees on private Bills should be accurately reported, it was ordered in 1572 "that in all matters preferred to this Court between any private persons, and wherein the Bill shall be thought good to be committed, those Committees shall make their reports thereof unto this House in presence of both the parties and their learned counsel."[3]

Reports of Committees, 1572.

[1] 97 Com. Journ. 449.
[2] Frere, p. 71.
[3] 1 Com. Journ. 97.

CHAPTER XXIII.

PROCEDURE AT BAR: OR IN COMMITTEE: POWERS OF COM-
MITTEES OVER PREAMBLE: HEARING GIVEN TO PETI-
TIONERS: COUNSEL: PARLIAMENTARY AGENTS.

Early proce-
dure on pri-
vate Bills in
House of
Lords not
recorded.

No light whatever is thrown upon procedure in private Bills
by the scanty records of Parliament during the reigns of
Henry VIII. and his son. We can only glean here and there
from the Lords' Journals during this period that Bills were
even referred to Committees.[1] No mention is made as to the
employment of counsel or hearings at bar. But as appeals are
likewise ignored, it may reasonably be assumed that private
Bills were considered with equal care, and that counsel were
heard for and against them.

Lady
Howard's
case, 1548.

That they were closely investigated appears from an entry
in 1548 upon an estate Bill of Lord Thomas Howard. As
its provisions affected Lady Howard, the Earl of Arundel
moved that " she should have warning to appear in the House,
and declare frankly whether she were content " with an appointment of certain lands to her husband and two youngest
sons. Accordingly, Lady Howard appeared and answered that
she was " very well content with the Bill," and "much desirous
that it should take effect, the children being as much hers as
was the eldest ; humbly thanking the Lords that it pleased
them to take pains in so simple a matter, and praying them
to continue their good mind to the conclusion of the same,
whereby she should be bound to pray unto God for the continuance of their estates in much wealth and honour."[2]

---

[1] 1 Lords' Journ. 12; A.D. 1511.   [2] Ib. 342.

Another proof to the same effect is given in 1548, by proceedings upon the Bill of attainder against the Lord High Admiral Seymour. There is no trace of evidence upon this Bill in the Lords until an entry appears :—" It was thought good to send down certain ministers of the Upper House to declare unto the Commons of the Nether House the manner after which the Lords had proceeded in this matter, and to declare unto them that in case they were minded to proceed in like sort, certain noblemen who had given evidence against the Admiral should be sent to them to declare, by mouth and presence, such matter as by their writing should in the meantime appear unto them."[1]

From this entry it appears that written evidence, probably copies of that taken in the Lords, was sent to the Lower House, with an offer that oral testimony should be forthcoming upon the Bill if it were desired. At first the Commons did desire it, for their Journals, after the second reading, record a resolution "that the evidence be heard orderly, as it was before the Lords, and also to require that the Lords which affirm that evidence may come hither and declare it *virâ voce*." Afterwards the Master of the Rolls declared to the Commons his Majesty's pleasure "that the Admiral's presence was not necessary in this Court;" and the House did not persist in its request for personal evidence.[2]

This was a public matter, but the proposal of a hearing at bar after the second reading corresponds with later practice in both Houses upon private Bills. References of these Bills to Select Committees are among the earliest entries in the Commons' Journals.[3] There is little clue, however, to methods of treating them. Written answers, corresponding with modern petitions, are mentioned in 1549, when the Dean of Wells was furnished at his request with a copy of a

Margin notes:
Attainder of Lord High Admiral, 1548.

Proceedings in Lower House.

Bill concerning Canons of Wells, 1549.

---

[1] 1 Lords' Journ. 346.
[2] Lord Seymour of Sudeley was beheaded in 1549.
[3] 1 Com. Journ. 58 *et seq.* ; A.D. 1548.

Bill promoted by "the canon residentiaries" concerning their "quotidians and dividends," and was ordered "to make answer on Saturday next, sitting the Court." He "brought in his answer in writing," and the Bill, which had been read a second time, was then committed.[1] Again, in 1552, after the second reading of a "Bill put in for Horsham and Sussex," it was ordered "that the suitors against the Bill shall appear here to-morrow, with their counsel, at eight of the clock." Accordingly, next morning. "Mr. Foskue, with his counsel Mr. Catlyn, exhibited certain articles in writing against the Bill,"[2] which was "to avoid more ironworks in Sussex" as injuring the roads and consuming too much timber for fuel.[3] Mr. Foskue was no doubt a petitioner whose interests were prejudicially affected by the Bill. This is the first notice of the appearance of counsel in private business; and his services appear to have been limited, as he merely handed in written reasons, and did not argue the case.

That counsel, however, were heard at bar may be inferred from an order of the House of Commons, in 1553, upon a Bill to repeal the Act attainting the Duke of Norfolk.[4] Certain grantees of the Duke's lands asked that their interests might be saved. At their request they were furnished with copies of the Bill, and directed to "be here ready to-morrow with their counsel at nine of the clock." Mr. Cholmley and Mr. Rich, counsel for the petitioners, appear then to have argued the case.[5] In 1558, the bishops and their counsel often appeared in the Commons against the Bills aimed at them in Elizabeth's first Parliament. Thus, the Bishop of Winchester, with his counsel, and counsel on the other side representing grantees of the episcopal lands, were directed to be in attendance. Then the bishop "in proper person" opened his title to certain manors, saying

Bill against ironworks in Sussex, 1552.

First notice of counsel in private Bills, 1552.

Bill to reverse Duke of Norfolk's attainder, 1553.

Bishops and their counsel; House of Commons, 1558.

---

[1] 1 Com. Journ. 13.
[2] Ib. 20; March 17, 1552.
[3] *Ante*, Vol. I. pp. 30-2.
[4] 1 Com. Journ. 32.
[5] *Ante*, p. 758.

" they had been parcel of the bishopric for 1,300 years; and required justice of this House." " The Queen's Attorney " (the Journals add) "hearing the talk of the bishop, required that he might be heard for the Queen touching certain lands late parcel of the bishopric." So a day was appointed, at half-past eight a.m., when Mr. Nowell and Mr. Bell argued for the bishop, and Mr. Attorney for the Queen.[1] A few days afterwards the Bishop of Worcester, also in proper person, " required the copy of a Bill exhibited against his bishopric and a day to make answer in writing or otherwise." The Bishop of Coventry and Lichfield made like petition. Both were granted and days fixed when the bishops should make answer; " other parties then to have their counsel here likewise, to hear the bishops." At the proper time " the Bishop of Worcester, with his counsel, declared that Hooper was not lawful bishop, by reason of the appeal of Bishop Heath ; and so the grant not good ; and prayed the House to consider it."[2] The Bishop of Coventry and Lichfield, and his counsel, were also heard, with counsel on the other side. On the same day " the Bishop of London, in proper person, required a copy of a Bill put in for confirmation of leases granted by Dr. Ridley, usurper of the bishopric, as he saith."[3] He was afterwards heard in person to show the untruth of the Bill, arguing that the commissioners for his deprivation " did not according to their commission, and yet by his appeal, as also by his letters patent from Queen Mary, he standeth still bishop, and the grants made by N. Ridley void."[4]

Other proceedings at bar before the House of Commons are reported in 1562 upon a Bill " to put down an iron mill near Guildford." After the first reading of this Bill, January 16, 1562, there is an entry, " For that it is said that T. Elrington hath interest in the iron mill in the town of Shere, in Surrey, whereof the Bill is to put down the

Bill to put down iron mill near Guildford, 1562.

[1] 1 Com. Journ. 56; March 1 and 6, 1558.

[2] Ib. 57 ; March 11, 1558.

[3] Ib. ; March 13, 1558.

[4] Ib. ; March 15, 1558.

same, it is resolved that Mr. Speaker shall direct his letter in the name of the House to come and show, if he will, for saving his estate therein."[1]   Elrington had therefore had no notice of the Bill affecting him.   Next day he appeared, asking for a copy of the Bill,[2] " and a day to answer with his learned counsel, two in number."   The House granted this request, and on a day fixed, " Mr. Elrington appeared, with Mr. Serjeant Harper and Mr. Plowden, being of his learned counsel, and showing great reasons that the Bill might be rejected."   The Bill was probably introduced by the desire of local authorities, for, after the argument, " certain articles delivered by the Mayor of Guildford for maintenance of the Bill were read; and the copy thereof awarded to Mr. Elrington."   Next day " Mr. Elrington came in with the Serjeant, requiring the order of this House, in what sort he should answer the articles; whereupon the whole matter was committed to twelve of the House to hear the parties and proofs on both sides, and then to certify this House."[3]

There is no further mention of the Bill, which must have dropped.   It is the first private measure sent to a Committee with specific instructions to hear evidence and counsel, for there can be little doubt that the parties were represented there by counsel as at the bar.   At the latter hearing it will be noted that the proceedings were partly in writing and partly oral.   In 1566 another hearing at bar occurred upon a Bill to take away sanctuaries for debt.   This measure was opposed in person by " Mr. Dean of Westminster," who " made his oration for the sanctuary, alleging divers grants by King Lucius and other Christian kings; and Mr. Plowden, his counsel, alleged the grant for sanctuary there by King Edward five hundred years past (viz.), dated 1066, with great reasons in law and chronicles.   Mr. Forde, a

Bill to take away sanctuary for debt at Westminster.

---

[1] 1 Com. Journ. 63; January 21, 1562.

[2] Persons injuriously affected had no certain means of knowing the contents of a Bill except by leave of the House.

[3] 1 Com. Journ. 64.

civilian, also alleged divers stories and laws for the same."
After these arguments the Bill "was committed to the
Master of the Rolls and others to peruse the grants and
certify the force of the law now for sanctuaries."[1]

Among many examples in 1604 of pleadings at bar in the
Commons, the most instructive is that upon a Bill affecting
the estate of Edward, late Duke of Somerset. The promoters and opponents were Lord Hertford and Mr. Seymour.
Counsel came to the bar by appointment at seven a.m.
"Mr. Serjeant Nicholls, for Mr. Seymour, began the argument," which was continued till nine o'clock, and then adjourned. "The Earl of Hertford, and Lord Henry Seymour,
his brother, came into the House, and were admitted to
come within the bar, and to sit upon stools with their heads
covered."[2] Three days afterwards the arguments were renewed, and the Journals show a surfeit of them. Counsel
for Mr. Seymour were "heard again at large. Mr. Richison
replies. Mr. Serjeant Altham rejoins. Mr. Walter pursues.
Mr. Serjeant Nicholls sur-rejoins." Even this piling-up of
argument was not enough, for the parties then intervened.
"The Earl himself was admitted to speak within the bar in
his own cause. Mr. Seymour to answer. The Earl to reply,
&c." Such is the clerk's notice of these remarkable proceedings, which show that in the House counsel adhered to their
tedious court-practice of statement, reply, rejoinder, and sur-
rejoinder, and also show either extraordinary patience on the
part of members or unwonted interest in the Bill.

From 1604, arguments at bar in the Lower House are
too frequent to need further mention.[3] A somewhat doubtful passage in the Journals seems to show that counsel were
also heard, by order of that House, before a Committee on the
Bill against Queen Mary.[4] Such orders, however, were rare.

Duke of Somerset's Estate Bill, 1604.

Bill against Mary, Queen of Scots, 1572.

[1] 1 Com. Journ. 74; October 16, 1566.
[2] Ib. 210; May 15, 1604.
[3] Four were appointed in one day in 1604. (1 Com. Journ. 187.)
[4] "Mr. Chancellor of the Duchy, Mr. Chancellor of the Exchequer, Mr. Serjeant Manwood, Mr. Attorney

Throughout the sixteenth century, the general practice probably was to leave evidence for Committees, and reserve arguments for the House. After 1600, both functions were somewhat oftener delegated to Committees. For example, in 1604, upon Lucas's Estate Bill, a Committee meeting in Middle Temple Hall was ordered to hear counsel on both sides.[1] Afterwards, in the same case, it was agreed that "all or any of the creditors who desire to be heard by their counsel shall be admitted at the Committee, and there be heard at large."[2] In the same Session, similar orders were made upon Bills sanctioning an exchange of lands between Trinity College, Cambridge, and Sir Thomas Monson; and to relieve "such as use the handicraft of skinners."[3]

Counsel before Committees, 1604.

There is a notice in 1604 that Mr. Bartlett, counsel, "was assigned by Mr. Speaker, *in formâ pauperis*, for Grys, being a very poor man."[4] Grys was a party to the Bill, and his counsel, with another for the promoter, were heard at the bar. Grys was probably the same person who in the following Session had a double hearing by his counsel, both at the bar and in Committee. The occasion was a "much disputed" Bill to carry out a decree made between Le Grys and Cottrell. The Committee first reported a desire of parties interested to be heard by counsel in the House. This request was granted, and after hearing Mr. Randall Crewe on one side, and Mr. Richison, of Lincoln's Inn, on the other, the Bill was recommitted, "and counsel on both parts to be heard there."[5]

Counsel assigned by Speaker to poor petitioner, 1604.

Counsel heard both at bar and in Committee.

It is not until the year 1562 that the Lords' Journals notice any arguments upon a private Bill:—"*Item, primò*

Arguments on private Bills first

---

of the Duchy, Mr. Attorney of the Court of Wards, Mr. Popham, Mr. Monson, Mr. Yelverton, and Mr. Norton, to have conferences for the understanding of the Bill against Mary, commonly called the Queen of Scots; and to meet this afternoon; and all arguments to be received, as upon the second reading of the Bill, until it shall be read the third time."—1 Com. Journ. 101: June 5, 1572 (15 Eliz.).

[1] Ib. 184; April 23, 1604.
[2] Ib. 202; May 7, 1604.
[3] Ib. 226, 235.
[4] Ib. 241; June 18, 1604.
[5] Ib. 273–5.

vice lecta est billa for the assurance of certain lands to Sir mentioned,
House of
Lords, 1562. Francis Jobson; upon which Bill the Lords took order that the learned counsel, as well of the said Sir Francis Jobson as of the Bishop of Durham, whom it touched, should, on Saturday the next following, be heard, what could on either side be said in furtherance or disallowing of the same."[1] According to a further entry, Sir Francis Jobson, with his counsel, came before the House on Saturday. Afterwards no further mention is made of the Bill.

Counsel are not again mentioned in the Upper House until 1580, but this appears to have been in litigation then pending.[2] Five years afterwards Lord Dacres and Lord Norris were Lord Dacres'
Bill, 1585. ordered to appear with their counsel upon a Bill affecting them.[3] Accordingly, after the first reading, there were read to the House " the reasons and allegations of Lord Norris why the Bill exhibited by the Lord and Lady Dacres should not be enacted." Counsel were then heard for all the parties, and Committee to
end contro-
versies. the case ended upon their agreement to refer all controversies to four peers and two judges, named by the parties. Lord Dacres named Lord Burleigh (Lord Treasurer), Earl of Leicester (Lord Steward), and Sir Roger Manwood, Lord Chief Baron. Lord Norris named the Earl of Kent, the Earl of Bedford, and Sir Gilbert Gerard, Master of the Rolls. The House then ordered that these peers and judges " should end the matters between the parties before the next Session of Parliament, if they could; and if they could not, then to make report thereof." Further, this Committee received Counsel
heard in
Committee. power to summon witnesses and " examine all parties upon their oaths if occasion so required."[4] The Committee appear to have heard counsel.[5]

[1] 1 Lords' Journ. 593; February 20, 1562 (5 Eliz.).

[2] Between the Marquis and Marchioness of Winchester, who were separately represented by counsel, and Mr. Oughtred, who appeared personally. In this case the matters in dispute were referred, by consent, to the Lord Chancellor and other peers.—2 Lords' Journ. 45.

[3] Ib. 72; December 14, 1585.

[4] Ib. 76; December 19, 1585. The same method was adopted in Hearne's Estate Bill of 1585, after hearing counsel on both sides. (Ib. 87, 104.)

[5] *Post*, p. 873.

In and after 1585, the hearing of counsel at bar by the Lords is frequently noticed.[1] This hearing seems to have generally occurred after the second reading. Sometimes when counsel had been heard, a Bill was committed.[2] In another case, in 1597, after arguments by counsel for the Marquis of Winchester against a Bill, and also for the promoter, Lord Mountjoy, " no just cause being found to hinder or stay the Bill, the same was read a third time." Lords' Committees at this period also heard counsel, without express powers to do so, as appears from a Bill to pay debts and legacies of one Molineux. Lord Shrewsbury reported " that the Committee on this Bill had heard counsel as well on the part of Mr. Molineux as against him, and finding some matter of difficulty in the Bill, counsel desired to be heard openly in the House." [3]

This double hearing was, in effect, an appeal to the whole House from the decision, or probable decision, of its Committee. Early in the seventeenth century there is evidence of a natural desire by the Lords to restrict the hearing of counsel to Committees. In 1610, upon a Bill to make void certain fraudulent conveyances of lands belonging to Sir Henry Crispe, the Archbishop of Canterbury, Chairman of the Committee, reported that although they had heard counsel on both sides, Lady Crispe, an opposing petitioner, now desired to be heard also by counsel at the bar. But the Archbishop represented that, as the Committee " arose satisfied " that this was a proper Bill, " it standeth not with the order of the House again to hear counsel at the bar"; and so the House determined.[4]

It is doubtful whether, until the seventeenth century, Committees in the Commons exercised like powers to hear counsel without special instructions. In 1623, these powers were

Lord Mountjoy's Bill, 1597.

Counsel heard in Committee and afterwards in House, 1597.

Double hearings restricted, 1610.

Crispe's Estate Bill, 1610.

[1] 2 Lords' Journ. 84, 85, 87, 204, 216, 218, 219, 222, 233, 246, 252.

[2] Hatch's Bill, 1597 (Ib. 207); Kettleby's Bill, 1601 (Ib. 237).

[3] 2 Lords' Journ. 212; Dec. 17, 1597.

[4] Ib. 589; May 7, 1610.

conferred. Upon a Bill injuriously affecting creditors of one Cope, the House of Commons ordered " to have these men heard by their counsel at the Committee, and to have their witnesses heard." On the same day a similar order was made upon Sir Richard Lumley's Estate Bill:—"Committee to have power to hear counsel and witnesses in this case. And all other Committees have the like power from the House." [1] No certain information is afforded by the Journals whether this resolution served as a rule, or grew into a custom, for all future Committees, or whether it merely held good for the Session or Parliament. However this may be, after 1623, no arguments in Committee on private Bills are mentioned until 1693.[2] Again, in 1698, the House ordered " that the City of London, and Company of Fishmongers, be heard by their counsel before the Committee " on a Bill to make Billingsgate a free market.[3] This Bill had been read a second time. There were similar orders in 1701 upon a Bill for improving Rye Harbour;[4] in 1711 upon a Divorce Bill,[5] and an Avon Navigation Bill.[6]

All Commons' Committees authorized to hear counsel and witnesses 1623.

During this interval of nearly a century, arguments at bar were frequent, and the House of Commons seems to have reserved to itself the right of hearing the arguments of counsel upon private Bills, generally before commitment.[7] Sometimes arguments were allowed at other stages, after the report of a Committee,[8] and upon the third reading,[9] even after they had been heard upon the second reading.[10] At the bar the order of proceedings in the Lords followed that observed upon appeals. In the Commons, if the House had directed that counsel should be heard, the Serjeant-at-Arms inquired whether any counsel were attending in the case. If they

Procedure in arguments at bar.

---

[1] 1 Com. Journ. 747; March 23, 1623.

[2] 11 Ib. 15.

[3] 12 Ib. 493.

[4] 13 Ib. 703.

[5] 16 Ib. 600.

[6] 17 Ib. 134.

[7] In 1 Com. Journ. 955 (April 24, 1604) is an entry, "Counsel always to be heard before the commitment."

[8] 1 Com. Journ. 1032-3; A.D. 1606-7.

[9] Ib. 355-7; Waller's Estate Bill, A.D. 1607.

[10] 17 Ib. 407.

were ready a motion was necessary " that counsel be called in ; " otherwise, although present by order of the House, they could not be heard. This motion was frequently opposed and negatived.[1] When admitted, counsel were placed on each side of the bar, and the Speaker inquired of each for whom he appeared. The Bill was then read by the clerk *pro formâ*; the petition against the Bill and order for hearing counsel were also read. No more than two counsel were heard on one side. First the petitioner's case was opened : in support of it witnesses were examined, and cross-examined by counsel for the Bill, questions being then put by any member. Evidence was then summed up for petitioners. Counsel for the Bill next made an opening speech, and called his witnesses. The right of final reply rested with petitioners. Counsel were then directed to withdraw, the Speaker " opened the Bill " (*i.e.* read his breviate of its contents), and, if opinions differed, a debate and division followed.[2]

Transfer of private business to Committees. These investigations by the whole House were unsatisfactory from all points of view. If the old Committees, with their local interests and shifting numbers, were bad tribunals, neither House could be a good one. Its judgment was seldom formed upon a competent knowledge of the facts or bearings in any case ; its impatience to pass to public business, though natural, was incompatible with any fair regard for the interests of suitors. Before the eighteenth century closed, this impatience made itself felt, and the House of Commons did not often constitute itself a Committee for hearing and deciding upon private Bills.[3] As trading ventures grew in importance and number, the unfitness of either House for inquiries so prolonged and elaborate became even more clear, and the increase of public business in Parliament

---

[1] Todd's Practice of Parliament, 209. Com. Journ. March 4, 1795 (Norwood and Paddington Canal Bill); Ib. March 2, 1796 (Pertenhall Enclosure Bill).

[2] Bramwell's Proceedings in Passing Private Bills; 2nd ed. 1816 : pp. 59, 60. The first edition of this work was published in 1809. Todd, 209-10.

[3] Eau Brink Bill; 1 Com. Journ. February 4, 1795.

made a complete delegation of these duties to Committees more necessary and inevitable.[1]

There was thus ready acquiescence in the gradual encroachments by Committees upon the power of both Houses over preambles. These encroachments seem to have begun early in the present century. The change was made by no specific resolution in either House, and can be marked by no exact date. After 1820, there are few instances in which counsel appeared before the whole House. Two orders, the last of their kind, that petitioners should be heard at the bar against private Bills, were made by the Commons in 1824. Neither took effect. In one case a large majority showed their sense of this irksome labour by rejecting the motion " that counsel be called in."[2] A Committee had already reported upon the Bill.[3] The other order for a hearing at bar was upon the second reading of a Bill to repeal, in favour of a new company, the then existing statutory prohibition of marine insurance by private associations. In this case, the petitioners did not avail themselves of the permission they had received.[4]

Last orders for hearing at bar upon private Bill, 1824.

Equitable Loan Bank Bill.

Marine Insurance Company, 1824.

Against public Bills counsel were heard more recently at the bar of both Houses. In 1835, counsel for the East India Company appeared against a Bill to compensate Mr. James Silk Buckingham for the suppression of a newspaper belonging to him at Calcutta.[5] Three years later, Mr. Roebuck was heard at the Commons' bar, as agent of the House of Assembly of Lower Canada, against the Lower Canada Government Bill.[6] In 1839, there were similar arguments upon the Jamaica Government Bill ;[7] and at the bar of the House of Lords so lately as 1844 upon the Sudbury Disfranchisement Bill.[8]

Later arguments at bar upon public Bills.

---

[1] Bramwell, in 1816, notes that it had lately become unusual for the House of Commons to hear counsel and witnesses on account of the interruption to public business (p. 60).

[2] Equitable Loan Bank Bill, 1824; 79 Com. Journ. 409.

[3] Ib. 416 ; May 26, 1824.

[4] *Ante,* pp. 579–81; 79 Com. Journ. 430.

[5] 90 Ib. 589.

[6] 93 Ib. 233.

[7] 94 Ib. 208.

[8] 99 Ib. 480 ; *post,* p. 874.

Divorce Bills.   Divorce Bills in the Commons continued to be referred to Committees of the whole House down to 1839; counsel were heard and witnesses examined in these cases at the bar.[1] In 1840, this jurisdiction was also surrendered by the House, and all divorce Bills were ordered to be referred to a select Committee of nine members; five, and afterwards three, to be the quorum.[2] Evidence as to substituted service, however, was still given at the bar, up to the passing of the Divorce Act.[3] The rare cases of divorce now submitted to Parliament are still heard by the Lords in Committee of the whole House,[4] the last survival of this ancient jurisdiction.

Old rule that opponents begin.   According to the rule of the House of Commons, three centuries ago, counsel against a Bill began first. This rule is expressly stated in the Journals of 1606 upon a measure relating to the parish of St. Saviour's, Southwark.[5] The Bill had been read a second time, and referred to a Committee; but the House also ordered that counsel on both sides should be heard at the bar.[6] Mr. Finch, against the Bill, then began: Mr. Goldsmith answered for the Bill. As "time was far spent" with arguments there, "the House appointed that the Bill should rest in Committee, and counsel be further heard there."

Arguments and evidence after second reading.   The reason why, after the second reading of a private Bill, opposing petitioners were called on to begin, becomes clear when we remember that, as the House had assented to the general principle, the onus of proof lay upon petitioners to show that

---

[1] Lardner's Divorce Bill, 1839; 94 Com. Journ. 250, 286. Napier's Divorce Bill, 1839; Ib. 250, 284. There were occasional exceptions to the rule stated. Allison's Divorce Bill, 1839, was referred to a Select Committee, which proceeded upon a printed copy of the evidence taken in the Upper House, without requiring oral testimony. (Ib. 381.)

[2] 95 Com. Journ. 74. This is the present constitution of Divorce Committees. (Commons' Standing Order,

189; Sess. 1887.)

[3] See Earl of Lincoln's Divorce Bill, 1850; Examination at Bar, 105 Com. Journ. 423.

[4] Lords' Standing Order 178, Sess. 1887.

[5] 1 Com. Journ. 349. The same order was observed in the arguments upon another private Bill of this Session. (Ib. 352.) See also Marshalsea Court Bill (Ib. 369 and 1040).

[6] Ib. 340.

their interests were so prejudicially affected by clauses that they were entitled to relief, or that the Bill ought not to pass. Hence it follows that Committees upon private as upon public Bills originally had no power over preambles. The ancient rule went further. If a member were opposed to preamble, he was excused or disqualified from service in Committee on the Bill for, as it was quaintly put, "the child is not to be put to the nurse that cares not for it."[1] In 1606, a member, Mr. Hedley, being nominated upon the Grand Committee then considering the Union with Scotland, "excused himself in that he was directly against the matter itself in opinion." It was thereupon "conceived for a rule that no man was to be employed that had declared himself against it."[2] Again, in 1640, the House of Commons "declared that those who speak against the body or substance of any Bill, Committee, or other thing proposed in this House, ought not to be of the Committee for that business."[3]

Members opposed to preamble not to serve on Committee.

This ancient rule of exclusion from Committees is no longer known in Parliament. But the principle on which it rested, that preambles were determined by the whole House, and that the powers of Committees were limited, remained in full effect until the present century. In conformity with this view, Committees on private Bills used to hold that they could not entertain objections to the general expediency of a measure, and that the sole object of the reference to them was to settle clauses, see that a Bill did not go beyond the objects stated by promoters, and that petitioners whose property or rights were interfered with received adequate protection. If, there- fore, opponents wished to call in question the principle of a Bill, they were bound to petition against preamble, stating

Former limited powers of Committees.

Petitions against preamble.

---

[1] 6 Grey's Debates, 373.

[2] 1 Com. Journ. 350; March 7, 1606.

[3] 2 Com. Journ. 14. This declara-
tion referred to a Committee upon the Lords' interference in matters of Sup-
ply.   "At this time" (the Journal adds), "though the King's Solicitor spake against the body of this last Committee, and desired himself in that regard to be exempted from it, yet, for some reasons then alleged, he was allowed to be of it."

their objections, and praying to be heard by counsel at the bar. They were then heard, if the House thought fit, upon a motion for the second reading, but at this stage no opposition was allowed to particular provisions. Promoters also might then be heard by counsel in defence of the principle.

Petitions against clauses.

After a second reading, petitions against preamble were no longer available. Another petition objecting to specific provisions in the Bill must then be presented, and was referred to the Committee on the Bill.[1] Opponents in Committee were then required to begin, the onus of proof being upon them to show that a measure approved in principle by the House contained clauses hurtful to their interests. Opponents, no doubt, were often astute enough to put a preamble into issue under cover of an attack upon clauses. It must always have been difficult for Committees to disentangle these questions. When, therefore, Parliament became unwilling to sacrifice its time in hearing counsel and evidence at bar, Committees by degrees were permitted, without demur, to usurp its functions, and decide upon the whole Bill, preamble as well as clauses. This departure from the constitutional rule that preambles should be sanctioned by the House alone was afterwards urged as a reason for maintaining in the Commons the old Committees with numerous members, so that the House might be adequately represented in each room. Authority to deal with the whole Bill could not, it was argued, be properly entrusted to a small tribunal of five members, whose decision, in the absence of full information as to what passed before them, could seldom be reviewed by the House.[2]

Present practice as to preambles.

The second reading of a public measure is still taken as affirming the general expediency of passing it. When, therefore, either House goes into Committee upon a public Bill, the preamble is postponed until clauses are considered.

---

[1] Sherwood, p. 28.

[2] Commons' Committee of 1838 on Private Business; Ev. of Mr. J. H.

Ley, clerk of the House of Commons.

If provisions vital to the Bill are then inserted or omitted, its preamble may be altered so as to correspond with these changes. Such alterations must have been necessary at a period when recitals in public Bills were long and argumentative, as they generally were. In modern drafting, preambles are put into the fewest possible words, avoiding, if possible, any opening for debate.

In private Bills, on the contrary, which from their very nature are exceptions to the general law, a preamble must explain, however shortly, the reasons why legislation is expedient on each of the more important subjects dealt with, and must also show, in certain classes of measures, that promoters have complied with Standing Orders or with general legislation, *e.g.*, that the approval of shareholders or of governing bodies and ratepayers has been given in the prescribed form. But the several statements thus made that legislation is expedient go to the root of each Bill, and are the very issues which Committees now try. The old practice, therefore, is now reversed. Promoters open with a statement of their case and with evidence to establish preamble. Petitioners follow with evidence and a speech, or a speech without evidence, in which case the promoters have no right of reply. If the preamble, as a whole, is not proved, there is an end of the Bill, but Committees alter preambles when the essential features of a Bill may still be preserved. This power of alteration is not limited by any order of Parliament, but Committees act upon the rule that either House assents by a second reading to the general lines of each Bill, provided the promoters prove their case in Committee, and therefore that the Bill they return to the House must not differ essentially in character from the Bill referred to them.[1] In the Court of Referees, petitioners are called upon to begin.

[1] Frere's Practice on Private Bills in House of Commons, 1846, p. 5. See also a case there referred to, Glasgow Police (No. 3) Bill (97 Com. Journ. 237), in which Mr. Tatton of Egerton reported to the House that the Bill, as submitted to them by the promoters, " was totally different from that referred to them, the allegations in the preamble being essen-

Speeches by counsel.   Up to the Session of 1845 counsel for promoters were entitled to make three speeches: in opening, summing up evidence, and replying. On the recommendation of a Committee, in 1845,[1] the right of summing up evidence was abolished. A proposal that the right of reply should also be put an end to was negatived, as were also resolutions that counsel should not be heard, except by special leave of a Committee, unless their attendance had been continuous.

Competing Bills.   Among numberless questions relating to procedure and the status of petitioners which have at various times been determined, a few may now be mentioned. Before the present system of grouping was adopted, competing Bills were often referred to separate Committees, who sometimes reported in favour of both, leaving the House to decide which should be preferred. This was the course taken upon the first docks proposed in the Thames in 1796-1800. While two Committees were occupied with two rival measures of this nature, a third Committee was appointed to inquire generally into the same subject.[2]

Status of petitioners.   By the common law of Parliament, landowners complaining of injury under a Bill which proposes actual interference with their land have a right to appear against it. This right arises from no Standing Order, but is based on immemorial usage, and extends to the whole contents of even an omnibus Bill; the sole limitation is that, like other parties, landowners can only be heard upon the allegations in their petition.[3] Further, the Costs Act of 1865 provides that no

---

tially altered, and every clause in the original Bill expunged." Under these circumstances the Committee considered that it was "not competent for them to proceed with the Bill."

[1] Committee on Railway Bills, 1845; Second Report, pp. 10, 11.

[2] *Ante*, pp. 646 *et seq.*, 660.

[3] In what is known as "the post case," decided in 1868 by the Court of Referees in a landowner's favour,

counsel for the promoting company asked:—"Am I to understand that your decision goes to this extent: if a landowner has a post in a field at Preston, and we take it, that he can be heard against all parts of an omnibus Bill, one of which may be for stopping up a footpath at Willesden?" The Chairman (Mr. Dodson): "If he is a landowner, we have no power to limit him." (1 Clifford & Stephens's Referee Reports, 63.)

landowner shall be liable to costs who "*bonâ fide* at his own sole risk and charge opposes a Bill" under which any part of his property will be taken.[1]

Mr. Cardwell's Committee, in 1853, recommended that if landowners alleged no general public ground, and were not liable to costs, they should not be heard upon general questions of public advantage, but that their cases should be limited to the residential or other damage which the proposed scheme would inflict upon them. Another suggestion afterwards made[2] was that the referees in the House of Commons should have a discretionary power to allow a hearing to landowners. Neither of these recommendations has been adopted. Earl Grey, in 1863, claimed the utmost latitude for landowners against railways :—" It is not true," he said, " that the interest of a landowner with respect to a railway is limited to the direct injury it may do to his property. . . . . Every person inhabiting a district has a great interest in having the best line of communication made which is practicable. . . . . Every landowner should therefore have an opportunity of opposing a Bill upon its general merits, as well as upon the manner in which it affects his own land, because the construction of one bad line through a particular country will almost invariably make the construction of a good one impracticable."[3] The fate of a railway is, in fact as well as in theory, involved in a single landowner's opposition if any lands proposed to be traversed are struck out of the Bill. The railway then is cut in two, and cannot be made as a continuous line of communication.

Committees on railway Bills used, indeed, to act upon this view : that if an owner's land was to be taken for a railway against his will, he was, at all events, entitled to require that the line should be the best. An instance was given in 1863 of beneficial results from this course, but only through

Margin notes: Suggested abridgment of landowners' rights. Earl Grey upon landowners and railways, 1863. Landowners' right to oppose railways on general grounds.

---

[1] 28 Vict. c. 27, s. 2.
[2] By Mr. Dodson, when Chairman of Committees. (1 Clifford & Stephens's Reports, p. 63.)
[3] Commons' Committee on Private Bill Business, 1863; Ev. pp. 105, 113.

the existence of a second tribunal. The Madeley, Drayton, and Newcastle-under-Lyme Railway Bill passed the Commons in 1862, but was afterwards thrown out in the Lords on Lord Crewe's opposition. He said that a line might come through his property, but that this line was not laid out in the best way for the public or himself. Evidence to this effect was not brought out very distinctly in the Commons. In the other House the opponent's case was better presented; and next year both parties adopted the line advocated by Lord Crewe, in preference to the original plan.[1]

Competition as ground for hearing in Parliament. In 1845 competition was not accepted as a valid ground of objection to railway or other Bills. Existing railway companies, therefore, were not allowed a hearing against new projects if the only injury they could allege was by loss of traffic. Some instances to the contrary occurred in 1844-5, but opposing petitions in those cases were heard by special order of the House, in consideration not of private but of public interests which were affected.[2] Owing to this restriction, railway companies who wished to oppose the making of a new railway used often to appear for landowners, as they were not heard against preamble, even when their own line was crossed or their land interfered with. On this point, however, there were conflicting decisions, some Committees allowing railway companies to oppose the whole policy of making a rival line, while other Committees confined them to protective clauses. Upon a recommendation by Mr. Cardwell's Committee, in 1853, Standing Orders were passed by the House of Commons, defining the cases in which railway companies should be allowed to appear against a new scheme, and giving them a right to be heard on the ground of competition, if Committees thought fit. This discretionary power is now exercised by the Referees in the Commons, and by Committees in the Upper House. It applies to dock, pier, and other forms of competition.

Railway companies opposing new lines for landowners.

Competition made a ground for *locus standi*, 1853.

[1] Commons' Committee on Private Bill Business, 1863; Ev. of Mr. G. P. Bidder, C.E., p. 229.

[2] Frere's Practice, p. 40.

Formerly, the House of Commons did not admit the right Shareholders.
of shareholders to petition, under any circumstances, against
Bills promoted by directors, unless they could show an
interest distinct from that of the company generally. The
ground for this view was, that shareholders had handed over
their interests, for good or for evil, to certain representatives,
and, according to the phrase used in these cases, could
not be heard against the common seal. It has been shown
that, in the House of Lords, Standing Orders were passed,
which for some time were peculiar to that House, providing
that companies promoting Bills should submit them to their
proprietors at what are known as Wharncliffe meetings.[1]
Dissentient shareholders at these meetings are now admitted
before Committees of either House in opposition to Bills.

Formerly, when private Bills were referred to Committees Local autho-
numerously constituted of local and other members, it was inhabitants.
assumed that inhabitants of the district and towns affected
were adequately represented, and, in practice, they were not
permitted to appear upon petition. This practice was continued, with extreme hardship to local interests, even after
Committees were freed from local influences, and inhabitants
or local authorities were no longer represented there.[2]
A Standing Order now gives the Court of Referees a discretionary power to admit local authorities or inhabitants
against a Bill, if they allege that it injuriously affects them.
In 1881, an absolute right was conferred on local authorities
to oppose any Bill relating to lighting or water supply, or the
raising of capital for any such purpose, if they allege that
their town or district may be injuriously affected.[3]

There used to be a Standing Order in the Lords that no Petitioners
petitioner should be heard there unless he had petitioned in against Bills.

---

[1] *Ante*, p. 784.

[2] Commons' Committee on Private
Bills, 1847, Third Report; Ev. of
Mr. C. H. Parkes, p. 91.

[3] On a division, this Standing
Order was carried in the Commons
by 311 votes to 56. (Standing Orders
134 and 134A, 1887.) As to the status
of Chambers of Commerce or Agriculture against railway rates and
fares, see Standing Order 133A;
and *ante*, p. 811, n.

the Commons.[1] This restriction has long since been abandoned. A petitioner can now intervene in both Houses, or
in either, but if he discusses clauses in Committee of one
House, he cannot, according to practice, be heard against
preamble in the other.   Usually, therefore, petitioners whose
first opposition to preamble has proved unsuccessful withdraw from the room when clauses are considered, reserving
their right to appear against the whole Bill in the second

**Petitioners
for Bills.**

House.   It was formerly necessary that petitions for a Bill
in the Commons should be " signed by the parties who were
suitors " for it,[2] and in the Lords " by all parties concerned."[3]
An odd rule prevented all persons from giving evidence who
had signed petitions either for or against Bills, on the
ground that they were interested in the issue.[4]   In 1844-5,
Committees adopted the more sensible rule, that such evidence
should be taken *quantum valeat*.[5]

**Reading
Bills in
Committee.**

There appears to have been a technical rule, probably
observed also in the Lower House, that Lords' Committees
should begin by reading the Bill referred to them.   When
Bills were in manuscript, and copies not generally accessible,
such a proceeding was necessary, and was observed in the
House itself, until breviates were introduced.   In 1610, a
demand was made for the rehearing of arguments addressed
to a Lords' Committee on a private Bill, because " the Bill
itself was not read " there.   This technical objection, put before the House by a petitioner against the Bill, was skilfully
evaded by the Archbishop of Canterbury, who had been
Chairman of the Committee, and said that, " forasmuch as the
Bill was formerly read in the House in the hearing of " the
peers appointed, " whereof they were so sufficiently remembered that they required not again to hear it ; therefore the
not reading of it at the time was not material."[6]

[1] Commons' Committee on Railway and Canal Legislation, 1858;
Ev. of Serjeant Wrangham, p. 96.

[2] Standing Order 2 (1832).

[3] Lords' Standing Order 98 (1832).
This Standing Order dated from 1705.

[4] In 1792 the Lords allowed petitioners to withdraw their names from
petitions in order to qualify as witnesses (32 Lords' Journ. 367, 455).

[5] Frere's Practice, p. 70.

[6] 2 Lords' Journ. 589; May 7, 1610.

Frequent mention has been made of counsel employed in Parliament. Their names are not recorded in the later journals, but during the sixteenth and seventeenth centuries a few names are repeated, and show that advocacy in Parliament even then was limited to certain members of the bar.[1] Draftsmen of petitions and Bills must have existed from a very early period. There is some evidence of these practitioners in the year 1372.[2] Instances have been given of preambles, both to public and private measures, almost equivalent to speeches of counsel, and setting forth the case for each Bill in flowing terms well chosen to show its public utility.[3] It was not, however, until great trading bodies arose, asking for statutory powers to make canals, docks, waterworks, gasworks, and, above all, railways, that sufficient business could have existed to support a distinct Parliamentary bar.

Probably, owing to the Imperial character of the tribunal, and the wide range of questions dealt with, counsel before Parliamentary Committees of either House have never possessed the right of exclusive audience which is conceded to them in the superior Courts of law. A Parliamentary agent, any solicitor who takes the trouble to put his name upon the list of agents, any member of the English, Scotch or Irish bars, and even, if necessary, the parties themselves, may appear before Committees and be heard. Perhaps the reason why, notwithstanding this open field, counsel are still generally retained, will best appear from some evidence given by a very able and experienced solicitor in 1863:—
' You may put a man of the first ability to the Parliamentary bar, and for a year or two he is of very little use. He has to learn the tone and temper of Committees;

Counsel in Parliament.

No exclusive right of audience.

---

[1] Plowden was often retained in Parliamentary cases during the reign of Elizabeth.

[2] *Post*, p. 872.

[3] It is clear from the language of some of the early Acts that they were modelled from the same draft. Examples will be found in the recitals and operative words of the Paving Bills promoted A.D. 1455–77 for Gloucester, Canterbury, Taunton, Cirencester, and Southampton. 5 Rot. Parl. 338; 33 Hen. VI. 6 Rot. Parl. 177–80; 17 Edw. IV. *Ante*, pp. 258 *et seq.*

he has to learn by experience what he may urge, and what he may not urge; and it is the keenness of perception, the nice judgment, and the talent in taking all the points of his case, which make the leaders of the Parliamentary bar so eminent. Only the other day I was remarking to one of them that he had got an advantage for his clients which was worth more than half a million of money; as I believe, by the simple fact of his holding the brief."[1] As Parliamentary Committees have to adjudicate upon far larger and more important interests than come before any other tribunals in the kingdom, it is natural that clients there should wish for special training and aptitude in those who represent them.

Some notices, necessarily scattered, will now be given of the position, at various periods, of counsel thus employed. A curious ordinance, or statute, passed about the year 1372,[2] is directed against what was then regarded as the abuse of petitioning on behalf of private interests, representing these as general grievances; in other words, against the attempt to obtain private relief by means of public Acts. The statute recites that men of the law who follow divers businesses in the King's Courts on behalf of private persons (" gentz de ley qui pursuent diverses busoignes en les Courts le roi pour singulers persones ") do procure and cause to be brought into Parliament many petitions in the name of the Commons which in no wise relate to them, but only to private persons for whom they are engaged. Parliament therefore directs, as a drastic remedy, that thereafter no lawyer shall be returned as Knight of the Shire; and those then returned are not to receive any wages.

Statute of 1372 against petitions promoted by lawyers in Parliament.

Power of members to plead in Lords, upon leave given.

Although, according to custom, members of the Commons, if also members of the bar, have always been unable to plead before their own House, they used, by leave, to appear upon Bills pending in the Upper House. This point

[1] Commons' Committee on Private Bill Business, 1863; Ev. of Mr. Robert Baxter, p. 314.
[2] 46 Edw. III.

was decided in 1607, when "Mr. Speaker[1] propoundeth to the House whether Sir John Bays and Mr. Brock, two counsellors at law but judges in this House, might be retained of counsel to attend a Committee of the Higher House in a private cause there in question. Urgeth a precedent of his own:—that in 27 Eliz., in the Lord Norris and Lord Dacres his case,[2] he himself had leave of the House to attend.   Mr. Solicitor and Mr. Recorder of London, in matter of title of honour between the Lord Lespencer and the Lord Abergavenny, had leave of the House the last Session. Leave granted upon this motion."[3] In the absence of such leave, Mr. Story, a burgess, was admonished, in 1558, that he "had not well used himself, being a member of this House, to go before the Lords, and be of counsel with the Bishop of Winchester against the patentees;[4] which by the House was taken to be a fault; whereupon Mr. Story excused himself, by ignorance of any such order; and nevertheless, since, had considered it, and doth knowledge it not well done: and therefore required (requested) the House to remit it; which willingly by the House was remitted."[5]

Case of 1585.

Story's Case, 1558.

In 1666 this privilege was revoked, and the Commons ordered "that such members as are of the long robe shall not be of counsel on either side in any Bill depending in the Lords' House before such Bill come down to this House."[6] This prohibition appears to have been limited to Bills, and for sufficient reason: that it would be unseemly if members were concerned as advocates in one House upon measures which afterwards came before them as legislators in their own House. Yet, in 1820, Mr. Brougham and Mr. Denman, the Queen's Attorney and Solicitor General, the King's Attorney and Solicitor General, and Dr. Lushington, were allowed to plead

Permission revoked as to Bills, 1666.

Exception made as to Bill against Queen Caroline, 1820.

---

[1] Serjeant Phillips, who sat for Somersetshire.

[2] *Ante*, p. 857.

[3] 1 Com. Journ. 373; May 15, 1607.

[4] This was a Bill, not a cause. *Ante*, pp. 852-3.

[5] 1 Com. Journ. 58-9; March 23, 1558.

[6] 8 Ib. 646.

before the Lords upon the Bill then pending against Queen Caroline.[1]   This leave was not to be drawn into a precedent, and it was understood that, if the Bill had come before the Commons, these five members would not have been allowed to vote upon it.[2]   It is also contrary to the law and usage of Parliament for any member, either by himself or any partner, to engage in promoting private Bills for pecuniary reward.[3]

Parliamentary agency by members.

Practice upon appeals.

When the House of Lords sat as a Court of appeal, the old practice was that members might plead before it, upon obtaining leave,[4] and specifying "the cause and parties, and whether on a writ of error or appeal."   In 1704 this permission was restricted by a resolution "that this House will not give leave to any of its members to plead at the bar of the House of Lords in cases of appeals from Courts of Equity."[5] No grounds are·stated for this distinction between common law and equity cases.   Since the year 1710 leave has been unnecessary in judicial cases.[6]

Leave given to member to plead upon public Bill, 1842.

Mr. Roebuck was allowed, in 1842, to plead as counsel at the bar of the House of Lords in support of a public measure, the Sudbury Disfranchisement Bill, which had then passed the Commons.[7]   There appears to be no similar case.   This precedent was quoted four years afterwards upon a motion

Leave asked by member to plead upon private Bill, 1846.

that Mr. Charles Buller should have leave to attend as counsel before the House of Lords upon the Bolton Waterworks Bill, which had then passed the Commons.[8]   To this motion Sir Charles Wood (Chancellor of the Exchequer) and Sir James Graham demurred, asking for time to examine precedents. In view of these objections, which were reinforced by Mr. Speaker, the motion was withdrawn.[9]

Counsel in the Lords.

In 1685 the House of Lords ordered "that for the future

---

[1] 75 Com. Journ. 444. 2 Hansard, p. 400.
[2] May, pp. 425–6.
[3] Ib. 425. 85 Com. Journ. 107.
[4] 9 Com. Journ. 104 ; A.D. 1669. 11 Ib. 22, 367 ; A.D. 1693–5.

[5] 14 Ib. 436 ; A.D. 1704.
[6] May, p. 426. 1 Hansard, N.S. p. 402.
[7] 97 Com. Journ. 499.
[8] 101 Ib. 627 ; May 4, 1846.
[9] 86 Hansard, pp. 93–4.

neither his Majesty's Attorney-General, nor any other assistant to this House, after having taken his place on the woolsack as such, shall be allowed to be of counsel at the bar of this House for any private person or persons whatsoever."[1] The restriction, no doubt, extended to appearances in Committee. In a case heard at the bar in 1742, this Standing Order was appealed to, but not enforced.[2]

The Attorney-General, as an assistant to the Lords, was entitled to a place on the woolsack, but not a voice. On this ground it was resolved by the House of Commons, in 1614, that Sir Henry Hobart, having been elected and having sat, though with much question and dispute, "shall for this Parliament remain, but that no Attorney-General shall serve as a member after this Parliament."[3] Accordingly, Attorney-Generals appear to have been excluded for nearly a century. The Solicitor-General was an attendant in the Lords, not an assistant, and his right to sit in the Commons was therefore admitted. It was a right, however, which, upon occasion, holders of this office sometimes ignored. On the Speaker's death, in 1566, a message was sent to the Lords that Richard Onslow, Esq., being a burgess for the borough of Steyning, and a member of the Lower House, might be restored to them to join in the election of a new Speaker. After some consultation among the Lords, Mr. Onslow was sent down, with the Queen's Serjeant-at-Law and the Attorney-General, "to show for himself why he should not be a member of the House." Accordingly he pleaded his office of Solicitor, and his writ of attendance in the Upper House; but he was adjudged to be a member and chosen Speaker. So, in 1580, John Popham, Solicitor-General, was brought down from the House of Lords by the Queen's Serjeant and Attorney-General, and being "restored to the House of

Attorney and Solicitor General.

Solicitor-General Onslow, 1566.

[1] Lords' Journ. June 13, 1685.
[2] Ib. May 13, 1742. 2 Hatsell, p. 28, note.
[3] Com. Journ. April 8, 1614. 2 Hatsell, pp. 26-8.

Commons as a member of the same," was immediately chosen Speaker.[1]

Under the Stuarts, the House of Commons was quick to resent attempts by any of its legal members to win credit with the Court by speeches in Parliament. Thus, upon a motion in 1604 to read a third time the Bill for confirming titles to Assart lands, which so much offended James I.,[2] a member, who was also a King's counsel, said "he hoped they would give him leave to speak in this that so much concerned the King, in respect to the place he held." It was replied "that every man here was as much of the King's counsel as he that spoke; that King's counsel in this House were never heard at the bar, as in other Courts, because the whole House is of the King's counsel."[3]

A narrow watch was also kept upon speeches made on private Bills by counsel who were not members. In his reply upon an estate Bill in 1605, counsel was sharply ordered to "utter nothing that was said yesterday," and "not wander in invectives."[4] It was especially necessary for counsel to measure their words in speaking of either House. In 1614 Mr. Martin was heard in the Commons on behalf of the Virginia Company, then petitioning Parliament. Lord Southampton, Lord Sheffield, and other peers interested in the company, were allowed to attend the argument, and there is this notice of the procedure:—"Ordered, there shall be great silence at the Lords passing here. Mr. Martin cometh in before the Lords. The bar, first down, taken up at the Lords' coming in. The Lords stood bare till after Mr. Martin had begun. Then Mr. Speaker spake to him to stay; and then, in the name of the House, spake to them signifying to them the pleasure of the House that they should sit down, and be covered."[5]

Margin notes:
King's counsel speaking for the King in Commons upon public Bill, 1604.

Repetition and invective forbidden.

Virginia Company, 1614.

---

[1] Com. Journ. January 18, 1580. 2 Hatsell, pp. 28-9.

[2] *Ante*, p. 721.

[3] 1 Com. Journ. 226; May 25, 1604.

[4] Ib. 270.

[5] Ib. 487; May 17, 1614.

Mr. Martin gave great offence by his speech, and imme- Exception by House of Commons to Mr. Martin's arguments at bar. diate exception was taken to it by several members, because it censured the last Parliament for what it had done or left undone towards colonization in North America. Sir Edward Montague thought the speech "the most unfitting ever spoken in this House." Sir Edward Hobby was of opinion that counsel should be called to the bar to answer for it. According to Mr. Duncombe, counsel had spoken "as a schoolmaster teaching his scholars." Next day, by order of the House, Mr. Martin appeared at the bar, and by reason of his former good service as a member was spared the humiliation of kneeling, then the usual attitude of delin- quents summoned there.[1] Mr. Speaker admonished him that Mr. Martin publicly re- buked by the Speaker. the House had taken his censure and advice "for a great presumption, and did despise and contemn it." Mr. Martin humbly confessed his error, but not with a dejected counte- nance, for there was comfort in acknowledging error, and not for fear of punishment. Zeal had outrun judgment; in his argument, "like to a ship that cutteth her cable and putteth to sea, so he had cut his memory and trusted to his inven- tion." Upon this acknowledgment, "though his offence was great and of a high pitch," the House "inclined to mercy, respecting his person, good affections, and former service here," and forgave him, "presuming he will sin no more in the like."[2]

So in the Upper House, in 1700, upon Lady Anglesea's Lady Angle- sea's case, 1700. Bill for a separation on the ground of her husband's cruelty, Mr. Beresford, her counsel, "spoke some words reflecting on the Earl." As the Countess declared that her life was en- dangered by her husband's violence, it must have been diffi- cult for her advocates to avoid such reflections. But the

---

[1] Until 1772, all persons were re- quired to kneel when they received orders or reprimands from the House. In that year, on the motion of Mr. Townsend, afterwards Lord Sydney, the House directed that persons brought to the bar should be permitted to stand, unless otherwise directed. (Com. Journ. March 16, 1772. 2 Hatsell, pp. 133–5.)

[2] 1 Com. Journ. 489.

House at once interposed, counsel were ordered to withdraw, and, upon their recall, the Lord Keeper (Lord Somers), by order, "reprimanded Mr. Beresford, telling him 'he must take care of his words for the future.'" Mr. Beresford then "went on to sum up his evidence," and, with a prudent regard for his client's interests, whatever his justification for the actual words used, "expressed his sorrow for anything he had said which might reflect on the Earl of Anglesea."[1]

Counsel reprimanded in House of Lords.

Parliamentary agents. Formerly clerks of each House.

For many centuries the work of soliciting private Bills in Parliament was performed by officers of each House, who took charge of Bills on behalf of promoters, saw that the required forms were complied with, made themselves responsible for the fees to which Bills were liable, and generally charged a fixed sum for this service. When private business increased in volume and importance, strong objections were taken to a system under which officers of Parliament received pay from persons seeking a *privilegium* there. In the year 1810, a select Committee of the House of Commons, in recommending the establishment of a Private Bill Office, also expressed their opinion that the clerks to be appointed for the business of that office "shall not be employed or act as agents in the management or conduct of any Bills in the House of Commons, nor be in partnership with any person so employed." But, although clerks in the new office were not allowed to undertake this service, their fellow-clerks continued to act as what were called House agents for more than a quarter of a century afterwards.

Recommendations of Commons' Committee, 1810.

Almost all the principal Committee clerks used to act in this capacity.[2] The senior deputy Committee clerk also acted as parliamentary agent to the Chief Secretary for Ireland, taking charge of Irish Bills.[3] There were out-door agents, who at a later period competed with the clerks; but

---

[1] 16 Lords' Journ. 640; April 1, 1700. *Ante*, Vol. I. pp. 433-6.
[2] Commons' Committee on Com-

mittee Rooms and Printed Papers, 1826; Min. of Ev. p. 15.
[3] Ib. p. 11.

the greater part, and at one time the whole, of this business, was conducted by officers of the two Houses. The system continued until the year 1836, when private business, through the growth of railways, so occupied the clerks' time that they could not properly perform their double duties. Accordingly, in 1836, the House of Commons passed a resolution requiring those of their officers who had acted as agents to elect whether they would retain their offices, confining themselves to their public work, or would retire with a view to private practice outside the House as parliamentary agents.[1] The House of Lords adopted the same course. Some of the officers preferred to retire, and established at Westminster firms most of which still bear their names.

Clerks in 1836 required to elect between private and public work.

From that time there has been a body of practitioners devoting themselves for the most part exclusively to the charge of Bills in Parliament, a business requiring for its proper discharge great tact and ability, with an exact knowledge of precedents and of the highly technical and complicated rules embodied in the Standing Orders and practice of the two Houses. It is part of an agent's duty to prepare Standing Order proofs, to draft most of the Bills which go before Committees, to frame notices, petitions, memorials as to non-compliance with Standing Orders, and all other documents required in promoting or opposing Bills at their various stages. Thus, having regard to the important interests at stake, the work involves grave responsibility, and in itself is one of great delicacy and difficulty.[2]

In theory an agent is still regarded as an officer of Parliament for purposes of private business,[3] just as a solicitor is

Agents still regarded as officers of Parliament.

---

[1] 91 Com. Journ. 819.

[2] "The profession of a parliamentary agent requires an accurate acquaintance with particular branches of the law, and especially with the practice of Parliament; also a sound knowledge of parliamentary drafting. It is at least as distinct from those of a barrister and a solicitor as those two professions are from each other, and several excellent agents have not belonged to either." (Report of Joint Committee of 1876 on Parliamentary Agency, p. 3.)

[3] Ib.; Ev. of Mr. Adam, p. 25:—"The agents' complete knowledge of the practice enables the officers of the two Houses to conduct the busi-

an officer of the High Court of Justice. Since the year 1836, any persons have been allowed to practise as parliamentary agents in the House of Lords, and no rules exist with regard to them. In the Commons the Speaker exercises

Speaker's rules of 1873. a certain control over all agents. Before they are allowed to act they must sign a declaration engaging to observe and obey the rules, orders, and practice of the House, and also to pay all fees due upon any petition or Bill on which they may appear. They may also be required to enter into a bond of 500*l.* to observe these conditions. No person is registered unless actually employed in promoting or opposing some pending Bill. Any agent wilfully acting in violation of rules, or wilfully misconducting himself in prosecuting any proceedings before Parliament, is "liable to an absolute or temporary prohibition to practise" at the Speaker's pleasure. No person who has been so suspended or prohibited from practising, or who has been struck off the rolls of solicitors, or disbarred by any of the Inns of Court, can be registered without the Speaker's express authority.[1]

Proposed test of fitness. From time to time opinions have been given in favour of some test of fitness for persons seeking to practise as Parliamentary agents, in analogy with the examinations imposed on admission to both branches of the legal profession. In 1875, the council of the Incorporated Law Society suggested such a

Joint Committee of 1876 on parliamentary agency. test in a letter to the Speaker;[2] and in 1876, a Joint Committee of both Houses, presided over by Lord Redesdale, was appointed to inquire into the subject. It had been proposed that agency in Parliament should be confined to barristers and solicitors. The Committee, however, thought that the training of barristers and solicitors did not afford in itself a

---

ness without difficulty, and at the least possible cost to the suitors. If any case of an unusual character arises, they form a body to whom the officers of Parliament can, and frequently do, apply for information and assistance."

[1] Rules sanctioned by the Speaker in 1873; Report of Joint Committee of 1876, App. B.

[2] See letter of Mr. Bircham in Appendix A. to Report of Joint Committee.

proof of qualification for this business, and they recommended a special examination in order to test the fitness of all new applicants for admission. They did not propose to apply this test in the case of any persons who might be merely conducting the opposition to a Bill. The recommendations of the Committee, however, were not adopted by either House, and, subject to the rules enforced by the House of Commons, the profession of parliamentary agent remains a perfectly open one.

CHAPTER XXIV.

EVIDENCE : SHORTHAND WRITERS : POWER TO ADMINISTER
OATHS : WITNESSES.

Mode of
examination
in Lords,
1641.

In Commons.

In the Lords one method of examination before Committees was by interrogatories; and it was therefore ordered, in 1641, " that when any Committee do return any examinations into this House, they shall return the interrogatories upon which the witnesses were examined."[1]   The same method was adopted by the Commons in examinations at the bar;[2] written questions, to be put to witnesses there by Mr. Speaker, were sometimes prepared by Committees, or agreed upon by the House.[3]   In the Committees of both Houses notes of the evidence were probably taken by the chairman or Committee clerk.   That some record was kept of statements made by witnesses there is clear from reports frequently made during the eighteenth century by Committees in the Commons, and entered in their Journals.   Evidence at the bar was sometimes given in writing;[4] or witnesses after examination at the bar were ordered to put their testimony in writing.[5]   Two members, Mr. White and Mr. Prideaux, were appointed to take notes of the evidence at the Earl of Strafford's impeachment in 1640; and power was given to the managers to employ two other persons for this purpose, " though they be not of the House." [6]

[1] 4 Lords' Journ. 442; November 16, 1641.

[2] 1 Com. Journ. 824; February 23, 1625.

[3] Ib. 827, 829; March 1 and 2, 1625. 9 Ib. 293; January 14, 1673 (Duke of Buckingham's case). Ib.

327; April 30, 1675 (Impeachment of Lord Danby).

[4] 9 Com. Journ. 322; April 23, 1675.

[5] 1 Ib. 584; April 20, 1621. 9 Ib. 643; October 30, 1680.

[6] 2 Ib. 108.

In the famous proceedings upon the Norfolk Divorce Bill in 1691, it was ordered [1]—"that the evidence shall be taken in writing by the clerk, who shall read what he hath taken to the witnesses before they go from the bar; and if counsel on either side observe anything to be omitted or mistaken, counsel may offer to have it rectified before the witness goes from the bar."

Norfolk Divorce Bill, 1691.

A great improvement upon this method of taking evidence was adopted in the same case eight years afterwards. Shorthand writers were then employed for the first time, nearly a century before any reference to them appears in proceedings of the other House. Upon the Norfolk Divorce Bill of 1699, the House of Lords ordered—"that the shorthand writers, who took the witnesses' evidence, do dictate to a clerk, in order to be transcribed, what the witnesses have said; and that the examinations, with the shorthand writers' books and papers, are to be sealed up and kept by the clerk until the next day the House shall proceed on this matter; and then what is transcribed shall be read at the bar in the presence of the witness." [2]   At this period the practice was that witnesses should sign the transcribed depositions when these had been read to them.[3] In 1700, Sir Edmund King's testimony upon Lady Anglesea's Separation Bill was also taken in shorthand, and the Lords ordered that it should be "transcribed from the shorthand writer, against to-morrow, at eleven o'clock; and that the witness then attend to have it read to him." [4]

Shorthand writers first engaged in Parliament, 1699.

Lady Anglesea's Separation Bill, 1700.

It is difficult to believe that an art of such utility in recording evidence and shortening proceedings should have been used in cases of this importance, and should then have been neglected. Yet, although commonly resorted to for the reports of civil and criminal trials throughout great part of the eighteenth century, in Parliament, where it would have rendered

Shorthand little used in Parliament during eighteenth century.

[1] 15 Lords' Journ. 50; January 24, 1691. *Ante*, Vol. I. 401–11.
[2] 16 Lords' Journ. 524; February
22, 1699. Ib. 535.
[3] Ib. 527, 537.
[4] Ib. 630, 634.

essential service, shorthand has left hardly any trace during that period.   Statements made before Committees must have been recorded, for in Lady Ferrers's Separation Bill, in 1758, evidence given by witnesses to the Committee on her petition was afterwards read at the bar, and confirmed by them there.[1] Probably these depositions were taken in longhand by the Committee clerk.[2]   Occasionally, this evidence, or part of it, was read in the House of Lords, if the proceedings in Committee were questioned, or to justify amendments in a Bill.[3] In one case witnesses corrected, before the whole House on the third reading of a Bill, part of their evidence in Committee.[4]

Trial of
Warren
Hastings.   It was upon the trial of Warren Hastings, in 1788-9, that the Commons' Journals first mention the use of shorthand. On this occasion again the House of Lords was beforehand with them, and ordered, " that the minutes of the verbal evidence, as taken by the clerk, which has been or shall be given upon the trial, and all the written evidence produced and read, be printed from day to day for the use of the members of this House only." [5]   The "evidence as taken by the clerk" was no doubt that taken by the shorthand writer employed by the clerk.   Light is thrown upon this statement by the mention of a now familiar name, upon a motion made soon afterwards in the Commons, " that Mr. Gurney, one of the shorthand writers of the notes taken at the trial of Warren Hastings, Esq., in Westminster Hall, be called in."   His evidence was desired in proof that certain words to which exception had been taken were used at the trial by Mr. Burke.[6]

[1] 22 Lords' Journ. 290.

[2] A Committee of the House of Commons recommended in 1821 "that it would be proper for the future not to admit any person as an assistant clerk who is not moderately capable of writing shorthand."   Committee on Private Business, Rep. p. 4.

[3] Calverton Enclosure Bill, 1782; 36 Lords' Journ. 1519.

[4] Bristol Gaol Bill, 1792; 39 Lords' Journ. 486.

[5] 38 Lords' Journ. 93; February 26, 1788.

[6] According to Mr. Gurney's evidence, Burke charged Warren Hastings with murdering Nuncomar by the hands of Sir Elijah Impey.   The House declared that it had not authorized the managers of the im-

Even after this striking service rendered upon an historical trial which lasted 145 days,[1] shorthand was only occasionally called to the aid of Parliament. It seems to have been first brought into prominent notice at inquiries into controverted elections before the Committees of the Commons, which were generally the signal for a lively struggle between parties. Shorthand writers were then found so useful that they obtained statutory recognition in an Act of 1802 for regulating these protracted trials.[2] This statute provided that every Election Committee should be or might be attended " by a person well skilled in the art of writing shorthand," who was to be appointed by the clerk of the House, and sworn by the chairman " faithfully and truly " to take down the evidence, and transcribe it for the use of the Committee. A Committee of the Commons appointed in 1803 reported that, according to information given to them by members who had served on Election Committees, " in all cases where this measure had been adopted much benefit had resulted to the parties " by expediting the inquiry and thereby lessening its expense. The Committee recommended a scale of charges, two guineas for the attendance of every shorthand writer, and one shilling per sheet of seventy-two words for a transcript of his notes ; these expenses to be defrayed by the parties.[3]

Controverted Elections Act, 1802.

So satisfactory was the experiment tried in 1803, that, during the same Session, shorthand writers were occasionally employed in Committees on private Bills.[4] In 1813, both Houses passed substantially the same resolutions for the appointment of a shorthand writer " who shall, by himself or sufficient deputy, attend when called upon to take minutes of evidence at the bar of this House or in Committees." Employment of a shorthand writer in Committees on

Appointment of shorthand writers to Parliament, 1813.

peachment to make such a charge, and that Mr. Burke ought not to have spoken these words.—34 Com. Journ. 320 ; May 4, 1789.

[1] The trial lasted over seven years, from February, 1788, to April, 1795, when an acquittal was pronounced by the peers.

[2] 42 Geo. III. c. 84.

[3] This scale, contained in the table of fees in 1803, is still in force.

[4] MS. letter of Mr. W. B. Gurney to secretary of Mr. Speaker, 1813.

private petitions or Bills was left to each chairman's discretion; the expenses were to be paid by promoters and opponents in such proportion as he should direct.[1]   Mr. Gurney and his assistants were appointed in all these cases, and the work begun by them for Parliament in 1788 remains in the same family, after the lapse of nearly a century.

As witnesses examined before Election Committees sometimes subjected themselves to indictments for perjury, the House of Commons resolved, in 1818, "that all witnesses examined before this House, or any Committee thereof, are entitled to protection in respect of anything said by them in evidence;" and with this view, no clerk, officer, or shorthand writer was allowed to give evidence elsewhere in respect of any proceedings in the House without special leave.[2]

Evidence in public and private Committees is now taken, transcribed, and printed day by day under the present admirably worked system with such speed and accuracy that it is difficult to picture the tedious delay and imperfect reproduction of oral statements when these were taken down by a clerk in longhand, like depositions before a magistrate or coroner's jury.   Some time passed, however, before the system took its present form.   Evidence taken on private Bills was not formerly printed unless upon a motion to that effect made in the House in which a Bill was pending.   It was then printed at the public expense, on the ground that it was printed for the convenience of the House and not of the parties.   In a case which occurred in 1836, Lord Wharncliffe suggested that this expense ought not to fall upon the public, but the existing practice was justified by the Duke of Wellington and Duke of Cumberland.[3]

Evidence on private Bills formerly not printed.

Supplied to parties in manuscript or lithographed.

Down to the year 1863, transcripts of shorthand notes of evidence taken on private Bills were handed over to the Committee clerks' Office in the House of Commons, and

---

[1] 68 Com. Journ. 497; 49 Lords' Journ. 449–82.

[2] 73 Com. Journ. 389.

[3] 33 Hansard, 511; Hull and Selby Railway Bill, 1836.

manuscript copies were made by law stationers employed by that department. These were supplied to promoters and petitioners at a charge of 1s. per folio. When more than five or six copies were required, reports were lithographed. All profits were handed over to the fee fund.[1] In any protracted inquiry the accumulation of these daily reports was bewildering; references were at all times difficult and often hopeless; the burden of carrying them was no light one. The printing of these notes was due to a recommendation by a Commons' Committee which sat in 1863. Each member of a Committee on a private Bill receives a print of the evidence daily; the expense is fairly divided among promoters and opponents. The result is generally considerable economy and always great convenience.

In proceedings against the Duke of Buckingham, in 1626, three members of a Commons' Committee were authorized to go to the houses of any witnesses who were ill, take their evidence in writing, and report it to their colleagues.[2] Similar powers were given to Committees on private Bills in the Lords, in 1807 to meet forthwith in order to take the evidence of a witness who was seriously ill, and in 1810 to appoint three of their number to examine a witness incapable of attending the House.[3]

Members of Committee deputed to take evidence of witnesses who were ill.

Although the House of Commons had no power to administer oaths, witnesses were examined at the bar on oath in 1604.[4] Power was also given to select Committees in 1650 to swear witnesses,[5] and one of these Committees reported to the House in 1645 that it had imposed a fine of 100l. upon a witness who had refused to take the oath.[6] In other cases members being justices of the peace were deputed

Examinations on oath by Commons.

---

[1] Commons' Committee on Private Business (1838); Minutes of Evidence, p. 6.

[2] 1 Com. Journ. 849, 851. Similar powers are recorded, 2 Ib. 49, 194; 13 Ib. 562.

[3] 46 Lords' Journ. 362; 47 Ib.

701.

[4] 1 Com. Journ. 200, 965. The clerk's entry is "an oath ministered." Ib. 203.

[5] 6 Ib. 529; 7 Ib. 55, 100, 287, 484.

[6] 4 Ib. 116.

to examine persons upon oath;[1] or witnesses were ordered to attend before the Lord Chief Justice for the same purpose;[2] or witnesses called to the bar were solemnly charged by the Speaker to tell the truth.[3]   In 1661, the Commons requested that witnesses upon Sir Edward Powell's Estate Bill should be sworn by the Upper House, in order to verify their evidence.   This request was considered in Committee of Privileges, and the Commons were told in conference that no precedents could be found to warrant such a proceeding.[4]

Power to swear witnesses on Private Bill Committees.

Election Committees were enabled by statute to administer oaths, and in 1858 the authority which the House of Commons had so long coveted was conferred, in certain cases, upon the Committees in both Houses.[5]   Before 1858, it was sometimes said in the Lords, when evidence taken before the other House was quoted, "that the inquiry there was a deficient and inferior inquiry, because the usual test had not been applied."[6]   It was not, however, competent for Committees in the Lords to administer oaths; witnesses were sworn at the bar, an inconvenient practice, productive of much expense.   Thus if a Committee on an opposed Bill were appointed to meet on Monday, it was often necessary, when the House of Lords did not sit for appeals on that day, that witnesses should attend on the previous Friday in order to be sworn.   The Act of 1858 put an end to this difficulty.   In 1871 a fuller statutory power of administering oaths was given to the House of Commons and its Committees.[7]

[1] 9 Com. Journ. 521 (A.D. 1678); 11 Ib. 110 (A.D. 1693).

[2] 11 Ib. 232 (A.D. 1694).

[3] 1 Ib. 599; Floyd's case; A.D. 1621. 5 Ib. 611.

[4] 11 Lords' Journ. 343-5.

[5] 21 & 22 Vict. c. 78, amended by 33 & 34 Vict. c. 1; 34 Vict. c. 3; 34 & 35 Vict. c. 83.

[6] Commons' Committee of 1847 on Private Bills, Third Report; Ev. of Mr. J. Parkes, p. 198.

[7] 34 & 35 Vict. c. 83. See also May, 479-81. "By the laws of England, the power of administering oaths has been considered essential to the discovery of truth. It has been entrusted to small debt courts, and to every justice of the peace; but until 1871 it was not enjoyed by the House of Commons, the grand inquest of the nation. From what

Witnesses prevaricating or refusing to answer have been repeatedly punished by the House of Commons. Thus, in 1694, Tracy Pauncefort persisted in refusing to answer questions put at the bar. The House thereupon resolved that he had violated the privileges and contemned the authority of the House, and committed him to the Tower.[1] In the course of proceedings taken in 1620 against one Dayrell, who had threatened a member, the accused was ordered to attend at the bar with his witnesses. One of these was a woman, and Sir Edward Coke opposed a motion to call her into the House, gravely objecting on the authority of St. Bernard "that a woman ought not to speak in the congregation." A Committee was therefore appointed to go out and examine her at the door.[2] In 1666, when evidence was taken at the bar upon an estate Bill, and a woman was tendered as a witness, counsel and the parties withdrew in order that this question might be debated. The question was then put and "resolved in the affirmative," so that the precedent of 1620 was reversed.

When witnesses are examined in the House of Commons, "the bar ought to be down; otherwise if the House be in Committee." This was declared "as a constant rule" in 1640.[3] During the proceedings in the Upper House in 1737 on the Bill punishing the City of Edinburgh for the murder of Captain Porteous, the Lords of Justiciary were examined at the bar; chairs were set for them there, and they appeared in their proper robes.[4]

Marginal notes: Prevarication or refusal to answer. Women as witnesses in the Commons. Precedent of 1620 reversed, 1666. Procedure on examination of witnesses. Porteous riots.

anomalous cause, and at what period, this power, which must have been originally inherent in the High Court of Parliament, was retained by one branch of it and severed from the other, cannot be satisfactorily established." Ib. 479–80.

[1] 11 Com. Journ. 230.
[2] 1 Com. Journ. 519; 1 Hatsell, 191.
[3] 2 Com. Journ. 26.
[4] Lords' Journ. May 2, 1737; 2 Hatsell, 141.

CHAPTER XXV.

PRELIMINARY INQUIRIES: ACTS OF 1846-51: FAILURE OF
SYSTEM: EXISTING INQUIRIES UNDER PUBLIC HEALTH
ACT: SUPERVISION OF PRIVATE BILLS BY PUBLIC DEPART-
MENTS: SUGGESTED CHANGES IN SYSTEM OF PRIVATE
LEGISLATION: FIXED TRIBUNALS: JOINT COMMITTEES:
JURISDICTION BY COUNTY OR LOCAL BODIES: OBJECTIONS
TO THESE PROPOSALS: ADVANTAGES OF COURT OF REVIEW:
CONTROL OF PARLIAMENT ESSENTIAL UPON QUESTIONS OF
POLICY AND EXPEDIENCY: REASONS FOR MAINTAINING
EXISTING SYSTEM.

*Commons'
Committee of
1846.*

IN the year 1846, a Committee, of which Mr. Hume was
chairman, recommended that, in order to elicit the facts of
each case with greater certainty and economy, and also save
the time of Committees, local inquiries should be made by a
department of the Government before certain classes of
private Bills were considered by Parliament.

*Preliminary
Inquiries
Act, 1846.*

Pursuant to the recommendation of this Committee an Act
was passed in the following Session " for making preliminary
inquiries in certain cases of applications for local Acts." [1]   This
Act directed the Commissioners of Woods and Forests in all
cases of Bills promoted for the establishment of waterworks,
or for draining, cleansing, paving, lighting, or otherwise improving any town, to send inspectors to hold a local inquiry,
after which the Commissioners were to report to Parliament
on each case.   The Lords of the Admiralty were authorized

---

[1] 9 & 10 Vict. c. 106.

to direct a like inquiry pending all applications for Bills affecting, directly or indirectly, any port, harbour, tidal water, or navigable river. If their inspectors reported that a Bill would prejudicially affect tidal waters, the Admiralty might withhold the consent of the Crown. In these cases an adverse report was conclusive; in all other cases reports from the two departments were laid before the Committee on each Bill, but had no binding authority.

It had been proposed by the Committee of 1846 that official inquiries should be made into all private Bills before their introduction into Parliament. With proper caution, Parliament preferred to confine the experiment, at first, to the classes of Bills above enumerated. This limitation was amply justified, for, within a year from the institution of preliminary inquiries, experience had shown that they were troublesome and expensive, and had secured none of the benefits expected from them.[1] A public Committee, which sat in 1847, thought it might be " necessary to provide some means of limiting the claims of individual inhabitants to interpose and delay proceedings now carried on at the promoters' expense;" which reads like a proposal to silence troublesome opponents in the interests of promoters. One obvious abuse was that opponents refused to state their objections to the inspector, and then went before Committees with the advantage of knowing all the promoters' case, while they had not disclosed their own. " That should not be allowed," the Committee naïvely said, but they did not add how it was to be prevented.[2] Although still of opinion that preliminary inquiries, with certain restrictions, might save expense and economize time, the Committee were alive to the fact that if the evidence were allowed to be reopened in Parliament, these advantages would be lost. Every witness concurred in this view. " The efficiency of preliminary inquiries," said a gentleman of great experience

Committee of 1847.

---

[1] Mr. Cardwell's Committee of 1853; Fifth Report, p. 14.

[2] Commons' Committee of 1847 on Private Bills, p. 15.

in directing them, "depends on their being final." [1]   If opposition were allowed, and evidence re-heard—if even new
evidence were received by Committees—there would be no
saving to anybody.   Local proceedings before inspectors
"must be considered so far final that parties will only be heard
in Committee on the effect of the printed evidence." [2]

View taken by   Experience, however, even at this period, had shown that
Committees.
Committees were not satisfied to decide, by means of printed
evidence only, the weighty issues, affecting both public policy
and private interests, which are raised in many private Bills.
As the Report of 1847 itself rightly declared, "from a desire
to do justice to parties, Committees" were "disposed to
inquire for themselves." As to the parties, they were not
likely, when great interests were at stake, to be satisfied with
an investigation conducted by a departmental officer; whether
promoters or opposing petitioners, they would seek, and justly
seek, to reopen such an inquiry.   If they succeeded in this
effort, the obvious results were doubled costs to them, with
no saving of time or trouble to Parliament.   And the Committee of 1847 thought it desirable that the House of Commons should abandon no portion of its jurisdiction which could
be useful in promoting private Bills and in securing the
interests of all parties. [3]

Act of 1848.   The inquiry of 1847 soon bore fruit.   In the following
Session the Act so lately passed was repealed, [4] and preliminary inquiries were partially discontinued.   The two departments received a discretionary power when they were of
opinion that a local investigation was superfluous.   At the
same time an attempt was made to make local inquiries, when
held, more complete.   This attempt also failed, and repeated
complaints of the system, even as amended, led to the ap-
Committee of   pointment of another Committee in 1850.   The evidence of
1850.

[1] Commons' Committee of 1847 on
Private Bills; Ev. of Captain Veitch,
R.E., consulting engineer to the Ad-
miralty, quoted at p. 17 of Report.

[2] Ib.; Ev. of Mr. Wingrove Cooke,
p. 16.
[3] Report, p. 17.
[4] 11 & 12 Vict. c. 129.

failure then taken was conclusive. "In very numerous cases," we are told, Committees on private Bills decided against the recommendations of the departmental inspectors who conducted the local inquiries. In no single instance was the evidence taken by those inspectors "judicially received by a Committee in proof of any matter" contested before them.[1] To the surveying officers' reports Committees could hardly help referring, because they were quoted as favouring one side or the other; to the local evidence Committees referred "very rarely"; in some instances minutes of evidence, and even reports, were returned to the Department of Woods and Forests with the seals unbroken.[2]

The reasons why official reports received so little attention were various. One was that they were often condemned in evidence by engineers whose position and authority were far higher than those of any inspectors whose services the departments were able to retain. The chief reason was one already indicated, namely, that the information laid before inspectors was incomplete, because both sides were unwilling to disclose their whole case in a mere preliminary skirmish. As neither promoters nor opponents were bound by local evidence, no more was offered than suited their purpose; all parties reserved their strength for the real contest in Parliament. Committees soon saw, therefore, that local investigations were illusory, that the information in official reports was incomplete, and the opinions founded on it by inspectors, through no fault of theirs, were more or less untrustworthy. Neglect of local evidence and official reports by Committees.

Some instructive cases were brought to the notice of the Committee of 1850. In 1847 the Corporation of Liverpool promoted a Bill to supply their city with water from the sources of the rivers Douglas and Darwen, both flowing into the Ribble, which is a navigable river up to Preston. It was proposed to impound water from streams on which there were extensive works, construct reservoirs occupying between 450 Liverpool Water Bill, 1847.

[1] Commons' Committee on Local Acts (Preliminary Inquiries), 1850;   [2] Ib.; Ev. pp. 19, 103.
Report, p. 5.

and 460 acres, and bring the water into Liverpool from a distance of about thirty-two miles. The scheme therefore affected many interests. Accordingly, twenty sets of opponents appeared at the preliminary inquiry, and were represented by twenty solicitors, as the surveying officers would not hear counsel. The opponents refused to state their case. Parties interested in water rights declined to specify the compensation they claimed, or even produce plans showing the position of their works; they said that they only came to watch the proceedings, but cross-examined the promoters' witnesses. Five days were occupied by the inquiry before inspectors of the Woods and Forests, at a cost to the corporation of 2,300l., although, to save expense, and knowing that the inquiry would not be conclusive, they did not call the greater number of their scientific witnesses from London. When these proceedings closed, Admiralty surveyors opened another investigation into the effect of the proposed works upon the tidal waters of the Ribble. On the whole, the inspectors' report was unfavourable, but the corporation persevered with their Bill. In the House of Commons they produced the same witnesses and many others; the Committee went into the case as though there had been no local inquiry at all, and sanctioned the Bill, after a struggle which lasted five weeks and cost 24,000l.[1]

Tyne Conservancy, and Belfast Improvement Bills, 1849–50.

Two other cases mentioned by the Committee were those of the Belfast Improvement Bill, 1850, and three Bills promoted in 1849-50, for establishing a Conservancy of the Tyne. There were costly local inquiries in all these cases, but they were followed by prolonged contests in Parliament; and it was stated in evidence that the surveyor's report on the Tyne Conservancy was made too late to affect the decision of the Commons' Committee. At Reading, a local inquiry into an improvement Bill promoted by the corporation lasted upwards of a month, and cost 6,000l.; alarmed at this expense, the

---

[1] Commons' Committee on Local Acts (Preliminary Inquiries), 1850; Ev. of Town Clerk of Liverpool, pp. 32–5.

inhabitants would not proceed with the Bill.[1] Two Bills, for waterworks and gasworks, came before the House of Commons unopposed, but with adverse preliminary reports. On hearing evidence, however, the Chairman of Committees passed both of them.[2] Not only were local inquiries ineffectual in saving labour to Parliamentary Committees; they also deranged the early and regular progress of private business through delays and uncertainty in laying the departmental reports before Parliament. Serious inconvenience was thus occasioned; in many cases it was necessary to postpone all the Bills in a group, at great expense to the parties.[3] Upon this and other evidence the Committee's conclusion will be best given in their own words:— *Delay in furnishing official reports.*

Conclusions of Committee.

"It appears that, however fully the whole case may have been inquired into and discussed by parties interested on the spot, the Parliamentary investigation has generally proceeded as if no such local inquiry had been held. The same witnesses who had been previously examined before the local inspectors have been again examined before the Committee, and it is especially deserving of remark that in numerous instances the principal witnesses at the local inquiry, more particularly the engineers and other scientific witnesses, were not connected with the locality to which the Bill related, but had been summoned from London and other distant places to give their evidence, at a great expense both to the promoters and opponents. *Double inquiry.*

Cost of bringing witnesses from London.

"In all these cases there have been two inquiries instead of one. Your Committee have taken pains to ascertain whether Parliamentary contests have been rendered less severe by preliminary inquiries, and whether the aggregate expense of the two inquiries may not have been less than if no local investigation had been held. Upon this point the witnesses have nearly all concurred in opinion that preliminary inquiries have not diminished the opposition of interested parties before Committees, or otherwise facilitated the passing of Bills through Parliament. On the contrary, some of the witnesses have *Parliamentary contests not abridged by local inquiry.*

---

[1] Ib.; Ev. p. 14. See also cases of Norfolk Estuary and Severn Navigation Bills; Ev. of Sir John Rennie and Mr. E. Leader Williams, pp. 51, 57.

[2] Commons' Committee on Local Acts (Preliminary Inquiries), 1850; Ev. p. 20.

[3] Ib.; Report, p. 6.

expressed their opinion that more time has been spent in the Committee in consequence of points raised by the reports of inspectors, and that, independently of the expense of the preliminary inquiry, the subsequent expense of carrying the Bill through Parliament has been increased instead of being diminished.

Expense increased.

"Your Committee, therefore, have come to the conclusion that, in saving Parliamentary expenses, and in economizing the time of members engaged in Committees, the Preliminary Inquiries Acts have been, on the whole, unsuccessful. To the ordinary expenses of a Parliamentary contest they have added the further expense of a local inquiry, and have not generally tended to shorten the proceedings of Committees.

Failure of system.

". . . In order to render any system of local inquiries effectual, it would be necessary to delegate to other tribunals much of the authority of Parliament. At present the inspector's position is anomalous, and the exertions of the parties who appear before him are without results. If his functions are to be useful, the evidence taken before him must be made final before the Committee as regards the points to which it refers.

Delegation of its authority by Parliament not recommended.

"Your Committee do not recommend to the House so extensive a delegation of its authority. While they are of opinion that every facility should be given to the public of availing themselves of the operation of general Acts for local improvements, yet when an application is made to Parliament for extraordinary powers, your Committee believe that no tribunal is generally so satisfactory as one constituted by Parliament itself."

Most satisfactory tribunal supplied by Parliament itself.

The Committee, which included amongst its members Sir John Pakington, Mr. Wilson Patten, Mr. Evelyn Denison, Mr. Hume, Mr. Brotherton, and Sir John Yarde Buller, was practically unanimous in its report. Accordingly Parliament in 1851 discontinued all preliminary inquiries by the Commissioners of Woods and Forests, but left this power with the Admiralty upon Bills which interfere with tidal waters.[1] In 1862,[2] these powers were transferred to the Board of Trade; but the Admiralty must be informed of pending schemes, and if they are of opinion that "the interests

Act of 1851.

---

[1] 14 & 15 Vict. c. 49. See also Harbours Transfer Act, 1862.

[2] 25 & 26 Vict. c. 69.

of her Majesty's naval service" require their direct interference, they may still hold the local inquiry originally
contemplated.[1]

Besides the local inquiries thus discontinued in 1851, a Local inquiries on railway bills.
similar experiment was tried by means of local investigations
and reports on railways, by the Railway Department of the
Board of Trade, under Lord Dalhousie and Mr. Laing, in
1845.[2] " Of both experiments," said the Speaker's counsel in
1863, " the result was unsuccessful, and from the same cause.
The Committees to which the Bills were referred declined to
be guided by the conclusions of the preliminary inquirers.
The reports carried no authority, and had even less weight
than, in some instances, their intrinsic merit entitled them to.
The two tribunals, Parliamentary and departmental, did not
work together. It may be anticipated that any other plan,
based on the same principle, would meet with similar failure.
If the auxiliary inquiry is to be regarded as conclusive, the
proceedings in Parliament become an empty form; if it is
not to be binding, it is useless. In practice, the interest of
the parties to whom the preliminary report may have been
adverse conspires with the jealousy of Parliament to set
aside the judgment of the inferior tribunal."[3] In the opinion
of other witnesses of authority, reports made by officers not
appointed under the immediate authority of Parliament are
always viewed with jealousy and disfavour by Parliamentary
Committees.[4]

[1] Ib. s. 4.

[2] *Ante*, Int. Vol. I. pp. 113-15.

[3] Commons' Committee on Private
Bill Business, 1863 ; App., Memorandum by Mr. Rickards, pp. 347-8.
See also Fifth Report of Mr. Cardwell's Committee in 1853, p. 14 ; and
Memorandum handed to Joint Committee of 1872 by Mr. Chichester
Fortescue, then President of the
Board of Trade, stating that experience had shown that the reports on
railways by this department " were

of no avail."

[4] Lords' Committee on Private
Bills, 1858 ; Ev. of Mr. T. Erskine
May, and of Mr. Booth, Secretary to
the Board of Trade, p. 13. At p. 120,
another witness, Mr. Swift, much
engaged in Parliamentary practice,
is asked his opinion of preliminary
inquiries, and answers, " They are
a total waste of money ; I never saw
a Committee that would listen to
them." Probably the main reason
for this disregard of departmental

Local
inquiries
before grant
of Provisional
Orders.

Another class of inquiries, instituted by public departments under various general Acts, before the grant of Provisional Orders, has been explained in a preceding Chapter.[1] Of these inquiries, it may be remembered, the most important are made by the Local Government Board under various sections in the Public Health Act,[2] designed to facilitate efforts by local authorities to provide water, improve drainage, or otherwise promote health in their respective districts. Besides the specific inquiries directed by this Act, the Board may make " such inquiries as they see fit in relation to any matters concerning the public health in any place, or any matters with

Costs of
general
inquiries
under Public
Health Act.

respect to which " the Act requires their consent.[3] They may order the costs of inquiries to be paid by any parties appearing before their inspectors, or may direct on what rates such costs shall be charged.[4] In conducting local investigations their inspectors can administer oaths, and have large powers for the

No discretion
as to local
inquiry in
certain cases.

examination of witnesses,[5] and the production of papers and accounts. When objection is taken to the making of any draft Order, the Local Government Board are not allowed a discretion: they are bound to hold a local inquiry, and permit all persons interested to attend and make objections.[6] In cases of comparatively small importance, when the Board's decision is likely to be accepted as conclusive, this preliminary investigation is proper and necessary. But there are cases in which the Board knows, and everybody knows, that, whatever may be their decision, parties will avail themselves of the appeal to Parliament which the Act provides.[7] In such cases, a local investigation is open to all the objections which led to the repeal of the Preliminary Inquiry Acts, namely,

reports has been that each really represents no more than the opinions of an individual employed by the department: opinions which may be outweighed by superior authority given before Committees.

[1] See Chapter on Provisional Order system, pp. 676 et seq.

[2] 38 & 39 Vict. c. 55.

[3] Ib. s. 293.

[4] Ib. s. 294.

[5] Ib. s. 296. See, as to powers of inspectors under this section, 4 & 5 Will. IV. c. 76, s. 12; 10 & 11 Vict. c. 109, s. 21.

[6] 38 & 39 Vict. c. 55, s. 297 (2).

[7] Ib. sub-s. (4).

that it may involve three expensive contests, instead of one or two, and does not save the time of Parliament.[1]

A suggestion by the Committee of 1846, that private Bills should be subject to departmental supervision, had then been to some extent anticipated. Before 1846, the Board of Trade exercised a general control over Bills which sought to incorporate trading companies, or related to docks, harbours, piers, canals, navigations, gas, and water. Railway Bills came within the jurisdiction of a distinct department of the Board. All these measures were examined to see that they contained nothing of a general nature injuriously affecting public interests.[2] With a view to extend this system, proposals were laid before the Committee[3] allocating various classes of Bills to other departments for like supervision. This plan has been substantially adopted, and by Standing Orders promoters are now required, on or before December 21, to lodge copies of all Bills at the Treasury and General Post Office, and of every railway and canal Bill, and every local Bill incorporating or giving powers to any company, at the Board of Trade. Bills relating to docks, harbours, navigations, piers, or ports, must be deposited at the same date with the Harbour Department of the Board of Trade; Bills relating to local Courts, stipendiary magistrates, and cemeteries, at the Home Office; Bills giving powers to local authorities, or relating to turnpike roads or trusts, highways or bridges, with the Local Government Board; and Bills which affect the boundaries of any school district or the jurisdiction of any school board, at the Education Office.[4]

By other Standing Orders in both Houses, every report made upon a private Bill by or under the authority of any

[1] See Lower Thames Valley Drainage case, *ante*, pp. 703–7.

[2] Commons' Committee on Private Bills, 1846; Ev. of Mr. J. G. Shaw-Lefevre, Joint Secretary to Board of Trade, p. 79.

[3] By Mr. Shaw-Lefevre. Ib. p. 224.

[4] Lords' and Commons' Standing Order 33, Sess. 1887.

Supervision of private bills by public departments.

Departmental reports referred to Committees.

public department stands referred to the Committee on the Bill;[1] and to ensure proper respect for these reports, the House of Commons resolved, in 1858, that whenever a Committee dissents from the departmental recommendations they contain, its reasons shall be stated to the House.[2] The House of Lords is satisfied to refer all official reports to its Committees, and assumes that they will not without sufficient cause disregard the recommendations they find there. In this way much has been done to harmonize and improve private legislation. Committees are informed of the views taken by responsible departments upon questions affecting public interests; and while, upon counter-statements by the parties, these views may for good reasons be set aside, they can no longer be ignored.

Commons' Committee dissenting from these recommendations to report their reasons.

In preceding pages there have been traced the chief improvements by which from time to time private legislation has been cheapened and made more speedy and efficient. It may now be useful to notice some of the very numerous suggestions to remodel the existing system or create a new jurisdiction. One of the earliest changes coming with authority was made by a Commons' Committee of 1858 on "the best mode of securing public interests and diminishing Parliamentary expenses." This Committee included among its members Mr. Gladstone, Sir James Graham, Lord Robert Cecil (Marquis of Salisbury), Mr. Cardwell, Mr. Henley, Mr. Lowe, and Colonel Wilson Patten, who presided. Many useful reforms are due to its report; but the House declined to adopt a recommendation that evidence taken before Committees in the Lords on

Suggested changes in system of private legislation.

Committees in second House to decide on printed evi-

---

[1] Lords' Standing Order 106; Commons' Standing Order 212; Sess. 1887.

[2] Com. Journ. March 24, 1858. Lords' Committee on Private Bills, 1858; Ev. of Mr. T. Erskine May, p. 26; see also pp. 120-1. Commons' Standing Order 150, Sess. 1887.

private Bills should be received by Committees in the Com- dence and counsel's speeches.
mons, and *vice versâ*, "under the same regulations heretofore
in force in Committees on divorce Bills." It is not probable
that Committees of either House would be satisfied to decide upon printed evidence and counsel's speeches.

Lord Brougham, in his later years, proposed a series of Lord Brougham's plan of re-form, 1860.
twenty-five lengthy resolutions, in which will be found a
detailed plan for the constitution of a Court or Board of five
legal members appointed by the Crown.[1] These judges were
to be highly paid, and removable only upon a joint address
by the two Houses. They were to be a Court of Record,
with powers to each member to sit separately, for greater
despatch, and at their discretion to call in aid a jury, if both
parties requested one, to decide on disputed facts. But while
Lord Brougham thought that such a tribunal would enable
Parliament to transact private Bill business "more expeditiously, more economically, and more satisfactorily," he at the
same time attached great importance to the necessity of still
securing "the control of each House over each enactment."
One of his resolutions therefore affirmed :—

"That it is nevertheless inexpedient, in a constitutional
view, for Parliament, or either of the Houses thereof, to
abdicate its functions and privileges in respect of private
legislation; but, on the contrary, that both Houses ought
jealously to retain their undoubted power of deciding upon
every proposed enactment, and of assenting to or dissenting
from such proposal."

As Lord Brougham's plan allowed petitioners to oppose, Plan dropped.
in each House of Parliament, a scheme approved by the new
Court, it would only have added another inquiry to those
already existing, and swollen costs instead of reducing
them, while it would have involved a large annual charge
for maintenance. After debate, therefore, his resolutions
were not again heard of. In 1863, this plan of a fixed
tribunal was much discussed by a Committee of great

---

[1] Lords' Journ. July 27, 1860.

Fixed tri-
bunal dis-
cussed by
Commons'
Committee,
1863.

authority, appointed by the House of Commons to inquire
whether any improvements could be made in private legislation. Mr. Milner Gibson, then President of the Board of
Trade, presided. Among the members were Mr. Lowe, Lord
Stanley, Mr. Walpole, Colonel Wilson Patten, Mr. Bouverie,
Mr. Adair, Mr. Massey, Mr. Charles Forster, and Mr. Liddell.
This Committee began their inquiry on March 3, and did not
conclude it till June 23. They sat on twelve days to hear
evidence, and on five to consider their report. It was therefore
a prolonged and careful inquiry, aided by evidence from witnesses of great experience in private legislation. Earl Grey
and Mr. Erskine May then suggested outside tribunals with
appeals to Parliament. But, warned probably by the recent
failure of the preliminary inquiry system, the Committee
were of opinion that on all contested Bills, " so great would
be the desire of the parties interested to avail themselves of
every chance, that the proposed plans would often merely add
one stage more to the inquiry."[1]

Objections
to fixed
tribunal
stated in
1863.

One objection to any fixed tribunal was clearly brought
out in the inquiry of 1863. At present, if promoters fail in
one Session, they come again to Parliament in the next
Session, provided that their scheme is substantially supported;
and schemes once rejected are often passed on a second
application, as circumstances change, the promoters' case is
stronger, or different Committees take different views upon
the expediency of proposed legislation. But, with a fixed
Court, composed of the same judges, striving for consistency, and attached to precedent, there would be little
encouragement to make a second attempt, however useful
and beneficial the undertaking. Fixed tribunals have fixed
opinions. That, indeed, is one of the reasons why such tribunals have been suggested, as their decisions would be uniform.
But it would be as absurd and as mischievous to stereotype
decisions upon private as upon public Bills; both involve

---

[1] Report, p. 4.

questions of policy; and the evidence and arguments on such questions sometimes present themselves, happily, in a different light to the minds of different Committees, and of Parliament itself, in successive Sessions. Thus, in the early history of railway legislation, Parliamentary Committees rejected Bills for the construction of some of our existing trunk lines. If a fixed tribunal had rejected the first railway Bill which was promoted, it would probably have kept to its view in successive years, and so projects of great public utility might have been defeated or long delayed. From the questions put to witnesses, it is clear that considerations of this nature weighed strongly with some members of the Committee, and led them to prefer, as they did, a fluctuating to a fixed tribunal.[1]

This view was placed before the Committee in writing by Mr. Booth, whose evidence has so often been quoted in this work, and whose experience of private legislation as Speaker's Counsel and afterwards as Secretary of the Board of Trade, gives to his opinions the highest value :— *Opinion of Mr. Booth, 1863.*

"For all open questions, *i. e.*, where the principle of decision cannot be reduced to a law, the Committee is, I think, better than a judicial tribunal. Its fluctuating character is not altogether a disadvantage. It varies with, and keeps progress with, the times. The public will permanently acquiesce in no other. A judicial tribunal, proceeding strictly on precedent, would be apt to stereotype the policy of a bygone age. One great recommendation of the judicial tribunal has been supposed to be the uniformity and consistency of its decisions. The Liverpool and Manchester, and the London and Birmingham Railway Bills were, I believe, both thrown out by Committees on their first introduction. Where would the railway system now have been under a course of uniform judicial decisions? A preliminary inquiry by officers on the spot, or by a judicial tribunal, who are not to have the final decision of the case, would, I think, in most contested cases, be merely adding to expense. It is sometimes said that the facts might usefully be investigated by officers in a local inquiry, and this might be so if you could define the facts requiring to be proved, as the condition on which the promoters of a scheme would be entitled to their

---

[1] Commons' Committee of 1863; Min. of Ev. pp. 51, 53.

Bill; but this is not the case, or you could reduce the matter to law, and no private Bill would be necessary."[1]

To the same effect was evidence given two years afterwards by one of the most experienced parliamentary agents at Westminster :—

"I am not much for fixed tribunals upon these questions [involving policy]. It has always been objected to Committees of both Houses that they are fluctuating bodies, and that one body tries the question in one year and another in the next year. I look upon that as a very great advantage. A fixed tribunal will have fixed opinions. Even members of the House of Commons are not without fixed prejudices, and there are always in the railway world some particular questions on which they may prevail more or less. There was the question of the gauges; there are the questions of amalgamation, running powers, competition, and so on. If you have a fixed tribunal, we, who represent the suitors, will know that a particular member presides over it, and that we have not a chance. I much prefer the present constitution of Committees when we do not know precisely before whom we shall go."[2]

Lord Monk Bretton, better known as Mr. Dodson, who was for some years Chairman of Ways and Means in the House of Commons, proposed there a series of resolutions, in 1872, with a view "to substitute as far as possible," for private Bills, an extended system of Provisional Orders, "obtainable in England, Scotland, and Ireland on application to a permanent tribunal of a judicial character, before which promoters and opponents should be heard in open court, and the decisions of which should be subject to confirmation by Parliament.[3]

---

[1] Commons' Committee on Private Bill Business, 1863; App., p. 356. The term "private Bill legislation" was first used in 1855. It was the title given by Mr. Serjeant Pulling to an article written by him, which appeared in the "Edinburgh Review" (vol. 101), describing the evils of the then system of private Bills. Being referred to in Parliament, it has gradually come into general use.

[2] Commons' Committee of 1865 on Court of Referees; Ev. of Mr. Coates,

p. 61. Advice from an expert engaged in Parliamentary practice has sometimes been deprecated, though in this instance it was sought by a Parliamentary Committee; but the question has with reason been asked, "why this should be the only business in the world which is better understood by those who do not conduct it than by those who do." (Sir Edmund Beckett, now Lord Grimthorpe, *The Times*, May 21, 1872.)

[3] 210 Hansard, 17.

Like Lord Brougham, Mr. Dodson did not propose to exclude an appeal to Parliament, but his appellate tribunal was a joint Committee of the two Houses. Although the tribunal of first instance was to be "of a judicial character," Mr. Dodson was not in favour of appointing judges, for "he doubted whether they would be disposed to undertake the work, and their habits and training would lead them to adhere to precedents, whereas this tribunal ought to allow amply for the variations of public opinion." Yet he proposed to choose for his new tribunal "eminent practitioners at the bar," and "saw no danger of men thus specially appointed adhering too strictly to precedents, and obstructing public improvements," while "the necessity of consulting public feeling would be kept alive in them by the power of appeal to Parliament."[1]

This plan was not pressed, for in the adjourned debate upon Lord Monk Bretton's resolutions strong objection was raised to a permanent tribunal, on the old ground that it would be wanting in the flexibility of a Parliamentary Committee, and, having once decided, would so decide again, no matter what the change of circumstances. *Withdrawal of scheme.*

Natural reluctance was also shown to abdicate the ancient power of Parliament in making and unmaking laws. Sir William Harcourt recognized that the right of appeal to Parliament should be absolute, and should not depend upon any intermediate tribunal.[2] Lord Monk Bretton proposed that all Provisional Orders considered by the new tribunal, whether granted or refused, should be laid before Parliament, "lest it should be possible that this tribunal, whether through error or some unfortunate bias by some of its members, should suppress some new invention or prevent a scheme of a novel character from being submitted to the legislature." In exceptional cases, Lord Monk Bretton admitted that Parliament could not properly dele- *Right of appeal to Parliament.*

---

[1] 210 Hansard, 21.   [2] Ib. 514; *post*, 911–12.

3 M 2

gate its functions at all, because when private Bills involved
" a new principle or matters of magnitude, such as to constitute a great question of public policy, in which it would
be apparent that neither the parties nor the public would
rest satisfied without a decision of the legislature," he suggested that his new Court should have a discretion " to remit
them at once to Parliament."

Questions of public policy and expediency, however, are
raised in greater or less degree by all private Bills. These
questions do not always appear on the surface. They are
sometimes only disclosed upon inquiry. And they are often
of higher importance in small Bills, affecting only small communities, than in Bills which interest wide districts and
involve a heavy expenditure. If all measures raising new
principles, or points of public policy, were really left for
decision by Parliament, along with all measures of exceptional magnitude, what percentage of contentious business
would be left for a permanent tribunal? And what per-
ceptible relief from its labours would be given to Parliament?

Prospects of relief to Parliament.

But the objections to a fixed tribunal, which influenced the
House of Commons in 1872, have seldom been more forcibly
stated than by Lord Monk Bretton himself. Speaking upon
the system of referees in the House of Commons in 1868, he
thus summed up these objections :—

Lord Monk Bretton on fixed tribunal, 1868.

" What are the questions before a Committee on a private
Bill ? It is not the interpretation of a law, the construction
of a document, or the ascertainment of a right and a wrong.
It is a question of expediency, a balancing of advantages
and disadvantages to the public. It is essentially a question
of policy; often a very important question. A judicial
tribunal must aim at consistency, and, from the very nature
of its being, always seek to uphold that which it has once
decided. Imagine our position if decisions respecting railways had, during the last five-and-twenty years, been left to
such a Court. The Court must either have broken away
from its own rules and precedents, in which case it would
have lost all weight and character as a judicial tribunal, or it

would have lagged behind, and found itself long ago in antagonism to the wants and opinions of the country." [1]

It is fair to mention that these were objections to a fixed tribunal whose decisions should be final; but Lord Monk Bretton added that, if Parliament fell into the habit of endorsing preliminary decisions by Courts or Departments, " we should be landed in all the evils of a fixed tribunal." This is most justly said. Parliament, therefore, in Lord Monk Bretton's view, is bound to retain and exercise an appellate jurisdiction. The record in this chapter of preliminary inquiries, and reports by public departments, shows that Parliament, when thus appealed to, will do its work thoroughly, and in its own way, not relying upon former inquiries or decisions, but determining each case upon evidence and argument addressed to itself through its Committees. Whether, therefore, a Court is created, or a department called into play, the result to suitors, when large interests are at stake, will be a double or treble hearing, with double or treble costs.

Experience of preliminary decisions.

These considerations probably determined the House of Commons to reject, by a large majority, a Bill introduced by Mr. Craig-Sellar, in 1885,[2] for the establishment of a permanent tribunal. This Bill was re-introduced in 1886,[3] but was not then considered. Substantially, it reproduced Lord Monk Bretton's plan. Three " Parliamentary Commissioners" were proposed, with salaries of 3,000*l.* a-year each, and 300*l.* each for clerks. This was a departure from the Bill of 1885, under which each of the judges would have received, for good reasons, 5,000*l.* a-year.[4] According to the scheme of 1886, all preliminary work now done in Parliament would

Mr. Craig-Sellar's Bills, 1885-6.

[1] 190 Hansard, 863; February 18, 1868.

[2] Hansard, February 25, 1885. The numbers were: ayes, 58; noes, 160; majority, 102. See also Debates of 1883 (276 Hans. 1611, 1645), and 1884 (285 ib. 1554).

[3] Bill 22, Sess. 1886.

[4] " That might appear to the Chancellor of the Exchequer a considerable sum: but it must be remembered that if they were to have good men, who alone could inspire confidence, they must not be afraid to pay them well." — Mr. Craig-Sellar; Speech on second reading of Private Legislation Bill, 294 Hansard, 1274 (February 25, 1885).

remain untouched; the Commissioners in England, judges of the Court of Session in Scotland, and of the High Court in Ireland, were to relieve Committees of their quasi-judicial but really legislative duties. Here, then, would be three separate tribunals: two purely judicial: all out of touch with Parliament, and with each other. Lord Monk Bretton more prudently suggested but one tribunal, on the ground that separate tribunals would prevent harmony and consistency of procedure, and that "there was not business enough in Scotland or in Ireland to justify the creation of separate tribunals" for those countries.[1]

Reports to Parliament.

Parliament was to receive the reports of the three tribunals. Each private Bill would then be dealt with by the House to which it belonged, by the light of these reports. Such an arrangement would be prolific of discussion in both Houses. The Bill of 1886 contemplated that any report might be referred back to the tribunal with special instructions. But there would be nothing to prevent either House from sending any Bill to a select Committee. Such a system would be little more than a revival, in a new form, of the old preliminary inquiry, with the old result of doubled inquiry and expense, and the added evil of a serious encroachment upon public time by frequent public debate. On this point a high authority upon private legislation may be quoted :—

If the report of a Committee is impugned in either House, "the members of the Committee are present to defend themselves, and enable the House to come to a right conclusion. But it is quite certain that the reports of persons not members, but only officers of the House, will invite much greater examination, and more frequent challenge. The reasons of the judgment will be before the House, but the judges themselves cannot be present to explain them; and the result will be habitual discussion on every report of importance, conducted under most unfair conditions and constant obstruction to the business of the House."[2]

---

[1] See on this point remarks and note, p. 749.

[2] Article on "Private Bill Legislation," by Mr. E. Leigh Pemberton, M.P., "Fortnightly Review," Aug. 1885, p. 231.

Answering elsewhere the argument that no real abdication of authority would occur under the Bill, the same writer remarks :—

"'Parliament would retain its power,' it was argued, 'inasmuch as each House would be at liberty to deal with the report of the justices, and to adopt, amend, or reject it, as the circumstances of each case required.' This argument appears to involve the following dilemma :—Either the Houses, upon the presentation of the report, will habitually go into its merits and examine for themselves the reasons of the justices for their decision—and, contrary to Lord Mansfield's advice, they are by the Bill required to state their reasons—in which case the inquiry before them will have been superfluous and amount only to a collection of evidence for other persons to examine and decide upon ; or the Houses will, as a matter of course, accept the report, and the abdication of authority will be complete." [1]

Another plan, free from the broad objections so often and so forcibly expressed to a permanent tribunal, is that of Committees appointed by the two Houses jointly, substituting a single inquiry for the existing double inquiry into contested Bills. This plan was much discussed by the Commons' Committee of 1858. Mr. Lowe, one of its members, moved "that the House of Lords should be invited to concur in some arrangement by which a private Bill may be investigated, at the same time and place, before a Committee of the two Houses, or by which one joint tribunal may be formed from both Houses." This plan was supported by Mr. Gladstone, Mr. Lowe, Lord Robert Cecil, Mr. Brown-Westhead, and Mr. Stuart Wortley. It was opposed by Sir James Graham, Mr. Cardwell, Mr. Henley, Mr. Turner, and Mr. Bouverie ; and, the numbers being equal, the chairman declared himself with the noes.[2] The same plan was sug-

Joint Committees on private Bills.

Discussed in Commons' Committee, 1858,

---

[1] Ib. p. 30. Mr. Pemberton's lengthened services when in Parliament, as chairman of the Court of Referees (*ante*, pp. 809-10), are a guarantee that he does not undervalue a permanent tribunal for determining questions properly within its sphere ; his emphatic condemnation of a fixed tribunal for dealing with private Bills therefore has peculiar weight.

[2] Report, p. 6.

and in Lords' Committee, 1858.

gested by witnesses examined before a Lords' Committee of the same year, but was not mentioned in their report. A Court of appeal, it was admitted, would be necessary in the case of a joint inquiry; and that being so, the economy or public advantage of such a system was doubtful.[1]

Single hearing in Parliament recommended, 1863.

In 1863, witnesses examined before the Commons' Committee on private business proposed a joint tribunal. The Committee also favoured a single hearing in Parliament, but adopted a plan of their own:—"That with a view of saving the expense and loss of time, now occasioned by the double hearing of contested cases by Committees of each House of Parliament, an arrangement ought to be come to by the two Houses by which a single hearing might be made to serve the purpose of the present double inquiry." Acting on evidence offered by one of its members, Mr. Massey, then Chairman of Ways and Means, the Committee also resolved: —"That opposed Bills having passed through a Committee of the House of Commons should be dealt with as unopposed Bills in the House of Lords, and *vice versâ*; but that each House should nevertheless retain the power of referring any Bill to a Committee, if from special circumstances that course should appear desirable." An amendment, that the practice which entitles petitioners to a second hearing in the second House " is a valuable security against unwise or unjust legislation," was rejected.[2] This proposal that one House should surrender its functions to the other in certain cases has not since found acceptance.

Joint Committee of 1869 on despatch of business.

A joint Committee of Lords and Commons was appointed in 1869 " to consider whether any facilities could be given for the despatch of business in Parliament." This Committee[3] considered it expedient that opposed private Bills

---

[1] Lords' Committee on Private Bills, 1858; Ev. p. 24.

[2] Minutes of Proceedings, p. 30.

[3] Its members were the Marquis of Salisbury, Earl of Derby, Earl Granville, Viscount Eversley, Viscount Halifax, Lord Redesdale, Sir George Grey, Mr. Disraeli, Mr. Bouverie, Mr. Walpole, Mr. Dodson, and Colonel Wilson Patten.

should be referred to a joint Committee, consisting of three members of each House, and were of opinion "that this change would introduce greater simplicity and rapidity of proceeding, and a corresponding economy." The plan also included joint Standing Order Committees and Committees of Selection, and a joint Court of Referees to decide cases of *locus standi*. Upon an opposed Bill, the chair was to be taken by a member of the House to which the Bill belonged. The chairman was to have only one vote; if the votes were equally divided the question would be negatived. A second hearing was not excluded by this plan. A Bill, after being reported, was to be "open to amendments and recommitment to the former or some other joint Committee" as might be expedient. Unless so referred it would become an unopposed Bill.

Second hearing before second joint Committee.

To leave the right of appeal from a single tribunal dependent upon the judgment of either House, would obviously waste public time by encouraging debates; it would also deny a right conceded outside Parliament to suitors with interests which, compared with those at issue in many private Bills, are infinitesimal. It is true that promoters whose Bill fails now have no appeal; but in the next Session they can renew their application, and may then reverse the former judgment against them. On the other hand, petitioners once denied a second hearing generally lose for ever their opportunity of redress. Sir William Harcourt, who once practised with success at the Parliamentary bar, told the House of Commons in 1872 that "over and over again he had known decisions on private Bills reversed by the House of Lords, and never recollected any in which that reversal was not right." That was natural, he added, because upon a second hearing mistakes were corrected, evidence was strengthened, and the case better understood. His conclusion, therefore, was that "it would be a mistake to make one standing Committee which could give only one hearing, because second hearings in cases of great importance were very valuable." The

Right of appeal should be absolute.

Sir William Harcourt on the value of second hearings, 1872.

"appeal should be as of right, and should not be left to the discretion of any intermediate tribunal. If you had a powerful Court of appeal, they would be disposed to support the decision of the Court below; and this prospect, with the liability to costs, would be a security against wanton and unnecessary appeals."[1]

Advantage of Court of review.

Besides the general testimony borne by Sir William Harcourt and other high authorities, several cases have from time to time been cited from evidence before Committees, showing the advantage of a Court of review.[2] A Parliamentary agent of great experience gave to the Committee of 1863 some then recent instances in which a second hearing of Bills had resulted in material alterations, generally believed to to be just and necessary. In 1856 the Mersey Docks Bill proposed to take away certain town dues from the Corporation of Liverpool without compensation. The Bill passed the Commons in this shape. Compensation amounting to 1,250,000l. was given to the Corporation by the Lords; their decision was accepted, and in a subsequent Session a Bill was submitted upon that basis, and became law. Again, in 1862, three railway companies, the Lancashire and Yorkshire, North Eastern, and South Yorkshire, brought forward rival Bills for obtaining access to Hull. The North Eastern succeeded in the lower House, but their Bill was opposed and defeated in the Lords, by the Lancashire and Yorkshire Company. In 1863, the three competing companies composed their differences, and joined in promoting a Bill which gave accommodation to all of them. In another instance the Lancashire and Yorkshire and East Lancashire Amalgamation Bill was altered in its progress through the Commons to the prejudice of the Midland Railway Company. That company appeared in the Lords, who threw out the Bill on the ground of these alterations. Next year it was reintroduced in a shape which removed nearly all opposition to it. In the opinion of this

---

[1] 210 Hansard, pp. 512–14.   [2] *Ante*, pp. 868, 903.

witness public interests would have suffered great injury in these instances had there been no Court of review; and public interests do not depend upon absolute rejection of a Bill by the second House, because equal advantage often results from material alterations made there for public or private benefit.[1]

Vague proposals have lately been current for allowing county Boards or other local authorities to decide at least upon some classes of private Bills. Such tribunals would be open to far greater objection than either of the two plans hitherto noticed. They would revive the old abuses of canvassing and of local influences, which led Parliament to discard open Committees and Speaker's list Committees.[2] There would be great risk of those scandals and suspicions from which even Parliamentary Committees were not free under the old system,[3] and of the lobbying and corruption which seem inseparable from similar methods in a kindred nation.[4] Private Bills often take the shape of valuable concessions. Rival promoters are willing to pay for them profusely, and would leave no means untried to obtain them. Not a whisper of suspicion attaches to existing tribunals, but Parliament appoints them with many safeguards suggested by lengthened experience. If the representatives of ratepayers in local bodies were even of the same class as representatives in Parliament, and always commanded the same public confidence, these safeguards could not in practice be enforced.

Private legislation by local authorities.

It is difficult, again, to see how, in local representative bodies, an adequate number of competent men could be found willing to give regular attendance throughout protracted

Continuous service, how to be enforced, on local tribunals.

[1] Commons' Committee on Private Bill Business, 1863; Ev. of Mr. Coates, p. 185. In the debate of 1872, Mr. Gregory mentioned a Bill of 1868, for the virtual amalgamation of the South Eastern, Brighton, and Chatham and Dover railways, which passed the House of Commons without much discussion. Strong feeling was afterwards aroused against this prospective monopoly; and in the House of Lords the Bill was withdrawn. (210 Hansard, 27.)

[2] *Ante,* pp. 827, 831-3.

[3] *Ante,* p. 831.

[4] *Ante,* p. 518, n.

proceedings, etc. to sacrifice the necessary time for these purposes, and likely to command the confidence of promoters and petitioners in determining the difficult questions of public expediency and of private interests which continually arise upon private Bills. Supposing this difficulty overcome, how would it be possible to exclude with certainty from tribunals composed of any local representative body the local bias and local and personal influences now so jealously kept out of Parliamentary Committees?[1]

There is the familiar case of a municipal corporation seeking to acquire gas or water works now in the hands of a company.[3] Could the company be expected to trust the impartiality of local representatives, whose interests were in common with those of the corporation, and who were perhaps looking forward to a similar transfer, upon favourable terms, to ratepayers in their own District? Assuming such a transfer to be by agreement, another familiar case is a contest between the municipal body who take over these works and the out-townships, sometimes in different counties, who are supplied from the same source. Shall these out-townships have the option of calling for a supply in bulk from the central works, and distributing it at a profit, or of purchasing the plant and works within their jurisdiction, or of simply continuing the present supply? If so, upon what terms; and, in the last case, subject to what differential rates, if any, compared with those paid inside the municipal boundaries?[4]

---

[1] Voting without hearing would probably be as common as in the old Committees of both Houses. *Ante*, pp. 827, 831, 838.

[2] See an instructive case, the Stone and Rugby Railway Bill of 1839, *ante*, pp. 837-8. On the first day of hearing, before a Commons' Committee of local and selected members, the Parliamentary agents had lists of the probable votes of local members on the last day, and were "not wrong in one vote."

[3] Stockton and Middlesbrough Water Bill, 1875; Stockton and Middlesbrough Corporations Water Bill, 1876; Wakefield Improvement Bill, 1877.

[4] Birmingham Gas and Water Bills, 1875; case of out-townships, *ante*, pp. 488-9. See also Stalybridge and Mossley Bill, 1885, and Oldham Corporation Bill, 1886 (*ante*, pp. 542-3). No fixed or local tribunal could have ventured to take without question the strong view taken and enforced by Committees in these two cases.

These are delicate and difficult questions often arising in practice, and always arousing a local feeling which extends far beyond the districts immediately affected. Could any local tribunal be trusted to decide these questions impartially? And if themselves impartial, would they be credited with impartiality by the parties whom their decisions affected?

Bills are now frequent, and with the rapid growth of suburban districts are likely to be often met with, for extending city or borough boundaries. Most large towns have sought, or would wish, to annex adjacent districts for municipal rate-paying purposes. It is a natural desire, but generally leads to a struggle between the municipality and the county or division whose territory will be absorbed, aided by inhabitants and railway companies, who say they do not profit by municipal expenditure, and should not be subjected to new and onerous taxation. Few questions are more keenly discussed in the locality, or excite greater feeling. In determining these antagonistic claims of town and county, what local representative body could be free from bias?[1] Glasgow has made repeated efforts to enlarge its boundaries, sometimes failing, sometimes succeeding; the Corporation of Dublin have long desired the inclusion of some of the prosperous townships around that city. It is not necessary to ask whether Lanarkshire or the county of Dublin could supply a representative body wholly impartial upon these burning questions. Could freedom from local or other influences be expected, even among representatives drawn from half-a-dozen counties in Scotland or Ireland?

Extension of municipal boundaries.

[1] The Leicester Extension Bill of 1886 was vigorously opposed by the county justices. In all cases of this kind the interests of outside districts sought to be annexed are most deeply affected, and deserve the most careful consideration by a tribunal lifted far above local controversies. Proposed extensions of municipal boundaries at Sunderland and Wakefield were rejected by Parliament in 1885. In the same Session Bury obtained a very moderate slice of the new territory it applied for, and that only subject to stringent conditions.

Appropriation of watersheds. Other typical cases of constant occurrence may be taken. Local authorities seek to appropriate a certain watershed. Their Bill is opposed by neighbouring local authorities, who say that, although they propose no immediate user, they wish to preserve for the district they administer its natural gathering ground.[1] Which population is entitled to possession? The first claimants, who may be sorely in need of additional sources for the service of a growing town? Or the authority which says: "We look forward to increased wants among our own population, and must not stand by and allow this encroachment"? Such appropriations excite the most legitimate jealousy among neighbouring communities, not only on the score of health and convenience, but because of the advantages to trade arising from an abundant and pure supply of water.

County bridge opposed by municipality and local authorities.

Joint drainage districts. Again, county justices propose to build a new bridge, but are much divided in opinion. A municipal corporation join with parochial authorities and landowners to oppose this plan, on the ground that the site is inconvenient for traffic.[2] A joint drainage board is formed, after vain objections from districts wishing to act separately. The board submits at various times schemes covering a wide area on both banks of the Thames. Constituent authorities oppose every one of these schemes. The Local Government Board approves of the last plan. Parliament then intervenes, disagrees with the department, rejects the scheme, and dissolves the drainage board.[3] What local representative body in Surrey, where this case occurred, or drawn even from all the home counties put together, could have been trusted to hold the balance

---

[1] This was the case of the Oldham Corporation Water Bill, 1886, opposed on some of the grounds indicated in the text by the Corporations of Ashton, Stalybridge, Mossley, and Stockport. In the same Session the Corporation of Leicester and Local Board of Loughborough were striving for possession of the same watershed.

[2] Penwortham Bridge Bill, 1885, promoted by Lancashire county justices; opposed by Corporation of Preston and other petitioners.

[3] See story of Lower Thames Valley Joint Drainage Board, *ante*, pp. 703-7.

equally between these numerous local authorities, all convinced that they were right, all anxious to do their duty to their constituents? And what representative body, or, indeed, what outside tribunal of any nature, would have had the courage and authority to act as Parliament did with general assent in this case?

For reasons which need no statement, Bills promoted by trading bodies are just as little suited for submission to local authorities, and would afford greater temptations, and greater opportunities for questionable decisions. Tramway companies have complained of the hindrances placed in their way by the mere powers of consent given under statute to local authorities.[1] What would be the result if the same local authorities had a share in the legislation which sanctioned tramways? It can hardly be supposed that Parliament would commit railways to local tribunals, leaving them to deal at their discretion with complicated questions of competition, of running powers, of leasing powers, of rates and fares, and with statutes upon the faith of which millions of money have been invested. Railways have ceased to be a mere local interest. Each trunk line, in its wide relations with other lines, its statutory obligations, its subventions and subscriptions, its enormous capital, and influence over transit, has become almost an Imperial interest. Even a small connecting link of what at first sight appears strictly a local line might have wide-reaching results, and might prejudice materially the revenue and position of some other railway company. The frequent improvements and shortening of distances on the rival East and West Coast routes to Scotland, the Great Western and South Western extensions into Devonshire and Cornwall, and the London, Chatham and Dover and South Eastern Companies' facilities for traffic to and from the Continent, are all examples of lines which, in one point of view are local, and, in another, of general importance.

Tramways.

Railways.

[1] *Ante*, Vol. I. pp. 190 *et seq.*

Other cases of
competition.

But leaving railways aside, large and difficult questions arise out of competition, or alleged competition, in other cases. Shall Birkenhead, in one county, establish docks in competition with Liverpool in another county? Shall Grimsby, in Lincolnshire, have docks which may ruin Hull, higher up the Humber and in Yorkshire?[1] How is a local representative body to be constituted which shall fairly decide upon questions of this type, vitally affecting different interests in different counties? Or can a judicial tribunal properly be trusted with these questions of expediency so vitally affecting many interests and communities? Yet such questions are frequently presented to Parliament, in connection with docks, piers, navigations, harbours, and other undertakings.

Private rights
and interests.

Parliamentary Committees have always been careful and considerate in their regard for private rights and interests, not allowing them to stand in the way of legitimate enterprise or public necessities, but taking care that they are only set aside for urgent reasons, and upon receipt of adequate compensation. The assertion of private rights is sometimes at the moment the sole or the best mode of questioning immature and mischievous projects, which are put forward for speculative purposes, and will only block the way for *bonâ fide* undertakings. It would be too much to expect from county boards or other local representatives the respect paid in Parliament to the due claims of property, and the patient hearing always given there to single petitioners who appear to protect themselves against injury. Before any local

---

[1] See, too, the questions of competition arising very recently upon Bills for constructing new docks in the Thames (Tilbury Docks, *ante,* p. 671). The Barry Dock and Railways Bill, 1884, in which traders promoted a new dock some miles away, competing with an existing dock at Cardiff, is another instance where large land-owning, coal-owning, railway and urban interests were concerned on one side or the other. Again, by the River Dee Conservancy Bills of 1885, two bodies of promoters, the Corporation of Chester and inhabitants and local authorities in the colliery district of Ruabon, sought to obtain control of the River Dee, and no effort was spared to enlist local influence in support of these rival interests.

tribunals an unpopular landowner, or any owner opposing a popular Bill, would fight an uphill battle indeed.

With forty counties in England alone, excluding divisions of counties, the county plan which has been suggested would demand at least forty tribunals, each costing something for staff and maintenance. Subject to any restrictions which might be imposed at starting, each court would be a rule to itself, both in procedure and principle, not knowing, or perhaps caring, what other courts were doing, and taking different views from its neighbours upon many issues of policy and expediency presented to it, so that promoters of similar Bills might, in one county, be sure to win, and in the next county to lose. This would be a system of local option indeed, if system of any kind it could be called. Private legislation so determined could only be kept from chaos, injustice and anomalies could only be prevented, by the continued control and interference of Parliament. But if this point is clear, and if railway business, with what appear to be, although they may not be, the most important local Bills, are reserved for decision by Parliament, all justification for a new tribunal disappears. It would relieve Parliament from little work; like other experiments here recorded,[1] it would only add another stage of litigation and expense.

Number and conflict of jurisdictions.

Control of Parliament necessary.

The existing Provisional Order system, while not free from blemish, supplies an inexpensive method of obtaining legislative sanction for small works by local authorities and promoters. This system has expanded so greatly that the number of Orders now annually confirmed almost equals the number of private Acts.[2] If any Orders or Acts are contested it is because they raise, in nearly all cases, questions of policy and expediency not suited for adjustment by any tribunal but Parliament; promoters and petitioners alike in these cases are satisfied with a decision by no lesser authority; and in depriving them of this decision Parliament

Extension of Provisional Order system.

[1] See Preliminary Inquiry Acts, *ante*, pp. 890 *et seq.* [2] *Ante*, pp. 708-9.

would abdicate its authority and probably commit much substantial injustice.

Legislative questions arising on private Bills.

Some of the issues presented in this Chapter and taken from actual practice, are clearly in their nature not judicial. It is still more clear that they are questions which should be withdrawn from any local arena. Others have been mentioned in the course of this work. One was the great project of the Corporation of Manchester to draw a supply of water from Lake Thirlmere.[1] In their application of 1879, the Corporation, having already bought land and water rights, asked, substantially, for a way-leave, a hundred miles long, from a neighbouring county to their own city. But Parliament intervened and required the Corporation to supply, upon request, towns past which the conduit was to run, and which, from their geographical position, might be supposed to have a prior claim upon Thirlmere for water.[2] Parliament alone could have enforced this claim and fastened upon any municipal body a like obligation. Again, under popular pressure, often temporary, or an honest conviction that they are consulting the welfare of constituents, local authorities sometimes propose to subscribe to railways, docks, or canals.[3] These proposals to pledge the rates for more or less speculative purposes are generally opposed by a considerable minority of ratepayers. Are Bills which raise these broad grounds of expediency fit for determination by any but the highest legislative body?

Thirlmere Water Bill, 1879.

Subscriptions by municipalities to railways, docks and canals.

Manchester Ship Canal.

The Manchester Ship Canal Bill will occur to many minds. It affected enormous interests. It divided into two

---

[1] *Ante*, pp. 481, 796.

[2] The Liverpool Water Act of 1880, to bring water from Welsh streams, diverting feeders of the Severn (*ante*, p. 474), raised another broad question of expediency. It was opposed by the Severn Conservancy Commissioners.

[3] The Corporations of Southampton, Newbury, and Winchester asked for powers in a Bill of 1882 to subscribe to the Didcot, Newbury, and Southampton Junction Railway; these powers were refused. The Corporation of Hull, in 1880, were allowed to subscribe towards the Hull and Barnsley line, being already interested in the docks. The Corporation of Salford proposed, in 1886, to subscribe towards the Manchester Ship Canal, but Parliament refused permission.

camps two great cities, with their subsidiary towns and districts. No one can doubt that, if the issues then pending had been decided by any inferior tribunal, Parliament would have been asked, by public discussion or by inquiry and trial in the existing forms, finally to settle all controversy.

In 1886, a Commons' Committee took cognizance of recent attempts to purchase the London water companies, and insisted, as a condition of passing Bills with new capital powers, that three of these companies should form a sinking fund, to be applied in "purchasing and extinguishing" share capital, or otherwise as Parliament might determine.[1] The promoters took time to consider whether they would withdraw their Bills, but ultimately yielded. Previous limitations upon the water companies' capital powers had been imposed, with a view of guarding against any future demand by them for higher terms of purchase.[2] Parliament alone could have enforced these strong measures in the public interest. Being decisions by Committees, they were accepted, as in the other cases which have been mentioned, without any public discussion or further demand upon the time of Parliament.

Metropolitan Water Acts, 1886.

Since 1882, the House of Commons has paid special attention to Bills of local authorities which seek to vary the general law, especially by police and sanitary clauses.[3] These Bills have not been left to the ordinary Committees, but in successive Sessions have been referred by the House to special Committees, who have disregarded precedents, summarily cut down many of the powers asked for, abridged the period for repayment of loans, and laboured with success to establish greater uniformity in local law, and abate its harshness to individuals. Special reports of their proceedings have been made by these Committees, so that the House has at once known that its instructions have been carried out. To what tribunal would Parliament be willing to entrust a similar authority; or what inferior

Police and sanitary legislation.

[1] *Ante*, pp. 543–4.   [3] *Ante*, pp. 536 *et seq.*
[2] *Ante*, p. 543.

authority would have been obeyed by the large and powerful communities affected by this legislation?

Advantage of Committees as tribunals.
Committees in both Houses enjoy great advantages: they are in constant touch with Parliament, reflect as a rule the current feeling of Parliament, can be called to account at once for any errors of judgment or misapprehension of facts,[1] and command out of doors the respect and authority due to members of the Imperial Legislature. Parliamentary inquiries and Royal Commissions have declared, one after another, that no other tribunal would command the same confidence. The Commons' Committee of 1863, described by Mr. Childers, when Chancellor of the Exchequer, as the strongest ever appointed upon private business,[2] reported

Testimony from Committee of 1863.
"that, considering the large discretion which must necessarily be vested in any tribunals, however constituted, to which may be entrusted the duty of reporting on opposed private Bills, and the absence of fixed rules for the guidance of such tribunals, it is not expedient that this duty should be performed otherwise than by Committees of this House."[3] A large majority of the witnesses examined before this Committee were also of opinion that no Court could be constituted which would on the whole be so satisfactory to the public as Committees of Parliament.[4] A more recent witness, possessing an intimate knowledge of the practice, writes:—

"After twenty years' experience I can unhesitatingly affirm that no satisfactory substitute for private Bill Committees can be found. There is not a Bill passed which does not necessarily interfere with existing rights, and very frequently with existing law; and no one would be, or ought to be, content that this should be done by anybody but the Legislature, nor could it justly or constitutionally be done. The double hearing secures full consideration, where it is needed; and from the fact that the tribunal is above suspicion, and that, with the rarest exceptions, the noblemen and

---

[1] See p. 697. A Lords' Committee had in this case rejected a Bill, but, after debate, the Bill was promptly reinstated in the orders, and proceeded with as a public measure.

[2] 294 Hansard, 1295.

[3] Report, p. 10; Min. of Proceedings, pp. 30, 37. This resolution was proposed by Lord Stanley.

[4] Report of Committee of 1863, p. 1. The Committee expressed their concurrence with this view.

gentlemen who compose it, sitting without fee or reward, are patient and painstaking, even the defeated feel no sense of wrong, while the uncertainty is one inherent in the subject-matter, for no two cases are alike. I, for one, have often found that when at the moment I have most strongly felt Committees have been wrong, I have afterwards thought them entirely right, in the light of experience." [1]

These legislative functions have for centuries been regarded as inseparable from Parliament. They include a strict appropriation of money borrowed by local authorities for local works.[2] Above all, they include a control of local taxation, and of tolls and rates charged for transit, for gas and water, for docks and navigation, affecting ratepayers, consumers and traders in many forms. It is no exaggeration to say that these taxes, and fares, tolls and dues far exceed, in their importance to the community, the whole burden of Imperial taxation. Yet, at a time when the interests of local ratepayers, and the interests of trade, more than ever require a close scrutiny of local taxation, and of tolls and dues, Parliament is asked to place this control substantially in other hands. Only thirty years since, the Commons resented any interference by the House of Lords with Bills imposing local rates, even for services rendered, and insisted that such measures should originate with their own body.[3] Between this constitutional assertion of privilege and a plan for handing over the jurisdiction to Commissioners, there is indeed a great gulf.

Control over local taxation, and of tolls and rates.

The House of Lords has shown no wish to rid itself of its share in private legislation, and has always discharged this duty with great care for public and private interests.[4]

Private equally with public legislation the duty of Parliament.

---

[1] "L.," *The Times*, February 15, 1884.

[2] *Ante*, Vol. I. p. 266; II. pp. 506 *et seq*.

[3] *Ante*, pp. 784-6. See especially resolutions passed by the House of Commons in 1661 upon an invasion of this privilege in a local Bill sent down by the Lords.

[4] Mr. Tyrrell, an eminent conveyancer of that day, told a Commons' Committee in 1839 that the forms of private Bills had been more considered in the Lords than in the other House. (Committee on Private Business, p. 11.) An acute and experienced solicitor, already mentioned in these pages, and often

The ... of the ... of members would, perhaps, ... or ... some from one who was then ... in Parliamentary business, and has taken even more ... ... in the work of private legislation. That time ... ... and ... and should be grudged ... ... is indeed little in keeping with the ... traditions and practice of Parliament recorded in these pages. If the jurisdiction be transferred, capital may easily ... from investments not directly sanctioned and ... ... by Parliament, and also deprived of the safeguards which Parliament, after long experience, has imposed.[1]

... by Committees, stated in ... that Lords' Committees were, as a rule, quicker in the despatch of business than those in the Lower House. "It is a remarkable fact," he said, "and one can only guess at the reason: but the truth is that a peer, generally speaking, is educated from earlier life as a chairman, and acquires habits of acting in that capacity with greater precision and accuracy than other people who have not had the same early practice." (Commons' Committee on Private Bill Business; evidence of Mr. Robert Baxter, p. 324.)

[1] Article on Private Bill Legislation; *Fortnightly Review*, August. 1885; by Mr. Pemberton, M.P.

[2] *Ante*, Vol. I. 262-66; II. 519-20.

New opportunities for public debate will be dearly purchased if undertakings are discouraged, funds for labour diverted, and means lost for providing employment and promoting trade.

Chiefly during the present century, Parliament has taken infinite pains to cheapen and perfect its procedure in passing private Bills. By abolishing the old Committees on petitions a double inquiry in both Houses has been abandoned, with a great saving to suitors.[1] Proof of Standing Orders no longer requires crowds of witnesses, delayed in London at enormous expense till their turn came.[2] Examiners now relieve members from this duty. The time of members has also been saved by largely reducing their numbers in Committees on Bills. Within the same period, these Committees have been made thoroughly impartial by the exclusion of all local and personal interests. They are selected by a method which is a guarantee against undue influences. They cost nothing to maintain. Fees from suitors pay for the private Bill staff in Parliament, and leave a considerable margin towards general establishment charges.[3]

Committees do a most useful and necessary work without payment. This work is part of the legislative functions of the High Court to which they belong, performed, it may almost be said, in the presence of Parliament, and subject to immediate check and revision from either branch of the Legislature. Committees are no more infallible than Parliament itself is. But suitors trust them, recognize their competence, and are satisfied with a right of appeal and a second hearing. The interests of suitors, however, are small in comparison with the public interests affected by this jurisdiction. For the Imperial Parliament to discontinue its ancient parliamentary tribunals, now reformed and cheapened,

Amendments in private Bill system.

Work of Committees.

---

[1] *Ante*, pp. 794-5.
[2] *Ante*, pp. 791-5.
[3] *Ante*, pp. 749–51. In 1845, the Chancellor of the Exchequer applied 220,000*l*. from the fee fund for public objects (*ante*, p. 750).

and delegate legislative functions, wholly or partially, to any inferior authority, would surely be a lamentable abandonment both of power and of duty.[1]

[1] In 1868, upon the Bill to transfer to judges the power over controverted elections, then exercised by the House of Commons, Mr. Bright expressed his hope that some other remedy might be provided, "without our being compelled to humble ourselves before the world, and say we have been obliged to transfer from ourselves the power which constitutionally belongs to us, and give it to another tribunal." (190 Hansard, p. 725.) But controverted elections involve questions of pure law and fact which can be determined by no persons so fitly as by judges. Mr. Bright's objections apply with tenfold force to any transfer by Parliament of its power over questions of expediency and policy.

APPENDIX A.

————◆————

WATER SUPPLY AND PROTECTION AGAINST FLOODS AT HULL, A.D. 1402.

THE following is a copy of a Commission issued in the reign of Henry IV. for inquiry into the means of draining and supplying the town of Kingston-upon-Hull with water[1] :—

Inquisition, 3 Hen. IV.

"Henry, by the grace of God King of England and France, and Lord of Ireland, to our chosen and faithful Henry de Percy le Fitz, Esquire; William Gascoigne, Esquire; Peter de Bukton, Esquire; John Scrop, Esquire; Robert de Hilton, Esquire; John Rouch, Esquire; John Holtrum, Esquire; Robert Tirwhit, William Godyngton, Hugh Arderne, John de Predenesse, and Richard Tirwhit greeting :

"Know ye that whereas, as we have learned, our chosen lieges the mayor, bailiffs, and commonalty of our town of Kingston-upon-Hull, hold the same town of us at a fee farm of sixty and ten pounds per annum, and that town is situated upon the river Humber, which is an arm of the sea; and there is need in these days of great charges and expenses for the protection of the same against the force of the water aforesaid; and so as well on account of charges and expenses of this kind there daily arising, to be sustained and supported, as that sweet water is not had coming or flowing to that town, except only by boats, and that at sumptuous cost, whereby the poor inhabitants of the town aforesaid in large numbers every year during the summer time, of necessity, on account of the scarcity and dearness of water of this kind, depart from the same town, and renounce and avoid it, to the injury of the town aforesaid, and in process of time to the final destruction of the same, unless a suitable and speedy remedy in this matter be speedily applied :

Protection against inroads of the Humber.

Obtaining supply of fresh water.

"We, considering the aforesaid, and that the said town is the key of the country there adjacent, and of all the county of York, and desiring therefore to treat with gracious favour the aforesaid

Inquiry into best means of providing for these objects.

---

[1] See Part II. Appendix to Second Report of Commission on State of Large Towns, &c. in 1845, p. 333.

mayor, bailiffs and commonalty in this matter, at the petition of the mayor, bailiffs and commonalty themselves, have assigned you, eleven, ten, nine, eight, seven, six, five, four and three of you, of whom we desire some of you (you the aforesaid Henry, William, Robert Tirwhit, William and Hugh to be one), to inform yourselves by all legitimate and honest ways and means by which, according to your sound discretions you shall best have known how or be able, and also to make inquiry, if it shall be necessary, upon the oath of good and lawful men of the county aforesaid, as well within as without the liberties, through whom the truth of the matter shall be able to be ascertained, how and in what manner the said town the better, the more speedily, and the more effectually shall be able to be relieved and sustained with sweet water of this kind, through parts there contiguous and adjacent, as well by sewer courses as by other mode; and to the full and due execution of all and of each (of the things) which shall happen to be devised in this matter, through information of this sort, or by inquiries, by you, eleven, ten, nine, eight, seven, six, five, four, or three of you (of whom we desire some one of you, you the aforesaid William, Robert Tirwhit, William and Hugh to be one), to be duly taken to be ordered, made and completed in the best and most discreet manner which you shall know or be able.

Ad quod damnum.

" And further to inquire by the order of good and lawful men of the same county, as well within as without the liberties, through whom the truth of the matter shall be better able to be known, whether the aforesaid matters to be ordered, made and completed in this business by you, eleven, ten, nine, eight, seven, six, five, four and three of you (of whom we desire some one of you, you the aforesaid Henry, William, Robert Tirwhit, William and Hugh to be one), what they shall have been so ordered, made and completed, be to our loss or prejudice or (to the loss or prejudice) of others or not; and if it be so, then what our loss and what our damage, and what the loss, and what the damage of others, and of whom, and how, and in what manner.

Return of inquisition into Chancery.

" And therefore we command you that at certain days and places which you, eleven, ten, nine, eight, seven, six, five, four or three of you (of whom we desire some one of you, you the aforesaid Henry, William, Robert Tirwhit, William and Hugh to be one) shall have provided for this purpose, you diligently attend respecting the aforesaid matters, and cause them to be inquired into, and examine them, and send without delay to us in our

Court of Chancery, and this briefly, the inquisitions thence distinctly and openly made under the seals of you, eleven, ten, nine, eight, seven, six, five, four or three of you, the aforesaid (of whom we desire some one of you, you the aforesaid Henry, William, Robert Tirwhit, William and Hugh to be one), and under the seals of those through whom they shall have been made.

"For we have commanded our sheriff of the county aforesaid, at certain days and places which you, eleven, ten, nine, eight, seven, six, five, four or three of you (of whom we desire some one of you, you the aforesaid Henry, William, Robert Tirwhit, William and Hugh to be one), may cause him to know, that he cause to come before you, eleven, ten, nine, eight, seven, six, five, four or three of you (of whom we desire some one of you, you the aforesaid Henry, William, Robert Tirwhit, William and Hugh to be one), so many and such good and lawful men of his bailiewick, as well within as without the liberties, through whom the truth of the business in the aforesaid matters shall be able the better to be known and inquired into.

Witnesses to be summoned by sheriff.

"In testimony of which thing we have caused these our letters to be made patent. Witness me myself at Westminster, the eighth day of March, in the second year of our Reign.

"By the King himself and Council,

"GAUNSTEDE."

[*Here follows the Return of the Inquisition of the Jury.*]

INDORSED.

" *The Answer of John Scrop Esquire, and of his Fellow Commissioners* within written appears in our Inquisition and Verdict (sewed to this Commission).

Return to writ.

"We, John Skrop, Hugh Arden, John Redeves, Richard Tirwhit, and our Associates, Commissioners of the Lord the King, being assigned by his letters patent to arrange, effect and determine how and in what manner the town of Kingston-upon-Hull shall be able to be better, more speedily and effectually relieved and sustained with sweet water, as well by sewer courses as by other mode, according to the force, forms and effect of the said letters to us, the aforesaid Commissioners directed, as in the same letters patent more fully appears:

Sewerage
works recom-
mended.

"By virtue of the aforesaid letters, and by good deliberation previously had, also through the information, assent and consent of the parts adjacent, and of very many trustworthy persons, we have for our decision decreed, ordained and determined that a certain ditch named a sewer be constructed anew in the pasture meadows and ground of Anlaby, in breadth twelve feet, and of the depth of five feet measured by the royal yard, in length from the spring called Julian's well, in the said pasture meadows and grounds of Anlaby, as far as the Wald Kerr of Swanland, and so descending from the Wald Kerr aforesaid, in the length, breadth, and depth aforesaid, as far as Miton Kerr-dike, and so descending by Miton Kerr-dike, on the north part of the field of Miton Kerr, as far as a certain ditch newly made near the common road which leads from the aforesaid town of Kingston towards Beverley, in length descending as far as the ditch called the Town-dike, under the walls of the said town of Kingston, and so thence descending, and by sufficient course, as far as the gate of the said town of

Dams for
warding off
salt water.

Kingston-upon-Hull; and that a sufficient dam for the warding off of the salt water may be made in the north end of a certain ditch lying between the pasture of Anlaby and the pasture of Swanland, called the Wald Kerr, for ever; and another sufficient dam, likewise made for the warding off of the salt water, at the north end of a certain ditch lying between the pasture of Swanland called the Wald Kerr, and a certain pasture called Miton Kerr, together with all other dams whatever hereafter to be made, wherever it shall appear necessary to the mayor, bailiffs and commonalty of Kingston-upon-Hull, now and in future, for the preservation of the sweet water aforesaid, and the warding off of all salt waters whatever coming there for ever; and that all the dams aforesaid made or in future to be made there, as well in constructing as repairing, be made by the aforesaid mayor, bailiffs and commonalty at their own proper cost, without injury, disturbance or obstruction of any persons whatever for ever.

Springs to be
conveyed for
public use.

"Through this sewer so to be newly constructed and afterwards to be called Julian-dike, all the courses of the sweet waters as well of the said spring called Julian-well as of all other courses of springs in Derrynghamynges in Anlaby, together with the course of a certain ditch in Derrynghamynges aforesaid, and the North Kerr of Anlaby, together with the courses of two springs existing in Anlaby and Hautempris, namely, from one spring in the ditch formerly (in possession) of Peter de Anlaby in Anlaby, thence descending as far as the aforesaid ditch called

Julian-dike, and from another spring in the field of Hautempris, in the Northwestynges, from thence descending by different courses, as far as the aforesaid ditch of Julian-dike, may have a direct course in the aforesaid ditch called Julian-dike, as is above written of the aforesaid matters, in the support, upholding and relief of the royal town aforesaid.

"Moreover, we, the aforesaid Commissioners, according to the tenour, force, form and effect of the Commission aforesaid, have caused diligent inquiry to be made by means of different Commissions, taken before us in neighbouring places and parts adjacent, in the presence of tenants making communications on the ground aforesaid, where the ditch aforesaid is ordered to be made, as in the verdicts of the said inquisitions, sealed and stitched to this letter more fully appears.

Course of dike to be constructed.

"All which things having been ordered, ordained, determined and adjudged, and also (as it is said) inquired into by us, the aforesaid Commissioners, the tenants of the ground aforesaid, with unanimous assent and consent, have defined and ordained that the aforesaid ditch should be made, as well in length and breadth as in depth, according to our order, determination, and decision aforesaid, and the verdict of the inquisition aforesaid.

Consent of tenants of land affected.

"In testimony, affirmation and approval of our aforesaid order, determination and decisions, to last for ever, for the improvement of the adjacent county, and the relief and support of the aforesaid royal town, according to the effect of the Commission of the Lord the King, we have affixed our seals to these presents.

"Dated the eighth day of October, in the third year of the reign of King Henry the Fourth after the Conquest."

APPENDIX B.

—◆—

SANITARY CONDITION OF MERTHYR TYDFIL,
1845-85.

Results of sanitary works at Merthyr Tydfil. IN 1885, Mr. Thomas Jones Dyke, Medical Officer of the Merthyr Tydfil Local Board of Health, presented an annual report, in which he showed the results of the various sanitary works completed by the Board since its establishment in March, 1850. Table A. of this report places the figures in a form adopted by Dr. Buchanan in his ninth annual report to the Privy Council, 1861. In the first column are (Mr. Dyke's preface is now quoted) "the proportions of deaths per 10,000 of total population yearly in the period of eleven years, 1845-1855, that is before any works of sanitation were commenced. In the second column, are the proportions during the six years while paving works were being done and inspection and removal of nuisances were attended to, the years 1856-61. In the third column, the period of four years, 1862-65, is taken, that is while the works above alluded to were being done, and while the water supply was being laid. In the fourth column are the proportions during the ten years 1866-75, when the water supply was perfected, and while the sewers and drains, and sewage disposal, were being made and completed. The fifth column gives the yearly proportion of deaths during the ten years 1876-85, when the whole of the sanitary works were completed, and sanitary inspections were in full operation.

Reduction of death-rate. " In referring to this Table A. you will not fail to notice the gradual and continuous reduction of the death-rate from all causes, from an average of 332 per 10,000 in 1845-55 to one of 231 in 1876-85, and also observe that the proportionate mortality of infants under one year was lessened from 80 to 45 per 10,000.

Fevers. " The various forms of contagious fevers, affecting children principally (measles, scarlet fever, whooping cough, diphtheria), do not seem to have been in any way affected by sanitary improvements; but with regard to other fevers (continued, typhoid, or enteric fevers), the former seems to have disappeared from the list of maladies fatal to our people, while the deaths due to the latter malady have been diminished from 21 to 3 per 10,000. The favourable effect of good sanitary work was distinctly shown in the death-rate from cholera, which in 1849 (when no sanitation had been attempted) was 267 per 10,000, was reduced in 1854, when refuse removal, house inspection, road and channel making were being done, to 83 per 10,000; and when, in 1865, a supply of good water was given, the death-rate sank to 20 per 10,000. Cholera.

" The death-rate from infantile diarrhœa was reduced from 11¼ to 4 per 10,000. The average age at death was increased from 17½ to 27½ years, a clear gain of ten years of life. Gain of life.

" The drainage of the subsoil by the construction of sewers, and making house closet and yard drains, and the consequent drying of the subsoil of houses, has borne fruit, as evidenced by the reduction of the deaths from phthisis or consumption (a disease particularly affecting persons living in damp houses) from 38 to 22 per 10,000. Consumption.

" Lastly, there remains to be noticed those diseases which have become more fatal during the last twenty years than they were during the previous fifteen years. I allude to acute and chronic bronchitis, and to pneumonia. The rates in the first period were 33, in the second period 45, per 10,000. I have in this report, and in many previous reports, stated that these maladies are proverbially most fatal in damp, unventilated dwellings, and I can only hope that laws may be enacted which may enable sanitary authorities to grapple more speedily with these prolific sources of this wasteful slaughter of hundreds of valuable lives annually. Bronchial disorders.

" In conclusion, I will here state the costs of the structural works made, and of the professional and other labour employed during the 35 years since the duties of the authority were commenced. Costs of works.

" The works for water supply have cost 155,000*l*., and the works for sewers, sewage irrigation and filtration, including the purchase of lands, 105,000*l*., making a total of 260,000*l*. To this sum should be added the charges for scavenging, gas-lighting, paving, channeling, interest on money borrowed, and establishment charges for the whole period, 240,000*l*.; in all 500,000*l*. The present income for water rents is 5,300*l*.; from

Income from works.

payments made by other authorities for the use of wide irrigation areas, from lands and houses, and profits of farming, 3,620*l.*; thus giving an annual income of 8,920*l.* The properties of the local board (that is, the water works, freehold lands, houses, &c.) are now estimated to be worth 300,000*l.*

Remunerative nature of sanitary works.

"A consideration of the various statistics of deaths from many causes which I have laid before you, and of the facts with regard to the costs incurred, show conclusively that sanitary works well planned, well executed, and thoroughly worked conduce to better health, and longer life, and become a source of profitable income to communities" :—

[TABLE A.

TABLE A.

Showing Deaths per 10,000 of Population annually in the Parish of Merthyr-Tydfil, during each of five periods of time.

YEARS.	1 1845—1855	2 1856—1861	3 1862—1865	4 1866—1875	5 1876—1885
Deaths from all Causes	332	280	262	261	231
Do. do. under 1 year	80 1/4	74 1/3	61	60	45 1/2
Do. Smallpox	10 2/3	14 2/3	4 2/3	7 1/5	0
Do. Measles	6 3/4	7 3/4	6 1/3	6 3/4	8 1/2
Do. Scarlatina	11 1/3	10	18	9 3/4	8
Do. Diphtheria	0 1/6	2	2 1/3	2	1
Do. Whooping Cough	6 1/3	7 2/3	4 1/4	8	4
Do. Continued Fever	23	12 2/3	9 2/3	0 1/10	0 1/4
Do. Typhoid Fever	21 1/3	12 2/3	8 2/3	6	3
Do. Typhus Fever	—	—	—	3 3/5	0 1/3
Do. Diarrhœa	11 1/4	11 2/3	6 1/4	4 2/3	4
Do. Cholera, &c.	1849—267 1/4	1854— 83 3/4	1866— 20 1/2	—	—
Do. Phthisis	38 2/3	41	34 1/3	26	22
Do. Lung Disease	28	38	32 1/2	43	47

INDEX.

LONDON :

PRINTED BY C. F. ROWORTH, GREAT NEW STREET, FETTER LANE, E.C.

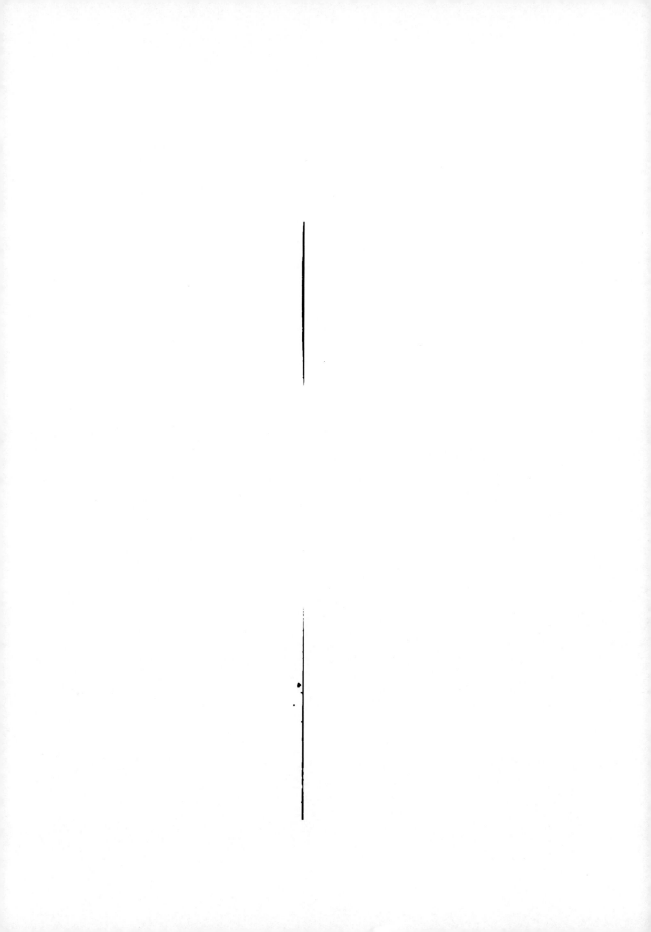